International Directory of

COMPANY HISTORIES

International Directory of
COMPANY HISTORIES

VOLUME 79

Editor

Jay P. Pederson

ST. JAMES PRESS
An imprint of Thomson Gale, a part of The Thomson Corporation

THOMSON
GALE

Detroit • New York • San Francisco • New Haven, Conn. • Waterville, Maine • London • Munich

THOMSON
GALE

International Directory of Company Histories, Volume 79
Jay P. Pederson, Editor

Project Editor
Miranda H. Ferrara

Editorial
Virgil Burton, Donna Craft, Louise Gagné, Peggy Geeseman, Julie Gough, Linda Hall, Sonya Hill, Keith Jones, Lynn Pearce, Holly Selden, Justine Ventimiglia

Production Technology Specialist
Mike Weaver

Imaging and Multimedia
Leslie Light, Michael Logusz

Composition and Electronic Prepress
Gary Leach, Evi Seoud

Manufacturing
Rhonda Dover

Product Manager
Jennifer Bernardelli

For more information, contact
St. James Press
27500 Drake Rd.
Farmington Hills, MI 48331-3535
Or you can visit our Internet site at
http://www.gale.com/stjames

Cover photograph Working Replica of Thomas Edison's Universal Stock Ticker, c. 1870. Courtesy of Stock Ticker Company.

LIBRARY OF CONGRESS CATALOG NUMBER 89-190943

ISBN 1-55862-583-6

This title is also available as an e-book
ISBN 1-55862-627-1

BRITISH LIBRARY CATALOGUING IN PUBLICATION DATA

International directory of company histories, Vol. 79
I. Jay P. Pederson
33.87409

Printed in the United States of America
10 9 8 7 6 5 4 3 2 1

Contents

Preface

The St. James Press series *The International Directory of Company Histories* (*IDCH*) is intended for reference use by students, business people, librarians, historians, economists, investors, job candidates, and others who seek to learn more about the historical development of the world's most important companies. To date, *IDCH* has covered over 7,850 companies in 79 volumes.

INCLUSION CRITERIA

Most companies chosen for inclusion in *IDCH* have achieved a minimum of US$25 million in annual sales and are leading influences in their industries or geographical locations. Companies may be publicly held, private, or nonprofit. State-owned companies that are important in their industries and that may operate much like public or private companies also are included. Wholly owned subsidiaries and divisions are profiled if they meet the requirements for inclusion. Entries on companies that have had major changes since they were last profiled may be selected for updating.

The *IDCH* series highlights 10% private and nonprofit companies, and features updated entries on approximately 50 companies per volume.

ENTRY FORMAT

Each entry begins with the company's legal name; the address of its headquarters; its telephone, toll-free, and fax numbers; and its web site. A statement of public, private, state, or parent ownership follows. A company with a legal name in both English and the language of its headquarters country is listed by the English name, with the native-language name in parentheses.

The company's founding or earliest incorporation date, the number of employees, and the most recent available sales figures follow. Sales figures are given in local currencies with equivalents in U.S. dollars. For some private companies, sales figures are estimates and indicated by the abbreviation *est.* The entry lists the exchanges on which the company's stock is traded and its ticker symbol, as well as the company's NAIC codes.

Entries generally contain a *Company Perspectives* box which provides a short summary of the company's mission, goals, and ideals; a *Key Dates* box highlighting milestones in the company's history; lists of *Principal Subsidiaries*, *Principal Divisions*, *Principal Operating Units*, *Principal Competitors*; and articles for *Further Reading*.

American spelling is used throughout *IDCH*, and the word "billion" is used in its U.S. sense of one thousand million.

Users of the *IDCH* series will notice some changes to the look of the series starting with Volume 77. The pages have been redesigned for better clarity and ease of use; the standards for entry content, however, have not changed.

SOURCES

Entries have been compiled from publicly accessible sources both in print and on the Internet such as general and academic periodicals, books, and annual reports, as well as material supplied by the companies themselves.

CUMULATIVE INDEXES

IDCH contains three indexes: the **Index to Companies**, which provides an alphabetical index to companies discussed in the text as well as to companies profiled, the **Index to Industries**, which allows researchers to locate companies by their principal industry, and the **Geographic Index**, which lists companies alphabetically by the country of their headquarters. The indexes are cumulative and specific instructions for using them are found immediately preceding each index.

SUGGESTIONS WELCOME

Comments and suggestions from users of *IDCH* on any aspect of the product as well as suggestions for companies to be included or updated are cordially invited. Please write:

The Editor
International Directory of Company Histories
St. James Press
27500 Drake Rd.
Farmington Hills, Michigan 48331-3535

St. James Press does not endorse any of the companies or products mentioned in this series. Companies appearing in the *International Directory of Company Histories* were selected without reference to their wishes and have in no way endorsed their entries.

Notes on Contributors

M. L. Cohen
Novelist and researcher living in Paris.

Jeffrey L. Covell
Seattle-based writer.

Ed Dinger
Writer and editor based in Bronx, New York.

Robert Halasz
Former editor in chief of *World Progress* and *Funk & Wagnalls New Encyclopedia Yearbook*; author, *The U.S. Marines* (Millbrook Press, 1993).

Frederick C. Ingram
Utah-based business writer who has contributed to *GSA Business*, *Appalachian Trailway News*, the *Encyclopedia of Business*, the *Encyclopedia of Global Industries*, the *Encyclopedia of Consumer Brands*, and other regional and trade publications.

Kathleen Peippo
Minneapolis-based writer.

Sara Poginy
Ohio-based writer.

Nelson Rhodes
Editor, writer, and consultant in the Chicago area.

Carrie Rothburd
Writer and editor specializing in corporate profiles, academic texts, and academic journal articles.

David E. Salamie
Part-owner of InfoWorks Development Group, a reference publication development and editorial services company.

Ted Sylvester
Photographer, writer, and editor of the environmental journal *From the Ground Up*.

Frank Uhle
Ann Arbor-based writer; movie projectionist, disc jockey, and staff member of *Psychotronic Video* magazine.

List of Abbreviations

¥ Japanese yen
£ United Kingdom pound
$ United States dollar
A.E. Anonimos Eteria (Greece)
A.O. Anonim Ortaklari/Ortakligi (Turkey)
A.S. Anonim Sirketi (Turkey)
A/S Aksjeselskap (Norway)
A/S Aktieselskab (Denmark, Sweden)
AB Aktiebolag (Finland, Sweden)
AB Oy Aktiebolag Osakeyhtiot (Finland)
AED Emirati dirham
AG Aktiengesellschaft (Austria, Germany, Switzerland, Liechtenstein)
ARS Argentine peso
ATS Austrian shilling
AUD Australian dollar
ApS Amparteselskab (Denmark)
Ay Avoinyhtio (Finland)
B.A. Buttengewone Aansprakeiijkheid (The Netherlands)
B.V. Besloten Vennootschap (Belgium, The Netherlands)
BEF Belgian franc
BHD Bahraini dinar
BRL Brazilian real
Bhd. Berhad (Malaysia, Brunei)
C. de R.L. Compania de Responsabilidad Limitada (Spain)
C.A. Compania Anonima (Ecuador, Venezuela)
C.V. Commanditaire Vennootschap (The Netherlands, Belgium)
CAD Canadian dollar
CEO Chief Executive Officer
CFO Chief Financial Officer
CHF Swiss franc
CIO Chief Information Officer
CLP Chilean peso
CNY Chinese yuan
COO Chief Operating Officer
COP Colombian peso
CRL Companhia a Responsabilidao Limitida (Portugal, Spain)
CZK Czech koruna
Co. Company
Corp. Corporation
D&B Dunn & Bradstreet
DEM German deutsche mark
DKK Danish krone
DZD Algerian dinar
EEK Estonian Kroon
EGP Egyptian pound
ESOP Employee Stock Options and Ownership
ESP Spanish peseta
EUR euro
FIM Finnish markka
FRF French franc
G.I.E. Groupement d'Interet Economique (France)
GRD Greek drachma
GmbH Gesellschaft mit beschraenkter Haftung (Austria, Germany, Switzerland)
HKD Hong Kong dollar
HUF Hungarian forint
I/S Interesentselskap (Norway)
I/S Interessentselskab (Denmark)
IDR Indonesian rupiah
IEP Irish pound
ILS new Israeli shekel
INR Indian rupee
IPO Initial Public Offering
ISK Icelandic krona
ITL Italian lira
Inc. Incorporated (United States, Canada)
JMD Jamaican dollar
K/S Kommanditselskab (Denmark)
K/S Kommandittselskap (Norway)
KG Kommanditgesellschaft (Austria, Germany, Switzerland)
KGaA Kommanditgesellschaft auf Aktien (Austria, Germany, Switzerland)
KK Kabushiki Kaisha (Japan)
KPW North Korean won
KRW South Korean won
KWD Kuwaiti dinar
LBO Leveraged Buyout
Lda. Limitada (Spain)
L.L.C. Limited Liability Company (United States)
Ltd. Limited (Various)
Ltda. Limitada (Brazil, Portugal)

Ltee. Limitee (Canada, France)
LUF Luxembourg franc
mbH mit beschraenkter Haftung (Austria, Germany)
MUR Mauritian rupee
MXN Mexican peso
MYR Malaysian ringgit
N.V. Naamloze Vennootschap (Belgium, The Netherlands)
NGN Nigerian naira
NLG Netherlands guilder
NOK Norwegian krone
NZD New Zealand dollar
OAO Otkrytoe Aktsionernoe Obshchestve (Russia)
OMR Omani rial
OOO Obschestvo s Ogranichennoi Otvetstvennostiu (Russia)
Oy Osakeyhtiö (Finland)
PHP Philippine peso
PKR Pakistani rupee
PLC Public Limited Co. (United Kingdom, Ireland)
PLN Polish zloty
PTE Portuguese escudo
Pty. Proprietary (Australia, South Africa, United Kingdom)
QAR Qatari rial
REIT Real Estate Investment Trust
RMB Chinese renminbi
RUB Russian ruble
S.A. Société Anonyme (Belgium, France, Greece, Luxembourg, Switzerland, Arab speaking countries)
S.A. Sociedad Anónima (Latin America, Spain, Mexico)
S.A. Sociedades Anônimas (Brazil, Portugal)
S.A.R.L. Sociedade Anonima de Responsabilidade Limitada (Brazil, Portugal)
S.A.R.L. Société à Responsabilité Limitée (France, Belgium, Luxembourg)
S.A.S. Societá in Accomandita Semplice (Italy)
S.A.S. Societe Anonyme Syrienne (Arab speaking countries)
S.R.L. Sociedad de Responsabilidad Limitada (Spain, Mexico, Latin America)
S.R.L. Società a Responsabilitá Limitata (Italy)
S.R.O. Spolecnost s Rucenim Omezenym (Czechoslovakia
S.p.A. Società per Azioni (Italy)
SAA Societe Anonyme Arabienne
SAR Saudi riyal
SEK Swedish krona
SGD Singapore dollar
Sdn. Bhd. Sendirian Berhad (Malaysia)
Sp. z.o.o. Spólka z ograniczona odpowiedzialnoscia (Poland)
Ste. Societe (France, Belgium, Luxembourg, Switzerland)
THB Thai baht
TND Tunisian dinar
TRL Turkish lira
TWD new Taiwan dollar
VAG Verein der Arbeitgeber (Austria, Germany)
VEB Venezuelan bolivar
VND Vietnamese dong
YK Yugen Kaisha (Japan)
ZAO Zakrytoe Aktsionernoe Obshchestve (Russia)
ZAR South African rand
ZMK Zambian kwacha

Aditya Birla Group

Worli
Mumbai, 400 025
India
Telephone: +91 56 52-5000
Fax: +91 56 52-5750
Web site: http://www.adityabirla.com

Public Company
Incorporated: 1870
Employees: 72,000
Sales: $7.59 billion (2005)
Stock Exchanges: India
Ticker Symbol: BIR
NAIC: 331491 Nonferrous Metal (Except Copper and Aluminum) Rolling, Drawing, and Extruding; 551112 Offices of Other Holding Companies; 423990 Other Miscellaneous Durable Goods Merchant Wholesalers; 331111 Iron and Steel Mills; 313210 Broadwoven Fabric Mills; 325120 Industrial Gas Manufacturing; 325131 Inorganic Dye and Pigment Manufacturing; 325221 Cellulosic Man-made Fiber Manufacturing; 327124 Clay Refractory Manufacturing; 313210 Broadwoven Fabric Mills; 322110 Pulp Mills; 322121 Paper (Except Newsprint) Mills; 325181 Alkalies and Chlorine Manufacturing; 327310 Cement Manufacturing

■ ■ ■

Aditya Birla Group is one of India's largest conglomerates and also claims to be the most international of the country's major corporations. The company acts as a holding company for more than 72 manufacturing and services subsidiaries throughout India, and in Thailand, Indonesia, the Philippines, Malaysia, Australia, China, Egypt, and Canada. Aditya Birla's major subsidiaries include Grasim, the world's leading producer of viscose staple fiber, and a manufacturer of rayon grade pulp, cement, sponge iron, textiles, and chemicals; Hindalco, a leading producer of aluminum and copper; UltraTech Cement, which produces portland cement and related products; Aditya Birla Nuvo, which manufactures clothing, textiles, and carbon black and is India's second largest producer of viscose filament yarn; Indo Gulf, a fertilizer producer; Birla NGK Insulators (a joint venture with NGK of Japan), which is the world's leading producer of insulators; and Idea Cellular Ltd., a mobile service provider jointly owned with fellow Indian conglomerate Tata Industries. The company also produces software and provides IT services, and operates a number of financial products subsidiaries. The company's Birla Sun Life Insurance Co. is the second largest private sector insurance company in India, and its Birla Sun Life Asset Management Co. is the country's fourth largest assets manager. In other areas, the company claims to be the world's eighth largest producer of cement and the world's fourth largest producer of carbon black. These operations combine to generate revenues of nearly $7.6 billion per year. The company is led by Kumar Mangalam Birla, son of Aditya Birla.

INDIAN FINANCIAL DYNASTY IN THE 19TH CENTURY

The Aditya Birla Group was founded in the 1960s by Aditya Birla, who started building his business empire at

COMPANY PERSPECTIVES

Our Vision: To be a premium global conglomerate with a clear focus on each business.

Our Mission: To deliver superior value to our customers, shareholders, employees and society at large.

Our Values: Integrity; Commitment; Passion; Seamlessness; Speed.

the age of 24. By then, however, the Birla family had been one of India's most prominent industrial and financial families for nearly a century. The origins of the Birla family fortunes lay in the second half of the 19th century, when in 1870 Seth Shiv Narayan Birla launched a cotton- and jute-trading business in the town of Pilani, in Rajasthan, India. Despite the British occupation, and the attempt to establish monopolies by the British trading companies, Birla succeeded in building the family's first fortune.

The next phase of the family's success came at the beginning of the 20th century, when Birla's grandson Ghanshyamdas took over as head of the family fortune. The younger Birla led the family into the industrial sector, setting up a jute mill in 1919. The Birla family also became important supporters of the independence movement led by Mahatma Ghandi. Ghanshyamdas Birla not only provided the financial backing for Ghandi, he also participated in the talks with the British that ultimately led to the country's independence. The company's wealth, and its intimate connection with the new Indian government, enabled it to emerge as one of a small number of Indian families that dominated India's quasi-socialist economy through the end of the century.

With independence, Birla began developing his industrial empire in earnest. The family quickly branched out into a number of sectors. Just days after the country's declaration of independence, for example, Birla founded Grasim Industrial Ltd., opening a small weaving plant in Gwalior. By 1950, Grasim had begun importing the recently developed rayon fiber, and it began producing rayon-based fabrics. In 1954, Grasim launched its own rayon production, opening a factory in Nagda. By the mid-1960s, Grasim also had launched production of the rayon pulp itself.

The family's interest in textiles and rayon in particular led it to acquire another branch, Indian Rayon Corporation, in 1966. That company had been founded just a decade earlier, and in 1963 had expanded with the construction of its own viscose filament yarn factory in Veraval. As part of the Birla family holdings, Indian Rayon, which later evolved into the Birla group's largest subconglomerate, Aditya Birla Nuvo, developed diversified operations, including the production of garments, textiles, carbon black, and insulators. The company also entered cement production, launching its own factory in 1985.

In the meantime, Birla's industrial interests had led it into a new area, the production of metals, and specifically aluminum. The family established a new company, Hindalco, in 1958 and began construction of their first smelter. That complex, in Renukoot, launched production in 1962. By 1967, the company had set up its own power plant, in Renusagar, described by the company as "a significant strategic move." The company later branched out into copper production as well.

The development of the family's business interests had been turned over to Ghanshyamdas Birla's sons, K. K. Birla, C. K. Birla, and B. K. Birla. While B. K. Birla took over the family's raw materials and related industrial operations, his brothers took charge of other Birla family holdings, including Hindustan Motors, part of India's big three automakers, and the *Hindustan Times,* one of the country's major newspapers.

INTERNATIONAL PIONEER: 1970-80

In the mid-1960s, Aditya Vikram Birla joined his father, B. K. Birla, in that branch of the family business, which by then consisted of Grasim, Hindalco, and Indian Rayon. By the end of the decade, Aditya Birla, then 24 years old, was placed in charge of these companies, which formed the basis of the Aditya Birla Group.

The younger Birla soon proved himself a visionary, leading the company's development from an India-focused industrial group to India's first and largest internationally operating conglomerate. The company enjoyed the advantages of India's "License Raj," a license-permit-quota system devised by the country's first prime minister, Jawarharal Nehru, that made it difficult for new domestic competitors to emerge. Although this system protected and reinforced the Birla family's interests, it also subjected the Birla group to strict capital controls. At the end of the 1960s, however, Aditya Birla recognized a means of skirting these controls, through the development of foreign interests.

In 1969, Birla launched its first subsidiary, Indo Thai Synthetics, to produce and export synthetic yarns in Thailand. Into the 1970s, the company continued to invest in Thailand, launching two new subsidiaries in 1974. The first of these, Thai Rayon, launched produc-

KEY DATES

1870: Seth Shiv Narayan Birla launches a cotton- and jute-trading business in the town of Pilani, in Rajasthan, India.

1919: Grandson Ghanshyamdas Birla sets up a jute mill, establishing the family's industrial holdings.

1947: The Birla family sets up the Grasim weaving plant, later adding production of rayon.

1958: The company establishes Hindalco for production of aluminum.

1966: Indian Rayon Corporation is acquired.

1969: Under Aditya Birla, the company launches international expansion, founding Indo Thai Synthetics in Thailand.

1978: Carbon black production is launched in Thailand.

1988: Indo Gulf is formed under Hindalco for the production of fertilizer.

1995: Aditya Birla dies and is succeeded by son Kumar Mangalam Birla, who later leads a restructuring and streamlining of the group; a joint venture, Birla AT&T, is formed.

1998: Info Gulf begins copper production; Birla enters Canada with the purchase of Atholville Pulp Mill in New Brunswick.

1999: Birla adds financial services through an insurance joint venture with Canada's Sun Life.

2000: Birla AT&T merges with Tata Communications; Hindalco acquires Indal.

2002: Hindalco restructures and spins off Indo Gulf Fertilizers; Anapurna Foils is acquired.

2003: Birla acquires Nifty Copper and Mt. Gordon Copper mines in Australia; the company enters China with the creation of the carbon black joint venture, Liaoning Birla.

2004: Indal merges into Hindalco.

2005: Construction of a new aluminum facility begins in Orissa, India; the St. Anne Nackawic Pulp Mill in Canada is acquired.

2006: The company announces plans to build a new viscose staple fiber plant in Laos.

tion of viscose rayon staple fiber, which it marketed on a global basis as Birla Cellulose. That company quickly grew into a major exporter, while also supplying the Thai textile industry. The company set up in 1974 was Century Textiles Co., which operated a weaving and dyeing plant, producing Centex-branded fabrics, including polyester, rayon, linen, and later lycra and others. By the end of the 1970s, the company's Thai holdings included Thai Carbon Black (TCB), founded in 1978. Carbon black, also known as soot and lampblack, was used as a black pigment for inks, food colorings, and especially for the production of rubber tires. TCB grew strongly, building the world's largest carbon black facility on a single location, and counting among its customers the global big three tire manufacturers. The company was particularly successful in Japan, where it captured more than half of the total carbon black market.

Birla's success in Thailand encouraged the group to extend its operations elsewhere in the region. In 1975, the company launched a joint venture in the Philippines, to produce spun yarn. The operation became the basis of the group's other Filipino holdings, grouped under the Indo Phil name. Malaysia became the company's next foreign market, with the opening of an edible oil production subsidiary in 1978. That business, Pan Century Edible Oils, became the world's largest single-location palm oil refinery.

STEADY GROWTH THROUGH THE END OF THE 20TH CENTURY

The Birla group's expansion continued through the 1980s. The company moved into Indonesia in 1982, setting up PT Indo Bharat Rayon. In Thailand, in 1984, the company expanded into the production of sodium phosphates for the detergents industry, establishing Thai Polyphosphates and Chemicals. The company added yet another Thai unit in 1987, deepening its interests in that country's textile sector with the founding of Thai Acrylic Fibre. The company also expanded into the chemicals market in Thailand, founding a joint venture, Thai Peroxide Co., with the United States' FMC Corporation in 1989.

In the meantime, Birla's Indian holdings continued to expand and diversify as well. Grasim, for example, added cement production in 1985, launching the Vikram Cement plant at Jawad, in Madhya Pradesh. By the beginning of the 1990s, that operation had tripled its production capacity. Through the 1990s, Grasim added other diversified businesses, including merchant exporter Birla International Marketing Corporation in 1992, and Vikram Ispat, a gas-based sponge iron factory, in 1993. Grasim also expanded its cement holdings, opening two new cement plants, Grasim Cement in Raipur and Aditya Cement in Shambhupura, in 1995. The growth of Grasim's cement operations led Birla to transfer its other cement production operations from Indian Rayon into Grasim.

This restructuring was launched under the leadership of Aditya Birla's son, Kumar Mangalam Birla, who took over the company after his father's death in 1995. Until then, the Birla group of companies had been described by *Institutional Investor International Edition* as a "murky empire." The younger Birla, who had been educated at the London Business School, now became determined to transform the company into a modern corporation. Birla now led a restructuring of the company's holdings, grouping all of its businesses under the single umbrella holding, Aditya Birla Group. Birla also continued to streamline operations, regrouping various industrial operations into a more coherent structure.

LEADING DIVERSIFIED CONGLOMERATE IN THE NEW CENTURY

Aditya Birla nonetheless remained committed to its structure as a highly diversified conglomerate. The company also took advantage of the liberalization of India's economy, launched during the country's economic crisis in 1991, to enter a number of new areas. In 1988, for example, the company launched a petroleum refining joint venture with Hindustan Petroleum Corporation. The company then entered the telecommunications market, forming a joint venture with AT&T of the United States, Birla AT&T, in 1995. That company merged with Tata Communications in 2000, becoming one of the country's leading telecom groups.

Through Hindalco, the company launched fertilizer production, under subsidiary Indo Gulf in the late 1980s; in 1998, Indo Gulf added the production of copper as well. In 2002, Hindalco was restructured, with its fertilizer production spun off into a separate company, Indo Gulf Fertilisers. Indo Gulf's copper business was placed directly under Hindalco. By then, Hindalco had acquired major rival Indal, an aluminum producer founded near Kolkata in 1938. That acquisition was completed in 2000; two years later, Indal boosted its aluminum foil production through the purchase of control of Anapurna Foils. Indal was merged into Hindalco in 2004.

Other new markets for Birla included software development and IT services, which were regrouped into Birla Technologies Ltd. in 2001. The company entered the power generation market through a joint venture with Powergen PLC. In 1999, Birla added financial services to its range, forming a joint venture with Canada's Sun Life Assurance.

Into the mid-2000s, Birla also continued to expand its international network. The company made its first entry into the North American market, acquiring the Atholville Pulp Mill in New Brunswick, Canada. The purchase, completed in 1998, established Birla as the world-leading producer of viscose staple fiber and also marked its first major foreign acquisition. In 2003, the company turned to Australia, buying up the Nifty Copper mines in Western Australia. The purchase enabled Birla to develop into an integrated copper group, supplying its factories in India with raw material. Later that year, the company bought up a second Australia copper mine, at Mt. Gordon. In that year, as well, Birla extended its reach into the mainland Chinese market, where it established a carbon black production unit, Liaoning Birla Carbon. Back at home, the company launched a project to build a new aluminum production complex in Orissa, beginning construction in 2005.

Birla's international expansion continued to drive the company's growth into the mid-2000s. In 2005, for example, the company reached an agreement to acquire the St. Anne Nackawic Pulp Mill in Canada. The company also sought out new markets; in March 2006, the company announced its plans to build a $350 million viscose staple fiber plant in Laos. Aditya Birla had grown into one of India's leading conglomerates, and a major player on the world market.

M. L. Cohen

PRINCIPAL SUBSIDIARIES

Aditya Birla Chemicals (Thailand) Ltd.; Aditya Birla Nuvo Ltd.; Alexandria Carbon Black Company S.A.E. (Egypt); Alexandria Fiber Company S.A.E. (Egypt); AV Cell Inc. (Canada); AV Nackawic Inc. (Canada); Birla Mineral Resources Pty. Ltd. (Australia); Birla Mt. Gordon Pty. Ltd. (Australia); Century Textiles; Grasim Industries Limited; Hindalco Industries Limited; Indo Gulf Fertilisers Limited; Indo Phil Textile Mills (Philippines); Indo Thai Synthetics; Liaoning Birla Carbon Co. Ltd. (China); Pan Century Edible Oils (Malaysia); PSI Data Systems Limited; PT Elegant Textile Industry (Indonesia); PT Indo Bharat Rayon (Indonesia); PT Sunrise Bumi (Indonesia); Thai Acrylic Fibre; Thai Carbon Black; Thai Peroxide; Thai Rayon; TransWorks Information Services Ltd.

PRINCIPAL COMPETITORS

RPG Enterprises; Tata Sons Ltd.; Murugappa Group; Jaypee Group; Amalgamations Ltd.; Dabur India Ltd.; Balmer Lawrie and Company Ltd.; Escorts Ltd.; HMT

Ltd.; Greaves Cotton Ltd.; Bombay Burmah Trading Corporation.

FURTHER READING

"AV Birla Group Charts 3-Pronged Growth Plan," *India Business Insight,* March 16, 2004.

"Birla Makes Changes," *Nonwovens Industry,* November 2004, p. 20.

"Birla Plans Expansion," *Mining Journal,* April 27, 2001, p. 315.

"Birla Renames Thai Unit," *Chemical Week,* January 25, 2006, p. 14.

Chandler, Clay, "Dealing with Dynasties," *Fortune International,* October 31, 2005, p. 56.

Clarke, Jo, "India's Birla in Deal to Buy Second Australia Copper Mine for $14.3M," *American Metal Market,* September 25, 2003, p. 4.

"India: High Profile Family-Owned Businesses," *International Market Insight Reports,* May 16, 2000.

Lachner, David, "Birla Breaks Ranks," *Institution Investor International Edition,* August 2000, p. 16.

Viscusi, Gregory, "India (the World's Billionaires)," *Forbes,* July 20, 1992, p. 186.

Advanced Medical Optics, Inc.

1700 East St. Andrew Place
Santa Ana, California 92705
U.S.A.
Telephone: (714) 247-8200
Fax: (714) 247-8672
Web site: http://www.amo-inc.com

Public Company
Incorporated: 2001 as Allergan Medical Technologies, Inc.
Employees: 2,865
Sales: $920.6 million (2005)
Stock Exchanges: New York
Ticker Symbol: EYE
NAIC: 339112 Surgical and Medical Instrument Manufacturing

■ ■ ■

Advanced Medical Optics, Inc. (AMO) is a leading manufacturer and marketer of medical devices and products for the eye. AMO's business is organized along two major product lines, ophthalmic surgical equipment and eye care products. The company's ophthalmic surgical business, which accounts for two-thirds of the company's annual sales, provides medical devices for use in the cataract, implant, and refractive, or laser, vision correction markets. Cataract and implant devices include foldable intraocular lenses, implantation systems, phacoemulsification systems, and viscoelastics. The refractive surgery line includes laser systems, diagnostic devices, treatment cards, and microkeratomes for use in laser eye surgery. The company's eye care product line comprises a full range of contact lens care products, including multipurpose cleaning and disinfecting solutions, daily cleaners, enzymatic cleaners, and rewetting drops. Both of AMO's two main product lines are sold in the United States and in more than 60 countries. International sales account for more than 67 percent of the company's revenue volume.

ORIGINS

AMO's history began with the history of Allergan Inc., an Irvine, California-based company that matured from a small ophthalmic laboratory founded in 1950 to become the third largest pharmaceutical company by the beginning of the 21st century, when it stood as a leader and pioneer in the eye care and specialty pharmaceutical industry. To Allergan, AMO owed much. AMO, in fact, was half of Allergan when it first greeted investors on Wall Street, a company whose expertise and product lines came from Allergan's half-century of innovation in its industry. AMO inherited Allergan's legacy of achievements, beginning when Allergan first entered the contact lens market in 1960 with Liquifilm, a wetting solution for hard contact lenses. The company steadily built a strong presence in the contact lens market, controlling 20 percent of the hard contact lens market by 1975 and maintaining a solid presence within the soft contact lens market through Hydrocare, a cleaning solution. By 1984, Allergan held a 20 percent share of the contact lens solutions market, a position that was strengthened three years later with the introduction of Ultrazyme Enzymatic Cleaner, the first weekly cleaner that could be used during disinfection.

COMPANY PERSPECTIVES

AMO is dedicated to advancing the science of vision through continuous development of innovative technologies that enhance patient outcomes and improve practitioner productivity. To that end, we strive to constantly access the best ideas through an operating structure whereby Research & Development and Corporate Development are managed together under a single corporate function called Strategy & Technology. This unique approach promotes a technological open-mindedness that ensures proper prioritization of our internal R&D resources in concert with the pursuit of progressive innovations from outside the company. Our R&D teams represent a full breadth of ophthalmic surgical technology skill and expertise, extensive knowledge of biomaterials and proficiency in eye care formulation chemistry. We believe our success depends on our ability to foster a stimulating environment that continues to attract the highest-caliber scientists and engineers who share our passion for creating technologies that optimize vision and quality of life for patients.

As Allergan entered the 1990s, the company's strategic focus began to change, subtly at first, gradually shifting toward the orientation that would necessitate the creation of AMO. A seminal event occurred in 1991 when Allergan acquired Oculinum Inc., a manufacturer of Type A botulinum toxin, a substance that would become more commonly known as BOTOX. The acquisition marked the beginning of the company's move toward specialty pharmaceuticals, but the future AMO continued to gain from Allergan's commitment to both pharmaceuticals and optical medical devices. Of particular importance to AMO was Allergan's 1994 acquisition of the intraocular lens product line from Ioptex Research. The acquisition was followed a year later by the purchase of Optical Micro Systems Inc., a manufacturer of cataract surgery equipment and Pilkington Barnes Hind's contact lens care product line. Although significant aspects of Allergan's business that later would benefit AMO continued to develop, including the introduction of a new contact lens lubricating solution, Refresh Contacts, in 2000, the seed that grew into AMO already was planted by 1998. That year, Allergan named David Pyott as president, chief executive officer, and chairman, marking the beginning of a restructuring program that eventually led to the creation of AMO.

ALLERGAN SPAWNS AMO IN 2002

"When I came here," Pyott said in a February 15, 2002 interview with *Ophthalmology Times,* "we were half pharmaceuticals, half medical devices. Basically, I found a jewel here. We have such a great pharmaceutical opportunity." His priorities were clear: Allergan would focus its efforts exclusively on its specialty pharmaceuticals business, a strategy that necessitated removing its ophthalmic surgical and contact lens care business. The separation, Pyott argued, would be better for both businesses. "As pharmaceuticals accelerate and lens care slows down, we have a dilemma: How to feed all the children?," he explained in his interview with *Ophthalmology Times.* "Pharmaceuticals tend to starve non-pharmaceuticals of resources." The decision to cut Allergan in half led to the organization of the company's ophthalmic surgical and lens care assets into a subsidiary named Allergan Medical Technologies, Inc., which was incorporated in October 2001. Next, Pyott announced in late January 2002 that Allergan would spin off Allergan Medical Technologies as a stand-alone company named Advanced Medical Optics, Inc. The spinoff, which took place in the form of a tax-free distribution to Allergan's stockholders, occurred in July 2002, "the most important event in the history of Allergan since our founding in 1950," Pyott wrote in the company's 2002 annual report.

On AMO's first day of business, it ranked as the second largest contact lens care company in the world and as the second largest ophthalmic surgical company in the world. The company was born a giant, boasting more than $500 million in revenue when it debuted as an independent company. Leading the company was a 22-year veteran of Allergan, James V. Mazzo, who was handed the titles of president and chief executive officer after serving as president of Allergan's Europe/Africa/Middle East region and global head of the company's ophthalmic surgical product line. AMO established its main offices in Santa Ana, California, the headquarters for more than 2,000 employees, direct sales operations in more than 20 countries, and distributors serving more than 60 countries. It marketed a broad range of lens care products under the names Complete, Oxysept, Consept One, UltraCare, and Ultrazyme, as well as medical devices such as foldable intraocular lenses for the cataract surgery market.

Although it was a market leader with an established track record, AMO failed to captivate Wall Street at first. On its first day of trading on the New York Stock

KEY DATES:

2002: Advanced Medical Optics (AMO) is spun off as a stand-alone company by Allergan, Inc.
2004: AMO acquires Pfizer Inc.'s surgical ophthalmology business for $450 million.
2005: AMO pays $1.27 billion for VISX, Incorporated, an acquisition that strengthens the company's position in the laser eye surgery market.

Exchange, the company's shares fell 71 cents to $10.29 per share. "It's not a growing business," an analyst said when asked about AMO in a July 2, 2002 interview with the *Orange County Register.* In response, Mazzo and his executive staff sought to invigorate the company's business, something they would accomplish through new product launches and by completing acquisitions. It did not take long for the company to introduce its first product as a stand-alone company, unveiling its Blink brand, which comprised Blink Contacts and Blink Revitalising drops, in the fall of 2002. A slew of new products followed, helping to refresh a stagnant sales record. The $538 million collected in revenue in 2002 represented a decline from the $543 million generated the previous year, but after a year on its own, buoyed by new product offerings, AMO recorded $601 million in revenue in 2003. From there, the company's annual sales volume swelled, as Mazzo turned to the most expedient way of achieving growth: acquiring other businesses.

MASSIVE ACQUISITIONS IN 2004 AND 2005

AMO embarked on the acquisition trail and pounced on two large targets in rapid succession, barely giving industry observers time to ponder the implications of one acquisition before completing another. The company announced the first acquisition in April 2004, when it revealed it was acquiring the surgical ophthalmology business owned by Pfizer Inc., the largest drug manufacturer in the world. The assets, which Pfizer had gained a year earlier when it merged with Pharmacia Corp., generated $150 million in sales in 2003. AMO completed the deal in June 2004, paying $450 million for a wide selection of eye treatment products, including the Healon ocular surgery brand and the CeeOn and Tecnis brands of foldable lenses used in cataract surgery and to a lesser extent in refractive surgery. The acquisition also added a new product line, the Baerveldt glaucoma shunt, which was a drainage device that paved the company's entry into the glaucoma market.

The acquisition of Pfizer's surgical ophthalmology business strengthened AMO's already strong cataract business. The cataract-related device market was deemed by analysts to be a fast-growing market, precisely the antidote for a company perceived to lack financial vitality. Analysts projected sales of cataract-related devices to collect $2.5 billion in sales in 2005, and they responded positively to AMO's purchase of the Pfizer assets, leading to a 12.6 percent increase in the company's stock to $28.05 per share the day the deal was announced. Within two years, the trading price of AMO's shares had nearly tripled, offering compelling evidence that the company was no longer viewed as an uninspiring castoff from Allergan. AMO's next deal only added to the heightening expectations for the company. "This one," AMO's chief marketing officer said of the company's next purchase in a November 11, 2004 interview with the *Daily Deal,* "was so big and so fast, right on the heels of the Pfizer acquisition, that it literally shocked people that we would be so bold in a manner so recent from our last deal."

The acquisition, announced in November 2004, opened up a wealth of opportunities in another fast-growing market. Unlike the Pfizer acquisition, which strengthened AMO's capabilities in a market where it already enjoyed considerable strength, the company's second massive purchase gave it strength in an area where it was relatively weak. The target was VISX, Incorporated, a designer and manufacturer of equipment systems used for laser eye surgery. The deal, hailed as joining two of the world's largest manufacturers of eye surgery equipment, married AMO, a leader in eye care surgical equipment with a focus on cataract surgery with VISX, a specialist in refractive eye surgery. AMO paid $1.27 billion for VISX, completing the transaction in May 2005. "This deal," an analyst was quoted as saying in the November 30, 2004 issue of the *America's Intelligence Wire,* "will put AMO on the map and give them the breadth and strength to be a big player."

AMO's sales neared $1 billion in 2005, confirming in the minds of many observers that the Allergan that entered the 21st century contained two powerhouse businesses. As the two companies prepared for the second half of the decade, the lines separating their market orientations were becoming blurred. AMO's entry into the glaucoma market, a field where Allergan liked to think of itself as major global competitor, was one example. The expiration of a non-compete agreement between AMO and Allergan represented another. When Allergan spun off AMO, AMO agreed that it would not launch any assault in the pharmaceutical eye care market until mid-2005, signing a contract that barred it from entering the fast-growing market for treating dry eye, a disease involving abnormalities and deficiencies in the tear film. The dry-eye treatment market was estimated to be worth between $500 and $700 million in sales, offering a promising avenue to pursue for growth in the future. An AMO spokesperson, quoted in the August 1, 2005 issue of the *America's Intelligence Wire,* was asked about the pending termination of the non-compete agreement, saying it would free his company "to explore such things as the dry eye market because it's considered more of a pharmaceutical venue. Until that time," the spokesperson added, "We're not able to do anything. We can't even get started until the non-compete ends."

The expiration of AMO's non-compete agreement with Allergan opened up an entirely new and vast business arena for the company to explore, fueling hopes for a profitable future. Although its net earnings suffered substantially from its aggressive approach to expansion, amounting to a loss of $129 million in 2004 and $453 million in 2005, AMO had opportunities and possessed the capabilities to leave behind a success story as impressive as Allergan's, setting the stage for a spinoff to usurp its parent company and thoroughly dominate the eye care sector.

Jeffrey L. Covell

PRINCIPAL SUBSIDIARIES

AMO Holdings, Inc.; AMO Nominee Holdings, LLC; AMO Spain Holdings, LLC; AMO U.K. Holdings, LLC; AMO USA, Inc.; Quest Vision Technology, Inc.; VISX, Incorporated; Advanced Medical Optics Australia Pty Ltd.; AMO Belgium BVBA; AMO Brasil Ltda. (Brazil); AMO Canada Company; AMO Global Holdings (Cayman Islands); AMO Ireland (Cayman Islands); AMO Puerto Rico Manufacturing, Inc.; VISX (Cayman Islands); AMO (Hangzhou) Co. Ltd. (China); AMO Denmark ApS; AMO France SAS; AMO Germany GmbH; AMO Asia Limited (Hong Kong); Advanced Medical Optics India Private Limited; Allergan Trading International Limited; AMO Ireland Export Ltd.; AMO International Holdings (Ireland); AMO Ireland Finance; AMO Regional Holdings (Ireland); AMO Italy SrL; AMO Japan KK; AMO Malta Limited; AMO Netherlands B.V.; AMO Groningen B.V. (Netherlands); Advanced Medical Optics Norway ASA; AMO Singapore Pte. Ltd.; Advanced Medical Optics Spain, S.L.; Advanced Medical Optics Norden AB (Sweden); Advanced Medical Optics Uppsala AB (Sweden); AMO United Kingdom, Ltd.

PRINCIPAL COMPETITORS

Alcon, Inc.; Bausch & Lomb Incorporated; CIBA Vision Incorporated.

FURTHER READING

"Advanced Medical Optics Wins $214M in Damages," *America's Intelligence Wire,* December 19, 2005.

"AMO Introduces Blink Contacts," *Asia Africa Intelligence Wire,* June 24, 2004.

Benesh, Peter, "Acquisition Gives Lens Maker New Identity," *Investor's Business Daily,* June 1, 2004, p. A9.

"Branding: AMO Enters Eye-Care Market with Blink," *Marketing,* October 31, 2002, p. 10.

Cohen, Judy Radler, "AMO Nears End of Allergan Non-Compete," *America's Intelligence Wire,* August 1, 2005.

Croft, Tara, "Advanced Medical Buys VISX," *Daily Deal,* November 11, 2004.

Galvin, Andrew, "Advanced Medical Optics' Stock Falls on Its First Day as Stand-Alone Company," *Orange County Register,* July 2, 2002.

Hahn, Avital Louria, "Mergers & Acquisitions: Eye-Care M&A Is on a Tear Thanks to Aging Peeps of Boomers," *America's Intelligence Wire,* November 30, 2004.

Klinec, Joe, "Allergan Spin-Off Places Focus on Pharmaceuticals," *Ophthalmology Times,* February 15, 2002, p. 1.

Morse, Andrew, "AMO Gets Pfizer Unit for $450M," *Daily Deal,* April 23, 2004.

AECOM

AECOM Technology Corporation

555 S. Flower Street
Suite 3700
Los Angeles, California 90071-2300
U.S.A.
Telephone: (213) 593-8000
Fax: (213) 593-8730
Web site: http://www.aecom.com

Private Company
Incorporated: 1990
Employees: 24,000
Sales: $2.4 billion (2005 est.)
NAIC: 541310 Architectural Services; 541310 Engineering Services; 541618 Other Management Consulting Services

■ ■ ■

Operating through more than a dozen subsidiaries, employee-owned AECOM Technology Corporation is a global provider of design, planning, engineering, consulting, program and construction management services, and operations and maintenance support. The Los Angeles-based private company is a leader in transportation and water and wastewater projects, and is also strong in such fields as design and construction; power generation and transmission projects; mine design, engineering, and infrastructure; and international development assistance, consulting with developing countries on such areas as public administration, municipal finance, political transition, and humanitarian response. Furthermore, subsidiary AECOM Enterprises, in conjunction with its equity partners, is involved in forging public-private partnership projects in the facilities, transportation, and environmental areas. AECOM maintains offices on five continents and employs some 24,000 people.

HERITAGE DATING TO 1910

AECOM traces its origins to Kentucky-based Ashland Inc., which in turn grew out of Swiss Drilling Company, founded in Oklahoma in 1910 by J. Fred Miles. Unable to survive on the low prices offered for the Oklahoma crude Swiss Drilling produced, Miles relocated to the newly discovered oil fields of eastern Kentucky in 1915. He gained control of some 200,000 acres and formed Swiss Oil Company in Lexington. In 1924 Miles launched a refining operation called Ashland Refining Company, headed by an ambitious young man named Paul Blazer. While the parent company struggled, leading to the ouster of Miles, Ashland prospered under Blazer's leadership, and in 1936 he was named chief executive officer of the reorganized company, Ashland Oil & Refining Company.

Blazer added refineries as well as a chain of gas stations to sell gasoline and motor oil under the Ashland name. Before he retired in 1957, the company became increasingly involved in the chemical and petrochemical businesses. He was succeeded as CEO by his nephew Rex Blazer, who would take Ashland into areas beyond petroleum. In 1966 Ashland acquired Warren Brothers and became involved in the highway construction and construction materials business. The company was now able to take fuller advantage of refinery byproducts used

> **COMPANY PERSPECTIVES**
>
> Across our operations, AECOM offers a unique blend of global reach, local knowledge, innovation, and technical excellence; and our operating companies are united by our shared vision, mission, and values.

to produce asphalt. Ashland grew into one of the nation's major road-construction firms and laid a future foundation for AECOM.

In the 1970s Ashland Oil & Refining became Ashland Oil, Inc. Five years later the company consolidated its construction assets into a construction division and also formed a coal subsidiary, indicative of a changing focus at Ashland. Although it generated more than $1 billion a year in sales, Ashland was a small player in the oil industry at a time when the cost of exploration had grown prohibitively expensive. By 1980 Ashland sold off its production assets, and a year later was reorganized as a modified holding company. A new corporate strategy was implemented as Ashland now focused on refining and marketing, and also looked to grow its non-refining businesses. In 1984 Ashland acquired Daniel, Mann, Johnson & Mendenall (DMJM), a global provider of transportation-related engineering services. Originally focused on military projects, after World War II it had become one of the first integrated engineering and architectural firms in the western United States. The acquisition of DMJM also included its president, Richard G. Newman, AECOM's future chief executive and chairman. In 1985 DMJM became part of a new subsidiary, Ashland Technology Corporation. Two years later Newman was named its new president.

Newman earned a B.S. in civil engineering from Bucknell University in 1956 and four years later earned a Master's in hydraulics and hydrology from Columbia University. In 1962 he went to work for Cahn Engineers, a small Connecticut firm that he helped to grow from a single office employing 16 to an eight-office operation employing more than 250. In 1971 Cahn was acquired by Genge, Inc., one of the first publicly traded architectural and engineering firms. Newman took over as president, and was later named CEO. By the time he left in 1977, Genge had become the third largest engineering firm in the country, according to *Engineering News Record*. Newman then joined DMJM, and under his leadership the firm tripled in size in six years.

FORMATION OF AECOM: 1990

In 1989 Ashland decided to focus on its core petroleum refining business and elected to divest itself of some assets, one of which was an Ashland Technology subsidiary, Williams Brothers Engineering Co., involved in the construction of pipelines and oil processing facilities. In the meantime, Newman prepared a management-led employee buyback proposal to acquire what remained of Ashland Technology. According to the *Los Angeles Business Journal,* "His proposal was both simple and unique; employees would create value for their clients, which would create value for AECOM and in turn deliver value back to the employees through stock ownership." In April 1990 Ashland sold a 58 percent stake in Ashland Technology to the employee stock ownership plan. All told, Ashland received a $97 million package in cash, stock, and subordinated debt, including the proceeds from the Williams Brothers sale. Ashland Technology now took on the name AECOM Technology Corp. and established its headquarters in Los Angeles, where DMJM was based. (AECOM was an acronym for architects, engineers, construction, operation, and maintenance). Newman was named president, CEO, and chairman of the holding company. Included under the AECOM umbrella in addition to DMJM, and operating independently, were Consoer Townsend Envirodyne Engineers, a Chicago company with offices in the Midwest as well as New York and California; Frederic R. Harris, Inc., a New York firm founded in 1927, specializing in transportation projects; Homes & Narver, Inc., an Orange County, California-based firm founded in 1933 which also did a great deal of transportation work; Turner Collie & Braden, Inc. (TCB), a Houston engineering firm established after World War II by a pair of former U.S. Army Corps of Engineers, maintaining offices in Texas, Pennsylvania, Colorado, and New York. TCB was involved in both transportation and environmental contracts, as well as land development projects.

AECOM's decision to allow its subsidiaries to operate independently was not a common industry practice, but it proved to be a wise choice, as AECOM outperformed its rivals over the next several years. Moreover, by the mid-1990s AECOM began offering design and build services and operation and maintenance services while casting its net around the world. It was involved in such projects as the renovation of FBI headquarters in Washington, D.C.; contracts with Kuwait's Ministry of Interior; architectural design services for the Korean Development Bank and construction management services for the City of Seoul subway system; design services for the Philippines' Metro

KEY DATES

1985: Ashland Oil forms Ashland Technology Corporation.
1990: Employees acquire controlling interest in Ashland Technology to create AECOM Technology Corporation.
1998: AECOM becomes 100 percent employee owned.
2000: Guy Maunsell International Limited is acquired.
2002: AECOM postpones initial public offering of stock.
2005: Richard Newman retires as CEO.

Manila Skyway; architectural, engineering, and program management services for Malaysian Airlines; design work for India's Port of Madras.

Revenues increased to nearly $725 million in fiscal 1997 (the year ending September 30) and net income totaled $2.8 million. In fiscal 1998 the firm was able to achieve 100 percent employee ownership, while revenues approached $860 million and net income more than doubled to $5.74 million. The firm was now ready to grow and diversify through strategic acquisitions. It also attempted to leverage the AECOM name while continuing to allow units to operate autonomously.

In March 1999 AECOM added Day & Zimmerman Infrastructure, Inc., an aviation project and construction management firm. Two weeks later AECOM acquired W. F. Castella, a San Antonio, Texas-based engineering and land surveying firm. Then, in May 1999, AECOM acquired Spillis Candela & Partners, a Coral Gables, Florida architectural and engineering firm. Altogether the three acquisitions cost AECOM $35.1 million in cash and stock.

The firm spent another $145 million in cash, stock, and notes on acquisitions in 2000. The first, completed in April of that year, was the purchase of Metcalf & Eddy, Inc., an environmental consultant founded in 1907 by Boston civil engineer Leonard Metcalf and the superintendent of the sewer department in Worcester, Massachusetts, Harrison Eddy. The firm became a pioneer in environmental engineering, especially in the treatment of industrial wastes, and went on to design the water treatment and wastewater plants in a number of North American cities. In the 1960s Metcalf & Eddy began to expand internationally and was eventually acquired by French water giant Vivendi. In August 1999 Vivendi acquired U.S. Filter Corp. in a $6.2 billion deal. Because of a potential conflict of interest, due to U.S. Filter selling water-related equipment and Metcalf & Eddy being in a position to recommend such equipment to its clients, Vivendi elected to sell Metcalf & Eddy, and AECOM was the beneficiary. Metcalf & Eddy had a great deal of brand recognition around the world in its area of expertise, and AECOM could now fold in its other environmental assets to maximize their value.

Also in April 2000, AECOM completed the acquisition of London, England-based Guy Maunsell International Limited, an infrastructure design firm and one of Europe's largest engineering and construction companies. It was founded in 1955 by an English marine engineer and was known for its bridge design work. Over the years Maunsell expanded overseas, first winning projects in Australia, and from there doing work in Hong Kong and throughout Asia, as well as Europe and the Middle East, all markets AECOM was targeting. With Maunsell in the fold, AECOM was able to add to the new unit the international offices of DMHM and Frederic R. Harris, while Maunsell was now able to do business in the United States, a market it was interested in. In addition, Maunsell provided Metcalf & Eddy with a way to reach new clients in a number of countries. Newman portrayed the Maunsell acquisition as a significant turning point for AECOM. "This merger positions us to compete effectively and grow across the globe," he told trade publication *ENR*. "We feel we are the preeminent infrastructure engineering firm in the world."

NEW CENTURY BRINGING REORGANIZATION

AECOM's acquisitions led to a reorganization in the fall of 2000, as assets were redistributed along functional lines. A new infrastructure group, DMJM Harris, was formed out of units taken from DMJ, Holmes & Narver, and Frederick R. Harris. DMJM Facilities and Holmes & Narver were merged to create DMJM Holmes & Narver. In addition, AECOM enterprises was formed to serve as a program integrator to help sister units obtain project financing and provide other development services. As a result of the acquisition spree, AECOM's balance sheet grew flush. Revenues reached $995 million in 1999 and topped $1.4 billion a year later. Net profits, in the meantime, increased from $10.4 million to more than $18.1 million.

AECOM completed six acquisitions in 2001 at a cost of nearly $21 million. One of the three major additions was the transportation planning practice of KPMG Consulting LLC, a Fairfax, Virginia firm. The addition of the KPMG unit was part of a corporate strategy to take advantage of the state and federal governments' likely investments in the United States long-neglected transportation infrastructure. Next, AECOM bought the remaining two-thirds of Halpern Glick Maunsell, an Australian engineering firm in which AECOM had picked up a stake in the Maunsell acquisition. Finally, in April 2001, AECOM acquired Warren Group, an English water engineering firm.

Two more acquisitions followed in fiscal 2002. In October 2001, another United Kingdom engineering firm, Oscar Faber plc, was acquired and combined with Maunsell. Faber, which did about $75 million in business, was mostly involved in design and transportation planning. Later in the month AECOM bought Alliance, a Denver-based consulting firm. The two deals cost AECOM $44.4 million in cash, stock, and notes. Also in fiscal 2002, in March 2002, AECOM filed for an initial public offering of stock, which it hoped would raise as much as $473 million. The proceeds would be earmarked to buy back stock from shareholders, pay down debt, and make more acquisitions. The market was not receptive to new offerings, however, and the sale was postponed indefinitely.

Despite being denied a chance to build up a war chest to fund further acquisitions, AECOM continued to pursue an expansion strategy. In April 2004, it added PADCO Inc., a Washington, D.C., consultant that mostly worked on World Bank and USAID economic development studies. In December 2005, AECOM spent $2.5 million on the Schaumberg, Illinois, and Houston offices of The Austin Co., a Cleveland, Ohio-based design and construction firm that recently filed for bankruptcy. These offices were combined with AECOM's subsidiary McClier Corp., and began doing business under the name of Austin AECOM. AECOM later attempted to purchase the rest of Austin but was outbid by Kajima Corp., a Japanese general contractor. AECOM was more successful in September 2005, when it acquired ENSR International, a Massachusetts-based environmental consulting, engineering, and remediation firm serving energy, oil and gas, chemical, and aerospace industrial clients. Three months later, AECOM added EDAW Inc., a San Francisco urban planning and design, landscape architecture, economics, and cultural and environmental services firm doing business around the world.

AECOM was now a $2.4 billion company and still growing. Newman, now 70 years of age, turned over the CEO post to 57-year-old John D. Dionisio, his chief operating officer. Newman stayed on as chairman, however. In a press release, Dionisio maintained, "AECOM has an impressive record of global growth and I intend to build upon that legacy."

Ed Dinger

PRINCIPAL SUBSIDIARIES

AGS; Austin AECOM; DMJM Aviation; DMJM H&N; DMJM Harris; EDAW; ENSR; Faber Maunsell; Metcalf & Eddy; PADCO.

PRINCIPAL COMPETITORS

ABB Ltd.; Bechtel Group, Inc.; The Louis Berger Group.

FURTHER READING

"Aecom Extends Internationally Through Merger with Maunsell," *ENR,* March 20, 2000, p. 19.

Belgum, Deborah, "Acquisition Raises Profile of AECOM," *Los Angeles Business Journal,* March 27, 2000, p. 3.

"Ernst & Young Entrepreneur of the Year," *Los Angeles Business Journal,* June 19, 2000, p. 35.

Kilgore, Margaret, "AECOM Technology Corporation," *Southern California Business,* December 1996, p. 8.

Korman, Richard, "AECOM Acquiring Metcalf & Eddy," *ENR,* April 10, 2000, p. 16.

Pettersson, Edvard, "Infrastructure Boom Gives Boost to Engineering Giant," *Los Angeles Business Journal,* January 1, 2001, p. 5.

Rubin, Debra, "AECOM Moves 'Up Front' with Link to Planning Firm," *ENR,* November 28, 2005, p. 13.

Affiliated Managers Group, Inc.

600 Hale Street
Prides Crossing, Massachusetts 01965
U.S.A.
Telephone: (617) 747-3300
Fax: (617) 747-3380
Web site: http://www.amg.com

Public Company
Incorporated: 1993
Employees: 974
Total Assets: $2.32 billion (2005)
Stock Exchanges: New York
Ticker Symbol: AMG
NAIC: 523920 Portfolio Manager

■ ■ ■

Boston-area Affiliated Managers Group, Inc. (AMG) is an asset management company with a controlling interest in more than 30 mid-sized investment management firms. Altogether these affiliates manage about $175 billion in assets in some 275 investment products, sold to both wealthy individuals and institutional investors. AMG's operating philosophy is to take an ownership position in affiliates between 50 percent and 70 percent, leaving the remaining equity with both senior and junior managers as an incentive to grow the business. In addition, affiliates are given a great deal of autonomy and allowed to retain their individual cultures and entrepreneurial spirit. By the same token, affiliates benefit from AMG's scale, realizing savings due to economies of scale in operations, distribution, and technology. AMG also has developed investment products that the affiliates market. AMG is a public company listed on the New York Stock Exchange.

FOUNDER, A PRACTICING LAWYER: 1970–80

AMG was founded by its chairman, William J. Nutt. The son of a western Pennsylvania dairy farmer, Nutt was able to gain his college education through full scholarships, first to Grove City College in 1963, then to the University of Pennsylvania law school. After earning his law degree in 1971 and clerking for a district court judge, Nutt began practicing corporate law for a Philadelphia law firm, making partner by the end of the decade. It was here that he began to learn the asset management field through his work for Wellington Management Company, Provident Capital Management, and other clients. In 1982 Nutt left to establish an administration, custody, and transfer agency business at Boston Company, a recent acquisition of Shearson/American Express that offered trust services primarily to wealthy individuals. Not only did Nutt begin making the transition from law to asset management, he came to appreciate how Shearson/American Express allowed Boston Co. a free hand at running its business with a minimum of interference.

When Boston Co. was sold to Mellon Bank Corp. in 1993, Nutt resigned. He had grown wealthy enough to retire at the age of 47, but decided to strike out on his own. During his days at Boston Co. he had taken an interest in the development of United Asset Management (UAM), a firm established in 1980 by Norton

COMPANY PERSPECTIVES

AMG's unique partnership approach creates powerful incentives for continued strong performance and excellent client service by providing Affiliate management with direct equity participation in their firms alongside AMG. AMG's growth strategy is to generate shareholder value through the internal growth of existing Affiliates, accretive investments in additional, growing mid-sized investment management firms, and strategic transactions and relationships designed to enhance our Affiliates' businesses and growth prospects.

Reamer to acquire independent asset management companies. Reamer acquired 100 percent interests but took a hands-off approach and shared about half the revenues with the managers. This was in stark contrast to banks and insurance companies, which made money managers paid employees and sapped their entrepreneurial spirit to the detriment of the funds' performance. Nutt's idea was to improve upon the UAM model, providing actual equity to talented fund managers and thus even greater incentive. Aside from philosophy, basic demographics favored Nutt's plan to acquire mid-sized asset management firms, many of whose founders were nearing retirement age. The Employment Retirement Income Security Act of 1974 had led to an increase in investment vehicles, and a large number of money managers at banks and insurance firms launched their own companies to manage pension funds. Some 20 years later these independent managers were faced with issues of succession and attaining liquidity to plan their estates. Hence they would be receptive to Nutt's concept, which would allow them to continue running their firms as they neared retirement, keep a large equity interest, yet address the problems of succession and estate planning.

Through investment banker R. Kendrick Wilson, Nutt was introduced to TA Associates, a Boston venture capital firm known for helping Federal Express get its start. More recently it had become involved in financial services and enjoyed success investing in money management firms. The people at TA agreed with Nutt that there was an opportunity to create a vehicle to snap up mid-sized money management firms, and in September 1993 TA hired Nutt as a consultant to flesh out a business plan, which then served to solidify their interest. Before the year was out TA agreed to back Nutt and invested $20 million in AMG for an 80 percent interest. Nutt contributed $1 million for a 10 percent stake, and the remaining 10 percent was used to recruit management talent. The most notable recruit would be Sean Healey, a Goldman Sachs veteran just two years shy of a potential partnership, who would come on board in the spring of 1995.

FIRST ACQUISITION: 1994

Not only did TA provide funding, its personnel helped Nutt by compiling a list of acquisition targets. In its first deal, in 1994 AMG paid close to $10 million in cash and notes for a 51 percent interest in New York-based J.M. Hartwell, and ultimately took a 75 percent position. Hartwell's business was trending downward, however, and the firm's performance fell far below expectations, not even keeping pace with the Standard & Poor's 500 index. AMG invested another $62 million in 1995 on stakes in four more money management firms. AMG gained majority interests in New Jersey-based Systematic Financial Management, Chicago-based Skyline Asset Management, and Cincinnati-based Renaissance Investment Management. In addition, AMG bought 30 percent of the New York firm Paradigm Asset Management Company, L.L.C. The performance of these new affiliates was at best spotty, with Systematic and Renaissance suffering declines in assets, while Paradigm and Skyline enjoyed strong gains.

AMG began to come of age in early 1996 when it acquired a Xerox subsidiary, Pasadena, California-based First Quadrant, a $10.3 billion firm that described itself as a "global quantitative investment manager." AMG's winning bid of about $50 million actually tied with another suitor, but Xerox sold to AMG because it was able to pay immediately. First Quadrant's managers thrived under AMG, which gave them one-third of the firm's stock and returned 70 percent of the revenues to them to reinvest at their own discretion. Assets under management grew to $28 billion in little more than two years. Also in 1996 AMG took a controlling interest in Chicago's The Burridge Group L.L.C.

In need of a fresh infusion of cash to fuel further growth and reach the size necessary to take the company public, Nutt raised $23 million in private equity from the likes of NationsBank and ITT Corp., and then arranged with AMG's syndicate of bankers to boost the firm's line of credit from $50 to $125 million. With a replenished war chest at his disposal, Nutt returned to acquisition mode. The first stop was Chicago, where in May 1997 AMG paid about $20 million for a 65 percent interest in Gofen & Glossberg, L.L.C., a $3.8 billion firm. Later in the year, AMG added GeoCapital Corp. to its portfolio, investing another $25 million in cash and stock for 60 percent of the $2.4 billion New York

KEY DATES

1993: The company is founded by William Nutt.
1997: The company is taken public.
2002: Third Avenue Management is acquired.
2004: Sean Healey is replaced by Nutt as CEO.
2005: AMG acquires interests in six Canadian firms.

firm. But the biggest deal of 1997, one that would turn the corner for AMG, was the $300 million cash purchase of a 71 percent position in New York-based Tweedy, Browne, a high-profile, and highly profitable, firm founded in 1920. AMG came along at the opportune moment, when Tweedy's three 50-something partners—brothers Christopher and William Browne and John Spears—were looking to plan their estates and sell at least a portion of the firm's stock, which the three of them controlled. Uninterested in selling out to a large organization, such as UAM, they found AMG more to their liking. They gained the liquidity they needed, but could continue to conduct their business as long as they chose to do so.

IPO: 1997

The addition of Tweedy added greatly to AMG's profitability. Moreover, it provided the spark Nutt had been waiting for to take AMG public. He struck quickly, and in November 1997 AMG made an initial public offering (IPO) of stock with Goldman Sachs serving as lead underwriter. Selling 48 percent of the company at $23.50 per share, AMG netted $187 million. Now the firm had new funds and a public stock to use in making further acquisitions. In addition, by the end of the year the banks increased its credit line to $300 million. With Tweedy in the fold, AMG was in a better position to attract other top-notch fund managers.

In March 1998, AMG paid nearly $70 million in cash plus stock for a 68 percent interest in Boston's Essex Investment Management Company L.L.C., owned by 64-year-old Joseph McNay, who then signed a ten-year employment contract to continue running his highly profitable growth equity investment firm with $6 billion in assets. At the end of the year AMG also bought the $3 billion Houston firm of Davis, Hamilton, Jackson & Associates, paying approximately $25 million for a 65 percent stake. AMG gained a similar position in Philadelphia's $3.7 billion Rorer Asset Management, investing $64 million for a deal that closed after the new year. As a result, AMG's stable now included 13 affiliates managing collectively $64 billion. For the year 1998, AMG recorded revenues of $238.5 million and net income of $25.6 million. AMG was hitting on all cylinders in 1999, as revenues soared to $518.7 million and net income increased to $72.2 million. The firm also raised more cash in another equity offering and made a key acquisition in April 1999, acquiring Norwalk, Connecticut-based The Managers Funds L.L.C., a family of nine, no-load mutual funds run by outside managers. These funds now became available for other AMG affiliates to market. In addition, in December 1999 AMG launched Managers AMG Funds, its own line of mutual funds made available to affiliates.

NEW CENTURY: FURTHER ACQUISITIONS

AMG closed on an acquisition in January 2000, paying a reported $105 million for a controlling interest in Frontier Capital Management Company, L.L.C., a Boston firm it had originally approached four years earlier. At the time Frontier's top executives were not concerned about retirement but had since begun to explore succession options with adviser Goldman, Sachs, which not surprisingly mentioned AMG as a possible solution. AMG now had 15 affiliates managing more than $90 billion. No other acquisitions were made in 2000, which proved to be a difficult year for the stock market. Despite a decline in revenues to $458.7 million, AMG recorded net income of $56.7 million. Poor economic conditions persisted in 2001, when AMG realized net income of $50 million on revenues that receded to $408.2 million. The firm continued to introduce products, such as funds managed by the experts of multiple affiliates. It also invested in Paris-based DFD Select Group to provide new affiliates with a way to sell some of their products in the European marketplace. In addition, AMG added a pair of affiliates to its portfolio, spending $247 million on a 51 percent stake in Delaware-based Friess Associates, L.L.C., and a reported $80 million to $120 million for the 163-year-old Boston firm of Welch & Forbes, which specialized as an adviser to wealthy families.

In 2002 AMG acquired another high-profile firm in New York's Third Avenue Management, owned by 77-year-old portfolio manager Martin J. Whitman, who took pride in calling himself a "vulture investor." The Third Avenue family of mutual funds placed a premium on buying stock in companies at highly discounted prices—an approach in keeping with the ongoing difficulties in the equity market. Conditions were such that AMG soon informed Wall Street that it was unlikely to make further acquisitions for the next year or so. Despite a softening in its stock price, AMG held steady, growing revenues to $482.5 million in 2002 and $495 million in 2003. Net income increased to $55.9 million in 2002 and $60.5 million in 2003.

With improved conditions, AMG resumed its acquisition activities in 2004, adding three affiliates. In June it acquired London, England-based Genesis Asset Managers, AMG's first foreign-based affiliate. With offices in Guernsey, Kenya, Chile, and Brazil it was also the first affiliate to focus on emerging markets. Then, in November 2004, AMG acquired AQR Capital Management, L.L.C., a Greenwich, Connecticut-based investment management firm and hedge fund manager with about $12 billion of assets under management. In that same month, AMG purchased the equity division of TimesSquare Capital Management. These additional affiliates helped to boost AMG's revenues to $660 million in 2004, when it also realized net earnings of $77.1 million. Also of note, at the end of 2004 Sean Healey became the firm's CEO, replacing Nutt, who remained chairman.

In 2005 AMG looked northward, acquiring equity interests in six Canadian asset management firms from First Asset Management Inc., a privately held Canadian holding company. The firms included Foyston, Gordon & Payne Inc.; Beutel, Goodman & Company Ltd.; Montrusco Bolton Investments Inc.; Deans Knight Capital Management Ltd.; Triax Capital Corporation; and Covington Capital Corporation. By all measure the year 2005 was highly successful for AMG, whose revenues increased to $916.5 million and net income totaled $126.5 million.

Ed Dinger

PRINCIPAL SUBSIDIARIES

First Quadrant Holdings, L.L.C.; Welch & Forbes, Inc.; Third Avenue Management L.L.C.; Tweedy, Browne Company L.L.C.

PRINCIPAL COMPETITORS

Asset Alliance Corporation; National Financial Partners Corporation; Old Mutual (US) Holdings, Inc.

FURTHER READING

Byrt, Frank, "Aging Founders May Seek to Sell Fund Concerns," *Wall Street Journal,* May 27, 1997, p. A13.

Der Hovanesian, Mara, "How AMG Is Growing Like Gangbusters," *Business Week,* January 10, 2005, p. 130.

Fraser, Katherine, "Allowing Money Managers Equity—and a Free Hand," *American Banker,* March 12, 1996, p. 11.

Kahn, Virginia Munger, "A Ticket to the Fast Lanes of Money Management," *New York Times,* November 16, 1997, p. 37.

Lappen, Alyssa A., "Nutt's House," *Institutional Investor,* January 1999, p. 95.

Santoli, Michael, "Toll Collectors," *Barron's,* July 11, 2005, p. L8.

Wyatt, Edward, "Buying a Fund Company Instead of Its Products," *New York Times,* April 26, 1998, pp. 3, 4.

Zuckerman, Gregory, "Goldman Banker Joins Acquirer of Money Management Firms," *Investment Dealers' Digest: IDD,* May 8, 1995, p. 8.

Akbank TAS

Head Office
Sabanci Ctr.
4 Levent
Istanbul, 80745
Turkey
Telephone: +90 212 270 00 44
Fax: +90 212 269 77 87
Web site: http://www.akbank.com.tr

Public Company
Incorporated: 1948
Employees: 10,592
Total Assets: TRL 54.2 billion ($40.46 billion) (2005)
Stock Exchanges: Turkey
Ticker Symbol: AKBNK
NAIC: 522110 Commercial Banking

■ ■ ■

Akbank TAS is one of Turkey's top two publicly held banking groups. The bank operates more than 600 branches throughout Turkey, as well as nearly 1,500 ATM machines. The company is also a member of the Golden Point ATM, extending its ATM services to more than 6,500 machines in the country. Since the early 2000s, Akbank, originally founded as a financial vehicle for the growing businesses of the Haci Omer Sabanci Holdings Group, has pursued a strategy of redeveloping itself as a truly full service bank. As part of that effort, the bank has added a new range of services, including pension funds, private banking, and assets management. In addition to its operations in Turkey, Akbank operates seven branch offices in Germany, one in Malta, and a subsidiary in the Netherlands. The bank also controls 65 percent of Sabanci Bank in London. In 2005, Akbank's total assets topped TRL 54.2 billion ($40.46 billion). The bank is listed on the Istanbul stock exchange. The Sabanci family directly controls 24.55 percent of the bank, and another 41.5 percent through the Haci Omer Sabanci Holdings conglomerate. Erol Sabanci serves as Akbank's managing director and chairman of the board.

FROM RAGS TO BANKER

Haci Omer Sabanci was born in Akçakaya, in Turkey's Kayseri region, in 1906. Sabanci's family was poor—his father died when he was only five—and at the age of 14, Sabanci set off on foot, walking 450 kilometers to find work in the Adana cotton fields. Before he turned 20, Sabanci had already begun to sharecrop his own parcel of land in the Adana region. Sabanci saved his money, which he invested in a cotton gin.

This investment provided the base for Sabanci's financial empire. Sabanci bought into a vegetable oil factory, later known as Yagsa, in 1943, and by the late 1940s had put together Toroslar Trading Company, which later became known as Marsa. The vegetable oils and margarine business later became one of the pillars of the Sabanci family conglomerate.

Sabanci's rising fortunes encouraged him to enter the financial markets as well. In 1948, Sabanci led a group of shareholders from the Adana and Kayseri regions in the creation of a bank, called Akbank after Sabanci's home village. Haci Sabanci and family remained Akbank's majority shareholder. From its base

COMPANY PERSPECTIVES

Akbank's vision is to be the leading multi-specialist bank in Turkey. Akbank's mission is to contribute to the development of the Turkish economy and the Turkish financial system by providing high-quality, specialized banking products and services that are innovative and comprehensive.

in Adana, Akbank grew quickly. By 1950, the bank had already begun to make equity investments elsewhere, starting with the Industrial Development Bank of Turkey. These investments helped Akbank emerge as a regional leader.

Akbank also began to build a branch network in the 1950s. The company's first branch was opened in Istanbul in 1950. That city became the growing company's headquarters in 1954. Less than a decade later, Akbank had already opened more than 100 branches. Akbank's success convinced the Sabanci family to deepen its financial interests, and in 1960 the family entered the insurance market, launching Aksigorta AS. That company initially operated as a subsidiary of Akbank, before being spun off as an independent business.

Akbank had also taken its first step into the international banking market. In 1964, the company opened a representative office in Frankfurt, Germany, serving the growing population of Turkish "guest workers" in Germany. The Frankfurt office served as a transfer point for workers sending their wages back to their families in Turkey.

The Sabanci empire in the meantime had grown considerably. Sabanci remained heavily involved in Turkey's cotton industry, buying up his own cotton farm in 1949, then extending this activity with the creation of a new cotton ginning mill, called Bossa. By 1951, Bossa had expanded to include the production of textiles as well. At the same time, Sabanci entered the real estate development market, leading the development of the Erciyes Palas complex in Adana, and then the construction market. The Sabanci family's holdings continued to grow strongly after Haci Omer Sabanci's death in 1966. By the early 1970s, the family-held conglomerate, now known as Haci Omer Sabanci Holdings and led by Sabanci's five sons, had become major producers and distributors of plastics products, cement, aluminum, buses and other vehicles, and automotive parts, including the Lassa tire company founded in 1974.

INTERNATIONAL MOVES

The Sabanci group was already one of Turkey's leading corporations by the early 1980s. As such, the holding company attracted the interest of a number of international companies seeking entry into the Turkish market. This enabled the Sabanci group to launch a series of partnerships, deepening its penetration of Turkey's industrial and financial markets. At the same time, Sabanci began building up its own international operations, such as the launch of the trading companies Exsa Handels, in Germany, Universal Trading in London, and Holsa in New York.

In support of this growth, Sabanci expanded its banking presence onto the international market as well. In 1981, the company opened an office in London. By 1983, this office had become a full-fledged bank. Originally known as Ak International Bank, the bank's name was later changed to Sabanci Bank. The bank, which operated as an Akbank subsidiary, was the first private sector Turkish bank to be established outside of Turkey. The company also continued to follow the development of the guest working community in Germany, opening representative offices in Hamburg, Essen, Hannover, Stuttgart, and Munich by the mid-1990s.

Akbank's status as a leading player in the Turkish banking sector was confirmed in 1985 when the company formed a joint venture with Banque Nationale de Paris, founding a new bank in Turkey, BNP-Ak Bank. The new bank was initially held at 51 percent by Akbank and 49 percent by BNP. In 1988, however, the partners broadened their ownership circle, bringing in a new partner, Germany's Dresdner Bank. The joint venture's name was then changed to BNP-Ak-Dresdner Bank.

Akbank's success reflected the success of the larger Sabanci conglomerate, which had continued to develop partnerships, such as the foundation of the Brisa tire joint venture with Bridgestone, and expanding its range of interests to include tobacco, hotel ownership and management, automobile manufacturing, dairy products, and even electricity generation. By the mid-1990s, the Sabanci family's holdings had long topped the $1 billion mark, and the conglomerate had become Turkey's largest privately owned business. Many of the companies within the Sabanci empire had gone public; by the mid-2000s, the holding company controlled some 13 public companies, including Akbank. Haci Omer Sabanci itself went public in 1997, in part as a means of moving family members out of key management positions.

KEY DATESS

1948: Haci Omer Sabanci founds Akbank in partnership with shareholders from Adana and Kayseri regions in order to provide financing for the development of Sabanci's other business interests.

1950: Akbank makes first equity investment, in the Industrial Development Bank of Turkey, and opens branch office in Istanbul.

1954: Akbank moves its headquarters to Istanbul.

1964: Company opens representative office in Frankfurt, Germany, to serve Turkish "guest worker" population there.

1983: Company founds Ak International Bank (later Sabanci Bank) in London, becoming first privately held international Turkish bank.

1985: Company founds BNP-Ak bank joint venture with BNP of France.

1988: Dresdner bank joins BNP-Ak-Dresdner Bank joint venture.

1994: Akbank becomes founding member of Golden Point ATM network in Turkey.

1996: Akbank gains exclusive franchise for American Express card in Turkey.

1998: Frankfurt office is converted to a branch office.

1999: Company converts offices in Hamburg, Essen, Hannover, Stuttgart, and Munich to branch offices; launches internet banking services.

2000: Akbank founds Ak Portfolio Management, the Private Banking Unit, and the Commercial Internet Branch in strategy to become full-service bank; opens branch office in Malta.

2001: Akbank forms subsidiary in the Netherlands, Akbank International NV; acquires Akhayat Insurance.

2002: Akbank launches $350 million branch restructuring program.

2003: Company converts Akhayat Insurance to Ak Pension Fund.

2005: Akbank increases holding in Sabanci bank to 65 percent; acquires full control of BNP-Ak-Dresdner joint venture.

TURKISH BANKING LEADER

Akbank continued to extend its branch office network in Turkey, and by the mid-2000s operated more than 600 branch offices. The company also rolled out ATM services, building up its own network of nearly 1,500 ATMs throughout the country. In 1994, Akbank was one of the driving forces behind the creation of the "Golden Point" ATM network, which shared ATM services among member banks. In this way, Akbank was able to extend its ATM services to more than 4,500 locations in Turkey, giving the company an 11 percent share of the total ATM market. Akbank also launched its own credit cards. In 1996, the bank's position as a leader in the Turkish market was further underscored when it acquired the exclusive franchise for American Express cards in the country in 1996.

Akbank expanded its international network further in the late 1990s. In 1998, the bank converted its Frankfurt office into a full-fledged branch. The success of that effort encouraged the bank to extend its branch network to its other offices in Germany. These were converted to branches in 1999. In that year, the company crossed another, albeit virtual, frontier, when it launched its own internet banking services. This was followed by the creation of a new banking vehicle, the Commercial Internet Branch, in 2000, which catered to the SME market. Also in 2000, Akbank created two new dedicated financial services subsidiaries, Ak Portfolio Management, and the Private Banking Unit. This move came as part of the company's effort to transform itself into a full-service bank for its next growth phase. As part of this change in group strategy, Akbank launched a vast branch restructuring program in 2002, earmarking an investment of some $350 million.

Akbank added to its international operations again in 2000, opening a branch office on the island of Malta. This was followed by the opening of a new branch office in Berlin in 2001, and the creation of a subsidiary in the Netherlands, Akbank International NV, to serve the large community of Turkish immigrants there. Back at home, the company extended its internet banking service to include a separate English-language site, in order to serve the large international community in Turkey as well. The company then acquired majority control of Akhayat Insurance, which it transformed into a pension fund called Ak Pension Fund, at the beginning of 2003, in a bid to take the leading share of Turkey's private pension fund market. In that year, also, Akbank launched a new credit card, the MasterCard-backed Axess, which became one of Europe's fastest-growing credit cards.

As it continued restructuring its branch network, Akbank also moved to take tighter control of other areas.

The bank boosted its direct shareholding in London's Sabanci Bank, from 37 percent to 65 percent in April 2005. By then, the company had also acquired full control of the BNP-Ak-Dresdner Bank joint venture.

By the mid-2000s, Akbank had clearly taken its place among Turkey's top four banks, boasting total assets of more than TRL 54 billion ($40 billion) to place it second among the country's publicly listed banks into 2006. Founded to provide the financial backing for the expansion of the Sabanci family's network of companies, Akbank had grown into a full-fledged international banking leader as one of Turkey's top lenders. Nonetheless, the bank remained intimately connected with the Sabanci family, which continued to hold more than 70 percent of Akbank's share both directly and through Haci Omer Sabanci Holding. Akbank looked forward to future growth as a Turkish banking leader.

Ed Dinger

PRINCIPAL SUBSIDIARIES

Ak Asset Management (99.99%); Ak Emeklilik Private Pension Fund (73.41%); Ak Investment Fund (45.72 %); Ak Securities (Ak Yatirim) Brokerage (99.80%); Akbank N.V.; AkLease (99.98%); BNP-AK-Dresdner Bank (39.99%); Sabanci Bank (65%); Turkiye Sinai Kalkinma Bankasi Development Bank (6.45%).

PRINCIPAL COMPETITORS

Turkiye Cumhuriyet Merkez Bankasi A.S.; Citibank Turkiye A.S.; Turkiye Cumhuriyeti Ziraat Bankasi; Akbank TAS; Turkiye Is Bankasi A.S.; Turkiye Garanti Bankasi A.S.; Yapi ve Kredi Bankasi A.S.; Turkiye Halk Bankasi A.S.; Turkiye Vakiflar Bankasi TAO; Finansbank A.S.; Kocbank A.S.

FURTHER READING

"Akbank: An Economic Overview," *Euromoney*, August 2005, p. S2.

"Akbank Sets Benchmark with $1.25bn Deal As Turkish Bank Refi Volumes Keep Growing," *Euroweek*, August 26, 2005, p. 33.

"Akbank Stretches Lenders with Request for a Revolver As Banks Oppose Garanti Price Drop," *Euroweek*, October 28, 2005, p. 51.

Kurtul, Zafer, "Akbank: See the Difference," *Banker*, September 2002, p. 112.

Norton, Guy, "Market Parched After Supply Dries Up," *Euroweek*, May 2, 2003, p. S5.

"Right on Track," *FDI Magazine*, February 5, 2004.

Timewell, Stephen, "Clean up Boosts Investors' Trust," *Banker*, February 1, 2004.

Aljazeera Satellite Channel

P.O. Box 23127
Doha,
Qatar
Telephone: +974 489 0777
Fax: +974 488 5333
Web site: http://english.aljazeera.net

Private Company
Incorporated: 1996
Employees: 1,400
Sales: $8 million (2002 est.)
NAIC: 513120 Television Broadcasting; 513210 Cable Networks; 513220 Cable and Other Program Distribution

■ ■ ■

Aljazeera Satellite Channel is the Arab world's leading news network. It claims a role as an independent alternative to government-controlled media in the region as well as to the West's corporate broadcasting giants. Aljazeera is no stranger to controversy, offending both local regimes and the U.S. government with its unflinching reporting. While some call it a propaganda mill for terrorists, others praise its balanced and in-depth look at topics other networks avoid. The name Aljazeera translates to "the island," a reference to the Arabian Peninsula. "The opinion and the other opinion," is written below the name in Arabic script.

Aljazeera was launched with support from the Emir of Qatar after the BBC closed down its Arabic language television in 1996. Ten years later, the launch of an English language cable channel was underway. The Aljazeera logo is already familiar to cable news buffs through news clips sold to other stations. The original Arabic language channel has about 200,000 subscribers in North America through Dish Network's Arabic tier. The satellite as well as terrestrial signals are free to those in the Arab world.

LAUNCHED IN 1996

Aljazeera Satellite Channel was launched in November 1996 following the closure of the BBC's Arabic language television station, a joint venture with a Saudi company. It had fallen apart after a year and a half when the Saudi government attempted to kill a documentary on executions under sharia law.

The Emir of Qatar, Sheikh Hamad bin Khalifa Al Thani, provided a loan of QAR 500 million ($137 million) to sustain Aljazeera through its first five years, Hugh Miles detailed in his book *Aljazeera: The Inside Story of the Arab News Channel That Is Challenging the West.* Shares were held by private investors as well as the Qatari government.

According to Miles, the Emir had been contemplating a satellite channel even before he deposed his father the previous year. A free press complemented his vision of the emirate as a center of commercial development and progress.

Sheikh Hamad bin Thamir Al Thani, previously Qatar's Deputy Minister of Information, was chairman of the enterprise, although Aljazeera maintained editorial independence. It was hoped the channel would break

COMPANY PERSPECTIVES

Free from the shackles of censorship and government control Aljazeera has offered its audiences in the Arab world much needed freedom of thought, independence, and room for debate. In the rest of the world, often dominated by the stereotypical thinking of news "heavyweights," Aljazeera offers a different and a new perspective.

even in five years through sales of advertising, news feeds and programs, as well as equipment rental. Much of the staff came from the 250 journalists displaced by the closure of BBC Arabic.

Aljazeera's first day on the air was November 1, 1996. It offered six hours of programming per day; this would increase to 17 hours by the end of 1997. It was broadcast to the immediate neighborhood as a terrestrial signal, on cable, as well as through satellites (which was also free to users in the Arab world). Ironically, notes Miles, Qatar (like many other Arab countries) barred private individuals from having satellite dishes until 2001.

At the time of Aljazeera's launch, Arabsat was the only satellite broadcasting to the Middle East, and for the first year could only offer Aljazeera a weak Ku-band transponder that needed a large satellite dish for reception. A more powerful C-band transponder became available after its user, Canal France International, accidentally beamed 30 minutes of pornography into ultraconservative Saudi Arabia.

Aljazeera was not the first such broadcaster in the Middle East; a number had appeared since the Arabsat satellite, a Saudi-based venture of 21 Arab governments, took orbit in 1985. The unfolding of Operation Desert Storm on CNN underscored the power of live television in current events. While other local broadcasters in the region would assiduously avoid material embarrassing to their home governments (Qatar had its own official TV station as well), Aljazeera was pitched as an impartial news source and platform for discussing issues relating to the Arab world.

In presenting "the opinion and the other opinion" to which the Arabic script in the network's logo refers, it did not take long for Aljazeera to shock local viewers by presenting the Israeli speaking Hebrew on Arab TV for the first time, according to Miles. Lively and far-ranging talk shows, particularly a popular, confrontational one called *The Opposite Direction*, were a constant source of controversy regarding issues of morality and religion. This prompted a torrent of criticism from the conservative voices among the region's press. It also led to official complaints and censures from neighboring governments. Some jammed Aljazeera's terrestrial broadcast or booted its correspondents. In 1999, the Algerian government reportedly cut power to several major cities to censor one broadcast. There were also commercial repercussions; Saudi Arabia reportedly pressured advertisers to avoid the channel, to great effect. Aljazeera was also becoming a favorite sounding board for militant groups such as Hamas and Chechen separatists. A source told Miles the range of complaints helped cancel out any allegations of bias.

Aljazeera was the only international news network to have correspondents in Iraq during the Operation Desert Fox bombing campaign in 1998. In a precursor of a pattern to follow, its exclusive video clips were highly prized by Western media.

AROUND-THE-CLOCK IN 1999

February 1, 1999 was Aljazeera's first day of 24-hour broadcasting. Employment had more than tripled in one year to 500 employees, and the agency had bureaus at a dozen sites as far as Europe and Russia. Its annual budget was estimated at about $25 million at the time.

However controversial, Aljazeera was rapidly becoming one of the most influential news agencies in the region. Eager for news beyond the official versions of events, Arabs became dedicated viewers. A 2000 estimate pegged nightly viewership at 35 million, ranking Aljazeera first in the Arab world, over the Saudi-sponsored Middle East Broadcasting Centre (MBC) and London's Arab News Network (ANN). There were about 70 satellite or terrestrial channels being broadcast to the Middle East, most of them in Arabic. Aljazeera launched a free Arabic language web site in January 2001. In addition, the TV feed was soon available in Britain for the first time via BSkyB.

POST-9/11 HEADLINES

Aljazeera came to the attention of many in the West during the hunt for Osama bin Laden after the September 11, 2001 terrorist attacks on the United States. The station aired videos it received from bin Laden and the Taliban, deeming new footage of the world's most wanted fugitives to be newsworthy. Some criticized the network, however, for giving a voice to terrorists. Aljazeera's Washington bureau chief compared the situation to that of the Unabomber's messages in the *New York Times.* The network said it had been given the tapes merely because it had a large Arab audience.

KEY DATES

1996: Aljazeera begins broadcasting after BBC closes its Arabic TV station.
1997: Aljazeera moves up to a C-band transponder on Arabsat and increases daily programming to 17 hours.
1999: Twenty-four-hour broadcasting begins.
2001: An Arabic language web site is launched; U.S. bombs destroy Aljazeera's Kabul office during the Afghan war.
2003: A U.S. missile strikes Aljazeera's Baghdad headquarters during the Iraq War, killing a reporter; an English language web site is launched.
2006: English language channel Aljazeera International launches.

The rest of the world's television networks were eager to acquire the same footage. According to Miles, CNN had exclusive rights for six hours before other networks could broadcast it (a provision that was broken by the others on at least one controversial occasion). Prime Minister Tony Blair soon appeared on an Aljazeera talk show to state Britain's case for pursuing the Taliban into Afghanistan.

Aljazeera's prominence was heightened during the war in Afghanistan since it had opened a bureau in Kabul before 9/11. This gave it better video than the others scrambling to cover the invasion, clips that sold for as much as $250,000. The Kabul office was destroyed, however, by U.S. bombs in 2001. Aljazeera then opened bureaus in other trouble spots, noted Miles, looking to stay ahead of the future conflicts.

According to Miles, the network remained dependent on government support in 2002, having a budget of $40 million and ad revenues of about $8 million. It also took in fees for sharing its news feed with other networks. It was estimated to have up to roughly 45 million viewers around the world. Aljazeera soon had to contend with a new rival, Al-Arabiya, an offshoot of the MBC, set up in nearby Dubai with generous Saudi backing.

MORE WAR IN 2003

Before and during the U.S. invasion of Iraq, where Aljazeera had had a presence since 1997, the network's facilities and footage were again highly sought by networks such as the BBC. The channel and its web site also were seeing unprecedented attention from viewers looking for alternatives to "embedded" reporting and military press conferences.

Aljazeera moved its sports coverage to a new, separate channel in November 2003, allowing for more news and public affairs programming on the other one. An English language web site had launched earlier in the year. The channel had about 1,300 to 1,400 employees, its newsroom editor told the *New York Times.* There were 23 bureaus around the world and 70 foreign correspondents, with 450 journalists in all.

In April 2003, a U.S. plane fired on Aljazeera's Baghdad bureau, killing reporter Tareq Ayyoub. The attack was called a mistake. Later reports that George W. Bush speculated to Tony Blair about bombing Aljazeera's Doha headquarters did not ease a feeling of mistrust and paranoia at the network. Aljazeera's troubled relationship with U.S. Central Command, which was based in Qatar, was profiled in *Control Room,* a documentary that aired at the Sundance Film Festival in 2004.

The broadcast of sometimes gruesome videos of hostages and torture victims from Iraq did not alleviate the network's image problem in the West. Organizers reportedly removed Aljazeera's banner from its media booth at the 2004 Democratic Convention. The network had its supporters, however, particularly in Qatar, and there was already talk of Aljazeera going public at some time in the future.

IN ENGLISH IN 2006

Aljazeera was launching an English language channel, called Aljazeera International, in 2006. It would count among its staff journalists hired from ABC's *Nightline* and other top news outfits. Josh Rushing, a former media handler for CentComm during the Iraq war, agreed to provide commentary. Britain's esteemed interviewer Sir David Frost was also on board. In an interesting technical feat, the broadcast of the new operation was going to be handed off between bases in Qatar, London, Washington, and Kuala Lumpur, Malaysia, on a daily cycle.

The new English language venture faced considerable regulatory and commercial hurdles in the North American market for its perceived sympathy with extremist causes. At the same time, others felt Aljazeera's competitive advantage lay in programming in the Arabic language. There were hundreds of millions of potential viewers among the non-Arabic speaking Muslims in Europe and Asia, however, and many others who might be interested in seeing news from the Middle East by local voices. If the venture panned out, it would extend the influence of Aljazeera, and tiny Qatar, beyond even what had been achieved in the station's first decade. In an interesting circle of fate, the BBC World Service was preparing to launch its own Arabic language station in 2007.

Frederick C. Ingram

PRINCIPAL COMPETITORS

Abu Dhabi TV; Arab News Network Limited; Cable News Network L.P.; Middle East Broadcasting Center.

FURTHER READING

Abt, Samuel, "For Al Jazeera, Balanced Coverage Frequently Leaves No Side Happy," *New York Times,* February 16, 2004, p. C2.

"Al-Jazeera: Making the News," *MEED Weekly Special Report,* October 17, 2003, p. 33.

"Al-Jazeera One Step Nearer to Going Public," *BBC Monitoring International Reports,* February 2, 2005.

Badge, David, *Casualty of War: The Bush Administration's Assault on a Free Press,* Amherst, N.Y.: Prometheus Books, 2004.

"Democrats Remove Aljazeera Banner," *AlJazeera.net,* July 26, 2004.

El-Nawawy, Mohammed, and Adel Iskander, *Al-Jazeera: How the Free Arab News Network Scooped the World and Changed the Middle East,* Cambridge, Mass.: Westview Press, 2002.

Khalaf, Roula, "Al-Jazeera's Global Aims Boost Qatar's Influence: Controversial TV Station Is to Start an English-Language Service Targeting a World Audience," *Financial Times* (London), October 25, 2002, p. 11.

Malik, Shiv, "Broadcast and Be Damned," *Independent* (U.K.), January 24, 2005.

Marozzi, Justin, "Get the Message from the Gulf: The US and Baghdad Both Criticise Al Jazeera, the Arabic Language Satellite Station. Perhaps It Is Doing Something Right," *Financial Times* (London), September 14, 2002, p. 2.

Miles, Hugh, *Al-Jazeera: The Inside Story of the Arab News Channel That Is Challenging the West,* New York: Grove Press, 2005.

Noujaim, Jehane, et al., *Control Room,* DVD, Artisan Home Entertainment, 2004.

Reed, Stanley, "Al Jazeera Meets American Resistance," *Businessweek,* April 3, 2006, p. 42.

Reporters Sans Frontières, "Watchdog RSF Condemns Harassment of Al-Jazeera TV," *BBC Monitoring International Reports,* January 28, 2005.

Tischler, Linda, "(Al Jazeera 1.0) A Decade of Discord," *Fast Company,* April 2006, p. 46.

———, "Al Jazeera's (Global) Mission: Can an English-Language News Network with Radioactive DNA Actually Be Good for Brand America? U.S. Business Better Hope So," *Fast Company,* April 2006, p. 42.

Vallely, Paul, "The New Power on the Small Screen; On a TV Near You: Al-Jazeera," *Independent* (U.K.), October 26, 2005.

Wallis, William, "It Is Not for Us to Decide Who Is the Good Guy and Who Is the Bad," *Financial Times* (London), May 18, 2005, p. 5.

Wells, Matt, "Al-Jazeera Accuses US of Bombing Its Kabul Office," *Guardian* (U.K.), November 17, 2001.

"World Service Confirms Arabic TV," *BBC News,* October 25, 2005.

Ampco-Pittsburgh Corporation

600 Grant Street, Suite 4600
Pittsburgh, Pennsylvania 15219
U.S.A.
Telephone: (412) 456-4400
Fax: (412) 456-4404
Web site: http://www.ampcopgh.com

Public Company
Incorporated: 1929
Employees: 1,234
Sales: $246.9 million (2005)
Stock Exchanges: New York
Ticker Symbol: AP
NAIC: 333911 Pump and Pumping Equipment Manufacturing

■ ■ ■

Ampco-Pittsburgh Corporation is an industrial metals concern operating in two business segments, forged and cast rolls and air and liquid processing. Ampco-Pittsburgh competes in the two business segments through four main subsidiaries, Union Electric Steel Corporation, Davy Roll Company Limited, Aerofin Corporation, Buffalo Pumps, Inc., and Buffalo Air Handling Company. Union Electric ranks as the world's largest manufacturer of forged hardened steel rolls, serving steel and aluminum manufacturers from its principal operations in Pennsylvania and Indiana. Davy Roll is a manufacturer of cast rolls with manufacturing facilities based in England. On the air and liquid processing side of Ampco-Pittsburgh's business, Aerofin Corp. produces heat exchange coils for customers in the electric utility, heating, ventilation, and air conditioning (HVAC), power generation, and industrial process industries. Buffalo Air Handling manufactures custom-designed air handling systems for commercial, institutional, and industrial building markets. Buffalo Pumps produces centrifugal pumps for the defense, refrigeration, and power generation industries. Ampco-Pittsburgh's air and liquid processing operations are located in Virginia and New York.

ORIGINS

The history of Ampco-Pittsburgh involves a series of acquisitions and divestitures orchestrated by two generations of the Berkman family. Although a publicly traded company for much of its existence, the company operated with the demeanor of a private company. Its officials avoided publicity, rarely took time to talk to analysts, and, atypically for a public company, advancement through its executive ranks flowed along familial lines, with leadership of the company passing from father to son to relatives through marriage. "Ampco-Pittsburgh," Patty Tascarella wrote in the May 1, 1995 edition of the *Pittsburgh Business Times,* "operated as privately as a public company could," and the analysts she spoke with concurred. "It's almost as if it were private," said one analyst. "I've always wanted to ask them if it wouldn't make more sense to be private," another analyst remarked.

The patriarch of the close-knit family that ran the taciturn company was Louis Berkman, an empire builder who made a rags-to-riches rise in the business world.

KEY DATES

1970: Louis Berkman creates Ampco-Pittsburgh through the merger of Screw and Bolt Corp. of America and Ampco Metal Co.
1979: Louis Berkman's son, Marshall Berkman, takes control of the company and completes $200 million worth of acquisitions during the ensuing five years.
1981: Aerofin Corp. and Buffalo Pumps, Inc. are acquired.
1984: Union Electric Steel Corp. is acquired.
1999: The Davy Roll Company is acquired.
2003: Ampco-Pittsburgh sells its plastics processing machinery business.
2004: Louis Berkman is named chairman emeritus.

Berkman, raised in Steubenville, Ohio, dropped out of school at the age of 15 to help his father. It was the mid-1920s and Berkman's education had been cut short so he could drive his father's horse-drawn wagon, a wagon filled with junk that the teenage Berkman peddled along the streets of his hometown. Berkman's humble start developed into something far more impressive during his adulthood. By the 1950s, he was in a financial position that enabled him to acquire other companies. He focused his efforts on what *Forbes,* in its October 30, 1989 issue, described as "mundane" steel companies in the Ohio River valley. Berkman, in an acquisition campaign that stretched into the 1960s, purchased numerous companies, including Parkersburg Steel, Follansbee Steel, and Ohio River Steel, but it was his purchase of Screw and Bolt Corp. of America, a "doddering" company according to *Forbes,* and Wisconsin-based Ampco Metal Co. that had a direct bearing on Ampco-Pittsburgh. In 1970, he merged the two companies to form Ampco-Pittsburgh, a company whose business interests would change frequently, as Berkman and his son, Marshall, demonstrated a decided penchant for purchasing other businesses.

As Louis Berkman began to build Ampco-Pittsburgh, he also acquired assets through other entities. Through privately owned Louis Berkman Co., he made investments in real estate, banking, and, later, cellular telephone companies. He purchased truck cab, snowplow, and lumber companies. He acquired a majority stake in Pittsburgh Screw & Bolt Co., expanded it by adding Pilgrim Drawn Steel and Wyckoff Steel to its operations, and built a communications arm to his empire by using a 30 percent stake in Rust Craft Greeting Card Co. that he acquired in 1959. Rust Craft, which became the foundation of a major printing and broadcast business, served as the training ground for the second generation of the family. When Louis Berkman sold Rust Craft in 1979, increasing revenues 500 percent during his 20 years in control, his son Marshall and his son-in-law Robert Paul, both of whom had begun their careers at Rust Craft, took over day-to-day control of Ampco-Pittsburgh.

RESTRUCTURING

Marshall Berkman became the principal executive at Ampco-Pittsburgh in 1979, exhibiting the same proclivity to acquire as his father. Unlike his father, Marshall Berkman received a complete education, earning degrees from Harvard College, Harvard Business School, and Harvard Law School. His academic background was impeccable, but when Marshall Berkman started putting his studies to practice, the streets of Steubenville appeared to offer a more effective business primer than the halls of academia. Berkman purchased a slew of companies, spending roughly $200 million on acquisitions during his first five years in charge, but the timing of the purchases spoiled any chance of the son replicating his father's success. Most of the acquisitions were completed just as an industrial recession set in, quickly hobbling Ampco-Pittsburgh. In 1982, the company recorded its first annual loss in more than two decades, as Marshall Berkman's bold attempt at expansion and diversification showed its first sign of being an imprudent move. Over the course of the next six years, the company lost $80 million as the acquisitions were written down, offering compelling evidence to Berkman that he had erred. In 1987, he began to undo much of what he had done, embarking on a divestment program as ambitious as his ill-fated acquisition program. In the sale spree that was underway for the next several years, industrial businesses that had accounted for approximately half of the company's total revenue were sold, but again Berkman's efforts suffered from bad timing. "Unfortunately," an analyst and Ampco-Pittsburgh shareholder said in an October 30, 1989 interview with *Forbes,* "they bought at the top of the cycle and sold at the bottom."

Marshall Berkman's missteps in the 1980s caused a fair bit of damage, but the accordion-like expansion and contraction of the company was not fatal. Ampco-Pittsburgh exited the decade with $250 million in sales and, after vigorous restructuring efforts, it was profitable, posting approximately $9 million in net income. Moreover, much of what constituted Ampco-Pittsburgh in the 21st century arrived during the 1980s. In 1981, the company's air and liquid processing business took shape with the acquisition of Aerofin Corporation and Buffalo Pumps, Inc. Founded in 1923, Aerofin manufactured heat exchange coils and related heat transfer equipment, which were sold to HVAC, power generation, pulp and paper, and industrial process industries. Buffalo Pumps, a manufacturer of centrifugal pumps since 1887, relied primarily on sales to the defense market, but the company also served the refrigeration, paper, and lube oil markets. In 1984, as Marshall Berkman's acquisition campaign wound down, Union Electric Steel Corporation was acquired, a company that served as a pillar of Ampco-Pittsburgh's forged and cast rolls business segment. Founded in 1923, Union Electric was regarded as a world leader in the forged steel roll market.

For a number of industry observers, Marshall Berkman's folly of the 1980s officially ended in 1993. That year, the last major transaction of his divestment program was completed when Ampco-Pittsburgh sold Buffalo Forge Company. According to the company's annual filing with the Securities and Exchange Commission (SEC), management looked at the divestiture as a turning point as well. In its March 1994 filing with the SEC, the company noted the sale "strengthened the corporation's financial position against economic uncertainties," freeing it to "concentrate on those companies that are better positioned to deal with both domestic and international business opportunities." Ampco-Pittsburgh was left with four principal businesses, Buffalo Pumps, Aerofin, Union Electric, and another forged cast rolls maker named New Castle Industries, Inc., which was based in New Castle, Pennsylvania. With these businesses, Marshall Berkman hoped to put the missteps of the 1980s behind him and make the 1990s a decade of unmitigated success. Tragically, he never had the opportunity to lead the restructured Ampco-Pittsburgh forward. The sale of Buffalo Forge Company marked the end of Berkman's divestment campaign and it represented the last significant deal he orchestrated on the company's behalf.

In September 1994, Marshall Berkman was aboard an airplane returning to Pittsburgh from Chicago, accompanied by Ampco-Pittsburgh's tax manager. On its approach to Pittsburgh International Airport, the airplane crashed, killing all 132 passengers aboard. As the Berkman family dealt with the loss, it was forced to address the leadership void created by Marshall Berkman's sudden death. Louis Berkman, in his mid-80s at the time, took over his late son's role as chairman. Robert Paul, Louis Berkman's son-in-law and Ampco-Pittsburgh's president, was appointed to the additional post of chief executive officer.

As Ampco-Pittsburgh pressed forward under the guidance of Berkman and Paul, the company was supported by three business segments. Its forged and cast rolls segment consisted primarily of Union Electric. Its air and liquid processing segment comprised Aerofin, Buffalo Air Handling, and Buffalo Pumps. The company's third business segment was its plastic processing machinery division, which included New Castle Industries and F.R. Gross Company, a Stow, Ohio-based producer of heat transfer rolls whose customers consisted primarily of manufacturers serving the plastics industry. Structured as such, the company proved to be a consistent money earner during the late 1990s. The company posted slightly more than $15 million in net income in 1997, 1998, and 1999, eclipsing the $200-million-in-sales mark by the end of the decade, when an important addition was made to the company's operations. In 1999, Union Electric acquired The Davy Roll Company, an England-based manufacturer of cast rolls that served the steel and metal industries. The same transaction included the purchase of Formet Limited, a producer of forgings for the oil and gas industry, and Turner Chilled Rolls Limited, a producer of cast rolls for use in the food industry. The three companies became part of Ampco-Pittsburgh's forged and cast rolls segment.

AMPCO-PITTSBURGH IN THE 21ST CENTURY

Ampco-Pittsburgh's financial health suffered as the company entered the 21st century. Recessive economic conditions in the industrial sector conspired against the company, causing profits to fall. After years of steadily posting around $15 million in net income, Ampco-Pittsburgh recorded a loss of $586,000 in 2001, followed by a profit of $2.5 million in 2002 and a loss of $2.1 million in 2003. Particularly hard hit was the company's plastics processing machinery business, which was hobbled by decreased demand and low levels of capital investment. The company responded to its difficulties by shedding its entire plastics processing machinery business in August 2003, a divestiture that stripped the company of less than 1 percent of its total revenue volume.

The sale of the company's plastics processing machinery business was the last transaction completed with Louis Berkman as chairman. In 2004, at age 96, Berkman was given the honorary title of chairman emeritus and Paul was named chairman, marking the end of Berkman's active control over the company. During this transition, the company began to exhibit the financial consistency that had characterized its performance during the late 1990s. After posting a $2.5 million loss in 2004, the company returned to the level of profitability it had become accustomed to, recording

$15 million in net income in 2005. In the years ahead, financial consistency was the goal, as the low-profile public company managed its assets in forged and cast rolls and air and liquid processing.

Jeffrey L. Covell

PRINCIPAL SUBSIDIARIES

Union Electric Steel Corporation; Davy Roll Company Limited; Aerofin Corporation; Buffalo Air Handling Company; Buffalo Pumps, Inc.

PRINCIPAL COMPETITORS

Cardo AB; Connell Limited Partnership; Roper Industries, Inc.

FURTHER READING

"Ampco-Pitt Realigns After USAir Crash," *American Metal Market,* September 22, 1994, p. 2.

"Ampco Sells Buffalo Forge to British Conglomerate," *Business First of Buffalo,* May 3, 1993, p. 16.

"Ampco Sells Forging Plant to Investors Led by Allen," *American Metal Market,* November 18, 1987, p. 2.

Beirne, Mike, "Ampco Seeking to Shed Wyckoff," *American Metal Market,* March 12, 1990, p. 2.

Gabriele, Michael C., "Ampco-Pittsburgh Sells Shepard Niles to Underwood," *Metalworking News,* March 7, 1988, p. 6.

Hannon, Kerry, "Education Marshall Berkman," *Forbes,* October 30, 1989, p. 72.

LaRue, Gloria, "Ampco-Pitt May Bid for Midway Airlines," *American Metal Market,* August 9, 1989, p. 2.

Lautenschlager, Scott, "Ampco-P'gh to Make Bid for Union Electric," *American Metal Market,* June 20, 1984, p. 16.

Tascarella, Patty, "Ampco Quietly Continues, Despite Losing Chief Executive," *Pittsburgh Business Times,* May 1, 1995, p. 12.

Weiss, Barabara, "Ampco-P'gh Tender Offer Set," *American Metal Market,* June 25, 1984, p. 5.

Arsenal Holdings PLC

Avenell Road
Highbury
London, N5 1 BU
United Kingdom
Telephone: (44) 20-7704-4000
Fax: (44) 20-7704-4001
Web site: http://www.arsenal.com

Private Company
Incorporated: 1893 as Woolwich Arsenal
Employees: 239
Sales: £138.4 million (2005)
NAIC: 711211 Sports Teams and Clubs

■ ■ ■

Arsenal Holdings PLC owns Arsenal Football Club, a competitor in the English Premiership and the primary source of its revenue. Arsenal Holdings' other interests are in property development, which accounts for slightly less than 25 percent of its revenue. Arsenal Football Club generates 35 percent of its revenue from broadcasting, 27 percent from gate receipts, and the balance from sponsorship deals and merchandise sales.

ORIGINS

To be a successful business enterprise, a sports team must first excel at its game. In the decades before sports teams became brands, a record of success offered virtually the only way for a sports team to survive financially. Championships and trophies attracted fans, giving the team the gate receipts to sustain itself. In the era after sports teams were regarded as brands, winning lost none of its importance, driving the marketing campaigns that helped pay for players' seven-figure salaries: the price of success in modern sports. Among the elite of the football world during both eras was Arsenal Holdings' jewel asset, Arsenal Football Club.

The catalyst for the club's formation was the arrival of Fred Beardsley and Morris Bates to the Woolwich Arsenal Armament Factory in October 1886. The two new employees arrived at the South London firm distinguished by their reputations, having both played football for Nottingham Forest, a club formed 20 years earlier. Their arrival convinced another Woolwich Arsenal employee, David Danskin, that he had the makings of a company football team. Danskin recruited 15 players for the squad, initially named "Dial Square" after one of the company's workshops, and set about the next order of business: buying a football. Each member of the newly formed team contributed toward the purchase of a football, pooling their money to give "The Gunners," as the team later would become informally known, its one indispensable piece of equipment. The modest means of the amateur club was underscored when it attempted to play its first game, a match scheduled for December 11, 1886, against the Eastern Wanderers. The site of venue, located on the Isle of Dogs, left much to be desired. The grounds-keeping debate of the day centered on whether one portion of the pitch was a ditch or an open sewer. Dial Square, evidently, was unaffected by the condition of the pitch, and began what would become a legacy of success by trouncing Eastern Wanderers 6 to 1.

Flush with victory, the team members assembled on Christmas Day to address three issues: a new team name,

KEY DATES

1886: Arsenal is formed by a group of factory workers at the Woolwich Arsenal Armament Factory.
1891: The club turns professional and joins the English Football League two years later.
1913: Arsenal relocates to Highbury.
1919: Arsenal is promoted to the First Division, beginning the longest uninterrupted stay in England's highest division.
1925: Herbert Chapman is hired as the club's manager, ushering in Arsenal's first era of dominance.
1930: Arsenal wins its first F.A. Cup, beginning a decade that would bring five First Division Championships and two F.A. Cups to the club.
1971: Arsenal wins the F.A. Cup and the First Division, a feat known as the "Double."
1986: George Graham is hired as manager and leads the team to a First Division Championship three years later, ending an 18-year drought.
1996: Arsene Wenger, Arsenal's first foreign manager, is hired.
1998: Arsenal completes its second Double, repeating the achievement four years later.
2004: Arsenal wins its 13th division title.
2006: Arsenal unveils Emirates Stadium.

a team kit (uniform), and finding a suitable pitch. The team members gathered at the Royal Oak next to the Woolwich Arsenal Station and used the site of their discussion as the inspiration for a new team name, settling on "Royal Arsenal." Fred Beardsley, who had played goalkeeper for Nottingham Forest, tackled the second issue facing the committee by writing to Nottingham Forest for help in securing a kit for the team. Nottingham Forest obliged, sending a complete set of red shirts and a football. For the third item on the agenda, a recreation area known as Plumstead Common was chosen as the club's new ground, where Royal Arsenal played its first official match in 1887, beating Erith 6 to 1.

Winning its first two games by an 11-goal margin, the group of armament employees likely was invigorated by the club's start. Victory encouraged meetings to discuss new team names, new kits, and any of a number of topics that added to the legitimacy of a team, fueling the desire to press forward as a viable enterprise. The first two games did much to perpetuate the existence of the club, but beyond the perspective of a small group of factory workers, much more was required to meet the standards of football excellence. The club became a team of distinction after navigating through several turning points in its early history. In later years, as history judged success, a football team was assessed by its achievements in two areas: its league standing and its progress in tournaments, or cups. Arsenal made its reputation by excelling in these two areas, achieving a record of success that elevated a group of 19th-century factory workers to a team of historical significance in the 21st century.

It was a half-century before Arsenal asserted itself as a dominant club, but the intervening years marked its progress toward dominance. The club won its first trophies in 1890, a year before it turned professional, capturing the Kent Senior Cup, the Kent Junior Cup, and, most significant, the London Charity Cup, a match it played in front of 10,000 people. Despite being the first "silverware" won by the club, the trophies paled in importance to the titles that would matter most as the 20th century progressed. Excellence was achieved by winning the First Division or winning the F.A. Cup, the most prestigious of English tournaments. On rare occasions, a club won both the division title and the F.A. Cup, which ran concurrent with the regular season in a single elimination format. The mediocre, "mid-table," teams usually won nothing. Those teams suffering from something more profound than mediocrity endured the ignobility and financial consequences of relegation, a process by which teams at the bottom of season-end standings were dropped to the league below. Every club in England, despite the rallying cry of its fans to "stay up!," experienced the desperation of relegation, but no club felt the sting of demotion less than Arsenal. The club, as the 20th century progressed, established the record for the longest uninterrupted tenure in the "top flight," but initially Arsenal struggled to keep its place in the First Division.

Before the club could subject itself to the process of promotion and relegation it had to join the English Football League in the first place, something it did in 1893. Competing as Woolwich Arsenal, the club joined the Second Division that year, the same year it formed a limited liability company in which 862 people purchased 1,552 shares at £1.00 per share. The club won promotion to the First Division in 1904, but never finished higher than sixth place before being relegated in 1913. Although the year marked the club's return to the Second Division, it also ushered in a new era, marking one of the crucial turning points in the history of the club. Woolwich Arsenal was having difficulty attracting spectators, a problem the club's chairman, Sir Henry Norris, attributed to its location in South London. After trying to merge the club with another London club, Fulham, and failing, a new home was found near a theological college in Highbury, North London. Tottenham Hotspur, located four miles away from the Highbury site, objected to the move, but Sir Henry Norris prevailed and moved his club into the residential area, sowing the first seeds of enmity between the two clubs. Arsenal dropped "Woolwich" from its name in 1914, settling on a permanent name as it settled into its permanent home, and made the leap into the First Division five years later, where it would stay for the remainder of the 20th century and into the next.

Rivalry between clubs was a natural occurrence in sports, but in the world of football the animosity took on an especially fierce quality. The severity of the antipathy drew its intensity, in part, from the identification of a specific target. The supporters of one football club regarded every other football club as an enemy, but to varying degrees. Nearly every club in the world had one enemy in particular, a rivalry that elicited the greatest passion between two teams and their supporters and became a mutual disdain handed down from one generation to the next. Arsenal, already viewed with disregard by Tottenham Hotspur supporters because it had encroached upon their home turf, made sure the ill feelings turned into deep-seated wrath by the way it gained promotion in 1919. After suspending play during World War I, the English Football Association (the F.A.) expanded the First Division from 20 to 22 clubs, which under normal circumstances would have resulted in the First Division's bottom clubs retaining their top-flight status and the top two Second Division clubs earning promotion. Instead, Tottenham Hotspur, which had placed 20th in the First Division in 1915, was dropped to the Second Division to make room for the top two Second Division teams and the Second Division's fifth-place team, Arsenal, a highly controversial selection made amid rumors of significant amounts of money changing hands. From that point forward, the feud between Arsenal and its North London neighbor, Tottenham Hotspur, became apoplectic.

A DOMINANT TEAM EMERGES

Arsenal's record-setting stay in England's highest division began with mediocrity, but soon after a new manager joined the club, it began to shine for the first time. Herbert Chapman, hired as the club's manager in 1925, brought a commitment to excellence to Arsenal, establishing the infrastructure to support an elite English club. Perhaps most important, he knew how to win, having turned Huddersfield Town into the dominant team of the late 1920s. Chapman led the effort to build a new stadium, a facility made with marble halls, undersoil heating, and outfitted with the best medical facilities in the country. He developed a youth program to train promising athletes and, although the F.A. rejected both proposals, he suggested putting numbers on players' shirts and using floodlights. His greatest achievement, aside from leading a winning side, was lobbying to change the name of the nearby underground train station from "Gillespie Road," to "Arsenal," a massive undertaking that required tickets, maps, and signage to be changed, providing his new club with a promotional coup. On the pitch, Arsenal excelled, becoming the dominant team of the 1930s. The club won its first major trophy, the F.A. Cup, in 1930 by beating Chapman's former team Huddersfield Town and added a second F.A. Cup in 1936. In the First Division, the club won its first title in 1931, establishing a point record (points are awarded for wins and draws) that would not be eclipsed for 30 years. Arsenal went on to claim four more division championships during the decade, including three in a row between 1933 and 1935, securing its fifth title in 1938.

The 1930s gave Arsenal its first taste of dominance, setting high expectations for the future. Following World War II, as football moved into the modern era, replicating the 1930s proved difficult. After winning the First Division title in 1948 and again in 1953, the club suffered an 18-year drought, failing to add another division title or win a major trophy until the beginning of the 1970s. To make matters worse, Tottenham Hotspur enjoyed its glory years while Arsenal struggled, becoming the first team in the country to win the F.A. Cup and the First Division in the same year, a feat known as the "Double." After years without fanfare, Arsenal stormed into the limelight, winning its first European trophy in 1970, the Inter Cities Fairs Cup, the predecessor to the UEFA Cup, and completing the Double in 1971. Arsenal supporters basked in the victory, with an estimated 250,000 fans lining the streets from Highbury to Islington Town Hall to watch the club display the two trophies from an open-top bus.

After the most successful season in the club's history, another long gap between division titles awaited Arsenal supporters. An F.A. Cup victory in 1979, the club's fifth, offered the only celebratory occasion until a member of the famed 1971 squad was named manager. George Graham, "Man-of-the-Match" in the 1971 F.A. Cup final, was hired in 1986, beginning an eight-year tenure in which Arsenal won six major trophies, including the club's ninth First Division Championship in 1989, ending another 18-year drought. During Graham's stewardship, the First Division was re-branded as the Premiership, a change in nomenclature that signaled the dawn of high-stakes football. The financial rewards to be won both on the pitch and on the business front grew enormously during the 1990s, becoming a new benchmark of success for the world's elite football organizations. Transfer fees, the amount paid for one club to purchase another club's player, salaries, and television revenues increased exponentially during the decade, driving the development of the sport into the realm of big business. Arsenal, after Graham's departure midway through the 1995 season and brief stints by two other managers, turned to Arsene Wenger to lead the club during the new era.

BEGINNING OF THE ARSENE WENGER ERA

Under Wenger's guidance, Arsenal established itself as an elite member of the Premiership. The club asserted itself as a domestic powerhouse during the late 1990s and the first years of the 21st century, completing the Double twice, in 1998 and in 2002. Its one glaring failure was a lack of distinction on the European stage, particularly the club's inability to win the most prized club trophy, the UEFA Champions League (formerly the European Cup). At home, however, Arsenal was a force to be reckoned with, establishing an unbeaten league record of 49 matches in 2005, a year that saw the club win its 10th F.A. Cup one year after capturing its 13th division title. As the club prepared to add to its impressive legacy of success, it also was preparing to move into a new home. Emirates Stadium, scheduled to be completed by August 2006, promised to provide a substantial boost to the club's revenue-generating capabilities. The £390 million, 60,000-seat stadium was one-third larger than Highbury, the site of the club's home games since 1913. Once the club moved into Emirates Stadium, its gate receipts, accounting for slightly more than 25 percent of Arsenal Holdings' total revenue, was set to increase significantly, giving The Gunners an ideal venue to showcase its winning pedigree.

Jeffrey L. Covell

PRINCIPAL SUBSIDIARIES

Arsenal Broadband Limited.

PRINCIPAL COMPETITORS

Tottenham Hotspur PLC; Chelsea Village; Manchester United Limited.

FURTHER READING

"Arsenal Football Club," *Marketing,* May 3, 2001, p. 10.

"Arsenal Plans Kick Off," *Estates Gazette,* February 28, 2004, p. 30.

Bradley, Mark, "Football: Arsenal Press on with New Stadium," *Independent,* May 1, 2003, p. 30.

———, "Football: Arsenal's Debts Spiral to £40M," *Independent,* May 1, 2003, p. 30.

Irwin, Mark, "Arsene Share Boost," *Sun,* July 16, 2001, p. 45.

"Wenger Will Have Money to Spend," *Journal* (Newcastle), February 19, 2005, p. 96.

Astec Industries, Inc.

1725 Shepherd Road
Chattanooga, Tennessee 37421
U.S.A.
Telephone: (423) 899-5898
Toll Free: (888) 451-5551
Fax: (423) 899-4456
Web site: http://www.astecindustries.com

Public Company
Incorporated: 1972 as Astec Industries, Inc.
Employees: 2,946
Sales: $616.07 million (2005)
Stock Exchanges: NASDAQ
Ticker Symbol: ASTE
NAIC: 333120 Construction Machinery Manufacturing; 333131 Mining Machinery and Equipment Manufacturing

■ ■ ■

Astec Industries, Inc. is a manufacturer of road building equipment. Its 13 manufacturing subsidiaries produce machinery to handle each step of the process, from crushing stone to applying road surfaces ("rock to road"). In addition, some units make construction and industrial equipment unrelated to roads. The company is the world's largest manufacturer of asphalt plants.

Astec's principal subsidiaries are organized into the Asphalt Group (Astec, Inc., Heatec, Inc., and CEI Enterprises, Inc.); the Aggregate and Mining Group (Telsmith, Inc., Kolberg-Pioneer, Inc., Astec Mobile Screens, Inc., Johnson Crushers International, Inc., Breaker Technology Ltd./Breaker Technology Inc., and Osborn Engineered Products, SA); the Mobile Asphalt Paving Group (Roadtec, Inc. and Carolson Paving Products, Inc.); and the Underground Group (Astec Underground, Inc. and American Augers, Inc.).

TENNESSEE ROOTS

Astec Industries, Inc. was incorporated in Tennessee on August 9, 1972. Its first president was J. Don Brock. Brock had earned a Ph.D. in mechanical engineering at the Georgia Institute of Technology in 1965, whereupon he moved back to help out at the Industrial Boiler Co. owned by his father.

Brock went on to head the asphalt division of CMI Corporation (later part of Terex Corporation) for three years after CMI bought Industrial Boiler. When CMI announced plans to relocate its asphalt plant business to its Oklahoma City home, Brock formed Astec, whose name is a contraction of "asphalt technology."

According to the *Chattanooga Times and Free Press*, Brock was joined in the Astec venture by three former schoolmates from East Ridge, Tennessee's Central High. Norm Smith was president of Astec Inc., the largest subsidiary, where one of his executives would be company cofounder Gail Mize. Albert E. Guth, later CEO of Astec Financial Services Inc., and Mike Uchytil, a transplant from Iowa, were also cofounders.

The five borrowed $400,000 to acquire a 24,000-square-foot building. Since the founders had a reputation in the industry, there was no shortage of work, Brock told the *Chattanooga Times and Free Press.* Sales

COMPANY PERSPECTIVES

Astec Industries, Inc. builds the equipment that moves America and the world from "Rock to Road and Beyond." Our roads are America's arteries. They carry our commerce, take us to work each day, transport us back to places in our memories and forward into the future. These thoroughfares, more than 90% of which are paved with asphalt, make up a 2.3 million-mile network linking 290 million people who always seem to be on the move.

were $5 million in the company's first year in business, producing a slender profit of $12,000. Based in Chattanooga, the company produced asphalt mixing and paving equipment.

Business was flat for a few years, but took off in the late 1970s. Annual sales reached $30 million by the early 1980s, according to *Crain's Chicago Business,* and were growing at a double-digit rate. The overall industry was entering several years of difficulty, however, which would thin out weaker competitors.

PUBLIC IN 1986

Astec Industries went public in June 1986 in a $12 million initial public offering. A portion of the proceeds was earmarked for reducing short term debt. Sales were more than $60 million for the year.

In January 1987 Astec took over a venerable rival, Barber-Greene Co. of Aurora, Illinois. Barber-Greene had been formed in 1917 but had lost leadership of the market for massive asphalt mixing plants (which sold for about $1 million each). While it had kept Astec from dominating the asphalt paver business (pavers were $100,000 items), Barber-Greene was financially weakened, burdened with a $32 million debt, and plants running at half capacity; employment was one-fourth its one-time peak of 2,500.

The purchase of Barber-Greene brought with it another venerable company, Telsmith, Inc., which had been formed in 1906. Telsmith was based in Mequon, Wisconsin, and produced aggregate processing equipment. Astec made an offer to buy another rival, Kansas City asphalt plant manufacturer Standard Havens Inc., in 1989, but canceled the offer, judging the price too high.

Unfortunately, Barber-Greene continued to lose money after Astec bought it. Most of Barber-Greene was sold off in April 1991, after overcoming initial reluctance from antitrust regulators. According to the *Legal Times,* Astec's plans to keep making asphalt pavers through its Roadtec division was key to the approval. After the deal, Astec was the fourth largest maker of large asphalt pavers, following Blaw-Knox Construction Equipment Co., Cedarapids Inc., and Caterpillar Paving Products Inc.

Barber-Greene's new owner, Caterpillar Inc., had entered the paver equipment manufacturing business three years earlier by acquiring Raygo Inc. from CMI Corporation (it had previously marketed CMI-made pavers under the Caterpillar brand). Caterpillar paid $25 million in cash for Barber-Greene, which then had revenues of about $40 million a year.

Astec Industries had posted sales of $135 million in 1990; it had a net loss of $13 million. Part of the damage was due to a $7 million judgment against Barber-Greene, which had been sued by CMI for patent infringement. However, Astec ultimately prevailed and 1994 income ($23 million on sales of $214 million) would include $15 million from this litigation.

In 1994 Astec attempted to acquire Georgia's Crown Andersen Inc., a manufacturer of pollution control products, but the two parties were unable to work out a price. Sales were $242.6 million in 1995. However, net income was hammered by losses from a German subsidiary.

Astec formed its own finance company in June 1996. Officials told the *Chattanooga Times and Free Press* that the company already had a long history of helping customers find equipment loans at other institutions.

SHOPPING SPREE

Business thrived in the late 1990s, helped by federal legislation (the Transportation Equity Act) to increase highway spending. Astec achieved record revenues of $364 million in 1998. Astec closed out the 1990s with a buying spree. Johnson Crushers was acquired in 1998. It had about 200 employees at two Oregon plants.

In August 1999, Astec bought Superior Industries of Morris Inc. for $17 million. Based in Minnesota, Superior built state-of-the-art conveyors for handling aggregates and had sales of about $25 million a year. It was sold off to management within a few years, however. Teledyne Specialty Equipment's construction and mining business, dubbed Breaker Technology, was acquired for $18.5 million soon after the Superior buy. It had sales of $30 million and operations in the United States and Canada. The former Allegheny Teledyne unit had been in business since the 1950s.

Astec made one more buy in 1999, picking up

KEY DATES

1906: Telsmith, Inc. is formed.
1972: Astec Industries is incorporated in Tennessee; first year sales are $5 million.
1986: Astec Industries goes public.
1987: Rival Barber-Greene Co., as well as Telsmith, are acquired.
1991: Most of Barber-Greene Co. is sold to Caterpillar Inc.
1998: Johnson Crushers is acquired.
1999: Superior Industries, Breaker Technology, and American Augers are acquired.
2003: Case New Holland trencher business is acquired.
2005: Astec eliminates its debt after 20 years.

American Augers Inc. for $14 million plus $6 million in assumed debt. The Salem, Ohio company made drills and boring equipment used primarily by utilities for underground construction. It had annual sales of $36 million. Astec had considered up to 40 potential acquisition candidates, Dr. Brock told the *Chattanooga Times and Free Press.* Astec typically retained existing management at acquired companies.

The company was riding high as it approached the turn of the millennium. Less than 10 percent of U.S. roads were paved with concrete; most were covered with blacktop, Astec's specialty. Astec had grown to 13 subsidiaries which were each typically leaders in their respective fields. Revenues continued to reach new heights, hitting $449.6 million in 1999. Net income rose 30 percent to $31.7 million, also a record.

PEAKS AND TRENCHES IN 2000 AND BEYOND

Employment hit a new high of 3,400 workers in 2000. However, the company was entering a period of global recession exacerbated by high oil prices and the effects of the terrorist attacks on September 11, 2001. In the cost-cutting that followed, the workforce was cut back by a fifth and Astec Financial Services was closed. In the midst of the downturn, Astec was supplying one of the country's biggest public works projects, the addition of a fifth runway at Hartsfield International Airport in Atlanta.

Some mergers and acquisitions activity, intent on extending Astec's "rock to road" reach, proved challenging to execute in the short term. It acquired Case New Holland's tracked trencher business for $12 million, and bought a Loudon, Tennessee plant from John Deere to consolidate its trencher lines. However, Astec was unable to sell its own Grapevine, Texas trencher plant immediately as planned. Astec Industries posted a $29 million loss for 2003.

A new $287 billion federal highway act signed into law in 2005 funded highway construction for six years and promised work for the company. Brock told the *Wall Street Transcript* that state and local governments accounted for most road construction and were likely to respond to the improving general economy, increasing their spending as well.

By this time, Astec was the leader in the world asphalt plant industry with an estimated 55 percent or better market share. It was also the largest manufacturer of crushing equipment in the United States (number two in the world), according to Brock. It also boasted the strongest balance sheet in the business, becoming debt free after 20 years by the end of 2005. Sales for the year were up 20 percent to $616 million for the year.

While federal spending emboldened customers to replace their roadmaking equipment, Astec was upgrading a few of its own facilities as well. Astec had to contend with rising prices for both oil and steel; however, renewed interest in energy exploration was increasing demand for its trenchers and drilling equipment. Since asphalt was a petroleum byproduct, increased oil costs made road building more expensive, leading some customers to defer purchases of new equipment, noted the *Investor's Business Daily.*

Astec had a reputation for producing the "luxury sedans" of roadmaking equipment. Its gear was innovative and efficient. The company was also responsive to environmental concerns and had developed economical processes for recycling asphalt onsite, a practice common in Europe but slow to catch on in the United States.

Jeffrey L. Covell

PRINCIPAL SUBSIDIARIES

American Augers, Inc.; Astec, Inc.; Astec Insurance Company; Astec Underground, Inc. (f/k/a Trencor, Inc.); Astec Mobile Screens, Inc. (f/k/a Production Engineered Products, Inc.); Breaker Technology, Inc.; Breaker Technology Ltd. (Canada); Buckeye Underground, Inc.; Carlson Paving Products, Inc.; CEI Enterprises, Inc.; Heatec, Inc.; Johnson Crushers International, Inc.; Osborn Engineered Products SA (Pty) Ltd. (South Africa); Kolberg-Pioneer, Inc.; Roadtec, Inc.; Telsmith, Inc.

PRINCIPAL OPERATING UNITS

Asphalt Group; Aggregate and Mining Group; Mobile Asphalt Paving Group; Underground Group.

PRINCIPAL COMPETITORS

Blaw-Knox Diamond Construction Equipment Corporation; Caterpillar, Inc.; Terex Corporation.

FURTHER READING

Beach, James, "Chattanooga, Tenn.-Based Astec Industries Forms Finance Company," *Chattanooga Times and Free Press,* June 6, 1999.

———, "Chattanooga, Tenn. Firm Announces Purchase of Salem, Ohio, Drill Maker," *Chattanooga Times and Free Press,* September 22, 1999.

———, "Chattanooga, Tenn., Road-Builder Astec to Acquire Minnesota Manufacturer," *Chattanooga Times and Free Press,* August 7, 1999.

———, "Tennessee-Based Astec Buys Teledyne Construction and Mining Unit," *Chattanooga Times and Free Press,* August 17, 1999.

———, "Tennessee's Astec Becomes Supplier of Choice for Nation's Road Builders," *Chattanooga Times and Free Press,* September 5, 1999.

"Breaking Through the Barriers," *Recycling Today,* June 1, 2005, p. 26.

"Chattanooga, Tenn.-Based Heavy-Equipment Maker Finds Smooth Road," *Chattanooga Times and Free Press,* February 23, 2000.

"Company Interview: J. Don Brock—Astec Industries, Inc.," *Wall Street Transcript,* June 21, 2004.

Elliott, Alan R., "Business Is Up at Equipment Maker, Ya Dig?" *Investor's Business Daily,* February 1, 2006, p. A7.

Ezell, Hank, "Proposed Crown Anderson Merger Called Off; Stock Falls," *Atlanta Journal and Constitution,* June 11, 1994, p. C1.

Gary, Bob, Jr., "Chattanooga, Tenn.-Based Road Equipment Maker Plans to Expand Operations," *Knight Ridder/Tribune Business News,* October 25, 2005.

———, "Chattanooga, Tenn., Businesses See More Job-Seekers Nowadays," *Chattanooga Times and Free Press,* May 5, 2001.

———, "Federal Law Benefits Chattanooga, Tenn.-Based Roadmaking Equipment Manufacturer," *Chattanooga Times and Free Press,* August 11, 2005.

———, "Five Chattanooga, Tenn., Friends Run Chattanooga, Tenn., Construction Firm," *Chattanooga Times and Free Press,* October 20, 2002.

———, "Tennessee-Based Roadbuilding-Equipment Maker to Post Loss of Over $29 Million," *Chattanooga Times and Free Press,* February 26, 2004.

———, "Two Executives to Depart Chattanooga, Tenn.-Based Road Materials Firm," *Chattanooga Times and Free Press,* December 11, 2002.

Klass, Michelle E., "Caterpillar Paving Products Inc./Barber-Greene Co.," *Legal Times,* April 29, 1991, p. 11.

Murphy, H. Lee, "Barber-Greene Buy Gives Cat Weight in Asphalt Paving Biz; New Parent Likely to Restore Black Ink to DeKalb Firm," *Crain's Chicago Business,* January 21, 1991, p. 36.

———, "Burdened by Debt, Barber-Greene Sells," *Crain's Chicago Business,* January 12, 1987, p. 17.

"Oregon-Based Rock-Crushing Equipment Maker Johnson Crushers Buys Factory," *Register Guard,* June 8, 1999.

ATI Technologies Inc.

1 Commerce Valley Drive East
Markham, Ontario L3T 7X6
Canada
Telephone: (905) 882-2600
Fax: (905) 882-2620
Web site: http://www.ati.com

Public Company
Incorporated: 1985 as Array Technology Inc.
Employees: 2,700
Sales: $2.22 billion (2005)
Stock Exchanges: NASDAQ Toronto
Ticker Symbol: ATYT; ATY
NAIC: 334112 Computer Storage Device Manufacturing

■ ■ ■

Based near Toronto, Canada, ATI Technologies, Inc. is one of the world's largest makers of computer graphic chips and boards. The company divides its business into two units: PC Business and Consumer Business. Serving the PC market with graphics processors has been ATI's focus since the start. The Radeon line of processors are used in desktop computers and workstations, while the Mobility Radeon line offers integrated graphics for notebooks. ATI's Imageon line of graphics processors serves the consumer market, which includes cell phones, set-top boxes for television, and the Nintendo GameCube video game console. ATI maintains research and development facilities in Canada and the United States, manufacturing is done in Taiwan as well as Canada, and sales offices are located throughout the Americas, Europe, and Asia. ATI is a public company listed on the Toronto Stock Exchange and the NASDAQ.

FOUNDER IMMIGRATES TO CANADA

The man most responsible for ATI's rise to prominence is cofounder and longtime CEO Kwok Yuan Ho. He was born in China in 1950, the son of a teacher, and grew up in a family where money was tight. Nevertheless, he was able to attend the National Cheng Kung University in Taiwan, where in 1974 he received a degree in electrical engineering. For the next decade he worked in Hong Kong for electronics companies, including National Semiconductor Corp., Philips Electronics, and Control Data Systems. Ho was involved in a wide range of areas—engineering, quality assurance, manufacturing, purchasing, and general management—providing him with a thorough knowledge of the industry. In October 1983, while on vacation, he paid a visit to Canada and fell in love with Toronto as well as his future wife. A year later he applied for immigrant status, but despite his experience in the technology sector he had a difficult time finding work. As a result, he joined forces with two other recent Hong Kong immigrants, Lee Lau and Benny Lau. They pooled their resources, raised CAD 300,000 in a bank loan, and in August 1985 launched their own company to produce graphics cards, and the graphics chips that powered them, for personal computers. At the time, personal computers used monochrome monitors, but Ho recognized early on that color would soon be coming and that computer graphics would stimulate the sale of PCs to the general public. Ho and his partners initially called the company Array Technology Inc.,

COMPANY PERSPECTIVES

From desktops to laptops, workstations to handheld devices, video game consoles to integrated solutions, ATI has established itself as a world leader in the design and manufacture of innovative 3D graphics solutions.

which soon became Array Technologies Inc. Before the year was out, however, they settled on an abbreviation, ATI Technologies Inc. Ho served as chief executive officer, while Lee Lau would become vice-president of strategic planning and Benny Lau vice-president of product planning.

In October 1985, Ho and his partners used application specific integrated circuit (ASIC) technology to develop a graphic controller, and unveiled the company's first graphics board product. In the first year of operation the company sold about CAD 10 million of these cards. ATI's first major success came in July 1987 with the release of the EGA WONDER and VGA WONDER cards, which were compatible with every computer monitor, graphics interface, and software on the market at the time. The company was soon doing about CAD 60 million in annual sales and billing itself as the largest graphics-board maker in the world. To keep up with its growth, ATI opened a new 35,000-square-foot facility in September 1988. Befitting its status as a major player in the graphics industry, ATI was one of nine video display adapter manufacturers who in 1989 founded the Video Electronics Standards Association (VESA), an international body that initially established a standard for 800x600 resolution video displays and went on to establish many other standards related to computer monitors and graphics.

ATI's next major product, released in May 1991, was the ATI Mach8. Available as a chip or a board, it was able to process graphics independent of the computer's CPU (central processing unit). The new product pushed sales to the CAD 100 million level and employment approached 300. More products followed in 1992, including the Mach32, which combined an integrated graphics controller and graphics accelerator in a single chip; and graphics cards for the VESA Local Bus (VLB) and peripheral component interconnect (PCI) slots of a personal computer, which had more of a direct connection to the CPU and therefore sent and received information faster. Also of note in 1992, ATI established a subsidiary in Munich Germany, ATI GmbH.

DIFFICULTIES AFTER GOING PUBLIC

With annual sales in the CAD 230 million range, ATI became a public company in November 1993 and its stock was listed on the Toronto Stock Exchange. But the company soon stumbled. When the fiscal year ended August 31, 1994, the company posted its first loss, CAD 2.7 million on sales of CAD 232.3 million. ATI's stock, which had traded around CAD 20, now slipped below CAD 5. To make matters worse, the company had not kept up with changes in chip design, which was now moving from 32-bit to 64-bit technology, allowing the processing of even greater amounts of information and resulting in better and faster graphics, including motion video. It was not until August 1994 that ATI introduced its Mach64 chip along with new graphics boards. To better keep pace with changes in the industry, ATI in 1995 established a 3-D engineering group, which would pay dividends throughout the decade.

ATI returned to profitability in 1995, when it also unveiled an Apple Macintosh-compatible graphics board, the first company in the industry able to serve both PC and Mac platforms. Later in 1995 ATI forged an agreement with United Microelectronics and other partners to build a semiconductor plant in Taiwan.

Innovations continued in 1996. ATI offered the graphics industry's first 3D chip for desktop computers, and later in the year unveiled a 3D chip for the notebook market. In addition, ATI became the first company to release a chip that could display computer graphics on a television, and also developed a video capture card, combining a graphics card with a TV tuner card to permit users to save analog TV signals. In another first, ATI now offered Macintosh PCI-based boards, something that only Apple had produced previously. Also of note, ATI established a European distribution headquarters in Ireland in 1996.

The efforts of the 3-D engineering group resulted in the 1997 release of the Rage Pro line of graphics accelerators. The 3D Rage II + DVD chip was the first graphic accelerator to offer motion compensation DVD software, and ATI became the first to offer hardware support for DVD acceleration and display. Moreover, ATI became the first graphics company that fully supported the Accelerated Graphics Port (AGP 2x), a high-speed channel connecting a graphics card to a computer's motherboard to accelerate 3D graphics. As a result of these advances, the company's graphic cards were now standard components in the top ten selling personal computers in the world. In 1997, ATI generated sales of more than CAD 600 million and recorded a net profit of CAD 47.7 million, but 1998 would be even better. Sales almost doubled to CAD 1.15 billion, while net

KEY DATES

1985: Company is founded.
1993: Company goes public and is listed on the Toronto Stock Exchange.
1999: ATI becomes largest chip maker in world.
2000: ATI is listed on the NASDAQ.
2004: Founder retires.

income increased almost fourfold to CAD 168.4 million, as ATI became the top graphics supplier in the world, according to International Data Corporation. ATI released a number of new products in 1998, including the All-in-Wonder Pro, an all-in-one television, video, and graphics upgrade card that could be installed in any Pentium computer with an open PCI slot. But to make sure it maintained its engineering edge ATI acquired the graphics design assets of Tseng Labs, Inc., picking up a 40-person engineering team. Then, in November 1998, it acquired Chromatic Research, Inc., which produced multimedia chips for use in low-end computers, set-top boxes, and other consumer electronics devices. Ho was also recognized in 1998, when he was named Canada's Entrepreneur of the Year.

ATI enjoyed another outstanding year in 1999. Now listed on the NASDAQ in addition to the Toronto Stock Exchange, the company began reporting its results in U.S. dollars. For the year, sales increased by 67 percent over 1998, totaling more than $1.2 billion. Net income improved by 50 percent to nearly $160 million. ATI would not be able to maintain this pace, however. Competition was stiff in the graphics industry, as chip makers spent a great deal of money developing ever more powerful chips. Moreover, Intel and other semiconductor makers were building in graphic capabilities, taking away sales from the low-end of the market. The end result was low prices and thin margins, and an end to the days of geometric increases in sales and profits. In 2000 ATI improved sales to $1.3 billion. ATI also faced increasing pressure from rival Nvidia Corp., now the fastest growing graphics chipmaker in the world. Investors, in typical what-have-you-done-for-me-lately fashion, punished ATI's stock, which lost about half its value.

DECLINING MARKET SHARE

While 2000 was clearly a challenging year, ATI did enjoy some advances. It acquired ArtX, Inc., a major developer of high-performance graphics for computers and appliances. The deal brought with it CEO Dave Orton, who would become ATI's president and chief operating officer. ATI also unveiled its Radeon graphics processor, which gave it entry into the high-end gaming and 3D workstation markets. But 2001 would see ATI surpassed in market share by Nvidia, which proved more nimble at launching new products and winning business from PC manufacturers and game console makers. In addition, Intel chopped away at ATI's share of the graphics market. By the third quarter of 2001, ATI's marketshare was 17 percent, a far cry from the 32 percent share it enjoyed in the halcyon days of 1999, while Nvidia now commanded 31 percent of the market and Intel 26 percent. At the end of 2001, ATI reported a drop in income to $1.04 billion and a net loss of $54.2 million. In a bid to rebound, ATI brought in new executives, and rather than make the add-in boards for its chips, it now licensed its technology to Taiwan board suppliers and returned the focus to chip design. In addition to increasing the budget, ATI established two chip-development teams, whose efforts were staggered to shorten the gap between products. The second team was, in essence, the ArtX R&D group. As a result, a process that once took 14 months now took about nine months.

The balance sheet continued to suffer in 2002, when ATI posted revenues of $1.02 billion and lost another $47.5 million, but its commitment to chips continued and began to bear fruit. In June 2002 the company acquired NxtWave Communications Inc. to expand its set-top chip business. A month later ATI released its Radeon 9700 Pro, the first major product to come from the ArtX design group. The new chip was twice as fast as any other graphic chip on the market, unseating Nvidia, and now became the gold standard for video game consoles. The technology was too costly, however, for most PC buyers, who opted for computers that relied on cheaper chips that integrated graphics with memory control and other functions.

ATI enjoyed greater success in 2003, bouyed by contracts with Microsoft's Xbox and Nintendo GameCubes video game consoles. For the year, ATI increased revenues to nearly $1.4 billion and returned to profitability, recording net income of $35.2 million. But ATI's comeback story was marred by accusations by the Ontario Securities Commission (OSC) that seven people connected to the company engaged in insider stock trading, including Ho and his wife along with two other ATI executives and their spouses. The charges stemmed from sales of ATI stock in early 2000, at a time when sales were beginning to sag and the company was on the verge of issuing an earnings warning to investors. On the day of that warning, ATI stock lost 42 percent of its value. Ho was under a great deal of pressure to step down, and he even had to use a back door to enter the Toronto hotel for the company's annual shareholder meeting in order to dodge photographers and reporters. But he refused to relinquish his post, expressing confidence that his conduct had been proper and would be judged so by the OSC. He would turn over the CEO role to Orton in June 2004, part of a succession plan that was already in place, but he would retain the chairmanship.

The insider trading case cast a shadow over ATI for years. Finally, in April 2005 a former ATI investor-relations director, Jo-Anne Chang, and her husband agreed to pay a CAD 1.5 million fine and accept a 20-year ban on trading in securities, and a ten-year prohibition on serving as a director or officer at a public company. Several months later, in October 2005, the OSC dismissed the charges against Ho and his wife. With the matter finally behind him, Ho now resigned as ATI's chairman and retired, something he said he had been planning to do since 1999. "I wanted to retire by the time I was 50. I failed," Ho told *Canadian Business.* "In the last 20 years I owe my family too much. I spent 99% of my time on ATI, ATI and ATI, and the other 1% on my kids and life. Right now, I should spend some time with my family, take care of them, but also take care of a lot of other interests."

Ho left ATI as it continued to battle Nvidia for supremacy in the graphics industry. In 2004 ATI continued to surge, as sales approached $2 billion and net income totaled $204.8 million. Nvidia staged a comback in 2005 by launching a popular dual graphics card, while ATI had nothing comparable to offer for several months. Although sales increased to more than $2.2 billion in 2005, net income plummeted to $16.9 million. ATI enjoyed strong business the first quarter of 2006, but the future would remain competitive and uncertain. Not only would it have to continue to slug it out with Nvidia at the high-end of computer-graphics chips, they both faced increasing competition from giant Intel, which was gaining market share by making performance improvements to its mainstream graphics chips.

Ed Dinger

PRINCIPAL SUBSIDIARIES

ATI Technologies (Europe) GmbH; ATI Research, Inc.; ATI Technologies Systems Corp.; ATI Research Silicon Valley Inc.; ATI Technologies Distribution Inc.

PRINCIPAL COMPETITORS

Creative Technology Ltd.; Intel Corporation; Nvidia Corporation.

FURTHER READING

Alpert, Bill, "Tech Trade: ATI's Moment of Glory," *Barron's,* August 18, 2003, p. T1.

"ATI Technology Corporation," *Canadian Shareholder,* May/June 1998, p. 19.

Berman, David, "Mr. Chips You Make Good Small Talk," *Canadian Business,* December 24, 1998 - January 8, 1999, p. 94.

Gray, John, "ATI Ho-Down," *Canadian Business,* February 17, 2003, p. 12.

Heinzl, Mark, "Graphics-Chip Pioneer Tries for Its Old Glory," *Wall Street Journal,* November 15, 2001, p. B6.

Holloway, Andy, "K.Y. Ho," *Canadian Business,* December 26, 2005 – January 15, 2005, p. 86.

Markoff, John, "For Chip Rivals, Slugfest Worthy of Video Game," *New York Times,* April 14, 2004, p. C1.

Roberts, Bill, "A Real Horse Race," *Electronic Business,* September 2002, p. 30.

Slofstra, Martin, "In Conversation (Interview with ATI Technologies Inc. Pres. K.Y. Ho)," *Computing Canada,* April 11, 1991, p. 11.

Wahl, Andrew, "Mortal Combat," *Canadian Business,* October 28, 2002, p. 99.

audible.com®

Audible Inc.

65 Willowbrook Boulevard
Wayne, New Jersey 07470
U.S.A.
Telephone: (973) 837-2845
Toll Free: (888) 283-5051
Fax: (973) 890-2442
Web site: http://www.audible.com

Public Company
Incorporated: 1995
Employees: 193
Sales: $62.97 million (2005)
Stock Exchanges: NASDAQ
Ticker Symbol: ADBL
NAIC: 511199 All Other Publishers; 512290 Other Sound Recording Industries; 514199 All Other Information Services

■ ■ ■

Audible Inc. is the leading provider of spoken audio in digital format. The company has worked out licensing deals with more than 225 content partners, allowing it to avoid the copyright complications that ensnared the music industry's relationship with the Web. Audible offers spoken versions of periodicals such as the *Wall Street Journal* in addition to a range of books and some original content produced for Audible.com. After nearly ten years weathering the hardware and financial issues that affected much of the tech world, the company finally achieved its first profit in 2004. Although it could not maintain profitability the next year, it did sustain the interest of investors.

ORIGINS

Donald Katz launched Audible Inc. in 1995 in Wayne, New Jersey. He was joined by Tim Mott, cofounder of Electronic Arts and Macromedia. Mott, who provided more than $400,000 in seed capital, would serve as chairman, while Katz was CEO. Other investors included a handful of venture capital firms (Kleiner Perkins Caufield & Byers among them) and the Thomson Corporation, who provided another $18 million within a couple of years.

Katz, a resident of New Jersey, had been a successful journalist for 20 years before launching Audible, publishing well-received books about Sears, Roebuck & Company and Nike. He continued contributing to publications such as *Esquire, Men's Journal,* and *Sports Illustrated* after starting the company.

In fact, according to *Business 2.0,* Katz was researching a book on the Information Superhighway for Random House (which had advanced him $400,000) when he became entranced with its commercial possibilities. Katz saw in the emerging technology of the Internet a cheap and convenient new medium for distributing spoken audio on demand. It was a marriage of high tech with the ancient simplicity of the human voice. "We want to be a leader in teaching the Internet to talk," Katz said in the *New York Times.*

Aside from saving the considerable expense of paper, printing, warehousing, and shipping, online delivery

COMPANY PERSPECTIVES

Audible (www.audible.com) is the Internet's leading provider of spoken audio entertainment, information, and educational programming. Content from Audible is downloaded and played back on personal computers, CDs, or AudibleReady computer-based mobile devices. Audible has 80,000 hours of audio programs from 270 content partners that include leading audiobook publishers, broadcasters, entertainers, magazine and newspaper publishers, and business information providers.

would allow almost immediate delivery and a vast selection. There was the added bonus on some titles of hearing the author's own voice. "Being read to is a very pleasurable experience, almost harkening back to bedtime stories," Katz later told the Associated Press. Finally, the population seemed to be turning away from books because they were too busy to sit down and read; spoken works could be consumed during commutes or workouts. Prior audiobook publishers had been constrained by the limitations of producing and shipping a physical product.

Audible claimed that its business model was one of the first designed around the Internet. It took Audible a couple of years to develop the technology for disbursing audio online while protecting the owners' copyrights, according to *Business 2.0.* Another critical part of the equation was the mobile playback device.

FIRST PORTABLE DIGITAL AUDIO PLAYER IN 1997

The company introduced the first Internet-ready portable digital audio player, called the MobilePlayer, in 1997. Although not up to the audio quality of the later iPod, or even AM radio, it was innovative enough for its day to land in the Smithsonian Institution. It could be listened to through headphones or via an unused frequency on a car stereo or other FM radio. It could store two hours of audio at a time. There were no removable disks; the MobilePlayer had to be reloaded via its docking station. The 3.5-ounce unit sold for more than $200, making it too pricey for the mass market.

For content, Audible turned to dozens of audiobook producers and educational content providers. Katz initially encountered resistance due to publishers' early failures with CD-ROM media. These partners, however, came to value the prospect of an efficient new sales channel. By the time of its product launch in 1997, Audible had more than 10,000 hours of spoken book and periodical material to offer for download, far more than most conventional audiobook outlets.

By September 1998, Audible had served more than 5,000 customers and had sold more than 3,000 players, noted the *New York Times.* Microsoft soon invested $5 million in the company, while agreeing to include Audible's software with the Windows CE operating system for handheld devices. Agreements with other hardware makers, including Compaq Computer Corp., soon followed.

PUBLIC, AND PRESSURED, IN 1999

Andrew J. Huffman, former head of multimedia software start-up Aimtech, was hired as Audible's CEO in March 1998, when the company had 35 employees. According to *Business 2.0,* the strain of constant cross-country flights to Silicon Valley was the reason Katz brought on the new hire. Tragically, in October 1999 Huffman died of a heart attack while playing basketball. He was 39.

Audible had had a successful initial public offering in July 1999, in which the share price opened at $9 and closed at $21 the first day. It also got another important new strategic partner during the year in Amazon.com, which acquired a 5 percent holding for $20 million.

Former Comcast executive Thomas Baxter was hired as Audible's president and CEO in February 2000. It was a precarious time to lead an Internet start-up, in spite of promising developments such as a new weekly comedy show from Robin Williams available only on Audible.com launched in April 2000. A strategic alliance was formed with Random House the next month, creating Random House Audible, said to be the first publishing imprint devoted to creating titles for digital distribution. Both of these projects aimed to use efficiencies of the Internet to connect with niche markets. Audible's downloads were priced at about $8, versus $20 for a book on CD.

The collapse of the high-tech bubble in the spring of 2000 stalled the company's efforts to find or make a cheaper, more capable audio player. The company's stock value was cut back, but not to the extent of other Internet start-ups. Nevertheless, Audible was posting some rising numbers. In 2000, content and services revenues more than quadrupled to $2.5 million, while the number of customers nearly tripled to 51,000. Total revenue, including hardware sales, was $4.5 million. Unfortunately, the company's net loss also increased, from $13.5 million in 1999 to $32.3 million in 2000.

KEY DATES

1995: Audible is launched by top nonfiction author Donald Katz and tech entrepreneur Tim Mott.
1997: Audible introduces the first portable digital audio player.
1999: Audible is valued at $538 million following its initial public offering but cancels production of its audio player after the death of its new CEO.
2000: Subscription service is introduced; total annual sales are $4.5 million.
2001: After the burst of the tech bubble nearly crushes Audible, the company is bailed out by a $10 million investment from Microsoft.
2002: Apple produces AudibleReady iPods.
2004: The company posts its first profit.

Microsoft acquired $10 million of the company's preferred stock in March 2001, allowing Audible to stay in business. (This holding was divested in 2003.) Amid growing losses, however, the company soon cut 40 percent of its staff, including Baxter, who later became CEO of Time Warner Cable. The company's web site was down for more than a week after its New York City server lost power following the September 11, 2001 terrorist attacks on the United States.

In spite of its obstacles, the company was able to avoid delisting on the NASDAQ as its share price dipped below $1, at least temporarily. It was among the tech companies that moved its national market to the small-cap market in 2002. It finally moved to the NASD Over-the-Counter Bulletin Board in February 2003. Fortunately, investors such as media giant Bertelsmann AG, parent of Random House, believed in the company and continued to help it survive.

INTRODUCING SUBSCRIPTIONS IN 2000

Audible was moving to a subscription-based business model. While it continued to offer individual downloads for $5 to $30, it introduced memberships beginning at about $13 per month. This encouraged greater consumer involvement and a steady income stream, Katz told the *New York Times.*

Audible brought out a new audio player, the Otis, in December 2001. It was available to subscribers for $49, and later for free, with a yearlong contract. Audible soon abandoned the Otis, however, in favor of off-the-shelf MP3 players.

It was the introduction of Apple's iPod in late 2002 that finally provided the means needed to connect Audible's content with a large audience. Audible soon worked out an exclusive deal with Apple to offer 6,000 of its downloads through the iTunes music store.

The venture's success, however, was attracting to the market established online players, noted *Business 2.0.* Amazon.com allowed Audible's exclusive agreement to provide its audiobooks to expire in 2003. Another former partner, Microsoft, also was developing its own online spoken audio business; Apax Partners acquired its Audible stock in 2003. Audible also had faced competition from others, such as Books on Tape Inc. and MediaBay Inc., for years. Still, Audible was the clear market leader for downloads of audiobooks.

According to figures in the *New York Times,* the audiobook industry had increased 360 percent in the previous dozen years, to $2 billion (compared with $12 billion for the U.S. music industry). Other sources pegged the figure at closer to $800 million. Audible itself seemed to be growing the market; more than half of its users had no previous exposure to audiobooks in any form.

A TASTE OF PROFITS IN 2004

By 2003, Audible's archives included more than 34,000 hours of material. This would double within two years. Net revenues were $34.3 million in 2004; the company posted net income of about $2 million. This milestone increased interest in its stock considerably; in fact, Standard & Poor's gave it its highest rating in 2005.

Sales were $63 million for 2005, though the company slipped into a loss. During the year, Audible began downloading content to mobile phones, beginning with the Treo. By this time, the company's content could be downloaded to more than 135 different devices. Audible also had signed a cross-marketing agreement to supply content to XM Satellite Radio Holdings Inc., while adding a subsidiary in the United Kingdom (its customers already came from more than 100 countries).

Frederick C. Ingram

PRINCIPAL SUBSIDIARIES

Audible Limited (U.K.).

PRINCIPAL COMPETITORS

Audio Book Club, Inc.; Audio Renaissance USA; Books on Tape Inc.

FURTHER READING

"Amazon to Sell Audible's Audio Books for Download," *Reuters News,* May 31, 2000.

"Audible Inc.—Move to NASD's OTC Bulletin Board," *Market News Publishing,* February 18, 2003.

"Audible Moving to Make Downloadable Audio More Accessible—But Will Consumers Care?," *BP Report,* February 11, 2002.

"Audible Sounds Off on a New Rival; CEO Donald Katz on Amazon Entering the Online Audiobook Biz: Offering a 'Happy Listening Experience' Is 'Different from Moving Boxes,'" *BusinessWeek Online,* June 6, 2005.

Barlas, Pete, "Audible Hums Along After Clamorous Start; Firm Weathered Dot-Com Crash, Nasdaq Delisting to Become Hot '04 Stock," *Investor's Business Daily,* January 31, 2005, p. A18.

Goad, Libe, "XM Satellite Radio Adds Audio Books to the Mix; XM Satellite Radio and Spoken-Word Content Provider Audible Enter into an Exclusive Partnership of Cross-Promotion," *PC Magazine,* June 7, 2005.

Gove, Alex, "Barely Audible—Audible's Deal with Microsoft Sounds Great, But Is It?," *Red Herring,* March 1, 1999, p. 64.

Gowrie, David, "CEO's Sudden Death Jolts Wayne Company; Audible Inc. Pledges Business As Usual," *Record* (New Jersey), October 6, 1999, p. L8.

Healey, Jon, "Open Mike on the Web; On a Screen Near You Are Stand-Up Comedy Routines by Robin Williams Aimed Specifically at a Web Audience," *Seattle Times,* April 30, 2000, p. C1.

Jackson, Tim, "When It Can Pay to Listen," *Financial Times,* August 4, 1997, p. 10.

James, Steve, "Random House Bookmarks Internet Spoken Word Company," *Reuters News,* May 11, 2000.

Keegan, Paul, "Audible Cranks It Up; An Acclaimed Writer Turned Entrepreneur Tries to Remake the Art of Storytelling for the Digital Era—And Boost the Volume on a Huge New Market He Helped to Create. Will His Tale Have a Happy Ending?," *Business 2.0,* March 1, 2006, pp. 104–10.

Kessler, Scott, "The Sweet Sounds from Audible; The Provider of Audio Books and Other Spoken Content Has Strong Offerings and a Jump on Its Market. That Earns It S&P's Highest Rating," *BusinessWeek Online,* June 21, 2005.

McKay, Martha, "Dot-Com Survivor; Demand for Spoken Books Keeps Audible on the Web," *Record* (New Jersey), December 2, 2003, p. L9.

———, "It's Cries and Whispers at Audible; Revenues Trumpeted; Profits Speak Softly," *Record* (New Jersey), October 31, 2002, p. B2.

———, "Stock-Stressed Firms Gain Breathing Room," *Record* (New Jersey), September 29, 2002, p. B1.

Marlowe, Chris, "Baxter Exits amid Audible.com Cuts," *Hollywood Reporter,* July 24, 2001, p. 4.

Napoli, Lisa, "Audio-Book Service Calls the Tune," *New York Times,* October 21, 2003, p. 16.

Redburn, Tom, "Forget Plastics. Go Find Subscribers," *New York Times,* December 9, 2001, p. 4.

———, "His Dream Is That We'll All Hear Little Voices," *New York Times,* September 23, 1998, p. G9.

Trachtenberg, Jeffrey A., "A Survivor's Story: By Offering Digital Audio Books on the Internet, Audible Inc. Has a Good Shot at a Happy Ending," *Wall Street Journal,* March 22, 2004, p. R3.

Zeitchik, Steven M., "Audible Names Baxter CEO," *Publishers Weekly,* February 21, 2000, p. 20.

Avantium Technologies BV

Zekeringstraat 29 1014 BV
Amsterdam,
Netherlands
Telephone: +31-20-586-8080
Fax: +31-20-586-8085
Web site: http://www.avantium.com

Private Company
Incorporated: 2000
Employees: 55
Sales: $6.5 million (2005)
NAIC: 541710 Research and Development in the Physical Sciences and Engineering Sciences

■ ■ ■

Avantium Technologies BV provides advanced chemical research services to the pharmaceutical, biotech, oil refining, and bulk and specialty chemicals industries. The Amsterdam-based company combines expertise in a wide array of fields, ranging from crystallography, catalysis, and organic chemistry, to robotics systems, process engineering, and statistics, to software development, with an emphasis on developing high-throughput processes for chemical research, development, and experimentation. The company has also established one of the world's largest catalysts libraries. Avantium has become a leader in developing and providing automated research and testing systems, in part through subsidiary Crystallics, which provides high-throughput polymorph screening services for solid state chemical applications. Avantium typically works in close partnership with its clients' research and development departments, both by providing outsourcing capacity, as well as placing employees in the field. Formed around core expertise developed by Shell, Avantium was founded by a consortium combining chemical groups, venture capital firms, the University of Leiden, and two other technical universities in the Netherlands. Members of the consortium include Shell, GSK, Eastman, Pfizer, Cazenove Private Equity, EDB Ventures, Akzo Nobel, and WR Grace, among others. Avantium Technologies remains a privately held company; Tom van Aken was named the company's chief executive officer in 2005.

ADVANCED CHEMICAL RESEARCH SERVICES PROVIDER

The development of new and ever more sophisticated research technologies, coupled with the need to increase the speed and efficiency of the research and development and testing cycles, stimulated the growth of a new market for outsourcing research at the end of the 1990s. The development of new high-throughput technologies, and high-speed experimentation and simulation technologies, provided the potential for a vast reduction in the research and development cycle. By combining multiple disciplines, the new technologies enabled huge gains in efficiency. Where traditionally experiments such as the testing of chemicals required that each variable be tested individually, the new technologies permitted the simultaneous testing of multiple variables, such as types of catalysts and solvents, influence of temperature and pressure, and the like. New advances in robotics, software development, and nano-technologies also enabled the

COMPANY PERSPECTIVES

Avantium Technologies provides innovative high-throughput R&D services and technologies to the pharmaceutical and chemical industries. Avantium innovation driven solutions combine high-throughput experimentation technology, novel research methodology and state-of-the-art software to accelerate R&D. Our mission is to increase the success rate and economics of the product and process development efforts of our customers. Using Avantium's proprietary technology platforms they will generate high-quality results much faster than using conventional research methods.

automation of research, development, and testing processes.

The increasing sophistication of technologies led a growing number of chemicals and pharmaceuticals companies, but also universities and chemical research software specialists, to seek out partnerships, as well as new sources of capital. These factors led Shell International Chemicals to form a technology partnership with the pharmaceuticals group SmithKline Beecham, informatics software developer GSE Systems, and three Dutch universities, the University of Leiden, Eindhoven University of Technology, and the University of Twente, to pool their experimental development of high-throughput hardware, software, and processes into a new company, called Avantium. Joining the partnership at the outset were the venture capital companies Alpinvest, The Generics Group, and SmithKline Beecham's own venture capital wing, SR One. Shell International Chemical's own technology formed the platform for Avantium's high-speed experimentation and simulation technology. Shell International Chemicals also provided Avantium's first CEO, Ian Maxwell, who had formerly been with the Dutch oil and chemicals giant as a technology manager. Avantium was also headquartered in Amsterdam, close to the Shell Chemical research laboratory, which itself had operated in Amsterdam since 1914. Avantium was launched in March 2000 with an initial capitalization of EUR 30 million ($28 million).

Avantium quickly attracted new partners to its shareholder consortium. By 2001, the company's backers included WR Grace, Akzo Nobel Chemicals, Pfizer, Eastman Chemical, and the newly formed Glaxo SmithKline. The company also added venture capital backing, including NIB Capital and Cazenove, among others. Many of the company's shareholders also became the company's partners. Avantium formed a catalyst development partnership with Eastman Chemical, for example, in 2001. Avantium received a strong boost in September 2001 when the Netherlands' government provided an NLG 10 million (approximately $5 million) grant in support of the company's university-based development program. By then, the company had already initiated 12 collaborative programs with its university partners. These programs focused especially on two promising areas, catalysts and high-throughput experimentation and simulation.

Avantium's high-throughput efforts took a step forward in 2001 as well when the company reached an agreement to acquire the VirtualPlant and VirtualLab software groups, developed in collaboration with GSE Systems. The acquisitions gave Avantium two new offices, in Maryland in the United States, and in Hexham, in Northumberland, England, and formed the basis of a new subsidiary, Avantium Technologies (US) Inc.

At the same time, Avantium's collaboration with the University of Leiden was also beginning to produce results. In 2000, that partnership had launched a subsidiary, Crystallics, which focused on developing high-throughput technologies for polymorph screening and protein crystallization, and providing research outsourcing services based on its technologies. By 2001, Crystallics had put into place a high-throughput polymorph screening system for the pharmaceutical market. The successful launch of Crystallics' high-throughput commercial operations led Avantium to take full control of the subsidiary in 2001. As part of that acquisition, Crystallics acquired the exclusive rights to deploy the high-throughput technologies produced through its collaboration with the University of Leiden. The high-throughput operations were moved to Crystallics laboratories at Avantium's Amsterdam headquarters. The collaborative effort in the field of protein crystallization remained at the University of Leiden.

Catalyst research became another major area of Avantium's operations in the early 2000s. In 2001, the company joined a catalyst research consortium, Combicar, based in Kuala Lumpur, Malaysia, in partnership with Berlin's Fritz Haber Institute, Spain's Institute of Chemical Technology, and three Malaysian universities. The new company focused its research on developing catalysts that could be used to transform raw materials such as palm oil and liquefied natural gas into high-value added products. Avantium's part in this effort consisted of providing its high-throughput technology and marketing support. In 2002, the company intensified its relationship with venture partner Universiti

KEY DATES

2000: Avantium is formed by a consortium including Shell International Chemicals, SmithKline Beecham, GSE Systems, three Dutch universities, and venture capital companies Alpinvest, The Generics Group, and SR One; Avantium forms Crystallics joint venture with University of Leiden.
2001: Avantium acquires Crystallics; joins Combicat research consortium based in Kuala Lumpur, Malaysia; acquires Virtual Plant and Virtual Lab from GSE Systems.
2003: Company merges Crystallics and Avantium Pharma to form new subsidiary, Avantium Life Sciences.
2004: Company opens new cytotoxic compound research unit.
2005: Company expands polymer process development capacity; launches Crystal16 system for parallel crystallization experimentation.
2006: Avantium signs collaboration agreement with Warwick Effect Polymers.

Malaya, forming a new collaboration to develop high-end products from palm oil, a chief Malayan resource.

Catalysts played an essential role in the development of new testing and screening procedures and high-throughput technologies. In response, Avantium began building its own "library" of catalysts, which were acquired from the major catalyst producers. This effort took on steam in October 2001, when Avantium reached a supply agreement with Degussa AG, a leading global catalyst producer.

PARTNERING FOR GROWTH

The forming of partnerships remained a major factor behind Avantium's growth into the mid-2000s. In 2002, for example, the company reached a chemical research collaboration agreement with DSM in order to develop computer-based chemical research simulations. As part of the agreement, DSM agreed to invest EUR 1 million in the project. The partnership was soon followed by the announcement of an agreement with Amcis, part of Solutia Inc., to develop plant modeling and simulation technologies for pharmaceutical synthesis and experimentation.

In 2003, Avantium merged its Crystallics subsidiary into another unit, Avantium Pharma, creating a new subsidiary, Avantium Life Sciences. The move combined the two units' technologies and research and development teams. Because both units targeted similar markets, and shared many of the same clients and facilities, the merger also allowed Avantium to streamline its marketing and sales operations.

Avantium also continued to seek out new partnerships. In 2003, for example, the company extended its relationship with shareholder Eastman Chemical Company. The new agreement called for the joint development of new catalytic systems focused on Eastman's own specialty chemical production. The company also continued to build up its catalyst library, forming a biocatalyst supply agreement with Novozymes, based in Denmark, in October 2003.

Avantium also invested in its own internal expansion. In January 2004, for example, the company opened a new cytotoxic compound research facility at its Amsterdam headquarters. The new unit was established to develop new polymorph screening procedures in support of pharmaceutical companies' efforts to produce higher-potency drugs.

Nonetheless, partnerships remained a major factor in Avantium's development into the middle of the decade. In 2004, the company added a new partnership, with Chiral Quest Inc., to add that company's chiral ligand catalysts to Avantium's catalyst library. In March 2004, the company teamed up with BP Petrochemicals, forming a collaborative effort to develop catalysts for the oil company's commodity chemicals operations. At the end of that year, the company signed a new research agreement with the Institute of OneWorld Health. The agreement called for Avantium to use its technologies to conduct studies on a new drug developed to treat Chagas' disease. By the end of 2005, Avantium had formed partnerships with some 40 of the world's major chemicals and pharmaceuticals companies. The company added to that list with a partnership with Germany's Boehringer Ingelheim.

The company also expanded its in-house capacity that year, adding a new workflow at its laboratory in Delft. The new unit enhanced Avantium's capacity in the polymer process development, and especially in petroleum derivatives such as polyethylene, polypropylene, and styrene. Also in 2005, the company launched a new parallel crystallization device, Crystal16, capable of running 16 experiments in parallel, developed in partnership with Pfizer.

Under newly appointed CEO Tom van Aken, Avantium continued developing its network of partnerships into 2006. At the beginning of that year, the company announced its latest collaboration, with Warwick Effect

Polymers based in the United Kingdom. The agreement called for Avantium to help develop and market Warwick's Polypeg polymer-based system for enhancing the uptake of drugs into the human body. In just half a decade, Avantium had established itself as a leading player in the rapidly growing technology services market.

M. L. Cohen

PRINCIPAL SUBSIDIARIES

Avantium Chemicals; Avantium Life Sciences.

PRINCIPAL COMPETITORS

Unilab Corp.; Quest Diagnostics Inc.; Medicus S.A.; Mds Inc.; Evotec AG; Inpharmatica; MDS Pharma; Genzyme Corp.; Nippon Flour Mills Company Ltd.; Laboratorio Medico del Chopo S.A. de C.V.; Takara Holdings Inc.; Lonza Group Ltd.; Diagnostic Medlab Ltd.; Sanofi Synthelabo Recherche; DixAmico; S.R.L. Inc.

FURTHER READING

"Avantium Adds Cytotoxics Capability," *Chemical Market Reporter*, January 5, 2004, p. 10.

"Avantium and WEP Enter into Collaboration for the Development of PolyPEG Technology for Pharmaceutical Applications," *Chemical Business Newsbase*, January 20 2006.

"Avantium in Catalyst Deals," *Chemical Market Reporter*, April 12, 2004, p. 4.

"Avantium Invests in New Cytotoxic Compound Research Facility," *Manufacturing Chemist*, January 2004, p. 9.

"Avantium Invests in Potent Facility," *Manufacturing Chemist*, December 2003, p. 18.

"Avantium Technologies," *Chemical Week*, March 13, 2002, p. S12.

"Avantium to Work with Degussa and BP," *Specialty Chemicals*, April 2004, p. 7.

"Crystallics Acquires HTS Rights," *Specialty Chemicals*, November 2001, p. 5.

"Degussa to Supply Avantium Technologies Catalyst Library," *Specialty Chemicals*, October 2001, p. 5.

"Drug Delivery Collaboration," *Chemical Week*, February 1, 2006, p. 32.

O'Driscoll, Cath, "Avantium Growth," *ECN European Chemical News*, February 28, 2005, p. 28.

Scott, Alex, "Avantium Forms Asian Consortium," *Chemical Week*, September 12, 2001, p. 42.

———, "Novel Catalysts Cut Costs, Increase Capability," *Chemical Week*, August 10, 2005, p. 24.

Banta Corporation

225 Main Street
Box 8003
Menasha, Wisconsin 54952-8003
U.S.A.
Telephone: (920) 751-7777
Toll Free: (800) 291-1171
Fax: (920) 751-7790
Web site: http://www.banta.com

Public Company
Incorporated: 1901 as George Banta Printing Company
Employees: 8,500
Sales: $1.54 billion (2005)
Stock Exchanges: New York
Ticker Symbol: BN
NAIC: 323110 Commercial Lithographic Printing; 323117 Books Printing; 541430 Graphic Design Services; 323119 Other Commercial Printing

■ ■ ■

Banta Corporation, one of the nation's largest printing and digital imaging companies, literally started in a small-town Wisconsin dining room in 1886. From its humble beginnings, Banta grew to become a technologically advanced, multifaceted reproducer of a wide variety of information, from small-run periodicals to educational and popular books to catalogs and direct marketing materials. Keeping pace with technology changes, Banta added software and services for managing digital content, online publishing, electronic commerce, and web site hosting and maintenance. By the late 1990s, Banta had acquired a diverse array of printing and digital imaging companies, reported sales of more than $1.3 billion, and maintained 33 production facilities in the United States and five in Europe located in Ireland, Scotland, and The Netherlands. Banta also diversified, entering into comprehensive supply chain management, from document printing through delivery to the end user, mainly for U.S. and European manufacturers of computer hardware and software. In the new century, Banta sold one of its other non-printing ventures, a healthcare products business, which made and distributed single-use healthcare products, such as examination gowns and dental bibs, and foodservice products, such as table covers and disposable bibs. The company intended to focus on its printing services and supply-chain management business, the latter an important driver of new growth for Banta.

FROM HUMBLE BEGINNINGS TO PIONEERING PRINTER

In the 1880s, company founder George Banta was a traveling agent for Phoenix Fire Insurance, based in Menasha, Wisconsin, some 80 miles north of Milwaukee. Banta was also a printing buff and, much to the distress of his new bride, Nellie, he brought a printing press into the only room in their house big enough to accommodate it. Two years, one house, and one baby later, Nellie Banta insisted on evicting the press to a shed built in the backyard. George bought a noisy gasoline engine to run the press and also hired one full-time worker for the tiny operation whose main business consisted of printing his insurance forms.

After a fire in 1901 burned down the shed, Banta

COMPANY PERSPECTIVES

Banta's growth strategy is focused and powerful: Drive Growth in our two business sectors by expanding value-added services, and pursuing acquisitions and alliances in our higher growth print, literature management and supply-chain management businesses.

moved his equipment to a Main Street store front, added a platen job press, and incorporated the business as George Banta Printing Company, with the purpose of "engaging in the business of job and newspaper printing, bookbinding, and manufacture of books and pamphlets." Two years later the corporation was renamed George Banta Publishing Company. The strain of running the shop along with his insurance job took its toll on George Banta, who had a history of malaria and lung problems. In 1904 his doctors ordered him West to recuperate. To save their business, Nellie stayed behind in Menasha and took over as manager. She proved a determined and effective entrepreneur. Meanwhile, George, who had been a Phi Delta Theta member at Indiana University and remained active in the fraternity's national organization, landed a contract to print the Phi Delta magazine, and in time also signed up a number of other fraternities and sororities.

George's educational contacts—his father was dean of the Indiana University law school—helped the company win orders for university catalogs and annuals, as well as some textbooks and magazines. Thus, Banta Publishing grew mainly as a specialist in book and periodical printing. Not that it turned away commercial customers; in its early days, it regularly printed large-volume promotional booklets for Quaker Oats. In 1910 Banta was ready for its own building, a two-story plant just across the Fox River. These facilities, vastly enlarged over the decades, remained the site of Banta Company's offices, the largest division of Banta Corporation, and a complex of printing facilities into the late 1990s.

In 1911, 18-year-old George Banta, Jr., dropped out of college and assumed charge of the office. The replacement of Nellie was somewhat brusque, wrote *Appleton Post-Crescent* contributor Kay Roberts, but while the "Founder's wife" reminisced that she "missed the five dollars a week she earned," she also maintained she had much to attend to at home and "left with few regrets." George, Sr., while periodically bothered by health problems, continued to be a major sales contributor and retained overall leadership as president until his death in 1935 at age 76. Nellie then assumed the presidency until she died in her 86th year in 1951.

The company continued to grow, with emphasis on the educational market. As a historical review in the 1990 annual report noted, Banta was emphatic on keeping "pace with technological change." However, "rather than attempting to serve many markets, the company focused initially on ones in which it could build special strengths and capabilities." Even though the company consistently ranked among the top five U.S. printers in the 1980s and 1990s, Banta liked to concentrate on numerous niche businesses and sought to be the leader or a strong contender in each market it entered.

By the onset of World War I, Banta was printing 184 scholarly, technical, and educational journals. The war years brought a harsher climate which lasted into the early 1920s, but then, as the decade progressed, Banta benefited from an "explosion in education." By the end of the decade, Banta found itself in the right place for an innovative concept. One of George, Jr.'s brothers-in-law, Russell Sharp, wrote an elementary school workbook and turned to Banta to produce it. The company soon became the leader in printing workbooks as these softcover scholastic aids became a major educational tool from first grade through graduate school. Eventually this expertise helped make Banta a leader in softcover books for the professional market as well as for "trade" books (general interest books sold through bookstores).

Always technically progressive, Banta acquired its first web offset press in 1940. In the early days, the prevailing state of the art in paper, platemaking, ink, and other printing supplies limited the jobs considered suitable for offset. Banta became a pioneer in pushing development of improved supplies as well as speedier and higher-quality presses. As web offset developed into the printing method of choice for many applications, the expanding Banta Company established itself as a major player in the industry.

In 1946 Banta expanded beyond its home complex with the 42,000-square-foot Midway plant, built halfway between downtown Menasha and nearby Appleton. Even as it kept expanding its printing business, the company contracted its name, dropping the "Publishing" to become George Banta Company, Inc. in 1954. The streamlined name also eliminated possible confusion about Banta's role: it did the production work for books and periodicals, while publishers (who create and market books) were its customers.

KEY DATES

1901: George Banta incorporates his printing business as George Banta Printing Company.
1903: Company is renamed George Banta Publishing Company.
1910: A two-story plant is completed in Menasha.
1940: Company purchases its first web offset press.
1946: A 42,000-square-foot Midway Plant is completed, located midway between Menasha and Appleton.
1954: Company's name is changed to George Banta Company, Inc.
1969: Acquisition program begins with purchase of Daniels Packaging.
1970: Sales reach $50 million.
1971: Company goes public through a $5.7 million initial public offering.
1989: Revenues surpass the half-billion mark; company name is streamlined to Banta Corporation.
1995: Company acquires Cork, Ireland-based BG Turnkey Services Ltd.; revenues top the $1 billion mark for the first time.
1998: Company's stock moves from the NASDAQ to the New York Stock Exchange.
1999: Company restructures; large supply-chain management contract is signed.
2002: New CEO guides company through tough economic times.
2005: Banta Healthcare Group is sold.

PRESSING FORWARD VIA ACQUISITIONS

Banta, which did barely $3.5 million in business at the end of World War II and $10 million in the mid-1950s, attained $33 million in sales by 1968. Family leadership had been interrupted in 1961 when John H. Wilterding, who had started at Banta in 1923, succeeded George Banta, Jr., as president. On Wilterding's retirement in 1965, however, George Banta III, the son of George, Jr., took over. Conglomeration had become the fashion throughout American enterprise, and the printing industry was no exception. George III related: "We had many beautiful offers to sell out . . . but we decided to remain independent." Banta set out to prepare itself for the new order. In 1968 it brought in Menasha-born Kimberly Clark executive William H. Fieweger as president, with George Banta III as chairman, a post he retained until his retirement in 1983.

Within a year, the Banta-Fieweger team had the company's first long-range expansion plan ready, based on the recognition that the industry was "becoming increasingly capital intensive" and hence required "larger economic units." The Banta plan aimed to: continue internal growth, "notably from educational sources"; acquire selected small firms to promote expansion; and encourage technological advancement not just by buying new equipment, but by innovating new methods and directions. The acquisition program began in 1969 with the $2.4 million purchase of Daniels Packaging of Rhinelander, Wisconsin, which specialized in producing foil and flexible film wrap for food and other grocery products. Somewhat ironically, this first acquisition also became the first major unit disposed of by Banta; in 1989 the greatly expanded Daniels was sold for an after-tax gain of $9.6 million.

In 1970, Banta added periodicals printer Hart Press of Minnesota and Menasha neighbor Northwestern Engraving, which prepared color separations for printers and for whom Banta had been a major customer. These acquisitions along with internal growth boosted Banta sales volume above $50 million for the first time. In March 1971 Banta was ready to go public, selling 455,000 shares (a 29 percent interest) at $12.50 per share. Over the next two-and-a-half decades, the share value multiplied more than 25-fold.

Acquisitions continued through the 1970s and 1980s. Ling Products of Neenah, Wisconsin, acquired in 1973, made disposable products for the health and foodservice industries, such as examination gowns, table covers, and bibs. KCS Industries of Milwaukee, purchased in 1975, produced point-of-sale displays. Moreover, R.J. Carroll of Harrisonburg, Virginia, bought in 1976 and later named Banta Harrisonburg, provided Eastern production facilities for Banta's basic education-oriented business. Banta's most important acquisition came in 1988, under the leadership of Chairman and CEO Harry W. Earle, when Minnesota-based Beddor Companies joined the fold. The move increased Banta's size by about two-thirds and put it into consumer catalogs and direct mail materials, among the fastest growing segments of retail merchandising. It also added to Banta's softcover capacity through printer Viking Press of Minneapolis (no relation to the well-known New York publisher Viking). The merger pushed sales above the half-billion mark in 1989 and brought Banta into the *Fortune* 500. At the same time, Banta further streamlined its corporate name to Banta Corporation.

COMMITTED TO PRINT

Acquisitions of "high-quality" companies remained high on the Banta agenda in the 1990s. Thus, in 1994, Banta added Danbury Printing and Litho of Connecticut, augmenting its capabilities in the direct marketing industry with a strategic manufacturing facility in the Northeast. Another 1994 acquisition was United Graphics of Kent, Washington, which gave Banta a second western printing plant to complement its Utah facility, Bushman Press, acquired in 1991. Through the United Graphics purchase, Banta also added software giant Microsoft Corporation to its already broad roster of top-level computer industry customers. Donald D. Belcher came to Banta as president in the fall of 1994 from office supplier Avery Dennison and took over the chairmanship and CEO position from retiring Calvin Aurand, Jr., in 1995.

All told, Banta added 23 companies during the first quarter century of its acquisition policy. Banta succeeded in obtaining strong growth from companies following their acquisition, which meshed into its overall plan for "aggressive and profitable growth" from internally developed new products and services.

Banta organized its many acquisitions into several product groups that operated as largely autonomous enterprises, an approach the company believed would make them "quicker, more nimble, and better able to respond to customer needs." The three largest groups in the mid-1990s, each with a little over one-fifth of total volume, were the Book, Catalog, and Direct Marketing units. The Banta Book Group handled both educational and general books, and also produced instructional games such as "Trivial Pursuit," a game wildly popular in the mid-1980s.

The Publications Group, which accounted for about one-eighth of total volume, put out more than 500 educational, trade, religious, and fraternal magazines with circulation mostly in the 15,000-to-350,000 range. Niche-conscious Banta specialized in this type of periodical rather than large-scale consumer magazines "because they are less subject to cyclical variation in number of advertising pages; also because regular planned growth is easier to achieve, since each new periodical adds only modestly to sales." Smaller groups were the Banta Digital Group, Information Services, and the more specialized KCS (signs, displays, etc.) and Ling (single-use products) units.

Banta planned to stay strong in the 1990s, noted Belcher, by "investing ahead of the curve in new technologies." Between 1990 and 1994, Banta reinvested $265 million in its operations, $87 million in 1994 alone. Such a figure represented around 10 percent of revenues, more than double the industry average. Capital acquired in the early 1990s included a $20 million printing press whose wide web permitted the printing of 50 percent more pages across the web of paper while running at nearly 50 percent greater speed. In another plant, a Xeikon full-color digital system printed entirely from digital information, requiring no film or plates. Other electronic and optical systems, often enhanced by proprietary software programs, sped prepress preparation and after-printing processing (addressing and distribution), enabling Banta to offer fast turnaround and highly customized service, such as catalogs or direct mail pieces with content tailored for specific recipients. Similarly, college texts could be custom-bound to match a professor's specific course curriculum.

Chairman Belcher expected Banta's core business to remain "imaging on paper," even as the design, production, and distribution processes which turned out these familiar print products were being "revolutionized by digital technologies." In addition, he predicted that a broad array of nonprint products, including CD-ROMs and "image archiving," would show proportionally faster growth than print. An example of the new kinds of jobs that were being taken on by Banta was an electronic catalog for a major business-to-business cataloger that was essentially a CD-ROM version of its printed catalog. For computer industry customers, Banta not only printed instruction manuals but provided on-demand electronic printing, duplication of floppies, diskettes, and CD-ROMs, and assembly of software kits.

NEW VENTURES

Though Banta had long expressed interest in the global market, foreign expansion had barely begun in the 1990s. In 1994 Banta established a software documentation unit in The Netherlands, which enabled domestic customers to download data for printing and distribution overseas. The following year came a much larger purchase, that of Cork, Ireland-based BG Turnkey Services Ltd. The Cork, Ireland-based company had annual sales of about $160 million and provided services to European computer industry customers similar to those offered by Banta's existing U.S. operations, including manual and promotional item printing, disk and CD-ROM duplication, software package assembly, and fulfillment. BG became part of the Banta Global Turnkey Group. Also in 1995, Banta moved into the burgeoning world of the Internet with the acquisition of New Frontiers Information Corp., a Cambridge, Massachusetts, software company specializing in the creation of online catalogs and ordering systems. Revenues for 1995 topped $1 billion for the first time.

Acquisitions continued in the late 1990s. In September 1997 Banta paid about $50.7 million in cash for the Omnia Group, a Troy, Michigan, supplier of single-use medical and dental products. The Omnia operation was merged into Banta's existing single-use products unit, which by this time was known as the Banta Healthcare Group. In October 1997 Banta acquired Greenfield Printing & Publishing Company, a printer of special interest and trade magazines based in Greenfield, Ohio, for about $21.3 million. Also in late 1997 Banta initiated a restructuring program, which entailed a $13.5 million charge and was completed in 1998. The company sold most of its KCS unit, including its point-of-purchase sign and display business; its interactive video operation; and three Banta Global Turnkey facilities in Sacramento and Irvine, California, and in Provo, Utah.

During 1998 Banta expanded into the Latin American market for the first time through the acquisition of a 30 percent interest in Morgan Impresores S.A., one of the largest printers in Chile with annual sales of about $45 million. Continuing to seek opportunities outside the United States, Banta in mid-1999 formed a joint venture with Grupo Imagen, a Queretaro, Mexico-based sheet-fed printer. During 1998 Banta made its first release of B-media, a digital content management system for storing, archiving, retrieving, and "repurposing" digital information for print or electronic distribution. In early 1999 leading educational publisher Houghton Mifflin Company selected Banta to develop two online education pilot programs to test Internet-based delivery of customized educational materials, as well as to begin development of a B-media system for the publisher that would encompass both textbook and Internet output. The company was also developing a B-commerce product which enabled Banta customers to sell and distribute their products through a web site.

Meanwhile, in January 1999 Banta signed a $100 million contract with IDG Books Worldwide, publisher of the bestselling "For Dummies" series and other trade titles. Banta committed to printing a variety of books for IDG, and also agreed to provide inventory management, order fulfillment, distribution, and returns processing. The company built a 250,000-square-foot distribution center in Harrisonburg, Virginia, which had a storage capacity for about 16 million books and was slated to be used exclusively for IDG products.

In April 1999 Banta announced a restructuring program aimed at generating annual savings of $18 million to $20 million by 2000. Underperforming facilities in Kent, Washington; Charlotte, North Carolina; and Berkeley, Illinois, were slated for closure, and 650 workers, representing about 9 percent of the overall workforce, lost their jobs. The restructuring, which resulted in a fiscal 1999 charge of about $50 million, was part of a three-part program to position Banta for the early 21st century, with the second and third parts both being partially funded through the restructuring savings. The company planned to step up its acquisitions program, as outlined by Belcher: "Recent acquisitions have boosted our technology and value-added service capabilities, and we are now accelerating our acquisition activities with the goal of aggressively growing our most profitable core print sectors and our healthcare business." The third part of the program was to continue the company's aggressive development of digital technology products, such as B-media and B-commerce.

ANOTHER HUNDRED YEARS: 2000 AND BEYOND

Banta struck a five-year deal with Compaq Computer Corp. late in 1999 to configure, test, package, and distribute hard drives and other storage components, according to a *Knight Ridder/Tribune Business News* article. To serve Compaq's domestic market, Banta opened a new facility in Houston. Additional facilities were planned in Asia and Europe for Compaq's international market.

Estimated at $600 million to $800 million, the ultimate value of the contract was dependent on "market demand and global production capacity," according to a *Houston Business Journal* article. Compaq hoped to reduce expenses and get product to customers more quickly through consolidating its distribution process with Banta, which already served Compaq in the United States and The Netherlands.

Banta's other turnkey manufacturing and distribution services clients included Microsoft, Intel, Sun Microsystems, Cisco Systems, and Dell Computer, but the new deal with Compaq raised the bar. "With Compaq, Banta graduated from supply chain management (the physical services of assembly, packaging, order fulfillment and distribution) to technology-enabled integration—their services and information are melded with its customer through a common information technology system," explained Joanne Zuhl in a November 1999 *Knight Ridder/Tribune Business News* article.

Banta's investment in facilities and technology amounted to more than $20 million in startup costs. The Banta Turnkey Group, which produced sales of about $250 million in 1998, was expected to contribute half again as much with the onset of the Compaq deal.

Even though the supply chain management end of business had made a leap forward, the printing segment of the business still was key to Banta's success. It produced an estimated 60-65 percent of total revenues for Banta about the time of the Compaq deal.

The company's book printing operation sales climbed 30 percent to $363 million in 2000. The acquisition of Southeastern Color Graphics and a strong educational publishing market helped drive the gains. But the next year, Banta's 100th anniversary, some glitches appeared on the screen. Book sales slumped for printers, including Banta and competitors Quebecor and R.R. Donnelley. All three implemented cost-cutting measures in response to the drop in demand for their services brought on by the economic downturn. In addition, Banta's investment in a dot-com business went sour, causing the printer to take an after-tax charge of about $7 million in the first quarter of 2001.

Banta President and COO Stephanie A. Streeter succeeded Belcher as CEO in 2002. Streeter, recruited by Belcher to succeed him, had come on board in January 2001: " I really credit Stephanie for the leadership role she has played since she came, " Belcher said in the *Milwaukee Journal Sentinel.* "She's had a responsibility for all of our operations worldwide and she has been a huge contributor in that leadership role to the positive growth and results that Banta has demonstrated in a very, very tough environment."

In 2003, Banta shut down an outdated catalog plant and reinvested in another now handling a greater workload. Banta also struck a deal with an engineering and software development company regarding the future development of B-media products, selling the intellectual property but retaining the right to market and sell the software. Two marginally performing chain-supply management operations, one in Mexico another in Ireland, were also closed.

Streeter succeeded Belcher as chairman in April 2004. Both had worked at Avery Dennison Corp. in the late 1980s to early 1990s, according to a *Knight Ridder/Tribune Business News* article. There Belcher observed Streeter's marketing savvy, which helped elevate her to group vice-president for worldwide office products, a $1.4 billion Avery Dennison division. In 2000, she left Avery Dennison for dot-com company Idealab! Belcher, and the board, had reason to be impressed with Streeter's performance at Banta, as well. "With printing industry prospects gloomy 16 months ago, Banta stock still outperformed its industry peers; the Dow Jones industrial average; and the S&P500. It maintained its earnings and grew its sales," Arlen Boardman explained in a May 2004 *Knight Ridder/Tribune Business News* article.

Among Belcher's legacy to Banta was the profitable supply-chain management operation. During his ten-year tenure, total Banta sales had climbed from $811 million to $1.4 billion, with supply chain management producing one-quarter of revenues. A significant share of those revenues came from the five-year supply-management contract with Compaq, which ultimately produced a total of about $600 million. Banta went on to earn a new deal with the computer maker. The segment also had facilitated Banta's global expansion. "Belcher joked that when he arrived in 1994, 'our most foreign operation was Mountain View, Calif.,'" wrote Boardman.

Under Belcher the company's stock price climbed by 250 percent but was still considered undervalued. Back in 1999, stock prices in the printing industry were down, as money funneled into the red-hot dot-com industry. Furthermore, the industry was hurt by predictions of its demise at the hands of the Internet revolution. Early in 2004, Banta bought back one million shares to boost its earnings per share.

In April 2005, Banta completed the sale of Banta Healthcare Group to an affiliate of Fidelity Capital Investors, Inc. for $67 million. Banta planned to tighten its focus on the printing services and supply chain management segments. The healthcare segment had produced about 7 percent of 2004 sales of $1.5 billion and 8 percent of the company's $136 million in operating income.

Meanwhile, the printing industry continued to face challenges. Over the past decade, 8,000 U.S. printing plants closed their doors, according to a February 2005 *Milwaukee Journal Sentinel.* An additional 4,000 to 8,000 were expected to shut down over the next ten years. Printing industry overall sales were up by less than 4 percent in 2004. But diversified Banta posted record earnings from continuing operations in the fourth quarter of 2005. "Banta had a great 2005 and an exceptional fourth quarter," Streeter said in the *Post-Crescent* in February 2006. "During the first half of the year we focused on investment and preparation for a strong second half of the year—and we achieved our expectations."

Henry R. Hecht
Updated, David E. Salamie; Kathleen Peippo

PRINCIPAL SUBSIDIARIES

Banta Direct Marketing, Inc.; Banta Europe BV (The Netherlands); Banta Europe Corporation (The Netherlands); Banta Healthcare Group, Ltd.; Banta Global Turnkey B.V. (The Netherlands); Banta Global Turnkey Ltd. (Ireland); Banta Global Turnkey Ltd. (Scotland); Banta Packaging & Fulfillment, Inc.; Banta Specialty Converting, LLC; Danbury Printing & Litho, Inc.; Banta Integrated Media—Cambridge, Inc.; United Graphics, Inc.; Wrapper, Inc.; Banta Publications-

Greenfield, Inc.; Greenfield Holdings Corp.; Type Designs, Inc.; Banta Holding Corp.; Banta Global Turnkey (Singapore) Pte. Ltd.; Banta Southeastern, Inc.; Banta Finance Corporation; Banta Global Turnkey—Guadalajara Sde RL de CV; BGT Services—Guadalajara Sde RL de CV; BGT-US, LLC; Banta Global Turnkey, Ltd.; Banta Global Turnkey Kft. (Hungary); Banta Global Turnkey, Limited (Hong Kong).

PRINCIPAL COMPETITORS

Dai Nippon Printing Co., Ltd.; Quebecor Inc.; R.R. Donnelley & Sons Company.

FURTHER READING

Bach, Pete, "Menasha, Wis.-Based Printing Firm Holds Strong in Catalog Production," *Knight Ridder/Tribune Business News*, January 1, 2003.

"Banta Celebrates 100 Years," *American Printer*, January 2002, p. 17.

"Banta Corp. Sets New Records," *Post-Crescent* (Appleton, Wisconsin), February 1, 2006.

"Banta Earnings Up," *Journal of Commerce Online*, January 26, 2005.

"Banta to Restructure in a Four-Part Plan," *Graphic Arts Monthly*, November 1997, p. 26.

Belcher, Donald D., Presentation on Banta Corporation to the New York Society of Security Analysts, company document, March 6, 1995.

Boardman, Arlen, "Menasha, Wis., Printing Company Names New CEO," *Knight Ridder/Tribune Business News*, May 23, 2004.

———, "Outgoing Chief of Menasha, Wis., Printing Company Helped Firm Expand Globally," *Knight Ridder/Tribune Business News*, May 23, 2004.

Byrne, Harlan S., "Banta Corp. Acquisition Doubles Sales, Moves It into Fast-Growing Field," *Barron's*, May 29, 1989.

———, "Banta Corp.: A Power of the Press," *Barron's*, March 20, 1995, p. 24.

Dresang, Joel, "Printers Find Growth in Niches," *Milwaukee Journal Sentinel*, February 21, 2005.

Elder, Laura, "Compaq Outsources Hard Drive Distribution to Wisconsin Firm," *Houston Business Journal*, October 29, 1999, p. 6A.

Hawkins, Lee, Jr., "Banta Shedding Parts of KCS: Firm to Close Printing Operation at Milwaukee Plant, Sell Display Business As Part of Restructuring Plan," *Milwaukee Journal Sentinel*, September 27, 1997.

———, "Menasha-Based Banta Corp. Lands $100 Million Publishing Contract," *Milwaukee Journal Sentinel*, January 28, 1999.

———, "Menasha, Wis.-Based Printing Company Names New President, CEO," *Milwaukee Journal Sentinel*, August 29, 2002.

———, "Menasha, Wis.-Based Printing Firm Banta Corp. to Lay Off 650 Workers," *Milwaukee Journal Sentinel*, April 13, 1999.

Joshi, Pradnya, "Banta Acquires Software Company," *Milwaukee Journal Sentinel*, October 10, 1995.

Key, Peter, "Digital Printer Runs Out of Cash, Files Chap.11," *Philadelphia Business Journal*, April 20, 2001, p. 3.

Matzek, MaryBeth, "Banta Healthcare Sold for $67 Million," *Knight Ridder/Tribune Business News*, February 15, 2005.

Milliot, Jim, "Difficult Market Leads to Slump in Printing Sales," *Publishers Weekly*, February 16, 2004, p. 52.

———, "Printers Report Soft Ending to Soft Year," *Publishers Weekly*, February 11, 2002, p. 76,

Olson, Jon, "Banta Corp. Makes Move into Europe," *Milwaukee Journal Sentinel*, August 29, 1995, p. D1.

———, "Banta Is Making an Imprint on Wall Street," *Milwaukee Journal Sentinel*, September 16, 1995.

Roberts, Kay, "The Founder's Wife," *Appleton (Wisc.) Post-Crescent*, February 4, 1979.

"Sales Up at Banta, Donnelley," *Publishers Weekly*, April 23, 2001, p. 17.

"Short and Sweet: Banta Digital Services Uses Digital Press Technology to Develop the On-Demand Print Market," *American Printer*, September 1995, pp. 36-38.

Stapel, Jeff, and Lorrie Potash, "Banta—90 Years of Growth," *Banta Company Magazine*, 1991, pp. 18-20.

Zuhl, Joanne, "Compaq Deal Gives Menasha, Wis.-Based Computer Firm New Dimension," *Knight Ridder/Tribune Business News*, November 24, 1999.

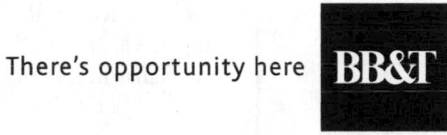

There's opportunity here BB&T

BB&T Corporation

200 West Second Street
Winston-Salem, North Carolina 27101
U.S.A.
Telephone: (336) 733-2000
Fax: (336) 733-2209
Web site: http://www.bbandt.com

Public Company
Incorporated: 1968 as Southern National Corporation
Employees: 27,700
Total Assets: $109.16 billion (2005)
Stock Exchanges: New York
Ticker Symbol: BBT
NAIC: 522110 Commercial Banking; 523920 Portfolio Management; 523991 Trust, Fiduciary, and Custody Activities; 524210 Insurance Agencies and Brokerages

■ ■ ■

BB&T Corporation is one of the leading banking groups in the Southeast. It is the parent company to North Carolina's oldest bank. The regional financial powerhouse also has substantial insurance, brokerage, and asset management businesses. BB&T has grown aggressively by acquisition since the 1980s; the company has a decentralized decision-making structure and strives for a community banking feel.

ORIGINS

BB&T traces its origins to 1872, when Alpheus Branch and Thomas Jefferson Hadley launched a bank called Branch & Hadley in the small farming town of Wilson, North Carolina. In the midst of the Reconstruction, the South was in political and financial chaos. As BB&T Chairman and CEO John A. Allison IV said in a Newcomen Society address, Branch and Hadley helped local cotton farmers stay in business. Branch bought out Hadley in 1887 and renamed the bank Branch & Company, Bankers.

According to Allison, the local economy was thriving by 1900, thanks to the addition of the more lucrative tobacco farming. By this time, the bank had received a North Carolina charter and had gone through a couple of different names (Wilson Banking and Trust Company and the State Bank of Wilson) before becoming known as Branch Banking Company. It was renamed Branch Banking and Trust Company (BB&T) in 1913.

The number of services offered increased steadily in the early decades of the 20th century. The bank began offering insurance and mortgages in the early 1920s. Around the same time, it became one of the first banks in the region to open branch offices. According to Allison, BB&T managed to triple its assets during the Great Depression, a time when many other banks failed.

BB&T handled government bonds during World War II and financed returning soldiers' postwar lifestyles with consumer loans, said Allison. It retained its emphasis on business banking as well.

SLOW GROWTH UNTIL 1981

BB&T had an office in Raleigh by 1959. A new headquarters building was constructed in Wilson, North Carolina, in 1971. These were highlights of a period of

COMPANY PERSPECTIVES

At BB&T we have two powerful passions. Our fundamental passion is our Vision: To Create The Best Financial Institution Possible—The "World Standard"—The "Best of the Best." We believe that the best can be objectively evaluated by rational performance standards in relation to the accomplishment of our mission.

To be the best of the best, we must constantly find ways to deliver better value to our clients in a highly profitable manner. This requires us to keep our minds focused at all times on innovative ways to enhance our productivity.

relatively slow growth. Assets were about $250 million in the early 1970s, and agriculture accounted for about one-quarter of its lending, according to the *Greensboro News-Record.* As North Carolina adapted to a changing, technology-driven economy, so would BB&T.

BB&T began the 1980s with deposits of $600 million. It had 81 branches, all in North Carolina. A policy of growth by acquisition was launched in 1981 with the purchase of Gastonia, North Carolina's Independence National Bank. By the mid-1980s, its branches stretched from the mountains to the sea.

BB&T entered South Carolina by merging with Greenville's Community Bancorporation Inc. in 1987, which was renamed BB&T of South Carolina. By the end of the decade, BB&T had assets of $4.7 billion. The holding company, which had been renamed BB&T Financial Corporation, had 187 branches in 105 communities in two states. Though it had grown considerably in the 1980s, it was a distant fourth to North Carolina's Big Three banking giants (NCNB Corp., First Union Corp. and Wachovia Corp.). It did, however, lay claim to the distinction of being the oldest operating bank in the state.

L. Vincent Lowe, Jr., became president and CEO in 1982 upon the death of Thorne Gregory. Lowe himself passed away in 1989. John A. Allison IV was named chairman and CEO after the death of Lowe, who had been his mentor. Allison had started working for the bank in 1971 while studying for an M.B.A. *Forbes* dubbed Allison the "Philosopher King" for his penchant for citing thinkers from the ancient Greeks to Ayn Rand.

A strong emphasis on reason would permeate the company's literature. Allison quoted Aristotle: "We are what we repeatedly do." What BB&T did repeatedly was buy banks, making it one of the leading consolidators in the Southeast. The company took advantage of the savings and loan crisis of the 1980s by acquiring healthy thrifts at bargain prices, once federal bailout legislation was expanded. Allison's management style stressed decentralization, striving for a community banking feel at the branch level. BB&T also became a specialist in lending to small to medium-sized businesses.

1995 SOUTHERN NATIONAL MERGER

BB&T combined with Winston-Salem's Southern National Corporation in a merger of equals in 1995. Southern National, the fifth largest bank in North Carolina before the merger (BB&T was number four), had been formed in 1897 in Lumberton.

The newly merged company had assets of $18 billion, making it the 35th largest bank in the United States and the sixth largest in the Southeast. While the BB&T brand was kept in use, Southern National Corporation, a holding company formed in 1968, was the surviving entity; it was renamed BB&T Corporation in 1997. Winston-Salem, where Southern National had been based, became BB&T's new home.

The mergers and acquisitions activity continued, bringing the company into Virginia with the January 1995 purchase of Commerce Bank of Hampton Roads. BB&T then bought Richmond's Fidelity Financial Bankshares Corporation.

In 1997, BB&T added Virginia First Financial Corporation, a thrift with a presence in southern and central parts of the state. Another Virginia acquisition, Craigie Inc. of Richmond, brought BB&T into investment banking for the first time, thanks to the loosening of a federal prohibition on banks selling securities. Another Richmond investment bank, the venerable Scott & Stringfellow (established 1893), was acquired later. BB&T set up its own venture capital firm in March 1998.

Sub-prime auto finance company Regional Acceptance of Greenville, North Carolina, was acquired in 1997. The march up the East Coast continued. Washington, D.C.'s Franklin Bancorporation Inc. was added in December 1997. Norfolk's Life Bancorp Inc. followed in March 1998. Several months later Maryland Federal Bancorp Inc. was acquired. The company also bought MainStreet Financial Corporation, a community bank which was based in the southwest Virginia town of Martinsville but had offices as far afield as Washington, D.C.

BB&T had a very busy year in 1999, as it expanded on all fronts. It arrived in metro Atlanta through the

KEY DATES

1872: Alpheus Branch and Thomas Jefferson Hadley begin banking in Wilson, North Carolina.
1897: Southern National is founded in Lumberton, North Carolina.
1913: Branch & Hadley is renamed Branch Banking and Trust Company (BB&T).
1921: BB&T begins opening branch offices.
1923: BB&T's assets exceed $4 million.
1968: Southern National Corporation holding company is incorporated.
1971: BB&T's assets are $250 million; new home office building is constructed.
1974: Holding company Branch Corporation is formed.
1987: BB&T enters South Carolina by merging with Greenville's Community Bancorporation Inc.
1988: Branch Corporation is renamed BB&T Financial Corporation.
1989: BB&T's assets are about $5 billion.
1995: BB&T merges with Winston-Salem's Southern National Corporation; company enters Virginia.
1997: BB&T acquires United Carolina Bancshares; company enters Washington, D.C. market, buys first investment bank.
1998: BB&T sets up venture capital firm.
1999: BB&T makes several acquisitions, enters metro Atlanta, West Virginia, and Kentucky.
2000: Company enters Tennessee via acquisition of Knoxville bank.
2002: BB&T enters the Florida Panhandle and Gulf Coast markets.
2003: After buying First Virginia for $3 billion, BB&T slows hectic M&A activity.
2005: Assets reach $109 billion.

purchase of Newman, Georgia's First Citizens Corporation. Macon's First Liberty Financial Corporation was also added. Premier Bancshares, an Atlanta commercial bank, followed.

At the same time, BB&T was buying Mason-Dixon Bancshares of Westminster, Maryland. The purchase of Williamson, West Virginia-based Matewan BancShares Inc. brought the company into West Virginia and Kentucky.

While making numerous acquisitions, BB&T introduced a number of online services in the latter half of the decade. It also instituted an aggressive sales process that was lifting its fee income faster than that of other major banks, Chairman and CEO John A. Allison IV said in a Newcomen Society address.

BB&T ended the 1990s as one of the two-dozen largest bank holding companies in the United States, with assets of about $43 billion. It employed 13,000 people at 620 branches in seven states in the Southeast and Mid-Atlantic region, as well as Washington, D.C. BB&T had a substantial presence in a number of fields besides commercial banking. It claimed the largest network of independent insurance agents in the Carolinas.

BB&T proposed merging with giant rival Wachovia Corp. in 2000. This fell through, but the shopping spree continued, at the rate of seven to ten banks a year. The purchase of Knoxville's BankFirst Corp. brought BB&T into Tennessee for the first time.

The company typically sought small to mid-sized banks with assets of $250 million to $10 billion. In acquiring banks, it looked for ways to cut costs through layoffs and the like. In August 2000, BB&T formed a special two-person team to ensure the conversions went smoothly, reported *American Banker.* The process required communicating with hundreds of branches and thousands of customers.

Some wondered if BB&T was paying too much for some of its acquisitions, exceeding the industry average for prices based on book value. However, BB&T defended its role as "acquirer of choice," and stressed the strategic nature of its acquisitions. It had developed a reputation as one of the most successful integrators of acquired banks in the industry. "Darn few have been able to get away with a consolidation strategy, but one of the best is BB&T," an SNL Securities analyst told the *Business Journal Serving Charlotte and the Metropolitan Area.*

BB&T continued to acquire more than banks. It picked up Cooney Rikard & Curtin (later renamed CRC Insurance Services Inc.), a Birmingham, Alabama-based insurance wholesaler, in January 2002 for stock worth $86 million. CRC specialized in excess and surplus insurance. Matching CRÇ with BB&T's existing retail agencies made sense for both parties, observed *American Banker.* BB&T announced the purchase of a large Birmingham insurance agency, McGriff, Seibels & Williams, in November 2003. By this time, the company owned 72 agencies in the South and Mid-Atlantic.

CUTTING DOWN ON M&A AFTER 2003

The pace of M&A activity was increasing, thanks in part to favorable changes in accounting rules. The company got a toehold in Florida with the acquisition of First South Bank in September 2002. However, after its largest deal yet, buying Virginia's largest independent bank, First Virginia Banks Inc., for $3 billion in 2003, BB&T announced it would largely curtail its acquisition activities.

The First Virginia buy made BB&T the nation's 13th largest bank holding company, according to *American Banker,* with assets of $91 billion. While it was an attractive investment due to its importance in the Virginia, Maryland, and Washington, D.C. markets (BB&T had been interested in it for ten years, according to Allison), the price of the First Virginia buy had some investors grumbling about price.

BB&T abstained from acquisitions altogether for nearly two years beginning in 2004, shelving a couple of deals in the high-priced Florida market. By the end of 2005, however, the company had already announced another purchase: Atlanta's Main Street Banks Inc., for stock worth about $600 million. The acquisition of another smaller bank, First Citizens Bancorp of eastern Tennessee, was announced in January 2006. BB&T was buying again, but no expensive mega-mergers were on the table.

While on a self-imposed M&A moratorium, the bank had begun to build dozens of new branches every year. The company decided to accelerate its construction even more after a consulting firm identified deposits as a more profitable area of activity than lending, where its traditional emphasis lay. The company had developed a special regimen in the Atlanta market for making new branches profitable within a year, three times faster than average, reported *American Banker.*

At the end of 2005, assets were up to $109 billion and the bank had 1,400 branches in 11 states and the District of Columbia. There were about 28,000 employees. In early 2006, BB&T was making headlines over Chairman and CEO John Allison's principled stance regarding property rights. He announced a policy of not financing private developments built on land seized through eminent domain.

Frederick C. Ingram

PRINCIPAL SUBSIDIARIES

Branch Banking and Trust Company; Regional Acceptance Corporation; Money 24, Inc.; Scott & Stringfellow, Inc.; SHDR Investment Advisors, Inc.; Mid-America Gift Certificate Company; BB&T Bankcard Corporation; BB&T Payroll Services Corporation; Grey Hawk, Inc.; BB&T Capital Trust I; Mason-Dixon Capital Trust; MainStreet Capital Trust I; Premier Capital Trust I; Berg Acquisition Company, LLC; First Virginia Services, Inc.; First Virginia Life Insurance Company; Sheffield Financial, LLC; BB&T Overseas Leasing, Ltd. (Bermuda); BB&T Asset Management, Inc.; BB&T Assurance Company, LTD. (Bermuda); Matewan Venture Fund, Inc.; Liberty Properties, Inc.; One Valley Square, Inc.; Branch Banking and Trust Company of South Carolina; Branch Banking and Trust Company of Virginia; Creative Payment Solutions, Inc.; Wilson Fiduciary Management Corporation; BB&T Charitable Foundation; Sterling Capital Management, LLC.

PRINCIPAL COMPETITORS

Bank of America Corp.; Wachovia Corp.

FURTHER READING

Ackermann, Matt, "BB&T Asset Unit Focuses on Ga.-Fla. Deals, Hiring," *American Banker,* February 2, 2006, p. 9.

Adams, Jerry, "Fast Start Marks Allison's Ascent; New Chief of BB&T Spurs Modernization," *American Banker,* July 6, 1987, p. 13.

Allison, John A., IV, "BB&T Corporation," New York: Newcomen Society of the United States, 1999.

"BB&T Chairman Lowe Dies at 53," *American Banker,* July 11, 1989, p. 6.

"BB&T's New Strategy: We Buy Harder," *Business-North Carolina,* August 1, 1990, p. 81.

Boraks, David, "The Evolution of a BB&T Deal," *American Banker,* August 5, 2003, p. 4A.

———, "Wholesale Division Changing BB&T's Philosophy," *American Banker,* October 7, 2003, p. 4A.

Davis, Paul, "After a Long Absence, BB&T Back to Buying: Price of Main Street Wins Over Wall Street," *American Banker,* December 16, 2005, p. 1.

———, "For BB&T, 2d Deal in Month After Long Layoff," *American Banker,* January 13, 2006, p. 1.

———, "A Surprising Study Turns BB&T's Focus to Deposits," *American Banker,* February 22, 2006, p. 1.

Donsky, Martin, "Banking's Eastern Star," *Business-North Carolina,* October 1, 1988, p. 38.

Fung, Amanda, "One Size Doesn't Fit All in BB&T Conversion Efforts," *American Banker,* May 29, 2002, p. 7A.

Gillam, Carey, "Whoops! Southern National Decides It Should Have Called Itself BB&T," *American Banker,* March 24, 1997, p. 6.

Gjertsen, Lee Ann, "BB&T Shifts Strategy in Its Biggest Deal Yet," *American Banker,* November 12, 2003, p. 1.

Grant, Lorrie, "BB&T, Southern National to Merge in $2.2 Billion Deal," *Reuters News,* August 1, 1994.

Hazard, Carol, "BB&T Acquiring First Va.," *Richmond Times-Dispatch,* January 22, 2003, p. A1.

Kline, Kenneth, "BB&T's Ads Break Taboo, Knock N. Carolina Brethren," *American Banker,* February 7, 1991, p. 10.

Nowell, Paul, "N.C. Banker Takes Maverick Stance on Eminent Domain Land Seizures," *Associated Press Newswires,* March 4, 2006.

Price, Dudley, "BB&T Leaving Town Where It Began; Economy, Civic Pride Are at Risk in Wilson," *News & Observer* (Raleigh), August 2, 1994, p. D1.

Rieker, Matthias, "Even for BB&T, Clear M&A Accounting Helps," *American Banker,* February 11, 2002, p. 1.

Sams, Rachel, "BB&T Corp. Making a Name for Itself in Florida Banking Market," *Knight-Ridder Tribune Business News: Tallahassee Democrat,* December 17, 2002.

Scism, Jack, "At 41, Allison Is Old Enough to Head BB&T," *Greensboro News & Record,* December 18, 1989, p. 4.

Tannenbaum, Fred, "BB&T Paying Top Dollar in Mergers," *Business Journal Serving Charlotte and the Metropolitan Area,* July 13, 2001, p. 1.

Thompson, Marie, "Allison, John A. IV 1948–," *International Directory of Business Biographies,* ed. Neil Schlager, Vol. 1, Detroit: St. James Press, 2005.

Vardi, Nathan, "Philosopher King," *Forbes,* June 11, 2001, p. 90.

Wyatt, Edward A., "Found: A Prosperous Bank—BB&T Financial Extends Its Growth," *Barron's,* July 23, 1990, p. 17.

Big A Drug Stores Inc.

12030 South Garfield Avenue
South Gate, California 90280
U.S.A.
Telephone: (562) 633-2026
Fax: (562) 633-3613
Web site: http://www.bigadrug.com

Private Company
Incorporated: 1971
Employees: 263
Sales: $114.4 million (2005)
NAIC: 446110 Pharmacies and Drug Stores

Big A Drug Stores Inc. owns a chain of 21 drugstores located in California operating under the names "Big A Drug," "Drug Emporium," "Camelot Drug," "Drug Fair," and "Drug Barn." The stores average 25,000 square feet and derive approximately 40 percent of their revenue from pharmaceuticals. Each store stocks a wide variety of merchandise, including food, office supplies, hardware, entertainment products, health and beauty products, pet food, and home health equipment. All of the company's stores are located in shopping malls or strip malls and offer home-delivery of prescription drugs. The stores also are equipped with service centers that allow customers to pay utility bills, use the U.S. Postal Service, and conduct transactions using Western Union. Big A's 14 Drug Emporium stores operate as deep-discounters. The composition of the rest of the chain comprises three Big A stores, two Drug Barn stores, one Camelot Drugs store, and one Drug Fair store. The company is owned by its founder, Edward Dallal, who serves as its president and chief executive officer.

ORIGINS

By the standards of the 21st century, Edward Dallal was an anomaly in the drugstore industry. His chain of drugstores did not follow the blueprint of success established by the industry's largest competitors, namely retail giants Walgreen Co., CVS Corporation, and Rite Aid Corporation, yet the Big A chain thrived: a diminutive, one-state company that was able to succeed in the shadow of giants. Together, the nation's three largest chains operated nearly 14,000 stores and generated a staggering $100 billion in annual revenue at a time when Dallal's chain comprised fewer than two dozen stores and collected just over $100 million a year in sales. Big A, in its various guises, succeeded because Dallal adhered to business practices his customers liked and had come to expect, creating a loyal customer base that allowed an irregular drugstore chain to remain financially healthy in the modern era of the retail industry.

Dallal, a pharmacist educated at the University of Southern California School of Pharmacy, decided to operate his own pharmacy in the early 1970s. In 1971, he purchased a drugstore in Long Beach, California, the beginning of the Big A chain. A chain of stores was slow to emerge, as Dallal adopted a measured approach to growth. During his first 25 years in business, he added a new drugstore to his operations at an average of one new unit every five years, expanding exclusively in the greater Los Angeles area, in shopping centers or along

COMPANY PERSPECTIVES

The philosophy of the Big A and Drug Emporium drugstores is to provide excellent customer service while remaining competitively priced. For example, the average large chain wait time can be as high as 1½ hours and our average wait time is usually ½ hour or less. We have some excellent relationships with local physicians and even offer delivery service in selected locations. This allows us to attract the insured customers as well as those who may be uninsured. Moreover, with increasing restrictions on drug formularies many patients are buying their non-formulary prescriptions from us. This not only provides the opportunity for growing the customer base, but also generates additional front end sales.

strip malls. Dallal's 25th year in business marked a turning point, however, ushering in a new era that embraced geographic expansion and a decidedly more rapid pace of expansion.

EXPANSION BEGINNING IN 1996

For a company that opened two stores a decade, adding two stores overnight represented an unprecedented surge in growth. In 1996, Dallal moved beyond the southern half of California for the first time when he purchased two, deep-discount stores operating under the banner Drug Barn. The stores, located in Colma and Sunnyvale, gave Dallal a northern division and added a new, larger format to his operations. Drug Barn's heavy discount pricing strategy, retained by Dallal after he acquired the stores, represented a new wrinkle to his business, a pricing strategy not followed by his other five stores, which operated under three names, Big A, Drug Fair and Camelot Drugs. The addition of a fourth name added to the eclectic quality of the small chain, but aside from the difference in pricing strategy, the entire operation had cohesion, held together by Dallal's retail philosophy.

Dallal preached customer service. Except for warehouse stores that functioned within a self-service format, every retailer claimed to emphasize customer service, but not all retailers put their words into practice. Dallal stressed service as the linchpin of his operating strategy, referring to the importance of his relationship with customers in nearly every discussion of his company. "We have our own clientele," he said in an April 26, 2004 interview with *Chain Drug Review.* "They've been coming to the stores for 20 or 30 years, and they know they'll get service." In an interview with *Drug Store News* on April 26, 1999, Dallal said, "Service is the name of the game. You can only compete with service." In a May 2, 2005 interview with *Chain Drug Review,* Dallal reiterated his refrain, explaining, "We have customers who have been shopping at our stores since they were children, and now they come in with their own children. They're not going to jump ship just because Wal-Mart or Walgreens opens a store down the road." A commitment to service bred customer loyalty, Dallal's only way to compete against much larger rivals whose size produced economies of scale against which the relatively tiny South Gate-based operation could not compete. Dallal knew his strengths and weaknesses; compete against Walgreen and other large competitors on price only, and he would be crushed, but if he could cultivate loyalty among his customers, his small retail chain had a chance to succeed.

The acquisition of Drug Barn seemed to awaken Dallal's desire for expansion, albeit in a conservative manner. He looked for additional stores to acquire in 1997, but he could not find any properties that met his criteria, the most important of which was store size. Dallal's stores typically were larger than 20,000 square feet, unusually large for a drugstore—one of several characteristics of the chain that distinguished it from most of its competitors. Dallal's search in 1997 failed to find any stores that met his size requirements, which would be a perennial problem because of the paucity of available real estate in many metropolitan markets in California. "We're still looking for acquisitions," Dallal said in an April 27, 1998 interview with *Drug Store News.* "My position is that I'm not in a hurry to expand unless it's the right store and the right location, and unless it comes at a very good price."

With no way to grow his business through external means, Dallal turned to internal improvements, looking for ways to increase business at his collection of seven stores. In 1997, he launched a marketing program with the help of Promotions Unlimited, distributing coupon books and placing advertisements for his stores. "It brings in business and I can compete in the market," he said in his April 27, 1998 interview with *Drug Store News.* Dallal also began experimenting with stocking variety and craft items, such as artificial flowers, adding a picture-framing self-service area, and a staffed, custom-framing service. The new features, which complemented the chain's service centers that allowed customers to pay their utility bills and send or receive money via Western Union, were intrinsic to increasing traffic at the stores, of particular importance to the Big A chain. Typically, drugstore chains relied on pharmacy business, referred to as "back-end" because of the location of the pharmacy,

KEY DATES

1971: Edward Dallal purchases his first store in Long Beach, California.
1996: Big A acquires two stores in northern California operating under the name Drug Barn.
2001: Big A acquires 15 Drug Emporium stores, tripling its store count.
2006: Big A launches its web site.

to generate nearly 70 percent of a store's business. Big A, in another departure from the norm, relied on back-end business for roughly half the business of a typical drugstore, generating the bulk of its sales from the "front-end," the groceries, health and beauty products, and sundry other merchandise stocked on the shelves leading to a store's pharmacy. Aside from offering a wide variety of merchandise, one of the advantages gained by operating large stores, Dallal added new, convenient services to lure customers into his stores, thereby bolstering the front-end of his business.

Without the aid of growth achieved by acquiring stores, Dallal made progress nevertheless. In 1998, the addition of new services and merchandise helped fuel a 10 percent increase in chainwide revenues to $55 million. Big A closed out the 1990s exuding strength, able to thrive as the industry's largest competitors expanded vigorously, establishing their stores, in some cases, only yards away from Dallal's stores. The company headed toward its 30th anniversary as something more akin to a mom-and-pop retailer than a chain, a drugstore operator without drive-through, prescription-drug service and without any stores opened 24 hours a day. Big A's diversion from the industry standard would continue, but the company's 30th anniversary marked an unprecedented increase in physical growth. Dallal's search for new stores found a large target in 2001, elevating the stature of his chain to a new level.

DRUG EMPORIUM ACQUISITION IN 2001

To the east, in Powell, Ohio, the fortunes of another drugstore chain drew Dallal's interest. Drug Emporium, a retail chain founded in 1977 in the Graceland Shopping Center in Powell, was in the headlines for all the wrong reasons. The company had spent the 1990s becoming one of the country's leading discount drugstore chains, assembling a roster of 137 company-owned stores and 42 franchised stores by the end of the decade. Aggressive expansion lifted sales to $1.2 billion, but rapid growth was achieved at the expense of profitability. The launch of DrugEmporium.com, the company's online pharmacy, in 1999 proved to be a particular disaster, recording an $8.1 million loss during the first quarter of 2000 and accumulating $22 million in losses during its first 15 months in operation. Drug Emporium soon headed toward financial collapse, as the chain, with stores concentrated in Pennsylvania, Ohio, Georgia, Michigan, and California, racked up crippling losses. The company prepared to file for bankruptcy in early 2001, but before it did so, Dallal moved in and acquired 15 of the company's California stores. The stores, which Dallal claimed were profitable, averaged 25,000 square feet, making a perfect fit to his enterprise. In early March 2001, Drug Emporium was delisted by the NASDAQ and filed for bankruptcy before the end of the month. Before the end of the year, 34 Drug Emporium stores were liquidated, two units were sold to Long's Drug, and 77 stores were sold to Snyder's Drug Stores Inc.

The acquisition of the Drug Emporium stores represented a massive addition to Big A, tripling the size of the chain. Almost immediately, Dallal began outfitting the 15 units with service centers, adding departments that increased store patronage considerably. The addition of bill-paying service centers, for instance, accounted for an average of 300 visits per store per day, while the presence of U.S. Postal Service stations attracted 150 customers per day and 600 per day during holidays. "An average drug chain might spend $26 to acquire a new customer or generate foot traffic," Dallal said in a June 25, 2001 interview with *Drug Store News.* "With these services, we're able to do it for free." Beginning in January 2002, he also began experimenting with 99-cents departments in several stores, scoring sufficient success to prompt a rollout of the department throughout the chain before the end of the year. By all measures the acquisition of the Drug Emporium stores proved to be a boon, but the same could not be said of Snyder's Drug Stores' experience with former Drug Emporium units. In 2003, the company, primarily because of its acquisition of 77 Drug Emporium units, filed for bankruptcy.

As Dallal looked ahead, his focus was on maintaining his stores' commitment to customer service and on adding new features and departments to keep new customers coming through the doors. Expansion in any substantial manner seemed unlikely given the lack of suitable real estate properties in California. Dallal's attitude toward further acquisitions in 2004 was much the same as it had been in 1998. "Unless it's a steal," he said in an April 26, 2004 interview with *Chain Drug Review,* "I'm not going to buy it." He was content to push ahead with his existing operation, an anachronism in the modern retailing world that was profitable nonetheless. In 2006, however, he bowed to the times in one respect by launching a corporate web site. He had purchased a domain name nearly six years earlier, and for nearly six years an "Under Construction" sign greeted online visitors. The launch of the web site, which was an information-only site, coincided with the company's 35th anniversary, an occasion that celebrated a successful past and pointed to a promising future.

Jeffrey L. Covell

PRINCIPAL COMPETITORS

CVS Corporation; Rite Aid Corporation; Walgreen Co.

FURTHER READING

"Big A Adds 99-Cents Depts.," *Drug Store News,* June 5, 2002, p. 2.

"Big A Earns Loyalty of Shoppers with an Unusual Approach," *Chain Drug Review,* May 2, 2005, p. 200.

Parks, Liz, "Acquisition Yields Greater Buying Clout Efficiencies," *Drug Store News,* April 29, 2000, p. 122.

———, "Big A: Traffic Building Is Job No. 1," *Drug Store News,* April 28, 2003, p. 118.

———, "Big A Upgrades Pharmacy System in Bid for Nursing Home Market," *Drug Store News,* September 23, 2002, p. 8.

"Service Is the Byword at Big A," *Chain Drug Review,* April 26, 2004, p. 196.

Symons, Allene, "Big A Expands Services, Plans for Growth," *Drug Store News,* April 26, 1999, p. 178.

———, "Big A Growth Plan Begins with Services," *Drug Store News,* April 27, 1998, p. 214.

Veiders, Christina, "Alternative Access," *Supermarket News,* October 24, 2005, p. 20.

BlackRock, Inc.

40 East 52nd Street
New York, New York 10022
U.S.A.
Telephone: (212) 810-5300
Fax: (212) 935-1370
Web site: http://www.blackrock.com

Public Company
Incorporated: 1998 as BlackRock, Inc.
Employees: 1,560
Total Assets: $1.84 billion (2005)
Stock Exchanges: New York
Ticker Symbol: BLK
NAIC: 523920 Portfolio Management; 523930 Investment Advice

BlackRock, Inc. is a leading investment management firm. Disciplined risk management is its trademark; in fact the firm markets its methods to others under the BlackRock Solutions brand. BlackRock had $452.7 billion in assets under management at the end of 2005; this would grow to a staggering $1 trillion upon successful completion of its merger with the investment management business Merrill Lynch, due by the end of 2006. BlackRock is indirectly controlled by Pittsburgh bank the PNC Financial Services Group, Inc. In addition to its New York base, the firm has offices in 14 cities in the United States, Europe, and the Pacific Rim. While BlackRock made its reputation on fixed income products, i.e. bonds, it has steadily developed an array of other investment capabilities.

ORIGINS IN MORTGAGE-BACKED SECURITIES

BlackRock's origins can be traced to 1988, when Blackstone Financial Management LP was formed by Laurence D. (Larry) Fink and a group of seven colleagues. A native of Los Angeles, Fink had earned an M.B.A. at UCLA before starting his Wall Street career at First Boston. There, according to *Fortune,* he turned a little-known mortgage-backed securities trade into a booming sideline for the bank's mortgage department. After weathering up cycles and down, Fink decided to become a buyer, rather than a seller, of bonds.

Fink then became a partner in the Blackstone Group, a New York investment firm. While the others in the group focused on leveraged buyouts, Fink offered clients such as pension funds customized portfolios of bonds based on the desired amount of risk. The asset management business would become known as Blackstone Financial Management.

Blackstone's first offering, reported *American Banker,* was a $100 million fund devoted largely to mortgage-backed securities. It was launched in 1988. An equity fund followed the next year. The firm preferred to invest in large, fiscally sound companies in growth industries.

Disciplined risk management, including computerized analysis, has always been a trademark of the firm, said *Fortune.* According to *Pensions & Investments,* the firm had started out with just one computer.

It began making its risk management expertise

COMPANY PERSPECTIVES

BlackRock's mission is to be a world-class provider of global investment management, risk management, and advisory services. We offer a broad range of investment products that target returns in excess of their benchmarks while efficiently managing risk. Our risk management products and services are developed from the same proprietary systems and analytics that support our own asset management business. We bring to asset management a practical, real world application of risk management techniques and analytics designed to maximize usability, consistency, efficiency, and flexibility.

BlackRock is committed to building long-term relationships by providing superior performance, excellent client service, and customized products and services to meet individual client needs. We continually and carefully evaluate new products and disciplines based upon market opportunities, investor needs, and their strategic fit with BlackRock's existing organization.

available to others in 1994, noted *Global Investor,* beginning with an analysis of Kidder Peabody's $10 billion collateralized mortgage obligation (CMO) portfolio that was being liquidated. This risk management business was branded as BlackRock Solutions in 2000. By 2004, the consulting business had annual revenues of $80 million.

By 1991, according to *Fortune,* Blackstone was managing $9 billion in assets for Chrysler, General Electric, and others. Blackstone Financial Management LP was renamed BlackRock Financial Management LP in July 1992. Its holding company, BFM Holdings Inc., filed for an initial public offering, but this would be deferred for a couple of years.

ACQUIRED BY PNC IN 1995

The PNC Financial Services Group, Inc., the Pittsburgh-based banking empire, acquired BlackRock Financial Management for $240 million in 1994. At the time, BlackRock's assets under management had blossomed to $23 billion, and it was just the beginning of a steep climb. They would increase more than sixfold in five years. After the takeover, PNC provided a special bonus pool to persuade fund managers to stay on the team. In 2001, when their contracts expired, PNC offered another $200 million as incentives, provided BlackRock maintained a 15 percent or better annual growth rate.

BlackRock added hedge funds to its products in 1996. Within three years of being acquired by PNC, BlackRock's assets doubled to about $46 billion, noted *Pensions & Investments* in 1997. According to *Crain's New York Business,* the affiliation with parent PNC gave BlackRock a source of retail customers to supplement its institutional investor client base, which in the late 1990s still accounted for about 80 percent of its assets under management.

BlackRock was reorganized as a corporation in February 1998. PNC granted its 22 partners 20 percent of its equity. PNC's own $108 billion asset management unit was merged into BlackRock later in the year.

1999 IPO

PNC sold 14 percent of BlackRock Inc.'s common stock to the public in an October 1, 1999 initial public offering (IPO). Priced at $14 a share, the IPO raised $126 million. Fink and other partners owned another 16 percent, leaving PNC with a 70 percent interest. At the time, BlackRock, valued at $895 million, was estimated to be the country's fifth largest publicly traded asset management firm. It then had 650 employees.

BlackRock planned to use the capital to be a leading consolidator in the crowded investment management field, while paying down debts related to the 1994 acquisition by PNC. Equities firms would be a particular area of interest for at least several years.

The tech stock speculation of the time largely escaped BlackRock, which was primarily focused on bonds, which were barely yielding 6 percent at the time. While its funds did not boast the stellar returns of the high-flying NASDAQ, after the bust its conservative management seemed inspired and, most importantly, safe. BlackRock steadily continued to grow into a monolith on Wall Street. The firm ended 2000 with $204 billion in assets under management. Revenue was $477 million.

Boston-based hedge fund manager Cylennius Capital Management was acquired in September 2002. It had $100 million in assets under management for institutions and high-net-worth individuals.

A few months later, in April 2003, BlackRock agreed to buy a majority interest in HPB Management LLC, a fund-of-hedge-funds company founded by veteran manager Howard P. Berkowitz, who went on to lead BlackRock's fund-of-hedge-funds business. HPB then had $150 million in assets. BlackRock, which had built

KEY DATES

1988: Blackstone Financial Management is formed at First Boston Corp.

1992: Blackstone Financial Management changes name to BlackRock Financial Management.

1994: BlackRock begins providing risk management systems to third parties.

1995: The PNC Financial Services Group, Inc. acquires BlackRock Financial Management.

1998: Partnership is reorganized as a corporation.

1999: PNC offers 30 percent of BlackRock shares to the public.

2005: BlackRock buys State Street Research & Management (SSRM) from MetLife, Inc.

2006: BlackRock and Merrill Lynch Investment Managers (MLIM) agree to merge to create $1 trillion giant.

its reputation on bonds, sought to offer more alternative investment products, a company source told *American Banker.* Institutional clients were looking for more potential for higher returns.

At the end of 2004, BlackRock was managing assets of $342 billion, up ten percent from the previous year. Most were managed in separate accounts, although the firm did have 27 percent in mutual funds such as BlackRock Funds and BlackRock Liquidity Funds. BlackRock ranked among the top 25 investment management companies in the world. By this time, its share price had more than quintupled to around $75.

In January 2005, BlackRock acquired MetLife, Inc.'s SSRM Holdings, Inc. in a deal worth $375 million ($325 million stock, $50 million of BlackRock common stock). SSRM had about $50 billion in assets under management through subsidiaries State Street Research & Management Company and SSR Realty Advisors.

Business Week chronicled the firm's attempts to build a reputation for stock funds as well as bonds, which were susceptible to losing value as interest rates increased. The SSRM acquisition was part of the plan; SSRM brought with it $17.6 billion in mutual funds. Fink was also manning existing funds with managers hired away from rivals. Even so, stocks accounted for less than 10 percent of BlackRock's assets. BlackRock ended 2005 managing assets of $452.7 billion. BlackRock was also aiming to increase its geographic diversity. In 2004, it added offices in Sydney and Singapore; London and Munich followed the next year.

MLIM MERGER PENDING IN 2006

In early 2006, Merrill Lynch was combining its asset management business, Merrill Lynch Investment Managers (MLIM), with BlackRock in exchange for a 49.5 percent holding in BlackRock valued at $6.8 billion. The merger, if completed successfully, would make not only a $1 trillion giant, second only to Fidelity in mutual funds, but would also bring BlackRock a long desired strengthening of its equities side. The merger was scheduled to close in the third quarter of 2006.

Frederick C. Ingram

PRINCIPAL SUBSIDIARIES

BlackRock Advisors, Inc.; BlackRock Financial Management, Inc.; BlackRock Institutional Management Corporation; State Street Research & Management Company; SSRM Holdings, Inc.

PRINCIPAL COMPETITORS

Western Asset Management Company; Pimco Advisors Holdings.

FURTHER READING

Ackerman, Matt, "BlackRock Bets on Alternative Products' Lure," *American Banker,* May 30, 2003, p. 10.

Appell, Douglas, "Money Management: BlackRock Seeks Incremental, Not Earth-Shattering, Changes," *Pensions & Investments,* May 2, 2005, p. 3.

———, "Pink Slips: BlackRock Slashes SSRM's Staff; 2 Chief Investment Officers Among 31% of Employees Let Go; CEO Davis Staying," *Pensions & Investments,* December 13, 2004, p. 1.

"BFM Holdings Files Initial Share Offer," *Reuters News,* May 20, 1992.

"BlackRock's Solution," *Global Investor,* November 2002, p. 22.

Boorstin, Julia, "The Hidden Beauty of Bonds: While You Were Watching the Stock Market, a Little-Known Bond House Called BlackRock Grew into One of the Biggest Players on Wall Street," *Fortune,* March 19, 2001, pp. 118+.

Burke, Kevin, "What the BlackRock/Merrill Deal Means to Advisors," *Registered Rep (Online Exclusive),* February 15, 2006.

Calio, Vince, " 'A Little More Scale': BlackRock Deal for SSRM Motivated by Mutual Funds," *Pensions & Investments,* September 6, 2004, p. 1.

Cardona, Mercedes M., "BlackRock Prospers with PNC As Owner," *Pensions & Investments,* June 9, 1997, p. 34.

Crawford, Gregory, "BlackRock's Solution; The Firm, Which Started Developing a Risk Management System from Its

1988 Inception, Offers a Broad Package," *Pensions & Investments,* July 11, 2005, p. 18.

Elstein, Aaron, "BlackRock Prospers amid Gloom; Unblemished by Scandal, Bond Firm Quietly Expands into Stock News," *Crain's New York Business,* October 18, 2004, p. 3.

Fraser, Katharine, "Offering by PNC's BlackRock Seen As Recipe for Growth," *American Banker,* May 17, 1999, p. 10.

Guerra, Anthony, "How BlackRock Stays Solid: BlackRock Vice Chairman Rob Kapito Describes How His Firm Stays on Top of the Fixed-Income World by Keeping Its Technology Architecture Simple," *Wall Street & Technology,* January 2004, p. 43.

Isidore, Chris, "In Shaky Market, BlackRock Looks for Risk-Averse Investors: Asset Manager Shifts Focus to Retail Clients; Looks to New Owner As Customer Source," *Crain's New York Business,* October 19, 1998, p. 16.

Keefe, John, "Steady As a Rock," *Global Investor,* December 2004, pp. 16+.

Marcial, Gene G., "BlackRock's Sale Will Line PNC's Pockets," *Business Week,* February 27, 2006, p. 96.

Mazzucca, Tim, "MS-BlackRock Deal Talk Stirs Worries About PNC," *American Banker,* January 30, 2006, p. 20.

"Merrill Lynch/BlackRock," *Financial Times* (London), February 16, 2006, p. 18.

Pressman, Aaron, "BlackRock Breaks Out of Its Bonds; Larry Fink Is Trying to Reduce Dependence on Fixed Income, But the Road Is Rocky," *Business Week,* July 4, 2005, p. 85.

Ring, Niamh, "PNC's Investment Chief Says Cultures Can Meld," *American Banker,* February 11, 1998, pp. 1+.

Serwer, Andy, "A Wall Street Star Hits the Even Bigger Time," *Fortune,* March 6, 2006, p. 37.

Stern, Gabriella, and Robert McGough, "PNC Agrees to Acquisition of BlackRock," *Wall Street Journal,* p. A4.

Talley, Karen, "BlackRock, Armed with Capital, Eyes Growth," *American Banker,* November 17, 1999, p. 8.

Tascarella, Patty, "Big Days at BlackRock: Andrew Damm Looks for Very Large and Very Healthy Companies with Above-Average Earnings Growth," *Pittsburgh Business Times,* October 2, 1998, p. 6.

———, "Future IPOs May Look to BlackRock," *Pittsburgh Business Times,* May 21, 1999, pp. 3+.

"TEAM, TEAM, TEAM," *Pensions & Investments,* January 7, 2002, p. 12.

Wallace, Evelyn, "Blackstone's First Offering Is Mortgage-Backed Fund," *American Banker,* June 28, 1988, p. 32.

Winokur, Cheryl, "Investment Unit of PNC Raises $126M in IPO," *American Banker,* October 4, 1999, p. 1.

Boots & Coots International Well Control, Inc.

11615 N. Houston-Rosslyn Road
Houston, Texas 77086
U.S.A.
Telephone: (713) 621-7911
Toll Free: (800) 256-9688
Fax: (281) 931-8392
Web site: http://www.bncg.com

Public Company
Incorporated: 1988 as Havenwood Ventures, Inc.
Employees: 66
Sales: $29.5 million (2005)
Stock Exchanges: American
Ticker Symbol: WEL
NAIC: 213112 Support Activities for Oil and Gas Operations

■ ■ ■

Boots & Coots International Well Control, Inc. serves the oil and gas industry, fighting well fires and blowouts, as well as offering services to prevent such "events." The Houston-based company also contains oil and hazardous materials spills that result from these emergencies and provides restoration services to return oil and gas wells to production. Boots & Coots' WELLSURE program, an alliance with Global Special Risks, a major international Managing General Agent, and Underwriters at Lloyd's of London, offers oil and gas clients an insurance package that includes a full range of prevention, well control, and well restoration services. Boots & Coots is a public company listed on the American Stock Exchange.

"HELLFIGHTING" DATING TO 1913

The history of Boots & Coots encompasses the history of "hellfighting," the dangerous task of extinguishing well fires, and includes the life story of the most famous hellfighter of them all, Red Adair. The well control industry got its start in 1913 when Myron M. Kinley and his father extinguished the first well fire using explosives. Kinley had learned about explosives by shooting wells with his father in the California oilfields. A highly dangerous occupation, shooting a well stimulated production by perforating the rock formations beneath the well. It was accomplished by lowering a torpedo filled with liquid nitroglycerin down the well shaft, then dropping a rock on it. In 1923 Kinley formed the M.M. Kinley Company to specialize in well control and established the basic principles of dealing with a well "blowout." Powerful streams of water were directed at the drilling rig and explosives were used to blow out the wellhead and deprive the blaze of oxygen. Once the fire was out, hellfighters had to move quickly to cap the well before it had a chance to reignite. Anything that might cause a spark was forbidden, and the workers even avoided talking, preferring hand signals, lest the fillings in their teeth create sparks, however minute, that could set the surrounding vapor cloud ablaze with fatal consequences.

Kinley worked out of Houston and in 1941 he first met a young man named Paul Neal Adair. "Red" Adair,

COMPANY PERSPECTIVES

Boots & Coots International Well Control, Inc. are the pioneers of oil well fire fighting and the most experienced blowout specialists.

as he was known because of his flaming red hair, stood just five-foot-seven but he was a fearless, tough, and athletic man, who as a teenager earned extra money boxing in semiprofessional bouts and never lost. He was born in Houston in 1915, the son of a blacksmith. He quit high school to help with the family finances, holding a number of jobs before going to work for the Southern Pacific Railroad in 1936. Two years later he first became involved with the oil industry, convincing a foreman at Otis Pressure Control Company to give him a chance. One of the jobs performed by Otis was the cleaning and adjusting of the large valves that prevented blowouts at the well head. Adair learned the business and worked sporadically in the oil patch. Then, in Smackover, Arkansas, in December 1940, he made a mark for himself at only his third job for Otis. A gas well his crew was working on blew, causing everyone to scatter, with the exception of Adair, who calmly sized up the situation, realized a flange on the blowout preventer was loose and that the space created allowed the escape of the gas. He also realized that if he did not act quickly and decisively the flange would soon come off, causing sparks and a massive explosion that would vaporize him. He managed to tighten the bagel-sized nuts of the flange and contained the flow of gas. He also created the start of a legend, which would grow a few weeks later when he stopped another blowout singlehandedly. In the spring of 1941 Adair was working with Otis when a well blew out and caught fire. Kinley was called in. He generally worked alone, taking on helpers on a short-term basis. He asked for a volunteer and Adair stepped forward. After two days of hard work they put out the fire and contained the blowout. Kinley would now hire Adair on occasion.

JOINING KINLEY AFTER WORLD WAR II

World War II interrupted Adair's hellfighting career, but he found an equally challenging and dangerous job to bide his time in the service, and one that provided valuable experience: He served in the Army's 139th Bomb Disposal Squadron. After the war in 1946 he went to work for Kinley full-time and became his trusted lieutenant. As if fighting oil well fires did not provide enough danger in his life, Adair also raced boats and automobiles. It was at Houston's Arrowhead Speedway that Adair met Asger "Boots" Hansen, another war veteran and a submarine crew member in the Pacific. In 1957 another man joined the Kinley crew: Edward "Coots" Matthew. He, too, courted danger during the war, serving as a tail gunner on a B17 bomber on 25 missions over Germany and France. After the war the Texas native went to work for Halliburton, and when he lost his job he used family connections to land a position with Kinley.

Boots and Coots were known as hard-drinking rabble rousers and would have likely been fired by Kinley, but they were both fearless and Adair vouched for them with the boss and promised to take responsibility for them. By this time injuries had caught up to Kinley, and it was Adair, assisted by Boots and Coots, who now showed up at a job to put out a well fire. In 1959 Adair decided to strike out on his own and formed the Red Adair Company, taking Boots and Coots with him. He now began to forge an international reputation that would extend far beyond the oil industry. In 1961 Adair tackled one of the world's most spectacular fires, the "Devil's Cigarette Lighter," a gas fire in Algeria that soared some 450 feet in the air. Some experts predicted it would blaze for several years, but Adair and his crew extinguished it in a matter of weeks. Adair received international acclaim for the achievement and made the cover of *Life* magazine. His story would also attract the attention of Hollywood, and in 1968 a movie called *Hellfighters* was released with the six-foot-four-inch John Wayne playing the five-foot-seven-inch Red Adair.

Red Adair now had a monopoly on the well fire business. He was called in to do a job with no price quoted. When the fire was out and the well capped, he submitted a bill for an amount that depended on his whim or need to finance some new toy, and his customers paid willingly because the amount of money they were losing due to a well fire far outweighed whatever Red charged. He did not face serious competition until 1975 when Joe R. Bowden formed Wild Well Control. Then, in December 1977, Adair gained further competition when Boots and Coots left to form their own company. The nature of their break with Adair was uncertain. They claimed that he fired them, while he maintained that they came to him with a set of demands he could not possibly meet and he suspected they already had a company set up. Whatever the circumstances, Adair and his erstwhile crew members began feuding in the press, creating bad blood that sometimes took a comical turn and became friendly badgering. Every December, for example, Boots and Coots sent Adair a telegram thanking him for firing them.

KEY DATES

1959: Red Adair launches a well firefighting company.

1977: Asger "Boots" Hansen and Edward "Coots" Matthews leave Adair to form Boots & Coots.

1994: Upon Adair's retirement, employees form International Well Control.

1997: International Well Control merges with Boots & Coots.

2004: Red Adair dies.

Red Adair Company, Boots & Coots, and Wild Well Control became fierce rivals. Adair's signature touch had been to revel in the color red, and his rivals followed suit with their own signature colors, even when it came to clothes and cars. According to a 1991 *People Weekly* article, "Red Adair's crew, for example, sport fire engine-red coveralls and drive identical red Cadillacs. That means the boys at Boots and Coots favor white coveralls and drive white Lincoln Continentals and BMWs. Not to be outdone, the team at Wild Well Control affect yellow coveralls with black trim and drive black Mercury Marquis."

There was enough work for all three companies and then some in 1991 after Iraq was expelled from Kuwait during the Persian Gulf War. As Iraqi forces left they set fires to some 700 wells. The three Texas firms were called in, along with Canada's Safety Boss, but the Kuwaiti government wanted faster action and asked for other bids. As a result, four more private companies as well as five government-sponsored crews joined the effort. The daunting task was completed in just nine months. Although Kuwait provided a windfall in profits for Red Adair and Boots & Coots, it also created even more competition, as the companies that put out fires in Kuwait now gained industry acceptance. The days of Red Adair naming his price after the job was done were long gone. To make matters worse for hellfighters, engineering had improved, making blowouts and well fires less common. They certainly could not count on a dictator to sabotage hundreds of oil wells very often.

In January 1994 the 78-year-old Adair sold his business to Global Industries Ltd., an oil-service company. A year earlier, Coots Matthews and Boots Hansen sold their company to employees. Adair's top people—Raymond Henry, Richard Hatteberg, Brian Krause, and Danny Clayton—had attempted to buy out Adair, but failed to reach a deal and went to work for Global. Although they received stock options, they soon chafed under Global's control. According to *Forbes,* Global's head, William Dore, "got cheap with his crews—no more imported beer and filet mignon and fancy cigars to celebrate after a big job—and he introduced time clocks. In a huff, Adair's four top guns quit and started a competing outfit." They called it International Well Control (IWC).

MERGER OF RIVALS IN 1997

To provide IWC with executive experience, Krause recruited Larry Ramming, a man with an extensive background in real estate, mortgage banking, and the investment banking industries. IWC now looked to expand its service offerings and to consolidate the fragmented well control industry. In 1995 the company took a major step in accomplishing the first end by forging an agreement with Halliburton Energy Services to create WellCall Alliance, which led to the WELLSURE program. As for the second goal, IWC also began talking in 1995 to Boots & Coots about a possible merger. Those talks came to fruition in July 1997 when IWC acquired Boots & Coots, and the company changed its name to Boots & Coots International Well Control, Inc. A month later Ramming took the company public by engineering a reverse merger with a shell company, Havenwood Ventures, Inc., an investment fund that made an initial public offering of stock in 1988.

To some on the outside, bringing together two fierce rivals was a recipe for difficulty, but as Ramming explained to *Houston Business Journal,* "Everybody forgot that they all learned under Red Adair. It was less a merger and more of a family reunion." The two companies complemented each other in a number of significant ways. For example, Boots & Coots had the equipment in Houston and South America that IWC lacked, while IWC boasted a deep roster of experienced personnel. Moreover, Boots & Coots had in recent years expanded its services to include industrial marine firefighting, in particular offshore drilling rig fires, an area in which IWC was interested.

After the merger and going public, Boots & Coots went on an acquisition binge in an attempt to consolidate the industry as well as achieve further diversity. In September 1997 it acquired ITS Environment Services/ASASCO, a Houston manufacturer of rapid-response oil and chemical spill containment products. Next, in January 1998 the company bought ITS Supply Corporation, an equipment, transportation, and logistics company with offices in Houston, South America, the United Kingdom, and the Middle East. A month later Boots & Coots added Code 3, Inc., an emergency response company. Baylor Co., a maker of industrial products for the drilling, marine, and power generation industries, was acquired in July 1998. Finally, in November 1998, Boots & Coots added HAZ-Tech Environmental Services, Inc., a provider of a full range of emergency prevention and response services, including environmental site audits, bio-remediation, and water treatment.

The expansion program did not work out as planned, however. The company ignored signs in 1998 that oil prices were collapsing, a situation that would result in reduced drilling activity and less need for the services Boots & Coots had to offer. Moreover, in order to grow, the company took on a great deal of debt, nearly $50 million. In 1999, sales dipped, the stock price tumbled, and Boots & Coots defaulted on its long-term debt. The company took measures to cut costs, including laying off a large portion of the workforce, but the struggles continued in 2000 when it undertook a restructuring and reached a new agreement with lenders in early 2001.

Difficulties continued for Boots & Coots, however. In June 2002 Ramming resigned, the company was on the verge of being delisted by the American Stock Exchange, and there was talk in the press about the company possibly filing for Chapter 11 bankruptcy protection. The price of Boots & Coots stock began to rebound in 2003 due to the pending war with Iraq and the expectation of many that once again there would be a great deal of oil well fires to extinguish. But the early days of the war were not a repeat of what happened in Kuwait a dozen years earlier, and there was far less work for Boots & Coots than anticipated, and the company continued to teeter on the verge of bankruptcy.

In 2004 Red Adair died at the age of 89 from natural causes, a surprisingly quiet ending for a man who spent decades handling explosives near fires that burned as hot as 2,000 degrees. The company that was the heir to his legacy, in the meantime, continued to barely scrape by. But after losing $300,000 in 2004, business improved in 2005, as Boots & Coots cast off some of its noncore assets and focused on its well control business. The effects of Hurricane Katrina on Gulf of Mexico wells also generated business, and as a result sales increased 22 percent to $29.5 million over the previous year, while the company turned a profit of $2.8 million. Whether this represented the start of a comeback or a transitory spike in business remained to be seen.

Ed Dinger

PRINCIPAL SUBSIDIARIES

IWC Services, Inc.; Hell Fighters, Inc.; Boots & Coots Special Services, Inc.; Boots & Coots Overseas, Ltd.; Boots & Coots Services, Inc.

PRINCIPAL COMPETITORS

Global Industries, Ltd.; Superior Energy Services, Inc.; Wild Well Control, Inc.

FURTHER READING

Carroll, Chris, "From Banking to Blowouts," *Houston Business Journal,* April 17, 1998, p. 14A.

Davis, Michael, "International Well Buys Rival Boots & Coots," *Houston Business Journal,* July 1, 1997, p. 1.

De Rouffignac, Ann, "Adair's Employees Made Attempt to Buy Company," *Houston Business Journal,* January 10, 1994, p. 1.

———, "Boots & Coots Lands in Hot Water," *Houston Business Journal,* August 30, 1999.

Dittrick, Paula, "Hellfighters Go Public," *Oil & Gas Investor,* April 1999, p. 43.

Flynn, Sean, "The Big Heat," *New York Times Magazine,* December 26, 2004, p. 46.

Severo, Richard, "Red Adair, 89, Conqueror of Oil Well Fires," *New York Times,* August 10, 2004, p. B8.

Singerman, Philip, *An American Hero: The Red Adair Story,* Boston: Little, Brown and Company, 1990.

Tarquinio, J. Alex, "Fighting Oil Fires, and Creditors," *New York Times,* March 30, 2003, p. 3.

Treen, Joe, "Fields of Fire," *People Weekly,* April 29, 1992, p. 42.

Bowne & Co., Inc.

55 Water Street
New York, New York 10041
U.S.A.
Telephone: (212) 924-5500
Fax: (212) 229-3149
Web site: http://www.bowne.com

Public Company
Incorporated: 1909
Employees: 3,131
Sales: $694.1 million (2005)
Stock Exchanges: New York
Ticker Symbol: BNE
NAIC: 323119 Other Commercial Printing

■ ■ ■

The world's largest financial printer and one of the oldest companies in the United States, Bowne & Co., Inc. operates corporate printing operations that print prospectuses, offering circulars, annual reports, stock certificates, and other legal documents. Bowne also ranks as the leading provider of EDGAR electronic filing services to clients. The company's clients include corporations, law firms, investment banks, and mutual fund groups. In addition to its core business, which traces its roots back to the 18th century, Bowne & Co. has become a provider of document-building solutions, Internet, and print on-demand services to its financial and legal clients. With offices throughout the United States and in strategic locations across the globe, Bowne recorded the most prolific growth in its more than two centuries of business during the 1990s. Annual sales swelled from $205 million in 1990 to more than $700 million in 1997. While Bowne continued to maintain market dominance in its core business, the first half of the 2000s were fraught with challenging circumstances.

18TH-CENTURY ORIGINS

A year and a half before the Declaration of Independence was signed, Bowne opened for business. On a February morning in 1775, Robert Bowne and his two business associates began carrying crates and boxes of merchandise through the door of Number 39 Queen Street, in New York City. Above the threshold of the door hung a placard that read, "Bowne & Co. Merchants." The name would endure for more than two centuries, earning its distinction as the oldest business operating under the same name in the history of New York commerce. The Bowne family, beginning with its patriarch, Robert Bowne, owned and operated the company for more than a century, developing a small street-side store into one of the nation's most venerable commercial institutions. The Bownes arrived on the shores of their future homeland in 1649, when Thomas Bowne left England and sailed to Boston. Four generations later, Thomas Bowne's great-great-grandson, Robert Bowne, was preparing to open the doors to his new general merchandise store, christening an enterprise whose formation predated the birth of the United States.

Robert Bowne was 31 years old when he opened his store on Queen Street, having left his family home in Flushing, New York, to start a mercantile business in the city. Inside the store, the shelves were stocked with writ-

COMPANY PERSPECTIVES

Bowne & Co. Strategy—Bownc & Co. has evolved in recent years from the world's largest financial printer into an integrated, diversified and global document and information management solutions provider. The company is focused on strengthening the market leadership of its individual core business units and in leveraging their capabilities to provide a combination of integrated solutions to individual customers in multiple locations anywhere in the world. Supporting Bowne's strategy and core businesses are company-wide platforms for operations, technology and corporate services, as well as a reputation for superior customer service that is second-to-none.

ing paper, account books, quills and pens, binding and printing materials, powder, furs, nails, glass, dry goods, and, among a list of other items, "a few casks of low-priced Cutlery," as announced in a 1775 newspaper advertisement. Business at Bowne & Co. was underway in February 1775, but before long the company fell victim to the first of many historic events that would occur during its long corporate life. When British troops led by General Howe defeated General George Washington's outnumbered forces at Brooklyn Heights in August 1776, the American Army retreated into Manhattan, prompting thousands of New Yorkers, Robert Bowne included, to flee from the battle front.

Bowne left New York with his wife and infant daughter, leaving the doors of Bowne & Co. closed behind him until it was safe to return. When New Yorkers were able to return, considerable rebuilding work awaited them. Many found their homes destroyed, lying in ruins from years of fire and battle. Bowne returned as well, and reestablished himself as a general merchant. During the post-Revolutionary War period, Bowne & Co. began doing printing work, making its foray into the type of work that would later become the company's mainstay business. More important to Bowne at the time, however, was the brisk sale of stationery supplies. It was during the post-Revolutionary War years that Bowne & Co. etched its identity as a stationery supply store. Although the company continued to sell a diverse range of merchandise, the increasing sales derived from stationery supplies were fueling the store's prosperity. Stationery figured as an essential facet of the company's business until it was abandoned in the early 20th century.

As Bowne built his store into a solid and reputable enterprise, he also spent considerable time building a reputation for himself as one of New York's prominent citizens. He was a prodigious organizer of philanthropic organizations and spent many evenings gathered around a table with some of the country's early luminaries organizing the basic institutions a fledgling nation required. Bowne helped organize New York's first bank, he fought against slavery, he served as governor of the New York Hospital for 34 years, he helped organize the first fire insurance company, and he promoted the development of the Erie Canal. His tireless efforts away from his store paid large dividends for Bowne & Co., because in many respects the company reflected the individual at its helm. Like its creator, Bowne & Co. blossomed during the early 19th century, securing itself as a fixture of the burgeoning city it served. Although stationery supplies figured large in Bowne & Co.'s business, the company was involved in a number of business activities, as wide-ranging as the extracurricular activities performed by its founder. Straying far beyond the sale of stationery and printing services, Bowne & Co. served as agents for other merchants; speculated in land; bought and sold commodities such as wheat, flour, wine, and brandy; and provided banking services.

Bowne died in 1818, leaving behind him a solid foundation upon which succeeding generations could build. He also left an ample number of heirs to expand upon the business foundation he created. Bowne, who came from a family comprising 14 brothers and sisters, had nine children of his own. After his death, Robert Bowne's genealogical legacy proliferated exponentially, giving him 50 grandchildren and 112 great-grandchildren. From this vast pool of direct descendants, Bowne & Co. would draw its leadership for the ensuing century.

BOWNE & CO. IN THE 19TH CENTURY

Control of Bowne & Co. after Bowne's death in 1818 fell to two of his sons, Robert H. Bowne and John L. Bowne. Their first great test arrived in 1835, when Bowne & Co. was destroyed by fire, as was most of New York, which lost 17 city blocks and nearly 600 buildings to a fire that started in a dry goods store. The mayor of New York referred to the "Great Fire" as "the most awful calamity which has ever visited the United States," a disaster that forced the Bowne brothers to rebuild Bowne & Co. on a new site at the corner of Wall, Pearl (formerly Queen), and Beaver streets. In its new quarters, the company gained a reputation as a manufacturer of leather-bound account books, one of the several special talents the company developed during its long record of business.

KEY DATES

1775: Bowne & Co. Merchants is founded in New York City.
1776: War disrupts operations.
1818: Upon Robert Bowne's death, Bowne's sons take control of business activities.
1835: New York's "Great Fire" destroys Bowne & Co. and most of the city.
1843: Three of the founder's grandchildren head company.
1898: Retirement of Robert Bowne, grandson of the founder, ends family management of company.
1909: Longtime employee Stanley M. Dewey is appointed president; company incorporates.
1922: Edmund A. Stanley guides company from stationery to printing business.
1933: Establishment of SEC lays groundwork for new printing opportunities.
1946: Sales exceed $1 million for first time.
1956: Edmund A. Stanley, Jr., becomes president upon the death of his father.
1968: Bowne debuts as a publicly traded company.
1974: Victor Simonte, Jr., works his way to the top.
1982: After a decade of growth, sales shrink with the computer age; Simonte exits Bowne.
1984: Bowne jumps aboard SEC's voluntary electronic filing program for corporations.
1997: Information management businesses help drive sales to $716 million.
2001: Hard times hit U.S. market and Bowne's sales and profits.
2004: Bowne Business Solutions is sold.
2005: Bowne Global Solutions sold.

By the 1850s, Bowne & Co. was headed by three of the founder's grandchildren, Robert, William, and John, the last generation of Bownes to manage the firm. During their tenure, which began in 1843 and ended in 1898, Bowne & Co. supplemented its thriving account book business with a variety of general printing work. Of the three Bownes who headed the company during the latter half of the 19th century, Robert Bowne's length of service was most enduring, encompassing a half-century. His retirement in 1898 signaled the end of Bowne family management and set the stage for the first non-family member to head the company, Stanley M. Dewey, who joined Bowne & Co. at age 16.

Dewey had been with Bowne & Co. for 30 years by the time he was appointed the company's fifth president in 1909, the year the business was incorporated for the first time. Much of the company's business at this stage in its history was realized from the sale of stationery supplies. Dewey himself visited banks and insurance companies during his years as a senior partner, noting whether or not customers were in need of ink, quills, sealing wax, account books, and other related items. This line of business, which had been a mainstay for the company since its inception, became less important after the 1909 incorporation. Eventually, the stationery business was abandoned altogether, as the company concentrated its efforts on developing its printing business.

A 20TH-CENTURY FINANCIAL PRINTER

Dewey retired as president in 1922, but stayed on as chairman of the board until his death in 1941. Upon his retirement in 1922, Dewey sold his interest in the company to a young Bowne & Co. associate named Edmund A. Stanley, who had joined the firm in 1908. Stanley took over as Bowne & Co. was in transition, gradually becoming less of a stationery supplier and more of a printing enterprise. To supplement the company's traditional work for banking and insurance companies, Bowne & Co. responded to the printing needs of the surrounding financial district, printing a substantial portion of the securities offering circulars of New York underwriters. Its printing operations received a major boost in business when the Securities and Exchange Commission (SEC) was formed in 1933. The SEC required, by law, stock issue prospectuses and instituted annual reporting requirements for publicly held corporations, creating a wealth of business for such companies as Bowne & Co. In the years after the SEC's formation, Bowne & Co. began specializing in meeting the precise printing demands of underwriters, attorneys, publicly traded corporations, and any party responsible for complying with SEC requirements.

The formation of the SEC established the framework for Bowne & Co.'s most important business during the 20th century, but the timing of the federal organization's debut could have been better from Bowne & Co.'s perspective. When the SEC was formed, the nation was in the midst of its most severe economic depression, a time when the fabric of the country's financial community was unraveling with alarming speed. Those companies able to stay in business during the Great Depression cut costs dramatically, reducing their advertising and promotional budgets to an absolute minimum. Bowne & Co. felt the sting of the harsh economic times and suffered along with nearly every other business in the country. Annual sales remained static during the decade-long crisis, hovering around $300,000. Annual financial losses occurred too frequently for any Bowne & Co. official to take lightly.

Bowne & Co. did not enjoy the full rewards of the SEC's presence until the 1940s, but once the economic climate improved, the company enjoyed an encouraging and much needed surge of growth. Sales exceeded $1 million for the first time in 1946 and remained at that level until the beginning of the 1950s.

By the 1950s, the next generation of Bowne & Co.'s executive management had joined the firm. Stanley was joined by his son, Edmund A. Stanley, Jr., in 1949. The younger Stanley rose swiftly through the company's executive ranks, becoming vice-president in 1953 and president of the company in 1956 when his father died. Victor Simonte, Jr., who succeeded Stanley in the 1970s, experienced a lengthier climb to the presidential post than Stanley, working the full gamut of jobs at Bowne before taking charge. Simonte joined the company in 1950 as a helper in the composing room when he was 17 years old. He subsequently held a variety of positions before being named president, laboring as an apprentice, journeyman, foreman, and plant superintendent. Together, Stanley, Jr., and Simonte would lead the company into the 1980s.

With Stanley, Jr., in charge, Bowne & Co. headed into the 1960s after a decade of measured financial growth. The $1 million in sales generated in 1950 rose to $3 million by 1961, the year the company moved to larger quarters on Hudson Street, where it would be located for the remainder of the century. Along with the move came the addition of new, modern printing equipment and new communications systems. With the aid of this new equipment and several important acquisitions, Bowne & Co. rose to the top of the financial printing industry in terms of annual sales, climbing from third to first during the 1960s. In 1966, the company acquired Garber-Pollack Co., a trade bindery, and two years later, when Bowne & Co. converted to public ownership, The La Salle Street Press, Inc. was purchased, giving the company the largest financial printer in Chicago. Following its debut as a publicly traded company, Bowne & Co. either started or acquired financial printing companies in Boston, Houston, Los Angeles, and San Francisco.

By 1974, as Bowne & Co.'s bicentennial approached and Simonte took over as president, annual sales stood at $38 million, far above the $3 million recorded in 1961. Under Simonte's watch, the company registered another decade of energetic financial growth and was generating more than $100 million in sales by the beginning of the 1980s. Although the sales growth recorded during Simonte's first decade of leadership kept Bowne & Co. ahead of all other rivals in the United States, its lead was diminishing as it headed into the 1980s. Pandick Press Inc., Bowne & Co.'s closest rival, was gaining ground during the 1980s, recording 20 percent annual gains in sales while Bowne & Co.'s sales volume shrank. Critics charged that Simonte had failed to make the transition into the computer age, and in late 1982 Bowne & Co.'s directors acknowledged this failure by announcing Simonte's retirement. Simonte left the company he had joined as a teenager at age 49 and was replaced by Franz von Ziegesar, ten years Simonte's senior. On the heels of this change in management, the benefits of embracing the computer age were made manifest by the SEC.

NEW TECHNOLOGY

In 1984, the SEC introduced a voluntary electronic filing program for corporations called EDGAR. Bowne & Co. was the first corporation to join the program and lent its assistance to the prime contractor in the development of the program. Although corporations were not obliged to file electronically at EDGAR's outset, participation eventually became mandatory. Bowne & Co., involved with the program from its start, found itself closely involved in what would prove to be a highly lucrative market, and one that underscored the importance of adapting to the changes engendered by the pervasive influence of computers in the business world.

By the 1990s, the ubiquity of computers had significantly altered the thinking of Bowne & Co.'s management. The company, after more than two centuries of business, was tailoring itself to be an information management company, a provider not only of the printing services to disseminate data and text but also a company capable of assisting its corporate clients in managing their endless flows of information through the latest technologies. The push to become this new type of company helped insulate Bowne & Co. from the cyclicality of its mainstay business. Historically, the financial printing business had been dependent on the economic cycles that influenced stock issues, mergers, and acquisitions, but by branching into providing corporate services for the Internet and helping clients manage information through computer-based technologies, Bowne & Co. could depend on business free from the economic fluctuations that affected financial printing.

With the movement toward becoming this new type of company underway as the 1990s began, Bowne & Co. started to record animated growth in earnings and sales, in proportions that never had been achieved before. The bulk of the financial growth was realized midway through the decade, after Bowne & Co. had established two subsidiary companies that represented its commitment to its new role as an information management company. Bowne Business Services, formed in 1996, was created to lead Bowne & Co.'s diversification into nonfinancial printing businesses. The company's intent was to manage customers' desktop publishing, word processing, and multimedia operations and also to offer services facilitating the creation and management of Internet and intranet sites. Bowne & Co. officials projected a potential $250 million in revenues in this area of business by the year 2000. The other subsidiary, Bowne Digital Services, was formed to take advantage of the emerging business created by the convergence of database processing and digital print technologies. Through Bowne Digital Services, Bowne & Co. positioned itself as a service provider for database management, on-demand printing, and digital print technologies.

With the addition of these new businesses, Bowne & Co.'s financial might was strengthened significantly. From $205 million in sales in 1990, the company's revenue total leaped to $501 million in 1996 and soared to $716 million in 1997. Bowne & Co.'s net income during the decade increased from 1990's $8.4 million to the record-setting $54 million registered in 1997.

Bowne & Co. continued to build on its nonprinting enterprises, acquiring Chicago-based Donnelley Enterprise Solutions, Inc., a technology outsourcing services business, in 1998. Yet the financial-transaction business, accounting for over half of earnings and about 45 percent of revenues, continued to drive the company's outlook. "While a strong economy breeds new security offerings and mergers and acquisitions activity, a downturn dampens it. A slowdown in printing documents related to financial transactions hurts Bowne disproportionately, since the work, especially in M&A, is particularly lucrative: Profit margins are between 20% and 40%," Lisa Sanders explained in *Crain's New York Business.*

Furthermore, hungry, smaller rivals had their designs on Bowne's new areas of business. CEO Robert M. Johnson, a lawyer and former publisher of *New York Newsday*, emphasized Bowne & Co.'s strong points. "We aren't an upstart Internet company," he told *Crain's.* "We have a real reputation for handling complex documents."

In 1999, some analysts saw a split-off of the new businesses as a ticket to improved stock valuation for Bowne & Co. The new ventures dragged down the worth of the traditional print end of the business, according to *Business Week.* Among the company's assets was a 12.6 percent stake in EDGAR Online, which had plans to go public.

Bowne ranked as the largest provider of EDGAR files with 39 percent of market share. Its closest competitors, Merrill Corp. and R.R. Donnelley & Sons, filed half as many documents as Bowne & Co., according to *InternetWeek.* As Bowne & Co. forged ahead with its e-filing business, the printing operations received attention as well, in the form of intranet technology to manage and track projects. During 1998, $697 million of the $848 million in revenue was derived from the traditional printing business.

Acquisitions bolstered the company's new tech activities. Bowne Internet Solutions, a web site builder for financial services companies, encompassed five companies purchased since 1997. Merrill Lynch Asset Management Group and Standard & Poor's were among its customers. Other acquisitions built a software localization business, which translated software and web sites into 15 different languages, according to *InternetWeek.* Customers for those services included Microsoft, Lotus, Novell, and Sun Microsystems.

"Johnson believes the Internet will bring all of Bowne's digital businesses together. 'I think you are going to see the digital print business and the globalization and localization business all merge into a segment that will be described as a Web-enabled communications segment in the next 24 months,'" the chairman and CEO of Bowne told *InternetWeek* in October 1999.

A NEW CENTURY TO MASTER

With shares trading at $11, down 28 percent from a year earlier, calls to split up the company grew louder, according to a January 2000, *Crain's New York Business* report. "Mr. Johnson, though, believes that all the units are integral to Bowne's long-term growth and that splitting them off could jeopardize the company's future. 'We are moving from being just a printer to being able to offer the full range of information delivery services,'" Johnson told *Crain's.* "In the long term, we are going to be better off if we end up owning 100% of all our business."

Nevertheless, Johnson had begun looking into the possible sale or spinoff of the software translating operation. Internet development and outsourcing businesses also could wind up on the trading block. During 1997 and 1998, Johnson had acquired 21 companies and business units now included: Bowne Internet Solutions, Bowne Business Solutions, and Bowne Global Solutions.

As electronically produced financial information undercut its hardcopy business, Johnson had moved to broaden its offerings. The company began contracting with companies such as Prudential and Charles Schwab to print and deliver clients' account statements. Printing plant reconfiguration also enabled Bowne to take on larger projects. When Metropolitan Life converted to a public company, Bowne had the capacity to produce its 11 million, 377-page prospectuses. Yet, Stephen Gandel reported for *Crain's* in January 2001, that "Johnson's efforts to diversify Bowne's sales have hurt the company's bottom line. The Internet division lost $12 million in the first nine months of last year. Analysts estimate the outsourcing division added more than $150 million in revenue in 1999, but under $1 million in profits. The company's expansion into printing mutual fund statements has lowered the company's historically high profit margin in its core financial printing operations."

Bowne cut into its workforce in 2001, first in January, and then in April with the elimination of its Internet consulting and development business. September proved to be another tough month on Bowne employees. The destruction of the World Trade Center on September 11 brought terror to Bowne's lower Manhattan offices and the country.

For the first time since 1976, the month of September produced no public offerings. Year-end results saw Bowne & Co.'s revenue down 11 percent. The rapid downturn in the capital market translated to a 40 percent drop-off in transactional financial printing revenue, although the company retained its market share position. Bowne & Co. attempted to mitigate the loss of business through consolidation of operations and a 10 percent reduction of staff during the 4th quarter. Bowne Business Solutions and Bowne Global Solutions fared better during the year, gaining market leadership in their respective segments of outsourcing and translation.

Mergers and acquisitions and initial public offerings during 2002 remained meager, but Bowne's market share continued to outpace the competition. Bowne claimed more than 40 percent of the significant M&A deals and 45 percent of the significant IPOs during the year. Companies distinguished with long, stable histories had started to look good to investors reeling from dot-com meltdowns and executive greed. At year-end, Bowne made a significant addition to its services for law firms, purchasing DecisionQuest.

The build-up to the invasion of Iraq had dampened the market during the last half of 2002 and continued to do so into the first couple months of 2003. But IPO activity picked up as the U.S. military showed early signs of success, and Bowne reaped the benefit. After slight declines in 2001 and 2002, Bowne posted an increase of 6 percent in revenues for 2003.

Into 2004, Bowne experienced an uptick in its electronic filing business, partially due to new government reporting standards. The Sarbanes-Oxley legislation, passed in response to the rash of corporate wrongdoing, required increased corporate disclosure.

In May 2004, Bowne & Co. faced a sudden shakeup in top management. Robert Johnson departed, citing personal reasons, according to *Information Week*. Senior Vice-President and General Counsel Phillip E. Kucera advanced as interim CEO. Then late in August Senior Vice-President and CEO of two Bowne business units, David J. Shea, stepped in as president. Shea, who joined Bowne in 1998, began his career at IBM, helping banks outsource technology projects. He later headed up R.R. Donnelley's information technology outsourcing unit.

At Bowne, outsourcing services produced $250 million in business or 24 percent of company revenue during 2003 compared to just 2 percent of revenue in 1997. "In the past 20 years, the outsourcing of labor has gone from a corporate America sideshow involving a handful of computer programmers or call-center staffs, to a main event, with banks, insurers and hospitals hiring thousands of people overseas to analyze balance sheets or assess medical test data," Aaron Elstein wrote for *Crain's New York Business* in October 2004.

During 2005 Bowne prepared to move its headquarters to a location just eight blocks from its original location. "The city development corporation and the Empire State Development Corporation announced this month that they had granted $1.63 million to Bowne under the job retention and creation program for Lower Manhattan. 'Bowne is a great candidate both for historical reasons and because it also helps diversify the economy downtown,'" Andrew M. Alper, president of the New York City Economic Development Corporation, said in the *New York Times* in March.

The company sold Bowne Global Solutions to Lionbridge Technologies in September 2005. (Bowne Business Solutions, the document outsourcing business, had been sold late in 2004.) Preliminary results for 2005, showed revenue gains for Bowne, but the company expected a net loss from continuing operations. Increased profits for the core financial print business during the fourth quarter of the year yielded some optimism.

In January 2006, Bowne announced it had paid Vestcom International, Inc. $30 million in cash for its Marketing and Business Communications division, which was to be combined with Bowne Enterprise Solutions. Named Bowne Marketing and Business Communications, the new entity produced estimated revenues of $140 million in the print-on-demand market during 2005.

Jeffrey L. Covell
Updated, Kathleen Peippo

PRINCIPAL COMPETITORS

Merrill Corporation; R.R. Donnelley & Sons Company; St Ives plc.

FURTHER READING

Bauer, Chris, "Bulls in a Bear Market," *Printing Impressions*, December 2003.

"Bowne Is Looking Juicier," *Business Week*, May 10, 1999, p. 122.

Dunlap, David W., "Printer Is Moving to Its (Very) Old Neighborhood," *New York Times*, March 21, 2005.

Elstein, Aaron, "Enlarging the Fine Print," *Crain's New York Business*," October 11, 2004.

Foley, John, "It's Never Business As Usual," *Information Week*, September 27, 2004.

Gandel, Stephen, "Investors See Red Over Printer's Redo," *Crain's New York Business*," January 31, 2000, p. 4.

Harrington, John, "Bowne Stock Pressing Toward High," *Crain's New York Business*," October 29, 2001, p. 46.

Henriques, Diana B., "Those Old-Time Shares Are Looking Good Again," *New York Times*," August 18, 2002.

Jaffe, Thomas, "Survivor," *Forbes*, September 4, 1989, p. 317.

McDougall, Paul, "Services Firms Boost Tech Dollars," *Information Week*, September 20, 2004.

Power, Christopher, "The Wrong Type?" *Forbes*, February 28, 1983, p. 2.

Sanders, Lisa, "Financial Printer Is Seeing Less Ink," *Crain's New York Business*," October 26, 1998, p. 40.

Stanley, Edmund A., Jr., *Of Men and Dreams*, New York: Bowne & Co., Inc., 1975, 83 p.

Schwartz, Jeffrey, "Bowne Moves Beyond Printed Word," *InternetWeek*, October 25, 1999, p. 33.

Roush, Matt, "Bowne Cuts Staff in Half, Blames Acquisitions," *Crain's New York Business*, October 19, 1998, p. 39.

The British United Provident Association Limited

BUPA House
15-19 Bloomsbury Way
London, WC1A 2BA
United Kingdom
Telephone: +44-20-7656-2000
Toll Free: 0800 00 10 10
Fax: +44-20-7656-2700
Web site: http://www.bupa.co.uk

Private Company
Incorporated: 1947
Employees: 40,000
Sales: £3.9 billion ($7.0 billion) (2004)
NAIC: 524114 Direct Health and Medical Insurance Carriers; 621491 HMO Medical Centers; 621493 Freestanding Ambulatory Surgical and Emergency Centers; 621498 All Other Outpatient Care Centers; 621512 Diagnostic Imaging Centers; 621999 All Other Miscellaneous Ambulatory Health Care Services; 622110 General Medical and Surgical Hospitals; 622210 Psychiatric and Substance Abuse Hospitals; 622310 Specialty (Except Psychiatric and Substance Abuse) Hospitals; 623110 Nursing Care Facilities; 623311 Continuing Care Retirement Communities; 623312 Homes for the Elderly; 623990 Other Residential Care Facilities

The British United Provident Association Limited (BUPA) is a leading provider of private health insurance in Great Britain. It has more than eight million customers in the United Kingdom and about 190 other countries, making it a leader in the highly fragmented global market. BUPA's largest foreign markets are Ireland and Spain, where its Spanish subsidiary Sanitas also runs a network of healthcare facilities. About one-third of BUPA's insurance is bought by individuals; the majority is provided by companies as a job perquisite. Other organizations, such as professional associations, also participate in group plans.

In addition to providing insurance, BUPA operates its own hospitals, clinics, and nursing homes. It is one of Britain's largest private companies. The insurance side operates on a nonprofit basis, and BUPA Hospitals is set up as a commercial company.

1947 FOUNDING

The British United Provident Association Limited (BUPA) was formed in 1947 by a number of regional provident associations. These were led by the Oxford District Provident Scheme, the Oxford University Provident Scheme, and others in Edinburgh and Birmingham. About 17 such associations joined. The insurer would be led for its first 30 years by Edward Webb, formerly a colonial civil servant in Tanzania. BUPA was a private company limited by guarantee. It had no shareholders, and would reinvest any surpluses in the business. (BUPA Hospitals would later be set up as a commercial company.)

The provident associations had helped to offset the risk of expensive medical treatment. As Webb later told a reporter, there was considerable doubt whether there would be any need for them after the launch of Britain's

COMPANY PERSPECTIVES

BUPA's vision is "Taking Care of the Lives in Our Hands." It's a succinct description of what its people do around the world every hour of every day.

National Health Service (NHS) in 1948 to provide free medical care to citizens. BUPA was not expected to last more than a few years. Its role, however, soon became clear: to provide choice for its customers. Thirty-eight thousand signed up for BUPA's coverage the first year. Subscription income was £74,000.

BUPA had 200,000 members by the mid-1950s; 2,000 companies were providing its insurance to their workers. In 1959, the group began allowing organizational members to provide coverage to their overseas employees.

In 1957, BUPA helped launch the Nuffield Homes Charitable Trust (later Nuffield Hospitals) to support endangered private hospitals and nursing homes. It acquired seven existing hospitals and built another half dozen. A dozen more were added by the 1970s. These smaller facilities dedicated to elective surgery became known as "mini hospitals."

A desire for privacy and personal treatment were two reasons for the success of BUPA and a couple of other provident associations, observed the *Times*. By 1966, BUPA was covering 1.1 million people, more than twice as many as its peers. BUPA had different levels of coverage, beginning at around £5 and eight shillings a year.

The main rationale for private healthcare, noted the *Times* in 1972, was avoiding the NHS's long wait for elective procedures, which then stood at around two years. BUPA embraced preventive healthcare in the 1970s. It opened its first wellness screening center in London in 1969 and launched research institutions. Its annual subscription income was £13 million in 1973.

BUPA also made its first ventures into countries overseas beginning in 1971. BUPA would become the largest private insurer of Britons abroad. Its coverage would ultimately be extended to those of other nationalities. A Hong Kong unit was formed in 1976.

The NHS made a few thousand of its beds available to private, paying patients. When their availability was threatened, in 1974 BUPA opened its first hospital for subscribers in St. Marylebone. Known as the Nightingale Bupa Hospital, its predecessor, once called "The Institute for Gentlewomen during Illness," was where nurse Florence Nightingale pioneered her revolutionary methods. BUPA was investing £1.5 million on upgrading the facility.

LAUNCH OF BUPA HOSPITALS IN 1978

Britons, alarmed at labor strikes in the NHS, were turning to BUPA in increasing numbers in the late 1970s. In 1978, the association formed BUPA Hospitals. This would become a competitor with the old BUPA spinoff, Nuffield Hospitals, which by then was operating about 25 facilities.

The association's hospital side grew rapidly in the 1980s through acquisitions and building. In 1981 it opened a £4.8 million facility in Manchester said to be the largest private hospital outside London. BUPA also joined the NHS in joint ventures such as the St. Thomas' Hospital and the National Hospital for Nervous Diseases.

BUPA CEO Bob Graham complained of hospital groups from the United States and Kuwait driving up healthcare costs with their new, for-profit hospitals. At the same time, BUPA was continuing its own international development. In 1988, BUPA acquired Sanitas, the largest private health insurance provider in Spain, a popular retirement destination for Brits.

A number of hospitals were acquired in the late 1980s. Ten facilities were acquired from the Hospital Corporation of America (HCA) in July 1989. With 27 hospitals and 1,500 beds in all, BUPA was the country's largest private owner of hospitals, with a 14 percent market share. BUPA posted a £38 million loss in 1990 but was soon in the black again, and growing.

BUPA embraced the fitness ethic in the 1990s, attaching its name to a number of sporting events, including a popular series of road races called BUPA Great Runs. The legendary BUPA Great North Run in Newcastle grew to become the world's largest half marathon, attracting 50,000 runners.

BUPA began offering dental insurance in 1993. Five years later, it acquired dental services provider Barbican Healthcare. While BUPA was diversifying, other insurers were beginning to offer competing healthcare coverage. By the mid-1990s, according to the *Times,* BUPA's market share had plunged to 44 percent. It was then operating 30 hospitals with 1,800 beds and 30 screening clinics.

GOODING CEO IN 1996

Free gym memberships were added to BUPA's preventive health prescription in 1996. In the same year, when

KEY DATES

1947: Regional provident associations join to create BUPA.
1950: BUPA is insuring one million people.
1957: BUPA forms the precursor of Nuffield Hospitals to ensure survival of threatened private hospitals.
1978: BUPA Hospitals is formed.
1988: Spain's Sanitas is acquired.
1989: Ten U.K. facilities are acquired from Hospital Corporation of America (HCA).
2000: Revenues exceed £2 billion.
2005: ANS Care Homes are acquired while nine hospitals are divested; insurance companies are acquired in Denmark and the United States.

turnover was £1.2 billion, a dynamic new chief executive replaced Peter Jacobs, who had led the company for five years. Much would be written of Val Gooding's influence on BUPA (and still more written on her compensation, which would make her "Britain's highest-paid woman").

Gooding was a 20-year veteran of British Airways. Her training techniques included making new management hires attend surgeries, noted *Campaign.* "It is one way of taking people right to the heart of what the business is about," explained Gooding.

Apart from the symbolic gestures, the organization was being recast from a simple insurance company to a comprehensive healthcare provider. Much effort would go into marketing and brand communications. BUPA also was restructured into five business units.

There was a great deal of international expansion in the late 1990s. It began operating in Ireland in 1996, where it was the first foreign health insurer allowed in the country. BUPA also set up joint ventures in Saudi Arabia (BUPA Middle East) and Thailand. A short-lived health center was launched in India but folded within a few years. BUPA entered the Australian market in 2003 by buying a local company.

BUPA's turnover exceeded £2 billion in 2000. Around 2002, BUPA became one of the private providers the NHS was employing to reduce its notoriously long waiting lists. The Redwood Diagnosis and Treatment Centre was dedicated to NHS work, but this represented a tiny fraction (1 percent) of BUPA's total revenues.

BUPA was thriving in 2003 and 2004, but company officials felt the need to update its image, reported *Campaign.* An ad campaign was launched to get customers to think about BUPA's products before they got sick. Making the insurer seem less corporate and more approachable was another goal, though more than 90 percent of Brits were familiar with the BUPA brand. The friendlier ads included cartoon characters interacting with BUPA staff.

BULLISH IN 2005

Revenues were up to £3.9 billion ($7.0 billion) in 2005, BUPA's sixth consecutive year of growth. Insurance accounted for £2.7 billion of the total. BUPA led the United Kingdom's private insurance market, with a 40 percent share. The group had 8.2 million customers. Claims paid exceeded £2 billion, a record. BUPA Hospitals were treating more than a quarter million patients a year. Cosmetic surgery procedures were particularly in demand. BUPA's surplus was growing 30 percent a year, its finance director told *Accountancy Age.* A source involved with its capital raising, however, told the *Banker* that the group was "reasonably highly" leveraged.

BUPA sold nine hospitals for £84 million and bought three companies. ANS Care Homes, which had 44 facilities, was acquired in a deal worth £334 million. BUPA spent £206 million on two foreign insurance companies, Denmark's International Health Insurance Danmark a/s (IHI) and Amedex Insurance Company of the United States. The purchase of Amedex, which was based in Miami, made BUPA the leading health insurance company in Latin America. It was also the market leader in Spain, Australia, Ireland, Hong Kong, Thailand, and Saudi Arabia.

Gooding was bullish about BUPA's prospects in a 2005 interview with the *Sunday Telegraph.* Although the government was launching another, much touted plan to improve the NHS, some of BUPA's healthcare lines would not be affected at all. In addition, the NHS, which received about £70 billion a year in taxpayer funds, was planning to outsource more treatments to private hospitals to cut waiting lists. As it evolved, BUPA was planning to sell off ten smaller facilities, while upgrading its remaining 25 hospitals.

PRINCIPAL SUBSIDIARIES

Blackrock Hospital Limited (Ireland; 56%); BUPA (Asia) Limited (Hong Kong); BUPA Australia Pty. Limited; BUPA Care Homes (CFG) PLC; BUPA Care Services Limited; BUPA Finance PLC; BUPA Hospitals Limited; BUPA Insurance Limited; BUPA Investments Limited;

BUPA Investments Overseas Limited; Sanitas, SA de Seguros (Spain; 99%).

PRINCIPAL COMPETITORS

AXA PPP Healthcare Limited; Nuffield Hospitals.

FURTHER READING

Bagnall, Sarah, "Prescribing a Run of Healthy Profits; BUPA: Sir Bryan Nicholson and Peter Jacobs," *Times* (London), April 2, 1994, p. 23.

Breckon, William, "London Leads with Check-Up Centres," *Times* (London), Health Sec., April 25, 1974, p. VI.

Brittain, Victoria, "The Facts Behind Private Medicine's Appeal As an Alternative to the National Health Service," *Times* (London), March 27, 1972, p. 12.

Bryant, Arthur W. M., *History of BUPA,* 1968.

"Bupa Opens First Subscribers' Hospital," *Times* (London), November 19, 1974, p. 3.

"Bupa Shows Its Friendly Side to Win Over Customers," *Campaign,* April 8, 2004, p. 14.

"Bupa's Quiet Revolutionary Values Its Compassion," *Campaign,* November 14, 2003, p. 16.

Busfield, Joan, "Medicine and Markets: Power, Choice and the Consumption of Private Medical Care," in *Consumption and Class: Divisions and Change,* eds. Roger Burrow and Catherine Marsh, New York: St. Martin's Press, 1992, pp. 71–88.

"Buyers Flock to Bupa Upper Tier Two with Optional Coupon," *Euroweek,* December 10, 2004, p. S3.

"Complex Operation Leaves Insurer in Rude Health," *Banker,* February 1, 2005.

"Edward Webb; Obituary," *Times* (London), October 18, 2005, p. 61.

Fielding, Rachel, "Ray King, the Man with His Finger on the Pulse at BUPA—Healthy Outlook," *Accountancy Age,* September 15, 2005, p. 22.

Gaselee, John, "Insurance Schemes Take the Sting Out of Treatment Charges," *Times* (London), Health Sec., April 25, 1974, p. VI.

———, "Provident Basis of Private Treatment," *Times* (London), Personal Finance Sec., September 27, 1974, p. IV.

Pfeifer, Sylvia, "Bupa Boss Is Highest-Paid Woman in UK," *Sunday Telegraph* (London), June 26, 2005.

———, "Will Blair Put Bupa in Intensive Care?," *Sunday Telegraph* (London), July 18, 2004, p. 9.

"Private Hospital Beds Preferred; Wider Membership of Insurance Schemes," *Times* (London), January 9, 1959, p. 13.

Robb, Douglas, *BUPA, 1968–1983: A Continuing History,* British United Provident Association Ltd., 1984.

Timmins, Nicholas, "BUPA Announces Further £20m Hospitals Scheme," *Times* (London), June 4, 1981, p. 3.

———, "Bupa Chief's Pay Soars to £623,000," *Independent Sunday* (London), September 1, 1996, p. 4.

———, "Bupa Sees Hospitals' Pursuit of Profit As Threat to Private Care," *Times* (London), December 11, 1985, p. 3.

———, "Real Growth But No Boom in Private Sector," *Times* (London), September 8, 1978.

Trompenaars, Fons, *21 Leaders for the 21st Century,* New York: McGraw-Hill, 2001.

"When BUPA Got Better," *Brand Strategy,* March 4, 2005, p. 20.

"Why the Insurers Were the First to Put the Brakes on Costs," *Times* (London), June 14, 1984, p. 17.

Wood, Patrick, "Encouraging a Partnership of State and Private Practice," *Times* (London), June 15, 1966, p. 13.

California Water Service Group

1720 North 1st Street
San Jose, California 95112
U.S.A.
Telephone: (408) 367-8200
Toll Free: (800) 750-8200
Fax: (408) 367-8430
Web site: http://www.calwatergroup.com

Public Company
Incorporated: 1997
Employees: 840
Sales: $320.7 million (2005)
Stock Exchanges: New York
Ticker Symbol: CWT
NAIC: 221310 Water Supply and Irrigation Systems; 551112 Offices of Other Holding Companies

■ ■ ■

California Water Service Group (CWSG) is the second largest, investor-owned water utility in the United States, operating as a holding company for five subsidiaries: California Water Service Company, CWS Utility Services, New Mexico Water Service Company, Washington Water Service Company, and Hawaii Water Service Company. Except for CWS Utility Services, which controls non-regulated water operations, CWSG's subsidiaries are regulated by state public utilities commissions and provide water utility services to more than two million customers. The largest and oldest of the subsidiaries is California Water Service Company, a provider of water service to more than 450,000 customers in 75 communities. Washington Water Service Company provides water service to 15,000 customers in Tacoma, Washington, and the state's capital, Olympia. The holding company's New Mexico operations serve nearly 6,500 water and wastewater customers in the Belen, Los Lunas, and Elephant Butte areas of the state. In Hawaii, the company serves nearly 500 customers on the island of Maui. Together, the three subsidiaries operating outside of California account for 4 percent of CWSG's annual revenues. CWSG's non-regulated operations consist of operating water systems owned by other companies, providing meter reading and billing services, brokerage services for water rights, and testing services for water quality.

ORIGINS

The formation of CWSG in 1997 created a corporate structure that facilitated profound changes for a 70-year-old business, a business that for decades had led a somewhat staid existence. The two eras had one common trait, supplying water to residential and commercial customers, but in all other respects glaring differences jumped out to the observer. CWSG was the agent of change, its formation ushering in a period of unprecedented expansion. Within a decade of the holding company's formation, a business that had constrained its activities within northern California spread its influence throughout the western United States, assuming the profile of a utilities giant. The executive who spearheaded the remarkable transformation, Peter C. Nelson, left an indelible imprint on the history of the California Water name, doing more to amplify the

COMPANY PERSPECTIVES

Looking at California Water Service Group through the eyes of a diverse group of stockholders, it is clear that our company appeals to investors for a variety of reasons. Some like the dividend; others look for long-term growth. Some buy our stock because of their confidence in our management; others are attracted by the reputation our employees have earned for providing excellent customer service. What they share, whether they are customers, retirees, employees, or business professionals, is an appreciation for our stability.

business's recognition than the cumulative effect of his predecessors.

The heart of the legacy inherited by Nelson was California Water Service Company. Formed in 1926, the company was based in San Jose, operating as a public utility serving communities surrounding its home base. During its first 60 years in business, the utility expanded across several counties, using a combination of wells and surface water to serve its customers. By the end of the 1980s, California Water Service Company provided water service in 21 water-service districts, a territory that comprised 38 northern California communities and boasted a customer base of slightly more than 335,000 customers. By using surface water for 52 percent of its annual production total of 98 billion gallons of water and wells for the remaining 48 percent, the company served its customers, representing a fundamental component of the infrastructure supporting residents and businesses in communities such as Cupertino, Los Altos Hills, Mountain View, and Sunnyvale, among others. Operating as such, the company concluded its last decade as a one-state utility. The 1990s ushered in a period of transformation, a decade that saw Nelson occupy the symbolic corner office at California Water Serve Company's San Jose headquarters.

In early 1996, California Water Service Company's directors were searching for a new chief executive officer. The criteria for their search, a recruitment effort overseen by the utility's chairman, Robert Foy, were specific. The directors demanded an executive with experience in public utilities, finance and marketing know-how, management expertise with an emphasis on social skills, and the ability to adapt to changing conditions in the water-service market. Their search chewed through candidates and eventually focused on one individual, a former executive at Pacific Gas & Electric Co. "It was a perfect fit," Foy said of Nelson in a September 23, 1996 interview with the *Business Journal*. "It was too good to be true." Foy was sold, but Nelson had his own stipulations, declining to accept the post before he assessed the companies he was asked to lead. Nelson, without revealing who he was, placed a service call to California Water Service Company to witness its response and he paid a visit to the company's main offices, asking employees what they thought of the company. His incognito research yielded evidence that pointed in the company's favor, encouraging him to accept the title of chief executive officer. The Pacific Gas & Electric Co. executive, with an undergraduate degree in engineering from the University of California's Davis campus and a master's in business administration from the University of Massachusetts, took the helm in mid-1996.

When Nelson took charge, California Water Service Company ranked as the largest private water company in California, serving 1.5 million customers. He soon sought to elevate the company's stature by using the formation of CWSG as his vehicle for expansion. In April 1997, shareholders voted to adopt a holding company structure at the board of directors' urging, agreeing that such a structure, according to an April 6, 1997 filing with the Securities and Exchange Commission, "will help the company to respond more effectively and efficiently to competitive changes occurring in the water industry and to new non-regulated business opportunities that may arise from these changes." After receiving regulatory approval from the California Public Utilities Commission, the holding company was formed, making its debut on the last day of 1997. When CWSG was incorporated, it became the parent company of two operating subsidiaries, California Water Service Company, and a newly formed entity, CWS Utility Services, which was created to provide non-regulated water operations and related services.

Nelson announced the first step in his expansion campaign within a year of orchestrating the formation of CWSG. In November 1998, CWSG announced what was believed to be the largest merger of private water utilities in the history of California business, the $53 million, all-stock purchase of Dominguez Services Corp. Dominguez Services Corp. operated Dominguez Water Co., a company formed in 1911 to irrigate the farmlands of one of the first Spanish land grants in California. The company also operated Antelope Valley Water Co., located in northern Los Angeles County, and Kern River Valley Water Co., a northern California water company. Additionally, Dominguez Service Corp. held a 20 percent stake in San Jose-based Chemical Services Co., a supplier of onsite chlorine generation equipment. Nelson explained the significance of the acquisition in a state-

KEY DATES

1926: California Water Service Company is formed.
1996: Peter C. Nelson is appointed chief executive officer of the company.
1997: California Water Service Group is created as a holding company for California Water Service Company and CWS Utility Services.
1998: Dominguez Services Corp. is acquired, the largest acquisition in the company's history.
1999: Washington Water Service Company is formed.
2000: New Mexico Water Service Company is formed.
2003: Ka'anapli Water Corp. is acquired.
2004: National Utility Company is acquired, strengthening the company's New Mexico-based operations.

ment quoted in the November 18, 1998 edition of *Knight Ridder/Tribune Business News,* saying, "The post-merger firm will be well-positioned to play an active role in the growth and consolidation taking place in the water industry." Nelson continued, "In combining our adjacent properties, we will pool our human resources and achieve economies of scale that will not only benefit our shareholders and customers, but also make us a more attractive and viable partner to public and private water providers."

GEOGRAPHIC EXPANSION WITH THE NEW MILLENNIUM

The Dominguez Services Corp. acquisition was completed in 2000 after receiving regulatory approval, making CWSG the fourth largest, investor-owned water utility in the United States. Nelson's next move put the holding company's structure to use, as he spearheaded the most aggressive geographic expansion in the company's history. For the first time, the California Water Service banner was unfurled outside California after the holding company purchased Harbor Water Company and South Sound Utility in 1999 and merged them to form its third operating subsidiary, Washington Water Service Company, in December 1999. The acquisitions and subsequent merger created the state's largest, investor-owned water utility, an entity that served two water districts with more than 12,000 customers. Several months after the subsidiary was created, its operations were expanded by an acquisition announced in April 2000. The purchase, a $500,000 deal, consisted of 700 metered connections in King County operated by Mirrormount Water Services.

As CWSG established a presence to the north in Washington, it also pressed to the east, adding another operating subsidiary to its holdings. New Mexico Water Service Company was created in 2000 to house the acquisition of Rio Grande Utility Corp., a utility that served 2,265 water and 1,600 wastewater customers in Valencia County, situated 30 miles south of Albuquerque. The acquisition, which was not approved by the New Mexico Public Regulatory Commission until June 2002, was completed for $2.3 million in cash and the assumption of $3.1 million in debt, giving CWSG a total of more than two million customers in 98 communities. The company's New Mexico operations were bolstered later by the acquisition of National Utility Company in 2004. CWSG paid $630,000 to gain 700 customers adjacent to New Mexico Water Service Company's Middle Rio Grande water system and 950 water customers residing 150 miles south of Albuquerque.

CWSG ENTERING HAWAII IN 2003

Nelson's next move represented the greatest geographic leap in the company's history. In August 2002, he signed an agreement to acquire Ka'anapli Water Corp., a water utility serving the island of Maui in Hawaii. The utility, which was acquired from AquaSource Utilities, Inc. for $8 million, gave CWSG approximately 500 customers, including six large resorts and eight condominium complexes. "We are thrilled to be entering our fourth state," Nelson said in an April 30, 2003 statement quoted by *Business Wire* that coincided with the completion of the acquisition. "This was a great opportunity that fit perfectly into our growth strategy, which is to seek good quality systems in the western United States that will add immediately to stockholder value."

As CWSG neared the end of its first decade in business, its acquisition campaign reflected an industry trend. The water utility industry was undergoing a period of consolidation during Nelson's first years in charge, pursuing a strategy aimed at attracting investors. Conservative investors typically were attracted to investor-owned water utilities, drawn to the sector because of regulated rates, consistent dividends, and the stability of the water business. An acquire-or-be-acquired mentality gripped water utility executives, winnowing the ranks of investor-owned water utilities to only 11 throughout the United States by the time CWSG expanded into Hawaii. Of these 11 utilities, CWSG ranked as the second largest by the mid-2000s, benefiting from Nelson's commitment to be a consolidator in the industry. The financial gains from his expansion campaign were not astounding: During CWSG's acquisition spree, its revenues only increased from $225 million in 1997 to $315 million in 2004, with the company's operations in Washington, New Mexico, and Hawaii generating just 4 percent of total annual sales. Perhaps of greater significance was the geographic diversity the acquisition campaign gave CWSG, enabling it to hold sway as the second largest company of its kind in the country.

In the years ahead, Nelson and his successors were expected to pursue a disciplined growth strategy, endeavoring to give the company's shareholders a low-risk, consistent return on their investment dollars. "After all," he wrote to CWSG's shareholders in the company's 2004 annual report, "we know why stockholders invest in California Water Service Group. They choose our company because of our people and the service they provide, because we are regulated and provide a basic necessity, because we have provided stability and growth over the long term, and because we have declared dividends for 60 consecutive years. In short," he concluded, "they invest in our company because we deliver a return on their investment."

Jeffrey L. Covell

PRINCIPAL SUBSIDIARIES

California Water Service Company; CWS Utility Services; New Mexico Water Service Company; Washington Water Service Company; Hawaii Water Service Company.

PRINCIPAL COMPETITORS

American States Water Company; American Water Works Company, Inc.; Southwest Water Company.

FURTHER READING

Bergstrom, Danna, "His Cup Runneth Over," *Business Journal,* September 23, 1996, p. 14A.

"Cal Water's Newest Subsidiary Announces Three New Acquisitions," *Business Wire,* April 12, 2000, p. 0600.

"California Water Service Company," *Business Journal,* June 27, 1988, p. 19.

"California Water Service Group Buys Water Company in New Mexico," *Business Wire,* November 15, 2000, p. 0595.

"California Water Service Group Completes Acquisition of Ka'anapli Water Corporation," *Business Wire,* April 30, 2003, p. 5698.

Cook, Bill, "California Water Service to Merge with Dominguez Services of Long Beach," *Knight Ridder/Tribune Business News,* November 18, 1998.

"New Mexico Regulation Commission Unanimously Approves California Water Service Group Purchase of Rio Grande Utility Corporation," *Business Wire,* June 12, 2002, p. 0318.

Canon Inc.

30-2, Shimomaruko 3-chome
Ohta-ku
Tokyo, 146-8501
Japan
Telephone: (+81-3) 3758-2111
Fax: (+81-3) 5482-5135
Web site: http://www.canon.com

Public Company
Incorporated: 1937 as Precision Optical Industry Company, Ltd.
Employees: 115,583
Sales: ¥3.75 trillion ($31.82 billion) (2005)
Stock Exchanges: Tokyo Osaka Nagoya Fukuoka Sapporo New York Frankfurt
Ticker Symbols: 7751 (Tokyo); CAJ (New York)
NAIC: 333314 Optical Instrument and Lens Manufacturing; 333315 Photographic and Photocopying Equipment Manufacturing; 334119 Other Computer Peripheral Equipment Manufacturing

■ ■ ■

Although it scarcely predates World War II, Canon Inc. has ranked as one of the world's leading manufacturers of electronics, principally optical electronics, since the late 1970s. Year in and year out one of the top three companies receiving U.S. patents, Canon has a history of innovation that has brought it a leadership position in copiers, laser and ink-jet printers, fax machines, scanners, multifunction devices, film-based and digital cameras, and camcorders. The company also manufactures and markets binoculars, camera lenses, liquid crystal display (LCD) projectors, calculators, semiconductor production equipment, LCD production equipment, and medical and broadcasting equipment. Canon has been involved in an important alliance with Hewlett-Packard Company (HP) since 1985 whereby Canon produces laser printers that are sold by HP under the HP LaserJet brand; approximately one-fifth of Canon's total revenues are derived from this partnership. The company is also linked with Toshiba Corporation in a joint venture focusing on surface-conduction electron-emitter display (SED) television sets, a high-definition alternative to plasma and LCD sets. Canon still manufactures the majority of its products in Japan, while also operating manufacturing subsidiaries in the United States, Germany, France, Taiwan, China, Malaysia, Thailand, and Vietnam along with a manufacturing joint venture in Korea. Fully 73 percent of the firm's revenues are generated outside Japan, with the Americas and Europe accounting for about 30 percent each.

EARLY HISTORY

The history of Canon dates back to 1933, when a young gynecologist named Takeshi Mitarai worked with some technician friends to develop cameras; to do so they founded Precision Optical Instruments Laboratory in Roppongi, Minato-ku, Japan. Their first major invention had applications that ranged far beyond the medical field. In 1934 Mitarai and his colleagues developed Japan's first 35-millimeter camera, closely patterned after the German Leica 35-millimeter camera, the industry

COMPANY PERSPECTIVES

The corporate philosophy of Canon is *kyosei.* A concise definition of this word would be "Living and working together for the common good," but our definition is broader: "All people, regardless of race, religion or culture, harmoniously living and working together into the future." Unfortunately, the presence of imbalance in our world—in areas such as trade, income levels and the environment—hinders the achievement of *kyosei.*

Addressing these imbalances is an ongoing mission, and Canon is doing its part by actively pursuing *kyosei.* True global companies must foster good relations, not only with their customers and the communities in which they operate, but also with nations and the environment. They must also bear the responsibility for the impact of their activities on society. For this reason, Canon's goal is to contribute to the prosperity of the world and the happiness of humanity, which will lead to continuing growth and bring the world closer to achieving *kyosei.*

standard. They named it the Kwanon, after a Buddhist figure representing mercy. In 1937 they incorporated their venture under the name Precision Optical Industry Company, Ltd.

In 1940 Precision Optical made a significant contribution to Japanese medical imaging technology when it developed the nation's first indirect X-ray camera, which played a major role in preventing the spread of tuberculosis in Japan. When Japan went to war with the United States, the Japanese economy was entirely given over to supporting the military.

The company barely survived World War II. It was unable to manufacture its mainstay 35-millimeter cameras for the duration of the war, and only Mitarai's tireless efforts kept it afloat in the economic desolation that followed Japan's surrender in 1945. With raw materials rationed and capital scarce, Mitarai had to scramble just to keep his production lines going and the company's finances in order. He also drilled into his workers the importance of producing high-quality products, but his most important move may have been persuading the Allied occupation forces to stock Precision Optical cameras in their post exchanges and ships' stores. This arrangement laid the groundwork for Canon's later success as an exporter; U.S. servicemen bringing their cameras home with them gave the company its first foothold in the U.S. market. In 1947 Precision Optical changed its name to Canon Camera Company, Inc., using a transliteration of the original Kwanon.

Another international breakthrough for Canon occurred in the early 1950s, when news photographers covering the Korean War found that the best Japanese lenses were every bit as good as German lenses. The export market began to open up, and Canon prospered throughout the decade. The company created a U.S. subsidiary, based in New York, in 1955 and two years later it formed a European subsidiary, Canon Europa, headquartered in Geneva. In 1956 Canon added an 8-millimeter movie camera to its product lines, and in 1959 it became the first company in the world to manufacture an 8-millimeter camera with a built-in zoom lens.

DIVERSIFYING INTO BUSINESS MACHINES

By the early 1960s Canon had become the dominant Japanese producer of middle-priced cameras, leaving the higher end of the market to Nikon. The company continued to grow, more than tripling in size between 1959 and 1963. In 1964 it ventured into business machines when it introduced the Canola 130 electronic calculator, the first in the world to use the now-standard ten-key keypad. In 1970 Canon and Texas Instruments produced the Pocketronic, the first all-electronic handheld calculator. After entering the photocopier market in 1965 with the Canofax 1000, Canon became an innovator in the field when it introduced its first plain-paper copier in 1968. Until that time Xerox Corporation had dominated the copier market with its own process, known as xerography. Canon's diversification moves were significant enough to prompt a name change; "Camera Company" was dropped from the name in 1969 and the company became simply Canon Inc.

In spite of the company's engineering successes, however, Canon was plagued by weaknesses in marketing strategy in the late 1960s and early 1970s. Although it was a part of the spectacular overall penetration of the U.S. market by Japanese calculator makers, the company failed for the most part to distinguish itself from its competitors. It also frittered away its technical advances by failing to exploit their sales potential before rivals could catch up to them. This problem affected its copier lines as well as its calculators. In 1972 it developed the "liquid dry" copying system—so named because it uses plain paper and liquid developer but turns out dry copies—but doubted its own marketing strength and feared that competitors would infringe on its patents. Therefore,

KEY DATES

1933: Led by Takeshi Mitarai, Precision Optical Instruments Laboratory is founded.
1934: Mitarai and colleagues develop Japan's first 35-millimeter camera, the Kwanon.
1937: The venture is incorporated as Precision Optical Industry Company, Ltd.
1947: Firm is renamed Canon Camera Company, Inc.
1955: New York branch is established.
1957: Canon Europa is formed, based in Geneva.
1964: An electronic calculator is introduced, Canon's first venture into business machines.
1968: Canon introduces a plain-paper copier.
1969: Diversification drive prompts name change to simply Canon Inc.
1976: The revolutionary AE-1 35-millimeter camera is introduced.
1982: Canon's personal copier debuts.
1985: Canon begins producing laser printers for Hewlett-Packard Company.
1987: Canon launches its EOS autofocus SLR camera.
1995: Fujio Mitarai takes over leadership of Canon.
1999: The ImageRunner line of high-end digital copiers is introduced.
2000: PowerShot Digital ELPH camera debuts.
2003: Canon launches the EOS Digital Rebel camera.
2006: Tsuneji Uchida succeeds Mitarai as Canon president.

instead of selling the system itself, it licensed the technology to other manufacturers, effectively wasting its earnings potential. These mistakes hindered Canon's financial performance, and in 1975 it failed to pay a dividend for the first time since World War II.

REVITALIZING NEW PRODUCT DEVELOPMENT AND MARKETING

Into this leadership void stepped Ryuzaburo Kaku, the company's managing director. He won approval from Mitarai, who was still chairman and president, to change management and sales practices. Under Kaku, Canon began to streamline its operations and chain of command and market its products more aggressively. In 1976 the company introduced its revolutionary AE-1 35-millimeter camera, which used a microprocessor to focus automatically and set the length of exposure, with an advertising blitz led by television commercials featuring tennis star John Newcombe. "It was a big gamble because 35-millimeter cameras had never before been advertised on TV," Mitarai said, but it paid off handsomely. According to *Fortune,* January 12, 1981, by 1981 the AE-1 had become so popular that one industry analyst called it "the Chevrolet of the 35mm market." Kaku's emphasis on faster new product development led to laser beam printing technology in 1975 and a new retinal camera that made pupil-dilating drugs unnecessary in 1976. In 1977 Kaku was named president of the company, succeeding Mitarai, who remained chairman.

In 1982 Canon introduced the first personal copier, so called because all the essential reproduction components were contained in a cartridge that users could replace themselves. Again, it was accompanied by a massive ad campaign, this time starring actor Jack Klugman. In less than a decade, Canon's salesmanship had undergone a radical change from passive to highly aggressive. When Canon overtook Nikon as Japan's camera sales leader in the early 1980s, former Nikon Chairman Kyojiro Iyanaga explained his rival's success by saying, "We still make the best cameras. Canon just outmarketed us."

Canon continued to introduce new products in the 1980s to compete effectively in mature markets. Much of its success, however, came in new markets, such as integrated office workstations and desktop publishing systems. Often that meant challenging large companies that were well entrenched in their markets. In 1982 it came out with an electronic typewriter, initiating a one-on-one competition with International Business Machines Corporation (IBM). Within a year, it captured 11 percent of that market, while IBM's share shrank from 26 to 17 percent. In 1983 it took on Xerox with a laser printer that offered similar quality at one-third the price. Canon also engaged Ricoh in a rivalry over facsimile machines in the early 1980s and laid the groundwork for a future duel with IBM in the computer business. It began a research push aimed at developing optical integrated circuits for personal computers of the future, and in 1984 Canon Sales started marketing the Apple Macintosh in Japan. Canon also joined with Apple to develop software for the Japanese market. Later in the decade, the company's optical chip efforts paid off when former Apple chief Steven Jobs chose Canon's chips for his new NeXT computer. In 1989 Canon acquired a 16.7 percent interest in NeXT Incorporated, along with the exclusive right to market the NeXT in Asia, for $100 million.

In the camera area, Canon dropped to the number two position worldwide in 1985 when Minolta introduced the popular Maxxum, whose automated features included autofocus. By the end of the decade Canon was back on top after the 1987 launch of the EOS (electronic optical system) autofocus SLR followed in 1989 by the high-end EOS-1 autofocus SLR.

In the meantime, Canon began a long-running partnership with Hewlett-Packard Company (HP) in 1985 when the two companies teamed up to develop HP's top-selling line of LaserJet printers. Canon produced the guts of the machines, including their high-quality laser motors, a key part of such printers, enabling HP to focus on its area of expertise, the software linking printers to PCs. Canon eventually derived as much as one-fifth of its total revenues from this alliance.

SLOWER GROWTH

Canon experienced rapid sales and profit growth from its low-water mark in 1975 through the end of the 1980s. Between 1975 and 1985, its annual sales grew sevenfold, to $3.3 billion, and its profits showed a 20-fold increase, to $136 million; by 1989, sales had reached $8.18 billion and profits hit $232 million. Following an exceptional year in 1990 that saw a 27.9 percent increase in sales (to $12.73 billion) and a near doubling in profits (to $452 million), succeeding years featured slower growth and reduced profits. Profit margins ranged from 1.1 to 1.9 percent from 1992 to 1994 after having ranged from 2.8 to 3.6 percent from 1988 to 1991.

The slowdown was partly attributable to the maturation of some of Canon's key product areas, notably copiers and cameras. The maturation in cameras, especially the SLR cameras Canon specialized in, affected Canon much less severely than other major camera makers (notably Minolta and Nikon), who relied on cameras for a much larger portion of overall sales than Canon did. In 1992, cameras comprised only 19 percent of overall Canon sales (compared to 44 and 43 percent for Minolta and Nikon, respectively), and by 1995 the percentage had dropped to 8.2 percent. Thus, the rapid growth in popularity of compact cameras, which began with Fuji's launch of the QuickSnap disposable camera in 1987 and was advanced by Konica's 1989 introduction of the Big Mini (the first super-compact camera), did not push Canon into the huge losses suffered by Minolta and Nikon in the early 1990s. Still, Canon quickly reacted to the new competition by developing its own compact camera, the Sure Shot, which grew into a full line of nearly a dozen models by the mid-1990s. In the meantime, however, Fuji had passed Canon as the world's top camera maker by 1992.

A larger factor in the 1990s slowdown was the recession in Japan and the appreciation of the yen, both of which affected all Japanese companies but hit the export-oriented electronic giants such as Canon especially hard. In response, the company made a major commitment to advance its globalization, in particular by moving production out of Japan whenever possible to where the products were sold. For example, Canon began to produce bubble-jet printers in Mexico in 1995, then started production of the same in Scotland the following year. The company also aggressively sought out new markets for its goods, setting a goal of increasing Asian-Pacific sales outside of Japan to 10 percent of overall sales, and marketing products to Russia for the first time in 1995 through the Finland-based Oy Canon AB subsidiary.

In the face of these years of slower growth, Canon continued its historic commitment to high expenditures on research and development (averaging about 5 percent of net sales) and risk-taking new product development. Back in 1977 a Canon engineer had accidentally invented the bubble-jet printing technology, which Canon then somewhat belatedly marketed successfully in the early 1990s. The BJC-820 full-color bubble-jet printer was introduced in 1992, followed in 1994 by the innovative notebook computer with built-in color bubble-jet printer, a product developed in partnership with IBM. Canon's determination to become a major player in the personal computer field was seen as particularly risky, given the failure of NeXT (which exited the hardware business in 1993) and the highly competitive nature of the personal computer market. Of course, Canon's partnership strategy, which continued in 1994 with another venture with IBM to develop small computers based on IBM's PowerPC chip, was designed to alleviate some of the risk. Nonetheless, evidence existed that Canon was still willing to venture into territory few dared enter, notably its research into the ferroelectric liquid crystal display (FLCD). Canon planned to invest more than ¥100 billion before seeing any return from its research into FLCD, an integral component to be used in flat, large-sized, high-definition computer and television screens—a projected replacement for the ubiquitous cathode ray tube.

RISING FORTUNES UNDER FUJIO MITARAI

In 1993 the founder's eldest son, Hajime Mitarai, succeeded Kaku as president of Canon, but the new leader died suddenly of pneumonia only two years later. Thrust into the leadership was Fujio Mitarai, a nephew of the founder, who would take the company to new heights. Mitarai's management style was a unique combination of Japanese and U.S. practices—consensus decision-making and job security from the former, merit-based pay and an emphasis on the bottom line from the latter—a style developed during the 23 years he spent at Canon U.S.A. During this stint, which included ten years as head of the unit, Mitarai boosted revenue at Canon U.S.A. sixfold, to $2.6 billion, which amounted to 35 percent of global sales. He returned to Japan in 1989 as executive director.

Mitarai took over a debt-ridden company managing only a razor-thin profit margin and losing ground in a range of fields to a host of competitors. He almost immediately shook up the company by pulling the plug on a number of money-losing operations, ordering the shutdown, between 1997 and 1999, of businesses producing personal computers, liquid crystal displays, photovoltaic batteries, electric typewriters, and optical memory cards. Canon was refocused on three core areas: copiers, printers, and cameras. While avoiding layoffs, particularly in Japan, Mitarai significantly cut costs (approximately $300 million in 1999 alone) by streamlining product development and manufacturing processes and through other initiatives. One big change on the manufacturing side came in 1998, when Canon began replacing the ubiquitous production line centered on a conveyor belt with an assembly process revolving around small groups called "cells," the members of which huddled together to perform multiple tasks. The new process aided teamwork, helped the workers feel more responsibility for their work, and was faster and more efficient. Canon also slashed its debt by using its own ample supplies of cash for capital investment instead of borrowing money, as was the practice at many Japanese companies; the firm's debt-to-assets ratio fell from 34 percent in 1995 to less than 11 percent in 2001.

At the same time, Mitarai did not skimp on research and development, investing about 7.5 percent of net sales each year, or ¥218.62 billion ($1.66 billion) in 2001, for example, to keep churning out new products and improving existing ones. In cameras, Canon joined in the Eastman Kodak Company-led consortium that developed the Advanced Photo System (APS) and introduced its ELPH APS camera in 1996. More importantly, Canon was one of the few camera makers that successfully made the transition from film to digital. The company introduced its first digital SLR camera, the high-end EOS DCS 3, in 1995, but Canon reached the top of the global digital camera market in 2004, surpassing Sony Corporation, following the introduction in 2000 of the PowerShot Digital ELPH (Digital IXY in some markets), an extremely compact and lightweight model, and the debut in 2003 of the EOS Digital Rebel, an entry-level SLR model. By 2005 Canon's share of the worldwide digital camera market was a leading 20 percent, while its share of the higher-margin digital SLR segment was a stunning 59 percent.

Canon also managed to surge past Xerox in the copier field by belatedly entering the digital market and by going after the U.S. firm on its own turf, corporate copying. In 1999 Canon introduced the digital ImageRunner copiers, which were smarter, more reliable, and faster than the comparable machines of its competitors. By 2001 the company had captured more than 22 percent of the market for high-end digital copiers, surpassing Xerox's 17 percent. Canon made further gains in the succeeding years by introducing color laser office printers/copiers, as the corporate world steadily began migrating from monochrome to color printing. Meanwhile, Canon remained heavily involved in the laser printer market, mainly through its continuing partnership with HP, although it also produced its own laser models that claimed a modest 5 percent of the global market. In inkjet printers Canon trailed far behind HP, which in 2005 held about 40 percent of the market, compared to Canon's 20 percent. Canon's photo printers were one bright spot, but in the arena of multifunction devices (printers also able to scan, fax, and/or copy) Canon was far behind the leaders, HP and Lexmark International, Inc.

In seeking to revitalize Canon's new product development efforts in its core business lines, Mitarai aimed to offset the price declines that had become commonplace in the world of high-tech products. By boosting sales of new products, Canon could lessen the impact of declining prices for its existing products. Between 2000 and 2005, Canon increased the proportion of its sales derived from new products from 44 percent to 66 percent.

Even more impressive were the overall results of the Mitarai era. Net sales increased from ¥2.17 trillion ($21.03 billion) to ¥3.75 trillion ($31.82 billion) between 1995 and 2005. Net income grew sevenfold, from ¥55 billion ($533 million) to ¥384.1 billion ($3.26 billion), amounting in 2005 to a profit of more than 10 percent, a huge advance over the minuscule margins of the early 1990s. By this time, Mitarai, widely considered to be the best Japanese CEO of his era, had been elevated to cultlike status in his home country. His prowess was recognized in 2006 when he was asked to head the Japan Business Federation, or Nippon Keidanren, the influential business lobby that serves as a representative of Japan's largest corporations. Because of the time commitment involved in this prestigious post, Mitarai announced that he would step down as president in mid-2006, while remaining chairman. Taking on the unenviable task of succeeding Mitarai was Tsuneji Uchida, who was selected in part for his strong technical background because Mitarai wanted the next leader to spearhead Canon's entry into new fields. As head of the camera division, Uchida had led the firm's ascendance to the top of the digital camera sector.

During this leadership transition, Canon was in the midst of further efficiency drives, including an effort launched in late 2004 to fully automate 25 percent of the company's plants within a three-year period. And in a bold but risky move, Canon had also partnered with Toshiba Corporation on a ¥200 billion ($1.82 billion) joint venture charged with producing surface-conduction electron-emitter display (SED) high-definition television sets. The SED technology was touted to offer both the flat panel design of LCD and plasma television and the same levels of brightness and color performance of bulky cathode-ray-tube televisions, while using much less power than LCDs and plasmas. Canon was hoping that the venture could capture 20 percent of the flat-panel television market by 2010, but the launch of the new technology was delayed until late 2007, or about 18 months, when the prices of flat-panel models began dropping faster than expected. Canon and Toshiba started seeking ways to cut production costs in order to maintain a sufficient level of profits. While this setback placed in jeopardy one of Canon's main engines for future growth, the company remained one of the world's leading electronics manufacturers, with leading or near-leading positions in cameras, copiers, and printers.

Douglas Sun
Updated, David E. Salami

PRINCIPAL SUBSIDIARIES

Canon Sales Co., Inc. (51.1%); Canon Electronics Inc. (54.2%); Canon Finetech Inc. (58.5%); Canon Software Inc. (57.7%); Canon Machinery Inc. (67.3%); Nisca Corporation (51.1%); Canon U.S.A., Inc.; Canon Europa B.V. (Netherlands).

PRINCIPAL COMPETITORS

Xerox Corporation/Fuji Xerox Corporation; Hewlett-Packard Company; Lexmark International, Inc.; Ricoh Company, Ltd.; Seiko Epson Corporation; Toshiba Corporation; Sharp Corporation; Konica Minolta Holdings, Inc.; Sony Corporation; Fuji Photo Film Co., Ltd.; Olympus Corporation; Nikon Corporation; Casio Computer Co., Ltd.; Matsushita Electric Industrial Co., Ltd.; Eastman Kodak Company; Sigma Corporation; Pentax Corporation; Victor Company of Japan Ltd.; ASML Holding N.V.

FURTHER READING

Baba, Kanji, "Canon Reaps Payoff for Tight Focus," *Nikkei Weekly,* July 14, 2003.

Beauchamp, Marc, "From Fuji to Everest," *Forbes,* May 2, 1988, p. 35.

Chandler, Clay, "Canon's Big Gun," *Fortune,* February 6, 2006, pp. 92+.

Cieply, Michael, "And Then We Will Attack," *Forbes,* March 26, 1984, pp. 42+.

Desmond, Edward W., "Can Canon Keep Clicking?," *Fortune,* February 2, 1998, pp. 98–100, 102, 104.

Eisenstodt, Gale, "Crazy Is Praise for Us," *Forbes,* November 7, 1994, pp. 174–84.

Friedland, Jonathan, "Nothing Ventured ...: Even Canon's Failed Products Serve a Purpose," *Far Eastern Economic Review,* February 24, 1994, pp. 76, 78.

———, "Out in Front," *Far Eastern Economic Review,* February 24, 1994, pp. 72–75.

Greenberg, Manning, "Canon Runs the Gamut from Video to Home Office," *HFD-The Weekly Home Furnishings Newspaper,* April 9, 1990, p. 150.

"Hard to Copy," *Economist,* November 2, 2002, pp. 63–64.

Heller, Robert, "What Makes Canon Boom," *Management Today,* September 1983, pp. 62+.

Helm, Leslie, and Rebecca Aikman, "Office Products: A Japanese Slugfest for U.S. Turf," *Business Week,* May 13, 1985, pp. 98+.

Holstein, William J., "Canon Takes Aim at Xerox," *Fortune,* October 14, 2002, pp. 215–16, 218, 220.

Johnstone, Bob, "If Anyone Can, Can Mitarai?," *Director,* July 1995, p. 17.

Kenward, Michael, "Canon Goes Flat Out," *Director,* March 1997, pp. 58–60.

Klebnikov, Paul, and Benjamin Fulford, "Canon on the Loose," *Forbes,* July 23, 2001, pp. 68–69.

Koyama, Takashi, "Strong Leadership, Top Tech Mean Healthy Canon Inc.," *Nikkei Weekly,* March 18, 2002.

Kunii, Irene M., "Making Canon Click: How Fujio Mitarai's East-West Style Revived the Company," *Business Week,* September 16, 2002, pp. 40–42.

Kyanon shi: Gijutsu to seihin no 50-nen, Tokyo: Kyanon, 1987, 422 p.

Landers, Peter, "Quality Counts: Technical Prowess and Global Reach Keep Japanese Giants on Top," *Far Eastern Economic Review,* February 5, 1998, pp. 46–48.

Martin, Neil A., "Copy This," *Barron's,* March 18, 2002, p. 14.

———, "Look Out, World," *Barron's,* January 24, 2000, pp. 26–27.

McCarthy, Joseph L., "Beyond the Box," *Chief Executive,* April 1995, pp. 32–35.

Murata, Taku, "Can Canon Become a PC Player?," *Tokyo Business Today,* January 1995, pp. 43–45.

Nakamoto, Michiyo, and David Pilling, "If Canon Can, Japan Can," *Financial Times,* September 24, 2003, p. 14.

NIKKEI, *How Canon Got Its Flash Back: The Innovative Turnaround Tactics of Fujio Mitarai,* translated by Mark Schreiber and Aaron Martin Cohen, Singapore: John Wiley,

2004, 221 p.

Port, Otis, "Canon Finally Challenges Minolta's Mighty Maxxum," *Business Week,* March 2, 1987, pp. 89+.

Rowley, Ian, Hiroko Tashiro, and Louise Lee, "Canon: Combat-Ready," *Business Week,* September 5, 2005, pp. 48–49.

"Tech-Savvy Uchida to Take Presidency," *Nikkei Weekly,* February 6, 2006.

Weigner, Kathleen K., "Xerox, Here We Come," *Forbes,* March 31, 1980, pp. 117+.

Centerplate, Inc.

201 East Broad Street
Spartanburg, South Carolina 29306
U.S.A.
Telephone: (864) 598-8600
Fax: (864) 598-8695
Web site: http://www.centerplate.com

Public Company
Incorporated: 1995 as VSI Acquisition II Corporation
Employees: 30,000
Sales: $643.1 million (2005)
Stock Exchanges: American Toronto
Ticker Symbol: CVP
NAIC: 722310 Food Service Contractors; 722110 Full-Service Restaurants; 722211 Limited Service Restaurants; 711310 Promoters of Performing Arts, Sports, and Similar Events with Facilities

■ ■ ■

Centerplate, Inc. is a leading provider of concessions, merchandise, catering, and management services for 135 of North America's best-known sports facilities, convention centers, and other entertainment facilities. Centerplate is one of the two largest food and beverage service providers to National Football League (NFL) facilities, the third largest provider to Major League Baseball (MLB) facilities, and the largest provider to minor league baseball and spring training facilities. High profile events over the years include 24 World Series games, ten Super Bowls, eight NCAA Final Four Men's Basketball Tournaments, 14 World Cup Soccer Games, and nine U.S. Presidential Inaugural Balls.

1929: ROOTS ESTABLISHED

Centerplate's roots date to 1929, when Nathaniel Leverone founded the Automatic Canteen Company of America. New Hampshire-born, Dartmouth educated, 45 years old and in the real estate business, Leverone got his idea for the business while waiting on a Chicago "L" platform. To pass the time, he put a penny into two different coin-operated weight machines and got readings of 106 pounds and 200 pounds. A gum machine ate another coin but a peanut machine rewarded him with a few moldy morsels. Penny-in-the-slot machines had been around a long time; in Chicago they were the province and turf of gangsters. The 155-pound man knew that he could do better.

The company's first big success came at Chicago's 1933-34 World's Fair, where his Automatic machines dispensed affordable sandwiches, cakes, pies, ice cream, candy, and cigarettes to the visiting masses. With Leverone at the helm, the first major national retail organization of its kind flourished in World War II by providing food service to workers at defense plants. Canteen landed its first major league baseball park concessions contract when the American League Athletics moved from Philadelphia to their new stadium in Kansas City in 1954, and established the New York Yankees and Yankee Stadium as clients in 1964.

The company changed its name to Canteen Corporation in 1966. When International Telephone and Telegraph Corporation (ITT) acquired Canteen in 1968 for $242 million, the cost of a vended coffee or soft drink was raised from 10 to 15 cents; sales that year were $340 million, with earnings of $32 million.

COMPANY PERSPECTIVES

Centerplate is in the business of creating something special for major and minor league sports facilities, convention centers and entertainment venues. And for the fans and guests of these facilities.

For more than forty years, we've provided catering, concessions, management and merchandise services for some of the most prominent venues in North America.

But what we do best is to combine our culinary talent with our extensive event management expertise to ensure that every guest at every event is treated to a unique experience that can't be duplicated anywhere else.

Concentrating specifically on the convention, and sports and entertainment industries, Centerplate's proficiency in serving premier, high-volume facilities with the highest-quality cuisine is unmatched.

One element that has enabled us—and our clients—to succeed is our ability to understand and build on the uniqueness of each facility. We add local favorites to menus in suites and banquet rooms. We develop proprietary gourmet concessions that take stadium fare to unexpected levels. We design and produce one-of-a-kind merchandise for team stores and souvenir kiosks. Tailoring our services to suit each individual venue and its clientele is how we continually fulfill our commitment to create something special.

Canteen continued to be headquartered in Chicago and, in the late 1960s and early 1970s, like many other vending businesses, shifted its focus to nonvended foodservices in fields such as restaurants, airline catering, fast-food franchises, and hotel and recreation area operations. In 1971, Canteen's Nationwide Concessions division operated in sports stadiums and recreation areas such as Yankee Stadium and Yellowstone National Park.

Citing antitrust regulations, the U.S. Justice Department forced ITT to divest a number of its holdings, including Canteen, and in 1973, Trans World Airlines, Inc. bought the company for a mere $132 million. In 1980 Canteen, officially a subsidiary of Trans World Corporation, had become the largest vending machine business in the United States with annual revenues of $850 million. As the industrial decline of the United States in the 1980s unfolded, Canteen saw its vending business feeding workers in the smokestack market diminish. By mid-decade, Canteen increasingly provided onsite foodservice to white-collar workers in corporate settings, and greatly expanded its food sales to leisure and recreation markets, and institutions such as schools, prisons, and hospitals. Canteen was now operating a number of different stadium concessions operations including its Volume Services unit, acquired when it bought Interstate United Corp. in 1985.

In 1990, Canteen's operations were moved from Chicago to Spartanburg, South Carolina, the new home of its parent company, now called TW Holdings, Inc., which also owned the Denny's Restaurant chain, 500 Hardee's, and 250 Quincy's. In 1992, Canteen had more than 11,000 food, vending, and recreation services accounts in 48 states, with sales of $1.28 billion. In 1993, TW Holdings Inc. changed its name to Flagstar Companies Inc., and because of heavy debt began selling off some of its businesses. In 1994, Flagstar agreed to sell Canteen's vending and foodservices businesses, except for its Volume Services division and TW Recreational Services, to London-based Compass Group PLC for $450 million.

VOLUME SERVICES EMERGING IN 1995

The company now known as Centerplate was officially founded in 1995 when a group of top-level managers of Volume Services, Inc. engineered a friendly buyout of the firm from its parent company. The new company registered as VSI Acquisition II Corporation but continued to do business under the "Volume Services" name, with the same logo, and in the same Spartanburg, South Carolina, headquarters. The sale of Volume Services by Flagstar was announced in November and completed by December 31, 1995. The company, which had 80 accounts and about $20 million in annual revenues in 1995, was sold for $75 million.

In 1996 Volume Services solidified its regional base of business in the Carolinas. In July, the company was selected to handle all food and beverage concessions as well as event booking, ticketing, and facility management of the planned BI-LO Center in Greenville, South Carolina, a $63 million sports and entertainment complex that was scheduled to open in September 1998. With 12 separate accounts, ranging from major amphitheaters to minor league baseball facilities, Volume Services was the largest concessions operator in the Carolinas when it secured a new NFL concessions contract for the expansion Carolina Panthers and their under-construction Carolinas Stadium in Charlotte.

By the mid-1990s, Volume Services found that it

KEY DATES

1929: Automatic Canteen Company of America is founded in Chicago.
1954: Canteen lands its first major league baseball park concessions contract in Kansas City.
1968: Canteen is sold to International Telephone and Telegraph Corporation.
1973: Trans World Airlines buys Canteen.
1985: Volume Services is acquired and folded into Canteen's sports and recreational foodservices operations.
1990: Canteen's headquarters is moved to Spartanburg, South Carolina.
1995: Management-led buyout establishes Volume Services as independent company.
1998: Service America Corporation is acquired; name is changed to Volume Services America.
2003: Unique public offering is launched; name is changed to Centerplate.

took quite a bit more than cold beer and warm hot dogs to impress a crowd, and once the novelty of nationally branded pizza and hamburger products had worn off, the company turned to the concept of regionalized branding. When the 1996 football season started, new menu items for fans included Carolina-style barbecue carved fresh from spit-roasted pork for Carolina Panthers fans, polenta-dusted fried Calamari and grilled Ahi tuna on a sourdough roll in San Francisco's Candlestick Park and fried Grouper Sandwiches at Houlihan's Stadium in Tampa Bay. In the same year, Volume Services helped design and construct an automobile-themed minor league baseball park and menu for the Lugnuts and their new Oldsmobile Park in Lansing, Michigan. They created a Hubcap Café, Filling Station, and Dashboard Diner, where fans could get a quarter-pound Ethyl Dog, a Diesel Dog, a Bore and Stroke bratwurst sandwich, or a High Octane Polish sausage dog.

In June 1997, the firm landed a 20-plus-year concessions, merchandise, and suite catering contract with the San Francisco Giants that would begin in 2000 when the team moved into the newly built Pacific Bell Park. Volume Services had been serving food and beverages to Giants' fans in Candlestick Park since 1993. Sometimes partnering with local companies, the company by the end of the year had a total of 90 contracts, including retail operations and concessions agreements at outdoor amphitheaters such as Hardee's Pavilion at Walnut Creek in North Carolina, and parks such as the Los Angeles Equestrian Center.

ACQUISITION OF RIVAL COMPANY: 1998

Volume Services nearly doubled its size in August 1998 when it acquired Service America Corporation, a rival company with a focus on convention center concessions. Service America had contracts for foodservice at more than 20 convention and entertainment centers, including Denver's Colorado Convention Center and the Jacob K. Javits Convention Center in New York City. In addition, the company provided foodservice at two MLB stadiums and two NFL arenas as well as the Rose Bowl in Pasadena, California, the Saratoga Racetrack in New York, the Los Angeles Zoo, and B.C. Place Stadium in Vancouver, Canada. With the acquisition came a name change from Volume Services to Volume Services America, and in October, a corporate name change from VSI Acquisition II Corporation to Volume Services America Holdings, Inc.

Service America had annual revenues of more than $170 million with 800 full-time and more than 10,000 part-time and seasonal employees. With combined annual revenues of more than $400 million and over 26,000 employees, the merger of the two privately held foodservice providers placed Volume Services America among the country's top four sports and recreation concessionaires. The expanded enterprise maintained an office in Stamford but continued to be headquartered in Spartanburg and led by Volume Services Chairman and CEO Lawrence A. Hatch, along with Service America President and CEO John T. Dee.

Despite being the largest foodservice provider to NFL stadiums, minor league baseball parks, and major convention centers, 1999 was a year of uncertainty for Volume Services America. The firm continued to retain and renew existing accounts and win new concession contracts but was evaluated negatively by financial analysts because of its $215 million debt load and the seasonality and event-driven nature of the recreational foodservice industry. In June, New York-based entertainment, aviation, and energy company Ogden Corporation entered into an agreement to buy Volume Services America for $127 million and its assumed debt but called off the deal in September. By April 2000, Volume Services America had realized $4.3 million in cost savings from the acquisition of Service America, and in the process regained more positive ratings from market analysts. The company's annual revenues jumped over 20 percent from $431 million in 1999 to $522 million in 2000, and then grew at 4 percent and 6 percent in

2001 and 2002, respectively. Sales for 2002 totaled $577 million, with a net income of $4.5 million.

UNIQUE PUBLIC OFFERING IN 2003

In February 2003, Volume Services America began doing business under the name Centerplate. On February 13, 2003, Volume Services America Holdings, Inc., the parent company of Centerplate, stunned Wall Street when it filed papers to raise $275 million in an initial public offering (IPO) of Income Deposit Securities (IDSs), a unit never before traded in any U.S. market. Based on what were called Income Trusts in Canada, IDSs had separate debt and stock components paired together into a single unit for trading purposes, with investors getting one common share and debt note for each security purchased. In turn, the buyer would receive income in two ways: a monthly interest payment on the notes and a monthly dividend on the stock.

On December 5, 2003, Centerplate made history when it began trading its IDSs on the American Stock Exchange under the ticker symbol CVP. On December 8, Centerplate IDSs began trading on the Toronto Stock Exchange under the ticker symbol CVP.up. By the time all IPO transactions closed on December 16, the company had raised $277 million, which it used to pay down debts, repurchase stocks, and establish cash reserves. The firm finished 2003 with $616 million in sales, but due to costs associated with refinancing and the IPO showed a loss of $4.4 million.

At the start of 2004, Centerplate had contracts with 68 sports facilities throughout the United States and Canada, as well as 30 convention centers and 31 other entertainment facilities in the United States. The bulk of its revenues came from food and beverage concessions at 18 major league sports facilities: ten NFL, six MLB, two National Basketball Association (NBA), and one National Hockey League (NHL). With 25 teams on its roster, Centerplate was also the largest foodservice and merchandise provider to minor league baseball and spring training facilities.

In October 2004, security holders approved an amendment that changed Centerplate's corporate name from Volume Services America Holdings, Inc. to Centerplate, Inc., completing a rebranding process that began in early 2003. The loss of the San Diego Padres contract, a sales decline at MLB and NFL facilities, and five fewer postseason games were responsible for a decline in annual revenues to $607 million for 2004. Centerplate ended the year serving 133 facilities, with $2 million in net income.

TURMOIL AT THE TOP IN 2005

In April 2005, the board of directors ousted Lawrence Honig, Centerplate CEO since 2002, for "conduct unrelated to the company's operating performance or financial condition." He was temporarily replaced by Janet L. Steinmayer, who had been with the company since 1993, and served as president since February 2004. The new management team pledged to go after big stadium contracts and in April won a credit agreement with GE Capital for $215 million to fund the new initiative as well as for efforts to build a branded company image with newly created in-house proprietary brands and concepts such as Top Dog at Qualcomm Stadium in San Diego and Flipside Grill at New York's Yankee Stadium.

In August 2005, Centerplate rejected an unsolicited takeover offer from Capital Management LLC and a former CEO, Lawrence Hatch. In late August, Hurricane Katrina affected four of the venues in which Centerplate operated food concessions, including the Louisiana Superdome, where the company lost $9.4 million in sales due to hurricane damage. In September 2005, Centerplate named Paul W. MacPhail, a former restaurant executive, to replace Honig as chairman and chief executive officer. At the same time it named acting CEO Janet L. Steinmayer as a director, president, and COO. The year ended with a net loss of $4.6 million on annual revenues of $643 million, up 5.9 percent from 2004. New contracts brought in $24.4 million and convention sales increased by $18.1 million, with 33 contracts bringing in 27.1 percent of total sales. Contracts in 72 sports facilities provided 63.7 percent of sales and 30 contracts in other entertainment venues comprised 9.2 percent of sales.

Turmoil at the top levels of Centerplate management continued in March 2006 as MacPhail, CEO for only six months, left the company. Centerplate named Janet L. Steinmayer, chief operating officer since September 2005, as chief executive officer. Contracts representing about 24 percent of Centerplate's revenue in 2005 were due for renewal in 2006 and the company was expected to raise its capital expenditures to secure these clients. Since Centerplate carried a heavy debt load, doubts were raised about whether the company could continue to pay its declared distributions on its IDSs in 2006 or 2007.

After a little more than a decade, the company that emerged from a giant in the vending industry in 1995 as an independent and more focused enterprise had established itself as a premier provider of concessions, merchandise, catering, and management services at some of North America's most popular venues, from Yankee Stadium, a customer for 41 years, to the Rose Bowl.

With veteran insider Steinmayer in place as CEO, Centerplate was expected to regain its focus as a major player in the highly competitive and fragmented recreational foodservices industry.

Ted Sylvester

PRINCIPAL SUBSIDIARIES

Volume Services America, Inc.; Volume Services, Inc.; Service America Corporation.

PRINCIPAL COMPETITORS

ARAMARK Corporation; Levy Restaurants, Inc.; Restaurant Associates Corp.; Delaware North Companies, Inc.; Compass Group PLC; Boston Culinary Group, Inc.; Sodexho, Inc.; SMG Management; Global Spectrum, L.P.

FURTHER READING

Allen, Robin Lee, "Service America, Volume in Merger," *Nation's Restaurant News*, August 10, 1998, p. 1.

"Another Change in CEOs at Centerplate," *Amusement Business*, March 6, 2006.

Bates, Patricia, "Volume Services Increasing Its Involvement in Baseball," *Amusement Business*, October 21, 1991, p. 19.

Elan, Elissa, "Centerplate Dishes up Better News for 1st Q, Offers Turnaround Plan," *Nation's Restaurant News*, May 16, 2005.

———, "Janet Steinmayer: Industry Vet Steps up at Centerplate with Renewed Focus on Culinary and Service," *Nation's Restaurant News*, March 27, 2006.

Ennis, Thomas W., Vending Industry Is Widening Its Horizons," *New York Times*, July 26, 1971.

"Hard Times in Vending Field," *New York Times*, May 31, 1969.

Hennessey, Raymond, "IPO Outlook: New Company, New Security to Make Debut," *Dow Jones News Service*, December 1, 2003.

Kalawsky, Keith, "Centerplate's Hot Dogs Come Up Short," *National Post*, March 10, 2006.

Marriott, Anne, "Bracing for Snack Attacks Workers Practice to Improve the Service at Cooke Stadium," *Washington Times*, September 26, 1997, p. B10.

Morris, Jack H., "Change for the Automatic Vending Industry Seen As Machines Become Less Important," *Wall Street Journal*, September 18, 1968.

"Nathaniel Leverone Dies at 84; Canteen Corporation Founder," *New York Times*, January 29, 1982.

Powell, Tom, "Volume, Restaura Hit Home Runs with Pair of Expansion MLB Teams," *Amusement Business*, April 13, 1998, p.18.

Scanlan, David, "CIBC to Raise up to US$625M for Two U.S. Firms: Bank Makes First Income Trust Sales to American Investors," *National Post*, October 28, 2003.

Waddell, Ray, "Volume Making Noise," *Amusement Business*, March 18, 1996, p. 24.

———, "Volume Services Picks up Four Baseball Accounts," *Amusement Business*, March 13, 1995, p 1.

Waddell, Ray, "Volume Services Puts Spin on Fare at Lansing Park," *Amusement Business*, April 29, 1996, p 16.

China Construction Bank Corp.

25 Finance St.
Beijing,
China
Telephone: +86 010 6759 8628
Fax: +86 010 6759 8544
Web site: http://www.ccb.com.cn

Public Company
Incorporated: 1954 as People's Construction Bank of China
Employees: 275,000
Total Assets: CNY 4.22 trillion ($521.8 billion) (2005)
Stock Exchanges: Hong Kong
Ticker Symbol: 939
NAIC: 522110 Commercial Banking

■ ■ ■

China Construction Bank Corp. (CCB) is one of China's big four banks, and is also one of the 40 largest banks worldwide, with total assets of CNY 4.2 trillion ($522 billion) in 2005. The bank is also the first of China's large, state-owned banks to be publicly listed; CCB's initial public offering (IPO) on the Hong Kong stock exchange was China's largest ever, and is also the world's largest bank IPO since 1980. Once responsible for the distribution of government infrastructure and construction spending, CCB began transforming itself into a commercial bank during the 1980s. The bank offers a full range of banking services to the private and corporate sectors, backed by a network of more than 14,000 branches and 275,000 employees. CCB also operates branch offices in Hong Kong, Singapore, Frankfurt, Johannesburg, and Seoul, and offices in New York and London. Subsidiaries include Jian Sing Bank Limited, in Hong Kong, and CCB Principal Asset Management Co., Ltd., a joint venture formed in September 2005. The bank also offers e-banking facilities, and boasts more than 26 million e-banking customers.

BACKING STATE INFRASTRUCTURE SPENDING

China Construction Bank was established as the People's Construction Bank of China in 1954. The body's primary role was to act as a central clearinghouse for government funding of the country's major infrastructure and industrial construction projects carried out under successive five-year plans. CCB's mandate literally included every phase of construction spending, encompassing every industry. As such, the CCB quickly developed a national organization.

Based in Beijing, the bank built a network of branch offices throughout the country. Many of these offices focused on specific areas of construction. By the end of the country's first five-year plan, CCB had opened 88 branches in 16 provinces, major cities, and autonomous regions specifically for the funding of major construction projects. Other specialized branches were placed as part of the country's major industrial complexes. These included ten branches located in the country's steel factories, another eight serving its heavy machinery production complexes, and branches dedicated to the mining and agricultural industry, as well as branches specifically governing the country's railroad system. Later

COMPANY PERSPECTIVES

CCB Essence: Teamwork, professionalism, innovation, and contribution. CCB Style: Faith, assiduity, truth, and motivation.

on, CCB continued to add new specialized branches, including offices governing such major industrial and infrastructure sites as Three Gorges and the Tsinghai-Tibet railroad.

CCB's banking operations remained limited to this role through the late 1970s. The drive toward economic reform and the first steps toward liberalization of the country's financial, commercial, and industrial sectors, led to a change in CCB's status. In 1979, CCB became one of the country's state-owned "special" banks, charged with helping the government implement the new reform policies.

The bank was placed under the direct control of the State Council. CCB's role then shifted from serving as a clearinghouse for governments to that of a more traditional banking role; instead of serving as a conduit for funding, the bank now became a lender. CCB completed its first loan, of CNY 34 million, to the Liaoyang Fiber Plant in 1979. By the beginning of the 1990s, CCB's total loan portfolio had topped CNY 300 billion. During this period, CCB's loan portfolio, while heavily based on construction loans, also expanded to include working capital loans and fixed assets investments. The bank also began lending to the newly emerging class of commercially operating enterprises, issuing its first working capital loans to this sector in 1987. In order to fund its newly expanded range of operations, CCB also began taking deposits; by the early 1990s, the bank boasted more than CNY 40 billion in self-financing deposits.

TRANSITION TO COMMERCIAL BANK

CCB's transition into commercial banking took another step forward during the decade as it expanded into consumer markets as well. The company entered the real estate market, and became a major player in the commercialization of the country's housing park, previously controlled by the various regional, provincial, and municipal government bodies. By the early 1990s, CCB had become one of the leading financial players in the country's real estate market.

The development of the special economic zones along China's coast and the opening of these zones to foreign investment and operations, led CCB to develop its own currency exchange and international finance operations, started in 1986. The bank's first success in this area came that same year when the bank's Shanghai branch helped arrange an international financing package for Shanghai Petro-Chemical. CCB began rolling out its international finance services elsewhere in its branch network, and by 1988 offered coverage through its branches in all of the major provincial markets and special economic development zones. Also during this period, CCB began issuing bonds, a service launched in 1986 with the backing of the Shandong Yantai Longkou Power stock offering.

Into the early 1990s, CCB built up a range of consumer services as well, and underwent a vast expansion of its branch network. By the beginning of the 1990s, CCB's network numbered more than 21,000 branches nationwide, and its employee base had grown to nearly 400,000. The bank began developing its first credit card in 1989 with MasterCard. That card was launched in April 1990, in Guangzhou province. The company then added a VISA card, and by 1993 had extended its credit-card issuing operations to nearly 270 branches. The company also began installing its own ATM network, and by the end of 1993 boasted some 7,000 machines.

The China government in the meantime had continued to carry out its economic reform policy. At the end of 1993, CCB prepared to enter into the third phase of its development, that of becoming a state-owned commercial bank. An important step in this process came in early 1994, when the CCB's policy making functions were separated from the bank and placed into a new entity, the China Development Bank. By August 1994, CCB had also shed its infrastructure construction loan operations. The bank's mandate turned fully toward commercial banking, with a focus on the mid- and long-term credit markets. To underscore its new independence from its former government function, the bank changed its name in 1996, formally adopting the China Construction Bank name. By then, CCB had grown into one of the country's top four banks, alongside its state-owned counterparts, Bank of China, Industrial & Commercial Bank of China, and Agricultural Bank of China.

LEADING THE CHINESE BANKING IPO MARKET

CCB adopted a new business strategy in the mid-1990s, calling on a shift toward performance-oriented operations. As part of that effort, the bank began put-

KEY DATES

1954: Chinese government establishes People's Construction Bank of China (CCB) to administer funding for infrastructure and industrial construction projects.
1979: CCB's status is converted to state-owned special bank as government launches economic reform policy; CCB begins transitioning to lending and taking deposits.
1990: CCB launches its first credit card.
1994: CCB cedes its policy business and infrastructure lending and becomes full-fledged commercial bank.
1996: Company changes name to China Construction Bank.
1999: China Cinda Asset Management Corporation is created, enabling CCB to shed its non-performing loan portfolio.
2001: Company adopts new customer-focused corporate culture.
2003: Chinese government announces intention to list CCB on Hong Kong Stock Exchange.
2004: CCB is reincorporated as a shareholding bank.
2005: CCB completes largest initial public offering in China's history.

ting into place a clear exit strategy for its lending operations. In 1995, the company also launched an effort to establish its own in-house credit-rating system, in order to develop more objective standards for its lending business. Nonetheless, CCB, like its other state-owned banking counterparts, remained saddled with huge levels of non-performing loans. In an effort to clean up the books of its four largest banks, the Chinese government launched a series of aid efforts, including establishing a number of new companies to absorb parts of the banks' non-performing loan portfolios. In 1999, for example, CCB transferred its own non-performing loans to a new state-owned vehicle, China Cinda Asset Management Corporation. Altogether, the Chinese government absorbed some $400 billion non-performing loans. The government also pumped in funds to enable the banks to balance their books. By the mid-2000s, the government had pumped nearly $260 billion into CCB and the other members of China's Big Four banking group.

The Chinese government continued to push ahead its economic reform policies in the run-up to the country's admission into the World Trade Organization in the mid-2000s. By the beginning of that decade, the government had also indicated its intention to transfer ownership stakes in its largest banks to the private sector. Yet the Chinese banking sector remained riddled with corruption (arrests of the sector's top executives for corruption and bribery charges were commonplace) while the banking industry was hampered by a lack of trained personnel. Indeed, into the 1990s, appointments to many top banking positions were still made according to political ties, rather than experience in banking.

In 2001, CCB adopted a new corporate culture position as it began its effort to transform itself into a modern, customer-focused operation. This effort came ahead of the announcement in 2003 that the Chinese government was preparing the initial public offerings (IPO) for CCB and for the Bank of China. Toward that end, in September 2004, the company was restructured as a shareholding bank, named China Construction Bank Corporation. The bank's major shareholders included The Central Huijin Investment Company, China Jianyin Investment Limited, State Grid, Shanghai Bao Steel (Group) Co., Ltd., and China Yangtze Power Co., Ltd., while the Chinese government retained its controlling stake in the company.

In the buildup toward its public offering, CCB turned to Citibank as its foreign partner and underwriter. Yet Citibank's involvement elsewhere in the Chinese banking sector led to a conflict of interest between the two banks, and Citibank was forced to withdraw. Instead, CCB found a new partner in Bank of America (BoA), which had only limited interest in China and agreed to spend some $3 billion for 8.7 percent of CCB's stock, with an option to increase its stake to nearly 20 percent. BoA also agreed to contribute some 50 staff members to provide technical advice and assistance to CCB. The backing of BoA was credited as a major factor in bringing CCB to the stock market.

As it prepared for its IPO, CCB also launched a massive streamlining effort; by 2005, the bank had trimmed its branch network by nearly one-third. The bank's 14,000 branches focused especially on the country's more economically vital areas, particularly its coastal regions. At the same time, CCB slashed its payroll, eliminating some 100,000 jobs.

CCB's IPO was completed in October 2005, with a listing on the Hong Kong Stock Exchange. The listing of just 10 percent of its shares had raised more than $8 billion, marking China's largest ever IPO, and also the largest IPO in the global banking sector since 1980. CCB continued its efforts to transform itself into a modern and efficient banking group. In September 2005, the bank set up a new joint-venture assets management wing, CCB Principal Asset Management Company, in partnership with the Principal Financial Group and

China Huadian Group. The bank also began stepping up its operations beyond mainland China. In late 2005, for example, CCB's Hong Kong branches launched personal banking services for the first time. CCB braced itself for the next phase in the China banking market's reform: the market's full liberalization was slated for the end of 2006. This meant that foreign banks were to be allowed to open their own branch networks in China and compete for banking customers for the first time. CCB appeared prepared to meet the challenges of what was expected to become one of the world's most competitive banking markets in the new century.

M. L. Cohen

PRINCIPAL SUBSIDIARIES

CCB Principal Asset Management Co., Ltd.; Jian Sing Bank Limited (Hong Kong).

PRINCIPAL COMPETITORS

Industrial and Commercial Bank of China; Agricultural Bank of China; Kreditanstalt fur Wiederaufbau Bank of China Ltd.; The Hongkong and Shanghai Banking Corporation Ltd.; China Development Bank; Bank of Communications Company Ltd.

FURTHER READING

Bremner, Brian, "Banking on China's Reforms," *Business Week Online*, February 6, 2006.

Bremner, Brian, Frederik Balfour, and Chester Dawson, "Betting on China's Banks," *Business Week*, October 31, 2005, p. 18.

"China Construction Bank Poised for Success," *Institutional Investor International Edition*, May 2002, p. SS3.

Low, Alvin, "Temasek Steps in As Citigroup Steps Aside," *Australian Banking & Finance*, August 30, 2005, p. 6.

Roell, Sophie, "Mission Accomplished," *Banker*, December 1, 2005.

Citizens Communications Company

3 High Ridge Park
Stamford, Connecticut 06905-1390
U.S.A.
Telephone: (203) 614-5600
Fax: (203) 614-4602
Web site: http://www.czn.net

Public Company
Incorporated: 1935 as Citizens Utilities Company
Employees: 6,103
Sales: $2.16 billion (2005)
Stock Exchanges: New York
Ticker Symbol: CZN
NAIC: 517110 Wired Telecommunications Carriers

■ ■ ■

Citizens Communications Company is a Stamford, Connecticut-based company that in the early 2000s made the switch from utilities to telecommunications. Under the Frontier brand, the company serves rural and small town customers with some 2.4 million access lines in 24 states, offering local and long distance telephone service, calling features, and high-speed Internet connections, as well as bundled satellite television through Dish Network. Frontier also offers voice, data, and Internet services, and telephone equipment to business customers. Citizens is a public company listed on the New York Stock Exchange.

ORIGINS DATING TO 1935

Citizens was incorporated in 1935 to reorganize Public Utilities Consolidated Corp., a subsidiary of W.B. Foshay Co. which had been forced into receivership. The man behind the company was Wilbur Burton Foshay, a prominent Minneapolis figure of the day. He parlayed a $6,000 loan received in 1916 into a business empire, which included finance and real estate interests. However, it was with utility companies that he made his mark, snapping up one after another during the Roaring Twenties, financing his deals by selling more and more stock in Public Utilities. By 1927 he was rich enough to build a new $3.7 million headquarters and a testament to himself: The 32-story Foshay Tower, as he named it, would become the tallest skyscraper west of the Mississippi River. The structure, made out of Indiana limestone, emulated the Washington Monument, with which Foshay had been fascinated since childhood. In August 1929 he was ready to dedicate the Tower, which featured "Foshay" etched in ten-foot-high letters on all four sides to be illuminated every night, and spent close to $120,000 on a three-day celebration, attended by a number of dignitaries. Foshay even commissioned legendary composer John Philip Sousa to write the "Foshay Tower Washington Memorial March," which the legendary composer then performed at the building's opening with his 75-piece band.

The dedication of the tower would be the highlight of Foshay's life, and the high-water mark for his business career. When the stock market crashed two months later, ushering in the Great Depression of the 1930s, Foshay's empire was revealed to be ethereal, nothing more than paper profits, a kiting scheme in which

COMPANY PERSPECTIVES

Our Mission: To be the leader in providing communication services to residential and business customers in our markets.

continuous sales of Public Utilities stock kept the enterprise afloat. Sousa's $20,000 check bounced, prompting the composer to refuse permission for the march to be played until he was paid. It was not revived until 1997, when Twin Cities residents chipped in to buy the rights and the "Foshay Tower Washington Memorial March" was performed once again. Foshay was convicted of three counts of mail fraud and sent to federal prison, serving three years before his sentence was commuted by President Roosevelt. President Truman fully pardoned Foshay in 1947, and ten years later, all but forgotten, the one-time utility mogul died in a Minneapolis nursing home.

Citizens Utilities maintained its headquarters in the Foshay Tower, which despite its builder's tarnished reputation became the civic symbol of Minneapolis. While Citizens Utilities managed to survive the 1930s, it was hardly a prosperous concern. After World War II came to a close it had revenues of $2.4 million and earnings of less than $180,000. At its height Public Utilities owned properties throughout the United States as well as in Central America, but many of these assets were shed during the reorganization, so that by 1946 Citizens owned a collection of electric, gas, and water utilities located in five states. Nevertheless, it attracted the attention of a young Wall Street Financier named Richard Laurence Rosenthal.

YOUNG FINANCIER ACQUIRES CITIZENS: 1946

Rosenthal was born in Canada in 1915 and came to the United States six years later. He earned an undergraduate degree at New York University (NYU), graduating summa cum laude in 1936. He then spent two years in postgraduate studies at NYU before taking a job with a Wall Street investment firm, Wertheim & Company. Unusual at the time, Rosenthal did not rely on company-provided information, preferring to personally visit acquisition candidates to conduct his own research. He impressed some Wall Street friends who formed an investment group and recruited Rosenthal, just 29 years old, to take charge of acquiring control of promising companies. He agreed and then decided to focus on an industry in which solid management could make a significant impact. In a 1980 *Barron's* interview he explained that his research experience had taught him, "if you wanted to find poor management, the utility industry was then a good place to look for it." Citizens would become Rosenthal's first acquisition, completed in 1946, and other purchases would follow: Michigan Gas and Electric in 1947 and the New York Water Service Corporation in 1948.

Rosenthal took over as president, chief executive officer, and chairman of Citizens, and soon moved the corporate headquarters from Minneapolis to Stamford, Connecticut, where he lived. He now faced the task of nurturing the business. "I had to decide either to liquidate much of what was there and have Citizens be a one-category, one-area utility company," he told *Barron's*, "or to extend what was in place and have it become more multi-state and more variegated. I chose the latter." As a result, Citizens became diversified by region, insulated from local economic cycles and not excessively impacted by the decision of regulators in a particular state.

Under Rosenthal, Citizens acquired more than 40 small companies in the electric, water, gas, wastewater, and telephone industries. In order to fund growth he implemented an innovative two-tier stock arrangement in 1955. According to the *New York Times,* "Instead of paying out most of the earnings in dividends, as most utilities do, he issued a special type of stock in which shareholders got stock as dividends. Investors enjoyed one of the highest annual rates of return in the utility industry during his tenure." During his 1980 *Barron's* interview, Rosenthal estimated that someone who invested $10,000 in the company in 1946 and then elected to take the stock dividend shares would have holdings worth $1.8 million. Rosenthal was also loathe to build new power plants to meet rising demand for electricity in his markets, electing instead to buy power from other producers. In addition to Citizens, he had a lot of other business interests, including a music publishing company and a Virginia Islands resort. Thus, he delegated a great deal of authority to the local utilities, although he paid regular visits and insisted on weekly reports to keep tabs on Citizen's growing number of assets.

The first acquisitions came in 1948 with the addition of Bangor Gas Co., based in Bangor, Maine. The 1950s saw scores of acquisitions, including Francis Land and Water Co., Ferndale, California, in 1954; Parkway Water Co., serving the Sacramento, California, area, in 1956; an Illinois company, Northwest Utilities Co., in 1956; California's Shasta Telephone Co. in 1956; Bluett Water Supply Co. of Roselle, Illinois, in 1958; and Ar-

KEY DATES

1935: Citizens Utilities Company is incorporated to acquire Public Utilities Consolidated Corp.
1946: Richard Rosenthal acquires company, moves it to Stamford, Connecticut.
1955: Two-tier stock arrangement is introduced.
1989: Rosenthal retires.
2000: Name is changed to Citizens Communications Company.
2004: Last utility asset is sold.

rowhead Water Co., serving suburban Chicago, in 1959. Rosenthal did not let up the pace in the 1960s and 1970s. A representative sampling of acquisitions included San Francisco-area Inverness Water Company; Sinking Spring Water Co., a Pennsylvania utility; Washington Water & Light Co., serving West Sacramento, California; Kauai Electric Co., which served the island of Kauai, Hawaii; Ohio Utilities Co., provider of water and wastewater services in the Columbus area; and Blue Mountain Consolidated Water Co., of Nazareth, Pennsylvania. Rosenthal continued to add to Citizens in the 1980s, acquiring such properties as Arizona's Oasis Utility Co. and Sierra Utility Co., and Glen Alsace Water Co., providing water service in Berks County, Pennsylvania.

Rosenthal retired in June 1989 having produced record earnings every year he was in charge of Citizens. All told, the company had more than 460,000 customers in over 500 communities in a dozen states. (Rosenthal would die in 1998 at the age of 82.) A year after Rosenthal's retirement, the company's president and chief executive, Ishier Jacobson, retired as well, after 35 years with the company and serving as president since 1970. Before leaving, he named a new president and chief operating officer, Daryl A. Ferguson, whom Jacobson recruited because of his significant experience in telecommunications, an indication of the direction Citizens was about to take. Within the month, Leonard Tow was named the company's new CEO, and he also assumed the chairmanship, which had been open since Rosenthal's retirement a year earlier.

FOCUS ON TELECOMMUNICATIONS

Under the new management regime, Citizens began to aggressively use its utility rights-of-way to expand its telecommunications business. One step taken in the early 1990s was a 1991 investment in Centennial Cellular Corp., a cellular telephone company. Two years later Citizens paid $1.1 billion to GTE Corp. for 500,000 access lines in nine states. More GTE lines were bought in Arizona, Montana, and California in late 1994. In 1995 Citizens acquired Flex Communications, provider of long-distance telephone, voice mail, paging, cellular, and private data services to 5,500 customers in Albany, Syracuse, Johnstown, Norwich, and Middletown, New York. Also in 1995 and 1996 Citizens bought access lines from ALLTEL Corp. in West Virginia, Oregon, Tennessee, Utah, New Mexico, and California.

The transformation of Citizens continued in the second half of the decade, as the Telecommunications Act of 1996 opened markets across the country. Conference-Call USA was acquired for stock in December 1996, and a year later Ogden Telephone Company was bought in a $23.5 million deal. In November 1998 Citizens spent another $80.9 million to acquire Rhinelander Telecommunications Inc., a holding company for a Wisconsin telephone company. By now, the telecommunications assets were branded under the Citizens Communications name, while energy and water operations were packaged under the Citizens Public Services banner. Citizens generated about two-thirds of its revenues from telecommunications and was looking to make an even greater commitment to the industry as the decade came to a close. In 1999 it paid $664 million for 187,000 access lines from GTE Corporation, and later in the year agreed to a $1.65 billion deal to acquire 530,000 rural phone lines in nine states from US West Communications Inc.

In June 2000 Citizens Utilities became Citizens Communications Co., and management began to actively divest its utility assets. Electric utility operations were sold for $535 million in February 2000. Louisiana Gas Service and sister company LGS Natural Gas Company, along with the Colorado Gas division, were sold in 2001. Early in 2002 Citizens sold its water and wastewater treatment operations to American Water Works in a $979 million transaction that was originally brokered in October 1999. Citizens' final utility sale came in April 2004 when it sold the Vermont Electric division for $21.4 million in cash.

Citizens' management had set a goal of owning five million access lines by 2005 and in the early 2000s appeared to be making considerable progress in realizing that vision, despite a setback in 2001. The $1.64 billion deal with US West fell apart after Citizens had second thoughts about the price and US West, since bought by Qwest Communications, refused to renegotiate, resulting in the termination of the acquisition. In the meantime, Citizens enjoyed better success with the $3.65

billion acquisition of Frontier Corp., a deal that added more than one million local access lines and gave Citizens the recognizable Frontier brand to build upon. But no major deals followed and Citizens produced lackluster results, although it still fared better than most in the troubled telecommunications sector.

In December 2003 Citizens announced that it would retain a financial advisor to explore "strategic alternatives," prompting speculation that the company would either be sold to a private equity firm or lopped off into individual pieces. In February 2004, J.P. Morgan Securities and Morgan Stanley were named financial advisors. A pair of suitors emerged, Kohlberg Kravis Roberts & Co. and the Blackstone Group, but by July 2004 both backed off, deeming the price of Citizens' stock to be too high. All speculation about a possible sale came to an end when Tow resigned as CEO and chairman in July 2004.

The Citizens board of directors found a new president and CEO in Maggie Wilderotter, who took over the posts in November 2004. In January 2006 she would also assume the chairmanship of the company. The 49-year-old Wilderotter was a seasoned executive in the telecommunications and cable industry. She learned the business by spending 12 years at U.S. Computer Services, Inc./Cable Data. She then became president-Western Region for McCaw Cellular and executive vice-president-National Operations for AT&T Wireless. Later she served as CEO of Wink Communications before joining Microsoft where she was a senior vice-president of Worldwide Public Sector.

Under Wilderotter's watch, Citizens added satellite video services in an agreement with Dish Network. The move allowed Frontier to bundle telephone, Internet, and video services, a single-bill offering that held great appeal to customers. Increasing product revenues was a key to Citizens' growth, because of the rural nature of its business. With customers spread far apart, the company could not fully take advantage of economies of scale but was required to provide universal telephone service to residents. Although it received a federal subsidiary for universal service, the amount the government paid continued to dwindle. In 2005, for example, the amount paid was $20 million less than in 2004.

Citizens' balance sheet showed marked improvement in 2005 over the prior year. The company generated sales of more than $2.16 billion, a slight increase over 2004, but net income grew 180 percent to $202.4 million. The company continued to adjust its business mix. In 2006 it liquidated its Rural Telephone Bank subsidiary and sold Electric Lightwave, primarily a provider of voice, data, and Internet services to portions of the western United States, for $243 million in cash.

Ed Dinger

PRINCIPAL SUBSIDIARIES

Citizens Cable Company; Citizens Capital Ventures Corp.; Frontier Subsidiary Telco LLC.

PRINCIPAL COMPETITORS

AT&T Inc.; Qwest Communications International Inc.; Verizon Communications Inc.

FURTHER READING

Alpukas, Agis, "Richard L. Rosenthal, a Utilities Entrepreneur, Is Dead at 82," *New York Times,* June 17, 1998, p. A29.

Farrell, Mike, "Leonard Tow Steps Down at Citizens," *Multichannel News,* July 19, 2004, p. 52.

"Founder of Century Joins Citizens Utilities," *New York Times,* June 26, 1990, p. D4.

Geiger, Bob, " Strother Communications Enjoys Plus Space in the Foshay," *Associated Press,* May 31, 2004.

"Poised to Buy: Private Equity Firms Consider Citizens Communications," *Fairfield County Business Journal,* March 8, 2004, p. 21.

"Utilities, Urges an Industry Lead, Should Fight Back," *Barron's National Business and Financial Weekly,"* August 18, 1980, p. 60.

Wagman, David C., "Citizens Seeks Market Share," *Public Utilities Fortnightly,* June 15, 1994, p. 10.

Compass Minerals International, Inc.

9900 W. 109th Street
Suite 600
Overland Park, Kansas 66210
U.S.A.
Telephone: (913) 344-9200
Fax: (913) 338-7928
Web site: http://www.compassminerals.com

Public Company
Incorporated: 2001 as Salt Holdings Corporation
Employees: 1,541
Sales: $742.3 million (2005)
Stock Exchanges: New York
Ticker Symbol: CMP
NAIC: 212399 All Other Nonmetallic Mineral Mining

■ ■ ■

Compass Minerals International, Inc. is a major producer of rock salt and evaporated salt, used for highway de-icing, consumer de-icing, water conditioning, and food preparation; and sulfate of potash (SOP), used to make specialty fertilizer. Compass products are sold in North America, which accounts for 85 percent of revenues, and Europe, where the United Kingdom is the dominant market generating 13 percent of Compass revenues. Although a low-margin item, highway de-icing salt is the company's most important product, generating nearly half of all revenues and representing three-quarters of all products shipped. Compass is composed of three subsidiaries devoted to the production and marketing of salt and one to the production and manufacture of SOP. A public company listed on the NASDAQ, Compass maintains its headquarters in Overland Park, Kansas. Some of its mines have been in operation since the mid-1800s.

COMPANY ROOTS DATING TO 1988

The bulk of Compass's assets were cobbled together by D. George Harris and his partners starting in the late 1980s. An Army brat, Harris attended high school in the 1940s in Beijing, where his father taught military strategy to calvary officers before the revolution when China became a Communist country. Harris graduated from Culver Military Academy and then earned a degree in chemical engineering from the University of Missouri at Columbia in 1954, at which point he served in the U.S. Army for a two-year stint. Harris then put his chemical engineering to use in building a business career. By 1966 he became International Sales Manager at Calgon Corporation, and later served as managing director for Chemviron S.A., Brussels; chief executive officer for Rhone-Poulenc's U.S. operations until the French company was nationalized in 1981; president of the chemical division of SCM Corp., and then president and chief operating officer at SCM. In 1986, Hanson Industries of the United Kingdom completed a successful hostile takeover of SCM. Although Harris could have stayed to work for the new organization, he felt his ability to shape strategy would be shackled and he elected to leave. With 30 years of experience in the chemical industry, he now became a senior investment advisor at Robert Fleming & Co., but in 1988 he chose to start

> **COMPANY PERSPECTIVES**
>
> Built on a foundation of over 100 years, Compass Minerals International is focused on supplying customers the best products and superior service—all at the right price.

his own company, which would one day evolve into Compass Minerals.

"Though the range of my experience was broad," Harris wrote in a 1994 *Chemical Business* article, "I had only built a company from scratch as a subsidiary of a larger organization. So I decided to capitalize on what I knew best and opted to start my own chemical company." Harris brought in a pair of former colleagues to help him: Anthony Petrocelli, his assistant at Rhone-Poulenc, and Richard Donohue, his assistant at SCM. They formed a leveraged buyout firm called D.G. Harris and Associates and began looking for acquisition opportunities to jumpstart their venture. They avoided pharmaceuticals and high-technology chemical companies because they were too expensive. Harris wrote, "We wanted a business with steady cash flow that would be recession and inflation resistant." They ultimately settled on salt, which had 14,000 uses and was an industry with proven staying power. Moreover, as Harris noted, "Though there were three major North American producers, our research uncovered a number of significant, established regional suppliers, all subsidiaries of much larger companies." Harris viewed the potential acquisition targets as "corporate orphans," business units whose products did not fit into the big-picture plans of their parent companies. As described by Harris in *Chemical Business,* these orphans "got just enough capital to exist, but not enough to change; just enough management attention to continue operations, but not enough to forge new markets or create new products; just enough strategic planning to keep them contributing to the structure; but not enough to bring them into the limelight." Harris's vision was to acquire corporate orphans in the salt industry and put "them into the hands of management for whom they are core operations, and who have a vested interest in their success." As a result, the neglected entities could become "mainstays of a new company."

Harris's first target company was Diamond Crystal Salt Company, a family-owned Michigan company, but in 1987 he was outbid by International Salt, a subsidiary of the Dutch chemical giant Akzo Chemie. Nevertheless, the endeavor brought him in contact with officials at Chase Manhattan Bank. They suggested he consider buying Kansas-based American Salt Company, which Diamond itself had attempted to buy from General Host Corp. in 1984. Harris liked what he saw at American Salt and in 1988, 13 months after its founding, D.G. Harris and Associates acquired American Salt Co. from General Host Corp. for $32 million. Later in the year a second Kansas-based company, Carey Salt, a subsidiary of Canadian Pacific, Ltd., was bought for $26 million.

FORMATION OF NORTH AMERICAN SALT CO. IN 1990

In 1990 Harris formed the North American Salt Co. (NAMSCO) to act as a holding company for American Salt and Carey Salt and to prepare the way for his next major acquisition later in the year: the Toronto, Canada-based Sifto Salt division of Domtar Inc. for $184 million. Sifto assets included a rock salt mine in Goderich, Ontario, three evaporated salt plants in Canada, the Nickell Salt Co. in Saskatoon, and distribution facilities. As a result, NAMSCO was well balanced between rock salt, evaporated salt, and solar salt. Harris told the press at the time of the purchase, "The addition of Sifto will bring North American Salt's annual sales to about $200 million and give us the size and geographic spread we need to be competitive in the North American salt market." The deal did not, however, completely pass muster with the U.S. Department of Justice, which cleared the acquisition of most of Sifto's assets but objected to NAMSCO adding a large rock salt mine in Louisiana, due to concerns of lessening competition in highway salt and salt for agricultural purposes in some markets in the United States. The matter was ultimately settled by NAMSCO divesting its salt mines in Hutchinson and Lyons, Kansas, which lacked the location advantage of the Louisiana mine. Both it and the company's other mine in Goderich, Ontario, were located on the water and possessed better access to transportation. Less expensive shipping translated into low pricing of salt and the ability to attract more business. The company, now the third largest salt company in North America, was especially strong throughout Canada and west of the Mississippi River in the United States.

In the course of assembling NAMSCO Harris and his partners became aware of another opportunity in a related field: Kerr-McGee Corp. was interested in selling its $200 million-a-year soda ash and boron products division, which included three chemical plants in Trona, California. Soda ash and boron were similar to salt in their limited competition. There were only a half-dozen soda ash producers in the United States and just one

KEY DATES

1988: D.G. Harris and Associates acquires American Salt Co. and Carey Salt.
1990: North American Salt Co. (NAMSCO) is formed as a holding company for American Salt, Carey Salt, and Sifto Salt.
1993: Great Salt Lake Minerals is acquired and folded into Harris Chemical Group with NAMSCO.
1997: IMC Global acquires Harris Chemical.
2001: Apollo Management forms Compass Minerals Group, and acquires IMC salt and soda ash assets.
2003: Compass Minerals is taken public.

maker of boron chemicals. Boron and soda ash also shared some similar markets with salt and provided an additional benefit by offering entrée to foreign sales. In December 1990 Harris acquired the Kerr-McGee unit for about $210 million and formed North American Chemical Co. (NACC).

In 1993 Harris acquired Great Salt Lake Minerals and Chemical Corp., an Ogden, Utah-based company that mined and produced sulfate of potash for specialty fertilizers, and packaged it, NAMSCO, and NACC into a new inorganic chemical holding company called Harris Chemical Group. Along the way, Harris also picked up some European businesses that were maintained under a separate corporate structure. They included a group of English salt companies called Salt Union; Germany's Matthes und Weber, maker of soda ash; and Societa Chimica de Laderoo, an Italian boron derivatives producer. Soon after forming Harris Chemical Group, Harris also created a specialty chemicals group.

In December 1997 Harris cast off the orphans he had collected into Harris Chemical Group Inc., selling the holding company to IMC Global Inc., a Northbrook, Illinois-based maker of fertilizers and animal feed ingredients. IMC also produced salt, but its annual output of 800,000 tons was just a fraction of the more than 11 million tons the Harris Chemical subsidiaries were able to turn out. The company now placed all of its salt assets in the IMC Salt unit. The deal was valued at $1.4 billion, with IMC Global paying 450 million in cash and assuming $950 million in debt.

FORMATION OF COMPASS MINERALS IN 2001

Little more than two years later, IMC Global put IMC Salt on the block after suffering through a rough patch for its core phosphate-based fertilizer products, troubled by weak demand and low prices. Even earlier IMC Global began trying to sell Great Salt Lake Minerals Corporation, acquired from Harris Chemical, which had taken the name of IMC Kalium Ogden. The buyer of IMC Salt was Apollo Management L.P., a New York private investment firm, which formed an entity in 2001 called Compass Minerals Group Inc. to buy an approximately 80 percent interest in IMC Salt and IMC Kalium Ogden while IMC Global retained a 20 percent stake. Another Apollo Management subsidiary, Salt Holdings Corporation, then acquired Compass Minerals Group and in November 2003 changed its name to Compass Minerals International, Inc. Compass Minerals paid $600 million for the IMC Global assets, including 13 salt-producing plants in North America and the United Kingdom, and the soda ash facility of IMC Kalium Ogden, which subsequently reverted to the Great Salt Lake Minerals name.

IMC Global cut its interest in Compass Minerals in 2003 by selling back a 15 percent stake for $60.5 million. Also included in the deal was the sale of a New Mexico SOP facility to Great Salt Lakes Minerals, with the proceeds used to pay down debt. IMC Global cashed out further in 2003 when Compass Minerals made an initial public offering of stock. The offering was underwritten by Credit Suisse First Boston and Goldman Sachs, and the proceeds went to existing shareholders rather than to the company, although the maneuver did create a public market for the stock to the benefit of Compass Minerals. At this point, Apollo Management owned 88.5 percent, IMC Global 5.8 percent, and officers and directors 3.9 percent. Because no money was put into the coffers of Compass Minerals, the $216.7 million "raised" was little more than a number used to calculate the registration fee. When it was over, Apollo Management retained a 38 percent share of the company and IMC a 2.5 percent interest. Additional offerings providing an exit strategy for Apollo Management were conducted in 2004. The first was a June secondary stock offering of nearly 6.9 million shares, a sizable portion of the firm's 11.5 million shareholding. Just three months later, Apollo Management filed a registration with the Securities and Exchange Commission to sell the rest of its shares in any manner it desired: through a public offering, a private sale, or any other means. Also covered in the registration were the shares still owned by IMC Global, soon to become Masaic after IMC Global merged with the fertilizer business of Cargill, Incorporated. By the end of 2004 both companies had reduced their interest in Compass Minerals to zero, necessitating some major changes to the company's board of ten directors, four of whom had been Apollo Management partners and a fifth who was IMC Global's CEO. When the shakeout was completed the size of the board was cut to eight.

Now a fully independent company, Compass Minerals looked to grow by increasing its capital investments by $5 million in 2005 and $14 million in 2006. A good portion of the money would be spent on expanding the magnesium chloride evaporation ponds at the Great Salt Lake, as well as upgrades on the production facility and the addition of a rail infrastructure. The company also began work on the installation of a new mill at a Canadian rock salt mine. To help pay for these and other capital improvements, Compass Minerals sold the evaporated salt business of British subsidiary Salt Union Ltd. due to changes in the chemicals industry in the United Kingdom. Management decided that the $36.3 million raised in the sale could be put to better use with the company's other operations.

Compass Minerals showed steady growth after breaking away from IMC Global. Sales that totaled $502.6 million increased to $742.3 million in 2005. Much of the company's success could be attributed to its CEO, Michael E. Ducey, a 30-year-veteran of Borden Chemical who in 2002 took the helm. In November 2005 he announced that he planned to retire at the end of 2006.

Ed Dinger

PRINCIPAL SUBSIDIARIES

North American Salt Company; Great Salt Lake Minerals Corporation; Sifto Canada Inc.; Salt Union Limited U.K.

PRINCIPAL COMPETITORS

Cargill, Incorporated; K&S Aktiengesellschaft; Rohm and Haas Company.

FURTHER READING

Comerford, Mike, "IMC Global Adds a Dash of Salt," *Daily Herald* (Arlington Heights, Ill.), December 13, 1997, p. 1.

"Compass Minerals Plans to Go Public," *Chemical Market Reporter,* November 10, 2003, p. 2.

Cuff, Daniel F., "A New Buyout Firm Finds Salt to Its Liking," *New York Times,* April 5, 1990.

Davis, Mark, "New York Group to Sell Shares in Overland Park, Kan.-Based Compass Minerals," *Kansas City Star,* September 28, 2004.

Fattah, Hassan, "Making a Family Out of Orphans," *Chemical Week,* January 22, 1997, p. 38.

Harris, D. George, "A Family of Corporate Orphans," *Chemical Business,* April 1994, p. 1.

Plishner, Emily S., "Harris Chemical Adopts 'Corporate Orphans,'" *Chemical Week,* June 1, 1994, p. 50.

Westervelt, Robert, "Compass Minerals Plans Secondary Offering," *Chemical Week,* June 16, 2004, p. 11.

Consorcio ARA, S.A. de C.V.

Avenida Bosque de Ciruelos 140
Colonia Bosque de Las Lomas
Mexico City, D.F. 11700
Mexico
Telephone: (525-5) 5246-3100
Fax: (525-5) 5291-2980
Web site: http://www.consorcioara.com.mx

Public Company
Incorporated: 1988
Employees: 6,733
Sales: MXN 6.77 billion ($621.1 million) (2005)
Stock Exchanges: Mexico City; OTC (ADRs)
Ticker Symbols: ARA; CNRF Y; CNRRF
NAIC: 236115 New Single-Family Housing Construction; 236220 Commercial and Institutional Building; 551112 Offices of Other Holding Companies

■ ■ ■

Consorcio ARA, S.A. de C.V. (ARA), one of the largest homebuilders in Mexico, is a holding company for operational subsidiaries engaged in the design, development, construction, and marketing of entry-level, middle-class, and upper-income houses. ARA also constructs housing for tourism and builds and operates commercial centers in some of the places where it has housing developments. The company also operates as a contractor for other parties in the construction, promotion, and marketing of commercial and industrial developments. It is active in 16 of Mexico's 31 states and in Mexico City.

FLEDGLING HOMEBUILDER: 1977–95

The enterprise was founded in 1977 by Germán and Luis Felipe Ahumada Russek, brothers who were both engineers. It was incorporated as Consorcio ARA in 1988. (ARA stands for Ahumada Russek y Asociados.) When, in late 1994, Mexico teetered on the brink of defaulting on its debts, ARA was one of the few homebuilders that survived the crisis. Because of fiscal prudence the company had not allowed its bank debt to rise above 44 percent of its assets, and hence it was able to continue making payments. Nevertheless, the ensuing year was an extremely difficult one for ARA. Interest rates on its debt rose to 120 percent. The company only built 1,722 houses, 30 percent fewer than in 1994. The number of houses it constructed for middle-income buyers, previously its main activity and a more-profitable market segment than government-subsidized housing, fell by about 70 percent.

SPECIALIZING IN SUBSIDIZED LOW-COST HOUSING: 1996–2001

Under these conditions, ARA made a necessary adjustment, focusing its efforts on building low-cost houses, mostly financed by government agencies. Armed with a $20 million credit line from an agency named Nafinsa, the company built 1,178 low-income homes in 1995 and 2,440 in 1996. These duplex-style homes sold for an average price of MXL 137,500 (about $17,000) in the latter year. In addition to Nafinsa (which took 10 percent of ARA's shares and exacted veto power over decisions by the board), the company depended on the

COMPANY PERSPECTIVES

Mission: To develop homes and communities for a style of life in which Mexicans will be proud to live.

mortgage loans at below-market interest rates extended to qualifying low-income buyers from agencies with the acronyms Infonavit and Fovi.

The Nafinsa credit carried another condition: that ARA become a publicly financed company within three years. Accordingly, the company sold 21.5 percent of its shares of common stock on the Mexico City stock exchange in September 1996, raising about $50 million. This made ARA the first non-exporting Mexican enterprise to make an initial public offering on the Mexico City stock exchange since the 1994–95 financial crisis. Its shares soon found even more favor among investors, and the company began selling American Depositary Receipts, the equivalent of shares, in the United States in 1998.

ARA was able to make healthy profits from low-cost housing for a number of reasons. Its modular method of construction enabled it to complete work in four or five months, while its competitors took up to 8 to 12 months to complete a project. Built of reinforced concrete, with small rooms, these houses were located amidst identical concrete structures on the periphery of Mexico City. ARA's development costs were low because it had purchased land cheaply in such areas for exactly this purpose. The company's debt was low because it built nothing on speculation, demanding, prior to construction, that the prospective buyer present evidence of a mortgage loan from a government program or commercial bank.

The 220 employees in ARA's offices were engaged in a number of essential tasks. Some acquired land and arranged for residential zoning. When a property owner rejected company offers to buy a desired tract, ARA would suggest a shared venture with shared profits. Other employees trolled for customers, offering, as an incentive, company support toward obtaining a mortgage. ARA's staff also solicited other developers, seeking construction contracts for projects that even included industrial plants.

ARA was the largest builder of affordable housing in Mexico City by 1997. It held more than 930 acres in the metropolitan area for future development, more than any other developer, and enough, it calculated, to build houses for a period of three to five years. It was showing off this fully-paid-for reserve by helicopter to potential foreign investors. The company also held land reserves in eight states. Beginning in early 1997, ARA's stock took off, almost doubling in value within six months. One attractive sign for market analysts was its backlog of 11,500 securely financed homes; another was its low debt, which now came to only 8 percent of its assets, lowest in the industry. In addition, ARA was planning on the eastern edge of Mexico City to build the largest housing development in Latin America: 20,000 homes for almost 100,000 inhabitants.

This kind of housing was desperately needed. Mexico's housing deficit was estimated at between four million and eight million units, and growing, since more than half the population was under 25 years of age. Primarily through Infonavit and Fovi, the federal government was providing more than 230,000 loans a year for new housing purchases by Mexico's poorest paid workers. In 1997 a new government program, Prosavi, was adopted to provide prospective buyers of affordable housing with cash subsidies, thereby, it was hoped, stimulating the private mortgage market. Competing for the trade of these new customers were more than 2,000 firms, none of which held more than 7 percent of the low-income housing market. The subsidized market, although significant, was overshadowed by construction for self-employed workers, who, not qualifying for mortgages, typically financed cheaply made homes out of their own pockets. Often they did much of the work themselves or hired contractors who used inferior tools and materials.

ARA's shares of stock reached three times the original price level before dropping precipitously in the summer of 1998. Analysts were disturbed because 96 percent of the homes that the company was building were for subsidized low-income buyers. This made it vulnerable, in the eyes of some, to funding cutbacks, although the company's chief financial officer described as "suicide" the possibility of the ruling party reducing support for the housing sector with a presidential election looming not far in the distance. Infonavit had been especially active on the border with the United States, where assembly plants were hiring 100,000 workers a year, thereby greatly stimulating the demand for new housing. Consorcio ARA and two of its rivals were building 200-to-300-home subdivisions in this region, hewing, according to Joel Millman, writing for the *Wall Street Journal,* "to a set of specifications so tight that some analysts dub them the Lego homes of Mexico."

Consorcio ARA, in 2001, initiated construction of 1,952 subsidized homes on a tract in Monterrey. The basic prototypes were a duplex three-bedroom house of about 860 square feet with 2½ baths, kitchen,

KEY DATES

1977: Founding of the enterprise by Germán Ahumada Russek and Luis Felipe Ahumada Russek.
1988: Incorporation of Consorcio ARA (Ahumada Russek y Asociados).
1994: ARA sells 2,543 houses, more than half built for middle-income buyers.
1995: ARA receives a $20 million credit from a government agency.
1996: The company raises about $50 million from an initial public offering of stock in Mexico.
1997: ARA is the leading builder of affordable housing in Mexico City.
1998: Ninety-six percent of the homes that ARA builds are for low-income subsidized buyers.
2000: ARA establishes a subsidiary to build commercial centers.
2002: ARA builds 15,000 homes a year and has a presence in 12 Mexican states.
2002: The company begins work on a 13,000-home development in the state of Mexico.
2004: Mexico's largest bank agrees to provide ARA with $175 million in financing.
2005: Completion of Centro Las Américas, the company's second commercial center.
2005: ARA has built 47 developments in 16 states.

combination living room-dining room, laundry area, and one with about 1,085 square feet, a separate living room in the back of the lower level, and a television room on the higher floor. Each could optionally be converted to a house with about 1,400 square feet of space. Prices ranged between MXL 300,000 and 400,000 (about $31,500 to $42,000).

HOMES AND COMMERCIAL CENTERS: 2002 TO 2005

However, nonsubsidized home buyers were hard to find, since Mexican banks, badly burned in the 1994 financial collapse and strapped for cash themselves, were extremely reluctant to lend money to anyone below a high-income level. By late 2001, the economic slump in the United States was affecting the ability of the Mexican government to continue funding its housing programs at existing levels. The result was that ARA, though now building more than 15,000 homes a year, was suffering from declining growth in its revenues. Rumors of quarrels between the Ahumada brothers also undermined investor confidence. The company's shares fell nearly 62 percent in value between early May and mid-July 2002. On the plus side, however, was its conservative financial management; an operating-profit margin in excess of 20 percent; and its growing presence now in 12 Mexican states.

By the end of 2002 the national economy was improving, and government-run housing trusts were planning a 23 percent increase in lending to home buyers. ARA was beginning work on Las Américas, a 13,000-home upscale development in Ecatepec, in the state of Mexico. This development came to include Centro Las Américas, the second ARA commercial center created by ARA's subsidiary Promotora y Desarrolladora de Centros Comerciales, S.A. de C.V. (PDCC) and O'Connor Capital Partners. Divided into a fashion mall and a "power center," it included a 142-room Fiesta Inn hotel, branches of banks and telecommunications companies, several department stores, 140 smaller stores, a 14-screen movie theater, a restaurant area, and an area for children's games. By late 2005, when the commercial center was opened, Las Américas included not only more than 13,000 homes but schools, parks, and a regional hospital center. ARA had licenses to build another 32,000 houses in the state of Mexico. In 2005 the company sold 19,015 units, of which 16,336 (86 percent) were subsidized housing. Its net profit that year was MXL 1.1 billion ($101 million).

By 2006 ARA had built and sold more than 140,000 homes since its inception. The company had 47 developments in 16 states, including Cancún, Guadalajara, León, Monterrey, Puebla, Tijuana, and Toluca. Its land reserves of 35.7 million square meters—the largest in the industry—in 2005 were deemed sufficient by the company to build 146,943 homes. PDCC, established in 2000, was operating more than 40,000 square meters of commercial centers. These consisted of three full-scale commercial centers: Centro Las Américas, Centro San Buenaventura, and Centro San Miguel; three smaller unicenters; and eight still-smaller minicenters. O'Connor Capital Partners became an equal partner to PDCC in the commercial centers in 2003.

A low inflation rate in 2004 resulted in a drop in interest rates, good news for the housing sector and for the shares of publicly traded homebuilders such as ARA. For the first time since the 1994–95 financial crisis, commercial banks accounted for a larger sum in mortgage loans than the specialized lenders known as Sofoles. Grupo Financiero BBVA Bancomer, S.A. de C.V. purchased Hipotecaria Nacional, S.A. de C.V., the largest of these lenders specializing in home mortgages. BBVA Bancomer also agreed to provide $175 million in financing for ARA. A market in mortgage-backed securities was established for the first time, and by early 2005 Infonavit and private lenders had sold about $400 million worth of these securities. Mexican policymakers were hoping that private institutional capital involvement would continue into secondary markets, which could greatly expand sources of financing.

The Ahumada Russek brothers owned 51 percent of ARA's shares of capital stock in 2005, with public investors holding the remainder. Germán was in charge of real estate and was chairman of the board of directors, while Luis Felipe was in charge of construction and was vice chairman of the board as well as director general of PDCC.

Robert Halasz

PRINCIPAL UNITS

Construction and Development; Real Estate.

PRINCIPAL SUBSIDIARIES

Asesoria Técnica y Administrativa GAVI, S.A. de C.V.; Comercialización y Ventas S.A.; Consorcio Integral, S.A. de C.V.; Constructora y Urbanizadora ARA, S.A. de C.V.; Inmobilaria ACRE, S.A. de C.V.; Promotora y Desarrolladora de Centros Comerciales, S.A. de C.V.

PRINCIPAL COMPETITORS

Corporación GEO, S.A. de C.V.; Consorcio Hogar, S.A. de C.V.; Desarrolladroa Homex, S.A. de C.V.; Urbi Desarrollos Urbanos, S.A. de C.V.

FURTHER READING

"Consorcio ARA: Invierte $586 milliones en Monterrey," *El Norte,* September 10, 2001, p. 1.

Fregoso Bonilla, Juliana, "Con cimientos firmes," *Expansión,* June 25–July 9, 2003, pp. 256, 259–60.

García, María Eugenia, "Lentos pero seguros," *Expansión,* July 10–24, 2002, pp. 78–81.

"Inauguran Consorcio ARA, PDCC y OCP el complejo 'Centro Las Américas,'" *Reforma,* November 13, 2005, p. 1.

León, Irina, "Se derrumban títulos de ARA por volatilidad," *Reforma,* October 15, 1998, p. 7.

Libaw, Oliver, "Affordable Housing: Bridging the Gap," *Business Mexico,* May 1997, pp. 26–28, 30.

Malkin, Elisabeth, "Can Fox Make Mexico a Nation of Homeowners?," *Business Week,* January 22, 2001, p. 55.

Millman, Joel, "In Cash-Short Mexico, Housing Is Scorned," *Wall Street Journal,* December 1, 1998.

Ortíz, Francisco, "Monopolizan 'boom' 5 empresas," *Reforma,* August 10, 2005, p. 8.

Ramírez Tamayo, Zacarías, "Los cantos del engaño," *Expansión,* September 10, 1997, pp. 40–44, 47–48, 51–52.

Ruiz, Ramon, "Mortgaging for Growth," *Business Mexico,* March 2005, pp. 18–21, 49.

Watson, Andrew, "Striking Gold," *Business Mexico,* December 2002/January 2003, p. 40.

CROSSMARK

5100 Legacy Drive
Plano, Texas 75024-3104
U.S.A.
Telephone: (469) 814-1000
Fax: (469) 814-1355
Web site: http://www.crossmark.com

Private Company
Incorporated: 1995
Employees: 13,000
Sales: $5.2 billion (2001)
NAIC: 414410 General Line Grocery Merchant Wholesalers

■ ■ ■

Privately owned, Plano, Texas-based CROSSMARK (Crossmark) is one of a handful of major sales and marketing agencies connecting the consumer packaged goods industry with supermarkets, convenience stores, and drugstores, offering the kind of services, and more, once handled by thousands of local food brokers. The company offers headquarters sales and support and retail services in an effort to convince shoppers to make a particular purchase; integrated services, including order processing, data synchronization, customer service, demand planning, third-party logistics, sales force automation, and software development; and private-label services, including marketing and promotion, category management, and order management. In addition to the United States, Crossmark does business in Canada, New Zealand, and Australia.

HERITAGE DATING TO THE EARLY 20TH CENTURY

Crossmark was created in 1995 when three companies merged: Sales Mark, The Gordon Company, and The Phillips Company. The oldest of the three was Sales Mark. It was founded by Willis Johnson and E. Leslie Hunt in 1905 in Fort Smith, Arkansas, as Johnson & Hunt Merchandise Brokers. They banked on the town's potential to become a major conduit to the western territories, but the destiny of Fort Smith would be inalterably changed when a tornado all but destroyed the central business district. It soon became apparent that the Fort Smith market would be taken over by nearby Little Rock brokers. Johnson elected to relocate to the larger town while Hunt remained in Fort Smith. On his own, Johnson established the Willis Johnson Company and began to build his brokerage business into a major player in the area. He also gained respect in the industry at large, so much so that in 1929 the small-market broker was elected chairman of the National Food Brokers Association.

Johnson was joined in the business by his son, Willis Johnson, Jr., who took over as president shortly before the United States entered World War II in 1941. He left to join the Navy, while the elder Johnson took a position in the government, serving with the National Office of Price & Administration. Back in Little Rock, son-in-law Bill Powell filled in and ran the company. After the war Willis Johnson, Sr., retired and Powell's son, Peter Powell, along with Austin Bell, became partners.

COMPANY PERSPECTIVES

Our mission is to be the best business services company within the CPG industry, delivering customized client solutions and unparalleled execution.

In the 1980s the company began to expand. Through acquisition, offices were opened in Memphis, Tennessee, and Jackson, Mississippi, in 1981. Then, in 1987, Fulcher-Evans-Welsh, with operations in both cities, was acquired. The company now became known as SALES MARK. In the late 1980s Austin Bell attended a Wal-Mart shareholders' meeting at which founder Sam Walton revealed his goal to become the largest food retailer in the United States. Bell and Powell recognized that this move would lead to consolidation among food retailers and ultimately the 2,500 food brokers operating in the United States at the time, because manufacturers would prefer to do business with brokers large enough to handle national chains. Sales Mark hitched its wagon to Wal-Mart, becoming the largest broker to service the giant retailer. In the 1990s Sales Mark continued to grow through acquisitions, picking up Little Rock's Gardner and Associates in 1990; Southern Food Brokerage, operating in Jackson and New Orleans, in 1991; and Southland and the H.S. Humphries Company in Memphis in 1993. Also during this period, the company launched the ALPHA One Division, which in the 1990s opened offices in Michigan, Minnesota, Alabama, and Canada.

Another southwestern broker that prospered by recognizing the opportunity inherent in Wal-Mart's aggressive move into food retailing was the Gordon Company. It was founded as The W.L. Gordon Company in Dallas, Texas, in 1944 by Red Gordon. Over the next 20 years he expanded his territory to include Oklahoma and New Mexico. Under the leadership of Fred Arnold, Gordon launched a growth spurt in the 1980s, opening offices in Houston and San Antonio and strengthening markets through several acquisitions.

The third company that joined forces to create Crossmark, The Phillips Company, was founded in 1953 in Birmingham, Alabama, by Bill Phillips. For an office he relied on his parents' kitchen table, but soon began to grow the business. A decade later Phillips opened a branch in Montgomery, Alabama, and then in 1970 expanded to Mobile, Alabama. Before becoming part of Crossmark, Phillips also acquired Birmingham's Knapp Sales.

FORMATION OF CROSSMARK IN 1995–96

In October 1995 Sales Mark, Gordon, and Phillips announced a merger, which would be completed in 1996. The combined companies took the name CROSSMARK. It established its headquarters in Dallas with Sales Mark's Butch Smith serving as chief executive officer. The company lost little time in doing its part to consolidate the industry. As Austin Bell had anticipated, Wal-Mart's move into groceries led to consolidation among supermarket chains and a multitude of mergers: Due to low interest rates, it was cheaper to buy existing stores than to open new ones. By the end of the 1990s the top five supermarket chains controlled 40 percent of all grocery sales. With only a handful of powerful supermarket chains to sell to, it was not surprising that manufacturers also began to consolidate in order to preserve their own competitive edge. It was inevitable that with large manufacturers selling to nationwide chains, both would want to deal with national brokers rather than scores of regional sales agents. As a result, brokers were forced to consolidate, with the weaker firms swallowed by the stronger until only a few survivors remained. Crossmark was determined to be one of those survivors.

In the space of five years Crossmark acquired 55 sales and marketing firms. The challenge was to find a way to roll up companies while still preserving the wherewithal to capitalize Crossmark. "Our model for the first half of that five-year period was to do, primarily, mergers that resulted in a tax-free stock swap," Smith told *Dallas Business Journal* in a 2001 profile. "That was terribly important, because it didn't obligate us to come up with significant amounts of cash at closing and the vast majority of these deals were non-interest bearing." Once it convinced a company to merge, according to *Dallas Business Journal,* "Crossmark then pooled its existing stock against the net asset value of the acquired company and reapportioned the stock relative to each company's contribution." With no actual value exchanged, the deal was tax-free.

Some of the early additions included the 1996 acquisitions of Retail Support Force, offering national retail services in supermarkets; FMS, Co., a firm servicing Nashville and eastern Tennessee; and the Dulin Company, whose markets included Atlanta, and Jacksonville, Miami, and Tampa, Florida. In 1997 Crossmark acquired Pfiester Company, which serviced Toledo, Columbus, and Cincinnati in Ohio and Detroit and Grand Rapids in Michigan; Paragon Marketing, doing business in the Carolinas; and the Bradshaw Group, handling accounts in markets such as San Francisco, Los Angeles, Seattle, Portland, Phoenix, Boise, Wyoming,

KEY DATES

1905: Willis Johnson cofounds John & Hunt Merchandise Brokers, which grows into Sales Mark.
1944: The Gordon Company is founded.
1953: The Phillips Company is founded.
1995: Sales Mark, Gordon, and Phillips merge to form CROSSMARK.
2002: David Baxley is named CEO.
2003: The company moves into new Plano, Texas, headquarters.

Montana, Alaska, and Hawaii. Crossmark also opened offices in Kansas City and Charlotte in 1997, and in Denver in 1998.

"As we got bigger," Smith explained to *Dallas Business Journal,* "the cash flowed beautifully. We had the ability to simply acquire businesses then—and we were, frankly, able to do that with virtually no public borrowing." Notable acquisitions in 1998 included Premier Sales, serving Alabama; Sell Group, handling accounts in Chicago, Milwaukee, St. Louis, Iowa, and Nebraska; and the Tom Flemming Company, doing business in Minnesota and the Dakotas. In 1999 Crossmark added Denver's D&F; Arizona's Action Brokerage; J.W. Riley Company, serving markets such as Philadelphia, Delaware, Baltimore, Richmond, and Washington, D.C.; and the Keystone Company, which served the New York metropolitan area, New Jersey, Boston, Buffalo, and Harrisburg, Pennsylvania. Crossmark also opened an office in Boston in 1999.

INDUSTRY CONSOLIDATION WITH NEW CENTURY

By the start of the new century there were four major sales and marketing specialists left standing. In addition to Crossmark, they included Jacksonville, Florida-based Acosta Sales Company, Inc., Advantage Sales and Marketing, L.L.C. of Los Angeles, and Marketing Specialists Corporation of Dallas. Crossmark's chief rival was Acosta, which also had found a way to realize growth without taking on debt. Marketing Specialists, on the other hand, borrowed money to finance a series of acquisitions after being incorporated in 1998. It compounded the problem by overpaying for many of the properties. When the new businesses failed to perform as hoped, Marketing Specialists was unable to keep up with debt payments, leading to a loss of $365 million in 2000 and a filing for Chapter 11 bankruptcy protection in May 2001. Acosta was quick to cherry-pick the company's top people and, in effect, acquired Marketing Specialists at no cost.

By the middle of 2001 there were only three sales and marketing firms, a situation that had a significant effect on the grocery, convenience store, and drugstore industries, and even more so on manufacturers. The top three brands of a particular category were able to find representation from Crossmark, Acosta, or Advantage, but it spelled problems for the number four brand and beyond since the big three could not take on a second brand due to conflicts of interest. According to a September 2001 *New York Times* article, "The consolidation also ties the hands of manufacturers of the three top-selling brands in any category because they have nowhere else to go. 'It's not like you can drop your broker if you don't like the service,' said a manufacturer of a top-selling snack food, who did not want his name used for fear of antagonizing his broker. 'The other two are working for your competitor.'" Manufacturers had the option of maintaining their own direct sales forces, but they would put themselves at a competitive disadvantage. According to the *Times,* "Most manufacturers use brokers to sell some or all product lines, paying them 2 to 5 percent of each product's wholesale price. Direct selling, by contrast, may cost as much as 10 percent." Supermarkets also were not especially pleased with the state of affairs, complaining that with no competition brokers had become complacent and that shelves were not as well maintained as in the past.

As a national company, Crossmark toyed with the idea of moving its headquarters, giving consideration to Chicago and New York, but in 2001 elected to build at an industrial park in Plano, Texas. Crossmark broke ground on a 150,000-square-foot facility in 2002 and relocated there in August 2003. By this time, it had a new CEO. Smith retired and was replaced by David Baxley, a Sales Mark veteran with 30 years of experience in the field. The former Marine and graduate of the University of Arkansas started out as a retail sales representative in Little Rock, and president of the Memphis Operating Division in 1981, before becoming president of the entire Food Brokerage Business six years later. When Crossmark was formed he moved to Dallas to become a vice-president and secretary of the board, and later became chief operating officer.

Aware that U.S. retailers had global aspirations, Crossmark began taking steps to expand beyond the U.S. borders. It entered the Australian market by acquiring Nationwide Brokers and New Zealand by acquiring SuperBroker Strategic Ltd. and Airtime Sales Ltd. Crossmark also established an office in the United Kingdom in London in 2002, but after it failed to acquire John Lusty Group, it pulled out of the market.

While it looked to international markets, Crossmark did not neglect to expand its domestic offerings. Crosscut, a marketing division, was established and was then merged with a Grey Advertising unit to form the J. Brown Agency. The joint venture helped a wide range of clients, including Kraft, NBA Basketball, and Circuit City, to market their brands. In 2002 Crossmark acquired Best Systems, renaming it Best Crossmark, a subsidiary that provided eBusiness solutions. Crossmark also established eXchangeBridge, an Internet supply chain gateway for the consumer packaged goods industry. Crossmark forged an alliance with ACNielsen to create Results@Retail, a monitoring system that prevented retailers and manufacturers from losing sales because a product was out of stock. As a result, Crossmark was well positioned to enjoy long-term growth.

Ed Dinger

PRINCIPAL SUBSIDIARIES

eXchange Bridge; BEST CROSSMARK; The J. Brown Agency (50%); Results@Retail (50%).

PRINCIPAL COMPETITORS

Acosta Sales Company, Inc.; Advantage Sales and Marketing, L.L.C.

FURTHER READING

"Firm Makes Its Mark ... CROSSMARK Style," *Today's Grocer,* January 2006.

Habal, Hala, "Rolling Up the Competition," *Dallas Business Journal,* April 6, 2001, p. 31.

Murphy, Kate, "Food Brokers Are Bigger, So Shelves Look Smaller," *New York Times,* September 2, 2001, p. BU4.

Quinn, Steve, "The Dallas Morning News Collin County Business Column," *Dallas Morning News,* June 13, 2002.

———, "Plano, Texas-Based Food Broker Takes on Marketing, Sales As Well," *Dallas Morning News,* June 17, 2001.

Spethmann, Betsy, "Going for Brokerage," *Promo,* March 1, 2004.

CSX Corporation

500 Water Street, 15th Floor
Jacksonville, Florida 32202
U.S.A.
Telephone: (904) 359-3200
Fax: (904) 359-3780
Web site: http://www.csx.com

Public Company
Incorporated: 1980
Employees: 35,000
Sales: $8.61 billion (2005)
Stock Exchanges: New York
Ticker Symbol: CSX
NAIC: 482111 Line-Haul Railroads; 486210 Pipeline Transportation of Natural Gas; 721110 Hotels (Except Casino Hotels) and Motels; 551112 Offices of Other Holding Companies

■ ■ ■

CSX Corporation is a leading transportation company boasting the largest rail system in the eastern United States, assets that are operated through the company's CSX Transportation Inc. subsidiary. The rail system comprises 22,000 miles of rail lines in 23 states and two Canadian provinces, utilizing 3,700 locomotives and more than 100,000 freight cars to deliver 5.2 million carloads of merchandise, coal, and automobiles annually. Aside from CSX Transportation, there are several other principal subsidiaries that flesh out the company role as one of the country's leading transportation concerns. CSX Intermodal Inc. serves customers from origin to destination with truck and terminal operations that also include a domestic container fleet. Total Distribution Services, Inc. serves the automobile industry, providing customers with distribution centers and storage facilities. TRANSFLO, Inc. provides logistical services for transferring products from rail to truck at more than 70 facilities. The company also controls several non-transportation subsidiaries. The Greenbrier Resort Management Company owns a resort in White Sulphur Springs, West Virginia. CSX Real Property, Inc. oversees the sale, lease, and development of CSX-owned properties. CSX Technology, Inc. operates as a provider of information technology services. CSX's rail system, the major part of its business over the years, is the end result of a long series of consolidations involving three historic railroad systems: the Seaboard Coast Line, the Chesapeake and Ohio Railway, and the Baltimore and Ohio Railroad, which together span nearly the entire history of railroading in the United States.

HISTORY OF THE BALTIMORE AND OHIO RAILROAD

The Baltimore and Ohio Railroad (B&O) was chartered in February 1827 by a group of leading Baltimore businessmen with one of their number, Philip E. Thomas, as the first president. Its purpose was twofold: to challenge major canals, especially the Erie Canal, for trade to the west and to provide more efficient and cheaper freight and passenger service than was then available. In Baltimore's case this traffic passed over the National Road, which ran from Cumberland, Maryland, to Wheeling, West Virginia, on the Ohio River, with an eastward extension to Baltimore. The railroad's

COMPANY PERSPECTIVES

At CSX, our confidence is strong and growing in light of anticipated changes in the economic landscape, notably the increased globalization of trade and the increasing congestion on the interstate highway system. CSX plays an integral role in the nation's economic development and the growth of the global economy. Globalization has resulted in longer international supply chains that will continue to benefit CSX. A strong global economy puts more raw materials and finished goods through the 70 ocean, river and lake ports served by CSX.

construction started on July 4, 1828, at an historic celebration presided over by Charles Carroll, the last surviving signer of the Declaration of Independence. The B&O's planners intended to use horses for motive power, but Peter Cooper's first locomotive used on the line, the diminutive *Tom Thumb,* made its first successful run in 1830, ending the railroad's need for horsepower.

Construction progress was slow, however, and the rail line from Baltimore to Wheeling was not completed until December 1852. A second western extension was completed to Parkersburg, West Virginia, in 1857, with connections to local railroads providing service to Columbus and Cincinnati, Ohio, and to St. Louis, Missouri. The Ohio and West Virginia connections fostered a great increase in coal traffic from mines in the Midwest to the East. By 1860 revenues from coal were about one-third of total rail freight revenue, a ratio that changed little over the years. More than a century later coal provided 32 percent of CSX's rail revenue.

The B&O played a key role in the Civil War, as did many other railroads, and the line suffered accordingly with substantial damage to track and equipment. Growth continued after the war under the presidency of John W. Garrett, who served from 1858 to 1884, providing sound management in an era when railroad mismanagement was all too common. Track mileage increased from 521 in 1865 to nearly 1,700 by 1885. As the B&O continued to expand through construction and acquisition of smaller railroads, mileage increased to 3,200 by 1900, reaching 5,100 by 1920 and achieving a peak of about 6,350 in 1935.

After Garrett's presidency, increasing debt and an over-generous dividend policy weakened the B&O financially while speculation in the company's stock hampered its fundraising ability. The financial panic of 1893 proved disastrous for the line, and in 1896 the B&O was placed in receivership. In the following decade and a half the reorganized railroad's mileage and revenues increased satisfactorily, but the B&O came under the control of the Pennsylvania Railroad, which had purchased a majority of its stock after the bankruptcy. The Pennsylvania involved itself briefly in the B&O's management, but sold its stock position in 1906 for fear of U.S. government antitrust action. Under the long presidency of Daniel Willard from 1910 to 1941, the B&O's physical plant and service were considerably improved, and the line, which now spread through western Pennsylvania, Ohio, West Virginia, Indiana, and Illinois, enjoyed increasing prosperity until the onset of the Great Depression in the 1930s.

The 1930s saw declining revenues, layoffs, and wage reductions. In 1932 dividends on the common stock were discontinued, not to be restored until 1952. Track mileage and locomotive and equipment rosters began a long decline that would continue until the B&O came under control of the Chesapeake and Ohio Railway (C&O) in 1963. Roy B. White, however, who served as president from 1941 to 1953, inherited from Willard a first-class railroad that offered excellent service. World War II provided renewed prosperity, but the B&O faced problems during the postwar years from inflation, debt for new equipment, declines in passenger traffic, and chronic labor disputes. U.S. President Harry Truman temporarily seized the nation's railroads in 1946 to offset a threatened nationwide strike, and similar crises occurred in 1948 and 1950.

During the B&O's last decade as an independent company, Howard E. Simpson served as president from 1953 to 1961, and Jervis Langdon, Jr., served from 1961 to 1964. Operating revenues and net income generally declined during the 1950s as did track mileage and employment. Labor costs grew because of constant union pressure for higher wages. In the late 1950s as the B&O's traffic and revenue position worsened, the railroad began to consider the idea of a merger with a stronger partner. The C&O and the New York Central Railroad vied briefly for dominance, but in February 1961 the C&O announced that it controlled 61 percent of the B&O's stock. In 1962 the Interstate Commerce Commission (ICC) approved the C&O's request to take over the B&O, and on February 4, 1963, the C&O finally took control. The affiliation produced an 11,000-mile rail system, stretching from the Atlantic to the Mississippi River and from the Great Lakes to the southern edges of Virginia, West Virginia, and Kentucky, and brought to the B&O's rescue a smaller but significantly

KEY DATES

1827: The Baltimore and Ohio Railroad is formed.
1852: Construction of the company's first rail line, connecting Baltimore and Wheeling, West Virginia, is completed.
1900: The railroad's rail network encompasses 3,200 miles.
1963: The company is acquired by the Chesapeake and Ohio Railway.
1972: The two railroads operate under a new name, Chessie System Inc.
1980: Chessie System and Seaboard Coast Line Industries Inc. merge, creating CSX Corporation.
1983: CSX Corp. diversifies, spending $1 billion to acquire Texas Gas Resources Corporation, one of the country's largest natural gas pipeline companies.
1986: Sea-Land Corporation, the largest U.S.-based ocean containership line, is acquired for $800 million.
1999: CSX and Norfolk Southern acquire Conrail Inc.
2000: CSX sells its international shipping line business, the first step in a plan to divest Sea-Land Corp.
2002: CSX sells its domestic shipping line business.
2004: The divestiture of the Sea-Land assets is completed with the sale of CSX World Terminal, marking the company's exit from the maritime business.
2005: As part of a five-year growth plan, CSX increases its capital improvement expenditures.

stronger railroad, not quite as old as the B&O, but with origins that also went back to the early years of railroading.

HISTORY OF CHESSIE SYSTEM

The C&O had its beginning in a short line railroad built to provide rail traffic to farmers and merchants in central Virginia. Chartered in 1836 as the Louisa Railroad, it originally covered 21 miles from Taylorsville to Frederick Hall, Virginia. In 1850 the line's name was changed to the Virginia Central Railroad, and by 1851 it extended eastward to Richmond, Virginia. A plan to extend westward to the Ohio River was delayed by the Civil War, during which the railroad served the Southern forces effectively but was heavily damaged. In 1867 the reorganized company changed its name to the Chesapeake and Ohio Railway Company and with financial backing from Collis P. Huntington, who subsequently became president from 1869 to 1888, the line was open from Richmond to Huntington, West Virginia, by 1873. The panic of 1873 ended in receivership for the C&O in 1875. In 1888 Huntington lost control to J. P. Morgan, who improved the railroad's performance such that, by 1900, the C&O was a solvent, well-managed 1,445-mile line connecting Newport News, Virginia, with Cincinnati, Ohio, and Louisville, Kentucky.

The C&O's history during the 20th century was characterized by conservative financial management supported by strong coal revenues. In 1947 the C&O made a major acquisition of the Pere Marquette Railroad with nearly 2,000 miles of track in the Midwest, New York, and Canada, and a sound base of merchandise traffic. The Pennsylvania and New York Central Railroads controlled C&O's stock from 1900 to 1909. During the 1920s and early 1930s control was exercised by Martis P. Van Sweringen and his brother, Oris P. Van Sweringen. From the mid-1930s, noted financier Robert R. Young owned a majority stock position, which he sold in 1954 to Cleveland investment banker Cyrus S. Eaton. By this time the C&O was a prosperous 5,000-mile line with $350 million in annual revenues and an exceptionally competent leader, Walter J. Tuohy, who had assumed the presidency in 1948. After completing the line's move to diesel engines in the mid-1950s, Tuohy moved aggressively to expand the C&O by acquisition, leading to the 1963 merger with the B&O.

The unification of the two railroads proceeded slowly and deliberately with a common annual report appearing in 1964 and senior administrative positions being gradually combined during the 1960s and 1970s. The continued separate operations of the lines avoided the confusion and errors that led to the failure of the Penn Central combination during the same period. It also avoided a downgrading of C&O debt securities because of the weaker financial position of the B&O before the merger, and maximized the benefits of operating two railroads whose traffic was, for the most part, complementary.

Hays T. Watkins became chairman and chief executive officer of the combined C&O and B&O in 1971. He was a strong administrator, firing President John Hanifin in 1975 for spending $2 million on tennis courts at the railroad's resort, the Greenbrier Hotel. Watkins adopted the name Chessie System Inc. in 1972 for the combined railroads and formally became CEO of Chessie System in 1973. By the late 1970s only 3 percent of Chessie's $1.5 billion in revenues were from non-rail sources, and Watkins was considering diversification and expansion. In 1978 Chessie proposed to the ICC a possible merger with the slightly larger southeastern railroad system, Seaboard Coast Line Industries Inc. Like the B&O and the Chessie, the Seaboard was a consolidation of several railroads whose history also reached back into the 19th century.

HISTORY OF SEABOARD COAST LINE

The Seaboard's key component, the Atlantic Coast Line Railroad (ACL), began as a series of small railroads running along a northeast-southwest line parallel to the Atlantic coast and connecting communities along the "fall line," the imaginary line joining towns at the heads of navigation of the coastal rivers. The oldest part of the ACL was the Petersburg Railroad, chartered in 1830 to run from Petersburg, Virginia, south to the North Carolina border. The corporate parent of the ACL, however, was the Richmond and Petersburg Railroad, chartered in 1836. These and similar, small independent railroads running along the fall line through Virginia, North Carolina, South Carolina, Georgia, Alabama, and Florida were joined after the Civil War in a holding company at first called the American Improvement and Construction Company, formed in 1889. In 1893 the name was changed to the Atlantic Coast Line Company. In 1902 the ACL bought a controlling share of the Louisville and Nashville Railroad (L&N) and, following a 1914 reorganization, the name was changed again to the Atlantic Coast Line Railroad Company.

In 1958 the ACL, by then a 5,300-mile railroad with revenues of about $163 million, proposed a merger with one of its southeastern competitors, the Seaboard Air Line Railroad with 4,100 miles and roughly similar revenues. The ACL, with its affiliates, the 5,700-mile L&N and the smaller Clinchfield Railroad, tapping the coal and merchandise markets of the Midwest, was the stronger of the two companies. The plan however, was to merge the ACL into the Seaboard to take advantage of the Seaboard's more modern corporate charter. The consolidation plan was filed with the ICC in 1960 but progress was slow, partly because of antitrust issues, with final approval not coming until 1967. The new company, eventually called Seaboard Coast Line Industries Inc., was the eighth largest railroad in the United States, with revenues of about $1.2 billion.

CREATION OF CSX IN 1980

The merger proposed in 1978 between the $1.5 billion Chessie and the $1.8 billion Seaboard offered benefits to both sides. It would give the Chessie a relatively inexpensive expansion into the booming Southeast and would provide a useful capital infusion for the Seaboard, especially for its maintenance and equipment-starved L&N subsidiary. The ICC approved the merger in September 1980 and the two systems were consolidated into CSX Corporation on November 1, 1980. The Seaboard's Prime F. Osborn III became chairman and the Chessie's Hays T. Watkins became president. Watkins was clearly the dominant figure, becoming chairman in 1982 on Osborn's retirement.

As in the case of the B&O and C&O, the operational consolidation of the two railroad systems proceeded gradually, again to avoid the internal stresses that had marred the Penn Central merger. It was not for another decade that all of the railroad operations of Chessie and Seaboard were consolidated under the CSX Transportation Inc. subsidiary.

DIVERSIFICATION

Meanwhile, diversification was in the air in the 1980s. In 1983 CSX made a deal with Southern New England Telephone Company to place a fiber optics telecommunication system along the CSX rights-of-way. A more significant diversification move in 1983 was CSX's "white-knight" $1 billion purchase of Texas Gas Resources Corporation, with $2.9 billion in revenues, one of the United States' largest natural gas pipeline companies with substantial gas and petroleum reserves. For CSX, with revenues of $5 billion, this was a major expansion into natural resources, adding oil and gas to its already large coal holdings. Texas Gas had as a subsidiary the American Commercial Lines Inc. (ACL), a large barge operator. On July 24, 1984, the ICC voted to allow CSX to keep and operate this shipping firm, a reversal of longstanding government policy against letting railroads own steamship or barge lines.

Continuing this precedent, the ICC in 1987 voted to approve CSX's 1986 $800 million acquisition of Sea-Land Corporation, the largest U.S. ocean container-ship line (later known as Sea-Land Service Inc.). This purchase was a continuation of Watkins's somewhat controversial policy of structuring CSX as an intermodal transportation company capable of serving both national and international markets. CSX became heavily involved in resort operations following its 1986 purchase of Rockresorts, Inc., owner and manager of several luxury resorts, which CSX bought from Laurance Rockefeller. Also in 1986, CSX purchased a 30 percent interest (increased to a majority stake two years later) in Yukon Pacific Corporation, which aimed to construct the Trans-Alaska Gas System to transport natural gas via pipeline from Alaska's North Slope to Valdez. In 1987 CSX further extended its array of transportation services by forming CSX/Sea-Land Intermodal (later known as CSX Intermodal Inc.), the nation's only transcontinental full-service intermodal company.

These acquisitions and initiatives were the last engineered by Watkins. The company's directors became disenchanted with CSX's low profits, declining return on investment, and stagnant stock price. Lagging rail profits, partially due to labor contracts and problems with the company's new acquisitions, resulted in major changes in management direction for CSX. A comprehensive restructuring program was announced by Watkins in 1988, but in April 1989 John W. Snow, a former federal highway official, was appointed president and chief executive officer of the company. Watkins continued as chairman until his retirement on January 31, 1991, when that position, too, was assumed by Snow.

CSX underwent a significant change in direction between 1988 and 1990. CSX's oil and gas businesses (with the exception of its Yukon Pacific stake) were sold in 1988 and 1989, resulting in a net gain of more than $200 million. Most of its resort properties and the telecommunications system were also sold, although CSX kept the Greenbrier Hotel and one smaller resort. A crew-reduction agreement was signed by the railroad with the United Transportation Union in 1989. This was a key step in Snow's plan to downsize the railroad, as well as other CSX operations, in order to increase profitability. CSX also improved its share earnings by using money from the gas and oil sale to buy back about 39 percent of its outstanding common stock. In his first years as chief executive, Snow installed a new management team determined to improve shipping and real estate profits and to focus on CSX's traditionally strong rail operations in order to earn a better return on the company's $12 billion asset base.

STRATEGIC ACQUISITIONS

With Snow's emphasis on improving both customer relations and profits, CSX's position grew ever stronger through the 1990s. Revenues increased steadily, from $8.21 billion in 1990 to $10.54 billion in 1996, while net earnings reached a peak of $855 million by 1996. Snow sought to leverage this strength by making selective, strategic acquisitions that would enhance and extend the company's core transportation operations.

In 1992 American Commercial Lines increased its barge capacity by more than one-third through the purchase of the Valley Line companies. Four years later, ACL acquired the marine assets of Conti-Carriers & Terminals Inc., adding 400 barges and eight towboats to a fleet that subsequently numbered 3,700 barges and 137 towboats. In early 1993 CSX acquired Customized Transportation Inc. (CTI), one of the leading logistics companies for the automotive industry, providing distribution, warehousing, and assembly on a contract basis for just-in-time delivery systems. CTI later added service in Europe and South America to its existing U.S. operations, and in 1996 began to service new industries, including electronics, retail, and chemicals. In 1996 Sea-Land entered into a global alliance with Danish shipping company Maersk Lines involving the sharing of vessels and terminals.

The company's acquisitions and initiatives of the early 1990s were largely overshadowed by CSX's attempted purchase of Conrail Inc., which began in October 1996. The 1990s had already seen the mega-mergers of Burlington Northern and Santa Fe to form Burlington Northern Santa Fe and of Union Pacific and Southern Pacific (whereby Union Pacific Corp. absorbed Southern Pacific). It appeared that Conrail and CSX would form the nation's largest railroad, including Conrail's lucrative routes to New York City, when Conrail agreed to CSX's $8.1 billion friendly takeover offer. But Norfolk Southern Corp., CSX's archrival and a fellow eastern U.S. rail power that had twice before attempted to buy Conrail, stepped in with a $9.1 billion hostile takeover bid, prompting CSX in November to raise its offer to $8.4 billion. By March 1996, after Norfolk had raised its bid twice more, CSX, Norfolk, and Conrail reached a three-way agreement for a $10.2 billion takeover, with CSX paying $4.3 billion for 42 percent of Conrail's operations and Norfolk paying $5.9 billion for the other 58 percent. Although the outcome was less than the full merger originally sought, CSX would still gain about 4,500 miles of rail, including lines to New York, Boston, and Montreal, giving it a 23,000-mile system in 23 states and the provinces of Ontario and Quebec. Pending approval by the Surface Transportation Board which was expected sometime in 1998, CSX and Norfolk Southern would operate the two dominant railroads in the eastern United States, with CSX having a slight edge over the 21,000-mile Norfolk system and thus remaining the nation's third largest railroad.

An increasing concern in the rapidly consolidating railroad industry of the mid-1990s was whether the mergers were compromising the system's safety. In the midst of CSX's seeking of regulatory approval of the Conrail takeover, a jury in New Orleans awarded damages of $3.37 billion, including $2.5 billion in punitive damages, against CSX in relation to a 1987 chemical-car fire. This September 1997 judgment was overturned two months later by the Louisiana Supreme Court, which sent it back to a lower court for reconsideration. CSX's safety record came under further fire when the Federal Railroad Administration issued a report in October 1997 criticizing CSX's safety procedures. The agency had started an investigation earlier in the year, following a collision between two CSX trains which killed one employee and injured another. The company paid $750,000 in fines for violations uncovered in the inquiry. More controversially, CSX Transportation hired the Federal Railroad Administration's safety chief shortly after release of the report, leading to criticism from safety advocates.

Assuming regulatory approval of the Conrail breakup, the consolidation of the company's newly acquired assets was likely to be CSX's number one priority into the 21st century. Just as the problems that resulted from the Penn Central merger led to the careful meshing of operations in previous CSX mergers, the kind of snafus encountered in the Union Pacific takeover of Southern Pacific would need to be avoided if CSX and Norfolk were to successfully divide Conrail. With the negotiation of the Conrail deal completed, the following question arose among industry observers: was railroad consolidation finally over? The next step, some felt, was the creation of two coast-to-coast giants, with CSX joining with either Southern Pacific or Burlington Northern Santa Fe and Norfolk Southern joining with the remaining partner. Whether or not further consolidation occurred, CSX was certain to remain at the center of the dynamic railroad industry.

CSX IN THE NEW CENTURY

The long-awaited takeover of Conrail occurred as CSX entered a new century, ushering in a period of structural reorganization and divestitures. CSX and Norfolk Southern took control of the Conrail assets on June 1, 1999, a day greeted with a mixture of joy and trepidation. The addition of the Conrail assets made CSX the largest rail system in the East, a momentous occasion in the history of the company, but there were grave concerns both inside and outside the company about its ability to effectively absorb the new assets. The merger of Union Pacific and Southern Pacific three years earlier was not handled properly, leading to delayed shipments, lost shipments, and traffic jams that lasted for a year and a half. John Snow, CSX's chairman, president, and chief executive officer, was mindful of the potential problems, assuring industry onlookers that the company was fully prepared to integrate the Conrail assets into CSX's operations. "We don't see anything that will create a cataclysm for us like it did Union Pacific and Southern Pacific," he said in a May 17, 1999 interview with *Industry Week.* "We've been over it and over it. We don't foresee a lot of problems." Despite Snow's assurances, CSX struggled to smoothly take over the Conrail assets, a fate suffered by Norfolk Southern as well. Although the problems were varied, one industry insider offered a broad assessment of the difficulties that arose in the wake of the merger. "Conrail service was a tough act to follow," an executive of an intermodal services firm said in a December 13, 1999 interview with *Traffic World.* "It seems that CSX has problems getting loads out, that they're just sitting in congested terminals. Once they're out, they seem to get to destination. Norfolk Southern gets their loads out, but they don't get to destination on time." As CSX dealt with the logistical problems related to the Conrail acquisition, problems that would persist for years, the company reorganized and shed some of its non-railroad assets. In 1999, the company sold the international shipping line business it had acquired through the Sea-Land acquisition. The deal, which included approximately 70 container vessels, 200,000 containers, and related container terminals, was brokered with the A.P. Moller-Maersk Line, which agreed to pay $800 million for the assets. Next, the company sold its CTI Logistx business unit to TNT Post Group, N.V. in 2000, gaining $650 million from the divestiture. In 2002, CSX shed another component of its Sea-Land business, selling its domestic shipping line business. The final aspect of Sea-Land's business was sold in late 2004, when CSX World Terminals was sold to Middle East port operator Dubai Ports International. The divestiture marked CSX's exit from the maritime business. The deal, valued at $1.2 billion, included nine terminals in Asia, Australia, Europe, and Latin America that generated $226 million in annual revenue.

The divestitures enabled CSX to sharpen its focus on its mainstay railroad business, the top priority of management as it plotted the company's future course. In 2005, the company announced a five-year growth plan that earmarked greater resources for improving different parts of its rail system, a move industry pundits believed was imperative for CSX to effectively compete in the East. Part of the plan involved increasing annual capital spending from $1 billion to as much as $1.4 billion. The investment was expected to be used to expand capacity in the Northeast and Southeast on rail lines between Chicago and Florida and between Albany, New York, and New York City. As the company pressed forward with the implementation of its growth plan, it was expecting annual revenue growth of between 4 percent and 6 percent until the end of the decade.

Bernard A. Block
Updated, David E. Salamie; Jeffrey L. Covell

PRINCIPAL SUBSIDIARIES

CSX Transportation Inc.; CSX Intermodal Inc.; CSX Technology, Inc.; The Greenbrier Resort Management Company; CSX Real Property, Inc.; Total Distribution Services, Inc.; TRANSFLO Corporation.

PRINCIPAL COMPETITORS

Burlington Northern Santa Fe Corporation; Norfolk Southern Corporation; Union Pacific Corporation.

FURTHER READING

Chambers, Sam, "Dubai Port Takes Control of CSX Hubs," *Europe Intelligence Wire,* February 25, 2005.

"CSX Completes Sale of Contract Logistics Unit," *Transportation & Distribution,* October 2000, p. 12.

"CSX Looking for Traction," *Traffic World,* September 5, 2005, p. 27.

Dilts, James D., *The Great Road: The Building of the Baltimore and Ohio, the Nation's First Railroad, 1828–1853,* Stanford, Calif.: Stanford University Press, 1993.

Dorin, Patrick C., *The Chesapeake and Ohio Railway, George Washington's Railroad,* Seattle: Superior Publishing Co., 1981.

Dozier, Howard Douglas, *A History of the Atlantic Coast Line Railroad,* Boston: Houghton Mifflin, 1920, reprint, New York: A. M. Kelley, 1971.

Fink, James, "CSX Battles High Costs, Negative Public Image," *Business First of Buffalo,* February 7, 2000, p. 5.

Finn, Edwin A., Jr., "On the Right Track?," *Forbes,* May 16, 1988, p. 105.

Gallagher, John, "Still Dark in the Tunnel," *Traffic World,* August 30, 2004, p. 27.

Gold, Jackey, "CSX: Stoking Up the Largest U.S. Railroad," *Financial World,* February 4, 1992, p. 18.

Hungerford, Edward, *The Story of the Baltimore & Ohio Railroad, 1827–1927,* 1928, reprint, New York: Arno Press, 1972.

Kimelman, John, "It's the Customer, Stupid?," *Financial World,* January 3, 1995, pp. 31–32.

Kizzia, Tom, "Chessie-SCL Industries: A Merger of Equals," *Railway Age,* March 30, 1981, p. 26.

Leach, Peter T., "Scaling New Heights," *The Journal of Commerce,* December 5, 2005, p. 32.

Lipin, Steven, and Daniel Machalaba, "CSX Agrees to Acquire Conrail for $8.1 Billion in Cash and Stock," *Wall Street Journal,* October 16, 1996, pp. 3A, 6A.

Machalaba, Daniel, and Anna Wilde Mathews, "How Norfolk's Chief Pulled Off Conrail Coup," *Wall Street Journal,* March 5, 1997, pp. 1B, 4B.

Machalaba, Daniel, and Steven Lipin, "CSX Raises Bid for Conrail to $8.4 Billion," *Wall Street Journal,* November 7, 1996, pp. 3A, 8A.

Martin, Justin, "The Great Train Game," *Fortune,* November 11, 1996, pp. 151–52, 154.

Mathews, Anna Wilde, "Jury Assesses CSX Punitive Damages of $2.5 Billion," *Wall Street Journal,* September 9, 1997, p. 6B.

Miller, Luther S., "The War Is Over. The Real Fight Begins," *Railway Age,* April 1997, pp. 31, 34, 36, 38.

Nomani, Asra Q., "CSX Unit Hires Safety Chief of Rail Agency," *Wall Street Journal,* October 21, 1997, p. 7B.

Norman, James R., "Full Steam Ahead," *Forbes,* June 7, 1993, pp. 14–15.

———, "'We've Got a Clock on It,'" *Forbes,* June 25, 1990, p. 116.

Richards, Gregory, "CSX Sells International Division," *Florida Times-Union,* December 10, 2004.

Stover, John F., *History of the Baltimore and Ohio Railroad,* West Lafayette, Ind.: Purdue University Press, 1987.

Toothman, Fred Rees, *Working for the Chessie System: Olde King Coal's Prime Carrier,* Huntington, W. Va.: Vandalia Book Co., 1993.

Turner, Charles Wilson, *Chessie's Road,* Richmond, Va.: Garrett and Massie Incorporated, 1956.

Verespji, Michael A., "Rail Deregulation Gives CSX a Boost," *Industry Week,* October 13, 1980, p. 31.

Watkins, Hays T., "CSX: A Bold New Course," *Railway Age,* January 1986, p. 36.

Weber, Joseph, "Highballing Toward Two Big Railroads," *Business Week,* March 17, 1997, pp. 32–33.

———, "This Railroad Is Weary of Getting Sidetracked," *Business Week,* October 17, 1988, p. 60.

Welty, Gus, "CSX Puts It All Together," *Railway Age,* January 1987, p. 27.

Cyberonics, Inc.

100 Cyberonics Building
Cyberonics Boulevard
Houston, Texas 77058-2072
U.S.A.
Telephone: (281) 228-7200
Toll Free: (800) 332-1375
Fax: (281) 218-9332
Web site: http://www.cyberonics.com

Public Company
Incorporated: 1987
Employees: 478
Sales: $103.4 million (2005)
Stock Exchanges: NASDAQ
Ticker Symbol: CYBX
NAIC: 334510 Electromedical and Electrotherapeutic Apparatus Manufacturing

■ ■ ■

Cyberonics, Inc. is a Houston-based medical device company, maker of the Vagus Nerve Stimulation (VNS Therapy) System, an implantable device that sends electrical pulsed signals to the vagus nerve in the left side of the neck. In 1997 the company received Food and Drug Administration (FDA) approval to use the device to treat epilepsy, and later gained FDA approval to treat depression, albeit not without a great deal of controversy. Cyberonics also is pursuing other uses for VNS Therapy, including a method to curb morbid obesity. In addition to the United States, the device is approved for use in Canada, Europe, and Australia. Cyberonics is a public company listed on the NASDAQ.

COMMENCING VNS RESEARCH IN 1971

Cyberonics grew out of the work of Jacob Zabara, a neuroscientist. The native of Philadelphia earned a doctorate at the University of Pennsylvania in 1959 and went on to establish a teaching career. He was a professor at Philadelphia's University School of Medicine in 1971 when he had an insight watching his wife control labor pains through breathing techniques while giving birth to their first child. He was well aware of the prevailing assumption in neuroscience that the vagus nerve provided a one-way connection to the organs of the body, but he now wondered if a reverse action were possible. In the case of his wife, was her breathing making a connection to the brain via the vagus nerve? Then, if this were true, could the vagus nerve serve as a pathway to the brain to control conditions such as seizures or nausea, an area of particular concern because Zabara served as a NASA consultant on space sickness? "Using medical research dating to the 1930s," according to *Business Week,* "he hypothesized that stimulation of the brain via the vagus nerve could create an anticonvulsion effect." Zabara began conducting research on the vagus nerve of lab animals, eventually succeeding in triggering a seizure in a dog, but his desire to work with human test subjects was greeted with derision from colleagues, and he was unable to persuade any scientific journals to publish his studies.

In the mid-1980s Zabara finally found someone interested in his work: Reese S. Terry. An electrical

> **COMPANY PERSPECTIVES**
>
> Cyberonics is a sharply innovative and progressive medical device company whose commitment to our mission is unsurpassed! Our products and achievements speak for themselves. We stand committed to our mission to improve the lives of people touched by epilepsy, depression and other chronic disorders that may prove treatable with our patented therapy, VNS.

engineer by training, Reese held a number of patents related to pacemakers and had become the vice-president of technology at Intermedics, a medical device company. Zabara gave him a demonstration of the vagus nerve stimulator that he had implanted in dogs. As described by *Fast Company,* "When the animals went into seizures, the device seemed to halt them. Terry was intrigued, but when Intermedics funded a study of the device in four monkeys, the outcome was cloudy." Only about half of the animals responded. Intermedics canceled the contract it had made with Zabara to develop a nerve stimulation device to control epilepsy, concluding that it would be too expensive and risky.

When Terry soon found himself a victim of a corporate restructuring effect that left him without a job, he decided to license Zabara's technology and develop the epilepsy product himself. In December 1987 he and Zabara incorporated Cyberonics. Relying on a book, Terry developed a business plan and began trolling for start-up funds. A newly formed Houston venture capital firm, Ventures Medical, kicked in $300,000 and promised several hundred thousand more as the company demonstrated progress. Other investors in this first round of fund-raising were the Vista Group and Dallas-based Sevin Rosen Bayless, the company that once provided seed money to Compaq Computer.

Well aware of how expensive it would be to bring a medical device to market, Terry husbanded his resources. According to *Fast Company,* "His rented office space was in a strip mall. Personnel matters were discussed in a booth at the Dairy Queen. … To save money, Terry and his medical-device consultants he hired tried to adapt off-the-shelf parts for their purposes instead of designing everything from scratch." Cyberonics soon developed a VNS prototype that could be used in human trials, and Terry managed to find a few doctors willing to give the device a try, but they lacked enthusiasm and some were more interested in disproving Zabara's theory than in validating it. The first device was implanted in a 25-year-old man in late 1988 at Wake Forest Bowman Gray Medical School in North Carolina by Dr. J. Kiffen Penry and neurosurgeon William Bell. The patient's seizure rate decreased by 80 percent, and a second patient, who had been suffering hourly seizures, experienced almost a complete eradication of the events. Over the next several months, another eight patients received the device. Although the improvements were less dramatic, Cyberonics was still able to pursue Phase II of the FDA's review process in which it tested the device on patients who did not respond well to epilepsy drug therapy. The company also attracted another $2 million in a second round of venture capital funding.

Terry brought in someone to take over as chief executive officer while he stayed on as chairman. He also succeed in raiding rival firms to bring in other talented executives, such as Ross G. Baker, Intermedics' former director of electronic design, who served as director of research and development. In addition to controlling epileptic seizures, the company was interested in testing VNS technology as a treatment in areas such as Parkinson's disease, cerebral palsy, circulation problems, bladder control, and intractable pain. The development of a VNS device appeared so promising at this point that pharmaceutical giant Pfizer invested $2.5 million in Cyberonics in 1990, and pledged another $5 million as the VNS device successfully navigated the FDA approval process.

INITIAL PUBLIC OFFERING IN 1993

The venture capital firms were, by now, eager to get their money out, and in 1990 it appeared that their best exit strategy was for Cyberonics to be sold to a major pharmaceutical company. Instead, the company was taken public in 1993. With Morgan Stanley & Co. acting as manager, Cyberonics held an initial public offering of stock, raising $24 million, despite some problems with its FDA application, which the company learned was incomplete. Cyberonics resubmitted its application in June 1993, but in 1994 it learned that the FDA wanted twice as many patients to be studied, 200 instead of 100. The rejection appeared to be nothing less than a death sentence for the independent company, even though in 1994 the company received approval to use the device on refractory epilepsy in Europe. However, the major money was to be found in the U.S. market, and with about $20 million remaining from the stock offering, the company lacked the money necessary to fund another year of FDA trials with twice as many patients.

According to *Fast Company,* "The CEO left, as did the vice president who'd come from Eli Lilly. Cyberonics shrunk from 50 employees to about 35. 'We had to

KEY DATES

1987: Cyberonics is founded.
1990: Pfizer invests in the company.
1993: An initial public offering of stock is completed.
1995: Skip Cummins takes over as CEO.
1997: VNS gains FDA approval to treat epilepsy.
2005: VNS gains FDA approval to treat depression.

cut back advanced development, lay off people, squinch by,' Terry says. 'It was the lowest point of my career.' But the company didn't go out of business." Terry raised more money through private placements of stock and then hired a new CEO to shepherd the device through the third attempt at FDA approval. But the former Johnson & Johnson executive had a last minute change of heart and backed out of the agreement, forcing Terry to step in as CEO.

It was at this delicate point in Cyberonics' history that Robert P. "Skip" Cummins became actively involved in the running of the company. A general partner at one of the venture capital firms that provided seed money, Vista Group, Cummins had served as a director on Cyberonics' board since 1988. In June 1995, according to *Fast Company,* he "was drafted to serve as acting chief. He took the job—temporarily, he thought—in part to help Cyberonics' investors to cash out. … One part of Cummins's mission as CEO was to scrounge enough money to keep the company moving toward FDA approval, but another was to find a corporate savior that would buy it."

Cummins was able to convince medical device manufacturer St. Jude Medical to invest $12 million in Cyberonics and take an option on buying the company. The money helped to complete the trials needed to satisfy the FDA. In April 1996 St. Jude agreed to pay approximately $72 million to acquire Cyberonics, but the trial results released in August of that year were not strong enough for the likes of St. Jude, which backed out of the deal. Although the price of Cyberonics' stock tanked, much to the displeasure of shareholders, the St. Jude interlude at least bought time for Cyberonics, which had enough cash available to complete the FDA submission.

Cummins became committed to the Cyberonics cause and accepted the CEO post on a permanent basis. He was a fiery leader. The *New York Times* offered a vivid description of the man: "The modern C.E.O. is supposed to be cool, calm, collected—imperturbable in the face of criticism. Skip Cummins is none of these things. Mr. Cummins is, to put it bluntly, a hothead. A 6'2" former Dartmouth football player, he favors the shaved-head look, which gives him an intimidating mien that he uses to great effect." Hedge fund manager and television host James Cramer called Cummins the "most antagonistic C.E.O. in America." But there was no doubting his passion and commitment to forwarding Cyberonics' agenda. In June 1997 he took a team of six doctors to Washington, D.C., to meet with the FDA advisory panel, which was then persuaded to make a unanimous recommendation to the agency to grant approval for the VNS system for use with epilepsy. A month later, after ten years of effort and $50 million, Cyberonics finally succeeded in gaining FDA approval. The company was now able to recoup that investment by raising $50 million in a secondary stock offering.

Cyberonics estimated that the epilepsy market could be worth as much as $200 million a year, but Cummins was not content with just this business. The company looked for new and possibly more lucrative applications for its VNS device, such as controlling depression, which it estimated could be worth $2 billion. During epilepsy trials a number of subjects who did not experience a reduction in seizures by using the device found themselves feeling happier, leading the researchers to pursue depression control through VNS. The company was also hopeful about using VNS to treat obesity, Alzheimer's disease, and anxiety, but decided to focus most of its resources on depression, an application it hoped could win FDA approval in a shorter time frame. A pilot study was launched in 1998 at the University of Texas Southwestern Medical Center, and a year later early results were encouraging. Of the 30 severely depressed patients, about 40 percent saw their symptoms cut by half in a matter of three months, and after nine months more than 50 percent of the patients benefited.

REJECTING A BUYOUT OFFER IN 2000

Once again Cyberonics was a company to be reckoned with. In 2000 Medtronics Inc., a major medical device company, tried to acquire the company for $480 million, even making the bid public in order to put pressure on Cummins, but in the end the Cyberonics board rejected the offer, electing to remain independent instead. In the meantime, a second study with a larger sample of depressed patients, 235 in all, was launched. To the surprise of Cummins and his management team, the preliminary results released in January 2002 showed no statistical difference between the patients receiving VNS treatment and the control group that never had their devices activated and continued to rely solely on drugs to control their depression. On release of the news, the price of Cyberonics' stock tumbled 17 points.

There was no shortage of opinions on why the numbers were so poor. Perhaps the patients in the second study were more depressed than the ones in the first, the electrical stimulation was too weak, or stimulation should have lasted longer than the eight weeks allotted to the trial. Cummins rejected the idea of starting all over, electing instead to hire experts to review the numbers and make changes to the trial already underway. In January 2003 a retooled application was submitted to the FDA, and in the spring of 2004 the FDA advisory panel recommended approval. In August 2004, however, the company received a "non-approval" letter from the agency. Once more the price of Cyberonics stock plummeted. The company also faced another takeover attempt, this time a $524 million bid from Advanced Neuromodulation Systems Inc. Again Cyberonics rejected and Cummins refused to accept the FDA ruling as the final word.

In July 2005 the FDA granted approval for the use of VNS therapy on depressed patients who failed to show improvement with at least four other available treatments. Cyberonics called it the "dawning of a new era" and Cummins was talking about revenues in excess of $1 billion by 2010, but there were also critics of the way the approval was granted, in particular the role played by Daniel Schultz, the director of the FDA's device center. According to a Senate investigation concluded in 2006, Schultz overruled the unanimous opinion of his scientific staff to grant approval. Nevertheless, the decision stood. Whether the market was as large as Cummins claimed and insurers could be persuaded to pay for VNS treatment to fight depression remained to be seen. With little more than $100 million in annual sales and a net loss of $12.2 million in 2005, it also remained very much an open question whether Cyberonics would ever reach the heights its backers had long predicted.

Ed Dinger

PRINCIPAL SUBSIDIARIES

Cyberonics Europe, S.A.

PRINCIPAL COMPETITORS

Athena Neurosciences; Shire PLC; Taro Pharmaceutical Industries Ltd.

FURTHER READING

Burton, Thomas M., "Cyberonics Rebuffs Bid from Medtronic, But Device Maker Is Effectively in Play," *Wall Street Journal,* September 12, 2000, p. B6.

Douglas, Michael, "Cyberonics Prepares Plan to Go Public with Initial Stock Offering," *Houston Business Journal,* February 3, 1992, p. 9.

Forest, Stephanie Anderson, "Epilepsy: The Advance of the Century," *Business Week,* August 4, 1997, p. 36.

Harris, Gardiner, "F.D.A. Staff Tried to Halt a Treatment, But in Vain," *New York Times,* February 17, 2006, p. A14.

Kirsner, Scott, "Fantastic Voyage," *Fast Company,* April 2004, p. 54.

Langreth, Robert, "Rewiring the Brain," *Forbes,* March 5, 2001, p. 160.

Mathews, Anna Wile, "Device to Treat Depression Wins FDA Approval," *Wall Street Journal,* July 18, 2005, p. B4.

McNamara, Victoria, "Houston Company Testing Epilepsy Treatment," *Houston Business Journal,* January 15, 1990, p. 1.

Nocera, Joseph, "A C.E.O. Who Carries a Big Stick," *New York Times,* October 8, 2005, p. C1.

Daiko Advertising Inc.

Nakanoshima Central Tower
2-2-7 Nakanoshima
Kita-ku
Osaka, 530-8263
Japan
Telephone: +81-6-7174-8111
Fax: +81-6-7174-8004
Web site: http://www.daiko.co.jp/en/index.html

Wholly Owned Subsidiary of Hakuhodo DY
Incorporated: 1944
Employees: 1,500
Sales: ¥181.03 billion ($1.52 billion) (2005)
NAIC: 541810 Advertising Agencies

■ ■ ■

Daiko Advertising Inc. is one of Japan's leading advertising agencies, and the largest agency targeting the western Japan market. Since 2003, Daiko also has formed part of Hakuhodo DY, Japan's second largest advertising group, behind market leader Dentsu. Like the other members of Hakuhodo DY, Daiko maintains independent operations, and boasts a number of prominent clients. The company's campaigns include television advertising for Matsushita Electric Industrial Co., the QP food group, Teijin, Suntory, Okinawa Meiji Milk Products, and Nintendo; newspaper campaigns for Asahi Broadcasting, Kubota, Matsushita, and Japan Post; magazine and poster work for Matsushita, Ezaki Glico, and Suntory; and web site advertising work for Nike Japan, among others. In addition to its advertising operations, Daiko provides a full-service offering, including public relations and promotional and event planning services. Daiko's focus remains primarily on the Japanese market; the company has established an international presence, however, targeting the Hong Kong and mainland Chinese markets. In 2006, the company established a new subsidiary in Vietnam, as well as its first wholly owned subsidiary in China, where it previously operated through a joint venture set up in 1995. Since 2000, Daiko has been involved in a partnership with The Interpublic Group of Companies and its Lowe & Partners Worldwide unit, giving Daiko access to some 82 countries worldwide. As part of the Hakuhodo DY, Daiko spun off its media buying operations into a new company, Hakuhodo DY Media Partners Inc., which became Hakuhodo DY's fourth major subsidiary. In 2006, the four companies joined together to form Hakuhodo DY Group i-Business Center, which focuses on advertising and related operations for the digital media market. Hideki Nakao is Daiko's president, and Chairman Takashi Adachi also serves as Hakuhodo DY's vice-chairman. In 2005, Daiko posted total billings of ¥181 billion ($1.5 billion).

JAPANESE ADVERTISING PIONEER IN 1944

Daiko Advertising originated in 1944 when a group of 14 advertising agencies in the Kinki region of western Japan joined together to form Kinki Advertising Corporation. A core member of the group was Kinsuido, however, by then one of the most well-known advertising agencies in the region, established around the dawn of the 20th century, and Daiko itself dated its

COMPANY PERSPECTIVES

Philosophy: As the market environment undergoes massive changes in the 21st century, methods of communication become increasingly important.

Our mission is to generate communications that create corporate and brand value by speaking directly to the hearts and minds of consumers.

Our core belief is that ideas are the bridges between a brand and its consumers. Communications solely focused on "effectiveness" and "efficiency" cannot inspire corporate or brand value: success only comes from exciting ideas that attract attention of consumers, which are drawn from every marketing channel.

Enthused with the bedrock belief that ideas bring success to clients and value to consumers, every member of Daiko is dedicated to the fashioning of creative ideas.

establishment back to 1893. The Japanese advertising industry of the post-World War II period remained relatively small, however; radio broadcasts had begun only in 1925, and the country saw little development in Western-style marketing techniques. Into the 1950s, Kinki limited itself in large part to the print advertising markets, which included purchasing space and placing advertisements in the region's magazines and newspapers.

The introduction of Western-style advertising and marketing techniques in Japan coincided with the launch of television broadcasting in the country, and opened new markets for the country's advertising agencies. While the Japanese government established two public-sector broadcast networks, private sector television networks were in large part owned by the country's print media groups. These in turn often controlled or held major stakes in advertising agencies, which had been responsible for the media group's magazine and newspaper advertising needs. The Kinki company, which adopted the new name of Daiko Advertising in 1960, also followed this pattern, boasting Asahi Shimbun as a major shareholder. That company also controlled Asahi National Broadcasting, the flagship of the Asahi Television Network. Backed by Japan's leading quality newspaper, Daiko emerged as one of the country's leading advertising groups, and became especially prominent in its core Kinki region. Daiko's headquarters remained in Osaka, the major city of the region, but the company also later established headquarters in Tokyo. Another major shareholder for the group was Kinki Nippon Tetsudo, part of the Kinki Group of some 160 companies.

In the early 1960s a new trend developed among Japanese advertising companies. The growing success of Japan's products, and later its brand names, on the international market, opened opportunities for the country's advertising companies to follow their major clients overseas. Rather than establishing their own global networks, however, advertising agencies turned to partnerships with major foreign advertising groups. At the same time, the foreign partnerships enabled the Japanese groups to gain experience working with Western firms entering the Japanese market. In 1960, for example, fast-growing rival and future partner Hakuhodo founded an alliance with McCann-Erickson Worldwide in 1960. That company later became a core member of the The Interpublic Group of Companies, a future shareholder in Daiko. In the meantime, Daiko launched its own international partnership, forming the Grey Daiko agency, in partnership with Grey International Inc. in 1963. This partnership signed up a number of important accounts, including Bristol Myers, Procter & Gamble, Wrigley, Lion, and in the early 1990s, Dell Computer. Like many relationships in the Japanese advertising industry, these partnerships tended to be extremely long-lasting. In Daiko Grey's case, the two founding companies remained partners until Daiko's exit in 1999.

Daiko expanded beyond its core Osaka base during the 1970s and 1980s. The company eventually grew to include offices in most of the country's major markets, including Osaka, Tokyo, Nagoya, Hokkaido, Sendai, and Niigata, supported by a network of branch offices and affiliated companies throughout Japan. By the late 1980s, Daiko had succeeded in capturing the number four position, with billings reported at more than $1.1 billion in 1988. Yet the company continued to trail far behind the clear market leader, Dentsu, and the number two in the market, Hakuhodo.

PARTNERSHIP FOR MARKET SHARE IN THE NEW CENTURY

Daiko remained focused on the domestic market into the 1990s. In this way, the company remained within the trend of the highly conservative Japanese advertising industry, which in large part avoided direct expansion into international markets. Nonetheless, the rapid consolidation of the global advertising industry, itself spurred by the development of large-scale, multinational giants in nearly every industry, encouraged Daiko to take its first steps internationally in the 1990s. The

KEY DATES

1893: The earliest part of Daiko Advertising is founded.
1944: Fourteen companies merge to form Kinki Advertising Corporation in Osaka.
1960: The company changes its name to Daiko Advertising.
1963: The Grey Daiko joint venture is formed with Grey International.
1995: A joint venture in Beijing is opened.
1999: The company exits the Grey Daiko joint venture.
2000: Interpublic acquires 20 percent of Daiko.
2002: Daiko, Hakuhodo, and Yomiko combine management.
2003: Hakuhodo DY is founded; Daiko remains an independent subsidiary.
2005: The company spins off its media business into Hakuhodo DY Media Partners Inc.
2006: The company joins in the creation of Hakuhodo DY Group i-Business Center; Vietnam subsidiary and wholly owned subsidiaries in Beijing and Guanzhou, China, are launched.

company's interests remained more or less limited to the Chinese market, however, where it established a Hong Kong office. In 1995, the company opened an office in Beijing as well, as part of a joint venture in keeping with Chinese rules that prevented foreign advertising agencies from opening wholly owned subsidiaries in that country. Daiko's international operations primarily provided support for its Japanese clients' own expansion into Hong Kong and mainland China.

In 1999, Daiko announced that it was pulling out of the Grey Daiko partnership, selling its nearly 41 percent in that agency in order to find a new international partner. Daiko's opportunity came later that year, when Kinki Nippon Tetsudo decided to sell off as much as 25 percent of its stake in Daiko. Interpublic, through its Lowes subsidiary, quickly stepped up, buying nearly 20 percent of Daiko. Interpublic and Daiko formalized their business alliance in 2000.

By then, however, Daiko had slipped in the ranks of Japan's largest advertising groups, back to fourth position. In the meantime, leader Dentsu had increased its dominance of the Japanese market, far outpacing number two Hakuhodo. At the same time, with the spate of mega-mergers among the global advertising industry at the end of the 20th century, both companies had plummeted in the international rankings. In Daiko's case, the company barely remained in the global top 20, holding on to 19th place.

In response, Hakuhodo, Daiko, and a third company, Yomiko Advertising, ranked number eight in Japan, announced their plans to join together at the end of 2002. By October of the following year, the three companies had integrated their management into a new holding company, Hakuhodo DY, which became the umbrella organization, while the three agencies retained their independent operations. The new company now had nearly caught up to market leader Dentsu, with ¥985 billion in revenues, versus Dentsu's nearly ¥1.4 trillion.

The integration of Hakuhodo continued into 2005, when the three companies spun off their media buying operations into a fourth company, Hakuhodo DY Media Partners Inc. In February 2005, Hakuhodo DY went public, listing on the Tokyo Stock Exchange. By February 2006, the partnership had found a new area of integration, when the four Hakuhodo DY companies joined together to found a new subsidiary, Hakuhodo DY Group i-Business Center. This operation specialized in developing advertising products specifically for the fast-growing digital media market. Hakuhodo DY also acknowledged its intention to continue the integration of its major subsidiaries, with the possibility of creating a single unified structure in the future.

Daiko remained on the lookout for growth opportunities, with a heightened interest in expanding its presence in the Asian market. In April 2006, the company set up a new subsidiary in Ho Chi Minh City, Vietnam. In this way, the company was able to provide support for Japanese companies entering the Vietnamese market. In the meantime, the Chinese government had relaxed its rule governing agency ownership. This allowed Daiko to establish its first wholly owned subsidiary in China, with a first office opened in Beijing. The company also planned to open a second subsidiary, in Guangzhou, by the end of April. As part of one of Japan's top advertising groups, Daiko remained one of the market's oldest and leading players.

M. L. Cohen

PRINCIPAL SUBSIDIARIES

Ad Daiko Nagoya Inc.; Advertising Daiko Gifu Inc.; Asahi Area Advertising Inc.; Chubu Asahi Advertising Inc.; Daiko Communications Asia Co., Ltd.; Daiko Hokuriku Advertising Inc.; Daiko Kobe Inc.; Daiko Kyoto Inc.; Daiko Kyusyu Advertising Inc.; Daiko Mie

Inc.; Daiko Pacific International Advertising Co., Ltd. (China); Daiko West Inc.; Kinki Koukokusha Co., Ltd.; Shanghai Daiko Maocu Advertising Co., Ltd. (China); Shanghai Daiko Maocu Advertising Co., Ltd. Guangzhou Branch (China); Taiyo Seimei Kagoshima Daini Bldg.

PRINCIPAL COMPETITORS

Sony Corporation; Odakyu Electric Railway Company Ltd.; Asatsu-DK Inc.; Dentsu Tec Inc.; DENTSU Inc.; Cyber Communications Inc.; Seven Seas Holdings Company Ltd.; Shinken-AD Company Ltd.; Tokyo Electron Agency Ltd.; Catalina Marketing Japan K.K.; Nippon Oil Trading Corporation.

FURTHER READING

"Daiko Sets Up Beijing Joint Venture," *ADWEEK Eastern Edition,* September 25, 1999, p. 9.

"Hakuhodo DY Holdings Inc., the Second Largest Japanese Advertising Agency, Fetched an Initial Price of ¥7,360 on Its Debut on the Tokyo Stock Exchange Wednesday, Up from the Initial Public Offering Price of ¥6,500," *Jiji,* February 16, 2005.

"Hakuhodo DY Stock Debuts 14% Above IPO Price," *Asia Pulse,* February 17, 2005.

"Hakuhodo, 2 Other Ad Agencies Integrate Management," *Japan Weekly Monitor,* October 6, 2003, p. 10.

Hatfield, Stefano, "Japan's New Ad Agency Group a Player to Be Reckoned With," *Advertising Age,* December 9, 2002, p. 24.

"Japan Ad Agency Daiko Launching Chinese, Vietnamese Units," *AsiaPulse News,* April 3, 2006.

Kilburn, David, "Big in Japan," *Campaign,* May 30, 2003, p. 10.

———, "Daiko Deal Offers IPG Little Spin Off," *Marketing Week,* April 13, 2000, p. 30.

Madden, Normandy, "Hakuhodo Readies Global Growth Plan," *Advertising Age,* May 19, 2003, p. 136.

Nakamoto, Michiyo, "Hakuhodo Joins with Smaller Agencies," *Financial Times,* December 3, 2002, p. 28.

Desnoes and Geddes Limited

214 Spanish Town Road
Kingston, 11
Jamaica
Telephone: (876) 923-9291
Fax: (876) 923-8599
Web site: http://www.redstripebeer.com

Public Subsidiary of Udiam Holdings AB
Incorporated: 1918 as Desnoes & Geddes Company Limited
Employees: 750
Sales: JMD 9.13 billion ($148 million) (2005)
Stock Exchanges: Jamaica
Ticker Symbol: DG
NAIC: 312120 Breweries

■ ■ ■

Desnoes and Geddes Limited (D&G) produces one of Jamaica's best-known exports, Red Stripe beer. It also brews other malt beverages for the local market under the Red Stripe Light, Dragon Stout, Malta (nonalcoholic), Smirnoff Ice, Guinness, and Heineken brand names. Only a small portion of D&G's shares are publicly traded. British beverage group Diageo PLC is the ultimate parent company. It has a 58 percent holding in D&G through Udiam Holdings AB of Sweden.

ORIGINS

Desnoes and Geddes Limited was formed in 1918 by Eugene Peter Desnoes and Thomas Hargreaves Geddes, who combined their two shops into one business. (According to a 75th anniversary retrospective in the *Gleaner,* the two had met earlier while Desnoes was employed as a 12-year-old "door opener" at the West Indies Mineral and Table Water Company.) The firm originally made soft drinks, or "aerated and mineral water," according to its prospectus in the *Gleaner,* but also sold alcoholic beverages shipped in from abroad. D&G was incorporated on July 31, 1918. A notable early product was "Kola Wine."

After about nine years, the pair opened the Surrey Brewery in downtown Kingston. The first Red Stripe beer was produced there in 1928. The famous brand was originally applied to an ale, which was too heavy to suit local tastes. The lager version, which would garner worldwide acclaim, was developed in 1938 by Paul H. Geddes, son of the company founder, and Bill Martindale. The lager would be described as light and refreshing, the perfect complement for the sultry Caribbean climate.

The British government tried taxing the beer in 1935 in order to protect sales of U.K. brews on the island. This proved very unpopular and was soon repealed.

Beer sales took off during World War II due to the influx of Allied soldiers to the island. In 1947, D&G was designated the Jamaican bottler for Pepsi Cola.

Peter S. Desnoes, son of the company founder, became chairman in 1952. He had started with D&G in 1928 as a salesman. A new plant was built to replace the Surrey Brewery in 1958. By this time, the sons of the founders were in charge of the business. In 1960, D&G began bottling Schweppes products under license.

COMPANY PERSPECTIVES

There is a growing appreciation of all things Jamaican. Red Stripe appeals to the trendsetters who say "apart from the quality, we love this beer because it is from a country where the people have rhythm, soul and live life to the fullest." People value the Irie Vibe that is Jamaica. Our strategy will focus primarily on allowing the quality and image of this great Jamaican product to do most of the talking.

Although Jamaica became free of British rule in 1962, one of the empire's fictional heroes would carry the Red Stripe banner to new world audiences. The beer was featured in Ian Fleming's James Bond spy novels and movies beginning with *Dr. No.* At this time, D&G had about 300 employees.

Writing on the occasion of Jamaica's independence, a local columnist referred to the beer as "far beyond the capacity of mere colonial dependence." A new plant was built in Montego Bay in 1966 to satisfy growing demand for soft drinks, which were mainly distributed locally. By 1967, annual profits were JMD 1 million.

1970 PUBLIC OFFERING

Desnoes & Geddes continued to grow and offered 8 percent of its shares to the public in 1970. Proceeds were earmarked to fund a JMD 3 million expansion. At the time, products included several varieties of soft drink, including Jamaica Dry Ginger Ale and a concoction called "Teem," which was produced under license. Turnover exceeded JMD 20 million for the year. In 1973, D&G began brewing Heineken beer through a joint venture with the Dutch brewer. It also started brewing U.K. stout brand Mackeson.

D&G launched the popular Ting Grapefruit Crush soft drink in 1976. The name was Jamaican dialect for "thing." Made with locally sourced grapefruit, it was soon being exported to more than 20 other countries, beginning with Barbados. Ting and Old Jamaica Ginger Beer, another naturally based beverage, were introduced to the United Kingdom in 1988, where they were instantly successful.

Ting's launch in the United States did not go as smoothly, reported the *Associated Press.* In 1985, D&G began exporting the drink to cosmopolitan areas with large ethnic Caribbean populations. Guinness had been unable to register the trademark in the United States, however. Several years later, Kraft General Foods, owner of the Tang brand of drink mix that was famous for going with the astronauts to space, sued D&G for trademark infringement.

Red Stripe beer entered the U.K. market in the late 1970s. A local brewer, Charles Wells of Bedford, made it under license; its distribution would extend to Italy and Spain, according to London's *Financial Times.*

The fortune of company heir Paul H. Geddes was subject to Jamaica's first palimony suit, launched after Geddes left his longtime lover Helga Stoeckert for a much younger American woman. In 1992 Stoeckert filed a claim on JMD 14 million (£200,000) in joint accounts at an English bank. She lost the case after a dozen years of legal arguments that extended as far as the United Kingdom's Privy Council. Geddes died in 1999 at the age of 89, leaving an estate worth $600 million in the charge of his widow, Margie.

Plant capacity was doubled around 1990, one of many expansions over the years. The company employed about 1,200 people at the time. D&G had continued to brew other brands under license. It started making Scottish & Newcastle PLC's new Strong Jamaican Ale around 1991. One of its relationships, however, was about to become much more involved.

GUINNESS CONTROL IN 1993

Guinness PLC, the U.K. beer and spirits giant, acquired a 51 percent holding in D&G for $62 million in September 1993. Civic leaders described it as the largest investment in Jamaica since the 1960s, reported the *Journal of Commerce.* The backing of the Guinness Group, later dubbed Diageo, greatly increased Red Stripe's international distribution.

Guinness had been shipping its own brews to the Caribbean since the early 1800s. D&G was one of a dozen brewers in the West Indies producing its trademark stout under license. D&G also had been producing its own brand, Dragon Stout, since 1961.

According to the *Financial Times,* Red Stripe was the United Kingdom's third favorite packaged lager by the early 1990s. While Red Stripe was popular in certain markets in the United States, such as New York, it was but a tiny player with about 500 competitors, noted the *Associated Press.* The beer's consumption in the United States took a dramatic rise, a reported 60 to 90 percent in one month, following a placement in the Tom Cruise film *The Firm* in the summer of 1993. Author John Grisham had written it into the novel of the same name. The beer also had shown up in another Tom Cruise movie, *Cocktail.*

KEY DATES

1918: Desnoes & Geddes Limited (D&G) is formed to produce soft drinks.
1928: The first Red Stripe beer is produced at D&G's Surrey Brewery.
1947: D&G becomes the Pepsi Cola bottler for Jamaica.
1958: A modern facility is constructed.
1961: Dragon Stout is introduced.
1970: D&G goes public.
1973: D&G begins brewing Heineken under license.
1976: Ting grapefruit drink is launched.
1993: Guinness acquires control of D&G.
1999: D&G divests wine and spirits and soft drink lines.
2003: Marketing spending is increased in the United States and the United Kingdom.
2005: Turnover reaches a record JMD 9 billion ($148 million).

D&G was working to improve productivity in the late 1990s to help it compete with imports. A $25.7 million rights issue was launched in 1997 to fund the expansion. According to Reuters, though D&G controlled 90 percent of the local beer and soft drink markets, Jamaica's rampant inflation was making it hard to stave off lower priced competition.

FOCUS ON BEER IN 1999

In 1999, D&G sold its wine and spirits business to Wray & Nephew Ltd., a Jamaican rum producer. Growing exports helped make up for falling domestic demand in 1999. Total turnover was up 2.6 percent to JMD 6.3 billion.

The local soft drinks business was getting more competitive. In 1999 D&G sold its soda pop plant to the Pepsi Cola (Jamaica) Bottling Company for an estimated $25 million, allowing it to concentrate on the brewing business. According to the *Gleaner,* Ting sales rose more than 200 percent within two years of the PepsiCo affiliate taking it over. Pepsi had invested in new bottling equipment and trucks.

A new product, Red Stripe Light, was introduced in Jamaica in 2000. Group turnover was JMD 5.1 billion in 2001. Pretax profit was $1.3 billion.

The company held a ceremony in February 2001 as its name changed from D&G to Red Stripe Limited. This was, in large part, a marketing gimmick designed to pitch D&G as the "world's coolest beer company." In spite of all the fanfare, the Desnoes & Geddes name remained in use on share certificates and annual reports.

2003 MARKETING PUSH

Whatever it was calling itself, the company doubled its marketing budget in 2003. Red Stripe over-the-top television ads in the United States revolved around the tagline, "Hooray beer!" They featured the brand's dapper "Ambassador of Beer" discussing the brand's merits in amusing situations. This was extended into a two-minute infomercial for late night television to great comedic effect.

The brand's U.K. brewer, Charles Wells Company, was acquiring London rock venues to reinforce a connection with live music. Wells, which had recently won back distribution rights, also was running a press campaign. In Jamaica, D&G was facing a tougher sell, as a 45 percent increase in Jamaica's Special Consumption Tax obliged the company to raise prices on all of its brews except for the nonalcoholic Malta.

D&G's total turnover rose 16 percent in 2005 to JMD 9.1 billion. Exports accounted for JMD 1.9 billion, a 50 percent increase. Gross profit remained a handsome 37 percent of turnover; in 2005 this amounted to JMD 3.4 billion. Pretax profit was JMD 2.5 billion. The company had 750 employees in 2005, 8 percent fewer than the previous year.

The company's main strategic goal was making Red Stripe a truly global brand. A push into Australia and Europe, where it was being relaunched in Sweden and Switzerland, helped raise exports 31 percent for the year. D&G also was investing JMD 378 million in capacity upgrades.

D&G continued to promote its brands at home by investing in sporting and music events. It was the largest single sponsor for soccer in the Caribbean. It sponsored the Jamaican national soccer team, the Reggae Boyz, as well as local clubs. The group invested JMD 18 million in the Red Stripe National Cricket Championship. Support for the massive Red Stripe Reggae Sumfest included the Red Stripe Big Break talent contest.

Frederick C. Ingram

PRINCIPAL SUBSIDIARIES

Foods of Jamaica (Export) Limited; Red Stripe Brewing Company Limited.

PRINCIPAL COMPETITORS

Banks Barbados Breweries Ltd.; Big City Brewing Company Ltd.; Carib Brewery Limited; Heineken N.V.; Labatt Breweries of Canada; Scottish & Newcastle PLC.

FURTHER READING

Beard, David, "Promo in 'The Firm' Produces Heady U.S. Sales of Jamaica's Top Beer," *Associated Press,* September 6, 1993.

Beaumont, Stephen, *Premium Beer Drinker's Guide,* Richmond Hill, Ontario: Firefly Books, 2000.

Bittar, Christine, "Tools of the Trade," *Brandweek,* August 18, 2003.

"Charles Wells Boosts Red Stripe Presence with Rock Venue Buyout," *Marketing Week* (U.K.), February 5, 1998, p. 8.

"The D&G Story," *Gleaner,* Desnoes & Geddes 75th Anniversary Supplement, July 7, 1993.

Davenport, Rosie, "Wells Puts Red Stripe Back on the Map," *Grocer,* February 8, 2003, pp. 50+.

"Desnoes & Geddes—Expansion Plans," *Sunday Gleaner,* November 29, 1970, pp. 21, 29.

"Desnoes & Geddes' Jamaican Ginger Drink Takes Root," *Grocer,* May 25, 1991, p. 76.

Desnoes & Geddes Limited, "Issue and Offer for Sale of 700,000 Ordinary Shares of $1.00 Each at a Price of $1.50 Per Share," *Daily Gleaner,* February 28, 1970, pp. 24–25.

———, "A Salute to Jamaica's Independence," *Times* (London), August 3, 1962, p. xi.

"Desnoes & Geddes Looking Good," *Cana Business,* October 1, 1999.

"Desnoes & Geddes Makes Name Change," *Modern Brewery Age,* December 4, 2000, p. 1.

"The Desnoes & Geddes-Pepsi Story," *Gleaner,* D&G "Pepsi 40" Supplement, May 27, 1987.

Dill, Mallorre, "Simply Red," *Adweek,* August 27, 2001, p. 22.

"From Darkness into Light," *Times* (London), April 26, 1971, p. V.

"Geddes Estate Wins Privy Council Palimony Suit," *Gleaner,* December 15, 2004.

"Geddes Takes on D&G," *Gleaner,* August 24, 2000.

Geitner, Paul, "Moon Drink Takes on Island Soda," *Associated Press,* January 13, 1992.

"Greater Focus on Brewing," *Cana Business,* October 1, 1999.

"Guinness Import Co. and Labatt U.S.A. Trade Key Brands: Red Stripe and Dos Equis," *Modern Brewery Age,* September 18, 1995, p. 1.

James, Canute, "Guinness Buys 51 Percent of Jamaican Brewer for $62 Million," *Journal of Commerce,* September 27, 1993, p. 4A.

K.A. Morgan Ltd., "Red Stripe: Jamaica's Famous Lager!," *Times* (London), advertisement, February 21, 1966, p. viii.

Khermouch, Gerry, "Labatt's Keeps Red Stripe Running with Promos," *Brandweek,* February 7, 1994, p. 11.

"Late Night Infomercial for Red Stripe Beer," *Beverage Aisle,* October 15, 2003, p. 14.

"Light Years of Laughter," *Gleaner,* May 16, 2003.

Luke, Peter D., "Inflation Hurts D&G," *Sunday Gleaner,* May 12, 1974, p. 17.

Rawstorne, Philip, "Guinness Silent on Red Stripe Stake Speculation," *Financial Times* (London), April 27, 1993, p. 25.

———, "Jamaican Purchase to Boost Stout Sales," *Financial Times* (London), September 24, 1993, p. 23.

"A Red Stripe Please! Lifetime Achievement Award," *Jamaica Observer,* June 1, 2003.

"Say Red Stripe Please!," *Gleaner,* February 22, 2001.

"Shareholders of Jamaican Brewer Approve New Stock," *Reuters News,* June 4, 1997.

Smikle, Patrick, "Jamaica: Local Bottler Prevails in Copyright Case," *Interpress Service,* November 5, 1997.

"Ting Launches Silver Anniversary," *Gleaner,* November 26, 2001.

Diageo plc

8 Henrietta Place
London, W1G 0NB
United Kingdom
Telephone: (020) 7927-5200
Fax: (020) 7927-4600
Web site: http://www.diageo.com

Public Company
Incorporated: 1997
Employees: 20,000
Sales: £9.04 billion ($16.18 billion) (2005)
Stock Exchanges: London New York
Ticker Symbols: DGE (London); DEO (New York)
NAIC: 312120 Breweries; 312130 Wineries; 312140 Distilleries

■ ■ ■

Diageo's brands are the platform from which its strategy will be delivered. The company's leadership position in premium drinks is based on its ownership of a number of the world's most important brands. Diageo manages nine of the world's top 20 premium distilled spirits brands as defined by *Impact,* a publication which compiles volume statistics for the international drinks industry.

The consumer appeal of Diageo's brands across broad geographies has enabled the company to build individual market-leading positions in some of the world's most profitable markets for premium drinks. Diageo's global business is managed as three regions, North America, Europe and International, led by market presidents who each report to the chief executive.

Diageo plc is the world's largest producer and marketer of premium spirits. Formed in December 1997 from the merger of Guinness PLC and Grand Metropolitan plc, Diageo (pronounced dee-AH-zhay-oh) manages nine of the world's top 20 premium spirits brands: Smirnoff, Johnnie Walker Red Label, Bailey's, Captain Morgan, J&B, José Cuervo, Gordon's, Johnnie Walker Black Label, and Crown Royal. Diageo leads the spirits market in the United States, Great Britain, Ireland, Russia, Brazil, India, Korea, and Australia. The firm is also a major player in the global beer and wine sectors, the former headed by Guinness stout, Harp Irish lager, Smithwick's ale, and Red Stripe lager and the latter by the Beaulieu Vineyard, Sterling Vineyards, Chalone Vineyards, and Blossom Hill brands. Diageo markets its products in more than 180 countries around the world, with Europe accounting for 43 percent of revenues and North America for 29 percent, while the remaining 28 percent is generated in the globe's other regions. Diageo also holds a 34 percent stake in Moët Hennessy, SNC, the wine and spirits business of LVMH Moët Hennessy Louis Vuitton S.A., a French luxury-goods and drinks giant.

EARLY HISTORY OF GUINNESS

Diageo's history begins with the formation of the Guinness empire. In 1759 Arthur Guinness, an experienced brewer, leased an old brewery at St. James's Gate in Dublin. Besides renting the brewery Guinness signed an unusual 9,000-year lease for a mill, storehouse, stable,

COMPANY PERSPECTIVES

Diageo's strategy is to generate consistent top line growth while enhancing its operating margins and return on invested capital.

house, and two malthouses. As it turned out, in just four years significant quantities of ale and table beer were emerging from the new workplace.

Soon after the brewery was in full operation, Arthur Guinness began to establish a reputation in both business and civic affairs. The company secured an active trade with pubs in towns surrounding Dublin and also became one of the largest employers in the city. As a vocal participant in public life, Guinness supported such diverse issues as penal reform, parliamentary reform, and the discouragement of dueling. Furthermore, although a Protestant, he strongly supported the claims of the Irish Catholic majority for equality.

The business nearly came to an abrupt end in 1775 when a dispute over water rights erupted into a heated exchange between Guinness and the mayor's emissaries. The argument centered around the City Corporation's decision to fill in the channel that provided the brewery with water. When the sheriff's men appeared at St. James's Gate, Guinness grabbed a pickaxe from a workman and with a good deal of "improper language" ordered them to leave. For fear of escalating violence, the parties to the dispute finally settled by means of a tenant agreement.

In 1761 Arthur Guinness married Olivia Whitmore; of the 21 children born to them only ten survived. Since the eldest son became a clergyman, the thriving company was passed on to the second son, Arthur, after the founder's death in 1803. Like his father, Arthur soon became active in both civic and political affairs. He served in the Farming Society of Ireland, the Dublin Society, the Meath Hospital, and the Dublin Chamber of Commerce. Most importantly, as an elected director in the Bank of Ireland, he played a significant role in settling currency issues. In politics, Arthur adhered to his father's beliefs by advocating the claims of the religious majority.

From the very beginning of his career, it appears that Arthur's main concern was not so much in managing the company as in pursuing his banking interests. Nonetheless, brewery records indicate that from the end of the Napoleonic Wars to the end of the Great Famine in 1850, the company's production output increased by 50 percent. For this reason, Arthur is often credited with making the Guinness fortune.

A great deal of that success, of course, can be attributed to Arthur Guinness's decision to shift most of the firm's trade from Ireland to England. Yet the growth of Guinness was a result not only of management's business acumen and the firm's financial strength but also of the myths surrounding the beverage: from its earliest days Guinness stout, a dark and creamy brew, was considered a nutritional beverage and promoter of virility. Although the company was once accused of mashing Protestant Bibles and Methodist hymn books into the brew in order to force ingestion of anti-Papal doctrine, Britain's leading medical journal during the mid-19th century claimed the drink was "one of the best cordials not included in the pharmacopeia." This notion formed the basis of the company's advertisement campaign of 1929, which suggested that drinking Guinness could lead to the development of "strong muscles," "enriched blood," and the alleviation of "exhausted nerves." Somewhat surprisingly, this tradition continued in Britain into the late 20th century, when the national health insurance system was underwriting the purchase of Guinness for nursing mothers.

When Arthur died in 1855, his son, Benjamin Lee, assumed control of the company. Fifty-seven at the time, he had already worked for nearly 30 years at the brewery. During his tenure as head of the firm, the St. James's Gate facility became the preeminent porter brewery in the world. Following the tradition of his family, he was also intimately involved in civic affairs. He was awarded a baronetcy in 1867 for his contributions to the restoration of St. Patrick's Cathedral and other services. He died a year later.

Although in his will Benjamin Lee Guinness divided the responsibility for running the firm equally between his two sons, Edward Cecil and Arthur Edward, Edward soon emerged as the more astute of the two. The younger of the brothers, he was said to be an energetic yet excitable man. His decisions were controversial and, apparently, overwhelming: after eight years Arthur decided to leave the brewing business, and the partnership between brothers was dissolved.

In the tradition of his family, Edward became a leading figure in both civic affairs and in English social life. After his marriage to his cousin Adelaide, he seems to have "arrived," and the young couple circulated freely in elite circles. Among the many dignitaries entertained at their opulent 23,000-acre estate in Suffolk was King Edward VII.

Edward Guinness's wealth, prestige, influence, and philanthropic work eventually earned him the title of Lord Iveagh. He drew heavily from the family fortune

KEY DATES

1759: Arthur Guinness leases an old brewery at St. James's Gate in Dublin, where he soon begins producing Guinness stout.
1886: Guinness becomes a public company and incorporates itself as Arthur Guinness Son and Co. Ltd.
1931: Grand Metropolitan plc (GrandMet) is founded by Maxwell Joseph.
1980: Ernest Saunders becomes the first non-family member to head Guinness.
1982: Guinness is converted to a public limited company under the name Arthur Guinness & Sons PLC.
1986: The newly named Guinness PLC acquires Distillers Company, gaining such liquor brands as Gordon's and Tanqueray gin and Johnnie Walker whiskey.
1987: Saunders is forced out at Guinness for his alleged part in a financial scandal; new head Anthony Tennant restructures the distilling operations as United Distillers; GrandMet's liquor unit, International Distillers & Vintners, is bolstered through the acquisition of Heublein Inc., maker of Smirnoff vodka.
1988: Guinness enters into an alliance with LVMH Moët Hennessy Louis Vuitton S.A.
1989: GrandMet acquires Pillsbury Company, owner of the Pillsbury and Green Giant food brands and the Burger King hamburger chain.
1997: Guinness and GrandMet merge to form Diageo plc; the two firms' liquor units are merged to form United Distillers & Vintners.
2001: Pillsbury is sold to General Mills, Inc.; Diageo and Pernod Ricard SA jointly acquire the Seagram spirits and wine group, with Diageo gaining several major spirits brands (including Captain Morgan and Crown Royal) and Seagram's wine business.
2002: Diageo divests Burger King.
2004: Company is reorganized into three divisions: Diageo Europe, Diageo North America, and Diageo International.

to contribute to worthy causes; he established the Iveagh Trust to provide basic necessities for 950 indigent families and donated money for the continuing restoration of St. Patrick's Cathedral. He was, as well, recognized as an enlightened employer, ahead of his time in providing pension plans, health services, and housing for his employees.

GUINNESS BECOMES PUBLIC COMPANY IN 1886

In 1886 Guinness became a public company (and incorporated itself as Arthur Guinness Son and Co. Ltd.), its shares traded on the London exchange (Dublin, at that time, lacked its own exchange). The company raised £6 million on its shares, and embarked on an ambitious period of expansion in Ireland, England, and abroad. Guinness's unique brewing process ensured that the quality of the product would not be impaired by long voyages to foreign markets. By the 1920s Guinness had reached the shores of East and West Africa and the Caribbean.

In 1927 leadership of the company passed to the next generation. The second Lord Iveagh was recognized primarily for his role in creating a modern brewery at Park Royal in London, built to service the company's growing business in southeast England. The facility became operational in 1936, and it is there that Guinness Extra and Draught Guinness were first brewed for the British market. By 1974 production at this plant exceeded that at St. James's Gate by 100 percent.

Construction of the Park Royal facility was completed under the supervision of a civil engineer named Hugh E. C. Beaver. He formed a close association with Managing Director C. J. Newbold, yet turned down Newbold's invitation to join the Guinness board of directors. After World War II Lord Iveagh personally asked Beaver to join the company as assistant managing director, and this time Beaver accepted. When Newbold died in the late 1940s, Beaver assumed the position of managing director. He is credited with modernizing the company's operations, introducing new management and research policies, increasing exports, and diversifying the company's product base. On his initiative the company was officially divided into Guinness Ireland and Guinness U.K. (control of both concerns remained with a central board of directors).

HARP AND *GUINNESS BOOK OF RECORDS* INTRODUCED

Beaver was also a strong advocate of generating new ideas through brainstorming sessions. One product to emerge from these meetings was Harp lager. When Britons began taking their holidays abroad during the 1950s, they returned home with a new taste for chilled lager. Beaver sensed this changing preference, and during one intensive company meeting, executives decided that Guinness should become the first local firm to market its own lager. Named for the harp on Guinness's traditional label, Harp lager soon became the most successful product in the growing British lager market.

Beaver is also recognized as the founder of the extraordinarily successful publication *Guinness Book of Records,* which appeared for the first time in 1955. Initially created as something of a lark, an aid to settling trivia disputes in pubs, the book was such a success throughout the world that it became a company tradition. By the late 1980s the renamed *Guinness Book of World Records* was selling some five million copies in 13 different languages.

GUINNESS DIVERSIFIES WIDELY: 1960–79

Beaver, now Sir Hugh, retired in 1960, but throughout the next decade Guinness continued to expand, notably abroad, in countries with warm climates. Consistent with this strategy, the company constructed new breweries in Nigeria and Malaysia, then a second and third brewery in Nigeria as well as breweries in Cameroon, Ghana, and Jamaica. Guinness also developed a new product during this period, Irish Ale, which was exported to France and Britain. To offset the declining market for stout, the company began to diversify into pharmaceuticals, confectionery, and plastics, as well as other beverages.

Although both sales and earnings per share had doubled between 1965 and 1971, Guinness entered the 1970s confronting a number of problems. Compared to those of its competitors, the company's shares sold at modest prices, largely because Guinness operated outside the tiedhouse system (the five largest brewers owned and operated most of the country's 100,000 pubs), and investors felt the other breweries had the advantage for growth. The London financial community reasoned that Guinness was at a disadvantage because the company had to absorb the added costs of retailing.

There were also problems at the St. James's Gate brewery. The Park Royal facility continued to outproduce the older Dublin site, and the company and its employees' union reached an agreement whereby the James's Gate workforce would be reduced by nearly one-half. This solution temporarily solved the problem of decreasing profits at the James's Gate facility and allowed operations to continue at the highly esteemed landmark facility. By 1976, however, the cost-cutting plan was seen to have achieved less than had been expected.

Diversification efforts during this period were also less than stellar; the company had gone on a purchasing spree in which 270 companies, producing a wide variety of products from baby bibs to car polish, had been acquired, and many of these companies were operating at a deficit.

Even in the base brewing business, Guinness had its share of troubles. The company's witty advertisements appealed to the middle class but ignored the working class that provided the bulk of Guinness's customers. A new product, designed to combine the tastes of stout and ale, was a £3 million mistake. The Guinness share price continued to decline.

SAUNDERS ERA BRINGS SCANDAL TO GUINNESS: 1980–87

To remedy the company's problems, Guinness executives called in the first non-family professional manager to take over leadership of the company. The sixth Lord Iveagh, as well as numerous Guinness relations, remained on the board, but Ernest Saunders, a former executive at J. Walter Thompson and Nestlé, stepped in as chief executive in 1980.

Saunders saw his first task as reducing the company's disparate holdings. He sold 160 companies, retaining only some retail businesses. He then reduced the workforce and brought in a new management team to develop and market the company's products in addition to investing in increased and more eclectic advertising. He also made canny acquisitions in specialty foods, publishing, and retailing (including the 7-Eleven convenience stores). Brewing, according to Saunders, would in the future comprise only half of Guinness's total volume. Financial analysts, and the City of London in general, were pleased with Saunders's efforts. The Guinness share price began noticeably to climb. In the meantime, the company was converted to a public limited company in 1982 under the name Arthur Guinness & Sons PLC.

By mid-1985 Saunders seemed to have conquered. During his tenure the company's profits had tripled, and its share price increased fourfold. In 1986, when the firm's name was shortened to simply Guinness PLC, Saunders accomplished a dazzling takeover of Distillers Company, gaining such liquor brands as Gordon's and Tanqueray gin and Johnnie Walker whiskey. That Guinness could, and would, pay £2.5 billion ($4.6 billion) for a company twice its size surprised many industry analysts, yet Saunders's wish to create a multinational company on the scale of Nestlé seemed to justify the expense. There were rumors that Saunders might be honored with a knighthood.

Within a matter of months, however, there were other kinds of rumors in the City, rumors concerning

Saunders's methods in pursuing the Distillers acquisition. In order to make the takeover possible, Saunders with two of his fellow directors, allegedly had orchestrated an international scheme to provoke the sale of Guinness shares and thereby raise their value. Outside investors were indemnified in various ways against any losses incurred in purchasing huge numbers of Guinness shares. Bank Leu in Switzerland purchased Guinness shares with the understanding that the company would eventually buy them back. In return, Guinness deposited $75 million (in a non-interest-earning account) with the bank. The bank's chairman happened to be Saunders's ex-boss at Nestlé and a Guinness board member. Ivan F. Boesky, the American arbitrageur who later admitted to insider trading in numerous deals, was cited as the primary source of information about the Distillers takeover. It was believed that Boesky himself played a large role in the takeover; Guinness made a $100 million investment in a limited partnership run by Boesky only one month after Boesky had made significant purchases of Guinness shares. Further investigation revealed that Boesky was seemingly only one of many international investors who bought Guinness shares in an effort to increase their value. The company's auditors discovered some $38 million worth of invoices for "services" rendered by various international investors during the takeover.

In December 1986 the British Trade and Industry Department instigated an investigation of Guinness. In January 1987 the Guinness board of directors asked for Saunders's resignation, and subsequently, in March, brought legal action against Saunders and one of his fellow directors, John Ward. In May the British government brought charges of fraud against Saunders: the claim was that Saunders knowingly destroyed evidence during the Trade and Industry Department investigation. Throughout these events, Saunders continued to deny all charges brought against him. In 1990, however, he was convicted of fraud and sentenced to two years in jail. Nine months into his incarceration he was released on the basis of a medical report claiming that he might be in the early stages of Alzheimer's disease. Subsequently, he twice tried and failed to have his conviction overturned on appeal. In December 1996 the European Court of Human Rights ruled that Saunders's rights had been violated during his trial, but it did not clear his name.

GUINNESS FOCUSES ON BREWING AND DISTILLING

Meanwhile, the survival of Guinness as an independent company was in peril. The company's share price tumbled as a result of the continuing scandal. To prevent any further decline, Anthony Tennant, Guinness's new chief executive, refocused the company on two core areas, brewing and distilling, jettisoning the bulk of the businesses outside these areas (a notable exception to all of the company's various purges of the later 20th century was the *Guinness Book of Records*). Tennant, along with Tony Greener, managing director of distilling operations, overhauled the unit, which was eventually renamed United Distillers, getting rid of numerous marginal brands and centralizing operations that had been organized into numerous separate companies. Distillers was also bolstered by the September 1987, $555 million acquisition of Schenley Industries Inc., which held the U.S. rights to Dewar's and Gordon's gin. Guinness further tightened its grip on the all-important distribution side of the liquor business through joint ventures, most notably a 1988 agreement with LVMH Moët Hennessy Louis Vuitton S.A., a French drinks and luxury-goods manufacturer. By 1989 each company had gained a 24 percent stake in the other, although Guinness's holding in LVMH was indirect.

In 1990 Guinness's brewing unit was beefed up through the acquisition of La Cruz Del Campo, the largest brewer in Spain, for £518 million. Two years later, Greener succeeded the retiring Tennant as chief executive. The company's alliance with LVMH was restructured in 1994 so that Guinness held a direct 34 percent stake in LVMH's Moët Hennessy champagne and cognac division, while LVMH's stake in Guinness was reduced to 20 percent (and by 1997 to about 14 percent). The following year Guinness sold 37 U.S. domestic liquor brands and two production facilities to Barton Inc., a division of Canandaigua Wine Company, for £111 million ($171 million), as part of an effort to concentrate on premium high-priced brands. Back on the brewing side, the early to mid-1990s saw Guinness build its flagship brand by helping investors around the world open up Irish-style pubs. The company did not own any of these houses, but encouraging their establishment helped to create a growing market for the quintessentially Irish Guinness stout.

In July 1996 Guinness denied that it was planning a takeover of Grand Metropolitan or considering divesting its brewing unit. Less than a year later, however, the two companies announced the merger that in late 1997 would create Diageo plc. In 1996, Guinness posted revenue of £4.73 billion and record profits before tax and exceptionals of £975 million.

GRAND METROPOLITAN FOCUSES ON FOOD AND DRINKS

Much like Guinness, Grand Metropolitan (GrandMet) had diversified widely in the 1970s and 1980s, before settling on a portfolio of food and beverage brands by the late 1980s. The company's roots extended to the early 1930s with founder Maxwell Joseph's investments in real estate. GrandMet eventually developed into a powerful European hotel firm; however, the last of the company's hotels were sold in the late 1980s. In the 1970s branded food businesses, restaurants and pubs, breweries, and distilling operations were acquired. The breweries were divested in 1991, while the restaurants and pubs were sold off piecemeal from 1989 to 1995. Other peripheral businesses acquired along the way included the U.S.-based Pearle Vision chain of optical shops, which were sold to Cole National Corp. in November 1996.

Under the leadership of Allen Sheppard, who became chief executive in 1987, and his eventual successor George J. Bull, GrandMet made three significant acquisitions of U.S.-based firms from 1987 through 1995. The brands and businesses gained thereby formed the very heart of the company that merged with Guinness. In 1987 GrandMet bolstered its liquor unit, International Distillers & Vintners, by acquiring Heublein Inc. from RJR Nabisco for £800 million ($1.3 billion), gaining such brands as Smirnoff vodka, Arrow liqueurs, and Harvey's Bristol Cream sherry in the process. Two years later, GrandMet completed a £3.2 billion ($5.68 billion) hostile takeover of Pillsbury Company, which featured the Pillsbury baked goods brand, the Green Giant vegetables brand, the Häagen-Dazs ice cream brand, and the Burger King hamburger chain, which Pillsbury had acquired in 1967. GrandMet in 1995 paid £1.8 billion ($2.6 billion) for Pet, Inc., which produced most notably the line of Old El Paso Mexican-food products, as well as Progresso soups.

By early 1997, when Bull was serving as chairman and John McGrath as chief executive, GrandMet had narrowed its packaged-food focus to four core international brands: Pillsbury, Green Giant, Häagen-Dazs, and Old El Paso. The company had by that time completed the sale of its various European-branded food businesses. For 1996, Grand Metropolitan posted revenues of £8.73 billion and profits before tax and exceptionals of £965 million.

DIAGEO FORMED IN DECEMBER 1997

In May 1997 Guinness and Grand Metropolitan announced that they would merge to form a new company, tentatively called GMG Brands. Seven months later the £12 billion ($19 billion) merger, the largest in U.K. history to that point, had been finalized, but not before a five-month battle with LVMH had ended peacefully. LVMH agreed to drop its opposition to the merger in return for receipt of £250 million upon the merger's consummation; the merged entity would retain Guinness's 34 percent stake in LVMH's Moët Hennessy champagne and cognac division, while LVMH would hold about 11 percent of the new company. Guinness and GrandMet also had to agree to divest the Dewar's Scotch whiskey and Bombay gin brands in order to gain approval from U.S. and European regulators. In late March 1998, the merged company, now named Diageo plc, announced an agreement to sell these brands to Bermuda-based Bacardi Ltd. for £1.15 billion ($1.94 billion) in cash. The name "Diageo" had been derived from the Latin "dia" (day) and the Greek "geo" (world). The company explained that the name was supposed to convey that "every day, all around the world, millions of people enjoy our brands."

Diageo was centered on brands. At its founding, the company had four main businesses: United Distillers & Vintners (UDV), Pillsbury, Guinness, and Burger King. UDV (which generated about 45 percent of overall revenue) was a combination of the numerous leading liquor brands of Guinness's United Distillers unit and GrandMet's International Distillers & Vintners unit; UDV became the world's number one distiller upon its formation. Pillsbury (29 percent) retained GrandMet's four packaged-food megabrands: Pillsbury, Green Giant, Häagen-Dazs, and Old El Paso. Guinness (18 percent) included such stellar brewing brands as Guinness, Harp, Kilkenny, Cruzcampo of Spain, Red Stripe, and Kaliber. Burger King (8 percent) trailed only McDonald's among the world's hamburger chains. Bull and Greener were named cochairmen of Diageo, while McGrath became Diageo's first chief executive.

As the integration of the liquor operations progressed in the late 1990s, Diageo saw its results hampered by the successive financial crises that hit Asia, Russia, and Latin America. In order to focus more on its top-selling international brands, Diageo sold a number of regional and national brands in 1998 and 1999, including eight Canadian whiskey brands (Black Velvet among them), Christian Brothers brandy, and Cinzano vermouth. Diageo also sold Cruzcampo, the Spanish brewing business, to Heineken N.V. in January 2000. On the new product front, Diageo introduced Guinness Draught in a Bottle in 1999, and that same year Smirnoff Ice was launched first in Britain and then in Ireland, the Canary Islands, Australia, and South Africa. The latter was a ready-to-drink vodka-and-lemon beverage that became a huge hit as part of the burgeoning "malternative" category, that is, alternatives to beer. Smirnoff Ice also proved popular in the U.S. market following its introduction there in January 2002 despite the fact that it contained no vodka in order to conform to state sales restrictions.

REFOCUSING ON PREMIUM DRINKS

By 2000 Diageo had endured three years of criticism from analysts unimpressed by the outcome of the Grand Met–Guinness merger. The company's sales were sluggish and its share price was sinking. A new management team took over that year, led by Lord Blyth, chairman of the Boots Company PLC, who was named nonexecutive chairman, and Paul Walsh, the new chief executive, who had previously headed Pillsbury. Walsh immediately began shaking up the firm. UDV and Guinness were combined into a single beverage division, Guinness UDV. More dramatically, Walsh narrowed the company to a single focus: premium drinks. In mid-2000 Diageo announced plans to divest both Pillsbury and Burger King. Pillsbury was ultimately sold to General Mills, Inc. in October 2001 for about $6 billion in stock and the assumption of $5.1 billion in debt. Diageo emerged with a 33 percent stake in General Mills, but by late 2005 Diageo had completely divested this holding. In December 2002, meantime, Diageo completed its exit from the food industry with the sale of Burger King to a consortium led by Texas Pacific Group Inc. in a £940 million ($1.5 billion) deal. Also divested during this period was the Guinness World Records business, which was sold in July 2001 to Gullane Entertainment for £45.5 million ($64.5 million).

As this refocusing on liquor, beer, and wine played out, Walsh simultaneously bolstered Diageo's core by joining with Pernod Ricard SA in an acquisition of the Seagram spirits and wine group from Vivendi Universal S.A. The purchase price totaled £5.62 billion ($8.15 billion), with Diageo contributing £3.7 billion ($5.4 billion). Diageo gained ten major spirits brands, including Captain Morgan rum, Crown Royal Canadian whiskey, Seagram's 7 Crown American whiskey, and Seagram's VO Canadian whiskey, as well as Seagram's wine business. The acquisition boosted the company's share of the U.S. liquor market from 16 percent to 25 percent and gave it a leading 29 percent share of the global market, with a portfolio featuring ten of the world's 20 top-selling spirits. In order to gain clearance from the U.S. Federal Trade Commission for the deal, which closed in December 2001, Diageo agreed to sell its Malibu rum brand. Malibu was sold to Allied Domecq PLC in May 2002 for approximately $796 million.

In the wake of the Seagram deal, Diageo launched an ambitious overhaul of its U.S. distribution system through which it aimed to have dedicated sales teams in each state. In September 2004 the company reorganized itself into three divisions (Diageo Europe, Diageo North America, and Diageo International), scrapping the Guinness UDV name. Several smaller-scale acquisitions followed. In February 2005 the Chalone Wine Group was acquired for £153 million ($285 million), giving Diageo a group of high-end wineries based in California with properties there, in Washington State, and in France. Chalone was subsequently merged into Diageo's North American wine business, Diageo Chateau & Estate Wines. Diageo also acquired the Old Bushmills Distillery Company Limited, the oldest licensed distillery in the world, dating back to 1608, and owner of Bushmills Irish whiskey, one of the world's leading Irish whiskey brands. This £200 million deal with Pernod Ricard closed in August 2005. Diageo shuttered its Park Royal brewery in London in June 2005, transferring its production of Guinness for the U.K. market to its St. James's Gate brewery in Dublin.

Updated, David E. Salamie

PRINCIPAL SUBSIDIARIES

Diageo Ireland; Diageo Great Britain Limited; Diageo Scotland Limited; Diageo Brands BV (Netherlands); Diageo North America, Inc. (U.S.A.); Diageo Capital plc; Diageo Finance plc; Diageo Capital BV (Netherlands); Diageo Finance BV (Netherlands); Diageo Investment Corporation (U.S.A.).

PRINCIPAL DIVISIONS

Diageo Europe; Diageo International; Diageo North America.

PRINCIPAL COMPETITORS

Pernod Ricard SA; Bacardi & Company Limited; Brown-Forman Corporation; Fortune Brands, Inc.; Heineken N.V.; SABMiller plc; Molson Coors Brewing Company; Carlsberg A/S.

FURTHER READING

Banks, Howard, "We'll Provide the Shillelaghs," *Forbes,* April 8, 1996, p. 68.

Beck, Ernest, "Bacardi to Buy Dewar's Label, Bombay Gin," *Wall Street Journal,* March 31, 1998, p. A18.

———, "Diageo Tries to Keep Its Spirits Up in Face of Falling Revenue and Volume," *Wall Street Journal,* March 17, 1999, p. B9B.

———, "Liquor Giants Brew New Name in Greek, Latin," *Wall Street Journal,* October 30, 1997, pp. B1, B11.

Beck, Ernest, and Jennifer Ordonez, "Diageo's Menu Brings Indigestion: Pillsbury, Burger King Clash with Success of Guinness, Johnnie Walker Brands," *Wall Street Journal,* May 12, 2000, p. B1.

Beck, Ernest, Tara Parker Pope, and Elizabeth Jensen, "GrandMet, Guinness to Form Liquor Colossus," *Wall Street Journal,* May 13, 1997, pp. B1, B8.

Blackwell, David, "Guinness Sells US Brands and Plants in $171m Deal," *Financial Times,* August 30, 1995, p. 17.

Brady, Rosemary, "Beyond the Froth," *Forbes,* March 28, 1983, p. 171.

Branch, Shelly, "Diageo, Pernod Sort Out Seagram Terms with Deal to Pay $8.15 Billion for Unit," *Wall Street Journal,* December 20, 2000, p. B10.

Branch, Shelly, Jonathan Eig, and Ernest Beck, "FTC Promises to Block Sale of Seagram," *Wall Street Journal,* October 24, 2001, p. A3.

Brown, Heidi, "Liquor Quicker," *Forbes,* April 15, 2002, pp. 114, 116.

Davidson, Andrew, "Paul Walsh," *Management Today,* September 2004, pp. 40–45.

Dennison, S. R., and Oliver MacDonagh, *Guinness, 1886–1939: From Incorporation to the Second World War,* Cork, Ireland: Cork University Press, 1998, 282p.

Deogun, Nikhil, and Jonathan Eig, "General Mills Agrees to Acquire Pillsbury," *Wall Street Journal,* July 17, 2000, p. A4.

"Diageo: The Morning After," *Economist,* December 12, 1998, pp. 64–65.

Donlon, J. P., "Blithe Spirits," *Chief Executive,* April 1992, p. 34.

Ellison, Sarah, and Robert Frank, "FTC Backs Diageo's Deal for Seagram's Liquor Unit," *Wall Street Journal,* December 20, 2001, p. B2.

Flynn, Julia, and Laura Zinn, "Absolut Pandemonium: As Liquor Sales Fall, Companies Are Battling for Premium Brands," *Business Week,* November 8, 1993, pp. 58–59.

Frank, Robert, "European Moguls Slug It Out U.S. Style," *Wall Street Journal,* August 4, 1997, p. A14.

Goldsmith, Charles, "Prefab Irish Pubs Sell Pints World-Wide," *Wall Street Journal,* October 25, 1996, pp. B1, B8.

"Grand Metropolitan: A British Giant Expands into U.S. Consumer Markets," *Business Week,* August 24, 1981, pp. 54+.

Guinness, Jonathan, *Requiem for a Family Business,* London: Macmillan, 1997, 390 p.

Heller, Robert, "Guinness's 'Brand New' Strategy," *Management Today,* December 1996, p. 25.

Jack, Andrew, "Adieu As Burger King Goes Off Menu in France," *Financial Times,* July 30, 1997, p. 1.

Jackson, Tony, "A New Spirit Is Brought into the World," *Financial Times,* May 13, 1997, p. 25.

Jackson, Tony, and John Ridding, "Heady Cocktail with Lots of Fizz," *Financial Times,* January 21, 1994, p. 17.

John, Peter, "Monster Plies U.S. As Europe Sobers Up," *Financial Times,* September 3, 2004, p. 21.

Jones, Adam, "Diageo Gives Back-up As Deal Clinched to Sell BK," *Financial Times,* December 14, 2002, p. 12.

Khermouch, Gerry, and Kerry Capell, "Spiking the Booze Business: Diageo's Bold Tactics Could Upend the Industry in the U.S.," *Business Week,* May 19, 2003, pp. 77–78.

Kirkland, Richard I., Jr., "Britain's Own Boesky Case," *Fortune,* February 16, 1987, p. 85.

Kochan, Nick, and Hugh Pym, *The Guinness Affair: Anatomy of a Scandal,* London: Helm, 1987, 198 p.

Lee, Peter, "Bending the Rules Till They Break," *Euromoney,* February 1987, p. 120.

Machan, Dyan, "A Liquid Lunch," *Forbes,* September 20, 1999, pp. 144–46.

Marcom, John, Jr., "The House of Guinness," *Forbes,* June 12, 1989, p. 85.

Maremont, Mark, and Amy Dunkin, "Guinness: A Lesson in Dealing with Drier Times," *Business Week,* June 27, 1988, pp. 52–54.

Mason, John, and Robert Rice, "Way Cleared for Saunders to Fight On," *Financial Times,* December 18, 1996, p. 10.

"Master of the Bar: Grand Metropolitan and Guinness," *Economist,* May 17, 1997, p. 70.

McInnes, Neil, "'Power and Goodness': They've Kept Arthur Guinness Son Flourishing for Over 200 Years," *Barron's,* December 11, 1972, pp. 9+.

Moss, Nicholas, and Charles Masters, "Merger on the Rocks," *European,* July 31, 1997, p. 8.

Murphy, Chris, "GrandMet Tries to Regain Its Concentration," *Marketing,* July 11, 1996, p. 16.

Oram, Roderick, "Finn's Tune Takes Time to Strike the Right Chord," *Financial Times,* November 9, 1995, p. 29.

———, "GrandMet Focuses on Core Brands," *Financial Times,* September 6, 1996, p. 17.

———, "Guinness Rules Out GrandMet Bid and Option for Demerger," *Financial Times,* July 8, 1996, p. 1.

———, "Resisting the Calls for a Flash of Pure Genius," *Financial Times,* July 8, 1996, p. 19.

———, "Sweeping the Shelves Clean," *Financial Times,* September 6, 1996, p. 19.

———, "An Unfinished Masterpiece," *Financial Times,* February 19, 1996, p. 17.

Palmer, Jay, "Stout Fellow: A New Head Man Brews Up a Recovery at Guinness," *Barron's,* March 4, 1991, pp. 12–13.

Racanelli, Vito J., "Diageo: Slipping from the Top Shelf," *Barron's,* January 31, 2005, p. MW9.

Rawstorne, Philip, "Guinness Restructures Alliance with LVMH," *Financial Times,* January 12, 1994, pp. 1, 18.

———, "Pure Genius Needed to Maintain Growth," *Financial Times,* December 12, 1992, p. 12.

Reier, Sharon, "Getting Scotch Off the Rocks," *Financial World,* August 6, 1991, p. 25.

Rembold, Kristin Staby, "Grand Met: $5.5 Billion British Giant Continues to Build and Diversify Its Foodservice-Lodging Empire, *Restaurants and Institutions,* May 15, 1981, pp. 90+.

Rice, Robert, "Success by Stealth," *Financial Times,* January 13, 1998, p. 12.

Seneker, Harold, "Watch Out, Seagram," *Forbes,* May 19, 1986, p. 200.

Sherrid, Pamela, "Britain's Business Elite Takes a Fall," *U.S. News & World Report,* February 2, 1987, p. 47.

"Stout Fellows," *Economist,* June 9, 1990, pp. 66, 68.

"A Stout Rebound for Guinness," *Business Week,* February 14, 1983, p. 42.

Syedain, Hashi, "Spirits Are Good for You: Guinness Has Now Emerged from Some Very Dark Times in the Company's History to Enjoy a More Golden Age," *Management Today,* October 1990, p. 64.

———, "Tony Greener," *Management Today,* September 1993, p. 48.

van de Vliet, Anita, "How Guinness Got Goodness," *Management Today,* May 1985, pp. 50+.

Wiggins, Jenny, "Diageo Gains a Shot at the Irish Whiskey Market," *Financial Times,* June 7, 2005, p. 20.

———, "Diageo Seeks Ways to Lift Its Spirits amid Poor European and U.S. Demand," *Financial Times,* February 16, 2006, p. 22.

Wilke, John R., "Grand Met and Guinness to Shed Lines," *Wall Street Journal,* December 3, 1997, pp. A3, A6.

Willman, John, "Adversaries Toast Outbreak of Peace," *Financial Times,* October 14, 1997, p. 24.

———, "Diageo Tops Global Spirits League Table," *Financial Times,* February 18, 1998, p. 36.

———, "Remarkably Relaxed and in Control of His Destiny," *Financial Times,* December 17, 1997, p. 25.

———, "Walsh Welcomed As New Chief of Diageo," *Financial Times,* October 8, 1999, p. 24.

Willman, John, Andrew Jack, and Emma Tucker, "LVMH Chairman Drops Opposition to Drinks Link-Up," *Financial Times,* October 14, 1997, pp. 1, 22.

Wilson, Derek A., *Dark and Light: The Story of the Guinness Family,* London: Weidenfeld & Nicolson, 1998, 319 p.

Diehl Stiftung & Co. KG

Stephanstr 49
Nuremberg,
Germany
Telephone: +49 0911 9 47 0
Fax: +49 0911 9 47 34 29
Web site: http://www.diehl.com

Private Company
Incorporated: 1902
Employees: 10,500
Sales: EUR 1.7 billion ($2.02 billion) (2005)
NAIC: 331111 Iron and Steel Mills; 332996 Fabricated Pipe and Pipe Fitting Manufacturing; 333512 Machine Tool (Metal Cutting Types) Manufacturing; 333513 Machine Tool (Metal Forming Types) Manufacturing; 334419 Other Electronic Component Manufacturing; 334518 Watch, Clock, and Part Manufacturing; 335999 All Other Miscellaneous Electrical Equipment and Component Manufacturing; 336412 Aircraft Engine and Engine Parts Manufacturing

■ ■ ■

Diehl Stiftung & Co. KG is one of Germany's major diversified industrial manufacturing companies. Based in Nuremberg, Diehl operates on an international level through three primary divisions: VA Systeme, Diehl Metall, and Diehl Controls. VA Systeme is the company's largest division, accounting for nearly 41 percent of its total revenues of EUR 1.7 billion ($2.02 billion) per year. The companies in the VA Systeme division produce ammunition, artillery rockets, fuses, guided missiles, and surveillance and warning systems; cockpit, aircraft cabin, and related display and utility systems; and flight and engine control equipment. The company, through subsidiary Diehl BGT Defence and others, has long been a major defense contractor for NATO and the United States, producing the Sidewinder missile, among others. Defense contracts continue to account for 33 percent of Diehl's total revenues. Under Diehl Metall, the group includes semifinished steel and metal products, including aluminum strips, copper and copper alloy cables, and wires; and brass and light alloys products, including keyblanks, profiles, tubes, and synchronizer rings. The Diehl Metall division, which includes a production joint venture in Wuxi, Jiangshu, China, and subsidiaries Griset SA in France and The Miller Company in the United States, accounts for 31.5 percent of group sales. Diehl Controls is a world-leading manufacturer of controls for home appliances, cooking equipment, thermostats, and other products, and represents 16 percent of group sales. Founded in 1902, Diehl remains 100 percent owned by the Diehl family; Thomas Diehl, great-grandson of the founders, serves as group chief executive officer.

FOUNDING A METAL WORKSHOP: 1902

Diehl's origins lay in the production of decorative fittings, including plaques, and wrought-iron and cast-iron fittings such as door handles. Founded by Heinrich and Margarete Diehl in Nuremberg in 1902, the company's production soon expanded to include semifinished items,

COMPANY PERSPECTIVES

Diehl Stiftung & Co. KG is one of the largest German corporations with an international orientation. 10,500 employees in more than forty independent companies, making up the three Divisions, Metall, Controls and VA Systems, are generating profits exceeding 1.7 billion Euros. The company has been an entirely family-run enterprise since its foundation one hundred years ago.

such as brass rods. With the outbreak of World War I, Diehl turned its production to the German war effort, producing shells for artillery and other ammunition. By 1917, the company had built a second, dedicated plant for its shell and related cast metal and casing production. In the interwar years, the company expanded again, adding an extrusion press in 1920, which enabled it to extend its production of rods, and add the production of tubes as well. The company emerged as a major producer of semifinished products for the German automotive and railroad industries, as well as a leading supplier to the plumbing market.

The Diehls were joined by son Karl, who quickly emerged as the driving force behind the company's expansion. The younger Diehl launched the company's shift from relatively unsophisticated semifinished products to a new range of mechanical precision products, such as watch and clock movements. The company set up this operation in a third factory in Nuremberg, which became the Diehl headquarters in 1937. Diehl continued to expand its semifinished products side, opening a new factory in Rothernbach in 1938. Founder Heinrich Diehl died that year, and son Karl took over as head of the company. By then, Diehl already counted nearly 3,000 employees.

Diehl entered a dark period during the war, when, classified as a strategic business, the company again turned its production to the German war effort. The company launched production of ammunition and fuses at this time, both of which would remain important products for the group. During the war, in order to supplement its workforce, Diehl also began using prisoner-of-war labor, and then slave laborers. (Diehl denied its use of slave forced labor during the war until the late 1990s.) By the end of the war, much of the company's production capacity had been destroyed.

POST-WORLD WAR II EXPANSION

The company rebuilt its factories in the aftermath of the war and in the immediate postwar period produced cookware. By 1946, however, the company had already resumed its production of mechanical components. Diehl now went further than producing simply the components for clocks, and in 1947 the company launched its first fully manufactured clock. This production led the company to develop a new branch of operations, and during the 1950s, the company also began producing calculators, preset timers, and other timepieces. In the early 1950s, Diehl took over development of the Archimedes brand of calculating machines. The company's first calculating machine debuted in 1952 and featured some 2,800 parts. The company quickly introduced a fully automatic version, and by the beginning of the 1960s had established itself as one of the world's leading producers of calculating machines.

In the meantime, Diehl's experience producing fuses and ammunition during the war enabled it to redevelop this activity again in the postwar era, with the formation of the Bundeswehr. As such, during the 1950s, Diehl already laid the basis for its three core divisions.

Diehl's drive to diversify its operations also led it to make the first of a number of acquisitions, including a majority control of Junghans, a timepiece specialist based in Schramberg, in 1957. The company added production of brass fittings in 1958, with the acquisition of Sundwiger Messingwerk, originally founded in 1698. The following year, the company bought a foundry, Remscheid Backhaus, followed by the purchase of a foundry in Mariahutte in 1960. Diehl continued to look for new diversification opportunities as well. In 1959, for example, the company launched an aircraft maintenance subsidiary. The company also succeeded in producing the world's first battery-driven timepiece, the "Mini Clock," that year.

Timepieces and calculating machines formed a major part of the group's operations into the early 1960s. Yet the company had already recognized a need to adapt to the future, noting the potential of the fast-developing electronics industry, and the threat the new technology posed to its mechanically driven components. As such, Diehl launched its own Data Technology and Text Systems operation in 1960, and began developing its own electronic products, notably in the fields of data and word processing. Diehl also began adapting its timepiece production, phasing out its mechanical movements in favor of new quartz crystal-based movements. The group slowly phased out its mechanical component operations, ending production of the last of its mechanical calculator line in 1972.

KEY DATES

1902: Heinrich and Margarete Diehl establish art foundry in Nuremberg.
1920: Company launches semifinished products business; begins production of metal rods and tubes.
1934: Karl Diehl joins company and leads it into production of precision mechanical components.
1939: Diehl begins production of fuses and ammunition for German military.
1947: Company enters clockmaking.
1952: Company produces first calculating machine.
1955: Company begins production for defense industry.
1957: Diehl acquires Junghans, a timepiece maker.
1973: Company phases out precision mechanical products division in favor of developing electronics business; founds Timer and Data Equipment division.
1975: Diehl acquires Eurostil, an integrated circuits maker in the United States.
1979: Company acquires Mauser Werke, adding subsidiaries in France and the Netherlands.
1989: Company forms Control Division; acquires Bodenseewerk Geratetechnik.
1993: Company acquires VDO Luftfahrtgerate in Frankfurt.
1994: Diehl acquires AKO Werke, becoming leading maker of control systems for European appliance industry.
1997: Diehl acquires Griset, semifinished products manufacturer in France.
1998: Company is renamed Diehl Stiftung & Co.
1999: Diehl opens plant in Shenzhen, China.
2000: Diehl acquires The Miller Company in the United States, and becomes world-leading producer of phosphor bronze strips.
2002: Diehl celebrates 100th anniversary.
2003: Company forms subsidiary in Kuwait.
2004: Company opens new control system manufacturing plant in Mexico.
2006: Diehl opens avionics development center in Rostock, Germany.

By then, Diehl had already established itself as a leading manufacturer of quartz-based and electronic-drive timepieces, a position that was highlighted when the company, through its Junghans subsidiary, was selected to provide the timekeeping equipment for the 1972 Munich Olympic Games. The following year, Diehl established a dedicated Timers and Data Equipment division.

DIVERSIFIED INDUSTRIAL GROUP

Diehl added a number of new acquisitions in the 1970s. In 1975, for example, the company purchased Konstanz-based CTM Computer Technik Muller, as well as majority control of Eurosil, based in the United States, which specialized in the production of integrated circuits. In 1977, Diehl purchased Emde KG, based in Bremerhaven, which specialized in rubber-metal components. Two years later, Diehl added Mauser Werke Oberndorf, which included subsidiaries in France and the Netherlands. By then, Diehl had also added a subsidiary in Brazil.

Diehl's control business began taking shape in the late 1970s and early 1980s as well. A significant step in this market came in 1977, when Diehl debuted its first electronic stove timer. The company quickly emerged as a leading producer of control systems for a variety of home appliances. In support of this, Diehl launched a dedicated controls division at the end of the decade, building a new headquarters and production facility for the division in Nuremberg in 1989. The company's developing control business was aided by its status as one of the world's timepiece innovators. For example, in 1984, Diehl unveiled the world's first solar clock, and also, through Junghans, produced its first clock that could be set and controlled remotely. By 1993, Junghans succeeded in combining and miniaturizing the two technologies, presenting a solar-powered, radio-controlled wristwatch, the Mega Solar.

Diehl's defense production was also preparing to undergo a transformation. The fading of the Cold War during the 1980s led to a drop in the group's traditional ammunition orders. In response, Diehl adapted its electronics expertise to its defense work, and began developing its capacity in guided missile production. This led to construction of a new automated factory for the production of the Multiple Launch Rocket System (MLRS) in 1988. Diehl further expanded its defense division with the acquisition of Bodenseewerk Geratetechnik in 1989, Friesen's IWS Industriewerke Saar in 1992, and then VDO Luftfahrtgerate, based in Frankfurt, in 1993. These acquisitions, which placed the company as the prime contractor for the NATO's AIM-9L air-to-air missile, helped refocus Diehl's defense operations onto the avionics and aerospace markets. Diehl began producing Sidewinder missiles under license through the 1990s as well. By the end of the decade, the group's defense and avionics operations, regrouped under the VA Systeme division, had become the largest part of its diversified businesses.

Diehl's Control Systems subsidiary achieved a major breakthrough in 1994 when the company acquired home appliance control maker AKO-Werke, based in Wangen, in 1994. As a result, Diehl emerged as one of the leading European producers of control mechanisms to the white goods. In addition to AKO's Wangen headquarters and production plant, the purchase also brought the company a new production facility in Kisslegg.

Diehl continued developing its semifinished products operations as well. In 1995, the company launched production of cadmium-free trolley wire. In 1997, the company expanded this division into France, where it purchased Griset SA. Founded in Paris in 1769, Griset had evolved into a pioneering producer of aluminum by the end of the 19th century, and later became one of France's leading independent producers of semifinished products.

THREE CORE DIVISIONS FOR THE NEW CENTURY

Diehl, which remained guided by Karl Diehl until 2002, reincorporated under a new family foundation in 1998, and changed its name to Diehl Stiftung & Co. In that year, the company faced international shame when Karl Diehl's claims that the company had never made use of slave labor were finally proven false. The company subsequently set up a fund to compensate the people it had brutalized during the war.

Diehl launched a restructuring of its operations at the end of the 1990s and into the early 2000s, selling its Junghans watchmaking division in 2000, to EganaGoldpfeil. The company briefly attempted to expand its defense operations with an entry into the repair of armored and other military vehicles. In support of this, the company acquired, then merged several companies, including FFG Flensburger Fahrzeugbau and Neubrandenburger Farhzeugwerke. However, this effort proved only temporary, and, with a downturn in the repair market, the company consolidated its repair operations to a single facility in 2001.

By the mid-2000s, Diehl's operations had been refocused onto three core divisions: VA Systeme, Diehl Metall and Diehl Control Systems. Diehl Metall continued to grow strongly, notably with an extension into mainland China with the establishment of a strip cutting plant in the Shenzhen development zone in 1999. The following year, the company acquired Connecticut-based The Miller Company, a specialty copper strip producer, with a strong capacity in phosphor bronze. The addition of this latter capacity placed Diehl as the world's leading producer of phosphor bronze strips. The company further expanded its metals production, notably its production of automotive components, with the opening of a new facility in Wuxi, in China.

Celebrating the company's 100th anniversary in 2002, Karl Diehl turned over the chairmanship of the company to his sons, Werner Diehl, who became company chairman, and Thomas Diehl, who emerged as the company's chief executive officer. As it entered its second century, the Nuremberg-based company continued to seek new expansion opportunities. In 2004, the company formed a joint venture with Raytheon to modernize the Sidewinder missile. In that year, also, the company's controls division established a new plant in Queretaro, Mexico. Into the mid-2000s, the company also began to target expansion in the Middle East, setting up a subsidiary in Kuwait in 2003. In February 2006, the company expanded its avionics operations with the opening of a new development center in Rostock, Germany. With strong growth in its core markets, Diehl remained committed to its tradition of family ownership and its position as a major German industrial group.

M. L. Cohen

PRINCIPAL SUBSIDIARIES

Diehl AKO Stiftung & Co. KG; Diehl Avionik Systeme GmbH; Diehl BGT Defence GmbH & Co. KG; Diehl Controls Italia S.r.l.; Diehl Controls Ltd. (U.S.A.); Diehl Controls Polska sp.z.o.o.; Diehl do Brasil Metalúrgica Ltda. (Brazil); Diehl Metall (Shenzhen) Co. Ltd. (China); Diehl Raytheon Missile Systeme LCC (U.S.A.); Diehl Synchro Tec Manufacturing (Wuxi) Co., Ltd. (China); Diehl VA Systeme Stiftung & Co. KG; EuroSpike GmbH; Franconia Industries Inc. (U.S.A.); Griset S.A. (France); SMH Süddeutsche Metallhandelsgesellschaft mbH; Sundwiger Messingwerk GmbH & Co.; The Miller Company (U.S.A.).

PRINCIPAL DIVISIONS

Diehl Metall; Diehl Controls; VA Systeme.

PRINCIPAL COMPETITORS

C Grossmann Eisen- u Stahlwerk AG; Arcelor S.A.; Corus Nederland B.V.; MAN AG; ThyssenKrupp Stahl AG; European Aeronautic Defence and Space Company EADS N.V.; Salzgitter AG; SKF (AB); Mittal Steel

Company N.V.; Honeywell International Inc.; Raytheon Company.

FURTHER READING

Kukeck, Anna Marie, "Diehl Stiftung & Co. Marks 101st Year," *Daily Herald*, September 18, 2003, p. 1.

"Raytheon Missile Systems and The Diehl Stiftung & Co.," *Journal of Electronic Defense*, April 2004, p. 40.

Yafie, Roberta C., "Diehl Metall Hits Phosphor Bronze Apex on Miller Buy," *American Metal Market*, May 10, 2000, p. 2.

East Penn Manufacturing Co., Inc.

Deka Road
Lyon Stations, Pennsylvania 19536
U.S.A.
Telephone: (610) 682-6361
Fax: (610) 682-4781
Web site: http://www.eastpenn-deka.com

Private Company
Incorporated: 1947
Employees: 5,000
Sales: $716 million (2004 est.)
NAIC: 336399 All Other Motor Vehicle Parts Manufacturing; 335912 Primary Battery Manufacturing

■ ■ ■

East Penn Manufacturing Co., Inc. is one of the world's leading manufacturers of lead-acid, gel-cell, and absorbed glass mat batteries. The private company, based in Lyon Station, Pennsylvania, is best known for its Deka brand of batteries, more than 4,000 different types in all, for cars, trucks, boats, farm equipment, and industrial uses. East Penn also makes specialty batteries for applications such as cell phone transmitters, military ordnance, backup power for solar and other renewable energy generators, golf carts, floor machines, wheel chairs, and alarm systems. The company also manufactures battery accessories, including battery terminals, battery cables, and booster cables, as well as general wire products such as starter cable, welding cable, trailer wire, speaker wire, and audio cable.

FOUNDING THE COMPANY AFTER WORLD WAR II

East Penn was founded by DeLight E. Breidegam, Jr., and his father, DeLight R. Breidegam, Sr. The elder Breidegam had little formal education, having left school after third grade, but he gained a practical education and became something of a jack of all trades, at one time earning his living as a farmer, salesman, painter, upholsterer, brass polisher, grocer, and battery case painter. His goal was to own his own business and, despite failing with a grocery store, he was determined to give entrepreneurship another try. He saved his money while learning the automobile battery business, employed in a variety of management positions at a pair of Berks County, Pennsylvania battery companies: Bowers Battery Company and Price Battery. The younger Breidegam was born in 1926 and he, too, gained knowledge of the battery business by working at Price Battery. When the United States entered World War II in 1941, he was not old enough to serve and began attending Gettysburg College before entering the Air Force as the war was beginning to wind down. While waiting to be discharged in 1946 he began writing to his father about launching a battery manufacturing business when he got home.

On the day he turned 20 years old, DeLight, Jr., returned home and he and his father quickly set to work implementing their plan. At the cost of $10 a month they rented a former creamery in Bowers, Pennsylvania, and their business idea became a reality. Because the military had commandeered so many of the raw materials they needed to make batteries, in the beginning the Breidegams rebuilt used car batteries, for which there was a great demand. The venture was very much a

COMPANY PERSPECTIVES

East Penn Manufacturing makes thousands of different sizes and types of lead-acid batteries, battery accessories, and wire & cable products for virtually any application. Since 1946, we have developed an enviable reputation for world-class quality products made in our state-of-the-art manufacturing facilities.

shoestring affair at this stage. DeLight, Sr., kept his job at Bowers and only stopped in at night to provide some help and prepare his son for the next day's work. DeLight, Jr., rebuilt the old batteries, using the scale at a grocery store across the street to weigh the lead, and took business calls from a nearby hotel. Both he and his father made sales calls to area service stations, selling their rebuilt batteries and buying old ones. The accounts were done on the family kitchen table by his mother and sister.

The Breidegams took on a partner in 1947, Karl Gasche, an MIT engineering graduate who worked at Bowers Battery. He became vice-president of the company, which was incorporated as East Penn Manufacturing Company. Raw materials were now becoming available and with Gasche's expertise—he would ultimately hold 21 battery-related patents—the company began to manufacture new automobile batteries. For a brand name they coined "Deka," which was a fusion of "DeLight" and "Karl," initially pronounced with a long "e." The company's original battery line included five automotive batteries, with the best labeled Deka Precision Built. The company also would sell batteries under the Berco and Hillcrest brands, but they did not stand the test of time as Deka did.

The partners needed to smelt lead for the new batteries, and so they built a small smelter on an 11-acre parcel of land located outside of Lyons, Pennsylvania, which they used at night while devoting their days to rebuilding old batteries and manufacturing new ones. It was also the first building of what would one day become two million square feet of operations on nearly 500 acres. By the start of 1948 the business was established enough that DeLight, Sr., was finally able to quit Bowers Battery and devote himself fully to East Penn. Business was steady and in 1950 the company, now employing six people, was able to move out of the creamery and add a 3,000-square-foot manufacturing facility at the Lyons site.

Once more the United States became involved in a war, although labeled a "police action," this time in Korea. Again raw materials, in particular lead, became difficult to obtain. East Penn managed to hang on, opened branch offices in Philadelphia and Ohio, and soon began to expand throughout the mid-Atlantic region. Key markets included Hartford, Baltimore, and Indianapolis, as well as the Pennsylvania cities of Harrisburg, Altoona, and Norristown. East Penn ventured far afield in 1954, establishing a manufacturing operation in Florida called Federal Battery, which initially received unformed batteries from the Pennsylvania facility and filled them with acid and finished them. Later, plates also were sent down for assembly.

ONGOING EXPANSION: 1960–90

East Penn continued its geographic expansion in the 1960s. A warehouse was opened in North Carolina in 1964, and a year later four warehouses were opened in the Washington, D.C., and Baltimore area. Then, in 1966 East Penn opened a new warehouse in New York. That year also saw the retirement of Karl Gasche, but while the company lost a brilliant engineer it did not lose its innovative spirit. During the 1960s East Penn diversified beyond automobile batteries. One of its major customers, Sears, Roebuck & Co., needed more plastic booster cable clamps, but East Penn was reliant on outside vendors to supply all of its plastic parts. When the supplier for the clamps was unable to meet Sears's demands, East Penn established an injection molding department at Federal Battery and began making its own plastic parts. East Penn also began to add to its product lines, first by offering battery cables and booster cables, and then by developing the industry's first lead terminal, a vast improvement over the brass terminals then on the market. East Penn successfully demonstrated the product to Sears and it was introduced to the market in 1967. Around this time Sears was looking to cut down on the number of suppliers it dealt with and asked East Penn to provide all its wire and cable products. As was the case with plastics, East Penn relied on an outside vendor unable to fulfill the contracts, and as a result East Penn set up its own operation to extrude wire. Sears proved to be a key catalyst for East Penn's growth. Not only did the retailer give East Penn an opportunity to diversify, it provided steady business, allowing the company to manufacture larger quantities and begin marketing its product lines to smaller distributors. Another key development for East Penn came in 1968 when it introduced an industrial battery line, used in applications such as lift trucks, personnel movers, diesel locomotives, and aircraft pushout vehicles. Mining batteries were also part of this segment and had already proven to be a major contributor to East Penn's balance

KEY DATES

1946: The company is founded by DeLight Breidegam, Sr., and DeLight Breidegam, Jr.
1947: Engineer Karl Gasche joins the company.
1954: Federal Battery is opened in Florida.
1966: Gasche retires.
1976: Lynx line battery accessories and cable are launched.
1988: Canadian distribution begins.
1992: DeLight, Sr., dies.
1994: Dan Langdon is named president.
2005: The automotive battery division of Douglas Battery Manufacturing is acquired.

sheet, accounting for about one-quarter of all sales in the mid-1960s.

When it celebrated its 25th anniversary in 1971, East Penn employed 350 people. Growth was so strong, however, that this number doubled within the next five years. The company acquired Philadelphia's Pioneer Auto Parts, which was folded into the warehouse operations in the city. East Penn also continued to add to its Lyons site, including a cable facility in 1974 and a wire operation in 1975. Then, in 1976, East Penn launched the Lynx line of automotive battery accessories and wire specialty products such as battery lifters and battery testers, which the company began to market through the automotive departments of mass retailers. Demand was so strong for these products that both the cable and wire facilities had to be expanded in 1977. In the meantime, East Penn produced more than a million batteries in a single year for the first time in 1976. To make deliveries of Deka batteries and Lynx accessories, East Penn added to its truck fleet and in 1974 built a garage in which to keep the vehicles serviced. Other plant expansion projects in the 1970s included the opening of an oxide facility and a new battery plant and laboratory, and the addition of a continuous automatic plate-making system. In the late 1970s East Penn introduced its "Kare-Free" line of calcium maintenance-free batteries; the line had so much potential that the company began making plans to build a second automotive plant for its production. To handle the wastewater created by battery manufacturing, East Penn also opened a treatment plant in 1977, able to process 100,000 gallons of wastewater each day.

East Penn expanded on a number of fronts in the 1980s. Battery design became the province of CAD (computer aided design), making the drafting tables obsolete. Engineers also turned their attention to new battery technology in the 1980s, such as absorbed-mat and gelled-electrolyte, nonspillable batteries, ideal for applications such as telecommunications. To keep pace with the demand for these new batteries and old product lines, East Penn continually expanded its Lyons site. In the early 1980s a new industrial batteries building was opened, a new maintenance building was opened to provide support services to all East Penn units, and later in the decade a new 135,000-square-foot distribution center and adjacent technical center were opened. New corporate offices were opened in 1985. Three years later, with the help of a state loan, East Penn opened a new automotive plant more than 100,000 square feet in size. It soon would be expanded to accommodate the production of the new gel cell batteries.

Manufacturing done by Federal Battery was brought to Pennsylvania in the early 1980s and the Florida location became a devoted warehouse. In addition, East Penn opened warehouses in Rhode Island and Virginia, and in 1984 acquired Batteries Unlimited, located in the Philadelphia suburbs, which became the new Pioneer Auto Parts warehouse. Other acquisitions in the 1980s included the 1986 purchase of Taylor Battery Company, based in Kentucky with a dozen warehouses in the Ohio River Valley, and the 1988 purchase of another Kentucky company, Holderfield Battery Co., which added four more warehouses. East Penn also turned its attention to the north and in 1988 began distributing its products in Canada, quickly carving out a significant share of the market.

NEW MARKETS: 1990 AND BEYOND

By the start of the 1990s East Penn was doing about $200 million in annual sales and each day its 2,000 employees produced about 20,000 car batteries and 1,400 industrial cells. By 1992 the company was producing five million batteries a year. East Penn continued to stay in the forefront of battery technology. In 1990 it introduced the Deka Dominator, a highly popular gel battery used in wheelchairs, golf carts, and marine and other applications. Two years later, the company introduced solar batteries, which became the foundation for the stationary battery division. These new batteries, providing emergency standby power, were suited to wind generation units, water pumping systems, and remote monitoring systems. A year later East Penn launched a line of stationary batteries for standby power applications such as telecommunications and UPS. Later in the 1990s stationary batteries were developed for the cable TV market. In 1995 East Penn opened a new 350,000-square-foot specialty battery plant to produce stationary and other batteries.

East Penn completed a pair of acquisitions in the 1990s. It bought independent battery specialist Electro Battery Company, a Midwest operation with four warehouses. In 1994 Power Battery Sales Ltd., an Ontario, Canada company, was acquired, adding nine Canadian warehouse operations.

East Penn saw some changes at the top ranks of management in the 1990s. DeLight, Sr., died in 1992, and in 1994 DeLight, Jr., turned over the presidency to Dan Langdon, who had joined the company in 1986 as controller and later became chief financial officer. DeLight, Jr., stayed on as chairman and remained active in East Penn's affairs. The entire company was challenged by a freak occurrence in January 1996 when a record storm dumped more than three feet of snow on the area and high winds caused drifting. The roof of the company's distribution center collapsed under the excessive weight, severing gas and electric lines, which led to a fire that required several days to extinguish, due in large part to the snow that prevented firefighters from making their way to combat the blaze. The company quickly rented an area warehouse and managed to cobble together orders, helped to some degree by competitors supplying product. In less than two months East Penn was able to resume normal operations.

As the twenty-first century dawned, East Penn continued to add new batteries, especially in the telecommunications field. When that sector struggled, East Penn was forced in early 2002 to lay off more than 100 workers until demand strengthened. The company was known for retaining employees; its workforce was composed of many people with tenures of 20 and 30 years and longer. East Penn was regularly recognized as one of the best places to work in Pennsylvania, and in 2005 *Fortune* magazine ranked it number 79 on its list of "100 Best Companies to Work For."

East Penn continued to pursue growth in the 2000s. In 2003 it forged a joint venture with Austrian company Banner GmbH, helping the partners to improve customer service in the other's home markets. East Penn acquired the automotive-battery division of Douglas Battery Manufacturing Co. in 2005, adding a North Carolina plant. With solid relationships with its customers and a committed workforce, there was every reason to believe that East Penn would continue to thrive for many years to come.

Ed Dinger

PRINCIPAL OPERATING UNITS

Standby Power; Stationary Power; Industrial Power; Automotive Power.

PRINCIPAL COMPETITORS

EnerSys Inc.; Exide Technologies; Johnson Controls, Inc.

FURTHER READING

Craver, Richard, "Winston-Salem, N.C.-Based Douglas Battery Manufacturing to Sell Automotive Unit," *Winston-Salem Journal*, January 12, 2005.

"DeLight E. Breidegam Jr. (Entrepreneur of the Year: Master—Winner)," *Philadelphia Business Journal*, June 25, 1990, p. 16C.

Fassnacht, Jon, "East Penn's Secret?," *Reading Eagle*, January 18, 2006.

Fineberg, Seth, "Snow Caused Collapse of Battery Facility Roof," *American Metal Market*, January 16, 1996, p. 2.

Espírito Santo Financial Group S.A.

231 Val des Bons Malades
Luxembourg, L-2121
Luxembourg
Telephone: +(442) 073324350
Fax: +(442)073324355
Web site: http://www.esfg.com

Public Company
Incorporated: 1869 as Caza de Cambio
Employees: 10,127
Total Assets: EUR 71.76 billion ($95 billion) (2006)
Stock Exchanges: New York
Ticker Symbol: ESF
NAIC: 522110 Commercial Banking; 551112 Offices of Other Holding Companies

■ ■ ■

Espírito Santo Financial Group S.A. is the Luxembourg-based holding company for the banking and insurance operations controlled by the Espírito Santo family. These operations focus primarily on the Portuguese market, especially through the Banco Espírito Santo (BES) and the Tranquilidade insurance group. BES is the third largest commercial bank in Portugal (and the second largest bank not owned by the Portuguese government). BES's operations include investment banking through BES Investimento, and fund management through ESAF—Espírito Santo Activos Financeiros. Espírito Santo also operates banking subsidiaries, directly or through BES, in several foreign markets, including Spain, France, Switzerland, Panama, Brazil, the Cayman Islands, the United States (in Florida), and in China and Angola. The company's insurance operations center on Companhia Seguros Tranquilidade, a nonlife, brokerage-based insurance group; Espírito Santo Seguros, which offers nonlife bancassurance products through BES; and Companhia de Seguros Tranquilidade Vida, which offers life insurance products in a bancassurance relationship with BES. In February 2006, Espírito Santo agreed to transfer half of its ownership of its bancassurance subsidiaries to longtime financial partner Credit Agricole, of France. Espírito Santo Financial Group is listed on the New York Stock Exchange. Ricardo Espírito Santo Silva Salgado serves as group president and chairman, and Jose Manuel Espírito Santo Silva serves as vice-chairman. In 2005, Espírito Santo posted total assets of EUR 71.76 billion ($95 billion).

PORTUGUESE FINANCIAL FAMILY IN THE 19TH CENTURY

The Espírito Santo (the name means "holy spirit") family's banking odyssey began during the late 19th century, when patriarch José Maria de Espírito Santo Silva set up a foreign exchange agency, Caza de Cambio, in Lisbon in 1869. Espírito Santo also acted as an agent for international and domestic credit bonds. Espírito Santo's major business, however, was as a sales agent for lottery tickets, and particularly for the distribution of Spanish lottery tickets in Portugal. Espírito Santo's success led him to move to larger quarters in the center of Lisbon in 1880.

The move inspired Espírito Santo to enter the banking sector proper. Starting in 1884, he formed a

COMPANY PERSPECTIVES

Mission: BES Group aims to be the leading Portuguese multispecialist financial group in terms of innovation, customer service, profitability and efficiency.

While maintaining strict risk management, BES is continuing organic market share growth fueled by anticipation of client needs and alliances with premier partners to leverage on our strong brand image.

number of banking and credit title agency partnerships, which ultimately led to the establishment of the Beirao, Pinto, Silva and Co. partnership in Lisbon. Espírito Santo gained control of the partnership in 1911, changing its name to JM Espírito Santo Silva & Ca. in 1915. After Espírito Santo's death that year, the company was taken over by his family and other shareholders. The bank was placed under the leadership of eldest son José Ribeiro do Espírito Santo e Silva and in 1918 the family changed the institution's name to Espírito Santo Silva and Banco Co. The bank was formally incorporated as Banco Espírito Santo (BES) in 1920.

BES launched a new phase of its growth, opening its first branch office in Torres Vedras in 1920. The following year, the bank opened a second branch, in Porto. Although the first two decades of the 20th century were a period of great political upheaval, during which time Portugal haltingly shifted via revolution from a monarchical form of government to a republican regime, the period between the two world wars was one of dramatic growth in Portugal's banking industry. The group continued to grow through the 1920s and into the 1930s, despite the harsh economic climate of the time, and by 1937 already operated some 13 branch offices.

By then, José Maria's eldest son, José Ribeiro do Espírito Santo e Silva, had been expelled from the Catholic country for getting a divorce in 1931. In his place, younger brother Ricardo defied the global depression of the 1930s to build a European banking empire. He found a willing supporter in Antonio de Oliveira Salazar, the prime minister who founded the "Estado Novo" (New State) in 1933. His virtual dictatorship endured over four decades, becoming Europe's most prolific authoritarian government. Salazar had acted as Portugal's finance minister in the late 1920s and had played an important role in the stabilization of the country's finances.

The Espírito Santo family expanded its banking empire into other financial markets in the 1930s, starting with the acquisition of Companhia de Seguros Tranquilidade, founded in Oporto in 1871. Toward the end of the decade, the bank grew again, this time through a merger with Banco Comercial de Lisboa in 1937. Founded in 1885, the Banco Comercial de Lisboa helped strengthen BES's presence in the capital city, boosting its size by more than 30 percent. Renamed as Banco Espírito Santo e Comercial de Lisboa (BESCL), the bank began expanding its network, opening its first branch office in Lisbon, where previously it had only had its main office, in 1939. By the end of the 1940s, BESCL's branch network had covered the entire Lisbon metropolitan region, and the bank boasted nearly 35 branches in all.

POSTWAR BOOM AND NATIONALIZATION

Salazar's strategies fostered Espírito Santo's growth during and after World War II. Portugal's neutrality during the war made it a haven for the wealthy of Europe, and postwar protectionism precluded foreign competition. Salazar's tenuous hold on Portugal's African colonies facilitated the Espírito Santo family's acquisition of major sugar, coffee, and palm oil plantations in Mozambique and Angola. BESCL extended its banking presence into the colonial regions, establishing branches in Angola and Mozambique. Back at home, the 1960s brought a veritable "boom" to what had historically been Western Europe's poorest nation, as economic growth surged at an annual rate between 5 and 7 percent. The fast-growing economy enabled BESCL to extend its banking network, and by the end of the 1960s the bank operated some 50 branches throughout Portugal.

BESCL also grew through acquisition, notably through its purchase of Cassa Bancaria Blandy Brothers, based on the island of Madeira and controlled by the Blandy wine-making family. The bank also entered Luxembourg, buying up shares in Banque Interatlantique. Into the early 1970s, the bank also became a partner in the establishment of two new banks, Libra Bank, formed in London in 1972 by a consortium including Chase Manhattan Bank, National Westminster Bank, Credito Italiano, and the Mitsubishi Bank; and Bank Inter-Unido, created in Angola in 1973 in partnership with Citibank.

By the early 1970s, the privately held, $2 billion-asset Banco Espírito Santo had become Portugal's largest bank, and its Tranquilidade subsidiary was the country's

KEY DATES

1869: José Maria do Espírito Santo Silva establishes a foreign exchange agency, Caza de Cambio, in Lisbon.
1884: Espírito Santo Silva forms a banking partnership, which later becomes Silva, Beirão, and Pinto & Ca.
1915: Silva, Beirão, and Pinto & Ca becomes Banco Espírito Santo.
1937: Banco Espírito Santo merges with Banco Comercial de Lisboa, and becomes Banco Espírito Santo e Comercial de Lisboa (BESCL).
1966: A subsidiary is established in Luxembourg.
1972: BESCL joins in the creation of Libra Bank Limited in London.
1973: Banco Inter-Unido in Angola is formed in partnership with Citibank.
1975: The Portuguese government nationalizes BESCL; the Espírito Santo family rebuilds financial holdings in Luxembourg, forming the company that becomes Espírito Santo Financial Group (ESFG).
1980: BESCL opens a London branch.
1985: BESCL opens branches in New York and Nassau.
1986: ESFG returns to Portugal and begins rebuilding investments in the country.
1989: The Portuguese government begins privatizing the banking and insurance industries, and ESFG reacquires control of the Tranquilidade insurance group.
1991: The first stage of BESCL privatization is initiated; ESFG acquires 40 percent of BESCL.
1992: BESCL privatization is completed, and ESFG acquires full control of BESCL; Banco Industrial del Mediterraneo in Spain and BES Venetie in France are acquired.
1994: BES Directo telephone banking service is launched.
1995: BESCL enters the Asian region with a banking subsidiary in Macao.
1997: A stake in Banco Boavista Inter-Atlantico in Brazil is acquired.
1998: BESNET online banking service is launched.
1999: BESCL changes its name to Banco Espírito Santo S.A.
2001: Banco BEST is launched in partnership with Portugal Telecom.
2004: Spain's Banco Inversion is acquired from Germany's HypoVereinsbank; two business units, Lusogest and Lusopensiones, are acquired from Banco Simeon Asset Management.
2006: The company agrees to transfer 50 percent of the Tranquilidade insurance group to Credit Agricole.

top insurance company. The family fortune was estimated to total $4 billion at its peak.

When Salazar suffered a debilitating heart attack in 1968, however, his successor, Marcelo Caetano, was unable to hold the Estado Novo together. By 1974, the pressure of colonial wars and deep economic recession precipitated a bloodless military coup. Although the new regime, the Movimento das Forcas Armadas (Armed Forces Movement, or MFA), instituted what has been characterized as "a moderate form of democracy," its communist leanings led to the nationalization of Portugal's biggest companies. Initially the government proposed a partial nationalization of a number of industries, with the government taking control of 51 percent stakes in the country's mining, oil and gas, electricity, steel, tobacco, and arms industries. The banking sector was initially left out of the original nationalization plan.

Yet the botched military coup of early 1975 led to an investigation of its backers, which included a number of members of the Espírito Santo family. The investigation uncovered evidence that the family, through BESCL, had diverted funds meant for the country's demobilized soldiers to its own accounts. The resulting scandal led the bank's own workers to strike, in part to prevent the removal of documents and the transfer of bank money outside of the country, and demand that it be nationalized. Within a week, both Portugal's bank and insurance industries were taken over by the new Portuguese government. Chief Executive Officer Manuel

Ricardo Espírito Santo was arrested at a meeting of the bank's board of directors and condemned to a 14-month prison sentence.

Battered but unbowed, the Espírito Santo family fled to Spain, then settled in London. The family took its meager settlement from the government and founded E.S. International Holding S.A. in Luxembourg with $20,000. They purchased a major stake in Florida's Biscayne Bank (later renamed Espírito Santo Bank of Florida) in 1978 and won a Brazilian banking license late in the decade. They began to reassert the well-recognized family name in 1983 with the creation of Bank Espírito Santo International Ltd. in the Cayman Islands. They also purchased equity in banks in London and Paris, and established a fund management company in Lausanne, Switzerland. The group was renamed Espírito Santo Financial Group (ESFG) in 1984. The company then listed its shares on the New York and London Stock Exchanges. By 1990, they had accumulated a $246 million enterprise.

During this period, BESCL continued its own growth, increasing its number of branches to 110 by the end of the 1970s, and then to more than 170. The group's assets made a substantial leap, growing from PTE 156 billion to nearly PTE 1.2 trillion. BESCL also launched new overseas operations, adding a London office in 1980. The bank then opened offices in New York and Nassau in 1985, before adding branches in Madrid and Madeira by the end of the decade.

In the meantime, the 1985 election of free-market Social Democrat Anibal Cavaco Silva heralded an era of reprivatization. When the new regime began to reprivatize financial institutions and insurance companies in 1986, the Espírito Santo family wasted no time in reentering their home country to begin the process of rebuilding their financial empire. The family's holdings quickly spread into the real estate, agroindustrial, communications, and services markets. ESFG also set up operations in assets management. The family's real target, however, was to regain control of their former financial holdings. In 1986, ESFG formed a commercial bank, Banco Internacional de Credito, as a joint venture with France's Credit Agricole. Espírito Santo used the proceeds of a Eurobond floatation to repurchase Tranquilidade, starting in 1989 and completed in 1990. The family then turned its sights on its former bank. ESFG's chance came in 1991, when the Portuguese government put 40 percent of BESCL up for sale. Backed by partner Credit Agricole, ESFG won the bid. Within a year, the Portuguese government had approved the sale of the remaining 60 percent of BESCL, and in February 1992, the Espírito Santo family took back full control of the bank.

While nationalization had weakened some of BESCL's competitors, Espírito Santo was fairly well managed throughout the period of state ownership. In 1993, Espírito Santo official Manuel Villas-Boas told *Euromoney*, "To a large degree the bank kept to the philosophies of credit and the systems implemented before the period of nationalization. The bank was fortunate in the choice of management it had under nationalization, and the bank had a strong and well provided balance sheet when we took it back."

PORTUGUESE FOCUS FOR THE NEW CENTURY

That did not mean that there was no room for improvement, however. For example, BESCL's employee roster had grown by 70 percent during the period of nationalization. Led by Chairman Ricardo Espírito Santo Silva Salgado, the family focused on restructuring the group and increasing efficiency. They called upon well-known management consultants McKinsey and Company to assist with the reorganization. The new management team increased productivity dramatically by reducing staffing levels from 6,800 in 1990 to 5,700 by 1994, while simultaneously increasing the number of branches from 177 to 332. The ratio of administrative costs to financial assets decreased by almost 18 percent and the number of employees per branch declined from 27 to 17 in the process. Assets per employee doubled from 1991 to PTE 400 million in 1994. In 1993, BESCL boosted its technological efficiency with a $12.8 million computer network upgrade from Unisys Corp.

The bank also shifted its strategic focus from corporate clients to private customers, who had proven loyal patrons during the exile. Espírito Santo's commercial bank, Banco Internacional de Credito, sought to increase its share of Portugal's mortgage business to 10 percent by the mid-1980s. In 1992, the financial group added a Spanish institution, Banco Industrial del Mediterraneo, to its growing roster of businesses, at an estimated price tag of ESP 5.5 billion ($55 million). The company's increasingly diverse interests, which included leasing, investment banking, and credit cards by the mid-1990s, allowed for cross-selling of products and services.

An unidentified Lisbon banker told *Euromoney*, "Espírito Santo represents old money in Portugal. Their bank is the last of the old commercial banks that has retained its power." That name recognition factor helped impart "an image of solidity and conservatism." BESCL continued to nurture that reputation in the early 1990s, employing a conservative lending policy and maintaining a highly diversified loan portfolio. That caution earned Espírito Santo the highest international credit rating given to a Portuguese bank. These strong appraisals, in turn, enabled BESCL to successfully float $76.9 million of its shares as American Depositary Receipts (ADRs) on the New York Stock Exchange in 1993.

In 1993, *Euromoney* noted, "Espírito Santo's biggest challenge is to adapt the style and organization of a bank which existed when Portugal was a small rural economy into one fit for a growing industrial and international environment." ESFG appeared to take this advice to heart, and in the 1990s began expanding and modernizing its range of financial services, as well as its geographic reach.

The company also added a new subsidiary in France, BES Vénetie. In 1993, ESFG added investment banking products to its lineup with the launch of Banco Espírito Santo de Investimento. The company also added a telephone banking service, BES Directo, in 1994. The group's banking services were later expanded again with the launch of an online banking service, BESNET, in 1998. The company changed the name of its bank in 1999, to Banco Espírito Santo, S.A.

In addition to building up its Portuguese holdings, ESFG expanded its operations elsewhere around the world. The company entered the Asian market for the first time in 1995, with the launch of a new subsidiary in Macao. The company later extended its presence in the region with a representative office in Shanghai.

Latin America remained an important market for ESFG as well. The company raised its profile in the region in 1997, when it acquired a major stake in Banco Boavista Inter-Atlantico, based in Brazil and serving especially the regions of São Paulo and Rio de Janeiro with more than 70 branches. In that year also, the company acquired a stake in Société Bancaire de Paris, then turned to Poland, where it bought a stake in Kredyt Bank PBI. The company continued to increase its Kredyt Bank PBI holding, to 10 percent in 1999, and then to nearly 20 percent in 2000. By then, ESFG had returned to Spain, where it bought ES Bank, as well as the investment banking groups Benito y Mionjardin and GESCapital.

ESFG attempted to merge BES with Banco Portugues de Investimento, which would have boosted BES into the lead in Portugal's banking sector. When that merger collapsed, however, the company switched its strategy, targeting the Internet for further growth. This led ESFG to form a partnership with Portugal Telecom in 2000 to launch e-finance projects. The first of these debuted in 2001, the online bank Banco BEST. The company also added a new bank in the Azores, Banco Espírito Santo dos Açores, in 2002. In that year, the company sold off its stake in Kredyt Bank.

ESFG returned to Spain in 2004, buying up Banco Inversion from Germany's HypoVereinsbank for EUR 11 million ($13.5 million). Also that year, the company acquired two business units, Lusogest and Lusopensiones, from Banco Simeon Asset Management. As it entered the second half of the decade, ESFG continued seeking additional growth opportunities, announcing in 2005 its interest in re-entering the Eastern European market through subsidiary Banco Espírito Santo de Investimento. At the beginning of 2006, ESFG restructured its holdings, agreeing to transfer 50 percent of its control of the Tranquilidade insurance group to Credit Agricole. Still controlled by the Espírito Santo family, ESFG had established itself as a fast-growing international financial group.

April Dougal Gasbarre
Updated, M. L. Cohen

PRINCIPAL SUBSIDIARIES

Banco Espírito Santo (Angola); Banco Espírito Santo (Cayman Islands); Banco Espírito Santo (U.S.A.); Banco Espírito Santo de Investimento; Banco Espírito Santo do Oriente (Panama); Banco Espírito Santo; Banco Internacional de Cridito; Bank Espírito Santo (International) Ltd. (Spain); Banque Espírito Santo et de la Vinitie (Macao); BES Investimento do Brasil; Compagnie Bancaire Espírito Santo (Switzerland); Companhia de Seguros Tranquilidade; Companhia de Seguros Tranquilidade Vida; ES Bank (Panama) S.A.; ESAF - Espírito Santo Activos Financeiros; Espírito Santo Activos Financieros (Spain); Espírito Santo Bank (France); Espírito Santo Companhia de Seguros; Espírito Santo Investment, SAU, SV (Spain); Europ Assistance.

PRINCIPAL COMPETITORS

UBS AG; HSBC Holdings PLC; Groupe BNP Paribas; The Royal Bank of Scotland Group PLC; Deutsche Bank AG; Allianz AG; Credit Agricole S.A.; Barclays PLC; Banco Santander Central Hispano S.A.; Societe Generale de Banque; Dexia S.A.; Banco Bilbao Vizcaya Argentaria S.A.; Fortis Bank.

FURTHER READING

"Espírito Santo Buys Spanish Wealth Player," *Private Banker International*, September 2004, p. 2.

Gilbert, Nick, "Espírito Santo: Kindred Spirits," *Financial World*, March 1, 1994, p. 18.

"Home Free and Looking to the Future," *Euromoney*, June 1993, p. 149.

Kraus, James R., "Big Foreign Banks Come Ashore to Raise Equity in U.S. Markets," *American Banker*, November 19, 1993, p. 24.

———, "More Banks Hopping on ADR Bandwagon," *American Banker,* September 7, 1993, p. 9.

"Portugal: Espírito Santo's 16-Year Odyssey," *International Management,* August 1990, p. 19.

"Portuguese Financial Group BESI Considers Investing in Czech Republic, *Czech Business News,* January 21, 2005.

Satterfield, David, "Miami Bank Ruffles Legal Feathers Over Use of Family Name," *American Banker,* March 10, 1987, p. 16.

Scherreik, Susan, "Looking Abroad for Stock Gains of 28 Percent or More," *Money,* January 1995, p. 68.

Wise, Peter, "BES Set for Global Online Expansion," *Financial Times,* July 26, 2000, p. 31.

Essar Group Ltd.

Essar House
11 K K Marg
Mahalaxmi, Mumbai 400 034
India
Telephone: +91 22 2495 0606
Fax: +91 22 2495 428391 261 832 6462
Web site: http://www.essar.com

Private Company
Incorporated: 1956
Employees: 5,000
Sales: INR 100 billion ($2.2 billion) (2005)
NAIC: 331111 Iron and Steel Mills; 213111 Drilling Oil and Gas Wells; 211111 Crude Petroleum and Natural Gas Extraction; 213112 Support Activities for Oil and Gas Field Exploration; 334220 Radio and Television Broadcasting and Wireless Communications Equipment Manufacturing; 532412 Construction, Mining and Forestry Machinery and Equipment Rental and Leasing; 483113 Coastal and Great Lakes Freight Transportation; 483111 Deep Sea Freight Transportation

■ ■ ■

Essar Group Ltd. is one of India's leading privately owned, diversified conglomerates, with a total asset base of more than $5 billion and annual revenues of INR 100 billion ($2.2 billion). Whereas Essar Group itself is controlled by the founding Ruia family, much of the company's diversified holdings fall under its publicly listed subsidiaries. The company's subsidiaries include Essar Steel, the second largest private sector steel company in India; Essar Oil, a fully integrated oil and gas producer, and the first private sector Indian company to enter the market since its liberalization in the early 1990s; Essar Power, which operates a 515 megawatt (MW) natural gas power plant in Hazira, with plans to increase its total output to 2,500 MW by the end of the 2000s; Essar Shipping, the group's original activity, the leading shipping group in India, with 30 vessels, including India's first Very Large Crude Carrier (VLCC) tanker, representing some 14 percent of the country's total fleet; Essar Teleholding, which, through its joint venture Hutchison Essar is the second largest cellular telephone provider in India; and Essar Construction, a leading construction company in India. Other Essar holdings include subsidiaries involved in magazine publishing, business process outsourcing, information technology, and flower and vegetable production. Essar Group is led by Shashi and Ravi Ruia, sons of the company's founder.

FROM EARLY 19TH-CENTURY TRADER TO LATE 20TH-CENTURY CONGLOMERATE

The Ruia family originated in the Rajasthan region of northwestern India. As members of the powerful Marwari trading community, which also produced such Indian financial dynasties as the Birla and Mittal families, the Ruia family's background in trading reached back to the early 19th century. The development of the modern Essar Group began in the 1950s, however, when Nand Kishore Ruia left Rajasthan to establish his own business in Chennai (also known as Madras), in the Tamil Nadu

COMPANY PERSPECTIVES

We insist on setting and surpassing world-class benchmarks in everything we do. No wonder we have the largest gas-based sponge iron plant and are one of the world's largest integrated sea logistics companies that owns India's largest double hull, double bottom VLCC. All our businesses are highly integrated across the value chain and use the latest technology to stay strong and agile. We have invested several billion dollars on exclusive state-of-the-art technology because we believe that it confers strong strategic advantages.

region. Ruia stuck to his trading roots, setting up an export business for the region's iron ore mining industry. By 1966, the group added stevedoring services, transporting the iron ore from the mines to the region's ports. By the end of the decade, the Ruia family had also entered the construction contracting market. Among Essar Group's first major construction contracts were the construction of an outer breakwater in Madras Port in order to support large tankers, completed in 1971, and the construction of a wharf and berth complex at Tuticorn port, completed in 1972.

By then, however, the family business had been placed under the control of Shashi and Ravi Ruia, after their father's sudden death in 1969. Both in their early 20s, the Ruia brothers set out to expand the family business, and develop it into one of India's most successful and most diversified conglomerates. Already at the end of the 1960s, the brothers targeted the shipping market, starting with the launch of Essar-Bulk Cargo Carriers in 1969. That operation originally served to transport the group's iron ore exports; by the mid-1970s, however, the company had begun providing a wider range of ship chartering and transport services. The shipping company grew strongly in the 1980s, notably through the 1983 acquisition of Karnataka Shipping Corporation. The enlarged operation was renamed as Essar Shipping Limited (ESL) in 1984.

The next phase of the shipping company's growth came in 1992, when ESL acquired South India Shipping Corporation (SISCO), adding that company's 14 vessels. The two companies were gradually merged, a process that was completed by 1996. At its height, Essar's shipping operations counted nearly 60 vessels; at the end of the 1990s, however, the company began trimming its fleet, back to 42 ships at decade's end.

Essar Construction continued to grow strongly through this period as well. The company completed a number of new major projects through the 1980s and into the 1990s. These included the construction of several new oil and ore berths at Mormugao Port, completed in 1977; the construction of two 7.2-kilometer pipelines near Bombay Port in 1983; a new 18-kilometer pipeline connecting a Bombay offshore facility to the Hazira Gujarat plant in 1985; and the dredging of the Mazgaon Docks in 1986. Pipelines and related construction became something of a company specialty as it completed a number of new projects into the 1990s, such as an order for 12 submarine pipelines for the Oil and Natural Gas Commission in Bombay, completed in 1989, and a one-kilometer ethylene pipeline crossing Panvel Creek, in Bombay, for Polyolefins Industries Ltd., completed in 1990. The following year, Essar Construction completed a new pipeline for Hindustan Petroleum Corp. in Baroda.

Essar also entered the steel industry, setting up Essar Gujarat, in the Gujarat region near Rajasthan, to take advantage of a new gas pipeline there. The company built a successful business producing sponge iron through the 1970s and into the 1980s. By the end of that decade, the company had added hot briquetting capacity, with the installation of two new sponge iron production modules imported from Germany in 1989. These modules began commercial production in 1990. A third module was then added the following year, and launched its commercial production in 1993.

By then, however, Essar, with the encouragement of the Indian government, was determined to enter the global steel business and become a vertically integrated steel producer. In 1989, Essar Gujarat, which later changed its name to Essar Steel Limited, began construction on a new $90 million cold-rolled steel mill. Originally slated for completion in 1992, the launch of the new plant was delayed when the group decided to expand the plant's production capacity. Commercial production at the plant finally took place only in 1997; by then, however, global steel prices had fallen sharply, and, amid the economic crises sweeping the Asian region, the company found itself in its own financial difficulties. In 1999, the group made headlines when it was forced to default on some $250 million in eurobond loans.

RENEWED GROWTH INTO THE 21ST CENTURY

Part of Essar Group's troubles came from its rapid diversification. As Ravi Ruia described the company's strategy to reporters in 1994, "We will get into any new business that will make us more money. ... Today the canvas is wide open. We must have an open mind. We should have basic synergies with what we do, but we

KEY DATES

1956: Nand Kishore Ruia moves to Chennai and establishes the Essar Group as a trading company.
1966: The company enters the stevedoring market for the region's iron ore mining industry.
1969: After Ruia's death, his sons Shashi and Ravi become heads of the company and launch a long diversification drive, starting with an entry into the construction market, through Essar Construction, and the shipping industry, through Essar Bulk Cargo Carriers.
1975: The company establishes Essar Gujarat (later Essar Steel) to produce sponge iron ore.
1976: The company establishes Essar Investment as a holding for the Ruia family's diversified investments.
1983: The company acquires Karnataka Shipping Corporation.
1984: Essar Bulk Cargo Carriers is renamed as Essar Shipping Limited (ESL) in 1984.
1989: The company establishes Essar Oil & Exploration with plans to develop integrated oil services.
1992: The South India Shipping Corporation is acquired.
1993: The company wins exploration bids for fields in Rajasthan and offshore Bombay; construction of a 510 megawatt (MW) power plant is launched in Hazira.
1995: The company enters the mobile telecommunications market.
1996: The company creates an alliance with Sterling Cellular Limited and rolls out the Essar Cellphone brand.
1999: Essar Group is forced to default on loan payments.
2001: Essar Oil begins developing its own service station network; Essar Steel forms a partnership to build a cold-rolled steel plant in Indonesia.
2002: The company merges cellphone operations into the Hutchison Essar joint venture.
2005: Hutchison Essar acquires BPL's cellular phone operations in India.
2006: Essar buys a new Very Large Crude Carrier (VLCC) tanker.

must not miss a major opportunity just because it does not fit in with our basic operations."

Essar attempted to enter the financial market in the late 1980s and early 1990s. In 1989, the company set up a new subsidiary, India Securities Limited, which began providing a range of financial services, including lease financing, bill discounting, capital management, and money market services. Essar also attempted to enter the banking market, making a bid to acquire Tamil Nadu Mercantile Bank, based in Tuticorin and serving, in large part, the Nadar community in the region. By 1994, Essar had gained control of more than 70 percent of the bank, but was ultimately forced to sell off its shareholding due to protests from the bank's Nadar clientele.

Essar took advantage of the liberalization of India's economy, carried out in 1991, by entering the oil and gas market. The company established Essar Oil & Exploration in 1989 with the aim of operating in three areas, those of energy production, offshore exploration, and petroleum refining. In 1993, the company became one of the first to bid for the country's first private sector exploration contracts. The company won its bid for the two onshore blocks in Rajasthan, as well as an offshore field near Mumbai. In that year, as well, Essar established its energy production division, Essar Power, with the construction of a 510 MW plant in Hazira, in the Gujarat region.

Through the 1990s, Essar also joined the race to capture India's telecommunications sector, which was liberalized in 1994. Essar formed a bidding partnership with Bell Atlantic to bid for cellular licenses in 1995. At the same time, Essar Gujurat formed a partnership with Sterling Cellular Limited to roll out the Essar Cellphone service in Delhi. The Essar Cellphone brand was later extended to the Rajasthan, Haryana, and Uttar Pradesh regions. The company added cellular stakes in the Punjab, Andhra Pradesh, and Karnataka regions through an alliance with JT Mobile Telecom Ltd.; the company also won a fixed line license in Punjab in the mid-1990s. By the early 2000s, Essar had found a new partner, Hong

Kong's Hutchison Whampoa, and in 2002, the two companies agreed to merge their cellular businesses in India into a new joint venture, Hutchison Essar. That company, with revenues of more than $2 billion, became one of India's leading mobile telecommunications groups, with operations in 26 of the country's main markets. In 2005, Hutchison Essar grew again, paying $1 billion to acquire the wireless operations of BPL Mobile.

In the meantime, Essar Group had emerged from its financial crisis at the beginning of the decade. Although its reputation had been somewhat tarnished, the company's foundations had proven financially solid. During the first half of the decade, the company moved to focus its diversified operations more closely around its core businesses in steel, oil, energy production, shipping, and construction.

The company expanded its oil business in 2001, with the opening of its first service stations. The company hoped to become a major player in that market, announcing its aim to open as many as 2,000 service stations in India. At the same time, the company expanded its exploration operations, focusing on the Rajasthan region. The company's construction wing also continued to grow. In 2003, for example, Essar won a $29 million contract to build a water supply system in the Rajasthan region.

By then, Essar had launched its first foreign operation, building a $35 million cold-rolling mill in Indonesia as part of a joint venture. Completed in 2003, the new facility's full-scale capacity was expected to top 400,000 tons per year. Closer to home, Essar also targeted its power generation operation for growth into the second half of the decade. By the beginning of 2006, Essar Group had announced its intention to expand its power generation capacity to 2,500 MW by 2010. The company also remained a heavyweight player in India's shipping industry; in 2006, the company announced that it was buying a new VLCC, solidifying the group as the country's leading private sector fleet operator. With total assets of more than $5 billion, and annual revenues of more than $2.2 billion, Essar Group had become one of India's leading and most diversified private sector conglomerates.

M. L. Cohen

PRINCIPAL SUBSIDIARIES

Essar Investments Ltd.; Essar Oil Ltd.; Essar Power Ltd.; Essar Shipping Ltd.; Essar Steel Ltd.; Essar Teleholdings Ltd.; PT Essar Dhananjaya (Indonesia).

PRINCIPAL COMPETITORS

RPG Enterprises; Tata Sons Ltd.; Murugappa Group; Jaypee Group; SKG Solvex Ltd.; Amalgamations Ltd.; Dabur India Ltd.; Balmer Lawrie and Company Ltd.; Escorts Ltd.; HMT Ltd.; Greaves Cotton Ltd.; Bombay Burmah Trading Corporation.

FURTHER READING

"Essar Doubles Indonesian Venture," *Steel Times International,* October 2001, p. 17.

"Essar Group," *Oil and Gas Journal,* October 22, 2001, p. 45.

"Essar Group Eyes Power Sector in Eastern Region," *Business Line,* November 6, 2003.

"Essar Inks $1.1 bn Deal with Trinidad," *Financial Express,* December 8, 2005.

"Essar to Go for DRI in Orissa," *Steel Times International,* May-June 2005, p. 6.

"Essar to Have 37% in Essar-Hutch Entity," *IPR Strategic Business Information Database,* March 11, 2002.

Guha, Krishna, "Payback Time for Essar Steel," *Financial Times,* July 21, 1999, p. 25.

Karmali, Naazneen, "When 13 Is Lucky," *Financial Times,* September 30, 1993, p. FTS16.

"Larger Lessons from the Essar Episode," *Hindu,* July 26, 1999.

Ruia, Ravi, "Where Modern India Stands," *American Metal Market,* August 15, 1994, p. 14.

"Shashi and Ravi Ruia," *India Business Insight,* November 30, 2005.

FEI COMPANY™
TOOLS FOR NANOTECH

FEI Company

5350 NE Dawson Creek Drive
Hillsboro, Oregon 97124-5793
U.S.A.
Telephone: (503) 726-7500
Fax: (503) 726-7509
Web site: http://www.feicompany.com

Public Company
Incorporated: 1973
Employees: 1,757
Sales: $427.2 million (2005)
Stock Exchanges: NASDAQ
Ticker Symbol: FEIC
NAIC: 333319 Other Commercial and Service Industry Machinery Manufacturing

■ ■ ■

FEI Company manufactures structural process management systems, essentially dual beam microscopy and transmission electron microscopy, and related software for three primary markets: nanoelectronics, serving semiconductor and data storage manufacturers; nanobiology, with traditional life-science research customers and emerging sales opportunities in the medical devices and pharmaceuticals industries; and nanoresearch, selling to research institutions and university laboratories. FEI uses electron beams, focused ion beams, or a combination of both to create high-resolution, three-dimensional reconstructions of objects smaller than the sub-Angstrom level (one hundred-millionth of a centimeter). As industries have delved further into nanotechnology, working with structures and devices that range in size from one to 100 nanometers (a nanometer is one billionth of a meter), they have found an increasing need to perform tests, and have turned to FEI for the systems needed to provide the necessary magnification. Chip makers, for example, pack an increasing amount of capabilities on a single tiny wafer, which might be worth $100,000. As a result, they are eager to avoid defects and to fix them when found. FEI systems are able to focus an ion beam to make a cross-sectional cut in the chip, and then with the help of software provide a slice-by-slice 3-D rendition, allowing engineers to isolate flaws and correct them. Developing markets for FEI systems include car and aircraft manufacturers who are beginning to use nanotechnology to develop lighter yet stronger materials; pharmaceutical companies in the development of new drugs and delivery systems; and energy companies interested in using the technology to develop alternative energy sources and improve the petroleum refining process. Based in Hillsboro, Oregon, FEI Company is a public company listed on the NASDAQ.

FOUNDER'S INTEREST IN FIELD EMISSIONS TECHNOLOGY BEGINS IN 1959

FEI was founded by Dr. Lynwood Swanson. He grew up in California with a career in medicine or pharmacy in mind, but he accepted a football scholarship to the University of the Pacific, which did not offer any majors in the health field. Instead, Swanson began to study chemistry and became enamored with it, ultimately earning a degree in chemistry and physics. He then

COMPANY PERSPECTIVES

With R&D centers in North America and Europe, and sales and service operations in more the 40 countries around the world, FEI is bringing the nanoscale within the grasp of leading researchers and manufacturers and helping to turn some of the biggest ideas of this century into reality.

earned a doctorate in physical chemistry at the University of California, Davis in 1959 and began doing postdoctoral work at the University of Chicago, involved in basic research in field emissions, the release of electrons from atoms. It was also in 1959 that Swanson met a pioneer in the field, Dr. Walter Dyke, a man who would become his mentor.

Dyke had earned a physics degree at Linfield in 1938, but his postgraduate studies at the University of Washington were interrupted by World War II. During these years he worked on radar research at the Massachusetts Institute of Technology and had to contend with the effects of emissions from the electron beam upon which radar relied. He sensed that if these emissions could be harnessed they might be exploited. After completing his doctorate following the war he returned to Linfield and began conducting field emission research. In 1955 the Linfield Research Institute (LRI) was formed in McMinnville, Oregon, to relieve the physics department of the burden Dyke's research placed upon it. LRI soon found a commercial application for its field emissions work: a flash x-ray system that could be used in stop-motion radiography and radiation research. In order to actually manufacture the system and other products that might result from LRI's research, Dyke formed Field Emission Corp. in 1958.

In 1961 Swanson joined Dyke at LRI and also began to teach at Linfield. He would form the second company to grow out of LRI, Field Electron and Ion, established in 1971 in a building on the Linfield campus with partners Noel Martin and Lloyd Swenson. Two years later the name would be abbreviated and the business incorporated as FEI Company. FEI was established to supply field emission researchers with high-purity, oriented single crystal materials. It operated quietly for several years and then became better known in its field, especially with the design and manufacture of electron and ion beam emitters. In 1981 it developed liquid metal ion (LMI) sources, improving focus beam technology and having a major impact on the semiconductor industry, which used focus beam technology to improve methods of failure analysis. A year later FEI began shipping its first LMI focusing column. The company began to take off, picking up major corporate customers such as Hewlett-Packard, Intel Corp., and Seagate Technology. FEI would eventually move its operations to Hillsboro, Oregon, to be closer to these customers.

MAJOR GROWTH SPURT BEGINNING IN 1987

Swanson was not fully committed to FEI as it rose in prominence. In 1973 he conducted surface physics research and advised students at the Oregon Graduate Institute, but by 1987 it was obvious that FEI was on the verge of major growth, due to changes in high technology. "When the semiconductor industry started talking in terms of nanometers," he told the *News Register* of McMinnville, "people needed tools to visualize that and create things. We had the technology ready at the right time." Not only in the semiconductor industry but also in structural biology and protein research were FEI microscopes of critical importance. Hence, Swanson decided to leave teaching in 1987, devoting himself full-time to running FEI.

To fuel its growth, in 1988 FEI raised $300,000 in a first round of funding from the Oregon Resource & Technology Development Corp. Fund, established by Northwest Technology Ventures. A year later the company achieved another milestone when it shipped its first complete ion beam (FIB) workstation. FEI closed the decade by recording sales of $4.5 million, a number that would increase to $7.5 million in 1990. The company also posted profits, something it had accomplished every year of its existence.

FEI started the 1990s employing around 85 people who worked in 25,000 square feet of leased space at Hillsboro's Oregon Graduate Center Science Park, later renamed AmberGlen Business Center. However, the company was growing so quickly at this stage that it needed to double its workforce and move to a larger space. Plans were announced in August 1991 to move into a larger custom-made building at AmberGlen, but a recession prompted FEI to be cautious. Instead, in December 1992, FEI signed a ten-year lease on a 43,300-square-foot building under construction in Hillsboro. It had been started seven years earlier but never got past the foundation stage when the area real estate market collapsed.

In the early 1990s FEI forged an alliance with Philips Electron Optics to develop an innovative new product. With experience in electron optics dating to

KEY DATES

1971: The company is founded as Field Electron and Ion by Dr. Lynwood Swanson.
1973: The company is incorporated as FEI Company.
1982: FEI ships the first LMI focusing column.
1995: FEI goes public.
1997: The company merges with Philips Electron Optics.
1999: The company merges with Micrion Corporation.
2004: Swanson retires.

the 1930s, Philips had built the world's first commercial transmission electron microscope in 1949 and had been responsible for a number of advances in the field in the years that followed. In 1990 Philips introduced a scanning electron microscope (SEM) suitable for use with six-inch semiconductor wafers. By directing a beam of focused electrons across an object and reading both the electrons deflected by the object and the secondary electrons produced by it, the microscope was able to create a three-dimensional image on a screen. FEI and Philips joined their technologies in 1993 to create the first DualBeam (FIB/SEM) workstation.

To support further growth, FEI looked to make an initial public offering (IPO) of stock in early 1994, but postponed it because of a rash of IPOs that depleted the resources of potential investors. It was not until June 1995 that FEI finally went public. With Black & Company Inc. and Pacific Growth Equities Shares serving as underwriters, the offering raised $23.8 million for the company. FEI's status as an independent public company would not last long, however. In September 1996 Philips Electronics N.V., parent company of Philips Electron Optics, acquired a 55 percent controlling interest in FEI. The operations of FEI and Philips Electron Optics would be merged under the FEI name in February 1997. While the merger was being sorted out Philips Electron Optics added some valuable assets that would become part of the business mix. ElectroScan and its ESEM (environmental scanning electron microscope) technology was acquired. ESEM did not require the high level of vacuum conditions in the specimen chamber as did conventional SEM. Philips also acquired a Czech company, Delmi S.R.O., in 1996.

In its first year of operation as an expanded company, FEI generated sales of $168 million. It was now a global enterprise employing close to 1,000 people in plants in the United States, The Netherlands, and the Czech Republic. FEI also was beginning to make the transition from equipment manufacturer to provider of customized solutions. In fact, almost one-quarter of its revenues came from service and components.

FEI experienced a change in leadership in 1998 when Vahe Sarkissian was named president and chief executive officer. Swanson remained as chairman. Sarkissian was a seasoned executive, the former president and chief operating officer of Silicon Valley Group and the president and CEO of an electron beam meteorology company, Metrologix Inc. During its first year under the new CEO, FEI launched a pair of new product families: the Tecnai transmission electron microscope and the xP860 DualBeam system for chipmakers' fabrication process control. Traditionally, FEI products had been used in the laboratory, but now they would go from lab to "fab," integrated into the fabrication process itself to provide ongoing verification. As a result, the market for FEI systems was expected to rise sharply. For the year sales increased to $178.8 million, but the company also took steps to grow its business even more quickly.

ACQUIRING MICRION IN 1999

In December 1998 FEI agreed to acquire Peabody, Massachusetts-based Micrion Corporation, a $70 million cash and stock deal that closed in 1999. With 200 employees Micrion manufactured FIB workstations, having shipped its first system in 1985. Micrion focused mostly on the high end of the FIB market, while FEI offered systems from the lower end and up. They often contended for the same business, so that by merging they created a near-monopoly in the FIB market. The consolidation actually served the interests of its customers, which were looking to deal with fewer companies and wanted the kind of integrated solutions to their problems that a combined FEI and Micrion could provide in the FIB arena.

With Micrion in the fold, FEI saw sales increase to more than $216 million in 1999. Another significant development in 1999 was the forging of a distribution agreement with Tokyo Electronics Ltd., an alliance that expanded FEI's product line while adding new markets. Revenues increased to $320.3 million in 2000 and $376 million in 2001. FEI also held a well-received secondary offering of stock in 2001, netting $89.3 million for the company. About $32.5 million was used to pay back a unit of the parent company, and a sizable amount was reserved for increased spending on research and development. Philips also sold some of its interest in FEI as part of the offering, so that it no longer held a controlling interest. With a 31 percent stake, however,

Philips remained a serious investor and supporter of FEI's effort.

FEI was adversely impacted by a serious downturn in the semiconductor industry but fared better than most equipment vendors because its systems were finding an increasing number of industrial and medical applications. Consolidation continued in the semiconductor equipment market, and FEI almost became part of that trend in 2002 when an agreement was reached with Veeco Instruments Inc. to sell FEI for nearly $1 billion in stock, a deal that would have resulted in the sixth largest company in the field. However, the merger would never come to fruition and ultimately was dropped in January 2003. In the meantime, FEI took steps to solidify its ties to Oregon, agreeing to buy a 27-acre campus in Hillsboro where it planned to employ 350 people in five buildings, including a 112,000-square-foot manufacturing and research and development facility and a 68,000-square-foot office facility.

While revenues dropped to $341 million in 2002, FEI continued to expand its product offerings and diversify its markets, part of an effort to push the company to the $1 billion annual sales mark. It completed a pair of strategic acquisitions in 2003, buying software product lines for manufacturing and semiconductor fabrication yield, and acquiring Revise Inc., maker of laser etching products.

FEI enjoyed a strong year in 2004, increasing sales 29 percent to $465.7 million and improving net income from $7.2 million to $16.6 million. The year also saw the retirement of Swanson, who turned over the chairmanship to Sarkissian. In 2005 FEI realigned its sales, marketing, and research operations to focus on three major nanotechnology markets—nanoelectronics, nanobiology, and nanoresearch—as it prepared to take advantage of future opportunities.

Ed Dinger

PRINCIPAL SUBSIDIARIES

FEI Asia Company; FEI Electron Optics International B.V.; FEI Deutschland GmbH; FEI Czech Republic S.R.O.; FEI Europe Ltd.

PRINCIPAL COMPETITORS

Applied Materials, Inc.; JEOL Ltd.; KLA-Tencot Corporation.

FURTHER READING

Earnshaw, Aliza, "FEI Puts Market Ahead of Products in Culture Change," *Portland Business Journal,* October 17, 2005.

———, "FEI's Strategy for Reaching Big Leagues," *Portland Business Journal,* August 18, 2003.

Fasca, Chad, "FEI, Micrion to Merge," *Electronic News,* December 7, 1998, p. 4.

Graham, Jed, "FEI Emerges As Defect Hunter," *Investor's Business Daily,* May 1, 2001, p. A04.

McIntyre, Jo, "FEI Is One of the Eyes of the Nan Science and Business Boom," *smalltimes, http://www.smalltimes.com/document_display.cfm?document_id=6949,* November 17, 2003.

Opdyke, Jeff D., "FEI CO. Is Moving Out of the Land and into New Growth Prospects," *Wall Street Journal,* January 13, 1999, p. NW2.

Pointer, Starla, "A Lead in His Field," *News-Register* (McMinnville, Ore.), May 14, 2005.

Saarinen, Yvette, "Field Emissions Research Finds a Home in Mac," *News-Register* (McMinnville, Ore.), November 4, 2000.

The Forzani Group Ltd.

824 41st Avenue N.E.
Calgary, Alberta T2E 3R3
Canada
Telephone: (403) 717-1400
Fax: (403) 717-1490
Web site: http://www.forzanigroup.com

Public Company
Incorporated: 1991
Employees: 9,516
Sales: CAD 1.13 billion ($984.3 million) (2006)
Stock Exchanges: Toronto
Ticker Symbol: FGL
NAIC: 451110 Sporting Goods Stores; 454110 Electronic Shopping and Mail-Order Houses; 421910 Sporting and Recreational Goods and Supplies Wholesalers; 533110 Lessors of Nonfinancial Intangible Assets (Except Copyrighted Works)

■ ■ ■

The Forzani Group Ltd. is the leading, and only national, sporting goods retailer in Canada. From the launch of a single outlet called Forzani's Locker Room by four Calgary Stampeder football players in 1974, the company has grown into an empire stretching across Canada and encompassing more than 450 stores, approximately 60 percent of which are company owned with the remainder being franchised outlets.

Forzani operates four company-owned retail chains: Sport Chek, Sport Mart, Coast Mountain Sports, and National Sports. Sport Chek outlets are large, typically about 20,000 square feet but with a few much larger, and are located primarily in enclosed malls and so-called power centers; their wide range of brand-name and private-label sporting goods are priced for the middle of the market. The smaller Sport Mart units, ranging from 5,000 to 11,000 square feet, are also located in shopping malls and power centers but their merchandise is priced for the lower to middle segment of the market; Sport Mart also runs an online store at www.sportmart.ca. Situated on the high end is Coast Mountain Sports, which offers outdoor technical gear; casual clothing, footwear, and accessories; and private-label apparel. National Sports, whose locations are centered in southern Ontario, focuses on team sports and the "athletic family." On the franchise side, Forzani administers a varicty of banners, including Sports Experts, Intersport, Atmosphere, RnR, Econosports, Tech Shop, Pegasus, Nevada Bob's Golf, Hockey Experts, and The Fitness Source.

Forzani also runs its own wholesaling operation, which oversees the development, manufacturing, and importing of private-label-brand products that are sold to Forzani's own corporate stores, to Forzani franchisees, and to other retailers. Approximately one-fourth of the company's total sales are generated by the wholesale side, which helps to counter the cyclical and seasonal nature of the retail operations. Western Canada is the origination point for about 39 percent of overall revenues, Ontario and Quebec are responsible for ap-

COMPANY PERSPECTIVES

Our mission is to provide the best customer shopping experience; to have the largest market share and buying power; to always remain the lowest cost competitor in any retail business that we participate in; and to offer branded and private-branded products in a manner that is unique, maintaining our Company's continued position as the most profitable sports/lifestyle retailer in Canada.

proximately 28 percent each, and eastern and northern Canada generate the remaining 5 percent.

BEGINNINGS AS OFF-SEASON VENTURE OF STAMPEDERS FOOTBALL PLAYERS

The driving force behind the Forzani Group throughout its history has been John Forzani, who was born in Calgary in 1947 and grew up in that city's Little Italy, part of a tight-knit family. Forzani's father had been a successful businessman himself as the owner of a prosperous service station, and when Forzani attended Utah State University on a full-ride football scholarship, he graduated in 1971 with a degree in business administration. Forzani was the middle brother of a football-playing Forzani trio that also included Joe and Tom. All three brothers attended Utah State and went on to star for the Calgary Stampeders of the professional Canadian Football League (CFL), John an offensive guard, Joe a linebacker, and Tom a running back. They became local heroes. During John's rookie season, the Stampeders won the Grey Cup, the CFL equivalent of the Super Bowl.

In 1974, in the middle of his CFL career, which extended from 1971 to 1977, John Forzani was inspired to open an athletic shoe store. He had noted that Calgary did not have a single outlet for athletic shoes and that he and other athletes typically bought their shoes in the United States. The spark that launched him into entrepreneurship was an article he read while working at his father-in-law's sporting goods store in Logan, Utah, during the off-season. The article focused on the owner of a sporting goods store who, lacking room for expansion, moved his shoe department into a separate location nearby, after which his shoe sales skyrocketed. Recognizing a good idea, Forzani pooled CAD 2,500 of his own money together with CAD 7,000 from his brothers Joe and Tom and the Forzanis' friend and Stampeders teammate Basil Bark to open the first Forzani's Locker Room, a 1,200-square-foot store in Calgary.

Forzani's timing could not have been better. Although Forzani had originally envisioned catering to full-time athletes, he quickly found that his venture had propitiously coincided with the start of the jogging and fitness craze and its legion of baby-boomer participants. The Nike brand of shoes had just been launched, and this and other highly technical footwear required experts to serve as salespersons. Forzani's Locker Room was staffed with hard-core athletes, who were able to provide expert guidance to the baby boomers taking up running and other sports to stay in shape. Soon, the store found itself maintaining waiting lists for particular models. During its first year, the venture netted CAD 10,000 on sales of CAD 214,000; sales proceeded to double for each of the next few years. Of these early years, Forzani told *Alberta Report* in 1995, "We had a winning formula, we had good people, and suddenly we were growing."

Although the venture was originally a part-time endeavor for Forzani, even, initially, somewhat of a lark, it eventually began to overshadow even football. "I'd go into the huddle and I wouldn't even listen to the quarterback—I would be thinking about my adidas shipment," he told *Report on Business Magazine* in 2003. After retiring following the 1977 football season, Forzani dedicated himself full-time to retailing. By the end of the fiscal year ending in January 1978, his company's sales had reached CAD 1 million, profits had reached CAD 150,000, and Forzani and company had expanded their operation into a seven-store chain.

FIRST ACQUISITIONS, GOING PUBLIC

Over the ensuing dozen years or so, the company steadily expanded, opening additional stores in western Canada. In the late 1980s the firm began launching additional retail concepts, including RnR—The Walking Store, which catered to aging baby boomers, and Jersey City, purveyor of pro sports merchandise. Forzani, however, recognized that the company needed to start pursuing acquisitions to keep growing and in particular to expand into eastern Canada. In 1991, the same year that The Forzani Group Ltd. was incorporated, the founder engineered the sale of a 35 percent stake in the company to Edmonton-based Vencap Equities Ltd., a venture capital firm. With this added backing, the Forzani Group completed its first deal, the acquisition of the ailing Sport Chek International Ltd. Founded in 1976 and also based in Calgary, Sport Chek was the first Canadian retailer to venture into the sporting goods superstore category. By the time of its acquisition, the Sport Chek chain consisted of eight locations, seven of which were

KEY DATES

1974: John Forzani and partners open the first Forzani's Locker Room, an athletic shoe store in Calgary.
1991: Company is incorporated as The Forzani Group Ltd.; Sport Chek International Ltd. is acquired.
1993: Forzani Group goes public.
1994: Sports Experts is acquired.
1996: Forzani reports the first net loss in the company's history.
1997: New management team is put in place to lead a turnaround.
2000: Forzani acquires Coast Mountain Sports Inc.
2001: Sport Mart Inc. is acquired.
2005: National Sports chain is acquired.

located in Alberta, each 20,000-square-foot store offering a wide and deep selection of merchandise at competitive prices.

The Sport Chek acquisition was followed in 1992 by the CAD 2.3 million purchase of Hogarth's Sport & Ski, which added six stores in British Columbia that were subsequently converted to the Sport Chek format. In 1992 Forzani's revenues reached CAD 55.6 million, a 21 percent increase over the previous year, while profits nearly tripled to CAD 1.1 million. To fund further growth, Forzani Group was taken public through an August 1993 initial public offering on the Toronto Stock Exchange that raised CAD 10.4 million.

Forzani next made a daring move, paying CAD 22 million to Univa Inc. in April 1994 for the Sports Experts chain, which Univa had been attempting to unload since 1991. Sports Experts, based in Montreal, was a franchiser of several sporting goods concepts and gave Forzani immediate entrance into the central and eastern Canadian markets. The 121-store Sports Experts chain consisted of all mall-based stores averaging 6,000 square feet in size and offering a wide variety of clothing and footwear and a select range of sporting goods. Among the other chains included in the deal was Podium, whose 43 outlets were located in smaller shopping centers and in rural communities and offered a variety of sporting goods, clothing, and footwear; some locales also featured extensive lines of outdoor gear for hunting, fishing, and camping. This acquisition of a much larger player transformed Forzani Group into a nationwide retailer and propelled its revenues to CAD 296.7 million for the fiscal year ending January 1995. Profits that year totaled CAD 7.7 million.

TURNAROUND FROM NEAR BANKRUPTCY

Acquiring Sports Experts, however, nearly proved to be Forzani's undoing. Integrating the corporate-owned Forzani's Locker Rooms and Sport Cheks with the franchised operations of Sports Experts proved quite difficult. Particularly troublesome was the launch of a new company-wide inventory management system. The system was fast-tracked once a new threat appeared on the horizon: the entrance of two U.S. "category killers," Sportmart, Inc. and the Sports Authority, Inc., into the Canadian market. The Forzani Group rushed to implement the expensive new system, leading to bogged-down deliveries, duplicate purchasing, and more than CAD 30 million of overstocking that eventually had to be dumped at deep discounts. Also adding to the operational woes was a huge and simultaneous expansion of the Sport Chek chain, which was taken national through the addition of another 32 stores in less than one year. This move too was aimed at fending off the encroaching U.S. competitors. The first Sportmart store opened in Toronto in March 1995, with Sports Authority arriving a few months later.

The operational difficulties, the increased competition, and a slowdown in consumer spending combined to create the first year in the red in company history, a CAD 5 million loss for the year ending in January 1996. John Forzani followed the lead of a number of outside consultants in quickly overseeing the completion of the new inventory system and in refinancing the firm's debt in order to stave off a possible bankruptcy filing. Perhaps most importantly in the long term, he agreed to shake up his management team. The old-timers who had been running the show simply did not have the experience to handle the enlarged and complex operations of the post–Sports Experts company. In early 1997, then, Forzani hired Bill Gregson as executive vice-president of corporate retailing and Bob Sartor as president and chief financial officer. Gregson was a turnaround specialist credited with rejuvenating the fortunes of Bata Industries Ltd.'s Athletes World chain. Sartor had previously served as corporate controller of Avenor Inc. and treasurer of Kraft Canada Inc. A third management change saw Tom Quinn, a Sports Experts veteran, promoted to head of the franchise operations.

These appointments were made just before Forzani announced a hefty loss of CAD 32.8 million for 1996, a result that included CAD 13.6 million in charges for asset writedowns and restructuring costs. The new management team focused relentlessly on the bottom line, placing real controls on inventory, adopting a penny-pinching approach to advertising, and closing down around 30 underperforming stores. The selection of products was overhauled as well, with an increased emphasis on that quintessential Canadian sport, hockey, including a full range of women's gear. The latter move was part of a larger strategy to carry more women's merchandise across the board, particularly casual fashions. Forzani shifted focus away from highly seasonal equipment toward clothing, which offered higher turnover, larger margins, and more growth potential. Forzani's Locker Room was relaunched as simply Forzani's, with the store size doubled to between 4,000 and 7,000 square feet in order to make it stand out from smaller mall competitors. Through these and other initiatives, Forzani turned the corner. The company returned to the black in 1998, posting a net gain of CAD 276,000, and then the following year reported record profits of CAD 8.1 million on revenues of CAD 378.6 million. Although its defense of its home turf had nearly turned suicidal, Forzani also succeeded in fending off the south-of-the-border encroachers. Sportmart abandoned the Canadian market in early 1997, and the Sports Authority did the same one year later.

LOOKING TO THE FUTURE

The results for 1999 were the start of a streak of four consecutive years of record results in both profits and revenues. During this period Forzani aggressively expanded its existing chains as well as its lineup of store formats. The company reached a deal with Austria-based Intersport S.A. to be the exclusive supplier of Intersport private-label products for the Canadian and U.S. markets, and also purchased a 6.7 percent stake in Intersport. Intersport, Europe's largest sporting goods retailer and distributor, ranked as the largest sporting goods buying group in the world. In 2000 Forzani converted all of its Podium stores and 14 Sports Experts outlets to the Intersport banner.

The company next added two more corporate-owned banners to its portfolio. In June 2000 the company acquired Vancouver-based Coast Mountain Sports Inc., operator of five stores in British Columbia, Alberta, and the Yukon offering high-end outdoor merchandise. This addition provided an entree for the Forzani Group into the fishing, hunting, hiking, and mountaineering markets. Forzani next went down market in the fall of 2000 with the launch of Save on Sports as a regional sports specialty store offering brand-name merchandise at everyday low prices. But this proved to be a short-lived venture following the August 2001 acquisition of Sport Mart Inc. for CAD 35 million. Based in Kamloops, British Columbia, Sport Mart (which was unrelated to the U.S.-based Sportmart) operated 36 stores in its home province, Saskatchewan, Manitoba, and Ontario. Its focus on the lower-end of the market provided Forzani with a quicker way to expand within this segment, and therefore the Save on Sports outlets were subsequently converted into Sport Marts. On the franchise side, Forzani in 2001 launched Atmosphere, seller of outdoor gear, in Quebec. By the end of the year, Forzani had grabbed about 15 percent of the Canadian sporting goods market, making it the leader of the CAD 6 billion category. It was by then operating or franchising 345 stores totaling 3.6 million square feet of retail space.

During 2002 Forzani opened 38 more corporate stores—14 Sport Cheks, 18 Sport Marts, and 6 Coast Mountain Sports. The company also began testing a new, larger format for Sport Chek that encompassed 42,000 square feet. In addition, it opened a new distribution center for western Canada located in Calgary. Revenues for the year surpassed the CAD 1 billion mark for the first time, and profits reached a record CAD 30.5 million. In February 2003 John Forzani stepped down as CEO but remained chairman. Sartor was named his successor, while Gregson was named president and chief operating officer.

Forzani's streak of full-year profit increases ended in 2003 with a 6.6 percent drop in earnings. Two of the factors contributing to this decline were the slowest growth in the sporting goods industry in several years and heightened competition in the casual clothing sector due in part to the entrance into the Canadian market of several U.S. casual clothing chains, including Old Navy and American Eagle. Forzani reacted quickly, shutting down the Forzani's chain and shifting the merchandise mix at its principal remaining chains to deemphasize nonathletic, nontechnical clothing. The firm's difficulties, however, continued over the next two years. A key factor was that the company had been concentrating so much on expansion that it was neglecting its existing stores. Both the older stores and the merchandise were looking tired. Renovations of existing stores were launched, particularly at the Sport Chek outlets, and the lines of merchandise were overhauled. By the second half of 2005 it appeared that the Forzani Group was well on its way to another comeback. Earnings for the fourth quarter were a record CAD 17 million, while revenues also reached a new high, CAD 438 million. Same-store sales (that is, sales at stores open at least one year) at the corporate stores increased a very healthy 10.1 percent.

Despite the struggles during this period, Forzani completed a series of acquisitions. In March 2004 the company bolstered its wholesale side by purchasing

Gen-X Sports Inc., a distributor specializing in selling excess merchandise from manufacturers. Forzani enhanced its position in the Ontario market in January 2005 by acquiring National Gym Clothing Limited, the operator of 19 National Sports stores in the province that collectively generated annual sales of about CAD 80 million. These outlets averaged 20,000 to 25,000 square feet of retail space and offered a wide variety of sporting apparel and equipment. As its opportunities for growth in the general sporting goods sector diminished, Forzani began venturing into the specialty sports retailing market. In the summer of 2004 the company gained the Canadian rights to the Nevada Bob's golf equipment chain, thereby acquiring 23 franchised Nevada Bob's outlets. In early 2006 Forzani acquired The Fitness Source Inc., operator of nine retail stores in Ontario selling home fitness products as well as commercial exercise equipment and accessories. By this time the company's franchise division had also launched two additional specialty sports banners: Hockey Experts and Pegasus, the latter focusing on running shoes.

David E. Salamie

PRINCIPAL SUBSIDIARIES

Sports Experts 2000 Inc.; Intersport North America Ltd.; Sport-Chek International 2000 Ltd.; Gen-X Sports Inc.; National Gym Clothing Limited; The Fitness Sources Inc.

PRINCIPAL COMPETITORS

Canadian Tire Corporation, Limited; Sears Canada Inc.; Wal-Mart Canada Corp.; Zellers Inc.; Costco Wholesale Canada Ltd.

FURTHER READING

Bhonslay, Marianne, "The Player," *Sporting Goods Business,* March 2002, pp. 32–33.

Brent, Paul, "Battered Forzani Bounces Back Off Ropes," *Financial Post,* May 8, 1996, p. 21.

———, "Forzani Jumps into Big Leagues of Sports Retailing," *Financial Post,* January 4, 1994, p. 12.

———, "Forzani Set to Expand Sports Empire," *Financial Post,* August 31, 1993, p. 12.

Brethour, Patrick, and Janet McFarland, "Forzani Agrees to Pay Record Settlement," *Globe and Mail,* July 7, 2004, p. B1.

Brooker, Kevin, "How Do We Do It? Volume! John Forzani Had a Simple Plan: Buy Big, It Worked," *Report on Business Magazine,* January 2003, pp. 66–70.

Flavelle, Dana, "National Sports Sale Tightens Sector," *Toronto Star,* January 21, 2005, p. E1.

Gaffney, John, "On Guard," *Sporting Goods Business,* August 1995, pp. 76+.

Hutchinson, Brian, "The Forzani Fortune," *Alberta Report,* September 13, 1993, p. 16.

Ingram, Mathew, "Forzani Builds a New Team," *Globe and Mail,* January 16, 1997, p. B2.

———, "Forzani Quietly Restructures," *Globe and Mail,* April 15, 1997, p. B2.

Koch, George, "First and Goal," *Profit,* April 1, 1997, p. 36.

———, "Forzani's Long Bomb," *Alberta Report,* May 15, 1995, p. 18.

———, "Forzani Turns the Corner," *Globe and Mail,* January 13, 1998, p. B2.

Lau, Michael, "Forzani's Ambitions Strictly Canadian," *Calgary Herald,* June 6, 2002, p. D1.

Motherwell, Cathryn, "Ex-Football Players Tackle Bigger-League Retailing," *Globe and Mail,* March 7, 1994, p. B1.

O'Brien, Greg, "On the Offensive," *Footwear News,* August 30, 1999, p. 28.

Olijnyk, Zena, "At the Top of Its Game," *Canadian Business,* April 29, 2002.

———, "Everything in Place at Forzani for a Turnaround," *Financial Post,* December 24, 1997, p. 11.

Onstad, Katrina, "Extreme Retailing," *Canadian Business,* September 26, 1997, p. 94.

Ramage, Norma, "Forzani Covers the Field," *Marketing Magazine,* September 9, 2002.

———, "Forzani Sticks to Offense," *Marketing Magazine,* October 9, 2000, p. 23.

Strauss, Marina, "Fierce Competition Still Battering Forzani," *Globe and Mail,* December 6, 1996, p. B1.

———, "Forzani Gets Back on Track for Turnaround," *Globe and Mail,* September 21, 2005, p. B6.

———, "Forzani Group Purchases Sport Mart," *Globe and Mail,* June 22, 2001, p. B3.

———, "Forzani Hires Bata Veteran to Lead Recovery," *Globe and Mail,* January 7, 1997, p. B1.

———, "Forzani Scores Deal to Buy National Sports, Targeting Key Ontario Market," *Globe and Mail,* January 21, 2005, p. B3.

———, "Forzani to Expand Test of Specialty Stores Despite Profit Woes," *Globe and Mail,* November 3, 2004, p. B1.

Toneguzzi, Mario, "Forzani CEO Predicts Year of Momentum," *Calgary Herald,* January 5, 2006, p. F1.

———, "Forzani Group Puts Up Record Fourth-Quarter Profit," *Calgary Herald,* March 25, 2006, p. C5.

———, "Forzani Predicts Worst Over After Posting $2.3M Loss," *Calgary Herald,* September 1, 2005, p. E3.

Fuji Photo Film Co., Ltd.

26-30, Nishiazabu 2-chome
Minato-ku
Tokyo, 106-8620
Japan
Telephone: (03) 3406-2111
Fax: (03) 3406-2193
Web site: http://www.fujifilm.co.jp

Public Company
Incorporated: 1934
Employees: 76,430
Sales: ¥2.53 trillion ($23.62 billion) (2005)
Stock Exchanges: Tokyo Osaka Nagoya
Ticker Symbol: 4901
NAIC: 325992 Photographic Film, Paper, Plate, and Chemical Manufacturing; 333314 Optical Instrument and Lens Manufacturing; 333315 Photographic and Photocopying Equipment Manufacturing; 334119 Other Computer Peripheral Equipment Manufacturing; 334613 Magnetic and Optical Recording Media Manufacturing; 339112 Surgical and Medical Instrument Manufacturing

Fuji Photo Film Co., Ltd. originated as a cinematic-film producer and has grown into a multidimensional manufacturer and marketer of imaging and information products. Fuji is by far the largest maker of photographic film in Japan while running neck-and-neck with Eastman Kodak Company for the lead in the world market. While still producing a wide range of film for still cameras, as well as motion picture film, photofinishing equipment, and color paper, chemicals, and services for photofinishing, Fuji has made a concerted push into the digital world, producing digital cameras, printers and office copiers, digital recording media, medical imaging products, and materials for flat panel displays. A little over half of revenues are derived in the Japanese market, while the Americas account for about 20 percent, Europe, nearly 14 percent, and the Asia-Pacific region (except for Japan), the Middle East, and Africa, another 14 percent.

EARLY HISTORY

In 1934 Dainippon Celluloid Company, Japan's first cinematic film manufacturer (and later renamed Daicel Chemical Industries, Ltd.), spun off its troubled photographic division. Named Fuji Photo Film Co., Ltd., the new company already employed 340 people and named Shuichi Asano as its first president. Its product line included motion picture film, dry plates, and photographic paper. The company struggled for three years, mainly because of the poor quality and high prices of its products relative to imports.

Fuji's first task was to build a reputation in the domestic market. Brand reliability proved critical in the photosensitive-materials industry, since buyers were not willing to risk losing a desired image to inadequate materials, regardless of cost. During its first three years, the company continued to lose sales, increase debt, and struggle to meet research expenses. Fuji could not expand without first addressing quality, so it employed a German specialist to assist in the area of emulsion technology.

COMPANY PERSPECTIVES

Fujifilm will constantly strive to develop superior technologies and to continue to cultivate an imaging and information culture. As a global company fully trusted by both customers and society itself, we aim to make innovative use of the most advanced technologies to create beautiful images and wide-ranging information and provide the imaging, information, and document solutions that will best meet the increasingly sophisticated needs of the world community.

The combination of outside consultation and its own research allowed the company to introduce its first film as an independent in 1936, as well as a motion picture negative film. The negative film was much harder to produce, and demonstrated Fuji's new technical competence to Japanese studios.

Fuji built a second factory in Odawara in 1938. Color research began in a new laboratory in 1939, but World War II halted such work. During the war the government set aside all sensitized materials for the military, so consumer-film development had to wait out the war. In 1945 Allied bombing raids partially damaged two Fuji factories, but recovery during the postwar era involved more than infrastructural repair.

The Allied Powers allowed civilian trade to resume in 1947, and Fuji immediately began exporting to outlets in South America and Asia. Japanese producers still enjoyed a good reputation in optical products, enabling Fuji to export its cameras and binoculars. In the area of film and other sensitized materials, however, Japanese technology still lagged behind U.S. and European producers.

Although it produced X-ray and cinematic film, Fuji did not produce large amounts of film for the amateur consumer market until the 1950s. In the meantime, it resumed color research and produced its first color film in 1948. In 1949 Indian buyers received a shipment of Fuji motion picture film, the company's first substantial postwar sale.

DOMESTIC AND OVERSEAS GROWTH

As the 1940s ended, so did a shortage of raw materials, including silver, paper, and petroleum-based chemicals, which kept Fuji from producing amateur photographic products in large quantities. Licensing agreements between Fuji and Eastman Kodak of the United States allowed Fuji to equal Western producers in terms of black-and-white amateur roll film quality. Fuji, now able to supply its products in large quantities, introduced its first amateur roll film in 1952. By 1958 Fuji had introduced three additional black-and-white roll films.

Fuji enjoyed burgeoning domestic demand for the next 20 years, due in part to tariffs on film imports. During the 1950s Fuji captured the Japanese market for consumer films, a market that would quickly comprise 15 percent of the world's total film sales. Branching out, Fuji joined forces with Xerox Corporation to create a Japan-based 50-50 joint venture called Fuji Xerox Co., Ltd., which concentrated on selling copies in Japan and the Pacific Rim.

After setting up an export sales division in 1956, Fuji reached 27 export agreements by 1958 in Asia, North America, and Central America. Fuji first entered North America in 1955, and established its U.S. subsidiary (Fuji Photo Film U.S.A., Inc.) ten years later.

As Fuji's international base grew, it still had to fight a perception of poor quality. In order to make a serious drive abroad, the company first had to develop film and paper compatible with the processing systems most commonly used worldwide. In 1966 Fuji introduced its first amateur slide film compatible with overseas processors. By 1969 all its films, photo paper, and chemicals were fully compatible. Employing the sales network it had established in the 1950s, exports began to flow.

In 1970 Fuji had nine overseas offices, and by the end of the decade it had 14 offices and subsidiaries abroad. These subsidiaries then branched out. Fuji's U.S. subsidiary, for instance, opened six offices between 1971 and 1982.

Recognition in these markets proved more difficult. Eastman Kodak's dominance in consumer films forced all producers to make compatible products in the postwar decades. Fuji learned this after it introduced a cartridge-film 8-millimeter home movie system in 1967. Fuji's product had the support of 14 Japanese and European manufacturers, including AGFA-Gevaert, Europe's largest photographic manufacturer. Kodak introduced its own system shortly after, which quickly gained control of the world market. Fuji had to abandon its system and rushed to develop compatible films. Fuji's overseas growth was slow during the 1970s, adhering to the industry's pace of product development.

In 1970 Kodak held more than 90 percent of the $400 million U.S. market, but Fuji's color films were already faster than Kodak's, meaning they required less

KEY DATES

1934: Dainippon Celluloid Company spins off its photographic division as Fuji Photo Film Co., Ltd.
1952: Fuji Photo begins producing film for the amateur consumer market.
1962: Fuji and Xerox Corporation create the joint venture Fuji Xerox Co., Ltd.
1965: U.S. subsidiary Fuji Photo Film U.S.A., Inc. is established.
1972: Company begins selling film under its own brand name in the United States.
1986: Fuji begins selling disposable cameras.
1988: Fuji produces its first digital camera.
1996: Production of specialized films for LCD screens commences.
2001: Company buys half of Xerox's stake in Fuji Xerox, increasing its stake to 75 percent.
2006: Fuji launches a major restructuring of its photo film and digital camera operations.

light for adequate exposure. In addition, Fuji films were better on warmer tones, including red, orange, and flesh tones. While Kodak pursued the convenience-based mass market, Fuji targeted professionals and serious amateurs. Although it would take several years before Fuji posed a serious threat to Kodak, its quality created a position of strength.

Relative to its competition, Fuji strengthened itself during the 1970s, partially due to the appreciation of the yen between 1971 and 1980. One factor in the growth of Fuji's non-Western markets was its development of manufacturing facilities. Operations in Brazil, Korea, and Indonesia began with Fuji assistance. The operations began with package assembly, but eventually produced presensitized materials, color processing chemicals, and optical products for export. Such manufacturing bases made the company less vulnerable to currency fluctuation and reduced overhead.

Where Fuji saved on manufacturing it spent heavily on research. Fuji began magnetic research in 1954, introduced products by 1960, and in 1963 produced videotape for domestic television. Magnetic products became the key to Fuji's long-term growth. In 1977 this research led to the introduction of Japan's first eight-inch floppy computer discs.

Fuji also developed products related to the photographic process for other industries. In 1967 for instance, Fuji, Mitsubishi Heavy Industries, and Konan Camera Institute developed a system to photographically trace blueprints onto construction materials. In addition to such new applications for heavy industry, Fuji continued to develop new technology for X-rays and other electronic systems for medical technology.

Fuji's core business continued to be film, however, and it pushed for additional access to lucrative Western markets just as Japanese film sales growth began to slow. Fuji had first entered the U.S. market as a private-label film supplier in 1960, and produced its first color film there in 1970. In 1972 it marketed the first film under its own brand name. Fuji went directly to retailers with its new film and received a 2 percent share of the American market, which more than doubled during the 1970s. Fuji's marketing was well-timed, and in 1976 Fuji also caught the attention of professionals and serious amateurs when it beat Kodak with an introduction of faster film (400 ISO speed), something it accomplished in 1984 as well (1600 ISO speed).

Fuji spent heavily to build its U.S. share but had relatively little success. Kodak's research expenditures were still large by comparison, and when Kodak introduced Kodacolor II film in 1972, Japanese companies had to hurry to put comparable films on the market. The recession during the late 1970s complicated Fuji's international drive. Industrywide production overcapacity and price increases for silver and oil-based chemicals cut into earnings.

While silver was still necessary for photographic imaging, its price jump demonstrated the wisdom of Fuji's research into electronic imaging technologies and its mid-1970s hiring campaign for electronics engineers. While many companies posted declines, Fuji's profits were only stagnant for 1977 and 1978.

Fuji was then the third largest filmmaker behind Kodak and AGFA-Gevaert, but the Japanese companies responded to the setbacks more aggressively. Fuji and its domestic competitor, Konishiroku (later Konica Corporation), raised their film prices only 7 percent, while competitors raised their prices from 10 to 30 percent, despite silver prices skyrocketing from $6 to $49 an ounce in 1979.

Silver inflation alone had cost Fuji ¥15 billion in 1979, and exchange losses on export sales cost an additional ¥4.6 billion. By 1979 consumer demand for magnetic products such as audio- and videotape began to climb dramatically, providing Fuji a faster recovery than its competition. Despite continued increases in raw material costs, Fuji's earnings improved quickly because of escalating demand served by the new magnetic-products division.

DIVERSIFICATION DRIVE

In 1980 earnings jumped 130 percent. Silver prices dropped, and sales for magnetic products still grew. Magnetic products, now 9 percent of sales, pushed exports up to 32 percent, where they remained for the entire decade. Fuji was well poised for a renewed assault on Western film markets.

In the 1980s the U.S. amateur film market changed rapidly. Consumers preferred higher-quality 35-millimeter over Kodak's disc, cartridge, or instant photography. Although the market changed to the advantage of manufacturers such as Fuji, who specialized in 35-millimeter films, consumers still demanded convenience. Autofocus cameras and faster film required more sophistication from manufacturers.

Despite this favorable shift in consumer preferences, the photo industry as a whole had matured. Further, while Fuji hoped to gain ground in the U.S. market, that market was only twice as big as the Japanese market in terms of photo sales. Fuji entered the 1980s resolved not only to increase its portion of film sales worldwide, but also to find growth for its products in imaging and electronics.

Minoru Ohnishi replaced Kusuo Hirata and became Fuji's youngest president ever in 1979. Ohnishi had worked for five years in the late 1980s as head of the U.S. subsidiary. His nontraditional appointment overlooked older officers, but he was able to use his experience in the U.S. market to establish a sales network for new products such as magnetic tape, optics, and hybrid electronic systems.

Fuji's growth through the early 1980s had come at the expense of smaller film manufacturers such as 3M and AGFA-Gevaert. By this time Fiji was the second largest firm in the industry, and it set its sights on Kodak's core. By 1982 Fuji's share of the U.S. market had slowly climbed to 5 percent, and Ohnishi set a 10 percent goal.

There were several factors behind Fuji's confidence. First, Kodak's product development in the 1970s was weak. Fuji had kept up with increasingly sophisticated demand by introducing faster and higher resolution films for both cinematic and amateur uses several times. Second, Fuji's research investments had been well placed. Kodak turned from chemical research to electronics late, while Fuji had already recognized the technology's long-term value in processing and imaging. Although Kodak's research expenditures dwarfed Fuji's, Fuji spent a larger share of its earnings on research. In 1979 Kodak applied for 255 patents in the U.S. and Japan, compared to Fuji's 270.

Fuji was the first non-U.S. company to produce videotape. The consumer and trade press praised Fuji tape quality from its introduction. By 1982 magnetic products were already 12 percent of revenues. With broad distribution, a good reputation, and a skyrocketing market, Fuji made large gains.

Magnetic products, like film, provided high margins. Unlike its position in the consumer film market, Fuji enjoyed a prominent role in the magnetic-products marketplace. Between 1978 and 1982 magnetic-division sales increased almost fivefold to $97 million. By 1983 films were only half of Fuji's business.

Newer areas such as biotechnology and office automation had been paid for not with debt but with cash generated from film products and stock sales. Electronic systems, including microfilm records for offices and electronic imaging for X-rays, began to contribute to earnings on their own. In addition, Fuji enjoyed high profit margins in all areas. Pretax operating margins increased one-third to 24.4 percent from 1976 to 1981. Fuji's film, tape, and computer-disc manufacturing was highly automated, allowing workers to circulate among factories for increased productivity.

The climate for high-technology industries proved intense in the 1980s, due in part to trade friction and yen appreciation. In addition, Fuji was relatively new to electronic systems, and other companies had a large lead in areas such as medical technology. In order to remain competitive in these new areas, Fuji had to keep cash available and increase momentum in film sales. Fuji steadily increased its U.S. advertising budget, peaking when it outbid Kodak as sponsor to the 1984 Olympics in Los Angeles. Eventually spending $7 million on the campaign, Fuji entered the event with a 6 percent share of the U.S. market. Meanwhile, Fuji had become a sponsor of soccer's World Cup in 1982, and has continued to sponsor the event from then on.

Simultaneously, the company strengthened distribution. In 1979 Fuji sold film in 30 percent of all film outlets in the United States; by 1984 it sold in 60 percent, expanding beyond specialty photo outlets. By the end of the Olympic year its share jumped to 8 percent, allowing Ohnishi to predict not only a 15 percent share in ten years, but also to carry out a more aggressive approach late in the decade. As Fuji stepped up its efforts to reach the professional market in 1986, its market share approached 10 percent.

Fuji did not face the same battle abroad that it faced in the United States. It already sold over half of the film and photo paper in southeast Asia, and the 1984 opening of a Chinese office gave it a lucrative foothold in an untapped and huge market. Brand loyalty was not as significant outside the United States, and in

1982 Fuji enjoyed a 10 percent share in Europe, Fuji's second largest market. One year later it captured 15 percent of that market, prompting the company to construct its first European plant, in the Netherlands, in 1984. Producing selected sensitized materials, the plant paved the way for continued growth on the continent and lessened difficulty with currency fluctuation.

EXPANDED U.S. PRESENCE

By the mid-1980s the U.S. market had begun to open to Fuji. Despite growth, profits there were still elusive. Videotape prices dropped sharply because of overproduction, and advertising costs continued to climb. While a U.S. market that declined overall was bad for Kodak, it helped Fuji, which was not as reliant on photography. Fuji could still pursue market share while continuing to find growth industries for other forms of imaging.

Fuji's renewed drive in the late 1980s came with more confidence. After a surprisingly successful introduction in Japan in 1986, Fuji was first on the U.S. market with a disposable camera. In Japan, a market less receptive to instant-photography items, Fuji sold 1.5 million cameras in six months. While the traditional market declined, Fuji managed to discover a completely new segment of consumer photography. By 1992, Fuji was the number one maker of cameras worldwide. In the meantime, Fuji was a pioneer in the field of digital cameras, introducing its first model, the DS-1P, in 1988.

By 1988 Fuji had achieved its 10 percent share and the exchange rate was favorable for building in the United States. The company built a plant in Greenwood, South Carolina, to make presensitized plates and related products. In 1989 a factory opened in Bedford, Massachusetts, to manufacture 3.5-inch floppy discs in a joint venture with BASF Corporation (Fuji bought out BASF in 1994 so that the facility was then wholly owned by Fuji). Another factory opened in Greenwood in 1991 to make videotapes. Moving production to the market served by the factory provided faster delivery and immunity from currency exchange losses, and eliminated charges of dumping.

With a double-digit market share firmly in place, Fuji sought to increase use of its processing systems, since Kodak's Colorwatch processing network still provided an obstacle, steadily enlarging its share of the photofinishing market. Launching its own system, Fujicolor Circle, Fuji offered technical support and promotional discounts. For the first time in 15 years of U.S. activity, Fuji put its logo on the back of its paper, no longer fearing consumer preference for Kodak. Fuji's distribution was now strong enough, and it had been successful with its mini-photoprocessing labs. Quicker to respond than retailing, processing systems allowed Fuji to capture 16 percent of the U.S. market for photo paper.

TURBULENT TIMES

Fuji entered the 1990s in a very strong position in its home market and enjoying increasing success in foreign markets as well. The company then posted three consecutive years of record sales in the early 1990s, culminating in 1992's ¥1.14 trillion in sales. Net income fell 18.7 percent in 1992 from 1991 levels, however, as Fuji began to feel the combined effects of the prolonged recession in Japan and the sharp appreciation of the yen. Nevertheless, Fuji continued to develop and introduce innovative new products, such as 1991's Fujix Digital Still Camera DS-100, which used a memory card to store images; the Fujix Simple-Hi 8 camcorder, introduced in 1993 as the smallest and lightest camcorder in the world; and the Pictrostat instant color print system, also launched in 1993, which could produce color prints from prints, slides, and objects in one minute without using any processing chemicals.

From 1993 to 1995, Fuji saw its sales stagnate. The company was affected overseas by the continuing strength of the yen and at home by unexpected competition, highlighted in 1994 when the largest Japanese supermarket chain, Daiei, began selling store-brand 35-millimeter film made by AGFA-Gevaert. Fuji's share of the Japanese film market fell from 74 to 69 percent from 1993 to 1994. Meanwhile, Kodak charged Fuji in 1993 with dumping color photographic paper in the U.S. market. To avoid having to pay threatened punitive tariffs, and to counter the effects of the strong yen, Fuji added to its Greenwood facility a factory to make color photo paper. This factory began operation in 1995. The Greenwood complex also saw the addition of a factory to produce Fujicolor QuickSnap disposable cameras that same year and a fifth factory, opening in 1996, for packaging and shipping 35-millimeter Fujicolor film manufactured at its plant in the Netherlands.

The long-term war between Kodak and Fuji was far from over, however. On the U.S. front, Fuji aggressively sought throughout the 1990s to capture more of the wholesale photofinishing market. It was largely successful as its network of U.S. photofinishing labs grew to 21 in 1996 when it spent $464 million to buy six labs from Wal-Mart Stores, Inc. The deal also included a ten-year contract through which Fuji was to supply all photofinishing services to the more than 2,250 Wal-Marts nationwide, taking business away from Kodak's photofinishing business, Qualex Inc. Wal-Mart was the leading photofinisher in the country at the time. Later in

1996, Fuji scored another coup when it signed an exclusive agreement with Ritz Camera Centers Inc. to supply paper to Ritz's chain of 550 minilabs, the third largest minilab chain in the country.

On the Japanese front, the battle was being conducted as another trade dispute. This time, Kodak accused the Japanese government and Fuji of illegally restricting access to the Japanese market for film and photographic paper. The U.S. government took the case to the newly formed World Trade Organization (WTO) in 1996, with the European Union soon joining the Kodak side. Fuji contended that Kodak's policies in pricing and marketing its products in Japan were to blame for the company's low market share, and that Kodak faced an environment in Japan similar to what Fuji faced in the United States. In fact, both companies held about 70 percent of their respective home markets, while Kodak held about 12 percent of the Japanese market and Fuji still only 10 percent of the U.S. market. Observers offered no consensus on how the WTO might rule in the case.

Ironically, while these battles were being waged, Fuji had joined the Kodak-led consortium of film and camera companies (the others were Nikon Corporation, Minolta Co., Ltd., and Canon Inc.) to develop the Advanced Photo System (APS), an effort to revitalize the stagnant still photography market. APS offered easy film loading and the ability to select from three photo sizes (4 inch by 6 inch, 4 inch by 7 inch, and a panoramic 4 inch by 10 inch) as photos are taken. In 1996 Fuji introduced a full range of APS products: films, compact cameras, disposable cameras, photofinishing equipment, a Digital Image Workstation, a Photo Player for displaying images on a television, and an Image Scanner for converting images to their digital equivalent for manipulation on a PC.

In 1996 Fuji enjoyed its best year since 1993, although it still had not recovered to the levels of the early 1990s. Also in 1996, Minoru Ohnishi became chairman and CEO; Masayuki Muneyuki, who had been one of two senior executive managing directors, became president. Under this leadership team, Fuji penetrated deeper into the U.S. market, boosting its market share as high as 20 percent during 1997, a year in which it cut the prices for its film in the U.S. market and began manufacturing color film at its Greenwood complex. In early 1998 Fuji won another battle in its long war with Kodak when the WTO issued a final ruling rejecting Kodak's claims that Fuji and the Japanese government had engaged in protectionism in the Japanese film market.

Throughout the late 1990s, Fuji pushed aggressively into the burgeoning digital camera market. The company not only developed innovative new cameras, including the MX-1700, which debuted as the world's smallest high-resolution digital camera, it also adopted a strategy of making many of the key components of digital cameras itself rather than relying on larger competitors. These included lenses, image processors, and signal-processing chips. Through its FUJIFILM Microdevices Co., Ltd. subsidiary, which was created in 1990, Fuji developed the Super CCD (supercharged coupled device), a small image-capturing chip that used octagonal pixels rather than rectangular ones in order to significantly increase the sharpness of a digital image while at the same time enabling the cameras themselves to be smaller in size overall.

DEALMAKING AND FURTHER DIVERSIFYING

While Ohnishi remained firmly in charge as chairman and CEO, Shigetaka Komori was named president in mid-2000. The early years of the new decade were marked by a series of significant deals. Early in 2000 Fuji Photo Film entered into an alliance with Xerox and Sharp Corporation whereby the three companies pledged to invest more than $2 billion over five years to develop a new line of inkjet printers. Xerox, meanwhile, in the midst of a huge restructuring, sold its subsidiaries in Hong Kong and China to the Fuji Xerox joint venture in late 2000 for about $550 million. Then in March 2001 Xerox sold half of its stake in Fuji Xerox itself to Fuji Photo Film for more than $1.3 billion in cash, increasing Fuji's interest in the joint venture to 75 percent. Fuji Xerox thus became a consolidated subsidiary of Fuji Photo Film, sparking a 73.6 percent increase in revenues in fiscal 2002 to ¥2.4 trillion ($18.05 billion). Fuji also continued its aggressive push into the Chinese market, establishing a holding company to invest in new businesses and entering into a joint venture involved in manufacturing and marketing digital cameras, both in April 2001. In July 2002 Fuji bolstered its stranglehold on the Japanese photo market by outbidding Kodak for Jusphoto Co., Ltd., one of the nation's leading film-processing chains. The price of the transaction was approximately ¥16 billion ($133 million). Fuji also gained a larger presence in the graphic arts systems area in April 2003 by acquiring Process Shizai Co., Ltd., which was subsequently renamed FUJIFILM Graphic Systems Co., Ltd.

As a result of Fuji's concerted diversification drive, by the end of 2003 the company's traditional line of products—silver-halide film, photo paper, developing chemicals, and the like—accounted for only 42 percent of sales. Chief rival Kodak, while itself moving aggressively into the digital world, still relied on film, paper, and processing for 61 percent of its revenue. In July 2003, meanwhile, Ohnishi retired as Fuji's CEO while retaining the largely honorary chairmanship. Komori was promoted to president and CEO. The new leader quickly set an ambitious goal of doubling profits by 2007, vowing to cut costs by $1.9 billion by then to help do so.

In another key growth area, Fuji by this time had become the world's largest supplier of specialized films for liquid crystal display (LCD) screens, a sector it had entered in 1996. Exploding demand for flat-panel computer monitors and televisions prompted Fuji in early 2005 to launch a massive capital investment program totaling ¥67 billion ($642 million) to build three new plants and two new production lines to increase the company's capacity to produce the specialized films. On the acquisition front, Fuji in November 2004 acquired U.S.-based Arch Chemicals, Inc.'s microelectronic materials division, producer of semiconductor-related chemical products. Fuji also acquired the U.K.-based Sericol Group Limited in February 2005, thereby gaining one of the world's top manufacturers of screen printing inks and industrial UV inks for inkjet use. About one year later, Fuji purchased another U.K. firm, Avecia Inkjet Ltd., maker of ink dyes for inkjet printers.

Aided by strong demand for materials used to make flat-panel displays, Fuji saw its net profits increase 2.7 percent in 2005, totaling ¥84.5 billion ($789.7 million). Revenues of ¥2.53 trillion ($23.62 billion) were a slight decrease from the previous year. Late in 2005 Fuji announced plans to turn itself into a holding company by October 2006. Responding to shrinking demand for photo film and slower growth in the global digital camera market, Fuji in early 2006 launched a dramatic restructuring of its operations in these areas involving 5,000 job cuts (4,000 abroad and 1,000 at home) and the streamlining of production, development, and sales functions. With demand for color film dropping at an annual rate of more than 20 percent, Fuji also began whittling down its range of photo film but said it had no plans to withdraw from the field altogether. This restructuring was expected to cost approximately ¥165 billion ($1.4 billion). In the meantime, Fuji also announced that it planned to bolster its research and development spending, earmarking ¥600 billion ($5.2 billion) for 2007 through 2009. The company was aiming to aggressively invest in such high-growth fields as flat-panel display materials, medical imaging products, electronic materials, and optical parts.

Ray Walsh
Updated, David E. Salamie

PRINCIPAL SUBSIDIARIES

Fujinon Corporation; FUJIFILM Techno Products Co., Ltd.; FUJIFILM Electronic Materials Co., Ltd.; FUJIFILM Microdevices Co., Ltd.; FUJIFILM Photonix Co., Ltd.; FUJIFILM Opto Materials Co., Ltd.; FUJIFILM Kyushu Co., Ltd.; FUJIFILM Medical Co., Ltd.; FUJIFILM Business Supply Co., Ltd.; FUJIFILM Imaging Co., Ltd.; FUJIFILM Graphic Systems Co., Ltd.; Jusphoto Co., Ltd.; FUJIFILM Logistics Co., Ltd.; FUJIFILM Techno Service Co., Ltd.; FUJIFILM Software Co., Ltd.; FUJIFILM Computer System Co., Ltd.; Fuji Xerox Co., Ltd. (75%); Suzuka Fuji Xerox Co., Ltd. (75%); Niigata Fuji Xerox Manufacturing Co., Ltd. (75%); Fuji Xerox Office Supply Co., Ltd. (75%); Fuji Xerox Information Systems Co., Ltd. (75%); Fuji Xerox Printing Systems Co., Ltd. (75%); Fuji Xerox Imaging Materials Co., Ltd. (75%); Fuji Photo Film U.S.A., Inc.; Fuji Photo Film Hawaii, Inc. (U.S.A.); FUJIFILM Medical Systems U.S.A., Inc.; Enovation Graphic Systems, Inc. (U.S.A.); Fujicolor Processing, Inc. (U.S.A.); Fuji Photo Film, Inc. (U.S.A.); FUJIFILM Microdisks U.S.A., Inc.; Fuji Hunt Photographic Chemicals, Inc. (U.S.A.); FUJIFILM Electronic Materials U.S.A., Inc.; Fuji Photo Film Canada Inc.; Fuji Graphic Systems Canada Inc.; Fuji Photo Film do Brasil Ltda. (Brazil); Fuji Photo Film (Europe) GmbH (Germany); Fuji Magnetics GmbH (Germany); Fuji Photo Film (U.K.) Ltd.; FUJIFILM Electronic Imaging Ltd. (U.K.); FUJIFILM Sericol UK Limited; Fuji Photo Film B.V. (Netherlands); FUJIFILM Medical Systems Benelux N.V. (Belgium); Fuji Hunt Photographic Chemicals, N.V. (Belgium); FUJIFILM France S.A.S.; Fuji Graphic Systems France S.A.S.; FUJIFILM España, S.A. (Spain); FUJIFILM Italia S.p.A. (Italy); FUJIFILM CZ, s.r.o. (Czech Republic); FUJIFILM Polska Distribution Sp. Zo.o. (Poland); Fuji Photo Film (China) Investment Co., Ltd.; FUJIFILM Imaging Systems (Suzhou) Co., Ltd.; FUJIFILM Starlight Co., Ltd. (China); Fuji Photo Film Printing Plate (Suzhou) Co., Ltd. (China); FUJIFILM Medical Systems (Shanghai) Co., Ltd. (China); Hong Kong Fuji Photo Logistics Ltd.; Fuji Photo Film (Singapore) Pte Ltd; Fuji Hunt Photographic Chemicals, Pte Ltd (Singapore); Fuji Photo Film (Malaysia) Sdn. Bhd.; Fuji Photo Film (Thailand) Ltd.; FUJIFILM Australia Pty Ltd; FUJIFILM NZ Ltd. (New Zealand).

PRINCIPAL COMPETITORS

Eastman Kodak Company; Agfa-Gevaert N.V.; Canon Inc.; Ricoh Company, Ltd.; Konica Minolta Holdings, Inc.; Olympus Corporation; Sony Corporation; Nikon Corporation; Hewlett-Packard Company.

FURTHER READING

Bandler, James, "Xerox Will Sell Half of Its Interest in Fuji Xerox in $1.34 Billion Deal," *Wall Street Journal,* March 7, 2001, p. B5.

Bounds, Wendy, "Fuji, Accused by Kodak of Hogging Markets, Spits Back: 'You Too,'" *Wall Street Journal,* July 31, 1995, pp. A1, A6.

———, "Fuji Will Buy Wal-Mart's Photo Business," *Wall Street Journal,* July 9, 1996, p. A3.

Dawson, Chester, "Fuji's Digital Picture Is Developing Fast," *Business Week* (international edition), February 23, 2004, p. 24.

Desmond, Edward W., "What's Ailing Kodak? Fuji," *Fortune,* October 27, 1997, pp. 185+.

Eisenstodt, Gale, "Sharply Focused," *Forbes,* December 24, 1990, p. 50.

"50 Years of Fuji Photo Film," Tokyo: Fuji Photo Film Co., 1984, 106 p.

"Fujifilm Snaps Up Market Share in U.S.," *Financial Times,* December 9, 1997, p. 27.

Fuji Fuirumu 50-nen no ayumi, Tokyo: Fuji Shashin Fuirumu Kabushiki Kaisha, 1984, 504 p.

"Fuji Photo: Lower Market Shares Forcing CEO Out," *Tokyo Business Today,* May 1995, pp. 18–19.

"Fuji Photo: Sharpening Its Image in the U.S. As It Develops New Products," *Business Week,* October 24, 1983, pp. 88+.

Greenberg, Jonathan, "Kodak's Japanese Shadow," *Forbes,* November 22, 1982, pp. 55+.

Greenberg, Jonathan, Laura Johannes, and Ross Kerber, "WTO's Kodak Ruling Heightens Trade Tensions," *Wall Street Journal,* December 8, 1997, p. A3.

Hamilton, David P., "United It Stands: Fuji Xerox Is a Rarity in World Business: A Joint Venture That Works," *Wall Street Journal,* September 26, 1996, p. R19.

Hechinger, John, "Xerox to Sell Its China Operations to Fuji Xerox Co. for $550 Million," *Wall Street Journal,* December 15, 2000, p. B4.

Kunii, Irene M., Geoffrey Smith, and Neil Gross, "Fuji: Beyond Film," *Business Week,* November 22, 1999, pp. 132–36, 138.

Martin, Neil A., "Good News, Bad News," *Barron's,* December 20, 1999, pp. 24, 26.

Mikawa, Tadahisa, "Shake-up at Top of Fuji Photo Forces Change of Direction for No. 1 Film Manufacturer," *Nikkei Weekly,* July 7, 2003.

Rosario, Louise do, and Jonathan Friedland, "Developing Negatives: Fuji Photo Film Feels the Pressures of Success," *Far Eastern Economic Review,* April 14, 1994, pp. 63–64.

"Shuttered: Photo Wars," *Economist,* August 5, 1995, pp. 59–60.

Smith, Lee, "The Little Pepper That's Got Kodak Hot," *Fortune,* August 22, 1983, p. 122.

Takahashi, Masatake, "Put the Facts in Focus: Another Look at the Kodak-Fuji Dispute," *Tokyo Business Today,* January 1996, pp. 12–15.

Turner, David, "Fuji Photo to Cut 5,000 Jobs," *Financial Times,* February 1, 2006, p. 30.

Gen-Probe Incorporated

10210 Genetic Center Drive
San Diego, California 92121
U.S.A.
Telephone: (858) 410-8000
Toll Free: (800) 523-5001
Fax: (858) 410-8625
Web site: http://www.gen-probe.com

Public Company
Incorporated: 1984
Employees: 866
Sales: $305.9 million (2005)
Stock Exchanges: NASDAQ
Ticker Symbol: GPRO
NAIC: 541710 Research and Development in the Physical Sciences and Engineering Sciences; 325411 Medicinal and Botanical Manufacturing

■ ■ ■

Gen-Probe Incorporated is a developer and manufacturer of nucleic acid, probe-based devices that are used for the clinical diagnosis of human diseases and for screening donated blood. To a lesser extent, the company also makes similar devices to detect harmful organisms in the environment and in industrial processes. Gen-Probe's diagnostic devices are sold to clinical laboratories, public health institutions, and hospitals in North America. The company's blood-screening products are marketed and distributed on a global basis through Chiron Corporation. Best known for its devices that detect the sexually transmitted diseases gonorrhea and chlamydia, the company also makes testing equipment for the detection of human immunodeficiency virus (HIV), certain types of cancer, various manifestations of hepatitis, and tuberculosis.

ORIGINS

A winner of the National Medal of Technology, the United States' highest honor for technological innovation, Gen-Probe pioneered the scientific and commercial development of nucleic acid testing (NAT). By relying on nucleic acid probes that specifically bind to nucleic acid sequences known to be unique to target organisms, NAT allowed laboratory technicians to identify microorganisms quickly, a capability that Gen-Probe first offered to the medical community in the mid-1980s. The company was formed in 1983, beginning as a partnership between Howard Birndorf, Thomas Adams, and David Kohne. Birndorf and Adams were successful entrepreneurs in the biotechnology field when they helped launch Gen-Probe, having founded a company named Hybritech, which became one of the most successful biotechnology companies in the San Diego area during the early 1980s. Hybritech was acquired by Eli Lilly Co. in 1986 for nearly $500 million, proof of its regard within the industry, but Birndorf and Adams left the company before the buyout, obtaining much of their start-up capital from the same company that would later buy Hybritech, Eli Lilly, which ranked as Gen-Probe's largest initial investor. Birndorf and Adams, skilled in the strategic and financial aspects of running a biotechnology company, were joined by David E. Kohne, a leading international authority on genetic-probe research. Kohne, who became the company's chief scientist,

COMPANY PERSPECTIVES

Over the past decade, major advances have been made in molecular diagnostic testing for infectious diseases. Many of those advances originated in the research laboratories of Gen-Probe, and have changed the basic methods of operation in microbiology laboratories around the world. Compared to traditional methods, molecular genetic assays offer better performance and shorter testing times. Most of all, clinicians are now able to provide patients and the community with more consistent, affordable, and higher-quality healthcare.

developed the science underpinning Gen-Probe at its inception, articulating the technical vision that Birndorf and Adams would help bring to market.

Gen-Probe began operating at a time of fevered interest in biotechnology ventures. Venture capitalists were quick to offer their financial support to almost any enterprise promising innovation in the sector, and Gen-Probe was no exception, creating a stir and fueling great expectations when it made its debut. The name of the company was a reflection of its commitment to the genetic probe, a novel diagnostic tool that drew its inspiration from the theory that all biological matter is encoded along the strands of a person's deoxyribonucleic acid (DNA). Kohne's scientific vision, paraphrased simply, was based on the assumption that indicators of various pathologies were present in a person's genes in much the same way that a person's genetic composition determined gender, eye color, and a host of other attributes. By using diagnostic kits incorporating genetic probes, Kohne reasoned, the presence of infectious microorganisms could be revealed, providing more rapid, sensitive, and specific diagnoses than traditional laboratory procedures, such as culture and immunoassays. Based on this belief, Gen-Probe was launched, sparking predictions of greatness in the biotechnology field. After preliminary work conducted under the auspices of the partnership among Birndorf, Adams, and Kohne, Gen-Probe was incorporated in June 1984 and shipped its first diagnostic kit six months later, a test for Legionnaires' disease.

Gen-Probe, as it developed, applied its science to identifying a broad range of diseases caused by bacteria, viruses, or fungi, but initially the company focused on pathologies afflicting the respiratory system. Test probes for pneumonia, Legionnaires' disease, and other similar pathogens took center stage, while the company's scientific staff worked on DNA probes related to tuberculosis (a family of organisms classified as mycobacterium), Acquired Immune Deficiency Syndrome (AIDS), sexually transmitted diseases (STDs), and cancer. The applications of the company's diagnostic kits were numerous, and applying the technology to a host of pathologies would be ongoing, but by the late 1980s kits to diagnose respiratory afflictions were usurped from their preeminent position by tests for STDs, specifically gonorrhea and chlamydia, the two most common STDs. The company became best-known for its work on identifying gonorrhea and chlamydia—"sexually transmitted diseases have been their franchise," a medical doctor and analyst summarized in a March 7, 2005 interview with *Investor's Business Daily*—but by the end of the 1980s not even the commercial introduction of what would become the company's franchise was enough to stave off financial difficulties. After starting its business life with much promise, Gen-Probe entered the late 1980s exuding far less luster than it had only several years earlier, having failed to live up to the industry's lofty expectations.

Venture capitalists, who had once flocked to the biotechnology sector, were backing away by the end of the decade, no longer convinced the new breed of companies could deliver a spectacular return on their investments. Gen-Probe's diagnostic kits faltered after their introduction, eliciting complaints about the radioactive isotopes around which the probes were designed. "It was not what you'd call inspired planning," Kohne conceded in the February 1990 issue of *California Business*. "We came along just as the controversy over disposal of hazardous wastes was peaking." The company also fell short of expectations because it was confronted by unexpected competition, as companies such as Gen-Zyme, Mycogen, Biograde, and AmGen joined the fray. The new entrants in the field committed their own miscues, which added to the disenchantment among venture capitalists, but their presence, nonetheless, diluted the market. Gen-Probe, its cash flow stagnating, struggled to obtain capital, and turned to Wall Street for help. In 1987, the company completed its initial public offering (IPO), raising $16.2 million from the offering, but the funds soon were exhausted. By late 1988, the company was forced to slash prices and furlough personnel it needed, leaving it in a precarious position as the decade ended.

THE END OF INDEPENDENCE IN 1989

Gen-Probe was rescued from its waning financial health by the intervention of another company. In 1988, Gen-Probe signed a $15.5 million, research-and-development

KEY DATES

1983: Gen-Probe is formed and is incorporated a year later.
1985: Gen-Probe ships its first product, the first FDA-approved diagnostic test using DNA probe technology.
1987: Gen-Probe completes its initial public offering of stock.
1989: Gen-Probe is acquired by Chugai Pharmaceutical Company Ltd.
1999: Gen-Probe begins developing devices to test for the West Nile virus.
2002: Gen-Probe is spun off from Chugai.
2003: Gen-Probe becomes the first company to market a screening test for the West Nile virus.
2005: Gen-Probe is awarded the 2004 National Medal of Technology Laureate.

deal with a Japanese pharmaceutical giant named Chugai Pharmaceutical Company Ltd. The deal involved eight viral products and two cancer products, all in diagnostics, that Chugai would sell in Japan and Gen-Probe would sell elsewhere, but the relationship soon became far more intimate. In 1989, Gen-Probe announced that it was being acquired by Chugai for $110 million, a union that joined Chugai's expertise in the therapeutic end of the business with Gen-Probe's emphasis on the diagnostic end of the business. Thomas Bologna, who was appointed president of Gen-Probe in 1987, commented on the transaction that would see Gen-Probe become a wholly owned subsidiary of Chugai. In a February 1990 interview with *California Business,* he referred to the 1988 research-and-development agreement, saying, "The point is, we'd already built up a good working relationship with the people at Chugai. We both really believe in genetic probe technology. The Japanese realize that biotech is a major opportunity. Besides," Bologna added, "the industry is shaking out. We're going to see more consolidations and we'll see them on a global basis."

Chugai acquired Gen-Probe for $110 million, a deal that offered Gen-Probe much needed assistance. When the company became a subsidiary of its Japanese parent, it had yet to record an annual profit, generating $2.7 million in revenue during its last year as an independent company. Chugai, supported by vast financial resources, offered relief to Gen-Probe's financial needs and it sheltered the company from the industry-wide consolidation set to take place during the 1990s.

Gen-Probe began the decade, and its relationship with Chugai, by introducing redesigned, "non-isotopic" probes, which found a much more receptive audience than the company's initial line and cured some of the problems plaguing it during its formative years. As the decade progressed, the NAT pioneer that produced the first Food and Drug Administration (FDA)-approved probe-based assay became a master at its craft. Gen-Probe's groundbreaking work thrust it into the most vital projects undertaken at the commercial level and those that concerned the health of the nation. In 1996, the National Institute of Health's National Heart, Lung and Blood Institute turned to Gen-Probe for the development of devices to screen donated blood, a program aimed at identifying blood infected with HIV, the virus responsible for acquired immune deficiency syndrome (AIDS). The response to the request by the National Institutes of Health (NIH) led to a strategic alliance with Chiron Corporation in 1998 to develop and market NAT-based products for the blood screening and clinical diagnostic market, a collaboration that would account for half of Gen-Probe's revenues a decade later. The NIH would turn to Gen-Probe again, offering development money to solve pressing health problems, but, at a corporate level, another significant event occurred as Gen-Probe's probe-based technology evolved. The company faced its second era as an independent company, a period it entered with far more strength than the floundering company that sorely needed the help of Chugai in 1989.

Gen-Probe's fate was decided in late 2001, determined by a joint announcement made in Basel, Switzerland, and Tokyo, Japan. Swiss pharmaceutical giant Roche AG and Chugai revealed plans to merge in a $2 billion deal that forced the divestiture of Gen-Probe. The union of Roche and Chugai, as it related to Gen-Probe, presented potential regulatory problems because of Roche's own diagnostics business, which ranked as the largest in the world. Accordingly, executives decided to spin off Gen-Probe as a separate, independent company and return the San Diego-based company to the public sector, where after a 13-year hiatus investors would be able to share in the success of the company's pioneering science. The spinoff was completed in September 2002, when Gen Probe began trading on the NASDAQ. At the time of the spinoff, the company had received clearances or approvals from the FDA for more than 40 devices, with its tests for gonorrhea and chlamydia still underpinning its business. Gen-Probe controlled 55 percent of the U.S. market for the two STDs. Revenue in 2001 reached $130 million, exponentially higher than the $2.7 million the company generated before being acquired by Chugai.

PROGRESS IN THE 21ST CENTURY

As Gen-Probe made the transition from a subsidiary to an independent company, its scientists were developing products for a number of markets. In 1999, the West Nile virus, transmitted to people and horses by mosquitoes, first appeared in the United States. The NIH offered grants to several companies to conduct early stage studies on potential vaccines and screening tests, Gen-Probe included, assigning the company one of its major challenges during its first years of independence. In June 2003, the company became the first to market a screening test for the West Nile virus, when the FDA approved the sale of its test as an investigational product. Late in the year, the company also achieved progress on two other fronts. In November, Gen-Probe signed a licensing deal for the rights to a gene marker called PCA3 that showed remarkable accuracy in identifying prostate cancer. Under the terms of the agreement brokered with Canada-based Diagnocure, a urine test was to be developed to detect PCA3, a test to be marketed by Gen-Probe. In December, the company was granted clearance from the FDA for its blood-testing platform, TIGRIS, which conducted tests for gonorrhea and chlamydia. By using TIGRIS, one laboratory technician could load 500 tests, leave for eight hours, and return for the results. Gen-Probe also was working on a testing platform called Ultrio that combined testing for HIV and hepatitis B and C in one product.

Gen-Probe's contributions to the advancement of science earned the company both recognition and an enviable financial record. In November 2005, Gen-Probe was named the 2004 National Medal of Technology Laureate for its tests that screened donated blood for HIV and hepatitis, an honor a company executive, in the November 16, edition of the *San Diego Union-Tribune,* hailed as "validation to our employees of their great efforts in achieving and applying some breakthrough technology to the service of mankind." Financially, the company was a roaring success as it completed its first 20 years in business, achieving substantial growth in terms of both revenue and net income. Between 2001 and 2005, the company's annual sales swelled from $130 million to $306 million. Its net income shot skyward from $4.6 million to $60 million. In the years ahead, further growth was expected as the company continued to turn its pioneering achievements into market success, providing vital services to hospitals, laboratories, and the nation at large.

Jeffrey L. Covell

PRINCIPAL SUBSIDIARIES

Gen-Probe Sales & Service, Inc.; Gen-Probe International, Inc.; Gen-Probe UK Limited (U.K.); Molecular Light Technology Limited (U.K.); Molecular Light Technology Research Limited (U.K.); Bioanalysis Limited (U.K.).

PRINCIPAL COMPETITORS

Abbott Laboratories; Ortho-Clinical Diagnostics, Inc.; Roche Holding Ltd.

FURTHER READING

Braude, Jonathan, "Roche Joins with Chugai Pharmaceutical," *Daily Deal,* December 10, 2001.

Dower, Rick, "IPO Imminent for Gen-Probe, Chairman Says," *San Diego Business Journal,* August 17, 1987, p. 1.

———, "New Financing, Products Help Gen-Probe Muscle Ahead," *San Diego Business Journal,* May 25, 1987, p. 6.

"Gen-Probe Begins Trading After Spin-Off from Chugai," *AsiaPulse News,* September 17, 2002, p. 5039.

Lau, Gloria, "For Now, Anyway, West Nile Virus Still Has the Upper Hand," *Investor's Business Daily,* September 15, 2003, p. A9.

———, "Gen-Probe Inc. San Diego, California; Medical Test Maker Takes on West Nile Virus," *Investor's Business Daily,* July 25, 2003, p. A6.

Salerno, Steve, "Making a Big Deal of Gen-Probe," *California Business,* February 1990, p. 46.

Shinkle, Kirk, "Gen-Probe Inc. San Diego, California; Its Blood Test Systems Help Labs Save Time and Money," *Investor's Business Daily,* March 25, 2004, p. A6.

Somers, Terri, "Blood-Screening Test Nets Medal for Gen-Probe," *San Diego Union-Tribune,* November 16, 2005.

Weeks, Katie, "FDA Grants Marketing Approval to Gen-Probe," *San Diego Business Journal,* December 12, 2005, p. 10.

Gentiva Health Services, Inc.

3 Huntington Quadrangle
Suite 200S
Melville, New York 11747-4627
U.S.A.
Telephone: (631) 501-7000
Fax: (631) 501-7148
Web site: http://www.gentiva.com

Public Company
Founded: 1971
Employees: 14,550
Sales: $868.8 million (2005)
Stock Exchanges: NASDAQ
Ticker Symbol: GTIV
NAIC: 621610 Home Health Care Services

■ ■ ■

Gentiva Health Services, Inc. is the largest home health-care services company in the United States, serving 500,000 customers in all 50 states, 36 through more than 400 company-operated locations and 14 through third-party providers. The company operates two brands: Gentiva and CareCentrix. Gentiva home services include nursing; social work; nutrition; disease management education; physical, occupational, speech, and neurorehabilitation services; and daily living assistance, such as providing housekeeping for the disabled or elderly. CareCentrix manages and coordinates the delivery of home nursing services for commercial insurance organizations and government health benefit plans. The 2006 acquisition of the Healthfield Group moved Gentiva into the hospice business. Based in Melville, New York, Gentiva is a public company listed on the NASDAQ.

FOUNDER, A POSTWAR PIONEER OF THE TEMPORARY STAFFING INDUSTRY

Gentiva grew out of the Olsten Corporation, founded by William Olsten. Born in 1919 he grew up in Yonkers just north of New York City. In 1940 he went to work at the General Motors assembly plant in Tarrytown, New York, which began making Avenger torpedo bombers to support the military buildup of World War II. Because so many men were called to military service, despite his young age he became a supervisor of a unit mostly staffed with women workers. He, too, was drafted in 1943 and eventually would find himself in Europe with the Third Army. After his discharge he worked in sales and marketing for a company that manufactured milk bottle caps. In 1950 he learned of a new industry, temporary staffing, which got its start in 1946 when Kelly Services was started. Manpower, Inc. followed in 1948. To take advantage of the demand for part-time office workers—legal secretaries, typists, clerks, and receptionists—Olsten opened a one-man employment office on West 42nd Street in Manhattan and began to place women, who since the war continued to join the workforce in increasing numbers. In the meantime he furthered his business education at the New York University's School of Commerce, earning a degree in 1951.

The demand for Olsten's services was so strong that he had trouble finding enough women employees. He

COMPANY PERSPECTIVES

Gentiva's mission: To improve quality of life and patient independence through the delivery of compassionate care and uncompromising service.

even created what he called the Olsten Mobile, a station wagon that aimed to attract women dropping off their children at bus stops in the Bronx, Brooklyn, and Queens. Olsten turned his New York operations into a national enterprise, and as the staffing industry began to expand in the 1960s, Olsten kept pace, offering workers outside of the secretarial field. In 1971 he became involved in home healthcare.

By the end of the 1970s Olsten Home Health Care had eight offices located across the country. But by the middle of the 1980s, the unit, generating about $20 million a year in revenues, was losing money. With the 1985 hiring of Robert Fusco, who would go on to become president of the unit, Olsten Home Health Care began to show dramatic improvements. Business was further helped in the late 1980s when a larger number of people became eligible to receive home healthcare services after a lawsuit by Medicare patients and home care providers resulted in a different interpretation of Medicare rules. By 1990 Olsten Home Health Care had 75 offices and was a profitable $100 million business. To accelerate growth it then acquired Upjohn Health Services Inc. for $58 million in December 1990, a deal that came at a very reasonable price and effectively tripled the size of the company, making it the second largest home healthcare provider in North America. Not only did Olsten Home Health Care add 200 offices and more than $180 million in revenues, it gained a footprint across North America. Prior to the acquisition Upjohn had been losing money, but within three months the operation was profitable. The combined company now operated under the name Olsten Healthcare.

Olsten Corporation viewed the home healthcare field as a major growth area, due in large part to the aging of the American population. Olsten Healthcare became the largest provider in May 1993 with the $525 million stock acquisition of publicly traded Boston-based Lifetime Corporation. Lifetime had begun to struggle a year earlier and Olsten Corporation attempted to buy a Lifetime temporary-worker business in England, Office Angels, but with no success. Then in March 1993, Lifetime received an unfriendly takeover bid of $23.50 per share from Abbey Healthcare Group, Inc. Lifetime brusquely rebuffed the offer, yet a month later announced that it was putting itself up for sale. Within a month Olsten Corporation and Lifetime reached a deal that called for a price of $33 per share and the assumption of $160 million in debt. The Lifetime acquisition brought with it 400 offices and boosted Olsten Healthcare's revenues from $338 million in 1992 to $1.2 billion. Moreover, Olsten Corporation picked up the Office Angels business it had originally wanted, providing the parent company with a presence in the European market.

LAUNCHING CARECENTRIX: 1995

In 1995 Olsten Healthcare launched CareCentrix to serve as an ancillary care benefit manager for insurers and government-related managed care payers. A year later, Olsten Healthcare entered the highly profitable home infusion business with the acquisition of Quantum Health Resources for $300 million in stock and assumed debt. Home infusion was especially important because of sharp reductions in the amount of money Medicare would pay for home nursing visits, changes that went into effect in October 1997. Home infusion was one of the few services to be reimbursed under the old payment schedule. However, Olsten Healthcare soon found itself saddled with a whistleblower lawsuit against Quantum, alleging that it overcharged Medicare, Medicaid, and a third health plan for services to hemophiliac patients from 1990 to 1997. Olsten Healthcare elected to settle the matter by agreeing to pay $4.5 million in October 1997. It was not the first time Quantum had courted trouble. In 1995 it settled similar claims with the state of California, and continued to be under investigation by the New Mexico attorney general. Olsten was itself coming under scrutiny at this time related to the Medicare billing practices of the Florida home healthcare operations of Columbia/HCA Health Corp. Olsten Healthcare had actually sold the 80 Florida offices to Columbia in 1993 but continued to operate them. That transaction became the focus of a second probe by the U.S. Justice Department, which would charge that Columbia bought the assets on the cheap and then inflated the fee it paid Olsten Healthcare subsidiary Kimberly Home Health Care Inc. to manage them in an effort to bilk Medicare. While the federal probe continued, Olsten Healthcare bought back the business for $34 million in 1998. Then, in July 1999, it reached a settlement with the Justice Department by agreeing to plead guilty to three felony charges, including conspiracy, mail fraud, and violation of the Medicare antikickback statute, and paying more than $10 million in criminal fines and almost $51 million as part of a civil settlement.

KEY DATES

1950: Olsten Corporation is founded as a temporary staffing company.
1971: Olsten begins providing home healthcare staffing services.
1990: Upjohn Health Services Inc. is acquired.
1993: Lifetime Corporation is acquired.
2000: Olsten spins off its healthcare assets as Gentiva Health Services, Inc.
2002: The Special Pharmaceutical Services division is sold.
2006: Healthfield Group is acquired.

FOUNDING OF GENTIVA HEALTH SERVICES AT THE START OF THE 21ST CENTURY

Not only did cutbacks on Medicare payments hurt Olsten Healthcare, the parent company also was encountering problems in the late 1990s. Falling profits and a slumping stock price led to a management shakeup at Olsten Corp. in early 1999. Later in the year the company agreed to merge its staffing and information-services business with Adecco S.A. As a result, it decided to split off its healthcare assets as an independent public company, which in 2000 took the name Gentiva Health Services, Inc. It legally broke away from Olsten Corp. in March 2000.

The first order of business for Gentiva's chief executive officer, Edward A. Blechschmidt, was to narrow the company's focus. It started out with four separate businesses: home healthcare, specialty pharmaceutical services distributing biopharmaceutical products, and one U.S. and one Canadian healthcare staffing operation. His goal was to sell off some of these assets and eliminate Gentiva's $120 million debt load. First he sold the U.S. staffing business for $66.5 million to Intelistaf Holdings Inc. A month later, in October 2000, he sold 81 percent of the Canadian staffing unit to Bayshore Health Group. This left Gentiva straddling two core businesses, home healthcare and specialty drugs, which together generated sales of $1.36 billion. For the year 2000 the company lost $104.2 million, but this was the result of writing off $119 million in accounts receivable. More important, Gentiva cut $100 million in debt and entered 2001 with a clean balance sheet. While revenues were essentially flat in 2001, totaling $1.38 million, the company recorded net income of $21 million in 2001. Home health services revenues dropped slightly in 2001 to $729.6 million, due to the company closing a dozen nursing branches and making the switch to Medicare's Prospective Payment System. The specialty pharmaceutical services business grew sales from $699.3 million in 2000 to $739.3 million in 2001, yet management decided to sell off this unit at the end of the year. In June 2002 when the deal closed, Gentiva sold the business to Accredo Health Inc. for approximately $415 million, split almost equally between cash and stock. Concurrent with the sale, Blechschmidt turned over the CEO and chairmanship posts to Ronald A. Malone, who had been with the company since 1994, serving as president of Olsten Staffing Services before it was divested.

No longer a hybrid company, Gentiva now devoted its attention to the home health services field. A major reason for selling off the pharmacy division and focusing on home healthcare was that the baby boom generation was reaching retirement age. According to the U.S. Census Bureau, the number of people aged 65 and older numbered 34.9 million in 2000. By 2020 that number was expected to grow by more than 50 percent to 53.7 million. Moreover, new medicines and technology allowed an increasing number of conditions to be treated at home rather than at a medical facility. There was also an increasing preference to recover and age at home. Added together it meant a steadily growing demand for the services Gentiva had to offer.

Gentiva continued to expand in 2003, completing a minor acquisition, buying Houston-area First Home Care, a five-branch home healthcare agency. More significant were internal developments, including the expansion of special programs, such as Gentiva Orthopedic Services, providing postoperative care for patients with joint replacements and other orthopedic needs, and Rehab Without Walls, a program to help patients recover from neurological problems at home. Gentiva made technological advances in 2003, deploying a new software-based scheduling system called CaseMatch, which connected patients to the most appropriate caregiver based on skills, geography, and availability. For the year, revenues improved 5.9 percent to $814 million. Net income approached $26.5 million.

Revenues continued to grow in 2004 to $846 million. CareCentrix was reconfigured and its network of providers expanded, and the unit also signed an important contract with TriWest Healthcare Alliance, a U.S. Department of Defense contractor that administered the TRICARE managed healthcare program in 21 states, covering more than two million active duty and retired military personnel and their families. In 2005 Gentiva recorded sales of more than $868.8 million and net income of $23.4 million.

Gentiva branched into the hospice field in 2006 with the $454 million cash and stock acquisition of Atlanta-based Healthfield Group. In one stroke Gentiva had become one of the top ten providers of hospice care, but Malone made it clear that Gentiva planned to aggressively grow the business in the markets where it already provided home healthcare services. Moreover, federal reimbursement levels had become more favorable, making it quite likely that in the years to come Gentiva would become even more aggressive on the acquisition front.

Ed Dinger

PRINCIPAL SUBSIDIARIES

Gentiva CareCentrix, Inc.; Gentiva Health Services (USA), Inc.; Quantum Health Resources, Inc.

PRINCIPAL COMPETITORS

Apria Healthcare Group Inc.; Coram Healthcare Corporation; Tender Loving Care Health Care Services, Inc.

FURTHER READING

Cameron, Tom, "Home Health Care a Growth Industry," *Long Island Business News,* July 15, 1991, p. 3.

Elliot, Alan R., "Chief Learns That Paring Down Is Not So Simple," *Investor's Business Daily,* March 15, 2001, p. A10.

Freudenheim, Milt, "Olsten in Deal for Lifetime; Will Be Giant in Home Care," *New York Times,* May 11, 1993, p. D1.

Hurtado, Robert, "Acquisition by Olsten May Gain It Some Respect on Wall Street," *New York Times,* July 20, 1993, p. D8.

Lagnado, Lucette, and Kelly Greene, "Olsten's Kimberly Home Unit Agrees to Plead Guilty to Criminal Counts," *Wall Street Journal,* July 20, 1999, p. 1.

Saphir, Ann, "Quantum Trouble: Olsten Bought More Than a Company in Infusion Deal," *Modern Healthcare,* November 23, 1998, p. 32.

Saphir, Ann, and Barbara Kirchheimer, "Olsten, Feds Reach Tentative Settlement," *Modern Healthcare,* April 5, 1999, p. 8.

Wolfgang, Saxon, "William Olsten, 72, Founder of Job Agency, Dies," *New York Times,* November 5, 1991, p. B8.

Zigmond, Jessica, "Gentiva Poised for Growth," *Modern Healthcare,* January 16, 2006, p. 11.

Gildemeister AG

Gildemeisterstrasse 60
Bielefeld,
Germany
Telephone: +49 05205 74 0
Fax: +49 05205 74 30 81
Web site: http://www.gildemeister.com

Public Company
Incorporated: 1870 as Gildemeister & Comp
Employees: 5,174
Sales: EUR 1.17 billion ($1.4 billion) (2005)
Stock Exchanges: Frankfurt Dusseldorf
Ticker Symbol: GIL
NAIC: 333512 Machine Tool (Metal Cutting Types) Manufacturing; 333513 Machine Tool (Metal Forming Types) Manufacturing; 333514 Special Die and Tool, Die Set, Jig, and Fixture Manufacturing; 333518 Other Metalworking Machinery Manufacturing

■ ■ ■

Gildemeister AG is a leading manufacturer of tools and machinery, focusing on turning and milling applications. The company's product line ranges from low-cost, mass-produced tools to highly specialized, high-tech machining systems. The company's lathes are marketed under the Gildemeister, Graziano, and Famot brand names, and its milling machines are marketed under the Deckel Maho brand. In addition to turning and milling machinery, Gildemeister has extended its reach to include laser technology and, since its acquisition of the Sauer brand in 2001, ultrasonic machining systems. These technologies enable the highly precise machining and engineering of precision components; the company's ultrasonic technology also enables the machining of traditionally difficult, brittle substances such as glass and ceramics. The adoption of these technologies comes as part of the company's shift from being a tools producer to becoming a leading provider of machining and engineering services. Gildemeister operates production subsidiaries in Germany, Poland, and Italy; the company added production facilities in Shanghai, its first outside of Europe, in 2003. Germany remains Gildemeister's largest market, at 60 percent of sales; the rest of Europe accounts for an additional 25 percent of sales. North America represents 8 percent of group revenues. Gildemeister has targeted the Asian markets for future growth; this region accounted for 6 percent of Gildemeister's revenues of EUR 1.17 billion ($1.4 billion) in 2005. Gildemeister is listed on the Frankfurt and Dusseldorf stock exchanges.

19TH-CENTURY TOOLING ORIGINS

Gildemeister was founded by Frederick Gildemeister in the town of Bielefeld, Germany, in 1870. The original factory, located at the Cöln-Minden Rail Station, began producing machine tools, and by the end of the century had established an extended range of tools. In 1899, Gildemeister reorganized the business as a limited liability company. After nearly 40 years in business, Gildemeister retired in 1906.

The direction of the company was then taken over by Wilhelm Berg, who remained as head of the company

COMPANY PERSPECTIVES

To remain successful in the market, customers expect highly reliable products and comprehensive services. To safeguard our future success, we have optimised our product portfolio and have developed further the group's orientation towards a full-line company in the turning, milling and laser/ultrasonic technologies as well as in services. The GILDEMEISTER group has the industry's most complete sales and services network. More than 5,000 employees in 58 group-owned sales and services companies are ready to serve our customers in 32 countries worldwide. The sales and services network stands out because of its consistent market proximity, direct selling covering all areas and customer-related services.

through World War II. Under Berg, the company began simplifying its range of machine tools, a process begun in 1907. The more limited range permitted the company to adopt the newly developing industrialized production techniques pioneered by Henry Ford. By 1915, Gildemeister had reduced its production to just four main product areas: automatic multi-spindle lathes; drum turret lathes; longitudinal milling machines; and vertical and horizontal machines.

The company's fortunes met a roadblock at the end of World War I, however, when the Allied powers placed the company on its banned companies list. Unable to continue production, Berg led the formation of a new company, Berg & Co., which specialized in the manufacture of tool components, specifically chucks and drives, rather than the machine tools themselves. Berg continued its production, even after Gildemeister was allowed to resume its operations in the 1920s.

Two factors enabled the company to grow during the economic crisis of the late 1920s and into the 1930s. The first was Wilhelm Berg's successful patent for a system for the clearance and disposal of wood chips created by its lathes and mills. The new tooling system also featured automated operations. The second factor was the rapid industrialization of the Soviet Union by the young Communist government. With large orders coming from Russia and elsewhere in the Soviet Union, Gildemeister was able to maintain continuous production throughout the crisis years. At its height, the company numbered some 600 employees.

The company was less fortunate during the war, when the factory was destroyed by Allied bombing raids. Once again on the wrong side of victory, the company faced the end of operations, and in 1945 was placed on the list of companies slated for dismantling by the Allied authorities. Gildemeister won a reprieve, however. In 1947, the company was placed under new management led by K. B. Grautoff, who had spent the war years interned in India. The company was allowed to resume operations and production got underway with just 25 employees in 1948.

POSTWAR MACHINE TOOL BOOM

Gildemeister quickly regained its former size, before growing into one of Europe's leading machine tools specialists. The company made its mark through the launch of a series of innovative products, such as the RV 50 turret lathe, introduced in 1950. In 1951 the company added two new product categories, a range of multi-spindle automatic bar machines, and a line of multi-spindle automatic chuck lathes. Toward the mid-1950s the company added the first eight-spindle automatic chuck lathe and, at the end of the decade, launched full-scale production of an economical single-spindle lathe.

Gildemeister's growth reflected the boom in the German economy in the 1950s and 1960s, as the country rebuilt itself into Europe's industrial powerhouse. The rising economy had stimulated an entirely new consumer market, which in turn stimulated the demand for a wide variety of products, most of which required Gildemeister's machining tools as part of their production process. As such, Gildemeister became an important supplier to the German automotive, automotive parts, machine construction, fittings, bicycle, and electrical industries.

The company's growth led it to purchase a new 300,000-square-meter site in 1961, in Sennestadt. The company began construction of new production facilities for itself and its subsidiaries, including Berg & Co., which were completed in 1965. By then, the company had begun to focus its production more specifically around lathes. In 1964, for example, the company discontinued its production of longitudinal milling machines. Instead, Gildemeister had begun to develop its first numerically controlled lathe, the RSA, which debuted in 1965. Featuring four coordinates, the RSA became the first on the market in 1967; at the same time, the company launched a smaller numerically controlled lathe, the RN.

ACQUIRING SCALE: 1969–89

Gildemeister also continued its external expansion. The company moved outside of Germany for the first time,

KEY DATES

1870: Frederick Gildemeister establishes a business producing machine tools in Bielefeld, Germany.
1899: Gildemeister & Comp. incorporates as a limited liability company.
1906: Wilhelm Berg takes over direction of the company and leads the streamlining of its product line.
1918: Gildemeister is banned from production by Allied authorities; Berg forms Berg & Co. to produce chucks and drives.
1928: Gildemeister grows based on a patented chip clearance system and contracts with the Soviet government.
1945: Gildemeister's factories, destroyed during the war, are placed on the Allied dismantling list.
1948: The company is taken over by KB Grautoff, and resumes production.
1951: The company introduces new multi-spindle automatic bar machines and a multi-spindle automatic chuck lathe.
1961: The company buys a new 300,000-square-meter site in Sennestadt.
1965: New production facilities open at the Sennestadt site.
1967: The company launches the first NC lathe, the RSA; the export operations of IMIS in Italy are acquired (later becoming Gildemeister Italiana).
1969: Gildemeister goes public.
1970: The company acquires Heidenreich & Harbeck, based in Hamburg.
1977: The company launches Elektropilot M computer-numerical-control system and microprocessor-controlled multi-spindle automatic lathes.
1982: A new subsidiary, Gildemeister Automation, is created for computer controlled and electronics-based products.
1989: The company acquires 50 percent of Witzig & Frank Turmatic, a maker of automatic drum transfer machines and flexible transfer lines based in Offenburg.
1993: The company restructures and creates Gildemeister Drehmaschinen GmbH.
1994: The company acquires most of Deckel Maho, adding contract lathe work and moulding engineering operations.
1998: The company acquires LCTec Laser- und Computertechnik.
1999: Gildemeister enters Poland through the acquisition of Famot Pleszew.
2001: The company acquires majority control of Sauer GmbH.
2003: A production facility is established in Shanghai.
2005: Sauer and Lasertec are merged.

taking over the global export operations of Italy's IMIS, a producer and exporter of small multi-spindle machines, in 1967. By 1969, Gildemeister had bought majority control of the Italian company, which then became known as Gildemeister Italiana S.p.A. The company continued buying up shares in Gildemeister Italiana through the 1970s. By then, Gildemeister itself had opened up its shareholding. In 1969, the company sold a minority stake to Westdeutsche Landesbank Girozentrale; following that sale, the company went public, listing its shares on the Dusseldorf and Frankfurt exchanges.

The public offering enabled Gildemeister to continue its expansion drive through the 1970s. The company bought up Heidenreich & Harbeck, based in Hamburg, in 1970. The new subsidiary's production was subsequently transferred to the group's Bielefeld site in 1972. In that year, Gildemeister added Langenhangen-based machine tool maker Max Muller Brinker.

Through the mid-1970s, Gildemeister launched a factory expansion program, adding new capacity to the Sennestadt site. By 1976, the company was able to transfer all of its production to the site, and ended production at its Bielefeld headquarters. That relocation was completed in 1977.

Gildemeister continued to innovate during this period. In the mid-1970s, for example, the company launched its Elektropilot M computer-numerical-control system. By the late 1970s, the company had begun development of a new generation of microprocessor-controlled multi-spindle automatic lathes. The first of these was introduced in 1977.

This effort, developed as part of a partnership with the Soviet Union's Ministry of Machine Tool Construction launched in 1972, fit in with the company's newly developed strategy, which called for its international expansion. The need to step up its presence in and development of foreign export markets came in the face of growing competition in Japan, and later Korea, Taiwan, and other fast-growing Asian markets.

Gildemeister developed a growing number of automatic and computer-controlled lathes in the early 1980s. The fast-growing electronics and automated product family was then spun off into a dedicated subsidiary, Gildemeister Automation, in 1982.

The company continued adding to its operations. In 1989, the company bought 50 percent of Witzig & Frank Turmatic, based in Offenburg, a maker of automatic drum transfer machines and flexible transfer lines. The company also acquired a stake in Varioline Handelsgesellschaft before the end of the decade.

NEW PRODUCTS IN THE LATE 20TH CENTURY

Into the early 1990s, Gildemeister remained focused on the production of lathes and lathes systems. This placed the company at somewhat of a disadvantage, particularly during the extended economic recession of the period. Gildemeister was particularly hurt by the slump in the automotive market, which accounted for as much as 40 percent of the group's sales.

To counter this, Gildemeister launched a restructuring exercise in 1993, merging several of its production units into a new subsidiary, Gildemeister Drehmaschinen GmbH. Gildemeister also sought to extend its production into new areas. This interest led the company to a major acquisition in 1994. In that year, the company took over most of Deckel-Maho, a maker of universal milling and boring machinery and machining centers, which had gone bankrupt in the early 1990s. The acquisition enabled the company not only to expand its product focus, but also to redefine itself, from a simple manufacturer to a full-service provider of assembly and engineering services.

The addition of Deckel-Maho helped shift the group's revenue balance. By the mid-1990s, 40 percent of the group's turnover now came from its contract lathe work/machine tool and moulding engineering operations. By then, the automotive industry accounted for less than 10 percent of total group sales.

Gildemeister's sales once again took off in the second half of the 1990s. The revitalization of the European economies helped drive the group's sales. Europe, together with Germany itself, continued to account for 85 percent of the company's revenues. Nonetheless, the company made increasing headway in its effort to establish a global presence. A step toward this direction came through the expansion of the company's technologies, notably through the acquisition of LCTec Laser- und Computertechnik in 1998. The addition of the Pfonten-based company allowed Gildemeister to develop a new generation of milling tools. By the end of that year, the company's revenues had passed the DEM 1 billion mark.

Gildemeister continued its expansion into the 2000s. The company moved into Poland in 1999, buying Famot Pleszew, that market's largest metal-cutting machine tool manufacturer. Also that year, the company bought full control of Gildemeister Italiana, which had previously operated as an independent public company. In 2001, Gildemeister once again added to its range of technology, buying up majority control of Sauer GmbH. That acquisition added new ultrasound technology to the group's range, enabling the machining of hard brittle materials. The company boosted its stake in Sauer to 95 percent in 2002.

Gildemeister next turned its target to the rapidly growing Asian, and especially Chinese, markets. In 2003, the company set up a production facility in Shanghai, its first manufacturing operation outside of Europe. In the meantime, the company's growing range of high-technology driven machine systems led it to merge its Sauer and Lasertec subsidiaries in 2005. In that year, the company celebrated its 135th anniversary, as its sales neared EUR 1.2 billion ($1.5 billion). Gildemeister remained one of the world's leading machine tool names in the new century.

M. L. Cohen

PRINCIPAL SUBSIDIARIES

a&f Stahl- und Maschinenbau; DECKEL MAHO Geretsried; DECKEL MAHO Pfronten; DECKEL MAHO Seebach; DMG Microset; DMG Shanghai Machine Tool; DMG Vertriebs und Service GmbH (Holding); FAMOT; GILDEMEISTER Drehmaschinen GmbH; GILDEMEISTER Italiana S.p.A.; GRAZIANO; SACO; SAUER GmbH.

PRINCIPAL COMPETITORS

DaimlerChrysler AG; Renault S.A.; ThyssenKrupp AG; Tata Sons Ltd.; NKMZ; Mondragon Corporacion Cooperativa; Giddings and Lewis Machine Tools L.L.C.; Johann A. Krause Inc.; ThyssenKrupp Technologies AG; Faur S.A.; Elabuzhskiy Light Vehicle Plant; Benteler AG; Liebherr-International AG.

FURTHER READING

"German Lathe Firm Invests in China," *AsiaPulse News,* May 27, 2002.

"German Machine Tool Maker Gildemeister Targets China Market," *AsiaPulse News,* November 1, 2000.

"Gildemeister Plans New Plants," *Metalworking Insiders' Report,* October 15, 2003, p. 6.

Houlder, Vanessa, "Gildemeister System to Speed Up High-Volume Production," *Financial Times,* May 27, 1999, p. 15.

Page, Michael, "Gildemeister on a Rebound, Picks Up a Laser-Machining Company," *Metalworking Insiders' Report,* March 5, 1999, p. 1.

"Performance Plus Thanks to Linear Technology," *Eurotec,* April 2001, p. 24.

Hindustan Lever Limited

Hindustan Lever House
165/166 Backbay Reclamation
Mumbai 400 020
India
Telephone: +91 22 2287 0622
Fax: +91 22 2287 1970
Web site: http://www.hll.com

Public Company
Incorporated: 1956
Employees: 41,000
Sales: $2.5 billion (2005)
Stock Exchanges: Mumbai
Ticker Symbol: 6261674
NAIC: 325611 Soap and Other Detergent Manufacturing; 311119 Other Animal Food Manufacturing; 311225 Fats and Oils Refining and Blending; 325620 Toilet Preparation Manufacturing

■ ■ ■

Hindustan Lever Limited (HLL) is India's leading consumer goods supplier, with a focus on the Fast-Moving Consumer Goods (FMCG) category that includes detergents, soap, shampoo, deodorant, toothpaste, and other personal care items, and cosmetics. HLL's personal care brands include soap brands such as Lux, Lifebuoy, Liril, Breeze, Dove, Pear's, and Rexona; shampoos and hair coloring brands including Sunsilk Naturals and Clinic; skin care brands Fair & Lovely and Pond's; and oral care brands Pepsodent and Close-Up. The company's cosmetic line is led by the Lakme brand; HLL also produces a line of Ayurvedic personal and healthcare items under the Ayush brand. In addition to the FMCG segment, HLL has developed a line of food items, primarily under the Kissan and Knorr Annapurna brands, as well as the ice cream brand Kwality Wall's. In the early 2000s, HLL also acquired baked goods producer Modern Food Industries. In addition to its domestic brand family, HLL sells bulk foods, including maize, rice, salt, and atta. HLL is also an active exporter, shipping its FMCG and food brands, as well as rice; marine products including surimi, shrimp, crabsticks, and others; and castor oil. HLL has completed a restructuring of its business in the first half of the 2000s, streamlining its brand portfolio, from 110 brands to 35 "power" brands, while exiting a number of businesses, such as teas (sold to the Woodbriar Group in 2006) and specialty chemicals. HLL maintains a strong manufacturing presence in India, with some 80 factories located throughout the country; the company also subcontracts to more than 150 third-party producers. HLL is itself a subsidiary of Unilever, which controls 51.55 percent of the group. HLL is listed on the Mumbai Stock Exchange.

INDIAN MANUFACTURING BASE STARTING IN 1931

England's Lever Brothers began importing their Sunlight brand soap into India in the late 1880s. By 1895, Lever had introduced another of its brands, Lifebuoy, which became the company's longest-running successful brand in India. Other Lever brands followed into the beginning of the next century, including the Lux soap flake brand in 1905; and scouring powder Vim as well as soap brand Vinolia in 1913. Lever Brothers, by then

COMPANY PERSPECTIVES

Mission: Unilever's mission is to add Vitality to life. We meet everyday needs for nutrition, hygiene, and personal care with brands that help people feel good, look good and get more out of life.

well into an international expansion that would see the company become one of the world's top multinationals, also acquired and introduced a number of other brands into the Indian market, including Pear's soap, in 1917. By 1930, Lever Brothers, which also had entered areas such as food production, including edible oils and margarine, had merged with The Netherlands' Margarine Unie, forming Unilever.

Unilever's Indian sales were based on imports into the early 1930s. The company had begun planning, however, to establish a manufacturing presence in the Indian subcontinent as early as 1923. The company began talks with the British and Indian authorities, and finally received permission to build its first factory in 1931. In that year, the company incorporated a new subsidiary, Hindustan Vanaspati Manufacturing Company, to produce edible oils. That company opened a production facility in Sewri in 1932.

Two years later, the company added another subsidiary, Lever Brothers India Limited, for the production of soap, and began construction of a factory next to its Vanaspati facility. That company launched production of Sunlight-branded soap at a factory in Bombay in 1934. In that year, as well, the company took over production at the Calcutta factory of another company, Northwest Soap, where it began producing the Lever brand family. That factory, known as the Garden Reach factory, added production of a line of personal care products in 1943.

In 1935, Unilever added a third subsidiary in India, United Traders Limited. This unit was created to provide marketing support for the company's other operations, tailoring the group's sales to the specifics of the Indian population. Through the 1940s, Unilever's Indian unit began extending its sales network throughout India, building up its own sales team, and adding sales offices in Mumbai, Chennai, Calcutta, Karachi, and elsewhere.

The transition of Unilever's multiple businesses to the single Hindustan Lever Limited began in the 1940s. In 1944, the three Indian companies were reorganized under a unified management. Nonetheless, the companies retained separate sales and marketing businesses. In the meantime, the company had launched an effort to transition the company from one led almost entirely by foreign and, in large part, European management, to one staffed primarily by Indians. This effort began in 1942, when the company began training Indians for its junior and then senior management positions. By 1951, the company appointed an Indian, Prakash Tandon, to the managing director's position. Tandon led the merger of the three Indian subsidiaries into a single entity, Hindustan Lever Limited (HLL), in 1956. By the end of the decade, Tandon had taken over the chairman's position as well. By then, nearly all of the group's management positions were filled by Indians. HLL was then taken public, as Unilever reduced its stake in the company in favor of domestic shareholders. By 1980, Unilever's stake in HLL had dropped to less than 52 percent.

NATIONAL CONSUMER GOODS GIANT IN THE SECOND HALF OF THE 20TH CENTURY

HLL already produced a wide range of consumer goods for the Indian market by the early 1960s. In 1962, the company launched its own export operations as well, in a move made in part to bring foreign exchange capital into the struggling Indian economy. HLL's exports reflected the company's own multifaceted operations. In addition to producing and supplying raw materials and finished products, including a number of specialty chemicals and tea, in the support of the international Unilever brand family, HLL also developed a bulk goods export business. For this the company focused on Indian-specific goods, such as castor oil, Basmati rice, and a variety of marine products, including shrimp and surimi.

HLL set up a new headquarters in Mumbai in 1963. The following year, the company entered the dairy industry, establishing its Etah dairy and launching the Anik brand of ghee (a prepared butter product used in Indian cooking). The company also began producing animal feed that year. Meanwhile, HLL launched a new shampoo, Sunsilk, for the Indian market. By the end of the decade, HLL had launched a number of other successful brands, including Signal toothpaste, Taj Mahal tea, Bru coffee, and Clinic shampoo, launched in 1971. By then, the company had firmly established itself as the leading producer of so-called "fast-moving consumer goods."

Part of the company's success came from its highly active sales network. A significant proportion of India's population, which would top one billion before the dawn of the 21st century, still lived in rural regions and in extreme poverty. For much of this population, personal care products remained luxury items. Yet the

KEY DATES

1888: Lever Brothers soaps are sold for the first time in India.
1931: Lever Brothers launches its first manufacturing subsidiary in India, Hindustan Vanaspati Manufacturing Company.
1933: A second Indian subsidiary, Lever Brothers India Limited, is established.
1935: A third subsidiary, United Traders Limited, is established.
1944: The three Unilever companies in India are placed under common management.
1956: A merger of the three companies forms Hindustan Lever Limited (HLL).
1962: Export operations are launched.
1969: HLL diversifies into fine chemicals production.
1971: Industrial chemicals production is added.
1980: Unilever reduces its shareholding in HLL to less than 52 percent.
1986: HLL launches an agri-foods unit.
1993: HLL merges with chief rival Tata Oil Mills Company.
1994: The company establishes Nepal Lever Limited in Nepal.
1995: HLL forms joint venture Lakme Lever Limited with Lakme, part of Tata, to produce cosmetics.
1998: HLL acquires full control of Lakme Lever.
2000: HLL acquires 74 percent of Modern Food Industries from the Indian government.
2002: Full control of Modern Food is acquired.
2006: The company undergoes a complete restructuring as part of the "power brand" strategy, selling Tea Estates India to a subsidiary of the Woodbriar Group.

company recognized the importance of building its brands in this region as well, and as such the company developed a vast sales network. Much of this network was based on an army of independent, direct sales agents, who hawked the company's products in the country's more than 150,000 villages.

Into the 1970s, HLL also began diversifying beyond its consumer goods operations. The company opened the Hindustan Lever Research Center, in Mumbai, in 1967. This led the group to begin producing fine chemicals in 1969. By 1971, the company had received permission from Unilever to enter the production of industrial chemicals. The company began construction of a pilot plant for this operation in Taloja in 1974. This unit was completed in 1976. In that year, HLL launched the construction of a larger chemicals complex, at Haldia. That facility began producing sodium tripolyphosphate in 1979. The production of these chemicals enabled HLL to begin producing synthetic detergents at Jammu in 1977.

Through the 1980s, HLL continued to develop its businesses. In 1986, the company set up an agri-products business, based in Hyderabad, which began producing hybrid seeds that year. HLL also added a new soap production facility in Khamgaon, and a personal products factory in Yavatmal that year.

HLL's growth had nonetheless been limited by restrictions put into place by the Indian government's quasi-socialist economic policies. In 1991, however, in the face of a major economic crisis, the government was forced to liberalize the country's economy. This opened up a new era of opportunity for HLL.

POWER BRAND FOCUS INTO THE 21ST CENTURY

A major step forward for the group came in 1993, when the company acquired its leading rival, Tata Oil Mills. By then, HLL also had met with new success in the detergents category, with the launch of its Surf Ultra brand. This brand targeted the country's middle class, which, with the liberalization of the country's economy, was also becoming one of the fastest growing segments of India's population. In a further move to target this population, the company launched a new, high-end detergent brand, Surf Excel, in 1996.

By the mid-1990s, HLL's revenues had topped $540 million. The company also had launched its first foreign subsidiary, establishing Nepal Lever Limited. That unit began producing soaps and detergents and other products within the HLL brand family, both for the Indian and Nepal market, as well as for the larger export market.

HLL also began developing a series of joint venture partnerships in the 1990s. In 1995, the company teamed up with Tata, this time forming a 50-50 joint venture with Tata's Lakme cosmetics group. HLL bought the Lakme brand family just three years later, taking full control of Lakme Lever. By then, the company also had formed a joint venture with Kimberly-Clark, which began marketing the Huggies diaper and Kotex sanitary pad brands in India.

HLL also deepened its food brands during the 1990s and into the 2000s. The company acquired Kwality and

Milkfood, which included the Kwality Wall's ice cream brand. In 2000, HLL marked the beginning of a new era in India's economy, when it acquired 74 percent of Modern Food Industries Limited. A major baked goods business in India, Modern Food had previously been owned by the Indian government, and marked HLL's extension into an entirely new product category. HLL subsequently acquired full control of Modern Food in 2002.

The first half of the 2000s nonetheless represented a difficult period for the company, which was faced with an economic slowdown in its core Indian markets. At the same time, HLL underwent a dramatic restructuring as part of the parent company's global "power brand" strategy. The company began streamlining its brand portfolio, which had grown to some 110 brands by the beginning of the decade, cutting that number back to just 35 brands by mid-decade. As part of this refocus, HLL also began selling off its noncore operations, including its chemicals businesses. That process was completed in large part with the sell-off of the last of HLL's tea plantation and production units, Tea Estates India, which was sold to a subsidiary of the Woodbriar Group in 2006.

By then, HLL appeared to have once again moved into a growth phase, posting revenue gains of 9 percent, and net profit growth of some 23 percent, over the previous year. HLL also prepared to enter a new management era; in 2006, the company appointed Douglas Baillie, who previously headed Unilever's operations in Africa, as the company's CEO. That appointment placed a non-Indian at the head of the company for the first time in more than 40 years. HLL appeared certain to clean up in India's consumer goods market for decades to come.

M. L. Cohen

PRINCIPAL SUBSIDIARIES

Bon Limited; Daverashola Tea Company Limited; Hindlever Trust Limited; Indexport Limited; Indigo Lever Shared Services Limited; International Fisheries Limited; KICM (Madras) Limited; Kimberly-Clark Lever Private Limited (50%); Lever India Exports Limited; Levers Associated Trust Limited; Levindra Trust Limited; Lipton India Exports Limited; Merryweather Food Products Limited; Modern Food and Nutrition Industries Limited; Modern Food Industries (India) Limited; Nepal Lever Limited (Nepal) (80%); Ponds Exports Limited; Quest International India Limited (49%); Thiashola Tea Company Limited; TOC Disinfectants Limited.

PRINCIPAL COMPETITORS

Nirma Ltd.; Jocil Ltd.; Nahar Industrial Enterprises Ltd.; Shrihari Laboratories P Ltd.; Ruchi Infrastructure Ltd.; Procter & Gamble Hygiene and Healthcare Ltd.; Amrit Banaspati Company Ltd.; Henkel SPIC India Ltd.; K S Oils Ltd.; Ultramarine and Pigments Ltd.; Vashisti Detergents Ltd.

FURTHER READING

Ananthanarayanan, Ravi, "New Improved HLL Rides the Bandwagon," *Economic Times,* February 18, 2006.

"Can Lever Get the Lather Back?," *Business Week,* December 4, 2000, p. 29.

Dadiseth, Keki, "Poor People," *Fast Company,* June 2001, p. 120.

Dinakar, S., "Choice and No Choice," *Forbes Global,* November 14, 2005, p. 40.

———, "A Penny a Packet," *Forbes,* November 28, 2005, p. 186.

"Future Perfect," *India Business Insight,* February 27, 2006.

"HLL Sells TEIL to Woodbriar Group," *Business Line,* March 3, 2006.

Lakshman, Nandini, "The New Broom at Hindustan Lever," *Business Week Online,* December 29, 2005.

Tanzer, Andrew, and Ghosh Chandrani, "Soap Opera in Bombay," *Forbes,* June 11, 2001, p. 129.

"Unilever Jewel," *Business Week,* April 26, 1999, p. 114.

Host America Corporation

2 Broadway
Hamden, Connecticut 06518
U.S.A.
Telephone: (203) 248-4100
Fax: (203) 230-8667
Web site: http://www.hostamericacorp.com

Public Company
Incorporated: 1986 as University Dining Service, Inc.
Employees: 470
Sales: $26.83 million (2004)
Stock Exchanges: Pink Sheets
Ticker Symbol: CAFÉ
NAIC: 722320 Caterers; 541330 Engineering Services; 541620 Environmental Consulting Services; 541690 Other Scientific and Technical Consulting Services; 561210 Facilities Support Services; 561790 Other Services to Buildings and Dwellings

■ ■ ■

Host America Corporation operates in two different business areas, foodservice management and energy and electrical services. The former consists of Host America Business Dining, which runs foodservice operations for the employees of more than 30 clients including Pitney Bowes and Oxford Health Plans; and Lindley Food Service Corp., which provides single serving and group meals to schools, senior citizen centers, Meals on Wheels, and emergency food programs. The company's electrical division, RS Services, Inc., manufactures and installs LightMasterPlus, a device that reduces energy usage of fluorescent light fixtures with minimal light loss. In the summer of 2005 the U.S. Securities and Exchange Commission began an investigation of the firm after a company press release that exaggerated its relationship with Wal-Mart Stores, Inc. caused the stock price to soar. Its stock was subsequently removed from the NASDAQ and CEO Geoffrey Ramsey was dismissed by the firm's board.

BEGINNINGS

Host America's roots date to 1986, when Geoffrey Ramsey and David Murphy founded University Dining Service, Inc. in New Haven, Connecticut. Both had worked for ARA Services and at several institutional dining facilities, and were then running the campus dining operations of New Haven University and teaching in its hotel/restaurant school. Together they had developed a new meal program called a declining balance system, in which students' meals were charged against a prepaid account rather than paying for a set number each week.

University Dining Service was founded to manage dining services for schools and colleges. Contracts were initially signed with only a few institutions, however, primarily small community colleges that yielded minimal revenues and had frequent down times, making labor retention difficult. Needing a steadier source of income, the firm soon began to seek work managing corporate dining facilities, which operated year-round.

In 1988 the company sold five million shares of stock to the general public, with Murphy and Ramsey

COMPANY PERSPECTIVES

Host America utilizes sophisticated technologies in its management services and energy conservation software products and systems. These products and systems enable us to design solutions to problems and develop cost reduction answers for building owners and managers. Host America employs a professional sales and marketing force that services both national and individual accounts and is headed up by a Management Team that has many years experience in food service and energy conservation management.

retaining controlling interest. The year 1990 saw the firm add vending and office coffee services, and two years later it began to focus exclusively on business dining. During the early 1990s the company (which had shortened its name to UDS) signed several *Fortune* 500 accounts, and by 1997 its annual revenues had grown to almost $6 million.

UDS now managed about two dozen corporate and manufacturing plant dining facilities in Connecticut, New Jersey, and New York, as well as providing them with vending, coffee, home meal replacement, and special event catering services. Its largest client was an office complex in Edison, New Jersey, called Twin Towers, which accounted for $1 million in revenue per year, and it was also running the foodservice operations of Pitney Bowes. Seeking further growth, in 1998 UDS management decided to make another public offering of stock. After effecting a 100-to-1 reverse split, in July the newly renamed Host America Corporation sold one million shares on the NASDAQ for $5 each, netting $3.8 million. President Geoffrey Ramsey and Executive Vice-President David Murphy continued to hold sizable stakes.

In the fall of 1998 the company formed a sports and recreational division, which subsequently opened dining facilities at an ice rink in Stamford, Connecticut. In 1999 new accounts were signed with the publisher of the *Hartford Courant,* Tyco Submarine Systems, Bayer Pharmaceutical, Oxford Health Plans, Staples, The Stanley Works, Trumpf, Inc., and Priceline.com. The latter had reportedly chosen the firm in part because of its home meal replacement program, which accommodated the long working hours of the new e-commerce firm's staff. Host America was now bidding on two contracts per week and winning about one in four.

ACQUISITION OF LINDLEY IN 2000

In July 2000 the firm bought Lindley Food Service Corp. for approximately $6.1 million, which was partially funded by a new $2.5 million loan from Webster Bank. Founded in 1982 by Gil Rossomando and Mark Cerreta, who would continue to run it after the acquisition, Lindley was the largest supplier of fresh and frozen single-serving meals for schools, day care centers, senior centers, and similar organizations in Connecticut. Some food was delivered via "Meals on Wheels" programs, and some served at large dining centers. Lindley's annual revenues of $8.4 million doubled Host America's total earnings, while positioning it for growth as the large baby boomer segment of the U.S. population neared retirement age.

The firm was also expanding its corporate foodservice work at a rapid rate, and in 2000 and early 2001 signed contracts to feed employees of JDS/Uniphase and Tellium, Inc., for whom it would provide cafeteria service, office coffee, and home meal replacement. As with Priceline.com, both offered products tied to the rise of the Internet and were building plush dining facilities in anticipation of rapid growth. Investors were already beginning to dump Internet stocks, however, and these firms soon cut back on amenities as their sales forecasts were downgraded.

August saw the purchase of Contra-Pak, Inc. of Dallas, Texas, a maker of shelf-stable meals that were used by Meals on Wheels and emergency feeding programs around the United States. Nearly 60 percent of its business came from the Northeast, and those orders were subsequently filled via Lindley's production facilities in New Haven, Westport, and Bridgeport, Connecticut. The firm had paid $160,000 in cash and 57,000 shares of stock.

In October Host America reached an agreement to buy SelectForce, Inc. of Oklahoma City for 700,000 shares of stock. SelectForce (which had annual revenues of $1.8 million) was an employee screening firm that looked into criminal histories and driving records, performed credit and employment verification, and later began administering drug tests. Its primary clients were healthcare and temporary staffing agencies. Continuing under its established management, SelectForce would perform work for corporate clients as well as become a part of Host America's dining service offerings, enabling the firm to certify to its clients that employees were of a high standard. For the fiscal year ended in June, Host America posted revenues of $21.6 million and a loss of $42,000.

In early 2002 several major contracts to provide food to senior citizens and children's Head Start

KEY DATES

1986: David Murphy and Geoffrey Ramsey found University Dining Service.
1992: Firm decides to focus exclusively on business dining.
1998: Company is renamed Host America Corp.; stock begins trading on NASDAQ.
2000: Lindley Food Service Corp. is acquired.
2001: SelectForce, Inc. and Contra-Pak are purchased.
2003: Energy management firm GlobalNet Investors is acquired.
2004: Electrical company RS Services and assets of Food Brokers, Inc. are purchased.
2005: SelectForce is sold; SEC inquiry is launched, stock is delisted, and Ramsey is fired.

programs in Indiana were signed, which would bring in $1.2 million per year. The company had also recently completed a restructuring of its operations, which was expected to save $250,000 annually.

In the fall of 2002 Host America defaulted on its loan from Webster Bank, and the company's auditor expressed doubts that it would remain a going concern. A new loan agreement was later reached, however. Earnings for the fiscal year ended in June had totaled $24.4 million, with a profit of $70,000 recorded. The firm was continuing to win new work from senior programs in Massachusetts, Rhode Island, and Florida, where it opened an additional office.

PURCHASE OF ENERGY BUSINESS IN 2003

In August 2003 Host America announced an agreement to acquire GlobalNet Energy Investors, Inc. in exchange for 550,000 shares of stock. GlobalNet manufactured and sold products and software licensed from Energy-Nsync, Inc. that reduced the energy usage in fluorescent lighting systems with minimal loss of visible light. In the fall the company also signed agreements to manage the foodservice operations of seven businesses in the Northeast, Florida, and Texas, including Honeywell's New Jersey facility.

Early 2004 saw acquisition of patents to a product called Fan Saver, which reduced the energy consumption of fans in refrigeration systems. The company's Lindley subsidiary also continued to win new work around the United States, including a five-year, $12.5 million contract to provide 3,500 meals per day in Massachusetts. For the year ended in June the firm reported revenues of $26.8 million and a loss of $4.9 million.

The company began installing its lighting energy conservation technology in test sites, including warehouses, a dormitory, and several chain restaurants. In July Host America received $8 million in new financing from Laurus Master Fund Ltd., after which it bought RS Services, Inc. of Duncan, Oklahoma, for $4.6 million. Founded in 2000 by Ronald Sparks, RS was an electrical installation company that employed 60 and would install Host America's energy management products, as well as perform contract work for outside firms. After the purchase, the GlobalNet name was dropped and the company's energy unit became known as RS Services.

In November the firm bought the assets and accounts of Food Brokers, Inc., a Bridgeport, Connecticut-based foodservice company, and early 2005 saw a joint venture formed with Innovative Performance Contracting of Texas and Oklahoma. The latter would market LightMasterPlus, as the firm's energy-saving technology was now known.

In the spring, Host America sold employment screening unit SelectForce to T.E.D., Inc. for $2.1 million. The company also announced that a U.S. Department of Energy test of LightMasterPlus had found it reduced electricity usage by 15 to 30 percent but had no negative effect on fluorescent fixtures and ballasts. May saw RS Services win a $6 million-plus contract to install Eaton Cutler-Hammer electrical controls in 400 Wal-Mart stores.

STOCK CONTROVERSY IN SUMMER OF 2005

On July 12, 2005, Host America issued a press release announcing that the firm would begin surveying ten Wal-Mart stores in preparation for installing LightMasterPlus in each, also filing an 8-K form with the Securities and Exchange Commission (SEC), which typically denoted an important material development. The press release quoted CEO Ramsey as saying, "This is a major event for our company, which we have been working towards since last year. We expect this prestigious customer will like the savings they receive from this first-phase roll-out and believe that the next phase will involve a significant number of stores." Investors jumped on the implication that Wal-Mart might install LightMasterPlus in many of its 3,725 U.S. stores, and the firm's stock price doubled to $6.35 that same day and topped $14 within a week.

After several of Host America's largest shareholders sold portions of their holdings, the SEC requested documents from the company supporting the claims of the July 12 press release, citing concerns that it had been "misleading." On July 22 trading was suspended for two weeks and a formal investigation was begun. The NASDAQ subsequently extended the trading suspension past the SEC's resumption date, while numerous lawsuits were filed against Host America, its top management, and certain shareholders, alleging misrepresentation. They were later consolidated into a class-action suit.

On August 31 the company admitted in a press release that the Wal-Mart agreement had been an "oral understanding" with no written contract, that the stores to be surveyed had not yet been determined, and that no agreement to buy LightMasterPlus had been reached. CEO and President Geoffrey Ramsey was then placed on administrative leave without pay, and resigned as board member and chairman. His place was taken on an acting basis by CFO David Murphy.

When the NASDAQ allowed Host America's stock to resume trading on September 1, its price plunged by 74 percent to $3.71 and kept falling thereafter. Two weeks later the stock was delisted by the exchange and began trading on the Pink Sheets information service. The firm subsequently notified the SEC that it would delay filing its annual report and the next quarterly report, citing the ongoing investigation and lawsuits. In late November the company fired Ramsey; his administrative assistant and wife, Debra Ramsey; and his sister Anne Ramsey, the company's human resources director and secretary (though she would remain a board member until the firm's shareholders met). News had recently surfaced that the fateful July 12 press release had been issued a day after the company granted stock options to its directors and top executives, exercisable immediately, though most had not sold any shares before trading was suspended.

In January 2006 Geoffrey Ramsey filed a $2.5 million claim against the company with the American Arbitration Association, alleging wrongful dismissal. His sister Anne and wife Debra also filed for a total of $2 million. In March, the firm issued a letter to shareholders vowing better future communication, though numerous matters continued to be unresolved including the Ramsey arbitration and the SEC investigation.

The 20-year history of Host America Corporation had seen the company branch out into several different business areas in an effort to become profitable. Reverberations from a 2005 stock scandal were still being felt, and its future status would depend to a large extent on management's ability to surmount a host of legal difficulties and a tarnished reputation among investors.

Frank Uhle

PRINCIPAL SUBSIDIARIES

Lindley Food Service Corp.; RS Services, Inc.

PRINCIPAL COMPETITORS

ARAMARK Corp.; Sodexho, Inc.; Guckenheimer; Epicurean Feast Cafes and Restaurants.

FURTHER READING

Brulliard, Nicolas, "Host America Dismisses CEO," *Dow Jones Corporate Filings Alert*, November 29, 2005.

Buzalka, Michael, "Paradigm Breakers," *Food Management*, September, 2002, p. 26.

Hemans, Donna, "Host America Auditor Doubts Co. Can Stay a Going Concern," *Dow Jones Corporate Filing Alert*, October 11, 2002.

Higgins, Steve, "After 6-Week Halt, Host America Stock Plummets 74 Percent," *New Haven Register*, September 2, 2005.

———, "Hamden, Conn.-Based Food Service Management CEO Resigns from Board," *New Haven Register*, September 1, 2005.

———, "Former CEO of Host America Corp. Seeks Damages After Termination," *New Haven Register*, January 5, 2006.

———, "Hamden, Conn.-Based Food Services Firm Buys Electronics Installer," *New Haven Register*, July 17, 2004.

———, "Hamden, Conn.-Based Host America Vows Better Communication with Shareholders," *New Haven Register*, March 10, 2006.

———, "Lighting Deal with Wal-Mart Drives Up Stock Price of Host America Corp.," *New Haven Register*, July 16, 2005.

"Host America Sees Profitable 2001, Helped by Lindley Unit," *Reuters News*, August 24, 2000.

"Host America Sells Screening Unit," *Associated Press Newswires*, April 4, 2005.

"Host America Shares Suspended After Run-Up, Sales," *Reuters News*, July 22, 2005.

"Host America Stock Offering Will Finance Growth Plan," *Vending Times*, July 25, 1998, p. 21.

"Host America Stock Surges on Acquisition Plans," *Reuters News*, August 7, 2003.

Kocik, Carrie, "Host America Corp. to Acquire Contra-Pak, Inc.," *Dow Jones News Service*, August 24, 2001.

Malone, Scott, "Host America Shareholders Cash in After Rally," *Reuters News*, July 19, 2005.

———. "Lifting the Lid—Host America Rally Shows Risks of Name Dropping," *Reuters News*, August 12, 2005.

Papiernik, Richard, "Host America Trims Losses to $42,000 in Fiscal 2001," *Nation's Restaurant News*, October 8, 2001, p. 12.

Troise, Damian J., "Host America Subsidiary Will Double Revenues with Wal-Mart Contract," *New Haven Register*, May 3, 2005.

Wang, Stone, "Host America Announces Merger Pact with Selectforce, Inc.," *Dow Jones News Service*, October 30, 2001.

Hubbard Broadcasting Inc.

3415 University Avenue
St. Paul, Minnesota 55114
U.S.A.
Telephone: (651) 646-5555
Fax: (651) 642-4103
Web site: http://www.kstp.com

Private Company
Founded: 1923
Employees: 1,100
Sales: $200 million (2004 est.)
NAIC: 515120 Television Broadcasting

■ ■ ■

Hubbard Broadcasting Inc. (HBI) operates one of the few remaining large family-owned television companies in the nation. An early innovator in its market, Twin Cities-based KSTP-TV nonetheless struggles with perennial news program ratings woes. Its subsidiary United States Satellite Broadcasting Company Inc. (USSB), an object of derision in its infancy, was purchased by Hughes Electronics Corporation for $1.3 billion in 1999. Conus Communications, its satellite-based news gathering organization, fared less well, shutting down most of its operations in 2002. The Hubbard family broadcasting legacy remains in the hands of a third generation.

ROOTS IN LOCAL RADIO AND TELEVISION

Minnesota native Stanley E. Hubbard, a pioneer of commercial radio and television broadcasting, established his first radio station in 1923. "WAMD–Where All Minneapolis Dances—broadcast part-time because Hubbard had to leave the microphone every few hours to go and sell advertising," wrote Kathy Haley in a 1997 *Broadcasting & Cable* article.

Interested in expanding his news coverage, Hubbard started his own news gathering bureau in 1925; Associated Press and United Press International did not yet serve the fledgling radio industry. WAMD merged with KFOY in 1928 to form KSTP. Hubbard broadcast the vaudeville acts of such performers as Jack Benny and the Marx brothers, live sporting events, and educational programs.

Among the first on the scene when television technology was being introduced, Hubbard experimented with closed-circuit broadcasts beginning in 1938 using one of the first RCA cameras. RCA formally presented television to the public during the 1939 New York World's Fair. World War II slowed development of commercial television, but in 1948 KSTP-TV began broadcasting.

KSTP-TV accumulated a series of firsts in the 1950s and early 1960s: the first television station between Chicago and the West Coast; the first independently owned NBC affiliate; the first station to carry a late evening local news program seven nights a week; and the first to do all-color broadcasting. Those early days of television were filled with sensational spot news stories, and Hubbard was known for aggressively seeking them out.

Hubbard expanded beyond the Minnesota borders late in the 1950s when he acquired a radio and televi-

COMPANY PERSPECTIVES

KSTP-TV Channel 5, the upper Midwest's first commercial television station, is owned by the pioneering broadcasting company Hubbard Broadcasting Inc. Channel 5 signed on the air April 27, 1948 and today remains the only locally owned locally operated broadcasting company in the Twin Cities. Eyewitness News is the station's hallmark, presenting local news, weather, and sports coverage daily for Channel 5 (ABC network affiliate) and its UHF sister station, Channel 45 (independent).

sion station in Albuquerque, New Mexico. In 1962, Hubbard Broadcasting Inc. was formed with Stanley E. Hubbard as president and general manager and son Stanley S. Hubbard as vice-president. Stanley S. Hubbard, who had been in and around the broadcasting business since his childhood, had come on board full-time in 1951.

Stanley S. Hubbard began making his own mark on the television industry in the 1960s with an operation in St. Petersburg, Florida. "Few independent station owners made money at all in 1968 and none had succeeded in making a go of a UHF in an all-VHF market, but the younger Hubbard had WTOG turning a profit within two and a half years," wrote Haley. Hubbard transformed the station by adding a much larger transmission tower and investing in popular programming.

A CHANGE OF LEADERSHIP

Minneapolis/St. Paul was a competitive market: both radio and television stations fought for the all-important ratings leadership. In the early 1970s, KSTP was losing ground to WCCO on both fronts. Stanley S. Hubbard brought in Marion, Iowa-based media consultant Frank Magid to help turn the tide. The action, initially opposed by founder Stanley E. Hubbard, "ushered in what was perhaps KSTP-TV's most successful era," according to Sandra Earley.

Among significant changes in the TV end of the business, according to Early, were the move to "personality driven newscasts" and the switch from the standard film format to easier to use videotape. The radio station switched to a rock-and-roll format and dropped its lengthy affiliation with NBC. The control of the business had clearly shifted from father to son.

A 1981 *Broadcasting* magazine article estimated Hubbard Broadcasting's worth at $200 million or more. The Hubbards owned three television and five radio stations, a marine radio-supply company, a production company, and a 148-room Miami Beach hotel. While often soundly criticized regarding their treatment of employees, the Hubbards were "held in generally high regard by other station owners," wrote Karl Vick in a March 1981 *Corporate Report Minnesota* article.

In 1984, continuing in their tradition of industry firsts, Hubbard Broadcasting initiated a satellite news gathering organization independent of the big three networks: ABC, CBS, and NBC. Conus (Continental U.S.) Communications bought and leased satellite transponders and then offered satellite access and newsfeeds to member stations. F&F Productions, a Hubbard subsidiary specializing in remote production, built the first satellite news gathering truck using the new Ku-band satellite technology.

Live offsite broadcasts became a practical reality for smaller stations. The C-band satellite systems in use at the time required huge receivers and were tightly regulated by the Federal Communications Commission (FCC) due to their disruptive effect on other signals, and ground-based microwave signals had a limited range and needed a clear pathway. Conus gained 60 member stations within the first few years of operation.

DIRECT BROADCAST SATELLITE

Stanley S. Hubbard was a true believer in the efficacy of satellite broadcasting, and his horizons expanded beyond news gathering applications. Back in 1981, when Hubbard Broadcasting was granted one of the first direct broadcast satellite (DBS) licenses, he had begun formulating plans for an advertising-supported home satellite service. The satellite-to-home concept had been tossed around since the early 1960s when Congress created the Communications Satellite Corp. (COMSAT).

The public effort to build a commercial television system around satellite technology failed due to lack of outside support and COMSAT was disbanded in the mid-1980s. Prudential Insurance, General Instrument, and shopping center developer Francesco Galesi formed United Satellite Communications in 1983 but had fewer than 10,000 subscribers when it folded a few years later, according to a 1991 *Forbes* article by Graham Button. SkyCable was shut down in June 1991. However, Hughes continued to develop the technology and linked up with Hubbard.

United States Satellite Broadcasting (USSB), a subsidiary of Hubbard Broadcasting formed in 1981, was also having trouble getting its satellite service off the

KEY DATES

1923: Stanley E. Hubbard establishes his first radio station.
1925: Company forms news gathering bureau.
1948: Company begins television broadcasting.
1951: Son Stanley S. Hubbard comes on board full-time.
1962: Hubbard Broadcasting Inc. is formed.
1981: United States Satellite Broadcasting (USSB) is formed.
1984: Company initiates a satellite news gathering service, Conus.
1991: Company buys transponders aboard Hughes satellite.
1994: Company begins broadcasting satellite television service.
1996: USSB goes public.
2002: Conus shuts down most of its operations.
2006: Moviewatch is expected to serve 26 million homes.

ground. USSB reformulated its earlier plan to include a mix of advertising, subscription, and pay-per-view programming to be transmitted via two RCA satellites and launched by 1988. Unfortunately, lack of financing foiled the endeavor. Many of the most promising potential investors were already involved in cable, a direct competitor to the satellite service, and others doubted Hubbard could succeed where much larger contenders had failed.

Yet, Hubbard persisted. Nationwide Mutual Insurance, Pittway Corp. (a fire alarm maker), and media investor Burt Harris came aboard as investors in the late 1980s. Technological advances improved the odds for success. Digital compression hiked the number of television channels that could be carried by a single transponder, and higher-powered satellites allowed receiver size to be greatly reduced.

In 1991, General Motors' Hughes Aircraft sold five of 16 transponders on its broadcast satellite to Hubbard in a deal valued at more than $100 million. DBS skeptics were quick to point out the market was already largely wired for cable service, and the initial cost to the consumer, about $700 for a receiving dish and signal converter, was much higher than cable. Furthermore, unlike cable, DBS did not transmit local programming.

Hubbard and other DBS supporters declared the higher capacity digital signals provided far better sound and picture quality than the standard analog signal used by cable and broadcast television. Cable companies themselves were gearing for costly upgrades to fiber optic cable which would carry digital signals and boost channel capacity. Moreover, many cable customers had grown frustrated with persistent service problems.

Thomson Consumer Electronics, a division of France-based Thomson S.A., developed and produced the 18-inch receiver and the converter under the RCA brand name. The consumer-friendly dish could pick up both USSB and Hughes's DirecTV signals. Competitor Primestar, which began service in 1990, required a higher-priced, larger, professionally installed dish and offered fewer channel choices.

Although they shared a satellite and receiving system, USSB and DirecTV were in competition for subscribers. DirecTV had more channels at its disposal than USSB, but Hubbard quickly acquired the right to carry popular premium channels such as Home Box Office (HBO), Showtime, Cinemax, and the Movie Channel. USSB planned to offer the All News Channel, a joint venture between Conus and Viacom International, as well. DirecTV got the jump on rural distribution when the National Rural Telecommunications Cooperative purchased the right to market the service to electric and phone customers. Areas that were not wired for cable were an important source of customers for both companies.

USSB began broadcasting satellite television service in June 1994 aided by funds from Microsoft cofounder Paul Allen, Dow Jones & Company, and Wall Street investor George Soros. More than a half million receiving systems were sold in the first year, making DBS the fastest-selling new consumer electronics product in U.S. history. USSB signed on more than 300,000 subscribers. Hubbard's vision had become a reality. He received further recognition for his accomplishments in 1995, when he and his late father were handed the Distinguished Service Award from the National Association of Broadcasters for their work in radio, television, and DBS.

The once scorned DBS became the darling of investors. In January 1996, AT&T paid $137.5 million for 2.5 percent of DirecTV, and MCI Communications Corp. and News Corp. paid $682.5 million for a DBS license. The activity boosted the value of satellite broadcasters' stock just as USSB prepared to make an initial public offering (IPO). USSB raised $224.1 million in February. The newly public company was valued at more than $3 billion, and the Hubbard family held more than 50 percent of the shares.

Expectations were sky high. But the early phenomenal growth rate cooled. USSB stock price fell steadily from a high of about $37 shortly after the IPO to about $11 per share just over a year after the offering. USSB lost $237 million in its first two and one-half years of operation. "The skeptics are again ascendant. Wall Street analysts, who have recently called for the sale of USSB, say that the company's value lies in the five transponders it owns on a satellite, not in its 1.2 million subscribers," Sandra Earley wrote in a May 1997 article.

While new satellite companies geared up—EchoStar Communications (DISH Network) merged with ASkyB and MCI Communications Corporation announced a partnership with News Corp. in 1997—cable remained USSB's main competition. The Digital Satellite Systems (DSS) which USSB shared with DirecTV were found in about 3.3 million U.S. households at the end of 1997 compared with tens of millions of cable subscribers. USSB continued to fine-tune its service in order to place itself in the best possible position in the market and contracted with Lockheed Martin for additional satellites.

BACK DOWN TO EARTH

By this time, a third generation of Hubbards was engaged in the family enterprise. Stanley E. Hubbard II served as president and CEO at USSB. Robert W. Hubbard led the television operation. Ginny Hubbard Morris headed the KSTP-FM and AM radio operations. Two other siblings also held spots on the HBI board. Hubbard concerns included KSTP-TV and Conus Communications in Minneapolis/St. Paul; seven television stations located in Minnesota, New Mexico, and New York; a television production company in Florida; and USSB and the radio stations.

Expanding use of digital technology, and the entry of electric utilities and telephone companies into market were among the changes taking place in the industry as the century wound down. Fifty-year-old KSTP-TV faced this new climate on the heels of a decade-long streak of third place finishes in the Twin Cities news market. A new team had been set in place to turn the tide.

"Could we give the station a facelift?," asked Vice-President and General Manager Ed Piette in the *Star Tribune* (Minneapolis) in April 1998. "Yes, we could. But if you put a new coat of paint on a wall, does that make the wall any stronger or any better? It has to have strength in the foundation. We believe we're putting strength in the foundation for the next 50 years."

In January 1999, Hughes Electronics Corporation acquired USSB for $1.3 billion. The Hubbard family's stake in the deal was estimated at $674 million, according to the *Star Tribune*. Hughes owned DirecTV, the nation's largest satellite broadcasting company.

The new century brought an economic and advertising slowdown in its wake. The situation worsened with the terrorist attacks on the United States on September 11, 2001. Carrying around-the-clock coverage from ABC News, KSTP-TV halted advertising for 36 hours. When regular programming resumed, some big advertisers in the market, such as Northwest Airlines, decided to cease their ad campaigns through year-end. Moreover, local stations' coverage of the events had racked up additional costs, and the prospect of U.S. retaliation against the attackers created further uncertainty.

The continuing post-9/11 downturn led to layoffs, wage freezes, and canceled local news programs. The Twin Cities broadcast market revenue was in a double-digit decline. Hubbard was forced to downscale ambitious growth plans for KSTC-TV, acquired in 1999.

Conus Communications staff also felt the ax in 2001, but news of more drastic changes came the next year. Hubbard planned to shut down most of Conus's operations by January 2003, phasing out satellite and production services business, television news service, and 24-hour news. The company would continue to sell satellite time to television stations and offer a video archive service. Terry O'Reilly, Conus president, attributed the change to media consolidation and the advertising climate, according to the *Star Tribune*. A rash of local stations dropped the fee-based service during the tough economic times. Moreover, since the founding of Conus many local stations had acquired their own satellite trucks.

Former Conus employees purchased the company's satellite services division, the *Business Journal* reported in January 2003. The division's activities ranged from webcasting to field producing. The company, for example, had provided early coverage of the Senator Paul Wellstone plane crash in northern Minnesota to Fox News, CNN, and CBS. The Conus News Service and the All News Channel operations had shut down in the fall of 2002. Conus, which also sold video clips to producers, had redirected its energy toward developing television network programming for DirecTV.

The FCC loosened ownership rules on media companies in 2003, opening the door for realignment of the industry. Prognosticators envisioned a paring down of independents including Hubbard Broadcasting, which was undergoing some stress.

During the previous three years, Hubbard Broadcasting had spent $81 million on the acquisition of two television stations and an AM/FM radio station, Eric Wieffering reported for the *Star Tribune* in June 2003. Audience building led to three years of losses. Hubbard was among a rare breed, which included independent stations in Boston, San Francisco, Seattle, and Atlanta. Media conglomerates, such as Viacom, Gannett, Fox, and Walt Disney, owned most major market television stations. On the radio side, ownership was even more concentrated. Texas-based Clear Channel Communications owned more than 1,200 radio stations nationwide, seven of them in the Twin Cities.

Wieffering wrote, "Hubbard's oldest son, Stanley, 42, said the new FCC regulations might present more of an opportunity than a threat, opening up the possibility of more acquisitions of TV or radio stations in some markets. Son Robert Hubbard agreed: 'I don't think the new rules are going to materially affect our ability to be competitive. At the end of the day, it's business as usual.'" Business as usual for the Hubbards included coming up with new ideas. Stanley E Hubbard was in the process of raising $100 million to fund a new cable and satellite service, Moviewatch.

Ed Piette, general manager of KSTP-TV, left the station for rival WCCO, owned by Viacom Inc., in 2003. Continuing to lag behind in news ratings, KSTP hired Ed Asner, who played news director Lou Grant on *The Mary Tyler Moore Show* to create some buzz in 2004. Low rankings translated to lower revenue. Top-ranked KARE-TV brought in $4,000 for a 30-second ad during the 10 p.m. news versus just about $1,400 for KSTP-TV, according to the *Star Tribune*. While increasingly costly to produce, news programming could bring in as much as half of a station's total advertising revenue.

In 2005, *Forbes* estimated Stanley S. Hubbard's worth at about $1.2 billion. The magazine also noted the 2006 debut of Hubbard Broadcasting's new venture Moviewatch, expected to serve 26 million homes.

Kathleen Peippo

PRINCIPAL COMPETITORS

Clear Channel Communications, Inc.; Granite Broadcasting Corporation; Sinclair Broadcast Group, Inc.

FURTHER READING

Alexander, Steve, "Hubbard's Satellite TV Subsidiary to Go Public," *Star Tribune* (Minneapolis), December 2, 1995, p. 1D.

Albiniak, Paige, "In the Family Business: Born into a Broadcasting Clan, Morris Found Radio a Good Fit," *Broadcasting & Cable*," July 15, 2002, p. 59.

Bork, Robert H., Jr., "Conus the Barbarian," *Forbes,* November 4, 1985, p. 111.

Brinkley, Joel, "As Digital TV Arrives, Cable's Picture May Not Be So Clear," *New York Times,* May 5, 1997.

Button, Graham, "Stan Hubbard's Giant Footprint," *Forbes,* November 11, 1991, pp. 344-50.

Chanen, David, "Stan Hubbard, Broadcasting Pioneer, Dies at 95 in Florida," *Star Tribune* (Minneapolis), December 29, 1992, p. 1A.

Covert, Colin, "In Twin Cities, the Digital Picture Is Still Fuzzy Among Broadcasters," *Star Tribune* (Minneapolis), April 4, 1997.

Earley, Sandra, "Stan the Man," *Corporate Report Minnesota,* May 1997, pp. 33-43.

Fiedler, Terry, "They Said Hubbard's Idea Couldn't Fly," *Star Tribune* (Minneapolis), March 12, 1996, p. 1D.

———, "TV Pioneer Conus to Go Dark," *Star Tribune* (Minneapolis), September 21, 2002, p. 1D.

———, "USSB to Drop Lifetime, 6 Other Channels in Favor of More Movies, Pay TV," *Star Tribune* (Minneapolis), January 7, 1998, pp. 1D, 5D.

Fiedler, Terry, and Ann Merrill, "USSB Prepares for Initial Public Stock Offering," *Star Tribune* (Minneapolis), January 30, 1996, p. 1D.

"Fifth Estate," *Broadcasting,* November 23, 1981.

Garrison, Nicole, "Employees Buy Conus Satellite Operation," *Business Journal* (Minneapolis/St. Paul), January 17, 2003, pp. 1+.

Gross, Steve, "Hubbard's TV Venture Via Satellite," *Star Tribune* (Minneapolis), June 14, 1993, p. 1D.

Haley, Kathy, "The Pioneering Spirit of the Hubbard Family," *Broadcasting & Cable,* March 31, 1997, pp. S1-S15.

Holston, Noel, "Once the Twin Cities' Pace-Setting News Station, KSTP-TV Is Playing Some Serious Catch-Up As It Approaches Its 50th Anniversary," *Star Tribune* (Minneapolis), April 26, 1998 p. 1F.

"Hubbard Broadcasting Inc.," *Corporate Report Fact Book 1998,* p. 574.

Hubbard, Stanley S., and Michelle Y. Green, "The Father of American DBS," *Broadcasting & Cable,* May 31, 1999, p. 26.

Justin, Neal, "KSTP-TV Manager Takes Over at WCCO," *Star Tribune* (Minneapolis), July 15, 2003, p. 1D.

Kamenick, Amy, "Hubbards Have $776M Stake in EchoStar-DirecTV Merger," *Business Journal,* June 7, 2002, pp. 1+.

Karrfalt, Wayne, "Where Integrity Rules: In Stanley S. Hubbard's World, the Work Begins with Localism and Public Service," *Broadcasting & Cable,* June 2, 2003, p. 4A.

Kearney, Robert P., "Shine On, Stanley Hubbard," *Corporate Report Minnesota,* June 1986, pp. 43-46.

Lambert, Brian, "Family Channels," *St. Paul Pioneer Press,* April 26, 1998, pp. 1E, 4E.

Madison, Cathy, "Launching into National Orbit," *Twin Cities Business Monthly,* April 1994, pp. 27-31.

Merrill, Ann, "Hubbard's Full Cupboard," *Star Tribune* (Minneapolis), April 21, 1995, p. 1D.

Meyers, Mike, "USSB Sale Means Windfall for KSTP Workers," *Star Tribune* (Minneapolis), September 22, 1999, p. 1D.

Montgomery, Leland, "Cable's Death Star," *Financial World,* May 11, 1993, pp. 32-33.

Motavalli, John, "Clash Brews Over Virtual Duopolies," *Television Week,*" July 19, 2004.

Reinan, John, "Oh, Mr. Grant," *Star Tribune* (Minneapolis), March 3, 2004, p. 1D.

"The Richest People in America," Special Issue: 2005 Edition *Forbes* 400, p. 113.

Schmickle, Sharon, "No Smooth Transition for High Definition TV," *Star Tribune* (Minneapolis), September 22, 1997.

Scully, Sean, "Countdown to DBS," *Broadcasting & Cable,* December 6, 1993, pp. 30, 34.

"United States Satellite Broadcasting Company Inc.," *Corporate Report Fact Book 1998,* p. 498.

Vick, Karl, "The Life and Prime Times of Stanley S. Hubbard," *Corporate Report Minnesota,* March 1981, pp. 85-88, 120-26.

Wieffering, Eric, "Independent-Minded," *Star Tribune* (Minneapolis), June 8, 2003, p. 1D.

———, "With Fewer Advertisers, Media Outlets Hurt," *Star Tribune* (Minneapolis), September 22, 2001, p. 1D.

Williams, Sarah T., "An Independent Bookstore's Last Chapter," *Star Tribune* (Minneapolis), April 28, 2005, p. 1B.

Zulgad, Judd, "Hubbard Cuts Jobs, Cancels Shows," *Star Tribune* (Minneapolis), October 31, 2001, p. 1D.

Inamed Corporation

5540 Ekwill Street
Santa Barbara, California 93111
U.S.A.
Telephone: (805) 683-6761
Toll Free: (800) 624-4261
Fax: (805) 692-5432
Web site: http://www.inamed.com

Public Company
Incorporated: 1961 as First American Corporation
Employees: 1,200
Sales: $384.4 million (2004)
Stock Exchanges: NASDAQ
Ticker Symbol: IMDC
NAIC: 339113 Surgical Appliance and Supplies Manufacturing; 339112 Surgical and Medical Instrument Manufacturing

■ ■ ■

Inamed Corporation is a healthcare products manufacturer focused on marketing breast implants, dermal fillers to correct facial wrinkles, and devices to treat severe and morbid obesity. The company operates through two divisions: Inamed Aesthetics and Inamed Health. Through Inamed Aesthetics, the company offers a broad range of breast implants that are used for therapeutic purposes in reconstruction surgeries but find their greatest use in breast augmentation procedures. The division also produces a line of dermal fillers, including Reloxin, a botulinum toxin under development that is billed as the company's competitive answer to Allergan, Inc.'s hugely popular Botox dermal filler. Inamed Health produces products for minimally invasive surgical solutions to obesity, including a device marketed under the name "Lap-Band," which is a less traumatic alternative to surgeries such as gastric bypass and stomach stapling. Inamed maintains manufacturing facilities in the United States, Costa Rica, and Ireland, marketing its products in more than 50 countries.

ORIGINS

The Inamed name first appeared in the mid-1980s, a decade after the business it represented was founded. The earliest predecessor to Inamed was a company incorporated in 1961, Florida-based First American Corporation, but the essence of the Santa Barbara, California-based enterprise was founded in 1974. That year, McGhan Medical Corporation was incorporated, a company founded to manufacture silicone products for plastic and reconstructive surgery. The formation of Inamed occurred after a series of transactions that took place during the ensuing decade. In 1977, Minnesota Mining and Manufacturing Company (3M) acquired McGhan Medical, controlling the silicone implant product line until a new McGhan Medical was formed in 1984 to purchase the assets acquired by 3M. In 1985, one year after the assets were spun off by 3M, McGhan Medical became the subsidiary of a publicly held company when First American Corporation became the new corporate parent of the silicone implant product line. The following year, McGhan Medical changed its name to Inamed, a corporate banner meant to convey the concepts of "innovation" and "medicine."

COMPANY PERSPECTIVES

Our vision is to become a leading healthcare company that develops and markets innovative, high-quality, science-based products and services that enhance the quality of people's lives. We will live by the Inamed values and create the best work environment where the best people choose to work. We aspire to deliver superior shareholder returns and to be a good corporate citizen in the communities where our employees live and work.

There was an element of risk involved in operating as a breast implant manufacturer, one that was known to Inamed executives when they first unfurled their corporate banner. By basing their financial sustenance on the breast implant market, management exposed itself to the possibility of lawsuits and the possibility that the Food and Drug Administration (FDA) would step in and use its regulatory powers to ban breast implants. Both possibilities existed when the Inamed name was born, and, to the company's disappointment, both threats materialized, presenting the overriding challenge facing Inamed during its first decades in business.

The controversy over breast implants centered on one of three types of implants. All implants essentially were envelopes of silicone, with the difference in types determined by the substance used to fill the shell of the implant. Implants held either silicone gel, saline solution, or a combination of the two substances. Litigation and FDA scrutiny centered on silicone-gel implants, the type overwhelmingly preferred by women because of their more natural look. The first lawsuit against an implant manufacturer was won in 1977, the year 3M acquired McGhan Medical, but the legal salvos volleyed at the breast implant industry did not pick up in intensity until after a San Francisco lawyer, Daniel Bolton, won a $1.5 million judgment for a Nevada woman in 1984. Bolton, who also won a $7.3 million settlement in 1991, based his arguments on complaints that the devices gave patients rheumatoid arthritis and other autoimmune diseases. A host of other accusations fanned a flurry of lawsuits, including complaints of migraine headaches, hair loss, facial paralysis, and memory loss. For its part, the FDA had begun looking into safety issues related to silicone-gel implants in 1982, but it found no evidence to suggest the devices were harmful. The FDA renewed its investigation in the early 1990s, however, when the regulatory agency's commissioner, David Kessler, launched an investigation amid a spate of lawsuits filed against breast implant manufacturers. In January 1992, Kessler ordered a three-month moratorium on the use of implants before banning them for cosmetic purposes in April 1992. Breast implants were used for therapeutic purposes such as breast reconstruction after a mastectomy, but most of the surgeries were performed for breast augmentation, a market that was taken from Inamed and all its fellow competitors.

The FDA ban dealt a stinging blow to silicone-gel implants manufacturers, but by the time Kessler issued his edict the industry already was crippled. Inamed was left with virtually no other rivals, having watched its fellow competitors fall off one by one, devastated by lawsuits and forced to retreat because of the promise of another wave of lawsuits following the FDA's ruling. Companies such as Bristol-Meyers Squibb and Bioplasty abandoned their breast implant businesses. Dow Corning, the world's largest manufacturer of breast implants, bore the most severe wound from the litigious war, a wound that proved fatal. Dow Corning exited the business in early 1992, facing lawsuits representing more than 300,000 plaintiffs. The company was ordered to pay $3.2 billion to settle its claims, which prompted it to declare bankruptcy in 1994. The combined influence of the FDA ruling and the numerous lawsuits reduced the population of the breast implant industry in the United States to two companies by the end of 1992: Inamed and its crosstown rival, Mentor Corporation.

SURVIVING THE 1992 FDA BAN ON SILICONE-GEL IMPLANTS

Although Inamed survived the assault on its industry, it did not escape unscathed. In 1997, by which point more than 170,000 lawsuits had been filed against implant manufacturers, Inamed paid $28.1 million to resolve its legal difficulties (the company generated $106 million in revenue during the year and posted a loss of $41 million). The litigation settlement exacted a heavy toll on the company, but Inamed remained in business, while others fled or shuttered their operations, by persevering and diversifying. The FDA ban did nothing to dampen the demand for breast augmentation procedures. Between 1992 and 2002 the number of breast enlargement procedures mushroomed from 32,000 to 237,000, nearly all of which were saline-filled implants, a type manufactured by Inamed. Further, the FDA ban did not apply to other countries. Silicone-gel implants remained the implant of choice overseas, particularly in Europe, where Inamed's silicone-gel-implant business continued to flourish. Accordingly, all was not lost in the wake of the FDA ban and industry-wide litigation. Inamed

KEY DATES

1961: First American Corporation is incorporated.
1974: McGahn Medical Corporation is founded and acquired by 3M three years later.
1985: First American acquires the assets purchased by 3M and changes its name to Inamed Corporation the following year.
1992: The Food and Drug Administration bans the sale of silicone-gel breast implants for cosmetic purposes.
1998: Inamed settles litigation with a $28.1 million payment.
1999: Inamed acquires Collagen Aesthetics Corporation, adding a line of dermal fillers to its product portfolio.
2001: The Lap-Band, a device to treat obesity, is launched.
2005: After agreeing to be acquired by Medicis Pharmaceutical Co., Inamed accepts a higher offer to merge with Allergan, Inc., effective March 2006.

persevered through the 1990s, and to ensure it could look forward to financial growth in the century ahead, the company diversified, giving it three pillars to support its growth in the 21st century.

Inamed's first diversifying move occurred one year before Kessler's ruling on silicon-gel implants. In 1991, the company acquired the patents for a device to treat morbid obesity and formed BioEnterics, which later became Inamed Health, a division devoted to developing and manufacturing medical devices for obesity and abdominal surgery. The device, dubbed the BioEnterics Lap-Band System, did not gain FDA approval until 2001, but once the Lap-Band was on the market it began to record encouraging sales growth. The Lap-Band, which essentially was a band that cinched off the stomach without damaging the tissue, offered morbidly obese patients a minimally invasive alternative to more traumatic procedures, such as gastric bypass and stomach stapling surgeries. Sales of Lap-Bands, which cost $3,000 each, rose 60 percent during their first three years on the market, giving Inamed a substantial new stream of revenue. A more immediate contributor to the company's balance sheet was the 1999 acquisition of Collagen Aesthetics Corporation, a purchase that was organized within the Inamed Aesthetics division. The acquisition added a third business line, injectable dermal-filler products, giving Inamed an increased presence in what was broadly referred to as the vanity medical market. Inamed added to Collagen Aesthetics' Zyderm and Zyplast lines of injectable collagen with brands such as Cosmoderm and Cosmoplast that the company developed after the acquisition. Perhaps the most promising facet of the company's dermal-filler business grew out of the 2003 acquisition of the rights to a wrinkle remover made by France-based Beaufour Ipsen Group. The product, a botulinum toxin A comparable to Allergan Inc.'s best-selling dermal filler Botox, was undergoing clinical trials to gain the FDA's approval midway through the first decade of the 21st century.

Thanks in part to a diversified product line, Inamed entered the 21st century exuding enviable strength. Once the Lap-Band was introduced, giving the company three principal revenue streams, Wall Street expressed its satisfaction, resulting in a 200 percent increase in the company's stock value between 2002 and 2003. Investors soon had more incentive to ally themselves with Inamed after the company completed a promising first step toward getting silicon-gel implants back on the U.S. market. Early in the decade, the FDA agreed to reconsider approving silicone-gel implants for cosmetic purposes amid growing skepticism that the implants were harmful. In October 2003, the FDA's General and Plastic Surgery Devices Panel, an advisory panel, recommended that the government approve the use of the implants for aesthetic purposes, but several months later the FDA rejected its panel's recommendation and denied Inamed's bid to reintroduce silicon-gel implants in the United States. The matter was revisited in April 2005, when the advisory panel rejected Inamed's application for the approval of the company's silicone breast implants, citing lingering questions about safety and durability. One day after Inamed's bid was rejected, the advisory panel voted in favor of recommending to the FDA that Mentor's silicone implants be approved.

THE POSSIBILITY OF A NEW CORPORATE PARENT FOR THE FUTURE

As Inamed continued to petition the FDA's advisory panel for approval, the company found itself involved in merger discussions that promised to mark the beginning of a new era. In March 2005, one month before the FDA's advisory panel rejected the company's application for silicone-gel implant approval, Medicis Pharmaceutical Co., a Scottsdale, Arizona-based leader in the dermatology industry, signed an agreement to acquire Inamed. The $2.8 billion deal, hailed as a marriage of a major dermatology company and a major plastic surgery company, was approved by the directors of both companies, but the merger was not completed. The deal collapsed after Allergan stepped in and offered $3.2 billion for Inamed, an offer that Inamed's board of directors, for obvious reasons, found more attractive than Medicis's offer. The intervention of Allergan led to the termination of the merger agreement between Inamed and Medicis in December 2005, the same month Inamed and Allergan executed their definitive merger agreement. The deal, concluded in March 2006, signaled the end of Inamed's independence and the beginning of a new chapter in its history as part of the $2.3 billion-in-sales, Irvine, California-based Allergan. The precise nature of the company's role within Allergan's organizational structure remained to be determined as both parties waited for regulatory approval and the consummation of the deal.

Jeffrey L. Covell

PRINCIPAL SUBSIDIARIES

Inamed Medical Products Corporation; McGhan Ltd.; Inamed Aesthetics; Inamed Health; BioEntrics Corporation.

PRINCIPAL DIVISIONS

Inamed Aesthetics; Inamed Health.

PRINCIPAL COMPETITORS

C.R. Bard, Inc.; iVOW, Inc.; Mentor Corporation.

FURTHER READING

Crowe, Deborah, "Santa Barbara, Calif. Based Medical Device Maker Promotes CEO to Chairman," *Ventura County Star,* August 2, 2002.

Darmiento, Laurence, "Comeback for Implant Maker Includes New Push for Silicone," *Los Angeles Business Journal,* August 4, 2003, p. 3.

Henderson, Diedtra, "California-Based Firm Gets FDA Approval to Widen Sales of Breast Implants," *Boston Globe,* September 22, 2005.

Marshall, Randi F., "FDA Rejects California-Based Inamed's Application for Silicone Gel Implants," *Newsday,* January 9, 2004.

Maurer, Harry, "The Cosmetic Medicine Catfight," *Business Week,* December 5, 2005, p. 33.

Nelson, Frank, "Inamed and Allergan Agree to Merger Plan," *Santa Barbara New-Press,* December 21, 2005.

———, "Inamed Officially Breaks Engagement with Medicis," *Santa Barbara News-Press,* December 14, 2005.

———, "Santa Barbara, Calif.-Area Implant Makers Seek to Reintroduce Silicone," *Santa Barbara News-Press,* September 1, 2004.

Reeves, Amy, "Inamed Corp. Santa Barbara, California; Bigger Breasts, Thinner Frames, Fatter Till," *Investor's Business Daily,* July 1, 2004, p. A5.

Todd, Michael, "Inamed's New Beau: Firm Made Merger Deal but Now Has New Proposal to Consider," *Santa Barbara News-Press,* November 17, 2005.

Intuitive Surgical, Inc.

950 Kifer Road
Sunnyvale, California 94086
U.S.A.
Telephone: (408) 523-2100
Toll Free: (888) 868-4647
Fax: (408) 523-1390
Web site: http://www.intuitivesurgical.com

Public Company
Incorporated: 1995 as Intuitive Surgical Devices, Inc.
Employees: 321
Sales: $227.3 million (2005)
Stock Exchanges: NASDAQ
Ticker Symbol: ISRG
NAIC: 339113 Surgical Appliance and Supplies Manufacturing

■ ■ ■

Intuitive Surgical, Inc. is a surgical robotics company that has developed and markets the revolutionary da Vinci Surgical System, which is installed in more than 350 academic and community hospitals in the United States as well as in Saudi Arabia, Australia, and throughout Europe. The $1.5 million system has received U.S. Food and Drug Administration (FDA) approval for use in procedures such as heart valve repair, prostatectomy, and hysterectomy. Da Vinci combines elements of virtual reality and video games to create a precise robotic surgical system. The surgeon performs work at a console across the room from the patient on an operating table, over which are suspended articulated robot arms that can be fitted with microsurgical instruments (sold under the EndoWrist label), such as scalpels, scissors, and clamps. The instruments are inserted into the patient through "ports," one-centimeter incisions. One of the arms includes a stereo endoscope, which sends visual information to the console where it is rendered into three dimensions and magnified. In this way, an artery can be made to appear the size of a hose. The surgeon positions the endoscope with foot controls and performs the surgical procedure using master controls beneath the console display. The system's software then translates the surgeon's motions into real-time manipulation of the surgical instruments inside the patient. The controls also provide some resistance to improve dexterity. The minimally invasive surgery performed by da Vinci lowers the risk of infection, leads to faster patient recovery, and shortens hospital stays. Based in Sunnyvale, California, Intuitive Surgical is a public company listed on the NASDAQ.

COMPANY ORIGINS: LATE 20TH-CENTURY RESEARCH

The original research that led to the development of da Vinci was performed in the late 1980s at the Stanford Research Institute, later known as SRI International. The goal was to improve the surgical tools available in the rising field of minimally invasive surgery (MIS). The concept of MIS dated to the ancient Greeks when Hippocrates made mention of a rectal speculum. The Romans also developed ways to inspect internal organs. The principles of endoscopy—using light, mirrors, and lenses to examine internal organs—were established in the 1800s. In the early 1900s the concept of laparoscopy

COMPANY PERSPECTIVES

Intuitive Surgical is proud to be fulfilling its mission to extend the benefits of minimally invasive surgery to the broadest possible range of patients, while providing extraordinary value for its customers, investors and employees.

was laid out, in which an incision was made, primarily in the navel, to allow for the inspection of abdominal and pelvic organs and the treatment of some conditions. In 1973 laparoscopy was first used on cancer patients for observation and biopsy of the liver. The introduction of video cameras in the early 1980s was a major advance in MIS, leading to surgeons using laparoscopy for the removal of gallbladders and ovarian cysts. However, the long instruments inserted in a patient were difficult to maneuver, moving in the opposite direction of the surgeon's hands, and the slightest movement was amplified on the other end. One surgeon compared the task to tying shoelaces with golf clubs.

SRI's efforts to improve microsurgery were aided in 1990 by funding from the National Institutes of Health. Researchers developed a prototype for a robotic surgical system that included major elements of da Vinci, including stereoscopic imaging, ergonomic design, and force feedback. The SRI System, as it was then known, came to the attention of the Defense Advanced Research Projects Administration (DARPA), which was no stranger to technological innovation, having played a key role in the development of the Internet (originally known as the DARPA-net). DARPA saw the SRI System as a way to perform "telesurgery" on the battlefield. The idea was that by using satellite transmission military surgeons hundreds of miles away could use a robotic surgery system to perform life-saving procedures on the wounded in remote locations and then evacuate the patients to a critical-care hospital.

In order to drum up interest in nonmilitary applications, SRI demonstrated the prototype to numerous venture capitalists and others in the early 1990s, but no one expressed serious interest until Dr. Frederick Moll in 1994. Moll received his medical degree from the University of Washington in 1981 and became fascinated by the rise of laparoscopy. He left his residency and developed the safety trocar, a tool that permitted surgeons to create a hole in the abdominal wall without risk of damaging organs. But Moll was as much an entrepreneur as a doctor, if not more so. He also held a bachelor of arts degree in economics from the University of California at Berkeley and a master of science degree in management from Stanford University. He cofounded a company called Endotherapeutics to market the trocar; the business ultimately was acquired by U.S. Surgical in 1992. Moll also cofounded Origin Medsystems, Inc. to develop laparoscopic tools, a company that would be bought by Eli Lilly for $100 million in 1992 and turned into an operating company of cardiac instruments subsidiary Guidant Corporation. Moll stayed on as chief medical officer of the unit.

According to *Forbes,* Moll initially did not think that the SRI System had much commercial value, just a lot of "wow factor." The more he thought about it, however, the more interested he became and he returned for a second demonstration. He knew that the telesurgery elements of the system could be applied to laparoscopic surgery. He told *Technology Review* in a 2000 article, "What got me excited wasn't the remote-surgery aspect, but the way the system eliminated the need for a hand to be directly connected to a surgeon's instruments. It offered new ways of solving the challenges in minimally invasive techniques." After failing to interest Guidant in licensing the technology, he approached Mayfield Fund, a venture capital firm that had backed him in the past. Mayfield then teamed up Moll with John Freund, who held both a Harvard medical degree and a Harvard M.B.A., to further examine the potential of Moll's idea. Freund was duly convinced and brought in an electrical engineer, Robert Younge, to provide the necessary technical expertise. Younge was also a Stanford graduate and in 1979 cofounded Acuson Corporation, a major ultrasound developer and manufacturer where Freund had been an executive since 1988. According to *U.S. News & World Report,* Younge "immediately realized that the technology existed to make a surgical robot feasible. 'It was like getting the stars in the skies to line up at the same time.'"

In 1995 Freund successfully negotiated a technology license from SRI, followed by other licenses for technology from IBM and MIT, and in November he, Moll, and Freund incorporated Intuitive Surgical Devices, Inc. Two years later the company adopted its current name. Mayfield and another venture capital firm, Sierra Ventures, supplied $5 million in seed money. Morgan Stanley Ventures joined in the next round of financing, followed by a number of private investors in subsequent rounds. All told, Intuitive raised $127 million by the end of the 1990s.

PROTOTYPE READY BY 1997

Younge went to work refining the SRI System into a viable piece of medical equipment, which was tested on

KEY DATES

1995: The company is founded.
1999: Da Vinci Surgical System is introduced.
2000: The company is taken public.
2003: The company merges with Computer Motion, Inc.

cadavers, and by March 1997 he had a prototype ready. It was called Mona, named after Leonardo da Vinci's painting *Mona Lisa.* Da Vinci also had invented the world's first robot and his name was ultimately applied to the commercial version of the system. In the meantime, Mona was taken to Belgium for tests on humans, performing such relatively simple procedures as peripheral vascular surgery. It was soon apparent that the imaging was not sufficient, which led to further investment in this area and the development of an endoscope that could provide a 3-D image. What was now known as da Vinci was again sent to Europe in 1998 for testing. In both Paris and Germany the system was used to perform abdominal surgery and several open heart operations.

While Intuitive began the process of seeking FDA approval, which would have to be done on a procedure-by-procedure basis, it began marketing da Vinci in Europe, selling ten systems there in 1999. Intuitive also began preparing to make an initial public offering (IPO) of stock. With Lehman Brothers serving as the lead underwriter, Intuitive completed its IPO in June 2000, netting the company $46 million, despite having been sued for patent infringement by a competitor, Computer Motion, Inc., just a month before the offering.

Intuitive was not the only company interested in robot surgery and was in fact a latecomer to the party. Computer Motion was founded in 1989 specifically to develop surgical robots, relying on NASA technology used to assemble equipment remotely in space. The company went public in 1997 and was the early leader in surgical robots. Its signature product was the ZEUS Robotic Surgical System, which also was approved for use in Europe and awaiting approval from the FDA. It, too, combined robotic arms (called Aesop), computer control, and a video console (called Hermes), as well as voice-recognition software to allow the surgeon to call out specific comments to the arms. A third player in the field, Integrated Surgical Systems Inc., had introduced RoboDoc to perform total hip arthroplasty and other orthopedic surgeries. It was Computer Motion that became Intuitive's chief rival, and in the early 2000s the two companies traded expensive lawsuits.

A short time after going public, Intuitive received FDA clearance to use da Vinci on gallbladder disease and gastroesophageal disease. The company's prospective cited gallbladder removals as a major use for da Vinci, but that promise did not pan out due to the far-less-expensive laparoscopic tools that were available to perform the relatively simple operation. The system was in need of an application and found it in prostate surgery, for which the FDA granted approval in June 2001. While the company enjoyed some U.S. sales in 2000, business picked up in 2001 as doctors began to realize the benefits of performing prostate surgery with da Vinci, achieving greater control and precision with less loss of blood and quicker patient recovery. The system also was being used in thoracic operations and mitral-valve heart repair.

In 2002 Moll and Younge left Intuitive to found another medical start-up, Hansen Medical, which developed a robotic system to move diagnostic catheters within a patient in order to perform procedures. Moll remained on Intuitive's board of directors until the beginning of 2003.

MERGER WITH CHIEF RIVAL IN 2003

Although da Vinci was receiving good review from doctors and a great deal of press coverage, sales were slow. The system was expensive and the microsurgery tools and microchips it employed could only be used several times before they had to be discarded. On average an operation consumed about $1,500 worth of these tools. Moreover, the litigation between Intuitive and Computer Motion was making potential customers nervous about a financial commitment to a company that might be the losing party in the patent disputes. The matter was resolved in June 2003 when Intuitive and Computer Motion agreed to merge. The merger proved to be a tremendous success on a number of levels. The Zeus system was phased out in favor of da Vinci, eliminating the difficulty customers experienced in choosing between the two, and the combined company was able to realize efficiencies of operations by now relying on a single sales force, a consolidated financial department, and other support areas. Sales picked up, aided in no small measure by the increasing number of procedures the FDA approved da Vinci to perform. While Intuitive was nearing profitability, however, the other major player in the field, Integrated Surgical Systems, was struggling to survive and in 2005 shut down.

In 2004 revenues increased 51 percent to $138.8 million and Intuitive recorded net income of $23.5 million, the company's first profitable year. Sales improved to $227.3 million in 2005 and net income soared to $94.1 million. Da Vinci was clearly establishing itself in the medical community, but it remained an expensive device and in the opinion of some was too large. Nevertheless, its potential remained enormous. In the spring of 2005 da Vinci received FDA approval to perform hysterectomies, a procedure performed five times more often than prostate surgery. Perhaps in the future da Vinci could be used to perform tele-surgery, as its original developers envisioned. Ideally, a specialist could perform several surgeries a day in scattered operating rooms far from his office, and perhaps military surgeons could indeed operate on soldiers hundreds of miles away. For the time being, however, such uses for da Vinci remained a future possibility, primarily due to the lag times caused by transmission delays over long distances, limiting the effective range to 30 miles by wireless communication and 200 miles by cable connection, as well as the unreliability of network communications. Intuitive's researchers continued to pursue the concept of telesurgery, but for the time being at least saw it as a way to speed up the training of surgeons learning to use robotic-assisted surgery by letting them work under the guidance of seasoned users. Regardless, Intuitive estimated that its market, in terms of selling da Vinci systems, consumable tools, and service contracts, could easily top $2 billion a year.

Ed Dinger

PRINCIPAL SUBSIDIARIES

Computer Motion, Inc.

PRINCIPAL COMPETITORS

Boston Scientific Corporation; Johnson & Johnson; Medtronic, Inc.

FURTHER READING

Alpert, Bill, "Cold Hands," *Barron's,* June 8, 1998, p. H26.

Barrett, Jennifer, "Cutting Edge," *Newsweek,* December 12, 2005.

Comarow, Avery, and Thomas Hayden, "Rob Younge & Frederic Moll: A Robot That Fixes Hearts," *U.S. News & World Report,* December 25, 2000, p. 50.

Ditlea, Steve, "Robo Surgeons," *Technology Review,* November 2000, p. 74.

Kichen, Steve, "Medical Renaissance," *Forbes.com,* July 27, 2005.

Moukheiber, Zina, "Dr. Robot," *Forbes,* March 6, 2000, p. 159.

Popolow, Gerry, "Robotic Systems Transform the Operating Room," *Robotics World,* November/December 1999, p. 32.

Salisbury, J. Kenneth, Jr., "The Heart of Microsurgery," *Mechanical Engineering,* December 1998, p. 46.

Wysocki, Bernard, Jr., "Robots in the OR," *Wall Street Journal,* February 26, 2004, p. B1.

JAFCO Co. Ltd.

1-8-2 Marunouchi, Chiyoda-ku
Tokyo,
Japan
Telephone: (+81 03) 5223 7536
Fax: (81 03) 5223 7561
Web site: http://www.jafco.co.jp

Public Company
Incorporated: 1973 as Japan Associated Finance Co. Ltd.
Employees: 360
Sales: ¥33.12 billion ($309.54 million) (2005)
Stock Exchanges: Tokyo
Ticker Symbol: J.JAF
NAIC: 523999 Miscellaneous Financial Investment Activities

■ ■ ■

JAFCO Co. Ltd. is Japan's leading private equity finance group. The company operations include venture capital, buyout investment, and the management of venture capital-oriented funds. The company's investments target four primary markets: Incubation investments, seeding new startups; Venture Investments of companies in the early development phase; Development Capital Investments of companies entering their growth phase; and Buyout Investments of established companies. JAFCO is an active investor; in 2005, for example, the company invested in more than 140 companies, nearly two-thirds of which were venture investments. As part of its investment operations, the company also creates funds, lining up a group of investors. Many of the companies backed by JAFCO are then guided toward their initial public offering (IPO). Since its founding in 1973, JAFCO has invested in nearly 3,000 companies, and has completed IPOs for nearly 750 of its investments, including 23 IPOs in 2005. The company has also overseen more than 60 venture capital funds. The company is especially active in the Japanese market, but is also present in the United States, China, Hong Kong, South Korea, Singapore, and Taiwan. JAFCO itself is listed on the Tokyo Stock Exchange. Nomura Holdings controls nearly 21 percent of the group's stock. In 2005, JAFCO posted revenues of ¥33.12 billion ($309.54 million).

PIONEERING JAPAN'S VENTURE CAPITAL MARKET: 1972–91

Japan's rapidly growing economy in the post-World War II era, and particularly the country's effort to establish itself as a global technological and manufacturing leader, created in its turn a strong venture capital investment market. Until the 1970s, however, Japan itself lacked a homegrown venture capital market, and instead tended to look overseas for investment capital. The first Japanese venture capital companies began to appear in the early 1970s. Between 1972 and 1974, some eight private venture capital firms were created. These firms were generally created as partnerships between Japan's largest financial companies, particularly banks and securities brokers, such as Mitsubishi, Nikko, Sumitomo, and Yamaichio.

In 1973, a group of some of Japan's largest financial institutions, including Nomura Securities, then the world's largest, as well as Nippon Life Insurance, the

COMPANY PERSPECTIVES

The JAFCO Group aims to build an earnings base that can absorb changes in the business climate, boost long-term profitability and underpin sustainable growth. To do this, JAFCO has implemented the following four processes: 1. The first is to encourage risk money through the launch of new funds. JAFCO obtains funds to maximize investment opportunities. As a result, JAFCO earns stable fund management fees. 2. The second is to implement full-line investment. JAFCO invests in high-quality companies and has constructed a well-balanced portfolio. 3. The third is to raise corporate value of investee companies. JAFCO actively supports the strengthening of investees' core business structure and corporate growth through our VA (Value Added) activities. 4. The fourth is to promote portfolio IPOs and increase capital gains through the establishment of a virtuous cycle of private equity investment. Finally, JAFCO carries out the above strategies based on an effective cost structure.

country's leading insurance company, and Sanwa Bank, the leading bank in Japan, joined together to form a new venture capital firm, called Japan Godo, or Japan Associated Finance Co. Ltd. (or JAFCO). While the company counted 15 in its group of investors, Nomura emerged as JAFCO's major shareholder.

From the start JAFCO targeted a range of industries, and by 1975, the company had already brought its first investment to the IPO market, listing appliance maker Shintom on the Tokyo stock exchange in July of that year. Also that year, the company brought Tateho Chemical Industries, which specialized in producing electrofused magnesia and other chemicals, to the JASDAQ stock exchange. Other successful IPOs completed during the 1970s included industrial valve producer Kitz; paint manufacturer Asahipen; Nippon Cable System; the supermarket groups Maretsu, Inageya, and Chujitsuya. JAFCO's string of IPOs continued into the early 1980s, and featured Sanshin, a civil engineering group; Chiyoda, a shoe retailer, and, in 1981, Aplus, a consumer finance group. JAFCO began its own geographical expansion, opening its first branch office, in Osaka, that same year.

The Japanese government had helped to facilitate the country's venture capital market by providing new vehicles enabling investors to exit their holdings more quickly, such as the creation of an over-the-counter market and the JASDAQ technology index. JAFCO itself helped pioneer another vehicle, the limited partnership investment fund, launching the country's first fund in 1982. Soon after, JAFCO, which had started out with a capital of ¥500 million, underwent a major capital increase, to ¥2 billion. In that year, also, the firm opened its second branch office, in Nagoya.

JAFCO soon began to target the international market as well, and in 1983 the company established its first foreign subsidiary, JAFCO International (Asia) Limited. The company's Asian region investments including Singapore Airlines, which made its IPO on the Singapore exchange in 1985; Jurong Shipyard, which went public in 1987, also on the Singapore exchange; Korea's Tae Il Media, which manufactured computer peripherals, in 1989; Ayala Land, in the Philippines; and Krung Thai Bank, in Thailand, in 1989.

Like most venture capitalists, JAFCO also developed a keen interest in the high-technology sector, and in 1984 the company moved closer to the global center of that market, opening its first U.S. subsidiary in San Francisco in 1984. The company's, and its own investors', relationship with Japan's industrial and technological markets made it an attractive partner for U.S. technology firms seeking entry into the Japanese market. JAFCO was characterized as a more patient, and less aggressive investor than typical U.S.-styled venture capital firms. While the U.S. groups often sought returns as high as 60 percent on their investment, JAFCO was willing to accept returns of just 25 percent. At the same time, the company leaned towards a hand-off investment approach. As then Managing Director Mitsuo Goto told *Electronic Business:* "Unless we are asked for help first, we never interfere with a company's management."

JAFCO quickly established itself as a primary source of Japanese investment capital for U.S. companies, accounting for some 80 percent of all such investments at the end of the 1980s. By then, the company had achieved a number of successful IPOs, such as Calgene, listed on the NASDAQ in 1987; Novellus Systems, which launched its IPO in 1988, and Cephalan, which went public in 1991. The company was also an early investor in hard drive leader Syquest, which launched its IPO on the NASDAQ in 1991.

INTERNATIONAL EXPANSION: 1986–99

In the meantime, JAFCO had continued to expand its geographical reach, opening a subsidiary in England in 1986. The company opened a second office in the United States, in New York, in 1987. In that year, the company

KEY DATES

1973: Japan Associated Finance Co. Ltd. (JAFCO) is founded.
1975: Company completes its first investment initial public offering (IPO).
1981: Company opens branch office in Osaka.
1982: Company launches first venture capital partnership fund in Jaan.
1982: Branch office opens in Nagoya.
1984: First U.S. subsidiary opens in San Francisco.
1986: Company opens office in the United Kingdom.
1987: Second U.S. office opens in New York.
1990: JAFCO forms joint venture with Nomura in Singapore.
1994: Company launches subsidiary in United Kingdom.
1997: Company changes name to JAFCO Co. Ltd.
1998: Branch opens in Hokkaido.
1999: JAFCO acquires full control of Singapore subsidiary.
2001: JAFCO goes public with listing on Tokyo exchange; establishes subsidiary in South Korea.
2002: Company establishes representative office in Beijing.
2004: U.S. subsidiary, JAFCO Ventures in Palo Alto, California, is established.
2005: JAFCO establishes five new investment funds for a total of $1.5 billion.

listed its own shares on the OTC market. During this period, JAFCO's capital base made a dramatic increase, jumping to ¥9.4 billion in 1988, and then past ¥20 billion in 1989.

Back home, JAFCO launched a new subsidiary, JAFCO BRAINS CO. in 1989. By then, the company had completed a number of other Japanese IPOs. These included Ryoyo Electro and Tokai Bussan, both involved in the sale of electronic materials and equipment; CSK Electronics, a computer retailer; Fuji Soft ABC, a software developer; Nihon Electric Wire & Cable; Sakata Seed; Kokusai Securities; consumer electronics distributor K's Denki; Funai Consulting; and software developer Japan Systems, among others.

The company's Asia operations were boosted in 1990 when the company joined with Nomura to establish a new joint-venture subsidiary in Singapore. In 1999, that joint venture became 100 percent controlled by JAFCO and changed its name to JAFCO Investment (Asia Pacific). In the meantime, JAFCO completed a number of IPOs in the region, including its first IPOs in Indonesia in 1990. Hong Kong became an attractive market for the company as well, and led to a number of IPOs, including computer game developer Magnum, in 1992; audio component producer Kosonic, in 1993; Innovative, an automobile parts group, in 1994; and footwear manufacturer Simphony Holdings, in 1995. By the end of the 1990s, JAFCO's Asia Pacific operations had included investments in the Philippines, Malaysia, Taiwan, and Australia as well.

JAFCO's European wing grew more slowly during the decade, despite the launch of a full-fledged subsidiary in the United Kingdom in 1994. The company's European investments focused especially on the biomedical research field, and led to investments in, and later IPOs by such companies as Celltech, Chiroscience, Biocompatibles International, Plasmon, and others in the United Kingdom, as well as Genset in France, Elekta Instrument in Sweden, and NV Innogetics in Belgium. By the end of the 1990s, the company had added investments in Germany, Israel, Switzerland, and Spain as well. The European market nonetheless remained a minor one for JAFCO. Meanwhile, JAFCO had continued to expand its presence in the United States, launching a new subsidiary, JAFCO Ventures, based in Boston and Palo Alto, California.

PUBLIC COMPANY: 2001

JAFCO changed its name, to JAFCO Co. Ltd., in 1997. The company began restructuring, merging its JAFCO BRAINS subsidiary with another subsidiary, JAFCO Consulting. The company took full control of the Asia Pacific subsidiary in 1999, then absorbed another of its subsidiaries, JAFCO Properties Co., that same year. In 2001, IPO-maker JAFCO launched its own full-fledged public offering, listing its shares on the Tokyo Stock Exchange.

JAFCO continued to expand its operational base as well. The company had opened a new Japanese office, in Hokkaido, in 1998. In 2001, JAFCO moved into the Korean market, establishing a dedicated subsidiary there. The company backed up this move with the launch of a new $178 million fund, the JAFCO Asia Technology Fund, some 15 percent of which was to be dedicated to investments in South Korea. At the same time, JAFCO had also been eyeing an entry into the fast-growing mainland China market. The company took its first step there in 2002 with the opening of a representative office in Beijing.

In 2003, JAFCO Ventures was spun off into a new company, Globespan Capital Partners, as part of a management buyout. JAFCO soon returned to the United States, however, establishing a new JAFCO Ventures subsidiary, based in Palo Alto, backed by its new $100 million JAFCO Technology Partners I Fund. The launch of the new fund fit in with an upswing in the investment market, which had been hit hard by recession at the beginning of the 2000s. By the end of 2004, however, JAFCO helped to signal the market's return to growth, with the establishment of five new investment funds with a total value of some $1.5 billion. The company also took advantage of the boom in the Asia investment market, and especially the growing shift of the global economy toward mainland China, adding a new fund targeting Asian investments in 2005.

By early 2006, JAFCO boasted an impressive record of investments. Since 1973, the company had invested in nearly 3,000 companies and had participated in nearly 750 IPOs. The company showed few signs of letting up. In 2005 alone, the company completed 23 IPOs. Meanwhile, it had completed its first IPOs for 2006, including Makoto Construction in Osaka, Felissimo in Hyogo, E-ton Solar Tech in Taiwan, and Acorda Therapeutics in the United States.

M. L. Cohen

PRINCIPAL SUBSIDIARIES

Beijing Representative Office; JAFCO America Ventures, Inc. (U.S.A.); JAFCO Consulting Co., Ltd.; JAFCO Investment (Asia Pacific) Ltd. (Singapore); JAFCO Investment (Hong Kong) Ltd.; JAFCO Investment (Korea) Co., Ltd.; JAFCOVEN Co., Ltd.; Taiwan Branch Office.

PRINCIPAL COMPETITORS

Nippon Venture Capital Corporation; Japan Asia Investment Co. Ltd.; SBI Holdings; Yasuda Enterprise Development.

FURTHER READING

"China: Chan Predicts Year Will Start with Bang," *Venture Capital Journal,* January 1, 2006.

Hayashi, Alden M., "Putting Japanese Venture Capital to Work in America," *Electronic Business,* July 1, 1988, p. 69.

"JAFCO Asia Enters Mainland," *SinoCast China Business Daily News,* October 11, 2002.

"JAFCO Launches $100m Fund," *Private Equity Week,* December 1, 2003, p. 6.

"JAFCO Planning Third Fund," *Private Equity Week,* July 11, 2005, p. 2.

"JAFCO Ventures Spins into Globespan," *Private Equity Week,* January 28, 2003, p. 12.

"JAFCO Ventures' Sun Rises in the West," *Venture Capital Journal,* January 1, 2004.

"Japan's JAFCO Procures $1.1 Billion for 5 Investment Funds," *Asia Pulse,* July 16, 2004.

"Japan's Largest Venture Capital Firm Opens Seoul Office," *Korea Herald,* June 12, 2001.

Moltzen, Edward F., "In Need of VC funds? See JAFCO," *Computer Reseller News,* July 24, 2000, p. 8.

Kao Corporation

14-10, Nihonbashi Kayabacho 1-chome
Chuo-ku
Tokyo, 103-8210
Japan
Telephone: (+81-3) 3660-7111
Fax: (+81-3) 3660-8978
Web site: http://www.kao.co.jp

Public Company
Incorporated: 1887 as Kao Soap Company, Ltd.
Employees: 30,002
Sales: ¥936.9 billion ($8.72 billion) (2005)
Stock Exchanges: Tokyo
Ticker Symbol: 4452
NAIC: 311225 Fats and Oils Refining and Blending; 322291 Sanitary Paper Product Manufacturing; 325188 All Other Basic Inorganic Chemical Manufacturing; 325199 All Other Basic Organic Chemical Manufacturing; 325611 Soap and Other Detergent Manufacturing; 325613 Surface Active Agent Manufacturing; 325620 Toilet Preparation Manufacturing; 325910 Printing Ink Manufacturing; 446120 Cosmetics, Beauty Supplies, and Perfume Stores

Kao Corporation, often called the Procter & Gamble of Japan, is one of Japan's leaders in personal care products, cosmetics, laundry and cleaning products, hygiene products, diapers, and bath additives. Kao (pronounced cow-OOH) also manufactures and markets fatty chemicals, edible oils, and specialty chemicals, including aroma chemicals and toner for copiers and printers. The company has operations in more than 70 countries around the world, including the U.S.-based Kao Brands Company (formerly The Andrew Jergens Company), a marketer of personal care products under the Jergens, Bioré, Curel, Ban, John Frieda, and Guhl brands. Back home, Kao expanded in early 2006 through the acquisition of Kanebo Cosmetics Inc., one of Japan's leading cosmetics companies.

EARLY HISTORY

Founded in 1887 as Kao (face) Soap Company, Ltd. by Tomiro Nagase, the company introduced its first soap product in 1890, selling it with the motto "A Clean Nation Prospers." That same year Kao adopted its crescent-moon logo, which was similar to the Procter & Gamble Company's logo registered eight years earlier; thus began a longtime rivalry. By the end of the 1920s, Kao had developed coconut alcohol-based synthetic detergents, and after World War II, began manufacturing heavy-duty detergents.

From early on, Kao employed at least 25 percent of its workers in research, particularly in the field of surface technology. Early research in the properties of oils and fats, the basic elements in soap, allowed Kao to expand its product line quickly to include finishing products, polishing agents, waxes, insecticides, antiseptics, fungicides, and deodorants.

Kao's early success was made possible not only by its dedication to R&D but also by its unique network of proprietary wholesalers. In the early 1960s the company

COMPANY PERSPECTIVES

Our mission is "to strive for the wholehearted satisfaction and enrichment of the lives of people globally" through the Company's core domains of cleanliness, beauty, health and chemicals.

Fully committed to this mission, all members of the Kao Group work together with passion to provide products and brands of excellent value created from the consumer/customer's perspective. In so doing, we "share joy with the consumer/customer."

persuaded its wholesalers to establish jointly owned companies, called *hansha,* which would exclusively distribute Kao products. This system greatly simplified the usually complicated way that products moved from manufacturers to consumers in Japan, and provided Kao with competitive advantages, such as getting products onto store shelves faster and maintaining lighter inventories.

In 1971 Yoshio Maruta became president of Kao and continued the company's emphasis on R&D. Maruta, holder of a doctorate in chemical engineering and 16 patents, invented a process for producing aircraft lubricant from vegetable oil during World War II, when Japanese supplies of petroleum were low. An aggressive and charismatic leader, Maruta often was criticized for his domineering style that left little room for open discussion. He had a fierce respect for consumers, however. As one of his assistants told *Forbes,* July 25, 1988, "You can cheat housewives once, but not twice."

SERIES OF SUCCESSFUL PRODUCT LAUNCHES

In the 1980s Kao's intense research operations paid off handsomely. In 1982 Kao entered the cosmetics market for the first time with its Sofina line of cosmetics, and rapidly advanced to the number two position in the Japanese cosmetic market, trailing only Shiseido Company, Limited. The following year the company's Merries brand of disposable diapers far outsold Procter & Gamble's in Japan, because Kao had developed a highly absorbent polymer that reduced diaper rash. Having expanded well beyond just soap, the company changed its name to simply Kao Corporation in 1985.

Kao's research in surface technology led the company into the electronics-software field as well. A research project on face powders resulted in the discovery of a dispersing system that was ideal for the management of magnetic particles spread over floppy discs, and Kao in 1985 established a U.S. subsidiary called Kao Infosystems Company to manufacture such discs. With the acquisition of West Coast Telecom in Portland, Oregon; Sentinel Technologies in Hyannis, Massachusetts; and the completion of a $60 million plant in Plymouth, Massachusetts, Kao Infosystems became in 1990 the largest North American maker of 3.5-inch floppy discs, although it was also consistently unprofitable. The company later branched out into CD-ROMs, hard disks, and digital audiotapes.

One of Kao's most successful introductions ever, Attack concentrated laundry detergent, came in 1987. Before Attack made its debut, Kao researchers collected dirt samples from around the world for four years in order to discover the bacteria that produces alkaline cellulose, an enzyme that cleans cotton. The researchers then spent two years synthesizing the enzyme through genetic engineering. The resultant detergent was four times as concentrated as cleaners that were then being sold; it was in fact the first concentrated laundry soap in Japan. Only six months after introduction, Attack commanded almost 50 percent of the Japanese detergent market. In spite of a price that was much higher than the competition, consumers appreciated the product's convenience—it was lighter to carry home and took up less space in the cabinet—and that it was better for the environment.

In 1990 Fumikatsu Tokiwa, who joined the company in 1965 in the research-and-development library, succeeded Yoshio Maruta as president. Around this time, Kao was the Japanese market leader in eight of its ten main product categories. It held more than half of the market in five categories: laundry detergents, fabric softeners, bleaches, skin cleansers, and household cleaners.

AGGRESSIVELY EXPANDING OVERSEAS

Beginning in the early 1970s, when Procter & Gamble (P&G) entered the Japanese market, Kao faced increasing competition at home from foreign companies. One of the company's responses to the encroachment of P&G, Unilever NV, and others into its home market was to turn the tables on the foreigners by aggressively expanding overseas itself. Kao began making serious moves into the U.S., European, and non-Japanese Asian markets in the late 1980s. The company's timing seemed particularly fortuitous when the Japanese bubble economy of the 1980s gave way to the prolonged recession of the 1990s. Nonetheless, Kao's overseas ventures met with only mixed results.

KEY DATES

1887: Kao Soap Company, Ltd. is founded by Tomiro Nagase.
1890: Company introduces its first soap and adopts a crescent moon logo.
1982: Kao enters cosmetics market through introduction of the Sofina brand.
1985: Company is renamed Kao Corporation.
1987: Attack laundry detergent is introduced.
1988: The Andrew Jergens Company, based in Cincinnati, Ohio, is acquired.
1989: Kao gains majority ownership of the German firm Goldwell GmbH.
2002: Jergens acquires John Frieda Professional Hair Care, Inc.
2004: Andrew Jergens Company is renamed Kao Brands Company.
2005: Molton Brown is acquired.
2006: Kao acquires Kanebo Cosmetics Inc.

In 1988 Kao acquired the Andrew Jergens Company, headquartered in Cincinnati, Ohio, and placed it within its main U.S. subsidiary, Kao Corporation of America. High Point Chemical Corporation, a specialty chemical company based in North Carolina that was acquired in 1987, supplied the raw materials for the Jergens toiletry and skin-care products. A move into Germany was made in 1989 when Kao purchased a 75 percent interest in Goldwell GmbH, a manufacturer and marketer of hair-care and beauty products through professional hairdressers around the world. Kao gained full control of Goldwell in the early 1990s, and the subsidiary was later renamed Kao Professional Salon Services GmbH.

These acquisitions greatly increased the amount of revenues Kao generated outside Japan (to about 20 percent by the mid-1990s), but the company encountered difficulty building upon the acquired firms' previous successes. Jergens, for instance, in 1989 introduced a line of bath tablets called ActiBath in an attempt to adapt for the U.S. market a Kao product extremely popular in Japan. ActiBath flopped in large part because Americans take fewer baths than the Japanese and take their baths less seriously. In addition to the challenge of understanding a new culture, Kao also faced fierce competition in the U.S. market from the already entrenched Procter & Gamble and Unilever. This competition was quite evident in the 1994 launch of Jergens Refreshing Body Shampoo, a line of liquid bath soaps. On the surface a product with more promise than ActiBath, the Body Shampoo, soon after its launch, had to contend with two rival products: Unilever's Caress Moisturizing Body Wash and P&G's Oil of Olay liquid soap. Overall, Kao's American and European operations were money-losing ventures into the mid-1990s.

Kao's forays elsewhere in Asia were more successful, and were as a whole profitable. By the early 1990s the company was holding its own alongside P&G and Unilever in Hong Kong, Malaysia, the Philippines, Singapore, Taiwan, and Thailand. As the decade progressed, Kao took an increasing interest in the newly opening markets of China and Vietnam. Overall revenue generated from the region increased at a 15 percent yearly clip from the early to mid-1990s. Nevertheless, Unilever and Procter & Gamble's deeper (R&D and marketing) pockets tended to place Kao at a decided disadvantage even this close to home. P&G, for instance, spent four times as much as Kao did on R&D in the mid-1990s, and was quickly able to capture 50 percent of the shampoo market in China and Taiwan. Meanwhile, Kao's market shares in these Asian countries ranged from 10 to 20 percent.

JETTISONING INFORMATION PRODUCTS; SUCCESSFUL BIORÉ LAUNCH

While the company's household products units defended their home turf from foreign invaders and attempted to gain beachheads overseas as vehicles for future growth, the information technology business continued to struggle thanks to fierce competition. By 1996 Kao Infosystems was still losing money. In response, a restructuring was initiated that year which initially involved the integration of operations in France and Germany into the subsidiary's facility in Ireland. In a second phase, facilities in the United States and Canada were restructured.

For the fiscal year ending in March 1996, Kao Corporation posted its 16th straight year of increased revenues *and* increased pretax profits. Kao found further success on the new product front with the April 1996 introduction in Japan of the Bioré Pore Pack, a facial skin blemish remover whose sales totaled ¥10 billion ($75 million) in its first year. When these facial strips reached the U.S. market in the summer of 1997 through the Andrew Jergens subsidiary, they quickly became the most popular product in their category, with sales of $55 million in just the first nine months following their launch. In a prime example of Kao's global marketing strategy, the Bioré product was also successfully launched in the United Kingdom through Andrew Jergens and in continental Europe through a strategic alliance with Beiersdorf AG, a German skin-care company.

In June 1997 Takuya Goto moved into the Kao presidency, taking over for Fumikatsu Tokiwa who became chairman. Goto came from Kao's chemicals side, perhaps indicating that Kao's board wanted some fresh ideas from senior management. Goto, a chemical engineer, joined the company in November 1979 as a manager of a plant in Thailand. After moving up Kao's chemicals management ladder, Goto became general manager of the chemical business division and purchasing division in July 1994.

Goto was quick to restructure Kao's operations. In early 1998 the company cut its production of floppy disks in half and also liquidated its U.S. holding company, Kao Corporation of America. The three U.S. operating companies—Andrew Jergens, High Point Chemical, and Kao Infosystems—became direct subsidiaries of Kao itself. In connection with these moves, Kao posted a special loss of ¥11.62 billion ($88.5 million) for fiscal 1998. As a result, the company recorded its first year-to-year decline in group net profits since Kao started keeping records of consolidated earnings in 1981. In May 1998 Andrew Jergens acquired the skin-care business of Bausch & Lomb, Inc. for $135 million, thereby bringing into the Kao fold Curel skin-moisturizing products and Soft Sense moisturizing lotion, and giving Jergens the number two position in the U.S. skin-care market, trailing Unilever. In December of that year, Kao took a step that at the time was unusual for a Japanese company: it withdrew entirely from one of its main operational areas. Kao completed its exit from the information technology business by selling most of the remaining assets to Zomax Optical Media, a U.S. compact disc maker. This divestment led to a further restructuring charge of ¥23.88 billion ($198.12 million), taken in 1999. Despite the charge, the continued doldrums in the Japanese economy, and economic travails elsewhere in Asia, Kao managed to achieve record net profits of ¥34.7 billion ($287.9 million). The following year, although profits jumped 50 percent, Kao saw its streak of consecutive years of increased revenues come to an end at 19 thanks to the sales lost through the jettisoning of the information technology business.

GROWTH THROUGH NEW PRODUCTS AND ACQUISITIONS

Its focus tightened to a three-legged core—consumer products, cosmetics, and chemical products—Kao continued to pursue both organic growth and growth through acquisition. In 1999 Kao introduced Healthy Econa cooking oil into the Japanese market. The product, touted to prevent the development of fat deposits, became a smash hit, despite a premium price tag, with sales reaching ¥10.4 billion ($83.9 million) by 2001. Kao later expanded the Healthy Econa line to include food products using the oil, such as mayonnaise and salad dressing. Nationwide distribution of the oil began in the United States in 2004, under the brand name Enova and through a joint venture with Archer Daniels Midland Company.

On the acquisition side, the Andrew Jergens unit completed two further acquisitions during this period. In September 2000 the Ban line of roll-on and stick antiperspirants and deodorants was acquired from Chattem, Inc. for $166.5 million. Jergens next acquired John Frieda Professional Hair Care, Inc. in September 2002 for $450 million, Kao's largest acquisition yet. Based in Stamford, Connecticut, John Frieda specialized in high-end shampoo, conditioner, and styling products. Its annual revenues were approximately $160 million. In between these deals, Kao lost out in the bidding in mid-2001 for the Clairol hair-care business, which was being auctioned by Bristol-Myers Squibb Company. Rival Procter & Gamble won out with its offer of nearly $5 billion, besting Kao's bid, which was believed to have been approximately $4.5 billion. In May 2003 Kao strengthened its chemicals business through the purchase of the aroma and fragrance operations of Cognis Deutschland GmbH & Co. KG. for approximately ¥4.7 billion ($39 million). Among the assets gained was Ambroxan, an aroma chemical with the scent of ambergris and a key ingredient used in soap, shampoo, and laundry detergent products around the world.

As Kao was building up its important North American business through acquisitions, the firm was also moving more aggressively into the burgeoning Chinese market. In 2001 four core products were selected for targeting to this market: face cleanser, feminine hygiene products, shampoos, and laundry detergent. The following year Kao (China) Holding Co., Ltd. was created as a holding company for its operations in China, and Kao increased its advertising in that nation. Then in 2004 Kao began selling Sofina cosmetics products in China. That same year, Andrew Jergens Company was renamed Kao Brands Company. The move was designed to reflect the increasing number of brands that were now managed by the U.S. subsidiary.

Following up on the success of its Econa oil, Kao in May 2003 launched Healthya Green Tea, whose high levels of tea catechin were said to reduce body fat. First-year sales totaled an impressive ¥19 billion ($180 million). Also successfully launched was the Asience line of hair-care products, which debuted in Japan in the fall of 2003. In mid-2004 Goto ended his tenure as Kao president and CEO, shifting into the nonexecutive chairman slot. Goto's emphasis on cutting costs, improving profitability, and more effectively using the firm's resources paid off: during his seven years at the helm, Kao's profit margin jumped from 3.1 percent to 7.2 percent, while return on equity more than doubled, increasing from 7.5 percent to 15.5 percent. Succeeding Goto as president and CEO was Motoki Ozaki, who had been in charge of the Global Fabric and Home Care division.

Under Ozaki, Kao's emphasis on new product development did not abate. In September 2004, for example, Kao pursued two additional segments of the Japanese cosmetics market. The Alblanc line of skin-care products was launched for distribution through general merchandisers and drugstores, while the ORIENA brand was targeted at the mail-order market. During Ozaki's first year, Kao achieved its eighth straight year of record profits: ¥72.2 billion ($672.1 million) on record revenues of ¥936.9 billion ($8.72 billion). Pretax profits rose for the 24th consecutive year.

Acquisitions continued in the Ozaki era as well. In July 2005 Kao purchased Molton Brown, a U.K. maker of luxury bath, skin-care, and cosmetics products, for £170 million ($298 million). Then in early 2006 Kao completed by far the largest acquisition of its history, the ¥427 billion ($3.7 billion) purchase of Kanebo Cosmetics Inc. The acquired company was the cosmetics arm of the financially troubled Kanebo, Ltd. Kao and Kanebo had two years earlier entered advanced discussions about a Kao takeover of the cosmetics business, but the deal fell through in early 2004. This time the deal was consummated, making Kao the second largest cosmetics maker in Japan and placing it in a better position to compete against market leader Shiseido. In Kanebo Cosmetics, Kao gained a company with annual revenues of about ¥212 billion ($1.8 billion) that sold its products in approximately 50 countries worldwide and also had an extensive network of retail outlets. Plans were immediately made to move more aggressively into the cosmetics market in China. Kanebo Cosmetics continued to operate independently as a wholly owned subsidiary of Kao Corporation.

Mary F. Sworsky
Updated, David E. Salamie

PRINCIPAL SUBSIDIARIES

Kao Hanbai Company, Ltd.; Kao Cosmetics Sales Co., Ltd.; Nivea-Kao Company Limited; Kao-Quaker Company, Limited; Kao Shoji Co., Ltd.; Kao Infonetwork Company, Limited; Kao Logistics Company, Limited; Niko Seishi Co., Ltd.; Kao Professional Service Co., Ltd.; Kanebo Cosmetics Inc.; Kanebo Cosmetics Sales Co., Ltd.; E'quipe, Ltd.; Lissage Ltd.; Kanebo Cosmillion, Ltd.; Inogami Co., Ltd.; Kao (China) Holding Co., Ltd.; Kao Corporation Shanghai (China); Kao Commercial (Shanghai) Co., Ltd. (China); Kao (China) Research and Development Center Co., Ltd.; Kao Chemical Corporation Shanghai (China); Zhongshan Kao Chemicals Limited (China); Shanghai Kanebo Cosmetics Co., Ltd. (China); Kanebo (Shanghai) Sales Co. Ltd. (China); Kao (Hong Kong) Limited; Kao Chemicals (Hong Kong) Limited; Kao (Taiwan) Corporation; Taiwan Kanebo Cosmetics Co., Ltd.; P.T. Kao Indonesia; P.T. Kao Indonesia Chemicals; Kao (Malaysia) Sdn. Bhd.; Fatty Chemical (Malaysia) Sdn. Bhd.; Kao Soap (Malaysia) Sdn. Bhd.; Kao Oleochemical (Malaysia) Sdn. Bhd.; Kao Plasticizer (Malaysia) Sdn. Bhd.; Pilipinas Kao, Incorporated (Philippines); Kao (Singapore) Pte. Ltd.; Kao Consumer Products (Southeast Asia) Co., Ltd. (Thailand); Kao Industrial (Thailand) Co., Ltd.; Kao Commercial (Thailand) Co., Ltd.; Kanebo Cosmetics (Thailand) Co., Ltd.; Kao Vietnam Co., Ltd.; Kao (Australia) Marketing Pty. Ltd.; Quimi-Kao, S.A. de C.V. (Mexico); Kao Brands Company (U.S.A.); Kao Specialties Americas LLC (U.S.A.); ADM Kao LLC (U.S.A.); Kanebo Cosmetics U.S.A. Inc.; Kao Corporation (France) SARL; Kanebo Cosmetics France S.A.R.L.; KPSS - Kao Professional Salon Services GmbH (Germany); Kao Chemicals GmbH (Germany); Kanebo Cosmetics Deutschland GmbH (Germany); Kanebo Cosmetics Italy S.p.A.; Kao Chemicals Europe, S.L. (Spain); Kao Corporation S.A. (Spain); Kanebo Cosmetics (Europe) Ltd. (Switzerland).

PRINCIPAL COMPETITORS

Shiseido Company, Limited; L'Oréal SA; Lion Corporation; The Procter & Gamble Company; Unilever.

FURTHER READING

"Efficient Corporate Resources Enhance Kao's Group Strengths," *Cosmetics International*, October 25, 1996, p. 10.

Friedland, Jonathan, "Lean and Clean: Japan's Kao Defies Taboos and Recession," *Far Eastern Economic Review*, May 19, 1994, pp. 50–51.

Fukui, Makiko, "Floppy Disks Are Hardship for Household Giant Kao," *Asian Wall Street Journal*, July 17, 1997, p. 20.

Fuyuno, Ichiko, "Japan's Kao Hopes to Exploit Fitness Game with Cooking Oil," *Wall Street Journal*, April 2, 2003, p. B4D.

"Goto Steering Kao for Future Growth," *Nikkei Report*, June 10, 2002.

Gray, James, "Turnarounds/United Appeal," *Canadian Business*, April 1988.

Harney, Alexandra, "Zen and the Subtle Art of Profit-Making," *Financial Times,* August 29, 2000, p. 13.

Hunter, David, "Kao Corp. Steps Up Its Overseas Presence," *Chemical Week,* May 29, 1991, p. 48.

An Inexhaustible Spring: Research and Development Activities at Kao, Tokyo: Kao Corporation, 1988.

Johnstone, Bob, "Attacking a Mature Market: Technology and Marketing Help a Japanese Soap Maker Clean Up," *Far Eastern Economic Review,* March 17, 1988, p. 82.

Kanabaysahi, Masayoshi, "Japan's Top Soap Firm, Kao, Hopes to Clean Up Abroad," *Wall Street Journal,* December 17, 1992, p. B4.

"Kao Crushes Rivals by Selling Premium Products, Shunning Price War," *Nikkei Report,* October 22, 2002.

"Kao, Kanebo Alliance Threatens Shiseido Dominance," *Nikkei Report,* December 19, 2005.

"Kao Selects Young Gun As Chief," *Nikkei Weekly,* April 19, 2004.

Luxenberg, Stan, "Here Comes—Gasp!—Kao," *Adweek's Marketing Week,* July 4, 1988, pp. 18+.

Martin, Neil A., "Jewel of Japan," *Barron's,* November 5, 2001, pp. 32–33.

Merris, Kathleen, "The Tao of Kao," *Financial World,* April 26, 1994, pp. 42–46.

Nagel, Andrea, and Koji Hirano, "Kao Jazzes Up Its Beauty Image," *WWD,* April 16, 2004, p. 12.

Neff, Jack, "It's Kao's Turn Now," *Advertising Age,* April 24, 2000, p. 28.

Ono, Yumiko, "Japan's Kao Reaps Benefits of Makeover," *Wall Street Journal,* August 31, 1999, p. A19.

———, "Kao's Plan to Expand Presence in U.S. May Be Hair Apparent," *Asian Wall Street Journal,* May 10, 2001, p. M1.

———, "Kao Tries to Sell Japanese Soap in U.S. Market," *Wall Street Journal,* August 8, 1994, pp. B1, B4.

Pilling, David, and Mariko Sanchanta, "Kao Seals Deal to Acquire Kanebo," *Financial Times,* December 19, 2005, p. 22.

Rahman, Bayan, "Kao in Cognis Fragrance Deal," *Financial Times,* March 18, 2003, p. 30.

Sanchanta, Mariko, "Japan's Kao to Pay $450m for John Frieda," *Financial Times,* August 2, 2002, p. 27.

"Should We Kow-Tow to Kao?," *Economist,* March 30, 1996, pp. 60–61.

Smith, Peter, "Kao Buys Molton Brown in £170m Deal," *Financial Times,* July 16, 2005, p. 4.

Takahashi, Yoshio, "Kao's Shine Dims in Some Eyes As Pricing Power Starts to Fade," *Asian Wall Street Journal,* August 2, 2004, p. M1.

Tanikawa, Miki, "Unilever, Procter & Gamble ... and Kao? The Japanese Manufacturer Wants to Be a Global Power," *Business Week,* March 8, 1999, p. 104D.

Tanzer, Andrew, "High Noon in Cincinnati," *Forbes,* July 25, 1988, p. 38.

Utsunomiya, Yuji, "Kao Cashes in on the Golden Elixir of Weight Loss," *Japan Times,* June 17, 2003.

van Raalte, John A., "A Visit with Kao," *HAPPI,* July 1990.

Kyocera Corporation

6 Takeda Tobadono-cho
Fushimi-ku
Kyoto, 612-8501
Japan
Telephone: (+81-75) 604-3500
Fax: (+81-75) 604-3501
Web site: http://www.kyocera.com

Public Company
Incorporated: 1959 as Kyoto Ceramic Co., Ltd.
Employees: 58,559
Sales: ¥1.18 trillion ($11.03 billion) (2005)
Stock Exchanges: Tokyo Osaka New York
Ticker Symbols: 6971 (Tokyo); KYO (New York)
NAIC: 327112 Vitreous China, Fine Earthenware, and Other Pottery Product Manufacturing; 327999 All Other Miscellaneous Nonmetallic Mineral Product Manufacturing; 333314 Optical Instrument and Lens Manufacturing; 333315 Photographic and Photocopying Equipment Manufacturing; 333515 Cutting Tool and Machine Tool Accessory Manufacturing; 334119 Other Computer Peripheral Equipment Manufacturing; 334210 Telephone Apparatus Manufacturing; 334413 Semiconductor and Related Device Manufacturing; 334414 Electronic Capacitor Manufacturing; 334417 Electronic Connector Manufacturing; 334419 Other Electronic Component Manufacturing; 336322 Other Motor Vehicle Electrical and Electronic Equipment Manufacturing; 339113 Surgical Appliance and Supplies Manufacturing; 339114 Dental Equipment and Supplies Manufacturing

■ ■ ■

Kyocera Corporation, founded in 1959, was one of the first companies to produce fine ceramic components. It has grown into one of the world's preeminent manufacturers of electronics, optical equipment, and other products that use sophisticated ceramics and electronics technology. Kyocera (pronounced key-OH-sarah) produces and sells information equipment (printers, copiers, and multifunction products); telecommunications equipment (cell phones, PHS ["personal handyphone"] handsets, PDAs, and wireless systems); applied fine ceramic products (cutting tools, medical devices, solar cells and modules, and recrystallized gemstones); fine ceramic products (components for the electronics, automotive, textile, paper, and other industries); electronic components (capacitors, connectors, input/output and display devices, and other components); and semiconductor parts (packages and other components used in advanced semiconductor devices). These products, many of which are manufactured outside of Japan, are sold around the world by the company's own sales force, as well as through a comprehensive network of distributors and dealers.

Although over the years Kyocera has been known more for its individualistic spirit than for a typical Japanese communal character, the company's corporate culture reflects a standard Japanese dedication to the manufacture of superior products. This philosophy was established and carefully cultivated by the company's entrepreneurial founder and chairman, Kazuo Inamori, who retired in mid-1997 to become a Zen Buddhist

COMPANY PERSPECTIVES

"To be a creative company that continues to grow"—that has been the Kyocera ("Kyocera" as a consolidated group) mission since Kyocera Corporation was founded in 1959, reflecting our unswerving commitment to shareholders. As we plan our future by "always seeking better ways," continuous growth will remain a top priority.

By continuously pursuing excellence while adhering to universal principles, we in the Kyocera Group will capitalize on our unique value system and technologies. Kyocera will lead the way to the value that rapidly changing markets demand. Not only will we create new technologies and new products, but entirely new markets. In so doing, every Kyocera Group company worldwide will create new value for society.

monk while remaining involved in the firm as chairman emeritus.

EARLY HISTORY

Upon graduation from Kagoshima University, where he studied applied chemistry, Inamori went to work as a ceramics engineer. When he was asked by his employer in 1959 to transfer to Pakistan and become the manager of an insulator factory, Inamori chose instead to take advantage of an opportunity offered by an outside investor to start his own company.

Kyoto Ceramic Co., Ltd. benefited from creative research ideas and methods that produced discoveries as much through accident as through pure scientific method. For example, during the development of an insulator made of magnesium oxide, a very dry, loose powder, the challenge facing the ceramics industry was to find a way to hold the magnesium oxide together during firing, a problem that leading researchers around the world had been unable to solve. When Inamori accidentally tripped over a block of paraffin wax as he walked across the lab, it struck him as he removed the wax that had stuck to his shoes that the wax might hold the key to the magnesium oxide problem. Inamori successfully mixed the magnesium oxide and the wax together using what is now humorously referred to in company annals as the "Inamori fried rice powder molding method."

From the very beginning, Inamori instilled a corporate philosophy that emphasized product excellence. To ensure the company's ability to grow without incurring further debt, since Inamori found debt unacceptable, all efforts were directed toward paying off the debt from the company's start-up. The pressure of meeting such ambitious objectives often required salespeople, production staff, and development personnel to work around the clock to fulfill product orders before deadlines.

In 1969, ten years after Kyoto Ceramic's birth, Kyocera International, Inc. was established as a sales company in the United States. Only two years later, this subsidiary entered into an agreement with Fairchild Camera and Instrument of San Diego, California, to acquire one of its factories to make ceramic components. On the other side of the ocean, Feldmühle Kyocera Elektronische Bauelemente GmbH was established in the same year as a joint venture with Feldmühle AG of West Germany for manufacturing semiconductor packages and electronic components. In 1971 Kyoto Ceramic's stock was listed on the Second Section of the Osaka Stock Exchange.

GROWING RAPIDLY

The late 1970s were a time of intense growth and expansion for Kyoto Ceramic both inside and outside Japan. In 1977 it established Crescent Vert Company, Ltd. to manufacture recrystallized jewels and Kyocera (Hong Kong) Ltd. to supply electronic components and equipment to southeast Asia. American Feldmühle Corporation and Cybernet Electronics Corporation became affiliates in 1979.

The acquisition of Cybernet, a Japanese manufacturer of citizens-band radios and audio equipment, was stimulated to a large extent by Inamori's desire to expand the company's base of business beyond ceramic packaging. Unfortunately, the merger created intense and conflicting company loyalties among the labor union workers inherited from Cybernet and hampered, for a time, the smooth transition Inamori sought.

REORGANIZING AND PURSUING ACQUISITIONS

The Kagoshima Central Research Laboratory was opened in 1979 to engage in fine ceramics research, particularly in the areas of applied and processing technologies. In 1984 Kyocera established its second research facility in Tokyo to study the areas of electronics, optoelectronics, and other new media. Meanwhile, in 1982, Kyocera Corporation was formed from the merger of Kyoto

KEY DATES

1959: Kazuo Inamori founds Kyoto Ceramic Co., Ltd.
1969: Kyocera International, Inc. is established as a U.S. sales company.
1982: Kyoto Ceramic merges with four of its subsidiaries to form Kyocera Corporation.
1983: Camera maker Yashica Co., Ltd. merges with Kyocera.
1984: Kyocera takes lead in the formation of the telecommunications firm Daini-Denden Kikaku Company, Ltd. (later DDI Corporation).
1989: Elco Corporation, maker of electronic connectors, is acquired.
1990: Capacitor producer AVX Corporation is acquired.
2000: Kyocera takes over photocopier maker Mita Industrial Co., Ltd., which is renamed Kyocera Mita Corporation, and also acquires the wireless phone business of Qualcomm Inc.
2005: Company announces its withdrawal from the digital camera market.

Ceramic with four of its subsidiaries, including Cybernet Electronics.

In 1984 Inamori formed a private telecommunications company called Daini-Denden Kikaku Company, Ltd. (later known as DDI Corporation) to enter into competition with Nippon Telegraph and Telephone (NTT). Funded by Inamori and 24 other institutional investors, this venture, NTT's first competitor, was launched in part in retaliation for NTT's successfully blocking an attempt by Kyocera to market its own line of cordless telephones in Japan the year before. NTT had been the only legal supplier. When Kyocera shipped 30,000 of its own units, rated superior to NTT's, NTT lodged an immediate complaint with Japan's Ministry of Ports & Telecommunications and forced Kyocera to recall its product. Subsequently, Daini-Denden, with Inamori as its chairman, rapidly expanded its business by adding public telecommunications services to its private network and by establishing subsidiaries to institute cellular mobile telephone services in several regions of Japan.

Subsidiary development continued in both North America and Europe during 1985 and 1986, culminating in the 1987 formation of Kyocera America, Inc. and Kyocera Electronics, Inc. to take over for Kyocera International, which became a holding company for seven other U.S. affiliates.

Following a 1983 merger that made camera and camera maker Yashica Co., Ltd. a Kyocera subsidiary, Yashica in 1987 successfully introduced the Samurai SLR camera, a breakthrough product integrating advanced technology, ease of use, and reasonable cost. Also in 1987 Kyocera Mexicana, S.A. de C.V. was incorporated, bringing the number of Kyocera's overseas manufacturing facilities to six.

Kyocera's growth was not free of setbacks. Many resulted from its chairman's continued resistance to the unspoken tenets of Japanese commerce as, for instance, his duel with NTT in 1984 shows. The following year, Inamori was criticized in the press for ignoring government exportation regulations and directly selling components to a leading U.S. defense manufacturer. A 1980 incident in which Kyocera began marketing a bioceramic medical implant prior to obtaining the official approval of Japan's Ministry of Health returned to haunt Inamori in 1985 when the company was accused of illegal activities by a member of Japan's parliament. Inamori was often a target of the Japanese press, which questioned both his strict managerial style and his judgment in doing such things as establishing a company cemetery.

Kyocera's partnership with the California-based LaPine Technology Corporation was another deal that brought bad press. In 1986 Kyocera invested more than $10 million to fund the manufacture of 3.5-inch hard disk drives for the Silicon Valley company. This arrangement enabled LaPine to obtain the necessary financing it sought from the Prudential-Bache Trade Corporation. Within months, however, the three-way partnership began to crumble, reducing all three companies to arguments over costs and shipment quantities. As this battle wore on, LaPine customers transferred their orders to other suppliers and employees were laid off in substantial numbers. In the end, Kyocera and Prudential-Bache squared off to fight over what little was left.

Nonetheless, Kyocera has been an active participant in its local and national community. The Inamori Foundation, established in 1984, awards the Kyoto Prize annually for achievements in science, technology, the creative arts, and the humanities. The foundation also funds a number of domestic research projects throughout Japan in a range of technological and cultural specialities.

MAJOR ACQUISITIONS IN 1989 AND 1990

During the late 1980s and early 1990s, Kyocera made major moves to bolster its overseas operations, particularly in Europe and North America. In 1988 a company reorganization set up head offices in Asia, the United States, and Europe, the latter of which, Kyocera Europe GmbH, was based in Germany. The following year the company spent $250 million to acquire Elco Corporation, a maker of electronic connectors based in the United States, which had annual sales of $152 million and operated two plants in Europe. This particular purchase did not go smoothly at first, as Elco soon lost most of its upper managers, who left after disagreements developed between them and Inamori.

Kyocera's 1991 $560 million acquisition of AVX Corporation, on the other hand, went smoothly. AVX, based in South Carolina and with six factories in Europe, manufactured multilayered ceramic and tantalum capacitors used in semiconductors, a perfect fit with Kyocera. Following the acquisition, Kyocera helped AVX cut costs and AVX also benefited from the two companies together being able to offer their customers a full range of electronics components. As a result, AVX revenues jumped from about $350 million in 1989 to about $1.2 billion in 1995; profits increased fourfold to about $130 million. In August 1995 Kyocera sold about 25 percent of AVX in an initial public offering, gaining a profit of more than $300 million in the process.

DIVERSIFYING

By 1993 DDI had grown rapidly, with sales reaching an estimated $3 billion, and was the clear number two telephone company in Japan. That year, DDI went public, after which Kyocera owned a 25 percent stake in it. Kyocera continued to expand its involvement in telecommunications, as evidenced by the 1995 debut in Japan of the personal handyphone system (PHS), a different type of cellular phone system, one that worked within a smaller area than that of cellular systems and that cost about one-fifth as much as cellular.

Kyocera expanded into multimedia in 1995, with the establishment in August of Kyocera Multimedia Corporation for the marketing via television of software for games, database information, and consumer products. The company also made a series of moves to pursue the burgeoning economy of China. In December 1995 Shanghai Kyocera Electronics Co., Ltd. was established to manufacture electronic components. The following year Kyocera entered into a joint venture with a Chinese company to form Dongguan Shilong Kyocera Optics Co., Ltd., which was charged with manufacturing and selling in China consumer optical instruments, such as cameras, lenses, and stroboscopes.

One of the most important developments of the late 1990s came in June 1997 when Kyocera's revered entrepreneurial founder, Kazuo Inamori, retired, becoming a Zen Buddhist monk in the Kyoto temple where he had years earlier set up the controversial tomb for Kyocera employees. Inamori nevertheless remained involved in the company as a board member and chairman emeritus. At this time Kensuke Itoh was serving as president, but he shifted into the chairmanship in mid-1999, when Yasuo Nishiguchi was promoted to president, having previously served as head of the telecommunications business.

In August 1998 Kyocera broadened its electronic component line by acquiring a minority interest in Kinseki, Ltd., a maker of quartz crystal oscillator products. Kyocera took full control of Kinseki in 2003 and subsequently renamed it Kyocera Kinseki Corporation. In the meantime, Mita Industrial Co., Ltd., a globally active maker of photocopiers, had run into financial problems and declared bankruptcy. During 1999 Kyocera stepped in to help Mita reorganize, hoping to save a major buyer of its electronic components. Having infused ¥12 billion ($117 million) into the troubled company, Kyocera in early 2000 took over Mita, changing its name to Kyocera Mita Corporation. In April 2002 Kyocera merged its printer operations into Kyocera Mita to take advantage of synergies between the two businesses. One major setback for Kyocera in this period was the high-profile failure of the much-hyped Iridium satellite-based phone system, the development of which had been led by Motorola Corporation. Kyocera was a major producer of Iridium handsets and was also involved in other aspects of the business. During 2000 Kyocera was forced to completely write off its Iridium inventory and investments, racking up losses totaling ¥15 billion ($146 million).

FURTHER EXPANSION IN TELECOMMUNICATIONS AND OTHER AREAS

By the early 2000s more than 80 percent of Kyocera's revenues were being derived from telecommunications- or information-related operations. The telecommunications side received a huge boost in February 2000 when the wireless phone business of Qualcomm Inc. was acquired for approximately ¥23 billion ($211 million). A new U.S.-based subsidiary called Kyocera Wireless Corp. was created to carry on the business, which quickly hit pay dirt in the form of the Smartphone QCP 6035, introduced in the United States in March 2001. This cell phone featured integrated personal digital assistant functions based on the Palm operating system, and it was released to stellar reviews.

Kyocera's telecommunications investments paid off in another way in 2001. In October 2000 DDI merged with KDD Corporation, the leading international-call carrier in Japan, and IDO Corporation, a provider of cell phone service, to form a company soon named KDDI Corporation. Kyocera's 25 percent stake in DDI was thus transformed into a 15.3 percent stake in KDDI, and in the process Kyocera added ¥98.2 billion ($779 million) to its net income for the year. Also in 2001, a year in which Kyocera's revenue surpassed the ¥1 trillion mark for the first time, the company acquired Tycom Corporation, a maker of carbide cutting tools for printed circuit boards, for $67.8 million. The acquired company was later renamed Kyocera Tycom Corporation. In addition, seeking inroads into the burgeoning Chinese and aiming to improve the profitability of its manufacturing operations, Kyocera began expanding its production in low-wage China by establishing a new plant in Shanghai. Kyocera later created additional production bases in Dongguan and Guiyang, established a sales company in March 2003, and formed a Chinese subsidiary that began assembling solar modules in November 2003.

Further cost-cutting in 2002 centered around the slashing of 10,000 jobs at its overseas subsidiaries, about 20 percent of its global workforce, mainly at Kyocera Wireless and Tycom. In August 2002 Kyocera sought to bolster its electronic components and materials businesses by acquiring Toshiba Chemical Corporation from Toshiba Corporation for about ¥9.4 billion ($80 million). The deal enabled Kyocera to pursue synergies between fine chemical technologies and fine ceramic technologies. The acquired unit was renamed Kyocera Chemical Corporation.

The year 2004 was marked by two further deals. Kyocera and Kobe Steel, Ltd. merged their respective medical divisions, each focusing on artificial joints and bones, into a new company called Japan Medical Materials Corporation, 77 percent owned by Kyocera and 23 percent owned by Kobe. The companies hoped to better compete against the U.S. and European firms that dominated the Japanese artificial joint sector. In October 2004 Kyocera joined with the U.S. investment firm Carlyle Group to take over DDI Pocket, Inc., the largest PHS (personal handyphone system) service provider in Japan. In a deal valued at approximately ¥220 billion ($2 billion), DDI was bought from KDDI, with Kyocera taking a 30 percent stake and Carlyle 60 percent, with KDDI retaining 10 percent. DDI Pocket changed its name to WILLCOM, INC. in February 2005. Although demand for PHS services had been disappointing in Japan, the market was growing rapidly abroad, particularly in Thailand, Taiwan, and China.

Continuing poor performance at Kyocera's optical equipment and telecommunications equipment groups prompted significant restructurings in 2005. Despite rapid growth in demand for digital cameras, brutal price competition and the company's weak camera brands made this sector a money-losing one for Kyocera. The firm thus decided to withdraw from the digital camera market, shifting focus toward camera modules used in cell phones. Kyocera Wireless, meanwhile, had failed to turn into a consistently profitable business for similar reasons: intense price competition and a lack of hot models. In yet another cost-cutting move, Kyocera shifted to outsourcing the manufacturing of all of Kyocera Wireless's phones, resulting in the layoff of almost 1,600 employees in San Diego and Tijuana. There were changes as well at the executive level. In June 2005 Nishiguchi was named chairman and CEO, while Makoto Kawamura was chosen to head the company as president. Kawamura had spent most of his 32 years at Kyocera in the cutting tool division. At the same time, Inamori stepped down from the company board, reportedly wanting to hand the company's management to a younger generation. It was nevertheless uncertain whether the founder's influence over management decisions would decline.

Updated, David E. Salamie

PRINCIPAL SUBSIDIARIES

Kyocera SLC Technologies Corporation; Kyocera Solar Corporation; Kyocera Elco Corporation; Kyocera Kinseki Corporation; Kyocera Display Institute Co., Ltd.; Kyocera Mita Corporation; Kyocera Mita Japan Corporation; Kyocera Optec Co., Ltd.; Kyocera Communication Systems Co., Ltd. (76.3%); Kyocera Chemical Corporation; Kyocera Leasing Co., Ltd.; Kyocera Realty Development Co., Ltd.; Japan Medical Materials Corporation (77%); Kyocera Precision Tools Korea Co., Ltd. (90%); Kyocera Elco Korea Co., Ltd.; Shanghai Kyocera Electronics Co., Ltd. (China; 90%); Dongguan Shilong Kyocera Optics Co., Ltd. (China; 90%); Kyocera Mita Office Equipment (Dongguan) Co., Ltd. (China; 90%); Kyocera Zhenhua Communication Equipment Co., Ltd. (China; 70%); Universal Optical Industries Limited (China); Yashica Hong Kong Co., Ltd. (China); Kyocera (Tianjin) Solar Energy Co., Ltd. (China; 90%); Kyocera Elco Hong Kong Ltd. (China); Kyocera Asia Pacific Pte. Ltd. (Singapore); AVX/Kyocera (Singapore) Pte. Ltd.; Kyocera (Malaysia) Sdn. Bhd.; Kyocera Wireless (India) Private Limited; Kyocera Mita Australia Pty. Ltd.; AVX Israel Ltd.; Kyocera International, Inc. (U.S.A.); Kyocera America, Inc. (U.S.A.); Kyocera Wireless Corp. (U.S.A.); Kyocera Telecommunications Research Corporation (U.S.A.); Kyocera Industrial Ceramics Corporation (U.S.A.); Kyocera Solar, Inc. (U.S.A.); Kyocera Mita America, Inc. (U.S.A.);

Kyocera Tycom Corporation (U.S.A.); AVX Corporation (U.S.A.; 70.42%); Kyocera Electronic Devices LLC (U.S.A.); Kyocera Mexicana, S.A. de C.V. (Mexico); Kyocera Yashica do Brasil Indústria e Comércio Ltda. (Brazil); Kyocera Mita Deutschland GmbH (Germany); Kyocera Fineceramics GmbH (Germany); Kyocera Mita (U.K.) Limited; Kyocera Fineceramics Limited (U.K.); AVX Ltd. (U.K.); Kyocera Mita France S.A.; Kyocera Fineceramics S.A. (France); Kyocera Mita Italia S.p.A. (Italy); Kyocera Mita Europe B.V. (Netherlands); AVX Czech Republic S.R.O.; Kyocera Solar Europe S.R.O. (Czech Republic).

PRINCIPAL DIVISIONS

Fine Ceramic Parts Group; Semiconductor Parts Group; Applied Ceramic Products Group; Electronic Device Group; Telecommunications Equipment Group; Information Equipment Group; Optical Equipment Group.

PRINCIPAL COMPETITORS

TDK Corporation; Murata Manufacturing Co., Ltd.; EPCOS AG; Nokia Corporation; Motorola, Inc.; International Business Machines Corporation.

FURTHER READING

Allen, Mike, "Sleeping Giant Kyocera Finally Wakes to Recognition," *San Diego Business Journal,* March 10, 1997, p. 1.

Anzai, Tatsuya, "Whither the Perfect Company—Can the 'Kyocera Myth' Be Revived?," *Tokyo Business Today,* February 1994, pp. 48–50.

Balint, Kathryn, "Cell Phone Simplicity: Kyocera Earns Profits, Brand Recognition After Emerging from Qualcomm's Shadow," *San Diego Union-Tribune,* July 13, 2004, p. C1.

———, "Kyocera Learns Lesson on Cell Phones," *San Diego Union-Tribune,* May 8, 2005, p. H1.

Bylinsky, Gene, "The Hottest High-Tech Company in Japan," *Fortune,* January 1, 1990, pp. 82–84, 86, 88.

Clark, Don, "Kyocera of Japan Agrees to Acquire Qualcomm's Wireless-Phone Business," *Wall Street Journal,* December 23, 1999, p. B10.

Crampton, Thomas, "Kyocera Chief Leaves Imprint on His Empire," *International Herald Tribune,* May 28, 2001, p. 9.

Dvorak, Phred, "Kyocera, Carlyle to Pay $2 Billion for DDI Pocket," *Asian Wall Street Journal,* June 22, 2004, p. A1.

Easton, Thomas, "A Smart Japanese Buy," *Forbes,* November 20, 1995, pp. 80, 83.

Friedland, Jonathan, "Samurai Sorcerer," *Far Eastern Economic Review,* June 3, 1993, pp. 60–62.

Fulford, Benjamin, "Kyocera's Pay Dirt," *Forbes,* September 20, 1999, pp. 113–14.

Halsema, Jane, "Kyocera America's New Driving Force," *San Diego Business Journal,* June 13, 1988, sec. 1, p. 10.

"The Heretic Who's a Hero to Japanese Business," *Business Week,* April 16, 1984, pp. 190+.

Hill, Roy, "Melding Human Relations with High Technology," *International Management,* March 1977, p. 33.

Inamori, Kazuo, *A Passion for Success: Practical, Inspirational, and Spiritual Insight from Japan's Leading Entrepreneur,* New York: McGraw-Hill, 1995.

"Japan's Other Maverick," *Chief Executive,* January/February 1993, pp. 38, 40–41.

Johnstone, Bob, "The Customer Is King: How to Win Friends and Keep the Orders Coming," *Far Eastern Economic Review,* June 3, 1993, pp. 62–64.

Jonishi, Arthur, "Kyocera Leader Outlines Success of Early Venture Business," *Business Japan,* October 1986, pp. 39+.

"Kyocera's Secrets: Flexibility, Spirituality, and Teamwork," *Business Japan,* January 1987, pp. 31+.

"Kyocera Thrives on High-Tech Edge," *Nikkei Weekly,* February 16, 2004.

Maeno, Masayo, "Multimedia Gives Kyocera a New Dimension: Ceramics Maker Ventures into Consumer Products," *Nikkei Weekly,* February 5, 1996, p. 8.

Martin, Neil A., "Can Kyocera Extend Its Rebound?," *Barron's,* June 10, 2002, p. T3.

Morris, Kathleen, "Born Again," *Financial World,* June 7, 1994, pp. 62–67.

Nee, Eric, and Cindy Kano, "Kyocera's Dilemma," *Fortune International* (Asia ed.), December 10, 2001, pp. 92+.

"The Parts Are Greater: Japanese Electronics," *Economist,* April 15, 1995, pp. 60–61.

Pollack, Andrew, "Eyes on Higher Things and on the Bottom Line: Not the Usual Retirement Ahead for a Master of Corporate Zen," *New York Times,* April 2, 1997, pp. D1, D6.

Taninecz, George, "Kazuo Inamori: 'Respect the Divine and Love People,'" *Industry Week,* June 5, 1995, pp. 47, 49–51.

Tanzer, Andrew, "The Shattering of Kyocera," *Forbes,* August 26, 1985, pp. 40–41.

Woodard, Kathy L., "Profiles in Ceramics: Kazuo Inamori—a Passion for Success," *American Ceramic Society Bulletin,* April 1999, pp. 74–81.

Lexmark International, Inc.

One Lexmark Centre Drive
740 West New Circle Road
Lexington, Kentucky 40550-1876
U.S.A.
Telephone: (859) 232-2000
Toll Free: (800) 539-627
Fax: (859) 232-2403
Web site: http://www.lexmark.com

Public Company
Incorporated: 1991
Employees: 13,600
Sales: $5.22 billion (2005)
Stock Exchanges: New York
Ticker Symbol: LXK
NAIC: 334119 Other Computer Peripheral Equipment Manufacturing; 325910 Printing Ink Manufacturing; 325992 Photographic Film, Paper, Plate, and Chemical Manufacturing; 333315 Photographic and Photocopying Equipment Manufacturing

■ ■ ■

Lexmark International, Inc. is one of the world's major designers, manufacturers, and suppliers of laser and inkjet printers and related supplies for both the office and home markets. Since being spun off from International Business Machines Corporation (IBM) in 1991, Lexmark has become a leader in the development and production of a broad line of printing and office imaging products, including color and photo inkjet printers, monochrome and color laser printers, inkjet and laser multifunction devices (offering some combination of printing, scanning, copying, and faxing capabilities), dot matrix printers, inkjet and toner cartridges, and other associated supplies and services. In addition to making products marketed under its own brand, Lexmark also produces items for other original equipment manufacturers (OEMs) that are sold under the OEM's name. An alliance with Dell Inc. accounts for fully 15 percent of Lexmark's overall revenues. Lexmark has manufacturing operations in Lexington, Kentucky; Boulder, Colorado; Geneva, Switzerland; Orleans, France; Juarez and Chihuahua, Mexico; and Lapu-Lapu City, Philippines. These sites, however, are mainly involved in the more technologically complex aspects of Lexmark's business, such as the production of toner, photoconductor drums, and inkjet cartridges. The production of the printers themselves is conducted through third-party manufacturers, many of which are located in China. As a spinoff from IBM ("Big Blue"), the company inherited a worldwide distribution network that management has built upon and expanded dramatically. Lexmark sells its products in more than 150 countries around the world, and approximately 55 percent of revenues originate outside the United States, more than 35 percent in Europe alone.

EARLY HISTORY

The birth of Lexmark International was a result of IBM's attempt to remain competitive in the intense atmosphere of the late 1980s, when so many smaller firms began chipping away at Big Blue's market share in the computer industry. When IBM initiated a strategic downsizing campaign to cut its workforce by selling or

COMPANY PERSPECTIVES

Lexmark International, Inc. (NYSE: LXK) makes it easier for businesses and consumers to move information between the digital and paper worlds. In doing so, we are guided by a simple vision: Customers For Life. To earn our customers' loyalty, we listen to them, anticipate their needs and act to create value in their eyes.

spinning off its peripheral businesses, the Information Products Division was designated as one of the targets. In the early part of 1991, IBM completed a deal to sell Lexmark ("Lex" as in "lexicon" and "mark" for "marks on paper"), its newly renamed Information Products Division, to the private investment group of Clayton, Dubillier, and Rice for approximately $1.5 billion. The leveraged buyout, arranged largely by Martin Dubillier, one of the founders of the investment firm, was financed mostly through bank loans that left the newly created company $1 billion in debt. Dubillier, knowing that Lexmark required astute and aggressive management if it was to survive and prosper with such a heavy debt load, hired Marvin Mann, an IBM vice-president with 32 years of experience, to serve as Lexmark's chairman, president, and chief executive officer.

Intimately knowledgeable about the successes and failures of IBM's business, Mann jumped into his new position with unbridled enthusiasm. Working 18-hour days, and starting with the outline of an organization, he began to reinvent a $2 billion operation. The leveraged buyout included the transfer of IBM's Lexington, Kentucky, plant to Lexmark. Mann made the plant the focus of the company's production facilities and immediately implemented a strategy to streamline its workforce. By means of generous benefits for voluntary retirements, transfers, or separations, including one-time assistance payments of $25,000, and one-time career retraining payments of $2,500 (also part of the agreement with IBM), Mann was able to reduce the plant's workforce from over 5,000 to only 1,200 employees. This downsizing significantly reduced Lexmark's operating costs.

At the same time, Mann began to hire virtually all of his management team from IBM. Part of the deal with IBM gave Mann the authority to approach IBM employees to work for Lexmark, and the new president had absolutely no qualms about bringing in experienced managers who were willing to reshape the business. Ultimately, Mann managed to recruit the heads of IBM's research and development, sales, marketing, production, and human resources departments. In order to increase efficiency and smooth the workflow, Mann decided not to establish the traditional "contention system," where staff members from different departments within the company challenge each others' proposals, a primary management strategy at IBM and its subsidiaries. Instead, Mann wanted his managers to focus their energies on positive suggestions that would keep Lexmark ahead of its competition.

Perhaps the most innovative management restructuring occurred in the area of manufacturing operations. Initially, small teams of employees were formed in order to make the production lines more efficient and to eliminate problems related to quality control. But the process of transferring responsibility for decision making from management to workers was not always a smooth one. In one instance, early on in the reorganization, a team of employees redesigned the laser printer production process and then presented their recommendations to management who asked the group to sign an approval form for the design. Realizing that the decision-making process, and all the responsibility that goes with it, was completely in their own hands, the group of workers shied away and refused to sign the document that would change the production process. One month later, the same group of workers returned with a more detailed redesign of the laser printer production process, and immediately supported it with their signatures. The two lessons Mann and his management team learned from this experience were that, first, empowerment does not work until workers believe that they can actually take ownership of the production process and, second, that involving employees in decisions that affect the production process takes time. These fundamental changes in management-employee relations went a long way toward establishing a highly motivated and effective workforce at Lexmark.

GROWTH AND DEVELOPMENT

After having reduced numerous layers of management, created highly independent product development teams, organized a brand new, extremely aggressive sales force, and discarded IBM's traditional appraisal and suggestion program, Mann was ready to take Lexmark to new heights. In 1992, as the company improved its product development time cycles and made its manufacturing processes more and more efficient, a new dot matrix printer was introduced for use at both work and home, along with an extremely lightweight battery-powered printer for portable personal computer users. Later that year, Lexmark introduced a PostScript-compatible inkjet

KEY DATES

1991: International Business Machines Corporation spins off its computer peripherals business as Lexmark International, Inc. through a leveraged buyout; Marvin Mann leads the new company.
1994: The use of the IBM brand is discontinued in favor of Lexmark.
1995: Company goes public.
1998: Paul Curlander succeeds Mann as president and CEO.
2003: Lexmark begins supplying Dell Inc. with Dell-branded printers.

printer, and also began to make a mark in the field of laser network printing. These laser printers were manufactured for Macintosh and were the first products bearing the Lexmark, rather than the IBM, name. At the same time, however, Lexmark retained its right under a licensing agreement to manufacture printers under the IBM logo.

In addition to expanding its product line with such items as color printers, Lexmark significantly increased the number of its original equipment manufacturer (OEM) printer customers, and was well on the road to doubling that number within its projected timetable of one year. Lexmark also aggressively expanded its IBM PC-compatible keyboard business, which, by the end of 1992, had grown to include over 40 original equipment manufacturers besides IBM. Lexmark was able to double its operating profits after only two years of operation. The company produced $1.8 billion in revenues during 1992 and, with a good cash flow and astute management of its financial resources, Lexmark was able to dramatically reduce its debt from $1.15 billion to approximately $700 million, an impressive accomplishment within such a competitive industry.

In 1993 Lexmark significantly enhanced its presence in the Pacific Rim with the acquisition of Gestetner Lasers. Arranged through its subsidiary, Lexmark Australia, the print maker Gestetner was the company's first acquisition and, like all subsequent purchases, was fully incorporated into the company's manufacturing operations. At this time, the company made a commitment to increase its business operations in the international sector and, after a restructuring plan implemented in 1992, improved manufacturing operations in France and built up distribution, marketing, and administrative operations throughout Europe. As a result of these measures, sales from the company's European business shot up to approximately $500 million. Through astute pricing and product sourcing decisions, management was able to minimize the effects of exchange rate fluctuations on the company's European revenues. Other major events during 1993 included the introduction of a new series of network laser printers, and a licensing agreement with Interlink Electronics to develop joystick technologies for a burgeoning market.

By the beginning of 1994, Lexmark had made its name in the laser printer industry. The sale of inkjet printers increased 27 percent over the previous year, much of this due to the entry of the company into the low-end color inkjet market. Associated printer supplies increased by 28 percent, attributed primarily to the continued growth of the company's installed printer base. Keyboard revenues increased only 6 percent, but the company's notebook computer line proved to be one of its most popular products in the retail market. In fact, Lexmark's presence in retail stores was growing at an astounding rate, with over 20 percent of the company's total revenues generated from retail sales. By the end of the year, Lexmark was ranked fourth in the retail market, closing in on such giants as Hewlett-Packard Company, Epson Corporation, and Canon Inc. in inkjet sales. A study conducted during this time indicated that consumer recognition of Lexmark and its products had grown from 36 percent to 41 percent in just three months.

In addition to the increase in revenues, Lexmark received a major endorsement from Microsoft Corporation when the software titan picked the company as its first partner for the WindowsAtWork printing environment. Pleased with Lexmark's innovative and aggressive style, Microsoft subsequently chose the company to work on a second generation of products which would be optimized to run in a Windows environment. The close of 1994 marked a milestone in Lexmark history as the IBM logo was finally removed from all company products to be replaced by the Lexmark name. Perhaps the most satisfying moment for Mann, however, arrived when Lexmark was able to reduce its debt to a mere fraction of the total amount by the end of 1994.

In 1995 Lexmark introduced one of its most successful products, MarkVision, the most thorough and comprehensive printer management system designed up to that time. Local area network (LAN) users within large corporations significantly increased their efficiency by installing MarkVision, which allowed staff to view all the available printers and check the print job status of each of them without leaving their desk. Another feature of MarkVision provided network administrators with access to the same information so that printer settings could be easily changed through a unique remote operator panel. The click of a mouse gave individuals the ability to remotely perform multiple tasks from their desktop, and simultaneously control and manage all printers across the entire network, regardless of whether the printer was on another floor in the building or across the country. Within a very short time, MarkVision had developed into one of the most popular network and systems management applications, used by many of the leaders in the network industry. With the success of MarkVision, Lexmark was able to introduce related applications such as the MarkNet IR, or infrared adapter. This highly compact product enabled a mobile printer to print, synchronize, and transfer files from an infrared-equipped notebook or laptop computer without the use of switch boxes or cables that required extensive hook-up procedures.

By the end of 1995, Lexmark was able to report nearly $2.2 billion in revenues, with approximately 70 percent of sales generated from printers and associated supplies. Nearly 40 percent of Lexmark revenues came from sales outside the continental United States, mostly derived from countries in Europe and around the Pacific Rim. With international sales up 25 percent over 1994, the company planned to continue expanding its presence overseas through a strategic effort to manufacture more competitive products, improve marketing, and intensify sales efforts. In November 1995 Lexmark went public through an initial public offering. In 1998 Clayton, Dubillier, and Rice divested its remaining 23 percent stake in Lexmark.

TARGETING THE CONSUMER AND SMALL OFFICE MARKET

During the late 1990s, while continuing to go after the corporate market and expanding its offerings for that market to include networkable color inkjet and laser printers, Lexmark began to increasingly target the consumer and small office market. The emphasis here was on affordable inkjet printers, and Lexmark broke new ground in 1997 when it began offering color inkjet printers that retailed for less than $100. The lower prices stimulated demand without affecting the company's bottom line because Lexmark made much of its money selling the cartridges required by its printers, in a replication of the razor-and-blades strategy pioneered by the Gillette Company. Further innovation came in 1998 when Lexmark introduced a color inkjet printer capable of editing, storing, and printing pictures from most digital cameras without needing to be connected to a computer or the camera itself. The company developed additional versions of so-called photo printers over the ensuing years. Also in 1998, Lexmark began supplying inkjets to Compaq Computer Corporation for bundling with Compaq PCs. These printers carried the Compaq brand but still required ink cartridges from Lexmark. In early 1999 Lexmark expanded its presence in the retail market by securing space for its printers on the shelves of three key retailers, CompUSA, Staples, and Office Depot.

The late 1990s also saw the first top management transition at Lexmark. In May 1998 Paul Curlander was named president and CEO, succeeding Mann, who remained chairman until April 1999, when Curlander assumed that position as well. Curlander had a Ph.D. in engineering and had developed IBM's first laser printer, shifting over to Lexmark upon its spinoff. Under Curlander's watch, Lexmark made its biggest product launch yet in late 1999, introducing six new laser printers aimed at the corporate market as well as new multifunction machines offering scanning, faxing, and copying functions in addition to printing.

Over the next two years, however, Lexmark suffered from the tech downturn, which severely depressed corporate information technology purchases. Sales of higher-end black-and-white laser printers in particular suffered, and consumers also cut back on their purchases of inkjet cartridges and printers. A series of restructurings followed. In 2000 the firm cut approximately 900 jobs from its workforce as it shifted production of its Optra line of laser printers from Lexington to plants in northern Mexico and southern China. A further cutback of 1,600 jobs, or about 12 percent of the workforce, followed in 2001. Lexmark was dealt a further blow in May 2002 when archrival Hewlett-Packard (HP) acquired Compaq, thereby ending the Lexmark-Compaq alliance. Despite this series of setbacks, Lexmark between 1998 and 2000 saw its installed base of laser printers increase from 2.9 million to 4.9 million, while the number of Lexmark inkjets skyrocketed from 10 million to 45 million. One result was that during this period revenues derived from the sale of cartridges and other supplies surpassed printer sales for the first time. The supplies business, which generated $836 million in sales in 1998, or 28 percent of the total, accounted for $2.3 billion of revenues in 2002, 54 percent of the record total of $4.36 billion.

Having lost its OEM deal with Compaq, Lexmark inked a pact with HP's archrival on the PC side, Dell. In 2003 Lexmark began supplying printers to Dell that the latter sold under the Dell brand. Revenue from the Dell partnership grew quickly, reaching $782 million by 2005, an amount representing 15 percent of Lexmark's total sales for the year. Overall results for 2005, however, were disappointing as revenues fell 2 percent to $5.22

billion, and profits fell from $568.7 million to $356.3 million. Lexmark blamed the results on a price war with its larger rivals and lower consumer demand, although some analysts contended that the company was not investing enough in research and development and thus not developing innovative new products. It was also possible that the company was beginning to feel the effects of cost-conscious consumers buying replacement cartridges from competitors rather than Lexmark, or having them refilled at the burgeoning number of outlets offering such services. Lexmark responded to the poor results by launching a restructuring in January 2006 that involved the elimination of 1,350 jobs, the closure of its inkjet cartridge manufacturing plant in Rosyth, Scotland, and other cost-cutting initiatives. The program incurred pretax charges of approximately $130 million. The company expected that these actions would result in annual cost savings eventually totaling $80 million.

Thomas Derdak
Updated, David E. Salami

PRINCIPAL SUBSIDIARIES

Blue Mark International SA (France); Lexmark Asia Pacific Corporation, Inc.; Lexmark Canada, Inc.; Lexmark Deutschland GmbH (Germany); Lexmark Espana, L.L.C. & Cia, S.R.C. (Spain); Lexmark Europe S.A.R.L. (France); Lexmark Handelsgesellshaft m.b.H. (Austria); Lexmark Internacional Mexicana S. de R.L. de C. V. (Mexico); Lexmark Internacional, S.A. de C.V. (Mexico); Lexmark Internacional Servicios, S. de R.L. de S.A. (Mexico); Lexmark International (Australia) PTY Limited; Lexmark International B.V. (Netherlands); Lexmark International (China) Limited; Lexmark International (Czech) s.r.o. (Czech Republic); Lexmark International de Argentina, Inc.; Lexmark International de Chile Ltda.; Lexmark International de Mexico, Inc.; Lexmark International de Peru, SRL; Lexmark International de Uruguay S.A.; Lexmark International do Brasil Limitada (Brazil); Lexmark International Financial Services Company Ltd. (Ireland); Lexmark International Hungaria Kft (Hungary); Lexmark International (India) Private Limited; Lexmark International, K.K. (Japan); Lexmark International (Korea), Inc.; Lexmark International Logistics, BV (Netherlands); Lexmark International Ltd. (U.K.); Lexmark International Manufacturing BV (Netherlands); Lexmark International (Philippines), Inc.; Lexmark International Polska Sp.Z.o.o. (Poland); Lexmark International (Portugal) Servicos de Assistencia e Marketing, Unipessoal, Lda.; Lexmark International Puerto Rico; Lexmark International S.A. (Belgium); Lexmark International S.A.S. (France); Lexmark International SCI (France); Lexmark International (Scotland) Ltd.; Lexmark International Service and Support Center Limited (Ireland); Lexmark International (Singapore) PTE LTD.; Lexmark International South Africa (Pty) Limited; Lexmark International S.r.l. (Italy); Lexmark International Technology S.A. (Switzerland); Lexmark Operaciones Mexico S. de R.L. de C.V.; Lexmark Printer (Shenzhen) Company Limited (China); Lexmark Research & Development Corporation (Philippines); Lexmark S.A. (Korea) LTD.; Lexmark (Schweiz) AG (Switzerland); Lexmark Solution Services (Australia) PTY Limited; Lexington Tooling Corporation; Pera Bilgi Islem Urunleri Ticaret A.S. (Turkey); Societe Printmark SA (France); Solution Services Europe GmbH (Germany); Technique Corporate Services (Pty) Ltd. (South Africa); Venture Computer Company (Pty) Ltd. (South Africa).

PRINCIPAL COMPETITORS

Hewlett-Packard Company; Seiko Epson Corporation; Canon Inc.; Ricoh Company, Ltd.; Xerox Corporation; Brother Industries, Ltd.; Samsung Electronics Co., Ltd.; Konica Minolta Holdings, Inc.; Kyocera Mita Corporation; Oki Data Corporation; Sharp Corporation.

FURTHER READING

Alpert, Bill, "Printing Money," *Barron's,* April 5, 1999, pp. 21–22.

Brown, Bruce, "An Ink Jet in Every Pot," *PC Magazine,* May 28, 1996, p. 301.

Bulkeley, William M., "Lexmark Slashes Profit Estimate, Blames Price War, Low Demand," *Wall Street Journal,* October 5, 2005, p. B3.

Butters, Jamie, "Lexmark's Executive Adapts with Changes," *Lexington (Ky.) Herald-Leader,* January 9, 2000.

Flanagan, Patrick, "IBM One Day, Lexmark the Next," *Management Review,* January 1994, p. 38.

Gillooly, Brian, "Lexmark Emerges from the Shadows in Printer Market," *Computer Reseller News,* June 10, 1991, pp. 2+.

Kellner, Tomas, "Protecting the Family Jewels," *Forbes,* December 8, 2003, pp. 66, 68.

Klein, Alec, "Lexmark to Launch Six Laser Printers in Bid to Grab Market Share form H-P," *Wall Street Journal,* September 21, 1999, p. B5.

Lavilla, Stacy, "Lexmark Makes Printers Manageable Through DMI," *PC Week,* March 4, 1996, p. 30.

———, "Lexmark Takes Aim at Low-End Printer," *PC Week,* January 29, 1966, p. 30.

———, "Lexmark Unleashes High-End Optra," *PC Week,* April 8, 1996, p. 31.

———, "Low-end Releases Pick Up Printer Pace," *PC Week,* July 29, 1996, p. 28.

McWilliams, Gary, and James Bandler, "Lexmark Will Make Cartridges and Printers Under Dell Brand," *Wall Street Journal,* September 25, 2002, p. B4.

Perenson, Melissa J., "It's All in the Speed," *PC Magazine,* May 14, 1996, p. 74.

Pinella, Paul, "Lexmark International Inc.," *Datamation,* June 15, 1993, p. 65.

Ryan, Ken, "Making a Mark: Lexmark Nipping at Heels of Major Printer Vendors," *HFN–The Weekly Newspaper For The Home Furnishing Network,* May 15, 1995, p. 75.

"Scotland Plant Planned," *New York Times,* October 4, 1995, p. C3.

Sharp, R. F., "Marvin Mann Discusses Lexmark, Compaq Deal, Stepping Down As CEO," *Lexington (Ky.) Herald-Leader,* May 8, 1998.

Shukovsky, Sam, "IBM Spin-off Lexmark Aims for Comeback," *PC Week,* January 6, 1992, p. 103.

Sloan, Scott, "Lexmark Looks Forward," *Lexington (Ky.) Herald-Leader,* March 27, 2006.

Stamper, John, "Lexmark Marks 10-Year Anniversary in Lexington, Ky.," *Lexington (Ky.) Herald-Leader,* March 27, 2001.

Tilton, Sarah, "Lexmark Computer Printers in China Certainly Aren't Run-of-the-Mill," *Wall Street Journal,* January 25, 1999, p. B9E.

"The Typing on the Wall," *Economist,* October 3, 1992, pp. 74+.

Veverka, Mark, "Printing Money," *Barron's,* May 10, 2004, pp. 17–18.

———, "Think Ink," *Barron's,* November 18, 2002, pp. 18–19.

Liquidnet, Inc.

498 7th Avenue, Floor 12
New York, New York 10018
U.S.A.
Telephone: (646) 674-2000
Fax: (646) 674-2003
Web site: http://www.liquidnet.com

Private Company
Incorporated: 2000
Employees: 142
NAIC: 522320 Financial Transactions Processing, Reserve, and Clearinghouse Activities; 523110 Investment Banking and Securities Dealing; 523120 Securities Brokerage; 523210 Securities and Commodity Exchange; 523910 Miscellaneous Intermediation

■ ■ ■

Liquidnet, Inc. manages an electronic marketplace for institutional trading that brings buyers and sellers together and enables them to anonymously trade large blocks of stock without intermediaries or information leaks. Liquidnet's global community is comprised of many of the more prominent buy-side financial institutions in the world. The company boasts an industry-leading average execution size of almost 42,000 shares of small-, mid-, and large-cap stocks since its launch. Liquidnet is registered as a broker/dealer with the Securities and Exchange Commission (SEC) and is a member of the NASDAQ. Liquidnet Europe Limited is regulated by the U.K. Financial Services Authority and is a member of the London Stock Exchange. Liquidnet Canada Inc. is regulated by the Ontario Securities Commission and Market Regulation Services Inc. and is a member of the Investment Dealers Association of Canada.

2000–01: THE BIRTH AND GROWTH OF AN ALTERNATIVE TRADING SYSTEM

Seth Merrin launched Liquidnet Inc. in April 2001 to bring together institutional buyers and sellers to trade large blocks of shares anonymously. After briefly considering a career in restaurant management, and having spent a year running a technology company in Silicon Valley, Merrin entered the training program at Oppenheimer Co. where he worked in the risk arbitrage group. As a risk arbitrage trader, Merrin worked closely with computer consultants to make it possible to spend less of his work time on manual tasks and more on trading. In 1985, at the age of 24, he founded Merrin Financial Inc., where, in 1987, he created the first order management system. *Wall Street and Technology* named Merrin one of the ten innovators of the decade for this development.

The year 1987 was a very tough one financially, Merrin recollected in a 2005 *Pensions and Investments* article. "At that point, nobody knew whether they were going to stay in business, and they certainly didn't want to hear from a 26-year-old kid that you could save them a few bucks. ... Going into 1990, we had all of nine clients ... not a raving success. But in 1990, the whole outlook changed, and people started investing money. In 1990, we signed 18 clients alone." In 1996, Merrin sold

COMPANY PERSPECTIVES

Liquidnet removes the barriers that erode trading performance, leaving members with seamless, efficient institutional-size executions. Members can easily access liquidity across 13 major markets through just one single access point.

Merrin Financial to Automatic Data Processing Inc. where he continued to work for a couple of years.

Then, in 1998, Merrin quit the company. While still uncertain what he would do next, he came up with the idea for Liquidnet. "I had tried to figure out the solution to institutions' liquidity problems. … The one missing piece that I couldn't figure out—nor could anybody else … was how to create a critical mass of liquidity on day one. ... I was lying in bed one night, not particularly thinking of anything, but it was that Eureka! moment that the final piece of the came together. … I drew everything out on a diagram. … That was October 1999."

Merrin's diagram laid out a specialized virtual marketplace within the market, where only block traders were allowed to meet. The Liquidnet model integrated closely with online order management systems, which most large money management institutions by then used. It used the aggregate quantities of all customers' orders to inform participants when there was liquidity available for trade on the network. A computerized process that resembled a bridge allowed a trader to let others in the network know that he wished to buy or sell a block of a particular stock. Without identifying the trader, the system let other institutional traders know that somebody wished to make a deal. Traders could then show each other the size of their interest and their terms. For all deals struck, Liquidnet as broker, charged a commission of two cents per share.

Merrin took his idea to Eric LeGoff, who had run operations at Michael Price's Mutual Series from 1986 to 1996. LeGoff and Merrin had founded VIE Systems, a middleware software vendor where LeGoff served as CEO, in 1997. Merrin and LeGoff spent the next couple of months talking to "industry bigwigs," among them the chairmen of CIBC Oppenheimer and Neuberger & Berman, asking them to "blow holes" in their idea or join their board of directors. In February 2000, Liquidnet acquired Armonie Software, a venture backed technology start-up which sped the new company's time to market and distinguished its architecture from other alternative trading systems. In March 2000, Merrin and LeGoff raised their first round of venture capital, and little more than a year later, having planned, built, tested, sold, and installed their product, they were up and running.

Liquidnet's arrival came at a crucial time. As the average institutional order had soared to more than 250,000 shares, the average trade size on NASDAQ had declined to 700 and on the New York Stock Exchange to somewhere between 1,000 and 1,200 shares. Block trades averaged 21,000 and 24,000, respectively. According to *Barron's*, no stock market has ever had the liquidity to absorb large block trades on the floor of its exchange. Posting a bid to buy 50,000 shares of even the biggest, most liquid stock is risky because of the large number of helpers entailed and the threat that the institution's intentions will leak out before the deal is complete.

Banks and mutual funds have tried two solutions, neither very satisfactory. They have engaged a large-block trader at a major brokerage to hunt down large-block sellers among his clients or through the worldwide rumor mill. They have also broken their order into relatively small retail pieces and fed the pieces into the market over time. On the way, they have encountered trade delays, missed trades, and market impact. Liquidnet, with its Internet-enhanced technology, promised to create institutional liquidity and eliminate the transaction costs of the standard system. Liquidnet also drastically undercut the traditional commission on institutional orders, which was about five cents a share on average, but with delayed and missed trades wound up closer to 45 cents on large-cap trades, and 81 cents on small-cap companies.

Liquidnet launched in April 2001 with about 38 institutions. First-day executed shares totaled 3,836,200 with an average execution size of 51,000. By the middle of May, 43 firms had signed on with 30 more committed, and the average trade was between 65,000 and 75,000 shares, somewhere around 90 times the industry average.

There was no cost to a member to sign on to Liquidnet, no service fee, no minimum commitment. All a company had to do was sign a two-page agreement, and Liquidnet arrived to do the half-hour software installation. For the most part, order management vendors facilitated their clients' integration process by constructing interfaces to Liquidnet's system, working with Liquidnet independent of their clients' involvement. In fact, by the end of 2000, Liquidnet had signed agreements with Advent Software, EZE Castle Software, and The MacGregor Group, three of the leading American order management system vendors, to couple their

KEY DATES

1999: Idea for Liquidnet is first formulated.
2000: Liquidnet, Inc. is incorporated.
2001: Liquidnet launches in the United States; Liquidnet Europe Ltd. is founded.
2002: Liquidnet Europe Limited is formed.
2004: Liquidnet Canada Inc. is established.

systems with Liquidnet's for those clients who wished to use its alternative trad ng system.

However, some vendors refused to do so on the grounds that sell-side firms, which sometimes shopped orders around to their best customers, might be less inclined to assist an institution that no longer regarded the involvement of brokers as beneficial. In fact, they were skeptical of the whole Internet-based block trading option on the grounds that it precluded other firms from injecting bids and offers, a step, they argued, that could result in an improved price for the customer.

2002–05: EXPANSION IN THE EUROPEAN AND CANADIAN BLOCK TRADING MARKETS

By April 2002, 89 institutions that collectively managed $4.3 trillion had joined Liquidnet. Of the nearly 16,000 trades that had been executed on the Liquidnet system, one out of every four had been for 100,000 shares or larger. By the end of 2002, with 125 members, Liquidnet ranked number one for large-block executions in both New York Stock Exchange (NYSE) and NASDAQ stocks. In November 2002, Liquidnet entered the European market with 33 participating firms in five distinct equity markets, the United Kingdom, France, Germany, Holland, and Switzerland, creating the possibility of cross border trading in Europe and the United States with a single broker, Liquidnet, instead of a broker for each separate market involved in a trade.

Liquidnet's membership grew steadily from its start. By the end of 2003, the online broker had 227 member institutions, representing 85 percent of the mutual fund industry, and was the 19th largest broker of NYSE shares. Collectively its membership managed the majority of equities in the United States (approximately $5.6 trillion) and included 62 percent of the top 50 buy-side firms.

Numbers continued to increase, and, in 2004, 271 institutions that collectively managed more than $6.6 trillion in assets had joined Liquidnet, now the 15th largest institutional broker of NYSE shares and the 17th largest for NASDAQ-listed stocks. Its average daily volume grew by more than 30 percent from 2003 to 2004, while NYSE's and NASDAQ's grew only 15 percent. The top-ranked broker for large trades, 50,000 shares or more, celebrated the good news when, in mid-2004, the Department of Labor's Division of Fiduciary Interpretations decided that Liquidnet could handle trades for Employee Retirement Income Security Act (ERISA) pension plans or their fiduciaries.

Liquidnet experienced further growth in 2004 as it launched Liquidnet Canada, Inc. in Ontario, a wholly owned subsidiary of parent Liquidnet Holdings, Inc. *Inc.* magazine named Liquidnet the fifth fastest growing private company in the United States based on its 10,406 percent growth from its inception. Head traders at 350 major money management firms voted the company one of the top ten institutional brokers in providing quality of execution for both NYSE and NASDAQ trades. By year's end, Liquidnet's average daily volume was 23 million shares, 77 percent greater than it had been just one year earlier.

The year 2005 saw five new European equity markets—Belgium, Denmark, Finland, Norway, and Sweden—join Liquidnet, by then the number one block trading firm in Europe. *Institutional Investor* magazine named Liquidnet its Leading Execution Venue as its liquidity pool topped 1.5 billion shares and the average daily volume traded set a new record at 33.3 million shares. From its launch in 2002 to 2005, Liquidnet's growth in principal traded in Europe had averaged more than 31 percent quarter-over-quarter.

By the end of 2005, Liquidnet had become the tenth largest NYSE institutional broker and the 11th largest NASDAQ broker. Fifty-two percent of the largest 100 U.S. buy-side institutions and 56 percent of the largest 50 companies (based on assets under management) were Liquidnet members. The company sold off a $250 million minority stake to two leading equity firms, Summit Partners and Technology Crossover Ventures, the proceeds of which went to some of its early investors. Estimates of the company's annual revenue were then around $145 million, not including its European business.

2005–06: MOVING INTO THE WHOLESALE MARKET FOR EQUITIES

Merrin and company were getting ready to take on a bigger challenge: building a wholesale market for equities trading that would intercept retail-size order flow. In September 2005, with 245 members in the United

States, 44 in Europe, and two in Canada, Liquidnet began rolling out Liquidnet H2O, a new version of its system, to about 20 buy-side firms. Like the original system, H2O pulled in liquidity suppliers from a variety of sources, expanding to include retail size orders. "Rather than have the institution go into a retail environment and try to satisfy the 250,000-share order at 400 shares a pop," Merrin explained in a 2005 *Wall Street & Technology* article, "imagine the power of having the 250,000 shares absorb a lot of those 400-, 300-, 200-share orders without putting pressure on the marketplace [and] without moving the marketplace."

The move to the sell-side was designed in large part to increase liquidity, which despite Liquidnet's growth in membership, was still in short supply. Ensuring adequate liquidity brought a slew of competitors, such as POSIT and Pipeline Trading Systems, looking to capture some of Liquidnet's volume, threatening to further fragment the institutional market for block trading. The idea behind H2O was that a buy-side trader, waiting to match a 250,000-share order in the traditional Liquidnet system, could trade with the "streaming liquidity" sources instead of leaving Liquidnet to search for another liquidity pool.

Industry analysts praised Liquidnet for maintaining its closed system while tapping into liquidity that had already been sent to the sell-side. Early results seemed promising as Liquidnet surpassed POSIT's volume in mid-2005. While still too early to determine whether or not H2O would prove as much of a splash as Liquidnet, it was certain that the company already had had an impact on Wall Street. While the NYSE was moving away from its human auction system toward a more electronic platform, NASDAQ announced steep price cuts for trades between its biggest-volume customers, from one-tenth to one-hundredth of a cent, and hiked the rebates it paid broker-dealers who brought in new business. Clearly Liquidnet had proved itself impressive competition for the old trading system and would continue to do so.

Carrie Rothburd

PRINCIPAL SUBSIDIARIES

Liquidnet Canada Inc.; Liquidnet Europe, Ltd.

PRINCIPAL COMPETITORS

Archipelago Holdings, Inc.; E*Trade Financial Corporation; NASD; New York Stock Exchange, Inc.

FURTHER READING

Birger, Jon, "Your Funds vs. Wall Street," *Money*, April 2004, p. 121.

Graham, Jed, "Peer-to-Peer Networks Could Alter Trading," *Investor's Business Daily*, February 9, 2001, p. 8.

Guerra, Anthony, "Will Liquidnet Catch the Buy Side,?" *Wall Street & Technology*, July 2001, p. 75.

"Observer: Will Liquidnet Live Up to Its Name?," *Global Investor*, February 2003, p. 1.

Santini, Laura, "New Online Stock Trading System Gets Street Interest," *Investment Dealers Digest*, April 30, 2001.

Schack, Justin, "Liquidnet in Talks with Investors," *Institutional Investor*, February 2005, p. 1.

Schmerken, Ivy, "Streaming Liquidity," *Wall Street & Technology*, November 2005, p. 34.

Marcopolo S.A.

Avenida Marcopolo 280
Caxias do Sul
Rio Grande do Sul 95086-200
Brazil
Telephone: (55) (54) 209-4000
Fax: (55) (54) 209-4010
Web site: http://www.marcopolo.com.br

Public Company
Incorporated: 1954 as Nicola & Cia. Ltda.
Employees: 10,959
Sales: BRL 1.71 billion ($700.82 million) (2005)
Stock Exchanges: São Paulo
Ticker Symbol: POMO3; POMO4
NAIC: 336211 Motor Vehicle Body Manufacturing; 336312 Gasoline Engine and Engine Parts Manufacturing; 811121 Automotive Body, Paint and Upholstery Repair and Maintenance

■ ■ ■

Marcopolo S.A. manufactures almost half of all buses and microbus bodies built in Brazil and is the third largest manufacturer of bus bodies in the world. Its production includes bodies for both urban and highway-transportation buses, and for motor coaches, vans, and recreational vehicles. The company also repairs these vehicles and makes automotive parts. Marcopolo sells its vehicles under such brand names as Volare, Fratello, Andare, Paradiso, Viaggio, Torino, and Viale, and it has factories in five other countries: Argentina, Colombia, Mexico, Portugal, and South Africa.

MOUNTING BUS AND TRUCK BODIES: 1949–92

The company was founded by Paulo Bellini and six other young mechanics in 1949. Under the name Nicola & Cia., it plated and painted cabins for trucks in Caixas do Sul, Rio Grande do Sul. Settled by Italian immigrants to Brazil's southernmost state, this city abounded in small-scale manufacturing enterprises, many of them founded by skilled metal and wood craftsmen working out of shops in backyards and basements. The first order came from a local commuter bus line, and Nicola built the body on a truck chassis. "It was all trial and error at first," Bellini recalled to Joel Millman, writing for *Forbes* almost a half-century later. "Everything was handmade." By 1954, when the company was incorporated, it was producing bus bodies; however, with only 15 employees, it essentially remained an artisanal enterprise, taking three months to make a single one. However, in 1957 it opened a real manufacturing facility in a suburb of Caixas do Sul.

Nicola & Cia. could not compete with bigger bodybuilders on price or delivery time, but it offered superior service. "We could make special seats," Bellini told Millman, "give the customer a bigger or smaller luggage rack, or fruit racks for buses in farm towns. Leather seats or plastic. Whatever the customer wanted." By contrast, he said, the company's rivals, "were arrogant with customers, setting the price and the style and telling the people, 'Take it or leave it.' We went out with our shirtsleeves up, looking for customers everywhere." Its first export order was in 1961, from a bus company in Uruguay.

COMPANY PERSPECTIVES

Mission: To offer solutions, goods, and services in order to satisfy customers and users with technology and performance; to provide adequate remuneration on investment, giving priority to the transport of passengers and contributing to better the quality of life of its contributors and society.

Nicola expanded in the 1960s and bought two other bodybuilders, one in Caixas do Sul, the other in Porte Alegre. By the late years of the decade it was turning out bodies for trucks with adaptable chassis. Production was doubling each year. In 1968 the company introduced a bus model called Marcopolo, and three years later it took that name for its own. Marcopolo began issuing stock shares on the São Paulo exchange in 1978. By 1980 it was making 15,000 units a year, but the oil-price and debt-crisis shocks that struck Brazil in this period reduced production to fewer than 6,000 vehicles in 1983. The company had to close the two factories it had acquired.

Under Bellini's direction, Marcopolo met calamity by seeking customers outside Brazil. In 1986 he and the company's production head went to Japan, visited many factories, and studied their manufacturing methods. When they returned, they began imparting what they had learned to the workers, organizing them into teams and stressing quality control. The company entered the U.S. market in 1988 with microbuses. In 1991 it established its first factory abroad, in Coimbra, Portugal. The following year it signed a contract with Dina Autobuses, S.A. de C.V. of Mexico to supply bus bodies and technology.

EXPANSION

By 1994, when Millman visited the Caixas do Sul factory, Marcopolo was making and assembling bus bodies on chassis made by Mercedes-Benz, Scania, and other big automakers. Half of its production was being exported to customers in 40 countries. Among them were Hertz Corp. and National Car Rental System Inc., which were using the vehicles as airport shuttles. Millman described Marcopolo as "obsessive about every aspect of its business, from the cleanliness of its factory floors to the mental health of its workers." Having adopted Japanese just-in-time inventory-control systems, the company carefully checked the ordering and installation of most of the 100,000 components needed, including seats, railings, dashboards, doors, and panels. No waste was tolerated; production teams were expected to monitor such details as how many liters of paint were being used on each bus.

Marcopolo lost BRL 2.8 million (about $2.5 million) in 1994, when a drastic national anti-inflation program made the company's exports uncompetitive in price. The company earned BRL 13 million (about $12.4 million) in 1995, however, and began selling American Depositary Receipts, the equivalent of shares of stock, that year (but later dropped its listing). A factory was opened in Río Cuarto, Córdoba, Argentina, in 1998. In addition, within Brazil, an automotive-parts factory was now in São José dos Pinhas, Paraná, and the main plant was also making fiberglass components. By this time Marcopolo had subsidiaries in Rio de Janeiro and São Paulo and representatives in 22 Brazilian cities and 15 abroad. The company was turning out 28 vehicles per day.

In 2000 Mercedes-Benz México, S.A. de C.V. took a minority share in Marcopolo's Mexican subsidiary, which had opened a production line in the city of Aguascalientes the previous year, when its contract with Dina lapsed. This facility moved to Mercedes-Benz's chassis plant in García, Nuevo León. A similar arrangement was made in 2000 to produce urban buses on Scania chassis in Pietersburg, South Africa, and on Volvo chassis in Bogotá, Colombia. By this time Marcopolo was the biggest manufacturer of bus bodies in Latin America, and its workforce, 3,300 in 1997, had swelled to 6,300. The company also acquired a plant in Duques de Caixas in the state of Rio de Janeiro, managed by a subsidiary, Ciferal Indústria de Ônibus Ltda.

Unlike its competitors, Marcopolo was vertically integrated, producing about 80 percent of the components and accessories it used in Brazil, including seats, windows, panels, and roof racks. Each highway bus was being turned out in an average of six days, compared to 20 in 1987. City buses took only four days. Another reason for Marcopolo's success was its traditional flexibility, allowing customers to choose a made-to-measure body on various chassis. In addition, because the customers of the Mexican subsidiary were in a hurry to get their vehicles, Marcopolo created a new system called PKD (partially knocked down), by which it shipped parts, already painted and finished inside as well as outside, from Brazil for reassembly abroad on a chassis. To speed delivery, Marcopolo transferred its port facilities from Itajaí, Santa Catarina, to Porte Alegre. By shipping from Brazil buses either partially assembled or in kit form rather than whole, Marcopolo was avoiding import duties. Always willing to oblige, for a Saudi Arabian client, Marcopolo fitted 95 of its buses with

KEY DATES

1949: Enterprise that later becomes Marcopolo is founded.
1957: Company opens a facility for manufacturing bus bodies.
1971: Company names itself Marcopolo for one of its models.
1978: Marcopolo makes its initial public offering of stock.
1980: Company produces 15,000 units of truck and bus bodies a year.
1988: Marcopolo enters the U.S. market with microbuses.
1991: Company opens its first foreign factory, in Portugal.
1996: Marcopolo's four chief shareholders turn over day-to-day management to professionals.
1998: Marcopolo has plants in Mexico and Argentina as well as Portugal.
2000: Company begins producing bus bodies in Colombia and South Africa.
2003: Marcopolo is cited as one of the ten best companies to work for in Brazil for the second year in a row.

removable roofs so that Muslim pilgrims to Mecca could feel themselves closer to Allah. This "haji bus" was, according to a *Newsweek* writer, the first mass-transit convertible.

MARCOPOLO IN THE 21ST CENTURY

Marcopolo's ventures in other countries were broadly successful, but the Argentine operation was hard hit by the recession that ended with the country defaulting on its debts and withdrawing support for its currency in 2001. "Our business in Argentina was excellent," José Rubens de la Rosa, Marcopolo's chief executive officer, told John Barham of *LatinFinance* in 2005. "We were doing well and it was our best market. Then along came 2001 and our market stopped. Sales went from 1,000 units to zero. We halted production at the plant in Argentina and all that was left there was a guard dog." Nonetheless even in Argentina, Marcopolo eventually rebuilt its business.

Marcopolo was evolving in other ways as well. In 1996 its four chief shareholders—Bellini, José Fernandes Martins, Valter Gomes Pinto, and Raul Tessari–turned over day-to-day management to professional executives, with de la Rosa as chief executive officer and Bellini as chairman of the board. After the professionalization of management came the professionalization of staff. By 2003, the company had divided its human resources needs into 202 job classifications, using a model adopted by some larger Brazilian enterprises. Applicants were evaluated not only on the basis of academic credentials and professional experience but also on personality and comportment, using a model created in the 1970s by David McClelland of Harvard University. Each of the 49 classifications on the factory floor was divided into up to five modules, or levels of competence, with performance rated once a year according to four criteria. Each favorable rating resulted in a promotion to the next module and an 8 to 10 percent salary increase. For executives, there were 62 classifications, rated in three segments: academic, professional, and emotional, with each subdivided into eight items. To reduce subjective evaluations, the assessor's evaluation was reviewed by that person's immediate chief and then by a committee.

Marcopolo was ranked among the ten best companies in Brazil to work in 2002 and 2003 by the business magazine *Exame*. It established a "school for professional formation" in 1990 to counter two problems: a lack of skilled workers in its Caxias do Sul plant and a surplus of unqualified youths in the community. Another program, founded in 1998, originally had as its purpose to prevent drug and alcohol use among the company's workers and family members, using such means as lectures and theater presentations. In 2001, Marcopolo executives decided to structure the different company projects in the social area into a "citizen's program" focused on volunteer aid by employees in community health and education institutions. Marcopolo also contributed to environmental programs, for which it won an award in 2002.

Marcopolo recorded consolidated sales of BRL 1.29 billion ($418.83 million) in 2003, of which exports represented 49 percent of the total. In 2004, revenues rose to BRL 1.61 billion ($549.49 million), and production of full-sized bus bodies increased to 15,938, of which 44 percent were exported and/or assembled in the company's plants abroad. However, the appreciation of about 50 percent for the Brazilian real in 2003–04 was raising the cost of selling goods abroad. As a result, Marcopolo began buying more raw materials and components from outside Brazil and then cutting production within Brazil while increasing production at its plants abroad. "This is not something we planned," de la Rosa told Jonathan Wheatley of the *Financial Times* in late 2005. "We simply saw the need and had to do it." Once made, the investments in manufacturing abroad would not be reversed, he said. "We cannot put the health of the company at risk by hoping the exchange rate will go back to where it was," he added. Marcopolo was reported to be planning to build plants in China, India, and Russia.

In spite of these problems, Marcopolo raised its net revenues to BRL 1.71 billion ($700.82 million) in 2005, although its net profit fell slightly. It raised the number of vehicle bodies that it produced to 26,983, of which 14,320 were for the Brazilian market. Forty-five percent of Marcopolo's revenues came from Brazil, and 55 percent from other countries.

Robert Halasz

PRINCIPAL SUBSIDIARIES

Ciferal Indústria de Ônibus Ltda.; Marcopolo Indústria de Carroçarias S.A. (Portugal); Marcopolo International Corporation (U.S.A.); Marcopolo Latinoamérica S.A. (Argentina); Marcopolo South Africa Pty Ltd.; MVC Components Plásticos Ltda.; Polomex S.A. de C.V. (Mexico; 74%); Poloplast Componentes S.A. de C.V. (Mexico); Superpolo S.A. (Colombia; 50%).

PRINCIPAL COMPETITORS

Agrale S.A.; Dina Autobuses, S.A. de C.V.; Daimler-Chrysler do Brasil Ltda.; Scania Latin America Ltda.; Volkswagen do Brasil Ltda.; Volvo do Brasil Ltda.

FURTHER READING

Barham, John, "Branching Out," *LatinFinance,* December 2005, pp. 30-31, 33.

Colitt, Raymond, and Richard Lapper, "Selling Brazil," *Financial Times,* September 15, 2004, p. 19.

Covarrubias, Benjamin, "Compran 26% de Marcopolo," *Reforma* (Mexico City), September 27, 2000.

Gianotti, Carlos Alberto, ed., *Histórias de Sucessos,* São Leopoldo, Rio Grande do Sul: Editora Unisinos, 1998, pp. 125-32.

Mano, Cristiane, "Quanto vale a competência?" *Exame,* February 26, 2003, pp. 64-67.

Margolis, Mac, "Flying South," *Newsweek* (International edition), December 26, 2005.

Millman, Joel, "'Evolving to Perfection,'" *Forbes,* November 7, 1994, pp. 298-99.

Naiditch, Suzana, "Marcopolo: Responsabilidade global," *Exame,* December 11, 2002, pp. 44-45.

———, "Podem me chamar de Dona Flor," *Exame,* November 29, 2000, pp. 46-49.

Wheatley, Jonathan, "Strong Real Raises Fears of Regression," *Financial Times,* December 16, 2005.

Middle East Airlines - Air Liban S.A.L.

BIA Airport Road
P.O. Box 206
Beirut,
Lebanon
Telephone: +961 1 628 888
Fax: +961 1 629 260
Web site: http://www.mea.com.lb

Private Company
Incorporated: 1945 as Middle East Airlines
Employees: 1,550
Sales: $250 million (2002 est.)
NAIC: 481111 Scheduled Passenger Air Transportation; 481211 Nonscheduled Chartered Passenger Air Transportation; 488190 Other Support Activities for Air Transportation

■ ■ ■

Middle East Airlines - Air Liban S.A.L. (MEA) is Lebanon's airline. The private company is owned by the Central Bank of Lebanon and operates on a commercial basis. Like the ancient cedar that forms its emblem, MEA has weathered many changes. Established soon after World War II, MEA pioneered many routes in the region as Lebanon enjoyed its heyday as a tourist destination and global aviation hub. Beginning in 1975, it had to contend with a 15-year civil war, earning it the title of "world's most resilient airline."

MEA has maintained a reputation for technical excellence, a relatively good safety record, and high customer service standards. Flight attendants are required to know three languages (Arabic, English, and French). An extensive restructuring program launched in the late 1990s trimmed the workforce while restoring the fleet with new, fuel-efficient planes. At the same time, deregulation opened Lebanon's skies to a slew of foreign carriers. MEA has appealed to customer loyalty through high standards rather than cut rates.

FOUNDED IN 1945

According to *A History of the World's Airlines,* the seminal tome by R. E. G. Davies, Middle East Airlines (MEA) was founded in September 1945 and launched its first service on November 20, 1945. Like many other carriers popping up after World War II, though controlled by local Moslems, it was initially dependent on technical expertise from the West, in this case advice and equipment from the British airline BOAC. Cofounders of MEA were Chairman Saeb Salaam and Technical Director Fawzi El-Hoss, who left the airline in 1951. Salaam resigned in 1956.

Sheikh Najib Alamuddin joined the airline as general manager in February 1952, was elected chairman in 1956, and remained on board until his retirement in 1977. He later published a book on his experiences called *The Flying Sheikh.* MEA had 166 employees at the end of 1945, he wrote.

Initial equipment included three 1930s-vintage de Havilland DH.89 Rapide biplanes; however, after BOAC declined MEA's request for bigger planes, MEA turned to the United States rather than Britain for technical support. Within a few months the Rapides were replaced with a couple of Douglas DC-3s sourced from an air

COMPANY PERSPECTIVES

Among MEA's distinctions: its ability to face challenges, crises and difficult circumstances with a strong resolve and an even stronger will, in order to develop its services, expand its horizons, and increase its security, safety, and leisure services for passengers on board its fleet.

base in Cairo. The planes were adorned with a logo of one of Lebanon's famous cedar trees.

In exchange for three more DC-3s plus spare parts, Pan Am received a 36 percent holding in MEA, which then had a registered capital of £1.25 million. Pan Am was interested in MEA as a feeder airline. In December 1954, however, Pan Am sold its shares as BOAC acquired a 78 percent interest. British-made turboprop-driven Viscounts upgraded the fleet beginning in late 1955. MEA entered the jet age by leasing Comets from BOAC in 1960.

Important early destinations included Baghdad and Cairo. Beirut was developing into a regional and global hub. In addition to becoming a tourist and trade center, Lebanon was exporting meat and produce by plane to countries in the Persian Gulf. MEA inaugurated service to London in June 1956.

There were two other passenger airlines operating out of Beirut. Local Christian interests established Air Liban, part owned by Air France, in the 1940s as Compagnie Générale de Transport (CGT). CGT brought MEA its first fare war (one of its pilots also crashed into one of MEA's first DC-3s, totaling it). Lebanese International Airlines (LIA) was set up in 1956 by the Arida family and later established ties to Belgian airline SABENA. Both, like MEA, had services to Europe. Air Liban had more coverage of Africa, noted Davies, while MEA had extended its reach east, to India.

Alamuddin reported guiding MEA through many difficulties in the late 1950s due to political unrest across the Middle East, which included the appearance of U.S. Marines in Beirut. The disruptions played havoc with MEA's finances. MEA recovered quickly, however, posting a profit of more than £4 million in 1961. BOAC subsequently sold its holdings in MEA to Lebanese investors in the early 1960s. MEA then tripled its capitalization to £18.75 million.

MEA established Jordan Airways in 1961 at the request of King Hussein. It was owned 35 percent by MEA. It was closed down by the Jordanians in 1963 in favor of a new venture with MEA rival Lebanese International Airlines (LIA).

1963 MERGER

MEA faced its first fatal accident in 17 years when a Turkish Air Force C-47 collided with one of its Viscounts over Ankara in February 1963. Eleven MEA passengers and three flight crew members were killed, as well as the three military airmen. Another 88 people died on the ground after the wreckage tore into a bank building. The accident was attributed to the military crew straying into Ankara Airport's approach while on instrument training.

MEA merged with Air Liban in early 1963. Air France emerged with a 20 percent holding in the merged company. It was soon carrying three million passengers a year, according to *Flight International.*

By 1967, MEA had a fleet of 11 aircraft, including larger, French-made Caravelle jets. By this time, it had cooperative arrangements with a dozen other airlines, while the well-established technical department served dozens of third parties.

In 1968, Israel destroyed eight of MEA's 13 aircraft, as well as five belonging to other Lebanese airlines, in a commando raid on Beirut Airport following a terrorist attack on an El Al airliner. MEA was able to maintain its flight schedule due to innovative routing and an outpouring of support from airlines in the Arab world, the West, and the Eastern Bloc, recalled Alamuddin. Fortunately no one was killed, and the $16 million loss was covered by insurance.

MEA acquired LIA's traffic rights in 1969. In the next few years, MEA itself would have to deal with hijackings from both Palestinian terrorists and the Israeli military, which in August 1973 intercepted one of its Caravelles flying a charter to Baghdad on behalf of Iraqi Airways. Although Israel said it was seeking to capture a Palestinian resistance leader, the skyjacking was roundly condemned.

1975–90 CIVIL WAR

MEA bought three Boeing 747 jumbo jets in 1975. The massive plane was the pinnacle of commercial aviation, and something of a status symbol among the world's airlines. Unfortunately, Lebanon was soon immersed in a civil war, which would last until 1990. Beirut Airport was closed for its duration and 12 of MEA's 23 planes were destroyed, seven of them in the 1982 Israeli invasion. MEA lost 40 employees to the violence. The company survived by wet leasing manned and fueled

KEY DATES

1945: Middle East Airlines (MEA) is established in Lebanon.
1955: Mideast Aircraft Services Company is established with BOAC.
1963: MEA merges with Air Liban.
1975: Civil war closes MEA's home airport for 15 years; the airline survives through leasing out planes and flying charters.
1996: Central Bank of Lebanon acquires MEA.
1997: Losses peak at $87 million.
2002: After restructuring, MEA posts its first annual profit in 20 years.

planes to other airlines, and by operating charter flights, sometimes from alternate bases such as Cyprus.

Asad Nasr, MEA's general manager since 1964, served as chairman from 1977 to 1982. He was succeeded by Managing Director Salim Salaam. After years of operating mostly Boeing 707s, MEA began ordering Airbus planes in the early 1980s. It would be forced to cancel these purchases, however, until after the war. The *Times* of London called MEA "arguably the world's most resilient airline" for its ability to keep functioning through difficult situations, such as President Ronald Reagan's efforts to isolate Beirut Airport in the mid-1980s.

CROWDED SKIES AFTER 1990

After the cessation of hostilities in October 1990, MEA methodically reconstructed its prewar route network. It also added flights to far-flung exotic destinations such as Sydney and São Paulo, and this apparently left it overextended. In spite of its many challenges, however, MEA retained a good safety record and a reputation for superior customer service.

MEA was not alone in the once again busy skies over Lebanon. Within two years, according to *Flight International,* 21 foreign airlines had resumed flights into Beirut Airport, which had implemented strict security measures after the lawless civil war period.

The Central Bank of Lebanon (Banque du Liban) acquired almost all of MEA's shares in 1996. According to the *Middle East Economic Digest,* this was in return for covering $375 million of the $720 million in losses MEA would accrue between 1981 and 2001. The airline's annual losses peaked at $87 million in 1997, followed by a deficit of $50 million the next year. Deregulation of Lebanon's airways was exposing MEA to many new competitors. The airline needed to evolve to survive among the lean, low-cost carriers of the day. MEA was then carrying one million passengers a year. It had only nine planes, but 4,500 employees, noted the *Middle East Economic Digest.*

MEA sold off the last of its Boeing 707s as well as its Boeing 747s in 1998. New Airbuses arrived to take their place; the company was also reviving its MASCO (Mideast Aircraft Services Company) venture, originally established in the mid-1950s, to capture a share of the region's maintenance revenues. Middle East Airports Services S.A.L. (MEAS) also was created, to provide terminal services at Beirut International Airport. A ground handling company, MEAG, was launched in 1999.

1998–2002 RESTRUCTURING

A new director general was appointed at this time: Mohamad El-Hout, a veteran of Central Bank. Hout soon implemented a number of practical measures to restore MEA to profitability. The most difficult, he told *Airways,* was letting go of about 1,600 employees in 2001, many through early retirement or assignments to affiliates. This left the carrier with a staff of about 1,200.

Hout also standardized the fleet and cut service on unprofitable routes, particularly to such distant destinations as Copenhagen, Sydney, and São Paulo. MEA directed this long-haul traffic into marketing arrangements with Air France and other foreign carriers, allowing it to connect with the Lebanese expatriates who had fled the region during the troubled 1980s.

PROFITABLE AGAIN IN 2002

In 2002, when revenues were $250 million, MEA posted its first annual profit in 20 years. It was only the beginning. Income increased from $3 million to $22 million in 2003, and exceeded $50 million the next year. The airline had a 36 percent share of the suddenly quite crowded local air travel market. According to *Airways,* there were 50 foreign airlines flying to Beirut. MEA was taking the high road, hoping to retain loyal customers through superior service rather than low-budget offerings.

Nine new Airbus aircraft, three of them leased, arrived in 2003. In 2004, a number of marketing agreements and code shares were added with KLM, Garuda, Royal Jordanian, and Egyptair. The next year, MEA added a code share on flights to Abu Dhabi with Gulf Air. At the same time, the cabin crew's uniforms were being updated. The dark blue was replaced with a turquoise symbolic of "a calm sea on a sunny day," according to the in-flight magazine *Cedar Wings*.

A possible partial flotation of shares had been discussed for the previous few years, and the company's strategic moves were made with privatization in mind. MEA was on a course of cautious expansion, El-Hout told *Airways*. It planned to add another two Airbus aircraft by 2008.

Frederick C. Ingram

PRINCIPAL SUBSIDIARIES

Mideast Aircraft Services Company (MASCO); Middle East Airlines Ground Handling (MEAG); Middle East Airports Services S.A.L. (MEAS).

PRINCIPAL COMPETITORS

Cyprus Airways Public Ltd.; Egypt Air; Gulf Air Company GSC; Royal Jordanian Airlines; Saudi Arabian Airlines.

FURTHER READING

Alamuddin, Najib, *The Flying Sheikh*, London: Quartet Books, 1987.

"Back in the Black: A Steady, Structured Approach to Problem Solving Has Paid Off for One of the Middle East's Longest-Established Airlines," *MEED Middle East Economic Digest*, December 5, 2003, pp. 33+.

Butt, Gerald, "Out of the Ashes," *Flight International*, May 13, 1992, pp. 30+.

"Central Bank Takes Over MEA," *MEED Middle East Economic Digest*, November 15, 1996, p. 27.

Davies, R. E. G., *A History of the World's Airlines*, London: Oxford University Press, 1967.

Fisk, Robert, "Lebanon Airline to Carry on Regardless; Middle East Airlines on US-Backed Efforts to Isolate Beirut Airport," *Times* (London), July 3, 1985.

Goold, Ian, "Middle East Airlines Considers Expansion," *Flight International*, January 13, 1993, p. 11.

Moxon, Julian, "Out of the Ashes," *Flight International*, May 20, 1998, p. 33.

Mroue, Haas, "Blue Skies for MEA," *Airways*, March 2006, pp. 45–49.

"The New MEA Cabin Crew Uniforms; A Whole New Blue, A Whole New Life," *Cedar Wings*, February-March 2005.

"Profits Surge Postpones MEA Sale," *MEED Middle East Economic Digest*, October 10, 2003, p. 22.

Milan AC S.p.A.

Via Filippo Turati 3
Milan,
Italy
Telephone: +39 02 62281
Fax: +39 02 6598876
Web site: http://www.acmilan.com

Wholly Owned Subsidiary of Fininvest S.p.A.
Founded: 1899 as Milan Cricket and Football Club
Employees: 144
Sales: EUR 250 million ($283 million) (2005 est.)
NAIC: 711211 Sports Teams and Clubs

■ ■ ■

Milan AC S.p.A. is one of the world's most recognized and most successful soccer clubs. The rossoneri ("red-blacks," after the team's red-and-black striped jerseys) are one of the world's winningest teams, boasting six European Championships, 17 "Scudetto" (national) championships, four European Super Cups, five Italian Super Cups, and three Intercontinental Cups, among its many victories since its founding in 1899. Milan AC shares the 85,700-seat Giuseppe Meazza stadium in Milan with arch-rival Inter. In 2005, however, Milan's CEO Adriano Galliani announced that the time had begun to plan a move to a new stadium. Milan AC also operates the world-famous training center Milanello, located on a parkland site of 160,000 square meters some 50 kilometers from Milan. Since 1992, Milan has operated the Milan Lab, one of the world's most sophisticated sports-oriented biomedical centers, which aims to predict potential player injuries. Milan AC is 100 percent controlled by Fininvest, which in turn is controlled by Italian media magnate and former Prime Minister Silvio Berlusconi, an avid Milan fan who named his political party, Forza Italy, after the popular team cheer. Belusconi's acquisition of Milan AC, which not only rescued the club from bankruptcy but permitted the club to regain its past glory, has been credited with aiding Berlusconi's political fortunes. Other companies in the Fininvest group include Mediaset, Italy's dominant media group, which also controls much of the broadcasting rights to the country's Serie A games; publishing group Mondadori; and film producer and cinema operator Medusa, among others. Milan AC posted revenues of EUR 250 million ($283 million) in 2005.

BRITISH BEGINNINGS AT THE END OF THE 19TH CENTURY

The British expatriate community in Milan at the end of the 19th century played a major role in the formation of one of Italy's most-loved football (also called soccer) clubs. Professional soccer was then in its early stages, with a first set of rules codified by a group called The Football Association in the United Kingdom in the 1860s. The name "soccer" was derived from "association" in order to distinguish the sport from another rapidly growing game, rugby football. By the 1890s, soccer had reached Milan, which saw the formation of the city's first team, called Mediolanum, which had been the Roman name for the city. Nonetheless, soccer in Italy remained a minor phenomenon.

> ## COMPANY PERSPECTIVES
>
> The team presents itself to its fans with a hundred years football tradition spent with constant commitment and high professional skills on the pitch and off it, ready to start a new season and face new, exciting challenges.

Much of the impetus toward the founding of Milan AC came through the efforts of Herbert Kilpin. Born in England in 1870, Kilpin, an avid cricket and soccer player, had traveled to Turin, where he found work at a textile company. By 1891, Kilpin had joined FC Torinese, one of Italy's first professional soccer teams, and he became the first from England to play soccer internationally as a professional.

Kilpin later moved to Milan, where he met two other British expatriates, Samuel Davies and Neville Allison, who both became star players on the early AC Milan team. Kilpin himself joined the Mediolanum team in 1898.

Avid crickets players, Kilpin, Davies, and Allison became interested in creating their own club to include that game as well, in an effort to popularize cricket among Italians. Kilpin had come into contact with another British expatriate, Alfred Edwards, a former vice-consul at the British embassy in Milan and a wealthy landowner. Edwards, a cricket player, had been active in organizing cricket matches on his property, and was also a well-known personality in the city.

One evening in December 1899, while drinking at the Fiaschetteria Toscana wine shop on Via Berchet, Kilpin, Davies, and Allison ran into Edwards and two of his friends. Kilpin approached Edwards with the idea of establishing a new cricket and soccer club; Edwards agreed to put up funding for the club, and was quickly joined by his companions. The group decided to name the club Milan Cricket and Football Club, with Edwards serving as its first president. Kilpin and Edwards then began putting together a board of directors, which included Pierro Pirelli, grandson of the founder of the Pirelli tire company. Pirelli later became president of the club as well as a major financial supporter of the team.

The club acquired a playing field, known as Trotters field, and registered with the Italian Football Federation. Although the club spent some time trying to attract members for its cricket team, the club failed to attract much interest for the sport. The idea was ultimately abandoned and Milan and the club decided to concentrate its energies on its soccer team, changing its name to Milan Football Club. Kilpin was credited with devising the team's uniform, choosing the colors red and black—red to emphasize the club's ferocity, black to portray its opponents' fear—and borrowed from the striped jersey already favored by many British rugby teams.

Milan played, and won, its first-ever game against Mediolanum in March 1900. The team already featured an international mix of players that was to highlight much of its success in later decades. By the end of 1901, the team had won its first Italian national championship, known as the Scudetto ("shield") because the winning team received the right to add a shield to their uniforms. That victory established Milan as a major force in the young Italian professional soccer league.

The team scored success again, winning two new Scudettos in 1906 and in 1907, under Herbert Kilpin. Kilpin retired from play that year, and was later killed during World War I. In the meantime, Pierro Pirelli had taken over as the club president, a position he held until the end of the 1920s. Pirelli's deep pockets were instrumental in financing the club, and its playing field. Yet the beginning of the Pirelli era was marked by controversy, as Italian players came to dominate the club. In 1908, a group of Milan players broke away and formed a rival team, Internazionale Football Club Milano, with the expressed purpose of accepting foreign players. The two teams met on the playing field that same year, with Milan winning the match. This became the start of a fierce and lasting rivalry between the two teams into the next century.

ENDING THE DROUGHT IN 1951

Pirelli's backing enabled the team to move into their own stadium in 1926. The stadium, called the San Siro after its neighborhood location, originally seated 10,000, already impressive in those days. The San Siro was later expanded several times. In 1939, the stadium could hold 55,000. Milan at first used the stadium exclusively; in 1947, however, rival club Inter began playing their home games at the stadium as well. This led to further expansion, and at its height the stadium's capacity reached 150,000, although a limit was set at 100,000 for security reasons. The San Siro stadium was renamed the Giuseppe Meazza stadium, in honor of the famed Inter player. Milan fans nonetheless continued to refer to the stadium by its original name. In 1989, in conjunction with Italy's hosting of the World Cup, the stadium was remodeled again, fitted with a glass roof, which reduced capacity to 85,000.

The new stadium failed to inspire the team, however, as Milan found itself without a championship for some

KEY DATES

1899: Milan Cricket and Football Club is founded by two British expatriates in Italy, Herbert Kilpin and Alfred Edwards; soon after the name is changed to Milan Football Club.
1900: Milan wins its first Scudetto title.
1926: The new San Siro stadium is inaugurated.
1963: The Milanello sports training center opens.
1986: Silvio Berlusconi rescues Milan from bankruptcy.
2002: The Milan Lab biomedical sports facility opens.
2004: Berlusconi is forced to resign the chairmanship of Milan.
2005: Milan announces plan to move to a new stadium.

44 years. A succession of presidents failed to spark the team's revival. In the meantime, under the Fascist government, the team was forced to adopt new team colors, and to change its name, to Associazione Calcio ("soccer") Milano. Following Italy's defeat in World War II, the team reverted back to its former colors, and re-adopted the British spelling of the name, becoming AC Milan.

The arrival of Umberto Trabattoni as team president following the war, and then of Andrea Rizzoli in the 1950s, produced a dramatic turnaround in Milan's standing. Trabattoni brought in a number of new players, notably the Swedish trio of Gren, Liedholm, and Nordahl. By 1951, Milan had ended its drought, capturing the Scudetto for the first time in decades. The team went on to win the Scudetto three more times that decade, as well as a number of other prestigious international cups.

Milan continued its winning streak during the 1960s, capturing the Champions League title at Wimbledon in 1963. Part of the team's success came through the efforts of the team's coach, Nereo Rocco, who was credited with developing a defensive style of play known as "catenaccio." Under Rizzoli, meanwhile, Milan opened a new sports training center, called Milanello, which featured state-of-the-art training facilities on a vast parkland.

The end of the 1970s provided a new low point in the club's history, however. In 1979, the team became embroiled in a match-fixing scandal. In the resulting sanction, Milan was dropped from the Serie A league and forced to play in Italy's Serie B. Although the team was accepted back into Serie A the following year, it suffered an even worse humiliation when it was relegated to the Serie B in 1981 because of its poor performance during the season.

BERLUSCONI ERA LEADING INTO THE 21ST CENTURY

By the mid-1980s, Milan was nearly bankrupt and on the verge of collapse. Fortunately for the team, however, one of its biggest fans was Silvio Berlusconi, who by then was already head of one of Italy's largest fortunes. Belusconi bought the team in 1986, and promptly steered Milan to its years of greatest triumph, which saw the team emerge as one of a small number of truly international teams. A major part of Milan's success came with its aggressive acquisition of new players, especially a new trio from The Netherlands, including Gullit, Rijkaard, and van Basten.

By the end of the 1980s, AC Milan was once again on the winning path, scoring a number of consecutive victories, including two Champions League titles and two Intercontinental Cup titles. Into the 1990s, the team reached even greater heights, scoring three consecutive Scudetto titles. The team also played in the Champions League finals for three consecutive years in the early 1990s. By the middle of the decade, Milan's popularity was credited with helping in another win, as Berlusconi, who named his political party Forza Italia ("Go Italy") after a popular Milan club chant, was elected Italian prime minister.

Into the 2000s, AC Milan added to its win record, capturing the Scudetti in 1999 and 2004, and the Champions League in 2003. By the middle of the decade, AC Milan ranked among Italy's most winning teams, trailing only Juventus. The company faced a financial setback in the early 2000s as well. Just days after signing star player Fernando Redondo to a contract worth more than $50 million, Redondo injured his knee, ending his career. In response, the team established a new sports biomedical center, Milan Lab, which sought to develop means of predicting, and avoiding, player injuries.

Berlusconi was forced to step down from the chairmanship of Milan in 2004, when the Italian government adopted new legislation restricting government officials from holding executive positions in private businesses. Little change was expected for Milan, which had already been under the de facto leadership of CEO Adriano Galliani for some time by then. In 2005, Galliani indicated that the club had begun examining plans to move Milan to a new stadium. In that year as well, the club reached a worldwide licensing agreement with Warner Bros. Consumer Products, in a move that was expected to help boost team revenues beyond 2005's EUR 250 million ($283 million). As one of the world's most well-known sports teams, AC Milan seemed certain to score many more goals in the new century.

M. L. Cohen

PRINCIPAL SUBSIDIARIES

Milan Lab; Milanello.

PRINCIPAL COMPETITORS

AS Roma S.p.A.; Inter Milan S.p.A.; Juventus.

FURTHER READING

Clendaniel, Edward, "Soccer Qualms," *Forbes ASAP,* October 7, 2002, p. 16.

"Italian Premier Leaves Helm of AC Milan," *Xinhua News Agency,* December 29, 2004.

"Italy's Uneven Playing Field," *Forbes,* April 4, 2006.

Plagenhoef, Scott, "Club Snapshot: AC Milan," *Soccer Digest,* November 2001, p. 14.

Sullivan, Ruth, "Why It Is Impossible to Wipe the Smile Off Berlusconi's Face," *European,* May 16, 1996, p. 23.

"Warner Bros. Consumer Products Ready to Kick It with AC Milan," *Licensing Journal,* June-July 2005, p. 36.

Nastech Pharmaceutical Company Inc.

3450 Monte Villa Parkway
Bothell, Washington 98021
U.S.A.
Telephone: (425) 908-3600
Fax: (425) 908-3650
Web site: http://www.nastech.com

Public Company
Incorporated: 1983
Employees: 106
Sales: $7.4 million (2005)
Stock Exchanges: NASDAQ
Ticker Symbol: NSTK
NAIC: 325412 Pharmaceutical Preparation Manufacturing

■ ■ ■

Nastech Pharmaceutical Company Inc. is a survivor. Founded on Long Island in the early 1980s and now based in Bothell, Washington, Nastech has rarely turned a profit and has lost far more money than it has ever taken in. It mostly focuses on intranasal drug delivery technology, adapting prescription drugs already available in oral or injectable forms, as well as developing new drugs to take advantage of the delivery method. Nastech has seen two of its products reach the market, Stadol (used for the relief of moderate to severe acute pain) and Nascobal (a vitamin B12 gel), but an obesity-fighting drug in clinical trials seeking Food and Drug Administration (FDA) approval has raised the company's profile, elevating Nastech from penny stock status to Wall Street darling. Other drugs in the pipeline include painkiller Morphine Gluconate; Calcitonin, used to treat osteoporosis; and a drug for erectile dysfunction, which the company hopes will offer competition to Pfizer's Viagra. In addition to nasal drug delivery, Nastech has become involved in tight junction biology, researching the way therapeutic drugs are passed from cell to cell, and RNA interference, a way to turn off the production of a protein in a cell to slow the spread of influenza and other respiratory diseases. Nastech is a public company listed on the NASDAQ.

1983 FORMATION COINCIDING WITH INCREASING INTEREST IN NASAL DELIVERY TECHNOLOGY

Using the nasal passages as a conduit for drug delivery gained interest with pharmaceutical researchers in the early 1980s. Sandoz Pharmaceuticals had introduced a nasally applied drug in 1957 to help nursing women with the flow of breast milk, and a few other applications followed, in addition to the common nasal sprays used to alleviate sinus conditions and treat head colds. The allure of nasally administered prescription drugs, although not the ideal delivery method for every drug, was manifold. First, the nose offers an abundant blood supply, allowing drug molecules to be absorbed into the bloodstream in as little as three minutes. The nasal delivery of some drugs could replace painful syringes. It was also well suited to replace some oral drugs, which were partially destroyed by enzymes or acids in the stomach before effectively entering the bloodstream. Moreover, holders of a drug patent could extend the usual 17-year life of the patent by developing a new way

COMPANY PERSPECTIVES

Nastech Pharmaceutical Company Inc. is an emerging pharmaceutical company dedicated to the development and commercialization of unique products to treat diseases in areas where our innovations will have the greatest impact on improving human health.

to deliver it. One of the medical researchers working in this field was Anwar A. Hussain, a professor of pharmaceuticals at the University of Kentucky Research Foundation. In March 1983 Nastech Pharmaceutical Company Inc. was incorporated in New York, and in June of that year it licensed seven patents from Hussain and the University of Kentucky Research Foundation for the nasal dosage of 21 pharmaceuticals.

Nastech's founders were Drs. Jeffrey Wenig and Martin J. Feldman, both of Long Island. Born and raised in New York City, Wenig earned a doctorate in pharmacology from New York University. He worked at a Long Island pharmaceutical, Endo Laboratories, before dabbling in politics. He made an unsuccessful bid to run for the New York State Assembly, then served on the pesticide board at Huntington, New York, before becoming the town's Environmental Protection Commissioner. He became Nastech's first chief executive officer. Feldman, a dentist born in Brooklyn, shared Wenig's interest in local politics, serving eight years in the Suffolk County Legislature. He was also an inveterate entrepreneur, although he never stopped practicing dentistry. During his undergraduate days in the 1950s, Feldman sold 78-rpm records, and after launching his dental practice in the 1960s managed a rock 'n' roll band, albeit with no success.

Nastech received funding from a dozen investors, many of them politicians recruited by Feldman. They paid 1/1,000th of a penny per share. Nastech then received FDA approval on five drugs to begin clinical testing on humans: a motion sickness medicine; an antinausea preparation; propranol, used to alleviate migraines and angina; Progesterine; and vitamin B-12. The company next went public in March 1984 at one penny a share and ground-floor shareholders began cashing out. Nastech's underwriter recommended that the company engage a public relations director, prompting Wenig to hire Michael Patterson, a former spokesperson for the Long Island Lighting Co. as well as a former press secretary to former New York Governor Hugh Carey. Patterson succeeded in interesting a wide swath of the media to take notice of Nastech, the only company solely dedicated to nasal delivery technology, which some of the larger pharmaceuticals were also actively pursuing. As a result, the company drummed up interest with investors, making the case that tiny Nastech was sitting on a gold mine. Articles appeared in magazines such as *Time, U.S. News & World Report, Fortune, Forbes,* and area newspapers, including Long Island's *Newsday,* the *New York Times,* and the *Daily News.* Wenig also made guest appearances on the Financial News Network and New York television stations.

Due in large measure to this attention, Nastech's stock increased to 48 cents a share, a major surge if you were an early backer who received one million shares for every ten dollars invested. According to filings with the Securities and Exchange Commission (SEC), between 1985 and 1988 Weinig sold more than 24 million shares, priced at two to 20 cents a share. In 1986 alone, Feldman sold 1.4 million shares at ten to 32 cents a share.

After the first three years of existence, Nastech had no products to sell and had lost $1 million, but Wenig continued to exude confidence. "We're certainly not years away from our first product," he told *Newsday* in 1986. "I think the potential rewards are mind-boggling. I have every hope we will be a much larger company." It was around this time that Feldman left the company. According to *Newsday,* "Friends of Dr. Feldman who insisted on anonymity said the founders had a falling out, largely because Dr. Feldman believed the stock was overly promoted and the two men had differing philosophies on how the company should proceed. An account executive of the F.S.G. Financial Services Group in Melville, Kirk Cronk, said, 'When Dr. Feldman left, a lot of people in his following also started selling, and that started to bring the stock down.'"

In the summer of 1988 Nastech agreed to sell $250,000 worth of B-12 gel doses for use in Pakistan, but it was no closer to gaining FDA approval to sell B-12 or any other drugs in the United States. The hype over the company faded, it was delisted from the NASDAQ because it could not meet minimum asset and equity requirements, and the stock was relegated to over-the-counter status. In an attempt to make the stock somewhat more appealing, Nastech engineered a 1-to-200 reverse stock split in January 1990, a move that raised the price to the 25 cent range.

COFOUNDERS' DEATHS IN 1991

As the 1990s opened, Nastech was just looking to hang on until it received FDA approval for a drug and could begin to bring in some much needed cash. Then, in the spring of 1991 it suffered a setback when Wenig died

KEY DATES

1983: The company is founded on Long Island.
1984: An initial public offering of stock is made.
1992: The first product is introduced.
1997: The second product is released.
2000: Atossa HealthCare, Inc. is acquired.
2002: Headquarters are moved to Bothell, Washington.

from a heart attack at the age of 54. Ironically, the 58-year-old Feldman had died of a heart attack the previous month. Wenig's son, just 25 years old, stepped in as chairman, while Senior Research Scientist Vincent Romeo took over as president and chief executive officer in August 1991. Romeo held a doctorate from St. John's University, where he taught pharmacology and remained on the faculty while heading Nastech.

Nastech's first product to receive FDA approval was Stadol, a migraine headache pain reliever, introduced in 1992 by Bristol-Myers Squibb, the company's licensee partner. At this stage in its history, Nastech licensed early stage products to marketing partners, who then invested their own money to finalize clinical trials. The partners also were required to assume the risk of regulatory approvals. The product generated sales of $15.9 million in the first year, resulting in royalties of $856,000 for Nastech. By keeping overhead low, the company was able to turn a profit of $208,000 in 1994 and another $119,000 in 1996, a year in which sales of Stadol reached $112.3 million.

In the autumn of 1996 Nastech introduced its second product, Nascobal, a vitamin B12 intranasal gel for vitamin B12 deficiency therapy. Schwarz Pharma served as a marketing partner for the product. At this stage the company changed its strategy, opting to now take the products in its pipeline to later stages of development. It was a riskier approach, requiring greater outlays of cash for research and development to the detriment of the balance sheet, but it also held out the possibility of greater long-term rewards. With no significant debt and more than $24 million in the bank, the company was well positioned to pursue this new strategy.

To ramp up its research and development effort, Nastech began constructing a new 28,000-square-foot research facility, which opened in 1999. The company was beginning to make progress in building a pipeline of new products when it suffered another setback. In May 2000, Romeo died at the age of 43, succumbing to leukemia, a disease he appeared to have overcome some nine years earlier. A three-person executive committee briefly took over at Nastech until an interim CEO could step in while the company looked for a permanent replacement. In August 2000 Nastech settled on its man, Dr. Steven C. Quay, who ran a one-person Seattle area company, Atossa HealthCare, Inc. Nastech acquired Atossa and Quay moved to Long Island to serve as Nastech's president, CEO, and chairman.

Quay was a well-respected research scientist and a seasoned executive. He was a graduate of the University of Michigan Medical School, where he received a master's and doctorate in Biological Chemistry in 1974 and 1975, followed by an M.D. in 1977. After postgraduate work at the Massachusetts Institute of Technology and a residency at the Massachusetts General Hospital, Harvard Medical School he became a faculty member at Stanford University School of Medicine. Even as he was teaching from 1980 to 1986, Quay began making a move to biotechnology. In 1984 he founded Salutar, Inc., which developed agents for magnetic resonance imaging, a field in which he would author more than 100 scientific papers. He received 24 patents in the field and also invented a pair of pharmaceuticals that gained FDA approval. Quay then founded Sonus Pharmaceuticals, Inc. in 1991 to expand the use of ultrasound testing technology. He served as chief executive until 1999, when he formed Atossa to develop women's health technologies, in particular a diagnostic test to assess the risk of breast cancer. It used a small pump to extract liquid through the nipple to test for the presence of cancer cells. It was while researching the mechanism for the pump that Quay first became aware of Nastech, whose nasal pumps relied on similar mechanics.

When Quay took charge of Nastech, he changed its approach, and soon moved its headquarters to Bothell, Washington, focusing on projects that offered high potential. "It's just as difficult to get a product through the FDA for a $50 million market as a billion-dollar market," he told *Newsday.* "You might as well grab for billion-dollar markets." According to *Newsday,* "Nastech has zeroed in on 10 compounds that can be given only by injection, that are generating more than a billion dollars each in annual revenue and that are marketed by at least two companies. Nastech's approach is to adapt a drug for nasal delivery and persuade one of the competing manufacturers to partner with Nastech for competitive reasons." The strategy worked, as Nastech was able to attract partners for three drugs. In February 2002 it reached a milestone agreement with Pharmacia Corp. to develop a Viagra-like product, using the drug apomorphine, that could be delivered by nose. The pump could be placed on a night table, where it could be used spontaneously, and by rapidly entering the bloodstream through nasal membranes could have the desired effect within 15 or 20 minutes.

MERCK DEVELOPMENT DEAL IN 2004

The sex-aid product and Quay's revamped business model caught the attention of investors, who gave Nastech a second look after having written off its chances 15 years earlier. It was still a highly speculative stock, one that investment managers were hesitant to buy for clients, but many were willing to buy it for themselves. They would become even more interested in 2004 when Nastech reached a deal with Merck & Co. to develop an experimental nasal spray treatment, PYY3-36 (PYY), for obesity. The *Wall Street Journal* estimated that the market of a successful product could be worth as much as $100 billion a year. One fund manager told the publication, "Obesity is like a lottery ticket, because if it really works and it's safe, it's off to the races."

Of course, there was no guarantee Nastech would develop a successful obesity drug, and in 2006 Merck was not satisfied with the early clinical results. Nastech disagreed, reacquired the rights to the drug, and elected to put its own money into the development of PYY. On other fronts in 2006, Nastech reached an agreement with Procter & Gamble Pharmaceuticals to commercialize a nasal spray treatment for osteoporosis, a deal that could garner Nastech significantly more than $500 million. Nastech also launched an RNAi therapeutics program to target influenza and respiratory diseases, an area bolstered by the acquisition of RNAi technology from Galenea Corp. of Cambridge, Massachusetts. RNAi, or RNA interference, is a method for turning off the production of a protein, which researchers hoped to use to ward off influenza or slow its spread. Not only was Nastech interested in developing therapies using the technology, RNAi could be used as a research tool in its study of "tight junctions," conduits for drug delivery between cells. Tight junction biology was of particular importance to Nastech because it involved the way nasal tissue worked.

Although Nastech lost $32.2 million in 2005 on sales of $7.4 million, most of that shortfall was due to a major increase in research and development spending, more than $30 million. The company still had nearly $60 million in the bank and appeared to be finally positioning itself for success after nearly a quarter-century of endeavor.

Ed Dinger

PRINCIPAL SUBSIDIARIES

Atossa HealthCare, Inc.

PRINCIPAL COMPETITORS

ALZA Corporation; Endo Pharmaceuticals Holding Inc.; Javelin Pharmaceuticals, Inc.

FURTHER READING

Baker, Isaac, "Somus Founder Quay Heads East," *Seattle Post-Intelligence* (Seattle, Wash.), August 12, 2000, p. B3.

Cooke, Tony, "Nastech Insiders Buy, Sell Shares After News of Obesity-Drug Deal," *Wall Street Journal,* October 13, 2004, p. C14.

Diamond, Stuart, "Medical Role for the Nose," *New York Times,* June 28, 1984, p. D2.

Marcial, Gene G., "Why Pros Have a Nose for Nastech," *Business Week,* June 10, 2002, p. 154.

Schreiber, Paul, "Nastech CEO Aiming for Nose with Drugs," *Newsday* (Long Island, N.Y.), March 12, 2002, p. A45.

Steinberg, Carol, "Ballyhoo on Nasal Drugs Meets Reality," *New York Times,* October 27, 1991, p. A1.

Wax, Alan J., "No Sales, No Profits, But 12 Rich Investors," *Newsday* (Long Island, N.Y.), April 14, 1986, p. O1.

———, "This Dentist Is Drilling for Gold," *Newsday* (Long Island, N.Y.), August 1, 1988, p. O1.

National Geographic Society

1145 17th Street NW
Washington, D.C. 20036-4688
U.S.A.
Telephone: (202) 857-7000
Toll Free: (800) 647-5463
Fax: (202) 775-6141
Web site: http://www.nationalgeographic.com

Nonprofit Organization
Incorporated: 1888
Employees: 1,400
Sales: $100 million (2005 est.)
NAIC: 511120 Periodical Publishers

Founded as a club of distinguished gentlemen devoted to promoting the study of geography, the National Geographic Society ranks among the largest nonprofit and educational organizations in the world. It is the publisher of one of the world's most widely circulated magazines, *National Geographic,* as well as *National Geographic Traveler* and *National Geographic Adventure.* National Geographic is also involved in book publishing, education, public service projects, and television production, though its flagship magazine remains its crowning achievement. Thanks in large part to the efforts of three generations of the Grosvenor family, *National Geographic* has become a staple of American mass culture. The Society's trustees have included such notables as Supreme Court Chief Justice Warren Burger, Lady Bird Johnson, Air Force General Curtis LeMay, astronaut Frank Borman, and businessman J. Willard Marriott, Jr. Having embraced new media and new techniques in publishing, the Society brought the far corners of the world to the doorsteps of millions of Americans. Frank Luther Mott, a journalism historian, observed that *National Geographic* has compiled "a fabulous record of success, especially since the magazine is founded on an editorial conviction that rates the intelligence of the popular audience fairly high." In the 21st century the National Geographic Society sought to build brand loyalty among international and more youthful audiences.

EMINENT ORIGINS

The National Geographic Society was founded in January 1888 in Washington, D.C., by a group of eminent citizens who wanted to promote geographic research and the popular distribution of the results of such research. The charter members of the Society included Alexander Graham Bell; Bell's father-in-law, lawyer Gardiner Greene Hubbard; explorers John Wesley Powell and A. W. Greeley; and scholar George Kennan, uncle of future ambassador to the Soviet Union George F. Kennan. Hubbard was one of Bell's early financial backers and had served as the first president of the Bell Telephone Company, the forerunner of AT&T. He was elected to serve as the Society's first president.

The first issue of *National Geographic* appeared in October and was sent to 200 charter members. It was published intermittently until January 1896, when monthly publication began. The early magazine bore little resemblance to the readable, eye-catching *National*

COMPANY PERSPECTIVES

After more than a century the National Geographic Society today is propelled by new concerns: the alarming lack of geographic knowledge among our nation's young people and the pressing need to protect the planet's natural resources. As our mission grows in urgency and scope, the Society continues to develop new and exciting vehicles for broadening our reach and enhancing our legendary ability to bring the world to our millions of members.

Geographic of later years. Its articles were written in a dry, academic style and bore titles such as "Geographic Methods in Geologic Investigation" and "The Classification of Geographic Forms by Genesis," and there were no illustrations. It is not surprising, then, that circulation remained limited, with less than 1,000 subscribers and negligible newsstand sales.

Gardiner Greene Hubbard died in 1897 and was succeeded as president by his famous son-in-law. When Alexander Graham Bell took the helm, he found the National Geographic Society in a precarious financial state, largely because its magazine had failed to provide a strong revenue base. He soon realized that *National Geographic* needed two things: a change in editorial policy that would make it a popular scientific magazine rather than a scholarly journal, and a full-time editor who would manifest the changes he sought. Bell hoped to fill both needs in 1899 when he wrote to his friend, historian Edwin Grosvenor of Amherst College, to ask if either of Grosvenor's sons might be interested in assuming editorship. Gilbert H. Grosvenor, then a 23-year-old prep school teacher in New Jersey, accepted.

Having grown up in Istanbul while his father researched his two-volume history of the Turkish capital, Gilbert Grosvenor had become fascinated with foreign lands and peoples at an early age, but he later confessed that he was also drawn to the job by his desire to be near Bell's daughter Elsie, whom he later married.

Grosvenor proved to be the catalyst behind the immensely successful popularization of the magazine. After studying such classic examples of travel writing as Darwin's *Voyage of the Beagle* and Charles Dana's *Two Year's Before the Mast,* Grosvenor concluded that *National Geographic* articles could be made more readable without sacrificing their educational value. Grosvenor then mandated some stylistic changes for the magazine, including eliminating academic jargon, keeping sentences short and punchy, and replacing scholarly formality and detachment with engaging first-person narrative.

Grosvenor also introduced photographs into the magazine, a step that would gain *National Geographic* more recognition than its newly accessible style. He knew well the impact that photographs would have; his father's history of Istanbul, published in 1895, was the first scholarly book published in the United States to make extensive use of photoengravings. Though some critics considered it vulgar to run photos in an academic work, the book sold well. Gilbert Grosvenor encountered much opposition from more conservative trustees of the National Geographic Society when the changes that he wished to make became known. He had, however, the firm backing of Alexander Graham Bell, which afforded him the time to prove the editorial merits of his innovations. Skyrocketing circulation (by 1906 the magazine could boast of 11,000 regular subscribers) confirmed his abilities.

Opposition from within the Society's board softened, too. In one incident in December 1904, Grosvenor faced a challenge when the next month's issue was about to go to press with 11 pages blank for want of copy. In that day's mail, however, he found an unsolicited packet containing the first photographs ever taken of the Tibetan capital of Lhasa. Awed by the photos and desperate for material, he used them to fill the blank pages. He later wrote that he expected to be fired for running an 11-page pictorial spread, but several days after the issue appeared, he was elected a trustee of the Society. Grosvenor ran *National Geographic*'s first color photos in 1910. The magazine remains a pioneer in the journalistic use of photography.

Alexander Graham Bell retired as president of the National Geographic Society in 1903, although he remained a contributor to the magazine and an influential member of the organization until his death in 1922. He was succeeded by a series of short-term chief executives: W. J. McGee served briefly, followed by Grove Karl Gilbert. Willis Moore served from 1905 to 1909. Henry Gannett, a charter member and chief geographer of the U.S. Geological Survey, succeeded Moore and served until his death in 1914. Gannett was succeeded by O. H. Tittman, who resigned in 1919. He was followed by John E. Pillsbury, who served less than a year before his death in December 1919. In 1920 the entire National Geographic Society and its expanding operations became Gilbert Grosvenor's responsibility when he succeeded John Pillsbury as president. Grosvenor remained editor of the magazine, which continued the readable, relatively upbeat style that he had created.

In these early years the Society began its sponsorship of high-profile exploratory, archaeological, and

KEY DATES

1888: First issue of National Geographic is sent to 200 charter members.
1898: Alexander Graham Bell succeeds his father-in-law as president.
1905: Eleven-page photo spread earns editor Gilbert H. Grosvenor unexpected praise.
1909: Organization supports Peary exhibition to North Pole.
1920: Grosvenor is named president, a position he holds for more than 30 years.
1930: National Geographic circulation reaches 1.2 million.
1941: Organization aids war effort by granting government access to photos and cartographic data.
1956: First undersea article by Jacques-Yves Cousteau is published.
1965: Melville Bell Grosvenor leads the Geographic to its first television special.
1970: Gilbert M. Grosvenor changes tone of National Geographic.
1985: National Geographic Explorer deal boosts television operations.
1995: "Local language" versions of magazine are introduced; National Geographic Television becomes separate, taxable unit.
1999: National Geographic Adventure magazine premieres.
2001: The Society adds a new purpose: to encourage better stewardship of the planet.
2005: Hurricane Katrina special issue reaches newsstands in record time.

naturalistic expeditions. In 1906 it contributed $1,000 to the Arctic expedition led by Commander Robert E. Peary, with whom the Society had a longstanding professional relationship. In 1909 Peary became the first documented explorer to reach the North Pole. (Years later, in 2000, the National Geographic Society posthumously awarded African-American Matthew Henson its highest honor, the Hubbard Medal, for accompanying Peary on the landmark expedition to the North Pole.) Another of the Society's early successes was Yale archaeologist Hiram Bingham's 1912 expedition to Peru, during which the Inca capital of Macchu Picchu was excavated.

As president of the Society, Grosvenor continued its sponsorship of extraordinary expeditions. The Society provided financial support for Commander Richard E. Byrd's various Arctic and Antarctic voyages between 1925 and 1930, during which he became the first person to fly to the North and South Poles. Byrd was aided by a special compass designed by Albert Bumstead, the Society's chief cartographer, which used the sun for navigation, since magnetic compasses would not work at the poles. In 1935 the Society and the U.S. Army Air Corps co-sponsored *Explorer II,* a helium balloon that set an altitude record for an occupied balloon that stood until the dawn of the Space Age. In 1939 the Society and the Smithsonian Institution co-sponsored an expedition to southern Mexico during which archaeologist Matthew Sterling uncovered a Mayan stela, an inscribed tablet, that was the oldest known human artifact from the New World.

National Geographic reached the mass readership that its founders had sought, with a circulation of 500,000 at the end of World War I, and the Society continued to expand its activities. In 1922, after receiving a request for geographical information from the National Education Association, the Society launched a weekly publication designed for classroom use, *Geographic School Bulletins.*

During World War II, the Society opened its photographic and cartographic archives to the U.S. military. Its vast library of photographs of foreign countries provided intelligence about infrastructure in enemy-held territory and also helped unveil camouflage when compared with the military's own reconnaissance photographs. The Society's maps of distant lands, which it had been accumulating since creating its own cartographic department in 1916, also proved valuable. After the war, the Society received a grateful letter from Fleet Admiral Chester Nimitz, one of the war's heroes, who reported that a National Geographic map of the South Pacific saved him considerable difficulty in 1942 when the crew members of the B-17 in which he was flying used it to get back on course after losing their bearings in a storm near Guadalcanal. Further, President Franklin Roosevelt asked the Society for a map, and was so impressed with the encased set that was given him that he later asked for and received a similar set to give to Prime Minister Winston Churchill. Churchill was so pleased with his maps that after the war, when the Society asked him to return the original set for a new and updated set in order to place the originals in the Society's museum, Churchill politely refused.

THE SPACE AGE

After the war, with so much of the Earth's land mass already explored and mapped, the Society turned part of its attention to the last remaining frontier: outer space. It co-sponsored with the California Institute of Technology the ambitious Sky Survey, which would produce the Sky Atlas, the first comprehensive photographic map of the heavens. Work on the Sky Survey began in 1949 and was completed in 1956, using the 48-inch "Big Schmidt" telescope at Palomar Observatory in California.

Almost concurrently, the Society also began its long and successful association with marine explorer Jacques-Yves Cousteau. The Society sponsored a number of Cousteau expeditions in the 1950s, including the 1956 dive during which he took photographs of the Romanche Trench in the Atlantic Ocean, the deepest point at which photographs had ever been taken. During another National Geographic-sponsored expedition in the mid-1950s, Cousteau shot footage for his Oscar-winning documentary *The Silent World.*

Gilbert Grosvenor retired in 1954 after 34 years as president of the National Geographic Society and 55 years as editor of *National Geographic.* He then became chairman of the Society and was succeeded in his former positions by his old friend and longtime assistant editor, John Oliver La Gorce. La Gorce served for three years, then retired and became vice-chairman of the Society. He was succeeded by Grosvenor's son, Melville Bell Grosvenor. Although his father remained the unquestioned sage of the board of directors, the title of CEO was given to the younger Grosvenor.

As editor of *National Geographic,* Melville Bell Grosvenor expanded the magazine's use of color photography, which regularly appeared on the cover beginning in 1959. As CEO of the National Geographic Society, he expanded the Society's book publishing operations and also led it into the increasingly ubiquitous medium of television. Film shot by National Geographic photographers had appeared on television since 1955, but always on network programs. Then, in 1958, Grosvenor and longtime staffer Luis Marden decided to produce the Society's own television programs. Three years later, the Society formed its documentary film department. The first Society-produced television special, "Americans on Everest," aired on CBS in 1965.

Gilbert H. Grosvenor died in 1966, and the next year his son retired and became chairman of the Society. In 1970, Gilbert M. Grosvenor, Melville's son, assumed the leadership position at *National Geographic.* He had joined the staff straight from Yale after winning the National Press Photographers Award for coverage of President Eisenhower's tour of Asia in 1951. Before long, Grosvenor became the center of controversy by enacting a subtle shift in *National Geographic's* editorial policy, easing it away from the uniformly upbeat tone and avoidance of sensitive topics that his father and grandfather had maintained. Under Gilbert M. Grosvenor, the magazine ran major stories on racial turmoil in South Africa, communism in Cuba, and social conditions in Harlem. Although the board of trustees publicly endorsed Grosvenor's editorship, some directors of the Society were scandalized, and conservative media critics accused *National Geographic* of contracting "a bad case of radical chic." Grosvenor became president of the Society in 1980, leaving the post of editor to his longtime assistant Wilbur Garrett.

Grosvenor took charge of an organization that was, in some ways, the envy of the publishing industry. In 1980 *National Geographic* boasted 10.7 million subscribers and a circulation of well over 30 million. That year, the Society announced a profit of $3 million on revenues of $217 million, yet the Society continued to refer to its annual profit as a "surplus" and its subscribers as "members," genteel terms used by nonprofit organizations. The Society retained its not-for-profit status and accompanying tax exemptions even though it published one of the bestselling magazines in the world and ran successful book publishing and television production operations. When the Society erected a new headquarters building in Washington, D.C., in 1981 at a cost of $30 million, it paid in cash.

The 1980s would not prove entirely kind to the Society, however. It fielded much criticism for a 1981 cover in which two Egyptian pyramids were digitally manipulated to appear closer together, a technique it promptly abandoned. Circulation figures and advertising revenues from *National Geographic* remained flat throughout most of the decade. Slowdowns in the economy and increased competition from other popular science magazines presented the greatest threat of decrease in readership since the Great Depression. The Society's television operations received a boost in 1985 when it signed an agreement with cable station WTBS to produce a weekly documentary series, *National Geographic Explorer.*

Gilbert Grosvenor had always focused on emerging technologies that could affect the Society's long-term future. In 1981 he speculated openly about the possibility of putting *National Geographic* and publishing books on video. In 1990 the Society published a multimedia software package called "GTV" in collaboration with Lucasfilm and Apple Computer. "GTV" was designed for use in middle schools and provided interactive lessons in U.S. history. Moreover, the Society was publishing its own catalog of merchandise and exploring the possibility of cooperative ventures, particularly with the catalog and retail firm The Nature Company, hoping to use merchandising as a new source of revenues.

NEW HORIZONS FOR THE NEXT CENTURY

By the mid-1990s, the Society had sold more than four million home videos. Its for-profit subsidiary, National Geographic Ventures, was producing educational materials in a variety of formats, including a Disney Channel television program called *Really Wild Animals.* The group was planning to air the National Geographic Channel on cable and satellite in cooperation with NBC. It also ran the Society's web site and online store, and had established theaters and exhibits at national parks.

One plan to issue *National Geographic's* entire back catalog on CD-ROM drew criticism from authors' rights groups, however, since no additional royalties were to be paid to writers and photographers for reuse of the work. The set, released on 30 CD-ROMs, retailed for $199.

Upon the retirement of Gilbert M. Grosvenor, Reg Murphy, formerly editor or publisher of the *Baltimore Sun, San Francisco Examiner,* and *Atlanta Constitution,* moved up to president and CEO of the Society in May 1996. Also during this time, in January 1994, Bill Allen became only the eighth editor in *National Geographic* magazine's history.

The Society began placing *National Geographic* on newsstands in 1998, breaking a century of its "members only" tradition. The group had actually tested some issues at the newsstand previously, and had recorded good sales figures in foreign retail outlets. Single-copy sales were expected to account for only a small fraction of total sales. The flagship's sister publication, *National Geographic Traveler,* introduced in 1984, had been sold at newsstands for seven years.

National Geographic Adventure, the Society's answer to *Outside* magazine, the leader in the burgeoning adventure travel category, debuted in April 1999. Initially a quarterly, *Adventure* was expected to be produced monthly by 2001. John Rasmus was the first editor at *Adventure*; he had previously held that position at *Outside* and *Men's Journal.*

As the National Geographic Society entered the 21st century, it boasted three magazines, programs for television and home video, an expanded web site, and two freestanding retail stores in Washington, D.C. Under development were new cable and international television channels and a new magazine. The Society was also seeking partners to capitalize upon the *National Geographic* brand name via toys, software, and other consumer goods. The Society's magazines were selling record levels of advertising and "local language" versions, begun in 1995, surpassed expectations abroad. The Society commemorated the millennium with a seven-part series on global issues.

As the world leaders continued to debate over the state of the global environment into the new millennium, the National Geographic Society added stewardship of the planet to its list of purposes in January 2001. Later in the year the organization added a new grant-making body, National Geographic Conservation Trust, to support conservation activities around the world.

In a different realm, the National Geographic Channel launched in January 2001 to about ten million U.S. homes. The operation had more than 12 million feet or 25,000 hours of material cached in its film and video collection dating back to 1965, according to *Electronic Media.* National Geographic Television had already engaged a digital asset management company to improve accessibility of material, both internally and for sale to outside users such as ad agencies.

The U.S. Supreme Court refused to hear National Geographic's appeal to overturn an appellate court decision in regard to digitalization of photographs, in October 2001. In a different case, the court had ruled in favor of freelance writers seeking intellectual property rights (Tasini v. the New York Times Company). Although the claim against National Geographic involved just one photographer while the writers' suit was class-action, common to both cases was the issue of compensation for dissemination of previously published information through new technologies.

The *National Geographic* put a name to a familiar face in March 2002. The organization located the "Afghan Girl," Sharbat Gula, seen on its most recognized magazine cover. While the National Geographic Society's own name recognition was enviable, translating the asset into new arenas was proving challenging. Audience awareness of National Geographic as a network unto itself needed work.

"When we ask viewers, 'Do you watch National Geographic?' they say, 'Oh sure, I watch it all the time ... on Discovery,'" Steve Schiffman, executive vice-president of marketing for National Geographic Channel told *Television Week* in 2003. "We get that a lot."

The three-year-old network had 50 million subscribers, but television specials and MSNBC's *National Geographic Explorer* were more generally known. Reality series *Worlds Apart,* which followed American families living with indigenous tribes, was one effort to increase network awareness.

Two-thirds owned by Fox, the challenge was to create buzz for the network without diluting the strong brand name. The National Geographic Society mitigated the potential problem through equal say in programming, marketing, and general operation decisions.

Through 2003, National Geographic Television & Film's new programming areas had produced mixed results. Mainstream feature films produced with partners produced tepid box office returns. Large format Imax films, with an inherently longer life span, were more successful endeavors. Programming for children was just getting off the ground.

"The whole point of an institution like Geographic is we want to have a voice," Tim Kelly, president and CEO of NGT&F told *Television Business International* in 2004. "People under 40 don't watch a lot of documentaries even if we enhance them with a lot of other elements. The entertainment genre is a way to reach those people, still with Geographic stories that are mission oriented."

In May 2004, the National Geographic Society added another dimension to its revenue stream with the introduction of the National Geographic Home Collection of Furniture. Consumer goods and programming revenue funded fieldwork of scientists and explorers, which in turn fed new programming and merchandise ideas.

In its signature *National Geographic*, 18 percent was devoted to advertising, well below the roughly 50-50 split in the U.S. magazine industry. But core advertiser camera maker Canon had spent $50 million on ads over 23 years, Lucy Aitken reported for *Campaign* in June 2004.

The society's mix of new media opened the door for the organization, and advertisers, to get their messages across in a variety of Geographic formats. The wholly owned and taxable subsidiary National Geographic Ventures handled content dissemination through means ranging from home video and DVD to international television to digital archives.

National Geographic gained a new editor-in-chief, Chris Johns, in January 2005. He began putting his mark on the title early in his tenure. The first edition completely under his leadership encompassed two Geographic rarities: a single topic and a cover sans photo. Then the magazine, with a normal lead time of about six months, hit the newsstands with an issue on Hurricane Katrina just weeks after the Gulf Coast disaster. "The special issue is meant to convey that the magazine can be nimble and relevant. 'We're tightening our monthly publication schedule constantly and becoming more agile,'" Johns told the *New York Times* in September 2005.

Meanwhile, the National Geographic Channel seemed to have made significant strides in making itself relevant to the 21st-century audience. In its fifth year, the channel was on top of the heap in terms of ratings growth among all U.S. broadcast and cable networks, according to a January 2006 *Adweek* article.

On the international front, the launch of a Slovenian edition of the *National Geographic* was planned for April 2006. Already printed in nearly 30 languages, the magazine was also seeking out a younger audience. The average Eastern European subscriber was about 30 years of age, while in the United States the average readers were about 20 years old, according to the *International Herald Tribune*. Typically produced under licensing agreements, the Geographic's foreign publishing partners also had begun mixing more local interest articles with American-produced content. The National Geographic Society had in some aspects transitioned from bringing the world to Americans, to bringing Americans to the world.

Douglas Sun
Updated, Frederick C. Ingram; Kathleen Peippo

PRINCIPAL SUBSIDIARIES

National Geographic Ventures.

PRINCIPAL COMPETITORS

Discovery Communications, Inc.; Rand McNally & Company; Time Inc.

FURTHER READING

Adams, Mark, "Geographic Shifts," *Mediaweek*, June 26, 1995, p. 18.

Aitken, Lucy, "National Geographic Finances Its Mission with Media Profits," *Campaign*, June 18, 2004.

Behr, Peter, "Geographic: The Wealth of Knowledge," *Washington Post*, December 7, 1981.

Brown, DeNeen L., "Picture This: Geographic's Africa Cover," *Washington Post*, August 18, 2005, p. C1.

Conaway, James, "The Geographic's Founding Family," *Washington Post*, December 19, 1984.

Friedman, Wayne, "National Geo Ready to Spin Brand into Gold," *Television Week*, October 20, 2003, p.15.

Granatstein, Lisa, "Looking for *Adventure*," *Mediaweek*, July 20, 1998, pp. 17-18.

Gremillion, Jeff, and Lisa Granatstein, "2000: A Space Odyssey," *Mediaweek*, February 2, 1998, p. 14.

Grosvenor, Gilbert H., *The National Geographic Society and Its Magazine*, Washington, D.C.: National Geographic Society, 1957.

Hays, Constance L., "Seeing Green in a Yellow Border," *New York Times*, August 3, 1997, Sec. 3.

Kerwin, Ann Marie, "Two New Titles Join Ranks of Adventure Travel Books," *Advertising Age*, March 8, 1999, p. 22.

"A Legacy Brand Expands: National Geographic Moves Borders to Four Corners of Media," *Adweek*, January 9, 2006, pp. S6+.

"National Geographic and Fox Cable: An Unlikely Match That Makes Uncommon Sense," *Adweek*, January 9, 2006, pp. S8+.

"National Geographic Ventures Announces Reorganization of Business Units," *Business Wire*, February 16, 2005.

"National Pride," *Television Buisness International*, May 1, 2004.

"NGC President, Role Model, World Series Champion: Laureen Ong Celebrates Five Years at the Reins," *Adweek*, January 9, 2006, p. S4.

Pfanner, Eric, "National Geographic Travels Far and Speaks in Many Tongues," *International Herald Tribune*, March 20, 2006.

Quint, Barbara, "A Second Tasini? National Geographic Loses to Freelance Photographers," *Information Today*, December 2001, p. 52.

Ringle, Ken, "Around the World in 25 Years," *Washington Post*, February 4, 1990.

Sawyer, Kathy, "Change at the Geographic," *Washington Post*, July 17, 1977.

Seelye, Katharine Q., "National Geographic, Known As Old and Venerated, Tries Fast and Hard-Hitting," *New York Times*, September 19, 2005, p. C6.

Trueheart, Charles, "Garrett, Grosvenor and the Great Divide," *Washington Post*, May 7, 1990.

Whitney, Daisy, "Geographic Opens Vaults," *Electronic Media*, October 22, 2001, p. 13.

National Medical Health Card Systems, Inc.

26 Harbor Park Drive
Port Washington, New York 11050
U.S.A.
Telephone: (516) 626-0007
Toll Free: (800) 251-3883
Fax: (516) 605-6981
Web site: http://www.nmhc.com

Public Company
Incorporated: 1981
Employees: 484
Sales: $800.5 million (2005)
Stock Exchanges: NASDAQ
Ticker Symbol: NMHC
NAIC: 524210 Insurance Agencies and Brokerages

■ ■ ■

National Medical Health Card Systems, Inc. helps institutional customers control costs related to the prescription drug coverage they offer their employees or members. National Medical offers its services to health maintenance organizations, corporations, unions, school districts, local government agencies, and employer groups. The company provides a full range of services to its customers, including pharmacy benefits management, health information management, home delivery pharmacy, and specialty pharmacy services. National Medical, through the plans offered by its customers, serves nearly nine million individuals. The company maintains service centers in Latham, New York; Little Rock, Arkansas; Dallas, Texas; and Sacramento, California. The company's home delivery facility is located in Miramar, Florida, and its specialty pharmacy is located in Portland, Maine.

ORIGINS

National Medical was not the first company started by Bert E. Brodsky, nor was it the last expression of his entrepreneurial talents. Once a top sales agent for Union Mutual Life Insurance, Brodsky began forming his own companies in 1970, more than a decade before he founded National Medical. His first company was named Medical Arts Services, Inc., a business formed to manage medical practices for hospital-based physicians, specifically anesthesiologists, who typically had no need to occupy their own offices and, consequently, welcomed assistance in bookkeeping. In 1973, Brodsky added software capabilities to the company's repertoire, making Medical Arts the first firm to offer computer-automated billing in its industry niche. In 1977, he sold the company to San Francisco-based Itel Corp., a claims processing company, gaining $3 million from the transaction. With the cash in hand, Brodsky began to demonstrate his penchant for starting his own companies, a predilection that soon led to the formation of National Medical. "Now I had the cash where I could do things," he said in an August 6, 2001 interview posted on the web site of E-Data Corp., one of numerous ventures Brodsky was involved with during the early 21st century.

Brodsky had capital and he also had the data center Medical Arts used to process claims. The assets were used to start Sandata, Inc. in 1978, a healthcare billing

COMPANY PERSPECTIVES

The focus of NMHC's Total Healthcare Solutions is on outcomes—better health outcomes for members and better cost outcomes for plan sponsors. This unique approach is based on our ability to access and analyze a rich set of pharmacy and medical claims data across the entire health plan. With this information and intelligence in hand, we can predict member health outcomes based on claims history and benchmarks, communicate with physicians, pharmacists and patients, and help intervene with improved care and cost-controlling strategies.

firm that later became one of the country's leading providers of advanced computer, telephony, and Internet-based technologies for the industry. Next, in 1981, he started National Medical, a company that would share resources with Sandata throughout its existence. In later years, Brodsky continued to form companies, launching Identification Data & Imaging; Mobile Health Management Services, Inc.; Brookhaven Magnetic Resonance Imaging, Inc.; several real estate holding companies; and a restaurant, Island Mermaid Inn, located on New York's Fire Island. "If the opportunity arises and it makes sense, I'm there," he said in a November 7, 2003 interview with *Long Island Business News*. Brodsky typified what the business press liked to refer to as a "serial entrepreneur."

National Medical began as a locally oriented enterprise. Brodsky started the company to provide automated processing services for prescription drug claims, setting his sights on customers in the greater Long Island, New York, area. Toward this end, he secured a valuable customer early on, signing ChoiceCare Long Island, Inc., later to become Vytra Health Plans Long Island, Inc. For years to come, Vytra Health would account for a substantial portion of National Health's business, sustaining the company during its first years in business and contributing more than 40 percent to its revenue total throughout the 1990s.

National Medical gradually expanded its services and its geographic reach, demonstrating a more conservative approach to expansion than it would after its first 15 years of business. The change in the company's demeanor was attributable, in part, to changing conditions in the company's market. National Medical developed into what was known as a prescription benefits management company, or PBM. Brodsky expanded upon the company's initial service offering, automated processing services for prescriptions, and fashioned National Medical into a full-service PBM: a company that helped its customers control costs related to prescription drug coverage by offering a host of services, including claims management; a pharmacy network; benefit design consultation; drug review and analysis; disease information services; and physician profiling. National Medical helped its customers save money, serving health maintenance organizations, corporations, local governments, unions, and other third-party administrators of prescription drug programs. The need for such services began increasing when healthcare costs began to escalate, becoming an issue of great concern during the 1990s and creating fertile ground for a company of National Medical's ilk to grow.

During the years when National Medical gradually developed into a full-service PBM, Brodsky took an active role in running the company on an occasional basis. Serving stints as the company's chairman and president, Brodsky did not occupy the posts on a long-term basis until 1998, several years after the company reached a turning point in its development. In 1995, the company decided to ramp up its efforts directed toward growth, articulating for the first time its desire to become a leading national PBM services provider. The proclamation set the company in motion, as new executives were hired, a national marketing program was begun, and information systems capabilities were enhanced. When the announcement was made, National Medical was a $45 million-in-sales company whose services were provided to approximately 230,000 individuals, figures that would increase substantially as the movement toward expansion gained momentum.

ACQUISITION CAMPAIGN BEGUN AFTER 1999 PUBLIC OFFERING

Another turning point in National Medical's development occurred at the end of the 1990s. Brodsky was firmly in charge by that time, having assumed the post of president in June 1998 and adding the title of chairman at the end of the year. His first major project was taking the company public. In early 1999, the company filed with the Securities and Exchange Commission (SEC) for a public offering, hoping to raise $15.7 million to enhance marketing efforts, update equipment, and, the most important reason for the initial public offering (IPO), to fund future acquisitions. "We are in an expansion mode and want to increase our capital," Brodsky explained in a February 26, 1999 interview with the *Long Island Business News*. "We have targeted several companies," he added. By the time the company completed its IPO in mid-1999, the number of

KEY DATES

1981: Bert Brodsky forms National Medical Health Card Systems.
1995: Brodsky and his managers decide to turn National Medical into a national, full-service pharmacy benefits management company.
1999: National Medical completes its initial public offering of stock.
2002: National Medical acquires Health Solutions Ltd.'s Centrus division, nearly doubling its size.
2004: Brodsky sells his majority interest in National Medical.
2005: National Medical acquires Pharmaceutical Care Network.

individuals it served had increased more than 90 percent, to 430,000. Sales, after a 40 percent increase in 1998, reached $100 million. The number of participating pharmacies comprising the company's network had increased to 42,000. The gains achieved since 1995 were substantial, but from 1999 forward acquisitions would accelerate National Medical's pace of growth, extending its geographic reach and increasing the ranks of those receiving its services.

As National Medical entered the 21st century, Brodsky led the company's acquisition campaign. He began targeting other PBMs, beginning with the purchase of two companies. The smaller of the two acquisitions was Provider Medical Pharmaceutical, a Tulsa, Oklahoma-based PBM with 90,000 participants covered by its prescription drug plan. The second acquisition was Pharmacy Associates Inc., a Little Rock, Arkansas-based PBM with 200,000 members. These two acquisitions, though meaningful, paled in size to the purchase made by Brodsky soon after the deals were completed.

Escalating healthcare costs underscored the need for the services offered by National Medical, stoking demand in the PBM market. The increase in market demand spurred consolidation within the industry, as PBMs began acquiring one another in an effort to seize control of new business. "This is clearly a game of scale," an analyst remarked in a July 1, 2002 interview with *Investor's Business Daily.* "The bigger you are, the more leverage you have." Brodsky understood the nature of the game, as demonstrated by a landmark acquisition he completed in early 2002. National Medical's third acquisition was the 14-year-old PBM division belonging to Health Solutions Ltd. Known as Centrus, the division generated $272 million in revenue in 2001, doubling National Medical's revenue volume. The addition of Centrus also nearly doubled National Medical's membership count, lifting it to 2.5 million. The total was far less than the membership counts of the industry's leaders, companies including AdvancePCS, Caremark Rx Inc., and Express Scripts Inc., who managed prescription benefit plans covering tens of millions of individuals, but the acquisition did much to elevate National Medical's stature.

As the company worked to integrate Centrus into its operations, it also adjusted to a change in leadership. In April 2002, Brodsky relinquished his responsibilities as chief executive officer, handing the duties to James Bigl, who had been serving as National Medical's president for the previous two years. Bigl, with nearly two decades of experience in the healthcare industry, continued the expansion campaign started by Brodsky, who stayed on to serve as the company's chairman. Before the end of 2002 another acquisition was completed, the purchase of Wellpartner Inc., a mail-order pharmacy based in Portland, Oregon. Founded in 1988, Wellpartner took prescription orders online, by telephone, and by fax, and delivered the orders to the customer's home. The acquisition marked the completion of the first step toward expanding the company's home-delivery business, following through on a plan announced earlier in the year.

BRODSKY ERA ENDING IN 2004

Fueled largely by acquisitions, National Medical's financial growth during the five years following its IPO was impressive. By the end of 2003, revenues reached $573 million, a more than fivefold increase in five years. By the end of the following year, National Medical had recorded nine consecutive years of double-digit sales gains, an enviable record that represented the legacy left by Brodsky. In March 2004, he and his family sold their majority interest in the company, selling their shares to New Mountain Capital, a private equity investment firm. The transaction, deemed a "seminal event" by Bigl, as quoted in the June 10, 2004 issue of *Investor's Business Daily,* provided a cash infusion of $80 million. The company used some of the money to acquire Inteq Group in June 2004, paying $31.5 million for the Dallas, Texas-based PBM.

In the management shuffle that occurred after Brodsky's departure, National Medical leadership for the future was established. Bigl was elected to the chairman's office, while James Smith, previously senior vice-president of healthcare services and government relations at CVS Corporation, was hired as president and chief executive officer. Under the leadership of Bigl and Smith, National Medical continued to expand through acquisitions, a strategy that was expected to be employed in the coming years. The first purchase completed with the team of Bigl and Smith at the helm occurred in March 2005. National Medical acquired Sacramento, California-based Pharmaceutical Care Network, which managed pharmacy benefits principally for California's Medicaid sector. Pharmaceutical Care was founded in 1984 as a subsidiary of the California Pharmacists Association. The $13 million deal, which increased National Medical's membership count to roughly nine million, offered tangible gains to the company. "We gain a West Coast presence and it's important for us to have a national footprint for all of our clients," a National Medical senior executive explained in the March 12, 2005 edition of the *Sacramento Bee.* "The addition of 1.3 million will give us more clout, more buying power, and more strength." In the years ahead, the company was expected to continue increasing its leverage and extending its geographic reach, endeavoring to join the industry's elite and rank as one of the country's largest PBMs.

Jeffrey L. Covell

PRINCIPAL SUBSIDIARIES

PBM Technology, Inc.; Interchange PMP, Inc.; Pharmacy Associates, Inc.; Specialty Pharmacy Care, Inc.; Centrus Corporation; NMHCRX Contracts, Inc.; NMHC Funding, LLC; National Medical Health Card IPA, Inc.; NMHCRX, Inc.; NMHCRX Mail Order, Inc.; Integrail Inc.; Ascend Specialty Pharmacy Services, Inc.; Portland Professional Pharmacy; Portland Professional Pharmacy Associates; Inteq PBM, L.P.; Inteq Corp.; Inteq TX Corp.; Pharmaceutical Care Network; PCN DE Corp.

PRINCIPAL COMPETITORS

Express Scripts, Inc.; Caremark Rx, Inc.; Medco Health Solutions, Inc.

FURTHER READING

Alva, Marilyn, "National Medical Health Card Systems Inc.," *Investor's Business Daily,* July 1, 2002, p. A10.

———, "National Medical Health Card Systems Inc.," *Investor's Business Daily,* June 10, 2004, p. A8.

Furfaro, Danielle T., "Port Washington, N.Y.-Based Pharmacy Benefits Management Firm Expands," *Times Union,* January 30, 2002.

Le, Thuy-Doan, "New York Firm Acquires PCN," *Sacramento Bee,* March 12, 2005.

"National Med Health Card Buying Mail-Order Pharmacy," *Long Island Business News,* August 23, 2002, p. 9A.

"National Medical Health Card Systems Inc.," *Crain's New York Business,* September 20, 2004, p. 31.

Pedone, Rose-Robin, "Health Card Company Readies Public Offering," *Long Island Business News,* February 26, 1999, p. 1A.

Solnik, Claude, "Brodsky Family to Sell Stock in National Medical Health Card Systems," *Long Island Business News,* November 7, 2003.

NCL Corporation

Norwegian Cruise Line
7665 Corporate Center Drive
Miami, Florida 33126
U.S.A.
Telephone: (305) 436-086
Fax: (305) 436-4000
Web site: http://www.ncl.com

Wholly Owned Subsidiary of Star Cruise Lines
Incorporated: 1968 as Norwegian Caribbean Lines
Sales: $1.6 billion (2005)
NAIC: 483112 Deep Sea Passenger Transportation

■ ■ ■

NCL Corporation is one of the pioneers of the modern cruise ship industry, and remains among the top cruise ship operators. Headquartered in Miami, Florida, and formerly known as Norwegian Cruise Lines, the company was acquired by Star Cruise Lines, a member of Malaysia's Genting Group, in 2000. In 2004, Star Cruise restructured NCL as its North American wing, including Norwegian Cruise Lines and NCL America. NCL operates 12 ships with more than 21,500 berths in 2006 (the company expects to take delivery on three new-build vessels by the end of 2007, adding more than 7,000 berths). Norwegian Cruise Lines is the largest part of NCL, operating its fleet in the Caribbean cruise market. NCL America is the only cruise line operator to sail ships under the U.S. flag, and is the only cruise line to serve the inter-island market in Hawaii. NCL also operates cruises to Alaska, and has developed a new cruise concept, "Homeland Cruising," offering year-round departures from New York. In the mid-2000s, NCL also has introduced another new cruise concept, "freestyle cruising," providing more flexible dining hours in a less formal atmosphere than traditional cruising. Once listed on the New York Stock Exchange, NCL remains wholly owned by Star Cruise Lines. The Malaysian parent has indicated its interest in a possible re-listing of NCL in the mid-2000s. David Colin Veitch is NCL's president and CEO.

MODERN CRUISE PIONEER IN 1966

NCL originated in Norway at the turn of the 20th century when Lauritz Kloster purchased a used steamship and founded a company shipping ice from Norway to the United Kingdom. Kloster filled his ship with coal for the return trip, and from this beginning built his company into a major shipping company, Klosters Rederi A/S. Based in Oslo, Klosters later added ferry services as well.

By the early 1960s, the company had come under the leadership of Kloster's son, Knut Kloster, who saw an opportunity to expand the group's ferry operations. In 1966, Klosters acquired a new vessel, the *Sunward,* which, at 8,600 grt (gross-register-tons) was capable of carrying up to 600 passengers and 500 cars. Kloster's idea was to provide ferry service to British vacationers from Southampton to points in Spain, Portugal, and Gibraltar.

Klosters launched the service in June 1966. The company was soon caught up in the long-running

COMPANY PERSPECTIVES

NCL Corporation Ltd. ("NCL") is one of the leading cruise ship operators in the world and is increasing the size and modernity of its fleet. NCL currently operates 12 ships with over 21,600 berths, which represents approximately 9.0% of the overall cruise capacity in North America in terms of berths. NCL is in the midst of a fleet renewal program which, by the end of 2007, will add three new ships to its fleet. The addition of these new ships will result in a fleet size of 15 ships with approximately 28,900 berths.

dispute between Spain and the United Kingdom over the island of Gibraltar, however. When Spain closed its border to cruise ships arriving from Gibraltar, the Klosters ferry service suddenly found itself on the brink of collapse.

Help came in the form of Ted Arison, an Israeli entrepreneur who had started out as a partner in an air-freight company before selling his stake in that operation to turn to a newly growing market, that of Caribbean cruises, in the mid-1960s. Until the late 1950s, the cruise ship market was more or less limited to larger vessels sailing intercontinental routes, and served foremost as a means of overseas transportation. The early cruise industry also was marked by a class system, from the luxury of first-class accommodations, to the relative squalor of third-class travel. The development of jet engines and the beginning of a true passenger airline service had begun to transform the cruise ship industry, however.

At the same time, the buoyant economy and the rapid growth of leisure time had begun to stimulate the travel and tourism industry. By the early 1960s, a number of shipping companies and other entrepreneurs had begun to offer shorter cruises. The short cruises provided transportation for vacationers traveling to their destinations, before rapidly evolving into becoming vacations themselves. Ferries, such as the *Sunward,* became sought-after vessels for the cruise industry.

Arison founded the Arison Shipping Company in 1966 and teamed up with another Israeli group that had begun operating ferry cruises between Miami and the island of Nassau in 1964. That group marketed its ferry service as "the world's first luxury one-class floating motel," distinguishing itself from the earlier cruise lines. By 1965, the group had added a second ferry service. Initially, these ships operated on short three- and four-day cruises. Joined by Arison, however, the company prepared to launch a new service, that of seven-day cruises, originating from Miami and traveling to Montego Bay and to Jamaica. In September 1966, Arison Shipping began marketing the new cruise, and began taking bookings from vacationers.

Arison's own company now found itself in jeopardy, when the ship owners went bankrupt and the two ferries were impounded. Yet Arison had heard of Klosters' problems with the *Sunward* and encouraged the Norwegians to bring their ferry to Florida. Klosters agreed, and the *Sunward* arrived in Miami in December 1966. Billed as "the Newest, Most Beautiful Cruise Liner," the *Sunward* was credited with establishing the modern cruise industry, and with placing Miami as the center of the global cruise market.

The success of the *Sunward,* and the rapid development of the cruise industry in the late 1960s, encouraged Klosters to invest in a new fleet. In 1968, the Kloster family founded a new company, Norwegian Caribbean Lines (NCL), and raised some $100 million to build four new ships. The new vessels were initially conceived along the lines of the *Sunward,* but on a larger scale. The company's second ship, the *Starward,* was launched in December 1958, with a gross-register-tonnage of 15,000, and capacity for 750 passengers. Yet the *Starward* still retained ferry capacity for 250 cars, in case of a potential collapse of the cruise industry.

By 1970, however, NCL had become convinced that the cruise industry was there to stay. In January of that year, the company launched its third ship, the *Skyward,* and the first in the company's fleet to feature all-passenger service, with no car-carrying facilities. As such, NCL became one of the leading pioneers of the modern cruise industry, developing a new range of services and facilities to cater to its vacationing passengers. The company began offering inexpensive year-round, seven-day cruises to the Caribbean. By 1971, the company had launched its fourth ship, the *Southward,* which became the first in the fleet to offer 14-day cruises. The company then completed its transition to full-fledged vacation cruise operations with the commissioning of the *Sunward II,* replacing the group's original vessel.

Into the 1970s, however, a dispute erupted between Arison and Kloster. With Kloster accusing Arison of misusing funds, the two companies separated in 1972. Arison once again found himself with bookings and no ships, and turned around and launched Carnival Cruise Lines. That company went on not only to rival NCL, but to become one of the world's top three cruise operators.

KEY DATES

1906: Lauritz Kloster founds Klosters Rederi in Norway.
1966: Klosters begins offering ferry services between the United Kingdom and Spain, Portugal and Gibraltar, but is forced to move to the Caribbean cruise market instead, forming a partnership with Ted Arison (later founder of Carnival Cruise Lines).
1968: Norwegian Caribbean Lines (NCL) is formed and an expansion program begins, with four ships added into the 1970s.
1979: NCL buys the S.S. France and converts it to cruise operations.
1984: The Royal Star Cruise Line is acquired.
1986: Kloster Cruises goes public on the Oslo Stock Exchange.
1987: NCL becomes Norwegian Cruise Lines.
1988: The Royal Viking Cruise Line is acquired.
1995: The fleet is consolidated under NCL, phasing out Royal Star and Royal Viking; Klosters becomes NCL Holdings.
1999: NCL Holdings goes public on the New York Stock Exchange.
2000: The company delists after its acquisition by Star Cruises of Malaysia; the Freestyle Cruise concept is launched.
2004: NCL America and inter-island Hawaii cruises are launched.
2006: Fleet expansion begins, with three new vessels added by the end of 2007.

A PERIOD OF DIFFICULTIES: 1979–95

NCL remained the market leader through the 1970s, notably through a string of innovations. The company began offering the industry's first air flight and cruise packages, providing low-cost flights to Miami. The company also played a role in developing new port destinations in the region, such as to the western Caribbean, Grand Cayman, and Mexico's Cozumel. These included the purchase of the company's own island, Great Stirrup Cay Island, in the Bahamas. The company then launched the first "out island" cruise—only NCL passengers were allowed onto the company's island—which later became an industry standard.

By the end of the decade, NCL had become a clear leader in the cruise market. In 1979, the company attracted international headlines when it purchased the *S.S. France,* the former pride of the French fleet, originally commissioned in 1962. NCL spent some $100 million to convert the ship, which joined the NCL fleet under the name *S.S. Norway.* Larger than every other cruise ship at the time, the *Norway* allowed NCL to greatly expand its range of onboard facilities and entertainment—the company later became the first to add full-scale Broadway shows to its cruises—establishing a new standard for the cruise industry.

Yet the purchase of the *S.S. France/Norway* was the start of a series of decisions made by Klosters that brought the family's shipping empire into difficulty. Although the *S.S. Norway* proved highly popular with NCL passengers, the newly renovated, large-scale vessel encouraged the company's rivals to build even larger vessels. While its competitors launched newly designed and built ships, NCL found itself saddled with the cost of maintaining the aging *Norway.*

The Kloster family company, which became Kloster Cruise A/S, went public in 1986, listing on the Oslo Stock Exchange. The public offering was meant to fuel the group's expansion in the mid-1980s. Observers later criticized Kloster's management, however, for developing an external expansion strategy during this period. By the late 1980s, Kloster had acquired two more cruise operations, Royal Viking Cruise Line and Royal Star Cruise Line. The addition of the new fleets established Kloster and NCL as the world's top cruise operators. The addition of the new fleets, some of the vessels of which were transferred to NCL, allowed NCL to begin operating in routes beyond the Caribbean for the first time. In the late 1980s, for example, the company began offering cruises to San Juan. In recognition of this expansion, NCL changed its name in 1987, to Norwegian Cruise Lines. The following year, Royal Viking Cruise Line was placed under NCL's management, while continuing to operate as a separate brand.

Nonetheless, NCL's expansion effort actually helped slow down the company's growth. Saddled with a fleet of older ships (the company had not commissioned a new-build vessel since the early 1970s), NCL watched its competitors steam ahead in the market with a new generation of modern "superliners." NCL attempted to play catch-up; in 1988, the company commissioned its first new-build in 17 years, the *Seaward.*

By the early 1990s, however, NCL's difficulties were compounded by the collapse of the international tourist market, amid the slumping economy and the repercussions of the Persian Gulf War. Adding to the group's troubles was a long series of management changes, and a succession of presidents, including Knut Kloster's brother Einar, and then his son Knut Kloster, Jr. In the meantime, the company had been slow to replace its aging fleet, launching its next new-build, the *Dreamward,* only in 1992, followed by the *Windward* in 1993. These were joined by the *Leeward* in 1995. By then, however, NCL had suffered through several years of losses.

CRUISING INTO THE NEW CENTURY

In 1995, Kloster was forced to consolidate its cruise ship operations, shutting down the Royal Viking and Royal Star lines. Most of these companies' fleets were then transferred to NCL, a move that allowed NCL to begin offering European cruises for the first time. During this time, the Kloster family lost control of the company, and Kloster Cruises was renamed as NCL Holdings.

Under new management and new ownership, NCL once again looked forward to expansion. The company acquired a new, single-ship cruise company, Orient Line, in 1998. In 1999, NCL went public, listing on the New York Stock Exchange. NCL soon took on a new major shareholder, Star Cruise Lines, part of Malaysia's Genting Group. Yet the company also faced down a hostile takeover attempt, from Carnival Cruise Lines.

By 2000, however, Star Cruise had gained full control of NCL, taking the company private again. Under Star Cruise and a new president and CEO, Simon Veitch, NCL launched a new period of growth. In particular, NCL appeared to have regained its position as cruise industry innovator. At the beginning of the decade, for example, the company launched the industry's first "Freestyle Cruise," a concept that provided more flexible dining, including a wider choice of restaurants, while dropping formal dining attire requirements in favor of more casual dress. In 2004, the company launched a new cruise concept, NCL America, which became the first to sail under the American flag in 50 years, and the first to provide inter-island cruises in Hawaii. In that year, NCL reincorporated as NCL Corporation. Star Cruise also announced its interest in taking NCL public in the near future.

By 2006, NCL had once again gained a place among the industry's top three, with a fleet of 12 ships and more than 21,500 berths. The company also had put into place a strong investment program, with plans to add three new ships, and more than 7,000 additional berths, by the end of 2007. The completion of this build schedule was expected to give the company the industry's youngest fleet. NCL Corp. appeared to have set sail for new successes in the 21st century.

M. L. Cohen

PRINCIPAL COMPETITORS

Carnival Corporation; Mitsui OSK Lines Ltd.; Carlson Companies Inc.; Neptune Orient Lines Ltd.; MyTravel Group PLC; PT Angkutan Sungai Danau Dan Penyeberangan; Royal Caribbean Cruises Ltd.; Wan Hai Lines Company Inc.; Stena Line Scandinavia AB; Seabourn Cruise Line; J Lauritzen A/S; Korea Line Corporation; Holland America Line Westours Inc.; Wallenius Lines AB.

FURTHER READING

Bertram, Cindy, "A Cruise Line of Innovation and 'Firsts,'" *Leisure Group Travel,* December 2003/January 2004.

"Carnival and Star Sever Tie Up After Buying NCL," *Travel Trade Gazette UK & Ireland,* March 27, 2000, p. 30.

Golden, Fran, "Kloster's Adam Aron: 'Dark Days Are Behind Us,'" *Travel Weekly,* March 28, 1994, p. 12.

Green, Marilyn, "NCL Will Target Asia," *Leisure Travel News,* October 16, 2000, p. 24.

Jordan, Allen E., "Humble Beginnings: Many of Today's Top Cruise Lines Grew from Hardscrabble Roots," *Cruise Travel,* January-February 2006.

Major, Brian, "Glory Days," *Travel Agent,* November 18, 1996, p. 44.

Mott, David, "Dynamic NCL Aims for the Youngest Fleet in the Industry," *International Cruise & Ferry Review,* Spring/Summer 2005, p. 43.

"NCL Gears Up for Five New Vessels by 2007," *Travel Trade Gazette UK & Ireland,* May 13, 2005, p. 17.

"NCL Parent Tweaks Corporate Setup," *Travel Weekly,* July 26, 2004, p. 6.

"NCL to Be Relisted on New York Exchange," *Travel Trade Gazette UK & Ireland,* February 18, 2005, p. 17.

"NCL to Take Agents to See Ship's Launch," *Travel Trade Gazette UK & Ireland,* March 17, 2006, p. 8.

NetIQ Corporation

3553 North First Street
San Jose, California 95134
U.S.A.
Telephone: (408) 856-3000
Fax: (408) 273-0578
Web site: http://www.netiq.com

Public Company
Incorporated: 1995
Employees: 1,332
Sales: $213.2 million (2005)
Stock Exchanges: NASDAQ
Ticker Symbol: NTIQ
NAIC: 511210 Software Publishers

■ ■ ■

NetIQ Corporation develops software that helps companies manage their computer networks, offering its customers control over performance, security, configuration, and vulnerability issues. The company's products are organized under four classifications: performance and availability management; security management; configuration and vulnerability management; and operational change control. NetIQ's performance and availability management software is designed to identify and to respond to application failures, system software crashes, hardware failures, slow response time, and insufficient resource capacity. Its security management software reduces exposure time to security breaches and identifies corporate policy violations. The company's configuration and vulnerability management software enables customers to assess network vulnerabilities and manage risk. The company's operational change control products allow companies to delegate administrative tasks and manage user accounts. NetIQ serves more than 60,000 customers through facilities located in 16 countries.

ORIGINS

Like most companies, NetIQ evolved during its first decade in business, beginning with a foundation that enabled it to establish itself as a going enterprise before using that foundation as a springboard to become something more than its founders originally conceived. NetIQ's foundation, set following its formation in September 1995, was in developing performance-monitoring software for companies with a presence on the Internet. Its reputation during its early years, the early years of the Internet as well, was built on a suite of products marketed under the name "AppManager." The AppManager found a receptive audience in the commercial sector because of its ability to monitor performance across large-scale networks. For a business keen on knowing the details of its web site's performance, as the online face of the business met a potential customer, AppManager provided useful information. The software measured server response time, registered minor idiosyncracies of the system, and alerted systems managers of potential problems. NetIQ established itself in the performance-monitoring niche, earning enough of a reputation to complete an initial public offering (IPO) of stock in July 1999, just as interest in any business related to the Internet was reaching fever pitch. To the company's credit, it foresaw the rapid maturation of

COMPANY PERSPECTIVES

NetIQ is a leading provider of integrated systems and security management solutions that empower IT with the knowledge and ability to assure IT service. NetIQ's Knowledge-Based Service Assurance strategy embeds knowledge and best practices to ensure operational integrity, better manage service levels and risk and ensure policy compliance. With NetIQ you know your IT service is assured.

its industry and cast a much larger net, evolving beyond a performance-monitoring software company.

The explosive growth of the Internet created a need for businesses to not only know how well their web sites performed, but also how visitors interacted with their web site. This was the major leap describing the difference between offering performance-monitoring software and systems-management software. NetIQ was able to make the leap because of its accomplishments as a performance-monitoring software provider, but the evolutionary step it chose to take was as much bold as it was the only viable option for survival. For virtually any company involved in anything related to computers or the Internet, Microsoft Corporation was an industry behemoth that at some point had to be confronted. Net-IQ did well as a performance-monitoring software developer, but its management realized it was only a matter of time until Microsoft turned its attention to the performance-monitoring niche and quickly dominated the market segment. The realization left NetIQ's management essentially with only two options: either fight on and most probably be crushed by Microsoft, or concede, get what it could from the technology it had developed, and redirect its focus to another, potentially more fruitful, business.

NETIQ CHANGING TACK FOR THE NEW CENTURY

NetIQ's senior executives chose to control their own destiny, expressing their decision via an acquisition and by ceding ground in its performance-monitoring niche. The first step toward developing a presence in a larger market was taken in February 2000, when NetIQ merged with Mission Critical Software Inc in a $1.4 billion deal. The two companies focused on separate, but related areas, with NetIQ targeting performance-monitoring business and Mission Critical targeting systems-management business, the future of the "new" NetIQ that emerged after the merger. The acquisition reflected NetIQ's realization that vast opportunities existed in the realm of applications management tools, a market the company intended to tap with Mission Critical's suite of One Point products. Developed for large-scale, Windows NT-based networks, One Point managed user traffic, user accounts, and network security, giving NetIQ a toehold in the systems-management market. A series of smaller acquisitions followed, including the purchase of Sirana Software Inc., Ganymede Software Inc., and Software Realization Inc., each of which added new systems-management components to NetIQ's product portfolio. After bolstering its systems-management business, the company "made what amounted to a sacrifice fly," according to the November 8, 2000 issue of *Investor's Business Daily.* In October 2000, NetIQ signed a $175 million product licensing deal with Microsoft, giving ground to obtain the resources to expand its systems-management capabilities further. "What you really have is, they sold the [performance-monitoring] product," an analyst explained in the November 8, 2000 issue of *Investor's Business Daily.* "They received $175 million to invest in extending their product portfolio and to help redefine themselves. That's what people are excited about."

The interest in NetIQ ratcheted up soon after the licensing agreement with Microsoft was signed. In January 2001, the company announced another mammoth deal, revealing that it intended to acquire Portland, Oregon-based WebTrends Corporation in an all-stock deal valued at $1 billion. WebTrends, known as an analytical software company, specialized in the analysis of log files, the principal resources from which Internet-based businesses derived information regarding how visitors used their web sites. Analyzing web logs was considered too complex and too costly for an Internet-based company to conduct internally, which meant that applying analytics to log files required the services of an application services provider (ASP) or the installation of software capable of gleaning pertinent information from the files in-house. With the addition of WebTrends, Net-IQ positioned itself to offer a range of software packages for which the company charged an annual license fee of between $700 and $10,000, and to compete as an ASP, creating a "powerhouse" that held sway as the "unquestioned leader in e-business infrastructure management and intelligence solutions," according to the May 21, 2001 issue of *123Jump.*

Despite *123Jump*'s glowing appraisal of the WebTrends deal, there was more than a modicum of investor pessimism about the merger. Within hours of the announcement, doubts about the deal's worth drove its value down by 20 percent. As the investing public grew increasingly disenchanted with the Internet sector, the

KEY DATES

1995: NetIQ is incorporated.
1999: NetIQ completes its initial public offering of stock.
2000: A merger with Critical Software Inc. paves NetIQ's entry into systems-management software development.
2001: NetIQ acquires WebTrends Corporation.
2002: Charles M. Boesenberg is named chairman, chief executive officer, and president.
2005: WebTrends is sold.

valuation, as measured by the trading price of NetIQ's stock, plummeted. By the time the deal closed in March 2001, what had been announced as a $1 billion merger ended up as a $250 million transaction.

As NetIQ progressed toward its tenth anniversary, the company continued to strengthen its capabilities by targeting rivals and bringing their expertise under the NetIQ banner. The acquisitions helped build the company's business along three fronts: system management, security management, and web analytics. To lead the company during its acquisitive phase, a new executive was brought in, marking a transition in leadership that saw one of NetIQ's founders end his stay at the company. Ching-Fa Hwang, who had helped start NetIQ and had served as the company's president and chief executive since its inception, named Charles M. Boesenberg as his replacement. An executive with 30 years of experience in the technology industry, Boesenberg held senior executive positions at Apple Computer and IBM before serving as chief executive officer and president of three companies: Central Point Software, Magellan, and Integrated Systems. Hwang stayed on as chairman of NetIQ for the first half of 2002, completing a planned succession of leadership that culminated with Boesenberg being named chairman in July 2002.

Under Boesenberg's control, NetIQ completed two acquisitions in 2002 that bolstered its security management business. In October, the company announced it had agreed to purchase PentaSafe Security Technologies, Inc., a Houston, Texas-based specialist in security management solutions. "This is a compelling and strategic combination that we are convinced will deliver strong results for customers and shareholders," Boesenberg explained in an October 1, 2002 NetIQ press release. "PentaSafe brings to our team a wealth of experience and knowledge in a fast growing market that will be instrumental in building on our strategy to become the leading provider of integrated cross-platform systems and security management solutions." The day after the $255 million deal was completed in early December 2002, Boesenberg announced a second acquisition meant to expand the company's security management business. Marshal Software Ltd., an Auckland, New Zealand-based company, was the target. Marshal developed software to safeguard networks, but its specialty was in providing security solutions for e-mail environments, giving administrators control over protecting confidential information, blocking e-mail-based viruses, and enforcing e-mail usage policies. The $23 million acquisition was completed before the end of the year, adding Marshal's customer base of 3,500 to NetIQ's expanding operations.

NETIQ PREPARING FOR THE FUTURE

In the final years before NetIQ's tenth anniversary, the company halted its acquisition campaign, directing its attention instead to integrating the assets it had purchased during the previous years. The period also was devoted to expanding the company's capabilities beyond serving Windows-based systems, as NetIQ broadened its product portfolio to embrace systems and security management products for UNIX and Linux operating systems. Against the backdrop of product upgrades and a focus on developing cross-platform solutions, NetIQ made a decision to shed its web analytics business. In the spring of 2005, the company announced it wanted to divest WebTrends, "undoing a deal from the final, fevered days of the Internet craze," as the March 29, 2005 issue of the *Oregonian* described it. The company, which had been operating in Portland as a division of NetIQ, was purchased by its managers with the financial backing of Francisco Partners, L.P., a California-based private equity firm. The deal was completed in May 2005 for $94 million, stripping an estimated $47 million from NetIQ's revenue volume.

As NetIQ celebrated its 10th year in business, the company stood as a far more comprehensive software developer than the company born a decade earlier. The evolutionary leap from providing performance-monitoring software to providing systems management and related software fueled energetic financial growth, lifting the company's revenue total from less than $400,000 in 1997 to $213 million in 2005. Although the increase in sales was substantial, the company could not claim similar success with its profitability. The process of maturing and redefining itself came at a cost, one that was evinced in NetIQ's bottom line. The company was a perennial money loser, racking up roughly $4 million in losses between 1999 and 2004. As the company prepared for its second decade of business, it began the journey on a positive note, recording a profit in 2005 of slightly more than $45,000. More of a symbolic victory than a substantial financial gain, the profit total perhaps marked the beginning of consistent profitability for NetIQ. To give his company a better chance at steady profitability, Boesenberg announced in mid-2005 that he would reduce the company's payroll by 15 percent and move certain operations from San Jose to Houston. Although the changes were expected to result in restructuring charges in 2006, Boesenberg was confident that the years ahead would confirm the prudence of the realignment and spark a successful start to NetIQ's second decade of business.

Jeffrey L. Covell

PRINCIPAL SUBSIDIARIES

NetIQ Pty. Ltd. (Australia); NetIQ do Brasil Ltda. (Brazil); NetIQ Europe Limited (Ireland); NetIQ deutschland GmbH (Germany); NetIQ Ireland Limited; NetIQ Software Internationl Limited (Cyprus); NetIQ K.K. (Japan); NetIQ Nederlands (Netherlands); NetIQ Benelux (Belgium); NetIQ Canada Corporation; NetIQ Denmark Aps; NetIQ France SARL; NetIQ Asia Limited (Hong Kong); NetIQ Italia SRL (Italy); NetIQ Asia Pty. Ltd. (Singapore); NetIQ Software Espana SL (Spain); NetIQ Limited (U.K.); NetIQ Sweden AB; Database Tools Development (Proprietary) Limited (South Africa); Marshal Software Limited (New Zealand); Marshal International Limited (New Zealand); Marshal Software LLC; Mission Critical Software, Inc.; PentaSafe Security Technologies, Inc.; PentaSafe Distribution Inc.; PentaSafe Security Technologies, Ltd. (U.K.); PentaSafe Security Technologies GmbH (Germany); PentaSafe Services, Inc.; PentaSafe Security Technologies A/S (Denmark).

PRINCIPAL COMPETITORS

BindView Development Corporation; BMC Software, Inc.; Internationl Business Machines Corporation.

FURTHER READING

Campanelli, Melissa, "Bugged Out," *Entrepreneur,* May 2003, p. 38.

Earnshaw, Aliza, "WebTrends Merger to Prove Self in the Future," *Business Journal-Portland,* January 26, 2001, p. 5.

Elliot, Alan, "NetIQ Corp.," *Investor's Business Daily,* November 8, 2000, p. A14.

Kemp, Ted, "The Many Flavors of Web Tracking," *InternetWeek,* November 26, 2001, p. 19.

Meyer, Cheryl, "IT Manager Ready to Deal," *Daily Deal,* September 23, 2004.

Rogoway, Mike, "WebTrends Managers Will Buy the Company," *Oregonian,* March 29, 2005.

Shabelman, David, "NetIQ Grabs PentaSafe for $251M," *Daily Deal,* October 2, 2002.

Silverman, Dwight, "Mission Part of 3-Way Deal," *Houston Chronicle,* February 29, 2000, p. 1.

Nexen Inc.

801 7th Avenue Southwest
Calgary, Alberta T2P 3P7
Canada
Telephone: (403) 699-4000
Fax: (403) 699-5800
Web site: http://www.nexeninc.com

Public Company
Incorporated: 1971 as Canadian Occidental Petroleum Ltd.
Employees: 3,247
Sales: CAD 4.82 billion (2005)
Stock Exchanges: Toronto New York
Ticker Symbol: NXY
NAIC: 211111 Crude Petroleum and Natural Gas Extraction

■ ■ ■

Nexen Inc. ranks as the fourth largest oil and gas company in Canada, conducting its exploration and production activities in the Gulf of Mexico, the North Sea, Yemen, Canada, and off the shore of West Africa. Nexen also holds a 61.4 percent interest in Canexus Income Trust, which controls the company's former chemicals division, a manufacturer of sodium chlorate and chlor-alkali products, such as chlorine, caustic soda, and muriatic soda. Nexen also holds a 7.23 percent interest in Syncrude Canada Ltd., a partnership that mines shallow oil sands deposits in Alberta.

ORIGINS

For decades, one of Canada's largest oil and gas companies was part of a Los Angeles-based conglomerate, Occidental Petroleum Corporation. Nexen was formed in mid-1971 when the crude oil, natural gas, and sulphur operations of Jefferson Lake Petrochemicals of Canada Ltd., which Occidental Petroleum had acquired in 1963, were combined with other Canadian crude oil, natural gas, and chemicals assets belonging to Occidental Petroleum, creating Canadian Occidental Petroleum Ltd., the name Nexen operated under during its first 30 years in business. When Canadian Occidental was formed, it joined a company that had recently established itself as one of the largest oil exploration firms in the world, a claim it could make after discovering massive reserves of oil in Libya in the late 1960s. Occidental Petroleum, and by extension Canadian Occidental, was the creation of a physician-turned-entrepreneur whom *Forbes,* in its April 11, 1994 issue, described as an "irrepressible autocrat," Armand Hammer.

Hammer did not found Occidental Petroleum, but his influence over the company was without rival. Through his aggressive expansion, he turned a little-known company into one of the largest conglomerates in the United States, creating an energy and chemicals behemoth with an eclectic array of interests built around its core businesses. Hammer was nearing retirement age when he first encountered Occidental Petroleum, having spent his career selling "medicinal" alcohol during Prohibition, dealing in Russian art, and breeding cattle, among various other pursuits. A search for a tax shelter

COMPANY PERSPECTIVES

From the ocean swells in the North Sea to the frosty north of Alberta's oil sands and desert heat of Yemen, our philosophy is to build sustainable businesses. Sustainable value comes from our solid core assets that provide superior returns and ongoing free cash flow. It also comes from strong development projects expected to generate attractive returns and high-impact exploration for long-term growth.

in the mid-1950s brought him into contact with Occidental Petroleum, a struggling oil exploration company founded in 1920 that had a net worth of only $34,000 when Hammer came across the company. He invested $100,000 in two of the company's exploration wells that soon struck oil, convincing him to buy up Occidental Petroleum's share and install himself as chief executive officer in 1957. Hammer was nearly 60 years old at the time, taking the helm of a company he would expand aggressively for the next 30 years, holding sway as the "irrepressible autocrat" until his death at age 92.

Under Hammer's direction, Occidental Petroleum developed into a sprawling conglomerate, building its portfolio of energy and chemical assets as it delved into far-flung ventures, such as meat packing and film production. "Whenever Hammer got interested in oil shale or art or hybrid seed technology, the Soviet Union or China, Occidental Petroleum Corp. got interested, too," a *Forbes* reporter wrote in the magazine's May 27, 1991 issue, "even if any chance of a return on its money seemed remote." Hammer's appetite for expansion created what stood as the 16th largest company in the United States by the time of his death in 1990, when Occidental Petroleum boasted nearly $22 billion in revenue. The company was awash in debt, however, partly because of Hammer's insistence on borrowing money to keep the company's dividend payments high. When his successor, Ray R. Irani, took control of the company, the primary objective was to bring fiscal responsibility to the table and pare down $8.5 billion of debt, a goal embraced by Irani who announced he would sell off $3 billion in assets and reduce debt by 40 percent within two years. It was this emphasis on downsizing and streamlining that led to the separation of Occidental Petroleum and Canadian Occidental later in the decade, a breakup that was not entirely amicable.

INDEPENDENCE IN 2000

By the end of the 1990s, Irani's restructuring efforts had reduced Occidental Petroleum to one-third its size at the beginning of the decade. Revenues stood at $7.8 billion. Canadian Occidental, led by President and CEO Victor Zaleschuk, posted nearly CAD 1.7 billion in revenue in 1999, deriving CAD 500 million of the total from its oil activities in Yemen. The Yemen assets, which comprised the 310,000-acre Masila field that produced 210,000 barrels of oil per day, was the single most important property in Canadian Occidental's portfolio, and it was coveted by Occidental Petroleum. Canadian Occidental, classified as the operator of the Masila Block, held a 52 percent interest in the property, while Occidental Petroleum held a 38 percent working interest in the field. In mid-1999, Occidental Petroleum revealed its desire to gain control of Canadian Occidental's interest in the Masila field, announcing it wanted to trade its 29.2 percent stake in Canadian Occidental, valued at an estimated $850 million, for full ownership of the Yemen assets. Canadian Occidental's management flatly rejected the offer, but Occidental Petroleum did not back away. The company reportedly approached rival oil companies in the United States and Canada, offering to assist in the takeover of Canadian Occidental in exchange for the Masila block, a strategy that failed because many rival companies were interested in Canadian Occidental for the same reason Occidental Petroleum was interested in the company: the 210,000 barrels per day being produced in Yemen. The discord between Canadian Occidental and its parent culminated in a shareholder vote in which Canadian Occidental shareholders were encouraged to approve a shareholder rights plan, a so-called poison pill, to fend off the advances of Occidental Petroleum. In February 2000, Canadian Occidental gained the support it needed to become independent. The following month, Occidental Petroleum sold its interest in Canadian Occidental to Canadian Occidental and a pension fund group, the Ontario Teachers' Pension Plan Board, for CAD 1.2 billion.

Canadian Occidental entered the 21st century as an independent company for the first time in its history. Following the company's separation from Occidental Petroleum, it searched for a new name, wanting to adopt a new identity to mark its separation from its parent. Zaleschuk, in a September 28, 2000 interview with *Canadian Corporate News,* explained the process of finding a new name for the company. "We looked at our entire business and asked for input from shareholders, staff, and consultants," he said. "Nexen, signifying a new energy, was the name we kept coming back to. Plus," he added, "it passed all of the international trademarking and linguistic checks."

KEY DATES

1971: Canadian Occidental Petroleum Ltd., Nexen's predecessor, is formed by Occidental Petroleum Corporation.
1991: Canadian Occidental's prime asset, an oil field in Yemen, is discovered.
1997: Canadian Occidental's Canadian oil production triples with the acquisition of Wascana Energy Inc.
2000: Occidental Petroleum sells its stake in Canadian Occidental.
2001: Charlie Fischer is named president and chief executive officer.
2004: Through a $2.1 billion acquisition, Nexen begins production in the U.K. North Sea.
2005: Nexen spins off its chemicals division as Canexus Income Trust.
2006: Nexen moves forward with the development of the Ettrick field in the North Sea.

The new Nexen corporate banner represented one of Canada's elite industrial concerns, an oil and gas giant with significant holdings in the chemicals business. At the heart of the company was the Yemen property, where oil was discovered on the first of 17 fields in 1991. Production at the Masila block commenced in 1993, yielding one million barrels of oil by the end of the year. Aside from Yemen, Nexen counted Canada and the U.S. Gulf of Mexico as its primary operating areas, although the company was involved in the exploration, development, production, and marketing of crude oil and natural gas in Nigeria, Australia, Columbia, and Indonesia as well. Its production in Canada was increased exponentially after the acquisition of Wascana Energy Inc., a CAD 1.9 billion deal that tripled production in its home country. The company derived 80 percent of its energy-related revenue from the production of oil and 20 percent from the production of natural gas. Nexen's chemicals business, which accounted for CAD 242 million of the company's CAD 1.7 billion in revenue in 1999, consisted of the manufacture and marketing of sodium chlorate, chlorine, and caustic soda. The company's chemical business established its first presence outside North America in 1999 through the acquisition of sodium chlorate facilities in Brazil.

Several months after adopting a new corporate title, Nexen gained a new leader. Charlie Fischer replaced Zaleschuk as president and chief executive officer in June 2001, completing his rise through Nexen's executive ranks which began in 1994 with his appointment as senior vice-president in charge of exploration and production in North America. Fischer inherited 37 million acres of land when he took the helm, and he promised to use it to double the company's size within five years, growth he intended to achieve largely without the aid of acquisitions. Fischer, as the November 19, 2001 issue of the *Oil and Gas Journal* noted, planned to grow "through the aggressive use of the drill bit."

RAPID EXPANSION IN THE 21ST CENTURY

The first years of the 21st century were highlighted by sound financial performance and promising oil discoveries that pointed toward a profitable future for the Calgary-based company. The fields in Yemen continued to underpin the company's financial growth, producing their 700 millionth barrel of oil in mid-2003, a year, not coincidentally, that resulted in record high net income of CAD 578 million. Nexen, by this point, ranked as the fourth largest oil exploration and production company in Canada, producing more than 220,000 barrels of oil per day from its worldwide operations.

As Nexen neared its 35th anniversary, the company's prospects were brightened by several significant moves. In 2004, the company entered the U.K. North Sea through a $2.1 billion acquisition that gave it access to the Buzzard field development, the region's largest discovery in a decade. Nexen, with a 43 percent interest in the project, operated as the lead partner, directing its efforts on the Scott and Telford fields. The acquisition prompted the company to announce a disposition plan in October 2004 to reduce its debt by CAD 1.5 billion. The plan, executed in 2005, consisted of spinning off its chemicals division as an income trust fund named Canexus Income Trust through an initial public offering of stock. The spinoff, valued at an estimated CAD 800 million, left Nexen with a 61.4 percent interest in Canexus.

The substantial boost to production resulting from expanding into the North Sea was followed by two promising events. In late 2005, industry observers reported what promised to be a massive oil field at Nexen's Knotty Head development in the U.S. Gulf of Mexico. Analysts estimated the field to contain 500 million barrels of oil in what ranked as the deepest well drilled in the Gulf. Nexen held a 25 percent stake in the project. In early 2006, Nexen approved a plan to develop the Ettrick field in the North Sea, where it maintained an 80 percent stake in a field estimated to have recoverable reserves of roughly 40 million barrels of oil in addition to natural gas. The company planned to drill three production wells, which were expected to begin producing in 2008. "This is a solid project that adds certainty to our production profile beyond 2007," Fischer commented in a February 22, 2006 interview with *Europe Intelligence Wire*. "The North Sea is important to our overall growth strategy and Ettrick is a stepping stone to growing a sustainable business in this area." As Fischer looked ahead, there was every indication that his stewardship of the company's assets would result in a legacy of success. Nexen, in an encouraging pattern, posted record high net income in 2004 of CAD 793 million. In 2005, with revenues nearing CAD 5 billion, the company registered an all-time high for the third consecutive year, eclipsing the CAD 1 billion mark for a total of CAD 1.15 billion in net income.

Jeffrey L. Covell

PRINCIPAL SUBSIDIARIES

Nexen Marketing International Ltd. (Barbados); Nexen Marketing Singapore Pte. Ltd.; Nexen Marketing U.S.A. Inc.; Nexen Petroleum Canada; Nexen Petroleum Offshore U.S.A. Inc.; Nexen Petroleum U.S.A. Inc.; Canadian Nexen Petroleum Yemen; Nexen E & P Services Nigeria Limited; Nexen Ettrick U.K. Limited; Nexen Exploration U.K. Limited: Nexen Petroleum Columbia Limited; Nexen Petroleum do Brasil Ltda. (Brazil); Nexen Petroleum Equatorial Guinea Limited; Nexen Petroleum Nigeria Limited; Nexen Petroleum U.K. Limited; Nexen Chemicals U.S.A.; Nexen Exploration Norge AS (Norway).

PRINCIPAL COMPETITORS

BP p.l.c.; Exxon Mobil Corporation; Petro-Canada Limited.

FURTHER READING

Cook, James, "The High Cost of Hammer," *Forbes,* May 27, 1991, p. 104.

Netzer, Baie, "A Leaner Oxy Looks for Fatter Profits," *Money,* March 1991, p. 70.

"Nexen Hoping to Move Forward with North Sea Project Proposals," *Europe Intelligence Wire,* February 22, 2006.

"Nexen Launches Ettrick with Partners' Blessing," *Europe Intelligence Wire,* February 28, 2006.

"Nexen to Raise $300 Million from Chemical Spin-Off," *Chemical Week,* August 17, 2005, p. 4.

O'Reilly, Brian, "Armand Hammer: Occidental Petroleum," *Fortune,* August 3, 1987, p. 58.

Pike, David, "CanadianOxy Braces for Fight with Parent," *Oil Daily,* December 17, 1999.

Sim, Peck Hwee, "CanadianOxy Becomes Nexen," *Chemical Week,* November 15, 2000, p. 18.

Stott, Jim, "Canada's Nexen Focused on Expanding Oil Production," *Oil and Gas Journal,* November 19, 2001, p. 36.

Wielaard, Robert, "Nexen Hints at Big Gulf Oil Find," *America's Intelligence Wire,* December 8, 2005.

NH Hoteles S.A.

Santa Engracia 120
Edificio Central
Madrid,
Spain
Telephone: +34 91 451 97 24
Fax: +34 91 451 97 30
Web site: http://www.nh-hoteles.es

Public Company
Incorporated: 1978
Employees: 14,000
Sales: EUR 980.89 million ($1.3 billion) (2005)
Stock Exchanges: Madrid
Ticker Symbol: NHH
NAIC: 721110 Hotels (Except Casino Hotels) and Motels

■ ■ ■

NH Hoteles S.A., or NH Hotels, is Spain's leading business-oriented hotel group, and is Europe's third largest and one of its fastest-growing corporate-focused hotel groups. NH Hoteles operates more than 260 hotels in 19 countries, primarily in Europe, but also in Latin America and in Africa. Altogether, the company counts more than 38,000 beds in its empire. The company also plans to add 20 new hotels into the second half of the 2000s, boosting its total room count by nearly 4,000. Spain remains the group's largest market, accounting for 34 percent of its hotel rooms. Germany (24 percent) and The Netherlands (15 percent) are the group's other major markets. In Europe, NH Hoteles is also present in Belgium, Switzerland, Austria, the United Kingdom, and Italy. The company's Latin American presence focuses on Argentina and Mexico, but also includes Brazil, Chile, Cuba, and Uruguay. The company's three Africa hotels are located in South Africa and Ghana. NH Hoteles owns 27 percent of the hotels in its chain, with a lease with call option on an additional 12 percent. Of its remaining hotels, 47 percent are leased and 14 percent are operated under management contracts. The company also owns 79 percent of luxury hotel resort operator Sotogrande S.A., and a 20 percent stake in Italy's four-star hotel operator Jolly Hotels. NH Hoteles' own hotels typically range in the three- and four-star categories; the company also specializes in smaller hotels, ranging from 80 to 200 rooms. Many of the company's hotels feature "Women Style" rooms designed specifically for the group's female clientele. NH Hoteles also has collaborated with star chef Ferran Adria to launch the "Fast Good" and Nhube dining concepts. Much of the group's strong growth came through a series of acquisitions, including the Hotel Krasnapolsky chain, based in The Netherlands, Astron Hotels in Germany, and Chartwell in Mexico, orchestrated by Chairman Gabriele Burgio. The change in the group's revenue mix has been dramatic: in 1999, the Spanish market represented more than 99 percent of the group's revenues. By the end of 2005, international operations accounted for 60 percent of the group's sales, which had more than tripled during this period, to top EUR 980 million in 2005. NH Hoteles is listed on the Madrid Stock Exchange. In January 2006, the company joined that exchange's IBEX 35 index.

COMPANY PERSPECTIVES

NH Hotels is known for its motto, "Eye for detail." Customers appreciate and have come to expect the difference in products and services provided by NH Hotels.

The just-squeezed orange juice in the buffet breakfast, the "Good Night" details in the guestroom, the choice of different size and shape pillows in all the hotels, or the complete complementary toiletry kit with "Agua de la Tierra," are just some of those details that try to improve the perception of value for money and increase our guests' satisfaction.

BECOMING A SPANISH LEADER IN THE LAST TWO DECADES OF THE 20TH CENTURY

NH Hoteles was founded in 1978 by Antonio Catalan Diaz, with the opening of a single hotel in Pamplona, in the Navarre region. Spain was just then emerging from decades under the Franco dictatorship. As the company began to liberalize its market and open its economy to foreign investment, Diaz recognized the potential for developing hotels catering more specifically to the needs of business travelers. Into the early 1980s, NH Hoteles shifted its interests to Spain's business centers, starting with the purchase of the Calderon in Barcelona in 1982.

The NH Hoteles format proved highly successful, and the company quickly added new hotels in the Madrid and then Zaragoza markets. By 1988, NH Hoteles operated 16 hotels in Spain and had emerged as one of the country's leading hotels groups focused on the buoyant business traveler market. In order to continue its strong growth, NH Hoteles began looking for outside investors.

Spain's fast-growing economy had by then attracted the attention of a number of international investors, particularly Italy's Carlo de Benedetti, one of that country's leading industrialists and investors. In 1987, de Benedetti's Cerus investment wing entered Spain, establishing Corporacion Financiera Reunida, S.A. (Cofir) with a number of other shareholders. In 1988, Cofir invested in NH Hoteles, acquiring 33.5 percent of the hotel group as part of a capital expansion. Other investments made by Cofir in the late 1980s included holdings in the winemaking sector, Banco Zaragozano, the Sotogrande resort development group, and Portugal's Cofipsa.

Cofir originally acted as a passive investment holding company, and as such provided the funding for the hotel group's continued expansion. NH Hoteles grew strongly into the next decade, building up a portfolio of 55 three- and four-star hotels, with more than 5,800 rooms covering all of Spain's major urban markets, by 1993. In addition to 17 hotels owned outright by NH Hoteles, the company acquired the leases to 29 hotels and management contracts for an additional nine hotels. By then, NH Hoteles had become Cofir's single largest holding.

With losses mounting, Cofir was doubly hurt by its exposure to the hotel market. For one, a vast building boom during the 1980s had led to massive overcapacity in the early 1990s. At the same time, the effects of the recession, combined with the chill cast over the international travel market following the first Persian Gulf War, had sunk occupancy rates to all-time lows. As a result of its losses, Cofir was forced to begin selling a number of its holdings. Many of the company's shareholders also were looking to exit their investment.

NEW LEADERSHIP IN 1992

De Benedetto installed new management at Cofir in 1992. Taking the lead of the company now was Gabriele Burgio, a native of Florence, Burgio had earned an M.B.A. at France's Insead business school, before working at Banker's Trust in New York, and the Manufacturers Hanover (an investor in Cofir) in Italy. When Manufacturers Hanover decided to exit its shareholding in Cofir, Burgio agreed to take charge of the company.

Under Burgio, Cofir changed strategy, adopting a hands-on approach as an "industrial operator," instead of as a passive investor. Burgio now targeted Cofir's hotel operations as its core focus, specifically the NH Hoteles business. Cofir now boosted its stake in NH Hoteles to 62 percent. Cofir then began investing heavily in the hotel operator through the 1990s. By 1999, the company had spent more than $140 million, raising NH Hoteles' portfolio to nearly 80 hotels. As part of the company's investment effort, it also had set out to redirect its mix of hotels to the three- and four-star category.

Yet, during the mid-1990s, Cofir also attempted to crack into the discount hotel market in Spain. The company initially sought to develop this operation through a partnership with France's fast-growing Accor group. In 1997, the two companies nearly set up a partnership that would have called for NH Hoteles to open 70 Ibis-branded two-star hotels in Spain. Yet the agreement fell through, and instead, Cofir attempted to

KEY DATES

1978: Antonio Catalan Diaz establishes NH Hoteles with the first hotel in Pamplona, Spain.
1982: The company adds a hotel in Barcelona, then shifts focus to major city markets, adding hotels in Madrid and elsewhere.
1988: Cofir acquires control of NH Hoteles, which by then holds 16 hotels.
1992: Gabriele Burgio takes over as Cofir CEO and steps up investment in NH Hoteles, which by then has 55 hotels.
1998: Cofir refocuses around a core of hotel and resort operations, transferring its holding in the Sotogrande resort development group to NH Hoteles.
1999: After Cofir sells off its winemaking holdings, it changes its name to NH Hoteles; the company enters the Latin American market; 20 percent of Jolly Hotels in Italy is acquired.
2000: NH Hoteles acquires the Krasnapolsky Hotel group in The Netherlands, doubling its number of hotels to 78.
2001: The company acquires 15 Chartwell Hotels in Mexico.
2002: Germany's Astron Hotels are acquired, adding operations in Germany, Austria, and Switzerland.
2003: The Nhube dining concept is launched.
2004: The Fast Good restaurant format is launched.
2005: The company acquires its first U.K. property, in London.
2006: Plans to acquire 20 more hotels are announced.

launch its own discount chain, called NH Express.

NH Hoteles by then accounted for some 90 percent of Cofir's earnings. In early 1998, the company decided to exit its non-hotels businesses and refocus itself as a pure-play hotel and resort operator. Ownership of Cofir's stake in Sotogrande was transferred to NH Hoteles, while the company's winemaking operations were sold off in 1999 for $125 million. Following that sale, Cofir changed its name to NH Hoteles S.A. At that time, the company's revenues neared EUR 270 million.

INTERNATIONAL GROUP IN THE NEW CENTURY

NH Hoteles, which already dominated the Spanish corporate hotel market, immediately turned its attention toward developing an international expansion strategy. In 1999, the company paid $31.9 million to acquire a 20 percent stake in Italy's four-star hotel group Jolly Hotels. The company then turned its sights to the Latin American market, buying up a number of properties as part of a $50 million investment program. The company initially targeted the Mercosur market, specifically hotels in Argentina, Uruguay, and Chile.

Back in Spain, NH Hoteles targeted further growth. The company bought up a 5 percent stake in the Madrid Movie World Theme Park, which opened in 2002. In 1999, the company paid $85 million to acquire the Hotel Princess Sofia in Barcelona from Inter-Continental. The company also earmarked an additional $80 million for expansion of its NH Hoteles brand, and its Hoteles Express brand, into the mid-decade.

The company's profile changed dramatically in 2000, however. In that year, the company bought up The Netherlands' Krasnapolsky hotel group, which included the flagship Grand Hotel Krasnapolsky in The Netherlands. The addition of the Krasnapolsky group doubled NH Hoteles' hotel portfolio to 168 hotels, adding operations in The Netherlands, Luxembourg, Belgium, and elsewhere. The deal restructured NH Hoteles' geographic presence, reducing its Spanish operations to just 66 percent of its total. Also in 2000, NH Hoteles entered the Portuguese market, buying up the Liberdade hotel in Lisbon.

Buoyed by the Krasnapolsky acquisition, NH Hoteles now began scouting for new foreign acquisition targets. In 2001, the company moved into Mexico, buying up five hotels from Grupo Chartwell. As part of that deal, the company established a new subsidiary, NH Mexico. That company then took over the management contracts for the remaining nine hotels in Mexico previously operated by Chartwell, which retained a 41.25 percent stake in NH Mexico.

Yet Europe provided NH Hoteles with its main stage for growth. The company struck again in 2002, reaching an agreement to pay EUR 130 million for an 80 percent stake in Germany's Astron Hotels. That acquisition gave the company control of 46 hotels in Germany, as well as six properties in Austria, and an additional hotel in Switzerland.

In the meantime, NH Hoteles had entered a collaboration with star chef Ferran Adria to develop new dining concepts for the group's hotels. That partnership resulted in the launch of a new in-hotel restaurant concept, Nhube (pronounced "noovay"). The new theme incorporated the needs of business clients traveling alone, combining a lounge, bar, and restaurant concept, providing diners with Internet access, television, and music, and reading materials. The Nhube concept, first opened in Madrid in 2003, proved so successful that the company quickly developed plans to open Nhube restaurants in 26 more hotels.

By then, the company's collaboration with Adria had led to the development of another restaurant concept, "Fast Good," which sought to merge fast service with quality food. The first Fast Good opened in Madrid in 2004. In addition to opening further Fast Good restaurants in its hotels in Spain, NH Hoteles planned to introduce the concept to its Latin American hotels, while also developing a stand-alone format.

NH Hoteles continued innovating into the middle of the decade. The company responded to the growing numbers of female business travelers by becoming a pioneer of new "Women Style" rooms, specially outfitted with amenities for the company's female clients. Similarly, NH Hoteles decided to launch its own line of toiletry items, Agua de la Tierra. Instead of buying items from third parties, in this way the company produced its own toiletries, which it also offered for sale.

The company continued to build its hotel network in Latin America. By 2006, NH Hoteles operated hotels in Chile, Argentina, Brazil, Uruguay, Cuba, and Mexico. Yet Europe remained the company's primary market, accounting for more than 75 percent of its total rooms, and some 94 percent of its total revenues of nearly EUR 981 million ($1.3 billion). In 2005, the company took its first step to develop itself as a true pan-European hotel group, buying up its first property in the United Kingdom, the Hotel Harrington in London, for $72 million. NH Hoteles also moved to extend its footprint into Italy, with two hotels in that market, while also eyeing an entry into the French market. With more than 260 hotels, NH Hoteles had far from exhausted its growth. Indeed, the mid-priced, corporate hotel market in Europe remained heavily fragmented, offering the company strong growth possibilities. NH Hoteles appeared confident of its future growth, announcing its plans to add another 20 hotels as it moved into the second half of the decade.

M. L. Cohen

PRINCIPAL SUBSIDIARIES

Cofi SL; European Golf Booking Center SL; Grupo NH Hoteles Participaties N.V. (The Netherlands); Hotel Albar Ciudad Albacete SL; Hotel Palacio Castilla S.A.; Hotelera Onubense S.A.; Hoteles Express SL; Latinoamericana de Gestion Hotelera S.A. y Sociedades Dependientes; Lenguados Vivos SL y Filiales; NH Aranzazu Donosti S.A.; NH Private Equity B.V. (The Netherlands); Nuevos Espacios Hoteleros; Retail Invest S.A.; Sotogrande S.A. y Sociedades Dependientes (79%); Toralo S.A. y Filal (Uruguay).

PRINCIPAL COMPETITORS

Rallye S.A.; Compass Group PLC; ACCOR S.A.; CIGA S.p.A.; Six Continents PLC; InterContinental Hotels Group (UK) PLC; The Rank Group PLC; Grupo Calinda S.A. de C.V.; Sol Melia S.A.

FURTHER READING

Burns, Tom, "Cofir Launches Hotel Network," *Financial Times,* July 10, 1998, p. 23.

———, "Cofir to Shift Focus to Hotels Business," *Financial Times,* December 11, 1998, p. 29.

Kirkman, Alexandra, "Affordable Iberian," *Forbes Global,* March 3, 2003, p. 52.

Milligan, Michael, "European Hotel Chain Seeks to Make Name in US," *Travel Weekly,* September 15, 2003, p. 24.

"NH Hoteles Aims for Pan European Expansion," *El Pais,* October 31, 2004.

"NH Hoteles Buys Its First UK Property," *Caterer & Hotelkeeper,* April 7, 2005, p. 6.

"NH Hoteles, Madrid, Continues to Transform Itself As It Grows from a Small, Regional Player to a Global Corner with 237 Hotels and More Than 34,000 Rooms in 18 Countries," *Hotels,* August 2002, p. 15.

"NH Hoteles Plans Growth," *La Nacion,* January 18, 2006.

"NH Hoteles to Branch Out into Toiletries," *Caterer & Hotelkeeper,* March 18, 2004, p. 8.

"NH sustituye a Mapfre en el indice Ibex 35," *El Pais,* December 16, 2005.

Sidron, Jorge, "NH Hotels to Make Big Investment," *Travel Weekly,* December 13, 2004, p. 50.

"Solo Dining Takes Center Stage," *Hotels,* October 2003, p. 11.

Weinstein, Jeff, and Mary Scoviak-Lerner, "NH Hoteles, Madrid Took Another Step Toward Its Goal of Pan-European Distribution with Its February Acquisition of an 80% Stake of Germany's Astron Hotels," *Hotels,* April 2002, p. 19.

"Who's Who ... NH Hoteles," *Caterer & Hotelkeeper,* November 13, 2003, p. 36.

NRG Energy, Inc.

211 Carnegie Center
Princeton, New Jersey 08540-6213
U.S.A.
Telephone: (609) 524-4500
Fax: (609) 524-4520
Web site: http://www.nrgenergy.com

Public Company
Founded: 1989
Employees: 3,682
Sales: $2.7 billion (2005)
Stock Exchanges: New York
Ticker Symbol: NRG
NAIC: 221121 Electric Bulk Power Transmission and Control

■ ■ ■

Based in Princeton, New Jersey, NRG Energy, Inc. is a wholesale power generation company with ownership interest in 58 power generating facilities located in the United States, Australia, Brazil, and Germany. These facilities are capable of generating nearly 25,000 net megawatts of electricity from a variety of fuel types, including oil, natural gas, nuclear, diesel, jet, and hydro. In addition to power generation, the company markets commodities such as coal, natural gas, and oil, and through subsidiary NRG Thermal L.L.C. operates co-generation facilities, providing both heat and power to customers, and district heating and cooling facilities, which supply steam, hot water, or chilled water to specific areas, such as an office building or factory, for heating, cooling, or industrial uses. Another subsidiary, NRG Engine Services, repairs and maintains power generating equipment. NRG is a public company listed on the New York Stock Exchange.

TIES TO THE 19TH CENTURY

NRG grew out of Minneapolis-based Northern States Power Company, whose founder, Henry Marison Byllesby, was a pioneer of power generation. An engineer, he went to work for famed inventor Thomas Edison in 1881 as a draftsman for a New York City power plant. Four years later, at the age of 26, he was lured away by another legendary inventor, George Westinghouse, who made Byllesby a vice-president and general manager of Westinghouse Electric. He first moved to the Minneapolis area in 1891 when he went to work for Thomson-Houston Electric Company and was put in charge of a St. Paul, Minnesota subsidiary. In 1902 Byllesby became involved with utility mogul Samuel Insull, buying and upgrading struggling Midwestern utilities. He became an owner himself, in 1912 acquiring Minneapolis General Electric of Minnesota. Four years later the company would take the name Northern States Power Company (NSP).

Over the first 20 years NSP acquired 25 Upper Midwest utility companies, emerging as one of the leading utility holding companies, but the Public Utility Holding Company Act of 1935 forced NSP to sell off interests and required many of its well-healed backers to sell their stock back to the company. NSP struggled through the rest of the 1930s and business did not pick up again until the demand for electricity surged with

COMPANY PERSPECTIVES

We generate power. Our assets are real and diverse. Our strategies provide value to our stakeholders and the electricity market. We're NRG Energy and we're proud of the work we do.

the United States' entry into World War II. NSP continued to grow in the postwar years and by the mid-1950s was one of the nation's top ten utilities.

In the late 1980s the game changed for government-regulated utilities including NSP. Deregulation was on the horizon, offering a myriad of opportunities for companies to take advantage of changing conditions. In 1989 NSP formed subsidiary NRG Energy to acquire, build, own, and operate nonregulated power and energy businesses in both the United States and overseas. The ten-person operation was headed by President Dave Peterson, an NSP veteran who had been vice-president, non-regulated generation, for NSP. NRG Energy, Inc. would then be incorporated in Delaware in May 1992.

NRG quickly displayed what Minneapolis' *Star Tribune* described as a "go-go, entrepreneurial culture." In the early years it became involved in a wide variety of projects, often in conjunction with partners. In 1991 it gained half-ownership of Jackson Valley Energy Partners. A year later it acquired 45 percent interests in three San Joaquin Valley Energy operations. All four of the facilities were cogeneration plants located near Fresno, California, which sold their power to Pacific Gas & Electric on long-term agreements. Another early venture was the ownership of three Minnesota steam lines, providing steam to two corporations as well as a Minnesota prison. NRG was also active internationally. In 1993 it became part of the Scudder Latin American Trust for Independent Power, an investment fund that bought and built power plants in Latin America and the Caribbean. NRG also acquired interests in power plants in Germany, the Czech Republic, and Australia.

Business began to accelerate for NRG in the second half of the 1990s, as deregulation began to spread across the United States. NRG would acquire primarily aging power plants around the country, put on the block by old-guard utility companies who in response to deregulation would be increasingly inclined to sell off generating capacity in order to focus on transmission and distribution. Once these plants became available, NRG was willing to take on an enormous amount of debt because the window of opportunity was limited. As Peterson explained to *CityBusiness,* a Minneapolis business publication, "Once these markets open up and these properties get sold, it usually doesn't happen a second time." According to *CityBusiness,* "Once power plants are in the stable, NRG's next challenge is to recreate them in its own entrepreneurial image. Often, the plants NRG buys were considered inefficient or environmental burdens to their previous owners. ... NRG usually cuts staff, adds performance incentives and makes each plant's management keep records of the facility's income." Until they came into the NRG fold, many of the plants' managers were disconnected from their parent company's accounting. "Most of them had no idea what kind of money they were making for their company," Peterson told *CityBusiness.*

STRONG GROWTH IN THE FINAL YEARS OF THE CENTURY

From 1996 to 1999, NRG grew its business 35 percent per year and began to focus on three core markets in the United States—the Northeast, South Central, and southern California markets—all of which were expected to lack enough generating capacity to meet rising demand in the near future. NRG started the new century in the same way it ended the last, by spending money on U.S. power plants in these core markets, especially the Northeast. It paid $550 million for Consolidated Edison Co. generating facilities in Staten Island and Queens in New York City, $445 million for three western New York generating plants, and another $460 million for plants in Connecticut. NRG also bought two other fossil-fuel facilities located in Delaware and Maryland, as well as minority stakes in a pair of Pennsylvania plants. In March 2000 NRG acquired power plants in Louisiana for about $1 billion.

Contributing about 20 percent of NSP's total revenues, NRG had become the largest growth vehicle for the parent company, whose stock was struggling as the 1990s came to a close. NSP made plans to merge with New Century Energies Inc. of Denver and began taking steps to spin off NRG in a public offering of stock. NSP would sell off 20 percent of the company, a move it hoped would untap the full value of NRG operating as a separate, independent company. The partial spinoff was completed in May 2000, and the initial public offering (IPO) of stock netted NRG $423 million, the largest IPO of a Minnesota company ever. Of that amount, about $300 million was earmarked to trim the company's massive debt and for general corporate purposes. Shares of NRG stock now began to trade on the New York Stock Exchange under the ticker symbol "NRG." NSP subsequently completed its merger with New Century Energies and took the name Xcel Energy, Inc.

KEY DATES

1912: Northern States Power Company is founded in Minneapolis.
1989: The company is formed as a subsidiary of Northern States Power Company.
2000: NRG is spun off as a public company.
2003: NRG restructures under Chapter 11 bankruptcy protection.
2004: The company moves its headquarters to Princeton, New Jersey.
2006: Texas Genco is acquired.

In the early months as an independent company, NRG soared. The price of its stock rose from the IPO price of $15 per share to $37 in the fall of 2000, and for the year NRG recorded revenues of $2.16 billion and net income of $182.9 million. Taking advantage of its momentum, the company conducted a secondary offering of stock to further repay debt and fund the development of pending projects.

NRG continued to fly high in 2001. It was now the United States' third largest independent power generator in terms of net equity in megawatts. In 2001 NRG grew sales to more than $2.4 billion and net income topped $265 million. But it also carried nearly $5 billion in debt, of which $3 billion was bond debt, another $1 billion unsecured bank debt, and about $900 million obligations in power plant financing. Moreover, NRG had another $5 billion of project financing on its plants, secured in large part by the plants themselves. By the end of the year there were rumblings of trouble ahead for NRG and the nonregulated power generation industry because of declining power prices and the collapse of Enron. In December 2001, NRG's debt was put under review for possible downgrade to junk status.

Thinking NRG's depressed stock price provided an opportunity to reacquire its growth engine at a reasonable price, in February, Xcel Energy tried to rescue NRG by announcing its intention to reacquire the company. Xcel Energy made a $300 million cash infusion in March 2002 in a feckless effort to prevent the downgrade of its debt. NRG backed out of pending acquisitions and began to shed assets; but nothing could prevent a downgrading of its corporate bonds to junk and the company defaulting on its debt payments. Peterson and other top executives either retired or resigned, and then filed an involuntary Chapter 11 suit against NRG when their severance and retirement packages went unpaid by Xcel. That matter was settled in February 2003 while NRG inched closer to bankruptcy.

BANKRUPTCY: 2003

NRG finally filed for Chapter 11 bankruptcy protection in May 2003 in what was, in effect, a prearranged settlement with unsecured creditors, who would receive about 54 cents on the dollar while secured creditors were paid 100 cents on the dollar, all in all an acceptable outcome. For its part, Xcel gave up its ownership interest in NRG and paid the former subsidiary $752 million to meet some creditor claims as well as provide some working capital. The reorganization plan was accepted by a federal bankruptcy judge in November 2003. When the dust settled, NRG retained about 14,000 megawatts of U.S.-based electric generating plants and another 3,000 megawatts in Australia, Germany, and Latin America. In December 2003, the company received a new CEO, David W. Crane, an energy industry veteran.

Given that the bulk of NRG's assets were located in the Northeast, Crane decided that it made sense for NRG to move its headquarters closer to the center of its business. A five-state search was conducted in the Northeast and the company finally settled on Princeton, New Jersey, an area familiar to Crane, who held a Bachelor of Arts degree from Princeton University's Woodrow Wilson School of Public and International Affairs. As an inducement, New Jersey provided a business employment incentive grant to NRG.

Crane succeeded quickly in turning around the new NRG, and in 2004 the company reported revenues of $2.36 billion and net income of $185.6 million, results that exceeded management's expectations. Progress continued in 2005, when sales increased to more than $2.7 billion and NRG posted net income of $84 million. Once again, the company was able to achieve external growth. In February 2006, it completed the acquisition of Texas Genco for $4.4 billion in cash, $2.7 billion in assumed Texas Genco debt, and 35.4 million shares of NRG common stock. As a result, NRG doubled its asset base and gained a much needed presence in Texas, complementing its energy assets in the Northeast, South Central, and Western regions of the United States.

Ed Dinger

PRINCIPAL SUBSIDIARIES

NRG Thermal L.L.C.; NRG Engine Services.

PRINCIPAL COMPETITORS

The AES Corporation; Calpine Corporation; Mirant Corporation.

FURTHER READING

Berman, Dennis K., Henny Sender, and Rebecca Smith, "NRG Is in Talks to Buy Texas Genco," *Wall Street Journal,* September 28, 2005, p. A3.

Pacelle, Mitchell, "NRG Proposed Chapter 11 Filing to Its Creditors," *Wall Street Journal,* November 8, 2002, p. A2.

Price, Dave, "Xcel Makes Last-Ditch Effort to Save NRG Energy," *Finance and Commerce Daily Newspaper* (Minn.), February 16, 2002.

Reilly, Mark, "A Power Surge," *CityBusiness* (Minneapolis, Minn.) March 10, 2000, p. 1.

St. Anthony, Neal, "NRG Raises $423 Million in Offering," *Star Tribune,* May 31, 2000, p. 1D.

———, "NRG Spinoff Could Turn Up Heat Under Shares of NSP," *Star Tribune,* February 1, 2000, p. 1D.

Smith, Rebecca, "NRG Is Cleared for Emergency from Chapter 11," *Wall Street Journal,* November 25, 2003, p. B5.

Nucor Corporation

2100 Rexford Road
Charlotte, North Carolina 28211
U.S.A.
Telephone: (704) 366-7000
Fax: (704) 362-4208
Web site: http://www.nucor.com

Public Company
Incorporated: 1955 as Nuclear Corporation of America
Employees: 11,300
Sales: $12.7 billion (2005)
Stock Exchanges: New York
Ticker Symbol: NUE
NAIC: 331111 Iron and Steel Mills

■ ■ ■

Nucor Corporation ranks among the largest steel producers in the United States. Its approach to steel production has been predicated upon drastically undercutting both foreign and domestic competition, a feat it accomplished through no small amount of hard work, risk-taking, and visionary thinking. For all practical purposes, Nucor launched the steel minimill industry in the late 1960s. Thereafter, minimills increasingly edged the large integrated steel companies out of most niche markets, and, led by Nucor in the late 1980s, made a bold entry into the flat-rolled steel market, the last domain of Big Steel. Maintaining profitability and a furious growth rate through difficult economic times, when the industry was virtually at a stand still, Nucor set its sights on becoming the nation's number one steelmaker by the year 2000. The company had been a perennial favorite of Wall Street into the mid-1990s; however, increasing competition in the areas that Nucor pioneered presented the company with significant challenges. But following a boardroom coup in 1999, Nucor headed into the 21st century full steam ahead.

ORIGINS DATING TO 1904

Nucor traces its origins to the early years of the 20th century, when automobile inventor Ransom Eli Olds founded the Olds Motor Works in Lansing, Michigan, with the considerable aid of venture capitalists. In 1904 Olds, dissatisfied with his lack of control over the business, abandoned it to found a new company, R. E. Olds Company; the name was quickly changed to Reo Motor Car Company to avoid a lawsuit over the use of the "Olds" name. From 1904 until 1924 Olds served as president of the company, before turning to real estate speculation, an unfortunate business move that ultimately led him to sell most of his Reo stock. When demand for the luxury cars manufactured by Reo plummeted during the Great Depression, the plant began making a number of other products, including lawnmowers and the Reo Speedwagon delivery truck. Olds died in 1950, and his namesake company, which had survived one bankruptcy, was now headed toward another. By December 1954 the company was all but dead; however, when stockholders were informed of plans for liquidation in 1955, a small, contentious group found a glimmer of hope in a tiny Reo business property, Nuclear Consultants, Inc. According to Nucor chronicler Richard Preston, what followed was "a forced takeover, an unusual move in corporate finance, wherein the dis-

COMPANY PERSPECTIVES

Management Philosophy—The company's success comes from its more than 11,300 employees. Nucor seeks to hire and retain highly talented and productive people. Nucor has a simple, streamlined organizational structure to allow employees to innovate and make quick decisions. The company is highly decentralized, with most day-to-day operating decisions made by the division general managers and their staff.

sidents forced Reo to take over Nuclear Consultants against Reo's wishes." When the paperwork was complete, Reo was reborn as Nuclear Corporation of America and became the first publicly traded nuclear company. Various publicity stunts and the power of the word "nuclear" propelled the company and its stock skyward. Yet its business endeavors in nuclear instrumentation, nuclear energy, chemicals, and electronics bordered on the illusory. A series of largely unrelated acquisitions, funded through stock offerings, sustained the company. One of these subsidiaries, Vulcraft, led to the establishment of Nucor.

In 1962 F. Kenneth Iverson, then a young mechanical engineer, became general manager of Nuclear's Vulcraft division in Florence, South Carolina. It soon became apparent that Vulcraft, a metal fabrication business specializing in steel joists and girders, was virtually the only healthy division in the conglomerate. A string of money-losing years led the Nuclear Corporation to the verge of bankruptcy in 1965. By this time Iverson had been elevated to group vice-president and transferred to the parent company's headquarters in Phoenix. Essentially, Nuclear was a business with $20 million in sales and $7 million in assets that was losing $400,000 annually. Two major loan defaults that year caused the president to resign and the board to appoint Iverson as the new president and CEO; the logic governing the decision was that Iverson had been in charge of the only divisions within the company that were profitable.

RESTRUCTURING

Taking over at mid-year, Iverson dumped half the divisions, reduced management positions from 12 to two, and posted the last loss ever for the company, some $2.2 million. Now came decisions regarding Nuclear's future operations. At this point, Vulcraft, with its South Carolina plant and another in Norfolk, Nebraska, held the greatest promise for growth. In 1966 Iverson committed himself to Vulcraft's steel joist industry, relocating to Charlotte and establishing corporate headquarters in a modest 2,000-square-foot office. During the first three years under his management, Nuclear's net sales rose from $21 million to $35 million, largely on the virtue of Vulcraft's dominant 20 percent share of the joist market. Although profits kept pace with this growth, Iverson was concerned with Vulcraft's dependency on others for its steel. Until Vulcraft graduated from steel fabricator to steel producer, its earnings were entirely dependent on steel prices outside its control.

In 1968 Iverson, in the first of several momentous decisions for the company, prepared Nuclear to become a minimill steel producer. His initial goal was to manufacture bar steel at a price competitive with foreign producers, who had been supplying up to 80 percent of the company's raw material. The goal was perhaps unrealistic, for Iverson would also be taking on such giants as U.S. Steel, a chief Vulcraft supplier. Furthermore, the construction cost for a traditional coke-and-iron steel mill was prohibitive. However, steel could be created another way: by melting scrap steel in electric-arc furnaces. Iverson took the gamble by effectively mortgaging the company for a loan of $6 million. The money was used to erect a plant in rural Darlington, South Carolina, and purchase the necessary equipment, a furnace, a continuous casting machine, and a rolling mill. According to *Success,* Iverson "recruited farmers, sharecroppers, and salesmen to do the dirty, often dangerous work of making steel. High technology and untrained troops made for a volatile mix, and delays and catastrophes caused stock prices to drop to pennies. But a legendary company culture was born: inventive, resourceful, team oriented, inspired by impossible challenges."

The delays and catastrophes centered around the plant's casting machine, which experienced regular breakouts of hot steel from the time production began in June 1969 until late 1970, and the newness of the venture in general. Depressed earnings finally rebounded spectacularly in 1971, jumping 140 percent. In 1972, they leaped another 70 percent. This same year, Iverson dropped the company's outmoded title and renamed the business Nucor Corporation. Nucor was now at the brink of the so-called golden era of the minimills. It had two successful operations: Vulcraft, which supplied joists to the construction industry, and Nucor Steel, which produced low-cost bar steel, largely for Vulcraft. Both posed a threat to the big steelmakers, but they were slow to respond. A flurry of minimills arose during the 1970s, following Nucor's lead and producing bar steel for the joist business at prices that eventually drove Bethlehem, Republic, and others out of the market.

KEY DATES

1955: Near demise of Reo Motor Car Company leads to first publicly traded nuclear company.
1966: F. Kenneth Iverson pins hope for the company's survival on metal fabrication operation.
1968: Minimill steel production plans set in motion.
1972: Company is renamed Nucor Corporation.
1974: Fatal accident leads to policies benefiting employee families.
1979: Company begins cold-finished bars manufacturing.
1986: Nucor embarks on effort to bring minimill into costly sheet steel market.
1990: Loss of life drives renewed safety effort by company.
1995: Despite looming uptick in industry capacity, Nucor continues aggressive growth drive.
1999: Company weathers management shakeup.
2002: Nucor acquires Birmingham Steel Corporation.

In 1977 Nucor launched its second assault on Big Steel by branching out into steel decking, for use in floors and roofs supported by its Vulcraft joists. Two years later the company again led the minimills by manufacturing cold-finished bars, employed in shafts and precision parts. By the end of the decade, Nucor ranked among the top 20 steel companies in the country, with sales of $430 million and net earnings of $42 million. Within a five-year span, it had more than tripled production through a series of new mill constructions. Its core business, Vulcraft, had also expanded through new plant openings and had virtually secured its position as the biggest steel joist producer in the United States. The one blemish on these years of fast-paced growth was a mill fire accident in 1974 that killed four Nucor employees.

The company would later face criticism from its competitors, the media, and community leaders that its operations were needlessly dangerous. Much of the criticism stemmed from the fact that Nucor's workforce remained nonunion and was therefore subject to lower wages and less assurance that a certain working environment would be maintained. Nevertheless, the dynamic Nucor work ethic and corporate culture, shared by management and employees alike, offered something unions would find impossible to provide during the 1980s: job security. In an industry plagued with plant closings, cutbacks, and layoffs, Nucor stood out as one company firmly committed to its steelworkers. No Nucor employee had ever been laid off; to hold down costs during difficult downswings, Nucor instead asked its workforce to reduce hours. As for wages, the company's stringent team performance standards offered incentives to employees to exceed production goals and, as a result, receive bonuses that could more than double their annual wages. The employees also benefited from such unusual policies as guaranteed college scholarships for their children, a policy first established when Iverson wanted to help the families affected by the 1974 accident. Nucor attributed much of its success to its nonunion, nonurban employees. As its brochure *The Nucor Story* stated: "A major ingredient in Nucor Corporation's success has been its commitment to locate its diverse facilities in rural locations across America. As a result of deliberately selecting non-urban locations, Nucor has been able to establish strong ties to its local communities and its work force. The ability to become a leading employer and pay a leading wage has been a key to attracting hard-working, dedicated employees."

Such simple, effective strategies became the trademark of the company and its CEO. Another important ingredient in the company's success was its sparse management staff. Only four management layers existed inside the company, beginning with the CEO and leading directly down through general managers, department heads, and foremen to the general laborers. All wore identical hard hats, as a tribute to teamwork and as a further sign of differentiation from unionized companies. The small staff, modest headquarters, and relentless drive to become a world-class competitor made for a supremely cost-conscious corporation in which new technologies were seized, decisions made swiftly, and production encouraged apace.

Iverson's races into new steel industries and new technologies during the 1980s were necessitated not by Big Steel, which was floundering, but by other American minimills and by the new world leader, Japan. In 1986 the CEO decided to tackle the last frontier, sheet steel, an expensive and prized market that no minimill had dared to consider. Start-up costs for manufacturing sheet steel were enormous, at more than a quarter of a billion dollars. At the time, Nucor's assets amounted to little more than twice that figure. Annual revenues stood at just $755 million. Nonetheless, Iverson took the plunge, first by exploring possibilities within the company to produce a state-of-the-art casting machine whose efficiency would trounce the competition. Although the in-house project held promise, Iverson was anxious to be the first to acquire and implement the technology, and an invention already in progress, by West German engineering firm SMS Schloemann-Siemag A.G., was chosen as the best candidate for Iverson's plans. Called the compact-strip-production machine (CSP), the invention was over 1,000 feet long and composed of some one million parts. Most experimental and most crucial to its success was a casting tower, supposedly capable of producing sheet steel just two inches thick instead of the conventional ten inches. According to Preston, "Inventors had been trying to invent a machine that would make an endless strip of steel since 1856, when Sir Henry Bessemer had tried it and failed. ... Any company that could solve the problem would by definition become the global leader in the manufacture of steel." Assembly of the machine began in 1988 at a new plant site in Crawfordsville, Indiana, and by mid-1989 the first experiments were begun. Throughout the period, the Crawfordsville Project and the CSP attracted a shower of criticism from the big steel companies, as well as a jumble of stock trading and public speculation.

SAFETY ISSUES

Under plant managers Keith Busse and Mark Millett the CSP was eventually completed, and despite delays, breakouts, and one fatal explosion in January 1990, the Crawfordsville plant was soon operating near capacity, producing flat-rolled steel in one-fourth the time of its competitors at $45 less per ton. Busse had said, "What we're doing in Crawfordsville is like taking a Conestoga wagon for the first time across the plains." Iverson, looking to the future, had remarked, "We are going to leapfrog Japan." Neither was overstating the enormity of the Nucor gamble. The freak accident, caused by a broken cable that sent a ladle of molten steel crashing to the plant floor, left one dead. OSHA (Occupational Safety and Health Administration) inspectors poured over the evidence before levying a $30,000 fine. The victim's family also sought settlement with the company. What arose from the tragedy was a renewed commitment to plant safety: a Nucor study undertaken a few years later showed that the company ranked in the top third among steel mills in terms of safety.

The company remained committed to aggressive growth, opening a second thin-slab sheet mill in Hickman, Arkansas, in September 1992. Soon, however, Nucor was facing a potential setback: the high-quality scrap on which its sheet-steel production relied was in short supply, with prices jumping 55 percent in 1993. The shortage was only expected to intensify as Nucor and other minimill operators increased their capacity. Seeking an alternative to high-quality scrap, Nucor, with its characteristic entrepreneurial flair, built an experimental $65 million plant in Trinidad and Tobago that would process cheap iron ore from Brazil to make iron carbide, an economical substitute for direct-reduced iron. The plant had an annual capacity of 320,000 tons.

Unfortunately, the plant was plagued by start-up woes. Although the conversion process itself worked flawlessly, the rapid transition from limited testing to full-scale operation encountered engineering snafus and mechanical breakdowns. A year behind schedule, the plant was registering cost overruns of 30 percent. Nucor's stock dropped precipitously on the news of the problems in Trinidad.

Domestically, Nucor continued its heavy investment and expansion. In 1993 the company opened a second mill in Blytheville, Arkansas, at a cost of $200 million, and spent $65 million to upgrade its plant in Darlington, South Carolina. While observers questioned whether Nucor could maintain its fast and flexible corporate culture as it expanded, employees and managers alike pursued the relentless innovations that kept it a step ahead of the competition. In just one example, from 1992 to 1994 employees reduced the time it took to melt steel from 72 minutes to 65 minutes, which allowed them to pour 25 additional tons of steel during a 12-hour shift. Larry Roos, manager at the Crawfordsville plant, maintained that there was so much experimentation in his shop that "half the time I don't know who's doing what out there."

At the same time, competitors in the minimill business were increasing dramatically in numbers and advancing rapidly in technical sophistication. By 1995, competitors had ten new minimills on the drawing board for launch by 1998, with an expected increase in total capacity of 40 percent. Undaunted, Nucor set its sights on being the largest steelmaker in the industry by the year 2000, in part by diversifying into new products and heavily targeting international markets.

Nevertheless, as the economy slowed and orders for sheet steel dropped off in mid-1995, Nucor was forced to cut prices, and its stock continued to take a beating. Its shares declined by more than 30 percent from 1994 to 1995.

In January 1996, COO John D. Correnti succeeded Iverson as CEO, with Iverson remaining on as chairman of the board. Said Correnti, "I just want to keep the train on track, steaming ahead."

Indeed, Nucor's growth continued unchecked. In 1997 the company announced that it would build a $150 million steel beam mill in Berkeley, South Carolina, to open in late 1998. Nucor also intensified its plans for international expansion, and, like many of its competitors, targeted India, China, and Brazil, markets where demand was expected to grow at three times the rate of

U.S. demand. Nucor's plans included a Brazilian joint venture to build a $700 million plant in the state of Cear, which Correnti called "a chance to whet our appetite in the international market, and to make money." Gunning for that number one position, Correnti would need both.

FIRED UP: 1999–2005

Nucor produced 9.6 million tons of steel in 1998, shipping 9.4 million tons. John D. Correnti was named Steelmaker of the Year by *New Steel* magazine. At yearend Iverson stepped down as chairman. H. David Aycock, who served as Nucor's president and COO from 1984 to 1992 and had continued as a director, was named chairman. Correnti was asked to leave, within six months of Iverson's exit, and Aycock added the roles of president and CEO. According to *Business* Week, Correnti and Iverson were pitted against an Aycock-led group of directors regarding the future direction of the company.

Aycock, the victor in the conflict, pulled the plug on Nucor's unprofitable Trinidad iron-carbide plant for starters and planned acquisitions in the bar products and engineered building sectors to provide new growth. Berkshire Hathaway doubled its stake in the company, during the year, to 4.1 million shares.

Nucor's net earnings climbed to a record $310.9 million in 2000, up from $244 million in 1999, according to *Business North Carolina*. In contrast, *Forbes* reported, six of the top eight publicly held steel makers lost money despite positive economic conditions. The industry, set back on its heels by a one-two punch of cheap imports and rising energy costs, had experienced a rash of bankruptcies since 1997.

In 2001, Nucor broke ground for a new plant boasting technology that might afford a boon for the $45 billion U.S. steel industry. The strip-casting operation in Indiana would be among the first to use the technology that cast molten steel directly into very thin sheets. "If it works, strip casting could reshape the industry, making steel faster, thinner, more cheaply and with fewer defects than conventional slab casting. Makers would be able to switch among multiple steel grades on the fly," Brett Nelson reported for *Forbes*. Nucor pioneered a successful thin-slab caster in the late 1990s, requiring less plant space and energy consumption; strip casting upped the ante.

Improvements in electronic controls and in materials had pulled steel makers around the world into a race to perfect the strip-casting technology. Australian mining concern BHP (Broken Hill Proprietary Co. Ltd.) had invested $200 million in development, producing a breakthrough in the early 1990s. Nucor joined with BHP in 2000 to form Castrip, a venture to license the technology. The pair each owned 47.5 percent and the Japanese equipment supplier held the remaining 5 percent.

Strip casting was just one part of Daniel R. DiMicco's master plan for the company, according to a September 2001 *Business North Carolina* article. As Nucor's president, CEO and vice-chair, DiMicco also looked to increased plant efficiency and acquisitions to drive up Nucor profits.

Aycock tapped the Nucor veteran as his successor and as the man to take his strip casting venture forward. DiMicco and Nucor were attempting what had yet to be accomplished, and naysayers questioned the likelihood of a commercial success. For his part DiMicco expressed confidence in the process but also acknowledged the potential for failure. "If it doesn't work, it will be another situation where Nucor took a risk on something," he told *Business North Carolina*. "It is not going to make or break the company. It won't make or break my career." Falling steel prices compressed sales and earnings during the year.

In February 2002, Nucor offered to buy Birmingham Steel Corporation for $500 million in cash. Former Nucor CEO Correnti had been at the helm of the struggling steel maker since December 1999. Nucor wanted to acquire four operating mills but did not want to be saddled with Birmingham's debt and idle facilities, nor did DiMicco wish to see his former rival within Nucor return to the fold.

Ultimately, Birmingham agreed to be purchased for $615 million in cash, a better deal than the initial offering but still shy of Birmingham's $626 million in debt. "Nucor got the deal done even though several other steel producers expressed interest in Birmingham Steel. The irony of his former company taking over, however, mattered little to Correnti in the final analysis. 'Nucor had the biggest checkbook,'" Correnti told *American Metal Market* in June 2002. "At the end of the day, you have to look out for everyone. You have to make the best deal for your shareholders, your lenders, your employees and your customers. Nucor had the biggest checkbook, and this was the best deal." As for Nucor, the additional capacity elevated the company to a position of national leadership in steel reinforcing bar production.

Demand for steel worldwide and in the United States markedly improved in late 2003 and into 2004. According to an October 2004 *Business Week* article, prices in some sectors of the industry had risen threefold during the past 12 months. The upswing was aided by an improved global economy. China, in particular, ramped up consumption in preparation for the 2008 Beijing Olympics.

In the United States, steel mills ran at near capacity. But remembering the worldwide steel surplus prior to 2000, the industry concentrated on improving existing facilities, forgoing new mill construction. While steel manufacturers' stock prices rose with the strengthening market, consumers of steel, such as automobile and heavy equipment manufacturers, felt the price pinch.

Minimills, while benefiting from the improved demand for steel, were up against scrap metal shortages and rising scrap prices. Some companies were able to alleviate the problem with surcharges; others had their hands tied by contract agreements.

"But even those minimills that have not seen profits dampened from increased scrap prices are uncertain that will continue to be the case. 'Up to this point input costs haven't dampened our profits but it is a concern,'" DiMicco said in a November 2004 *Steel Times International* article. As the price of scrap rose, minimills' advantages over integrated mills began to erode.

U.S. scrap shortages coincided with worldwide demand. Domestic scrap was being shipped abroad, while other nations created barriers to metal scrap leaving their shores. Moreover, integrated steel mills, experiencing shortages of materials necessary to their production processes, had upped their use of scrap. Nucor, already seeking scrap alternatives, moved forward with development of iron substitute projects in Australia, Brazil, and Trinidad during 2005.

Nucor's earnings exceeded Wall Street's expectations in the fourth quarter of 2005. The quarterly results combined with news that the world's largest steelmaker, Mittal Steel Co., had set out to buy its closest competitor, Arcelor SA., drove Nucor stock to record levels. Combining the Rotterdam-based Mittal and Luxembourg-based Arcelor would result in an entity that controlled 10 percent of the world's steel, according to the *Tribune Review* of Greenburg, Pennsylvania. Mittal's move for Arcelor sparked speculation regarding takeovers involving other industry players, Nucor among them.

Driven by increased commercial construction, Nucor reported a second straight year of record earnings. At $1.31 billion, the 2005 figure was 17 percent higher than in 2004 and more than four times the earlier peak of $310.9 million in 2000. The gains were made despite a dramatic increase in natural gas prices. Anticipating continuing high energy costs, Nucor moved to mitigate the dilemma through bringing in new energy efficient equipment and hedging future natural gas purchases. But even as Nucor posted those record earnings for 2005, speculation regarding another global steel glut arose. Some industry watchers foresaw a time when China would begin dumping excess production into the world market.

Jay P. Pederson
Updated, Paula Kepos; Kathleen Peippo

PRINCIPAL SUBSIDIARIES

Nucor-Yamato Steel Company (joint venture); Castrip LLC (joint venture).

PRINCIPAL COMPETITORS

Commercial Metals Company; Mittal Steel USA; United States Steel Corporation.

FURTHER READING

Armel, Anne Lobel, "Competition Thins out As Iverson Casts Nucor's Lot," *Iron Age,* August 1991.

Aston, Adam, and Michael Arndt, "Suddenly Steel Has Industrial Strength," *Business Week,* October 18, 2004, p. 133.

Baker, Stephen, "Can Nucor Forge Ahead—And Keep Its Edge?" *Business Week,* April 4, 1994.

———, "From Blueprints to Grand Design," *Business Week,* January 8, 1996.

———, "Striking While the Iron Is Hot," *Business Week,* January 11, 1993.

———, "Testing Nucor's Mettle," *Business Week,* June 5, 1995.

Beirne, Mike, "The Bridges Steel Is Building," *Business Week,* June 2, 1997.

———, "Nucor Sets Iron Carbide Plant," *American Metal Market,* January 8, 1983.

Clifford, Mark, "Like Big Steel, Like Little Steel," *Forbes,* May 20, 1985.

Curran, Rob, "Nucor's Profit Slips but Outlook Is Upbeat on Solid Steel Demand," *Wall Street Journal,* January 28, 2006, p. A6.

Fortney, David L., "The Little Steel Mill That Could," *Reader's Digest,* August 1985.

Gendron, George, "Steel Man Ken Iverson," *Inc.,* April 1986.

Glader, Paul, "Journal Exclusive: Increase in Steel Prices to Slow, Analysts Say," *Wall Street Journal Europe,* April 6, 2006, p. 3.

Karmin, Monroe W., "Where Shift to High Tech Already Pays Dividends," *U.S. News & World Report,* September 3, 1984.

Kirkland, Richard I., Jr., "Pilgrims' Profits at Nucor," *Fortune,* April 6, 1981.

Love, Martin, "Steel from the Workshop," *Forbes,* April 30, 1984.

"Meet the New Revolutionaries," *Fortune,* February 24, 1992.

"Melding of Steel Industry Likely," *Tribune Review* (Greensburg, Penn.) January 28, 2005.

Metzger, Mark K., "F. Kenneth Iverson of Nucor: Man of Steel," *Inc.,* April 1984.

Milbank, Dana, "Minimill Inroads in Sheet Market Rouse Big Steel," *Wall Street Journal,* March 9, 1992.

———, "Nucor to Build Iron-Carbide Plant to Aid Minimills," *Wall Street Journal,* January 7, 1993.

"Minimills, Maxiprofits," *Time,* January 24, 1983.

Nelson, Brett, "An All-New Cast," *Forbes,* April 16, 2001, p. 318.

"Nucor Advantage: A New Way of Thinking," *Inland Steelmaker,* January 31, 1992.

"Nucor: Meltdown in the Corner Office," *Business Week,* June 21, 1999, p. 37.

"Nucor Ups Sheet Tags by $10 to $15 Per Ton," *American Metal Market,* January 29, 1993.

Oliver, Regina, "F. Kenneth Iverson of Nucor Corp.: Forging a New Steel Age," *North Carolina,* November 1992.

Parmar, Arundhati, "Doubts Nag at Nucor Performance: Steelmaker Beats Forecast, but Oversupply Looms," *Journal Gazette* (Ft. Wayne, Ind.), February 5, 2006, p. 1H.

Pinkham, Myra, "North American Minimills–the Quest for Iron," *Steel Times International,* November 2004, pp. 24+.

Preston, Richard, *American Steel: Hot Metal Men and the Resurrection of the Rust Belt,* New York: Prentice Hall Press, 1991.

Robertson, Scott, "Aycock's Nucor Focus: Aggressive, Acquisitive," *American Metal Market,* June 9, 1999, p. 1.

———, "Nucor Hopping As 'Leapfrog' Iron Alternate Plans Progress," *American Metal Market,* July 25, 2005, pp. 1+.

———, "Nucor Lays Its Cards, $500m on the Table: DiMicco Sees No Role for Correnti," *American Metal Market,* February 18, 2002, pp. 1+.

———, "Nucor Secures Birmingham Steel: Irony Not Lost on John Correnti," *American Metal Market,* June 3, 2002, p. 1.

Rohan, Thomas M., "The 'Other' U.S. Steel Industry Is Booming," *Industry Week,* July 13, 1981.

Schriber, Jon, "The Solution That's Not a Solution," *Forbes,* January 5, 1981.

Scredon, Scott, "Iverson: Smashing the Corporate Pyramid," *Business Week,* January 21, 1985.

Simon, Ruth, "Nucor's Boldest Gamble," *Forbes,* April 3, 1989.

Speizer, Irwin, "Roll Dice, Not Steel," *Business North Carolina,* September 2001, p. 24.

"Strike the Underbelly," *Success,* January/February 1992.

Wells, Edward O., "Bootstrapping for Billions," *Inc.,* September 1994.

Wrubel, Robert, "The Ghost of Andy Carnegie?" *Financial World,* September 1, 1992.

Zellner, Wendy, "Go-Go Goliaths," *Business Week,* February 13, 1995.

Open Text Corporation

275 Frank Tompa Drive
Waterloo, Ontario N2L 0A1
Canada
Telephone: (519) 888-7111
Fax: (519) 888-0677
Web site: http://www.opentext.com

Public Company
Incorporated: 1991
Employees: 1,900
Sales: $414.8 million (2005)
Stock Exchanges: NASDAQ Toronto
Ticker Symbols: OTEX; OTC
NAIC: 511210 Software Publishers; 518210 Data Processing, Hosting, and Related Services; 541511 Custom Computer Programming Services; 541512 Computer Systems Design Services; 541519 Other Computer Related Services; 611420 Computer Training

■ ■ ■

Open Text Corporation is one of the leading providers of enterprise content management software and services in the world. The firm's flagship offering, Livelink, enables corporations, government agencies, and other organizations to securely manage, share, and store electronic documents as well as video, audio, and graphics files. Livelink, which can be purchased with many variations and add-ons, is used on more than 20 million computers by 13,000 clients in 114 countries. Open Text's revenues are derived from software licensing fees as well as customer support and other professional services.

BEGINNINGS

The origins of Open Text date to the mid-1980s, when an international project to create a computerized version of the massive Oxford English Dictionary (OED) was begun. Work on developing software that could search for specific words or phrases in the text was performed at the University of Waterloo in Ontario, Canada, starting in 1984, and completed in 1989.

Recognizing other potential uses for the program, Waterloo professors Frank Tompa, Timothy Bray, and Gaston Gonnet secured commercial rights and founded a company called Open Text to market it in June 1991, making their first product shipment in September. The following year saw the seven-employee company create a CD-ROM for the Canadian Pharmaceutical Association and reach an agreement with Nissho Iwai to distribute its products in Japan.

In 1993 Open Text shipped its first Windows-based applications to UBS of Switzerland and also began working with Infodata Systems on the EarthLaw environmental database, which boosted its presence in the United States. The company now employed 20 and had opened a second office in Vancouver, British Columbia. In addition to a search engine, Open Text also offered an online browser display module called LECTOR. Its products had been sold to more than 2,500 clients around the world.

In 1994 the Open Text 4 search engine was released, and the company began working with Booz-Allen and

COMPANY PERSPECTIVES

Open Text is the market leader in providing Enterprise Content Management (ECM) solutions that bring together people, processes and information. Our software seamlessly combines collaboration with content management, transforming information into knowledge that provides the foundation for innovation, compliance and accelerated growth.

Our legacy of innovation began in 1991 with the successful deployment of the world's first search engine technology for the Internet. Today, Open Text supports 20 million seats across 13,000 deployments in 114 countries and 12 languages worldwide.

As a publicly traded company, Open Text manages and maximizes its resources and relationships to ensure the success of great minds working together.

signed an agreement to perform services for Universal Document Management Systems. Customers now included Blue Cross/Blue Shield of Oregon, Caterpillar, General Dynamics, and Grolier Publishing, as well as the Ontario Legislative Assembly. The year 1994 also saw the company's board appoint a new management team, with Tom Jenkins named president and CEO.

In April 1995 the firm introduced the Open Text Index, a search tool that used automated "Web crawler" software to continuously index the Internet. Though the company had originally sought to supply its search engine to users of databases and other self-contained information resources, the emergence of the World Wide Web as a source of seemingly unlimited information gave Open Text and other companies like it a new opportunity. Unlike other software of its type, which omitted common words such as "and" and "the," the OED assignment had required that everything be indexed, which allowed users to search for specific phrases.

During 1995 the firm also raised CAD 25 million from investors, which helped fund the purchase of browser software from MKS, Inc. of Waterloo, as well as the assets of Intunix AG of Switzerland. In September Open Text also announced a deal to provide its web searching software to Yahoo! of Mountain View, California, where it would be used to complement that firm's own hierarchical index of Internet resources.

ACQUISITION OF LIVELINK IN FALL OF 1995

In November Open Text purchased a company called Odesta Systems Corp. of Northbrook, Illinois, for CAD 29.8 million. Odesta was developing software called Livelink, which allowed electronic documents to be accessed by multiple users over a company's internal network, called an intranet. The web-based program supported multiple file types and software programs. The company now employed 100, and in 1995 it recorded sales of $10.6 million, up from just $3 million in 1994.

In January 1996 Open Text went public on the NASDAQ with an offering of 4.6 million shares priced at $15 each, netting $61 million. By now the company was embroiled in a lawsuit filed by departed cofounder Gaston Gonnet, who was asking for $90 million and 391,000 shares of stock over his claim to own the Open Text 5 software.

Early 1996 also saw the company introduce its new Livelink Intranet software, early users of which included the Ford Motor Co. and Qualcomm, Inc. The introduction of Livelink came as the market for search engines was collapsing, and the company would soon make the document management product its primary offering. In the summer the firm also settled Gonnet's lawsuit with a payment of CAD 300,000 and release of the disputed shares of stock.

Acquisitions made during 1996 included software development companies Nirv Centre and InfoDesign; Softcore, a European reseller; and a stake in MiningCo.com, Inc. (later known as About.com). Alliances were formed with Siemens Nixdorf and web browser maker Netscape as well.

The year 1996 also saw Open Text initiate a restructuring which included layoffs of 12 percent of its 300-person workforce, the moving of its Web index office from California to Toronto, and closure of its Paris office. Competition was fierce in the development of new software products, and the firm had not turned a profit since going public. The company was continuing to sign up new clients, however, including Thomson Corporation and the U.S. Government Printing Office, which would use its software to index government documents.

In early 1997 an International Data Corp. survey ranked Open Text the world leader in web-enabled electronic document management software, with 64 percent of the market. June saw Netscape Communications Corp. begin bundling Livelink with a product called SuiteSpot, while the firm named former Oracle Corp. vice-president Brett Newbold to the title of

KEY DATES

1991: Open Text is founded in Waterloo, Ontario, to produce search engine.
1995: Livelink document management software maker Odesta is acquired.
1996: Initial public offering brings firm $61 million.
1998: Information Dimensions acquisition boosts employment to more than 570.
2002: Centrinity purchase adds FirstClass voice mail, email, fax integration software.
2004: Merger with Ixos Software AG of Germany doubles company's size.
2005: Firm cuts 15 percent of workforce, closes offices; Artesia is acquired.

president, with Jenkins remaining CEO. For the fiscal year ended June 30, 1997, the company recorded $22.6 million in revenues and a net loss of $13.2 million.

In October 1997 Open Text paid $6.7 million to buy OnTime client-server scheduling software maker Campbell Services, and the following January launched Livelink Online, a subscription service in which the company hosted other firms' documents. That month the firm recorded its first quarterly operating profit as a public company.

Open Text now had a total of 18 offices around the world and was focusing on expansion in Europe, where it had a presence in the Netherlands, Switzerland, and the United Kingdom. Eighteen percent of sales came from that continent and 1 percent from Asia, with the bulk taking place in North America.

In early 1998 the firm signed its biggest contract to date with the Ford Motor Co., where 135,000 workers would use Livelink. It followed on the heels of a 60,000-worker contract with Motorola. The company's clients paid about $100 per user, with various packages available so that some could have full access and others "read-only" access to documents in a Livelink system, with easy upgrades available at additional cost. The software was particularly useful for large multinational firms that had staff in far-flung locations working on projects together.

News of the company's new contract with Ford helped boost its stock price to more than $20 from a recent low of $5, and in March Open Text issued special warrants for 1.75 million new shares to Canadian institutional investors to raise $35 million. The same month saw the firm introduce a new business-friendly search engine, Livelink Pinstripe.

INFORMATION DIMENSIONS PURCHASED IN SUMMER OF 1998

In June Open Text acquired Information Dimensions, Inc. of Dublin, Ohio. That firm, which employed 170 and had revenues of $20 million, was considered the company's closest competitor after market leader Documentum, Inc. of California. After the sale Open Text would draw even with the latter, employing 570 and selling its products in 31 countries.

Results for the fiscal year ended in June (when the firm's shares had also begun trading on the Toronto Stock Exchange) showed revenues doubling to $45.3 million, with a loss of $23.5 million largely due to the $18.4 million spent to acquire Information Dimensions. Livelink was now being used at 2.5 million "seats," the industry term for individual users.

In October Open Text appointed John Shackleton to take over the president's role from Brett Newbold, and in late November the company made an offer to buy PC Docs Group International, Inc. The latter firm offered a similar product to Livelink that was installed at one million seats, which analysts cited as the primary reason Open Text was seeking the acquisition. The $162 million proposal was rejected as a "Grinch-like stunt" by PC Docs, however, and the offer was later retracted. Soon afterwards Open Text bought the assets of bankrupt document management firm Lava Systems, Inc. and introduced MyLivelink, which would serve as a web search engine for companies' internal web-based documents.

In April 1999 the firm, whose stock had doubled in price since December, sold two million additional stock warrants for $34 each to investment dealers, and then offered CAD 235.5 million in cash to buy PC Docs, which had tentatively accepted a lower offer from Hummingbird Communications Ltd. The latter firm subsequently boosted its offer, however, and Open Text withdrew. Not long afterwards the company acquired MicroStar Software, Ltd. for approximately $7 million, and bought a 15 percent stake in Communities.com, which operated chat rooms where users could share video, audio, or text.

In early 2000 Open Text created a new unit to operate a web site through which companies could exchange documents and perform transactions. The firm also began to offer Livelink through application service providers including British Telecom and KPNQwest, which enabled smaller companies to lease the software rather than buy it. For the year ending in June 2000,

Open Text reported revenues of $112.9 million and a profit of $25.1 million.

The year 2000 had also seen the company form an alliance with BlackBerry maker Research In Motion and acquire Bluebird Systems of California and part of LeadingSide, Inc. of Massachusetts. According to some observers, small acquisitions such as these were primarily made to obtain new employees. Finding talented workers had become difficult, and in 2001 Open Text launched a recruiting effort that sought to add 400 new employees to its staff of 1,100.

After the September 11, 2001 terrorist attacks on the United States caused business travel to plummet, the firm's software became even more attractive to companies with geographically dispersed units, and despite the worsening North American economy Open Text's sales remained strong. The firm also began ramping up development of secure document storage and viewing options for new clients that included U.S. government agencies, and it subsequently won certification from the U.S. Department of Defense for its secure software. Over the next several years a newly formed government operations division would grow to produce more than 10 percent of revenues.

In December Open Text bid $68.5 million for electronic form producer Accelio Corp., which had 8.5 million users, but that firm's board voted unanimously to reject the offer. Accelio was later purchased by Adobe Systems, Inc. for a much higher figure, while Open Text, which had acquired an 18 percent stake, made a substantial profit.

In 2002 the firm paid $30 million to acquire Centrinity, Inc., whose FirstClass Communications Platform gave integrated access to voice mail, email, and fax content for educational and business users. The Livelink software suite was also in the process of being upgraded, and recently added options included Records Management 2.0 and Livelink MeetingZone 2.0, which enhanced physical records management and online conferences, respectively. Installations of Open Text's flagship product, now available in the improved version 9.1, reached six million seats during the year.

Acquisitions continued in 2003 with business-communications software maker Eloquent, Inc. of California, web portal software company Corechange, Inc. of Massachusetts, and Web content management software maker Gauss Interprise AG of Germany.

IXOS ACQUISITION DOUBLES FIRM'S SIZE IN 2004

Open Text's largest purchase to date came in October 2003 when a $230 million deal was reached to buy Ixos Software AG of Germany, a document management and email archiving technology firm. The adoption of the Sarbanes-Oxley Act in the United States had made archiving of emails a necessity for corporations, while also increasing the complexity of record-keeping. After the sale closed in early 2004 it doubled the size of the company to 2,000 employees, though 130 Ixos workers were let go. The merged firms would have total revenues of $375 million.

The summer of 2004 saw Open Text form an alliance with Siemens AG of Germany to provide consulting and support services in Europe. The company also paid $24 million to buy Quest Software, Inc.'s Vista Plus software management and storage product line during the year.

In July 2005 President John Shackleton took over as CEO from Tom Jenkins, who would continue to serve as chairman. The firm subsequently announced a restructuring that included layoffs of 15 percent of its workforce of 2,200 and the closing of 27 offices, which was expected to save CAD 40 million per year. Some operations would be consolidated, with primary business locations continuing to be Ontario, Chicago, and Munich, Germany. According to several observers Open Text was having trouble combining its operations with Ixos, though the firm itself cited slowdowns in Europe and Japan, currency price fluctuations, and delays in completing several major transactions.

In August the company bought Artesia Technologies, Inc. of Maryland, which made software to manage large digital video, audio, and graphics files. Several months later Open Text announced that Microsoft would offer Artesia as an option in its SQL Server 2005 database platform, and the program was later purchased for use by the National Collegiate Athletics Association.

Fall also saw Open Text move into a new headquarters facility in the University of Waterloo Research and Technology Park, on a street named Frank Tompa Drive in honor of one of the company's founders. Sales for the year totaled $414.8 million, with a profit of $20.4 million recorded. Revenue from software licenses accounted for $136.5 million, customer support $179.2 million, and service $99.1 million.

Open Text, which had recently bought back one million shares of its stock, now had no debt and a war chest of more than $80 million. Its software products were installed in some 20 million seats in 114 countries around the world. Expansion was continuing, and early 2006 saw the company form an alliance with European technology consulting giant Atos Origin to market Livelink.

In 15 years Open Text Corporation had grown into one of the top makers of electronic content management software in the world, taking in nearly half a billion dollars a year from a category that did not exist when it was formed. The company's products were essential tools for organizations that required multi-user access and secure storage of a wide range of electronic file types.

Frank Uhle

PRINCIPAL SUBSIDIARIES

Open Text, Inc. (U.S.); Artesia Technologies, Inc. (U.S.); Open Text Eloquent, Inc. (U.S.); Open Text GmbH (Germany); Ixos Software AG (Germany); Gauss Interprise AG (Germany).

PRINCIPAL COMPETITORS

FileNet Corporation; EMC Corporation; Hummingbird Ltd.; Interwoven, Inc.; International Business Machines Corporation; Microsoft Corporation.

FURTHER READING

Alphonso, Caroline, "Open Text a Light in Tech Gloom," *Globe and Mail,* August 30, 2001, p. B14.

Avery, Simon, "Analysts Closing the Book on Open Text," *Globe and Mail,* July 13, 2005, p. B11.

———, "Open Text Seeks SEC Extension for Filing Results," *Globe and Mail,* September 16, 2005, p. B7.

Brethour, Patrick, "Open Text Buys Information Dimensions," *Globe and Mail,* June 4, 1998, p. B3.

———, "Open Text Tops Up Its Talent," *Globe and Mail,* August 13, 1997, p. B10.

Chu, Showwei, "Open Text Agrees to Buy Centrinity," *Globe and Mail,* September 20, 2002, p. B5.

———, "Why Techs Keep Bids Friendly," *Globe and Mail,* January 16, 2002, p. M1.

Damsell, Keith, "Open Text Sales to Soar with Deal for Rival," *Globe and Mail,* October 22, 2003, p. B1.

Deruyter, Ron, "Open Text Loses $12.9 Million US," *Kitchener-Waterloo Record,* November 4, 2005, p. D4.

Evans, Mark, "Open Text Rides Internet-Mania," *Globe and Mail,* April 16, 1999, p. B11.

Hamilton, Tyler, "Open Text Shares Dive After Quarterly News," *Globe and Mail,* October 30, 1999, p. B8.

Hercz, Robert, "High Browse," *Canadian Business,* June 1, 1996, p. 74.

Leitch, Carolyn, "Open Text Clicks with Investors," *Globe and Mail,* March 5, 1998, p. B16.

Maurino, Romina, "Open Text Says Partnerships Will Help Profitability," *Canadian Press,* December 15, 2005.

———, "Open Text Slashes Jobs, Closes Offices to Offset Slump," *Globe and Mail,* September 9, 2005, p. B4.

McCarthy, Shawn, "Security Foray a Prized Open Text Chapter," *Globe and Mail,* June 29, 2004, p. B9.

Mulqueen, John T., "The Trading Gets Complex," *Communications Week,* January 29, 1996, p. 93.

Nadile, Lisa, "Open Text Books Private Intranets," *PC Week,* February 19, 1996, p. 14.

"Open Text Shares Soar," *Kitchener-Waterloo Record,* January 25, 1996, p. B6.

Rowan, Geoffrey, "Open Text Teams Up with Yahoo," *Globe and Mail,* September 19, 1995, p. B3.

Wheelwright, Geof, "Technology Triangle," *Financial Post,* October 18, 1997, p. IT01.

PagesJaunes Groupe SA

7 Ave. de la Cristallerie
Sevres,
France
Telephone: 33 01 46 23 30 00
Fax: 33 01 46 23 32 86
Web site: http://www.pagesjaunes.fr

Public Subsidiary of France Telecom
Incorporated: 1946 as Office d'Annonces
Employees: 4,762
Sales: EUR 1.06 billion ($1.24 billion) (2005)
Stock Exchanges: Euronext Paris
Ticker Symbol: PAJ.PA
NAIC: 323119 Other Commercial Printing; 541810 Advertising Agencies

■ ■ ■

PagesJaunes Groupe SA is France's leading publisher of printed and online telephone directories, as well as the country's leading business web site developer. The company controls the French yellow pages, and is also responsible for printing its white pages, formerly known as the Pages Blanches but now rebranded as L'Annuaire in coordination with its parent company, France Telecom. Both L'Annuaire and the Pages Jaunes are present in print, online, and via France's Minitel system. Each year the company publishes more than 356 editions of its directories, with a total circulation of nearly 68 million. The company's directories represent one of the most widely used advertising platforms in France, with average monthly consultations of some 169 million. Formerly part of internet access provider Wanadoo, also a France Telecom subsidiary, PagesJaunes maintains an active web site development wing, targeting the business market. At the beginning of 2006, PagesJaunes was responsible for more than 26,000 business web sites. The company also controls the Mappy online map and itinerary service, as well as Wanadoo Data, which markets business-oriented databases and services. PagesJaunes has made some inroads in its attempt to expand outside of France: the company controls PagesJaunes Liban, where it publishes Lebanon's official telephone directory; Eurodirectory SA, which publishes the telephone directory for the Luxembourg market; and QDQ, which publishes an alternative yellow pages for the Spanish market. PagesJaunes also publishes the Kompass business directories in Belgium, Luxembourg, and Spain. PagesJaunes Groupe is listed on the Euronext Paris stock exchange. France Telecom controls 54 percent of the company. In 2005, PagesJaunes generated revenues of EUR 1.06 billion ($1.24 billion).

GROWING WITH THE FRENCH TELEPHONE IN THE 20TH CENTURY

The first telephone exchange in France was built in 1883 by the private company SGT (Société Générale du Telephones), under license from the French government. By the end of the decade, the country already counted some 15,000 telephones, and by the beginning of World War I, that number had already topped 300,000. While the penetration of the country's telephone system remained proportionally modest, and particularly limited to the major metropolitan areas, the growing numbers

COMPANY PERSPECTIVES

Innovation—a daily challenge. PagesJaunes has come up with new solutions to meet the needs of developing technologies. The Group is already France's leading business website developer, with a portfolio of 25,600 sites.

of subscribers presented the need to develop a directory service. While early directories featured simply names, the development of automated switching systems in the late 1890s, and the rapidly growing subscriber numbers, produced the need for full-fledged directories featuring names, numbers, and addresses. The first directories began to appear in the 1890s, and in the late 1890s, the French government formed a new organization, called the Service national des annuaires téléphoniques, or Snat.

By then, many directory publishers had already begun to publish separate directories or directory sections for residential customers and commercial customers. In larger markets, independent business-to-business directories also became popular. By tradition, the commercial directories were printed on yellow paper. Legend had that the first "yellow page" directory appeared in 1883, when a directory printer ran out of white paper and used yellow paper instead. Later research established that black type was easier for customers to read against the yellow paper. Before long, the yellow page format had been adopted by directory publishers throughout the world.

In addition to their utility, the directories, which were provided for free in France, also became a highly prized advertising medium. Since the directories were distributed to nearly every household and business with a telephone, they boasted significantly deep advertising penetration rates. By selling space, including a business's listing itself, in the yellow page directory, publishers were able to generate significant revenues. In France, these revenues helped offset the cost of printing and distributing the telephone directories.

In 1946, the French government decided to separate the telephone directories' publishing and printing wing from its advertising side. In that year, the sale of advertising space in the yellow pages was turned over to the Office d'Annonces (ODA), which was placed under control of the government-owned Havas advertising group. The Snat and the ODA remained separate throughout the following decades before being joined in the 1990s. While the Snat, attached to the French PTT (which later became France Telecom), held the monopoly on directory printing and publishing, the ODA gained the monopoly on editing (including advertising sales) and diffusion of the directories.

ODA's early revenues were modest, reaching the equivalent of just EUR 1.6 million at the middle of the 1950s. Yet the French government became determined not only to modernize the country's telephone system, which had suffered a great deal of damage during World War II, but also to extend it to every part of the country. With the PTT legally obligated to extend its reach to as much as 100 percent coverage of the population, the growth of the telephone network was accompanied by the growth in Snat's directory publishing activities. By the mid-1980s, the PTT had connected 96 percent of the population. In turn, ODA's revenues grew strongly, and by the early 2000s directory advertising revenues neared EUR 850 million.

A significant factor in ODA's growth in the 1980s, however, came through the development of the Minitel system. Developed by the PTT and launched in 1982, the Minitel was the world's first modem-based consumer online service. From the start, the Minitel featured the country's telephone directories, generating revenues both from advertisers as well as from consumers, who paid fees to access the directories. As a result, the Minitel represented a major source of revenues not only for ODA but also for the future France Telecom, which acquired a 45 percent stake in the ODA. Havas's stake was reduced to 45 percent, while the remainder was held by the Société des Investissments.

The Snat and the ODA's positions were challenged in the late 1980s, however, when the French government passed legislation ending the company's respective monopolies on directory publishing and advertising sales. Indeed, the ODA soon found itself faced with competition, notably from Communication Media Service (CMS), a company established by a former ODA director. CMS succeeded in producing a number of directories, yet never rose to become a serious rival to ODA's domination of the French market. Nonetheless, the appearance of competition led the French government to weigh the possibility of launching ODA as a public company in the early 1990s.

PUBLIC COMPANY

The success of the Minitel service gave France Telecom less incentive to invest in the newly developing internet access market. Yet as internet usage began to grow in France, the telephone monopoly recognized a new opportunity for placing its directory services online. In

KEY DATES

1896: Snat is formed to publish telephone directories in France.
1946: Advertising sales in telephone directories are placed under control of ODA, a Havas subsidiary.
1982: Minitel telephone directory service is launched.
1987: New legislation ends telephone directory monopoly in France.
1996: Pagesjaunes.fr online directory begins operating through France Telecom subsidiary Wanadoo.
1998: France Telecom acquires control of ODA.
1999: Wanadoo acquires Kompass franchises in Spain, the Benelux countries, and France.
2000: ODA and Snat merge as PagesJaunes, which becomes Wanadoo subsidiary; PagesJaunes acquires Indice Multimedia in Spain.
2004: Wanadoo transfers ownership of Kompass franchise and Wanadoo Data to PagesJaunes, which goes public; PagesJaunes acquires full control of Eurodirectory in Luxembourg.
2005: PagesJaunes acquires e-sama through Wanadoo Data.
2006: France Telecom transfers ownership of L'Annuaire to PagesJaunes.

1996, France Telecom founded its own internet access service, Wanadoo, which then became responsible for the implementation and access to the new online version of the PagesJaunes.

ODA's ownership had made a number of changes in the 1990s, with Havas taking 100 percent control toward the end of the decade. In 1998, however, Havas transferred its shares in ODA to a France Telecom subsidiary, Cogecom. By 2000, France Telecom decided to merge ODA with most of Snat, forming a single company, then named PagesJaunes. Ownership of this company was then transferred to Wanadoo. The transfer in ownership played an important role in Wanadoo's successful initial public offering (IPO) that year. Indeed, throughout most of the 1990s, and into the 2000s, PagesJaunes represented some two-thirds of Wanadoo's total operations. As part of the restructuring, PagesJaunes also took over responsibility for the editing and advertising sales of L'Annuaire, the renamed Pages Blanches, as well as the Minitel service PagesJaunes 3611. These operations, however, remained under the ownership of France Telecom.

In the meantime, PagesJaunes had begun expanding its own directory portfolio. In 1999, PagesJaunes acquired the French, Spanish, and Belgian franchises for the Kompass directories. Founded in Switzerland in the 1940s, Kompass had established itself as one of the world's leading business directory groups, notably through establishing international franchise partnerships.

PagesJaunes continued seeking opportunities for its international expansion. The company targeted Spain at the end of 2000, buying up that country's second largest online and print directory publisher, Indice Multimedia. That business was subsequently renamed QDQ Media, and the name of its core directory adopted the new brand QDQ, LQ Guia Util. In 2001, Wanadoo entered the Lebanese internet market; PagesJaunes followed later, producing a yellow pages for that market. PagesJaunes also entered Luxembourg, teaming up with Italian counterpart SEAT Pagine Gialle to buy up Eurodirectory, which controlled 49 percent of Editus Luxembourg, the publisher of that country's telephone directories.

Expansion into foreign markets, however, brought PagesJaunes head-to-head with those markets' dominant players, which, like PagesJaunes, tended to be offshoots of the region's former telecommunications monopolies. This meant the company's hopes of penetrating new markets in a meaningful way were limited; however, the company continued to enjoy the fruits of its own dominant status in France. That country continued to represent nearly 80 percent of the company's sales into the mid-2000s.

In the meantime, Wanadoo's internet access business, spurred by the development of ADSL technologies, had been growing rapidly. By 2003, PagesJaunes represented just 10 percent of Wanadoo's total sales. Nonetheless, PagesJaunes was enjoying its own brisk growth rate, with revenues rising by more than 50 percent per year.

In 2004, France Telecom, which had remained Wanadoo's majority shareholder, decided to buy back full control of the company. In an agreement with Wanadoo's minority shareholders, France Telecom announced it would then float the PagesJaunes directory business as a separate company. To sweeten the directory publisher's IPO, Wanadoo also transferred its Kompass franchise and its business-to-business database service wing, Wanadoo Data, to PagesJaunes.

PagesJaunes's IPO came in July 2004, when France Telecom placed 36.9 percent of its shares on the Euronext Paris Stock Exchange. The public offering raised more than EUR 1.4 billion ($1.7 billion). The newly public company then moved to strengthen its own shareholdings, notably through buying out partner SEAT Pagine Gialle in order to take full control of Eurodirectory.

At the beginning of 2005, in a new move to expand its range of services, PagesJaunes acquired e-sama, a specialist in database hosting and customer relationship management services. The new subsidiary was placed under Wanadoo Data, boosting its relationship marketing offering. At that time, France Telecom, which had recently acquired Equant, announced its intention to sell more of its shares in PagesJaunes. The secondary offering, made in February 2005, raised an additional EUR 440 million, while reducing France Telecom's stake in the directory group to 54 percent. At that time, France Telecom acknowledged its intention ultimately to reduce its holding in Pages Jaunes to just over 50 percent.

In January 2006, France Telecom transferred ownership of L'Annuaire to Pages Jaunes. The company in the meantime continued developing the services offering of its PagesJaunes internet operation, which was rapidly becoming the company's most important business. The company added a number of features, such as embedded voice and video applications, and, at the beginning of 2006, formed a partnership with eStara, a specialist in internet-based telephony applications, to add "click-to-call" services. In February of that year, the company announced new partnerships with Institut Géographique National and Allociné to add content to the pagesjaunes.fr site. By then, PagesJaunes's online site had become one of the most widely visited web sites in France.

M. L. Cohen

PRINCIPAL SUBSIDIARIES

Edicom SA; Editus (Luxembourg); E-Sama; Eurodirectory SA (Luxembourg); Kompass Belgium; Kompass France; Mappy SA; PagesJaunes Liban; PagesJaunes Outre-Mer; PagesJaunes SA; QDQ Media; Wanadoo Data SA.

PRINCIPAL COMPETITORS

Edward Thompson (Printers) Ltd.; News Corporation Ltd.; Bertelsmann AG; Daily Mail and General Trust PLC; Caverswall Holdings Ltd.; Giesecke and Devrient GmbH; The Polestar Group Ltd.; Yell Group PLC.

FURTHER READING

"Eurodirectory Now Fully Owned by PagesJaunes," *RDSL Europe*, October 15, 2004.

"France Telecom Sells Pages Jaunes for EU440m," *Euroweek*, February 11, 2005, p. 26.

Négréanu, Gérard, "ÓDA: une truffe en bourse," *L'Expansion*, May 6, 1993.

Neville, Laurence, "PagesJaunes Targets Transparency," *Corporate Finance*, February 2005, p. 24.

"Pages Jaunes fait du web qui rapporte," *L'Expansion*, November 8, 2001.

"PagesJaunes Increases Revenues 12.6% in 3Q, Buys Directories," *Yellow Pages & Directories Report*, November 12, 2004.

Reece, Damian, "France Telecom Unveils Plans to Float Directories Business," *Independent*, June 23, 2004, p. 38.

Tieman, Ross, "France Telecom Plans Directory IPO," *Daily Deal*, June 23, 2004.

———, "PagesJaunes Makes Flat Debut," *Daily Deal*, July 9, 2004.

"Votre vieil annuaire est une mine d'or," *L'Expansion*, March 15, 2001.

"Wanadoo Directories Surpasses Targets, Expands in Middle East," *Yellow Pages & Directory Report*, February 14, 2001.

PDQ Food Stores Inc.

8383 Greenway Blvd.
Middleton, Wisconsin 53562
U.S.A.
Telephone: (608) 836-3335
Toll Free: (800) 972-3817
Fax: (608) 836-8233
Web site: http://www.pdqstores.com

Private Company
Founded: 1949
Employees: 675
Sales: $154 million (2005 est.)
NAIC: 445120 Convenience Stores; 447190 Other Gasoline Stations

■ ■ ■

PDQ Foods Stores Inc. owns and operates more than 40 convenience stores in Wisconsin, Minnesota, and California. The company ranks among the top 100 privately held companies in its home state of Wisconsin. In an era of sprawling superstores, PDQ lures time-crunched customers with the promise of convenience: convenient parking, convenient locations, convenient hours, and convenient shopping. Over the years, the family-owned operation has shifted strategy, first expanding then contracting geographically. During the last decade and a half, PDQ has been expanding the size of individual units, part of a national trend for convenience stores.

MADISON MERCHANT MAKING MOVES

Sam Jacobsen opened his first store, Tri Dairy, in 1948. A slow start-up, Jacobsen improved business by adding groceries, beer, soft drinks, and other merchandise. He operated a single unit for 13 years, until he had enough money to add a second store in 1962. Jacobsen's wife Mary adopted a World War I era saying, "Pretty Darn Quick," for the new store's name. The Tri Dairy store also changed its name to PDQ.

Madison, Wisconsin-based PDQ grew along with the rapid expansion of convenience stores across the United States. According to the *Madison Capital Times*, in 1986, PDQ bought 52 Kwik Way stores in southern Colorado. Operating 109 outlets in Wisconsin, Minnesota, Colorado, and Florida by 1991, Sam Jacobsen determined it was time to sell the business to his sons Jeff and Chris. But the chain would change its growth plan during the next few years.

Regional refiner and marketer of petroleum Diamond Shamrock purchased the Colorado operations of PDQ Food Stores in 1994. Twelve convenience stores/retail gas units were located in the greater Denver area, two in Colorado Springs, two in Pueblo, one in Falcon, and one in Canon City. The Colorado stores, which employed about 125 people, would be renamed Diamond Shamrock Corner Stores and join approximately 2,000 other branded outlets in eight states. According to the *Journal Record* (Oklahoma City), PDQ President Jim Shelton said the sale to the $2.6 billion San Antonio-based company allowed "PDQ to focus on our primary position outside of Colorado." Diamond

COMPANY PERSPECTIVES

Quick, Courteous Service is our goal and our Mission Statement. We strive to provide the highest quality products and services coupled with quick friendly service at the most convenient locations around town. We are a privately held family run company with over 50 years in the convenience store business.

Shamrock had been looking for an opportunity to expand in Colorado, where it already held about 100 locations. PDQ turned attention to its stores in Wisconsin and Minnesota.

RE-SHELVING

Seeking time-saving measures, PDQ eliminated the lottery in 14 of its 18 stores in 1995. While customer traffic fell off by 5 to 7 percent per week during the first few weeks, same store sales stayed steady. "From the start, we knew we did the right thing," PDQ Marketing Director Terry Dehring told *National Petroleum News*. "Before long, the numbers of customers returned to their normal levels. Then we found that turnaround time of customer transactions had improved 25% without lottery. The flow was much improved at the checkout area."

Dehring speculated lost lottery customers had been replaced by the return of people driven away by long lottery lines. Moreover, lottery ticket purchasers often bought little else. Other convenience store chains were evaluating the value of low commission lottery sales to their operations. PDQ had analyzed the effects of the lottery program on the stores prior to their elimination and had given customers notice of the pending change.

PDQ moved to protect its sales through the court system in the late 1990s. According to a January 1999 *Supermarket News* article, the company filed suit against Woodman's Supermarkets, a competing seven-store chain, over cheap gas sales. The state of Wisconsin imposed a 9.18 percent markup per gallon over the daily wholesale rate, which PDQ claimed Woodman's had failed to adhere to on a number of occasions in 1998. The markup was intended to create a level playing field for smaller players, by prohibiting below cost sales of certain products. An amendment to The Wisconsin Unfair Sales Act of 1939 allowed competitors to sue one another for injuries related to violations of the act. Woodman's denied the charges. Opponents sought repeal of the minimum markup law.

With gross sales for 1998 at $110 million, a survey by accounting firm Arthur Andersen ranked PDQ as the 79th largest privately held company in Wisconsin. The Jacobsen family continued to lead the operation. Jeff Jacobsen chaired the three-member board, which also included President Dave Savich and retired President Jim Shelton. Sixteen of the 40 PDQ stores were located in Madison, 14 in the Minneapolis/St. Paul area, and ten in the Milwaukee area. Employees numbered about 500.

After a half-century of operation, PDQ had become a fixture in the Madison area, successfully operating stores even in close proximity of one another. Obtaining hot locations, even when near an existing store, presented an opportunity. With two stores relatively close to each other but on opposite sides of a highway, customers could drop into a PDQ without the hassle of crossing over lanes of heavy traffic. "The market is there. We might as well be our own competition," Randy Manning, director of real estate for PDQ, told Mike Ivey with the *Madison Capital Times*.

But not everyone in the Madison area wanted a PDQ on the street where they lived. Detractors rejected the company's claims to being a close relation to the old neighborhood corner-grocery store. With all PDQ stores selling gasoline, 60 percent of total revenues were generated by fuel sales, according to the *Madison Capital Times*.

The National Association of Convenience Stores said about 93 percent of convenience stores opened in 1998 sold gas. Trucks and sport utility vehicles had helped drive up the nation's gasoline consumption. U.S. convenience store gross sales climbed 5 percent in 1998 to $164 billion and profit was up 37.8 percent over 1997. National convenience store chains included Dallas-based 7-Eleven, North Carolina's The Pantry Inc., and Marathon Oil Company division SuperAmerica. PDQ's competitors also included Madison-based Stop N Go Stores and LaCrosse-based Kwik Trip Inc.

Even though convenience stores had established themselves as part of the American landscape, over the years they had struggled with blows to their reputation. Open all hours, convenience store employees were more vulnerable to crime, putting a store's name on the front page. In addition, at times the merchandise they carried raised the ire of communities. "John Becker, president and CEO of Stop N Go Stores, said the industry in general is headed away from its beer and pornography reputation," Ivey wrote for the *Madison Capital Times*. The PDQ stores in Madison, for example, did not sell adult magazines or rolling papers.

KEY DATES

1948: Sam Jacobsen opens first store as Tri Dairy.
1949: PDQ Food Stores Inc. is founded
1962: Company opens second store, first under the PDQ name.
1986: Company buys convenience stores in Colorado.
1991: Sam Jacobsen sells business to sons Jeff and Chris.
1995: PDQ eliminates lottery sales to improve customer service.
1999: PDQ celebrates a half-century of operation.
2005: Company is now operating stores up to 6,000 square feet in size.

PDQ had moved to differentiate itself from the run of the mill convenience store in other ways. In 1991, a relatively spacious 3,400 square foot format had been launched. The store was 50 percent larger than most of its competitors. Amenities included ATM machines, larger bathrooms, wider aisles, and designer coffee.

BIGGER AND BETTER

PDQ Food Stores, like any commercial venture, ran up against some obstacles in its path to growth. Some of those were peculiar to a particular location. In 2001, for example, PDQ faced an unwritten policy: beer and milk do not mix. Although there was nothing formal, lawmakers in a town southeast of Madison traditionally refused requests for beer licenses from food stores. In another matter, in the early 2000s, PDQ engaged in a legal battle over property polluted by a landfill in a town near Milwaukee.

In addition to adding to its number of stores, PDQ continued expanding their size. At least one visitor was impressed following a trip to a 6,000-square-foot PDQ store opened in August 2005. "Wow. I wished they'd build one out by us," Sharon Kelter told the *Wisconsin State Journal.* "We want more, more, more. We're all in a big hurry." PDQ customers at the chain's larger stores certainly did get more: 20 gas pumps, a double-bay automatic car wash, made-to-order sandwiches, and a walk-in beer cooler.

For the 21st-century convenience store, what was inside mattered just as much if not more than what was outside. According to the Virginia-based National Association of Convenience Stores (NACS), inside sales drove profitability. "You don't make your money on gas," NACS spokesman Jeff Lenard said in the *Wisconsin State Journal.* "You can make more on selling a doughnut." But convenience stores had to lure people inside to sell those doughnuts. For a customer to use plastic to pay for gas at the pump was just not enough to keep the operations in the black in days of volatile gas prices.

As some stores grew to 10,000 square feet, complete with restaurants, the NACS's definition of convenience stores had been outstripped. "A convenience store is defined by the association as a shop with off-street parking, extended hours of operation and seven-day-a-week service, more than 500 different items for sale and less than 5,000 square feet," Barry Adams explained in his *Wisconsin State Journal* article. In 2004 the nation had 138,205 convenience stores and reported record revenues of $394 billion. Retailing giant Wal-Mart produced $285 billion in U.S. sales that year.

As neighborhoods lost traditional grocery stores, some of those many convenience stores became the sole source of food for low-income shoppers. While PDQ emphasized the benefits of its operation for the neighborhoods it entered, others had a wait-and-see attitude.

"We certainly are happy to see redevelopment in that area," Middleton city planner Eileen Kelley told the *Wisconsin State Journal.* "One thing we're hoping is that there are uses that help meet the daily needs of those who live there." The site under development for Middleton, on the northwest side of the city of Madison, would be Dane County's 21st PDQ store.

PDQ was a bigger player compared to some competitors in its own neck of the woods, yet smaller than others. More than half of the convenience stores in the state were one-store operations. Kwik Trip, on the other end of the spectrum, was the Badger state's largest operator with 227 stores. PDQ had yet to announce plans for the development of additional stores in the Madison area, but during 2005 the privately held company acquired three properties, spending more than $2.5 million, according to the *Wisconsin State Journal.*

Even though convenience stores were trying harder to win food customers, the executive director of the Wisconsin Grocers Association could not see the day when convenience stores would replace grocery stores offering larger selection and lower prices. "Certainly it's competition, but you have to take into account what a consumer is looking for," Brandon Scholz told the *Wisconsin State Journal.* "In reality, there are more grocery stores than there have been in the past. The difference is there are fewer independents." PDQ for its part intended to make sure consumers looking for something in a big hurry equated them with "Quick, Courteous Service."

Kathleen Peippo

PRINCIPAL COMPETITORS

7-Eleven, Inc.; Exxon Mobil Corporation; Kwik Trip, Inc.; Valero Energy Corporation.

FURTHER READING

Adams, Barry, "Fast and Tempting; Quik-Stop Stores Get Bigger, Flashier," *Wisconsin State Journal,* February 5, 2006, p. C1.

"Diamond Shamrock Signs Agreement to Acquire 18 PDQ Food Stores Sites," *Journal Record* (Oklahoma City), June 25, 1994.

Doege, David, "PDQ Store Owners Want Suit Dismissed," *Milwaukee Journal Sentinel,* January 19, 2005, p. 2.

Dwyer, Steve, "Minus Lottery, PDQ Hits Jackpot," *National Petroleum News,* April 1996, p. 20.

Harrison, Michael, "C-Store Sues Woodman's on Gas Price," *Supermarket News,* January 18, 1999, p. 4.

Ivey, Mike, "Pretty Darn Busy Area PDQ Stores Still Growing After 50 Years," *Madison Capital Times,* September 18, 1999, p. 1E.

"Milk and Beer Mix for First Time in Stoughton," *Wisconsin State Journal,* October 23, 2001, p. D2.

"MW Marketers Score Below-Cost Victories," *Oil Express,* November 13, 2001, p. 23.

Penzeys Spices

Penzeys Spices, Inc.

P.O. Box 924
Brookfield, Wisconsin 53045
U.S.A.
Telephone: (262) 785-7676
Toll Free: (800) 741-7787
Fax: (262) 860-1777
Web site: http://www.penzeys.com

Private Company
Incorporated: 1988 as Penzeys Spice House, Ltd.
Employees: 250
Sales: $22 million (2005 est.)
NAIC: 311942 Spice and Extract Manufacturing; 445299 All Other Specialty Food Stores

■ ■ ■

With stores in 18 states and headquarters in Brookfield, Wisconsin, Penzeys Spices, Inc. grinds, blends, packs, and ships spices to customers nationwide, and sells it aromatic wares at 30 retail locations around the country. The company imports cooking ingredients that are available as dried leaves or whole seeds, coarsely ground or finely powdered, from growers around the world.

1957–86: FROM LOCAL SPICE STORE TO MAIL-ORDER SPICE BUSINESS

In 1957, Ruth and Bill Penzey, Sr., started a coffee and spice business in Milwaukee, Wisconsin. Their son, Bill Penzey, joined the business when he was ten, working in the family store. Later on, the Penzeys narrowed their business to focus solely on herbs and spices, calling it the Spice House. While definitions vary, generally speaking, a spice is a root or seed, and an herb is a leaf.

In 1986, the younger Penzey spun off the mail-order aspect of the company as Penzeys Spice House, Ltd. He refused to take out a bank loan, and instead put all profits back into the business, surviving at first on a weekly budget of about $8. Armed with an Acer personal computer and a daisy wheel printer, the 22-year-old Penzey published his own spice catalog. For the first three years, he was the company's sole employee, living on about $10,000 per year. Penzey, Jr., also began traveling to such places as Bali and Turkey for four months of each year to establish contacts with new suppliers and to inspect the quality of spices coming in from existing suppliers. While overseas, he liked to photograph spices growing in the fields for use in the company's sales catalog.

Fortunately for Penzey, the late 1980s were a time when, inspired by travel, nostalgia, and an interest in culinary roots, Americans were taking more of an interest in ethnic cooking and wanted to learn the recipes of their grandmothers. "Our grandmothers knew more about spices than our mothers," Penzey said in a 2005 *Oregonian* article, going on to explain that, up until the 1930s, Americans used a fair amount of spices. But in the 1940s, ships were diverted from importing spices to transport war supplies, and sales of spices slacked off for the rest of the decade. In the 1950s, processed foods became more popular, and the general interest in spices declined still further.

COMPANY PERSPECTIVES

We have tried to build our business on these feelings of caring that we see every day in our customers. We know that if you want to get people to cook you have to show them the value in it and we are pretty convinced the real value is in the lifetime of relationships it creates.

1990–99: STEADY GROWTH AND THE DEBUT OF STORES IN WISCONSIN

In 1987, Penzey moved his mail-order business to an 8,000-square-foot building in Oak Creek, Wisconsin, and, in 1990, moved it again to a new 25,000-square-foot facility in Waukesha, Wisconsin. Throughout the 1990s, the mail-order business grew steadily, mostly by word of mouth. In 1994, the company branched out, opening the first Penzeys Spices store in Milwaukee, Wisconsin. "With spices you want to be able to compare things, smell things to see which ones you like," Penzey explained about opening the store, looking back in a 2005 *Boston Globe* article. "It's a very sensory sort of experience you can't exactly get with a catalog."

By 1997, there were two retail Penzeys stores, one on Blue Mound Road in Brookfield, Wisconsin, and one on University Avenue in Madison, Wisconsin, which together did about 10 percent of the company's business. Penzeys Spice House, Ltd. had grown to a point where the warehouse in Waukesha, Wisconsin, was cramped and chaotic. Warehouse shelves contained more than 250 different herbs and spices that were ground and packaged for shipping at small work stations scattered throughout the building. The firm employed about 40 people, having grown from 13 people in 1992. "For the past three years, we've been growing at a rate of about 50 percent annually," announced Penzey in a 1997 *Milwaukee Journal Sentinel* article.

By the late 1990s, nationally, per capita consumption of herbs and spices had increased from two decades earlier by more than 50 percent annually, from two pounds to more than three pounds, according to the American Spice Trade Association. The then current trend in spices was hot spices, which as a group accounted for 41 percent of Americans' spice consumption. Consumption of white pepper and of mustard seed had increased 58 percent since 1980, while consumption of red pepper was up 125 percent.

2000–06: NATIONAL EXPANSION VIA COMPANY-OWNED OUTLETS

In 1999 Penzeys Spices, Ltd. opened a sister business, Penzeys Spices, Inc., to take charge of its outlet operations. These stores, which began to appear in 2000 under the name Penzeys (without the apostrophe), allowed the company to sell a fresh, high-quality product less expensively than in grocery stores where shelf space was very expensive. The outlet stores were designed to have an old-fashioned, homey atmosphere. Wooden crates formed the aisles, with containers of blends, herbs, and spices of all sizes arranged alphabetically by category. There was a special section of flavors for baking, including multiple varieties of cinnamon. Large jars contained samples of products for sniffing with labels that explained the origin and use of each spice or herb. A year later, the company moved production to another new 90,000-square-foot facility in Brookfield, Wisconsin.

In January 2002, the company opened stores in Pittsburgh, Pennsylvania, and Columbus, Ohio, locations chosen because of the large number of mail-order customers in the area. Between 2002 and 2004, Penzeys opened a total of 11 more stores. At first, the company brought people in to open the new outlets, but soon switched to hiring people rooted in the community. All stores closed at 5:30 so employees could go home and have a home-cooked meal with family.

Toward the end of 2004, Penzeys debuted *PenzeysOne*, a bimonthly magazine that was a natural outgrowth of the company's catalog, which by then had garnered a cult following, in large part because of the dozen or so recipes included in each issue. It sold to Penzeys' 300,000 mail-order customers at a subscription cost of $19.95 per year. Penzey was optimistic about the future of *PenzeysOne*, despite the fact that other cataloguers had failed in similar publishing attempts. "We have a great relationship with our customers. We hear great stories, get cooking tips in our call center and stores, and we're going to focus more on the content we're already creating," he said in a 2004 *Catalog Age* article. In keeping with the company's "everyman" philosophy, *PenzeysOne*'s motto became "The food magazine by and for everyone," and shared stories, recipes, and photographs of ordinary American home cooks. "People see spices and think we must only be for gourmets. But we have plenty of things for the everyday cook," Penzey further explained in a 2005 *Boston Globe* article.

In early 2005, having launched one or two stores every year since 1994, the company, by now called Penzeys Spices, Inc., opened its 22nd store in Boston after more customers from the Boston area lobbied for an outlet than anywhere else in the United States. Penzeys decided upon this unique approach to expansion after

KEY DATES

1957: Ruth and Bill Penzey, Sr., start a coffee and spice business in Milwaukee, Wisconsin.
1986: Bill Penzey, Jr., spins off the mail-order aspect of the company.
1987: Penzey moves his mail-order business to Oak Creek, Wisconsin.
1990: The business moves again to a new facility in Waukesha, Wisconsin.
1994: The company opens the first Penzeys Spices store in Milwaukee, Wisconsin.
1999: Penzeys Spice House, Ltd. adds a sister company, Penzeys Spices, Inc., for its outlet business.
2001: The company moves to a new production facility in Brookfield, Wisconsin.
2004: Penzeys debuts PenzeysOne, a bimonthly magazine.
2006: The company purchases a new 300,000-square-foot warehouse in Wauwatosa, Wisconsin, with a projected moving date of January 2007.

noticing that it took a year or two for word of mouth to advertise the presence of a new store and to bring customers in after it opened. In light of this phenomenon, the company decided to try to create the buzz of publicity in advance of each new opening. Ten more new stores were planned by the end of the year, also in places "picked" by Penzeys customers.

Despite reaching revenues of $22 million in 2005, and operating 27 retail stores in 18 states, most of the employees at Penzeys' headquarters still wore several different hats. The people who did packaging would rotate in to take phone orders and also worked in the store outlet. The reason for this was that Penzey believed it was important for all employees to know the company's customers and how they used its products.

With plans in the works to move operations from the company's 90,000-square-foot building in Brookfield to a larger facility in Wauwatosa in 2006, and confirmed leases on stores in Torrance, California; Grand Central Terminal, New York; Philadelphia, Pennsylvania; and Alexandria, Virginia, Penzey was optimistic, but also reflective about the future of his company. Regarding what it meant to have a growing enterprise, he said in a 2005 *Star Tribune* article, "I know there is a time limit on all of this ... so I have to continually remind myself that I might as well do something fun with the time that I'm given. I don't know how many people have as much fun as I have, doing what I do."

Carrie Rothburd

PRINCIPAL COMPETITORS

McCormick & Company, Incorporated.

FURTHER READING

Durbin, Barbara, "Spice World," *Oregonian*, August 9, 2005, p. FD1.

Klink, Luke, "Firm Knows Sweet Smell of Success: Penzeys Spice House Says Business Has Grown 50 Percent Each Year for Three Years," *Milwaukee Journal Sentinel*, March 20, 1997, p. 5.

Nelson, Rick, "From Mail Order to Outlet, His Spice of Life: As Penzeys Spices Celebrates Its 20th Year, Founder Bill Penzey Reflects on the State of Spices and His Far-flung Influence," *Star Tribune*, December 26, 2005, p. 1E.

Retzlaff, Heather, "Penzeys Cooks Up Magazine," *Catalog Age*, December 1, 2004, p. 13.

Rhonde, Marie, "Penzeys Spices Opening in Glendale; Outlet Store Is 26th in 16 States," *Milwaukee Journal Sentinel*, July 30, 2005, p. 3.

Yonan, Joe, "Penzeys Has a Nose for Selling Spices," *Boston Globe*, March 16, 2005, p. E4.

Petrohawk Energy Corporation

1100 Louisiana
Suite 4400
Houston, Texas 77002
U.S.A.
Telephone: (832) 204-2700
Fax: (832) 204-2800
Web site: http://www.petrohawk.com

Public Company
Incorporated: 1997 as Beta Oil & Gas, Inc.
Employees: 154
Sales: $258.0 million (2005)
Stock Exchanges: NASDAQ
Ticker Symbol: HAWK
NAIC: 211111 Crude Petroleum and Natural Gas Extraction

■ ■ ■

Petrohawk Energy Corporation (PEC) is an independent oil and gas company with properties concentrated in Texas, New Mexico, Oklahoma, Kansas, and Louisiana. PEC controls total proved oil and gas reserves of 437.3 billion cubic feet equivalent. An aggressive acquirer, PEC is managed by Floyd C. Wilson, who serves as its chairman, chief executive officer, and president and holds a 67 percent stake in the company.

ORIGINS

Massive, multibillion-dollar mergers in the oil and gas industry tend to attract much of the public's attention, but the small and mid-sized competitors in the industry engage in meaningful deal-making as well, orchestrating the acquisitions, dispositions, and mergers that propel the industry forward. PEC was an enterprise created at the negotiating table, an oil and gas concern that represented a combination of assets drawn from two companies, Beta Oil & Gas, Inc. and Petrohawk Energy L.L.C. Although the driving force behind the company's management and mission came from Petrohawk Energy, its origins were embedded in Beta Oil.

Beta Oil was formed in 1997, beginning its involvement in the oil and gas market at an opportune juncture in the industry's development. Between 1997 and 1999, commodity prices plummeted, causing the price of oil and gas assets to fall as well. Beta Oil swept in, spending its first years in business purchasing assets at depressed prices. The company quickly and cheaply assembled a collection of properties, forming an asset base that leaned heavily toward the exploration end of the oil and gas business. To strike more of a balance between exploration and production, the company purchased Red River Energy in September 2000, gaining a foundation of producing assets to provide a consistent source of cash flow to fund its exploration activities, a so-called "portfolio approach." By 2001, the company's strategy was beginning to deliver its desired results, as Beta Oil commenced an active drilling schedule. Roughly 55 percent of the company production output came from the purchase of Red River, while the remaining 45 percent was produced through its exploration projects. In all, the company owned interests in more than 275 wells primarily in Texas, Oklahoma, Louisiana, and Wyoming, by mid-2001, enjoying robust gains in production as it found its footing. Beta Oil's production

COMPANY PERSPECTIVES

Petrohawk's business strategy focuses on achieving increases in the per share value of our common stock through the combination of attractive acquisitions and further development of existing properties, complemented by potentially significant exploration projects.

total in 1999 amounted to 486 million cubic feet equivalent (Mmcfe) of gas production before jumping to 1.9 billion cubic feet equivalent (Bcfe) in 2000. By the end of 2001, the company was projecting a 100 percent increase in its production volume to 3.85 Bcfe.

Beta's production volume continued to record exponential increases during the first years of the 21st century, expanding by a factor of ten by the time PEC's other organizing entity, Petrohawk Energy, was founded. The principal figure behind Petrohawk Energy was a 30-year veteran of the energy industry named Floyd C. Wilson, an executive with a wealth of experience in starting up oil and gas ventures. In his career as an entrepreneur in the energy sector, Wilson demonstrated a penchant for forming a company, building up its assets, and then selling the company to another oil and gas company. In 1987, he founded Hugoton Energy Corporation, took it public in 1994, and sold it in 1998 to Chesapeake Energy Corporation for $450 million. Next, in 1999, he formed 3TEC Energy Corporation, serving as its chairman and chief executive officer until he sold the venture to Plains Exploration & Production Corporation in June 2003 for $350 million, a transaction that left him free to pursue his next start-up, Houston, Texas-based Petrohawk Energy L.L.C.

A REVERSE MERGER IN 2004

In forming Petrohawk Energy, Wilson solicited the help of former 3TEC executives. To help finance the venture, he gained the backing of EnCap Investments and Liberty Mutual, an affiliate of Liberty Energy Holdings L.L.C. The mission of the company was specific and, if executed according to plan, relatively short-lived: build up assets, convert to public ownership, and sell the company to another company. Like Hugoton Energy and 3TEC, Petrohawk Energy embraced a build-and-sell strategy, vowing, in filings with the Securities and Exchange Commission (SEC) "to monetize at an appropriate time with the goal of providing superior returns to stockholders." Wilson accomplished his first two goals, acquiring assets and taking the company public, at roughly the same time. He took the most expedient route to converting to public ownership by approaching Beta Oil in late 2003, proposing to execute a reverse merger. Under the terms of the agreement, Petrohawk Energy said it would invest $60 million in the stock of Beta Oil, which would give Wilson majority control over the Tulsa, Oklahoma-based company. "Petrohawk is a new company that was started earlier this year," Beta Oil's president and chief executive officer, David Wilkins, said in a December 16, 2003 interview with *Tulsa World.* "They definitely have the ability to raise capital." Wilson, in the same edition of *Tulsa World,* said, "We intend to use this investment to provide a platform of future growth." When the reverse merger was completed in June 2004, the entity that emerged was PEC, a Houston-based company with Wilson serving as its president, chief executive officer, and chairman. The company represented an amalgamation of Beta Oil's 30 Bcfe and Petrohawk Energy's three Bcfe.

While officials were finalizing the reverse merger in June 2004, Wilson was in Dallas, Texas, working on completing his next goal. His objective was to expand his newly formed company taking shape in Houston, and he had heard that Ronald Wynn, who was in Dallas, might be interested in selling his company, Wynn-Crosby Energy Inc. Wynn-Crosby was the operator of eight partnerships formed between 1995 and 2002, a venture backed by roughly 60 investors that controlled 200 Bcfe of proved reserves in southern and eastern Texas, the Permian Basin in Texas and New Mexico, and the Arkoma Basin in Oklahoma and Arkansas. The discussion between the two energy executives progressed smoothly. "We used those meetings to come to an understanding of the range of value that would lead to a deal until we could get into the technical data," Crosby reflected in a March 2005 interview with *Oil and Gas Investor.* "If I were starting a company and trying to build a public entity, our property base would be a great one to start with," he added. Wilson evidently concurred, agreeing with a handshake in Dallas to push forward with the deal. The deal, revealed to be a $425 million transaction, was announced to the public in November 2004, joining Wynn-Crosby Energy's 200 Bcfe with PEC's 33 Bcfe, which provided a substantial increase to PEC's profile. "This is a transforming event for Petrohawk," Wilson noted in a statement quoted in the November 2004 issue of *Oil and Gas Investor.* "We believe these high-quality, long-lived assets include significant upside, and we will attempt to boost recovery rates within an accelerated development program. We will continue to pursue our combined growth strategies—acquisitions complemented by an aggressive drilling program."

KEY DATES

1997: Beta Oil & Gas, Inc. is formed.
2000: Beta Oil acquires Red River Energy, substantially increasing the number of producing wells it owns.
2003: Petrohawk Energy L.L.C. is formed.
2004: In a reverse merger, Beta Oil and Petrohawk Energy L.L.C. are united, creating Petrohawk Energy Corporation.
2005: After paying $425 million for Wynn-Crosby Energy the year before, Petrohawk Energy doubles in size by acquiring Mission Resources Corporation for $500 million.
2006: Winwell Resources, Inc. is acquired for $208 million.

ACQUISITION OF MISSION RESOURCES IN 2005

True to his word, Wilson pressed ahead with expansion following the Wynn-Crosby Energy deal. In February 2005, PEC completed the purchase of Proton Oil & Gas Corporation, paying $53 million for the company's proved reserves of 28 Bcfe located in Louisiana and Texas. Wilson's next acquisition was much larger, rivaling the size of the Wynn-Crosby Energy purchase. In April 2005, he announced that PEC was acquiring Mission Resources Corporation, a Houston-based company with proved reserves of 226 Bcfe. The $500 million acquisition, completed in July 2005, doubled PEC's size in terms of reserves and production, achieving growth in a manner chosen by many of its rivals. "Companies want to grow production," an analyst explained in an April 5, 2005 interview with the *Houston Chronicle,* "and a lot of them have expressed difficulty achieving the growth rate they want from drilling only—so they turn to acquisitions." The Mission Resources acquisition included three significant fields in the Permian Basin, as well as interests in the Gulf Coast and the south Texas regions.

Acquisitions fueled energetic financial growth during PEC's first years in business. Oil and gas sales leaped from $12.9 million in 2003 to $258 million in 2005, making PEC roughly twice the size of Hugoton Energy and 3TEC when Wilson sold the companies. By August 2005, the company was reportedly searching for a suitor, seeking to sell the assets it had acquired during its first two years in business. "We prefer to grow a smaller cap company because once it reaches a certain size you start getting into the treadmill," a PEC executive remarked in an August 6, 2005 article in *Corporate Financing Week,* before adding, "We hope to do a couple more deals." The sale of PEC was not imminent, but it was on the horizon. In the interim, Wilson and his team worked to make PEC a more desirable company, efforts that included acquisitions and dispositions.

As PEC entered the second half of the decade, it likely entered its last years as an independent company. In early 2006, it moved in two directions as it prepared for its eventual sale. In January 2006, the company acquired Winwell Resources, Inc. for $208 million. The purchase gave PEC 106 Bcfe of proved reserves in northern Louisiana. On the same day it purchased Winwell Resources, the company added to its holdings in northern Louisiana by paying $86 million for assets belonging to Redley Company. In early February 2006, the company countered its increased involvement in northern Louisiana by severing its ties to the Gulf of Mexico. PEC reached an agreement with Northstar GOM, L.L.C. to sell nearly all of its Gulf of Mexico properties for $52.5 million. The divestiture stripped PEC of approximately 25 Bcfe. As Wilson looked to the immediate future, further acquisitions and dispositions were possible, but in the longer term only the company's sale to another oil and gas company appeared certain. PEC executives were expected to be done with their building efforts by the end of the decade, at which point the history of PEC would become part of the history of another energy concern.

Jeffrey L. Covell

PRINCIPAL SUBSIDIARIES

Petrohawk Operating Company; P-H Energy, L.L.C.; Red River Field Services, L.L.C.; Petrohawk Holdings, L.L.C.; Petrohawk Properties, LP.

PRINCIPAL COMPETITORS

BP PLC; Comstock Resources, Inc.; Royal Dutch/Shell Group of Companies.

FURTHER READING

"Beta Oil & Gas," *Oil and Gas Investor,* August 2001, p. 2S4.

Darbonne, Nissa, "Big Fish," *Oil and Gas Investor,* March 2005, p. 45.

Kelly, Andrew, "Petrohawk Expands with $425 Million Deal, Seeks Further Growth Opportunities," *Oil Daily,* October 14, 2004.

Maxwell, Taryn, "Petrohawk Expands in North Louisiana," *Oil and Gas Investor,* February 2006, p. 79.

Patel, Purva, "Petrohawk Strikes Mission Deal," *Houston Chronicle,* April 5, 2005, p. 3.

"Petrohawk Buying Growth Platform for $425MM," *Oil and Gas Investor,* November 2004, p. 101.

"Petrohawk Circles Takeover Prey," *Investment Dealers' Digest,* December 5, 2005.

"Privately Held Petrohawk Energy LLC, Houston, and Beta Oil & Gas Inc., Tulsa, Okla., Have Agreed to Petrohawk's Purchase of $60 Million of Beta Common Stock, Warrants and a Convertible Note," *Oil and Gas Investor,* February 2004, p. 93.

Ray, Russell, "Houston Energy Firm Buying Beta Oil & Gas of Tulsa, Okla.," *Tulsa World,* December 16, 2003.

Pfizer Inc.

235 East 42nd Street
New York, New York 10017-5755
U.S.A.
Telephone: (212) 573-2323
Fax: (212) 573-7851
Web site: http://www.pfizer.com

Public Company
Incorporated: 1900 as Charles Pfizer & Company Inc.
Employees: 106,000
Sales: $51.29 billion (2005)
Stock Exchanges: New York London Euronext Swiss
Ticker Symbol: PFE
NAIC: 325412 Pharmaceutical Preparation Manufacturing; 325411 Medicinal and Botanical Manufacturing; 325320 Pesticide and Other Agricultural Chemical Manufacturing; 424210 Drugs and Druggists' Sundries Merchant Wholesalers; 339113 Surgical Appliance and Supplies Manufacturing; 541710 Research and Development in the Physical, Engineering, and Life Sciences

■ ■ ■

Pfizer Inc. is the largest research-based drugmaker in the world. The company operates in three business segments: healthcare, animal health, and consumer healthcare. Pfizer is the company behind well-known consumer products such as Listerine, Rolaids, Sudafed, and Visine, but the company's greatest revenue producers are its prescription drugs. Pfizer's marquee pharmaceuticals include Viagra, a treatment for erectile dysfunction, Zoloft, an antidepressant, and Lipitor, a cholesterol-lowering pharmaceutical that is the bestselling drug in the world. Pfizer's products are marketed in more than 150 countries.

PFIZER'S EARLY HISTORY

In 1849 Charles Pfizer, a chemist, and Charles Erhart, a confectioner, began a partnership in Brooklyn to manufacture bulk chemicals, Charles Pfizer & Company. While producing iodine preparation and boric and tartaric acids, Pfizer pioneered the production of citric acid, a product Pfizer continues to market to soft drink companies, using large-scale fermentation technology. By the end of the 19th century, Pfizer was producing a wide range of industrial and pharmacological products and had offices in New York and Chicago. In 1900 the company was incorporated in New Jersey as Charles Pfizer & Company Inc.

While Pfizer technicians became experts in fermentation technology, across the ocean Sir Alexander Fleming made his historic discovery of penicillin in 1928. Recognizing penicillin's potential to revolutionize healthcare, scientists struggled for years to produce both a high quality and large quantity of the drug. Experimentation with production became an imperative during the Nazi air raids of London in World War II. In a desperate attempt to solicit help from the community of American scientists, Dr. Howard Florey of Oxford University traveled to the United States to ask the U.S. government to mobilize its scientific resources.

Because of its expertise in fermentation, the government approached Pfizer. Soon afterward, Dr. Jasper Kane

COMPANY PERSPECTIVES

The cycle of renewal drives everything we do at Pfizer. With several Pfizer medicines now coming to the end of their life cycles, we are doing what Pfizer people have done many times since our founding in 1849—build a new platform for extended growth. Pfizer colleagues around the world are putting into place the next-generation Pfizer, one that will meet fast-changing needs in health and healthcare. We are working hard to both transform our business and to be partners in transforming healthcare itself. Our focus remains on our core business—innovation in the medicines that are integral to good healthcare. But our strategy goes further—to help create entire new directions in health and healthcare, exploring systems that start with the simple question: "How can we best help people before disease strikes?"

from the company laboratory began his own experiments. Initially using large glass flasks, Dr. Kane's experimentation then led to deep-tank fermentation. Later, the company announced its entrance into large-scale production with the purchase of an old ice plant in Brooklyn. Refusing government money, the company paid the entire $3 million for the purchase and within four months John McKeen (future chairperson and president) had converted the ancient plant into the largest facility for manufacturing penicillin in the world.

Early production, however, was not without its difficulties. The first yields of penicillin required constant supervision, and yet quality and quantity remained low and inconsistent. In one of those inexplicable quirks of history, however, a government researcher browsing in a fruit market in Peoria, Illinois, discovered a variant of the "Penicillium" mold on an overripe cantaloupe. Using this variant, production suddenly increased from ten units per millimeter to 2,000 units per millimeter. By 1942 Pfizer divided the first flask of penicillin into vials for the medical departments of the Army and Navy; this flask was valued at $150,000. Mass production began in 1944, when Pfizer penicillin arrived with the Allied forces on the beaches of Normandy on D-Day. Meantime, in June 1942, Pfizer reincorporated in Delaware and went public with an offering of 240,000 shares of common stock.

Even as the government controlled production of the drug for the sole use of the Armed Forces, the public, aroused by miraculous results of penicillin, asked Pfizer to release the drug domestically. In 1943 John L. Smith, Pfizer president, and John McKeen, against the explicit regulations of the federal government, supplied penicillin to a doctor at the Brooklyn Jewish Hospital. Dr. Leo Lowe administered what was thought of as massive dosages of penicillin to several patients and cured, among others, a child suffering from an acute bacterial infection and a paralyzed and comatose woman. Smith and McKeen, visiting the hospital on Saturdays and Sundays, were witness to penicillin's curative effects on the patients.

POSTWAR EXPANSION FOR PFIZER: TERRAMYCIN AND BEYOND

Nevertheless, it was not until the end of the war when the federal government realized its mistake in restricting production of the drug. In 1946 Pfizer purchased Groton Victory Yard, a World War II shipyard, in order to renovate it for mass production of the new publicly accessible medicine. This marked Pfizer's first official entrance into the manufacturing of pharmaceuticals. In a few years the five-story building, equipped with 10,000 gallon tanks, produced enough penicillin to supply 85 percent of the national market and 50 percent of the world market. In 1946 sales already had reached $43 million.

Competition from 20 other companies manufacturing penicillin soon resulted in severe price reductions. The price for 100,000 units dropped from $20 to less than two cents. Furthermore, although the company could boast ownership of fermentation tanks "exceeded in size only by those in the beer industry," Pfizer's bulk chemical business decreased as former customers began establishing production facilities of their own. Pfizer's instrumental role in developing antibiotics proved beneficial to society, but a poor business venture.

All this was to change drastically under the new direction of President John McKeen. In 1949 McKeen, whose career at Pfizer began the day after he graduated from the Brooklyn Polytechnic Institute in 1926, was elevated to president and, later, chair of the company. Already responsible for increasing sales by an impressive 800 percent between 1939 and 1950, McKeen's business acumen became even more evident during the marketing campaign for Terramycin, which was launched in 1950. In the postwar years, pharmaceutical companies searched for new broad-spectrum antibiotics useful in the treatment of a wide number of bacterial infections. Penicillin and streptomycin, while helping to expand the frontier of medical knowledge, actually offered a cure

KEY DATES

1772: Henry Nock founds the business that eventually becomes Wilkinson Sword.
1849: Charles Pfizer and Charles Erhart found Charles Pfizer & Company.
1866: Parke-Davis is founded in Detroit by Hervey C. Parke and George S. Davis.
Dr. Joseph Lawrence develops the original formula for Listerine.
1877: Wilkinson Sword begins making straight razors.
1881: Lawrence sells his formula to Jordan Wheat Lambert, who founds Lambert Pharmacal Company.
1886: William R. Warner founds William R. Warner & Company.
1899: Several major U.S. gum producers merge to form American Chicle.
1900: Charles Pfizer & Company Inc. is incorporated in New Jersey.
1916: Warner & Co. acquires Richard Hudnut Company, a cosmetics firm.
1921: Colonel Jacob Schick invents the Magazine Repeating Razor, forerunner of the Schick Injector razor.
1942: Pfizer goes public.
1944: Pfizer begins mass production of penicillin, primarily for the war effort.
1950: Pfizer launches Terramycin, an antibiotic; Warner & Co. is renamed Warner-Hudnut, Inc.
1955: Warner-Hudnut merges with Lambert Pharmacal to form Warner-Lambert Company.
1962: Warner-Lambert acquires American Chicle.
1970: Charles Pfizer & Company is renamed Pfizer Inc.; Warner-Lambert acquires Schick and Parke, Davis.
1984: Agouron Pharmaceuticals, Inc. is founded.
1989: Pfizer launches Procardia XL.
1992: Pfizer launches Novasc, Zoloft, and Zithromax.
1993: Warner-Lambert acquires Wilkinson Sword.
1995: Pfizer acquires the animal health unit of SmithKline Beecham.
1997: Warner-Lambert launches Lipitor through a marketing alliance with Pfizer.
1998: Pfizer divests its Medical Technology Group; Pfizer launches Viagra.
1999: Pfizer begins comarketing Celebrex; Warner-Lambert acquires Agouron Pharmaceuticals.
2000: Pfizer acquires Warner-Lambert.
2002: Pfizer's Lipitor ranks as the best-selling drug in the world.
2003: Pfizer merges with Pharmacia Corp., making it the largest drugmaker in the world.
2006: The FDA approves Exubera, the first inhaled insulin therapy to be granted approval.

for only a limited number of infections. Pfizer's breakthrough came with the discovery of oxytetracycline, a broad-range antibiotic that soon would prove effective against some 100 diseases.

The drug's remarkable capture of a sizable portion of the market was not due entirely to its inherent curative powers. Rather, it was McKeen's ability to promote the new drug that actually propelled Pfizer into the ranks of top industry competitors. McKeen's first accomplishment was the timely decision to market the antibiotic under a Pfizer trademark. Thus Terramycin, the drug's chosen name, launched Pfizer into its first ethical drug campaign. Lacking the resources other pharmaceutical companies had to promote their drugs, McKeen announced the "Pfizer blitz," whereby the company's small sales force used an unusual array of marketing strategies.

For the first time, the company circumvented traditional drug distributing companies and began selling Terramycin directly to hospitals and retailers. Pfizer's minuscule retail force (pharmaceutical salespeople) would target one small region at a time and promote their product to every accessible healthcare professional. The sales force left generous samples of the drug at every sales call, sponsored golf tournaments, and ran noisy hospitality suites at conventions. Surprised at the success of this tiny band of salespeople, which eventually would grow into a 4,000-person army, industry competitors reluctantly increased their own sales forces and, similarly, began promoting their products directly to physicians.

Taking the calculated risks of insulting the entire medical community, Pfizer ran lavish advertisements in the conservative *Journal of the American Medical Association.* The ad was greeted with a large degree of reservation and threatened the drug industry's abhorrence of "hard sell" marketing. In an unprecedented move, the company had paid a prohibitive $500,000 to run the multipage ad. In two years the entire Terramycin campaign cost $7.5 million, and Pfizer became the largest advertiser in the American Medical Association's journal.

After 12 months on the market, Terramycin's sales accounted for one-fourth of Pfizer's total $60 million in sales. Yet problems with the company's advertising strategy were to surface soon. In 1957, while promoting a new antibiotic called Sigmamycin, a Pfizer advertisement used the professional cards of eight physicians to endorse the drug. John Lear, science editor of the *Saturday Review,* denounced this advertisement in a scathing attack. Not only were the names of the eight physicians fictitious, Lear claimed, but the code of Pharmaceutical Manufacturers Association prohibited soliciting endorsements from physicians. Moreover, Lear used the Pfizer ad to underscore and criticize what he saw as a trend toward the overprescription of antibiotics, exaggerated claims on drug effects, and concealment of possible side effects.

Pfizer was quick to defend their advertisement. The company upheld the reputability of the ad agency, William Douglas McAdams Inc., a highly respected firm responsible for the Sigmamycin campaign. While defending the drug and the clinical reports supporting the drug's efficacy, Pfizer admitted that the business cards were purely symbolic and, therefore, fictitious and, as a result, may have been misleading. The company accordingly changed the campaign.

John Lear's final attack on Pfizer expressed an unspoken industry complaint. Not only was it disturbing that such "hard sell" tactics should actually prove successful, but so was Pfizer's status in the industry; as the company's recent past was in bulk chemical production, it was a relative newcomer to the industry of ethical drugs. Lear argued that the young company should have shown respect for the industry's formal and restrained method of conducting business. Pfizer, however, was not intimidated by the industry's attitude toward its advertising campaign; it was interested in claiming and maintaining a share of the market. If it meant breaking tradition, it was clear Pfizer was not going to hesitate.

Aside from its modern marketing campaigns, Pfizer was very successful at developing a diversified line of pharmaceuticals. Whereas many companies concentrated their efforts on developing innovative drugs, Pfizer generously borrowed research from its competitors and released variants of these drugs. Although all companies participated in this process of "molecular manipulation," whereby a slight variance is produced in a given molecule to develop greater potency and decreased side effects in a drug, Pfizer was particularly adept at developing these drugs and aggressively seizing a share of the market. Thus the company was able to reduce its dependence on sales of antibiotics by releasing a variety of other pharmaceuticals.

At the same time Pfizer's domestic sales increased dramatically, the company was quietly improving its presence on the foreign market. Under the methodical directive of John J. Powers, head of international operations and future president and chief executive officer, Pfizer's foreign market expanded into 100 countries and accounted for $175 million in sales by 1965. It would be years before any competitor came close to commanding a similar share of the foreign market. Pfizer's 1965 worldwide sales figures of $220 million indicated that the company might possibly be the largest pharmaceutical manufacturer in the United States. By 1980 Pfizer was one of only two U.S. companies among the top ten pharmaceutical companies in Europe, and the largest foreign healthcare and agricultural product manufacturer in Asia.

Pfizer's crowning success to its unorthodox business procedures involved McKeen's quest for diversification through acquisition. While competing companies within the industry preferred to keep $50–$70 million in savings, Pfizer not only kept a meager $25 million in cash, but was the only major pharmaceutical to use common equity to borrow capital. "Not to have your cash working is a sort of economic sin," McKeen candidly stated. Between 1961 and 1965 the company paid $130 million in stock or cash and acquired 14 companies, including manufacturers of vitamins, antibiotics for animals, chemicals, and Coty cosmetics.

McKeen defended this diversification strategy by claiming that prodigious growth had decreased overall profits while competitors, on the other hand, had neither grown nor profited from their conservative investments. Furthermore, Pfizer's largest selling drug, Terramycin, generated only $15–$20 million a year and thus freed the company from a dependence on one product for all its profits.

In 1962 Pfizer allotted $17 million for research and that same year McKeen announced plans for his "five by five" program, which included $500 million in sales by

1965. Obviously, sales would not come from new pharmaceuticals, but from the company's accelerated rate of acquisitions.

McKeen never actually saw the company reach this goal during his presidency. In 1964 sales did surpass $480 million, but the following year Powers replaced McKeen as chief executive officer and president and inherited a company with almost half its sales generated from foreign markets and wide product diversification from 38 subsidiaries.

For the next seven years Powers continued to preside over the company's comfortable profits and sizable growth. In the absence of McKeen's style of conducting business, Powers directed Pfizer toward the more conservative and methodical approach of manufacturing and marketing pharmaceuticals.

Powers also guided the company in a new direction with an increased emphasis on research and development. With increased funds allocated for research in the laboratories, Pfizer joined the ranks of other pharmaceutical companies searching for the innovative and, therefore, profitmaking, drugs. Vibramycin, an antibiotic developed in the 1960s, was very profitable; by 1981 it generated sales of $250 million.

EMPHASIZING R&D AT PFIZER

In 1970 the company changed its name to the more modern-sounding Pfizer Inc. In the early 1970s Edmund Pratt, Jr., stepped in as company chairman and Gerald Laubach took over as Pfizer president. Although company assets reached $1.5 billion and sales generated $2 billion by 1977, Pfizer's overall growth was much slower through the period of the late 1970s and early 1980s. Increased oil prices caused comparable increases in prices for raw materials; low incidents of respiratory infections slowed sales for antibiotics; and even a cool summer in Europe reduced demands for soft drinks and, consequently, the need for Pfizer citric acids. All of these factors contributed to the company's slow rate of growth.

In light of this, the two new top executives significantly changed company strategy. First, funds for research and development reached $190 million by 1981; this marked a 100 percent increase in funding from 1977. Second, Pfizer began a comprehensive licensing program with foreign pharmaceutical companies to pay royalties in exchange for marketing rights on newly developed drugs. This represented a noticeable change from the years Powers supervised international operations. Under his directive, Pfizer chose to market its own drugs on the foreign market and establish joint ventures or partnerships only if no other option was available.

The two new drugs—one called Procardia, a treatment for angina licensed from Bayer AG in Germany for its exclusive sale in the United States, and the other called Cefobid, an antibiotic licensed from a Japanese pharmaceutical company—promised to be highly profitable items. Furthermore, drugs discovered from Pfizer's own research resulted in large profits. Sales for Minipress, an antihypertensive, reached $80 million in three years, and Feldene, an anti-inflammatory, generated $314 million by 1982.

By 1983 sales reached $3.5 billion and Pfizer was spending one of the largest amounts of money in the industry on research ($197 million in 1983). Pratt, in a final move to shed Pfizer of its former idiosyncracies, began selling some of its more unprofitable acquisitions.

Interestingly, one Pfizer product acquired through a company acquisition in the 1960s experienced a market rediscovery during the 1980s. Ben Gay, a well established liniment marketed for relief of arthritis pains through the late 1970s, found new patrons in the health-conscious 1980s. Discovering that sales for Ben Gay were increasing when marketed as a fitness aid, Pfizer began an advertising campaign by employing athletic superstars to endorse the drug. This campaign cost the company $6.3 million in 1982.

By 1989, Pfizer operated businesses in more than 140 countries. Net sales that year were $5.7 billion, but net income declined. Research and development expenditures had quadrupled during the 1980s, and Pfizer planned to continue investing heavily in research and development. Procardia XL was launched in 1989, and Diflucan, an antifungal agent, received Food and Drug Administration (FDA) approval. Globally, Pfizer chalked up $150 million in sales, in 14 countries, of its Plax dental rinse.

BLOCKBUSTER INTRODUCTIONS FOR PFIZER

Pfizer headed into the 1990s with numerous drugs in development, including preparations in the areas of anti-infectives, cardiovasculars, anti-inflammatories, and central nervous system medications. Net sales in 1990 reached $6.4 billion. Procardia rapidly became the most widely prescribed cardiovascular drug in the United States. Research and development costs rose 20 percent, in keeping with Pfizer's determination to invest heavily in new drugs.

Pfizer International launched 37 new products worldwide in 1990. The company's antifungal drug, Diflucan, became the world's leading drug of its kind during this time. Sales of Pfizer's newest products accounted for 30 percent of all pharmaceutical sales, up from 13 percent in 1989.

Pfizer entered the decade facing controversy about heart valves produced by Shiley, Inc., a Pfizer subsidiary. In 1990, 38 fractures of implanted valves were reported. Pfizer instituted a policy of compensating those with fractured valves. Shiley was sold later in the decade to Sorin Biomedica S.p.A., a subsidiary of Fiat S.p.A., for $230 million.

In 1992, Pfizer received final FDA approval for Norvasc, used in treating angina and hypertension. Zithromax, an antibiotic developed to treat outpatient pneumonia, tonsillitis, and pharyngitis, also hit the market that year after FDA approval, as did the antidepressant Zoloft. By the late 1990s, all three of these drugs had reached blockbuster status, achieving annual sales of more than $1 billion. Net sales in 1992 were $7.2 billion, with a net income of $811 million, and research and development expenses hit $863 million. Pfizer's chairperson and CEO of 19 years, Ed Pratt, retired and was succeeded by William C. Steere, Jr.

Although the early 1990s were marked by a wave of mergers and acquisitions in the global pharmaceuticals industry, Pfizer declined to join in, and was instead content to build its product pipeline organically rather than through acquisition. By 1995, in fact, the R&D budget hit $1.3 billion. The one major acquisition that the company did complete during this period came not in the area of human pharmaceuticals but in the animal health realm. In 1995, Pfizer spent $1.45 billion for the animal health unit of SmithKline Beecham plc, the largest acquisition in Pfizer history. The purchase transformed the company's Animal Health Group into one of the largest providers of medicines for both livestock and pets, with remedies for more than 30 species, including anti-infectives, antiparasitics, anti-inflammatories, and vaccines.

Not content with its own rich product pipeline, Pfizer entered into a series of partnerships whereby it co-marketed drugs developed by smaller pharmaceutical firms, firms that were attracted by Pfizer's powerful sales force. In 1997 Pfizer helped Warner-Lambert bring Lipitor, a cholesterol-lowering pill, to market. Lipitor soared to the top of the anticholesterol niche in the United States, achieving sales of $865 million in 1997 and $2.2 billion in 1998. Another 1997 introduction of a comarketed drug was Aricept, which was developed by Japan's Eisai and quickly became the leading drug prescribed to treat the symptoms of Alzheimer's disease.

Focusing ever further on pharmaceuticals, Pfizer in 1998 sold its Medical Technology Group in four separate transactions: Valleylab was sold to U.S. Surgical Corporation for $425 million; AMS to E.M. Warburg, Pincus & Co., LLC for $130 million; Schneider to Boston Scientific Corporation for $2.1 billion; and Howmedica to Stryker Corporation for $1.65 billion. These transactions, however, were overshadowed that year by Pfizer's introduction of Viagra, a pill for treating male impotence, or what the company called "erectile dysfunction." By far the most famous of the new "lifestyle drugs," Viagra was an instant blockbuster: more than 350,000 prescriptions were written in the first three weeks, and sales for 1998 totaled $788 million; sales exceeded $1 billion in 1999. Less than a year after the launch of Viagra, Pfizer began comarketing Celebrex, which had been developed by G.D. Searle & Co., then a unit of Monsanto Company. Celebrex, the first of a new category of pain drugs called Cox-2 inhibitors, was approved for the treatment of arthritis pain and inflammation. The new drug became the most successful pharmaceutical launched in U.S. history, with 19 million prescriptions written in the first 12 months; sales during 1999 alone exceeded $1.4 billion.

Having participated in three record-setting launches in the late 1990s, Pfizer was one of the fastest growing drug companies in the world in revenue terms. Sales increased from $11.31 billion in 1996 to $16.2 billion in 1999. The overall growth for the 1990s was even more impressive as revenues increased 284 percent from the 1989 total of $4.2 billion. During this same period, Pfizer increased its R&D budget sixfold, reaching nearly $2.8 billion by 1999, or more than 17 percent of sales, among the top levels in the industry.

The company was not without its problems, however, particularly as a series of setbacks beset its drug development efforts. Trovan, an antibiotic that Pfizer hoped would be a blockbuster, ran into trouble during clinical studies following reports that it killed some patients. Development stopped on an experimental drug for diabetic nerve damage. Zeldox, an antipsychotic drug, and Relpax, a migraine treatment, saw their development delayed. In addition, sales of Viagra suffered at least a temporary setback following reports that some users of the drug had died of heart attacks. It was with this somewhat shaky product pipeline as a backdrop that Pfizer entered into a battle for control of Warner-Lambert in late 1999, a battle that Pfizer won early the following year.

EARLY HISTORIES OF WARNER AND LAMBERT

Warner-Lambert Company was the product of the 1955 merger of Warner-Hudnut, Inc. and the Lambert Pharmacal Company. Warner was founded in the late 19th century by William R. Warner, a Philadelphia pharmacist who had earned a fortune by inventing a sugar coating for pills. In 1886 he formed William R. Warner & Company and began making drugs. In 1908, several years after Warner's death, the company was acquired by Gustavus A. Pfeiffer & Company, a patent medicine company from St. Louis. Pfeiffer retained the Warner company name, moved its headquarters to New York, and began a series of acquisitions that included Richard Hudnut Company, a cosmetics firm acquired in 1916, and the DuBarry cosmetic company. By the 1940s, some 50 companies had been acquired during the Warner company's history.

Elmer Holmes Bobst arrived at Warner in 1945, already a veteran executive of the pharmaceutical industry and a multimillionaire. As president of Hoffmann-La Roche's U.S. office, he had proved instrumental in acquiring for the Swiss company a large share of the U.S. drug market. Many observers were surprised that Bobst accepted the position at Warner; he was then 61 years old, wealthy, and could have settled into a comfortable retirement.

Nevertheless, when Gustave A. Pfeiffer, Warner's chairperson and the only surviving member of the original founding family, approached Bobst with an offer of the presidency, he accepted. Nearly 30 years earlier, Bobst had been asked to join Warner as the head of its pharmaceutical division but declined when the Pfeiffer family refused to sell Bobst any of the company stock (the family held all the common stock). By the mid-1940s, however, Bobst had proved his abilities, and Pfeiffer readily offered the job on Bobst's terms; Bobst was hired and allowed to purchase 11 percent of the common stock. By 1955, Bobst's holdings were worth more than $3 million.

What Bobst inherited with his new position was a family-operated company suffering from an aging product line and antiquated facilities. Although the Hudnut cosmetic line accounted for most of the company's $25 million in sales, that product line was barely turning a profit. In an effort to improve the image of the cosmetics production, Bobst renamed the firm Warner-Hudnut in 1950.

Bobst's managerial style was well suited to the company's policy of growth through acquisition. Moreover, his experience with high-level industry and political affairs enabled him to hire a new management team of accomplished executives and public figures. Successful investment bankers, business executives, and political officials were brought in, notably Anna Rosenberg, the company's manager of industrial and public relations, who was once the U.S. assistant secretary of defense, and Alfred Driscoll, later Warner's president, who had served as governor of New Jersey for seven years.

In 1952, Bobst made his first major acquisition, purchasing New Jersey Chilcott Laboratories, Inc. Chilcott earned its reputation as a manufacturer of ethical drugs in large part through its development of Peritrate, a long-acting "vasodilator," which enlarged constricted blood vessels. Three years later Bobst arranged a merger between his company and Lambert Pharmacal.

Lambert Pharmacal's history is tied to that of the oral antiseptic Listerine. Dr. Joseph Lawrence developed the original formula for Listerine in the 1870s. Lawrence sold his formula in 1881 to Jordan Wheat Lambert, who founded the Lambert Pharmacal Company to make and sell Listerine. The product became widely popular, particularly under the advertising strategy of Gordon Seagrove, who joined Lambert in 1926 after leaving his job as a calliope player in the circus. Seagrove made Listerine a household staple by promoting its ability to cure halitosis, sore throats, and dandruff. The advertising copy for one magazine ad depicted a man encouraging a woman to continue massaging Listerine into his head, with the tagline "Tear into it, Honey—It's Infectious Dandruff!"

Bobst had met the president of Lambert, Edward Williams, at a meeting of the American Foundation for Pharmaceutical Education, and the two decided that their operations, each producing different but reputable products, would complement one another. Bobst was particularly interested in gaining access to Lambert's well-organized distribution network, which incorporated modern marketing techniques previously unavailable at Warner-Hudnut's. Furthermore, Williams brought a strong background in the management of pharmaceutical companies, enhancing Bobst's accomplished executive team, which had little experience in the pharmaceutical industry. When Warner and Lambert merged in 1955 to form Warner-Lambert Company, former governor Alfred Driscoll was named president of the new company.

GROWING THROUGH ACQUISITION: WARNER-LAMBERT, 1960–79

The new company quickly outgrew its New York headquarters and so relocated to Morris Plains, New Jersey, a suburb of New York City, in 1956. Acquisitions were soon to follow. Warner-Lambert acquired Emerson Drug, maker of Bromo-Seltzer, in 1956. Six years later, the company acquired American Chicle, maker of Chiclets and other chewing gums, for about $200 million in stock. American Chicle had been formed in 1899 through the merger of several major U.S. gum producers. Many industry analysts criticized the high price paid for American Chicle; in 1962, the company's net income for the year was less than $10 million. By 1983, however, after expanding into foreign markets, Chiclet sales were reaching the $1 billion mark. Ward S. Hagan, chairperson of American Chicle, called its gum and mint business "the largest in the world."

Meanwhile, the success of Peritrate, the drug that had come to Warner-Hudnut through that company's purchase of Chilcott Laboratories, was the cause of some controversy. Peritrate proved useful in a wider application of treatments than originally allowed, and the FDA approved of Peritrate's "new drug" usages in 1959. Over the next several years, however, Warner embarked on a controversial Peritrate advertising campaign. Appearing in several medical journals, including the *Journal of the American Medical Association,* ten-page ads advocated the use of Peritrate not only for the treatment of angina, but as a "life-prolonging" prophylactic for all cardiac patients. The advertisement, based on the results of one study, was released at a time when the FDA had initiated an increasingly aggressive policy of evaluating claims for drug effectiveness. Even as the director of the study refuted the advertisement claims, Warner-Lambert executives stood by the claims for the effectiveness of their drug. By 1966, however, when an estimated 56 percent of the 3.1 million people afflicted by heart disease used Peritrate, the government, under the directive of the FDA, seized a shipment of the drug, bringing charges against the company's unapproved advocacy of an even wider usage for the drug.

Concurrently, Listerine continued to increase in popularity under its new ownership; by 1975, the oral antiseptic held a sizable portion of the $300 million market. Warner-Lambert continued to invest heavily in advertising for Listerine. For years, Listerine had been advertised as a preventive measure against colds and sore throats, and, during the Asian flu epidemic of 1957, Bobst personally placed an ad in *Life* magazine promoting Listerine's ability to resist the sickness. The company's advertising agency had rejected the ad earlier, since its claims were unsubstantiated, but the promotion resulted in sales increases of $26 million for the year.

By 1975, the Federal Trade Commission (FTC) had begun to investigate the Listerine advertisements. The FTC disputed the cold prevention claims of Listerine as insupportable and ordered the company to embark on a disclaimer ad campaign amounting to $10 million, a figure equal to the company's average annual advertising expenditure between 1962 and 1972. The FTC argued that only corrective disclaimers could educate the consumer, and, in 1978, the Supreme Court upheld the FTC's order.

During the 1970s and 1980s, Warner-Lambert made several acquisitions, including cough drop manufacturer Smith Brothers, American Optical, and Schick Shaving. The latter, which was acquired in 1970, traced its origins to the 1920s when Colonel Jacob Schick, inspired by the repeating rifle, invented the Magazine Repeating Razor, which eventually was redubbed the Schick Injector razor.

Warner-Lambert also acquired Parke, Davis & Co. in 1970. The company was founded in Detroit in 1866 as Parke-Davis by Hervey C. Parke and George S. Davis. Among the numerous medical innovations marking the history of Parke, Davis were the 1938 development of Dilantin, which became the drug of choice for the treatment of epilepsy; the 1946 introduction of the first antihistamine, Benadryl; and the 1949 discovery of chloromycetin, a broad-spectrum antibiotic.

The acquisition of Parke, Davis met with some resistance. The Antitrust Division of the Justice Department launched an investigation of the proposed merger. According to the chair of the House Judiciary Committee, the merger would raise "serious problems" because it had the potential to limit competition and create a monopoly. Upon approval, the merger would result in combined revenue of $1.7 billion and would rank the new company among the 100 largest industrial companies in the United States.

On November 12, 1970, the Justice Department announced that it would not challenge the merger despite the Antitrust Division's recommendation to the contrary. The department referred the matter to the FTC, which held concurrent authority to enforce the Clayton Act. A day later, the merger was completed. By 1976, however, the FTC ordered the company to sell several units of its Parke, Davis subsidiary that produced specified drugs. Those units producing thyroid preparations, cough remedies, cough drops and lozenges, normal albumin serum, and tetanus immunoglobulin would have to be sold to restore competition in those product lines.

Satisfied with the FTC's actions, S. Burke Giblin, chair and CEO of Warner-Lambert at the time of the ruling, nevertheless faced several other challenges in the ensuing years. In 1976, Warner-Lambert disclosed figures to the Securities and Exchange Commission (SEC) concerning illegal payments abroad, announcing that more than $2.2 million "in questionable payments" had been uncovered in 14 of the 140 countries in which Warner-Lambert conducted business. Only months later an explosion at an American Chicle plant in Queens, New York, killed six people and injured 55. After a year of investigation, a grand jury indicted the company and four of its officials on charges of reckless manslaughter and criminally negligent homicide. The charges were based on reports that the fire department had warned the company about the explosive potential of magnesium stearate dust used as a gum-machine lubricant. Contending that the charges were "outrageous" and unwarranted, company executives appealed the case. In 1978, a state judge dismissed the charges, citing "crystal clear and voluminous evidence" that the company had tried to eliminate the danger of an explosion. The following year, however, the New York State court's appellate division voted to restore the indictments. Finally, in 1980, the state's highest court once again dismissed all charges in connection with the explosion.

Another controversy involved Warner-Lambert's Benylin cough syrup product, which was made available without a prescription in 1975. In response to questions regarding the cough syrup's effectiveness, the FDA ordered the drug back on a prescription-only status, and, after seven years of deliberation, a settlement finally was reached in which the FDA approved the reinstated over-the-counter sale of the drug.

In 1978, Warner-Lambert purchased Entenmann's Bakery for $243 million in cash. By 1982, Entenmann's had become Warner-Lambert's most profitable consumer division, with sales reaching $333 million and an annual growth rate of 19 percent. During this time, however, a rumor was started that Entenmann's profits were supporting the Reverend Sun Myung Moon's Unification Church. Since the source of the rumor was said to have come from Westchester County in New York, Warner-Lambert took out an ad in the county newspaper denying the alleged connection. Nevertheless, the rumor continued to circulate and actually received a large amount of publicity in the Boston, Massachusetts area. It was reported in some places that Entenmann's delivery and sales staff were being harassed, and one Rhode Island church urged a boycott of the baked goods. When sales growth began to slip, Warner-Lambert mailed a letter to 1,600 churches in New England describing Entenmann's history as a family-owned business for 80 years before it was purchased. As Entenmann's profits continued to slip, Warner-Lambert sold the bakery to General Foods for $315 million in 1982.

The late 1970s had proved financially unstable for Warner-Lambert. Profit margins were off by 40 percent in 1979, the majority of revenues came from the sale of consumer goods, and the company was considered a potential takeover candidate. One critic characterized it as a "floundering giant." That year, Ward S. Hagan replaced Bobst as chairperson, while Joseph D. Williams assumed the chief executive office. Hagan and Williams then embarked on a restructuring program with the goal of revitalizing the pharmaceutical operations and trimming unprofitable and noncore businesses.

RESTRUCTURING AND REFOCUSING ON CORE AREAS: 1980–99

Five unprofitable subsidiaries, including American Optical and Entenmann's, were divested between 1982 and 1986, providing Warner-Lambert with capital of nearly $600 million. At the same time, such company programs as the "Total Production System" aimed to increase productivity by cutting downtime, reducing paperwork, and creating a more flexible work environment. Hagan and Williams closed or consolidated 24 plants in foreign and domestic locations, while reducing the company labor force by almost half, from 61,000 to 32,000. Research for new drugs at the Parke, Davis division was supported by a 20 percent increase in budgetary funds during 1983 to $180 million.

Despite its improved financial condition, Warner-Lambert came under criticism, particularly for its 1982 purchase of IMED Corp., a small hospital supply manufacturer. Many found Warner-Lambert's $468 million purchase, 23 times IMED's earnings, exorbitant. IMED was the market leader, with 35 percent of sales in the hospital supply field and continued annual sales growth of 50 percent. The company, however, was beset with problems. IMED's executives apparently concentrated on short-term sales goals, at the expense of new product development. In fact, a management conflict between IMED's manufacturing and research and development executives caused many important employees to resign in frustration. In 1986, Warner-Lambert sold IMED and some of its affiliates to the Henley Group, Inc. for $163.5 million.

Williams, who was given the additional duties of chairperson during Warner-Lambert's turnaround period, was able to report that return on equity had increased from 9 to 32 percent from 1979 to 1986, as sales diminished through divestments and profits held fairly steady. Investing in research and development and luring industry talent from competing companies, Williams hoped to develop and increase sales of high-margin prescription drugs, such as Lopid, a cholesterol-reducing drug that received positive publicity in the late 1980s. A trend among consumers toward treatment without medication, however, as well as swelling support for reform of the healthcare industry, and the attendant possibility of price controls, caused uncertainty among ethical drug producers. Business also was threatened by a late 1980s recession and discounting in the consumer goods segment.

In anticipation of these potentially adverse market forces, a new chairperson and CEO, Melvin R. Goodes, announced yet another reorganization of Warner-Lambert late in 1991. The plan called for a 2,700-person layoff, reorganization of the global management scheme, and consolidation of operations into two groups: pharmaceuticals and consumer products. Goodes also began to concentrate the company's marketing efforts on three primary geographic markets: North America, Europe, and Japan. The company invested $1.3 billion in advertising and promotion and $473 million in research and development, apparently banking on its consumer goods, which still constituted 60 percent of annual sales in 1992.

That year, Warner-Lambert became the fourth company to enter the competitive and controversial market for transdermal nicotine patches. Its prescription smoking cessation device, branded Nicotrol, was strongly promoted through direct consumer advertising, and the product enjoyed early success. Sales, however, quickly declined in 1993; Warner-Lambert's late entry into the segment, chronic product shortages, a lower than expected success rate, side effects, and, especially, reports that some users had suffered heart attacks, all led to declines in sales.

In 1993, the company became the first to win approval from the FDA for a drug (Cognex) that retarded the progression of Alzheimer's disease. Warner-Lambert also formed joint ventures with Glaxo Holdings plc and Wellcome plc to orchestrate the movement of the companies' drugs from prescription to over-the-counter and generic markets. Another development in 1993 was the acquisition of Wilkinson Sword, a maker of shaving products and toiletries and a business that fit well alongside Schick. Wilkinson Sword traced its origins back to 18th-century London, where in 1772 Henry Nock began making guns and bayonets. James Wilkinson, a son-in-law of Nock, soon became a partner in the enterprise and then inherited the company in 1805. Wilkinson's son Henry joined the firm and expanded the business into sword making. The manufacturing of straight razors began in 1877.

The critical drug development front showed only mixed results for Warner-Lambert in the early 1990s. Lopid, whose sales had peaked at $556 million in 1992, went off patent in January 1993, resulting in significant and immediate generic competition and plummeting sales. Meantime, sales of Cognex were disappointing. Neurontin, which had been approved for the treatment of epilepsy, also got off to a slow start, although by 1998 sales had hit a solid $514 million. Sales of Accupril, a cardiovascular drug, were $175 million in 1994; by 1998 sales had increased to $454 million. In the OTC realm, Warner-Lambert helped the newly merged Glaxo Wellcome plc bring Zantec 75 heartburn treatment to market in 1996. The alliance ended in 1998, however, when Warner-Lambert bought the U.S. and Canadian rights to the product, which that year achieved sales of $168 million.

Two key pharmaceutical introductions marked 1997. Following its approval by the FDA in December 1996, Lipitor was launched in February of the following year. This drug was used to reduce cholesterol levels and proved to work faster and more effectively than other available remedies. As a result, Lipitor became the blockbuster pharmaceutical long sought by Warner-Lambert and was in fact the first prescription drug to achieve $1 billion in worldwide sales in its first year on the market. Sales in 1998 reached $2.19 billion.

The other 1997 launch, Rezulin, also got off to a fast start, posting $750 million in 1998 sales, but then ran aground. Launched in March 1997 as a breakthrough treatment for the most common kind of diabetes, type 2 diabetes, Rezulin was by March 1999 the subject of an FDA investigation into its safety, after 30 people in the United States who were taking the drug died after developing liver problems. The FDA at first allowed the drug to continue to be sold with a change in the labeling requiring strict monitoring of liver function. In 2000, however, Rezulin was pulled from the market.

The Rezulin setback and the lack of any blockbusters in the pipeline that were close to market provided the impetus for Warner-Lambert's acquisition of Agouron Pharmaceuticals, Inc. for about $2.1 billion in stock in May 1999. Agouron had been founded in 1984 by several University of California at San Diego scientists who pioneered in computer-aided drug design. The method employed by Agouron involved first understanding the structure of disease-causing proteins in the body and then using computers to design pharmaceuticals that can inhibit the proteins' activity. Agouron had been focusing its development efforts in the areas of oncology and virology, and its first product was Viracept, one of the so-called protease inhibitors being used to treat HIV/AIDS. Viracept was soon considered the top drug in its class because it was more convenient to use and had slightly fewer side effects; sales thereupon totaled $530 million in 1998. Agouron's product pipeline was filled with promising new drugs, including treatments for cancer, macular degeneration (which affects the eyesight), and the common cold, in addition to more AIDS therapies.

PFIZER'S TAKEOVER OF WARNER-LAMBERT IN 2000

Goodes retired from his position as CEO and chairman of Warner-Lambert in May 1999, with the company's president, Lodewijk J. R. de Vink, taking on Goodes's titles as well. In early November of that year, as drug industry consolidation was continuing, Warner-Lambert agreed to a nearly $70 billion merger with American Home Products Corporation (AHP). Pfizer, not wanting to lose its 50 percent of the revenues from the sale of the blockbuster Lipitor, with sales nearing $4 billion per year, and seeking to bolster its product pipeline through the addition of Agouron, stepped in within hours with a hostile bid exceeding AHP's offer. Warner-Lambert attempted to fend Pfizer off, even bringing in a third party, the Procter & Gamble Company (P&G), to discuss a three-way deal with P&G and AHP. P&G soon dropped out of the picture when its stock price plummeted on news of the talks. Finally, in early February 2000, Pfizer and Warner-Lambert reached agreement on what was initially an $84 billion merger, ending the largest hostile takeover action in U.S. history. AHP received a breakup fee of $1.8 billion, which was believed to be the largest such payment ever made.

The merger was completed in June 2000 in what ended up being a $116 billion stock swap. The combined company retained the Pfizer Inc. name, with the consumer product lines of the two firms combined within a unit called Warner-Lambert Consumer Group. The FTC forced the firms to complete a number of relatively minor divestitures. The new Pfizer boasted pro forma 1999 revenues of $27.3 billion, making it the world's number two drug company, trailing only Aventis. The company had the industry's largest R&D budget, totaling $4.7 billion in 2000, as well as what was generally considered to be the industry's top sales and marketing operation. In terms of prescription drugs, Pfizer marketed eight products with annual sales in excess of $1 billion. The Warner-Lambert Consumer Group was a leading marketer of OTC healthcare, confectionery, and shaving brands, with 1999 pro forma revenues of $5.5 billion. The Pfizer Animal Health Group was the world leader in medicines for pets and livestock, with 1999 sales of $1.3 billion. William C. Steere continued at the helm of Pfizer in the initial months following the merger, but was slated to retire in early 2001 and be replaced by the company's president and COO, Henry McKinnell. The company veteran, who joined Pfizer in 1971, was faced with the challenges of integrating the staffs and cultures of Pfizer and Warner-Lambert, healing whatever wounds might be left over from the bruising takeover battle, and restoring investor confidence in the company's product pipeline. McKinnell was aiming to achieve annual cost savings of $1.6 billion by 2002 through the elimination of redundant activities and the centralizing of such operations as the two companies' distribution systems. Two major product launches were anticipated to occur in 2001: Zeldox, an antipsychotic drug, and Relpax, a migraine treatment.

PFIZER AND PHARMACIA MERGER: 2003

Pfizer's appetite for massive mergers was not sated by the Warner-Lambert deal, making for an eventful start to the 21st century. In the months after the merger, the company quickly integrated Warner-Lambert's consumer products lines into its own and, symbolically, removed the Warner-Lambert name in 2001 from its consumer health division to create "Pfizer Consumer Healthcare," one of seven divisions focused on three broad business segments: healthcare, animal health, and consumer healthcare. The assimilation of Warner-Lambert's assets barely was completed before the company announced another major transaction. In June 2002, exactly two year after the Warner-Lambert merger was completed, Pfizer announced it was merging with Pharmacia Corp. in a $60 billion deal. Approved by shareholders in December 2002 and completed in April 2003, the merger gave Pfizer a new strength in oncology and ophthalmology, expanded its consumer healthcare offerings, and made its animal health business the largest in the world. The merger also made Pfizer the largest drug maker in the world, with annual revenues nearing $50 billion.

In the wake of the momentous merger with Pharmacia, Pfizer applied its energies to its all-important prescription drug business. Lipitor ranked as the company's greatest moneymaker at the time of the Pharmacia merger and as the best-selling drug in the world, generating $8.6 billion in revenue. In the years to follow, demand for the cholesterol-lowering drug only increased, pushing sales past $12 billion by 2005. The drug was expected to generate $13 billion in revenue in 2006. Lipitor was the consummate blockbuster drug, and Pfizer needed to find others of its breed. One potential candidate was inherited through the Pharmacia merger, a painkiller, classified as a Cox-2 inhibitor, known as Celebrex. The drug generated $3.3 billion in revenue in 2004, but hopes for increased sales were dashed when the FDA pulled Merck's drug Vioxx, also a Cox-2 drug, from the market in October 2004. Studies revealed that Vioxx caused cardiovascular problems, which led to a government-run study of Celebrex. The FDA decided against pulling Celebrex from the market—the study found a less definite link to cardiovascular damage and a much lower risk—but concerns about Cox-2 drugs delivered a decisive blow to Celebrex's stature. "Pfizer is now feeling Merck's pain," *Business Week* noted in its December 20, 2004 issue. Sales of Celebrex fell to $1.7 billion in 2005, severely hampering the drug's chances of becoming the company's next blockbuster.

As Pfizer worked to rehabilitate Celebrex's image, there were several promising products that pointed to a profitable future. In January 2006, the FDA approved the Exubera, the first inhaled insulin therapy to reach the market. Worldwide sales of inhaled insulin products were expected to achieve sales of $4.8 billion by 2010, and Pfizer hoped Exubera would lead the way. Among a host of drugs in the company's development pipeline was Torcetrapib, a drug developed to raise high-density lipoprotein, or HDL, more commonly referred to as "good cholesterol." Pfizer was expected to release data concerning the drug in late 2006. Other candidates slated to be money earners were Aricept, a treatment for Alzheimer's disease, Indiplon, a treatment for insomnia, and Fragmin, a therapy developed for cancer patients.

Marinell Landa; April Dougal Gasbarre
Updated, David E. Salamie; Jeffrey L. Covell

PRINCIPAL SUBSIDIARIES

Pfizer (China) Research and Development Co. Ltd.; Pfizer (Malaysia) Sdn Bhd; Pfizer (Perth) Pty Limited (Australia); Pfizer (S.A.S.) (France); Pfizer (Thailand) Limited; Pfizer A.G. (Switzerland); Pfizer A/S (Norway); Pfizer AB (Sweden); Pfizer Afrique de L'Ouest (Senegal); Pfizer Asia Pacific Pte Ltd. (Singapore); Pfizer B.V. (Netherlands); Pfizer Beteiligungs-G.m.b.H. (Germany); Pfizer Canada Inc.; Pfizer Chile S.A.; Pfizer Corporation (Panama); Pfizer Corporation Austria Gesellschaft m.b.H. (Austria); Pfizer Deutschland GmbH; Pfizer Egypt S.A.E.; Pfizer Export Company (Ireland); Pfizer Group Limited (U.K.).

PRINCIPAL DIVISIONS

Pfizer Consumer Health Care; Pfizer Global Research and Development; Pfizer Animal Health Group; Pfizer Corporate and Divisional Functions; Pfizer Global Manufacturing; Pfizer Global Pharmaceuticals; Pfizer Pharmaceutical Sales.

PRINCIPAL COMPETITORS

Bayer AG; Merck & Co., Inc.; Novartis AG.

FURTHER READING

Alger, Alexandra, "Viagra Falls," *Forbes,* February 7, 2000, pp. 130–32.

Barrett, Amy, "Another Blockbuster Is Busted," *Business Week Online,* December 20, 2004.

———, "The Formula at Pfizer: Don't Run with the Crowd," *Business Week,* May 11, 1998, pp. 96–97.

Baum, Laurie, "A Powerful Tonic for Warner-Lambert," *Business Week,* November 30, 1987, pp. 144, 146.

Benway, Susan Duffy, "Just What the Doctor Ordered: 'Restructuring' Revives Warner Lambert," *Barron's,* December 30, 1985, pp. 35+.

Boles, Tracey, "FDA Warning on Celebrex Adds to Pfizer's Woes," *Sunday Business,* December 19, 2004.

Bradford, Stacey L., "Sweet Dreams: Gum and Mints May Help Warner-Lambert Become a Bigger Success in Drugs," *Financial World,* October 21, 1996, pp. 44–45.

Byrne, Harlan S., "Warner-Lambert: On the Mend," *Barron's,* January 2, 1995, pp. 19–20.

"Cadbury-Schweppes Snaps Up Adams from Pfizer," *Investors Chronicle,* December 19, 2002.

Campanella, Frank W., "Healthy Turnaround: Warner-Lambert Is Poised for an Earnings Recovery," *Barron's,* February 1, 1982, pp. 35+.

Crabtree, Penny, "Pfizer, San Diego Biotechnology Firm Join in $400 Million Alliance," *San Diego Union-Tribune,* December 20, 2002.

Davenport, Caroline H., "Glowing Prospects: New Products Will Keep Pfizer Growing at a Healthy Clip," *Barron's,* December 22, 1980.

"Did Warner-Lambert Make a '$468 Million Mistake'?" *Business Week,* November 21, 1983, pp. 123+.

Gibson, W. David, "R&D = Rx for Growth: That's Warner-Lambert's New Corporate Formula," *Barron's,* February 20, 1984, pp. 13+.

Hayes, John R., "Pill Selling 101," *Forbes,* November 21, 1994, p. 64.

Hensley, Scott, "Pfizer Appoints McKinnell to Top Posts," *Wall Street Journal,* August 11, 2000, p. B10.

"Irrational Exubera-nce of Pfizer?" *Business Week Online,* February 15, 2006.

Krauskopf, Lewis, "Cadbury to Acquire Parsippany, N.J.-Based Candy Division from Pfizer," *The Record,* December 18, 2002.

LaBell, Fran, "Fat Extenders in Salad Dressings," *Food Processing,* May 1992, p. 64.

Langreth, Robert, "Behind Pfizer's Takeover Battle: An Urgent Need," *Wall Street Journal,* February 8, 2000, p. B1.

———, "Pfizer's Warner-Lambert Purchase Contains Big Prize: Pipeline of Biotechnology Unit Agouron Is Stuffed with Potential Blockbusters," *Wall Street Journal,* April 24, 2000, p. B4.

———, "Pfizer, Warner-Lambert Agree on Terms," *Wall Street Journal,* February 7, 2000, p. A3.

Langreth, Robert, and Michael Waldholz, "Pfizer Pins Multibillion-Dollar Hopes on Impotence Pill," *Wall Street Journal,* March 19, 1998, p. B1.

Loynd, Harry J., *Parke-Davis: The Never-Ending Search for Better Medicines,* New York: Newcomen Society in North America, 1957.

Lubove, Seth, "Failure Focuses the Mind," *Forbes,* November 8, 1993, pp. 76–78.

Mahar, Maggie, "Legal Heartbreak?: Pfizer Faces Huge Liability If It Loses a Key Lawsuit," *Barron's,* April 2, 1990, pp. 8+.

Mines, Samuel, *Pfizer: An Informal History,* New York: Pfizer, 1978.

Morse, Andrew, "Pharmacia Shareholders Approve Pfizer Deal," *Daily Deal,* December 10, 2002.

O'Reilly, Brian, "The Pills That Saved Warner-Lambert," *Fortune,* October 13, 1997, pp. 94–95.

"Pfizer and Pharmacia Merger Goes Ahead," *Chemist & Druggist,* April 19, 2003, p. 9.

"Pfizer: Counting on 'Spare Parts' to Keep Up Its Momentum," *Business Week,* January 9, 1984, pp. 109+.

"Pfizer Joins with Other Drug Makers on Price Control," *Chemical Marketing Reporter,* February 1, 1993, p. 7.

"Pfizer Making Significant Contribution to Pharmaceutical Industry Health Partnerships in Developing Countries," *PR Newswire,* March 10, 2006.

"Pfizer's Disappointing Prognosis," *Business Week Online,* February 13, 2006.

"Pfizer Steps Up Launches from Global Portfolio," *Economic Times,* March 3, 2006.

"Pfizer Wins U.S. FDA Approval for Norvasc," *European Chemical News,* August 17, 1992, p. 23.

Pratt, Edmund T., Jr., *Pfizer: Bringing Science to Life,* New York: Newcomen Society of the United States, 1985.

Rodengen, Jeffrey L., *The Legend of Pfizer,* Ft. Lauderdale, Fla.: Write Stuff Syndicate, 1999.

Roman, Monica, "Pfizer Finally Sees Its Payoff," *Business Week,* July 1, 1991, pp. 86+.

———, "Pfizer's Pipeline Is Full, But Will the Drugs Flow Fast Enough?," *Business Week,* September 11, 1989, pp. 74+.

Rundle, Rhonda L., and Waldholz, Michael, "Warner-Lambert Agrees to Buy Agouron," *Wall Street Journal,* January 27, 1999, p. A3.

Schroeder, Michael, "Heart Trouble at Pfizer," *Business Week,* February 26, 1990, pp. 47+.

Shinkle, Kirk, "Pfizer's Shares Dive As Celebrex Study Shows Heart Risks," *Investor's Business Daily,* December 20, 2004, p. A1.

Starr, Cynthia, "First-Ever Alzheimer's Drug Brings Some Hope to Millions," *Drug Topics,* October 11, 1993, pp. 16–18.

Stipp, David, "Why Pfizer Is So Hot," *Fortune,* May 11, 1998, pp. 88–90, 92, 94.

Tanner, Ogden, *Twenty-Five Years of Innovation: The Story of Pfizer Central Research,* Lyme, Conn.: Greenwich Publishing, 1996.

"Turning Warner-Lambert into a Marketing Conglomerate," *Business Week,* March 5, 1979, p. 60.

"Warner-Lambert: Reversing Direction to Correct Neglect," *Business Week,* June 15, 1981, pp. 65+.

Weber, Joseph, "Curing Warner-Lambert—Before It Gets Sick," *Business Week,* December 9, 1991, pp. 91, 94.

Weber, Joseph, et al., "The New Era of Lifestyle Drugs," *Business Week,* May 11, 1998, pp. 92+.

Wiriyapong, Nareerat, "Enlarged Pfizer Expects More Subdued Local Growth," *Asia Africa Intelligence Wire,* April 19, 2003.

Zipser, Andy, "Beyond Shiley: A Vote for Pfizer," *Barron's,* May 27, 1991, pp. 28+.

Power-One, Inc.

740 Calle Plano
Camarillo, California 93012
U.S.A.
Telephone: (805) 987-8741
Fax: (805) 388-0476
Web site: http://www.power-one.com

Public Company
Incorporated: 1973 as Power CA
Employees: 2,422
Sales: $261.6 million (2005)
Stock Exchanges: NASDAQ
Ticker Symbol: PWER
NAIC: 334419 Other Electronic Component Manufacturing

■ ■ ■

Listed on the NASDAQ, Power-One, Inc. is one of the world's leading manufacturers of power-conversion equipment for the telecommunications, networking, and technology markets. Its products are used in routers, data storage and servers, semiconductor-test equipment wireless communications, medical diagnostic equipment, and railway and industrial applications. The Camarillo, California-based company offers DC (Direct Current) to DC converters, AC (Alternating Current) to DC converters, and power systems. Major customers include Cisco Systems, Ericsson, Lucent, Motorola, Nortel Networks, Siemens, and Teradyne. In addition to its U.S. facilities, Power-One maintains operations in Europe and Asia.

ORIGINS

Although Power-One did not come into its own until the 1990s, it was founded in Chatsworth, California, in 1972 to make AC/DC power supplies. A year later the family-owned business was incorporated as Power CA and in the late 1970s relocated to Camarillo. The company opened a factory in Isabela, Puerto Rico, in 1981 and seven years later added a plant in San Luis, Mexico. Most of the Puerto Rican operations were relocated to Santo Domingo, Dominican Republic, in the 1990s where labor was cheaper.

In 1982 Power CA hired an engineer named Steven J. Goldman, who would play a major role in the growth of Power-One. With a degree in electrical engineering from the University of Bridgeport in 1979, he began working his way up through the ranks. After heading Power CA's research and development division, he turned his attention to executive-level posts and supplemented his education by earning a master's of business administration from Pepperdine University in 1989. He became Power CA's chief financial officer, and then in 1990 was named president.

Goldman led a management-team buyout of the company, now known as Power-One L.L.C., a Delaware entity that acquired Power CA in preparation for a sale, in September 1995, backed by the Little Rock, Arkansas investment firm of Stephens Group Inc. Stephens took a 66 percent stake in the company, with senior management dividing up the remaining interest. The deal was brokered by Power-One's investment banker, Los

COMPANY PERSPECTIVES

Power-One has evolved over 30 years into an industry leader, competitive on a world-class level. Power-One's structure provides business units with access to substantial financial, logistical, and technical resources, and the flexibility to adapt to changing market conditions.

Angeles-based F.M. Roberts and Co. Its president, Fred Roberts, was a friend of Stephens chief executive officer, Warren Stephens, who was attracted to Power-One because its market was booming and sales were growing at a 30 percent clip, totaling close to $75 million in 1995.

Power-One also had developed a flexible operation, imperative because it combined dozens of power modules to satisfy the different needs of some 10,000 customers. As described by *Electronic Engineering Times,* "Carmillo headquarters acts as the nerve center for its entire planning, organization and process operation, while its factories in Mexico, the Dominican Republic and Puerto Rico make the physical products. These facilities are optimized for manufacturing a wide array of its current products and not designed for the high-volume component-type DC/DC converter manufacturing." The publication further explained that Power-One, which was strong in AC/DC switchers and linears, needed a financial partner such as Stephens in order "to become a diversified manufacturer and a global marketer of products. The two areas in which Power-One has been lacking are DC/DC converters and an international presence." The company's strategy, as developed by Goldman, was to provide "a complete power-supply solution to a worldwide customer base." Rather than a route to prosperity, it was in some respects a survival plan. Most of Power-One's customers were original equipment manufacturers (OEMs), and changes in the way they did business were having a profound impact on the power supply industry. Because OEMs were outsourcing more and more production processes, shortening the time-to-market of their products, and cutting the number of suppliers with which they dealt, component manufacturers across the board were forced to grow larger. This meant consolidation in the power supply industry, which numbered some 300 companies in North America. Hence, Power-One needed to grow larger or risk being left by the wayside.

1997 IPO

In order to fuel growth plans, Power-One was prepared to be taken public and make an initial public offering (IPO) of stock. In January 1996 the company was reorganized as a Delaware corporation, and later in the year it licensed new technology from Calex Manufacturing Co. to expand its line of AC/DC products. "That's really where the new Power-One started," Goldman told *Electronic Buyers' News.* "Previously, we were operating in a conservative environment focused on North America. We took no real risks, there were no acquisitions, and no strategic alliances." The IPO was completed in October 1997, raising more than $80 million. Of that amount $38 million was earmarked to pay down bank debt, and the rest was set aside for acquisitions and the upgrading of existing facilities. In order to expand capacity, the company soon broke ground on a new 110,000-square-foot manufacturing facility in Mexico, which would open in 1998.

Power-One's first acquisition took longer than most investors expected. It came in August 1998 when Power-One paid $43.4 million and assumed $11 million in debt for Melcher Holding AG, a group of Swiss companies with three locations. Melcher was an attractive addition because there was almost no overlap in products—Power-One focused on AC/DC power products and Melcher on DC/DC power products—and it provided Power-One with a gateway to Europe's $2 billion power supply market. Moreover, Melcher brought with it a highly desirable expertise in the fast-growing telecommunications market. Power-One's vice-president for finance and logistics, Ed Schnoop, told *Electronic Buyers' News* that Melcher was "more into telecom and transportation, and we were more into test equipment and datacom. So the communication aspect of it interested us, as well as the geographical and product-line synergies." Melcher would also benefit from the breadth of Power-One's operations. Melcher had outsourced a number of processes that Power-One was able to do in-house, such as magnetics, harnesses, and sheet metal.

The Melcher acquisition also demonstrated the unique attributes of Power-One's chief executive. One securities analyst quoted by *Electronic Buyers' News* explained, "Goldman comes with an engineering background, so while some people tend to look at acquisitions for size considerations, he's taken more of an engineer's viewpoint in determining what product capabilities he needs." He also brought a team approach to the process. "I have a philosophy, which is that, as a rule, [my staff] must never let me make a mistake," he told *Electronic Buyers' News.* "If they think I'm wrong, they have the right to constantly disagree with me. The

KEY DATES

1972: The company is founded as Power CA.
1981: The plant opens in Puerto Rico.
1988: The plant opens in Mexico.
1995: Stephens Group Inc. acquires a controlling interest.
1997: The company is taken public.
1998: Melcher Holding AG is acquired.
2000: HC Power, Inc. is acquired.
2003: The company completes the acquisition of di/dt Inc., maker of high-density DC/DC converters called "bricks."

central thing we've learned as we work through our disagreements is that people have to be considered in the decisions we make as a company."

Sales were strong in the first half of 1998, but economic conditions soured, due in large part to an Asian recession, resulting in poor sales during the second half of the year. Revenues increased from $93 million in 1997 to more than $102 million in 1998, but net income dipped from $8.2 million to $5.7 million. Management anticipated a turnaround in the near term and took steps to position the company to take full advantage, including a greater investment in research and development to broaden the Power-One product line.

Power-One's second major acquisition came in January 1999 with the $31.8 million purchase of International Power Devices Inc. (IPD), a Boston-based manufacturer of high-density DC/DC board-mounted converters, the fastest-growing type in the industry and one in which Power-One had little representation. Moreover, IPD owned a 49 percent interest in a People's Republic of China distributor, providing Power-One with entry into the promising Chinese communications marketplace. In order to realize economies of scale and make its products more competitive, Power-One transferred production to the new Mexico facility.

Power-One's increasing focus on the telecommunications market, in which the company hoped to ultimately achieve three-quarters of its sales, paid off in 1999. Revenues more than doubled in 1999 to $205.4 million, and net income kept pace, increasing to more than $10 million. The year also brought a new president and chief operating officer, William T. Yeates, whose arrival allowed Goldman to devote more of his attention to acquisitions and big picture considerations.

In February 2000, Power-One completed another acquisition, the $98.4 million stock purchase of Irvine, California-based HC Power. Once again, the deal added new products and provided Power-One with access to a lucrative market. In this case, the company became involved in the high-end power systems for telecommunications and Internet service providers, a $3 billion market. For HC, joining forces with Power-One offered a number of dividends. It would be able to tap into Power-One's larger sales force, which offered greater geographical coverage, and by moving production to Power-One's Dominican Republic plant, where labor costs averaged about $1 per hour instead of the $14 paid to workers in California, HC's products could be priced cheaper and gain a competitive edge.

Another acquisition came just three months later in 2000 when Power-One paid $72 million in cash and stock for Powec A.S. of Norway. In a related transaction, Power-One spent another $14 million to add the telecommunications product line of the Crane Company. These deals opened up the telecommunications power supplies markets in Europe and Asia. In all, the year 2000 was a breakthrough year for Power-One. Revenues soared to $511 million and net income followed suit, increasing to $43.9 million for the year. As a result, the company was added to the S&P 500 and recognized by *Forbes* as one of the best 200 companies in the United States.

POOR BUSINESS CONDITIONS AT THE START OF THE 21ST CENTURY

To keep pace with demand, Power-One added about 275,000 square feet of manufacturing space to its Dominican Republic and Mexico plants, and in the spring of 2001 it replaced a small research and development center in Limerick, Ireland, with a new 35,000-square-foot facility. The company also looked to make further acquisitions, primarily targeting Asia, but such plans would have to be shelved as the telecommunications market began to falter and the global economy lapsed into recession. Demand for power supply products weakened as OEMs cut back on manufacturing to sell off excess inventory, and their problems were passed on to suppliers including Power-One. With 70 percent of its revenues derived from communications, Power-One suffered significant losses. Revenues dropped off 28.8 percent to $363.7 million as the company suffered a net loss of $185.9 million.

Difficult conditions continued in 2002, leading to a cost reduction effort at Power-One that included laying off almost one-quarter of the workforce. This news, along with an announcement that the company planned to take nearly $200 million in restructuring charges in the third quarter of the year, resulted in the price of Power-One stock tumbling below the $2.50 mark. Company executives, who believed the industry had reached bottom and was due for a rebound, eagerly snapped up shares of Power-One stock at these distressed prices. When the year ended, Power-One recorded a 36.6 percent drop in revenues to $230.7 million and a net loss of $212 million.

Power-One completed an acquisition in 2003, using stock to buy di/dt Inc., maker of high-density DC/DC converters called "bricks." Whereas this addition helped to fill out Power-One's product lines, the company also took steps to become involved in silicon-based DC/DC power modules, which it believed communications customers were likely to embrace in the years to come because they were smaller and less expensive than brick-type converters, while offering comparable performance. Power-One formed the Silicon Power Systems unit and also unveiled a new corporate logo, the first redesign since the company was founded three decades earlier. The new unit would soon develop the industry's first digital power products.

Business began to pick up for Power-One in 2003, as revenues increased to $256.3 million, but the company posted a net loss of $18.2 million. Sales increased to $280.3 million in 2004, when the company lost another $21.2 million. Sales dipped to $261.6 million in 2005, and Power-One recorded a net loss of $38.3 million. The company believed, however, that the costs of restructuring were now complete and that prospects for the future looked better. There would be a slight change in the management ranks going forward, however, as Goldman turned over the CEO position to Yeates while retaining the chairmanship and continuing to guide Power-One's growth strategy. The company also increased its focus on the data storage and server markets, becoming less dependent on the volatile telecommunications industry.

Ed Dinger

PRINCIPAL SUBSIDIARIES

Power-Electronics, Inc.; Melcher Inc.; HC Power, Inc.

PRINCIPAL COMPETITORS

Artesyn Technologies, Inc; Ault Incorporated; Transistor Devices, Inc.

FURTHER READING

Chin, Spencer, "Power-One Plan Aspires to Spin Silicon into Gold," *EBN,* May 12, 2003, p. 1.

Haman, John, "Stephens Takes Power Supply Firm Public," *Arkansas Business,* October 6, 1997, p. 1.

Lewis, Nicole, "Steve Goldman—Power One—Hard Work, Risk-Taking Transform Power-One into a Powerhouse," *Electronic Buyers' News,* December 18, 2000, p. 56.

Liotta, Bettyann, "Power-One to Acquire the Melcher Group," *Electronic Buyers' News,* August 31, 1998, p. 12.

Mankikar, Mohan, "Power-One at a Crossroad," *Electronic Engineering Times,* November 6, 1995, p. 84.

Moreau, Andrew, "Stephens Buys Majority Stake in Maker of Power Converters," *Arkansas Democrat-Gazette,* October 25, 1995, p. 1D.

Sullivan, Ben, "Power-One of Camarillo to Buy Swiss Companies," *Daily News* (Los Angeles), August 26, 1998, p. B1.

Quanta Services, Inc.

1360 Post Oak Boulevard, Suite 2100
Houston, Texas 77056
U.S.A.
Telephone: (713) 629-7600
Fax: (713) 629-7676
Web site: http://www.quantaservices.com

Public Company
Incorporated: 1997
Employees: 1,450
Sales: $1.86 billion (2005)
Stock Exchanges: New York
Ticker Symbol: PWR
NAIC: 238210 Electrical Contractors

■ ■ ■

Quanta Services, Inc. is a Houston-based public company that on an outsourcing basis provides network infrastructure design, engineering, construction, and maintenance services to the electric power, gas pipeline, telecommunications, and broadband cable industries. The company also provides specialty services to other private-sector and government clients, including airport fueling, emergency restoration engineering, intelligent highway systems, light rail control systems, rock trenching, vegetation control, and wind generation. Listed on the New York Stock Exchange, Quanta maintains operations in all 50 states and Canada.

FOUNDER: A VIETNAM VETERAN

The man behind the creation of Quanta Services was its longtime chief executive officer and chairman, John R. Colson. Growing up on a farm in Blue Spring, Missouri, he became accustomed at an early age to hard work, which he used to his advantage later in life. "Unfortunately, I wasn't born the smartest guy in the world, so I have to work a lot harder than some of my contemporaries," he once told *Investor's Business Daily.* "I've found that I can make up for things I don't know if I just work hard at it." After earning a degree in geology from the University of Missouri at Kansas City, Colson entered the military and served one year in Vietnam. He was discharged from the Army in 1971 and returned to Kansas City, taking temporary employment at Par Electrical Contractors, Inc., which built high-voltage transmission lines, distribution lines, and substations, and provided other electric utility infrastructure services. His job was to carry stakes for a survey team, a menial task given that as a geology major he had surveying experience. Nevertheless he took the job seriously and because of his diligence was kept on after the stint was up. Colson was interested in the oil business and sent out his resumes while working with Par, but he never did leave the company and launched an unintended career in the electrical contracting business.

Soon after becoming a permanent employee at Par, Colson was put in charge of work crews installing utility lines in Missouri, and he took advantage of his military training to organize his men into a coordinated unit. His abilities and dedication to the work caught the eye of his superiors who began to promote him through the

COMPANY PERSPECTIVES

With more than 13,000 employees, major offices in 40 states, and field and support offices in all 50 states and Canada, Quanta Services has the manpower, resources and expertise to complete projects that are local, regional, national or even international in scope.

organization. Within three years he was named manager of engineering services, and after six he had worked his way up to vice-president of operations. After becoming executive vice-president and general manager in the early 1980s, he began buying the company, became president in 1991, and ultimately emerged as its owner.

In the 1990s a number of factors came together that led to the creation of Quanta Services and other companies that participate in a consolidation of the electrical contracting industry, populated by more than 50,000 companies, the vast majority of which were small, owner-operated enterprises. Deregulation in the electric utility industries in a number of states prompted utilities to become more cost-competitive, leading to the outsourcing of infrastructure work to contractors who could do the job more efficiently. Moreover, much of the transmission and distribution infrastructure in the United States was aging and in need of repair or replacement. In 1997 Colson spearheaded the combination of four contractors to form Quanta Services, Inc., which then established its headquarters in Houston with Colson as its head.

In addition to Par, Quanta consisted of Union Power Construction Co., Trans Tech Electric Inc., and Potelco, Inc. By this time Par was generating more than $42 million a year in revenues while doing business in 11 states, including Colorado, California, and Hawaii. Union Power, based in Englewood, Colorado, operated in six western states and did about the same amount of business as Par. The third partner, Trans Tech, was based in South Bend, Indiana, and served customers in Indiana, Kentucky, and Michigan. It added about $24 million in annual sales. Finally, Seattle-based Potelco contributed about $14.5 million in business from customers in Washington, Oregon, and Idaho.

Quanta's initial vision was to focus on outsourcing opportunities with electric utilities, but it soon became apparent that the old boundaries between transmission industries were becoming blurred, as utilities now launched telecommunications subsidiaries. The buzzword became "convergence," as electric power, telecommunications, cable television, and, to some extent, gas pipelines were becoming parts of larger enterprises. Hence, Quanta soon began expanding into the telecommunications and cable TV fields.

A major part of Quanta's business plan was to grow through acquisitions, and Colson now had to decide if it was wise to take Quanta public in order to raise money and have stock to use in making purchases. According to *Investor's Business Daily,* Colson pondered his decision by going hunting in 1998. After some reflection he decided to try for an initial public offering (IPO) of stock, although he had some misgivings about dealing with Wall Street. "Then he decided that all he had to do was change his attitude toward investors," wrote *Investor's Business Daily.* "He'd treat them like a new group of customers. All he had to be, he saw, was honest. 'The best thing is to tell the story just as straight as you can. There's no magic, no science to it,' he said. 'We know what we're doing, and we just need to tell Wall Street what we're doing and why we're doing it and why we think it will work.'"

1998 IPO

With BT Alex Brown Incorporated, BancAmerica Robertson Stephens, and Sanders Morris Mundy Inc. serving as underwriters, Quanta completed its IPO in February 1998, raising $45 million. Of that amount $21 million was used to pay the cash portion of the buyouts of the four founding companies. Much of the balance, along with a $175 million line of credit arranged with a consortium of nine banks, was used on a dozen acquisitions completed in 1998. They included telecommunications contractors Manuel Bros., Inc. of Grass Valley, California; Minnesota-based Smith Contracting; Telecom Network Specialists, Inc., operating out of Kirkland, Washington; North Pacific Construction Co., based in Woodland, California; Oregon's NorAm Telecommunications, Inc.; Spalj Construction Company, located in Deerwood, Minnesota; and Golden State Utility Co., a Turlock, California company. Electric contractors included Las Vegas-based Harker & Harker, Inc.; Sumter Builders, Inc. of Sumter, South Carolina; and Environmental Professional Associates, Ltd., a Marysville, California company. In addition, Quanta acquired Wilson Roadbores, Inc., a Princeton, Missouri-based company involved in both electric and telecommunications contracting, and Underground Construction Co., Inc., a Benecia, California company that served the telecommunications, transportation, commercial, and industrial markets. Of these acquisitions, three-quarters were considered platform companies, averaging $24 million in annual sales and 34 years in business.

KEY DATES

1997: The company is formed.
1998: An initial public offering of stock is made.
2000: Sales reach $2 billion.
2002: A hostile takeover bid is defeated.

Another significant development in 1998 was the acquisition of the patent to the Linemaster Robotic Arm, a remote control device that could safely perform work on energized high-voltage power lines. Because the lines did not have to be shut down to perform maintenance work, customers were not only spared an inconvenience, they saved money because the utility did not have to contend with as many costly outages. Quanta also forged what, at the time, it perceived to be an important alliance when it established a partnership with Enron, which was beginning to install thousands of miles of fiber optic cable. Enron also invested $50 million in Quanta. When the results for 1998 were posted it revealed that revenues for Quanta jumped from $179.4 million in 1997 to more than $333.8 million in 1998. Net income improved from $9.8 million to $16.8 million. The company was also well diversified in its mix of customers. About half of Quanta's revenues came from the electric utility sector, 37 percent from telecommunications, and 9 percent from transportation.

Investors were impressed with Quanta's quick start and snapped up shares of stock that became available in a secondary offering completed in late January 1999. The company had planned to sell 3.5 million shares at $21 per share, but interest was so strong that in the end 4.6 million shares were sold at $23.25 per share. All told, Quanta realized $101.1 million, money used to fund the acquisition of 40 additional companies, which in total cost $323.6 million in cash and notes and 15 million shares of stock. Many of these additions were made to expand Quanta's business in gas transmission and cable television. As a result, the company's business mix experienced a significant shift by the end of 1999, when it recorded sales of $925.7 million and net income of nearly $54 million. Now just 30 percent of sales were from the electric power sector, while 35 percent came from telecommunications, 13 percent from cable television, and 22 percent from ancillary services, which included transportation services, gas pipeline work, and rock-boring and trenching for water and sewer lines.

The acquisition binge continued in 2000 when Quanta paid $282.4 million in cash and issued 4.4 million shares of stock to add another 25 companies. As a result of these new assets and internal growth, Quanta increased revenues to the $2 billion mark in 2000 and net income increased to $85.8 million. The company was now more committed to telecommunications than to any other sector, contributing 43 percent of sales. Electric utilities accounted for 19 percent and 15 percent came from Cable TV. As a result, the sagging fortunes of the telecommunications industry, as well as a struggling economy, would begin to cause a drag on Quanta's growth.

DECLINING REVENUES AT THE START OF THE 21ST CENTURY

Quanta completed a pair of acquisitions in 2001, adding Utility Construction & Technology Solutions L.L.C. and North Houston Pole Line Corp., but for the most part the company looked to improve the integration of the operations already in the fold. The executive team was beefed up and a regional management structure was implemented to allow operating units to create business opportunities for one another. Although revenues in 2001 dipped to $1.79 billion in 2001, the company was able to improve its profits to $105.7 million.

Quanta experienced a more difficult year in 2002; not only did business conditions not improve, the company found itself the target of a hostile takeover bid after the price of its once high-flying stock languished.

In 2001 UtiliCorp United Inc., an energy company with whom Par Electrical had been doing business since the 1950s, began taking steps to gain control of Quanta. UtiliCorp owned a sizable stake in Quanta, about 36 percent, an investment that was originally part of a strategic alliance between the two companies when UtiliCorp outsourced all of its maintenance needs to Quanta. Quanta resisted UtiliCorp's overtures to increase its stake, and in October 2001 the two parties signed a standstill agreement.

A month later Quanta adopted a so-called "poison pill" plan to prevent a takeover, prompting UtiliCorp to sue, claiming that its three Quanta directors had not been properly notified of the board meeting at which the plan was approved. An all-out proxy fight ensued in the spring of 2002. Quanta maintained that UtiliCorp, which was enduring difficult times, wanted to gain a controlling interest in order to consolidate Quanta's earnings with its own balance sheet to keep its number in line with Wall Street expectations and buoy the price of its own stock. This agenda, Quanta insisted, was not in the best interests of its shareholders. In the proxy fight, UtiliCorp told shareholders that it wanted to gain control of the board in order to improve the value of Quanta for the benefit of all shareholders, listing an outright sale of the company as a possible strategy. The fight came to an end in May 2002, as Quanta fended off the takeover bid. But the effort cost Quanta $12 million and also proved to be a major distraction for management.

Quanta's customers continued to be wary of new capital spending in 2003. As a result, revenues fell to $1.64 billion and the company lost $32.9 million. Quanta took steps to control costs and reorganized its operations along industry lines, but beyond that there was nothing management could do until customers began spending money again. Sales dipped slightly to $1.63 billion in 2004, and Quanta narrowed its loss to less than $10 million. The company appeared to turn the corner in 2005 when it returned to profitability, recording net income of $29.6 million on sales of $1.86 billion. A good portion of that revenue was attributed to work performed in response to the hurricanes that lashed the Gulf Coast in the autumn of 2005, but the industries Quanta served were also beginning to ramp up spending. Given that maintenance work could not be postponed indefinitely, the long-term prospects for Quanta remained positive.

Ed Dinger

PRINCIPAL SUBSIDIARIES

Par Electrical Contractors, Inc.; Trans Tech Electric, L.P.; Potelco, Inc.

PRINCIPAL COMPETITORS

EMCOR Group, Inc.; Integrated Electrical Services, Inc.; MYR Group Inc.

FURTHER READING

"Aquila, Quanta Agree to End Proxy Fight for Board Control," *Wall Street Journal,* May 21, 2002, p. B6.

Greer, Jim, "Quanta Leap: Power Surge Propels Telecom Company's Stock Price," *Houston Business Journal,* March 31, 2000, p. 14A.

Korman, Richard, "Big Investor Fights Contractor for Control of the Company," *ENR,* February 18, 2002, p. 17.

———, "Quanta: We Won't Overpay," *ENR,* May 11, 1998, p. 19.

McGough, Robert, and Rebecca Smith, "Investors Think That UtiliCorp's Quanta Stake Makes the Utility's Stock a Buried Treasure," *Wall Street Journal,* May 25, 2000, p. 1.

"Quanta Finds Big New Partner," *ENR,* July 12, 1999, p. 15.

Shinkle, Kirk, "Quanta Services' John Colson—His Hard-Wired Dedication Helped Build Up Contractor," *Investor's Business Daily,* May 11, 2000, p. A04.

Sidel, Robin, "Proxy Fight for Quanta May End in TKO—In Strange Scenario, UtiliCorp Doesn't Plan a Takeover Bid," *Wall Street Journal,* February 22, 2002, p. C14.

Quiksilver, Inc.

15202 Graham Street
Huntington Beach, California 92649
U.S.A.
Telephone: (714) 889-2200
Fax: (714) 889-2315
Web site: http://www.quiksilver.com

Public Company
Incorporated: 1976 as Quiksilver U.S.A.
Employees: 4,350
Sales: $1.78 billion (2005)
Stock Exchanges: New York
Ticker Symbol: ZQK
NAIC: 315223 Men's and Boys' Cut and Sew Shirt (Except Work Shirt) Manufacturing; 315228 Men's and Boys' Cut and Sew Other Outerwear Manufacturing; 315232 Women's and Girls' Cut and Sew Blouse and Shirt Manufacturing; 315999 Other Apparel Accessories and Other Apparel Manufacturing; 339920 Sporting and Athletic Goods Manufacturing

■ ■ ■

Quiksilver, Inc. designs, produces, and distributes casual sportswear, footwear, winter sports apparel and equipment, and golf equipment, selling its merchandise in surf shops, department stores, specialty stores, and in the company's own stores, a chain of 158 Boardriders Club stores. Quiksilver's merchandise is sold under numerous brand names, including Quiksilver, Roxy, Raisins, DC Shoes, Radio Fiji, Gotcha, Fidra, Hawk Clothing, Rossignol, Dynastar, Lange, Leilani, Lib Technologies, Gnu, and Bent Metal. The company generates roughly one-fifth of its revenue from the sale of T-shirts, its most important product category. Quiksilver relies on international business for slightly more than half of its revenue.

ORIGINS

The Quiksilver name first appeared in the United States thanks to the entrepreneurial efforts of two inveterate surfers, Robert B. McKnight and Jeffrey Hakman. Hakman was the more accomplished surfer of the two, having won several international surfing championships, but McKnight shared an equal passion for the sport and its attendant lifestyle. Born and raised in Pasadena, California, McKnight graduated from the University of Southern California with a degree in business in 1976, the year he decided to move to Oahu, Hawaii, and spend his days surfing on the island's world renowned north shore. While on Oahu McKnight renewed his friendship with Hakman and together the two surfing addicts discussed their desire to start a business that could finance their days on the beach. They decided to try to get the licensing rights for Quiksilver, a seven-year-old company based in Torquay, Australia, where it was founded by two surfers, Alan Greene and John Law.

For McKnight and Hakman, obtaining the licensing rights to Quiksilver represented a perfect opportunity to turn their favorite pastime into a vocation. The company's boardshorts and swimsuits, which were tight-fitting and outfitted with velcro straps, were quickly becoming the rage among surfers in Australia, turning

COMPANY PERSPECTIVES

Quiksilver has developed from a 1970s boardshort company into a multinational apparel and accessory company grounded in the philosophy of youth. Our mission is to become the leading global youth apparel company; to maintain our core focus and roots while bringing our lifestyle message of boardriding, independence, creativity and innovation to this global community. Individual expression, an adventurous spirit, authenticity and a passionate approach are all part of young people's mindset and are the essence of our brands. Combine this with the aesthetic appeal of beaches and mountains, and a connection is established that transcends borders and continents. Include thirty-plus years of quality, innovation and style, and you have Quiksilver.

the Quiksilver brand name into a highly coveted, trendy label. McKnight and Hakman hoped to achieve commensurate success with the Quiksilver name in the United States, but neither of the two aspiring entrepreneurs thought of creating a beach wear apparel empire, particularly McKnight, whose business intentions were modest. Reflecting on his entry into the business world, McKnight explained, "I thought I could make a few shorts and stay near the beach and party." Despite his less than grandiose plans, McKnight soon found himself guiding the fortunes of a rapidly growing, flourishing enterprise. "I never thought the business would fail," McKnight remembered, "I just didn't expect it to get so big so quickly."

McKnight and Hakman's surprising success with the Quiksilver brand name began in April 1976, when Hakman entered a surfing competition in Australia. Hakman won the event, and as luck would have it, he met Greene and Law and sat up all night with Quiksilver's owners eating, drinking champagne, and discussing the possibility of securing the U.S. licensing rights to the Quicksilver name. After plates of food and bottles of champagne, Greene and Law agreed to sell Quiksilver's U.S. rights to McKnight and Hakman on one condition, a unique proviso that became the first obstacle the two Americans had to hurdle in order to launch themselves into business. The duty of fulfilling Greene and Law's demand fell solely to Hakman; McKnight, back in Hawaii, could be of no assistance. Greene and Law informed Hakman that they would agree to the proposal provided Hakman ate the large paper doily under his plate, which Hakman promptly did. After swallowing the plate-sized piece of paper, Hakman shook hands with Greene and Law and placed a call to Oahu to tell McKnight of the good news.

McKnight, who spearheaded the business end of the venture, offered the specifics of the proposal to Greene and Law. McKnight and Hakman invested no money, but agreed to pay a royalty of 1 percent of sales for three years, which jumped to 3 percent after three years, and an additional 1 percent of sales to support international promotions. Next, McKnight hurried to secure the capital required to launch the business. He returned to California and asked his father, who was a sporting goods importer, to lend him $20,000 to finance a production run of Quicksilver apparel. McKnight's father agreed, and a few months after Hakman's all-nighter with Quicksilver's Australian owners, the two young Americans were ready to start production for their new company, Quiksilver U.S.A.

McKnight and Hakman debuted their first line of apparel in the summer of 1976. They bought some fabric on credit and manufactured 600 pairs of boardshorts, featuring six separate designs, for their first season. The two entrepreneurs then took their boardshorts, which were priced higher but were more colorful than similar merchandise produced by established rivals Ocean Pacific and Hang Ten, and peddled them to three surf shops in Southern California. With their product distributed, all McKnight and Hakman could do was wait and see if they had made a prudent move. In nine days, the 600 pairs of boardshorts were nowhere to be found on the shelves and racks of the three surf shops, having sold out with encouraging speed.

Several years after their remarkably successful inaugural year of business, McKnight and Hakman found themselves surrounded by a wealth of new competitors, as start-up after start-up entered the active beach wear industry. The influx of new competition created a contentious marketing environment for such companies as Quiksilver, but McKnight and Hakman kept their operation lean, eschewing debt, and remained tightly focused on producing the type of merchandise that first launched them toward success. Describing this period in the company's history, McKnight noted, "While everyone else was making swimwear, we were setting the standard for surfwear," an approach that would hold Quiksilver in good stead in the decades ahead. "We've been successful," McKnight went on to explain, "because our philosophy has always been to bring the image off the beach and into the stores. Since we were all surfers, we knew what kids wanted."

KEY DATES

1969: Quiksilver is founded in Torquay, Australia.
1976: Robert B. McKnight and Jeffrey Hakman acquire the licensing rights to Quiksilver and form Quiksilver U.S.A.
1985: Quiksilver begins distributing merchandise to department stores.
1986: Quicksilver completes its initial public offering of stock.
1988: Quicksilver launches a skiwear line.
1993: The Raisin Company, Inc. is acquired, which adds a line of women's swimwear and sportswear.
1997: Quiksilver acquires Mervin Manufacturing, Inc.
2000: Quiksilver acquires Quiksilver International Pty Ltd., part of the company's bid to secure control over the worldwide rights to the Quiksilver brand.
2004: Quiksilver acquires DC Shoes, Inc.
2005: Quiksilver acquires Groupe Rossignol SA.

EXPANSION

McKnight's commitment to his business strategy successfully carried Quiksilver through its fledgling years, creating a firmly established company by the beginning of the 1980s. The 1980s witnessed a host of sweeping changes that reshaped Quiksilver as it maneuvered through its corporate adolescence, beginning in 1981 when Hakman exited the business, leaving on amicable terms with McKnight to return to Australia and surf. Four years later, a turning point in Quiksilver's history occurred when McKnight took Quiksilver to the next plateau of the retail apparel business and began distributing Quiksilver merchandise to department stores.

The foray into the retail mainstream began gradually and conservatively, manifesting two defining characteristics of Quicksilver's development during its first decade. The move into department stores marked the beginning of the company's evolution into a more sophisticated enterprise. As the 1980s progressed, Quiksilver became more than a business whose chief objective was to finance McKnight's surfing and partying at the beach. A full-fledged corporation was in the making, propelling Quiksilver's growth forward at a substantially faster pace and engendering the attendant pitfalls of rapid growth.

Following McKnight's decision to expand Quicksilver, the company celebrated the conclusion of its first decade of business by completing its initial public offering (IPO) of stock in December 1986, when annual sales were up to $19 million and the stock market was receptive to small-sized companies such as Quiksilver. McKnight and his minority partners sold 50 percent of the company to the public, raising $16 million to bolster Quiksilver's financial foundation as it developed its department store business. With the proceeds gained from the public offering, McKnight bought the Quiksilver trademark for the United States and Mexico, paid off all the company's short- and long-term debts, and expanded Quiksilver's line of production runs in preparation for greater department store business. From 1986 the company operated under the name Quiksilver, Inc.

As Quiksilver intensified its involvement with department stores, eventually distributing its merchandise to retailers such as Macy's, Marshall Fields, Dayton Hudson, and the Dillard Group, McKnight decided to a bring in someone with greater experience in dealing with department stores. In July 1987, McKnight hired John C. Warner, who at the time was senior vice-president and general merchandising manager of Macy's Department Stores' Denver operation. Initially, Warner was hired as head of sales, but he quickly proved to be a tremendous asset and seven months after joining the company was named chairman and chief executive officer of Quiksilver.

With Warner occupying the two top managerial posts and McKnight serving as president, Quicksilver moved headlong into fostering the growth of its department store business. Sales in 1987 amounted to $30 million and shot up the following year to $48.3 million, while earnings rose to $3.7 million. Sales to department stores made up 40 percent of Quiksilver's $48.3 million in sales in 1988, and offered tangible evidence that the company had made commendable progress into the retail mainstream. The company's range of merchandise had expanded substantially as well, growing well beyond the original line of six styles of boardshorts. Once the sole source of revenue for the company, boardshorts by the late 1980s accounted for only 18 percent of total annual sales, while the balance was derived from a host of different apparel items. T-shirts accounted for 15 percent of total sales, shirts 11 percent, pants 12 percent, fleece wear 9 percent, walking shorts 27 percent, jackets 4 percent, and surfing accessories another 4 percent.

In addition to these products, the company also was moving beyond purely surfing-related merchandise, diversifying its business as the strength of the Quiksilver brand name increased. In 1988, the company introduced six skiwear designs, offering the same number of styles as it had 12 years earlier with boardshorts. The initial success of the skiwear line nearly matched the initial success of the boardshort line, selling out in five weeks and grossing $500,000.

The growing spectrum of Quiksilver products appeared in roughly 2,000 stores nationwide during the late 1980s, including in the original three surf shops that purchased the company's first line of boardshorts in 1976. Fueled by this vast distribution system, annual sales leaped from the $48 million registered in 1989 to more than $70 million in 1989. By this point, when sales to department stores accounted for nearly 50 percent of total sales, some industry observers predicted that the company would become too big and low-price retailers would begin selling their merchandise, a development that would erode profitability and potentially tarnish the appeal of the Quiksilver name to the hard-core surfing set. Aware of the problem, Warner confided to a *California Business* reporter in 1989, "We have no illusions that our growth as Quiksilver in our existing businesses is limited somewhat down the road, but we want to continue growing and will do so by acquisition, start-up, or licensing."

DIVERSIFICATION

As the company entered the 1990s, it continued to record robust sales gains. Sales in 1990 neared the $100 million mark, fueled by the continued success of the company's traditional line of surfing apparel, but the early years of the decade signaled a disruption in Quiksilver's rousing 1980s rise. Two trends emerged during the early 1990s, both of which negatively affected Quiksilver. First, a nationwide economic recession developed, sending many retailers reeling, particularly the large department stores that accounted for the bulk of Quiksilver's business. To combat the recession, department stores reduced the amount of square footage devoted to selling young men's apparel among other things, which caused Quiksilver's sales to dip. Exacerbating this development was the growing popularity of the "grunge" look during the early 1990s, a fashion style that embraced muted, earthy hues rather than the flashy, colorful styles that had predicated Quiksilver's popularity during the 1980s. As a result, Quiksilver's neon boardshorts were no longer the rage of the day, and the company began to suffer.

To beat back the effects of the recession and changing fashion tastes, Quiksilver diversified its apparel lines and refocused its efforts toward selling to specialty stores. In 1991, the company acquired Na Pali, S.A., the European licensee of the Quiksilver brand in Europe, and established a subsidiary headquartered in France to design and produce Quiksilver apparel for all countries in Western Europe. By the mid-1990s, Quiksilver was collecting more than 30 percent of its total annual revenues from its European operation, a definite contribution to the company's resurgence by the middle part of the decade. Help came from elsewhere as well, including the company's foray into producing snowboard clothing and its entrance into the market for women's sportswear. Women's sportswear became a key facet of Quiksilver's business following the company's November 1993 acquisition of The Raisin Company, Inc., a manufacturer of women's swimwear and sportswear. Aided by the addition of a strong European business, a return to the specialty and surf shops, and the expansion of its apparel lines, Quiksilver survived the recession and stood firmly positioned as a market leader by the mid-1990s.

During the mid-1990s, Quiksilver derived roughly 40 percent of total revenues from surf shops and nearly 45 percent from specialty shops. After building its department store business significantly during the latter half of the 1980s, the company had largely abandoned these retailers by the mid-1990s, deriving less than 15 percent of total sales from department stores. This shift back to the company's roots was perceived as a positive step by a number of industry analysts, as was the company's encouraging financial growth. Between 1992 and 1995, annual net income rose from $371,000 to more than $10 million, while sales leaped from $89 million to $172 million. As the company prepared for the late 1990s in the wake of this robust growth, expectations were high, fueling confidence that years ahead would strengthen Quiksilver's market position as a dominant force.

1995–2005: CREATION OF AN INDUSTRY GIANT

Few industry observers could have predicted the phenomenal growth Quicksilver achieved as it progressed toward its 30th anniversary. The company, in the course of a decade, evolved from a surf brand into a global leader in the outdoor sports lifestyle market, completing a leap in stature that evoked comparisons to industry behemoth Nike, Inc. The magnitude of Quicksilver's financial and physical growth was staggering: The company that was flirting with the $200 million-in-sales mark during the mid-1990s had the $2 billion plateau within sight a decade later; the ranks of Quiksilver employees increased by a factor of ten, exploding from 400 to more than 4,000; international operations grew with a flourish, fanning out from France to encompass all of Europe before spreading into Asia and the Pacific region. The relentless charge forward was led by McKnight.

To increase the breadth and depth of his company McKnight assumed the posture of an aggressive acquirer. Internal growth accounted for a meaningful portion of the growth achieved—gains made through the expansion of the company's existing product lines, the establishment of international subsidiaries, and the creation of a retail arm—but the purchase of other companies highlighted Quicksilver's rise. Acquisitions provided entry into new lines of business, giving Quiksilver an established presence in new markets literally overnight, and they provided nearly immediate financial benefits, enabling McKnight to point to surging sales and profit totals far sooner than if he had relied solely on internal means of expansion. As the company's acquisition campaign progressed, Quiksilver became the promoter of an ever expanding roster of brands, beginning with the purchase of Mervin Manufacturing, Inc. in 1997. Mervin manufactured Lib Technologies and Gnu snowboards, as well as Bent Metal snowboard bindings, paving Quiksilver's entry into the snowboard market. In 2000, Quiksilver acquired Hawk Designs, owner of the famed Tony Hawk skateboarding name for apparel and related accessories, and created Hawk Clothing, but the year's most significant move took the company back to its roots.

As Quiksilver entered a new century, McKnight seized control over the empire he was building. In July 2000, he acquired Quiksilver International Pty Ltd., the company that had originally created the Quiksilver brand. The acquisition gave McKnight all international rights to use the Quiksilver and Roxy trademarks, a right that previously was limited to use in the United States and Mexico. Another step toward gaining global control over the two brands was completed at the end of 2002, when McKnight acquired Ug Manufacturing Co. Pty Ltd. and Quiksilver Japan KK, which had licensed through Quiksilver International to operate in Australia, Japan, New Zealand, and additional southeast Asian territories. By the end of 2003, after one full year of controlling the Quicksilver and Roxy brands, the company revenues pressed toward the $1 billion mark, reaching $975 million.

McKnight completed two more acquisitions before Quiksilver's 30th anniversary, adding substantially sized operations that enabled the company to hurtle past $1 billion in sales and nearly reach $2 billion. In May 2004, Quiksilver purchased DC Shoes, Inc., a designer and manufacturer of footwear, apparel, and accessories that catered to consumers drawn to skateboarding. The acquisition increased the company's revenues by 7 percent in 2004, helping lift its revenue total to $1.23 billion. Roughly a year after the DC Shoes purchase, McKnight added more than $600 million to Quiksilver's revenue volume by acquiring Voiron, France-based Groupe Rossignol SA, a leader in the ski industry that also owned a golf equipment manufacturer. For approximately $320 million, McKnight acquired a host of new brands, including Rossignol, Dynastar, Look, Lange, and Cleveland Golf. Rossignol ranked as the world's largest maker of skis and bindings and the third largest producer of ski boots, but perhaps the most appealing facet of the company's business was that it only generated 7 percent of its revenue from the sale of apparel, Quiksilver's specialty. Rossignol's relatively small apparel business offered Quiksilver room for growth, a potential the company perceived in many of its other businesses. Accordingly, as the company prepared for the future, it was expected to rely on internal means of growth to continue its evolution into a sports lifestyle giant. "If you do the math," a Quiksilver executive said in a May 2, 2005 interview with *Footwear News,* "without any more acquisitions we should be able to get to $3 billion or $4 billion in sales in the next five to seven years. We think there is lots of growth potential there. If some incredible deal shows up and it makes sense, then we'd have to look hard at it, but we're not looking for a big deal to do in the near future."

Jeffrey L. Covell

PRINCIPAL SUBSIDIARIES

Fidra, Inc.; Hawk Designs, Inc.; Mervin Manufacturing, Inc.; Mt. Waimea, Inc.; QS Optics, Inc.; QS Retail, Inc.; Quiksilver Entertainment, Inc.; Quiksilver Wetsuits, Inc.; DC Shoes, Inc.; DC Direct, Inc.; Quiksilver Americas, Inc.; QS Wholesale, Inc.; UMTT Pty Ltd. (Australia); Carribean Pty Ltd. (Australia); Pavilion Productions Pty Ltd. (Australia); QSJ Holdings Pty Ltd. (Australia); Quiksilver Australia Pty Ltd.; Quiksilver International Pty Ltd. (Australia); Ug Manufacturing Co. Pty Ltd. (Australia); Watermoons Pty Ltd.; DC Australia Pty Ltd.; Andaya SARL (France); Cariboo SARL (France); Emerald Coast SA (France); Infoborn SARL (France); Kokolo SARL (France); Na Pali SAS (France); Na Pali Entertainment SARL (France); Na Pali Europe SARL (France); Omareef Europe SAS (France); Tavarua SCI (France); DC Europe SARL (France); Zebraska SARL (France); Kauai GmbH (Germany); Makaha GmbH (Germany); Quiksilver Asia Sourcing Ltd. (Hong Kong); Quiksilver Greater China Ltd. (Hong Kong); DC Shoes International Ltd. (Hong Kong); PT Quiksilver Indonesia; Namotu Ltd. (Ireland); Haapiti SRL (Italy); Moorea SRL (Italy); Quiksilver Japan K.K.; QS Holdings SARL (Luxembourg); Urban Surf (Malaysia); Pukalani BV (Netherlands); Tuvalu BV (Netherlands); Ug Manufacturing Co. Pty Ltd. (New Zealand); Rawaki sp z.o.o. (Poland); Kiribatti Lda

(Portugal); Tarawa Lda (Portugal); Bakio SL (Spain); Quiksilver Europa, SL (Spain); Sumbawa SL (Spain); Town Surf (Thailand); Escatade Ltd. (U.K.); Lanai Ltd. (U.K.); Molokai Ltd. (U.K.); Sunshine SA (Switzerland); Longboarder GmbH (Switzerland).

PRINCIPAL COMPETITORS

Billabong International Ltd.; NIKE, Inc.; Pacific Sunwear of California, Inc.; Burton Snowboards Inc.

FURTHER READING

Bailey, Lee, "Quik Expands in SOHO," *Daily News Record,* November 14, 2005, p. 1.

Barron, Kelly, "Quiksilver Surfwear Explains Its Third-Quarter," *Knight-Ridder/Tribune Business News,* September 13, 1996, p. 9.

Basas, M. Susan, "Quiksilver Inc.," *Investor's Business Daily,* February 19, 2003, p. A8.

Buchalter, Gail, "Do What You Wanna Do," *Forbes,* October 3, 1988, p. 82.

———, "Fun, Fun, Fun," *California Business,* July 1989, p. 16.

Cuneo, Alice Z., "Quiksilver Aims to Cash in on Pop-Culture Surf Craze," *Advertising Age,* June 9, 2003, p. 18.

David, Gregory E., "Quiksilver: Don't Catch This Wave," *Financial World,* January 17, 1995, p. 18.

Driscoll, Marie, "Quiksilver Catches a Growing Wave," *Business Week Online,* April 27, 2004.

Gorrell, Mike, "Outdoors Retailer Chooses Park City," *Salt Lake Tribune,* September 7, 2005.

Kletter, Melanie, "Quiksilver Establishes Global Corporate Team," *WWD,* July 8, 2005, p. 19.

Luna, Nancy, "Surfwear Giant Quiksilver Confirms That It's Buying the Rossignol Ski Empire," *Orange County Register,* March 23, 2005.

Marsh, Emilie, "Global Surfin' Safari," *WWD,* June 30, 2005, p. 1.

Martinez, Brian, "Quiksilver CEO: Board-Sport Industry Unlimited," *Orange County Register,* June 23, 2005.

Nelson, Alexandra, "Sadeghi Exits Post at Quiksilver, Inc.," *Daily News Record,* July 21, 1992, p. 2.

Nguyen, Hang, "Quiksilver Posts Almost 30 Percent Jump in Net Income," *Orange County Register,* September 9, 2005.

Niemi, Wayne, "Quiksilver, DC Moving Fast," *Footwear News,* May 2, 2005, p. 4.

Pallay, Jessica, "Quiksilver Opens Single-Sex Store," *Daily News Record,* August 25, p. 16.

Price, Shawn, "Surfwear Giants Billabong, Quiksilver Take to Skies in Latest Stage of Rivalry," *Orange County Register,* December 15, 2004.

"Quiksilver Buys Rossignol," *Sporting Goods Business,* April 2005, p. 12.

"Quiksilver Earnings Up 10 Percent, Sales Jump 15 Percent in 2nd Quarter," *Daily News Record,* September 26, 1996, p. 5.

Slovak, Julianne, "Quiksilver," *Fortune,* February 26, 1990, p. 90.

Tschorn, Adam, "Quiksilver Heads for the Hills," *Daily News Record,* March 28, 2005, p. 2.

Empresas RANDON®

Randon S.A. Implementos e Participações

Av. Abramo Randon 770
Caxias do Sul, Rio Grande do Sul 95055-010
Brazil
Telephone: (55 54) 3209-2000
Toll Free: (0800) 512158
Fax: (55 54) 3209-2566
Web site: http://www.randon.com.br

Public Company
Incorporated: 1952 as Mecânica Randon Ltda.
Employees: 7,100
Sales: BRL 1.94 billion ($795.08 million) (2005)
Stock Exchanges: São Paulo
Ticker Symbols: RAPT3; RAPT4
NAIC: 336211 Motor Vehicle Body Manufacturing; 336212 Truck Trailer Manufacturing; 336330 Motor Vehicle Steering and Suspension Components; 336390 Motor Vehicle Brake System Manufacturing; 336510 Railroad Rolling Stock Manufacturing; 551112 Offices of Other Holding Companies

■ ■ ■

Randon S.A. Implementos e Participações is a Brazilian holding company that, through subsidiary and joint-venture companies, is engaged in the manufacture, sale, and export of trailers, semi-trailers, railroad cars, and more specialized vehicles such as off-highway trucks, mining trucks, and aerial-work lift cranes; auto parts and systems; and services such as maintenance and sales financing. All of its eight industrial plants are in Brazil except for one in Argentina. Randon represents itself as the world manufacturer with the most diversified portfolio of equipment and vehicles for the transportation of road cargoes, and it is the largest manufacturer of road-vehicle implements in Latin America. It occupies more than 40 percent of the Brazilian market for trailers and semi-trailers and is among the five leading world manufacturers in this sector. Randon sells its products in over 100 countries.

WORKSHOP TO FACTORIES: 1952–80

Raul Anselmo Randon, son of Italian immigrants, was a poor student who left school to become an ironworker in Caixas do Sul, Rio Grande do Sul, Brazil's southernmost state, in 1943, when, at the age of 14, he began helping his father make farm implements. In 1949, after returning from compulsory military service, he began repairing engines for his brother Hercílio, who had bought a small lathe. They also formed a company with an outside partner to build typesetting machines, but the shop burned down in 1951. In 1952, with the backing of a different partner, they founded Mecânica Randon Ltda., for the production of road equipment and air brakes for trailers. Soon after, this enterprise turned to manufacturing the third axle for trucks.

In the late 1950s work began on Brazil's BR-111 highway, which fostered road transport and, consequently, the production of road vehicles. Mecânica Randon began converting and adapting truck chassis for use in buses and, in 1961, built its first two semi-trailers, on the basis of a design developed in Hercílio's own workshop. By 1965 the enterprise was producing a semi-

COMPANY PERSPECTIVES

Mission: To coordinate, represent, and orient the Randon businesses, optimizing the disposable resources.

trailer per day. Randon established a São Paulo branch in 1969 in order to install third axles on General Motors Corp. and Ford Motor Co. trucks. The company also took out a patent on third axles for semi-trailers. It also began publishing Informativo Randon, a house organ that, 30 years later, was available in Spanish and English as well as Portuguese, with nearly 50,000 copies per issue.

Visits to Germany and Italy stoked Raul Randon's ambition. In 1970 the company changed its name to Randon S.A. - Indústria de Implementos para o Transporte, and the following year it became a publicly traded corporation. Raul and Hercílio continued to hold majority control, and Raul became director-president. The money they raised by selling shares of stock went to buy land for a new factory. They also received financing for this purpose from government development agencies. When the factory opened in 1974, Randon introduced a 25-metric-ton off-road vehicle, the RK 424, and thereby became the first totally Brazilian enterprise to build automotive vehicles in the south of the country. Accordingly, the company was renamed Randon S.A. - Veículos e Implementos in 1975.

Randon joined with a French firm in 1976 to introduce a new enterprise. Based in Rio de Janeiro, it built platforms with axles modulated to carry cargoes from 100 to 700 metric tons. In the same year, it began establishing a post-sale network of authorized service shops that eventually grew to almost 70 in number. Randon had begun exporting on a very small scale to neighboring Uruguay in 1973. Four years later, it sent more than 1,000 semi-trailers to Algeria. The following year it acquired its principal competitor, Mêcanica Rodoviária S.A.

In 1979 Randon entered a business far afield from its usual concerns: it established Randon Agro-Pastoril Ltda., under government incentives, to grow and sell apples. This subsidiary, located in an orchard in Vacaria, Rio Grande do Sul, began as a kind of hobby for Raul Randon (who also delighted in making Italian-style cheeses from the milk yielded by cows imported from the United States) but became one of the nation's largest producers of the fruit. It later began producing and selling grapes as well, and was part of Rasip, an enterprise that included about 14,000 acres sown in corn, wheat, and soybeans, plus a herd of 5,000 short-horned cattle, and even capivaras, wild boar, and fish. Rasip Agro-Pastoril S.A. became a separate company in 1998.

NEW VENTURES: 1980–99

By 1981 Brazil could no longer sustain an economy marked by triple-digit annual inflation and heavy debt obligations. Randon's sales fell by half that year. The company was forced into receivership for two years, and many of the 6,000 employees lost their jobs. By the mid-1980s, however, Brazil and Randon had recovered. The company was now looking for foreign partners to help it sell to markets abroad, and in 1986 it formed a joint venture, Freios Master Equipamentos Automotivos Ltda., with Rockwell International Corp., to make brakes and other automotive products for buses, trucks, trailers, and semi-trailers. Another joint venture, Carrier Transicold Brasil Ltda., a unit of Carrier Corp. of the United States, was formed in 1993 to produce air conditioning for buses and refrigeration units for trucks and semi-trailers. A third, Jost Brasil Sistemas Automotivos Ltda., was organized in 1995 with Germany's Jost Werke AG to manufacture parts such as spare wheels and towing hookups for trucks and automobiles.

Hercílio Randon died in 1989, leaving Raul in sole direction of the enterprise. Randon's revenues reached $134 million that year, not counting revenue from joint ventures, and its products included not only road vehicles and parts but even cranes and other moving hoists. About 15 percent of its sales volume came from customers in 40 countries. As a third-world manufacturer, Randon was doing well in poor countries such as Algeria, Ethiopia, and Kenya. Management saw Africa as a back door to nearby Europe. But the recession in Brazil during the initial years of the 1990s resulted in a $12 million loss in 1991 and the dismissal of about 1,000 employees.

With the aim of raising productivity, Randon responded to this challenge in a number of ways, investing in new equipment, training new personnel, and stimulating production by means of monthly prizes. Special attention was given to bettering communication, by satellite, with the company's eight joint ventures, 45 distributors, and 60 points of sale. Another part of the effort was the transfer to outside contractors of some of Randon's functions. The first services to be contracted out were food, cleaning, and legal affairs. Within two months, expenses had been reduced by one-fifth. Next, the company was looking at contracting out other areas, especially transport. It also continued its longstanding

KEY DATES

1952: Hercílio and Raul Randon begin making road equipment and air brakes for trailers.

1961: The Randon brothers' enterprise builds its first two semi-trailers

1969: The company has begun installing third axles on General Motors and Ford trucks.

1971: Randon makes its initial public offering of stock.

1977: The company opens a post-sale network of authorized service shops.
Brazil's economic problems put Randon into receivership.

1986: Randon enters a joint venture to make brakes and other products for heavy vehicles.

1994: The company holds half of Brazil's market for trailers, semi-trailers, and truck bodywork.

1995: Randon is also taking part in three other joint ventures to produce automotive equipment.

1997: Formation of the Suspensys unit, which becomes a leading auto-parts manufacturer.

2002: A U.S.-based company now holds half of Suspensys and the brake joint venture.

2005: Randon is rated the fourth best company to work for in Brazil.

effort to raise export levels. In 1991 it established another joint venture to make and sell trailers and semi-trailers in Portugal, followed the next year by a Portuguese subsidiary to sell the company's heavy vehicles in Europe, Africa, and Asia. But in spite of these measures, Randon's revenues fell again in 1992.

Randon was restructured in 1993. Four Randon companies that had been publicly traded were folded, along with six others, into a holding company, Randon S.A. Implementos e Participações. With the revival of the Brazilian economy in 1994, Randon's revenues rose by 50 percent, and the value of the holding company's shares of stock shot up almost eightfold. The company now held half of the Brazilian market for trailers, semi-trailers, and truck bodywork. Its off-road vehicles, used in quarries and mines, held 60 percent of this sector. Randon also established, in a joint venture with local businessmen, a manufacturing plant in Rosario, Argentina. The company bought out these partners the following year.

Randon, in 1996, purchased a majority interest in deficit-ridden Fras-le S.A., Brazil's leading producer of abrasive materials, which Randon returned to fiscal health. Fras-le was one of the world's leading manufacturers of brake linings and friction pads. In 1997 Randon created the company which became Suspensys Sistemas Automotivos Ltda. Located in Randon's Caxias do Sul industrial park, Suspensys immediately became the leading independent Brazilian manufacturer of heavy suspension for trucks, buses, trailers, and semi-trailers. It also produced axles, brake drums, and wheel hubs, becoming the nation's fifth largest auto-parts manufacturer. Suspensys, in 2005, was 23 percent owned by Randon and 53 percent-owned by the brake joint venture. Randon also introduced the Sistema Bimodal Transtrailer, which allowed a vehicle to travel either by road or rail.

RANDON IN THE 21ST CENTURY

Randon commemorated, in 1999, its founder's 50 years in business, as a group of companies with customers in 80 countries, served by a sales-and-assistance network of more than 100 offices in Brazil and abroad. But the company shared in Brazil's next economic downturn, losing money in 1999 and 2000. Once again, there had to be a restructuring. The company sold its Portuguese subsidiary and, in 2001, its interest in Carrier Transicold Brasil, returning to profitability that year. In 2002, Randon signed a new joint-venture agreement with Arvin-Meritor Inc. of Troy, Michigan, which by this time had replaced Rockwell in the brake joint venture, now called Master Sistemas Automotivos Ltda. Randon agreed to convert Suspensys into a 50-50 partnership with Arvin-Meritor to build and sell truck and trailer suspensions and trailer axles. Thus, Fras-le produced linings, drums, and friction pads for Master's brakes, which were joined to axles and suspensions produced by Suspensys.

By the end of 2003 Randon had made an extraordinary recovery, raising its revenues more than 40 percent from the previous year and its profit more than fourfold. Production reached record levels, too. The company was a leader in Brazil in everything to which it turned its hand. In the 1980s Randon had been a company more than 80 percent verticalized, that is, producing components for its own vehicles. Now, however, it was producing 90 percent of its components for others. The company was, for example, in addition to its own vehicles, making Fras-le brake pads for Honda and Yamaha motorcycles; Jost pneumatic suspensions, Suspensys auxiliary axles, and Master brakes for Volvo NH 12 6x2 trucks; brakes, brake drums, and wheel hubs for buses made by Volkswagen AG in Brazil; and Fras-le brake pads and linings for General Motors Corp.'s Corsa and Celta automobiles.

Auto parts and automotive systems were accounting for more than half of Randon's revenues in 2004. The group's strategy was to search for alliances with global companies that had the resources to support its technology and, above all, to allow it to enter new markets. Two of its transport businesses, producing rail cars and off-road vehicles, also illustrated this principle, since both were built on the same platform and with common basic components and engineering. Randon saw the rail market as sure to grow, because of the need to transport Brazil's grains, minerals, wood, and steel.

Raul Randon had spoken in the past of retiring at the age of 60, then at 65. He continued at the helm, however, until finally, in 2004, at the age of 75, fulfilling earlier pledges to step down in favor of the two eldest of his five children. His plan called for the two to take turns as chief executive officer, while himself filling the position of chairman of the board. Randon's third and youngest son was a manager for a subsidiary in São Paulo. All three, unlike their self-made father, had been trained in engineering and business administration. A controlling group that included Randon family members held 41 percent of the shares of Randon S.A. Implementos e Participações, the holding company that, in turn, owned the subsidiaries and held stakes in the joint ventures.

A 2005 supplement of the Brazilian business magazine *Exame* ranked Randon as the nation's fourth-best company in which to work. A five-module apprenticeship program consisted of leadership development, technological empowerment, incentives, formal education, and assignment to teams. Another program offered courses by Internet. About 10 percent of the employees in Caxias do Sul had been working there for 20 or more years. Twenty-five years or more earned a trip to Europe for two; 35 years, a gold watch; and 40 years, a lifetime health plan. At 57 years of age, employees began a program of preparation for mandatory retirement at 60. The work environment at Randon was ranked especially high for "respect," "pride," and "camaraderie."

Another *Exame* supplement ranked, for the second consecutive year, Master as the best-performing company in Brazil's automotive sector in 2004. In that year the company raised its sales to $99.3 million, a 45 percent increase. Its exports almost doubled. Especially useful for the firm was its leadership in air brakes for trucks and buses, two of the fastest-growing parts of the Brazilian automotive sector because of heavy demand from agribusiness and foreign countries.

In 2005, Randon turned out 14,543 semi-trailers in Brazil, almost half the total, and 665 in Argentina. It also built 494 rail cars, 133 off-road trucks, and 155 excavating vehicles. Master manufactured 469,731 brakes, and Fras-le turned out 51,389 metric tons of refractory materials. Road, rail, and special vehicles accounted for 49 percent of net revenues. Auto parts and systems also accounted for 49 percent, and services and others for the remaining 2 percent. Sales between Randon enterprises represented 14 percent of revenues. Only Randon Argentina lost money. With regard to commercial vehicles, according to Randon, Master held 55 percent of the Brazilian market for air brakes, and Fras-le held 95 percent for heavy-vehicle brake linings. Jost Brasil was the leader in coupling components and articulation between tractor and towed vehicles. Suspensys was the leader in axle girders and suspensions for commercial vehicles.

Robert Halasz

PRINCIPAL SUBSIDIARIES

Jost Sistemas Automotivos Ltda. (51%); Master Sistemas Automotivos Ltda. (51%); Randon Administradora de Consórcios Ltda; Randon Argentina S.A.; Randon Veículos Ltda.

PRINCIPAL COMPETITORS

Cinpel Cia. Indústria de Peças para Automóveis; Dana-Alborus S.A. Industrial e Comércio; Delphi Automotive Systems do Brasil Ltda.; Featherline, Inc.; GKN Sinter Metals Ltda.; Maxion Components Automotivos S.A.; TRW Automotive Ltda.; Valeo Sistemas Automotivas Ltda.; Visteon Sistemas Automotivas Ltda.; Wabash National Corp.

FURTHER READING

"ArvinMeritor Forms Venture in S. America," *Automotive News,* August 26, 2002, p. 22J.

"De passaporte na caçamba," *Exame,* January 8, 1992, p. 43.

Gianotti, Carlos Alberto, *Histórias de Sucessos,* São Leopoldo: Editorial Unisinos, 1998, pp. 145–49.

Lorini, Arlete, "Uma idéia puxa a outra," *Exame,* August 4, 2004, pp. 64–65.

Naiditch, Suzana, "A saída pode estar bem ao seu lado," *Exame,* July 15, 1998, pp. 62–63.

———, "Cara de blue chip," *Exame,* February 15, 1995, p. 75.

———, "Eternos, só os diamantes," *Exame,* September 5, 2001, pp. 72–74.

———, “Os hobbies viram um bom negócio,” *Exame,* April 8, 1998, pp. 65–66.

Oliveira, Maurício, “Tratamento vip,” *Exame,* September 24, 2005, supplement, pp. 46–47.

“Oportuna opção pelos pobres,” *Exame,* January 10, 1990, p. 35.

Pinto de Almeida, Edson, “Com o pé no acelerador,” *Exame Melhores e Maiores 2005,* p. 154.

“Um pé, cá, outro lá,” *Exame,* January 6, 1993, p. 44.

Renner Herrmann S.A.

Avenida Carlos Gomes 111
Porto Alegre, Rio Grande do Sul 90480-003
Brazil
Telephone: (55 51) 378-2410
Toll Free: (0800) 51-2380
Fax: (55 51) 378-2422
Web site: http://www.renner.com.br

Private Company
Incorporated: 1927 as Renner Koepke & Cia., Ltda.
Employees: 3,000
Sales: $270 million (2004 est.)
NAIC: 321114 Wood Preservation; 325510 Paint and Coating Manufacturing; 332431 Metal Can Manufacturing; 488310 Port and Harbor Operations; 551112 Offices of Other Holding Companies

Renner Herrmann S.A. is a holding company for interests in the manufacture of industrial paints, varnishes, and allied products in Brazil and other South American countries. The most important is Renner Sayerlack S.A., one of the largest manufacturers of industrial paints in Latin America. Other units include "operational" Renner Herrmann S.A., which makes maritime paints and metal cans and conducts industrial maintenance in the port cities of Curitaba, Paraná, and Porto Alegre, Rio Grande do Sul. Tintas Renner, which is part of Renner Sayerlack, has manufacturing plants in Chile and Uruguay as well as Brazil.

LEADING PAINT MANUFACTURER: 1927–90

Born in 1884, Antônio Jacob Renner was descended from German immigrants to Brazil's southernmost state, Rio Grande do Sul, where his father owned grain mills and a meatpacking plant. A. J. Renner pioneered in the manufacture and sale of waterproof ponchos for gauchos and experimented with flax raising for linen, developing three varieties suitable for growing on his own tracts of land. The energetic A. J. eventually became a textile magnate whose enterprises led Brazil in turning out ready-made clothing. But there were other Renner companies as well. Most were based on the raw materials of Rio Grande do Sul, including a tannery; felt, shoe, porcelain, and lime-mortar plants; and a factory that made concrete tubes. The Renner group dominated the economy of the state. In addition, there was a Renner company that made sewing machines; a retail chain, called Lojas Renner; and a Banco A.J. Renner. (Lojas Renner was sold to J.C. Penney in 1998.)

In 1927, A. J.'s sons Waldemar and Leopoldo Renner founded, with Arthur Koepke (or Koepcke), a company to manufacture powder paints in Porto Alegre. This was an artesanal process at first and involved manually grinding colored earth, minerals, and charcoal, then combining them with pigments and boiled linseed oil. The resulting mixture was then filtered, pressed, dried, and ground into powder. Waldemar retired in 1935, and Ernesto Herrmann joined the firm in 1941, when Koepke retired. In 1947 Hugo Herrmann, who was married to A. J. Renner's sister, entered the firm as an industrial chemist. This enterprise became Renner Herrmann S.A. - Indústria de Tintas e Óleos. On Le-

KEY DATES

1927: Waldmar and Leopoldo Renner found a company to make powder paints.
1947: Hugo Herrmann enters the firm, which becomes Renner Herrmann.
1980: The company buys Sayerlack, which specializes in varnishes for wood finishes.
1986: Renner Herrmann has become the largest paint manufacturer in Brazil; DuPont do Brasil takes a stake in the Tintas Renner joint venture.
1993: The company opens franchised "paint boutiques" for the home.
1995: Renner Herrmann and DuPont restructure their joint venture, called Renner DuPont.
1997: Renner Herrmann forms a coatings joint venture with The Valspar Corporation of Minneapolis.
2001: The company merges Sayerlack and Tintas Renner to form Renner Sayerlack.
2002: Renner Herrmann sells its stake in the Valspar venture and becomes a private company.
2004: DuPont purchases Renner Herrmann's share of the Renner DuPont joint venture.

opoldo's death in 1952, Hugo Herrmann became its director.

Renner Herrmann opened other Tintas Renner plants in the 1960s in the states of São Paulo and Bahia. It expanded greatly in the 1970s by purchasing rivals, including, in 1977, Ideal Tintas, and, in 1980, Sayerlack S.A. Indústria Brasileira de Vernizes, which specialized in varnishes for wood finishing. During the 1970s the company pioneered in introducing polyurethane acrylic paints for buses. The company bought a factory in Curitiba in 1982. Then, in 1984 and 1986, respectively, it purchased two São Paulo companies, Oxford and Polidura, thereby vaulting to first place among some 300 paint manufacturers in Brazil. It also acquired Tintura, a company in the state of Pará, and opened another plant in Gravataí, Rio Grande do Sul. Renner Herrmann was, in 1987, the first paint manufacture in Brazil to introduce a "tintometric" multicolor system enabling customers to choose the color they wanted in their homes, boasting that it could double the colors offered by competitors. For repainting automobiles, this system enabled some 25,000 variations to be prepared by the dealer from 50 basic products in a few minutes.

By this time Tintas Renner S.A. was no longer wholly owned by Renner Herrmann. By 1985 the giant German firm Hoechst AG had taken a stake in the company, which had become a joint venture. The following year DuPont do Brasil S.A. exchanged its shares of its Polidura paints and coatings operation, which it had acquired in the early 1970s, for a 23 percent equity interest in Tintas Renner. Hoechst had an equivalent equity share, leaving Renner Herrmann with the majority stake.

NUMEROUS CHANGES

In 1990 Tintas Renner had annual revenue of $400 million. Pinturas Renner Uruguay S.A. in Montevideo, formerly Sintéticos del Plata, was making paints for the automotive industry and exporting to other Latin American countries, and headquarters in Brazil had just bought an Argentine site for a similar plant. Renner also opened a distribution center in Paraguay and secured a license to make paint products in Bolivia for Espintbol, the leader of the market in that country. In 1993 it purchased a controlling share of a Chilean paint manufacturer, Pinturas Blundell S.A., and purchased two Argentine producers, Pintcol S.A.I.C.F. and Pamex - Pinturas Americanas de Exportación. These latter acquisitions were in connection with a partnership formed with Sevel, which was then the leading automobile manufacturer in Argentina.

In Brazil itself, Renner held 60 percent of the market in paints for the automotive industry in 1990. It also held 40 percent of the market in paints for electric home appliances and about 10 percent of the market for civil construction. The following year, in conjunction with Oxiteno Nordeste S.A. Indústria e Comércio, it established a joint venture, Oxiquímica S.A., to make acrylic acid and acrylates, prime materials for the manufacture of acrylic paints, in Triunfo, Rio Grande do Sul. In 1993 it opened its first franchised retail units. These units, "paint boutiques," were equipped with terminals which enabled customers to look at a house exterior or interior that they wanted to paint and experiment with colors based on the company's multicolor system. Also that year, the company spent $7 million to open a Porto Alegre shopping center in an area where it had its headquarters. The venture failed to thrive and was sold in 2003.

Tintas Renner was going through a restructuring during the early 1990s, a recessionary period for the Brazilian economy. Marcos Bier Herrmann, its executive director, described the company to Suzana Naiditch of the Brazilian business magazine *Exame* as harboring "a babel of cultures." Its brands were redefined, with the poorest performers eliminated. Its five industrial plants were rationalized so that each would specialize in a particular line of products. Its production and administrative processes were reformulated in order to adopt the most modern management methods. A quality-control program was instituted. The company had seven training centers for concessionaires and auto workers who used its plants. A toll-free number was added so that employees could field customer complaints.

In late 1995 DuPont do Brasil and Renner Herrmann restructured their existing joint venture, which was now Renpar S.A., in order to focus on industrial coatings, original-equipment manufacturers, and refinish automotive coatings in South America. (Hoechst had sold its stake in Renpar the previous year.) The new joint venture, Renner DuPont Tintas Automotivas e Industriais S.A., did not include Renpar's architectural, marine, and wood-coating lines, all of which reverted to Renner Herrmann. DuPont dedicated its entire manufacturing capacity from its coatings plant in Valencia, Venezuela, to the venture. Renner Herrmann contributed two plants in Brazil, in Guarulhos and São Bernardo, São Paulo, and one in Argentina.

Renner Herrmann formed another joint venture in 1997, this time with Valspar Corp. of Minneapolis, a leading coatings manufacturer. The new company for the manufacture and sale of coatings for metal packaging, that is, paint for aluminum cans, in South America was named Valspar Renner Revestimento para Embalagens Ltda., with each partner holding a 50 percent share. A securities analyst said the joint venture had made Valspar the largest packaging coatings company in the world. In addition, besides being a holding company, Renner Herrmann formed, in 1997, an operational division with two business units. One, based in Curitaba, was for maritime paints and industrial maintenance, providing coatings to protect against corrosion from salt water. The other was for making metal cans in Porte Alegre. Also in 1997, Renner Herrmann created software that enabled customers using its multicolor paint system to view the results on computer.

A Brazilian bank issued an unfavorable analysis on Renner Herrmann in 1998. While acknowledging that Renner DuPont ranked first in Brazil in painting for original equipment manufacturers (including automakers), automobile repainting, and painting for industry in general, it noted that the joint venture's main competitors were four huge multinational firms and that the automotive-painting sector was characterized by global competition and "intense downside price pressure." The same firms were providing stiff competition in Renner Herrmann's architecture and house paints segment, which was represented by its Tintas Renner subsidiary. Sayerlack, the national leader in furniture paints and coatings, was doing better, but was only 60 percent owned by Renner Herrmann. The printing-ink segment, also first in its field, was represented by Companhia Química Industrial Brasileira, another subsidiary. Renner Herrmann sold this enterprise in 1999.

DOWNSIZING IN THE NEW CENTURY

Renner Herrmann's gross revenues came to BRL 852.25 million ($465.71 million) in 2000. The largest share, 42 percent, came from Renner DuPont. Sayerlack contributed 27 percent, and Tintas Renner, soon to be united with Sayerlack in Renner Sayerlack, 21 percent. The operational Renner Herrmann division accounted for 6 percent, Valspar Renner for 2 percent, and other sources of revenue, 2 percent. All these units lost money in 2000, and only Sayerlack made a profit in 1999. Twenty-seven percent of Renner Herrmann's revenues came from wood finishes, 21 percent from decorative uses, 20 percent from painting of original equipment manufacturers, and 16 percent from repainting automotive equipment.

Brazil's economic difficulties, and Argentina's as well, presumably contributed to Renner Herrmann's loss of BRL 8.8 million BRL ($4.8 million) in 2000. That year it sold its stake in Oxiquímica and reduced its participation in Renner DuPont to 51 percent. Renner Herrmann also merged Tintas Renner with Sayerlack, creating, on the first day of 2001, Renner Sayerlack S.A., which was now 75 percent-owned by Renner Herrmann. This merger was made in the interests of maximizing the use of distribution and to gain synergies in administrative areas. Renner Herrmann lost BRL 12.5 million (about $5.3 million) in the first half of 2001. Later in the year, it delayed a $3 million investment intended to raise paint production at the Gravataí plant from 100,000 metric tons to 150,000 metric tons a year. A company executive told *Coatings World,* "We have idle capacity and could double production now."

At the beginning of 2002, Renner Herrmann sold its stake in the joint venture with Valspar for $15 million. Three weeks later, it delisted its stock and became a private company. In 2004, DuPont purchased Renner Herrmann's stake in Renner DuPont and renamed brands such as Multicolor. This joint venture was doing about $130 million worth of business a year at the time.

Gravataí remained Renner Sayerlack's plant for manufacturing Tintas Renner paints for real property and interior decoration, and for manufacturing paints for industrial machinery under the name Renner Tintas Industriais. Cajamar, São Paulo, was Renner Sayerlack's plant for a complete range of solutions for coating wood surfaces. Tintas Renner was emphasizing the products of its Renner Tintas Industriais unit for buses, agricultural implements, construction machinery, and industry in general. Renner Sayerlack had sales of $253.2 million in 2004 and employment of 2,510.

Robert Halasz

PRINCIPAL SUBSIDIARIES

Alpha - Administração e Participações Ltda.; Pinturas Renner Chile S.A. (92%): Pinturas Renner Paraguay S.A.; Pinturas Renner Uruguay S.A.; Renner Sayerlack S.A. (75%).

PRINCIPAL COMPETITORS

Akzo Nobel S.A.; BASF S.A.; PPG Industrial do Brasil Ltda.; Tintas Coral Ltda.

FURTHER READING

"Brazil Investments Continue, More Cautiously," *Coatings World,* December 2001, p. 23.

"Du Pont Co., Inc. to Merge Brazilian Paint Operation," *American Paint & Coatings Journal,* December 23, 1985, p. 22.

"Du Pont's Brazil Unit to Merge," *Journal of Commerce,* December 3, 1985, p. 21B.

Fattah, Hassan, "DuPont, Renner Restructure Paints JV," *Chemical Week,* December 20, 1995, p. 18.

Fortes, Alexandre, "As Indústrias Renner," *Historia,* 2002, pp. 163–93.

Gain, Bruce, "Valspar and Renner Herrmann Form Brazilian Alliance," *Chemical Week,* June 4, 1997, p. 13.

Kannebley, Andrea, "Renner Herrmann," *Votorantim Brazil Research,* January 28, 1998.

"Latin Painting," *Chemical Week,* May 24, 1995, p. 45.

Maia Neto, J., *Homen e Progreso,* Porto Alegre: Livrania Salina, 1963.

Naiditch, Suzana, "A Renner quer pintar o sete lá fora," *Exame,* October 27, 1993, pp. 60–62.

"O que pinta de novo na Renner," *Exame,* February 7, 1990, p. 69.

"Valspar Enters Brazilian JV," *Chemical Market Reporter,* June 2, 1997, p. 3.

Rounder Records Corporation

1 Camp Street
Cambridge, Massachusetts 02140
U.S.A.
Telephone: (617) 354-0700
Toll Free: (800) 768-6337
Fax: (617) 354-4840
Web site: http://www.rounder.com

Private Company
Incorporated: 1970
Employees: 90
Sales: $50 million (2005 est.)
NAIC: 512220 Integrated Record Production/ Distribution; 512120 Motion Picture and Video Distribution; 511130 Book Publishers

■ ■ ■

Rounder Records Corporation is one of the top three independent record companies in the United States. The firm's releases range from country and bluegrass to folk, zydeco, reggae, blues, world music, and rock and roll, and appear on a variety of imprints including Heartbeat, Philo, Zoe, Bullseye Blues, Marsalis Music, and Rounder Kids. The company also releases videos and operates a book unit whose subjects range from music to baseball. Distribution of many music and video releases are handled by a division of NBC Universal, while others are sold through independent distributors or by the label itself. Rounder's best-known artists include bluegrass fiddler Alison Krauss, rock group Cowboy Junkies, jazz vocalist Madeleine Peyroux, New Orleans soul legend Irma Thomas, western band Riders in the Sky, and children's performer Raffi. The firm is owned by its three founders, Ken Irwin, Marian Leighton-Levy, and Bill Nowlin.

EARLY YEARS

Rounder Records was founded in Massachusetts in 1970 by friends Ken Irwin, Marian Leighton, and Bill Nowlin. Irwin and Nowlin had met at Tufts University, where they shared a room and a passion for folk and old-time country music. A year after their 1966 graduation (Irwin with a degree in political science, Nowlin in psychology), Irwin began dating Clark University student Leighton, and the three eventually began sharing an apartment in Somerville, Massachusetts.

The trio enjoyed traveling together to folk and bluegrass music events around the United States, and after spending time with the founders of a small record label at one such gathering, they decided to try releasing records themselves. The name Rounder was suggested by Nowlin and chosen for its multiple meanings, which included the shape of a record and a nickname for a hobo or traveler, as well as being a tribute to underground folk band The Holy Modal Rounders. The new label's goal was to document the work of older musicians as well as to record new groups that performed in traditional styles.

In 1970 the young entrepreneurs released their first album, a three-year old recording by septuagenarian North Carolina banjo player George Pegram which they had purchased for $125. When stores in nearby Cambridge, Massachusetts, were hesitant to stock it, they

COMPANY PERSPECTIVES

Despite the massive growth that Rounder has achieved, the three original founders still maintain an active role in Rounder's operations. Whether going over figures in the office; mastering, mixing, or producing albums; or taking to the road to seek out new talent, Ken Irwin, Marian Leighton-Levy, and Bill Nowlin remain at the center of it all. "The reason we remain involved," says Nowlin, "is that Rounder has held true to its overriding ideal—to present good and even important music and to try to spread the word about the music to the broadest audience we can. That remains energizing. We feel we are doing work of real value, truly contributing something of real significance to the broader culture."

decided to begin distributing other small folk labels to boost their credibility, and also started selling albums at music festivals.

Over the next several years more releases were issued by artists including guitarist Norman Blake, while other members joined the loose Rounder collective. A typical release might sell only a few thousand copies, with more popular performers such as Blake reaching the low five figures. The firm was only marginally profitable, however, and all three founders continued to work day jobs, Nowlin as a political science professor at the University of Lowell.

In 1974 the Rounders (as the three were often called) finally began earning enough from the label to pay themselves each $400 a month, and as their catalog expanded they hired a few employees to perform distribution and other chores. In addition to releasing new recordings, the firm was also beginning to reissue rare 78 rpm discs from the 1920s and 1930s, including a compilation of classic Hawaiian guitar songs.

THOROGOOD A ROCK HIT

In 1977 Rounder signed Delaware-based blues-rock group George Thorogood and the Destroyers, who started to sell more records for the label than any previous act. Their second album, *Move It On Over,* became a national hit and sold over 500,000 copies, which earned the label its first gold record. This success pushed Rounder into the world of national promotion and distribution, and the firm hired more employees and moved into larger quarters in Cambridge, its fifth location to date. After a third album for Rounder Thorogood left for a major label, EMI America, though the company formed a partnership with him that brought it a percentage of his royalties.

In 1979 Rounder's employees decided to form a union, a move that was strongly opposed by the firm's owners. Though having long espoused the left-leaning politics associated with the folk scene, the company hired a Boston law firm to fight the effort. After a heated battle the workers voted to join Local 25 of the Service Employees International Union, after which relations between owners and staff would be strained for some time.

In 1981 an imprint called Heartbeat Records was founded in partnership with Rounder Distribution manager Duncan Browne, which would release both new and vintage Jamaican reggae music. The success of the venture later led the firm to purchase an 80 percent stake in Washington D.C.-based Ras Records, which focused on current reggae styles.

The early 1980s also saw Rounder begin recording zydeco, blues, and rhythm and blues music from New Orleans and elsewhere under producer Scott Billington. In 1982 the label won its first Grammy award for Texas blues guitarist/violinist Clarence "Gatemouth" Brown's *Alright Again* album. By this time the firm had also founded Varrick Records to release rock, blues, and folk albums that did not quite fit the Rounder mold.

In the wake of Thorogood's success Rounder's staff had grown to 24, but without his hit-making power the company's revenues dropped and by 1984 it was losing $1,000 a day. The firm's owners decided they needed professional advice to develop a business plan, and consulted with volunteers from SCORE and the Small Business Administration. They soon realized they would have to cut their payroll, but rather than issue pink slips they asked for volunteers. Eight staffers were willing to leave, and with the three owners giving up their own salaries for more than a year costs were reduced enough to keep going. The year 1984 also saw the firm acquire a bankrupt label called Philo Records, whose output consisted of such singer/songwriters as Utah Phillips, Dave Van Ronk, and Mary McCaslin.

Rounder released its music on long-playing vinyl albums, as well as cassette tapes when that format became popular. With digital technology beginning to gain favor, in 1987 the firm began to issue its recordings on compact discs.

During the 1980s Rounder's best sellers included albums from soul singer Solomon Burke, Cajun group Beausoleil, and Philo folk singers Christine Lavin and Nanci Griffith. As Thorogood had done, Griffith and

KEY DATES

1970: Rounder Records is founded to issue country and bluegrass recordings.
1979: George Thorogood and the Destroyers win label its first gold record.
1981: Heartbeat Records is formed to issue reggae albums.
1984: Singer/songwriter label Philo Records is acquired.
1987: Bluegrass violinist Alison Krauss is signed; first compact discs are released.
1991: Bullseye Blues is founded; Krauss wins her first Grammy award.
1994: Music For Little People distribution is acquired and renamed Rounder Kids.
1995: European distribution unit is formed; Flying Fish label is purchased.
1997: A 100-disc reissue series of historic Alan Lomax recordings is launched.
1998: Distribution pact is signed with Mercury (later Universal); Zoe imprint is founded.
2004: Rounder Books is formed.

other popular acts including The Dirty Dozen Brass Band and Buckwheat Zydeco eventually left for larger labels. However, many others preferred to stay with the smaller company because of the greater artistic freedom it offered.

ALISON KRAUSS TAKES OFF

In 1988 Rounder won its second Grammy award for an album of previously unreleased recordings by the late New Orleans piano legend Professor Longhair, and in 1991 the firm took home a third for 19-year-old bluegrass fiddler Alison Krauss's second solo album, *I've Got that Old Feeling.* The latter spawned one of the label's rare singles as well as several music videos that received heavy exposure on the CMT and TNN cable networks, and the album went on to sell nearly 200,000 copies. Originally signed in 1987, youthful prodigy Krauss was nurtured by the firm and remained loyal to Rounder after achieving national success.

In 1991 the label partnered with musician and producer Ron Levy to form Bullseye Blues, which would release music by such legends as Lowell Fulson and newer acts including Smokin' Joe Kubek. By now Rounder had a total of 75 employees and three warehouses in the Cambridge area, with annual sales approaching $16 million. In addition to its own releases, the firm continued to distribute the recordings of other independent labels to stores and via an extensive mail-order catalog.

In the fall of 1991 Rounder opened a Midwest warehouse in Olathe, Kansas, that had belonged to a bankrupt firm called House Distributors. A few months later Rounder Distribution merged with Rykodisc distribution unit East Side Digital to form the REP Co., though Rounder later pulled out and formed Distribution North America (DNA), which would handle the releases of 400 smaller labels in addition to its own product. The firm was adding more staff to its promotion department and expanding its marketing efforts via monthly genre-centric sales and bargain-priced sampler discs.

The label had continued to release archival projects over the years, and in 1993 it began a series of reissues of the complete late 1920s/early 1930s RCA recordings of the Carter Family, considered by many to be the founders of country music. The recordings were licensed from major label BMG, which had several years earlier allowed Rounder to re-release the catalog of Jimmy Rodgers, another key early country figure. The firm's business model enabled it to make a profit on special projects like these which might sell only a few thousand copies, while larger companies such as BMG needed to move many times that number just to break even. The prolific firm was now releasing as many as 100 albums per year.

In 1994 DNA formed a joint venture with leading "one-stop" operator Valley Record Distributors, which would boost the regional coverage of both. The year also saw acquisition of the distribution arm of Music For Little People, which handled more than 150 children's labels. Renamed Rounder Kids and expanded to 250 labels, it would distribute both music and video titles to toy, book, and gift stores. The firm would later sign Raffi, the best-known children's performer in North America, as well as releasing albums of music based on the popular *Arthur* series on PBS television.

KRAUSS ALBUM GOES PLATINUM IN 1995

In January 1995 Rounder partnered with BMG's Nashville unit BNA records to push a new Alison Krauss single, "When You Say Nothing at All," which appeared on her new album *Now That I've Found You,* as well as a BNA compilation. She was touring heavily (including opening for star Garth Brooks), and the release became Rounder's first top-ten country chart entry and was later certified double platinum for sales of more than two million units. Krauss was later honored with a Grammy and several Country Music Association awards.

In February the company formed a distribution unit in the Netherlands called Continental Records Services, and in the fall bought Chicago-based Flying Fish Records, which had been founded in 1974 by early Rounder associate Bruce Kaplan. It had a catalog of 500 records by artists such as Sweet Honey in the Rock and Doc Watson. The company also celebrated its 25th anniversary during the year by sponsoring a touring package of popular acts Marcia Ball, Beau Jocque, and Steve Riley and the Mamou Playboys, and was profiled in an independently produced documentary film called *True Believers*.

In January 1997 Rounder sold its stake in the DNA distribution joint venture to partner Valley Record Distributors, though its labels would continue to be handled by the latter firm. Spring saw the release of the first in a series of compact discs documenting the work of legendary folklorist Alan Lomax, who had recorded musicians around the world since the 1930s. More than 100 discs would be released over the next decade. In October Rounder General Counsel John Virant was named president and CEO of the firm, though all three founders remained heavily involved with its management. For 1997 the company had sales of approximately $24 million.

MERCURY DISTRIBUTION PACT SIGNED IN 1998

In June 1998 Rounder signed a distribution agreement with major label Mercury Records, whose PolyGram Group Distribution affiliate would handle more than a third of the firm's catalog of 2,500 titles. It was expected to help boost sales of new releases by such artists as country singer Heather Myles and folkie Juliana Hatfield, who would appear on newly launched Rounder pop music imprint Zoe. The firm would continue selling lower-profile titles via DNA and another distributor, Bayside.

In April 1999 the company signed an agreement with Liquid Audio, Inc. for digital distribution of its music over the Internet. By now Mercury parent PolyGram had been acquired by Universal, Inc. (later NBC Universal), whose Universal Music and Video Distribution unit would handle Rounder's bigger titles.

In 2002 Rounder signed a deal with Provident Music Distribution to sell Rounder products to Christian retailers, and began marketing the recordings of jazz saxophonist Branford Marsalis's Marsalis Music label, whose artist roster included its founder as well as New Orleans pianist/vocalist/heartthrob Harry Connick, Jr. The firm also had another smash during the year with a live Alison Krauss album that sold more than two million copies. Popular acts of the early 2000s included former Geffen act Cowboy Junkies, quirky pop group They Might Be Giants, Canadian folkie Sarah Harmer, Texas honky tonk singers Joe Ely and Jimmie Dale Gilmore, multi-Grammy winning polka singer Jimmy Sturr, and cowboy act Riders in the Sky, who had started out on Rounder in the 1970s but left for larger labels before returning in 1995.

In 2003 the firm signed a licensing agreement with online music listening service MusicMatch, Inc., and released a music/DVD hybrid disc on Zoe, which contained live concert videos by Kathleen Edwards on one side and music tracks on the other. Rounder was now releasing videos by traditional musicians as well as stars including Alison Krauss and heavy metal rockers Rush, whose live concert DVD sold more than 200,000 copies in 2004. That year also saw formation of a new division, Rounder Books, to publish titles on a range of topics from music to baseball, including some written by cofounder Bill Nowlin.

In 2005 the company launched the Rounder Archive, which offered limited edition CDs of out-of-print albums from the label's now 3,000-plus title catalog. They could also be downloaded over the Internet for a fee.

Rounder artists had been awarded a sizable number of Grammy Awards since the 1980s, and 2006 saw the firm win six including three for Krauss and two for a Lomax recording of jazz pioneer Jelly Roll Morton, produced in partnership with the Library of Congress Archive of Folk Music. The year also brought "Rock for Relief," a various artists album whose proceeds were earmarked for hurricane, earthquake, and tsunami relief efforts.

In just over 35 years Rounder Records Corp. had become one of the top independent record companies in the United States. Its large roster of artists included some of the most popular and critically-acclaimed performers in a variety of different roots-music genres, while its extensive archival offerings kept musical treasures available for new generations to discover.

Frank Uhle

PRINCIPAL SUBSIDIARIES

Heartbeat Records; Philo Records; Zoe Records; Bullseye Blues Records; Flying Fish Records; Rounder Books; Rounder Kids; Rounder Archive.

PRINCIPAL COMPETITORS

Shanachie Entertainment Corp.; Welk Music Group; Arhoolie Productions, Inc.; Rykodisc, Inc.

FURTHER READING

Bessman, Jim, "Rounder Embarks on Lomax Collection," *Billboard*l March 29, 1997, p. 9.

———, "Rounder Philosophy Draws Artists to Pop Imprint Zoe," *Billboard,* March 31, 2001, p. 1.

Christman, Ed, "Rounder, Mercury Ink P&D Deal," *Billboard,* July 4, 1998, p. 6.

———, "Valley, Rounder Form Unusual Partnership," *Billboard,* May 21, 1994, p. 48.

Cobb, Nathan, "Easy Rounder," *Boston Globe,* August 20, 1989, p. 22.

Ferguson, Laura, "Rounder's Fellow Rebels," *Tufts Magazine,* Spring, 2005.

Henderson, Richard, "Rounder's Contract with America's Music: It's in the Genres," *Billboard,* May 6, 1995, p. R6.

Horak, Terri, "Rounder Gives All for Alison Krauss," *Billboard,* January 21, 1995, p. 8.

Morris, Chris, "Rounder Flies at Chance to Purchase Flying Fish," *Billboard,* September 2, 1995, p. 6.

Morse, Steve, "Godsmack on Rounder? Much Has Changed at Cambridge's Independent Label," *Boston Globe,* December 5, 2004, p. N10.

———, "Rounder Marks 25 With Vintage Cuts," *Boston Globe,* February 5, 1995, p. 47.

Peterson, Anne M., "Independent Record Label Still Produces After 21 Years," *Associated Press,* July 3, 1991.

The St. Paul Travelers Companies, Inc.

385 Washington Street
Saint Paul, Minnesota 55102-1309
U.S.A.
Telephone: (651) 310-7911
Toll Free: (800) 328-2189
Fax: (651) 310-3386
Web site: http://www.stpaultravelers.com

Public Company
Incorporated: 1853 as St. Paul Mutual Insurance Company
Employees: 31,900
Total Assets: $113.19 billion (2005)
Stock Exchanges: New York
Ticker Symbol: STA
NAIC: 524126 Direct Property and Casualty Insurance Carriers; 524130 Reinsurance Carriers

■ ■ ■

The St. Paul Travelers Companies, Inc. is Minnesota's oldest business corporation and one of the oldest insurance companies in the United States. Known as The St. Paul Companies, Inc. prior to its acquisition of Travelers Property Casualty Corp. in April 2004, the company is one of the leading providers of commercial and personal property and casualty insurance in the United States. St. Paul Travelers distributes its insurance products principally through U.S. independent agents and brokers, ranking as the second largest writer of automobile and homeowners insurance through this channel. The firm remains headquartered in Saint Paul, Minnesota, with a major secondary base in Hartford, Connecticut, where Travelers had its home; additional offices are located in the United Kingdom, Ireland, and Canada.

EARLY HISTORY

In the years preceding the founding of The St. Paul, people living in the Minnesota Territory were insured primarily by agents representing eastern insurance companies. Most wintertime claims and claim payments had to wait for spring, when travel and communication resumed.

In 1853 Alexander Wilkin, the secretary of the territory, and The St. Paul's first and youngest president, approached his neighbors, George and John Farrington, with the idea of starting a Saint Paul, Minnesota-based insurance company. The need for local fire insurance was particularly great, and George Farrington, a local banker, saw the opportunity to stem the flow of cash out of the territory. Farrington introduced a bill of incorporation in the territorial legislature that same year, and St. Paul Mutual Insurance Company was incorporated.

The St. Paul was to operate as a mutual company, but it also sold traditional, or stock, policies. Mutual policyholders were to share in both the profits and losses of the company; stock policyholders would not. The company's charter permitted it "to make insurance on all descriptions of property against loss or damage by fire," and "to make insurance on all descriptions of boats and vessels, the cargoes and freights thereof."

The company needed to sell $100,000 of insurance

COMPANY PERSPECTIVES

We begin 2006 with distinct advantages. We have an impressive, broad national reach—built upon excellent relationships with our distributors at a local level—making us a "go-to" market in our agents' and brokers' offices. While our relationships are deep in many individual product lines, they do not always reflect the breadth of insurance products and services that we offer. Therefore, one of our best opportunities for growth lies in our ability to increase distributor access to our range of products, which is among the broadest in the industry. We are pursuing strategies designed to make it easier for distributors to tap into our many products and services. These strategies are based upon the foundation of offering quality products and services, delivered at competitive prices.

to raise the capital to begin business. To accomplish this end, the company's ten founders each applied for $10,000 policies on their own property. Shortly thereafter it was discovered that none of the founders possessed property worth $10,000. The members of the board rejected their own applications and rewrote them for $5,000 each. In February 1854 the company issued its first policy, a mutual policy for $800. It insured the home and furnishings of Robert A. Smith, the territory's librarian and private secretary to Governor Willis A. Gorman, who in turn purchased the company's first stock policy.

The St. Paul sustained its first fire loss in April 1855 when a row of offices and a bakery burned to the ground, resulting in $3,000 in claims. This loss was followed by a much greater problem, the panic of 1857, in which many New York companies folded. In Saint Paul all but three of the local banks were forced to close. The St. Paul and other insurance companies were forced to accept "notes of indebtedness" as premium payments. These notes could not be converted into cash to cover day-to-day operating expenses and, as a result, 47 fledgling insurance companies closed. The St. Paul, faced with severe cash flow problems, elected not to issue any new policies for a time and was forced to sell its office furniture to maintain operations.

A period of stagnation occurred starting in 1861, during the Civil War. The St. Paul's president, Alexander Wilkin, died on a Mississippi battlefield. He was succeeded by James C. Burbank, the company's first full-time president, in April 1865. Also in 1865, The St. Paul reorganized as a stock company and changed its name to St. Paul Fire and Marine Insurance Company. One of Burbank's first duties was to oversee The St. Paul's expansion into the Canadian market. By 1866 the company was writing business in Manitoba. A shareholder-elected board voted to pay semiannual dividends, and in July 1867 the company issued its first stock dividend, of $1.50 per share. Following the Civil War, The St. Paul grew. It constructed a new corporate headquarters. A model for fire-resistant structures of the future, the building was built of metal and stone.

REPUTATION GROWS OUT OF THE GREAT CHICAGO FIRE OF 1871 AND THE SAN FRANCISCO EARTHQUAKE OF 1906

In 1871 the Great Chicago Fire strained the company's resources. The fire left 275 people dead and 100,000 people homeless and destroyed more than 17,000 buildings. More than 200 insurance companies experienced fire-related losses and many were financially ruined; about one-quarter of the 200 companies went out of business and most that survived paid as little as four cents on the dollar to settle their claims. At a meeting of The St. Paul's board, it was agreed that all claims would be paid in full. President Burbank predicted that this decision ultimately would bring a return as word got out that the company was covering its losses. In that year claims submitted by policyholders exceeded by 165 percent the amount the company collected in premiums. The St. Paul paid a total of $140,000 to cover losses. The St. Paul's assets were greatly reduced, and it paid no dividends that year. The company's sales did improve as a result of the decision to pay all claims, however, and The St. Paul recouped its losses.

Burbank died in 1876, and the company's secretary, Charles H. Bigelow, was elected president. Shortly thereafter The St. Paul was faced with the insurance price war of 1877. The insurance market was becoming more competitive as the country grew and prospered. The result was too many insurance companies offering lower prices to compete. Under Bigelow's leadership the company dropped unprofitable agencies, introduced new products such as cyclone insurance and crop hail coverage, and instituted more stringent guidelines in accepting new customers. The St. Paul rode out the price war intact, without lowering its rates. Insurance buyers were not only affected by the price; product and service diversity were also important to a successful business plan.

During the late 19th century, the company expanded into new types of insurance coverage. The San

KEY DATES

1853: St. Paul Mutual Insurance Company is founded by Alexander Wilkin and George and John Farrington, based in Saint Paul, Minnesota.
1865: Company reorganizes as a stock company and renames itself St. Paul Fire and Marine Insurance Company (The St. Paul).
1871: The St. Paul enhances its reputation by paying, in full, all claims from the Great Chicago Fire.
1926: Firm begins offering liability coverage through a newly formed subsidiary, St. Paul Mercury Indemnity Company.
1957: With acquisition of the Western Life Insurance Company, The St. Paul enters the life insurance market.
1968: Company reorganizes under a holding company, The St. Paul Companies, Inc.
1974: John Nuveen & Co. is acquired.
1992: Record losses from catastrophic storms, particularly Hurricane Andrew, and a goodwill write-down connected with a troubled U.K. subsidiary send The St. Paul into a net loss for the year.
1998: In a deal valued at approximately $3.9 billion, The St. Paul acquires USF&G Corporation.
2001: The St. Paul's losses stemming from the terrorist attacks on September 11, 2001 total $941 million.
2004: In a $17.9 billion deal, The St. Paul acquires Travelers Property Casualty Corp. and then renames itself The St. Paul Travelers Companies, Inc.
2005: Nuveen is divested.

Francisco Earthquake and Fire of 1906 took a heavy toll on The St. Paul's new product development plans, however. Claims in excess of $1.2 million were paid, in full, and the company's reputation grew. In 1911 Charles Bigelow died, and his son, Frederic Bigelow, succeeded him as president. In the years following Frederic Bigelow's appointment, the United States prepared for World War I. The St. Paul adjusted its charter to include losses incurred resulting from acts of war. In 1917 The St. Paul covered the loss of 260 vessels, totaling more than $4 million, most of which was repaid by Germany over 50 years. During the war The St. Paul began overseas expansion in a modest fashion, when it began to issue policies in Great Britain to cover losses incurred as a result of bomb damage, but in a relatively short period of time the British government cut the rates charged by U.S. companies by about 50 percent. The St. Paul, however, continued to insure against bomb damage in England for the duration of the war. The St. Paul also added automobile insurance to its product line during this period.

As a result of massive losses incurred during World War I, most European insurance companies were all but paralyzed. The St. Paul became a charter member of the American Foreign Insurance Association (AFIA), a group of companies that pooled its resources, and with combined capital of $135 million, began to market insurance abroad. The company was soon doing business in 25 foreign markets, and another period of diversification and new product development began.

Throughout the 1920s The St. Paul introduced all-risk coverage for the jewelry trade and for other "priceless objects" of artistic and historical significance. The policy insured items in transit from almost every known risk, except theft, because fire and marine insurance companies were prohibited from writing liability coverage. The St. Paul's leadership decided, therefore, that a liability company was needed, and in 1926 a subsidiary, St. Paul Mercury Indemnity Company, was formed. The St. Paul also added aircraft insurance and surety bonds to its product line in 1929.

After serving as The St. Paul's president for 27 years, Frederic Bigelow became chairman in 1938, and Charles F. Codere became The St. Paul's fifth president. Shortly thereafter, the United States entered into World War II. At the onset of the war, U.S. insurance companies wrote marine insurance through a specially formed syndicate, but as losses grew, the U.S. government assumed the burden of covering the staggering war losses. The War Damage Corporation, a company financed by the federal government and run by private insurance companies, wrote more than nine million policies and collected close to $250 million in premiums by the war's end.

CONTINUING TO DIVERSIFY IN POSTWAR PERIOD

In 1948 Codere became chairman, and A. B. Jackson was elected The St. Paul's new president. Codere and Jackson worked well together, and the company greatly expanded its product lines and services. Liability insurance was offered to real estate brokers, insurance agents, and hospitals. The St. Paul refined its package policy program, allowing its agents to offer more and diverse coverage in one policy. Package policies had been introduced during World War II to provide the military with an insurance package to cover liability, shipping, and fire insurance. This method of issuing coverage continued after the war, with The St. Paul offering packages for a variety of commercial risks. Jackson also was instrumental in the organization of two new associations to insure nuclear reactors.

In 1957, with the acquisition of the Western Life Insurance Company of Helena, Montana, The St. Paul broke into the life insurance market. By 1964 Western Life sales had more than doubled. The St. Paul's agents were now able to sell all forms of insurance, sales volume continued to increase, and The St. Paul acquired several general agencies, which sold the insurance products of many different companies, to work with its independent agents more effectively. Management training programs were also initiated in 1958, computers were installed in 1956 to speed up the handling and processing of information, and in 1961 The St. Paul rebuilt and enlarged its offices.

When Codere retired in 1963, Jackson succeeded him and Ronald M. Hubbs became The St. Paul's next president. During the 1960s the emphasis was on customer service. Hubbs was instrumental in the development of more than 40 property and liability service centers nationwide. Each center was self-contained; it had its own underwriters, risk management staff, marketing, claims and policy services, and office support personnel. The company believed decentralization would bring it closer to its customers.

In 1968 The St. Paul reorganized. St. Paul Fire and Marine Insurance Company became The St. Paul Companies, Inc. The name St. Paul Fire and Marine Insurance Company was retained for the property-liability insurance subsidiary. In the years following the reorganization, The St. Paul Companies diversified its insurance-related business and branched into other areas of consumer and business services.

In 1970 St. Paul Guardian Insurance Company was formed to market personal lines of insurance. Two years later St. Paul Investment Management Company, an investment management firm, was started, and in 1973 St. Paul Life Insurance Company, whose purpose was to market life insurance through independent agents representing St. Paul Fire and Marine, was formed.

In 1973 Jackson retired as chairman. He was succeeded by Hubbs, and Carl B. Drake became the eighth president of The St. Paul Companies. Less than one year later, The St. Paul acquired John Nuveen & Co., a trader, marketer, underwriter, and distributor of securities. Nuveen was founded in Chicago in 1898 and had been a pioneer in tax-exempt bonds for individual investors, which it introduced in 1961. The St. Paul also added St. Paul Risk Services Inc., which provided consulting services to self-insure institutions and firms, and St. Paul Surplus Lines, which again broadened the coverage offered by St. Paul Fire and Marine.

In the midst of this growth the public was becoming more concerned about the quality of the products and services it was receiving. This concern, combined with changes in the medical field—in particular, new drugs, transplants, the growth of large group medical practices and group medical plans, and less personal doctor-patient relationships—contributed to an increased number of medical liability claims. Insurance companies selling malpractice coverage began to suffer massive losses. Medical cases often took years to settle, and court awards continued to grow.

The St. Paul, the largest carrier of medical liability insurance, stopped accepting new policies for a short time. When the company began to write new business again, it based premiums on the practitioners' past record. This "claims made" standard had been used in other types of liability for many years. It led to more accurate pricing and seemed to stabilize the market. The company also raised its malpractice premiums. The company later created a medical services division, which brought together The St. Paul's underwriting, marketing, and administrative expertise in healthcare-related fields. The company introduced simplified language policies, starting with its personal liability catastrophe coverage, with the hope that it would reduce claims.

PERIOD OF RETRENCHMENT

In 1980 Chairman Drake refocused mainly on insurance-related businesses. The company began to divest most non-insurance subsidiaries (with the exception of the John Nuveen asset management and investment banking unit) and resumed expansion of its insurance-related interests. Under a new president, Robert J. Haugh, these divestitures were completed by 1984, when The St. Paul's net loss was $210 million. The company then undertook a new series of acquisitions. Among these purchases were Seaboard Surety Company, a provider of fidelity and surety bonds, and Swett & Crawford Group, a Los

Angeles-based wholesale broker in excess and surplus lines. Atwater McMillian (renamed St. Paul Specialty Underwriting in 1988), a company handling specialty risk accounts and surplus lines, was formed in 1981.

During the 1980s more demanding consumers, an evolving marketplace, and government deregulation resulted in another price war that hurt The St. Paul's liability business. During the same years The St. Paul also expanded its involvement in European markets. The company acquired the London-based Minet Holdings PLC in 1988, making The St. Paul the seventh largest insurance brokerage firm in the world. Shortly after the Minet acquisition, The St. Paul established St. Paul (U. K.) Limited.

On May 1, 1990, Haugh retired and was replaced by The St. Paul's new chairman, president, and CEO, Douglas W. Leatherdale, who continued the company's strategy for an increasing presence in the European market. The St. Paul also formed Minet Europe Holdings Limited, as part of the Minet Group, to manage the expansion of The St. Paul's European market.

After two and a half bitter years of litigation and regulatory oversight, The St. Paul in mid-1990 successfully ended an attempted hostile takeover by Alleghany Corporation. In May 1992 The St. Paul completed an initial public offering for the highly successful, and newly renamed, The John Nuveen Company, selling eight million shares at $18 per share and leaving The St. Paul with a 74 percent stake (which increased to 77 percent by mid-1997). For the year, John Nuveen enjoyed record revenues of $221 million, 23 percent higher than the previous year, but The St. Paul as a whole did not fare as well. Record catastrophic storms that year, including Hurricanes Andrew and Iniki and Typhoon Omar, led to a record $445 million in catastrophe losses, which when coupled with a $365 million write-down on the goodwill associated with the continuously troubled Minet Group subsidiary, resulted in the worst operating loss in company history: $333.8 million.

In May 1993 The St. Paul launched a restructuring of its U.S. underwriting businesses (known collectively as St. Paul Fire and Marine Insurance), partly in response to the losses of the previous year. Nearly two dozen departments were streamlined into three new entities: St. Paul Specialty, which housed such niche underwriting operations as medical services; St. Paul Personal & Business, responsible for underwriting personal insurance for individuals and commercial insurance for small business owners; and St. Paul Commercial, responsible for midsized commercial customers. In August 1993 the St. Paul Personal & Business unit was bolstered through the $420 million purchase of Economy Fire & Casualty from Kemper Corporation. With no repeat of the spate of catastrophic 1992 storms, The St. Paul returned to profitability in 1993, posting record operating earnings of $386.6 million, with records following for 1994 ($413.9 million) and 1995 ($464.9 million) as well.

Results for 1996 were not nearly so rosy, as the company suffered its second worst catastrophe losses in history, $207 million, stemming in large part from an East Coast blizzard, flooding in the West and Southwest, and Hurricane Fran. In July of that year, St. Paul Fire and Marine strengthened its position in the small to midsized commercial underwriting market with the purchase of Northbrook Holdings, Inc. from Allstate Insurance Company for $190 million. Then in December The St. Paul decided to sell its loss-making Minet Group, finally unloading it in May 1997 to the insurance brokerage firm Aon, based in Chicago. Meanwhile, John Nuveen added $13.6 billion to its assets under management through the acquisitions of Flagship Resources in January 1997 and of Rittenhouse Financial Services in July 1997. St. Paul International Underwriting, the underwriter of non-U.S. property and liability insurance, was active as well, opening new offices in France, Germany, Canada, Mexico, and South Africa and acquiring the Botswana General Insurance Company of South Africa in October 1997.

In the rapidly consolidating insurance industry of the 1990s, The St. Paul Companies continued to be on the side of the acquirers. With the company's strong balance sheet backing him, Leatherdale next engineered a blockbuster deal: the April 1998 acquisition of USF&G Corporation for approximately $3.9 billion in stock and assumed debt. In buying the Baltimore-based USF&G, a firm founded in 1896, The St. Paul propelled itself from the 13th to the eighth largest property and casualty insurer in the nation. The companies' operations meshed well geographically, with The St. Paul's strength in the Midwest, and USF&G's in the South and Northeast. To integrate the USF&G operations, The St. Paul launched an 18-month plan to slash 2,600 jobs from the combined workforce.

The St. Paul barely eked out a profit of $89.3 million in 1998 as it again suffered catastrophic losses—$418.7 million pretax from a battery of hurricanes, tornadoes, and other storms. In the wake of these results, Leatherdale elected to focus the company on the more profitable commercial side of its business, and more specifically the specialty commercial sector, jettisoning several individual insurance units over a two-year period. The St. Paul sold its personal property and casualty lines to MetLife Auto & Home for $600 million in 1999, its nonstandard auto insurance unit to the Prudential Insurance Company of America in 2000 for $200 million, and its Fidelity & Guaranty Life Insurance unit to the U.K.-based Old Mutual PLC for $635 million in 2001. In the meantime, The St. Paul bolstered its healthcare business in April 2000 by acquiring MMI Companies for $320 million in cash and debt. MMI, based in Deerfield, Illinois, specialized in services for the healthcare industry, including clinical risk management, operational-consulting services, and insurance and reinsurance in the United States and London. Later in 2000 The St. Paul elected to sell an unprofitable subsidiary of MMI, Unionamerica Insurance Co., a London-based unit focusing on medical-liability reinsurance. In what turned out to be the final deal of the Leatherdale era, The St. Paul acquired Toronto-based London Guarantee Insurance Company, Canada's second largest specialty property and casualty insurer, for $80 million in late 2001.

2001 AND BEYOND: THE FISHMAN/TRAVELERS ERA

As a result of the terrorist attacks on the United States of September 11, 2001, The St. Paul incurred claims totaling approximately $941 million. This propelled the firm into a net loss for the year of $1.09 billion. Shortly after 9/11, in the middle of the following month, Jay S. Fishman was brought onboard as chairman and CEO, succeeding Leatherdale. Fishman had been the head of Travelers Insurance Group, a unit of Citigroup Inc., but elected to leave for an opportunity to run his own company rather than wait for a chance to succeed Citigroup's Chairman and CEO Sanford Weill.

Fishman quickly put his stamp on The St. Paul. In a reversal of one of his predecessor's moves, The St. Paul once again began seeking out general commercial property and casualty business, concentrating on small and midsize businesses, ones with revenues under $500 million. The company also substantially reduced its international operations, retaining only its businesses in the United Kingdom, Canada, and Mexico, and in December 2001 began a gradual pullout from medical-malpractice insurance, a business in which it was paying out more in claims than it was collecting in premiums. In reinsurance, the company narrowed the types of reinsurance it offered and then converted the remaining reinsurance operation into a separate Bermuda company with The St. Paul as a major investor. Fishman also slashed about 1,100 jobs from the workforce. On the downside, The St. Paul reached a settlement in a legacy asbestos case inherited through the takeover of USF&G. In mid-2002 the company settled a case involving Western Asbestos, agreeing to a $987 million payment, which resulted in a net charge of $380 million for 2002.

Fishman's blockbuster move, however, was the $17.9 billion stock-swap acquisition of Travelers Property Casualty Corp., Fishman's old company, which Citigroup had spun off into a separate company in 2002. Announced in November 2003 and completed in April 2004, the deal created the second biggest commercial property and casualty insurer in the United States, trailing only American International Group, Inc. It also brought homeowners and auto insurance back into The St. Paul fold and combined Travelers' more extensive general commercial lines with The St. Paul's stronger specialty insurance business. Upon the deal's completion The St. Paul changed its name to The St. Paul Travelers Companies, Inc. and retained its Saint Paul headquarters, and Travelers became a subsidiary while staying based in Hartford, Connecticut. Fishman remained CEO but temporarily relinquished the chairmanship to Robert I. Lipp, head of Travelers. In late 2005 Fishman succeeded Lipp as chairman.

As St. Paul Travelers moved ahead with integration plans that included cutting 3,000 jobs from the combined workforce of 30,000 and aims to save $350 million in annual operating costs, the merger got off to a rough start. In July 2004 the company announced a reserve charge of $1.625 billion, a charge about twice as large as analysts had been expecting, that officials said was needed to reconcile differing accounting treatments at the two merged entities. The company also lost some commercial business as independent agents who had been selling products of The St. Paul chafed at the more stringent underwriting policies and sales practices of Travelers. Moreover, the string of major storms that hit the southeastern United States in 2004 resulted in before-tax claims of $612 million at St. Paul Travelers. Net income thus totaled just $955 million on revenues of $22.54 billion.

In 2005 the combination of catastrophic claims and special charges was even higher than the previous year. The former figure, largely attributable to the devastation wrought by Hurricane Katrina, amounted to $1.5 billion after-tax, while the company also added $548 million to its asbestos reserves. Needing to raise cash, St. Paul Travelers elected to sell off its majority stake in Nuveen, garnering $2.4 billion in the process. Coupled with improving performance in the company's core operations, the Nuveen divestment helped St. Paul Travelers bump up its net income for the year to $1.62 billion.

The year 2006 started out inauspiciously, as a U.S. Circuit Court of Appeals ruling exposed the company to potential additional asbestos liabilities of more than $1 billion in a case involving ACandS Inc., a former distributor and installer of asbestos products. As St. Paul Travelers continued to wrestle with its asbestos claims and made plans for the prospect of another round of devastating hurricanes and tropical storms, surprising speculation about another merger emerged. In March 2006 the *Wall Street Journal* reported that St. Paul Travelers was in the early stages of discussing a takeover of Zurich Financial Services, one of Europe's largest insurers and a firm that was also a major U.S. property and casualty insurer. Any such deal promised to be highly complex and take months to complete, but in the meantime St. Paul Travelers issued a denial that any such talks were taking place.

William R. Grossman
Updated, David E. Salamie

PRINCIPAL SUBSIDIARIES

Travelers Property Casualty Corp.; The Standard Fire Insurance Company; The Travelers Indemnity Company; The Northland Company; The Phoenix Insurance Company; Travelers Casualty and Surety Company; St. Paul Guarantee Insurance Company (Canada); St. Paul Fire and Marine Insurance Company; St. Paul Mercury Insurance Company; United States Fidelity and Guaranty Company; St. Paul Reinsurance Company Limited (U.K.); USF&G Financial Services Corporation.

PRINCIPAL DIVISIONS

Commercial Lines; Specialty Lines; Personal Lines.

PRINCIPAL COMPETITORS

American International Group, Inc.; The Chubb Corporation; The Hartford Financial Services Group, Inc.; Nationwide Mutual Insurance Company; Allianz AG; Zurich Financial Services; AXA; ING Groep N.V.

FURTHER READING

DePass, Dee, "Fishman: 'I'm Going As Fast As I Can': The St. Paul's New CEO Says Significant Changes Are Coming," *Minneapolis Star Tribune,* October 24, 2001, p. 1D.

———, "St. Paul Companies to Sell Life Insurance Unit for $635 Million," *Minneapolis Star Tribune,* April 27, 2001, p. 3D.

———, "The St. Paul Companies Will Buy USF&G Corp.," *Minneapolis Star Tribune,* January 20, 1998, p. 7B.

———, "The St. Paul Cos. Plans to Grow by Shrinking," *Minneapolis Star Tribune,* January 11, 1999, p. 1D.

———, "The St. Paul Finds New CEO in New York," *Minneapolis Star Tribune,* October 12, 2001, p. 1D.

———, "St. Paul-Travelers Merger Creates Insurance Giant," *Minneapolis Star Tribune,* November 18, 2003, p. 1A.

Dorfman, John R., "Laughing in the Storm," *Forbes,* November 7, 1983, p. 270.

Dykewicz, Paul, "St. Paul Restructures Comp, Reinsurance," *Journal of Commerce and Commercial,* May 6, 1993, p. 10A.

Fletcher, Meg, "St. Paul, Alleghany Truce Could Curtail Hostile Insurer Bids," *Business Insurance,* June 4, 1990, pp. 3, 45.

Francis, Theo, and Robin Sidel, "St. Paul Agrees to Stock Deal with Travelers," *Wall Street Journal,* November 18, 2003, p. C1.

Hays, Daniel, "St. Paul Travelers Loses $1B-Plus Asbestos Decision," *National Underwriter Property and Casualty-Risk and Benefits Management,* January 10, 2006, p. 7.

"A History of the St. Paul," St. Paul, Minn.: The St. Paul Companies, 1988.

Kunz, Virginia Brainard, "Fires, Hurricanes, Diamonds, Elephants: St. Paul Companies' Colorful History," *Ramsey County (Minn.) History,* Fall 1996, pp. 3–32.

Laing, Jonathan R., "Sins of St. Paul," *Barron's,* May 16, 2005, pp. 32, 34.

Lee, Thomas, "$800 Million Hit for St. Paul Travelers," *Minneapolis Star Tribune,* September 24, 2005, p. 1D.

Moylan, Martin J., "St. Paul Cos.' Restructuring Puzzles Analysts, Worries Staff," *Journal of Commerce and Commercial,* November 24, 1993, p. 8A.

Mullins, Ronald Gift, "Aon Acquires Minet Group from St. Paul," *Journal of Commerce and Commercial,* April 14, 1997, p. 10A.

———, "St. Paul Says '92 Big Storms Cost Company $305 Million," *Journal of Commerce and Commercial,* January 21, 1993, p. 11A.

"An Old-Fashioned Marriage," *Economist,* November 22, 2003, p. 70.

Oster, Christopher, and Paul Beckett, "St. Paul Cos. Names Fishman of Citigroup As Chief Executive," *Wall Street Journal,* October 12, 2001, p. C13.

Phelps, David, "The St. Paul Aims to Sharpen Focus: MetLife Pays $600 Million for Unit," *Minneapolis Star Tribune,* July 13, 1999, p. 1D.

St. Anthony, Neal, "Sale of Unit May Mean New Opportunities for St. Paul," *Minneapolis Star Tribune,* July 16, 1999, p. 1D.

"St. Paul Cos.: Bucking an Industry Trend by Moving More Deeply into Insurance," *Business Week,* February 28, 1983, pp. 92+.

Schifrin, Matthew, "The Artful Contrarian," *Forbes,* February 17, 1992, p. 184.

Scism, Leslie, "St. Paul to Pay $2.8 Billion for USF&G," *Wall Street Journal,* January 20, 1998, p. A3.

Singer, Jason, Charles Fleming, and Dennis K. Berman, "Prospect of Trans-Atlantic Merger Reflects Ferment Among Insurers," *Wall Street Journal,* March 17, 2006, pp. A1, A9.

Stavro, Barry, "Risk Is Relative," *Forbes,* March 10, 1986, p. 63.

Treaster, Joseph B., "Citi Man Is Thinking Big but Thriftily in the Midwest," *New York Times,* March 27, 2002, p. C1.

———, "$16 Billion Deal Joins St. Paul and Travelers," *New York Times,* November 18, 2003, p. C1.

Willoughby, Jack, "Winning Policies," *Barron's,* September 8, 2003, p. 23.

salesforce.com, Inc.

1 Market Street, Suite 300
San Francisco, California 94105
U.S.A.
Telephone: (415) 901-7000
Toll Free: (800) 667-6389
Fax: (415) 901-7040
Web site: http://www.salesforce.com

Public Company
Incorporated: 1999
Employees: 1,304
Sales: $280.6 million (2006)
Stock Exchanges: New York
Ticker Symbol: CRM
NAIC: 511210 Software Publishers; 518111 Internet Service Providers

■ ■ ■

salesforce.com, Inc. operates in the customer relationship management, or CRM, market, providing web-based applications that allow companies to share information related to their sales efforts, such as sales leads, customer information, and customer interaction. The company's service, available exclusively online, competes with CRM software that companies purchase and install on their own hardware, as well as other on-demand CRM providers. salesforce.com charges its customers a monthly fee on a per user basis, which is typically much less expensive than buying enterprise software, installing it, configuring it, and maintaining its operation. One of the first companies to offer web-based CRM services, salesforce.com serves more than 20,000 customers representing approximately 400,000 subscribers in 70 countries. Notable salesforce.com customers include IBM, Microsoft, PricewaterhouseCoopers, Nokia, Kaiser Permanente, and Dow Jones Newswires.

ORIGINS

No single individual had a greater influence over salesforce.com during its formative years than its founder, Marc Benioff, an impassioned pitchman for a start-up venture whose lifeblood was salespeople, or rather, the companies who employed salespeople. Described as brash, gregarious, irreverent, among a long list of other flattering and unflattering adjectives, Benioff was a showman who chased publicity, preaching the dawn of a new age in the software industry. He was initially dismissed by many of his peers, who viewed his business model as incapable of generating any sort of success. A short time later, more than a few his critics were following his lead, employing the same market approach they had earlier disparaged.

Before Benioff assumed a revolutionary role in the software industry, he distinguished himself as one of the industry's rising stars. Raised in Hillsborough, California, Benioff grew up creating computer games on his Commodore 64, making enough money to buy a car, a Toyota Supra, and to put himself through college. He attended the University of Southern California, where he earned a degree in business administration while working as a programmer and salesman for Apple Computer. After college, he joined Oracle Corp., a leading developer of business software led by industry dignitary Larry Ellison.

COMPANY PERSPECTIVES

We're setting the standard for on-demand CRM. And winning the most repeat awards in the industry in the process. The customer-driven success of salesforce.com is based on delivering more than just run-of-the-mill product features. Instead, we listen to users like you—and translate your ideas into the kind of simple-to-use, indispensable CRM you've always dreamed possible.

Benioff began working at Oracle in 1986, rising quickly through the company's executive ranks. He was named the company's "Rookie of the Year" at age 22, and at age 25 he became Oracle's youngest vice-president. Benioff went on to hold a number of executive positions in marketing and development, taking a particular interest in CRM software, software that enables companies to manage every aspect of their relationship with a customer. When a friend and Oracle colleague, Tom Siebel, left the company in 1993 to start a CRM software developer, Siebel Systems, Inc., Benioff invested $50,000 in the start-up venture. Unknowingly, his investment helped launch what would be his fiercest rival.

After a decade at Oracle, Benioff was ready for a change. He took a sabbatical in 1996 and traveled throughout Asia and India. Not long after his return to Oracle, Benioff began planning the start of his entrepreneurial career. His idea was to start a CRM company, but instead of selling packaged software to businesses Benioff proposed to offer CRM services on the Internet, using central servers to store customers' data. The idea ran counter to convention, prompting many industry pundits to look askance at Benioff's strategy. "People were saying, 'This stuff will never fly. Companies will never let anyone host their data,'" an early salesforce.com executive recalled in an October 2005 interview with *Technology Review.* "The word 'control' came up a lot." Benioff envisioned a web-based service capable of connecting salespeople, enabling users to track contacts, conversations, and other relevant client information online, eliminating the need to pay for hardware and software, as well as the installation, customization, and maintenance of the software.

Benioff hired three programmers and formed salesforce.com in March 1999. Few in the investment community paid much attention to the start-up CRM venture that was based mainly in Benioff's house, despite the accomplishments of its founder. The CRM market was a $3.2 billion business when Benioff entered the fray, and most of the attention from industry experts was paid to companies such as Siebel Systems, whose Siebel Sales Enterprise software system had created an industry titan. Benioff was well aware of the success of his former colleague: The $50,000 investment he had made in the company in 1993 had been parlayed into more than $20 million by the time he started salesforce.com, giving him the financial resources to fund his company's development. Without his own personal fortune, Benioff would have had a difficult time establishing salesforce.com, at least in the way he envisioned the company. Venture capitalists insisted that Benioff offer his customers a choice, a web-based CRM service and a self-contained CRM software package, believing that the hosted, online version would attract customers who soon would want to purchase packaged software. Benioff steadfastly refused to alter his strategy to obtain financial backing from venture capitalists. "We've taken plenty of big bets," a salesforce.com senior executive explained in an October 2005 interview with *Technology Review,* "and the bet we took in 1999 was that we were not going to play that game. We were going to go whole hog into the hosted model. Marc [Benioff] felt that the control issue was just an emotional issue, not really a rational issue." Benioff used $6 million of his own money and obtained $2 million from Oracle's Ellison to start salesforce.com, wholly committing himself to hosting all of his customers' data in one place.

SALESFORCE.COM LAUNCHES ITS SERVICE IN 2000

It took nearly a year before Benioff could begin pointing to the superior logic of what he called "software as a service," or on-demand software. salesforce.com officially launched its service on February 7, 2000, when small businesses, the company's target audience, began signing up for online assistance in automating their sales forces. The year also marked the launch of Oracle's on-demand CRM applications, prompting Benioff to demand that Ellison vacate his seat on salesforce.com's board of directors, not the last time Benioff would clash with former colleagues. salesforce.com, which Benioff planned to take public sometime in 2000, charged $50 per five users on a monthly basis as it started out, initially limiting its service to automating sales processes online, giving salespeople the ability to click on tabs to navigate from their contact list to account information, and to sales leads. Within four months, the company's customer base totaled 5,000, with the number of clients expected to increase to 15,000 by the end of the year, a year that would pass without salesforce.com completing an initial public offering (IPO) of stock.

KEY DATES

1999: salesforce.com is founded by Marc Benioff.
2000: salesforce.com launches its web-based service in February.
2003: salesforce.com records its first profitable quarter.
2004: salesforce.com completes its initial public offering of stock.
2005: salesforce.com releases AppExchange.

As Benioff set out to prove the merits of web-based CRM services, he did so with a swagger, generating as much publicity as he could to aid in his assault on convention in the CRM industry. He had his sights set squarely on Siebel Systems, which had developed into a $790 million-in-sales company by the time salesforce .com was formed. "Our objective," Benioff proclaimed in a February 21, 2000 interview with *Business Week,* "is to put Siebel Systems out of business." The battle against Tom Siebel, in which Benioff went as far as to stage a fake protest outside a Siebel Systems customer conference, was a two-sided affair, with Siebel firing his own salvo at salesforce.com. "There's no way that company exists in a year," he said in a June 25, 2001 interview with *Fortune.* Despite Benioff's bravado, he chose to be a hands-off chairman, handing the duties of running the company to another former Oracle executive, John Dillon. Dillon, who was named salesforce.com's chief executive officer in September 1999, joined the company after leading Sunnyvale, California-based Hyperion Solutions. Under Dillon's rule, the company began expanding the capabilities of its services, developing beyond sales-processes automation to present CRM tools as comprehensive as those offered by Siebel Systems and Oracle. In March 2001, the company launched a full suite of CRM applications, including new tools for customer service and marketing that enabled it to begin targeting medium-sized businesses, companies in the 5,000- to 10,000-user range.

As salesforce.com's approach to the CRM market began to win over customers, the company gained its financial footing. The company generated $5 million in revenue in 2001, a figure that would more than triple by the next year, reaching $21.5 million. The company was losing money, however, incurring a $31.8 million loss in 2001 and a $29 million loss in 2002, which, combined with the spectacular collapse of the high-technology sector, made an IPO out of the question. Just as the company began to market its CRM services to larger companies and record its first substantial gains in revenue, the relationship between Dillon and Benioff quickly fractured, leading to Dillon's resignation as chief executive officer in November 2001. Benioff stepped in, assuming day-to-day control over the company, and presided over the jump to $21.5 million in revenue in 2002, holding the titles of chairman and chief executive officer. Under his leadership, salesforce.com recorded its first profitable quarter, a momentous event announced in mid-2003, when the company registered $188,000 in net income. A second consecutive profitable quarter followed, when the company posted $127,000 in net income in the fall of 2003. Dillon, nearly two years after he left, found the results unimpressive. "I find it hard to believe that Marc is doing a good job as chief executive officer," he said in a September 1, 2003 interview with *Business Week.* "He's not operational. He doesn't have the wherewithal to manage people."

PUBLIC OFFERING IN 2004

Benioff did not lack detractors, but as salesforce.com entered the mid-2000s, the performance of his company offered a powerful riposte to those who dismissed or denigrated his actions. With profits starting to come in, Benioff could entertain the idea of completing an IPO, something he had wanted to do since salesforce.com first launched its subscription service. The financial results for 2004, announced in the spring of 2004, showed the company's first annual profit, a gain of $3.5 million that prompted Benioff to file with the Securities and Exchange Commission for a conversion to public ownership. salesforce.com completed its IPO in June 2004, selling 11.5 million shares at $11 per share, netting $113.8 million from the offering. Benioff retained a 26 percent stake in the company following its IPO, which was worth an estimated $500 million by the end of 2004.

salesforce.com was beginning to hit its financial stride following the IPO. After recording $85.7 million in sales in 2004, the company collected $157.9 million in 2005, a year that saw its net income increase from $3.5 million to $7.3 million. Towards the end of the year, during the first week of October, Benioff celebrated what he referred to as "the most exciting week of my career," according to the October 5, 2005 edition of the *Financial Times.* Benioff explained: "Not only have we introduced our most important product, but our top competitor just disappeared." The battle between salesforce.com and Siebel Systems ended with Benioff emerging victorious, resolved when Oracle announced it was acquiring Siebel Systems. The announcement of the $5.8 billion acquisition, which was completed in early 2006, coincided with the release of AppExchange, the product hailed by Benioff. AppExchange allowed salesforce.com users to create their own applications with the company's architecture and sell them to others. "Someone in Bangalore might go home one evening and develop an application on our service," Benioff explained in an October 5, 2005 interview with the *Financial Times.* "They save it to a directory and charge others. Once we had two on-demand applications and now we have 70 and soon we will have thousands."

As salesforce.com prepared for the future, the business model once dismissed as unviable stood as a model copied by a host of competitors. The company faced stiff competition not only from industry giants such as Oracle but also from other web-based CRM companies, each jockeying for market share in a rapidly growing market. Spending on on-demand software was expected to grow 25 percent per year during the second half of the decade, reaching $9 billion by 2008, or nearly three times the volume of business recorded when Benioff formed salesforce.com. As Benioff marshaled his forces to grab market share from his competitors, the release of the company's annual financial results in March 2006 provided compelling evidence that the company stood on a sound foundation. Revenues swelled to $280.6 million, up markedly from the $157.9 million generated in 2005, but the year's most impressive result was the increase in net income, which nearly quadrupled, reaching $28.4 million.

Jeffrey L. Covell

PRINCIPAL SUBSIDIARIES

Kabushiki Kaisha salesforce.com (Japan); SFDC (EMEA) Limited (Ireland); SFDC International Limited (Ireland); SFDC Ireland Limited; salesforce.com SARL (Switzerland); SFDC UK Ltd.; SFDC Luxembourg SARL; SFDC Australia Pty. Limited; SFDC Singapore Pte. Ltd.; salesforce.com Canada Corporation; salesforce.com Information Technology (Shanghai) Co. Ltd. (China); salesforce.com Germany GmbH; salesforce.com Hong Kong Ltd.; salesforce.com India Pvt. Ltd.; SFDC International Ltd. (U.K.); salesforce.com, LLC; SFDC Mexico S. de R.L. de C.V.; salesforce Spain, S.L.; SFDC Sweden AB.

PRINCIPAL COMPETITORS

Oracle Corporation; FrontRange Solutions Inc.; Sage Software, Inc.

FURTHER READING

Drachman, Elizabeth, "Salesforce.com Vying for Its Piece of the Industry Pie," *San Francisco Business Times,* June 23, 2000, p. 29.

Hamm, Steve, "Who Says CEOs Can't Find Inner Peace?," *Business Week,* September 1, 2003, p. 77.

Liedtke, Michael, "Salesforce.com's Stock Soars in IPO Debut," *America's Intelligence Wire,* June 23, 2004.

Lohse, Deborah, "CEO's Interview Leak Stalls IPO for Software Leaser Salesforce.com," *San Jose Mercury News,* June 5, 2004.

Panja, Tariq, "Salesforce.com Runs Up Against the Big Dogs," *America's Intelligence Wire,* March 7, 2006.

Roush, Wade, "The Customer Is Sometimes Wrong," *Technology Review,* October 2005, p. 36.

"Sales-Force.com: An Ant at the Picnic," *Business Week,* February 21, 2000, p. 76.

Temple, James, "Salesforce.com Hooks Big Fish with New Apps.," *San Francisco Business Times,* March 9, 2001, p. 6.

Wilson, Lizette, "Salesforce.com Switches from Small Fry to Big Guy," *San Francisco Business Times,* October 5, 2001, p. 19.

SeaChange International, Inc.

50 Nagog Park
Acton, Massachusetts 01720
U.S.A.
Telephone: (978) 897-0100
Fax: (978) 897-0132
Web site: http://www.schange.com

Public Company
Incorporated: 1993 as SeaView Technology, Inc.
Employees: 500
Sales: $126.26 million (2006)
Stock Exchanges: NASDAQ
Ticker Symbol: SEAC
NAIC: 334220 Radio and Television Broadcasting and Wireless Communications Equipment Manufacturing; 511210 Software Publishers

■ ■ ■

SeaChange International, Inc. is the leading supplier of digital video server systems to cable system operators, cable TV networks, and television stations in the United States and abroad. The firm's products are used for video-on-demand (VOD) services, storage and playback of video content, and to automate the insertion of advertisements into programming. The publicly traded SeaChange is run by cofounder and CEO William Styslinger, who owns about 7.5 percent of its stock.

BEGINNINGS

SeaChange International was founded in Massachusetts by a group of former Digital Equipment Corp. (DEC) employees led by William Styslinger. University of Buffalo applied mathematics graduate Styslinger had worked for DEC since 1978, most recently as head of its newly formed Cable Television Business unit. His staff had been seeking a way to store video digitally with compression software so it could be transmitted over cable television networks, but when financially strapped DEC cut the project's funding in 1992, Styslinger decided to quit and, with coworkers Edward Delaney, Jr., and director of engineering Ed McGrath, formed a new company they called SeaView Technology, Inc. After getting DEC's permission to continue their research, they borrowed more than $300,000 from family and friends and set up shop in McGrath's dining room in July 1993. They soon recruited several other key engineers from their former employer, and subsequently amended the company's name to SeaChange when the name SeaView was found to be in use.

The new firm's goal was to develop equipment that would enable cable television service providers to send different advertisements simultaneously to as many as a dozen separate geographic areas, or zones, in their systems. The cable firm could determine which demographic groups were most populous in each zone, and thus better serve advertisers seeking to reach audiences in a more precise manner. Several firms already offered tape-based analog systems for this purpose, but SeaChange's new digital technology was potentially more reliable and could offer quicker system upload times, as well as cost savings, because no physical tapes were involved.

The company's staff worked on the project for little pay until July 1994, when the first system was shipped

COMPANY PERSPECTIVES

SeaChange International, Inc. is a leader in the market for digital video systems for television. We create powerful server and software systems that manage, store, and distribute professional-quality digital video. Our innovative products are based on a scalable, distributed software architecture and standard technology components. As a result, we enable broadband, broadcast, satellite and new media companies to streamline operations and reduce costs, allowing for expanded services, new applications, and increased revenues.

We're providing the foundation that is allowing the television industry to meet the ever-increasing market for on-demand entertainment and information.

to Time Warner Manhattan. Additional sales of the new Spot advertising insertion system followed over the next year to clients that included cable giants Tele-Communications, Inc., Cox Communications, and Continental Cable. By the summer of 1995 systems were operating in 40 cities, and the rapidly growing 45-employee company had relocated to a facility in Concord, Massachusetts. In addition to manufacturing the products from off-the-shelf hardware, the firm also offered 24-hour technical support with a guaranteed two-hour response time.

The success and reliability of the Spot product quickly brought SeaChange close to 60 percent of the U.S. market for ad insertion technology, and in the fall of 1995 the company created an international sales unit to pursue the European, African, and Middle Eastern markets. The year also had seen introduction of the new VideoServer 100 storage device, which boosted the capacity of the Spot system. Sales for 1995 jumped to $23 million from $5 million a year earlier, and the company recorded a profit of $1.2 million.

In March 1996 the firm changed its name to SeaChange International, Inc. as it sought to further position itself as a worldwide entity. Its headquarters were moved to a new 25,000-square-foot site in Maynard, Massachusetts, though manufacturing would continue to be performed in Acton, Massachusetts, and video server development in Greenville, New Hampshire.

The spring of 1996 saw the firm sign a multimillion-dollar deal with the largest cable company in the United Kingdom, Telewest PLC, and form a partnership with IBM, which would market the Spot system as part of its TV industry product line. In July the company added new features to Spot that automated the management of advertising traffic control and billing, using software licensed from Summit Software Systems of Boulder, Colorado.

INITIAL PUBLIC OFFERING IN THE FALL OF 1996

In November 1996 SeaChange went public on the NASDAQ with the sale of 2.3 million shares of stock for $15 each (representing 13 percent of the total), netting $24 million. The funds would be used for various purposes including development of a product that allowed television stations to geographically target ads through cable providers, as well as to expand into such new business areas as video-on-demand (VOD). The latter was a technology that enabled video content to be streamed over a cable network to individual users on request, typically for a fee. Although initially tape-based and controlled from the provider end, when offered through new interactive digital networks the ability to pause, fast-forward, and rewind would eventually become possible, along with a much greater breadth of content.

Shortly after the IPO, the firm partnered with IPC Interactive, Inc. to develop a VOD service for hotels and other multiple-dwelling units. SeaChange also bought Horizon Systems, Inc., a Colorado-based maker of software to manage ad traffic and billing, which would replace the licensed Summit product. For the year the company's revenues more than doubled, to $49.3 million, and it recorded a profit of $4.3 million.

The year 1997 saw the introduction of a satellite-based ad distribution system for broadcasters as well as the new Movie System for multichannel operators that broadcast long-form video programming. The latter used the firm's patent-pending MediaCluster storage technology to link multiple Video Server 100s together. Early customers included cable systems in The Netherlands and Austria.

In August 1997 the world's first fiber-optic VOD network system was launched in New York. SeaChange equipment was at the heart of the Time Warner Hotel Network, which would allow several different Manhattan hotels to offer multiple cable channels and pay-per-view movies.

In November the company formed an agreement to work with U.K.-based OmniBus Systems, a maker of broadcast operations automation software for use in newsrooms and similar facilities. The firm was starting to post quarterly losses as research-and-development costs rose above expected levels, sales

KEY DATES

1993: SeaView (later SeaChange) Technology, Inc. is founded in Massachusetts.
1994: The company ships the first digital ad insertion system to Time Warner Manhattan.
1996: MediaCluster is introduced; an initial public offering is made on the NASDAQ.
1997: IPC Interactive, Horizon Systems are purchased.
1998: SeaChange ITV System for video-on-demand is unveiled.
1999: MediaCluster is awarded a patent; Digital Video Arts, Ltd. is acquired.
2001: SeaChange wins an Emmy Award for MediaCluster.
2002: New Broadcast MediaLibrary, High-Definition video-on-demand products debut.
2004: ZQ Interactive is purchased.
2005: SeaChange acquires Liberate Technologies' non-U.S. business and On Demand.

growth slowed due to cable operators' uncertainty about converting to digital, and international markets proved harder than expected to enter.

Year's end saw acquisition of IPC Interactive Pte. Ltd. of Singapore and its U.S. subsidiary in a stock swap deal worth $6.7 million. Founded in 1984, IPC's tape-based Guestserve interactive television network system was the leading VOD product for the hospitality and commercial property markets, and would be converted to SeaChange's digital delivery systems following the purchase. After IPC's operations were consolidated, the firm would have a total of 270 employees.

In March 1998 the company introduced the Broadcast MediaCluster System, which would allow television stations and other users to store and play large amounts of digital video. In April a joint venture was formed with AMX Corp. to develop digital video products for use outside the television industry in places like corporate boardrooms.

INTRODUCING THE SEACHANGE ITV SYSTEM: FALL OF 1998

Spring also saw an alliance formed with cable software and set-top box maker Scientific-Atlanta to provide VOD equipment to cable operators. Early VOD experiments had failed because of the high per-subscriber start-up costs, but the SeaChange system cost half as much or less, though it was limited to fiber-optic cable systems, which then comprised only 15 percent of the U.S. total. In November the new SeaChange ITV System, the firm's first comprehensive digital VOD product, was officially made available. Trials were soon undertaken by Time Warner Cable and Comcast in the United States as well as other major companies in Canada and the United Kingdom.

In 1999 the firm bought Pennsylvania-based Digital Video Arts, Ltd., a developer of set-top software for digital video and interactive television, won a U.S. patent for MediaCluster, and began working with a firm called Optibase to develop video encoding systems. Revenues for the fiscal year ended January 2000 topped $85.2 million and net income was $1.1 million.

During early 2000 SeaChange launched a new satellite-based digital distribution service for commercials called MediaExpress and partnered with TV Guide, Inc. to market a version of the latter's interactive electronic program guide with VOD capability. In May an agreement was reached with Microsoft to develop a system to simultaneously encode video for television broadcasting or streaming over the Internet. Microsoft would also spend $18 million to buy a 2 percent stake in the firm.

In June 2000 SeaChange filed suit against a rival company called nCube, alleging patent infringement of its MediaCluster technology. A jury found in its favor that September, after which nCube revised its system to avoid using the patented program. In October SeaChange announced that it had been selected to provide set-top VOD software for 2.9 million users in New York, New Jersey, and Connecticut by Cablevision Systems Corp., and in December Comcast Corp. bought a $10 million stake in the firm, as well as signing a long-term agreement to buy its VOD systems and services.

In January 2001 nCube filed its own suit against SeaChange, alleging the company's VOD system infringed one of its patents. Meanwhile SeaChange was beginning to ramp up business in this area, with orders from the likes of Time Warner Cable helping sales top $10 million per quarter, about a third of the firm's total revenues. The year also saw the company begin working with 24/7 Media to integrate that firm's software and SeaChange's ITV System into a set-top box developed by Pace Micro Technology.

In December the company issued 2.79 million new shares of stock in a secondary offering that netted more than $80 million, and for the fiscal year ending January 31, 2002, reported sales of $115.8 million and income of $381,000. VOD systems accounted for $43 million of the total, with a similar amount coming from advertising systems. The firm also had won an Emmy Award for MediaCluster during the year.

INTRODUCING BROADCAST MEDIALIBRARY, HD-VOD IN 2002

Early 2002 saw the introduction of the Broadcast MediaLibrary, which could store huge amounts of video, as well as a new VOD system that could handle High-Definition (HD) television content. SeaChange claimed that it had spent $20 million in research costs developing the latter. In May nCube's patent infringement suit was found against the company, and it quickly appealed the verdict and began development of a way to eliminate the disputed patent, which was soon completed.

In the fall SeaChange announced a new VOD offering that would allow DVDs to be streamed on demand complete with bonus features, and the company also invested $2.3 million to buy part of a U.K.-based firm called On Demand Group that provided VOD services in Europe. The following March a judge ordered SeaChange to pay nCube double the original damages assigned by the jury, or $4 million, as well as two-thirds of that firm's lawyers' fees, though the award was appealed.

VOD now accounted for half of SeaChange's revenue, and ad insertion systems just 16 percent. The company continued to be the industry leader in both categories, with deployments in 86 of 171 North American VOD markets (compared to nearest rival Concurrent Computer Corp., with 52), and an estimated 80 percent share of the ad insertion market. For the fiscal year ended January 31, 2004, the company recorded sales of $146.1 million and net income of $5.6 million. During the fourth quarter VOD sales had accounted for two-thirds of revenues.

The firm's VOD system was facing a new challenge from personal videorecorders including TiVo, however, which could record programs on a computer-like hard drive for playback. Rather than offering content on demand, the relatively inexpensive devices could be programmed to record and store up to 30 hours of material with minimal effort and no tapes. Cable providers were still eager to add VOD, however, because rival satellite broadcasters, who charged less to subscribe, did not have the technical capability to offer VOD services. Cable providers also began to make increasing amounts of VOD content free, rather than pay-per-view, and broadened the content available.

In 2004 the firm introduced the High-Definition enabled VOD Recording System 2.0, which allowed cable operators to automatically record and store HD broadcasts for later playback on demand, with insertion of ads also possible. SeaChange had recently won new work from NTL, Inc. to build Europe's largest VOD network to date, several large Israeli firms, and major telecommunications companies including Verizon and Japan's NTT, which were seeking a piece of the VOD pie as well. The year 2004 also saw the company acquire a China-based software developer called ZQ Interactive for $2 million. Profits for the year ending January 31, 2005, hit $9.9 million on revenues of $157.3 million.

VOD sales were now falling off, however, and the company was working hard to expand its product and service offerings in several different areas. In the spring of 2005 SeaChange bought the international business of Liberate Technologies for $23.5 million, which included contracts, patents, and other intellectual property. Liberate provided software for digital cable systems for European networks. The company also formed a partnership with several other firms to create a digital video system for use in courtrooms, and began working with Visible World and Atlas to develop new digital ad insertion capabilities. In June a new VOD recording system was introduced that allowed playback while a program was still being aired, enabling viewers to see a show that had started at 10:00 p.m. as soon as 10:01. The Recording System 2.5 device could handle hundreds of channels simultaneously. A federal appeals court also overturned the decision in SeaChange's 2000 lawsuit against nCube (now owned by C-COR, Inc.) and upheld the results of the 2001 nCube suit that SeaChange had lost. The total award was $7.8 million.

August saw the company join a global consortium to offer Internet protocol television (IPTV) equipment to telecommunications firms and reach an agreement with video encoder maker EGT, Inc. to provide VOD services to television companies. In September SeaChange also acquired full ownership of the London-based On Demand Group for $13.4 million. On Demand provided movies and other programming for VOD and pay-per-view services throughout Europe, and owned a stake in leading European VOD content provider FilmFlex. It had 50 employees and revenues of $10.7 million. A 19.8 percent stake also was acquired in Massachusetts-based video streaming software firm Casa Systems during the year.

The fiscal year ended in January 2006 saw a huge drop in earnings, with revenues falling to $126.3 million and a loss of $12.1 million posted. VOD system sales were off 51 percent, but CEO Styslinger nonetheless tried to paint an encouraging picture in a conference call to stock analysts, citing an uptick in sales late in the year, increasing VOD content choices, and the dramatic growth of HD, which required five times the storage of standard definition television. Another encouraging sign was that 40 percent of the firm's business now came from international sales, up from less than a quarter in fiscal 2005.

Early 2006 saw the company outfit Los Angeles PBS station KCET with digital broadcast equipment, bringing to nearly 30 the number of public TV stations that utilized its MediaCluster and MediaLibrary systems. SeaChange also was introducing new products for streaming video content to mobile phones, iPods, laptops, and other portable equipment. In March, the company moved its headquarters from Maynard to neighboring Acton, Massachusetts.

In slightly less than 15 years SeaChange International, Inc. had grown to become the leader in video-on-demand and advertising insertion equipment for cable providers and broadcasters. The market was evolving rapidly as technology changed and consumers began to sort out the many choices available, but the company had weathered numerous storms and with experienced management and engineering teams in place was well-positioned to continue as an industry leader in future years.

Frank Uhle

PRINCIPAL SUBSIDIARIES

Digital Video Arts, Ltd.; ZQ Interactive (China); On Demand Group (U.K.)

PRINCIPAL COMPETITORS

C-COR, Inc.; Concurrent Computer Corporation; Broadbus Technologies Inc.; Leitch Technology Corporation; Avid Technology, Inc.; Sony Corporation.

FURTHER READING

Ackerman, Jerry, "Bringing Home 'Video-on-Demand' SeaChange Chief Stakes Company's Future on Making It Possible," *Boston Globe,* November 11, 1998, p. C1.

Dawson, Fred, "Microsoft Deal Signals Standards Sea Change," *Multichannel News,* May 15, 2000, p. 8.

Dickson, Glen, "SeaChange Demos Mobile Content Delivery," *Broadcasting & Cable,* April 10, 2006.

———, "A SeaChange to VOD," *Broadcasting & Cable,* May 8, 2000, p. 112.

Donohue, Steve, "SeaChange Wins Big with Cablevision Deal," *Multichannel News,* November 6, 2000, p. 51.

Howe, Peter J., "SeaChange Soars in Struggling Market," *Boston Globe,* May 17, 2005, p. F22.

Iler, David, "VOD Leaves Drawing Room, Crashes Cable Homes," *Multichannel News,* January 3, 2000, p. 27.

Judge, Paul C., "SeaChange International: Cable Ads, By Special Delivery," *Business Week,* May 26, 1997, p. 98.

Knell, Michael E., "Concord Firm Wins $2M Contract to Supply TCI," *Boston Herald,* August 12, 1995, p. 12.

Moss, Linda, "SeaChange Purchases Ad-Software Vendor Horizon," *Multichannel News,* November 25, 1996, p. 53.

———, "SeaChange Targets Broadcast Market, Satellite Delivery," *Multichannel News,* September 30, 1996, p. 46.

———, "SeaChange to Launch Ad-Management Software," *Multichannel News,* July 1, 1996, p. 16.

Rosenberg, Ronald, "SeaChange Is on Target for Cable TV Operators," *Boston Globe,* June 26, 1996, p. 55.

Santo, Brian, "VOD Patent Battle Turns Bitter," *Cable World,* January 15, 2001, p. 36.

Scanlon, Mavis, "Patent Ruling Goes Against SeaChange," *Cable World,* June 3, 2002, p. 10.

"Scientific Atlanta, SeaChange Hope to Revive VOD," *Video Technology News,* May 4, 1998.

"SeaChange Reports Q4 Revenue of $33.2M, Up 11% Year-on-Year, for Net Loss of $2.9M or 10¢ Per Share," *Optical Networks Daily,* March 15, 2006.

Sheng, Ellen, "SeaChange Faces Tough Rivals in Video-on-Demand Service," *Wall Street Journal,* June 11, 2003.

Spooner, John, "CEO Goes Through Sea of Change," *Boston Herald,* July 21, 1997, p. 27.

Thomas, Jennifer, "C-COR Wins Case on Patent Infringement," *Centre Daily Times,* January 11, 2006.

Vittore, Vince, "SeaChange Fills in Content Play," *Primedia Insight,* September 27, 2005.

"VOD Companies Hope Cable Puts Service on Fast Track," *DV Business,* November 30, 1998.

Semitool, Inc.

655 West Reserve Drive
Kalispell, Montana 59901
U.S.A.
Telephone: (406) 752-2107
Toll Free: (800) 548-8495
Fax: (406) 752-5522
Web site: http://www.semitool.com

Public Company
Incorporated: 1979
Employees: 958
Sales: $190.4 million (2005)
Stock Exchanges: NASDAQ
Ticker Symbol: SMTL
NAIC: 333298 All Other Industrial Machinery Manufacturing

■ ■ ■

Semitool, Inc. designs and manufactures sophisticated equipment used by semiconductor manufacturers. The company's equipment handles a process called wet chemical processing, which semiconductor manufacturers use to put layers onto silicon wafers. The fabrication of semiconductors, or "chips," typically requires several hundred manufacturing steps. Semitool's products address more than 150 of these manufacturing steps. The company's customers include industry heavyweights such as Advanced Micro Devices, Intel, Sony, IBM, and Texas Instruments, among a host of other leading chipmakers. International sales account for nearly three-quarters of Semitool's revenue volume. Nearly all of the company's manufacturing activities take place in Kalispell, Montana.

PRIVATE COMPANY: 1978–94

Raymon Thompson, a mechanical engineer with a background in semiconductor equipment, purchased a machine shop in Orange County, California, in the 1970s and founded Semitool there in 1978. The company's first product was a horizontal on-axis spin rinser/dryer that removed chemicals from the surfaces of silicon wafers being imprinted with computer chips. In 1979 Thompson moved the fledgling company to his hometown of Kalispell, Montana.

Semitool introduced the company's spray-solvent and spray-acid tools in the early 1980s and its first automated tool in 1984. Thompson then founded Semitherm, a partnership with a group of former Texas Instruments engineers, to develop vertical furnace systems for "baking" silicon wafers. This company was merged with Semitool in 1994. During the 1980s Semitool introduced several generations of its spray-solvent and spray-acid tools for chemical processing and its vertical furnaces for thermal processing and began to market its products to manufacturers outside the semiconductor industry. Exporting abroad began in 1981.

In fiscal 1991 (the year ended September 30, 1991) Semitool, together with Semitherm, had net sales of $25.1 million and total assets of $15.1 million but a net loss of more than $1.1 million and debt of $3.1 million. There were approximately 200 employees. For a 1991 survey Thompson told *D&B Reports,* "I have an absolutely outstanding workforce, from software

COMPANY PERSPECTIVES

We are a leader in the design, development and manufacturing of advanced, wet chemical processing equipment. We leverage our years of experience in designing and manufacturing production-proven semiconductor manufacturing equipment to deliver solutions that enable the fabrication of increasingly higher performance semiconductor devices. We have several key technological core competencies, including advanced computational modeling, and have assembled a development team with extensive engineering and modeling expertise to capitalize on these competencies.

engineers right down to the gal who cleans the floor. I think it's largely an ethic of our area here in this part of Montana. People love living here, and they come to work with an internal peace of mind. They're ready to participate as a creative human being, not as a monkey." In 1995 Semitool employees were working weekly four-day, ten-hour work shifts; the third weekend shift was putting in a three-day work week.

Semitool lost $303,000 on nearly $28 million of net sales in fiscal 1992 and $447,000 on net sales of $42.8 million in fiscal 1993. The company's first profitable year was 1994, in which it had net income of $2.1 million on net sales of $55.8 million. Total assets reached $37.1 million. That year Semitool doubled the size of its plant and introduced three new products: Equinox, Magnum, and Storm.

PUBLIC COMPANY: 1995–96

Semitool's debt, however, reached $13.5 million at the end of 1994, so Thompson decided to take the company public. About 30 percent of the outstanding common stock was offered to the public in February 1995 at $13 a share, with 60 percent of the money raised to be used for debt reduction.

Although a *Barron's* analysis indicated that the offering was pricey, Semitool's stock reached $36.75 a share, nearly triple the offering price, in July. With nine-month sales in 1995 double that of the same period in the previous year, Semitool announced a three-for-two stock split on July 24. Demand for Equinox, Magnum, and Storm had contributed heavily to a $63 million backlog of orders. Also in 1995, the company won a contract from the research-and-development consortium Sematech for the creation of a new furnace to cook batches of silicon-chip wafers and a $7.7 million contract to supply furnaces to a domestic manufacturer. It also agreed to acquire Semy Engineering, Inc., in 1996 and opened offices in Oregon, Italy, and Japan. During the year Semitool's factory was expanded again.

Semitool recorded net income of $14.9 million on sales of $128.3 million in 1995. With a five-year average annual return on equity of 42.6 percent, it placed ninth on *Forbes*'s 1995 list of the 200 best small companies in the United States. Company debt had dropped to $4.9 million by the end of the fiscal year.

Semitool's stock plummeted, however, in September 1995 and was trading at only $11.50 a share one year after reaching its peak. In a class-action suit filed in March 1996, a stockholder charged that the company's executives had issued false and misleading information while unloading their own shares, thereby enabling themselves to pocket $8.3 million before the stock fell in value. Thompson, who had been chairman, president, and chief executive officer of Semitool since its inception, held, with his wife, Leila, 51.2 percent of the stock at the end of 1995.

In February 1996 Thompson announced the largest sale in Semitool's history, a $23 million multi-year order for the VTP 1500 vertical furnace from a domestic semiconductor manufacturer. The company ended fiscal 1996 with net income of $15.1 million on sales of $174.2 million, both figures topping the previous year's totals. In October, however, Semitool announced it was reducing its workforce by about 10 percent because of soft demand in the semiconductor-equipment industry.

SEMITOOL'S PRODUCTS

Semitool's batch chemical processing tools were incorporating centrifugal spray technology to process wafers and substrates by exposing them to a user-programmable, sequenced spray of chemicals inside an enclosed chamber. The wafers, and the cassette and chamber in which they were loaded, were dried by centrifugal spinning coupled with a flow of warm nitrogen. Semitool's batch chemical processing products included the spray-acid and spray-solvent tools. They were also being used in the manufacture of a variety of products other than wafers. The purchase price of these tools ranged from $150,000 to $700,000, with prices (as for other Semitool products) depending on configuration.

The spin rinser/dryer was being used primarily for removing chemical residues from substrate surfaces with deionized water and utilized the same enclosed-chamber, spray-processing, and centrifugal-drying technologies employed by the spray-acid and spray-solvent tools.

KEY DATES

1978: Raymon Thompson founds Semitool in Orange County, California.
1979: Semitool moves its headquarters to Kalispell, Montana.
1981: Semitool begins shipping its products overseas.
1994: Manufacturing capacity is doubled.
1995: Semitool completes its initial public offering of stock.
1999: Sales plummet amid a severe downturn in the semiconductor industry, falling to $122 million.
2005: Financial consistency returns, as the company continues to focus on producing copper-circuit processes.

More than 20,000 of Semitool's spin rinser/dryers had been sold since the company's inception. The purchase price ranged from $10,000 to $150,000 in 1995.

The Magnum was a multi-module chemical processing tool that clustered the company's solvent, acid, and spin rinser/dryer capabilities into a single automated unit. It incorporated a company-designed advanced robot that employed fiber-optic communications, absolute positioning, and a linear motor track to ensure precise, reliable, and particle-free automated wafer handling. The purchase price ranged from $900,000 to more than $2 million.

The Equinox was being employed for substrate processing. Its capabilities included immersion, spray, ultrasonics, hydrofluoric vapor, and infrared heating, to address cleaning, stripping, etching, developing, and gold-plating applications. In addition to its customary silicon-wafer applications, the Equinox was being used to process ceramic substrates, thin film heads, and photo masks. It was selling for between $175,000 and $730,000.

The Storm wafer carrier-cleaning system was being used to clean and dry the cassettes and plastic boxes in which the wafers were being transported and stored. It employed a unique rinsing/spinning process that occurred inside an enclosed chamber. The price ranged from $190,000 to $400,000.

Semitool's VTP 1500 vertical furnace was designed to avoid variances in the process exposure times of individual wafers, thereby avoiding the nonuniformity inherent in traditional vertical furnace processing. Semitool's patented double-lift chamber design also permitted the heating element to be lifted away from the sealed process chamber, allowing wafers to cool more rapidly in a controlled environment and thereby saving time. The VTP 1500 also had the flexibility to be quickly reconfigured for varying processes and to be easily upgraded to accommodate larger wafer sizes. The price ranged from $550,000 to $950,000.

Semitool also was fabricating frames, consoles, and the components to fill them itself, rather than subcontracting for these materials. "All this is engineered here, and it's all built here," Thompson told a Montana newspaper. "It's very unusual for a company like ours to actually build the robots [but] we don't hesitate to design products and build products that require workmanship. We know it's tough for the other guys to do that."

At the end of 1995 Semitool had U.S. sales offices in Arizona, California, Colorado, New Hampshire, New York, North Carolina, Oregon, Pennsylvania, and Texas. There were also offices in France, Germany, Great Britain, Ireland, Israel, Italy, and Japan. (Customers outside the United States accounted for about 43.5 percent of sales in fiscal 1995.) The company's chief property was a 170,000-square-foot facility on a 110-acre site in Kalispell. It planned to build a facility in Cambridge, England, in 1996 for its European sales, service, and customer-demonstration operations.

STUMBLING INTO THE 21ST CENTURY

As Semitool progressed toward its 20th anniversary, it endured unprecedented hardship, watching record-setting results plummet spectacularly. Financially, the company peaked in 1997, when it registered $194 million in revenue, a banner year that was followed by a drop to $180 million in 1998 and a severe plunge to $122 million in 1999. Net income, which stood at $12.5 million in 1997, was obliterated by the end of the decade, resulting in a nearly $7 million loss in 1999. If it was any solace to Thompson and his management team, the cause for the drastic drops in financial figures did not arise from any wrongdoing on Semitool's part. The semiconductor industry, to which the company was inextricably wed, suffered its deepest downturn in more than 20 years, delivering a direct and crippling blow to Semitool's business. Thompson found some encouragement at the close of the century, reporting an increase in new bookings and shipments at the end of 1999 that seemed to suggest the worst was over. Semitool's financial performance for the next two years supported the belief that the notoriously capricious semiconductor industry was on the mend. The company's sales swelled to $239 million in 2000 and $256 million in 2001 and profits returned, but the recovery was swiftly followed by another devastating crash. The $256 million in sales recorded in 2001 plunged to $123 million in 2002, a year Thompson, in his annual letter to shareholders, referred to as "without a doubt, one of the most challenging years for Semitool." The company posted a numbing $14 million loss for the year, one year after it had reported a profit of $25 million. Again, conditions in the semiconductor industry were to blame, casting a pall over the company's offices in Kalispell.

Although the financial side of Semitool's business presented a bleak picture to industry onlookers at the time, the period also included some promising developments that provided some encouragement for the future. Semitool threw itself into the development and promotion of copper instead of aluminum as the metal of choice for the tiny metal line etched on chips. Copper, with greater conductive properties than aluminum, represented the future in Thompson's mind, enabling faster running chips because of its superior ability to conduct electricity and because it lowered manufacturing costs; copper circuits, for instance, only required room-temperature processes, while aluminum processes required an ultrahigh vacuum environment. The shift from aluminum to copper for semiconductor interconnects was a gradual one, a movement still underway midway through the decade. As Semitool prepared for the future, the eventual adoption of copper circuits by chipmakers promised to bolster the company's business. In the meantime, Thompson and his managers worked on repairing the company's business. Profits returned in 2004 and 2005, while revenues climbed from their nadir of $117 million 2003 to $190 million in 2005.

Robert Halasz
Updated, Jeffrey L. Covell

PRINCIPAL SUBSIDIARIES

Rhetech, Inc.; Semitool Europe Ltd. (U.K.); Semitool France SARL; Semitool Halbleitertechik Vertriebs GmbH (Germany); Semitool Japan Inc.; Semitool Austria GmbH; Semitool Israel, Ltd.; Semitool Italia SRL (Italy); Semitool Korea, Inc.; Semitool (Asia) Pte. Ltd. (Singapore); Scientech Corporation (Taiwan).

PRINCIPAL COMPETITORS

Applied Materials, Inc.; Novellus Systems, Inc.; Tokyo Electron Limited.

FURTHER READING

"Asian Troubles Mean Tight Cost Control for More Firms," *Electronic News (1991),* February 2, 1998, p. 60.

Cohen, Judy Radler, "Applied Materials Circles Semitool?," *America's Intelligence Wire,* November 9, 2004.

Detar, James, "Move to Copper Chips from Aluminum Brightens Semitool's Outlook," *Investor's Business Daily,* May 29, 2002, p. A8.

Dorsch, Jeff, "Semitool, SpeedFam Partner on Copper Interconnect," *Electronic News,* February 22, 1999, p. 10.

Fasca, Chad, "Semitool Scores Success with 300mm ECD Copper," *Electronic News (1991),* June 1, 1998, p. 67.

Malo, Patrick J., "New Chip-Furnace Deal Will Fuel Growth," *Investor's Business Daily,* July 11, 1995, p. A6.

"Montana Manufacturer Takes Dim View of U.S. Leadership," *D&B Reports,* November/December 1991, p. 30.

Schwennesen, Don, "Semitool Brass Accused of Lying, Insider Trading," *Missoulian,* March 9, 1996, p. B1.

———, "A Sweet 16: The Years Have Been Good to Ray Thompson and Semitool Inc.," *Missoulian,* June 18, 1995, p. F1.

"Semitool," *Barron's,* January 9, 1995, p. 29.

"Semitool Engineering Sells SEMY Subsidiary to Brooks Automation for $38.8 Million," *Electronic News (1991),* February 26, 2001, p. 29.

"Semitool Reports Drop in Orders, Headcount Reduction," *Electronic News (1991),* November 18, 2002, p. 15.

"Semitool Revises Financial Outlook," *Electronic News (1991),* March 26, 2001, p. 30.

"Semitool Stokes 3Q Sales; Stock Split Is Planned," *Electronic News,* August 14, 1995, p. 14.

The Stanley Works

1000 Stanley Drive
New Britain, Connecticut 06053-1675
U.S.A.
Telephone: (860) 225-5111
Fax: (860) 827-3895
Web site: http://www.stanleyworks.com

Public Company
Incorporated: 1852
Employees: 15,800
Sales: $3.29 billion (2005)
Stock Exchanges: New York Pacific
Ticker Symbol: SWK
NAIC: 332212 Hand and Edge Tool Manufacturing; 332213 Saw Blade and Handsaw Manufacturing; 332439 Other Metal Container Manufacturing; 332510 Hardware Manufacturing; 333991 Power-Driven Handtool Manufacturing; 335999 All Other Miscellaneous Electrical Equipment and Component Manufacturing; 561621 Security Systems Services (Except Locksmiths)

■ ■ ■

The Stanley Works is a manufacturer of a broad range of tools, hardware, and security products for the consumer, industrial, professional, commercial, and institutional markets. Stanley is a global manufacturer, with production facilities in 17 U.S. states and 14 foreign countries, and is one of the world leaders in hand tools. Approximately 40 percent of its revenues are derived outside the United States. Stanley is an old and successful company in a hidebound industry, metalworking, that has proven extremely vulnerable to foreign competition since the 1960s. The early 2000s have seen the company diversify further into the security business through a string of acquisitions; security products and services now generate a full quarter of overall sales.

STANLEY BROTHERS FOUNDED COMPANY IN MID-19TH CENTURY

The company was founded in 1843 by Frederick T. Stanley, a 41-year-old merchant and manufacturer whose previous work experience included stints as a clerk on a Connecticut River steamboat and as an itinerant peddler in the South. In 1831, Stanley, in partnership with his younger brother William Stanley, had opened a small facility in New Britain, Connecticut, for the manufacture of house trimmings and door locks. Though the business failed to survive the Panic of 1837, it seemed to have served as the prototype for a second manufacturing venture in New Britain, Stanley's Bolt Manufactory, which Frederick Stanley, again in concert with his brother, established in 1843.

The establishment of this "manufactory" marks the official beginning of the Stanley story. The company's name was adopted in 1852, when the Stanley brothers, along with five neighbors, were granted a charter of incorporation by the state of Connecticut for a newly organized firm, The Stanley Works. This corporation, initially capitalized at $30,000, was to be directed by Frederick T. Stanley, who was named its first president.

COMPANY PERSPECTIVES

In 1843, an enterprising businessman named Frederick Trent Stanley established a little shop in New Britain, Connecticut to manufacture door bolts and other hardware from wrought iron. Stanley's Bolt Manufactory was only one of dozens of small foundries and other backyard industries in town struggling to make a go of it by turning out metal products. But Stanley possessed a special innovative spirit and an uncommon passion for doing things right and his modest enterprise prospered and grew as The Stanley Works.

Today, 160 years after the company's founding, The Stanley Works is a worldwide manufacturer and marketer of tools, hardware and specialty hardware products for home improvement, consumer, industrial and professional use. The company stills bears not only Frederick Stanley's name but also the spirit and passion that drove him to succeed where others failed. The essence of that drive was summed up in 1877 by a widely read trade publication, Asher & Adam's *Pictorial Album of American Industry:* "The secret of this company's success is an open one--all who will may avail themselves of it, and all who do so will succeed--one word tells it all and that one word is: Excellence."

During its early years Stanley was one of hundreds of similar companies in antebellum America producing hardware and builders' goods. Frederick Stanley was not unique in perceiving an entrepreneurial opening for such goods in a nation growing and industrializing as rapidly as the United States. There were scores of shops similar to his in Connecticut alone.

If Frederick Stanley had an early competitive advantage, at least locally, it may have been in his manufactory's power source, a single-cylinder high-pressure steam engine, which he had purchased from the firm of William Burdon of Brooklyn. This relatively sophisticated engine enabled Stanley's Bolt Manufactory and, later, The Stanley Works, to produce goods—whether bolts, T-hinges, or wrought-iron straps—in a more capital intensive and efficient way than was the case in less automated shops in the area.

Nevertheless, the firm's early growth was not exceptionally rapid. Total sales were $7,328 in 1853 and $21,371 in 1854, and rose to about $53,000 in 1860, on the eve of the Civil War. Only after that conflict ended would the dramatic rise of The Stanley Works begin.

To say that the firm's rise postdated the Civil War is not to imply that the war itself was directly or fundamentally responsible. More significant than any war-induced demand for Stanley's products were deep-seated economic forces related to industrialization and increased market size and integration. Productivity gains made possible through mechanization and the creation, via the railroad, of an embryonic national market transformed the U.S. business environment in the late 19th century, presenting new opportunities to, and posing new problems for, most U.S. manufacturers. Alfred D. Chandler describes this transformation in his *The Visible Hand: The Managerial Revolution in American Business.*

In order to exploit new production and marketing possibilities and to overcome problems arising from oversupply and greater competition, Stanley developed new business strategies and structures. In so doing, it integrated and expanded its operations, and employed new productivity-enhancing and competition-dampening methods of production, marketing, and organization.

Such policies resulted in the dramatic growth of The Stanley Works. Frederick T. Stanley seems to have had little to do with the company's rapid postwar ascent; from the 1860s to the time of his death in 1883, he increasingly withdrew from active business operations, devoting more of his time to politics and civic affairs in New Britain. The animating spirit behind Stanley's rise was William H. Hart, whose career with the firm stretched from 1854 to 1918.

WILLIAM H. HART OVERSEES COMPANY'S DRAMATIC EARLY GROWTH

Prior to joining Stanley in 1854 at the age of 19, Hart, like a number of 19th-century industrialists, had worked in the railroad industry, as a freight agent and assistant station manager. Hart rose quickly at Stanley, assuming the position of secretary-treasurer a few months after joining the firm and in 1856, before he had reached the age of 21, winning election to the board of directors. From there, he gradually took on more direct managerial responsibility, eventually rising to the position of president, a post he held from May 1884 to February 1915.

Under Hart's leadership, the firm pursued a number of successful strategies that enabled Stanley to thrive even in the fiercely competitive business environment of the day. Hart expanded hardware production facilities in

KEY DATES

1843: Frederick T. Stanley founds Stanley's Bolt Manufactory in New Britain, Connecticut.
1852: Stanley incorporates his firm as The Stanley Works.
1884: William H. Hart begins long stint as company president.
1920: Company acquires The Stanley Rule & Level Company.
1962: Donald W. Davis takes de facto control of Stanley, beginning quarter-century at helm in which he revitalizes the firm.
Early 1970s: Stanley launches aggressive push into the consumer hand-tool market.
1997: New CEO John M. Trani launches major restructuring.
2002: Stanley acquires Best Lock Corporation, doing business as Best Access Systems.
2005: Facom S.A. is acquired for $486 million.

New Britain in 1866, for example, and in 1909 opened new facilities in Niles, Ohio, strategically located in the steel belt of northeastern Ohio, and in Canada in 1914. He helped to reduce Stanley's production costs by mechanizing operations to a greater degree and by repositioning equipment in his factories. Manufacturing technology improved dramatically under his helm (Stanley was particularly important in the development of a process for the cold rolling of wrought-iron strip) and the firm came to hold several significant manufacturing patents, including one issued in 1889 for the development of the first hinge to use ball bearings.

At Hart's urging, the firm made several small but noteworthy innovations in the marketing of hardware, packing installation screws along with the firm's hinges and shipping hardware in labeled boxes. In 1870, when Stanley opened a sales office in New York City, the firm began to devote attention to developing export markets for its products, a precocious strategy for the time.

Hart also tried to diversify the company and to develop a fuller product line. By moving into the production of steel strapping around 1900, for example, Stanley was able to not only diversify its operations but also vertically integrate to a degree. The move into steel strapping was to prove of major consequence to the company; Stanley was one of the nation's leading manufacturers of this product before moving out of the industry in 1987.

Stanley had an impressive record of expansion in the period between the beginning of the Civil War and the end of World War I. The company's net sales by 1872 had already reached $480,000, a ninefold increase over the figure for 1860. By 1919, the year after Hart stepped down as chairman of the board, net sales were over $11 million. Nor was Stanley's a case of growth at any cost; in 1877 the firm began an unbroken streak of yearly dividends. During World War I Stanley produced belt buckles, gas mask components, and ammunition tubes.

Although William H. Hart was the central figure in the rise of The Stanley Works—the company's trademark was heart-shaped for a time—Stanley survived his departure. By the time Hart retired as chairman in 1918, he had created a corporate culture and strategy conducive to continued growth.

ACQUISITIONS FUEL GROWTH: 1920–29

Stanley's efforts to reduce costs, often through external integration, and to diversify did not abate with Hart's retirement. For example, after years of trying, the firm was able to cut energy costs by purchasing, and later rebuilding, a hydroelectric power plant on the Farmington River near New Britain. Even more important, however, was the firm's 1920 merger with its crosstown neighbor in that city, The Stanley Rule & Level Company, an old-line manufacturer of measuring devices and hand tools, which had been founded in 1857 by a cousin of Frederick Stanley. The acquisition of Stanley Rule & Level, at the time one of the largest and most respected companies in its field, allowed The Stanley Works to increase its labor force by some 1,200 workers, its capitalization by 50 percent, and its net sales by $6 million. In addition, it brought Stanley the benefits of diversification, without distancing the company from its historical roots or its areas of experience and expertise: hardware, hand tools, and measuring devices were naturally complementary.

Stanley Rule & Level had long been active in the merger and acquisition business itself. As early as 1863 the firm had acquired a competitor, the Brattleboro, Vermont, rule factory of E.A. Stearns & Company. Two later acquisitions, that of the Atha Tool Company of Newark, New Jersey, in 1913 and that of the Eagle Square Manufacturing Company, a Shaftsbury, Vermont maker of carpenters' steel squares, in 1916, contributed significantly both to the company's growth and to its appeal.

Although similar strategies were being employed elsewhere as well, the consolidation of Stanley Rule &

Level into The Stanley Works, and the success of this consolidation, clearly spurred the development of one of Stanley's principal growth strategies in the post-1920 period, the aggressive pursuit of competing or related companies through merger or acquisition. Other, less dramatic, growth strategies were also employed. During the interwar period, the company continued to expand operations into new geographical areas, both at home and abroad. Stanley opened a woodworking plant in 1923, for example, in Pulaski, Tennessee, near timberlands which the company had acquired previously. By 1926 Stanley was producing hardware in Germany, and in 1937 the firm opened a factory in Sheffield, England, for the manufacture of hand tools.

Technological innovations also continued under Hart's immediate successors, at times furthering the company's efforts to develop a fuller product line and to diversify. Perhaps the most impressive individual innovation during the interwar years was Stanley's introduction in 1931 of the first automated entranceway in the United States, a technology the company patented under the name Magic Eye. The Magic Eye, which opened doors through the activation of a photoelectric cell, and other devices based on similar technology became mainstays of Stanley's product line. A number of other products were also introduced during the period, most notably a line of electric tools, which were produced under a new division established in 1929.

GREAT DEPRESSION BRINGS ON DECLINE

If Stanley's culture and strategy were still conducive to profits and growth, they were not enough to assure either. Between roughly 1930 and 1945, economic and political conditions were at work that minimized the difference corporate culture and strategy, good or bad, could make. Stanley's fortunes declined sharply during the Great Depression, which hit manufacturing and construction, and thus the tool and hardware industries, extremely hard. The company's net income was negative in 1932, for example, and, after paying out dividends, Stanley ran a deficit on its income account in 1934 as well.

Stanley's performance in the 15 years after 1930 was neither fundamentally shaped nor adversely affected by corporate decision-making. The four men who successively followed William Hart as president—his son, George P. Hart, who served from 1915 to 1918; E. Allen Moore, whose term began in 1918 and ended in 1923; Clarence F. Bennett, who was president from 1923 until 1941; and Richard E. Pritchard, who served between 1941 and 1950—each performed ably, but to little effect.

With the advent of World War II Stanley, of necessity, had been forced to retool, transforming itself for the most part into a manufacturer of military hardware. Annual sales rose significantly as a result, reaching $44 million in 1943. Yet wartime sales were just that; Stanley sold 460 million belt links for machine gun bullets and 36 million cartridge clips during World War II, but this contribution did not boost its postwar performance.

STRUGGLE DURING IMMEDIATE POSTWAR YEARS

The same management strategy that had helped the firm to succeed earlier limited the company's performance in the decades after the war. In emphasizing manufacturing matters, key decision makers tended to neglect the marketing and financial dimensions of Stanley's operations. This situation was particularly true between 1945 and the early 1960s.

Despite the fact that Stanley, like many traditional New England manufacturers, continued to produce high-quality products during this period, the company's expansion was slow and its earnings erratic. For example, Stanley's annual net sales, already over $90 million in 1951, had grown only to $95.4 million by 1960; moreover, the company's earnings for 1948, $5.25 million, were surpassed only twice between that year and 1965.

Stanley's sluggish performance in this period was shaped in part by structural factors. Much of the nation's basic manufacturing sector, the principal market for Stanley's products, was not mature, which dampened opportunities for rapid growth. Even when opportunities did present themselves in basic manufacturing—some segments of the metalworking industry did, in fact, grow rapidly during this period—Stanley, entrenched in its traditional lines, could not always move quickly. Indeed, were it not for the postwar baby boom, which boosted the U.S. construction industry and thus the demand for builders' tools, Stanley's record might have been worse.

While Stanley's management neglected certain key business functions, they were not totally inert and their policies were not ineffectual. Under the leadership of John C. Cairns, chief executive officer from 1950 to 1966, the company made several important acquisitions and continued efforts to expand to modernize existing operations. During the 1950s Stanley acquired the Humason Manufacturing Company of Forestville, Connecticut, a maker of springs and screw machine parts; the H. L. Judd Company of Wallingford, Connecticut, a large producer of drapery hardware; and the Florida-based Denison Corporation, a manufacturer of aluminum window frames and doors. In addition, in 1957 Stanley opened a 115,000-square-foot, state-of-the-art steel-strapping plant in New Britain, which nearly doubled the firm's manufacturing capacity for this product.

COMPANY REVITALIZED BY DONALD W. DAVIS

Nonetheless, as Stanley entered the decade of the 1960s, its management's recent performance had been disappointing. Fortunately for Stanley, a bright and energetic young executive, Donald W. Davis, the most important figure in the company's history since William H. Hart, was coming to the fore.

Born in Springfield, Massachusetts, in 1921, Davis joined The Stanley Works in 1948. He rose rapidly at Stanley and in 1962 was promoted from his position as general manager of the steel-strapping division to executive vice-president of the firm. With this promotion Davis took de facto control of the company, functioning as Stanley's chief operating officer between 1962 and 1966, when he was named president and chief executive officer.

In the quarter century between 1962, when Davis assumed control, and 1987, when he turned over day-to-day managerial responsibilities to Richard H. Ayers, Davis was able not merely to rouse Stanley from its long postwar slumber, but to transform the company into an aggressive leader in the globally competitive tool and hardware industry.

Stanley's rejuvenation program under Davis can be broken down into several distinct parts. Each part of the program was shaped by his recognition that if Stanley was to remain a central player in the industry, the company would have to become more competitive and would have to assume a more aggressive, growth-oriented posture. Davis believed that as world markets became more integrated, Stanley, as well as The Black & Decker Corporation, Snap-On Tools Corporation, and other U.S. tool and hardware companies, would have to face the harsh reality of global competition for the first time.

Davis called for increased competitiveness and faster growth at The Stanley Works. Under his leadership the company rationalized production and modernized plant facilities; aggressively pursued mergers and acquisitions, while at the same time divesting itself of poorly performing or nonstrategic divisions and product lines; identified new markets and penetrated such markets once identified; devoted much more attention to marketing and advertising; and exploited more fully international manufacturing and marketing opportunities.

In order to see these policies through, Davis, along with Garth W. Edwards, vice-president for finance, overturned company policy in the mid-1960s by taking Stanley into long-term debt. This gambit proved extraordinarily successful; over time, borrowed funds helped to accomplish Davis's goals without compromising Stanley's financial integrity through excessive leveraging.

Davis used retained earnings, equity capital, and borrowed funds to build a number of new plants (the hand-tool plant that Stanley opened in New Britain in 1964 was the largest in the world at the time) and to upgrade existing facilities. Between 1979 and 1983 the company spent about $55 million yearly on upgrades alone. In part as a result of such efforts, Stanley was able over time to substantially improve both its capital-labor ratio and its overall manufacturing productivity.

During Davis's tenure Stanley made more than 25 major acquisitions, including Berry Industries (maker of garage doors and operators; acquired in 1965); Volkert Stampings (stampings and components in the television, radio, spacecraft, and electronic equipment industries; 1966); Ackley Manufacturing Company (hydraulic tools; 1971); Compo-Cast ("dead blow" striking tools; 1980); Mac Tools (auto-repair tools; 1980); Taylor Rental Corporation (tool rental centers; 1983); Proto Industrial Tools (specialty industrial tools; 1984); National Hand Tool (mechanic's hand tools; 1986); and Textron's Bostich Division (fasteners and fastening tools; 1986). During the 1980s Davis streamlined the company by selling off its garden-tool and electric-tool businesses, its drapery-hardware business, and its steel and steel-strapping divisions. In 1986 Stanley sold its South African interests to local management.

SUCCESSFUL PURSUIT OF DO-IT-YOURSELF MARKET

Stanley's modernization, acquisition, and rationalization strategies under Davis were impressive. More impressive still were the company's efforts during the same period to identify and penetrate new markets. In particular, Stanley's early and aggressive push during the early 1970s into the so-called do-it-yourself (DIY), or consumer, hand-tool market paid handsome returns. This market, propelled by such factors as inflationary building and repair costs, a shortage of skilled tradesmen, and the movement of upscale baby boomers into older homes, became one of Stanley's largest and most profitable markets and one of its most important in strategic terms. Because the DIY market, unlike Stanley's others, was countercyclical, the chances that a general economic downturn would spell disaster to the firm were now significantly reduced.

In order to establish itself in the DIY market, and for other strategic reasons as well, Stanley, formerly a production-driven company, committed itself under Davis to developing its marketing capabilities. By working more closely with wholesalers and retailers of its products, increasing its market research, and, perhaps most importantly, making a sizable investment in television advertising, the company over time did just that. The phrase "Stanley helps you do things right," coined by Davis, became familiar in different languages around the world.

Stanley became a much more international company under Davis. Not only did the firm increase its commitment to exporting but it also expanded foreign production by acquiring facilities in Latin America, Canada, France, and Germany. Perhaps most significant of all, given geopolitical trends, was Stanley's 1986 move into the Pacific Rim with its acquisition of Taiwan-based Chiro Tool Manufacturing Corporation.

By the time Davis stepped down at Stanley—Richard H. Ayers, who had risen through the ranks since joining Stanley in 1972, succeeded him as president and chief executive officer in 1987 and as board chairman in 1989—the company bore little resemblance to the one Davis had taken over in the early 1960s. Stanley had not merely survived, but had flourished under his helm, with net income and earnings at all-time highs in 1989.

DIFFICULT YEARS

Unfortunately for The Stanley Works (and Ayers) the optimistic ending of the 1980s was quickly succeeded by the dark days of the early 1990s. First weak economic conditions contributed to flat revenues in both 1990 and 1991 and earnings declines of 9 percent in 1990 and 11 percent in 1991. Then the very future of Stanley as an independent company came into serious doubt through the appearance of a hostile takeover bid.

Stanley had itself taken over numerous companies in its long history but always companies interested in a merger, so it was somewhat ironic that the Newell Company initiated a hostile takeover attempt of Stanley in mid-1991. After initial friendly talks between executives of the two firms led nowhere, Newell, desirous of the respected Stanley brand name, began buying Stanley stock, acquiring a less than 1 percent stake, then filing a notice that it intended to boost this stake. Stanley responded in June 1991 by filing a federal antitrust lawsuit against Newell. Subsequently the state of Connecticut's attorney general, Richard Blumenthal, filed a similar lawsuit, which served to persuade Newell to abandon its hostile bid. In October 1992 a court agreement was reached whereby Newell promised to sell its Stanley stock within one year and not to purchase any additional Stanley securities or "seek to control or influence Stanley for 10 years." In return Stanley agreed to drop its lawsuit.

As he battled to keep Stanley independent, Ayers also sought out expansion opportunities through joint ventures and acquisitions, the most notable of which increased the company's overseas presence. A 1991 joint-venture agreement created Stanley Poland Ltd. to manufacture tools in the newly opened Eastern Europe. Among 1991 acquisitions were Mosley-Stone, a U.K. maker of paint brushes, rollers, and decorator tools; Nirva, a French manufacturer of closet systems; and Sidcrome Tools, the leading maker of mechanics tools in Australia. The following year brought Stanley a controlling interest in Tona a.s. Pecky, a major Czech manufacturer of mechanics tools. The domestic area was not neglected, however. In 1992 Stanley acquired American Brush Co., Inc., manufacturer of paint brushes and decorator tools; LaBounty Manufacturing, Inc., a maker of large hydraulic tools; Mail Media, a catalog marketer of precision tool kits consisting of Jensen Tools, Inc. and Direct Safety; and Goldblatt Tool Co., which manufactured masonry, tile, and drywall tools.

These acquisitions helped Stanley enter another period of sales growth, as revenues increased each year (to record levels each year) from 1992 through 1996, with the $2 billion sales mark reached for the first time in 1992 and $2.5 billion in 1994. Unfortunately, earnings did not keep pace with sales, and instead bounced up and down during this period.

Starting in 1993, the year Stanley celebrated its 150th anniversary, Ayers began making some restructuring moves in an effort to boost earnings. That year the company's 23 divisions were streamlined into 11. Ayers also sought to make selective divestments of units with low margins, and in 1993 sold the franchise operations of Taylor Rental, then sold the company-owned outlets the following year.

Ayers embarked upon a more aggressive divestment strategy in July 1995 as part of the "Four by Four" program. Over a four-year period Stanley sought, in addition to increasing revenues to $4 billion, to save $400 million by reducing operating costs by $150 million and assets by $250 million. In 1995 and 1996 Stanley exited from eight product categories; closed six factories, three distribution centers, and two support facilities; and eliminated about 550 jobs. In early 1997 the company completed the divestiture portion of "Four by Four" when it sold its garage-related operations to Whistler

Corporation. Stanley incurred 1995 charges of $85.5 million and 1996 charges of $47.8 million related to these restructuring moves.

RESTRUCTURING UNDER TRANI: 1997–2003

To reach $4 billion in sales by the year 2000, Stanley had to increase revenues 10 percent a year. Sales for 1996, however, grew less than 2 percent, and Ayers decided early that year to retire at year-end. Analysts quoted in *Business Week* felt that Stanley needed to bring someone in from the outside to shake things up and reinvigorate the company. Stanley's board did just that when it hired John M. Trani as CEO and chairman at the beginning of 1997. Trani had led the turnaround at General Electric Company's GE Medical Systems and had a reputation as a cost-cutter and tough leader.

Trani wasted no time getting started on a possible Stanley turnaround. In April 1997 the company announced a reorganization into a product management structure, aimed at strengthening the Stanley brand, focusing more on customers, improving new product development, and enhancing efficiency. As part of the plan, Stanley was reorganized into eight new product groups, supported by centralized manufacturing, engineering, sales, and service, along with a newly created corporate marketing and brand development function. Stanley also embarked on a massive cost-cutting program. From 1997 to 1999, 50 manufacturing and distribution facilities were closed, resulting in the termination of 5,300 employees, more than a quarter of the overall workforce. In step with the trend of the times, the company shifted a great deal of manufacturing overseas to locations where labor costs were lower. Restructuring costs of $238.5 million led to a net loss of $41.9 million in 1997.

As the restructuring was implemented, Stanley completed a couple of acquisitions. In November 1997 the firm paid $46.3 million for Atro Industriale S.p.A., an Italian maker of pneumatic fastening tools, collated nails, and staples, mainly for the industrial market. The following August, Stanley acquired ZAG Industries Ltd. for $129.3 million. Based in Israel, ZAG produced plastic storage products for the consumer market, including tool boxes, bulk storage containers, and shelving systems. Also during this period, Trani overhauled the firm's product lines, concentrating more on the best-selling products and introducing hundreds of new products. Among the most successful of the latter was the FatMax line of professional tools, which debuted in 1999 with the 25-foot FatMax tape rule.

Trani continued restructuring in the early 2000s. In 2001 a further round of plant closings was launched, involving 13 facilities and the layoff of another 2,200 employees. Restructuring charges for the year totaled $72.4 million. Completing its first acquisition in nearly three years, Stanley spent $79.3 million in April 2001 for Contact East, Inc., a North Andover, Massachusetts, distributor of tools and supplies for assembling, testing, and repairing electronics.

The most controversial move of Trani's tenure occurred in 2002 when he proposed reincorporating Stanley in Bermuda in a tax-avoidance scheme through which he predicted the firm would save $30 million per year. Arguing that the shift to Bermuda was necessary to enable Stanley to better compete in the global market, Trani soon gained shareholder approval for the move. But, amid the burgeoning corporate scandals of the time, pressure from the U.S. Congress and state officials in Connecticut forced Stanley to abandon the plan in August.

In a more positive legacy of the Trani era, Stanley began positioning security products and services as a major vehicle for growth in 2002. In November of that year, the company completed its largest acquisition yet, spending $316 million for Best Lock Corporation, which conducted business as Best Access Systems. Based in Indianapolis, Best Access produced both mechanical and electronic locks and related products as well as offering related security services. Best Access was combined with Stanley's existing security offerings, which included Stanley locks and StanVision video-based door opening and closing systems, in a unit that was eventually called Stanley Security Solutions.

In April 2003 Stanley began yet another restructuring, this one involving the closure of nine more plants, the elimination of more than 1,000 jobs, and $50 million in charges. The following month, Trani announced that he would retire effective at the end of the year. He left at a time when the company seemed poised to shift from restructuring mode to a more growth-oriented phase. In his final year, Stanley saw its revenues rise 12 percent, to $2.68 billion, but net income, under the impact of the restructuring charges, fell 3 percent, to $255 million.

2004 AND BEYOND: GROWTH THROUGH INDUSTRIAL TOOLS AND SECURITY, OVERSEAS EXPANSION

Under interim leadership headed by John D. Opie as chairman, Stanley completed several important deals in early 2004. Electing to concentrate on industrial tools and security solutions as its growth vehicles, Stanley sold its residential entry door division to Masonite

International Corporation in January 2004 for $161 million. That same month, two acquisitions were consummated. On the tools side, Chicago Steel Tape Co. and its affiliates (CST/Berger) were bought for $64 million. Based in Watseka, Illinois, CST/Berger specialized in laser and optical leveling and measuring equipment. In security, Stanley acquired Blick plc for $177 million, gaining a leading U.K. provider of security-integration, communication, and time-management solutions for the commercial and industrial sectors. In March 2004 Stanley purchased Frisco Bay Industries, Ltd. for $39 million. Frisco Bay was headquartered in St. Laurent, Quebec, and was a leading Canadian provider of security systems and equipment for financial institutions, government agencies, and major industrial corporations.

Also in March 2004, the search for a new CEO ended when John F. Lundgren came onboard as both chairman and chief executive. Lundgren had been president of European consumer products for Georgia-Pacific Corporation. Continuing his predecessor's focus on industrial tools and security solutions, Lundgren sold the firm's home decor business to Wellspring Capital Management LLC for $87 million in December 2004. The divested unit, which produced mirrored closet doors, closet organization products, and wall decor items, had contributed annual sales of approximately $150 million. During 2005 Stanley's security operations were bolstered through the purchases of Security Group, Inc., parent company of Sargent & Greenleaf and SafeMasters, and Precision Hardware, Inc. For the year, security sales amounted to fully 25 percent of the $3.29 billion in overall revenues, a huge jump from the 6 percent figure of 2000. Also acquired in November 2005 was National Manufacturing Co. for $173.6 million. Headquartered in Sterling, Illinois, and better known under its brand name, National Hardware, the acquired firm was a leading North American manufacturer and supplier of builders' hardware that served more than 25,000 outlets and had annual sales of about $100 million.

Lundgren's next move, the largest acquisition in Stanley's 162-year history, served both the objective of growth in industrial tools as well as a new goal: increasing overseas sales. In January 2006 Stanley acquired Facom S.A. from Fimalac S.A. for $486 million. Based in France, Facom specialized in hand and mechanics tools principally for the professional automotive and industrial markets and recorded 2004 revenues of approximately $445 million. Facom's focus on the professional and industrial sectors meant that there was little overlap with existing Stanley operations in Europe, which concentrated on the consumer and construction markets. All of Facom's revenues were generated outside the United States, which helped increase Stanley's total sales abroad from 30 percent to 40 percent, and also reduced the firm's dependence on retail customers in the United States. Having dramatically bolstered its presence in Europe, Stanley was likely to next target Asia, though Lundgren cautioned against the expectation of any immediate blockbuster acquisitions there. While revenues generated in Asia were growing rapidly, having doubled between 2002 and 2005, the $186.8 million total for the latter year amounted to less than 6 percent of overall sales.

Peter A. Coclanis
Updated, David E. Salamie

PRINCIPAL SUBSIDIARIES

Contact East, Inc.; National Manufacturing Co.; Precision Hardware, Inc.; Sargent & Greenleaf, Inc.; Blick International Systems Limited (U.K.); Facom S.A. (France); Frisco Bay Industries, Ltd. (Canada); Stanley Canada Corporation; Stanley de Chihuahua S. de R.L. de C.V. (Mexico); Stanley do Brasil Ltda. (Brazil); Stanley France S.A.S.; Stanley Iberia S.L. (Spain); Stanley Italia S.r.l. (Italy); Stanley Nordic ApS (Denmark); Stanley Svenskas Aktiebolag (Sweden); Stanley Technology Co. Ltd. (China); Stanley Tools (N.Z.) Limited (New Zealand); Stanley Tools, S.A.S. (France); Stanley Tools S.r.l. (Italy); Stanley UK Limited; Stanley Works Asia Pacific Pte. Ltd. (Singapore); Stanley Works (India) Private Limited; Stanley Works Limited (Thailand); Stanley Works (Malaysia) Sdn Bhd; Stanley Works (Nederland) B.V. (Netherlands); Stanley (Zhongshan) Hardware Co., Ltd. (China); Suomen Stanley OY (Finland); The Stanley Works Japan; The Stanley Works Limited (U.K.); The Stanley Works Pty. Ltd. (Australia); The Stanley Works (Shanghai) Co., Ltd. (China); The Stanley Works (Zhongshan) Tool Co., Ltd. (China); Z.A.G. Industries Ltd. (Israel).

PRINCIPAL DIVISIONS

Consumer Products; Industrial Tools; Security Solutions.

PRINCIPAL COMPETITORS

The Black & Decker Corporation; Makita Corporation; Danaher Corporation; Snap-on Incorporated.

FURTHER READING

Abelson, Reed, "Investors Wait for Stanley to Rebound," *New York Times,* April 11, 2000, p. C1.

Barmann, Timothy C., "Stanley Tools Up for Future with Acquisition," *Providence (R.I.) Journal,* April 13, 2001, p. F1.

Canedy, Dana, "Stanley to Cut 4,700 Jobs in Revamping," *New York Times,* July 19, 1997, sec. 1, p. 33.

Carlo, Andrew M., "Stanley Bows to Pressure, Backs Off Bermuda Plan," *Home Channel News,* September 2, 2002, pp. 3, 29.

———, "Stanley Works Acquires National Hardware," *Home Channel News,* October 3, 2005, p. 4.

———, "Stanley Works Sells Its Home Decor Business," *Home Channel News,* November 8, 2004, pp. 3, 33.

———, "Vive le Stanley: Acquisition Strengthens Tool Maker's Position in Europe," *Home Channel News,* August 8, 2005, pp. 3, 6.

Chandler, Alfred D., *The Visible Hand: The Managerial Revolution in American Business,* Cambridge, Mass.: Belknap Press, 1977.

Davis, Donald Walter, *The Stanley Works: A 125 Year Beginning,* New York: Newcomen Society in North America, 1969, p. 24.

Dubashi, Jagannath, "Donald W. Davis, The Stanley Works," *Financial World,* April 21, 1987, p. 60.

Gordon, Mitchell, "Tooling Ahead: Acquisitions Are Helping Stanley Works to Another Record Earnings Year," *Barron's,* September 23, 1985, pp. 60+.

Green, Hardy, "Once a Company Town, Always a Company Town," *Business Week,* September 27, 1993, pp. 28D–28J.

Haar, Dan, "Stanley Adds to Tool Box," *Hartford (Conn.) Courant,* July 19, 2005.

Hussey, Allan F., "Handyman's Friend: Stanley Works Maintains Growth As Toolmaker for Home, Industry," *Barron's,* October 3, 1983, pp. 59+.

Jackson, Susan, and Tim Smart, "Will the GE Magic Work at Stanley?," *Business Week,* April 21, 1997, pp. 144, 148.

Jacob, Walter W., "The Man Who Turned The Stanley Works Around: The Story of William H. Hart," *Chronicle of the Early American Industries Association,* December 2005, p. 162.

Johnston, David Cay, "Stanley Hails Bermuda Vote, but Employees Cry Deception," *New York Times,* May 10, 2002, p. C1.

———, "Stanley Voids Bermuda Vote and Promises to Try Again," *New York Times,* May 11, 2002, p. C1.

Kennedy, Julie, "Stanley Works: It's Nailing Down a Sizable Piece of the Do-It-Yourself Market," *Barron's,* August 10, 1981, pp. 50+.

King, Resa W., "Stanley Falls Off Its Ladder," *Business Week,* March 11, 1985. pp. 82C+.

Leavitt, Robert Keith, *Foundation for the Future: History of The Stanley Works,* New Britain, Conn.: Stanley Works, 1951.

Moran, John M., "Georgia-Pacific Executive to Be Chairman of Stanley Tool Works," *Hartford (Conn.) Courant,* February 6, 2004.

Plitch, Phyllis, and Glenn R. Simpson, "Bowing to Pressure, Stanley Works Drops Plan for Bermuda Tax Move," *Wall Street Journal,* August 2, 2002, p. A1.

"Proud of Our Past: 150 Years of Growth Through Excellence at The Stanley Works," New Britain, Conn.: The Stanley Works, 1993.

Rodengen, Jeffrey L., *The Legend of Stanley: 150 Years of The Stanley Works,* Fort Lauderdale, Fla.: Write Stuff Syndicate, 1996, 191 p.

Rosenberg, John S., "Focus on Consumers Helps Stanley Works Thrive," *New York Times,* October 5, 1980, p. CN21.

"Stanley Revamp May Close Some Plants," *Providence (R.I.) Journal-Bulletin,* April 30, 1997, p. F1.

"Stanley Tries the Faster Track," *Business Week,* November 5, 1966.

"Stanley Works to Cut 4,500 Jobs," *Providence (R.I.) Journal-Bulletin,* July 19, 1997, p. B10.

"Stanley Works Tooled Up for Brisk Operating Gains," *Barron's,* May 23, 1977, pp. 38+.

"Trani to Leave Stanley at Year's End," *Home Channel News,* June 16, 2003, p. 3.

Uchitelle, Louis, "Only the Bosses Are American," *New York Times,* July 24, 1989, p. D1.

———, "The Stanley Works Goes Global," *New York Times,* July 23, 1989, p. F1.

Weiner, Steve, "How Do You Say 'Tape Measure' in Chinese?," *Forbes,* June 25, 1990, pp. 96, 99.

Welsh, Jonathan, "Stanley Works Picks GE Official As Chief in Apparent Bid to Boost Overseas Sales," *Wall Street Journal,* January 3, 1997, p. B3.

Woods, Chelsie, "Best Access Retools; Here Comes Stanley," *Security Systems News,* November 2002, pp. 1, 12.

StarTek, Inc.

100 Garfield Street
Denver, Colorado 80206
U.S.A.
Telephone: (303) 399-2400
Fax: (303) 388-9970
Web site: http://www.startek.com

Public Company
Founded: 1987 as StarPak, Inc.
Employees: 6,700
Sales: $216.4 million (2005)
Stock Exchanges: New York
Ticker Symbol: SRT
NAIC: 561499 All Other Business Support Services

■ ■ ■

Denver-based StarTek, Inc. provides process management outsourcing services to major corporations in the telecommunications and computer industries, including supply chain management, provisioning management, customer care, product and technical support, and e-commerce fulfillment. The public company, listed on the New York Stock Exchange, maintains 20 North American operational facilities, seven of which are located in Canada. StarTek also owns Domain.com, a subsidiary that owns a number of Internet domain names, including wedding.com and airlines.com.

ORIGINS

StarTek was cofounded by Arthur Emmet Stephenson, Jr. He was born in Louisiana in 1945, the son of a businessman, Arthur Emmet Stephenson, Sr., who owned real estate, an automobile dealership, a manufacturing company, and a bank. The younger Stephenson was exposed to the world of commerce at an early age. By 12 he was sitting in on bank board meetings with his father. As he recalled later in life, "It never occurred to me to do anything other than start my own business." He graduated first in his class at Louisiana State University, receiving a bachelor's degree in finance in 1967, and while at LSU spent some time in Washington, D.C., working as an administrative aide to U.S. Senator Russell Long. Stephenson then entered Harvard Business School, earning a Master's of Business Administration two years later. During his time in Boston he picked up some practical business experience by serving as a security analyst for Fidelity Funds. After graduating from Harvard, he went into business for himself, eventually launching a dozen companies, one of which was StarTek.

StarTek was founded as StarPak, Inc. in 1987 by Stephenson, who provided the money, and Michael W. Morgan, 15 years younger, who provided the expertise. Like Stephenson, Morgan got an early start in business. When he was just 12 he made a successful bid to service his father's arcade business. Later he worked in a variety of jobs, including sign painting and the training of Arabian horses. He also became involved in a venture in California that packaged and distributed software. When that business shut down, he recognized that the trend of downsizing in the software publishing industry would open up an opportunity for a company to provide software packaging and distribution services on an out-

COMPANY PERSPECTIVES

Our Company mission is to provide our clients and their customers with the highest level of professionalism and service as we continue to find innovative ways to grow and improve profitability and shareholder value in a dynamic and fun environment.

sourcing basis. Stephenson put up the money and Morgan did the legwork in setting up the business in Greeley, Colorado. In 1990 Morgan became president and chief executive officer, and Stephenson served as chairman of the board.

Initially, StarPak duplicated customers' software, packaged it, and shipped it. The company soon moved toward offering complete product fulfillment. In 1989 a phone order service was added, followed in 1991 by technical support services. Corporate customers included Federal Express, IBM, Hewlett-Packard, and Sony. Work was done out of a pair of Greeley sites, a former health club and a former mobile-home factory. As the business expanded in the 1990s, StarPak bought the old Western Electric building in nearby Aurora, Colorado. A 1996 *Denver Post* article offered a glimpse of the way the business worked, using a CD-ROM commemorating Ohio State University's football history as an example. The independent software company "promotes the CD with a telephone number that rings in one of StarPak's Greeley buildings. The consumer pays for the disk by credit card and as the order is entered, a mailing label is printed, the disk is pulled from inventory and can be shipped within hours." For software that required technical support, StarPak trained people to provide help via toll-free telephone lines.

StarPak opened a facility in Singapore and gained a foothold in the European market by establishing a subsidiary in the United Kingdom. During the mid-1990s, StarPak also branched into the Internet field. Subsidiary Domain.com was formed and the company secured the rights to some three dozen web site addresses, paying $50 apiece. Stephenson kept the web site names close to the vest, but some of his favorites were gifts.com, wedding.com, and airlines.com. He also bided his time looking for partners to commercialize the sites, convinced that by having the right domain name a company did not have to spend nearly as much money in building the brand. According to a 1999 *Wall Street Journal* article, "That logic hasn't been lost on others pursuing Internet entry. I've been offered millions for some of these names, well into seven figures for some of them."

1996 IPO

StarPak's revenues grew steadily in the early 1990s, totaling $23 million in 1993 and increasing to $71.6 million in 1996. On December 30, 1996, Stephenson incorporated StarTek, Inc. in Delaware and two days later it acquired StarPak in preparation for taking the business public. With Morgan Stanley & Co. and Donaldson, Lufkin & Jenrette Securities Corp. serving as underwriters, the initial public offering (IPO) of stock, priced at $15 per share, netted the company more than $40 million. Nearly $10 million of that amount was earmarked to pay down debt, another $5.5 million repaid Stephenson, and more than $31 million became working capital to support StarTek's strong growth. In 1997 some of that money would be put to use in building a new Colorado facility and expanding the United Kingdom operation. When its first year as a public company was completed, StarTek reported a 25 percent increase in revenues to $89.1 million, and a 51 percent increase in net income to $5.9 million.

Expansion continued for the rest of the 1990s. StarTek brought three more new facilities into operation in 1998. The largest was a 305,000-square-foot manufacturing and distribution center that opened in Clarksville, Tennessee. StarTek also opened a 35,000-square-foot, state-of-the-art call center in Greeley, and a similar high-tech call center in Laramie, Wyoming. Three additional operations were opened in 1999. A 46,000-square-foot facility was built in Grand Junction, Colorado, to serve Internet, software, and communications clients. A 30,000-square-foot building was opened in Big Spring, Texas, to bolster StarTek's Internet support services. In addition, to keep pace with its rapidly growing provisioning management and E-commerce support operations, StarTek bought an 88,000-square-foot building in Greeley.

On another front in 1999, StarTek found a partner for its gifts.com web site, creating a joint venture, Gifts.com, Inc., with The Reader's Digest Association, Inc., which took an 80.1 percent stake, leaving StarTek with a 19.9 percent interest. The site was launched in the fall of 1999. After the announcement of the Reader's Digest alliance, the price of StarTek's stock jumped from $37 to $55 a share, an improvement even more dramatic given that shares were trading in the $8 range just a year earlier. About the only concern investors had was Star Tek's increasing reliance on business from Microsoft, which accounted for about three-quarters of its business.

KEY DATES

1987: The company is founded as StarPak, Inc. by Arthur Emmet Stephenson, Jr., and Michael W. Morgan.
1989: Phone order service is added.
1991: Technical support services are added.
1996: StarTek, Inc. is incorporated.
1997: StarTek acquires StarPak, and is taken public.
2001: Morgan resigns as CEO.
2006: Stephenson retires as chairman.

The company maintained, however, that it did business with a dozen different, independent Microsoft units, so that it was not likely to lose that entire amount of business in one stroke. The situation also was mitigated because in 1999 StarTek began doing work for another giant corporation, AT&T. StarTek closed the 1990s very much on the upswing, topping the $200 million mark in revenues in 1999 and posting net income of $13 million, a 52 percent increase over the prior year.

In the year 2000, StarTek experienced a slight decline in revenues, but net income improved 49 percent to $19.4 million due to improved efficiencies and a better mix of services. The company gained membership in the Russell 2000 Index and the Standard and Poor's 600 Small Cap Index. Moreover, in May 2000 *Business Week* recognized StarTek as one of the nation's 100 fastest-growing small companies, and later in the year *Fortune* magazine listed it among its fastest-growing companies as well, ranking it number 73. The year also saw the opening of two more facilities. A 48,000-square-foot building for technical support/customer care was opened in Enid, Oklahoma. StarTek's provisioning management operations also were strengthened with the addition of a new 54,000-square-foot facility in Grand Junction, Colorado. Furthermore, in 2000 StarTek struck a deal with WeddingChannel.com to exploit the wedding.com domain site.

StarTek expanded into Canada in 2001, opening three facilities—two in Kingston, Ontario, and a third in Cornwall, Ontario—and hiring and training 1,000 employees to provide call center support. But the year was the most challenging one the company faced since the early days. The economy began to sag, and then the terrorist attacks of September 11, 2001, severely impacted business for several days. Uncertain of demand for its services, the company kept its call centers fully staffed but realized little revenue during this time. When the accounting on the year was completed, Startek experienced a 9 percent drop in revenues in 2001 to $182.6 million, and net income fell to $4.9 million. The year also brought changes at the top ranks of management. StarTek's chief financial officer, Dennis Swenson, retired, and cofounder Morgan retired as president and CEO, although he stayed on as vice-chairman. He was succeeded by William E. Meade, Jr., who had a dozen years of experience with the American Express Company, where he rose to the rank of senior vice-president of Business Development and Global Operations and was involved in a number of strategic, planning, and re-engineering programs. After leaving American Express he became CEO of WebMiles, Inc. Another major addition to StarTek's management ranks was Michael Burke, hired as senior vice-president of Marketing and Sales.

CHANGING FOCUS IN THE EARLY 21ST CENTURY

Meade and Burke were brought in to help StarTek adapt its business model and marketing approach to a changing world. In particular, the company began to place even greater emphasis on outsourcing, which it considered to be a growth sector. Meade explained to *Customer Inter@ction Solutions,* "In the post-9/11 world, budgets have been cut, but we foresee that in 2003 companies are going to even more closely examine what their core competencies are, which means continued growth in outsourcing." Meade also forged an alliance with Novantas, a New York-based management consulting firm, serving industries such as finance, energy, publishing, and technology. Novantas used proprietary technology, such as Mindswift software, to help companies' call center personnel to test a variety of dialogue strategies to determine the best way to converse with a customer. Through the partnership agreement, Novantas gained StarTek's call center capabilities, while StarTek was able to enter some new industries and make available additional consulting options to its clients.

In general, Startek enjoyed a bounce-back year in 2002. Revenues increased to $207.9 million and net income more than doubled to $10.3 million. Business was even better in 2003. Revenues increased to a record $231.2 million, and net income approached $22.2 million. The trend continued early in 2004, and sales for the year reached the $250 million mark for the first time. The company even opened three new process outsourcing call centers to meet increased demand, located in Alexandria, Louisiana, and Lynchburg and Collinsville, Virginia. However, problems also began to develop, as the company lost volume in some of its more profitable services. The price of StarTek's stock suffered and the company began taking action. In order to focus its resources on the North American business process outsourcing market, StarTek chose in 2004 to sell its U.K. supply chain management operations. Business continued to slip in early 2005 and in February 2005, the company began laying off employees. The *Greeley Tribune* reported that the company had "security guards on Feb. 10 escort employees to their cars after suddenly laying them off." A week later Meade resigned. According to the *Rocky Mountain News,* he was "unexpectedly ousted." When the first quarter numbers were released several weeks later, it was revealed that StarTek had experienced a 14.2 percent decline in sales over the same period the prior year.

Chief Financial Officer Steve Butler took over as CEO on an interim basis and began the process of getting costs and headcounts in line with the current economic reality. In June he was named the permanent chief executive. By the end of 2005 he completed the sale of the company's Supply Chain Management Services platform, as StarTek now elected to focus on its Business Process Management Services platform. For the year, StarTek reported sales of $216.4 million and net income of $12.8 million. Changes continued in 2006, highlighted by Stephenson's retirement as of the end of May.

Ed Dinger

PRINCIPAL SUBSIDIARIES

StarTek USA, Inc.; Domain.com, Inc.; StarTek Canada Services, Ltd.

PRINCIPAL COMPETITORS

ClientLogic Corporation; NewRoads, Inc.; Sykes Enterprises, Incorporated.

FURTHER READING

Berry-Helmlinger, Lyn, "Call Center Staffing Company Dials 'S' for 'Success,'" *Denver Business Journal,* December 30, 2002.

"Emmet Stephenson: Profile of an Entrepreneur," *Harvard Business School,* October 21, 1997.

Fillion, Roger, "StarTek Abruptly Ousts CEO," *Rocky Mountain News,* February 22, 2005, p. 4B.

Freeman, Diane, "StarPak Wraps Up 1995 with 65% Revenue Hike," *Denver Business Journal,* April 12, 1996, p. 15C.

Graham, Sandy, "To Boldly Go," *ColoradoBiz,* December 1999, p. 42.

Greim, Lisa, "Software Service Firm Plans $14 Million IPO," *Rocky Mountain News,* February 11, 1997, p. 7B.

Leib, Jeffrey, "Job Growth Creates New Challenges," *Denver Post,* January 28, 1996, p. H-O3.

Locke, Tom, "As StarTek Draws Attention, Its Stock Climbs," *Wall Street Journal,* August 23, 1999, p. 5F.

Tehrani, Rich, "Everything Old Is New Again," *CustomerInter@ction,* November 2002, p. 10.

Straumann Holding AG

Peter Merlan-Weg 12 4002
Basel,
Switzerland
Telephone: +41 061 965 13 21
Fax: +41 061 965 11 03
Web site: http://www.straumann.com

Public Company
Incorporated: 1954 as Dr. Ing. R. Straumann Research Institute AG
Employees: 1,342
Sales: CHF 509.55 million ($388.95 million) (2005)
Stock Exchanges: Switzerland
Ticker Symbol: STMN
NAIC: 339112 Surgical and Medical Instrument Manufacturing

■ ■ ■

Straumann Holding AG is one of the world's leading specialists in the development, manufacture, and distribution of dental implant systems and regenerative tissue compounds. Based in Basel, Switzerland, Straumann invests actively in developing new implant technology, such as SLActive, the first hydrohilic implant surfacing technique that has provided significant reductions in patient healing times. Straumann has been expanding strongly, opening several new manufacturing plants, including a new state-of-the-art facility in Andover, Maryland, which also serves as the company's U.S. subsidiary's headquarters. Straumann has also been actively expanding its core range, notably through the purchases of Switzerland's Kuros Therapeutics and Sweden's Biora. These purchases formed the basis of the company's new biomaterials division, which develops soft and hard tissue regenerative products, such as Straumann Bone Ceramic, launched in 2005. Straumann has also instituted a policy of taking tighter control over its distribution operations. The strategy has included the purchases of its former distributors in a number of markets, including Italy, Korea, and, in January 2006, Denmark, and the establishment of new subsidiaries in Australia and Mexico. Straumann is listed on the Swiss stock exchange and is led by President and COO Gilbert Achermann and Chairman Rudolf Maag. Thomas Straumann, grandson of the founder, remains the company's largest shareholder, with nearly 39 percent of shares.

WATCHMAKER ORIGINS

Like many families in the Waldenthur region, the Straumann family was originally involved in watchmaking. Following World War I, the family, led by Reinhard Straumann, focused its interest in the materials used for the manufacturer of watches. Starting in 1920, Straumann lent his background in engineering to the development of new alloys that could be used for the production of watch movement. Straumann succeeded in producing alloys that provided such properties as resistance to fatigue and corrosion, while remaining non-magnetic. Straumann's alloys later found their way into watches produced by such famous watchmaking names as Rolex and IWC. Straumann's alloys were particularly important in the development of new spring types.

COMPANY PERSPECTIVES

Our vision is to become the world leader in the field of implant dentistry and dental tissue regeneration, and to be the provider of choice to dental professionals. Our mission is to enable dental professionals to restore their patients' oral function and esthetics through effective, reliable and safe treatment methods in implant dentistry and dental tissue regeneration.

Straumann set up a dedicated laboratory for his alloys research in 1938. By 1954, Straumann had succeeded in developing a commercially viable alloy and founded a new company, Dr. Ing. R. Straumann Research Institute AG. The company also launched a second activity, that of laboratory testing. Later, the company also added another offshoot, that of the production of ski jumping equipment. Over the next decades, the company's alloys played an important role in supporting the Swiss watchmaking industry's reputation as the center of the global watchmaking market as it came under heavy pressure from Japanese competitors in the 1970s.

In the late 1950s, Straumann, now led by the founder's son Fritz Straumann, began looking at new areas to extend its alloys technologies. The company teamed up with the Swiss Association of Internal Fixation (AO/ASIF), which had been looking for new materials and fixation systems for treating bone fractures. Straumann and the AO/ASIF began working together to adapt Straumann's alloy process for use in internal bone fixation devices. The partnership represented a breakthrough in orthopedic surgery, and Straumann quickly became a world leader in the production of internal fixation systems.

The seeds for the later Straumann Holding were sown in the early 1970s, when Straumann identified a new market, that of dental prostheses, for its growing range of implant technologies. By 1974, the company had produced its first dental implant using its alloys, conducting clinical trials at the University of Berne. The company's involvement in the new field deepened in 1980 when it became one of the founding members of the International Team for Oral Implantology, or ITI. The ITI, which originally started with 12 founding members, later grew to include more than 400 members by 2000, with more than 15 branches internationally.

Straumann began its own international expansion in the 1980s. The company began the decade with the establishment of a subsidiary in Germany. By the end of the decade, the company had also launched a subsidiary in the United States. The company also debuted an important advance in dental implant technology, known as the Morse taper connection, in 1986. Straumann's dental division remained quite small, however.

DENTAL IMPLANT TECHNOLOGIES LEADER

The death of Fritz Straumann in 1990 brought about the transformation of the company his father had founded less than 40 years earlier. At that time, the Straumann family decided to sell off the company in a management buyout. The new company, called Stratec, took with it only Straumann's osteosynthesis operations, which represented the major part of its business. Stratec later merged with Synthes, becoming Synthes-Stratec.

Instead of abandoning the company's small, but promising dental implant activities, however, Thomas Straumann, son of Fritz Straumann, led a second management buyout of this unit. The new company retained the Straumann name, becoming Institut Straumann. Under the younger Straumann, then in his mid-20s, the company now refocused itself as a specialist producer of dental implant systems.

Straumann set out to solve a major complication in dental implant surgery, namely the long recuperation period needed for the bone to integrate with the implant. This period lasted for as long as 24 weeks using competitors' implant systems. By the mid-1990s, however, Straumann had reduced its own system's recovery period to 12 weeks. Then, in 1997, Straumann achieved a new breakthrough, with the launch of its SLA implant system. SLA, which stood for "sandblasted, large grits, acid-etched," enabled a reduction of the integration process to just six to eight weeks, placing Straumann at the forefront of dental implant technology at the time.

The successful launch of the SLA system encouraged the company to prepare for a new period of expansion. As part of this effort, the company went public in 1998, listing its shares on the Swiss stock exchange. While Thomas Straumann remained the company's principal shareholder, a new management team was brought in to guide the group's new growth strategy.

As part of that strategy, the company began construction of a new state-of-the-art production facility at Villeret, Switzerland, near Berne. That facility was completed in 2000. The company also opened a new Technology Center at its Waldenburg home base that year, allowing the company to step up its research and

KEY DATES

1920: Reinhard Straumann begins researching the development of new alloys for the Swiss watchmaking industry.
1938: Straumann sets up a dedicated lab for alloy development in Waldenthur.
1954: Dr. Ing. R. Straumann Research Institute AG is founded for production of alloys, laboratory testing, and ski jumping equipment.
1960: Under son Fritz Straumann, company begins adapting alloys for use in internal bone fixture procedures.
1974: Straumann produces first dental implant, which undergoes clinical testing at the University of Berne.
1980: Company establishes subsidiary in Germany; becomes a founding member of International Team for Oral Implantology (ITI).
1986: Company debuts new implant technology using Morse taper connection.
1989: Straumann forms U.S. subsidiary.
1990: After Fritz Straumann's death, main osteosynthesis operations are spun off into Stratec in a management buyout; Thomas Straumann leads management buyout of dental implant operation, which becomes Institut Straumann.
1997: SLA implant technology debuts.
1998: Straumann goes public, lists on Swiss stock exchange.
2000: Company opens new state-of-the-art production facility in Villeret, Switzerland.
2002: Company adds second major operational division, Biomaterials, with acquisition of Kuras Therapeutic AG.
2003: Straumann acquires Biora, based in Malmo, Sweden, which is merged with Kuras Therapeutic.
2004: Company acquires Bio srl, the company's Italian distributor, as it begins expanding its direct distribution network.
2005: Company launches SLActive, which reduces implant recovery time to just four weeks; establishes distribution subsidiaries in Australia and Mexico; moves U.S. headquarters to expanded facility in Andover.
2006: Straumann acquires Danish distributor Dentech.

development effort. The success of the SLA system also drove the increasing adoption of implants, as an alternative to crowns, bridges, and dentures. By the early 2000s, the company was already forced to expand the Villeret facility.

EXPANDING TECHNOLOGIES

Straumann had also begun to look for new opportunities to augment its operations, while remaining focused on the field of dental care. In 1997, the company added further surgical capacity when it purchased the MODUS@System for maxillofacial surgery. This business remained just a small part of the group's overall revenues, which were instead driven by the rapid growth of the global implant business.

In the early 2000s, Straumann recognized another potential market, that of the development of biomaterials that could be used for the regeneration of soft and hard tissues lost to periodontal and other diseases. Rebuilding the bone support structure was an essential component in the successful implementation of implants. In 2002 the company made its first biomaterials acquisition, of Kura Therapeutics, based in Switzerland. That purchase was followed in 2003 by the acquisition of Sweden's Biora. The Malmo-based company's flagship product was the protein-based Emdogain, a breakthrough product used to treat periodontal disease. Following the acquisition, Biora and Kura were merged to form Straumann's second major division, Biomaterials.

Straumann moved its own headquarters to Basel in 2004, as it began to reposition itself as a truly international group. With the growing and rapid acceptance of implant technologies, the company adopted a new strategy of developing a direct relationship with its customers. As such, Straumann began expanding its sales and distribution network into new markets, while boosting its presence in its established markets. As part of this effort, the company began acquiring a number of its existing distributors, such as BIO srl, in Italy, acquired at the end of 2004, and DenTech.in Denmark, the acquisition of which was completed in 2006. The company also strengthened its presence in Korea, and established new distribution subsidiaries in Australia and

Mexico in 2005. The company also responded to its rising sales in the United States by moving its U.S. subsidiary's headquarters and production plant to a new facility in Andover, Maryland, in 2005. By then, the company's international network included some 18 subsidiaries, with sales to more than 60 countries.

At the same time, Straumann's research and development effort continued to turn out innovative products; indeed, by the end of the 2005, the company had completely renewed its product line. One new product came in 2005, with the launch of Straumann Bone Ceramic, a synthetic bone-graft substitute. That product was joined by another breakthrough, the launch of the SLActive system. The new generation of implant technology, which boasted the industry's first hydrophilic surface system, once again halved the osseointegration recovery period. Straumann had proved itself a driving force behind the fast-developing oral implant market in the 2000s.

M. L. Cohen

PRINCIPAL SUBSIDIARIES

Institut Straumann AG; Straumann AB (Sweden); Straumann AS (Norway); Straumann Brasil Ltda. (Brazil); Straumann BV (Netherlands); Straumann Canada Ltd.; Straumann Denmark ApS; Straumann GmbH (Austria); Straumann GmbH (Germany); Straumann Italia srl (Italy); Straumann Ltd (U.K.); Straumann Mexico SA de CV; Straumann OY (Finland); Straumann Pty Ltd. (Australia); Straumann SA (Spain); Straumann SA/NV (Belgium); Straumann SARL (France); Straumann USA, LLC.

PRINCIPAL COMPETITORS

Siemens AG; Fresenius Medical Care AG; B Braun Melsungen AG ; Centerpulse Orthopedics AG; Stada Arzneimittel AG; GN Store Nord A/S; Nobel Biocare.

FURTHER READING

"Sirona, Straumann to Develop Individualized Implant Prosthetics," *Dental Lab Products*, January 2005, p. 33.

"Straumann Group Relocates Headquarters," *Chemical Business Newsbase*, November 5, 2001.

"Straumann Holding," *Business Week*, October 24, 2005, p. 68.

"Straumann Is Growing Rapidly," *Chemical Business NewsBase*, August 13, 2004.

"Straumann Takes over Biora," *Chemical Business Newsbase*, April 26, 2003.

Stryker Corporation

2725 Fairfield Road
Kalamazoo, Michigan 49002
U.S.A.
Telephone: (269) 385-2600
Fax: (269) 385-1062
Web site: http://www.strykercorp.com

Public Company
Incorporated: 1946
Employees: 15,891
Sales: $4.9 billion (2005)
Stock Exchanges: New York
Ticker Symbol: SYK
NAIC: 339112 Surgical and Medical Instrument Manufacturing; 339113 Surgical Appliance and Supplies Manufacturing; 334517 Irradiation Apparatus Manufacturing

■ ■ ■

Stryker Corporation, founded by an orthopedic surgeon, makes the vast majority of its annual sales in the worldwide orthopedic implant and equipment market. Other business segments include the global endoscopic market, domestic outpatient rehabilitation services market, and the North American medical bed and stretcher market. Descendants of the founder own about one-quarter of the company.

1940–77: INNOVATIONS IN PATIENT CARE

Stryker Corporation was founded by Dr. Homer Stryker, an innovative orthopedic surgeon from Michigan. Stryker, born in 1894, started his medical career as a general practitioner in his hometown of Kalamazoo. After spending eight years in general practice, however, he decided to enter the field of orthopedics. He spent three years in an orthopedic residency at the University of Michigan Medical School at Ann Arbor before returning to Kalamazoo in 1940 to practice his specialty. He was 45 years old.

As an orthopedist, Stryker discovered that some of the medical products used in his field were less effective than they could be, in terms of both caregiver efficiency and meeting patient needs. While this was, no doubt, a common complaint of many physicians, Stryker's response was somewhat atypical. He began designing new devices to replace those that he found inefficient. His first such device was the Wedge Turning Frame, a mobile hospital bed with a frame that pivoted from side to side. This turning frame, which came to be known in the industry as the "Stryker Frame," allowed doctors to position injured patients as needed while still keeping them immobile. When his invention proved to be successful, Stryker formed the Orthopedic Frame Company, the predecessor to Stryker Corporation, to manufacture and sell the beds.

Stryker continued to pursue his medical career while at the same time overseeing his small company. As before, he found various aspects of patient care that needed improvement, and, as before, he designed and built

COMPANY PERSPECTIVES

At Stryker, we believe results speak louder than words. Since the Company's founding in 1941, that philosophy has made us a leader in the worldwide orthopedic market and placed us at the forefront of medicine's most promising solutions. Today we are one of the preeminent medical products and services companies in the world.

solutions. One of his next inventions was the Cast Cutter, a motorized saw that cut through patients' casts without cutting the skin underneath. As his company grew and began to manufacture a more diverse line of medical devices, Stryker insisted that each product either improve the efficiency of the caregiver or reduce the cost of providing treatment. In 1964, the name of the company was changed to Stryker Corporation.

Stryker's son, Lee, who became general manager in 1955 and then president of the company in 1969, ran it in much the same fashion as had his father. Stryker worked to improve and market the company's line of hospital beds and stretchers, which made up almost 70 percent of total sales. He also focused on the development of a series of innovative medical devices, including the first medical pulsed irrigation system and the first flume evacuator for bone cement. As Stryker grew the company's product line and sales presence, he maintained a very centralized form of management, keeping a close hold on all decision making.

In the mid-1970s, one of his top-down decisions had very negative results. After tinkering with his salespeople's compensation arrangement, switching them from commission to salary, Stryker found himself with virtually no sales force at all. While it was still in the middle of this sales force crisis, the company was dealt an even worse blow. Lee Stryker was killed in a plane crash in July 1976.

It was into this turbulent atmosphere that Stryker's new president and CEO, John W. Brown, entered in 1977. Brown, a 43-year-old native of Tennessee, had previously been in charge of a subsidiary of Bristol-Meyers Squibb that manufactured surgical instruments. When he was first offered the Stryker position in 1976, he declined. He was happy at Squibb, satisfied with his progress and thoroughly entrenched in the corporate culture. The Stryker board was persistent, however, offering Brown a second chance at the CEO position in 1977. That time he accepted, although apprehensively.

1977–83: JOHN BROWN'S COMPANY

Brown had definite ideas about what Stryker needed, and he moved quickly to realize them. One of his first moves was to rebuild the decimated sales force, changing the compensation structure back to commission. He also set up a formal budget, worked to trim operating costs, and established a procedure for managerial goal-setting. After instituting more formal management controls, Brown turned his focus to Stryker's product line. In addition to expanding the line of surgical power tools, Brown added a new category to the company's product line with the 1979 acquisition of Osteonics Corp. The three-year-old Osteonics was a maker of hip implants for joint replacement surgeries.

Also in 1979, the Stryker family decided to sell some of their stock in the company, and Stryker was taken public. It was at this time that Brown announced an ambitious goal for the company: a 20 percent annual growth rate from then on. He chose this goal because he had been told that emerging growth companies had growth rates of no less than 20 percent. Brown did not soft-pedal his expectations, referring to his 20 percent growth goal as "the law" and demanding that each and every employee do his or her part to achieve it.

Overall, Brown's early years at Stryker were not smooth ones. His style of management and straightforward attitude clashed with many of the existing executives, and his changes were not always met with enthusiastic acceptance. Rocky transition notwithstanding, Brown delivered on his promises; Stryker consistently showed no less than 20 percent annual growth. In 1981, it was named to the *Forbes* list of the Best 200 Small Companies in America, where it would remain for ten consecutive years.

1983–85: SWEEPING CHANGES

While Stryker was struggling through its own personal transitions, the healthcare industry itself was undergoing even greater upheavals. Since the passage of the Medicaid and Medicare bills in the mid-1960s, healthcare costs had skyrocketed. Between 1970 and 1980, U.S. annual medical care expenditures had more than tripled, triggering a social and governmental backlash. Concerned with excessive spending under the Medicaid and Medicare plans, the federal government began looking for ways to control those costs. In 1983, the Reagan administration instituted a new payment system for hospital patients on Medicare, which was designed to reduce unnecessary treatments and hospitalizations. Under this system, the Prospective Payment System, hospitals were reimbursed for the cost of care determined

KEY DATES

1941: Homer Stryker starts medical products business.
1946: Orthopedic Frame Company is incorporated.
1964: Name is changed to Stryker Corporation.
1969: Lee Stryker, son of Homer, becomes company president.
1977: John W. Brown heads company, a year after Lee Stryker is killed in plane crash.
1979: Company completes initial public offering, enters into orthopedic implant market.
1983: New Medica payment system undercuts sales to hospitals.
1985: Company embarks on collaborative research into osteogenic protein (OP-1).
1986: Company enters arthroscopy and endoscopy fields via acquisition.
1992: Stryker buys French spinal implant system maker.
1993: Stryker gains part ownership of a Japanese medical device business.
1996: Company enters trauma market with acquisition of Swiss company.
1998: Company nearly doubles in size through acquisition of Howmedica.
2001: OP-1 is launched commercially.
2002: Sales reach $3 billion; company is listed on *Fortune* 500.
2004: Stryker enters artificial disc market.
2005: Stephen P. MacMillan succeeds Brown as CEO.

by diagnosis rather than by length of hospitalization or actual services performed.

The Prospective Payment System took its toll on hospitals and on patients. Many treatments and procedures that had formerly required hospital admission became outpatient procedures. Hospital admissions dropped, patient stays became much shorter, and healthcare providers had to look for ways to contain their own costs. Unfortunately for Stryker, fewer hospital admissions meant the need for fewer hospital beds, the company's main source of revenue. To offset this slowdown, Brown led Stryker into new product areas that would be less affected by healthcare cost controls.

One such area was biotechnology. In 1985, Stryker entered into a long-term collaborative research program with Creative BioMolecules, Inc. The purpose of the collaboration was to develop an implant that utilized an osteogenic protein. The protein, OP-1, occurred naturally in humans and helped to promote natural bone growth and healing. Using DNA engineering, Stryker and Creative were able to produce this protein and began testing its use in animals. Early trials indicated that OP-1 stimulated the formation of new bone when it was implanted in bony areas that were not healing properly.

A year later, Stryker again added to its product portfolio with the acquisition of Syn-Optics, Inc. Syn-Optics specialized in endoscopic systems: medical video cameras, light sources, powered instruments, and disposable materials used in minimally invasive surgical procedures. Unlike the hospital bed market, the demand for endoscopic equipment was growing rapidly. Endoscopic procedures, which were usually done on an outpatient basis, were increasingly replacing traditional, more invasive procedures for a wide range of diagnostic and surgical applications. Stryker's newly acquired endoscopy business soon became one of its fastest growing divisions.

As the company's product line grew more diverse, Brown made a radical departure from Stryker's traditional management style. He completely decentralized the company, breaking it into several fully autonomous operating divisions. Each division head became responsible for setting the division's goals, establishing its manufacturing operations, and managing its sales and marketing efforts. Brown believed that in a business operating in diverse markets, decentralization was a natural choice. "Decentralization allows each division to run like its own business, and make quicker decisions about product and strategy," he said in a November 1994 interview with *Sales & Marketing Management.* "We want each autonomous division to enjoy all the thrills of success and all the anxieties of failure. There's nothing like running your own business," he observed.

1986–97: NEW PRODUCTS, NEW DIVISIONS

One byproduct of Stryker's decentralization was a closer relationship between sales staff and customers. Whereas previously sales reps had been responsible for selling the whole gamut of Stryker's products, the decentralization allowed them to narrow their focus. They became better acquainted with a smaller product portfolio and thus better able to understand and respond to their customers' needs. From these closer customer relationships, salespeople began to garner ideas for new products and for ways to improve existing ones. Stryker responded to this influx of product ideas by sinking more money into research and development. Between 1986 and 1991, the company almost quadrupled its research and development (R&D) budget, and doubled its product line.

The 1990s ushered in a flurry of acquisitions for Stryker. In 1992, the company acquired Dimso S.A., a French maker of spinal implant systems used for patients with degenerative spinal diseases and spinal injuries. Another acquisition followed in 1993, when Stryker bought an interest in Matsumoto Medical Instruments, Inc. Matsumoto was one of the largest distributors of medical devices in Japan. In 1994, the company purchased a product line called Steri-Shield from a private company. Steri-Shield was a personal protection system that helped protect operating room personnel from infectious diseases. Stryker entered the market for orthopedic trauma treatment systems in 1996 with the acquisition of Osteo AG. The Switzerland-based Osteo was a maker of equipment used to set bone fractures.

At the same time Stryker was expanding via acquisition, its existing businesses were meeting Brown's goal of growing by 20 percent each year. The company's revenues steadily ratcheted up, increasing from sales of $280.6 million in 1990 to $980.1 million in 1997. Net earnings followed suit, from $33.5 million in 1990 to $125.3 million in 1997. Its consistent success won high favor from Wall Street pundits, industry analysts, and even a U.S. president. In 1992, President George H. W. Bush paid a visit to Kalamazoo to recognize Stryker for its achievements. "Stryker is celebrated across the nation and around the world for the quality of your work and the excellence of the management, the way it's handled," Bush said in an address to Stryker employees. "You're leaders in an innovative industry that makes our country proud."

BECOMING A BIG PLAYER

Near the end of 1998, Stryker acquired Howmedica, the orthopedic division of Pfizer, Inc., for $1.65 billion. Howmedica developed and manufactured specialty medical products used to treat musculoskeletal disorders. Its main products included hip and knee implants, bone cement, and trauma systems for bone repair. Through its subsidiary, Leibinger, Howmedica also manufactured products and instruments used in craniofacial surgery. Howmedica was integrated with Stryker's Osteonics division, which was renamed Howmedica Osteonics.

The purchase of Howmedica was highly significant in that it transformed Stryker from a small player into a very large one. Brown's decision to make this jump had much to do with the changing face of the healthcare marketplace. For the prior several years, a trend toward consolidation had been sweeping the industry. Increasingly, independent hospitals and surgery centers were being absorbed into large healthcare conglomerates. As a result, purchasing power was often centralized, and physician preference became less significant than economies of scale. Stryker, who had built its sales approach on personal relationships with individual decision-makers, realized that it could not compete effectively as a small company any longer. "Larger institutions and buying groups are demanding ever-higher quality at ever-lower cost, and they prefer to deal with clearly identified market leaders," Brown wrote in his 1998 letter to shareholders, adding, "In this environment, only companies that offer scale and superior efficiency will succeed."

As Stryker wound down its sixth decade in business, it remained true to its growth goal. Although the purchase of Howmedica broke its 21-year streak of 20 percent net earnings increases, the company expected to return to its historical growth rate as early as the year 2000. Its long-term growth strategy centered around the global marketing of diversified product lines with an orthopedic core. With well-developed markets in the United States and Asia, Stryker planned to improve its position in Europe, Australia, and the rest of the world. It also planned to continue aggressively developing and marketing new, innovative products within its key markets, as well as improving and expanding its existing lines.

Late in the 1990s, Stryker Corporation was developing and manufacturing specialty surgical and medical products for healthcare markets around the world. The company's product lines included various powered surgical instruments, orthopedic implants, trauma systems for use in bone repair, endoscopic systems, and patient care and handling equipment such as stretchers and hospital beds. Stryker also provided outpatient rehabilitative physical therapy through its Physiotherapy Associates Inc. subsidiary, and was engaged in clinical testing of a patented bone growth protein through its Stryker Biotech subsidiary. The company was broken into ten discrete operating divisions: Howmedica Osteonics; Stryker Endoscopy; Stryker Instruments; Stryker Medical; Physiotherapy Associates; Stryker Pacific; Stryker Europe; Matsumoto Medical Instruments; Stryker Americas; and Stryker Biotech. Each division operated as its own entity and produced its own line of health-related products or services. In 1999, annual sales reached $2.1 billion, and by January 2000 Stryker's earnings had rebounded from the Howmedica purchase.

GOING FOR FLUID MOVEMENT: 2001–05

Brown's formula for success continued to produce results. Michael A. Verespej wrote for *Chief Executive (U.S.)* in

June 2002: "Last year Stryker's net income increased 21 percent, matching the compounded annual growth rate of the past decade and pushing its 25-year compound growth rate to near 24 percent. In this year's first quarter, net earnings were 27 percent higher than the first quarter of 2001. 'They are hitting on all cylinders right now,' asserts Katherine Martinelli, medical technology analyst in the New York office of Merrill Lynch. 'Their earnings are well above the industry average of 13 to 14 percent.'"

External factors favored Stryker in the early years of the new century. With many high growth technology companies down and out, investors began flocking to the medical equipment sector. Stryker and its competitors stood to be the beneficiaries of ailments inherent to an aging U.S. population; moreover, they engaged in product sales relatively independent to swings of the economy.

While demand for knee and hip replacements was expected to continue to grow, pricing faced a drop-off. The cost of implants had risen an estimated 90 percent since the early 1990s, according to *Business Week Online.* In terms of product development, the industry was keyed in on improving existing products.

The device manufacturers continued to be attentive to crucial relationships with surgeons inserting their products. Patients, meanwhile, benefited from technology changes, undergoing less invasive procedures using longer lasting and more maneuverable artificial joints.

Stryker and competitor Zimmer Holdings Inc. engaged in advertising directed at the public in the fall of 2003. Golf legend Arnold Palmer touted Stryker's ceramic and titanium implant in a television ad run during *60 Minutes.* Departing from industry norm, ads for the complex medical device drew critics. According to the *New York Times,* patient advocates voiced concerns over the lack of information about risks inherent to such implant surgery. The Food and Drug Administration required pharmaceutical companies to follow strict guidelines for their ads, but the agency regulated ads for artificial hearts and pacemakers, only, with other devices falling under the Federal Trade Commission rules.

Historically, device makers marketed their products to surgeons, often making first contact during their medical training. Many of the leaders in the field helped companies improve their products and also trained students in implant procedures.

John Brown relinquished his management position at the end of 2004. During his 27 years at the helm, Stryker produced average annual earnings growth of 22 percent. The anticipated change put pressure on the stock during the later half of 2004. Additionally, investors were cashing in on the recent upswing in stock price. Costs related to the purchase of a spinal device company and delays in a new product also took a toll, according to *Business Week.*

Former pharmaceuticals executive Stephen P. MacMillan succeeded Chairman Brown as CEO. MacMillan joined Stryker in June 2003, coming from Pharmacia Corp. Prior to that he marketed consumer products, including Tylenol, for Johnson & Johnson. He envisioned a new source of growth through biotech products, such as OP-1, which was commercially launched in 2001. Selective additional acquisitions and increased in-house product development rounded out his game plan for Stryker.

However, the competition had plans in motion. Johnson & Johnson's DePuy and Zimmer had introduced products comparable to Stryker's longer lasting, higher priced ceramic and titanium joints. OP-1, although used in Europe and Asia, had FDA approval for only very limited use as U.S. clinical trials continued.

Although Stryker held a 24 percent share in the artificial hip and 19 percent in the artificial knees markets, artificial spine disk products brought on board through the 2004 SpineCore, Inc. acquisition were still in clinical trials. Powerhouse medical device maker Medtronic Inc. held nearly half of the spinal products market.

Orthopedics remained Stryker's biggest moneymaker midway through the first decade of the twenty-first century. Stryker and DePuy led the market followed by Zimmer. While Stryker continued along a track of solid growth other factors came into play. "Actually, 20 percent earnings per share growth is our second most important metric," MacMillan told the *New York Times* in March 2005. "The most important thing we need to do is to make sure we continue to run the company in an ethical manner where we don't bend the rules to meet our goals."

The Justice Department had begun looking into the practices of large orthopedics manufacturers in 2005 in respect to their relationships with hip and knee surgeons, as well as medical students. DePuy, Biomet Inc., and Stryker were among the companies under scrutiny. As for the highlights of the year, Stryker's net sales and net earnings continued their upward trajectory.

Shawna Brynildssen
Updated, Kathleen Peippo

PRINCIPAL SUBSIDIARIES

Howmedica Osteonics.

PRINCIPAL COMPETITORS

DePuy, Inc.; Smith & Nephew plc; Zimmer Holdings, Inc.

FURTHER READING

"Bigger Niche at Stryker," *New York Times,* December 16, 1980.

Brewer, Geoffrey, "20 Percent—or Else," *Sales & Marketing Management,* November 1994, p. 66.

Feder, Barnaby J., "A Parts Supplier to an Aging Population," *New York Times,* March 26, 2005, p. 1C.

———, "Subpoenas Seek Data on Orthopedics Makers' Ties to Surgeons," *New York Times,* March 31, 2005, p. C12.

Gowrie, David, "Giving Back the Ability to Walk," *Hackensack (New Jersey) Record,* October 28, 1998.

Jones, John A., "Stryker Keeps Moving with Strong Research Commitment," *Investor's Business Daily,* January 20, 1992.

Kerwin, Kathleen, and Michael Arndt, "Knees and Hips—And Now What?" *Business Week,* December 6, 2004, p. 64.

Kramer, Farrell, "Stryker Becomes a Synonym for Consistency," *Investor's Business Daily,* July 6, 1990.

"Medical Technologies Company Reports Q4 2005 Net Sales Up 10.6% Over 2004," *World Disease Weekly,* February 9, 2006.

Peterson, Melody, "Campaign for Medical Device Bypasses Doctors," *New York Times,* October 30, 2003, p. C1.

Rogers, Doug, "Stryker Skillfully Handles a Steady Run of New Products," *Investor's Business Daily,* March 21, 1991.

Sawaya, Zina, "Focus Through Decentralization," *Forbes,* November 11, 1999, p. 242.

Seebacher, Noreen, "Stryker Products: Just What the Doctor Ordered," *Detroit News,* May 6, 1991.

Stavro, Barry, "The Hipbone's Connected to the Bottom Line," *Forbes,* December 3, 1984.

Stroud, Michael, "Stryker: Another Play on Endoscopy Boom," *Investor's Business Daily,* October 25, 1991.

Tsao, Amy, "Online Extra: Biomet and Stryker: Stocks with Legs," *Business Week Online,* April 21, 2003.

Verespej, Michael J., "Recession? What Recession? Southern Gentleman John Brown Achieves 20 Percent Earnings Growth Annually—No Matter What," *Chief Executive* (U.S.), June 2002, pp. 45+.

SunOpta Inc.

2838 Bovaird Drive West
Norval, Ontario L0P 1K0
Canada
Telephone: (905) 455-1990
Fax: (905) 455-2529
Web site: http://www.sunopta.com

Public Company
Incorporated: 1973 as Stake Technology, Ltd.
Employees: 1,800
Sales: $426.1 million (2005)
Stock Exchanges: NASDAQ Toronto
Ticker Symbols: STKL; SOY
NAIC: 424490 Other Grocery and Related Products Merchant Wholesalers; 311222 Soybean Processing; 115114 Postharvest Crop Activities (Except Cotton Ginning); 562111 Solid Waste Collection

■ ■ ■

SunOpta Inc. is one of Canada's largest publicly traded food producers, primarily focusing on natural, organic, kosher, and specialty foods. SunOpta's food ingredients and packaged products are sold worldwide in the retail private label, foodservice, and industrial markets and can be found in many popular grocery stores across North America such as Kroger, Whole Foods, Meijer, Trader Joe's, and Loblaws. SunOpta also operates an industrial materials recycling business and has a division that makes steam explosion technology systems for the bio-fuel, food processing, and pulp industries.

EARLY YEARS OF EXPERIMENTATION AND COLLABORATION

From its beginnings as Stake Technology Ltd. in Ontario, Canada, in 1973, SunOpta Inc. has always tried to be environmentally friendly. The pioneering enterprise was founded on patented technology designed to convert agricultural and forestry byproducts such as wood chips, corn stalks, and straw from low-grade wasted biomass into usable products.

Stake's first commercial venture with its proprietary "steam explosion" technology involved turning hardwood trees into food for cattle, sheep, and goats. With a company sales brochure that declared, "Trees are really only tall grass," Stake's product claimed to replace the traditional use of corn, hay, or potatoes as roughage additives for livestock diets. With help from the Canadian government, Stake had set up its first commercial biomass conversion plant in Maine by 1980.

In 1990, Stake announced a joint venture with a Venezuelan company to produce cattle feed from sugarcane bagasse (what's left of the stalk after its juice has been extracted) using Stake equipment in a South American facility. Stake also formed Recoupe Recycling Technologies, a partnership with Chesapeake Corp. of Richmond, Virginia, to advance Stake's steam explosion process for recycling paper. Stake claimed its technology lowered capital and operating costs, and reduced energy and chemical consumption over traditional recycling methods.

Stake's first big contract came in 1992 in a CAD 2.75 million deal with Consumer's Paper to supply a

COMPANY PERSPECTIVES

To rapidly grow our revenues, profits and shareholder value through an effective balance of internal growth and acquisition, with a focus on integrated business models in the natural, organic and specialty food markets.

steam explosion pulping system to recycle mixed office waste into toilet paper, paper towels, and napkins at a Consumer's facility in Red Cliff, Alberta. In 1992, a Stake steam explosion digester also became part of a new technology demonstration plant for the production and recycling of biobased materials. DeNovo Corporation, in which Stake was the majority shareholder, entered into a joint venture with the Biobased Materials Center of Virginia Tech, in Blacksburg, Virginia. The plant marked the first in the United States where research, development, and testing of environmentally friendly technologies using renewable and recyclable resources were conducted.

The first quarter of 1992 produced a 15-fold increase in sales, to CAD 980,000 and record net profits of CAD 872,000, compared to a profit of CAD 58,000 in the previous year's first quarter. The gains were attributed to a project to supply an advanced biomass separation demonstration plant to ENEA, the Italian Commission for New Technology for Energy and the Environment. The plant, located in Trisaia, Italy, was near completion at the time.

1995: STAKE BUYS INDUSTRIAL RECYCLING BUSINESS

In January 1995, Stake invested CAD 800,000 to acquire 51 percent of Barnes Environmental Inc., a company formed to buy the assets of Barmin Inc., a failed industrial recycling business. Barmin, an Ontario-based company that specialized in recycling and the sale of industrial minerals, had sales of CAD 14.7 million before succumbing to substantial debt from investments into unsuccessful non-core businesses.

In a complicated deal, Barnes purchased the assets and business of Barmin with a loan, and then Stake bought a majority of Barnes with CAD 800,000 that it borrowed from its principal banker. With the purchase, Stake's management saw an opportunity to combine the recycling technology of their steam explosion process with Barnes's industry knowledge of recycling markets in North America.

In August, Stake made its first sale to the pulp and paper industry, a deal with Weyerhaeuser Co. of Tacoma, Washington, to supply its pulping system to one of Weyerhaeuser's major operating facilities. After raising $3.5 million in October from DGC Entertainment Ventures Corp., an investment fund looking to diversify its portfolio, Stake in November purchased the remaining 49 percent of Barnes Environmental Inc.

The acquisition of Barnes proved a great success for Stake as it saw its sales for 1995 soar to CAD 10.8 million compared to a paltry CAD 174,000 for 1994. Most of the growth was fueled through sales of Barshot, the market name for specular hematite, a recyclable abrasive product used in cleaning metal surfaces. A sharp-edged, high-density, non-rusting iron ore, Barshot, according to Barnes, not only cleaned rust and paint from metal more quickly than other blasting materials, but was free of heavy metals and silica, which had been directly linked to various forms of silicosis, a potentially debilitating lung disease. The popularity of Barshot led to the November 1997 opening of a distribution center for the company's abrasive products in New Orleans, thus adding a third location to Barnes's existing operations in Ontario and in Lachine, Quebec.

In 1998, hoping to expand its markets, Stake acquired AJF Inc. of New Boston, Michigan, a manufacturer of industrial products including chromite ore used in the foundry and steel industries. Like Stake's acquisition of Barnes, and virtually all future acquisitions, AJF's management, employees, and corporate structure remained in place, while only a handful of employees continued to oversee company operations at Stake's corporate offices in Norval, Ontario. By the end of 1998 Stake's annual sales revenue had more than doubled from 1995 to over CAD 22 million.

1999: LAUNCH OF HEALTH FOODS BUSINESS

The acquisition in August 1999 of Sunrich Inc., an agritech company headquartered in Hope, Minnesota, was Stake's first significant step in launching its food business. Sunrich supplied major food producers in the United States and Japan with specialty grains and premium food ingredients and had sales of $30 million in 1998. Its product line included non-GMO (non-genetically modified organisms), organic, and identity preserved varieties of corn and soybeans, soy powders and concentrates, and organic starches.

Stake's investment in Sunrich received a significant boost in October 1999 when the U.S. Food and Drug Administration declared that soy protein could help reduce the risk of heart disease, the leading cause of

KEY DATES

1973: SunOpta is founded as Stake Technology Ltd. in Ontario, Canada.

1992: Stake's first big contract is to supply its patented steam explosion pulping system for paper recycling.

1995: Stake acquires Barnes Environmental Inc., an industrial recycling business.

1999: Stake buys Sunrich Inc., a major U.S. soybean producer.

2003: Stake changes name to SunOpta to better reflect "environmental and organic commitment."

2004: SunOpta leads North America in soymilk concentrate sales; company ranks as world's largest supplier of oat fiber.

2005: SunOpta completes Canada's first national distribution network for natural and organic foods.

death in the United States, and recommended 25 grams of soy protein a day as part of a healthy diet low in saturated fat and cholesterol. Stake's total 1999 sales rose 116 percent to CAD 47.5 million from CAD 22 million the year before and Stake was named by *Profit* magazine in its 1999 "Profit 100" as the fifth fastest growing company in Canada over the previous five years.

With Sunrich as the anchor, Stake began further expansion of its food business in September 2000 with the acquisition of Northern Food and Dairy, Inc., a producer of 65 percent of the soymilk sold in the United States, with manufacturing facilities in Alexandria and Bertha, Minnesota. At about the same time, Stake bought a separate soymilk-packaging facility, also in Alexandria.

March 2001 saw Stake acquire First Light Foods Inc., a Minneapolis-based marketing firm and a supplier of soymilk to major retailers. In September, Stake and Northern Food & Dairy created a joint venture called Star Valley Natural Foods and purchased a plant and equipment to manufacture soymilk in Afton, Wyoming, for the West Coast market. Together they also opened a plant in Fosston, Minnesota, that produced a natural preservative for the European market. By the middle of October, Stake had to double the capacity of its soymilk plant in Wyoming due to greater than expected demand.

Stake launched a new division in March 2002, Sunrich Valley, to promote its entry into the organic milk market with "MU," the brand name for a full range of organic milk and butter products. With plenty of new products to sell, Stake in 2002 sought to shore up its distribution needs and in October signed an agreement with Quebec-based Natrel, which had a network of 83 distribution centers that serviced more than 30,000 retail outlets. By the end of the year Stake had acquired two more distributors of organic and natural food products, Wild West Organic Harvest Co-operative Association, in Vancouver, British Columbia, and the Toronto-based Simply Organic Co. Ltd.

Stake closed out 2002 by buying Opta Food Ingredients, Inc., of Bedford, Massachusetts, a supplier of food ingredients to more than 350 food companies, which included 12 of the largest U.S. consumer packaged food companies and three of the world's largest quick-service restaurant chains.

2002: FOOD BUSINESS GROWING DOMINANT

The early 2000s saw Stake's annual sales growth continue to explode due to the purchase of Sunrich and the strategy of expanding through internal growth and acquisitions. The firm showed growth rates of 116 percent in 2000, 42 percent in 2001, and 37 percent in 2002, when annual sales reached $121 million, four times the 1999 figure. More than two-thirds of the company's sales came from its Sunrich Food Group.

Most of the company's remaining sales came from its newly named Environmental Industrial Group, anchored by Barnes International Environmental and the 2000 purchases of George F. Pettinos Limited, also known as PECAL, in Ontario, and Temisca, Inc., in Quebec. PECAL was a direct competitor of Barnes in the sand, coated-sand, and industrial minerals businesses, and Temisca, Inc. produced specialty sands for the golf course, filtration, and commercial product markets.

In 2001 Stake's Environmental Industrial Group had also added Virginia Materials and Supplies, Inc. of Norfolk, Virginia, and a 51 percent interest in International Materials & Supplies, Inc., of Keeseville, New York. Virginia Materials supplied abrasives to the shipbuilding and repair industry, and International Materials produced industrial garnets for sale to the water filtration, water jet cutting, and abrasives markets.

The StakeTech patented steam explosion technology continued to play a small but steady role in company operations and in April 2002 the division landed a $4 million contract for its first sale to China of a StakeTech Steam Explosion Pulping System, designed to produce pulp for paper from straw.

Recognizing that its future was in the natural and organic food business, Stake's Chairman and CEO

Jeremy N. Kendall explained the company's June 2003 shareholder approval of a name change in a press release: "We believe the name SunOpta reflects our environmental and organic commitment to products nourished in the 'sun' with 'optimal' nutritional value and environmental responsibility. The inclusion of 'Technology' in our name is no longer appropriate to our focus in the growing integrated natural and organic food business." The company maintained its corporate trading symbols of "STKL" on the NASDAQ and "SOY" on the Toronto Exchange and in August 2003 raised $49 million with its biggest share offering to date, which would be used to help finance future acquisitions.

2003: SUNOPTA CONTINUING BUYING SPREE

The years 2003 through 2005 were marked by continued strong internal growth and an aggressive buying spree, as SunOpta gobbled up over a dozen natural and organic food distributors, branded and private label food suppliers, organic fruit and vegetable producers, technical processing firms, and specialty food distribution facilities and networks.

In 2003 SunOpta acquired SIGCO Sun Products Inc., a worldwide supplier of sunflower products; Sonne Labs Inc., a manufacturer of natural and organic soy, corn, and sunflower snack foods; Pro Organics Marketing Inc., a leading distributor of organic fresh foods with distribution facilities in Vancouver, Toronto, and Montreal; and Kettle Valley Dried Fruit Ltd., a producer of branded and private label natural and organic fruit bars for markets in North America and the United Kingdom.

SunOpta increased its pace in 2004, buying five more companies and a General Mills Bakeries & Foodservice oat-fiber-processing plant, which included an agreement to supply oat fiber to General Mills, Inc. Four of the acquisitions were Canadian distribution companies: Distribue-Vie Fruits & Legumes Biologiques Inc., Supreme Foods Limited, Snapdragon Natural Foods Inc., and kosher grocery products specialists Kofman-Barenholtz Foods Limited.

In January 2005 SunOpta consolidated three of its distributors (Supreme, Snapdragon, and Kofman-Barenholtz) into a 135,000-square-foot, state-of-the-art facility in Toronto. In December, SunOpta bought another kosher foods distributor, Les Importations Cacheres Hahamovitch Inc., and achieved its objective of creating Canada's first national distribution network for the company's more than 4,500 natural, organic, kosher, and specialty food products.

2005: CREATION OF $100 MILLION FRUIT GROUP

In 2005 SunOpta launched a new Los Angeles-based division, the SunOpta Fruit Group. With Kettle Valley Dried Fruit Ltd. in hand since 2003, SunOpta in April 2005 added Organic Ingredients, Inc., a California organic fruit and vegetable trader and provider with worldwide sourcing and manufacturing capabilities. The summer brought two more California purchases, natural and organic frozen fruits and vegetables producer Cleugh's Frozen Foods, Inc., and Pacific Fruit Processors, Inc., a manufacturer focused on fruit-based ingredients for the dairy, bakery, and beverage industries. The Fruit Group was expected to generate total annualized revenues of approximately $100 million.

In November 2005, SunOpta underwent a corporate realignment and re-branding and emerged organized into three business units: the SunOpta Food Group, the Opta Minerals Group, and the SunOpta BioProcess Group. The Food Group was divided into four operating groups: Grains and Foods, Ingredients, Fruit, and Canadian Food and Distribution. Operating out of over 30 facilities in Canada and the United States, the SunOpta Food Group accounted for 90 percent of SunOpta's 2005 sales of $426 million.

The Opta Minerals Group, formerly called the Environmental Industrial Group, accounted for about 9 percent of SunOpta's 2005 revenues. In February 2005, Opta Minerals Inc., at the time a wholly owned subsidiary of SunOpta, completed an initial public offering and raised about CAD 17 million and began listing under the trading symbol "OPM" on the Toronto Stock Exchange and the NASDAQ Small Cap Market. SunOpta retained a 70.6 percent share in the unit. The Group's head office remained in Waterdown, Ontario, with production and distribution facilities in Ontario, Quebec, Louisiana, South Carolina, Virginia, Maryland, and New York.

SunOpta's BioProcess Group, formerly its StakeTech Steam Explosion Group, accounted for only 1 percent of SunOpta's revenues in 2005. In 2006, SunOpta's over-30-year-old "pet project" got a boost with a CAD 7.1 million contract to supply its patented steam explosion equipment and process technology to a subsidiary of Abengoa, the largest ethanol producer in Europe and the second largest in the world. Located in Spain, the world's first commercial production facility to convert wheat straw into ethanol was scheduled to be operational in the fall of 2006.

After more than 30 years of peddling its biomass conversion technology without great success, SunOpta Inc. had found its place as a leading player in the highly fragmented healthy-foods industry. The company's strategy in the late 1990s and early 2000s to expand by acquiring many diverse yet compatible health-food businesses had put it into a good position to exploit a continuing consumer trend towards choosing healthier diets in search of more healthy lifestyles.

Ted Sylvester

PRINCIPAL SUBSIDIARIES

Sunrich, Inc. (U.S.A.); Northern Food and Dairy, Inc. (U.S.A.); First Light Foods Inc. (U.S.A.); Wild West Organic Harvest Co-operative Association; Simply Organic Co. Ltd.; Opta Food Ingredients, Inc. (U.S.A.); Kettle Valley Dried Fruit Ltd; Pro Organics Marketing, Inc.; SIGCO Sun Products, Inc. (U.S.A.); Sonne Labs, Inc. (U.S.A.); Distribue-Vie Fruits & Legumes Biologiques Inc.; Supreme Foods Limited; Snapdragon Natural Foods Inc.; Kofman-Barenholtz Foods Limited; Organic Ingredients, Inc. (U.S.A.); Earthwise Processors, LLC (U.S.A.); Cleugh's Frozen Foods, Inc. (U.S.A.); Pacific Fruit Processors, Inc. (U.S.A.); Les Importations Cacheres Hahamovitch Inc.; Opta Minerals Inc. (70.6%).

PRINCIPAL COMPETITORS

Tree of Life, Inc.; Ag Processing Inc.; Bunge Limited; Saskatchewan Wheat Pool Inc.; Allied Waste Industries, Inc.

FURTHER READING

Adams, Scott, "This Stake Sprouts Roots in Friendly Markets: Organic Food Company," *Financial Post*, July 30, 2003.

Davidson, Andrew, "Organic Food Firm SunOpta's Shares Drop As Q2 Profit Slips to US$3.3M," *Canadian Press*, August 9, 2005.

Flavelle, Dana, "Small Firm Aims to Grow Bigger Organically; Stake Technology Plans Offering, U.S. Health Food Market Targeted," *Toronto Star*, August 13, 2003.

Kirby, Jason, "SunOpta: Hungry or Not Hungry Enough?: Acquisitive Organic Food Producer Has No Appetite for Big Purchases," *Financial Post*, July 18, 2005.

Linecker, Adelia Cellini, "Low-Carb Diet Craze A Natural Fit for Producer of Soy, Oat Products," *Investor's Business Daily*, April 5, 2004.

Perkins, Tara, "SunOpta Swallows California Organic Strawberry Packer Cleugh's Frozen Foods,"*Canadian Press*, June 20, 2005.

Shaw, Hollie, "Ontario Company Milking the Health Business," *Financial Post*, April 25, 2002.

Wulf, Gary, "FOCUS: World's First Commercial Cellulosic Ethanol Plant," *Dow Jones International News*, February 8, 2006.

———, "Spain: World's First Cellulosic Ethanol Plant Prepares for Operations," *Automotive World*, February 14, 2006.

———, "SunOpta Inc. - Segmented Reporting Realignment and Corporate Branding Initiatives," *Market News Publishing*, November 29, 2005.

TIBCO Software Inc.

3303 Hillview Avenue
Palo Alto, California 94304
U.S.A.
Telephone: (650) 846-1000
Toll Free: (800) 420-8450
Fax: (650) 846-1005
Web site: http://www.tibco.com

Public Company
Incorporated: 1997
Employees: 1,505
Sales: $445.9 million (2005)
Stock Exchanges: NASDAQ
Ticker Symbol: TIBX
NAIC: 511210 Software Publishers

■ ■ ■

TIBCO Software Inc. develops software that enables the various applications, databases, and platforms used by companies to work together. The company's products are known as integration software, the "middleware" that bridges the computer systems within a business and connects the business's software to outside suppliers, vendors, and customers. Integration software is regarded as a vital part of operating a business online. TIBCO serves companies in the energy, manufacturing, retail, healthcare, and financial services industries. The company operates on a global basis, maintaining two dozen offices outside North America in Asia, Europe, the Middle East, Africa, and South America.

ORIGINS

Vivek Ranadive, described as "a true visionary in a valley full of seers," by the August 10, 2004 issue of *Information Age,* left Bombay at age 17 with enough money to last two months. The year was 1958, and Ranadive was headed to Cambridge, Massachusetts, where he had been accepted at the Massachusetts Institute of Technology (MIT). Ranadive excelled in the academic world, earning an undergraduate degree in electrical engineering and computer science and a master's degree in engineering at MIT before crossing the Charles River to Allston, Massachusetts, where he earned a master's degree in business from Harvard Business School. After completing his education, Ranadive joined Ford Motor Co., where he served as a manager and an engineer. Stints as a senior executive at Fortune Systems and M/A-COM Linkabit followed, leading to the start of his entrepreneurial career and the genesis of TIBCO.

A quarter-century after leaving his native India, Ranadive was ready to launch his own information technology company. He was interested in technology that allowed the delivery of electronic information to users as the information became available, which described the essence of what later became Ranadive's "The Information Bus," or TIB. It was the mid-1980s, a point in Ranadive's career at which a well-paying investment banking position was offered to him, but he rejected a job at Goldman, Sachs & Co. and directed his energies toward starting his own company. While a friend worked on developing a prototype TIB, Ranadive began searching for start-up capital in northern California, registering little success until he approached Teknekron Corp. in late 1985. The company, described as an

COMPANY PERSPECTIVES

TIBCO is focused on leveraging and extending the capabilities of its software to help companies move toward predictive business: an exciting new way of doing business that lets companies anticipate customer needs, create opportunities and avoid potential problems. As the basis of the real-time movement of data across the enterprise, TIBCO's software is uniquely capable of correlating information about a company's operations and performance with information about expected behavior and business rules so they can anticipate and respond to threats and opportunities before they occur.

"entrepreneurial hothouse" in the February 1994 issue of *Wall Street & Technology,* agreed to back Ranadive's venture, but not in the usual fashion. "Teknekron isn't a venture capital company," Ranadive explained to *Wall Street & Technology.* "They told me the operating model and set a level of profitability. They said, 'You have to hire people smarter than you.'" According to the agreement between Ranadive and Teknekron, if profits failed to materialize after a set date, the venture would be shuttered and Ranadive could walk away debt free. If profits did materialize, Teknekron would recoup its investment and retain an ownership stake in the company. Under the terms of the agreement, Teknekron Software Systems Inc. (TSS) was formed in 1985, the company that later became TIBCO.

TSS succeeded during its early years because of a combination of talent and technology. Ranadive, following his financial backers' order to find people smarter than himself, solicited help from faculty members and friends at MIT. He also turned to the nearby talent pool at Stanford University and the University of California at Berkeley, gathering a small staff of academics to finish work on TIB technology. Under Ranadive's direction, the team developed software infrastructure to integrate and to deliver market data under the name Marketsheet, a product that used TIB technology to deliver stock quotes, news, and other financial information in trading rooms of large banks and financial institutions. The product proved to be an immediate success, embraced by the financial institutions who clamored for real-time information. In little more than five years, TSS's software could be found on more than 10,000 desktop computers worldwide, used by brokers and analysts at financial firms such as Salomon Brothers, Goldman, Sachs & Co., Fidelity Investment Services, and J.P. Morgan & Co. By 1992, revenues reached $39 million, from which the company earned $8 million in profits.

THE TIBCO NAME IS BORN IN 1996

Encouraged by the initial success of his venture, Ranadive began to address a larger audience, leading TSS in a direction that would later describe TIBCO's business. In 1992, the company expanded its product line to include software solutions for companies outside the financial services sector. TSS began to develop software that helped companies manage the often disparate software applications that supported their business. "Our vision was that it be an information highway, providing a mechanism to tie software applications together, not just to trade and provide market data," Ranadive explained in a February 1994 interview with *Information Age.* The event that eventually led to the birth of the TIBCO name occurred shortly before Ranadive's interview with *Information Age.* In December 1993, Ranadive sold TSS to the global financial news and information group Reuters Holdings PLC for $125 million. Reuters, the world's leading provider of real-time market data, international news, and transaction services, wanted to integrate Ranadive's TIB technology with its Triarch 2000 trading system. Under the terms of the deal, Ranadive was given the authority to run TSS independently. In 1996, TSS changed its name to reflect the patented technology that served as its backbone, adopting TIBCO Inc. as its official corporate title.

In the wake of the name change, Ranadive pushed for the division of his company, the final step in the process that gave birth to the TIBCO of the 21st century. Ranadive wanted to pursue the development of integration software for customers outside the financial services sector, a desire that led to the formation of TIBCO Software Inc. in January 1997. TIBCO Software became a separate entity from TIBCO Inc., which changed its name to TIBCO Finance Technology Inc. after the split. TIBCO Finance remained a wholly owned subsidiary of Reuters, focusing its business on providing TIB technology-based software to the financial services and insurance industries. TIBCO Software, with Ranadive serving as president, chief executive officer, and chairman, licensed TIB-technology from Reuters, which retained a 49 percent stake in the newly formed company.

In moving TIB technology off the trading floor, Ranadive offered corporate clientele what he perceived as an indispensable tool. Companies typically used a variety of applications to handle different corporate functions,

KEY DATES

1985: Teknekron Software Systems Inc., which later created TIBCO Software Inc., is formed.
1992: Teknekron Software begins courting customers outside the financial services sector.
1993: Teknekron Software is acquired by Reuters Holdings PLC.
1996: Teknekron Software changes its name to TIBCO Inc.
1997: TIBCO Inc. is split into two companies, TIBCO Finance Technology Inc. and TIBCO Software Inc.
1999: TIBCO Software completes its initial public offering of stock.
2004: Reuters cuts its ownership interest in TIBCO Software from 49 percent to less than 10 percent.
2005: Revenues reach a record high of $445 million.

but the disparate pieces of software often did not communicate with each other effectively. Ranadive, through TIB technology, sought to write code to connect the motley assortment of software programs used by companies, creating a seamless platform that operated efficiently on a real-time basis. A single purchase, for instance, could affect information related to order entries, logistics, inventories, and budgets, all of which had to be tied together. "You can have all the pretty pictures you want on the front end," an analyst remarked in a June 6, 2001 interview with *Investor's Business Daily,* "but if they don't connect to the back end to complete a transaction, you've got nothing. This stuff isn't sexy," the analyst said of integration software, "but it's the glue."

TIBCO's role as an intermediary that provided the middleware to help companies manage their businesses became increasingly important as the 1990s progressed. By carving out the sales recorded within the financial services sector by its predecessor, TSS, the company generated $8 million in revenue in 1992, the first financial figure recorded by the business TIBCO Software later represented. By 1996, the total reached $30 million, as the complexity and diversity of applications used by businesses increased. The spark that ignited an unprecedented rate of financial growth was the rapid development of e-commerce, which created a greater need for integrated software to not only enable a company to operate its assortment of applications and databases in concert, but also to extend its system to business partners and to customers. As online business ratcheted up during the late 1990s, TIBCO's sales grew robustly, reaching $52 million by 1998, when it was promoting its TIB/ActiveEnterprise suite of products. The software facilitated the distribution of data and the integration of business processes across local or wide-area networks, including the Internet, allowing multiple and distinct applications, web sites, databases, and other content sources to be managed in real-time within a common framework. Touting the benefits of such technology, the company cashed in on the burgeoning growth of e-commerce and completed an initial public offering (IPO) of stock in 1999.

The months before and after TIBCO's IPO encompassed the most energetic growth the company had ever experienced. The increased need for integration software attracted a host of competitors, such as webMethods Inc. and SeeBeyond Technology Corp., but the biggest rival to TIBCO was International Business Machines Corporation (IBM), which controlled an estimated 25 percent of the market with its MQSeries software. The rewards to be won in the race for market share were escalating at a rapid pace, with global sales of integration software totaling $1.6 billion in 2000 and expected to reach nearly $9 billion by 2004. Ranadive forged ahead with highly regarded technology, an asset that he strengthened by fleshing out his company's expertise via acquisitions. In 1999, TIBCO bought InConcert Inc., a developer of integration software geared for telecommunications companies. When Ranadive acquired software vendor Extensibility Inc. the following year for $100 million, TIBCO's market valuation towered at more than $30 billion. One year later, in 2001, revenues reached $322 million, more than six times the total registered three years earlier.

TIBCO largely escaped the devastation caused by the collapse of the high-technology sector at the turn of the millennium. The company's market valuation incurred the most severe blow when the Internet "bubble" burst, plummeting from $30 billion to slightly more than $1 billion in less than three years. Sales fell as well, dropping by 20 percent, but the company soon recovered, avoiding the brunt of the storm. In 2002, the company returned to an acquisition mode, purchasing two companies. The first and the larger of the two was Talarian Corp., a developer of infrastructure software. TIBCO paid $155 million for Talarian in April, gaining access to the company's 300 customers, which included prominent firms such as Boeing, Hewlett-Packard, and Southwest Airlines. In September, TIBCO signed an agreement to acquire Praja, Inc., a developer of business-activity monitoring software, which enabled users to assess real-time business operations against key performance indicators. TIBCO paid nearly $3 million for Praja.

2004: ACQUISITION OF STAFFWARE

In the final years before its 10th anniversary as an independent company, TIBCO continued to expand and to strengthen its business under the watchful eye of Ranadive. By 2004, the company ranked as the largest, independent integration software developer. Sales for the year reached $387 million, surpassing for the first time the record high posted in 2001. Early in the year, the company's prospects brightened when Reuters reduced its ownership stake from 49 percent to 8.8 percent, a move that allowed TIBCO to return to its roots and begin seriously assaulting the financial services sector. In April 2004, the company announced another acquisition, its first since purchasing Praja. The $217 million transaction involved Staffware PLC, a U.K.-based developer of workflow-management and integration software. The addition of Staffware broadened TIBCO's product offerings, adding roughly 700 customers in the banking, insurance, and telecommunications industries, but perhaps the most significant benefit of the deal was Staffware's strong presence overseas. "We are stronger outside North America and parts of Asia," Staffware's chairman and chief executive officer, John O'Connell, explained in an April 23, 2004 interview with the *Daily Deal.* "TIBCO is clearly stronger in North America," O'Connell added, "and we can help them more outside the United States." The addition of Staffware helped TIBCO generate $445 million in revenue in 2005. Profits for the year totaled $72.5 million, up substantially from the $44.9 million posted the previous year, making for a highly profitable end to the company's first decade of business.

Jeffrey L. Covell

PRINCIPAL SUBSIDIARIES

3301 Hillview Holdings Inc.; TIBCO BPM (U.K.).

PRINCIPAL COMPETITORS

BEA Systems, Inc.; International Business Machines Corporation; webMethods, Inc.

FURTHER READING

Bonasia, J., "Business Software Integration Field Gets Crowded," *Investor's Business Daily,* June 6, 2001, p. A6.

"An Internet Company That Makes Money," *123Jump,* May 1, 2001.

Keri, Jonah, "TIBCO Software Packs Growing Sales Punch," *Investor's Business Daily,* February 25, 2005, p. B8.

McGuire, Craig, "TIBCO Full Speed Ahead Following IPO," *Wall Street & Technology,* September 1999, p. 10.

Meyer, Cheryl, "TIBCO Snags Staffware for $218M," *Daily Deal,* April 23, 2004.

"The Renaissance of TIBCO," *Information Age,* August 10, 2004.

"TIBCO Software Reaches Milestone in Financial Services Sector," *Asia Africa Intelligence Wire,* June 21, 2004.

Vizard, Michael, "TIBCO to Challenge IBM Portal Play," *InfoWorld,* November 1, 1999, p. 12.

Zecher, Joshua, "All Aboard the 'Information Bus,'" *Wall Street & Technology,* February 1994, p. 64.

TOKYOPOP Inc.

5900 Wilshire Boulevard, Suite 2000
Los Angeles, California 90036-5020
U.S.A.
Telephone: (323) 692-6700
Fax: (323) 692-6701
Web site: http://www.tokyopop.com

Wholly Owned Subsidiary of TOKYOPOP, K.K.
Incorporated: 1997
Employees: 100
Sales: $40 million (2003 est.)
NAIC: 511130 Book Publishers; 512110 Motion Picture and Video Production; 512230 Music Publishers

■ ■ ■

TOKYOPOP Inc. is a leading publisher of manga and anime, or Japanese comic books and animation. Within a few years of its launch, the company had helped turn an Asian cultural phenomenon into one of the biggest publishing sensations in U.S. history. Sister companies are also active in Europe. TOKYOPOP's investors include Trans Cosmos USA Inc., Japan's Softbank Finance Corporation, Mitsui Venture Capital, Nissho Inter Life Company Limited, Nippon Venture Capital Corporation, Tekinvest K.K., Impress Group, and Rentrak. "Manga for us is a lifestyle," TOKYOPOP executive Mike Kiley told online publication *ICv2 News.* "It's a way of characterizing the world, it's a way of expression that isn't specific to Asia, although it has its roots there, so we see ourselves at the forefront of the manga-ization of the country."

JAPANESE ORIGINS

TOKYOPOP Inc. was incorporated in California in early 1997, a subsidiary of a Japanese parent formed the previous year. Its founder, entrepreneur Stuart Levy, was introduced to Japan's $4 billion comic book phenomenon, called manga, while working as a consultant in the country's multimedia industry.

Manga differs from traditional American comic books in a number of ways. The artwork is highly stylized; characters typically have outsized eyeballs and pupils and spiky hair. Manga also portrays a wide array of subject matter, far beyond the traditional superhero theme. Plots tend to be complex.

Levy had launched Mixx Entertainment Inc. in 1996 with a reported $500,000 raised from Mitsui Venture Capital Corp. and Nippon Venture Capital Co. Based in Japan, Mixx would be the parent company for the U.S. business; it was renamed TOKYOPOP, K.K., in 2003.

According to the *Los Angeles Business Journal,* Mixx started with a magazine to bring Asian pop culture to the United States. Later, another $2 million in capital was raised from the original investors as well as Trans Cosmos USA and Rentrak Corp.

LAUNCH OF TOKYOPOP.COM IN 1999

Around 1999, the web site Tokyopop.com was launched. It was expanded as a kind of Asian culture portal, offering e-mail and instant messenger services. It had both paid and free levels of membership. It acquired another Asian culture site, GoldenSilk.com, in 2000.

> ## COMPANY PERSPECTIVES
>
> TOKYOPOP is hailed as a leading youth-oriented entertainment brand and an innovator of manga creation, with a revolutionary artistic vision that transcends countless platforms. From the introduction of the first-ever extensive manga publishing program in North America, to the development of its manga-originated intellectual properties into film, television and digital entertainment, TOKYOPOP has changed the way teens experience pop culture.

TOKYOPOP.com was a product of the University of Southern California's Annenberg Incubator Project (EC2).

John Parker, president and chief operating officer, told the *Los Angeles Business Journal* the company was not growing entirely smoothly, however. It decided to focus on traditional retailing channels rather than the magazine and e-commerce. TOKYOPOP also got a new investor, Softbank Finance Corp., a major shareholder in Yahoo, which provided about $10 million (¥1 billion).

Sailor Moon was TOKYOPOP's first product to be translated and export to the United States, according to the *Nikkei Report.* The Japanese language version had been a huge hit for Kodansha. TOKYOPOP was not the first to publish manga in the United States, but it became a major force in bringing manga to the mainstream. Part of the trail to youth acceptance had been blazed by animated video game characters (especially Nintendo's Pokémon).

One of TOKYOPOP's biggest anime and manga titles was *Initial D,* the story of a tofu delivery boy turned street racer. A phenomenal ($300 million) hit in Asia, it even spawned a remote-controlled model of the hero's Toyota Corolla and other autos from the series. Other huge manga hits for TOKYOPOP included *Love Hina* and *Chobits.* Cine-manga, introduced in the late 1990s, would be one of TOKYOPOP's greatest areas of mainstream success. It was based on existing characters from movies and television.

TOKYOPOP expanded into anime (animated) DVDs and video game soundtracks around 2000. However, the diversion pushed the company into red for a couple of years, noted the *Los Angeles Business Journal.* Revenues were $7 million in 2001, and were expected to more than double as the company accelerated its product releases to one per day. By early 2002, TOKYOPOP was distributing its manga comics and anime DVDs to 100 U.S. retailers, including Suncoast Motion Picture Co., Borders, and Best Buy.

The company experimented with the format of its products before it found a bestselling formula for the U.S. market. It eventually settled on what would become known as the "manga format," according to *Publishers Weekly.* This was a five- by seven-inch paperback. It helped TOKYOPOP keep retail prices below $10.

An important change was adopting the traditional Japanese layout of books: essentially the reverse of Western style, reading "back" to front (i.e., the spine of the book on the right) and right to left. This differentiated the product and added an exotic feeling. It also simplified production for licensed Japanese books, since they only had to be translated, not reformatted, from the original version. Further, the layout change also tapped into the spirit of adolescent rebellion. "It's something they understand and their parents don't," COO John Parker told the *Los Angeles Business Journal.*

LAUNCH OF RISING STARS IN 2002

TOKYOPOP was known for licensed productions it imported to the United States from Japan, beginning with those of the publisher Kodansha Limited. It also began to foster American talent with its Rising Stars of Manga contest, launched in 2002 to discover new artists in the United States, and develop an inventory of original English language (OEL) manga. The Rising Stars program was soon expanded to other areas of the world. The company had also found success with Korean comics, called *manwha.*

By 2002, Mike Kiley told *ICv2 News* that large bookstore chains were accounting for most of the company's sales growth. Around this time, TOKYOPOP introduced a video game–style rating system to advise readers of potentially alarming content in some titles.

TOKYOPOP had successfully brought some of its titles to hundreds of mainstream bookstores by 2003. The next year, it tried its hand in the mass retail market, testing sales in a handful of department stores including Wal-Mart and Fred Meyer, reported *Publishers Weekly.*

Manga was evolving to suit different audiences. *Shojo,* specifically tailored towards "tween" girls (ages 11 to 17), was one of the most popular subgenres. *Marmalade Boy,* a complicated type of Brady Bunch story, and *Fruits Basket* were among its biggest hits. The *Stray Sheep* series of children's books debuted in the fall of 2003.

The parent company, TOKYOPOP, K.K., had revenues of ¥53 million in 2003. TOKYOPOP founder

KEY DATES

1996: Parent company Mixx Entertainment, later dubbed TOKYOPOP, K.K., is established in Japan.
1997: Subsidiary TOKYOPOP Inc. is formed in California.
1999: TOKYOPOP.com is launched.
2002: Rising Stars of Manga contest is launched to discover new U.S. talent.
2003: TOKYOPOP manga storms mainstream bookstores; U.K. subsidiary is launched.

Stuart Levy told the *San Diego Union-Tribune* that sales had doubled every year since its founding, to about $40 million in 2003. In an interview with *Publishers Weekly,* Levy estimated the size of the U.S. manga market at about $150 million in 2003, with females making up 60 percent of readership. Manga's popularity in Europe had also been growing over the previous decade. A London subsidiary, TOKYOPOP U.K., Ltd., was launched by 2003, followed by a German unit.

MORE COMPETITION AFTER 2003

By 2004, TOKYOPOP was publishing 500 titles a year. While it was a leader in the manga field, it was not alone in the United States. It faced competition from VIZ LLC, a San Francisco-based outfit with Japanese backers that had been publishing since the 1980s. Major publishers were also muscling their way in, such as Random House with its imprint Del Rey. In 2004 TOKYOPOP was estimated to have a 3 percent share of the total U.S. market for comic books, magazines, and graphic novels. The company had a 50 percent market share of manga exports to the United States, according to the *Nikkei Report.*

In January 2006, explaining a round of layoffs at the company, which employed 100 people, Kiley acknowledged to *Publishers Weekly* that the manga market was becoming more competitive. Even Archie Comics and DC Comics had begun to produce manga titles. TOKYOPOP's growth rate had slowed to 40 percent in 2003, according to the *Journal of Japanese Trade & Industry.*

In February 2006, the *New York Times* reported several New York publishers were courting TOKYOPOP for its distribution rights, looking for a way to offset lagging sales among traditional publications. Client Distribution Services (CDS) had handled fulfillment for TOKYOPOP since 2002. They apparently understood its business. "We're radical, crazy, teen-pop-culture guys who do a lot of wild stuff and who have to turn on a dime," Kiley told the *Times.*

In spite of backing from its new parent company, Perseus Books Group, CDS lost the distribution deal to HarperCollins Publishers. According to TOKYOPOP publisher Mike Kiley, the company had grown 800 to 1,000 percent in just a few years and needed a larger distributor. There were also creative synergies involved; TOKYOPOP agreed to produce manga spinoffs of certain HarperCollins titles, including works by teen author Meg Cabot. HarperCollins CEO Jane Friedman told the *New York Times* that her company was especially interested in manga since it had a larger appeal among females than other types of comic books. TOKYOPOP continued working to put its products in front of new audiences. Its manga was beginning to appear in newspaper comics sections.

Frederick C. Ingram

PRINCIPAL COMPETITORS

A.D. Vision, Inc.; Dark Horse Comics, Inc.; Del Rey Manga; VIZ Media, LLC.

FURTHER READING

"Anime Merchandising Straddles Three Markets," *Video Store,* September 1, 2002, p. 8.

"Anime Supplier TokyoPop Is Expanding into the United Kingdom," *Video Store,* April 20, 2003, p. 16.

Baker, Tom, "Is North American Manga Mania a Generational Thing?" *Daily Yomiuri* (Tokyo), November 27, 2004, p. 12.

Clack, Erin E., "Typical 'Boy' Interests Start to Entice Girls," *Children's Business,* August 1, 2004, p. 28.

De La Cruz, Edwin, "Anime Rules! The Latest News from the World of Japanese Animation," *Video Store,* Special Merchandising Guide: Anime Videos, January 26, 2003, p. 20.

Green, Frank, "Genre of Japanese Comic Books Rival Traditional U.S. Titles," *San Diego Union-Tribune,* July 20, 2003.

Hein, Kenneth, "TokyoPop Enters U.S. with a Bang," *iMarketing News,* January 17, 2000, p. 11.

Helbling, Brigitte, "Liebe, Lust, Tränen und Hoffnung - Der Hamburger Verlag Tokyopop ist mit japanischen Comics für Mädchen erfolgreich," *Berliner Zeitung,* July 22, 2005, p. 27.

"ICv2 Talks to Tokyopop Publisher Mike Kiley About the HarperCollins Alliance," *ICv2 News,* March 28, 2006, http://www.icv2.com/articles/news/8431.html.

"Interview with Tokyopop Publisher Mike Kiley," *ICv2 News,* October 6, 2005, http://www.icv2.com/articles/home/7623.html.

"Interview with Tokyopop VP Mike Kiley," *ICv2 News,* July 11, 2002, http://www.icv2.com/articles/news/ 1614.html.

"JMPR Hired to Push Tokyopop Cartoon into US Auto Media," *PR Week* (US), May 26, 2003, p. 4.

Katsumi, Yukiko, "Multimedia Firm Anxious to Blend Culture," *Daily Yomiuri/Yomiuri Shimbun* (Japan), October 1, 1997.

Keough, Christopher, "Japanese Content Importer Angles for a Backwards Hit," *Los Angeles Business Journal,* March 11, 2002, p. 16.

"Leading Gen Y Online Network Adds Proven Business Leadership to the Mixx; Mixx Entertainment Names John Parker President and Chief Operating Officer," *Business Wire,* August 24, 1999.

MacDonald, Heidi, "Manga Sales Grow; So Do Worries; Despite Concerns About Title Glut, Quality and Censorship, Manga and Anime Sales Continue to Boom," *Publishers Weekly,* March 15, 2004, p. 29.

———, "Manga Sales Just Keep Rising; Manga Publishers Scramble to Meet a Steady Rise in Demand," *Publishers Weekly,* March 17, 2003, p. 24.

"Manga Exports at TOKYOPOP Grow into ¥7bn Business," *Nikkei Report,* July 3, 2004.

Reid, Calvin, "Manga Is Here to Stay: Tokyopop's Format Leads Manga into the Bookstore Market," *Publishers Weekly,* October 20, 2003.

———, "Tokyopop Goes Mass Market, Signs Rising Star," *Publishers Weekly,* December 22, 2003, p. 8.

———, "Tokyopop Plans Manga TV Spots," *Publishers Weekly,* May 10, 2004, p. 10.

"Reorg at Tokyopop," *Publishers Weekly,* January 30, 2006, p. 5.

Thuresson, Michael, "Love on the Run," *Los Angeles Business Journal,* September 22, 2003, p. 6.

"Top Comic Book Publishers, 2004," *Market Share Reporter,* February 18, 2005, http://newsarama.com/pages/2004 Numbers.htm.

"What Lies Behind the Global Success of Manga?" *Journal of Japanese Trade & Industry,* May 1, 2005.

Wolk, Douglas, "Tokyopop Goes Left," *Publishers Weekly,* March 18, 2002, p. 36.

Wyatt, Edward, "Comic Book Publisher Switches a Deal to HarperCollins," *New York Times,* March 28, 2006, p. C7.

———, "Publishers Find Growth in Comics," *New York Times,* February 13, 2006, p. 1.

Travelzoo Inc.

590 Madison Avenue
21st Floor
New York, New York 10022
U.S.A.
Telephone: (212) 521-4420
Fax: (212) 521-4230
Web site: http://www.travelzoo.com

Public Company
Incorporated: 1998 as Travelzoo.com Corporation
Employees: 49
Sales: $50.8 million (2005)
Stock Exchanges: NASDAQ
Ticker Symbol: TZOO
NAIC: 541512 Computer Systems Design Services

■ ■ ■

Travelzoo Inc. is one of the few Internet media companies to survive the dot-com meltdown of the early 2000s and achieve profitability. Even so, the travel-related business has not skirted controversy or avoided regular predictions of its demise. Based in New York City, Travelzoo recommends the best available deals on airline tickets, hotels, cruises, and vacation packages on its web site, the Travelzoo Top 20 e-mail newsletter sent to nine million subscribers, and the Newsflash e-mail publication. The emphasis is on advertisers' current specials. Subscribers do not actually book tickets on the Travelzoo site. Rather, they connect to the travel company itself. Travelzoo acts as a clearinghouse and makes money from its more than 500 advertisers, which include travel agencies as well as stalwarts of the industry such as American Airlines, Avis Rent A Car, Caesars Entertainment, Liberty Travel, Marriott Hotels, and United Airlines. Travelzoo is known to be scrupulous about the offers it recommends from advertisers, portraying itself as a consumer advocate by making sure there is enough product and "test booking." Representatives, for example, call to see how long it takes to reach a sales agent. Travelzoo also has been known to lobby a travel company to make more product available. The company does business in North America and Europe, maintaining offices in Chicago, Las Vegas, London, Miami, Munich, Silicon Valley, and Toronto. Although Travelzoo is a public company, listed on the NASDAQ, it is 80 percent owned by founder, Chairman, and CEO Ralph Bartel.

COMPANY'S FOUNDING IN 1998

A native of Germany, Bartel earned a number of degrees before launching his business career. He received a master's degree in journalism from the University of Eichstaett in Germany, and a Master's of Business Administration from Switzerland's University of St. Gallen, where he also earned a Ph.D. in economics. He earned a second doctorate in communications from the University of Mainz, Germany. In 1996 he went to work as a managing assistant at Grunner und Jahr, the magazine division of the Germany media giant Bertelsmann AG. In 1998, according to the *New York Post,* "He hit upon an idea for an internet-based travel business that in retrospect looks both obvious and brilliant: start a Web site containing nothing but advertisements for the one thing every traveler wants to know—namely,

COMPANY PERSPECTIVES

At Travelzoo our mission is to give you the best and smartest information.

what's the cheapest flight (or car rental, or hotel room, or package tour, you name it) to anywhere."

Bartel chose the odd but memorable name of "Travelzoo" for his business, and registered the company in the Bahamas for $850. Then using a personal computer at his parents' home in Hamburg, Germany, he set up his web site. Bartel's next task was to build a subscriber base in order to attract advertisers. What he devised was a gimmick that became the subject of Internet newsgroups, chain e-mails, and media scrutiny: He offered to give away three shares of Travelzoo stock to anyone who submitted their first name and e-mail address. He also promised not to sell the information, and to perhaps one day pay dividends. There were questions about the legality of the free offer, prompting a cursory look by the Securities and Exchange Commission (SEC). In general, it was dismissed by virtually everyone as a mere stunt. There was no chance, experts maintained, that Travelzoo would ever declare a dividend and make good on its promise. Nevertheless, the ploy at the very least generated interest in Travelzoo and Bartel had a base of subscribers with which to work. The people who signed up for stock would receive Travelzoo's newsletter of travel deals and be urged to at least check out the deals as a way to enhance the value of their stock in Travelzoo. Altogether, about 5.2 million "Netsurfer" shares were given away.

Bartel "soon found out, however," wrote *Business Week,* "that building an audience was the least of his problems. His Web site was virtually empty, and he had no experience in the travel business. … 'I was too busy to think about that,' says Bartel. 'In the beginning, we had lots of problems just keeping one server up.'" Later in 1998 he established Silicon Channels Corporation in California to run the Travelzoo web site, with Mark Foster serving as president of the operation, setting up shop in the former headquarters of Lotus Corp. in Mountain View, California. To drum up advertisers and populate the web site with content, *Business Week* reported, he hired a former account executive from Budget Rent-A-Car, who offered free trial advertisements. The free offer worked well enough that Travelzoo soon began to attract paying customers. From May 21, 1998, when the web site first engaged in actual business through the end of the year, the company generated sales of $84,000. It was not enough to allow Bartel and Foster to quit their day jobs, but a promising beginning, nonetheless.

Business grew at a steady clip in 1999 and Bartel was now joined by his brother, Holger Bartel, who took over as vice-president of sales and marketing. He held an M.B.A. in finance and accounting and a Ph.D. in economics from the University of Gallen. In the early 1990s he came to the United States to serve as a research fellow at Harvard Business School, and then in 1995 went to work in Los Angeles for the consulting firm of McKinsey & Company before being lured away by his brother. By the end of 1999 Travelzoo had signed up more than 150 travel companies as advertisers, including American Express Vacations, American Airlines, Radisson Hotels, and Hilton, as well as local travel agents. They paid about $200 a month to post as many as ten deals on the Travelzoo site. To help them determine the winners, Travelzoo introduced a software program called Hitmaster, which provided real-time information on how many people were clicking on a particular posting. Advertisers could access the information on a password-protected web site and then adjust their postings to improve performance. Airline tickets were the top draw for the company, but Travelzoo also did well on cruises and Caribbean and Hawaiian vacations. In 1999, Travelzoo added a ski category, which quickly proved popular with consumers. When the year came to a close, Travelzoo recorded more than $950,000 in sales and net income of $105,000.

Over the next two years Travelzoo continued its strong growth. Revenues increased to $3.95 million in 2000 and $6.15 million in 2001. Net income grew to $362,000 in 2000 and $364,000 in 2001. As could be expected, the company enjoyed a commensurate improvement in the size of its subscriber base, which increased to 700,000 in 2000 and 1.5 million in 2001.

One of the provisions in the 1998 stock giveaway required that Netsurfer recipients certify that they were U.S. or Canadian residents at least 18 years of age. After two years Travelzoo reserved the right to cancel shares that had not been properly certified. Although that two-year period had passed, the company did not yet move to cancel shares, a decision that would have repercussions later. In the meantime, Travelzoo took steps to become a U.S. public company. In January 2001 Travelzoo Inc. was incorporated in Delaware as a subsidiary of the Bahamas-based Travelzoo.com Corporation. Also in that month Silicon Channels merged with the new corporation. Next, in March 2002, shareholders, in effect Ralph Bartel, voted to merge Travelzoo Corporation and Travelzoo Inc., with the latter becoming the surviv-

KEY DATES

1998: The company is incorporated in the Bahamas.
2001: The U.S. entity is incorporated in Delaware.
2002: The company is taken public.
2004: Company stock soars nearly 1,000 percent.
2005: A European office is opened in London.
2006: An office is opened in Toronto.

ing entity. Netsurfer shareholders were given another two years to exchange Travelzoo Corporation shares for Travelzoo Inc. shares.

GOING PUBLIC IN 2002

On August 28, 2002, Travelzoo made an initial public offering of stock priced at $6.50 per share. It was then quoted on the OTC Bulletin Board, where it attracted little notice. Only 14,500 shares were traded on the first day. Travelzoo began to catch the notice of investors in 2003, however, as the business continued to grow. In addition to its Silicon Valley technical operation, Travelzoo established its corporate headquarters in midtown Manhattan, and then in May 2003 opened an office in Miami to better serve its important advertising clients in Florida, a key tourism state. Three months later Travelzoo opened a fourth office, this one in Chicago to provide a presence in the middle of the country. When 2003 ended, Travelzoo increased the number of subscribers to more than four million. Revenues also approached the $10 million mark and net income totaled $853,000. Moreover, in late December 2003 Travelzoo stock graduated from over-the-counter status and began trading on the NASDAQ Smallcap Market.

The price of the stock soared to incredible heights in 2004. By all accounts, Bartel had nurtured a respectable little business, but the price of the stock was clearly not in keeping with the actual value of the company. Shares started at $8.70 and reached $18.30 by early June. The company announced that the stock would be moving to the NASDAQ National Market and by the end of August the share price reached $41, meaning that the company now had a market capitalization of $730 million. When the price of Travelzoo stock reached $71 in the middle of September, Ralph Bartel was a billionaire, on paper, at any rate.

What was driving Travelzoo's skyrocketing stock price were shortsellers, investors who borrowed shares of Travelzoo in the expectation that the stock would fall. They sold the borrowed shares in the expectation that they could buy them back cheaper later on and return the borrowed shares. In this way they would pocket the difference between the price of the stock when they sold it and the price at which they bought it. As Travelzoo stock began to shoot up in the spring of 2004, short-sellers, according to the *New York Post,* "began to circle." The way the newspaper described it, they were actually stepping into a trap laid by a crafty Bartel, who announced "that of the roughly 19 million shares outstanding, more than four million were being cancelled because the recipients had never bothered to certify their ages and countries of residence. This automatically reduced the public float by 80%, lifting Bartel's control back to more than 87%, while causing suddenly anxious short-sellers to begin chasing the stock that still remained public in order to close out their positions, which of course simply caused the stock's rise to accelerate. It was the start of a classic short squeeze."

STOCK PRICE PEAKS IN LATE 2004

The price of Travelzoo stock peaked in December 2004 at $106, chalking up a gain of 997 percent for the year. The price would steadily deflate over the months to come as, in the words of the *New York Post,* "one short-seller after the next gets carried out, feet-first, reducing demand for the shares accordingly." Unconnected to the price of its stock, Travelzoo carried on its steady growth. Sales approached $18 million in 2003 and totaled $33.7 million in 2004. Net income improved from $2 million in 2003 to more than $6 million in 2004, and the number of Travelzoo subscribers reached seven million.

Travelzoo opened a London office in April 2005 to do business in Europe. Later in the year the company opened an office in Las Vegas. For the year, revenues increased to $50.8 million while net income approached $8 million. Expansion continued in 2006, with a second European office opening in Munich, Germany. In April Travelzoo opened an office in Toronto, part of what Bartel called a strategy to build Travelzoo into a global media brand. In the process Bartel may have been forging an exit strategy, making Travelzoo into an acquisition target for perhaps Google or Yahoo. On the other hand, those giant Internet companies could opt to emulate the Travelzoo format and use their heft to put the squeeze on Bartel, threatening the life of the Internet company.

Ed Dinger

PRINCIPAL SUBSIDIARIES

Travelzoo.com Canada, Inc.; Travelzoo (Europe) Ltd.

PRINCIPAL COMPETITORS

AOL L.L.C.; Google Inc.; Yahoo! Inc.

FURTHER READING

Anderson, Karen M., "It's a Zoo Out There," *Travel Agent*, November 29, 1999, p. 36.

Berman, Dennis, "Can Travelzoo's Keeper Survive the Online Jungle?," *BusinessWeek Online*, June 7, 2000.

Byron, Christopher, "Travelzoo's Skidoo," *New York Post*, October 18, 2004.

Elstein, Aaron, "Travelzoo's Wild Ride Destined to End Poorly," *Crain's New York Business*, December 5, 2005, p. 4.

Limone, Jerry, "Travelzoo: It's the Real Deal," *Travel Weekly*, May 10, 2004, p. 1.

Napoli, Lisa, "Free Stock Shares from the Internet," *New York Times*, July 27, 1998, p. D4.

Savitz, Eric J., "Animal House," *Barron's*, August 30, 2004, p. 13.

———, "Rattling the Cage," *Barron's*, February 7, 2005, p. 13.

Tsuruoka, Doug, "After Roaring '04, Travelzoo Quiets," *Investors' Business Daily*, February 9, 2005, p. A05.

———, "Highflying Travelzoo Brought to Earth by Prove, Q4 Results," *Investor's Business Daily*, January 25, 2005, p. A06.

———, "Travelzoo Success May Breed Competition," *Investor's Business Daily*, September 23, 2004, p. A05.

TreeHouse Foods, Inc.

Two Westbrook Corporate Center
Suite 1070
Westchester, Illinois 60154-5744
U.S.A.
Telephone: (708) 483-1300
Fax: (708) 409-1062
Web site: http://www.treehousefoods.com

Public Company
Incorporated: 2005
Employees: 1,727
Sales: $707.7 million (2005)
Stock Exchanges: New York
Ticker Symbol: THS
NAIC: 311421 Fruit and Vegetable Canning; 311423 Dried and Dehydrated Food Manufacturing; 311941 Mayonnaise, Dressing, and Other Prepared Sauce Manufacturing; 311999 All Other Miscellaneous Food Manufacturing

■ ■ ■

TreeHouse Foods, Inc. is a leading U.S. maker of pickles, nondairy creamers, and other food products. Formerly the Specialty Foods Group of Dean Foods Company before being spun off in June 2005, TreeHouse and its main operating subsidiary, Bay Valley Foods LLC, market a wide array of shelf-stable products to the retail and foodservice channels and also sell ingredients to other food manufacturers. The company's largest business, generating approximately 45 percent of total sales, is its pickles segment, which is the largest pickle and pepper supplier in the United States and is also the top supplier of private-label pickles for the retail market. In addition to supplying private-label pickles, relish, peppers, and related products to retailers, TreeHouse sells pickle products to retailers under its own brands, including Farmans, Nalley's, Peter Piper, and Steinfeld, and to foodservice customers. The firm's pickles segment also sells sauces and syrups to retail grocers under the Bennett's, Hoffman House, and Roddenberry's Northwoods brand names. Approximately 37 percent of sales are attributable to the nondairy powdered creamer segment, which sells creamer under private labels and under TreeHouse Foods' proprietary Cremora brand, principally to retailers. The remaining 18 percent of revenues are generated by the sale of other food products, including Mocha Mix nondairy liquid creamer, Second Nature liquid egg substitute, and aseptic cheese sauces and puddings for the foodservice market, aseptic products being ones that have been processed under heat and pressure in a sterile environment, producing a product not requiring refrigeration before use. TreeHouse Foods operates 10 main production plants, which are located in California, Illinois, Indiana, Iowa, Michigan, North Carolina, Oregon, and Wisconsin. The firm's major retail customers include Wal-Mart Stores, Inc., the Kroger Company, and Topco Associates LLC, while major foodservice customers include U.S. Foodservice Inc., UniPro Foodservice, Inc., and McDonald's Corporation.

From its founding, TreeHouse stated its intention to grow through acquisitions. In March 2006 the company agreed to acquire from Del Monte Foods Company its private-label and foodservice soup busi-

COMPANY PERSPECTIVES

TreeHouse Foods is dedicated to being a leader in supplying high quality products and services to the private label and foodservice industries. Our business is based on the following propositions: Private label food and beverage is a $38 billion sector that has grown at approximately twice the pace of branded products over the past six years. Foodservice channels now account for approximately 50% of total food industry sales and continue to gain share from grocery and other retail channels. Consumer needs and customer demands for improved quality, value, availability and service should favor private label food manufacturers with low cost production, a responsive supply chain, a trusted reputation and excellent service. The fragmented private label and foodservice manufacturing industries should continue to consolidate, as greater scale and national distribution are required to compete. We believe that TreeHouse is ideally suited to address the challenges and seize the opportunities posed by these long term trends and strategic developments. Our mission is to create superior value for our customers, their consumers and you, our shareholder, through a combination of superb quality, service, innovation and execution.

nesses and the Nature's Goodness baby food business, for approximately $275 million.

THE ROAD LEADING TO TREEHOUSE

The original Dean Foods Company, at the time known as Dean Milk Company, had entered the specialty food segment in 1962 when it acquired pickle producer Green Bay Food Company. Green Bay, based in Green Bay, Wisconsin, traced its roots back to the 1862 founding of Alart and McGuire Co., a pioneer in the pickle industry that built the first pickle tank in the United States. Alart and McGuire built a pickle-making plant in 1917 before being bought out by Arnold Brothers Pickle and Preserve Co. in 1925. When Leslie Kelly took control of Arnold Brothers in 1930, he renamed the company Green Bay Food Company. Over the ensuing years, Green Bay expanded its product range, until by 1949 it was making pickles, vinegar, mustard, sauerkraut, and salad dressing.

Under the Dean umbrella, Green Bay expanded considerably, in part through acquisition. In early 1993, for example, Dean acquired W.B. Roddenberry Co. Inc., a processor of pickles, peanut butter, and syrup based in Georgia that generated approximately $57 million in annual sales and owned a stable of brands with widespread regional name recognition. The following year, Green Bay's name was changed to Dean Pickle & Specialty Products.

In December 2001 Dean Foods, then the number two milk processor and distributor in the country, was bought by the number one milk firm, Suiza Foods Corporation, in a $1.7 billion deal. Suiza brought to the combined company two of the brands which were part of the original TreeHouse Foods portfolio. In November 1997 Suiza bought The Morningstar Group, Inc., whose assets included Mocha Mix nondairy liquid creamer and Second Nature liquid egg substitute. Mocha Mix had been introduced in 1950 by Presto Food Products, Inc., which was acquired by Morningstar in December 1996. Suiza assumed the Dean Foods Company name after its acquisition of the old Dean.

A final piece of the TreeHouse Foods puzzle was added late in 2003 when the new Dean's Specialty Foods Group bought the Cremora brand of nondairy powdered creamer from Eagle Family Foods, Inc. Eagle had been spun off from the now defunct Borden Foods Corporation in 1996, and the Cremora line of products continued to sport the Borden name and an image of Elsie, the famous spokescow. Borden had introduced Cremora in 1962.

CREATION OF TREEHOUSE FOODS IN 2005

Eventually Dean Foods elected to narrow its focus in order to concentrate on its two core areas, its Dairy Group and the WhiteWave Foods Company subsidiary. In January 2005, then, Dean transferred the following assets to a newly formed subsidiary called TreeHouse Foods, Inc.: its Specialty Foods Group, which produced pickles, peppers, and relishes; its Mocha Mix, Second Nature, and Cremora product lines; its foodservice salad dressings operations; and its shelf-stable, aseptic cheese-based sauces and puddings. In June 2005 TreeHouse became a completely separate, standalone company when it was spun off to the shareholders of Dean Foods. Its stock was listed on the New York Stock Exchange. TreeHouse started with about 1,700 employees, and its headquarters were established in Westchester, Illinois, a suburb of Chicago.

The name of the new company harkened back to Keebler Foods Company and the home of its mythical

KEY DATES

1862: Pickle maker Alart and McGuire Co. is established in Green Bay, Wisconsin.
1925: Arnold Brothers Pickle and Preserve Co. acquires Alart and McGuire.
1930: Arnold Brothers is renamed Green Bay Food Company.
1962: Dean Milk Company (soon renamed Dean Foods Company) acquires Green Bay Food.
1993: Dean acquires W.B. Roddenberry Co. Inc., a Georgia-based pickle processor.
1997: Suiza Foods Corporation acquires The Morningstar Group, Inc., whose assets include Mocha Mix nondairy liquid creamer and Second Nature liquid egg substitute.
2001: Dean Foods is acquired by Suiza Foods, which assumes the Dean name.
2003: Dean's Specialty Foods Group acquires the Cremora brand of nondairy powdered creamer.
2005: Dean forms TreeHouse Foods, Inc., which is spun off to Dean Foods shareholders, becoming an independent company based in Westchester, Illinois; Bay Valley Foods LLC is established as TreeHouse's main operating subsidiary.
2006: TreeHouse agrees to pay Del Monte Foods Company $275 million for its private-label and foodservice soup businesses and the Nature's Goodness brand of baby food.

elves. A five-member team of former Keebler managers, led by Sam K. Reed, the CEO of Keebler from January 1996 to March 2001, were tapped to lead the Dean spinoff. Reed's team was credited with turning around Keebler before selling it to Kellogg Company in a deal valued at $4.4 billion, a huge increase over the $450 million that Keebler had fetched in a 1996 transaction. Collectively, the new executives invested $10 million in TreeHouse for a 1.67 percent stake. While establishing their headquarters in Westchester, Reed and company kept the main operational base in Green Bay, through a subsidiary called Bay Valley Foods LLC. In August 2005 Joe Coning was named president of Bay Valley. Coning had 34 years of experience in the food industry, most recently as vice-president of contract packing and custom sales at Kellogg.

The initial strategies at TreeHouse were to focus particularly on expanding the private-label businesses and to pursue acquisitions within existing product areas and into new lines related to existing products. An extremely low debt load, just $6.1 million at the end of 2005, left the firm in a strong position to make deals. As it worked on these efforts, the company also took some steps to rationalize its operations. In November 2005 TreeHouse announced plans to close a pickle plant in La Junta, Colorado, that was operating less efficiently than its other plants. Upon its closure in February 2006, production was reallocated among the five remaining pickle plants. TreeHouse in 2005 also sold a production facility in Cairo, Georgia, where its predecessor had manufactured aseptic nutritional drinks.

A $9.9 million charge associated with the La Junta closure helped lead to a net loss of $5.6 million for the fourth quarter of 2005. For the full year, TreeHouse reported net income of $11.6 million on sales of $707.7 million. A 5.6 percent decline in sales of the firm's pickles segment was more than made up for by increased sales of nondairy powdered creamer and other products. Prices were increased in the fourth quarter across all of the company's segments in an effort to offset rising energy and raw material costs.

FIRST ACQUISITIONS IN 2006

TreeHouse's pursuit of acquisitions began to come to fruition in early 2006. In February of that year the company acquired the trademarks and customer base of Oxford Foods, Inc., a food processor based in Deerfield, Massachusetts, that produced pickles, peppers, relishes, and barbecue sauce for the foodservice industry. The acquired firm's brands included Oxford, Cains, and Max's Deli Dills. Oxford's distribution center and plant were not included in the deal, and TreeHouse shifted production of the purchased product lines to its plant in Faison, North Carolina.

Following this bolt-on acquisition, TreeHouse next reached an agreement in March 2006 on a major deal to add a third main category to its stable of private-label operations. The firm agreed to pay Del Monte Foods Company $275 million in cash for its private-label soup business, its foodservice soup business, and the Nature's Goodness brand of baby food. The private-label soup business, which produced both condensed and ready-to-eat canned soups, along with broths and gravies, was the most important part of the deal, as TreeHouse instantly gained a business with an estimated 70 percent share of the private-label soup market. Soup fit in well alongside TreeHouse's two other core private-label categories, pickles and nondairy powdered creamer, as all three were "dry" grocery, center-of-the-store businesses.

Nature's Goodness, meanwhile, ranked as the third largest brand in the U.S. infant feeding sector. The Del Monte businesses were expected to generate nearly $300 million in sales in the 12 months following the acquisition. The deal was slated to be financed out of the company's existing $400 million line of credit.

This acquisition was unlikely to be TreeHouse's last. While for the short term focused on bringing the new operations in line with the business model created at TreeHouse and Bay Valley Foods, the TreeHouse management team was determined to continue seeking bolt-on acquisitions similar to that of Oxford Foods and to keep their eyes out for bigger opportunities in other food categories, particularly for businesses specializing in private-label products.

David E. Salamie

PRINCIPAL SUBSIDIARIES

Bay Valley Foods LLC.

PRINCIPAL COMPETITORS

H. J. Heinz Company; Kraft Foods North America, Inc.; Nestlé USA, Inc.; Ralcorp Holdings, Inc.

FURTHER READING

Jargon, Julie, "TreeHouse Dips into Soup: Dean Foods Spinoff to Take on Industry Leader Campbell," *Crain's Chicago Business,* March 13, 2006, p. 4.

O'Connor, Patrick, "Pickle Plant Closing," *Northampton (Mass.) Daily Hampshire Gazette,* February 24, 2006, p. A1.

Schmeltzer, John, "Dean Says Specialty-Foods Spinoff to Find Home in Area," *Chicago Tribune,* January 28, 2005.

Shiers, Leslie, "Food Processor Sees Private Label As Way to Go," *Chicago Daily Herald,* October 7, 2005, p. 2.

"TreeHouse Foods, Inc.," *Wall Street Transcript,* February 27, 2006.

Tucker, Jeff, "La Junta Pickle Plant to Shut Down," *Pueblo (Colo.) Chieftain,* November 17, 2005.

Troutman Sanders L.L.P.

600 Peachtree Street NE
Suite 5200
Atlanta, Georgia 30308-2216
U.S.A.
Telephone: (404) 885-3000
Fax: (404) 885-3900
Web site: http://www.troutmansanders.com

Private Partnership
Incorporated: 1897
Employees: 600
Sales: $206.5 million (2004)
NAIC: 541110 Offices of Lawyers; 541199 All Other Legal Services

■ ■ ■

Troutman Sanders L.L.P. is a leading Atlanta law firm. It has offices in Washington, D.C., Virginia, North Carolina, New York, London, and Hong Kong. The firm is active in a number of areas and has significant lobbying activities. Former Georgia governor Carl E. Sanders has lead the firm after joining his practice with Atlanta's venerable Troutman, Sams in 1971. Troutman, Sams brought with it longtime client the Southern Company, and utilities have remained a prime focus of the group.

ORIGINS

Troutman Sanders L.L.P. was formed by the 1971 merger of Troutman, Sams, Schroder & Lockerman with that of former Georgia governor Carl E. Sanders, who had launched his own firm in 1967. By the time of the merger, it had about two dozen attorneys and was known as Sanders, Ashmore & Boozer.

Sanders, who was governor from 1963 to 1966, was a Democrat and a leader of the New South movement. Sanders was raised a Southern Baptist in Augusta, Georgia; his father worked a white collar job for the Swift & Co. meatpacking plant. After a World War II stint in the Army Air Corps, Sanders earned a law degree and joined local attorneys Hammond & Kennedy. He later formed a firm with G. Bertrand Hester and C. B. Thurmond.

After leaving politics Sanders terminated his practice with his remaining Augusta partner, Eugene Holley, and established a new firm in downtown Atlanta's historic Candler Building. Within a few years its roster of clients included First Georgia Bank, whose holding company Sanders founded in the late 1960s. No mere figurehead, Sanders actively built it into one of Atlanta's top law firms, notes biographer James F. Cook. At the same time, the former governor was involved in a number of business and civic ventures.

The Troutman firm dated back to 1897. It had 15 attorneys at the time of the merger. Georgia Power Company, an electric utility, had become a major client in 1930, when the firm was called Colquitt, Parker, Troutman and Arkwright. In fact, two of Troutman's partners, Preston Arkwright, Jr., and Harlee Branch, would go on to become presidents of the utility.

Carl Sanders later told the *Atlanta Business Chronicle* that the idea to merge the two firms came from Georgia

COMPANY PERSPECTIVES

Troutman Sanders attorneys are experienced in virtually every aspect of commercial law and public policy. We maintain a solid reputation for our international work, with offices in Hong Kong and London. From managing litigation to trying cases, our attorneys have the skills to bring virtually any matter to a successful resolution. Whether it's sophisticated transactional work or government regulatory issues, we have the depth and breadth to handle your case. You'll find that no matter what your legal needs are, we have a skilled lawyer capable of meeting them.

Power President Ed Hatch. The Southern Company, the parent of Georgia Power and then the largest utilities holding company in the United States, hired Troutman Sanders as its own general counsel in 1979, replacing its New York attorneys Winthrop, Stimson, Putnam & Roberts. These accounts were worth $3 million a year, according to the *American Lawyer.*

Sanders headed the newly merged firm as chief partner. Troutman Sanders had 85 attorneys by the early 1980s. The largest segment of its practice was litigation (including bankruptcy litigation), with 27 lawyers, according to *The American Lawyer Guide to Law Firms 1981–82.* It also was involved in real estate, general business (including media and sports), utilities, corporate finance, tax and estate planning, and administrative law.

GAINING ACCESS FOR CNN IN 1981

Clientele included a number of Atlanta sports teams as well as Ted Turner's growing media empire, including Turner Broadcasting System, Inc. and the Cable News Network (CNN). In 1981, Troutman Sanders filed the antitrust lawsuit against the three main broadcast TV networks that ultimately granted CNN access to the White House news pool.

The broadcasting empire controlled by Sanders' longtime friend J. B. Fuqua was an enduring client, as was Cousins Properties, owner of Atlanta's Omni Coliseum and Omni Hotel. According to the *American Lawyer,* Sanders also attracted a number of international businesses to his firm, including Belgium's Food Giant grocery chain.

NEW HQ IN 1992

By the early 1990s, Troutman Sanders had 175 attorneys and was billing $40 million a year, Sanders told Cook. In 1992, Troutman Sanders moved its headquarters into seven floors in the new 55-story NationsBank Plaza (later called Bank of America Plaza) on Atlanta's Peachtree Street. It was the tallest building in Georgia.

At the same time, the firm's name was officially shortened from Troutman, Sanders, Lockerman & Ashmore to Troutman Sanders. In 1993, the firm adopted an executive committee structure, headed by Carl Sanders, while tapping Robert W. Webb, Jr., for the newly created position of managing partner.

A Washington, D.C., office was opened in September 1993. During the course of the decade, it would grow to more than 50 lawyers.

By the late 1990s, Troutman Sanders was the third largest law firm in Atlanta, based on the number of local attorneys, according to the *Atlanta Business Chronicle.* Public, corporate, litigation, and real estate law were its main areas of emphasis.

The overseas acquisitions of client Southern Co. kept Troutman Sanders busy in international law. The firm opened a small office in Hong Kong in May 1997, just before the British handed the colony over to the People's Republic.

According to *Fulton County Daily Report* figures cited by *Georgia Trend,* Troutman Sanders had revenues of $77 million in 1998 and net income of $29.5 million. It was growing fast in spite of increasing competition among law firms, Webb told *Georgia Trend.*

MAYS & VALENTINE MERGER IN 2001

At the turn of the millennium, Troutman Sanders employed 300 attorneys and about 300 other staffers at offices in Atlanta, Washington, and Hong Kong. The firm grew 50 percent by combining with Virginia's Mays & Valentine, L.L.P. in a merger that was completed on January 1, 2001. Mays & Valentine was based in the state capital of Richmond and also maintained offices in Tysons Corners, Norfolk, and Virginia Beach in northern Virginia's high tech corridor. It had been founded in the 1920s. According to the *Fulton County Daily Report,* both firms were "lifestyle-focused," encouraging attorneys to have a life outside the office.

Both Troutman Sanders and Mays & Valentine had settled upon a course of regional expansion. "We believe that creating a regional footprint is in the best interests of our clients, who expect practice depth and regional coverage," said Troutman Sanders Managing Partner Robert W. Webb, Jr., in a statement.

KEY DATES

1897: The Troutman law firm is established.
1967: Former Georgia governor Carl Sanders launches a law firm in Atlanta.
1971: The Troutman and Sanders law firms merge.
1981: Troutman Sanders represents CNN in a lawsuit to gain access to White House press conferences.
1992: The firm moves into Bank of America Plaza.
1993: The Washington, D.C., office is opened.
1997: The Hong Kong office is opened.
2001: The firm merges with Virginia's Mays & Valentine.
2005: The New York office is launched.

Troutman opened an office in London in 2001, again drawn by utilities work. It was considering other locations in Europe as well.

Troutman Sanders also was preparing to expand in North Carolina, although the proper opportunity to enter the financial center of Charlotte proved elusive. An office did open in Raleigh, North Carolina's high-tech center, in March 2003. As was its custom, Troutman Sanders typically hired local lawyers for its new offices, rather than relocating large numbers of staff. By this time, the firm also had offices in Hong Kong, London, Washington, and four cities in Virginia. It had considered Dallas, Nashville, south Florida, and Europe for future sites.

By 2003, the firm had roughly 500 attorneys altogether. It also had a thriving lobbying practice, signing up Coca-Cola Co. as a client in late 2002. Other public affairs clients included Microsoft, General Electric, and Merck. Total annual revenues rose from $194 million to $206.5 million in 2004, reported the *Fulton County Daily Report.*

MORE SPACE IN 2004

Rather than join the exodus of law firms abandoning downtown Atlanta for the burgeoning midtown district, in 2004 Troutman Sanders decided to renew its lease while expanding its offices by 22,000 square feet to 307,000 square feet. Troutman Sanders committed to the Bank of America Plaza, which was owned by longtime client Cousins Properties, until 2020.

Troutman Sanders launched a New York office in 2005 with 90 lawyers from Jenkens & Gilchrist Parker Chapin L.L.P. Jenkens & Gilchrist was formed in 1934 as Parker Chapin & Flattau and had been acquired by Jenkens & Gilchrist of Dallas in 2001.

While the Atlanta office was staying put, Troutman was moving its Richmond, Virginia, staff (who had also been housed in a building named for Bank of America) to a new development called Riverside on the James. The 15-story building was the downtown area's first skyscraper in 15 years, noted the *Richmond Times-Dispatch.*

Frederick C. Ingram

PRINCIPAL DIVISIONS

Corporate; Finance; Litigation; Public Law; Real Estate.

PRINCIPAL COMPETITORS

Alston & Bird L.L.P.; Kilpatrick Stockton L.L.P.; King & Spalding L.L.P.

FURTHER READING

Abramson, Jill, "'Cuff Links Carl' Builds an Empire," *American Lawyer,* September 1982, pp. 14, 16.

Bentley, Tim, "High-Wire Juggling Act," *Georgia Trend,* August 1, 1999, p. 57.

Coleman, Zach, "Atlanta Law Firms Head into International Waters," *Atlanta Business Chronicle,* May 16, 1997.

Conley, Janet, "Suddenly, Troutman Isn't the Only Game in Town," *Fulton County Daily Report,* May 30, 2003.

Cook, James F., "From Politics to Business," *Carl Sanders: Spokesman of the New South,* Macon, Ga.: Mercer University Press, 1993, pp. 341–58.

Cooper, Alan, "Mays & Valentine Eyes Merger," *Richmond Times-Dispatch,* July 13, 2000, p. B8.

Donner, JoAnne, "I've Been Very Lucky," *Georgia Trend,* September 1, 2000, p. 73.

Gray, Julia D., "Troutman Call Came at Right Time," *Fulton County Daily Report,* February 25, 2003.

Hazard, Carol, "Law Firm's Demand Was Key to Downtown Richmond Mixed-Use Project," *Richmond Times-Dispatch,* June 13, 2005.

Lin, Anthony, "Atlanta Firm Acquires N.Y. Office of Jenkens & Gilchrist," *Recorder,* March 4, 2005, p. 2.

Newkirk, Margaret, "Law Firm in Middle of Mirant-Southern Spat," *Atlanta Journal-Constitution,* June 24, 2005, p. F1.

Quinn, Matthew E., "Troutman Sanders Expanding in China," *Atlanta Journal, Atlanta Constitution,* June 30, 1998, p. B2.

"Renowned Atlanta Law Firm to Defend Georgia Power in Discrimination Case," *Constitution – Georgia,* October 15, 2000.

Salter, Sallye, "C&S Plaza Snares Premier Law Firm As Tenant," *Atlanta Journal, Atlanta Constitution,* December 13, 1989, p. C1.

Schreiber, Lisa Kiersky, "Troutman Back in the Game After 2003 Slump," *Fulton County Daily Report,* June 20, 2005.

Sidden, Jennifer Boyd, "Atlanta Law Firm on Merger Hunt," *Charlotte Business Journal,* April 18, 2003.

Sinderman, Martin, "Troutman Sanders Reels in Deal to Stay at Home," *Atlanta Business Chronicle,* November 5, 2004.

Stephens, Erica, "Legacy of Law," *Atlanta Business Chronicle,* June 9, 2000.

"Troutman Opens in New York with Jenkens Coup," *Lawyer,* March 14, 2005, p. 7.

"Troutman, Sanders, Lockerman & Ashmore," *The American Lawyer Guide to Law Firms 1981–82,* New York: Am-Law Publishing Corporation, 1981.

"Troutman Sanders to Attack Euro Energy Work from City," *Lawyer* (U.K.), May 28, 2001, p. 4.

"Troutman Sanders Will Ring in 2003 with a New Lobbyist and a New Marquee Public Affairs Client, The Coca-Cola Co.," *Fulton County Daily Report,* December 10, 2002.

"Welcome to Firm Where Billing Too Much Causes Concern," *Fulton County Daily Report,* October 31, 2000.

Woods, Walter, "Law Firm Will Stay Downtown; Troutman Sanders Extends Lease at Bank of America Plaza Through 2020," *Atlanta Journal-Constitution,* September 17, 2004, p. F1.

———, "Troutman Sanders Law Firm May Join Downtown Atlanta Exodus," *Atlanta Journal and Constitution,* March 19, 2004.

True Religion Apparel, Inc.

1525 Rio Vista Avenue
Los Angeles, California 90035
U.S.A.
Telephone: (323) 266-3072
Fax: (323) 266-8060
Web site: http://www.truereligionbrandjeans.com

Public Company
Incorporated: 2001 as Gusana Explorations Inc.
Employees: 95
Sales: $102.6 million (2005)
Stock Exchanges: NASDAQ
Ticker Symbol: TRLG
NAIC: 315224 Men's and Boys' Cut and Sew Trouser, Slack, and Jean Manufacturing

■ ■ ■

True Religion Apparel, Inc. is a designer of premium denim wear, selling its apparel to fashion-conscious customers in North America, Asia, and Europe, where the company's signature emblem of a smiling Buddha strumming a guitar has attracted a loyal following. The product line, built around jeans that retail for as much as $465 per pair, comprises denim jeans, jackets, and shirts; corduroy jeans, jackets, and shirts; and velvet jeans and jackets for men. For women, True Religion designs denim jeans, jackets, shirts, skirts, and shorts; corduroy jeans and jackets; twill jeans; and velvet jeans and jackets. The company also sells denim jeans and corduroy jackets for children. The brand is sold primarily in specialty retail stores through 300 accounts that generate roughly 75 percent of the company's sales. The merchandise is also available in department stores such as Neiman Marcus, Bergdorf Goodman, and Saks Fifth Avenue. True Religion operates one retail store under the True Religion name, a 900-square-foot unit in Manhattan Beach, California. Sales abroad, led by markets in Japan, Germany, Canada, and the United Kingdom, account for 46 percent of the company's sales. True Religion apparel is made by third-party manufacturers based in the United States and Mexico.

ORIGINS

Jeffrey Lubell spent more than 20 years working in the textile industry before he launched his entrepreneurial career. The experience soon turned into a nightmare. With his wife Kymberly, Lubell launched two lines of jeans under the Bella Dahl and Jefri Jeans labels in the late 1990s, but the venture became ensnarled in financial and legal difficulties that likely left the Brooklyn native pining for a return to his days as a fabric salesman. Lubell's company, Bella Dahl Inc., fell behind in payments to its factor—a financial intermediary that purchases accounts receivable as security for short-term loans—and was forced into bankruptcy. Bitterness over the collapse of the company quickly turned into a legal battle: "We got no ownership and got hung out to dry with our liability with CIT Commercial Services, our factor," Lubell fumed in a September 25, 2001 interview with *WWD.* "We feel like two children were stolen from us, two prestigious denim labels," he said. "We're suing for our ownership interest and what was promised to us."

Anger flared and lawsuits were filed soon after CIT foreclosed on Bella Dahl Inc. in November 2000. Jolna

COMPANY PERSPECTIVES

Our strategy is to build brand recognition by marketing our products to fashion conscious, affluent consumers who shop in high-end boutiques and department stores and who want to wear and be seen in the latest, trendiest, jeans and related apparel. We plan to limit distribution to the more exclusive boutiques, specialty stores and department stores in an effort to maintain the unique nature of our brand and our True Religion Brand Jeans sell in the range of $170 to $300 per pair at retail. We utilize contract manufacturers located in the United States so that we can brand our products as having been "Made in the U.S.A.," and because it helps us control our costs and keep fixed overhead to a minimum. We plan to update our product offerings—style, fit, washes—every six months to be seen as a trend setter in the contemporary better jeans market.

Design Group Inc., led by brothers Kerry Jolna and Steve Jolna, purchased the trademarks and partial assets of Bella Dahl Inc. that month and began marketing the Bella Dahl and Jefri Jeans lines. In June 2001, the Jolna brothers were the first to strike, filing a lawsuit against the Lubells that alleged misappropriation of trade secrets and unfair competitive practices related to the Lubells' new line of jeans, Hippie Jeans. The Lubells fired back, filing a ten-count countersuit charging the Jolnas and CIT with fraud and conspiracy. "Kerry Jolna and Steve Jolna engineered a default of Bella Dahl Inc. under the factoring agreement," the lawsuit, as quoted in the January 28, 2002 issue of *WWD,* stated, "such that Kerry Jolna and Steve Jolna would be able to acquire cross-complainants' [the Lubells'] IP [intellectual property] and other valuable property." In the end, the Lubells lost the battle, forcing them to start from scratch with their next venture, True Religion Apparel.

The lessons learned from the Bella Dahl debacle dictated the Lubells' approach with True Religion. "With my other two brands," Jeffrey Lubell said in a September 4, 2003 interview with *WWD,* "I made bad decisions. I said, 'I'd rather do things myself than to sell out and go through that again.' When you find a partner, you have to answer to someone else's rules and regulations because people who put money in think they deserve majority ownership." Lubell was careful not to make the same mistakes again when he and his wife launched the True Religion line in December 2002. He registered the company's trademarks to himself and he sought an arrangement that would provide an infusion of capital without forcing him to give up majority ownership of the company. Lubell's stipulations led to an odd corporate marriage, a deal that would see his company, Guru Denim Inc., a designer of high-fashion, high-priced denim wear, wed a beleaguered Canadian company prospecting for gold in British Columbia.

UNION OF A GOLD MINER AND A DENIM DESIGNER: 2003

The deal was a reverse merger, a transaction in which a private company is folded into a public company and managed by executives from the private company. Not uncommon, reverse mergers avoid the legal and underwriting expenses associated with taking a privately owned company public. For Lubell, a reverse merger answered his need for capital and met his desire to maintain control, a logical solution provided by an incongruous corporate union.

In April 2001, Gusana Explorations Inc. was incorporated as an exploration entity to mine for minerals and valuable metals in British Columbia. Incorporated in Nevada and occupying main offices in Vancouver, British Columbia, Gusana held titles to six mineral claims north of Vancouver, where it hoped to prospect for gold. The company never became a going enterprise. A registration statement filed with the Securities and Exchange Commission (SEC) on March 5, 2002, came across as particularly despondent, exceeding the usual cautionary tone adopted by companies in presenting their case to the U.S. regulatory body. "We have no known ore reserves," the statement read. "We have not identified any gold on the property and we cannot guaranty that we will ever find any gold. Even if we find that there is gold on our property, we cannot guaranty that we will be able to recover the gold. Even if we recover gold, we cannot guaranty that we will make a profit. If we cannot find gold or it is not economical to recover the gold, we will have to cease operations." Such was the outlook, when the company, unable to attract enough investors to finance its exploration efforts and having never generated any revenues, was forced to face its own collapse. The directors, presiding over a company with debts of $9,773 and assets of $2,819, looked for a way to save the corporate shell they controlled, deciding in May 2003 that something had to be done.

While Gusana's directors mulled over their options in Vancouver, down south, in El Segundo, California, Lubell was exploring his own options. He solicited the help of a friend to secure a direct investment in Guru

KEY DATES

2001: Gusana Explorations Inc. is incorporated.
2002: Jeffrey Lubell forms Guru Denim Inc.
2003: In a reverse merger, Gusana and Guru Denim unite, creating True Religion Apparel, Inc.
2004: True Religion records its first annual profit, posting $4.2 million in net income.
2005: True Religion opens its first retail location, a 900-square-foot boutique in Manhattan Beach, California.

Denim, and his friend introduced him to the investment bankers backing a forlorn operation up north, Gusana. In June 2003, Lubell agreed to sell his denim company to Gusana, gaining the leverage he demanded after his experience with Bella Dahl. Gusana, unable to make its mark as a mining concern, became a clothing company, a super-premium denim designer headed by Lubell, who held the titles of president and chief executive officer. To further assuage any concerns on Lubell's behalf of a repeat of the Bella Dahl experience, he was given a 62 percent stake in the company, holding sway as the company's majority owner. The pot was sweetened by the $250,000 Lubell was given to support the apparel line's expansion, the price of selling Guru Denim to Gusana. The reverse merger was made complete in August 2003, when Gusana changed its name to True Religion Apparel Inc., an El Segundo-based company with Guru Denim as its mainstay subsidiary.

2003–05: A HOT TREND FUELING FINANCIAL GROWTH

By the time True Religion's corporate structure was in place, the company already had made a name for itself in the fashion world. Lubell and his three employees—his wife Kymberly, a production supervisor, and a product designer—created a buzz in the industry within months of launching the company's line, a line comprising "super-premium" denim wear. The company's jeans, bearing an emblem of a smiling Buddha strumming a guitar and, in some occasions, elaborately embroidered, were at the highest end of the price spectrum, wholesaling for between $100 and $200 and selling at retail for as much as $465. "Today's customer is about the product," Lubell said in a March 17, 2005 interview with *WWD*. "It's not about the price point. If you want to buy a price point, you go to Wal-Mart and Target." The line quickly attracted a following of celebrities, providing invaluable exposure. True Religion apparel was worn by Madonna, Gwyneth Paltrow, Bruce Willis, among a host of other luminaries, including the entire cast of the television program *Desperate Housewives.* The brand was featured in films such as *Cake, The Fog, Domino,* and *Dukes of Hazzard,* and appeared in a long list of fashion magazines, including *Elle, Vogue,* and *Bazaar.* "Anybody who's alive and kicking is a True Religion customer," Lubell exclaimed in the April 2006 issue of *Kiplinger's Personal Finance Magazine,* and many answered his call, eagerly paying for the prestige associated with the brand.

Lubell succeeded in generating hype about his apparel brand, and he also set up the means to get the most out of the public's desire for the True Religion label. During his first year in business, Lubell established distribution and licensing deals in Japan, Canada, Italy, Spain, Germany, Australia, and New Zealand, creating an international network that soon accounted for approximately half of the company's annual sales. Abroad and in the United States, the company's apparel was available at department stores, but Lubell relied heavily on specialty shops for showcasing the brand. From Italy's Gio' Moretti to France's Martine Chambon to New York City's Anik, prestigious boutiques represented the primary retail outlet for True Religion attire, accounting for two-thirds of all sales. Structured as such, the company's distribution and retail network generated explosive financial growth during the first few years of the True Religion brand. In 2003, the company collected $2.4 million in sales and recorded a net loss of $10,700. In 2004, the previous year's loss was turned into a $4.2 million gain, as sales swelled to $27.6 million. In 2005, revenues shot upward, jumping by nearly fourfold to $102.5 million. The company's net income for the year posted an even greater gain, leaping to $19.5 million. As the company's financial stature increased so too did its esteem among the investment community. True Religion's shares first began trading on the NASDAQ over-the-counter bulletin board, when the company essentially was a penny stock. In August 2005, the company's shares began trading on the main NASDAQ market, reaching a high of $17.77 per share during the year.

Looking ahead, there was every reason to expect further robust growth from True Religion, and there was the not-to-be-overlooked chance that the True Religion fad could sputter away as quickly as it began. Lubell catered to the most capricious of tastes, occupying a market niche that quickly enriched the successful and summarily discarded those who failed to captivate consumers. Some analysts wondered whether Lubell would take his company to the next level by developing True Religion into a so-called "lifestyle" brand and thereby endeavor to strengthen the financial potential and longevity of the True Religion name. The company was exploring one new avenue of growth as it entered the second half of the decade, opening its own retail location. In July 2005, the company opened a 900-square-foot True Religion store in Manhattan Beach, California, giving it a new, potentially massive business area to exploit. No plans were announced for additional store openings, however. In the years ahead, much remained to be seen in regard to True Religion's staying power in the business world, but there was certainty about the company's first years in business: True Religion created a stir in the fashion world, an achievement whose worth was not to be underestimated.

Jeffrey L. Covell

PRINCIPAL SUBSIDIARIES

Guru Denim, Inc.

PRINCIPAL COMPETITORS

Calvin Klein, Inc.; Innovo Group Inc.; Levi Strauss & Co.

FURTHER READING

Bowers, Katharine, "Hippie Jeans Designers Countersue Jolna Group," *WWD,* September 25, 2001, p. 11.

Brown, Rachel, "Jeans Makers Sew Up $24 Million Stock Deal," *Los Angeles Business Journal,* October 3, 2005, p. 3.

———, "One-of-a-Kind Boutiques Find Growth Comes Easier in Pairs," *Los Angeles Business Journal,* July 11, 2005, p. 8.

Cunningham, Thomas, "True Religion CEO: We're Not Behind Newsletter Hype," *Daily News Record,* December 1, 2003, p. 1.

———, "True Religion Stock Soars, Drops Midweek," *Daily News Record,* September 29, 2003, p. 5.

Goldberg, Steven T., "What Price Denim?," *Kiplinger's Personal Finance Magazine,* April 2006, p. 66.

Greene, Joshua, "Bella Dahl Countersued," *WWD,* January 28, 2002, p. 4.

Malone, Scott, "Lubell Finds Independence," *WWD,* September 4, 2003, p. 8.

———, "Lubell Founds True Religion," *WWD,* August 28, 2003, p. 7.

———, "True Religion Takes Off," *WWD,* March 17, 2005, p. 6.

Tran, Khanh T. L., "True Religion Begins Trading on NASDAQ," *WWD,* August 19, 2005, p. 24.

"True Religion Apparel to Open First Retail Store in California," *DSN Retail Fax,* April 18, 2005, p. 2.

Tschorn, Adam, "True Religion Settles Suit with Former Partner," *Daily News Record,* October 4, 2004, p. 2.

———, "The Wrath of True Religion," *Daily News Record,* June 27, 2005, p. 4.

Tucker, Ross, "True Religion's 3Q Sales Triple," *WWD,* November 22, 2005, p. 10.

"USA: Strong Demand Drives True Religion's Q1 Growth," *just-style.com,* April 27, 2005.

Vesilind, Emili, "True Religion Makes Low-Key Retail Debut," *WWD,* December 21, 2005, p. 12.

Union Pacific Corporation

1400 Douglas Street
Omaha, Nebraska 68179
U.S.A.
Telephone: (402) 544-5000
Toll Free: (888) 870-8777
Fax: (402) 271-6408
Web site: http://www.up.com

Public Company
Incorporated: 1969
Employees: 48,000
Sales: $13.57 billion (2005)
Stock Exchanges: New York
Ticker Symbol: UNP
NAIC: 482111 Line-Haul Railroads; 484121 General Freight Trucking, Long-Distance, Truckload; 551112 Offices of Other Holding Companies

■ ■ ■

Union Pacific Corporation (UP) is a holding company whose principal operating subsidiary is Union Pacific Railroad Company. UP's railroad business is the largest in North America, linking every major West Coast and Gulf Coast port through more than 32,000 miles of track crossing 23 states. UP ranks as the largest hauler of chemicals in the country, but the company also transports substantial amounts of coal, food, forest products, grain, intermodal (truck trailers and containers), metals and minerals, and automobiles and parts. The railroad also runs a large commuter train operation in Chicago. UP's largest customer is APL Limited, a steamship company that operates in the Pacific, and its second largest customer is automobile manufacturer General Motors.

TRANSCONTINENTAL ORIGINS

Union Pacific came into existence in response to the widely held belief, fully formed by the 1850s, that the United States needed a rail link between its older, eastern states and the distant but rapidly growing states of the far West. Various proposals were made for northern, southern, and central routes, but the U.S. Congress could not agree on a plan. Following the South's secession from the United States in 1861 the remaining congressmen from the North quickly agreed upon a route, and U.S. President Abraham Lincoln signed the Pacific Railroad Act of 1862, urged on by military considerations as much as by those of economics. The act called for the creation of a public corporation, called Union Pacific Railroad Company, to build a railroad from Nebraska to the California-Nevada border and there to meet the Central Pacific, building east from Sacramento, California, and later linked with San Francisco. Later, the meeting place of the two railroads was set at Promontory Summit, Utah Territory. As amended by a second piece of legislation, the act specified that the company would be supported by a loan from the federal government of U.S. bonds, to be paid back in 30 years, and by the issuance of its own bonds and capital stock. Further, the company would receive land grants in the amount of 6,400 acres on alternating sides of every mile of track laid, a checkerboard swath of land across the middle of the country that would eventually total around 12 million acres of valuable

COMPANY PERSPECTIVES

Since its inception, Union Pacific has been a company whose activities have always been associated with the land—first as a key transportation link spanning the West, later as a developer and guardian of its natural resources. The strategic planning and investment decisions of the modern Union Pacific Corporation stem from this heritage. The corporation concentrates on businesses that it knows, using the specialized knowledge acquired over the years in fields of endeavor critical to the American economy and the nation's future.

minerals, grazing land, and metropolitan real estate. The government retained the right to inspect each section of track laid before releasing the allotted number of bonds, and it would keep two directors on UP's board, but the company was to be otherwise a private sector venture.

While the logic and value of a railroad across the western United States was obvious in the early twenty-first century, it was much less so in 1864. The men who became involved in the leadership of the UP, chiefly Thomas C. Durant and the Ames brothers, Oliver and Oakes, did so largely in order to make handsome profits off the railroad's hurried construction. Durant was the vice-president and dominant figure in the company's early years, and it was he and a handful of others who formed a construction company called Credit Mobilier of America (CMA) to receive contracts from UP for the building of its vast railroad. Estimates vary as to precisely how inflated these contracts were, but later congressional investigations left no doubt that the backers of CMA intentionally siphoned off far more of the UP's capital than was fair to its investors or good for its future financial health. The investigations of the early 1870s also revealed that the CMA principals bribed members of Congress with company stock.

Still, the railroad they built was a splendid success, and so vast a project might never have been undertaken without the promise of equally vast profits to be made. In five years the UP crews laid more than 1,000 miles of rail between Omaha, Nebraska, and Promontory Summit, Utah Territory, where on May 10, 1869, a golden spike completed the first transcontinental rail line. The railroad's completion supplied a critical impetus to the development of the American West, which to that time had been settled only on the Pacific Coast and in areas of unusual mineral wealth, such as Colorado. With the coming of the railroad, farmers, ranchers, and manufacturers were able to transport their goods to the great eastern metropolitan markets cheaply and quickly, and the West began to fill with pioneers. As the area's most significant railroad for almost 15 years, UP enjoyed rapid growth and excellent earnings for its scandal-ridden promoters, who were dominated from 1873 to the mid-1880s by financier Jay Gould.

EXPANSION IN 19TH CENTURY

Gould's direction of UP was notable for two things. First, the railroad expanded considerably during the decade of the 1870s. Its main route from Omaha, Nebraska, to Ogden, Utah, was soon joined by a host of feeder lines extending into the neighboring territory, some of them of substantial length; and from its Ogden terminus the company acquired control of two new branches, the Utah and Northern running to Montana, and the Utah Central progressing in the general direction of Los Angeles, which it reached in 1901. More immediately significant was the 1880 annexation by the UP of one of its rivals, the Kansas Pacific. The Kansas line ran from Kansas City, Kansas, to Cheyenne, Wyoming, via Denver, Colorado, and although its finances were in even worse condition than UP's it added an important link to the company's midwestern network. Finally, UP defended its transcontinental business by building a bridge to the Pacific Ocean through Idaho and Oregon, a system of new and existing lines that eventually fell under the aegis of UP's Oregon Short Line Railway Company. UP's original link to the ocean, the Central Pacific line to San Francisco, became a part of its most formidable rival, Southern Pacific, and was therefore lost to UP's purposes until late in the 20th century.

The second legacy of Jay Gould's years at UP was less beneficial. Beginning about 1875, Gould used the railroad's considerable income to pay an extremely high dividend on its common stock, of which he happened to own about two-thirds. As a result of Credit Mobilier's excessive construction contracts, UP was already badly overcapitalized and faced stiff periodic interest payments on its own bonds as well as an eventual lump sum reimbursement to the federal government of about $76 million of principal and interest on the latter's bond loan. Instead of taking prudent steps to provide for these liabilities, Gould bled UP of its cash flow, drove up the company's stock price by means of the huge dividends, and then sold the bulk of his shares in 1878 for a bulging profit. UP staggered on until 1884 with Gould and others of like persuasion in charge of its failing finances, at which time the company tried to make a fresh start under its newly elected president, Charles

KEY DATES

1862: The Pacific Railroad Act calls for the formation of a public corporation to build a railroad connecting the eastern United States to the western United States.
1866: Southern Pacific Railroad is chartered by the U.S. Congress to build rail lines from San Francisco to San Diego.
1869: The first transcontinental rail line is completed.
1901: Union Pacific Railroad acquires a 46 percent interest in Southern Pacific Railroad.
1913: The U.S. Supreme Court rules that Union Pacific must sell its stake in Southern Pacific to comply with antitrust legislation.
1969: Union Pacific Corporation is formed as a holding company.
1982: Union Pacific merges with the Missouri Pacific and Western Pacific railroads.
1986: Union Pacific enters the trucking business through the acquisition of Overnite Transportation Company.
1988: Southern Pacific is acquired by Philip Anschutz and becomes part of Rio Grande Industries.
1995: Union Pacific Corp. completes the $1.1 billion acquisition of the Chicago & North Western Railway.
1996: Union Pacific Corp. and Southern Pacific merge, creating the largest railroad company in the United States.
2003: Union Pacific Corp. exits the trucking business by spinning off Overnite in an initial public offering of stock.
2006: James R. Young is appointed president and chief executive officer.

Francis Adams, Jr., a Bostonian of impeccable credentials with a scholar's grasp of the railroad business.

GOVERNMENT RECEIVERSHIP: 1893

Adams faced a doubly difficult situation. UP's actual and reputed past sins made it nearly impossible to convince Congress and the public that the new president was in fact taking commendable steps toward reducing the company's debt and improving its efficiency. As a result, Adams's efforts were often thwarted, and UP continued to struggle under the burden laid upon it by its founders. At the same time, UP was by then no longer the sole provider of transcontinental rail service. Competition from three rival lines had cut severely into UP's operating income by the mid-1880s, further complicating Adams's task. The combination of looming government debt, fresh competition in the market, and a skeptical legislative climate proved too much for the company when the financial panic of 1893 strained the U.S. economy to the utmost. In October of that year UP went into government receivership.

It was not until the end of 1895 that a satisfactory resolution of UP's debt was accomplished, during which interval the railroad lost many of its most important branch lines to local receiverships. In 1895 a reorganization committee representing UP's first-mortgage bondholders and backed by the New York investment banking house of Kuhn, Loeb and Company came up with a plan to foreclose on the railroad and sell its assets to a new company of the same name. The foreclosure sale was held in November 1897, and Kuhn, Loeb was able to raise the capital needed to pay off most of the government's $71 million in remaining debt and launch the new corporation on a solid financial basis. Quickly asserting himself on the UP's board of directors was an astute New York financier, Edward H. Harriman, who used his chairmanship of UP as the centerpiece of a remarkable railroad empire. Harriman was as brilliant a dealmaker as Jay Gould, but he also represented a new class of industrial magnate, one who was more interested in the construction of vast and durable business combines than in the clever manipulation of capital for immediate profit. Under Harriman's leadership, UP became one of the best run as well as one of the largest of U.S. railroads.

HARRIMAN'S REIGN, 1898–1909

Harriman first set about retrieving the various pieces of UP lost during the receivership and soon reassembled the company's three basic networks: those running between Omaha and Ogden, Ogden and the Pacific Northwest, and Ogden and Los Angeles. Between 1898 and Harriman's death in 1909, the UP increased its track miles from 2,000 to 6,000, and when the chairman became frustrated by UP's failure to gain control of the old Central Pacific run between Ogden and San Francisco's bay area, he wasted no time in buying up Central's owner, Southern Pacific (SP). SP was UP's chief rival and equal, the owner of three main routes between San Francisco and Portland, Oregon; San Francisco and Ogden; and San Francisco and the entire Southwest to New Orleans. SP also owned a series of steamship lines extending from California to Japan and Panama, and from New Orleans to New York. UP's purchase of 45 percent of SP's stock in 1901 for $90 million virtually merged the two giants of western rail transport into a single, monopolistic entity dominating the markets from Kansas City to San Francisco and Denver to New Orleans, Louisiana.

E.H. Harriman was a man of unlimited ambition. Shortly after sealing the Southern Pacific merger, he entered into a complicated series of maneuvers that resulted in the purchase by UP of a strong minority position in Northern Pacific, owner of vital Chicago connections operated by the Chicago, Burlington and Quincy Railroad. In turn, Northern Pacific and Great Northern Railroad became a part of a holding company known as Northern Securities Corporation, which was ordered dissolved by the U.S. Supreme Court in 1904. When the pieces of this gigantic, short-lived combination were sorted out, UP emerged as the owner of 20 percent of both Northern Pacific and Great Northern and a substantial amount of cash profit as well. With the proceeds of this wrangling, Harriman bought sizable shares of many of the other important railroads in the western United States, in particular the Illinois Central and the Atchison, Topeka and Santa Fe, the latter providing the UP-SP's sole competition in the Southwest. The empire of E. H. Harriman and UP-SP thus comprised large numbers of railroads, railroad stocks, steamship lines, increasingly valuable real estate holdings, and uncounted tons of coal, iron, and other minerals.

Harriman was a prudent administrator of his roads, reinvesting the bulk of their net income in extensive renovation and new rolling stock. In 1906, however, he began paying an unusually large dividend of 10 percent, raising widespread accusations that Harriman was another profiteer out to gouge the public for his own benefit. The Interstate Commerce Commission (ICC) initiated an investigation into Harriman and UP that resulted in a 1913 decision by the U.S. Supreme Court that the company was inhibiting competition and must divest itself of its Southern Pacific holdings. Harriman did not live to see UP thus reduced roughly to the size and shape it had been in 1900, the company's lines once again restricted to the three main routes between Omaha and Ogden, Ogden and the Northwest port cities, and Ogden and Los Angeles. Lost was the prized route between Ogden and San Francisco, but in the meantime UP had beefed up its branch system and added new lines between Portland and Seattle.

Although Harriman died in 1909, his family retained a powerful influence at UP, Harriman's sons W. Averell Harriman and E. Roland Harriman sitting on the company's board for many years and both serving as chairmen. Furthermore, so successful was the elder Harriman that the company he left behind became a model for the railroad industry of financial strength and unexcelled performance. From 1916's gross revenue of slightly more than $100 million, UP more than doubled sales to $211 million by 1923, where they remained for much of that prosperous decade. Earnings were steadily excellent in the 1930s and 1940s, an increasing portion of them in the 1930s generated by UP's oil and gas holdings and industrial real estate. A long-term problem for the railroad industry had by then made itself felt, however; truck and automobile traffic was eroding the railroads' share of both freight and passenger miles. This trend, which would intensify during much of the 20th century, was especially painful when the Great Depression of the 1930s curtailed the heavy industrial transport upon which the railroads had come to depend. UP revenues did not approach their former heights until World War II recharged the industrial economy after 1940, and in the early 1930s they barely topped $125 million annually.

Averell Harriman was chairman of UP for most of the 1930s, and did an excellent job of keeping expenses down during the lean years while also investing needed capital in technological developments such as the diesel locomotive. With the outbreak of World War II the Harrimans had little to worry about in the financial realm. The need to shuttle huge amounts of personnel and heavy equipment around the United States gave UP all the business it could handle, company employment nearly doubling to 60,000 and revenue pushing to more than $500 million by war's end. Between 1914 and 1944 alone, UP purchased 2,270 new locomotives, including a number of Big Boys, the world's largest steam locomotive designed for the most taxing Rocky Mountain routes. The end of the war in 1945 caused only a temporary drop in sales for UP, and by the early 1950s revenue was again exceeding $500 million annually and the company remained in generally excellent financial health.

STEPPING UP RESOURCE DEVELOPMENT ACTIVITIES

The next few years were not as kind, however. UP faltered in the late 1950s, its income, dividend, and stock price all falling between 1956 and 1961. Part of the problem lay in the rapid depletion of the company's best oil well, outside Los Angeles, and part in the continuing loss of railroad freight sales to the trucking industry. In response, UP restructured its holdings into three divisions—transportation, land development, and natural resources—and in the mid-1960s began a concentrated program of mineral, oil, and gas exploration. The reorganization into divisions helped UP pursue what had grown into three very distinct businesses, each one with the potential to add significant dollars to the company's bottom line. Only a small percentage of the railroad's 7.8 million acres of remaining land had been fully explored and utilized, but even so by 1967 the firm operated five oil and gas fields and was the owner of the world's largest known deposit of trona soda ash ore; vast reserves of coal; and sizable holdings of iron, titanium, and uranium. In a further step toward the exploitation of these resources, in 1969 UP acquired Champlin Petroleum Company and Pontiac Refineries from Celanese Corporation for $240 million, thus completing the formation of a fully integrated oil and gas business. Champlin would eventually operate three refineries, in Texas, Oklahoma, and California, and to ensure that its plants were kept busy UP also signed a joint-venture agreement allowing a subsidiary of Standard Oil Company of Indiana to drill for oil on its acreage, with UP getting royalties and retaining a quarter interest in whatever oil was found.

Overseeing this diversification at UP was chief executive officer Frank Barnett, the first CEO without intimate ties to the Harriman family to run the company in the 20th century. Barnett, who became CEO in 1967, had as his goal to develop equally strong transportation and nontransport divisions at UP. In 1969 UP established a holding company called Union Pacific Corporation, with Union Pacific Railroad Company becoming one of the subsidiaries of this holding company. With oil prices soaring after the oil crisis of 1973–74, UP's revenue quadrupled during the 1970s to $4 billion, more than half of which was provided in the late 1970s by the nontransportation businesses. The company's coal reserves also became more valuable during the energy-conscious 1970s, when UP upped its production tenfold. Less successful was the company's 13-year effort, begun in 1962, to win ICC approval of a merger with Chicago, Rock Island & Pacific Railroad (CRI&P) and thereby secure a valuable link between UP's Omaha terminus and both Chicago and St. Louis, Missouri. The merger was opposed by rivals of UP who feared the impact of its entry into Chicago, the nation's busiest rail center. The CRI&P subsequently ceased operations in 1980, and many of its lines were sold to other railroads, including the Missouri Pacific and the Missouri-Kansas-Texas Railroad.

MERGER WITH MISSOURI PACIFIC AND WESTERN PACIFIC IN 1982

In 1982 UP gained a Chicago gateway in another way. In a move reminiscent of E.H. Harriman's reign, the company took advantage of U.S. President Ronald Reagan's deregulation of the railroads to accomplish an important merger with the Missouri Pacific and Western Pacific railroads. Missouri Pacific operated some 11,500 miles of track in Texas, Oklahoma, and Missouri, and also provided the crucial bridge between Chicago and Omaha long sought by UP, along with three key gateways to Mexico; while Western Pacific operated a route between Ogden, Utah, and the bay area of San Francisco.

The merger was a major undertaking, and it signaled a new era of consolidation in the U.S. railroad industry. While the move would benefit all three partners in the long run, it also presented UP with a massive organizational problem. With suddenly bloated employee and management ranks and a doubling of track mileage, UP slipped to dead last in operating profitability among U.S. railroads in 1984, although profits were up nearly 30 percent. The company's problems were not helped by the steadily falling price of oil, which was especially hard on domestic producers trying to squeeze the last drop out of older oil wells; but its basic need was for a drastic pruning of its labor force. This was accomplished by Drew Lewis, U.S. secretary of transportation in the early 1980s and UP chairman starting in 1987, and his railroad president, Michael Walsh, who together cut nearly 12,000 employees from UP's ranks. The cuts had resulted in far greater productivity from line workers as well as a more responsive management, whose ranks were thinned from nine administrative levels to only three. In another cost-saving move, Union Pacific Corporation in 1988 relocated its headquarters from New York City to Bethlehem, Pennsylvania. Walsh resigned in 1991 to become CEO of Tenneco. He was succeeded by Richard K. Davidson.

Meanwhile, UP gave up trying to beat the truckers and instead joined them, buying Overnite Transportation Company, a national trucking company, in 1986 and stepping up its capacity for intermodal services. Union Pacific Corporation in 1987 combined its Champlin oil and gas unit with its Rocky Mountain Energy mineral unit to form Union Pacific Resources Group. In 1988 UP further expanded its railroad operations through the acquisition of the Missouri-Kansas-Texas. The following year the Harriman Dispatching Center opened in Omaha, providing a central location for all train dispatching. Also in 1989 UP acquired a 25 percent stake in the Chicago & North Western Railway (C&NW).

CONCENTRATION ON RAILROAD OPERATIONS: 1990–95

As the 1990s, a decade of intensified railroad consolidation, unfolded, Union Pacific Corporation increased its concentration on its railroad operations. In 1994 UP gained minority control of the C&NW, then acquired it outright the following year for $1.1 billion. UP subsequently had great difficulty integrating the C&NW, leading to service problems, including widespread delays for Midwest shippers, and an apology from UP management to its customers. Also in 1994 UP entered into a battle with Burlington Northern for control of the Atchison, Topeka & Santa Fe (the Santa Fe). UP's bid failed, and Burlington Northern and the Santa Fe merged in 1995 to form Burlington Northern Santa Fe, which thereby became the number one U.S. railroad. UP was able, however, to gain significant trackage rights from Burlington Northern as a merger concession.

Pennzoil Company, a major energy company best known for its motor oil, approached Union Pacific Corporation in 1995 about purchasing Union Pacific Resources, an overture that UP rejected. That year UP combined all of its natural resource operations into Union Pacific Resources, then sold a minority stake to the public. UP then sold its remaining 83 percent stake in 1996. It was during this period when it was divesting its noncore resources operations that Union Pacific made its boldest railroad acquisition yet in the consolidating 1990s: Southern Pacific.

SOUTHERN PACIFIC'S CENTRAL PACIFIC ORIGINS

The history of Southern Pacific begins with the efforts of Theodore D. Judah to build an earlier railroad, the Central Pacific. Judah was a Connecticut engineer experienced in railroad construction who moved to California in 1854 and immediately became absorbed by the possibility of a rail link between that state and the East. Not a financier, Judah lobbied Congress for help with his grand project, and around 1860 became acquainted with four ambitious businessmen from Sacramento. This quartet, whose members would go on to build and own the Southern Pacific, were Collis P. Huntington, proprietor of a large hardware store; Leland Stanford, lawyer and in 1861 governor of California; Charles Crocker, dry goods merchant; and Mark Hopkins, partner to Huntington. Along with Judah and a few other investors, the four promoters created the Central Pacific Railroad of California on June 28, 1861, and then set about finding the cash infusions that would be needed even to begin the mammoth construction project from Sacramento, California, to the East.

The bulk of these funds were eventually provided by the U.S. government, which under the terms of the railroad acts of 1862 and 1864 agreed to loan to Central Pacific a varying amount of government bonds for every mile of road built, depending on the difficulty of terrain traversed, and to grant it a checkerboard pattern of land on alternate sides of the railroad that would eventually total millions of acres of urban and range property. An important caveat deprived the railroad of most mineral rights to this land, a category generally interpreted by the courts to include oil. In addition to this federal aid, Central Pacific was empowered to sell stocks and bonds of its own, but in the early years few buyers for these could be found. The four original promoters were therefore continually scrambling for enough money to support the road's construction, which began in January 1863. To ease its chronic financial burden, Central Pacific persuaded municipalities to buy its bonds, threatening bluntly that if such support were not forthcoming the railroad would simply be built around the town in question, destroying its economic viability. In this way, Central managed to raise a substantial amount of money to complement its federal funds. However, as it became clear that the partners would succeed in their project, public optimism about the benefits thus gained was tempered by the realization that there would be one and only one major rail system in northern California.

Further blackening the reputation of the Central Pacific was the widespread belief that the promoters of the road were skimming profits. They awarded lucrative contracts to construction companies owned by themselves, contracts calling for payments in the form of both cash and Central Pacific stock and so liberal in terms that by the time the road was completed in 1869 the construction company was, in effect, its owner. The net result was that a railroad had been built over the Sierra mountains to Ogden, Utah, with government funds, but was now owned by four individuals.

SOUTHERN PACIFIC SUPPLANTS CENTRAL PACIFIC BY 1884

Once the road was finished the promoters decided to remain in the railroad business, foreseeing that with a modicum of effort they could establish a virtual monopoly over the state of California. They began an intensive campaign of acquisition and expansion, rapidly solidifying their hold on rail transport throughout the state's midsection. In particular, Central Pacific's attention was drawn to a new government railroad venture known as the Southern Pacific, chartered by Congress in 1866 to build rail lines from the San Francisco Bay area to San Diego, California, thence eastward to California's eastern boundary. The Central Pacific promoters gained control of this new road in 1868, recognizing that such a project would allow them to duplicate their construction profits and also grow to be the dominant railroad in the far West. In the following 15 years the Southern Pacific spread its myriad lines from Sacramento all the way to New Orleans, having effected a number of mergers in the process, and as early as 1877 the Central Pacific-Southern Pacific combination controlled 85 percent of all rail traffic in the state of California as well. In that year the combined companies had sales of $22.2 million and capital of $225 million, soon greatly enlarged by the additional tracks reaching out to Texas and New Orleans.

In 1884 the three remaining promoters, Hopkins having died in 1878, took steps to ensure their control of the rapidly expanding Southern Pacific. Having sold the bulk of their holdings in Central Pacific, which by then was clearly of secondary value, they formed a new corporation, Southern Pacific Company of Kentucky, with which they acquired all of the stock of the old Southern Pacific and its subsidiaries while agreeing to lease the use of Central Pacific's roads. This arrangement not only further concentrated their hold upon Southern Pacific, but it also distanced the promoters from California's laws of incorporation, under which stockholders' liability was unlimited.

SP and its owners remained extremely unpopular for many years. The railroad's early bullying of municipalities, its discriminatory pricing, suspected trafficking in legislative votes by means of bribery, and monopoly power fueled popular resentment. Various legal remedies were attempted by the state of California, including the creation of a state Railroad Commission in 1876, but all were undermined by the Southern Pacific. In the 1890s the federal government also became increasingly involved in the regulation of railroads. The source of its concern was not only the public welfare but the more tangible fact that the transcontinental railroads owed the U.S. government a great deal of money, in the form of the 30-year bonds they had borrowed for construction and due to mature in the mid-1890s.

None of the roads, including Southern Pacific, had made provision for the repayment of these huge debts, operating income instead ending up in the hands of promoters. Partly in response to this crisis, the Interstate Commerce Commission (ICC) was created in 1887 as a federal agency charged with general regulation of the railroads; more specifically, by the mid-1890s it was clear that SP was unable to pay its debts and would require refinancing. So unpopular was the company in its home state of California that a San Francisco newspaper gathered 195,000 signatures, more than 10 percent of the state population, on a petition asking the government to foreclose on the railway and to run it as a public service. This the government was disinclined to do, preferring to get its money back rather than enter the railroad business, and after long negotiations the debt was refunded until 1909 and SP was instructed to have it paid off by that date. As the Southern Pacific was by then already the largest railroad in the United States, with 7,300 miles of track, and a profitable company when managed properly, it was able to meet the new debt schedule and was by 1909 financially independent of the government.

SP BRIEFLY CONTROLLED BY UP IN THE EARLY 20TH CENTURY

In 1901, shortly after the death of the last of Southern Pacific's founders had left the company vulnerable, the rival Union Pacific bought a controlling interest in the road and in effect merged the two great western rail systems. The railroad monopoly of California thus became part of an even larger corporate giant, stretching from Portland to New Orleans and Los Angeles to St. Louis, Missouri, and including a fleet of steamships traveling between California and the Far East and between New Orleans and New York. E.H. Harriman, Union Pacific's chairman, was a far more prudent administrator than the previous generation of rail magnates, and under his direction both the Union Pacific and Southern Pacific were run according to a conservative philosophy of low dividends, the reinvestment of income in capital improvements, and a tight lid on debt accumulation. As a result, SP was able to pay off the federal government while strengthening its physical assets and generally to grow into a mature, efficient corporation.

Congress and the U.S. populace were less interested in Harriman's skills than in the monopolistic status of his railroads. As two monopolies do not make a market, an ICC investigation was followed in 1911 by a federal antitrust suit against the Union Pacific–Southern Pacific combination. The Supreme Court agreed that the combine inhibited competition and in 1913 ordered the sale of SP stock, much of which ended up in the hands of the Pennsylvania Railroad. As of that date, then, the Southern Pacific Railroad was restored to the general configuration it had had before the 1901 merger, its three principal routes being those between San Francisco and Portland, San Francisco and Ogden, Utah, and San Francisco and New Orleans. A second antitrust action deprived SP of its Ogden lines for a number of years, but these were eventually restored. Other litigation forced Southern Pacific to give up most of the oil-producing land included in its original grants, oil falling under the rubric of mineral rights, as well as its timberland.

Southern Pacific survived, however, and enjoyed a decade of unbroken prosperity in the 1920s. Buoyed by a strong national economy and the rapid growth of its two main markets, California and Texas, Southern's net income steadily rose to its 1929 peak of $48 million, despite having lost to the ICC the right to fix its own freight rates. These results were misleading, however, for in the meantime the nature of U.S. transportation had undergone a fundamental change as great as that of the railroad itself. Truck and auto traffic trebled during the 1920s, and along with the airplane would soon wrest from the railroads most long-distance passenger service and many types of freight, except those bulk items for which rail transport is ideal. The impact of these changes was not really felt by SP until the Great Depression brought to an end the era of plentiful business for all; reeling from these double blows, SP watched its net decline to $4 million in 1931 and then disappear altogether for the next four years.

The age of railroads had come to an end, and under new President Angus McDonald the Southern Pacific began the long evolution needed if it were to survive in a truly competitive marketplace. The former monopoly became far more responsive to the needs of its customers, offering a much more flexible schedule of service and the use of the railroad's own short-haul trucking company, Pacific Motor Trucking Company. Although the latter was barred by law from competing with full-service truck lines it became an integral adjunct to SP's rail system, transporting goods between the rail depots and customer warehouses. SP also fought a well-publicized if losing battle for passenger business, offering low-priced tickets on a number of famous routes between California and the East. These efforts may well have kept the Southern Pacific name before the public eye, but it proved simply impossible to move passengers by rail as cheaply and directly as by car and airplane, and for many years passenger travel was a money-losing burden on all railroads.

Despite these generally gloomy developments, Southern Pacific remained a true giant among U.S. corporations. Its 1936 assets of $1.95 billion were exceeded by only two other U.S. industrial corporations; it retained ownership of millions of acres of land that would some day become extremely valuable; and with 16,000 miles of track and $200 million in annual sales, Southern Pacific was among the three largest U.S. railroads by any measure chosen. Although the industry as a whole faced new competition, SP itself continued to enjoy the benefits of its relatively uncrowded western territory, where only Union Pacific and Santa Fe offered any challenge to its supremacy. The company was thus well positioned to take advantage of the enormous upsurge in heavy freight caused by the outbreak of war in 1939. With every segment of the industrial economy straining to meet the requirements of war, the railroad entered a period of unprecedented prosperity. SP's net income reached an all-time high of $80 million in 1942 and remained strong for several years, despite a vigorous program of debt reduction and capital outlays for new rolling stock and track.

POSTWAR PROSPERITY FOR SP

Following the war, Southern Pacific settled into a long period of sedate good fortune. Business lost to the truckers and airlines was more than replaced by the overall economic growth of its western home. Passenger revenue continued to decline, except for commuter service, but under the regulatory regime of the ICC the railroads were ensured a living wage in the bulk freight business, and since neither mergers nor rate wars were permitted the competitive environment was stable and modestly profitable. Under Donald J. Russell, Southern Pacific's chief from 1952 through the mid-1960s, revenue rose from $650 million to $840 million, and the company expanded its trucking service as well as added a profitable oil pipeline along a segment of its track in the Southwest. Russell spent liberally on maintenance of track and rolling stock, and SP generally built a reputation as one of the country's soundest railroads, although the sheer size of its operations forced the company to incur debt for capital expenditures at a level higher than Wall Street thought prudent. The tremendous growth of California's population and agricultural production kept SP healthy, along with the rapid increase in intermodal (rail-to-truck and truck-to-rail) transport and a booming oil business in Texas and Louisiana. The latter portion of the SP system had been solidified years before by the acquisition in 1932 of the "cotton belt" lines extending northward to St. Louis from Dallas, Texas.

While SP's market area and rate structure were both fixed, it could and did increase efficiency by means of technological innovation and consequent labor cuts. By 1969 the entire railroad was under the guidance of a computerized information system which helped to cut down on idle cars and switching delays. By means of such changes Southern Pacific was able to reduce its labor force from 76,000 in the mid-1950s to 45,000 by 1970, while substantially increasing its volume of rail traffic. This trend continued; in 1990 SP employed about 21,000 workers.

In 1972 SP diversified into telecommunications. Using its existing network of microwave transmitters, the company became a carrier of long-distance telephone and data communications, first to large corporate users and later to the general public under the Sprint name. In 1979 it also bought Ticor, the largest title insurer in the United States. Neither venture was particularly successful, however. Telecommunications was a world all its own, one that demanded expertise and more capital than Southern Pacific could spare from its own vast physical plant; and the Ticor purchase had barely been signed when a severe recession all but killed the residential real estate market on which the title business depends. As a result, both companies were eventually sold off. In 1982 two of SP's chief rivals announced a potentially devastating merger: Union Pacific and Missouri Pacific (along with a third merger partner, Western Pacific) would soon form the largest rail combine since the days of E.H. Harriman.

The merger of Union Pacific and Missouri Pacific was made possible by U.S. President Ronald Reagan's deregulation of the railroad industry and presented Southern Pacific with grave problems. The new Union Pacific would be able to offer longer through service and lower rates than Southern Pacific in nearly every market area, and Southern Pacific immediately began casting about for a merger partner of its own. In 1983 Santa Fe Industries Inc. purchased Southern Pacific with the intention of merging SP with the Atchison, Topeka & Santa Fe Railway (known as the Santa Fe), one of SP's main competitors. The proposed merger elicited immediate opposition from government officials and Santa Fe's competition, and the Interstate Commerce Commission in 1987 blocked the Santa Fe–SP merger as anticompetitive. Robert Krebs, the chairman of Santa Fe Industries, was forced to sell one of his lines and chose SP, which he felt was the weaker of the two.

ACQUISITION OF SP BY ANSCHUTZ IN 1988

In October 1988 Southern Pacific found a new home among the holdings of Denver billionaire businessman Philip Anschutz, whose Rio Grande Industries already owned the Denver and Rio Grande Western Railroad. Anschutz, who had used his political influence to help block the Santa Fe–SP merger, paid $1 billion for Southern Pacific, which thus became a part of Rio Grande Industries, a group of railroads that functioned as cooperating but distinct rail systems.

In the initial years after the purchase, SP suffered from declines in its traditional accounts in auto parts, lumber, and food; increased competition from UP and the Santa Fe; and more rigorous safety inspections in California, where SP trains were involved in two chemical spills in July 1991. SP continued to show operating losses after the merger and was profiting mainly from the proceeds of real estate sales. Its railroad operations were bolstered, however, by improving the quality of its service through heavy expenditures to maintain its track. As trade between the United States and Mexico increased in the early 1990s, SP was positioned to profit from it with its six Mexican gateways in California, Texas, and Arizona. The company's strategy appeared to be working as an operating loss of $347.7 million in 1991 had been reduced to $24.6 million in 1992. Nevertheless, in 1993, SP slid back to a loss of $149 million. Contributing to the loss was $14 million incurred from the settlement of a class-action lawsuit stemming from one of the 1991 derailments which had contaminated the Sacramento River with weed killer.

In the summer of 1993, Anschutz turned to a railroad company veteran, Edward Moyers, to assist in turning SP around. Moyers had retired after a very successful four-year stint at Illinois Central, where he cut its operating ratio (operating expenses as a percentage of revenues) from 98 percent to 71 percent. Anschutz hired Moyers as chief executive, and Moyers immediately focused on SP's operating ratio, which stood at 96.5 percent in 1993. In an effort to reduce SP's debt load, 30 million shares of common stock were offered to the public in August 1993. Although the initial offering price was estimated at $20 per share, the actual price of the shares as issued was $13.50. Still, that the offering was successful at all was attributed by many to the hiring of Moyers. Investor interest in Southern Pacific increased in the several months that followed, so that by February 1994, when a secondary stock offering of 25 million shares was initiated, they sold for $19.75 per share. Following these sales, Anschutz owned 41 percent of the shares outstanding.

Moyers started a multipronged strategy for revitalizing Southern Pacific. First, he worked to cut costs by reducing the employee ranks through a buyout program and a reorganization. In his first year, he reduced the labor force by more than 3,000 to about 19,000 jobs. Second, Moyers focused on service to SP's customers, putting pressure on his subordinates to improve the operations. This initiative saved a lucrative Georgia-Pacific account by increasing on-time Georgia-Pacific deliveries from 0 percent to 80 percent in three months. Overall, on-time deliveries were up by more than 50 percent in his first year. Moyers also sought to bolster Southern Pacific's equipment through the purchase of new locomotives, the rebuilding of existing locomotives, and better maintenance of both trains and track. Although SP was still in weak financial condition, Moyers had managed to make a number of improvements, and in February 1995 he once again retired. Moyers was succeeded as president and CEO by veteran railroader Jerry R. Davis.

UNION PACIFIC-SOUTHERN PACIFIC MERGER IN 1996

By 1995, the consolidation that followed the deregulation of the railroad industry in the early 1980s had reduced the number of large, Class 1 railroads from 40 to 10, but the mergers were not over yet. In November 1995 Union Pacific filed an application with the ICC to acquire Southern Pacific in a $3.9 billion takeover. One month later the U.S. Congress abolished the ICC, creating the Surface Transportation Board (STB) as the new railroad industry oversight body. The UP-SP deal was fiercely opposed by the Justice, Transportation, and Agriculture departments and by such rival railroads as Kansas City Southern and Consolidated Rail. In spite of this opposition, in July 1996 the STB approved the merger, with the only major stipulation being that UP grant trackage rights to Burlington Northern Santa Fe over about 4,000 miles of track. The combined UP-SP railroad, which would operate under the Union Pacific name, was once again the nation's largest, with more than 30,000 miles of track and about $10 billion in revenue. The merger was expected to result in $627 million in annual savings through the consolidation of operations. In late 1996 Lewis retired as chairman and CEO of Union Pacific Corporation, and was succeeded by Davidson, who had most recently been president and COO of the UP holding company. Davidson was also named CEO of Union Pacific Railroad, while Davis became president and COO of the railroad.

Unfortunately, the integration of Southern Pacific into UP was no smoother than that of the Chicago & North Western. In fact it was far worse. Starting in the summer of 1997 and extending into 1998, Union Pacific's rail network suffered from gridlock, particularly along the Gulf Coast. By March 1998 delays in shipments had cost rail customers approximately $1 billion in curtailed production, reduced sales, and higher shipping costs. The STB in November 1997 ordered UP to temporarily open a part of its freight business in its Houston hub to Kansas City Southern. In February 1998 UP and Burlington Northern Santa Fe reached an agreement to create a joint dispatching center for their Gulf Coast operations, share ownership of line between Houston and New Orleans, and allow UP to use Burlington Northern tracks between Beaumont and Navasota, Texas, as needed, to bypass Houston congestion. In addition to its difficulties digesting SP, Union Pacific was also under fire for its safety record. Following three fatal accidents, a joint safety team was formed in August 1997 to review safety across the UP system. The team consisted of UP managers, union employees, and Federal Railroad Administration representatives. Meanwhile, UP moved its headquarters from Bethlehem, Pennsylvania, to Dallas in September 1997.

In May 1998 Union Pacific Corporation announced that it planned to divest its Overnite trucking unit through an initial public offering (IPO), in order to further focus on its core rail business. However, the IPO was abandoned following a deterioration in market conditions. An attempt to find a third-party buyer failed as well. In the fourth quarter of 1998 the corporation recorded a $547 million charge to reflect an impairment in Overnite's goodwill, leading to a net loss of $633 million for the year, a loss that was also due to UP railroad's service problems and system congestion. Another outcome of the railroad's service difficulties was the August 1998 announcement of a plan to decentralize its railroad management. The railroad was reorganized into three regions: southern, based in Houston; northern, based in Omaha; and western, based in Roseville, California.

In September 1998 Ike Evans was named president and COO of Union Pacific Railroad, succeeding Davis, who became vice-chairman until his retirement in March 1999. Evans had previously been a senior vice-president at Emerson Electric Company, a manufacturer of electrical, electromechanical, and electronic products and systems. In July 1999 UP moved its headquarters again, this time landing in Omaha, where its main subsidiary, Union Pacific Railroad, was located. The corporation continued to look for an opportunity to divest Overnite through an IPO or sale to a third party and was likely to be busy assimilating Southern Pacific well into the 21st century.

ENTERING A NEW CENTURY

The Southern Pacific merger presented UP with arguably the most difficult challenge in its history. Difficulties with absorbing the assets persisted for years, continuing to plague the company a decade after the deal was completed. If it was any comfort, UP was not the only railroad to stumble through a megamerger: The acquisition of Conrail Inc. in 1999 by CSX Corp. and Norfolk Southern created profound operational problems for both of the acquiring railroads, but UP struggled far more than its rivals struggled. The company suffered from capacity problems during the first years of the 21st century, experiencing particular difficulties with the 760-mile "Sunset Route" it inherited from the Southern Pacific merger. Connecting El Paso, Texas, and Los Angeles, the route was used by Southern Pacific as a low-price alternative to faster, better-run service offered by competitors. Under UP's control, the Sunset Route became a bottleneck, forcing the company to turn away cargo originating from ports in the Los Angeles area and scheduled to move eastward. The cause for the capacity problems was the layout of the track, less than a quarter of which was double-tracked when UP acquired it from Southern Pacific. UP had added a second track to 100 miles of the route by 2005, enabling trains to move in both directions without idling on a side track to wait for a passing train, but the capital improvement project, slowed by low-paying customers using the route, still had much to accomplish a decade after the merger. In the short term, UP planned to invest $105 million to add 69 miles of double-track to the route, which was expected to be completed by 2007.

The problems along the Sunset Route represented a microcosm of broader operational inefficiencies UP experienced during the first years of the 21st century. In some respects, the lack of fluidity across the vast UP network was a function of ranking as the largest railroad, the price the company paid for being the industry behemoth. The company was able to devote more attention to smoothing out the wrinkles hobbling its progress after it disposed of its trucking business. In November 2003, after years of contemplating the divestiture, UP spun off Overnite in an initial public offering, making it what industry analysts referred to as a "pure" railroad company. Midway through the decade, there was evidence that UP was turning a corner, as the company posted encouraging results concurrent with a change in leadership. James R. Young became UP's president and chief executive officer at the beginning of 2006, succeeding Richard Davidson. Young, who joined UP in 1978 in the company's finance department, assumed day-to-day control over the company two years after being appointed president and chief operating officer of the railroad subsidiary. He inherited a company that posted record profits and revenue in 2005, gains that were attributed to a more efficient rail network that enabled UP to make more money per carload. In the years ahead, Young hoped his legacy would add another chapter of success to the history of one of the country's most powerful transportation companies.

Jonathan Martin
Updated, David E. Salamie; Jeffrey L. Covell

PRINCIPAL SUBSIDIARIES

Union Pacific Railroad Company

PRINCIPAL COMPETITORS

CSX Corporation; Norfolk Southern Corporation; Burlington Northern Santa Fe Corporation.

FURTHER READING

"Back to Railroading for a New Era," *Business Week,* July 14, 1980.

Bailey, Ed H., *The Century of Progress: A Heritage of Service, Union Pacific, 1869–1969,* New York: Newcomen Society in North America, 1969, 24 p.

Barrett, Amy, "The Bull Pen: Union Pacific's Drew Lewis Says He's Fed Up with Politics," *Financial World,* January 8, 1991, pp. 24+.

Barrows, Matthew, "Judge's Order Puts Union Pacific Trains Back on Track," *Sacramento Bee,* January 28, 2001.

Bell, Ted, "Contract Complaint Prompts Strike at Omaha, Neb.-Based Union Pacific," *Sacramento Bee,* January 27, 2001.

Berman, Phyllis, and Roula Khalaf, "'I Might Be a Seller, I Might Be a Buyer,'" *Forbes,* February 3, 1992, pp. 86–87.

Byrnes, Nanette, "The Waiting Game," *Financial World,* September 13, 1994, pp. 32–34.

Cook, William S., *Building the Modern Union Pacific,* New York: Newcomen Society of the United States, 1984, 24 p.

Daggett, Stuart, *Chapters on the History of the Southern Pacific,* New York, Kelley, 1966.

Gallagher, John, "Young's Unified UP Plan," *Traffic World,* June 6, 2005, p. 9.

Galloway, John Debo, *The First Transcontinental Railroad: Central Pacific, Union Pacific,* New York: Simmons-Boardman, 1950; reprint, Westport, Conn.: Greenwood Press, 1983.

Greenberg, David, "Union Pacific Losing Market Share over Capacity Problems," *Los Angeles Business Journal,* August 1, 2005, p. 11.

Hamel, Stacie, "Railroad Expects Good Year in 2006," *Omaha World-Herald,* January 19, 2006.

———, "Union Pacific's CEO Sees Need to Keep Raising Rates," *Omaha World-Herald,* January 16, 2006.

Howard, Robert West, *The Great Iron Trail: The Story of the First Transcontinental Railroad,* New York: Putnam, 1962.

Huneke, William F., *The Heavy Hand: The Government and the Union Pacific, 1862–1898,* New York: Garland, 1985.

Jordon, Steve, "Union Pacific Income Affected by Economic Downturn, Severance Expenses," *Omaha World-Herald,* January 19, 2001.

Kenefick, John C., *Union Pacific and the Building of the West,* New York: Newcomen Society of the United States, 1985, 18 p.

Klein, Maury, *Union Pacific: Birth of a Railroad,* New York: Doubleday, 1987.

———, *Union Pacific: The Rebirth, 1894–1969,* New York: Doubleday, 1990.

Kupfer, Andrew, "An Outsider Fires Up a Railroad," *Fortune,* December 18, 1989, pp. 133+.

Machalaba, Daniel, "A Big Railroad Merger Goes Terribly Awry in a Very Short Time," *Wall Street Journal,* October 2, 1997, pp. A1, A13.

———, "Union Pacific and Burlington Northern to Coordinate Some Train Dispatching," *Wall Street Journal,* February 9, 1999, p. A6.

———, "Union Pacific Reverses Course with Burlington Pact," *Wall Street Journal,* February 17, 1998, p. B4.

———, "Union Pacific to Reverse Centralization," *Wall Street Journal,* August 20, 1998, pp. A3, A9.

Machalaba, Daniel, and Anna Wilde Mathews, "Union Pacific Tie-Ups Reach Across Economy," *Wall Street Journal,* October 8, 1997, pp. B1, B17.

Machalaba, Daniel, and Asra Q. Nomani, "More Rail Deals May Be Down the Track," *Wall Street Journal,* July 5, 1996, p. A2.

Machan, Dan, "The Man Who Won't Let Go," *Forbes,* August 1, 1994, pp. 64–65.

Mathews, Anna Wilde, "Union Pacific's Burns Resigns Positions, Davidson, Davis Named to Succeed Him," *Wall Street Journal,* November 7, 1996, p. B10.

Mongelluzzo, Bill, "Peak Performers: Investment, Lower Import Growth Help Railroads Keep Congestion at Bay," *The Journal of Commerce,* August 15, 2005, p. 16.

O'Reilly, Brian, "The Wreck of the Union Pacific," *Fortune,* March 30, 1998, pp. 94+.

Palmeri, Christopher, and Ann Marsh, "Can Drew Lewis Drive the Golden Nail?," *Forbes,* December 18, 1995, pp. 52+.

"Southern Pacific," *Fortune,* November 1937.

"SP's Strategy for Success," *Railway Age,* May 1993, pp. 31–32, 34, 36, 38.

Trottman, Nelson, *History of Union Pacific,* New York: Ronald Press, 1923.

"Union Pacific: The Story Behind the Statistics," *Railway Age,* December 1992, pp. 19–23.

Weber, Joseph, et al., "Union Pacific's Uphill Haul," *Business Week,* July 1, 1996, pp. 52, 54.

Welty, Gus, "Railroader of the Year: SP's Ed Moyers," *Railway Age,* January 1995, pp. 29–31.

———, "SP Battles Back to Respectability," *Railway Age,* November 1994, pp. 22–23, 25–26.

Willoughby, Jack, "The Rebuilding of Uncle Pete," *Forbes,* November 14, 1988.

Zellner, Wendy, "An Old Brakeman Faces His Ultimate Test," *Business Week,* October 6, 1997, pp. 110+.

———, "The Rails: Trouble Behind, Trouble Ahead," *Business Week,* November 24, 1997, pp. 40, 42.

Zellner, Wendy, and Kathleen Morris, "A Desperate Effort to Clear the Tracks," *Business Week,* March 2, 1998, p. 46.

United Negro College Fund, Inc.

8260 Willow Oaks Corporate Drive
P.O. Box 10444
Fairfax, Virginia 22031-8044
U.S.A.
Telephone: (703) 205-3400
Toll Free: (800) 331-2244
Fax: (703) 205-3507
Web site: http://www.uncf.org

Private Company
Incorporated: 1944
Employees: 257
Operating Revenues: $182.2 million (2005)
NAIC: 813219 Other Grantmaking and Giving Services; 813410 Membership Organizations

■ ■ ■

United Negro College Fund, Inc. (UNCF) provides financial assistance primarily to African Americans for the purposes of higher education. The UNCF is the oldest and largest minority higher education assistance program in the United States, raising over $2 billion and providing support to over 350,000 students since its inception in 1944. In addition to offering scholarships and internships to students at about 900 institutions, the UNCF also provides funds and services for 39 member historically black colleges and universities, as well as faculty and administrative professional training.

EARLY ROOTS

The story of United Negro College Fund, Inc. begins long before its incorporation in 1944. In fact, one could say that the first chapters were actually written decades before, when the schools that would later become the UNCF's charter members took the steps necessary to educate former slaves. In the mid- to late 1800s, because few states would support the education of African Americans with public funds, private colleges became necessary for instruction of black students. According to the UNCF, "by 1870, there were three times as many private black colleges as there were public. These schools often served a multitude of purposes, educating young children, college students, and adults just learning to read."

In 1928, a young Frederick D. Patterson began his tenure at Tuskegee University as the head of the veterinary division. Born in 1901 and orphaned at the age of two, Patterson was well-educated, having received two doctorate degrees in veterinary medicine, one from Iowa State College and another from Cornell University, and a master's degree in science from Iowa State College. In 1935, Patterson became the third president of Tuskegee University.

Dr. Patterson rapidly realized that without proper funds it would be difficult to run Tuskegee in an efficient manner because so many of the school's students lacked the means to pay their tuition. While qualified for the position, he "quickly acknowledged that he lacked the fundraising skills and personal ties of past Tuskegee Presidents Booker T. Washington and Robert S. Moton," according to *Educational Foundations*. Additionally,

COMPANY PERSPECTIVES

Our mission is to enhance the quality of education by providing financial assistance to deserving students, raising operating funds for member colleges and universities, and increasing access to technology for students and faculty at historically black colleges and universities. Since its inception in 1944, UNCF has grown to become the Nation's oldest and most successful African American higher education assistance organization.

the trustees of Tuskegee seemed to have grown used to the strong fundraising skills of past presidents and turning to them for new insight became an exercise in futility. Driven by frustration, Patterson began to correspond with presidents of other black colleges. He received letters in return telling stories of financial hardships and detailing the difficulties of fundraising. Through this correspondence, he realized that black colleges were "competing against each other by soliciting the same organizations and donors, usually the large industrial philanthropies." On January 30, 1943, Patterson publicized this fact in an article in the *Pittsburgh Courier.* He pled with his colleagues by suggesting that they "pool their small monies and make a united appeal to the national conscience."

THE FIRST CAMPAIGNS: 1944–72

On April 25, 1944, the UNCF was incorporated with 27 member colleges. The first fundraising campaign was highly successful, "raising three times more money for the UNCF supported schools than the schools raised independently the previous year," according to the UNCF. Creating more awareness of the organization were its early supporters who included President Franklin Delano Roosevelt and John D. Rockefeller, Jr.

By 1963, civil rights were at the forefront of American issues. It was a time of great unrest with many Americans showing their views in the form of demonstrations and protest. One of the most famous of these Americans was Dr. Martin Luther King, Jr., a graduate of a UNCF member school Morehouse College. It could be argued that it was partly because of King's vocalizations that President John F. Kennedy, Jr., decided to take stronger action to help the civil rights struggle. It was also in this year that the UNCF launched its second capital campaign, kicking it off with a reception at the White House, hosted by President Kennedy. The president also made a special contribution to the UNCF, the Pulitzer Prize money he won for his book *Profiles in Courage.*

A PHRASE IS COINED: 1972

In 1972, an advertising executive at Young & Rubicam, Inc. created the new slogan for the UNCF. The tagline, "A mind is a terrible thing to waste," was created pro bono and would become one of the most successful themes of all time. The slogan was important for the UNCF because, according to *Verde Gallery,* "if improperly handled, the advertising campaign for the UNCF could have presented blacks as charity cases, or it could have been viewed as patronizing to the black community. Instead, the creators of the advertisements focused on the potential inherent in the African American community, potential that had been denied due to discrimination and prejudice." Thirty years later, the tagline would become perhaps one of the most recognized in history.

The first of many telethons to support the UNCF was launched in 1974. Called "Something Special" and hosted by singer Nancy Wilson and actor/composer Clifton Davis, it raised $300,000. Later, in 1979, actor/singer Lou Rawls hosted an expanded version of the telethon, the first annual "Lou Rawls Parade of Stars" telethon. The program featured singers and entertainers, as well as compelling stories from the UNCF students and inspiring messages about historically black colleges and universities. The show's name would change one last time in 1998, becoming "An Evening of Stars" and, throughout its history, would raise over $200 million in support of the UNCF's efforts.

In 1983, another brainchild of Dr. Patterson came to fruition. Based on the UNCF's College Endowment Funding Plan, Congress enacted the Challenge Grant Act Amendments. This was a fundraising program that depended on donations from private organizations that were matched with federal monies. The program was important, according to the UNCF, "because it was the first matching grant program for small college endowments, especially the nation's historically black colleges and universities."

The UNCF launched its most ambitious capital campaign ever in 1990. "CAMPAIGN 2000: An Investment in America's Future" was kicked off by a reception hosted by President George H. W. Bush and by a pledge of $50 million by billionaire publisher Walter H. Annenberg. The campaign concluded in 1996, exceeding its goals by 12 percent and generating $280 million for historically black colleges and universities and their students. The success of CAMPAIGN 2000 was

KEY DATES

1944: The United Negro College Fund, Inc. (UNCF) is incorporated.
1972: Young & Rubicam coins the phrase, "A mind is a terrible thing to waste."
1974: UNCF's first telethon is held.
1983: Congress enacts the Challenge Grant Act Amendments.
1994: UNCF celebrates its 50th anniversary.
1996: UNCF announces creation of the Frederick D. Patterson Research Institute.
2001: UNCF launches Liberty Scholarship Program for children of victims of September 11, 2001 terrorist attacks on the United States.
2004: William H. Gray III resigns from position as president and CEO; Dr. Michael L. Lomax takes his place.

celebrated at a White House reception hosted by President William J. Clinton.

The year 1994 brought the 50th anniversary of the UNCF. Again, the organization was able to exceed its fundraising goals. According to *Black Enterprise*, "fundraising hit a record high and administrative costs dipped below 17 cents per dollar raised, giving the UNCF one of the best such ratios of any educational nonprofit group." Although the year saw a decrease in the rate of charitable gifts, the UNCF was able to raise a record $58 million in its annual campaign. The organization expressed excitement and cited their success as coming from a balance, maintaining a connection with corporate America, while also preserving the support of prominent Americans, many of whom were alumni of the UNCF's historically black colleges and universities. The UNCF also acknowledged that its biggest challenge would always be fundraising. "We must provide assistance to our institutions at every level. We have to put them in a position to be competitive with other schools," said William H. Gray III, president and CEO of the UNCF. Also in 1994, the UNCF moved from its location in New York to offices in Fairfax County, Virginia, moving closer to its colleges and universities and thereby reducing administrative costs.

PAVING THE WAY: 1996

In 1996, the UNCF continued with its legacy of taking first steps in the black community by announcing the creation of the Frederick D. Patterson Research Institute. The Institute was founded by Gray and was named to honor the originator of the UNCF. According to the Frederick D. Patterson Research Institute, "the Institute was the first African American led research institute in the country to design, conduct, analyze, interpret and disseminate research on blacks in education and provide essential information to the public, policymakers, and educators." Also in 1996, the Institute released the first of its research results in the form of a Data Book. The book, called *The African American Education Data Book,* was a three-volume reference that compiled statistics on the status, performance, and progress of African Americans in education from preschool to the postgraduate level. It was the first of its kind and would become one of several reports released from the institution.

NEW FUNDING SOURCES: 1998–99

The UNCF received a $41.7 million grant from the Lilly Endowment in 1998, forming The Lilly Endowment-United Negro College Fund Historically Black Colleges and Universities Program. According to *Knight Ridder/Tribune Business News*, this grant would be "the largest single grant in the 61-year history of the endowment." The Lilly Endowment's relationship with the UNCF went back to 1944 and this grant, though significant, simply continued the Endowment's support of the independent schools. In its first round of funding, nine private historically black colleges and universities were approved for funding.

In 1999, the UNCF began its involvement with another important funding source, the Gates Millennium Scholars Program. In partnership with the Hispanic Scholarship Fund, the Organization of Chinese Americans, and the American Indian Graduate Center Scholars, the UNCF was named administrator of the $1 billion program. The Gates Millennium Scholars Program was funded by a grant from the Bill & Melinda Gates Foundation and was aimed at expanding opportunity to those students whose backgrounds reflected diversity in society.

NEW SCHOLARSHIP OPPORTUNITIES AND CONTINUED FUNDRAISING SUCCESS: 2001–02

In 2001, the UNCF launched several new scholarship programs. The first, called the New Jersey Law Scholars Program, was formed to provide scholarships to deserving students from historically black colleges and universities in order to attend certain New Jersey law schools. The program was funded by Richard and Lois Rawson. Rawson, a senior vice-president and general counsel at Lucent Technologies, Inc., was a 1977 graduate of Rutgers School of Law-Newark. The scholarship program was created as part of an effort to increase diversity in the legal profession. "There are many young people for whom the dream of higher education does not stop with college," said Gray. "The New Jersey Law Scholars Program means that students attending UNCF schools who dare to set goals of becoming lawyers one day have another resource available to them to help achieve those goals."

Another scholarship program launched in 2001 was the UNCF Liberty Scholarship Program. The program was formed to provide scholarship aid to children of victims of the September 11, 2001 terrorist attacks on the United States. Ex-New York Mayor Rudolph Giuliani announced the program, saying that the UNCF's generosity would "transform the lives of many innocent victims." The program made full scholarships available to all children of victims of the attacks, "regardless of age, race, creed or color," according to the UNCF.

In the fall of 2002, the UNCF was able to announce that it had another strong fundraising year. Finishing the 2002 fiscal year with $168.9 million in revenues, the organization reached its campaign goal. In addition, it was able to maintain a low ratio of administrative costs to funds raised, meaning that a majority of the money raised would go directly to deserving students.

NEW LEADERSHIP: 2004

After the resignation of William H. Gray III in 2004, the UNCF announced a new president and CEO. The new head of the UNCF, Dr. Michael L. Lomax, previously held a position as president of Dillard University in New Orleans. He brought "an impressive background in education, management and fund-raising," according to Michael Jordan, chairman of the UNCF's board of directors. Though he held a notable resume, Dr. Lomax faced some challenges in filling Gray's shoes. Gray resigned after an unforgettable tenure. "Under his leadership," according to *Jet*, "UNCF's fund-raising results will have accounted for approximately 70 percent of the more than $2.2 billion that will have been raised over UNCF's 60-year history."

In 2005, solid fundraising continued with a Black & White Ball in Chicago. Some 1,200 guests gathered to celebrate the UNCF, raising over $800,000. The celebration also honored Nancy Wilson, original cohost of the UNCF's telethon, *Something Special,* for her three decades of support. Wilson received the Legacy Award.

After over 60 years of support to over 350,000 students, the UNCF was still going strong. Though the UNCF had raised billions, its legacy as a "helping" organization extended far beyond the money. It lived on in the graduates of the UNCF's member institutions who continued to make lasting contributions to the world.

Sara Poginy

PRINCIPAL COMPETITORS

American Indian College Fund; Scholarship America; Hispanic Scholarship Fund.

FURTHER READING

Allen, Jodie T., et al., "Gates's $1 Million Boon to Minority Students," *U.S. News & World Report*, September 27, 1999, p. 12.

Chambers, Dr. Jason, "Introduction: A Mind Is a Terrible Thing to Waste: A Retrospective of the Advertising Campaign for the United Negro College Fund," *Verde Gallery*, April 12, 2004, http://verdant-systems.com/mind.htm.

"Dr. Michael L. Lomax Named New President and CEO of UNCF," *Jet*, March 1, 2004, pp. 48+.

Lowery, Mark, "50 Years and Going Strong," *Black Enterprise*, September 1994, pp. 132+.

Reagan, President Ronald, "Remarks on Signing the Challenge Grant Amendments of 1983," September 26, 1983, http://www.reagan.utexas.edu/archives/speeches/1983/92683e.htm.

United Negro College Fund, "Roots That Run Deep: An Historical Look at the Impact of the United Negro College Fund and Its Member Colleges on American History," *United Negro College Fund, Inc.*, http://uncf.org/history/roots.asp.

"UNCF Launches New Jersey Law Scholars Program," *Black Issues in Higher Education*, June 21, 2001, p. 15.

"UNCF Offers College Scholarships to Children of Terrorist Attack Victims," *Black Issues in Higher Education*, November 22, 2001, p. 21.

"UNCF Raises More Than $800,000 at Black and White Ball," *Jet*, July 11, 2005, pp. 22+.

The University of Chicago Press

1427 E. 60th Street
Chicago, Illinois 60637
U.S.A.
Telephone: (773) 702-7700
Fax: (773) 702-9756
Web site: http://www.press.uchicago.edu

Private Company
Founded: 1891
Employees: 150
Sales: $50 million (2005 est.)
NAIC: 511120 Periodical Publishers; 511130 Book Publishers

■ ■ ■

The University of Chicago Press is one of the oldest continuously operating university presses in the United States, and has earned a reputation for not only exceptional scholarly works but general fiction as well. Founded in 1891 as an integral part of the University of Chicago, the Press moved beyond its duties to print course selections and college forms, publishing world renowned and prize-winning authors. The Press publishes books (both hardcover and paperback), distinguished journals, and runs an extensive warehousing and distribution system with thousands of titles stored in its high-tech BiblioVault repository. Among its longstanding bestsellers are the *Chicago Manual of Style,* first published in 1906, and Kate Turabian's seminal work *A Manual for Writers of Term Papers, Theses, and Dissertations,* originally published in 1937. Both reference titles sell thousands of copies each year and continue to be used worldwide.

IN THE BEGINNING

In the last decade of the 19th century more and more young men, along with a few women, were able to seek higher education. In the state of Illinois there were 25 colleges and universities by 1891, a phenomenal number considering there were only four million residents at the time. According to the *Chicago Daily* newspaper, Illinois had "too many" institutions of higher learning when there were only 23 universities in all of Germany, serving 53 million people, and 15 in France, serving 40 million inhabitants.

Chicago was home to Northwestern University and the recently defunct Chicago University, which had closed in 1886. Yet oil baron John D. Rockefeller believed Chicago needed a prestigious new university, chartered in the manner of the East Coast's renowned Harvard and Yale. He approached Dr. William Raney Harper, chair of the Semitic Languages department at Yale, to be a trustee of the proposed university and its first president. Once Harper agreed, the two collaborated and established the University of Chicago in 1891.

The University of Chicago was to be no "ordinary" university; part of its formation included the University of Chicago Press. Originally, the Press was more of a printing and public relations unit, creating forms and schedules for the University's professors and news about the university. Its earliest noncourse-related publications were journals, the first being the *Journal of Political Economy.*

COMPANY PERSPECTIVES

Since its founding in 1891 as one of the three original divisions of the University of Chicago, the Press has embraced as its mission the obligation to disseminate scholarship of the highest standard and to publish serious works that promote education, foster public understanding, and enrich cultural life.

Within a year of the Press's creation, Dr. Harper had signed prominent publisher D.C. Heath to establish the Press as a leading academic publisher. Heath would run the Press and be responsible for the printing, publishing, and selling of books. As part of the deal, Heath relocated its headquarters from Boston to Chicago. Local publisher R.R. Donnelley became part of the Press operations as well.

By 1893 the Press was operating a bookstore and had added several more journals including the *Journal of Geology, Biblical World,* and *Hebraica,* the latter two of special interest to Harper, a noted scholar in Hebrew and biblical studies. Unfortunately, by 1894 there were mounting difficulties with D.C. Heath and R.R. Donnelley amidst complaints of mismanagement and inflated pricing. Heath withdrew its operations and the Press began to fend for itself, under the watchful eye of Harper and the University's board of trustees.

Harper firmly believed the Press was destined for greatness, commenting at the University's spring convocation address in 1894, "The [Press] is to be considered as truly part of a university's equipment as the machinery of the physicist or the microscope of the biologist," Harper told his audience, as quoted in the *Chicago Daily Tribune* (February 23, 1896). "Its possibilities in connection with university work have never been fairly tested. When, ten or twenty years hence, the story shall be written of what the university press has done for the university, men will begin for the first time to realize that its establishment at the period of the University's beginning was no foolish dream or idle vision."

In 1895 the Press introduced the *American Journal of Sociology,* the first to exclusively cover the burgeoning field of sociology. The first book published by the Press was the three-volume *Assyrian and Babylonian Letters Belonging to the Kouyunjik Collections of the British Museum* by Robert Francis Harper. According to the University of Chicago's web site, the book sold five copies during its first two years in print. It was followed by a translation of *Finanzwissenschaft* by Thorstein B. Veblen, and John Dewey's *The School and Society,* published in 1899, which remained in print for more than a century.

EARNING ACCOLADES

By 1900 the Press, despite difficulties with funding and management since severing ties with Heath and Donnelley, had published 127 books. Its scholarly journals numbered an impressive 11, including such disparate studies as the *Astrophysical Journal* and the *Journal of Near Eastern Studies.* In addition, Rockefeller gave the Press a sizeable gift of $1.5 million. Though two-thirds of the money went into an interest-bearing endowment fund, a chunk of the other $500,000 was earmarked for a new Press building, which would also house a library.

By 1901 land parcels for the new Press building were donated by Rockefeller and trustee Martin A. Ryerson. The new property, comprising half a block at Ellis Avenue and 58th Street, was worth an estimated $90,000. Construction on the new Press building was completed in late 1902, with a mailroom and Press operations on the first floor; a reading room, library, and offices on the second floor; and additional office space and "composing" rooms for the Press on the fourth floor. The building was outfitted with skylights, hardwood trim, and a state of the art elevator.

The new home came at an opportune time as the burgeoning Press had more than doubled its output within four years, generating over $200,000 for the 1901-02 academic year. Some of the year's success was due to a new scholarly imprint, Decennial Publications, which began publishing articles and monographs by the University's increasingly acclaimed staff.

By the end of 1904 the University of Chicago and its Press thrived; in President Harper's biennial address and statement, released in May 1905, the University itself was worth an estimated $18 million (the majority represented by $9.1 million in investments and $7.1 million in buildings and grounds), while the Press was considered an asset worth more than $120,000. In 1905, for the first time, the Press published books by scholars outside the University, including *The Silver Age of the Greek World* by J. P. Mahaffy of the University of Dublin and *One Year of Sunday School Lessons for Young Children* by Florence U. Palmer.

The next year, 1906, marked an important milestone for the Press with the publication of the *Chicago Manual of Style,* which set comprehensive standards for academic publishers nationwide. More than a century later, the *Chicago Manual of Style* remained an industry staple for all writers and publishers. Another milestone, though

KEY DATES

1891: The University of Chicago is established.
1894: The University takes control of the Press from publisher D.C. Heath.
1901: Land for a new press building is donated to the University.
1902: The Press building opens its doors at Ellis Avenue and 58th Street.
1906: The first edition of the *Chicago Manual of Style* is published.
1937: Kate Turabian's *A Manual for Writers of Term Papers, Theses, and Dissertations* is published.
1951: The Press separates books, journals, and University printing operations.
1966: Morris Philipson begins a 33-year term as Press director.
1982: Philipson wins the PEN Publisher Citation for the Press.
1992: Norman Maclean's *Young Men and Fire* becomes a national bestseller.
2000: Retiring director Philipson wins the AAUP's Curtis Benjamin Award for excellence.
2001: Book storage and distribution at the Press goes digital.
2003: The 15th edition of the *Chicago Manual of Style* is issued.
2006: The Press celebrates 115 years in operation.

devastating to the University and the Press, was also met in 1906 with the burial of Dr. Harper. A memorial, dedicated to the tireless champion of the University and Press, was planned for the campus.

In the 1910s and 1920s the Press broadened the scope of its works though titles in the social sciences and religion were plentiful. Books of the era included Edgar Goodspeed Johnson's *The Story of the Bible* (1916); Arthur W. Ryder's Sanskrit translation of *The Panchatantra* (1925); Joseph Warren Beach's *The Outlook for American Prose* (1926); Shirley Jackson Case's *Jesus: A New Biography* (1927); and *The Life of George Rogers Clark* by James Alton James (1928).

CHANGE AND EXPANSION

By the beginning of the 1930s the Press had become an actual business entity of the University and its operations were transferred from the supervision of the trustees to the school's business manager. Sales had grown to nearly $200,000 as the Press gained momentum and publishing accolades. The majority of the books published in the 1930s and 1940s reflected the issues of the time in religion, social sciences, and a growing awareness of the arts, including *Movements of Thoughts in the Nineteenth Century* by George Herbert Mead and Charles W. Morris (1936); *The Professional Thief* by Chic Conwell and Edwin H. Sutherland (1937); *Edna St. Vincent Millay and Her Times* by Elizabeth Adkins (1936); and *The Story of the Apocrypha* by Edgar Goodspeed Johnson (1939).

Following the success of its *Chicago Manual of Style* came a similar title for university papers, Kate Turabian's *A Manual for Writers of Term Papers, Theses, and Dissertations.* Originally a pamphlet to guide students, it was published in book form in 1937 and became an enduring bestseller. At the time of Turabian's book, the Press became a member of the newly rechristened Association of American University Presses (AAUP), formerly known as the National Association of Book Publishers. The AAUP had become a unifying force for the nation's academic presses, and its support brought many of the member publishers from obscurity to mainstream success.

In 1951 the operations of the Press were formally separated: the books and journals were put under the direction of an academic board, while the printing operations remained with the University's business manager. Although the printing division was absorbed into the business office, it had generated a healthy income for the Press. To help make ends meet, the business office gave the Press an annual stipend for the next four years. By 1955 the Press was wholly independent and in good financial shape with several bestsellers; a year later, the Press began publishing its own paperback editions. Rather than farm its hardcover titles out to a mainstream publisher, the Press began producing its own "trade," or larger-sized, softcover editions under the name of Phoenix Books. This decision, along with joint ventures with foreign publishers to translate international works, set the University of Chicago Press apart from other presses of the era.

The turbulence of the 1960s had little effect on the Press, other than further expanding the scope of its works. In 1961 a new journal, *The History of Religions,* began publication, the first periodical to compare the world's religions. In 1966 the Press proved its diversity with numerous publications, including Daniel J. Boorstin's study of American history *An American Primer;* Claude Lévi-Strauss' sociological study *The Savage Mind;* and Chicago sports commentator Mike Royko's *Chicago Tribune* columns, called *Time: The Best of*

Mike Royko. While readers were accustomed to the Press delivering a variety of intellectual titles, Royko's popular book earned the Press praise for issuing a nonscholarly title. The same year, 1966, the Press appointed a new director, Morris Philipson. Philipson took the reins at a time when the Press had reached annual sales of about $4 million. Philipson realized the importance of the Press's backlist titles, committing to keep as many of these titles in print as possible. Though it was often an expensive endeavor, it paid off in the long-term, with many titles still selling decades after their original publication dates.

PHILIPSON'S REIGN

Like the late Dr. Harper, Philipson enjoyed taking risks with the Press, holding quality far above quantity and pushing the limits of what a university press should be. Philipson took the Press to new levels by literally mixing it up, publishing books as disparate as John Franklin Hope's *Racial Equality in America* (1976), Norman Maclean's *A River Runs Through It* (1976), Klaus J. Hansen's *Mormonism and the American Experience* (1981), John Boswell's *Christianity, Social Tolerance, and Homosexuality* (1980), and Jane J. Mansbridge's *Why We Lost the ERA* (1986).

Philipson also enjoyed the challenge of producing complicated multivolume works such as Muriel St. Clare Byrne's *The Lisle Letters* (1981) about Viscount Arthur Plantagenet Lisle, which went on to win several awards, including *Publishers Weekly*'s Carey-Thomas award and a PEN America Center's Publisher Citation for Philipson himself in 1982.

By the 1990s the Press was the largest university press in the nation, publishing over 200 titles per year and maintaining a backlist of thousands. In 1992 the movie of Norman Maclean's acclaimed novel, *A River Runs Through It,* hit theaters as another Maclean book, *Young Men and Fire,* about the smokejumpers of Mann Gulch in Montana, climbed the national bestseller list and the Press gained worldwide attention. By 1995 the Press had more than 4,500 titles in print and handled the marketing, printing, and distribution of dozens of books for other regional presses and small publishing houses.

The Press prepared to ring in the new century with major changes: Philipson announced his imminent retirement and the search began for a new director. For 1999 the Press brought in revenues of $42 million from 172 new titles as well as numerous paperback originals, reprints, and reissues.

NEW CENTURY, NEW ERA

By the dawn of the 21st century the University of Chicago Press was one of the oldest continuously operating university presses in the nation. In early 2000 Philipson retired after 33 years at the helm; he had not only taken the Press from sales of under $5 million to $42 million, but had steered it to a number of awards and citations. Philipson himself was awarded AAUP's Curtis Benjamin Award for Creative Publishing for his leadership.

Philipson's replacement was Paula Barker Duffy, former publisher at the Free Press. When she took over the Press, it was producing 49 journals and about 260 titles per year, two-thirds new books and the remaining third paperback reissues. Its longtime bestselling reference titles, the *Chicago Manual of Style* and Kate Turabian's *A Manual for Writers of Term Papers, Theses, and Dissertations,* had sold millions of copies and continued to sell more than 60,000 copies per year combined. Barely a year into Duffy's tenure came an overhaul and modernization of the Press' distribution services. With a grant from the Andrew W. Mellon Foundation, the Press went digital, creating the BiblioVault to store its vast backlist of titles. Both new and backlist books were stored in the Vault, enabling employees to search titles and order short-run printings quickly and efficiently.

The BiblioVault allowed the Press to keep backlist titles in print longer and produce books in record time. With the Vault, the Press was also able to offer fulfillment services to more than three dozen presses and publishers nationwide, as well as international houses looking to issue titles in North America. A sampling of Press books published in the 2000s included Howard Gillman's *The Votes That Counted: How the Courts Decided the Presidential 2000 Election* (2001); Allan H. Meltzer's *A History of the Federal Reserve* (2003); Margaret Morganroth Gullette's *Aged by Culture* (2004); David Schmid's *Natural Born Celebrities: Serial Killers in American Culture* (2005); Sylvia Lovegren's *Fashionable Food: Seven Decades of Food Fads* (2005); Jeffrey C. Goldfarb's *The Politics of Small Things: The Power of the Powerless in Dark Times* (2006); and Mario Biagioli's *Galileo's Instruments of Credit: Telescopes, Images, Secrecy* (2006).

In its 115-year history, the Press published nearly 12,000 books on a wide range of topics, from politics, science, religion, and the arts, to pop culture, biography, and fiction. The University of Chicago Press had more than reached the lofty goals of its founders; even Dr.

Harper, its staunchest proponent, had no idea the Press would have such a profound influence beyond Chicago's windy shores.

Nelson Rhodes

PRINCIPAL COMPETITORS

Columbia University Press; Harvard University Press; New York University Press; Northwestern University Press; Oxford University Press; Yale University Press.

FURTHER READING

"Chicago University Press," *New York Times,* May 20, 1892, p. 4.

"Dined by the Baptists," *Chicago Daily,* November 6, 1891, p. 6.

"Duffy to Head University of Chicago Press," *Publishers Weekly,* April 24, 2000, p. 9.

Goddard, Connie, "University of Chicago Press Celebrates Its Centennial," *Publishers Weekly,* July 25, 1991, p. 15.

"Harper Funeral Plans Complete," *Chicago Daily Tribune,* January 12, 1906, p. 2.

"Its Wealth Still Grows," *Chicago Daily Tribune,* May 23, 1905, p. 5.

Milliot, Jim, "University Presses to Embark on Digital Initiative," *Publishers Weekly,* November 5, 2001, p. 10.

Monaghan, Peter, "For the 15th Time, Look It Up: The Chicago Manual of Style Enters 21st Century," *Chronicle of Higher Education,* July 25, 2003, p. A14.

"New Press Building at the University of Chicago," *Chicago Daily Tribune,* September 5, 1902, p. 2.

"Pay East Tribute at Harper's Funeral Bier," *Chicago Daily Tribune,* January 6, 1906, p. 3.

"Press of the University of Chicago a Power," *Chicago Daily Tribune,* February 23, 1896, p. 28.

"Rockefeller Gives $1,500,000," *New York Times,* December 19, 1900, p. 1.

"Sketch of President Harper," *Chicago Daily Tribune,* October 2, 1892, p. 26.

"University Press Will Dissolve," *Chicago Daily Tribune,* May 27, 1894, p. 1.

Van Lanschot NV

Postbus 1021
's-Hertogenbosch
Netherlands
Telephone: +31 073 548 35 48
Fax: +31 073 548 36 48
Web site: http://www.vanlanschot.com

Public Company
Incorporated: 1737
Employees: 2,000Total Assets: EUR 18.3 billion ($20 billion) (2005)
Stock Exchanges: Euronext Amsterdam
Ticker Symbol: LANS
NAIC: 522110 Commercial Banking; 522293 International Trade Financing

■ ■ ■

Van Lanschot NV is The Netherlands' oldest independent private bank, with a history dating back to 1737, and is also one of the country's largest private bankers, with total assets of more than EUR 18 billion, and net profits of more than EUR 152 million in 2005. Van Lanschot offers highly personalized financial services and a range of financial products, including assets management, securities brokerage, insurance, and other products. Van Lanschot also offers corporate banking services, as well as banking services tailored to the institutional investment community, including associations, religious organizations, insurance companies, and the like. Van Lanschot has avoided the Internet banking market, and instead focuses its operations on its branch network, which includes 33 branches in The Netherlands, eight branches in Belgium (including one branch in Brussels), and offices and subsidiaries in Switzerland, Curacao, Jersey, and Hong Kong. In The Netherlands, Van Lanschot caters to a relatively broad market, for a private banker; the bank's average customer deposits just EUR 100,000, and the company accepts initial accounts as low as EUR 50,000 for promising young customers. In Belgium and elsewhere, however, Van Lanschot limits its operations to the high net-worth category. In the mid-2000s, Van Lanschot has achieved strong growth, in part through the purchase of rival CenE Bankiers in 2004. Listed on the Euronext Stock Exchange since 1999, Van Lanschot's major shareholders include Friesland Bank, NIB Capital, Delta Lloyd, and La Dou du Midi. The founding Van Lanschot family also remain significant shareholders in the bank.

TRADING HOUSE IN THE 18TH CENTURY

Cornelius Van Lanschot established a trading firm in 's Hertogenbosch, near Amsterdam, in 1737. The Van Lanschot family remained focused on the commercial trade, shipping goods to and from The Netherlands' colonial possessions, until well into the 19th century. The Netherlands' waning influence in the international trade market, however, encouraged the Van Lanschot family to develop interests in the relatively new commercial banking sector in The Netherlands. By the end of the second half of the century, the Van Lanschot family's operational focus had shifted completely to banking.

COMPANY PERSPECTIVES

Van Lanschot provides personal services where other institutions can no longer do so due to their size. The personal relationship with clients is at the core of Van Lanschot's business. Independence, flexibility and confidentiality are important pillars for how we want to do business. Our co-entrepreneurial approach has proved to be the most important link to our corporate clients. With 32 branches in the Netherlands, Van Lanschot is represented in most large cities. This network enables us to offer a comprehensive package of banking and insurance services throughout the country.

The Van Lanschot banking business was originally set up to provide private banking services to the Van Lanschot family fortune, including the family's investments in The Netherlands' rapidly growing industrial sector. Even as the bank began to develop a larger client base, the bank itself remained quite small, with just the single building in 's Hertogenbosch, and a focus on that city and its surrounding region.

This focus began to broaden following World War II, especially after 1954, when Van Lanschot began opening its first branches. The bank's expansion initially targeted the country's southern regions. Into the 1960s, however, the bank also had begun to establish operations in the country's financial and political centers in The Hague in Amsterdam. In 1960, for example, the bank acquired majority control in Amsterdam's Vermeer & Co., adding banking facilities in that city. By 1966, the bank had formed a partnership with a prominent Hague bank, Staal & Co.

During the 1970s, Van Lanschot turned toward acquisitions to build further scale, and into the 1980s the bank made a series of small acquisitions, adding a presence in a number of new local markets. The expansion of the group's client base allowed the bank to offer a wider ranger of financial services, in turn attracting a growing number of clients. The company continued its organic growth as well, expanding into the country's central region with the opening of a number of new branches during the 1980s.

To fuel the bank's expansion, the Van Lanschot family turned to outside investors during the early 1970s. In 1973, the bank sold 25 percent of its shares to National Westminster, which remained a major shareholder in the bank into the late 1980s. In 1978, Van Lanschot sold a further 25 percent to Rabobank. In the mid-1980s, Rabobank and Westminster joined together to acquire an additional 30 percent of Van Lanschot, in a transaction completed in 1986. The Van Lanschot family, including the bank's management, together with Delta Lloyd, nonetheless retained control of 20 percent of the bank.

National Westminster bought out Rabobank's stake in the bank in 1990, strengthening its own position to 79 percent. The British bank then sought to take over Van Lanschot entirely, and merge the bank into its own operations. The Van Lanschot family resisted this effort; finally, unable to agree on a common strategy, the two sides agreed to separate. In 1994, National Westminster sold its stake in Van Lanschot to a consortium of Dutch financial groups, including ABN AMRO Group and ING Group. As part of that sale, the Van Lanschot family agreed to list the bank on the stock exchange before the end of the decade. Van Lanschot completed its initial public offering in 1999.

LEADING INDEPENDENT PRIVATE BANKING FIRM INTO THE 20TH CENTURY

Although Van Lanschot remained focused, in large part, on its domestic market, building up its branch network to 33 offices in The Netherlands by the mid-2000s, the bank began developing its international private banking market. The bank's first step in this direction came in 1989, when it launched a subsidiary in Luxembourg. Into the 1990s, the bank turned its attention to the neighboring Belgian market, opening its first branches in the Flemish-speaking region. By 2006, the bank had opened eight branches in Belgium, including an office in Brussels. In contrast to its Dutch operations, which developed a larger client base, the bank's foreign subsidiaries targeted especially the high net-worth category.

In response to the needs of its growing clientele, the bank also added offshore banking services, launching subsidiaries in Jersey and Curacao. Van Lanschot also opened a subsidiary in Switzerland, with branches in Geneva and Zurich. Van Lanschot next turned to the Asian market, opening its first representative office in that region, in Hong Kong, in 2003. By then, Van Lanschot had grown into The Netherlands' sixth largest private banker, with nearly EUR 11 billion in total assets.

Van Lanschot boosted its profile still higher in 2004. In that year, the bank paid an estimated EUR 250 million to acquire rival CenE Bankiers, formerly the affinity wealth management division of the ING Group. Van

KEY DATES

1737: Cornelius Van Lanschot founds a trading company in 's Hertogenbosch, The Netherlands; by the late 19th century, Van Lanschot has converted to a private bank.

1954: Van Lanschot begins expansion beyond the 's Hertogenbosch area.

1960: Van Lanschot acquires a majority stake in Vermeer & Co. te Amsterdam.

1966: A partnership is formed with Staal & Co. in The Hague.

1974: National Westminster acquires a 25 percent stake.

1978: Rabobank acquires a 25 percent stake.

1986: Rabobank and National Westminster each acquire an additional 15 percent stake.

1989: Van Lanschot launches a subsidiary in Luxembourg.

1990: National Westminster buys out Rabobank's share.

1994: National Westminster agrees to sell its control of Van Lanschot to an institutional investor consortium.

1999: Van Lanschot goes public on the Amsterdam Stock Exchange.

2003: Van Lanschot opens a representative office in Hong Kong.

2004: CenE Bankiers is acquired from the ING Group.

2006: A team of private bankers is added from MeesPierson, part of Fortis.

Lanschot began integrating CenE's network into its own operations. By the end of 2005, that process had, in large part, been completed. As part of the integration process, CenE was refocused in order to target exclusively the healthcare market.

At the time of its public offering, Van Lanschot had taken on a new group of institutional shareholders, including Friesland Bank, which acquired nearly 20 percent of Van Lanschot. The two banks entered into a shareholding agreement at that time. In 2005, the banks formed a new agreement, in which Friesland Bank confirmed its intention to respect Van Lanschot's independence. As part of that agreement, Friesland Bank agreed to limit its shareholding to a maximum of 29 percent, and agreed not to help another shareholder gain more than 20 percent of Van Lanschot. In this way, Van Lanschot guaranteed its continued independence.

By the end of 2005, Van Lanschot had raised its total assets past EUR 18 billion. Into 2006, the bank affirmed its commitment to further growth when it acquired an entire team of highly experienced private banking specialists from MeesPierson, the wealth division of the Fortis bancassurance group. The new nine-member team joined Van Lanschot's Amsterdam office at the beginning of April 2006, targeting the high-end bracket. After more than 250 years, the Van Lanschot name remained one of the most prominent in The Netherlands' financial market.

M. L. Cohen

PRINCIPAL SUBSIDIARIES

CenE Bankiers N.V.; Efima Hypotheken B.V.; F. van Lanschot Bankiers (België) N.V.; F. van Lanschot Bankiers (Luxembourg) S.A.; F. van Lanschot Bankiers (Schweiz) AG; F. van Lanschot Bankiers N.V.; F. van Lanschot Beheer B.V.; F. van Lanschot International Trust Company B.V.; F. van Lanschot Overseas NVTE Curaçao; F. van Lanschot Participaties B.V.; F. van Lanschot Trust Company Ltd. (Jersey); Family Ohce B.V.; Van Lanschot Asset Management B.V.; Van Lanschot Assurantiën B.V.

PRINCIPAL COMPETITORS

Fortis N.V.; Bank Nederlandse Gemeenten N.V.; SNS Reaal Groep N.V.; Eureko B.V.; SNS Bank Nederland N.V.; Nederlandse Waterschapsbank N.V.; NIBC Bank N.V.; Achmea Bank Holding N.V.; Kas Bank N.V; ABN AMRO Bank N.V.; Friesland Bank N.V.; Delta Lloyd Bank N.V.

FURTHER READING

"CenE Bankiers wordt grotendeels Van Lanschot," *Hugin,* September 23, 2005.

Cramb, Gordon, "Van Lanschot Share Offer Values Group at [EURO] 1bn," *Financial Times,* June 21, 1999, p. 29.

Harris, Clay, "Club Atmosphere in a Dutch Way," *Financial Times,* November 16, 1999, p. 7.

JMG van Lanschot, et al., *De balans van 225 jaar. Een korte schets van de geschiedenis: F. van Lanschot, bankiers,* 's Hertogenbosch: F. Van Lanschot, 1962.

"Lanschot in Private Banking Acquisition," *Private Banker International,* August 31, 2004.

"Netherlands' F. van Lanschot Bankiers Sets Up Office in HK," *AsiaPulse News,* February 20, 2003.

"2005 an Outstanding Year for Van Lanschot," *Hugin,* March 16, 2006.

"Van Lanschot Builds Up," *Private Banker International,* March 22, 2006.

"Van Lanschot in Private Banking Acquisition," *Private Banker International,* August 2004, p. 2.

"Van Lanschot versterkt Private Banking," *Hugin,* March 1, 2006.

VASCO Data Security International, Inc.

1901 South Meyers Road, Suite 210
Oakbrook Terrace, Illinois 60181
U.S.A.
Telephone: (630) 932-8844
Toll Free: (800) 238-2726
Fax: (630) 932-8852
Web site: http://www.vasco.com

Public Company
Incorporated: 1984 as VASCO Corp.
Employees: 112
Sales: $29.8 million (2004)
Stock Exchanges: NASDAQ
Ticker Symbol: VDSI
NAIC: 541512 Computer Systems Design Services; 511210 Software Publishers

■ ■ ■

VASCO Data Security International, Inc., designs and markets hardware and software identity authentication products for private enterprise networks and public networks, such as the Internet. The company's products, as well as those of its competitors, often are referred to as "security tokens." The company's main line of devices is marketed under the name "Digipass." VASCO primarily serves banking customers, deriving the bulk of its revenue from serving customers based overseas. The company's operational headquarters are located in Brussels, Belgium, where the software to support its product is developed. Next, the software is sent to Samsung Group, the manufacturer of VASCO's chips, before being sent to one of two manufacturers in mainland China, where final assembly takes place.

ORIGINS

VASCO's development during its first 20 years of business traveled along two separate paths. The distinction between the two courses of development represented more than just two eras of existence. VASCO jumped from one path and headed in an entirely different direction, metamorphosing from one company into a distinctly different company, effecting a transformation that made the original VASCO irrelevant to the company bearing the VASCO banner in the 21st century.

The company began operating in 1984 under the name VASCO Corp., an enterprise that provided consulting, training, and software services to corporate clientele and government agencies. Although the company's consulting and technical training business, marketed as VASCO Performance Systems, endured for a decade, the event that caused VASCO Corp. to become VASCO Data Security International, Inc. occurred early in the company's history. In late 1989, the company acquired an option to purchase a majority interest in ThumbScan, Inc., which it exercised at the beginning of 1991. The acquisition led VASCO into the data security business, a signal moment that provided the compass point leading to the company's future. In 1993, ThumbScan was renamed VASCO Data Security, Inc., a wholly owned subsidiary of VASCO Corp. In 1996, all matters related to the company's future strategic orientation were resolved. The metamorphosis was made

COMPANY PERSPECTIVES

We believe we have one of the most complete lines of security products and services for Identity Authentication available in the market today and we intend to become a leading worldwide provider of these products and services. A key element of our growth strategy is to demonstrate to an increasing number of distributors, resellers and systems integrators that, by incorporating our security products into their own products, they can more effectively differentiate themselves in their marketplaces and increase the value of their products. In addition, we will demonstrate to our corporate users that our products provide mission critical security to their internal and external security infrastructures. Following this active marketing and promotion effort, we will work with these resellers and integrators to support their sales of solutions that include our products. Also, we plan to expand our direct sales marketing program to new and existing blue chip customers.

complete through disposition and acquisition, resulting in the VASCO tracked by analysts and onlookers in the 21st century.

A NEW VASCO IS BORN

VASCO built its future base before it disposed of its past. In early 1996, the company expanded its computer security business by purchasing a 15 percent interest in Lintel Security NV/SA, a company based in Brussels, Belgium, the future operational headquarters of VASCO. The purchase of a minority interest in Lintel Security NV/SA spawned a VASCO subsidiary named Lintel Security, also based in Belgium, that took hold of assets associated with the development of security tokens and security technologies for personal computers and computer networks. In June 1996, VASCO acquired full control over Lintel Security NV/SA for $4.4 million, acquiring a company that figured as one of its competitors. The following month, VASCO paid $8.2 million for Digipass NV/SA, another Brussels-based company that posed a competitive threat to VASCO. Digipass, like Lintel, developed security tokens and security technologies for personal computers and computer networks, but its addition to the VASCO fold was significantly more important. In the years ahead, VASCO's leading product was marketed under the Digipass name. The company's original line of business, the consulting and technical training services business marketing under the name VASCO Performance Systems, was sold in August, one month after the Digipass NV/SA purchase, cutting all ties to the company formed a decade earlier.

VASCO, in a corporate sense, formally acknowledged its metamorphosis through a series of moves between 1997 and 1998. The two Belgian companies, Lintel and Digipass, were combined in 1997 to form VASCO Data Security NV/SA. In July 1997, VASCO Data Security International, Inc. was incorporated as a subsidiary of VASCO Corp., setting the stage for the final step in the company's reorganization plan. In March 1998, the two companies swapped positions through a public offering in which VASCO Data Security International acquired VASCO Corp., making VASCO Corp. a subsidiary of VASCO Data Security International. In October 1998, VASCO Corp. was merged into VASCO Data Security International and ceased to exist.

Wholly committed to operating as a data security provider, VASCO entered the late 1990s at an important juncture in the development of its new industry. The emergence of electronic commerce, and electronic banking in particular, created burgeoning demand for the technology offered by VASCO and its fellow competitors. VASCO approached the market touting its Digipass device, an identity authentication product designed to combat fraud and theft during electronic transactions conducted on private enterprise networks and public networks, such as the Internet. The Digipass, a pocket-calculator sized device, used software capable of generating electronic passwords specific to individuals at specific times and places. When a customer logged onto a secure web site, the Digipass prompted the user to enter a personal identification number and responded by generating a password valid for one-time access to the user's account.

As VASCO dived headlong into identity authentication technology, the company relied heavily on the banking industry for its business. Banking customers accounted for roughly 80 percent of the company's business, and, more specifically, primarily foreign banking customers. The dependence on overseas business, which prompted the company to establish its financial headquarters in the United States and its operational headquarters in Belgium, stemmed from differing attitudes toward security issues in the United States and abroad, particularly in Europe. "Europe has taken more of a comprehensive approach from the beginning and has gotten security taken of, which is why the tokens are

KEY DATES

1984: VASCO Corp. is founded.
1991: The acquisition of ThumbScan marks VASCO's entry into the data security business.
1996: The purchase of Lintel Security NV/SA and Digipass NV/SA gives VASCO a Belgian base in the data security market.
1997: VASCO Data Security International, Inc. is incorporated and acquires VASCO Corp. the following year.
1999: First Union Bank agrees to use Digipass devices, greatly strengthening VASCO's U.S. business.
2006: VASCO delivers its 20 millionth Digipass unit.

more widely used there," an analyst explained in a June 19, 2000 interview with *American Banker.* Consequently, VASCO's early years were spent trying to promote the acceptance of Digipass in the United States, while deriving 80 percent of its financial sustenance from abroad. A breakthrough moment for VASCO and for the U.S. banking industry occurred in early 1999, when First Union Corp., a $234 billion-in-assets bank based in Charlotte, North Carolina, began deploying the Digipass 300 to its customers, the first time a major U.S. bank had agreed to use the breed of security tokens made by VASCO. The deal, which involved roughly 20,000 units of the Digipass 300, did much to foster acceptance of identity authentication technology in VASCO's home country, an event to be celebrated by the company's leaders. In a January 21, 1999 interview with *American Banker,* T. Kendall Hunt, VASCO's chairman and chief executive officer, offered his assessment of the significance of the First Union contract. "A very visible, prestigious name like First Union is going to make the road ahead a lot faster," he said, adding, "This is very big for us."

Shortly after the landmark First Union contract was secured, VASCO underwent a change in leadership, producing the executive team that would be responsible for tackling the challenges ahead. In a nod to the importance of the company's European business, Mario Houthooft, the leader of Belgium-based VASCO Data Security NV/SA, was named president and chief executive officer of the entire company in mid-1999. Hunt remained chairman, taking on responsibilities related to long-term strategic issues while Houthooft, ten years his junior, assumed day-to-day control over the company, splitting his time between Brussels and suburban Chicago. Looking ahead, Houthooft and Hunt faced two major challenges: increasing the company's presence in the U.S. market, its "Achilles heel," according to the July 5, 1999 issue of *Crain's Chicago Business,* and increasing the overall size of the company. VASCO, when Houthooft took the helm, was generating $15 million in revenue, more than seven times the total registered four years earlier, in 1994, but hardly a revenue volume to impress analysts and industry pundits. VASCO's main U.S. rival, Bedford, Massachusetts-based RSA Security, controlled 60 percent of the hardware security token market, boasting a revenue volume more than ten times larger than VASCO's, having developed into an industry giant by supplying security tokens used mainly by employees to access corporate systems. VASCO needed to get bigger, not only in the United States, but in any region that offered opportunities for growth. The identity authentication market was emerging, escalating in importance with each passing year. Market dominance depended on the actions of all competitors in the next few years, presenting the overriding challenge facing Houthooft and Hunt as they pursued expansion.

EXPANSION ENTERING 2000

Houthooft and Hunt expanded VASCO by stepping up marketing efforts in the United States, by maintaining progress abroad, and by completing acquisitions. The first purchase after the promotion of Houthooft strengthened the company's greatest weakness. In October 1999, VASCO acquired Intellisoft Corp., an Acton, Massachusetts-based supplier of identity authentication products to a number of U.S.-based customers, including John Hancock, 3M, Liberty Mutual, and Allmerica Financial. In August 2000, VASCO acquired Invincible Data Systems, Inc., a privately held security products company with sales and research development operations in Sunnyvale, California. Next, VASCO purchased Indentikey Ltd., completing the purchase in March 2001. Indentikey, a privately held company based in Brisbane, Australia, developed security software for corporations, financial institutions, and government agencies on a global basis.

As VASCO fought for new business during the first years of the 21st century, the company was beginning to show the first signs of developing into a more prominent competitor. The efforts directed toward expansion lifted revenues to nearly $30 million in 2004, but the total was dwarfed by the volume of business generated by its largest competitor, RSA Security, which recorded $310 million in revenue during the year. The company needed to become much larger, and much of its growth potential was located in the largely untapped U.S. market. To reach a higher plateau, VASCO needed the U.S. market to embrace identity authentication technology, something some industry pundits believed was about to occur midway through the century's first decade. "Europe has always been more security conscious than the United States, but the United States is going to catch up," an analyst said in a June 27, 2005 interview with *Crain's Chicago Business.* "You're going to see their [VASCO's] business in the United States grow with all the security breaches now occurring," the analyst added. "The time is right for VASCO."

Based on the escalating sales of the company's Digipass devices, there was a sense that the company was turning a corner. It took VASCO seven years to deliver its first one million security tokens, but by late 2004 it was selling one million units in a three-month period. In 2005, the company sold more than seven million Digipass units, a record number that more than doubled the total sold in 2004. "We're really starting to accelerate on the retail side," Hunt said in a November 3, 2005 interview with *USA Today.* In early 2006, a milestone was reached when the company delivered its 20 millionth Digipass device. Hunt, naturally, was excited by the surge in business, but he was mindful that much remained to be completed. "RSA is still the Coca-Cola in this industry and we're the RC Cola," he said in a June 27, 2005 interview with *Crain's Chicago Business.* In the years ahead, VASCO's success largely would be determined by its ability to elevate its stature substantially and stand eye-to-eye with its largest rival.

Jeffrey L. Covell

PRINCIPAL SUBSIDIARIES

VASCO Data Security, Inc.; VASCO Data Security Europe S.A.; VASCO Data Security NV/SA; Lintel Security SA/NV; VASCO Data Security Development, Inc.; VASCO Data Security Asia-Pacific Pte Ltd.

PRINCIPAL COMPETITORS

RSA Security Inc.; ActiveCard Corp.; Litronic, Inc.

FURTHER READING

Byron, Acohido, "Two Security Token Makers Vie for Consumer Market," *USA Today,* November 3, 2005, p. 2B.

Domis, Olaf de Senerpont, "Secure Transaction Device for 20,000 1st Union Clients," *American Banker,* January 21, 1999.

Magee, C. Max, "Demand Grows for Security Company," *Daily Herald,* February 13, 2005, p. 1.

Murphy, H. Lee, "VASCO Taps into Fraud Fear," *Crain's Chicago Business,* June 27, 2005, p. 12.

"Tech Bytes: Data Security Merger," *American Banker,* October 19, 1999, p. 17.

"Tech Bytes: VASCO Data Security Splits Itself in Two," *American Banker,* January 10, 2000, p. 9.

"VASCO's Key to Domestic Sales," *Crain's Chicago Business,* January 1, 2001, p. 10.

Walkers Shortbread Ltd.

Aberlour-On-Spey, AB38 9PD
Scotland
Telephone: +44 01340 871555
Fax: +44 01340 871355
Web site: http://www.walkers-shortbread.co.uk

Private Company
Incorporated: 1898
Employees: 870
Sales: £69.12 million ($117 million) (2004)
NAIC: 311821 Cookie and Cracker Manufacturing; 311812 Commercial Bakeries

■ ■ ■

Walkers Shortbread Ltd. has baked one of Scotland's, and the world's, favorite shortbread recipes for more than 100 years. The company, based in Aberlour, in northeastern Scotland, continues to produce its shortbread and other baked goods from the same recipes developed by founder Joseph Walker in the late 1890s. Shortbread remains the company's flagship product, and the company produces a variety of shortbread recipes and packaged assortments. Other company products include oatcakes, fruitcakes, tarts, cookies, and biscuits. The company produces a successful assortment of cookies for the Weight Watchers brand; in 2005, the company added a line of Weight Watchers-branded biscuits as well. Walkers also produces and distributes a line of organic biscuits for Duchy Originals, a company established by Prince Charles to promote organic farming in the United Kingdom. Walkers Shortbread also produces products for third party and private supermarket labels. The company distributes its products through various channels in the United Kingdom, including supermarkets, small grocers, and gift shops. Walkers Shortbread is also one of the United Kingdom's top-selling export brands, in terms of overall proportion of sales, generating some 45 percent of its turnover overseas. Major markets include the United States and Canada, continental Europe, Australia, New Zealand, and India; the company also sells its products in China, Thailand, and elsewhere. Walkers operates production facilities in Aberlour and Elgin, and has launched plans to build a second factory in Aberlour as early as 2006. The company also operates a distribution subsidiary in the United States. Walkers remains 100 percent owned by the founding Walker family; James and Joseph Walker, grandsons of the founder, serve as co-managing directors. The next generation of the Walker family have also entered the company, which remains committed to its private, family-owned status. In 2004, Walkers Shortbread produced revenues of more than £69 million ($117 million).

SHORTBREAD SUCCESS IN 1898

Joseph Walker was 21 years old when he borrowed £50 and opened his own bakery in Torphins, Scotland, in 1898. Walker began developing his own recipe for shortbread, a traditional favorite in the United Kingdom. By the end of his first year in business, Walker had perfected his recipe, using no more than flour, sugar, butter, salt, and water.

The Scotsman's shortbread quickly established its reputation as one of the finest in the region. Before

COMPANY PERSPECTIVES

Walkers Shortbread is baked from the finest ingredients, with no artificial flavouring, colouring or preservative in sight—just as it has always been. The irresistible range of varieties is beautifully presented in Walkers distinctive tartan packaging, making it a reliably welcome gift.

long, the original shop had grown too small, and Walker moved to larger premises in the Speyside village of Aberlour. The move was important in establishing the company as one of the finest shortbread producers, in part due to its water, which also provided the basis for the village's famed whiskey. Walker also bought a horse and carriage and began his first deliveries. In the meantime, Walker continued to develop new recipes, extending his range of shortbread varieties while adding other treats, such as oatcakes, cookies, and biscuits.

Walker, described by *Grocer* as "fierce," laid the foundation of the future Walkers Shortbread with his recipes, many of which remained company mainstays into the next century. However, Walker's two sons, James and Joseph, were chiefly responsible for the company's growth from a small bakery into a true baked goods manufacturer. As grandson James Walker told *Grocer*: Walker "gets the credit for founding the company, which is a difficult and brave thing to do. But the biggest credit goes to our father and uncle who had to put up with him for 30 years."

The two Walker sons joined their father in the 1930s and quickly began to develop the bakery from a local to a regional basis. The brothers introduced new products, including cakes and confectionery items. In 1936, also, the bakery motorized its delivery, adding the first of a fleet of vans with which it could extend its distribution throughout the region.

The family bakery's growth was slowed during World War II, when many of its core ingredients were placed under strict rations. During this time, the company developed its oatcake recipe, which became a popular favorite and took its place in the group's permanent product range. Following the war, the bakery's production returned to its previous level. Yet the Walkers faced continued shortages in raw ingredients, including butter. The company nevertheless remained true to its original shortbread recipe, refusing to replace butter with margarine. Walkers also became noted for its refusal to use artificial colorings, flavorings, and preservatives.

Joseph Walker died in 1954 and his sons took over as the owners of the bakery. James and Joseph began transforming the bakery into a full-fledged food company. The pair were joined by the next generation, James's children James, Joseph, and Marjorie, who all began working with the company by the beginning of the 1960s. The growing number of family members allowed the company to expand, adding shops in Grantown and Elgin. By the early 1960s, also, the bakery operated a fleet of 14 delivery vans.

MODERN COMPANY

By then the first supermarkets had begun to appear in Scotland, and the company had also begun to distribute its goods through the region's local grocers. The increasing demand encouraged the company to add new employees, and by the middle of the decade, Walkers employed over 100 people. Nearly all of these came from Aberlour itself, as the company and the village developed a close-knit relationship. In an interview with the *Sunday Herald*, James Walker, grandson of the founder, described the relationship in this way: "We fit beautifully into the demographics of the village. The rest of the village are mainly employed in the distilleries but there are no women on the production side of distilling so we provide alternative jobs for the women. We need the village and the village needs us. They'd literally walk through fire for us."

Walkers also began investing in machinery in order to satisfy the growing demand for its products. Despite the industrialization of its production, the company took care to maintain the quality of its shortbread. A major factor in the group's success in fulfilling its quality commitment came from its insistence on baking its shortbread and other recipes in small batches. In this way, the company was able to retain its original recipes, and its products preserved not only their flavor, but their appearance as well.

The rise of the supermarket and the growing dominance of large-scale, nationally operating supermarket chains played a role in Walkers' shifting focus from the local and regional levels to a national and then international level in the 1970s. Helping establish the company's reputation were its contracts to supply such noted British retailers as Harrods, Selfridges, Fortnum & Mason, and others. These London-based department stores also attracted a large international clientele, which led the company to begin eyeing the export market in the early 1970s.

KEY DATES

1898: Joseph Walker opens bakery in Torphins, Scotland, and develops his own shortbread recipe, then moves to a larger bakery in Aberlour.
1936: Walker is joined by his sons, James and Joseph, who add new recipes and motorized delivery vehicles.
1972: Company begins exports to France and Germany, then to North America.
1975: Walkers builds second production facility in Aberlour.
1987: Third generation of Walkers takes over as co-managing directors after death of James Walker.
1995: Company builds third production facility in Elgin; acquires U.S. distributor and establishes Walkers Shortbread Inc.
2003: Company acquires site next to Aberlour factory for future expansion.
2005: Walkers applies for permission to build new 70,000-square-foot factory in Elgin.

The company launched its first exports, to France and Germany, in 1972. Soon after, the company began distributing to North America. The company began a distribution partnership with Europa Foods in the United States, which helped developed the Walkers brand into one the leading imported cookie types in North America. The group's international expansion, as well as the increased shelf space available in supermarkets, also encouraged it to develop new recipes. As such the company launched a number of new products, such as shortbread featuring chocolate chips for the U.S. market, and macadamia nut shortbread for the Australian markets, and other specialties during the 1970s and 1980s.

The increasing demand forced Walkers to move out of its original bakery facility, and into a new, custom-built, state-of-the-art production facility in Aberlour. The company nevertheless kept the original bakery in operation, for "sentimental reasons," as Marjorie Walker told *Grocer*, and also because the bakery was "a part of village life." The bakery also provided a proven testing ground for the company's new recipes, allowing the company to test new products with the local population before launching full production. As the company described it, "Customers around the world are enjoying a range of products that were first given the seal of approval by the villagers of Aberlour."

LEADING EXPORT BRAND

Walkers continued adding to its line of recipes, producing more than 80 products by the mid-1990s. By then, the next generation of Walkers had taken the leadership following the senior James Walker's death in 1987. The younger Walkers took up positions as co-managing directors, with each assigned specific responsibilities in the company. As such Joseph Walker directed the group's production, purchasing, and distribution operations, while Marjorie Walker handled the company's administration and finance. James Walker provided the company's public face, responsible for marketing and sales.

The younger generation remained true to company tradition. As James Walker told *Grocer*: "Tradition is an obsession and quality is a god. And I don't say it lightly. We can maintain that because the three directors are so close to the company and the product. The product has been run by bakers, not accountants." Joseph Walker also confirmed the group's continued commitment to its tradition-based production process, adding: "We're almost fanatical about tradition, continuity and consistency. We never make changes unless absolutely necessary. The objective is to make everything in a simple, straightforward fashion."

The Walkers also remained true to their region. As James Walker expressed it: "We're more than an employer to a lot of people. We're often good friends, and have grown up with a lot of them." As such, when the company sought to expand its production capacity, it went only so far as the village of Elgin, just 15 miles away, where it built a 44,000-square-foot factory in 1995. The new facility enabled the company to step up its product range, in part through the production of private label products for the supermarket groups. Walkers also entered licensing partnerships with a number of companies, including Disney, the Thornton's chocolate brand, and, into the 2000s, Weight Watchers and Duchy Original. By the mid-2000s, Walkers' product range had grown to more than 200 items.

Walkers saw strong growth into the 2000s, notably on the export front. By the early 2000s, 45 percent of the group's sales came from international markets, with the United States, Canada, Europe, and Japan forming its major international markets. The company's North American presence was backed up in 1995 when Walker took over its North American distributor, establishing a new subsidiary, Walkers Shortbread Inc. This percentage placed the company among the leaders of the United

Kingdom's food brand exporters. The company continued to seek out new markets, such as Thailand in 2003, and mainland China as well.

Walkers also prepared for its future. In 2003, the company purchased a former private school located next to its main Aberlour facility, announcing the possibility of adding new offices on the site. In 2005, the company acquired a new site in Elgin, a former sawmill. The company applied for permission to build a new 70,000-square-foot factory on the site, which was to become part of a new £16 million retail development.

At the same time, the Walker family was preparing for the future change in company leadership. Marjorie Walker retired in 2005. Later that year, James Walker revealed the company's plans to turn over its direction to the succeeding generation over the next ten years. Three of the new generation had already joined the company's management in the mid-2000s.

The announcement came as part of the company's commitment to remain a privately held, family-run concern. As James Walker told *Aberdeen Press & Journal*: "It will be a gradual process. But our absolute aim is to secure the company as an independent, privately owned and family-run business. We think that is very important, not just for the firm, but for the local community. It allows us to take a long-term view of things, which might not be the case if it was owned by a group of investors." With the Walker family at the helm, Walkers Shortbread appeared certain to remain a leading baked goods brand during the new century.

M. L. Cohen

PRINCIPAL SUBSIDIARIES

Walkers Shortbread Inc. (U.S.A.).

PRINCIPAL COMPETITORS

United Biscuits Holdings PLC; Associated British Foods PLC; Northern Foods PLC; Goodman Fielder Proprietary Ltd.; George Weston Foods Ltd.; Arnotts Biscuits Ltd.; British Bakeries Ltd.

FURTHER READING

Darroch, Valerie "Valerie Darroch Talks to One of the Family Trio Who Have Made Their Shortbread a Market Leading Product," *Sunday Herald*, October 12, 2003, p. 11.

Gannaway, Belinda, "The Past Is the Future," *Grocer*, August 26, 2000, p. 40.

McClintock, Linda, "Secrets of the 'Small Loaf,'" *Grocer*, March 15, 1997, p. 20.

"Understanding WeightWatchers Is Key to Motivation," *Grocer*, October 29, 2005, p. 19.

"Walkers Bake New Generation of Family Heirs to Business," *Aberdeen Press & Journal*, November 3, 2005.

"Walkers Factory Plans to Create 200 New Jobs," *Aberdeen Press & Journal*, September 3, 2005.

"Walkers Shortbread," *Gourmet Retailer*, December 2000, p. 158.

"Walkers Shortbread Takes the Biscuit," *Food Trade Review*, June 2005, p. 436.

"Walkers Shortbread Tins Celebrate Scottish History," *Candy Industry*, September 2005, p. 40.

Wise Foods, Inc.

245 Townpark Drive
Suite 450
Kennesaw, Georgia 30144
U.S.A.
Telephone: (770) 794-2720
Fax: (770) 528-0668
Web site: http://www.wisesnacks.com

Private Company
Founded: 1921 as Wise Potato Chip Company
Employees: 2,000
Sales: $325 million (2005 est.)
NAIC: 311919 Other Snacks Food Manufacturing

■ ■ ■

Wise Foods, Inc. is a private company based in Kennesaw, Georgia, that makes and sells snacks through retail food outlets in 15 eastern seaboard states as well as Vermont, Ohio, West Virginia, Kentucky, Tennessee, and Washington, D.C. Best known for its potato chips—which come in several varieties, including jalapeno, unsalted, wavy, and all-natural under the Kettle Cooked label—Wise also offers Cheez Doodles, varieties of bagged popcorn, tortilla chips, pork rinds, cheez waffles, onion rings, Dipsy Doodle chips, Nacho Twisters, Quinlan brand pretzels, and French onion and nacho cheese dips. Wise is majority owned by Palladium Equity Partners, a New York City-based private equity firm specializing in middle market companies.

ORIGINS OF THE POTATO CHIP DATE TO THE MID-19TH CENTURY

A multitude of sources agree that the potato chip was invented in the summer of 1853 in Saratoga Springs, New York, the upstate summer destination for the well-healed who gathered for the prestigious horse racing season and other gaming and resort pursuits, including dining. One of the restaurants of the area, Moon's Lake House, boasted an irascible chef named George Crum who did not take kindly to criticism from the patrons. Should a diner have the temerity to return something to the kitchen, he was known to send back to the table the worst dish his fevered mind could concoct at the moment. It was during the 1853 season that a customer, alleged in some quarters to be Cornelius Vanderbilt, was dissatisfied with the fried potatoes he ordered, maintaining they were not crispy enough, and had them sent back to the kitchen. To gain revenge, Crum was determined to present his new nemesis with the crispiest fried potatoes imaginable. He sliced the potatoes in thin wafers, cooked them in hot grease, and as a final measure, according to some accounts at least, salted them excessively. Unaware apparently that he was being insulted, the diner tried the potatoes and loved them. The owner of the Moon's Lake House recognized an opportunity and put Crum's "potato crunches" on the menu. Later when he opened his own restaurant, Crum called them "Saratoga Chips," and as other restaurants across the country began to imitate him the name changed to potato chips.

Potato chips became available in grocery stores in the 1890s. The first potato chip factory was generally

COMPANY PERSPECTIVES

Our mission is simple, to make real food for real people ... great tasting snacks made from the finest ingredients and backed by exceptional customer service. From our familiar favorites to our newest varieties, we strive to be the snack you are proud to share with your friends and family.

credited to William Tappendon of Cleveland, Ohio, who outgrew his home kitchen and converted his barn into a chip-making operation. More productive potato chip factories opened in the early years of the 20th century, including the plant opened by the Leominster Potato Chip Company in Leominster, Massachusetts.

Wise Foods started out as Wise Potato Chip Company, founded in Berwick, Pennsylvania, in 1921 by a young man named Earl Wise, Sr. He owned Wise Delicatessen and began making potato chips as a way to make use of excess potatoes, initially cooking them in his mother's kitchen, and then selling them to customers in brown paper bags. At the time, potato chips were generally kept in glass display cases or cracker barrels, and scooped into paper bags for customers. The bags developed grease spots and did not keep the chips fresh for very long, eventually leading to the development of waxed paper bags. Wise's chips proved an immediate hit with customers and soon the delicatessen owner became a regional potato chip mogul, remodeling a garage to serve as his initial factory. He had his first delivery truck by 1922. For a logo he decided on a picture of an owl, a creature known to be "wise."

Potato chips had become a favorite across the country, leading to a number of entrepreneurs getting involved in the potato chip business. Located in Hanover, Pennsylvania, rival Utz also was launched in 1921 by Bill and Salie Utz. A relative latecomer to chips, Herman Lay, would start out as a distributor for the Atlanta-based Barrett Potato Chip Co. before buying Barrett's Atlanta and Nashville factories and introducing Lay's Brand Potato Chips in 1938. It would be Lay who became the powerhouse in the fledgling snack industry, the only one to develop a national potato chip brand.

The snack industry and the fortunes of the Wise Potato Chip Company improved dramatically after World War II. Per capita consumption of potato chips in the United States increased from 1.91 pounds in 1945 to 2.56 pounds a decade later. According to a 1956 article about the rise of the snack food industry published in *Barron's National Business and Financial Weekly* in 1956, it was not just potato chips that benefited from Americans' love affair with snacks: corn chips, pretzels, popcorn, peanut butter sandwiches, crackers with cheese, and fried bacon rinds were also popular. Only peanuts dropped in sales, perhaps due to a backlash from consumers who had eaten more than they cared to during the food rationing years of World War II. *Barron's* speculated about the upward trend of snack foods: "The spread of the supermarket, for one thing, has permitted the prominent display of items in appealing transparent packages. ... 75% of all snack food purchases are made on impulse. The buyer spots the potato chips or popcorn and decides to take a package or two home with her detergent, frozen spinach and corn flakes." The impact of television also was cited. "Its grip, in fact, has been so strong as to encourage what might be called sustenance by snack—that is, nibbling tid-bits before the TV set rather than eating a full-course meal at the table. This factor is pointed up by the increase in sales of various dip preparations over the past two years. These preparations, of course, have boosted further the overall sales of the chips, crackers and other food bits that are dipped into them." Whatever the reason, the popularity of potato chips and other snack foods continued to grow into the 1960s.

SOLD TO BORDEN IN 1964

In 1964 the Wise Potato Chip company passed out of the Wise family, attracting the attention of Borden Condensed Milk Co. Founded in 1858 by Gail Borden to manufacture condensed milk, Borden became a top dairy company in the 20th century, spurred in part by the introduction of its Elsie the Cow marketing mascot in the 1930s. After World War II the company became involved in chemicals, in 1947 introducing the first household adhesive, Elmer's Glue-all. In the 1950s and 1960s Borden acquired a variety of companies involved in chemicals, paints, wallpaper, textile coatings, paper, and plastics. Borden's lucrative home milk delivery business came under pressure by the 1960s from private-label dairy products sold at the supermarket, prompting the company to assemble a slate of supermarket products, mostly packaged foods, in a diversification effort. Borden added familiar brands such as ReaLemon lemon juice, Cremora coffee creamer, Cracker Jack caramel popcorn, and Campfire marshmallows, and in 1964 it bought the Wise Potato Chip Company, the leading potato chip company in the eastern United States.

In 1968 Borden Condensed Milk, now highly diversified, shortened its name to Borden, Inc. In a similar vein Wise Potato Chip company, which now sold popcorn, Cheez Doodles, Bravos Tortilla Chips,

KEY DATES

1921: The company is founded as Wise Potato Chip Company.
1964: The company is sold to Borden Condensed Milk Co.
1969: The name is changed to Wise Foods, Inc.
1995: Kohlberg, Kravis, Roberts & Company acquires Borden and Wise.
2000: Wise is sold to Palladium Equity Partners.

and other snack foods, changed its name to Wise Foods, Inc. In 1989 Wise acquired Moore's Quality Snack Foods, which also produced a full line of salty snacks, including potato chips, marketing mostly in Virginia and the Carolinas. Over the years, Borden acquired a number of other regional snack food businesses: Chicago-based Jays Foods, Indiana's Seyfort Foods, Humpty Dumpty Foods serving eastern Canada, Utah-based Clover Club Foods, and Guy's in Missouri. At its peak, Borden's snack foods business was second only to Pepsi-Co's market leader Frito-Lay.

Borden had assembled a wide range of food products that could have benefited from the company's national distribution system to become national brands, Wise Foods serving as a prominent example. However, starting in the mid-1960s, Borden was headed by chief executives with backgrounds in chemicals and little feel for the food industry. One of these CEOs, Romeo Ventres, launched a massive buying spree in the mid-1980s, spending about $1.9 billion to pick up scores of small regional food brands, including many snack food assets. According to *Forbes,* "The diversification plan was sensible enough, the execution disastrous. Sales grew to over $7 billion, but debt ballooned to over $2 billion. … Borden became an inefficient patchwork of declining brands and loosely related products. By the early 1990s Borden had one of the lowest profit margins and returns of any company in the food business."

Finally in 1993 Borden hired a CEO with a background in packaged foods, but the company was in such poor condition that when he put it up for sale later in the year Borden received no bids. Instead it began a divestiture program, which was slated to include Wise Foods and other snack food assets. Before buyers could be lined up, a subsidiary of buyout firm Kohlberg, Kravis, Roberts & Company (KKR) acquired the troubled Borden. While the $2 billion stock deal was receiving approval from the Securities and Exchange Commission (SEC), Borden arranged in October 1994 to sell the Wise and Moore's brands to Pittsburgh Food and Beverage, whose businesses included Iron City beer and Clark candy bars. The sale had been rumored for months, yet it was never completed. The agreement expired at the end of January 1995, and as a result Wise stayed in the Borden family, albeit on the periphery. The Wise assets were broken off to form Wise Holdings Inc. and became majority owned by B.W. Holdings L.L.C., an affiliate of Borden Inc. and KKR.

Now based in Kennesaw, Georgia, Wise invested a reported $55 million to rebuild its presence on the East Coast, which had eroded in recent years. The company also brought in executive talent, in 1997 hiring Terry E. McDaniel, who brought 18 years of food industry experience, holding positions at Ragu Foods, Tropicana Products, Inc., and Pillsbury Company subsidiaries Alpo Petfoods, Inc. and Haagen Dazs, Inc. He soon became acting president and in the spring of 1999 was named president and CEO. By the end of the 1990s Wise estimated that it held about a 10 percent share of the salty-snack business in its markets, a far cry from Frito-Lay, which boasted a 62 percent share across North America. In 1999 Wise generated sales of about $336 million, and operated four plants, located in Berwick and Denver, Pennsylvania; Spartanburg, South Carolina; and Bristol, Virginia.

NEW CENTURY, NEW OWNER

In October 2000 the company finally changed hands, bought by the private New York investment firm of Palladium Equity Partners L.L.C. for $96 million. Formed in 1997, Palladium had invested more than $700 million in a number of industries, including radio, television, and automotive components. Because Wise represented the firm's first involvement in the food business, Palladium teamed up with a specialist in the field, Ardale Enterprises, whose principals, J. Robert Hall and Keith Lyon, both had more than 20 years of food industry experience. As Palladium's cofounder, Timothy Mayhew, explained to *Private Equity Week,* "I've had enough humbling experiences to realize that I've never run a potato chip company. … It's very useful to have that experience on the investment team."

Palladium made sure that McDaniel and his management team were kept in place, giving them equity in Wise as an inducement. According to the *Wall Street Journal,* "The new ownership would help the company strengthen its share of the $19.38 billion snack-food business in the U.S. and expand into new snack categories." McDaniel also maintained that Wise was beginning to realize the fruits of its investments in the late 1990s, adding, "This is the third-largest and second-most-profitable category for supermarkets. There's a lot of opportunity for growth for everyone to enjoy."

For years the snack industry had to contend with questions about nutrition as it remained very much a part of Americans' eating habits. To assuage some of these concerns, potato chip makers introduced fat-free products using Olestra, but Wise took a wait-and-see attitude and avoided the not-so-profitable fad. It did, however, add new flavors to its chip lineup. All told, Wise entered the new century as number three in national market share in potato chips at 3.1 percent, trailing private-label chips with 6.4 percent, and Frito-Lay's towering 68 percent share.

Wise made some changes in the 2000s to improve its competitiveness. It closed the Quinlan Pretzel Co. plant in Denver, Pennsylvania, in 2002 and contracted with another area company to make pretzels under the Quinlan name. More important, in 2004 Palladium began infusing cash to help Wise in its efforts to cut into Frito-Lay's share in Wise's key markets, including the introduction of new packaging for all of its products. "We will take them on. We're not a globally, mass-produced chip maker like Frito-Lay," Wise's vice-president of marketing Jordi Ferre told *Brandweek*. "We make real chips for real people because our tightly-targeted grass roots efforts bring us closer to consumers." Much of the money would be spent on the New York City metropolitan area, Wise's largest market. The company linked itself to the popular New York Yankees baseball team by inking an endorsement deal with catcher Jorge Posada. In the summer of 2005 Wise forged direct ties to the New York Mets through a multi-tiered, three-year sponsorship deal that made Wise the Official Potato Chip of the Mets. As such, Wise products would be sold exclusively at Shea Stadium, where Wise also would receive extensive signage in center field. In addition, Wise would air frequent radio spots on the team's Spanish-language radio broadcasts. There was every indication that Wise would fortify its position in traditional markets, but whether it could successfully compete against Frito-Lay on a larger stage remained in doubt.

Ed Dinger

PRINCIPAL SUBSIDIARIES

PEP Snack Foods Inc.

PRINCIPAL COMPETITORS

Frito-Lay, Inc.; Kellogg Snacks Division; Kraft Foods Inc.

FURTHER READING

McKay, Betsy, "Palladium Affiliate Agrees to Buy Wise for $96 Million," *Wall Street Journal,* September 6, 2000, p. B8.

Reyes, Sonia, "Frito-Lay Gets Wise to Rival's Revamp," *Brandweek,* June 21, 2004, p. 9.

Schifrin, Matthew, "Last Legs," *Forbes,* September 12, 1994, p. 150.

Wilkes, Ann Przybyla, "A Century and a Half of Crunch: The Potato Chip Turns 150!," *Snack Food & Wholesale Baker,* January 2003, p. 30.

Willatt, Norris, "Profits in Nibbling," *Barron's National Business and Financial Weekly,* June 4, 1956, p. 336.

Yell Group PLC

Queens Walk
Oxford Rd.
Reading,
United Kingdom
Telephone: +44 01189 592111
Fax: +44 01189 509888
Web site: http://www.yellgroup.com

Public Company
Incorporated: 1999
Employees: 11,400
Sales: £1.29 billion ($2.4 billion) (2005)
Stock Exchanges: London
Ticker Symbol: YELL.L
NAIC: 511140 Database and Directory Publishers

■ ■ ■

Yell Group PLC is the United Kingdom's leading publisher of print and online telephone advertising directories and the leading independent publisher of directories in the United States. Yell Group focuses on four primary products: print directories, including Yellow Pages and Business Pages in the United Kingdom and Yellow Book in the United States; online directories and related services, including the United Kingdom's Yell.com and the United States' Yellowbook.com; and, in the United Kingdom, telephone-based directory assistance, through Yellow Pages 118 24 7. Altogether the company publishes nearly 900 directory editions, distributing some 200 million copies each year. The company's U.K. operations publish 111 editions, while its fast-growing U.S. unit numbers 790 editions, reaching nearly every state in the country. While the company's print directories operation in the United Kingdom, based on the former Yellow Pages unit of British Telecom, is relatively mature, the company has found new channels for expansion, including its online service, and rolling out mobile Internet and SMS-based directory services for cellular phone users. In the United States, Yell has become the fastest growing directories group through an aggressive acquisition drive. Between 2000 and 2006, the company completed more than 25 acquisitions, including its largest to date, of TransWestern Holdings L.P. for $1.58 billion in 2005. The acquisition helped boost the company's revenues to £1.29 billion ($2.4 billion) for the year. Yell is listed on the London Stock Exchange and is led by CEO John Condron.

U.K. YELLOW PAGES

The first telephone directories in the United Kingdom appeared soon after the installation of the country's first telephone exchanges in London. By the end of 1880, the initial directory counted more than 300 telephone numbers. In the United States, the development of telephone directories led to the creation of the "yellow pages," that is, directories specifically oriented toward providing the telephone numbers and addresses for businesses. As legend has it, the first yellow pages appeared as early as 1883, when a directory printer ran out of white paper and substituted yellow paper instead.

Later, researchers determined that the black type on yellow paper was easier for consumers to read, and the

COMPANY PERSPECTIVES

Yell creates value by putting buyers in touch with sellers through an integrated portfolio of simple to use, cost-effective advertising products available as printed, online and telephone media.

We aim to be the best business information bridge between buyers and sellers, regardless of channel, time or location. Yell seeks to understand, anticipate and meet the changing demands of advertisers and users and to take advantage of new technologies and communication methods in the development of world class products and services.

use of yellow paper for commercially oriented, classified directories became an industry standard, not only in the United States, but across the world. Yellow page directories became commonplace throughout the United States. That market was largely dominated by the country's telephone operators; however, a number of independent directory publishers appeared in the early part of the century. Among these was a directory published by the Merchants Advertising Service Inc. covering local businesses in Long Island, New York. That company began publishing in 1930; by 1949, the company had changed its directory's name to Yellow Book.

In the United Kingdom, where the country's telephone system was placed under a monopoly controlled by the General Post Office, the directory market developed more slowly and remained limited to white page directories into the 1960s. In 1966, however, the General Post Office decided to test its own classified directory. The first of these appeared in Brighton that year. The success of that initial directory led the Post Office to proceed with a general rollout of yellow page directories by 1973. While the initial yellow pages directory was geared toward the home customer, the Post Office soon rolled out a specifically business-to-business directory, the Commercial Classified, in 1969.

The new directories quickly represented a major source of new income for the Post Office through the 1970s. The success of the Yellow Pages brand in the country led the post office to change the name of the Commercial Classified directory as well, which became known as Industrial and Commercial Yellow Pages in 1979. The Yellow Pages also played a role in the launch of the United Kingdom's earliest dialup information service, Prestel, which debuted in 1980 and featured an online version of the Yellow Pages. The new service also provided an extra revenue stream for the Post Office, as it collected fees not only from advertisers, but also from customers consulting the directory.

In 1981, the General Post Office was split up into its separate parts, and the telecommunications wing was spun off as British Telecommunications. The Yellow Pages became a division of the new telephone company, which remained under government control into the early 1980s. In 1984, British Telecom was privatized, at which point the directories division was established as a separate subsidiary, Yellow Pages.

NEW TECHNOLOGIES

In that year, also, Yellow Pages launched a new directory product, called Business Pages. The first of these were produced for the Bristol and South Wales markets. The company then prepared to launch the Business Pages on a wider scale, releasing a London edition in 1985. By the end of 1986, Business Pages directories had appeared in seven major markets. Yellow Pages parlayed the success of the Business Pages into a new service, the Business Database, in 1986. This division provided direct marketing and related support services.

While Prestel had failed to capture the British consumer's interest, in part because customers were required to purchase the needed set-top box, the Yellow Pages had not lost interest in developing an online version of its directories. The spread of personal computers and the development of a new generation of dialup modems enabled the company to roll out a new online directory service in 1987. This time around, existing Yellow Pages advertisers received online listings as part of their subscription service, while consumers were charged only for the telephone connection.

Yellow Pages in the meantime had begun development of another delivery technology, providing extended directory information over the telephone. The new service debuted in 1988 as Talking Pages; among the features of the new system was the ability to obtain commercial directory assistance outside of one's local calling area. The Talking Pages service was first tested in the Brighton and Bristol markets, before launching on a national scale in 1992. By 1993, British Telecom had initiated a single, nationally available telephone number of the Talking Pages, which provided the service at local calling rates. Two years later the company added a number for users of the FreePhone cellular telephone service as well.

Yellow Pages continued to adapt to and adopt new technologies into the mid-1990s. In 1995, the company

KEY DATES

1930: Merchants Advertising Service, which becomes Yellow Book in 1949, is founded in the United States.
1966: General Post Office (GPO) in Britain publishes first yellow pages in Brighton.
1969: GPO publishes first Commercial Classified directory.
1973: Yellow Pages is launched nationally.
1979: Yellow Pages is added to Prestel service.
1984: GPO's telecoms business becomes British Telecom (BT); Yellow Pages becomes subsidiary of BT.
1988: Talking Pages telephone directory service debuts.
1996: Yell.co.uk online directory service begins operation.
1999: Yellow Pages acquires Yellow Book.
2000: Company changes name to Yell Group.
2001: Company is spun off in management buyout.
2002: Yell Group acquires McCleod Directory Publishing in the United States.
2003: Yell Group launches new telephone directory service, 118 24 7, to replace Talking Pages; Yell goes public on London stock exchange.
2004: Company acquires Feist Publications in the United States.
2005: Company pays $1.5 billion to acquire Trans-Western Holdings in the United States.

launched an extension of the Talking Pages service with the Nationwide Film & Cinema service, offering film and theater scheduling information. The following year, the Yellow Pages reached the Internet with the creation of a new online version, Yell.co.uk. That site was extended to include e-commerce capabilities, linking customers to advertiser products, with the creation of Shop Yell in 1997.

The company continued to broaden its print business as well. In 1998, for example, Yellow Pages published its first Business Pages for the Scottish market. The company also began developing a new design format for its directories, publishing its first "new look" directory in Northern Ireland in 1998. The successful test of the design led to a national revamp of the many Yellow Pages editions. By the end of the 1990s these reached more than 90, including the latest, in Gloucester and Swindon, added in 1999. In 2000, the company added new Business Pages for the Thames Valley and Central regions. Further growth of the Business Page brand continued into the mid-2000s, including the launches of editions for the eastern, southern and southwest, and South Wales regions in 2004. By then, the company's core Yellow Pages directory had completed its national coverage, with a launch of an edition in Hull. By the middle of the decade, the company counted more than 110 directory editions across the United Kingdom.

INDEPENDENT AND INTERNATIONAL FOR THE NEW CENTURY

Yellow Pages' success story had only just begun, however. In 1999, the company crossed the Atlantic and acquired Yellow Book USA for $655 million. The purchase instantly placed the U.K. company among the leaders in the U.S. independent directory publishers market. Yellow Book had grown into the country's largest independent directory publisher serving a largely eastern seaboard market. Acquisitions had formed a major part of Yellow Book's growth, especially in the 1990s, when it made a series of acquisitions in New York, New Jersey, and Pennsylvania, before landing RH Donnelley Proprietary East in 1997. That purchase raised Yellow Book's directory list to more than 250 editions covering seven states.

Yellow Book continued its acquisition spree, buying up several more directory publishers and boosting its total editions to nearly 300 by the time of its acquisition by Yellow Pages. The purchase also brought in Yellow Book's own online directory service, Yellowbook.com. The U.S. division continued to grow strongly into the 2000s, buying up Sprint Publishing, and its 55 directories, along with several other publishers in 2000. In 2001, Yellow Book made its first move west of the Mississippi region, acquiring CGC directories.

Yellow Pages changed its name to Yell Group in 2000 as it prepared to claim its independence in the new decade. This came in 2001, when British Telecom sold Yell in a management buyout backed by an investment partnership between Apax Partners & Co. and Hicks, Muse, Tate & Furst. That deal valued Yell at nearly $3 billion.

Under its new ownership, Yell quickly returned to the acquisition trail. The United States remained the company's key expansion target, and in 2002 the company struck big again, buying that market's second largest independent publisher, McCleod US Publishing. The deal, worth $600 million, firmly placed Yellow Book at the head of the fast-growing independent directory market in the United States. The McCleod purchase also enabled Yellow Book to double its national presence, to 38 states, as well as the Washington, D.C., market.

By the end of 2002, Yellow Book's acquisition drive had enabled it to reach the United States' West Coast, with the purchase of California's National Directory Company. More acquisitions followed in 2003 and 2004, including Dag Media, Directory Publishers Inc., Feist Publications, FYI Directories, as well as selected directories from CGC, Pioneer Telephone Directories, and Cannon Publishing, among others. Yellow Book also launched a number of entirely new directories, adding editions in New York, Florida, Virginia, North Carolina, Connecticut, and elsewhere. Yell's strong growth in the meantime encouraged its financial backers to cash in on their investment, and in 2003 Yell was listed on the London Stock Exchange.

The company continued making a stream of smaller, bolt-on acquisitions through 2005, even as it prepared its next large-scale acquisition. This came in July 2005, when the company agreed to pay more than $1.5 billion to acquire its chief rival in the United States, TransWestern. That purchase not only raised Yell's total number of directories, including its U.K. operations, to nearly 900, it also transformed Yellow Book into the United States' fifth largest, and Yell itself into the world's third largest, directory publisher. Yell appeared likely to remain a leading force in the fast-growing directory market for some time to come.

M. L. Cohen

PRINCIPAL SUBSIDIARIES

Yellow Book USA.

PRINCIPAL COMPETITORS

AT&T Inc.; Microsoft Corporation; BellSouth Corporation; Mindscape; Telecommunications Inc.; R.R. Donnelley and Sons Co.; The First American Corporation; Verizon Information Services; Harte-Hanks Shoppers Inc.; SEAT Pagine Gialle S.p.A.

FURTHER READING

Atkinson, Simon, "End of an Era Now Yellow Pages Is Printed Abroad," *Birmingham Post*, January 17, 2006, p. 10.

Bevens, Nicks, "Yell Buying US Rival for £829 Million," *Scotsman*, May 18, 2005, p. 51.

Brooks, Greg, "Yell.com: Mellow Yellow," *New Media Age*, September 1, 2005, p. 18.

Clow, Robert, and Juliana Ratner, "Yell to Buy US Directories Company McLeod," *Financial Times*, January 22, 2002, p. 19.

Dalla-Costa, Julie, "Problem Child Yell Makes the Big Time," *Euromoney*, August 2003, p. 28.

"Directories Business Has Plenty to Yell About," *Journal*, February 8, 2006, p. 39.

Duckers, John, "US Buys Do Not Slow Yell," *Birmingham Post*, November 9, 2005, p. 19.

Fagan, Mary, "Yell's Hard Sell," *Sunday Telegraph*, June 2, 2002, p. 6.

Killgren, Lucy, and Kate Mackenzie, "TransWestern Acquisition Strengthens," *Financial Times*, February 8, 2006, p. 22.

Loades-Carter, Jonathan, "Yell Poised for £861m US Growth," *Financial Times*, May 18, 2005, p. 22.

McIntosh, Bill, "BT May Abandon Yell Float in Favour of Full Demerger," *Independent*, January 29, 2001, p. 16.

Sabbagh, Dan, "Internet Allows Yell to Shout About Aims for Growth," *Times*, November 9, 2005, p. 51.

"Yell Expands Telesales into Northern Ireland," *Property Week*, July 8, 2005, p. 81.

"Yell Launches Yell.com Mobile," *Internet Business News*, October 13, 2004.

"Yell Out to Show Its Expansion," *Birmingham Post*, December 24, 2002, p. 13.

"Yell Turnover Soars After US Acquisitions," *News Letter*, February 14, 2003.

Index to Companies

Listings in this index are arranged in alphabetical order under the company name. Company names beginning with a letter or proper name such as Eli Lilly & Co. will be found under the first letter of the company name. Definite articles (The, Le, La) are ignored for alphabetical purposes as are forms of incorporation that precede the company name (AB, NV). Company names printed in **bold** *type have full, historical essays on the page numbers appearing in bold. Updates to entries that appeared in earlier volumes are signified by the notation* **(upd.)***. Company names in light type are references within an essay to that company, not full historical essays. This index is cumulative with volume numbers printed in bold type.*

A

Automatic Manufacturing Corporation, **10** 319
Automatic Payrolls, Inc. *see* Automatic Data Processing, Inc.
Automatic Retailers of America, Inc., **II** 607; **13** 48
Automatic Sprinkler Corp. of America *see* Figgie International, Inc.
Automatic Toll Systems, **19** 111
Automatic Voting Machine Corporation *see* American Locker Group Incorporated.
AutoMed Technologies, Inc., **64** 27
Automobiles Citroen, 7 35–38
Automobili Lamborghini Holding S.p.A., 13 60–62; 34 55–58 (upd.)
Automotive Components Limited, **10** 325; **56** 158
Automotive Diagnostics, **10** 492
Automotive Group *see* Lear Seating Corporation.
Automotive Industries Holding Inc., **16** 323
AutoNation, Inc., **41** 239; **50 61–64**
Autonet, **6** 435
Autonom Computer, **47** 36
Autophon AG, **9** 32
Autoroutes du Sud de la France SA, 55 38–40
Autosite.com, **47** 34
Autotote Corporation, 20 47–49 *see also* Scientific Games Corporation.
Autoweb.com, **47** 34
AUTOWORKS Holdings, Inc., **24** 205
AutoZone, Inc., 9 52–54; **26** 348; **31 35–38 (upd.)**; **36** 364; **57** 10–12
AVA AG (Allgemeine Handelsgesellschaft der Verbraucher AG), 33 53–56
Avado Brands, Inc., 31 39–42; **46** 234
Avalon Correctional Services, Inc., 75 40–43
Avalon Publishing Group *see* Publishers Group, Inc.
AvalonBay Communities, Inc., 58 11–13
Avantel, **27** 304
Avantium Technologies BV, 79 46–49
Avaya Inc., **41** 287, 289–90
Avco *see* Aviation Corp. of the Americas.
Avco Corp., **34** 433
Avco Financial Services Inc., 13 63–65
Avco National Bank, **II** 420
Avdel, **34** 433
Avecia Group PLC, 63 49–51
Avecor Cardiovascular Inc., **8** 347; **22** 360
Aveda Corporation, 24 55–57
Avedis Zildjian Co., 38 66–68
Avendt Group, Inc., **IV** 137
Avenor Inc., **25** 13
Aventis Pharmaceuticals, **34** 280, 283–84; **38** 378, 380; **63** 232, 235
Avery Communications, Inc., **72** 39
Avery Dennison Corporation, IV 251–54; 17 27–31 (upd.); 49 34–40 (upd.)
AvestaPolarit, **49** 104
Avex Electronics Inc., **40** 68
Avfuel, **11** 538
Avgain Marine A/S, **7** 40; **41** 42
Avia Group International, Inc. *see* Reebok International Ltd.
Aviacionny Nauchno-Tehnicheskii Komplex im. A.N. Tupoleva, 24 58–60
AVIACO *see* Aviacion y Comercio.
Aviall, Inc., 73 42–45
Avianca Aerovías Nacionales de Colombia SA, 36 52–55
Aviation Corp. of the Americas, **9** 497–99; **11** 261, 427; **12** 379, 383; **13** 64
Aviation Inventory Management Co., **28** 5
Aviation Power Supply, **II** 16
Aviation Sales Company, 41 37–39
Aviation Services West, Inc. *see* Scenic Airlines, Inc.
Avid Technology Inc., 38 69–73
Avimo, **47** 7–8
Avion Coach Corporation, **11** 363
Avionics Specialties Inc. *see* Aerosonic Corporation.
Avions Marcel Dassault-Breguet Aviation, I 44–46 *see also* Groupe Dassault Aviation SA.
Avis Group Holdings, Inc., 6 356–58; 22 54–57 (upd.); 75 44–49 (upd.)
Avista Corporation, 69 48–50 (upd.)
Avisun Corp., **IV** 371
Aviva PLC, 50 65–68 (upd.)
Avnet Inc., 9 55–57
Avocent Corporation, 65 56–58
Avon Products, Inc., III 15–16; 19 26–29 (upd.); 46 43–46 (upd.)
Avon Rubber plc, **23** 146
Avondale Industries, Inc., 7 39–41; 41 40–43 (upd.)
Avondale Mills, Inc., **8** 558–60; **9** 466
Avonmore Foods Plc, **59** 205
Avril Alimentaire SNC, **51** 54
Avro *see* A.V. Roe & Company.
Avstar, **38** 72
Avtech Corp., **36** 159
AVTOVAZ Joint Stock Company, 65 59–62
AVX Corporation, 21 329, 331; **67** 21–22; **41–43**
AW Bruna Uitgevers BV, **53** 273
AW North Carolina Inc., **48** 5
AWA *see* America West Holdings Corporation.
AWA Defence Industries (AWADI) *see* British Aerospace Defence Industries.
AwardTrack, Inc., **49** 423
AWB Ltd., 56 25–27
Awesome Transportation, Inc., **22** 549
Awrey Bakeries, Inc., 56 28–30
AXA Colonia Konzern AG, III 210–12; 49 41–45 (upd.)
AXA Financial, Inc., **63** 26–27
AXA Private Equity *see* Camaïeu S.A.
AXA UK plc, **64** 173
Axe-Houghton Associates Inc., **41** 208
Axel Johnson Group, I 553–55
Axel Springer Verlag AG, IV 589–91; 20 50–53 (upd.)
Axon Systems Inc., **7** 336
Ayala Corporation, **70** 182
Ayala Plans, Inc., **58** 20
Aydin Corp., 19 30–32
Aynsley China Ltd. *see* Belleek Pottery Ltd.
Ayr-Way Stores, **27** 452
Ayres, Lewis, Norris & May, Inc., **54** 184
AYS *see* Alternative Youth Services, Inc.
AZA Immobilien AG, **51** 196
Azcon Corporation, 23 34–36
Azerbaijan Airlines, 77 46–49
Azerty, **25** 13
Azienda Generale Italiana Petroli *see* ENI S.p.A.
AZL Resources, **7** 538
Azlan Group Limited, **74** 338
Aznar International, **14** 225
Azon Limited, **22** 282
AZP Group Inc., **6** 546
Aztar Corporation, 13 66–68; 71 41–45 (upd.)
Azteca, **18** 211, 213

B

B&D *see* Barker & Dobson.
B&G Foods, Inc., 40 51–54
B&J Music Ltd. *see* Kaman Music Corporation.
B & K Steel Fabrications, Inc., **26** 432
B & L Insurance, Ltd., **51** 38
B&M Baked Beans, **40** 53
B & O *see* Baltimore and Ohio Railroad.
B&Q plc *see* Kingfisher plc.
B&S *see* Binney & Smith Inc.
B.A.T. Industries PLC, 22 70–73 (upd.) *see also* Brown & Williamson Tobacco Corporation
B. B. & R. Knight Brothers, **8** 200; **25** 164
B.B. Foods, **13** 244
B-Bar-B Corp., **16** 340
B.C. Rail Telecommunications, **6** 311
B.C. Sugar, **II** 664
B.C. Ziegler and Co. *see* The Ziegler Companies, Inc.
B. Dalton Bookseller Inc., 25 29–31
B-E Holdings, **17** 60
B/E Aerospace, Inc., 30 72–74
B.F. Goodrich Co. *see* The BFGoodrich Company.
B.F. Walker, Inc., **11** 354
B.I.C. America, **17** 15, 17
B.J.'s Wholesale, **12** 335
B.J. Alan Co., Inc., 67 44–46
The B. Manischewitz Company, LLC, 31 43–46
B. Perini & Sons, Inc., **8** 418
B Ticino, **21** 350
B.V. Tabak Export & Import Compagnie, **12** 109
BA *see* British Airways.
BAA plc, 10 121–23; 33 57–61 (upd.)
Bålforsens Kraft AB, **28** 444
Baan Company, 25 32–34; **26** 496, 498

Banco Credito y Ahorro Ponceno, **41** 312
Banco da América, **19** 34
Banco de Chile, 69 55–57
Banco de Comercio, S.A. *see* Grupo Financiero BBVA Bancomer S.A.
Banco de Credito Local, **48** 51
Banco de Credito y Servicio, **51** 151
Banco de Galicia y Buenos Aires, S.A., **63** 178–80
Banco de Londres, Mexico y Sudamerica *see* Grupo Financiero Serfin, S.A.
Banco de Madrid, **40** 147
Banco de Mexico, **19** 189
Banco de Ponce, **41** 313
Banco del Centro S.A., **51** 150
Banco del Norte, **19** 189
Banco di Roma, **II**, 257, 271
Banco di Santo Spirito, **I** 467
Banco di Sicilia S.p.A., **65** 86, 88
Banco do Brasil S.A., II 199–200
Banco Español de Credito, **II** 198
Banco Espírito Santo e Comercial de Lisboa S.A., 15 38–40 *see also* Espírito Santo Financial Group S.A.
Banco Federal de Crédito *see* Banco Itaú.
Banco Frances y Brasiliero, **19** 34
Banco Industrial de Monterrey, **19** 189
Banco Itaú S.A., 19 33–35
Banco Mercantil del Norte, S.A., **51** 149
Banco Nacional de Mexico, **9** 333; **19** 188, 193
Banco Opportunity, **57** 67, 69
Banco Pinto de Mahalhãhes, **19** 34
Banco Popolar *see* Popular, Inc.
Banco Português do Brasil S.A., **19** 34
Banco Santander Central Hispano S.A., 36 61–64 (upd.); **42** 349; **63** 179
Banco Santander-Chile, **71** 143
Banco Serfin, **34** 82
Banco Sul Americano S.A., **19** 34
Banco União Comercial, **19** 34
BancOhio National Bank in Columbus, **9** 475
Bancomer S.A. *see* Grupo Financiero BBVA Bancomer S.A.
Bancorp Leasing, Inc., **14** 529
BancorpSouth, Inc., **14** 40–41
Bancrecer *see* Banco de Credito y Servicio.
BancSystems Association Inc., **9** 475, 476
Bandag, Inc., 19 36–38, 454–56
Bandai Co., Ltd., 55 44–48
Bando McGlocklin Small Business Lending Corporation, **53** 222–24
Banesto *see* Banco Español de Credito.
Banfi Products Corp., 36 65–67
Banfield, The Pet Hospital *see* Medical Management International, Inc.
Bang & Olufsen Holding A/S, 37 25–28
Bangkok Airport Hotel *see* Thai Airways International.
Bangkok Aviation Fuel Services Ltd. *see* Thai Airways International.
Bangladesh Krishi Bank, **31** 220
Bangor and Aroostook Railroad Company, **8** 33
Bangor Mills, **13** 169
Bangor Punta Alegre Sugar Corp., **30** 425
Banister Continental Corp. *see* BFC Construction Corporation.
Bank Austria AG, 23 37–39; 59 239
Bank Brussels Lambert, II 201–03, 295, 407
Bank Central Asia, **18** 181; **62** 96, 98
Bank du Louvre, **27** 423
Bank für Elektrische Unternehmungen *see* Elektrowatt AG.
Bank Hapoalim B.M., II 204–06; 54 33–37 (upd.)
Bank Hofmann, **21** 146–47
Bank Leumi le-Israel B.M., 60 48–51
Bank of America Corporation, 46 47–54 (upd.)
The Bank of Bishop and Co., Ltd., **11** 114
Bank of Boston Corporation, II 207–09 *see also* FleetBoston Financial Corporation.
Bank of Britain, **14** 46–47
Bank of China, 63 55–57
Bank of Delaware, **25** 542
Bank of East Asia Ltd., 63 58–60
Bank of England, **10** 8, 336; **14** 45–46; **47** 227
Bank of Hawaii Corporation, 73 53–56
Bank of Ireland, 50 73–76
Bank of Italy, **III** 209, 347; **8** 45
The Bank of Jacksonville, **9** 58
Bank of Lee County, **14** 40
Bank of Mexico Ltd., **19** 188
The Bank of Milwaukee, **14** 529
Bank of Mississippi, Inc., 14 40–41
Bank of Montreal, II 210–12, 231, 375; **26** 304; **46 55–58 (upd.)**
Bank of Nettleton, **14** 40
Bank of New England Corporation, II 213–15; 9 229
Bank of New Orleans, **11** 106
Bank of New South Wales *see* Westpac Banking Corporation.
Bank of New York Company, Inc., II 216–19, 247; **34** 82; **46 59–63 (upd.)**
Bank of North Mississippi, **14** 41
The Bank of Nova Scotia, II 220–23, 345; **59 70–76 (upd.)**
Bank of Oklahoma, **22** 4
The Bank of Scotland *see* The Governor and Company of the Bank of Scotland.
Bank of Sherman, **14** 40
Bank of the Ohio Valley, **13** 221
Bank of the Philippine Islands, 58 18–20
Bank of Tokyo-Mitsubishi Ltd., II 224–25; 15 41–43 (upd.)
Bank of Tupelo, **14** 40
Bank of Wales, **10** 336, 338
Bank One Corporation, 36 68–75 (upd.)
Bank-R Systems Inc., **18** 517
BankAmerica Corporation, II 226–28 *see also* Bank of America.
BankAtlantic Bancorp., Inc., **66** 273
BankBoston *see* FleetBoston Financial Corporation.
BankCard America, Inc., **24** 394
Bankers and Shippers Insurance Co., **III** 389
Bankers Corporation, **14** 473
Bankers Life and Casualty Co., **10** 247; **16** 207; **33** 110
Bankers Life Association *see* Principal Mutual Life Insurance Company.
Bankers National Life Insurance Co., **10** 246
Bankers Trust Co., **38** 411
Bankers Trust New York Corporation, II 229–31
Bankhaus August Lenz AG, **65** 230, 232
Banknorth Group, Inc., 55 49–53
Bankruptcy Services LLC, **56** 112
Banksia Wines Ltd., **54** 227, 229
BankWatch, **37** 143, 145
Banner Aerospace, Inc., 14 42–44; 37 29–32 (upd.)
Banner International, **13** 20
Banner Life Insurance Company, **III** 273; **24** 284
Banorte *see* Grupo Financiero Banorte, S.A. de C.V.
Banpais *see* Grupo Financiero Asemex-Banpais S.A.
BanPonce Corporation, **41** 312
Banque Bruxelles Lambert *see* Bank Brussels Lambert.
Banque de Bruxelles *see* Bank Brussels Lambert.
Banque de France, **14** 45–46
Banque de la Société Générale de Belgique *see* Generale Bank.
Banque de Paris et des Pays-Bas, **10** 346; **19** 188–89; **33** 179
Banque Indosuez, **II** 429; **52** 361–62
Banque Internationale de Luxembourg, **42** 111
Banque Lambert *see* Bank Brussels Lambert.
Banque Nationale de Paris S.A., II 232–34, 239; **III** 201, 392–94; **9** 148; **13** 203; **15** 309; **19** 51; **33** 119; **49** 382 *see also* BNP Paribas Group.
Banque Paribas *see* BNP Paribas Group.
Banque Sanpaolo of France, **50** 410
La Banque Suisse et Française *see* Crédit Commercial de France.
Banque Worms, **27** 514
Banta Corporation, 12 24–26; 32 73–77 (upd.); 79 50–56 (upd.)
Bantam Ball Bearing Company, **13** 522
Bantam Doubleday Dell Publishing Group, **IV** 594; **13** 429; **15** 51; **27** 222; **31** 375–76, 378
Banyan Systems Inc., 25 50–52
Banyu Pharmaceutical Co., **11** 290; **34** 283
Baoshan Iron and Steel, **19** 220
Baosteel Group International Trade Corporation *see* Baosteel Group International Trade Corporation.
BAP of New York, Inc., **15** 246
Bar-S Foods Company, 76 39–41
Bar Technologies, Inc., **26** 408
Barastoc Stockfeeds Pty Ltd., **62** 307
Barat *see* Barclays PLC.

Brother International, **23** 212
Brothers Foods, **18** 7
Brothers Gourmet Coffees, Inc., 20 82–85
Brotherton Chemicals, **29** 113
Brotherton Speciality Products Ltd., **68** 81
Broughton Foods Co., 17 55–57
Brown & Bigelow, **27** 193
Brown & Brown, Inc., 41 63–66
Brown & Haley, 23 78–80
Brown & Root, Inc., 13 117–19; **38** 481 *see also* Kellogg Brown & Root Inc.
Brown & Sharpe Manufacturing Co., 23 81–84
Brown and Williamson Tobacco Corporation, 14 77–79, 33 80–83 (upd.)
Brown Boveri *see* BBC Brown Boveri.
Brown Brothers Harriman & Co., 45 64–67
Brown Cow West Corporation, **55** 360
Brown-Forman Corporation, I 225–27; 10 179–82 (upd.); **12** 313; **18** 69; **38 110–14 (upd.)**
Brown Group, Inc., V 351–53; **9** 192; **20 86–89 (upd.)** *see also* Brown Shoe Company, Inc.
Brown Institute, **45** 87
Brown Jordan International Inc., 74 54–57 (upd.)
Brown Printing Company, 26 43–45
Brown-Service Insurance Company, **9** 507
Brown Shipbuilding Company *see* Brown & Root, Inc.
Brown, Shipley & Co., Limited, **45** 65
Brown Shoe Company, Inc., 68 65–69 (upd.)
Browning-Ferris Industries, Inc., V 749–53; 20 90–93 (upd.)
Browning International, **58** 147
Browning Manufacturing, **II** 19
Browning Telephone Corp., **14** 258
Broyhill Furniture Industries, Inc., 10 183–85; **12** 308
BRS Ltd. *see* Ecel plc.
Bruce Foods Corporation, 39 67–69
Bruce Power LP, **49** 65, 67
Bruce's Furniture Stores, **14** 235
Bruckmann, Rosser, Sherill & Co., **27** 247; **40** 51 *see also* Lazy Days RV Center, Inc.
Bruegger's Corporation, 29 171; **63 79–82**
Brugman, **27** 502
Brummer Seal Company, **14** 64
Bruno's Supermarkets, Inc., 7 60–62; **13** 404, 406; **23** 261; **26 46–48 (upd.)**; **68 70–73 (upd.)**
Brunswick Corporation, III 442–44; **22 113–17 (upd.)**; **77 68–75 (upd.)**
Brunswick Mining, **64** 297
The Brush Electric Light Company, **11** 387; **25** 44
Brush Electrical Machines, **III** 507–09
Brush Engineered Materials Inc., 67 77–79
Brush Moore Newspaper, Inc., **8** 527
Brush Wellman Inc., 14 80–82
Bruxeland S.P.R.L., **64** 91
Bryce Brothers, **12** 313
Brylane Inc., **29** 106–07; **64** 232
Bryn Mawr Stereo & Video, **30** 465
Brynwood Partners, **13** 19
BSA *see* The Boy Scouts of America.
BSB, **IV** 653; **7** 392
BSC *see* Birmingham Steel Corporation; British Steel Corporation.
BSH Bosch und Siemens Hausgeräte GmbH, 67 80–84
BSkyB, **IV** 653; **7** 392; **29** 369, 371; **34** 85
BSN Groupe S.A., II 474–75, 544; **22** 458; **23** 448 *see also* Groupe Danone
BSN Medical, **41** 374, 377
BT Group plc, 49 69–74 (upd.)
BTG, Inc., 45 68–70; **57** 173
BTI Services, **9** 59
BTM *see* British Tabulating Machine Company.
BTR Dunlop Holdings, Inc., **21** 432
BTR plc, I 428–30; **8** 397; **24** 88
BTR Siebe plc, 27 79–81 *see also* Invensys PLC.
B2B Initiatives Ltd. *see* O.C. Tanner Co.
Bubbles Salon *see* Ratner Companies.
Bublitz Case Company, **55** 151
Buca, Inc., 38 115–17
Buchanan Electric Steel Company, **8** 114
Buck Consultants, Inc., 32 459; **55 71–73**
Buck Knives Inc., 48 71–74
Buckaroo International *see* Bugle Boy Industries, Inc.
Buckbee-Mears Company *see* BMC Industries, Inc.
Buckeye Business Products Inc., **17** 384
Buckeye Partners, L.P., 70 33–36
Buckeye Technologies, Inc., 42 51–54
Buckhorn, Inc., **19** 277–78
The Buckle, Inc., 18 84–86
Buckley/DeCerchio New York, **25** 180
BUCON, Inc., **62** 55
Bucyrus Blades, Inc., **14** 81
Bucyrus-Erie Company, **7** 513
Bucyrus International, Inc., 17 58–61
Bud Bailey Construction, **43** 400
Budapest Bank, **16** 14
The Budd Company, 8 74–76; **20** 359
Buderus AG, III 694–95; **37 46–49**
Budgens Ltd., 57 257; **59 93–96**
Budget Group, Inc., 25 92–94
Budget Rent a Car Corporation, 9 94–95
Budgetel Inn *see* Marcus Corporation.
Budweiser, **18** 70
Budweiser Budvar, National Corporation, 59 97–100
Budweiser Japan Co., **21** 320
Buena Vista Home Video *see* The Walt Disney Company.
Buena Vista Music Group, **44** 164
Bufete Industrial, S.A. de C.V., 34 80–82
Buffalo Forge Company, **7** 70–71
Buffalo News, **18** 60
Buffalo Paperboard, **19** 78
Buffalo Wild Wings, Inc., 56 41–43
Buffets, Inc., 10 186–87; **22** 465; **32 102–04 (upd.)**
Bugaboo Creek Steak House Inc., **19** 342
Bugatti Industries, **14** 321
Bugle Boy Industries, Inc., 18 87–88
Buhrmann NV, 41 67–69; **47** 90–91; **49** 440
Buick Motor Co. *see* General Motors Corporation.
Build-A-Bear Workshop Inc., 62 45–48
Builders Concrete *see* Vicat S.A.
Builders Emporium, **13** 169; **25** 535
Builders Square *see* Kmart Corporation.
Building Materials Holding Corporation, 52 53–55
Building One Services Corporation *see* Encompass Services Corporation.
Building Products of Canada Limited, **25** 232
Buitoni SpA, **II** 548; **17** 36; **50** 78
Bulgari S.p.A., 20 94–97
Bulgheroni SpA, **27** 105
Bulkships, **27** 473
Bull *see* Compagnie des Machines Bull S.A.
Bull Motors, **11** 5
Bull Run Corp., **24** 404
Bull S.A., III 122–23; **43 89–91 (upd.)**
Bull Tractor Company, **7** 534; **16** 178; **26** 492
Bull-Zenith, **25** 531
Bulldog Computer Products, **10** 519
Bulletin Broadfaxing Network Inc., **67** 257
Bulley & Andrews, LLC, 55 74–76
Bullock's, **31** 191
Bulova Corporation, 12 316–17, 453; **13 120–22**; **14** 501; **36** 325; **41 70–73 (upd.)**
Bumble Bee Seafoods L.L.C., 64 59–61
Bundall Computers Pty Limited, **56** 155
Bundy Corporation, 17 62–65
Bunge Ltd., 62 49–51
Bunte Candy, **12** 427
Bunzl plc, IV 260–62; **12** 264; **31 77–80 (upd.)**
Buquet, **19** 49
Burbank Aircraft Supply, Inc., **14** 42–43; **37** 29, 31
Burberry Ltd., 17 66–68; **41 74–76 (upd.)**
Burda Holding GmbH. & Co., 20 53; **23 85–89**
Burdines, Inc., 9 209; **31** 192; **60 70–73**
Bureau de Recherches de Pétrole, **7** 481–83; **21** 203–04
The Bureau of National Affairs, Inc., 23 90–93
Bureau Veritas SA, 55 77–79
Burelle S.A., 23 94–96
Burger and Aschenbrenner, **16** 486
Burger Boy Food-A-Rama, **8** 564
Burger King Corporation, II 613–15; 17 69–72 (upd.); **56 44–48 (upd.)**
Burgess, Anderson & Tate Inc., **25** 500
Burgundy Ltd., **68** 53
Bürhle, **17** 36; **50** 78

C

CART *see* Championship Auto Racing Teams, Inc.
Carte Blanche, **9** 335
Cartem Wilco Group Inc., **59** 350
CarTemps USA *see* Republic Industries, Inc.
Carter & Sons Freightways, Inc., **57** 278
Carter Hawley Hale Stores, V 29–32
Carter Holt Harvey Ltd., 70 41–44
Carter Lumber Company, 45 90–92
Carter Oil Company, **11** 353
Carter-Wallace, Inc., 8 83–86; 38 122–26 (upd.)
Carteret Savings Bank, **III** 263–64; **10** 340
Carterphone, **22** 17
Cartier, **27** 329, 487–89
Cartier Monde, 29 90–92
Cartier Refined Sugars Ltd., **II** 662–63
Cartiera F.A. Marsoni, **IV** 587
Cartiers Superfoods, **II** 678
Cartocor S.A. *see* Arcor S.A.I.C.
Carton Titan S.A. de C.V., **37** 176–77
Cartotech, Inc., **33** 44
Carvel Corporation, 35 78–81
Carver Pump Co., **19** 36
Cary-Davis Tug and Barge Company *see* Puget Sound Tug and Barge Company.
CASA *see* Construcciones Aeronautics S.A.
Casa Bancária Almeida e Companhia *see* Banco Bradesco S.A.
Casa Cuervo, S.A. de C.V., 31 91–93
Casa Ley, S.A. de C.V., **24** 416
Casa Saba *see* Grupo Casa Saba, S.A. de C.V.
Casablanca Records, **23** 390
Casalee, Inc., **48** 406
Casarotto Security, **24** 510
Casas Bahia Comercial Ltda., 75 86–89
Cascade Communications Corp., **16** 468; **20** 8; **24** 50
Cascade Corporation, 65 90–92
Cascade Fertilizers Ltd., **25** 232
Cascade General, Inc., 65 93–95
Cascade Natural Gas Corporation, 6 568; **9 102–04**
Cascade Steel Rolling Mills, Inc., **19** 380–81
Cascades Inc., 71 94–96
CasChem, Inc. *see* Cambrex Corporation.
Casco Northern Bank, 14 89–91
Casden Properties, **49** 26
Case Corporation *see* CNH Global N.V.
Case Technologies, Inc., **11** 504
Casey's General Stores, Inc., 19 79–81
Cash & Go, Inc., **57** 139
Cash America International, Inc., 20 113–15; 33 4; **61 52–55 (upd.)**
Cash Wise Foods and Liquor, **30** 133
Casino, **10** 205; **23** 231; **26** 160; **27** 93–94
Casino America, Inc. *see* Isle of Capri Casinos, Inc.
Casino Frozen Foods, Inc., **16** 453
Casino Guichard-Perrachon S.A., 59 107–10 (upd.)
Casino USA, **16** 452
Casinos International Inc., **21** 300
CASIO Computer Co., Ltd., III 448–49, 455; **16 82–84 (upd.)**; **40 91–95 (upd.)**
Casite Intraco LLC, **56** 156–57
Caspian Pipeline Consortium, **47** 75
Cassa Risparmio Firenze, **50** 410
Cassandra Group, **42** 272
Cassco Ice & Cold Storage, Inc., **21** 534–35
CAST Inc., **18** 20; **43** 17
Cast-Matic Corporation, **16** 475
Castel MAC S.p.A., **68** 136
Castex, **13** 501
Castings, Inc., **29** 98
Castle & Cooke, Inc., II 490–92; 9 175–76; **10** 40; **20 116–19 (upd.)**; **24** 115 *see also* Dole Food Company, Inc.
Castle Cement, **31** 400
Castle Communications plc, **17** 13
Castle Harlan Investment Partners III, **36** 468, 471
Castle Rock Entertainment, **57** 35
Castle Rock Pictures, **23** 392
Castle Rubber Co., **17** 371
Castlemaine Tooheys, **10** 169–70
Castleton Thermostats *see* Strix Ltd.
Castorama S.A. *see* Groupe Castorama-Dubois Investissements.
Castro Convertibles *see* Krause's Furniture, Inc.
Castrorama, **10** 205; **27** 95
Casual Corner Group, Inc., 43 96–98
Casual Male Retail Group, Inc., 52 64–66
Casual Wear Española, S.A., **64** 91
Caswell-Massey Co. Ltd., 51 66–69
CAT Scale Company, **49** 329–30
Catalina Lighting, Inc., 43 99–102 (upd.)
Catalina Marketing Corporation, 18 99–102
Catalogue Marketing, Inc., **17** 232
Catalyst Rx *see* HealthExtras, Inc.
Catalyst Telecom, **29** 414–15
Catalytica Energy Systems, Inc., 44 74–77
Catalytica Pharmaceuticals Inc., **56** 95
Catamaran Cruisers, **29** 442
Catamount Petroleum Corp., **17** 121
Cataract, Inc., **34** 373
CATCO *see* Crowley All Terrain Corporation.
Catellus Development Corporation, 24 98–101; 27 88
Caterair International Corporation, **16** 396
Caterpillar Inc., III 450–53; 15 89–93 (upd.); **63 93–99 (upd.)**; **69** 167, 169
Cathay Insurance Co., **III** 221; **14** 109
Cathay Pacific Airways Limited, 6 78–80; 18 114–15; **34 98–102 (upd.)**
Catherines Stores Corporation, 15 94–97; 38 129
Cathodic Protection Services Co., **14** 325
Catholic Charities USA, 76 82–84
Catholic Digest, **49** 48
Catholic Order of Foresters, 24 102–05
CatiCentre Ltd. Co, **48** 224
Cato Corporation, 14 92–94
Catteau S.A., **24** 475
Catterton Partners, **62** 137
Cattleman's, Inc., 20 120–22
Cattles plc, 58 54–56
Cattybrook Brick Company, **14** 249
CATV, **10** 319
Caudill Rowlett Scott *see* CRSS Inc.
Caudle Engraving, **12** 471
Cavalcade Holdings, Inc., **53** 146
Cavallo Pipeline Company, **11** 441
Cavco Industries, Inc., 65 96–99
Cavendish International Holdings, **IV** 695
Cavenham Ltd., **7** 202–03; **28** 163
Caves Altovisto, **22** 344
Caves de Roquefort, **19** 51; **24** 445
Caviton Ltd. *see* Harvey Norman.
Caxton Superannuation Fund Trustee Limited, **70** 43
Cazenove Group plc, 72 63–65
CB&I, **7** 76–77
CB&Q *see* Chicago, Burlington and Quincy Railroad Company.
CB&T *see* Synovus Financial Corp.
CB Commercial Real Estate Services Group, Inc., 21 94–98
CB International Finance S.A.R.L. *see* Constellation Brands, Inc.
CB Richard Ellis Group, Inc., 70 45–50 (upd.)
CBE Technologies Inc., **39** 346
CBI Industries, Inc., **7** 74–77; **22** 228; **48** 323
CBN *see* The Christian Broadcasting Network, Inc.
CBN Cable Network, **13** 279–81
CBN Satellite Services, **13** 279
CBOT *see* Chicago Board of Trade.
CBPI *see* Companhia Brasileira de Petróleo Ipiranga.
CBR-HCI Construction Materials Corp., **31** 253
CBRL Group, Inc., 35 82–85 (upd.)
CBS Corporation, II 132–34; 6 157–60 (upd.); **28 69–73 (upd.)** *see also* CBS Television Network.
CBS.MarketWatch.com, **49** 290
CBS Musical Instruments, **16** 201–02; **43** 170–71
CBS Radio Group, **37** 192; **48** 217
CBS Records, **22** 194; **23** 33; **28** 419
CBS Television Network, 66 44–48 (upd.)
CBSI *see* Complete Business Solutions, Inc.
CBW Inc., **42** 129
CC Beverage Corporation, **48** 97
cc:Mail, Inc., **25** 300
CCA *see* Container Corporation of America; Corrections Corporation of America.
CCA Industries, Inc., 53 86–89
CCAir Inc., **11** 300
CCB Financial Corp., **33** 293
CCC Empreendimentos e Participaçoes, **74** 48
CCC Franchising Corporation *see* Primedex Health Systems, Inc.

Chittenden & Eastman Company, 58 61–64
Chiyoda Fire and Marine, **III** 404
Chock Full o'Nuts Corp., 17 97–100; 20 83
Chocoladefabriken Lindt & Sprüngli AG, 27 102–05; 30 220
Choice Hotels International Inc., 14 105–07; 26 460
ChoiceCare Corporation, **24** 231
ChoicePoint Inc., 31 358; **65 106–08**
Chorion PLC, **75** 389–90
Chorus Line Corporation, 30 121–23
Chouinard Equipment *see* Lost Arrow Inc.
Chovet Engineering S.A. *see* SNC-Lavalin Group Inc.
Chr. Hansen Group A/S, 70 54–57
Chris-Craft Industries, Inc., 9 118–19; 26 32; **31 109–12 (upd.); 46** 313
Christensen Boyles Corporation, 19 247; **26 68–71**
Christensen Company, **8** 397
Christiaensen, **26** 160
The Christian Broadcasting Network, Inc., 13 279; **52 83–85; 57** 392
Christian Dalloz SA, 40 96–98
Christian Dior S.A., 19 86–88; 23 237, 242; **49 90–93 (upd.)**
Christian Salvesen Plc, 45 10, **100–03**
The Christian Science Publishing Society, 55 99–102
Christian Supply Centers, Inc., **45** 352
Christiana Bank og Kredietklasse, **40** 336
Christie, Mitchell & Mitchell, **7** 344
Christie's International plc, 15 98–101; 39 81–85 (upd.); 49 325
Christofle Orfevrerie, **44** 206
Christofle SA, 40 99–102
Christopher & Banks Corporation, 42 73–75
Christopher Charters, Inc. *see* Kitty Hawk, Inc.
Chromalloy American Corp., **13** 461; **54** 330
Chromalloy Gas Turbine Corp., **13** 462; **54** 331
Chromatic Color, **13** 227–28
Chromcraft Revington, Inc., 15 102–05; 26 100
Chromium Corporation, **52** 103–05
Chrompack, Inc., **48** 410
The Chronicle Publishing Company, Inc., 23 119–22
Chronimed Inc., 26 72–75
Chronoservice, **27** 475
Chrysalis Group plc, 22 194; **40 103–06**
Chrysler Corporation, I 144–45; 11 53–55 (upd.) *see also* DaimlerChrysler AG
Chrysler Financial Company, LLC, **45** 262
CHS Inc., 60 86–89
CHT Steel Company Ltd., **51** 352
CH2M Hill Ltd., 22 136–38
Chubb Corporation, III 220–22; 14 108–10 (upd.); 37 83–87 (upd.)
Chubb, PLC, 50 133–36
Chubb Security plc, **44** 258
Chubu Electric Power Company, Inc., V 571–73; 46 90–93 (upd.)
Chuck E. Cheese *see* CEC Entertainment, Inc.
Chugach Alaska Corporation, 60 90–93
Chugai Boyeki Co. Ltd., **44** 441
Chugai Pharmaceutical Co., Ltd., 8 215–16; **10** 79; **50 137–40**
Chugai Shogyo Shimposha *see* Nihon Keizai Shimbun, Inc.
Chugoku Electric Power Company Inc., V 574–76; 53 101–04 (upd.)
Chugoku Funai Electric Company Ltd., **62** 150
Chunghwa Picture Tubes, Ltd., 75 100–02
Chuo Rika Kogyo Corp., **56** 238
Chuo Trust & Banking Co. *see* Yasuda Trust and Banking Company, Limited.
Chupa Chups S.A., 38 133–35
Church & Company, **45** 342, 344
Church & Dwight Co., Inc., 29 112–15; 68 78–82 (upd.)
Church and Tower Group, **19** 254
Church's Chicken, 7 26–28; **15** 345; **23** 468; **32** 13–14; **66 56–59**
Churchill Downs Incorporated, 29 116–19
Churchill Insurance Co. Ltd., **III** 404
CI Holdings, Limited, **53** 120
Cia Hering, 72 66–68
Cianbro Corporation, 14 111–13
Cianchette Brothers, Inc. *see* Cianbro Corporation.
Ciba-Geigy Ltd., I 632–34; 8 108–11 (upd.) *see also* Novartis AG.
CIBC *see* Canadian Imperial Bank of Commerce.
CIBC Wood Gundy Securities Corp., **24** 482
Ciber, Inc., 18 110–12
Ciby 2000, **24** 79
CIC *see* Commercial Intertech Corporation.
CIC Investors #13 LP, **60** 130
CICI, **11** 184
Cie Continental d'Importation, **10** 249
Cie des Lampes, **9** 9
Cie Générale d'Electro-Ceramique, **9** 9
Cie.Generale des Eaux S.A., **24** 327
CIENA Corporation, 54 68–71
Cifra, S.A. de C.V., 12 63–65 *see also* Wal-Mart de Mexico, S.A. de C.V.
Cifunsa *see* Compania Fundidora del Norte, S.A.
Ciga Group, **54** 345, 347
Cigarrera La Moderna, **21** 260; **22** 73
Cigarros la Tabacelera Mexicana (Cigatam), **21** 259
CIGNA Corporation, III 223–27; 22 139–44 (upd.); 45 104–10 (upd.)
CIGWELD, **19** 442
Cii-HB, **III** 678; **16** 122
Cilbarco, **II** 25
CILCORP Energy Services Inc., **60** 27
Cilva Holdings PLC, **6** 358
Cima, **14** 224–25
CIMA Precision Spring Europa, **55** 305–06
Cimaron Communications Corp., **38** 54
Cimarron Utilities Company, **6** 580
CIMCO Ltd., **21** 499–501
Cimeco S.A. *see* Grupo Clarín S.A.
Cimenteries CBR S.A., **23** 325, 327
Cimentos de Portugal SGPS S.A. (Cimpor), 76 92–94
Ciments Français, 40 107–10
Ciments Lafarge France/Quebec *see* Lafarge Cement
Cimos, **7** 37
Cimpor *see* Cimentos de Portugal SGPS S.A.
Cinar Corporation, 40 111–14
Cincinnati Bell, Inc., 6 316–18; 29 250, 252
Cincinnati Electronics Corp., **II** 25
Cincinnati Financial Corporation, 16 102–04; 44 89–92 (upd.)
Cincinnati Gas & Electric Company, 6 465–68, 481–82
Cincinnati Lamb Inc., 72 69–71
Cincinnati Milacron Inc., 12 66–69 *see also* Milacron, Inc.
Cincom Systems Inc., 15 106–08
Cine-Groupe, **35** 279
Cinecentrum, **IV** 591
Cinemark, **21** 362; **23** 125
CinemaSource, **58** 167
Cinemax, **IV** 675; **7** 222–24, 528–29; **23** 276
Cinemeccanica S.p.A., 78 70–73
Cinemex, **71** 256
Cineplex Odeon Corporation, 6 161–63; 23 123–26 (upd.)
Cinerama Group, **67** 291
Cinnabon Inc., 13 435–37; **23 127–29; 32** 12, 15
Cinquième Saison, **38** 200, 202
Cinram International, Inc., 43 107–10
Cinsa *see* Compania Industrial del Norte, S.A.
Cintas Corporation, 21 114–16; 51 74–77 (upd.)
Cintra *see* Concesiones de Infraestructuras de Transportes, S.A.; Corporacion Internacional de Aviacion, S.A. de C.V.
Cinven, **49** 451; **63** 49–50
Cipal-Parc Astérix, **27** 10
Ciprial S.A., **27** 260
CIPSCO Inc., 6 469–72, 505–06 *see also* Ameren Corporation.
CIR *see* Compagnie Industriali Riunite S.p.A.
Circa Pharmaceuticals, **16** 529; **56** 375
Circle A Ginger Ale Company, **9** 177
Circle International Group Inc., **17** 216; **59** 171
The Circle K Company, II 619–20; 20 138–40 (upd.)
Circle Plastics, **9** 323
Circon Corporation, 21 117–20
Circuit City Stores, Inc., 9 120–22; 29 120–24 (upd.); 65 109–14 (upd.)
Circus Circus Enterprises, Inc., 6 203–05; 19 377, 379

Compagnie Financière Belge des Pétroles *see* PetroFina S.A.
Compagnie Financiere De Bourbon, **60** 149
Compagnie Financière de Paribas, II 259–60; 21 99; **27** 138; **33** 339 *see also* BNP Paribas Group.
Compagnie Financière de Richemont AG, **29** 90
Compagnie Financière de Suez *see* Suez Lyonnaise des Eaux.
Compagnie Financière du Groupe Victoire, **27** 54; **49** 44
Compagnie Financiere pour l'Amerique Latine, **67** 326
Compagnie Financière Richemont AG, 27 487; **29** 91–92; **50 144–47**
Compagnie Financière Sucres et Denrées S.A., 60 94–96
Compagnie Française Chaufour Investissement, **27** 100
Compagnie Française de Manutention, **27** 295
Compagnie Française des Pétroles *see* TOTAL S.A.
Compagnie Fromagère de la Vallée de l'Ance, **25** 84
Compagnie Générale d'Électricité, II 12–13; 9 9–10
Compagnie Generale de Cartons Ondules, **IV** 296; **19** 226
Compagnie Générale des Eaux *see* Vivendi SA.
Compagnie Générale des Établissements Michelin, V 236–39; 19 508; **42 85–89 (upd.); 59** 87
Compagnie Générale Maritime et Financière, 6 379–81
Compagnie Industriali Riunite S.p.A., **IV** 587–88; **54** 21
Compagnie Industrielle de Matérials de Manutention, **27** 296
Compagnie Industrielle des Fillers *see* L'Entreprise Jean Lefebvre.
Compagnie Internationale Express, **25** 120
Compagnie Laitière Européenne, **25** 83, 85
Compagnie Luxembourgeoise de Télédiffusion, **15** 54
Compagnie Monegasque du Banque, **65** 230, 232
Compagnie Nationale à Portefeuille, **29** 48
Compagnie Nationale de Navigation, **27** 515
Compagnie Parisienne de Garantie, **III** 211
Compagnie Transcontinentale de Reassurance, **57** 136
Compagnie Union des Assurances de Paris (UAP), **49** 44
Compal, **47** 152–53
Companhia Brasileira de Distribuiçao, 76 111–13
Companhia Brasileira de Petróleo Ipiranga, **67** 216
Companhia de Bebidas das Américas, 57 74–77; 67 316
Companhia de Celulose do Caima, **14** 250
Companhia de Electricidade da Bahia, **49** 211
Companhia de Seguros Argos Fluminense, **III** 221
Companhia de Seguros Tranquilidade Vida, S.A. *see* Banco Espírito Santo e Comercial de Lisboa S.A.
Companhia de Tecidos Norte de Minas - Coteminas, 77 116–119
Companhia Energética de Minas Gerais S.A., 53 18; **65 118–20**
Companhia Industrial de Papel Pirahy, **52** 301
Companhia Nordeste de Participaçoes, **73** 244
Companhia Siderúrgica de Tubarao, **IV** 125
Companhia Siderúrgica Mannesmann S.A. *see* Mannesmann AG.
Companhia Siderúrgica Nacional, 76 114–17
Companhia Vale do Rio Doce, IV 54–57; 43 111–14 (upd.); 67 85–86
Compania Cervecerias Unidas S.A., 70 61–63
Compañía de Nutrición General S.A., **72** 128
Compania Electro Metaluurgica, **67** 13
Compañia Española de Petróleos S.A. (Cepsa), IV 396–98; 56 63–66 (upd.)
Compania Fresnillo, **22** 286
Compania Fundidora del Norte, S.A., **54** 152
Compania General de Aceptaciones *see* Financiera Aceptaciones.
Compania Hulera Euzkadi, **21** 260; **23** 170
Compania Industrial de San Cristobal, S.A. de C.V., **54** 186
Compania Industrial del Norte, S.A., **54** 152
Compañia Mexicana de Transportación Aérea, **20** 167
Compania Minera de Penoles *see* Industrias Penoles, S.A. de C.V.
Compania Minera Las Torres, **22** 286
Compania Siderurgica Huachipato, **24** 209
Compañía Telefónica Nacional de España S.A. *see* Telefónica Nacional de España S.A.
Compaq Computer Corporation, III 124–25; 6 221–23 (upd.); 26 90–93 (upd.) *see also* **Hewlett-Packard Company.**
Comparex Holdings, **69** 127
Compart, **24** 341
Compass Airlines, **27** 475
Compass Bancshares, Inc., 73 92–94
Compass Design Automation, **16** 520
Compass Group PLC, 6 193; **24** 194; **27** 482; **34 121–24**
Compass Minerals International, Inc., 79 109–112
CompDent Corporation, 22 149–51
Compeda, Ltd., **10** 240
Competence ApS, **26** 240
Competrol Ltd., **22** 189
CompHealth Inc., 25 109–12
Complete Business Solutions, Inc., 31 130–33
Complete Post, **50** 126
Completion Bond Co., **26** 487
Components Agents Ltd., **10** 113; **50** 43
Composite Craft Inc., **I** 387
Composite Research & Management Co., **17** 528, 530
Comprehensive Care Corporation, 15 121–23
Compression Labs Inc., **10** 456; **16** 392, 394; **27** 365
Compressor Controls Corporation, **15** 404; **50** 394
Comptoir Général de la Photographie *see* Gaumont SA.
Comptoir Métallurgique Luxembourgeois, **IV** 25
Comptoirs Modernes S.A., 19 97–99
Compton Foods, **II** 675
Compton's MultiMedia Publishing Group, Inc., **7** 165
Compton's New Media, Inc., **7** 168
Compu-Notes, Inc., **22** 413
CompuAdd Computer Corporation, 11 61–63
CompuChem Corporation, **11** 425
CompuCom Systems, Inc., 10 232–34, 474; **13** 176
CompuDyne Corporation, 51 78–81
Compumech Technologies, **19** 312
CompuPharm, Inc., **14** 210
CompUSA, Inc., 10 235–36; 35 116–18 (upd.)
Compuscript, Inc., **64** 27
CompuServe Incorporated, 10 237–39 *see also* America Online, Inc.
CompuServe Interactive Services, Inc., 27 106–08 (upd.) *see also* AOL Time Warner Inc.
Computer Associates International, Inc., 6 224–26; 10 394; **12** 62; **14** 392; **27** 492; **49 94–97 (upd.)**
Computer City, **12** 470; **36** 387
The Computer Company, **11** 112
Computer Consoles Inc., **III** 164
Computer Data Systems, Inc., 14 127–29
The Computer Department, Ltd., **10** 89
Computer Discount Corporation *see* Comdisco, Inc.
Computer Discount Warehouse *see* CDW Computer Centers, Inc.
Computer Engineering Associates, **25** 303
Computer Factory, Inc., **13** 176
Computer Learning Centers, Inc., 26 94–96
Computer Motion, Inc. *see* Intuitive Surgical, Inc.
Computer Network Technology Corporation, **75** 256
Computer Peripheral Manufacturers Association, **13** 127
Computer Power, **6** 301
Computer Renaissance, Inc., **18** 207–8

Cullman Bros. *see* Culbro Corporation.
Culp, Inc., 29 138–40
Culter Industries, Inc., **22** 353
Culver Franchising System, Inc., 58 79–81
Cumberland Farms, Inc., 17 120–22; 26 450
Cumberland Federal Bancorporation, **13** 223; **31** 206
Cumberland Newspapers, **7** 389
Cumberland Packing Corporation, 26 107–09
Cummings-Moore Graphite Company *see* Asbury Carbons, Inc.
Cummins Cogeneration Co. *see* Cogeneration Development Corp.
Cummins Engine Co., Inc., I 146–48; 12 89–92 (upd.); 40 131–35 (upd.); 42 387
Cummins Utility Supply, **58** 334
Cumo Sports, **16** 109
Cumulus Media Inc., 37 103–05
CUNA Mutual Group, 11 495; **62 84–87**
Cunard Line Ltd., 23 159–62
CUNO Incorporated, 57 85–89
CurranCare, LLC, **50** 122
Current, Inc., 37 106–09
Currys Group PLC *see* Dixons Group PLC.
Curtas Technologie SA, **58** 221
Curtice-Burns Foods, Inc., 7 17–18, **104–06; 21** 18, **154–57 (upd.)** *see also* Birds Eye Foods, Inc.
Curtin & Pease/Peneco, **27** 361
Curtis Circulation Co., **IV** 619
Curtis Homes, **22** 127
Curtis Industries, **13** 165; **76** 107
Curtis 1000 Inc. *see* American Business Products, Inc.
Curtis Restaurant Supply, **60** 160
Curtis Squire Inc., **18** 455; **70** 262
Curtiss-Wright Corporation, 10 260–63; 35 132–37 (upd.)
Curver-Rubbermaid *see* Newell Rubbermaid.
Curves International, Inc., 54 80–82
Cushman & Wakefield Inc., **58** 303
Cussons *see* PZ Cussons plc.
Custom Academic Publishing Company, **12** 174
Custom Building Products of California, Inc., **53** 176
Custom Chrome, Inc., 16 147–49; 74 92–95 (upd.)
Custom Electronics, Inc., **9** 120
Custom Expressions, Inc., **7** 24; **22** 35
Custom Hoists, Inc., **17** 458
Custom, Ltd, **46** 197
Custom Organics, **8** 464
Custom Primers, **17** 288
Custom Publishing Group, **27** 361
Custom Technologies Corp., **19** 152
Custom Thermoform, **24** 512
Custom Tool and Manufacturing Company, **41** 366
Custom Transportation Services, Inc., **26** 62
Custom Woodwork & Plastics Inc., **36** 159
Customized Transportation Inc., **22** 164, 167
AB Custos, **25** 464
Cutisin, **55** 123
Cutler-Hammer Inc., **63** 401
Cutter & Buck Inc., 27 112–14
Cutter Precision Metals, Inc., **25** 7
CVC Capital Partners Limited, **49** 451; **54** 207
CVE Corporation, Inc., **24** 395
CVG Aviation, **34** 118
CVI Incorporated, **21** 108
CVN Companies, **9** 218
CVPS *see* Central Vermont Public Service Corporation.
CVRD *see* Companhia Vale do Rio Doce Ltd.
CVS Corporation, 32 166, 170; **34** 285; **45 133–38 (upd.); 63** 335–36
CWA *see* City of Westminster Assurance Company Ltd.
CWM *see* Chemical Waste Management, Inc.
CWP *see* Custom Woodwork & Plastics Inc.
CWT Farms International Inc., **13** 103
CXT Inc., **33** 257
Cyber Communications Inc., **16** 168
CyberCash Inc., **18** 541, 543; **76** 370
Cybermedia, Inc., 25 117–19
Cybernet Electronics Corp., **II** 51; **21** 330
Cybernex, **10** 463
Cyberonics, Inc., 79 128–131
Cybershield, Inc., **52** 103, 105
CyberSource Corp., **26** 441
CYBERTEK Corporation, **11** 395
CyberTrust Solutions Inc., **42** 24–25
Cybex International, Inc., 49 106–09
Cycle & Carriage Ltd., **20** 313; **56** 285
Cycle Video Inc., **7** 590
Cyclops Corporation, **10** 45; **13** 157
Cydsa *see* Grupo Cydsa, S.A. de C.V.
Cygna Energy Services, **13** 367
Cygne Designs, Inc., 25 120–23; 37 14
Cygnus Business Media, Inc., 56 73–77
Cymbal Co., Ltd. *see* Nagasakiya Co., Ltd.
Cymer, Inc., 77 125–128
Cynosure Inc., **11** 88
Cypress Amax Minerals Co., **13** 158; **22** 285–86
Cypress Insurance Co., **III** 214
Cypress Management Services, Inc., **64** 311
Cypress Semiconductor Corporation, 20 174–76; 48 125–29 (upd.)
Cyprus Amax Minerals Company, 21 158–61
Cyprus Minerals Company, 7 107–09
Cyrix Corporation *see* National Semiconductor Corporation.
Cyrk Inc., 19 112–14; 21 516; **33** 416
Cytec Industries Inc., 27 115–17
Cytyc Corporation, 69 112–14
Czarnikow-Rionda Company, Inc., 32 128–30

D

D&B *see* Dun & Bradstreet Corporation.
D&D Enterprises, Inc., **24** 96
D&F Industries, Inc., **17** 227; **41** 204
D&K Wholesale Drug, Inc., 14 146–48
D&N Systems, Inc., **10** 505
D&O Inc., **17** 363
D&W Computer Stores, **13** 176
D & W Food Stores, Inc., **8** 482; **27** 314
D Green (Electronics) Limited, **65** 141
D.B. Kaplan's, **26** 263
D.C. Heath & Co., **36** 273; **38** 374
D.C. National Bancorp, **10** 426
D. de Ricci-G. Selnet et Associes, **28** 141
d.e.m.o., **28** 345
D.E. Shaw & Co., **25** 17; **38** 269
D.E. Winebrenner Co., **7** 429
D.G. Calhoun, **12** 112
D.G. Yuengling & Son, Inc., 38 171–73
D.H. Holmes Company, Limited *see* Dillard's Inc.
D.I. Manufacturing Inc., **37** 351
D.K. Gold, **17** 138
D.L. Rogers Group, **37** 363
D.L. Saslow Co., **19** 290
D.M. Nacional, **23** 170
D.R. Horton, Inc., 58 82–84
D.W. Mikesell Co. *see* Mike-Sell's Inc.
Da Gama Textiles Company, **24** 450
D'Addario & Company, Inc. *see* J. D'Addario & Company, Inc.
Dade Behring Holdings Inc., 71 120–22
Dade Reagents Inc., **19** 103
DADG *see* Deutsch-Australische Dampfschiffs-Gesellschaft.
DAEDUK Techno Valley Company Ltd., **62** 174
Daewoo Group, III 457–59, 749; **18 123–27 (upd.); 30** 185; **57 90–94 (upd.)**
DAF, **7** 566–67
Daffy's Inc., 26 110–12
NV Dagblad De Telegraaf *see* N.V. Holdingmaatschappij De Telegraaf.
D'Agostino Supermarkets Inc., 19 115–17
Dagsbladunie, **IV** 611
DAH *see* DeCrane Aircraft Holdings Inc.
Dahill Industries *see* Global Imaging Systems, Inc.
Dahl Manufacturing, Inc., **17** 106
Dahlberg, Inc., **18** 207–08
Dahlonega Equipment and Supply Company, **12** 377
Dai-Ichi *see also* listings under Daiichi.
Dai-Ichi Bank, **I** 511
Dai-Ichi Kangyo Asset Management Co. Ltd., **58** 235
Dai-Ichi Kangyo Bank Ltd., II 273–75
Dai-Ichi Mokko Co., **III** 758
Dai-Ichi Mutual Life Insurance Co., **III** 277, 401; **25** 289; **26** 511; **38** 18
Dai Nippon *see also* listings under Dainippon.
Dai Nippon Brewery Co., **I**, 282; **21** 319

Dunn Manufacturing Company, **25** 74
Dunnes Stores Ltd., 58 102–04
Dunning Industries, **12** 109
Dunphy Holding Pty. Ltd., **64** 349
Dunwoodie Manufacturing Co., **17** 136
Duo-Bed Corp., **14** 435
Dupey Enterprises, Inc., **17** 320
Duplainville Transport, **19** 333–34
Duplex Products, Inc., 17 142–44, 445
Dupont *see* E.I. du Pont de Nemours & Company.
Duquesne Light Company *see* DQE.
Duquesne Systems, **10** 394
Dura Automotive Systems Inc., **53** 55; **65** 282, 284
Dura Convertible Systems, **13** 170
Duracell International Inc., 9 179–81; 71 127–31 (upd.)
Durachemie *see* Hexal AG.
Duraflame Inc., **58** 52
Duramed Research Inc. *see* Barr Pharmaceuticals, Inc.
Durametallic, 21 189–91
Durango-Mapimi Mining Co., **22** 284
Duravit AG, **51** 196
Duray, Inc., **12** 215
D'Urban, Inc., **41** 169
Duriron Company Inc., 17 145–47
Durkee Famous Foods, **7** 314; **8** 222; **17** 106; **27** 297
Dürkopp Adler AG, 65 131–34
Duro-Matic Products Co., **51** 368
Duron Inc., 72 91–93
Dürr AG, 44 158–61
Durr-Fillauer Medical Inc., **13** 90; **18** 97; **50** 121
Dürrkopp Adler AG, **62** 132
Dutch Boy, **II** 649; **10** 434–35
Dutch Crude Oil Company *see* Nederlandse Aardolie Maatschappij.
Dutch State Mines *see* DSM N.V.
Dutchland Farms, **25** 124
Duttons Ltd., **24** 267
Duty Free International, Inc., 11 80–82 *see also* World Duty Free Americas, Inc.
Duval Corp., **7** 280; **25** 461
DVI, Inc., 51 107–09
DVM Pharmaceuticals Inc., **55** 233
DVT Corporation *see* Cognex Corporation.
DWG Corporation *see* Triarc Companies, Inc.
Dyas B.V., **55** 347
Dyckerhoff AG, 35 151–54
Dycom Industries, Inc., 57 118–20
Dyersburg Corporation, 21 192–95
Dyke and Dryden, Ltd., **31** 417
Dylex Limited, 29 162–65
Dymed Corporation *see* Palomar Medical Technologies, Inc.
DYMO *see* Esselte Worldwide.
Dynaction S.A., 67 146–48
Dynalectric Co., **45** 146
DynaMark, Inc., **18** 168, 170, 516, 518
Dynamem Corporation, **22** 409
Dynamic Capital Corp., **16** 80
Dynamic Controls, **11** 202
Dynamic Foods, **53** 148
Dynamic Health Products Inc., **62** 296
Dynamic Homes, **61** 125–27
Dynamic Microprocessor Associated Inc., **10** 508
Dynamics Corporation of America, **39** 106
Dynamit Nobel AG, **III** 692–95; **16** 364; **18** 559
Dynamix, **15** 455
Dynapar, **7** 116–17
Dynaplast, **40** 214–15
Dynascan AK, **14** 118
Dynasty Footwear, Ltd., **18** 88
Dynatech Corporation, 13 194–96
Dynatron/Bondo Corporation, **8** 456
DynCorp, 45 145–47
Dynea, 68 125–27
Dynegy Inc., **47** 70; **49 119–22 (upd.)**
Dyno Industrier AS, **13** 555
Dyson Group PLC, 71 132–34
Dystrybucja, **41** 340

E

E&B Company, **9** 72
E&B Marine, Inc., **17** 542–43
E. & J. Gallo Winery, I 242–44; 7 154–56 (upd.); 28 109–11 (upd.)
E&M Laboratories, **18** 514
E & S Retail Ltd. *see* Powerhouse.
E! Entertainment Television Inc., 17 148–50
E-Mex Home Funding Ltd. *see* Cheshire Building Society.
E-mu Systems, Inc., **57** 78–79
E-Pet Services, **74** 234
E-Stamp Corporation, **34** 474
E-Systems, Inc., 9 182–85
E*Trade Financial Corporation, 20 206–08; 60 114–17 (upd.)
E-II Holdings Inc. *see* Astrum International Corp.
E-Z Haul, **24** 409
E-Z Serve Corporation, 17 169–71
E A Rosengrens AB, **53** 158
E.B. Badger Co., **11** 413
E.B. Eddy Forest Products, **II** 631
E.C. Snodgrass Company, **14** 112
E.C. Steed, **13** 103
E. de Trey & Sons, **10** 270–71
E.F. Hutton Group, **II** 399, 450–51; **8** 139; **9** 469; **10** 63
E.F. Hutton LBO, **24** 148
E.H. Bindley & Company, **9** 67
E.I. du Pont de Nemours and Company, I 328–30; 8 151–54 (upd.); 26 123–27 (upd.); 73 128–33 (upd.)
E.J. Brach & Sons *see* Brach and Brock Confections, Inc.
E.J. Longyear Company *see* Boart Longyear Company.
E. Katz Special Advertising Agency *see* Katz Communications, Inc.
E.M. Warburg Pincus & Co., **7** 305; **13** 176; **16** 319; **25** 313; **29** 262
E. Missel GmbH, **20** 363
E.On AG, 50 165–73 (upd.); **51** 217; **59** 391; **62** 14
E.piphany, Inc., 49 123–25
E.R.R. Enterprises, **44** 227
E. Rabinowe & Co., Inc., **13** 367
E. Rosen Co., **53** 303–04
E.S. International Holding S.A. *see* Banco Espírito Santo e Comercial de Lisboa S.A.
E.V. Williams Inc. *see* The Branch Group, Inc.
E.W. Howell Co., Inc., 72 94–96*see also* Obayashi Corporation
The E.W. Scripps Company, IV 606–09; 7 157–59 (upd.); 28 122–26 (upd.); 66 85–89 (upd.)
E. Witte Verwaltungsgesellschaft GmbH, **73** 326
EADS N.V. *see* European Aeronautic Defence and Space Company EADS N.V.
EADS SOCATA, 54 91–94
Eagel One Industries, **50** 49
Eagle Airways Ltd., **23** 161
Eagle Credit Corp., **10** 248
Eagle Distributing Co., **37** 351
Eagle Family Foods, Inc., **22** 95
Eagle Floor Care, Inc., **13** 501; **33** 392
Eagle Gaming, L.P., **16** 263; **43** 226; **75** 341
Eagle Global Logistics *see* EGL, Inc.
Eagle Hardware & Garden, Inc., 16 186–89
Eagle Industries Inc., **8** 230; **22** 282; **25** 536
Eagle Managed Care Corp., **19** 354, 357; **63** 334
Eagle-Picher Industries, Inc., 8 155–58; 23 179–83 (upd.)
Eagle Plastics, **19** 414
Eagle Sentry Inc., **32** 373
Eagle Thrifty Drug, **14** 397
Eagle Trading, **55** 24
Eagle Travel Ltd., **IV** 241
Earl Scheib, Inc., 32 158–61
Early American Insurance Co., **22** 230
Early Learning Centre, **39** 240, 242
Earth Resources Company, **17** 320
Earth Wise, Inc., **16** 90
Earth's Best, Inc., **21** 56; **36** 256
The Earthgrains Company, 36 161–65; 54 326
EarthLink, Inc., 33 92; **36 166–68; 38** 269
EAS *see* Engineered Air Systems, Inc.; Executive Aircraft Services.
Easco Hand Tools, Inc., **7** 117
Easi-Set Industries, Inc., **56** 332
Eason Oil Company, **6** 578; **11** 198
East African External Communications Limited, **25** 100
East African Gold Mines Limited, **61** 293
East Hartford Trust Co., **13** 467
East Japan Railway Company, V 448–50; 66 90–94 (upd.)
The East New York Savings Bank, **11** 108–09
East Penn Manufacturing Co., Inc., 79 154–157

Education Loan Processing, **53** 319
Education Management Corporation, 35 160–63
Education Systems Corporation, **7** 256; **25** 253
Educational & Recreational Services, Inc., **II** 607
Educational Broadcasting Corporation, 48 144–47
Educational Computer International, Inc. *see* ECC International Corp.
Educational Credit Corporation, **8** 10; **38** 12
Educational Development Corporation *see* National Heritage Academies, Inc.
Educational Loan Administration Group, Inc., **33** 420
Educational Publishing Corporation, **22** 519, 522
Educational Supply Company, **7** 255; **25** 252
Educational Testing Service, 12 141–43; 42 209–10, 290; **62 116–20 (upd.)**
Educor *see* Naspers Ltd.
Educorp, Inc., **39** 103
Edumond Le Monnier S.p.A., **54** 22
EduQuest, **6** 245
EduServ Technologies, Inc., **33** 420
Edusoft Ltd., **40** 113
EduTrek International, Inc., **45** 88
Edw. C. Levy Co., 42 125–27
Edward D. Jones & Company L.P., 30 177–79; 66 101–04 (upd.)
Edward Hines Lumber Company, 68 131–33
Edward J. DeBartolo Corporation, 8 159–62
Edward P. Allis Company, **13** 16
Edward Smith & Company, **8** 553
Edwards & Jones, **11** 360
Edwards and Kelcey, 70 81–83
Edwards Food Warehouse, **II** 642
Edwards George and Co., **III** 283
Edwards Theatres Circuit, Inc., 31 171–73; 59 341–42
Edwardstone Partners, **14** 377
EEC Environmental, Inc., **16** 259
EEGSA *see* Empresa Eléctrica de Guatemala S.A.
EEX Corporation, **65** 262
eFamily *see* Marchex, Inc.
EFM Media Management, **23** 294
Efnadruck GmbH, **IV** 325
Efrat Future Technology Ltd. *see* Comverse Technology, Inc.
EFS National Bank, **52** 87
EFTEC, **32** 257
EG&G Incorporated, 8 163–65; 18 219; **22** 410; **29 166–69 (upd.)**
EGAM, **IV** 422
EGAT *see* Electricity Generating Authority of Thailand (EGAT).
Egg plc, **48** 328
Egghead Inc., 9 194–95; 10 284
Egghead.com, Inc., 31 174–77 (upd.)
EGL, Inc., 59 170–73
EGPC *see* Egyptian General Petroleum Corporation.
eGrail Inc., **62** 142
EgyptAir, 6 84–86; 27 132–35 (upd.)
Egyptian General Petroleum Corporation, IV 412–14; 32 45; **51 110–14 (upd.)**
EHAPE Einheitspreis Handels Gesellschaft mbH *see* Kaufhalle AG.
eHarmony.com Inc., 71 135–38
eHow.com, **49** 290
Ehrlich-Rominger, **48** 204
Eiffage, 27 136–38
Eiffel Construction Metallique, **27** 138
800-JR Cigar, Inc., 27 139–41
84 Lumber Company, 9 196–97; 39 134–36 (upd.)
Eildon Electronics Ltd., **15** 385
Eileen Fisher Inc., 61 85–87
Einstein/Noah Bagel Corporation, 29 170–73; 44 313; **63** 81
eircom plc, 31 178–81 (upd.)
EIS, Inc., **45** 176, 179; **62** 115
Eisai Company, **13** 77
EJ Financial Enterprises Inc., **48** 308–09
Ek Chor China Motorcycle, **62** 63
Eka Nobel AB, **9** 380
Ekco Group, Inc., 16 190–93
Eko-Elda A.B.E.E., **64** 177
Ekoterm CR *see* Dalkia Holding.
EKT, Inc., **44** 4
El Al Israel Airlines Ltd., 23 184–87
El Camino Resources International, Inc., 11 86–88
El Chico Restaurants, Inc., 19 135–38; 36 162–63
El Corte Inglés, S.A., V 51–53; 26 128–31 (upd.)
El Dorado Chemical Company*see* LSB Industries, Inc.
El Dorado Investment Company, **6** 546–47
El-Mel-Parts Ltd., **21** 499
El Nasr Petroleum Co., **51** 113
El Paso Corporation, 66 105–08 (upd.)
El Paso Electric Company, 21 196–98
El Paso Healthcare System, Ltd., **15** 112; **35** 215
El Paso Natural Gas Company, 10 190; **11** 28; **12 144–46; 19** 411; **27** 86 *see also* El Paso Corporation.
El Pollo Loco, Inc., 69 138–40
El Portal Group, Inc., **58** 370
El Taco, **7** 505
Elamex, S.A. de C.V., 51 115–17
Elan Corporation PLC, 63 140–43
Elan Ski Company, **22** 483
Elanco Animal Health, **47** 112
Elano Corporation, 14 179–81
Elantis, **48** 290
Elastic Reality Inc., **38** 70
Elcat Company, **17** 91
Elco Corporation, **21** 329, 331
Elco Industries Inc., **22** 282
The Elder-Beerman Stores Corp., 10 281–83; 19 362; **63 144–48 (upd.)**
Elders IXL Ltd., I 264, **437–39**, 592–93; **7** 182–83; **21** 227; **26** 305; **28** 201; **50** 199
Elders Keep, **13** 440
Eldorado Gold Corporation, **22** 237
ele Corporation, **23** 251
Electra Corp., **III** 569; **20** 361–62
Electra Investment Trust, **73** 340
Electra/Midland Corp., **13** 398
Electra Partners, **75** 389, 391
Electrabel N.V., 67 169–71
Electric Boat Co. *see* General Dynamics Corporation.
Electric Bond & Share Company, **6** 596
Electric Clearinghouse, Inc., **18** 365, 367
Electric Fuels Corp. *see* Florida Progress Corporation.
Electric Light Company of Atlantic City *see* Atlantic Energy, Inc.
Electric Lightwave, Inc., 37 124–27
Electric Storage Battery Co., **39** 338
Electric Transit, Inc., **37** 399–400
Electricidade de Portugal, S.A., 47 108–11; 49 211
Electricité de France, V 603–05, 626–28; **41 138–41 (upd.)**
Electricity Generating Authority of Thailand (EGAT), 56 108–10
Electricity Metering Distribucion, S.A. DE C.V., **64** 205
Electro-Flo, Inc., **9** 27
Electro Metallurgical Co., **11** 402
Electro-Motive Engineering Company, **10** 273
Electro Refractories and Abrasives Company, **8** 178
Electro Rent Corporation, 58 108–10
Electro String Instrument Corporation, **16** 201; **43** 169
Electrocomponents PLC, 50 174–77
Electrolux AB, 53 124–29 (upd.)
Electrolux Group, III 478–81
Electromagnetic Sciences Inc., 21 199–201
Electromedics, **11** 460
Electronic Arts Inc., 10 284–86
Electronic Banking Systems, **9** 173
Electronic Book Technologies, Inc., **26** 216 **29** 427
Electronic Data Systems Corporation, III 136–38; 28 112–16 (upd.) *see also* **Perot Systems Corporation.**
Electronic Engineering Co., **16** 393
Electronic Hair Styling, Inc., **41** 228
Electronic Processing Inc. *see* EPIQ Systems, Inc.
Electronics Boutique Holdings Corporation, 72 102–05
Electronics Corp. of Israel Ltd. *see* ECI Telecom Ltd.
Electronics for Imaging, Inc., 15 148–50; 43 150–53 (upd.)
Electrowatt Ltd., **21** 146–47
Elekom, **31** 176
Elektra *see* Grupo Elektra, S.A. de C.V.
Elektra Entertainment Group, 64 115–18
Elektra Records, **III** 480; **23** 33
Elektriska Aktiebolaget *see* ABB Asea Brown Boveri Ltd.
Elektrizitäts-Gesellschaft Laufenburg *see* Elektrowatt AG.

Elektrizitätswerk Wesertal GmbH, **30** 206
Elektrocieplownie Warszawskie S.A., **57** 395, 397
Elektrowatt AG, 6 489–91
Elementis plc, 40 162–68 (upd.)
Eletropaulo Metropolitana, **53** 18
Eletson Corp., **13** 374
Elettra Broadcasting Corporation, **14** 509
Elettrofinanziaria Spa, **9** 152
Elf Aquitaine SA, 21 202–06 (upd.) *see also* Société Nationale Elf Aquitaine.
Elfa International, **36** 134–35
Elgin Blenders, Inc., **7** 128
Elgin Exploration, Inc., **19** 247; **26** 70
Eli Lilly and Company, I 645–47; 11 89–91 (upd.), 47 112–16 (upd.), 50 139
Eli Witt Company, **15** 137, 139; **43** 205
Elior SA, 49 126–28
Elisra Defense Group, **68** 222, 224
Elite Acquisitions, Inc., **65** 150
Elite Microelectronics, **9** 116
Elizabeth Arden, Inc., 8 166–68; 40 169–72 (upd.)
Eljer Industries, Inc., 24 150–52
Elkay Manufacturing Company, 73 134–36
ElkCorp, 52 103–05
Elke Corporation, **10** 514
Elkjop ASA, **49** 113
Elko-Lamoille Power Company, **11** 343
Ellanef Manufacturing Corp., **48** 274
Ellen Tracy, Inc., 55 136–38
Ellerbe Becket, 41 142–45
Ellesse International S.p.A. *see* Reebok International Ltd.
Ellett Brothers, Inc., 17 154–56
Ellington Recycling Center, **12** 377
Elliot Group Limited, **45** 139–40
Elliott & Co. (Henley) Ltd. *see* Gibbs and Dandy plc.
Elliott Automation, **13** 225
Elliott Bay Design Group, **22** 276
Elliott Paint and Varnish, **8** 553
Ellipse Programmes, **48** 164–65
Ellis & Everard, **41** 341
Ellis-Don Ltd., **38** 481
Ellis Paperboard Products Inc., **13** 442
Ellis Park Race Course, **29** 118
Ellisco Co., **35** 130
Ellos A.B., **II** 640
Elmendorf Board, **IV** 343
Elmer's Products, Inc. *see* Borden, Inc.
Elmer's Restaurants, Inc., 42 128–30
Elmo Semiconductor Corp., **48** 246
Elna USA *see* Tacony Corporation.
Elphinstone, **21** 501
Elrick Industries, Inc., **19** 278
Elron Industries, **75** 304–05
Elscint Ltd., 20 202–05
Elsevier NV, IV 610–11 *see also* Reed Elsevier.
Elsinore Corporation, 36 158; **48 148–51**
Eltra Corporation, **I** 416; **22** 31; **31** 135
Eltron International Inc., **53** 374
Elvirasminde A/S *see* August Storck KG.
Elvis Presley Enterprises, Inc., 61 88–90
ELYO, **42** 387–88
eMachines, Inc., **63** 155
Email Ltd., **62** 331
EMAP plc, 35 164–66
Embankment Trust Ltd., **IV** 659
Embassy Suites, **9** 425; **24** 253
Embedded Support Tools Corporation, **37** 419, 421
Embers America Restaurants, 30 180–82
Embotelladora Andina S.A., 71 139–41
Embotelladora Central, S.A., **47** 291
Embraer *see* Empresa Brasileira de Aeronáutica S.A.
Embraer-Liebherr Equipamentos do Brasil S.A., **64** 241
Embrex, Inc., 72 106–08
EMC Corporation, 12 147–49; 20 8; **46 162–66 (upd.)**
EMC Technology Services, Inc., **30** 469
Emco, **III** 569; **20** 361
EMCOR Group Inc., 60 118–21
EMD Holding, Inc., **64** 205
EMD Technologies, **27** 21; **40** 67
Emerald Technology, Inc., **10** 97
Emerson, 46 167–71 (upd.)
Emerson-Brantingham Company, **10** 378
Emerson Electric Co., II 18–21
Emerson Foote, Inc., **25** 90
Emerson Radio Corp., 30 183–86
Emery Worldwide Airlines, Inc., 6 388–91; 25 146–50 (upd.)
Emge Packing Co., Inc., 11 92–93
Emhart Corp., **III** 437; **8** 332; **20** 67; **67** 67
EMI Group plc, 22 192–95 (upd.); 24 485; **26** 188, 314; **52** 428
Emigrant Savings Bank, 59 174–76
Emil Moestue as, **51** 328
Emil Schlemper GmbH *see* Acme United Corporation.
The Emirates Group, 24 400; **39 137–39**
Emmis Communications Corporation, 47 117–21
Empain, **18** 472; **19** 165
Empaques de Carton Titan, **19** 10–11
Empex Hose, **19** 37
Empi, Inc., 27 132–35
Empire Blue Cross and Blue Shield, III 245–46 *see also* WellChoice, Inc.
Empire-Cliffs Partnership, **62** 74
The Empire District Electric Company, 77 138–141
Empire Family Restaurants Inc., **15** 362
Empire Hanna Coal Co., Ltd., **8** 346
Empire Iron Mining Partnership, **62** 74
Empire of America, **11** 110
Empire of Carolina Inc., **66** 370
Empire Resorts, Inc., 72 109–12
Empire State Pickling Company, **21** 155
Empire Steel Castings, Inc., **39** 31–32
Empire Stores, **19** 309
Employee Solutions, Inc., 18 157–60
employeesavings.com, **39** 25
Employers General Insurance Group, **58** 259
Employers Insurance of Wausau, **59** 264
Employers' Liability Assurance, **III** 235
Employer's Overload, **25** 432
Employers Reinsurance Corp., **II** 31; **12** 197
Emporsil-Empresa Portuguesa de Silvicultura, Lda, **60** 156
Empresa Brasileira de Aeronáutica S.A. (Embraer), 36 182–84
Empresa Colombiana de Petróleos, IV 415–18
Empresa Constructora SA, **55** 182
Empresas Almacenes Paris S.A., 71 142–44
Empresas CMPC S.A., 70 84–87
Empresa de Distribucion Electrica de Lima Nortes SA, **73** 142
Empresa de Obras y Montajes Ovalle Moore, S.A., **34** 81
Empresa Eléctrica de Guatemala S.A., **49** 211
Empresa Nacional de Telecomunicaciones, **63** 375
Empresas Copec S.A., 69 141–44
Empresas Emel S.A., **41** 316
Empresas Frisco, **21** 259
Empresas ICA Sociedad Controladora, S.A. de C.V., 34 82; **41 146–49**
Empresas La Moderna, **21** 413; **29** 435
Empresas Penta S.A., **69** 56
Empresas Polar SA, 55 139–41 (upd.)
Empresas Tolteca, **20** 123
Emprise Corporation, **7** 134–35
EMS-Chemie Holding AG, **III** 760; **32** 257
EMS Technologies, Inc., **21** 199, 201; **22** 173
Enbridge Inc., 43 154–58
ENCAD, Incorporated, 25 151–53
Encompass Services Corporation, 33 141–44
Encon Safety Products, Inc., **45** 424
Encor Inc., **47** 396
Encore Acquisition Company, 73 137–39
Encore Computer Corporation, 13 201–02; 74 107–10 (upd.)
Encore Distributors Inc., **17** 12–13
Encryption Technology Corporation, **23** 102
Encyclopedia Britannica, Inc., 7 165–68; 39 140–44 (upd.)
Endata, Inc., **11** 112
Endeavor Pharmaceuticals Inc. *see* Barr Pharmaceuticals, Inc.
Endemol Entertainment Holding NV, 46 172–74; 53 154
ENDESA S.A., V 606–08; 46 175–79 (upd.); 49 210–11
Endevco Inc., **11** 28
Endicott Trust Company, **11** 110
Endo Pharmaceuticals Holdings Inc., 71 145–47
Endo Vascular Technologies, Inc., **11** 460
ENDOlap, Inc., **50** 122
Endovations, Inc., **21** 47
ENECO *see* Empresa Nacional Electrica de Cordoba.
Enerchange LLC, **18** 366
Enercon, Inc., **6** 25

F

First Express, **48** 177
First Federal Savings & Loan Assoc., **IV** 343; **9** 173
First Federal Savings and Loan Association of Crisp County, **10** 92
First Federal Savings and Loan Association of Hamburg, **10** 91
First Federal Savings and Loan Association of Fort Myers, **9** 476
First Federal Savings and Loan Association of Kalamazoo, **9** 482
First Federal Savings Bank of Brunswick, **10** 92
First Fidelity Bank, N.A., New Jersey, 9 221–23
First Fidelity Bank of Rockville, **13** 440
First Financial Insurance, **41** 178
First Financial Management Corporation, 11 111–13
First Hawaiian, Inc., 11 114–16
FIRST HEALTH Strategies, **11** 113
First Healthcare, **14** 242
First Heights, fsa, **8** 437
First Hospital Corp., **15** 122
First Industrial Realty Trust, Inc., 65 146–48
First Insurance Agency, Inc., **17** 527
First International Computer, Inc., 56 129–31
First Interstate Bancorp, II 288–90
First Investment Advisors, **11** 106
First Investors Management Corp., **11** 106
First Leisure Corporation plc *see* Esporta plc.
First Liberty Financial Corporation, **11** 457
First Line Insurance Services, Inc., **8** 436
First Madison Bank, **14** 192
First Maryland Bancorp, **16** 14
First Mississippi Corporation, 8 183–86 *see also* ChemFirst, Inc.
First Mississippi National, **14** 41
First National Bank, **10** 298; **13** 467
First National Bank and Trust Company, **22** 4
First National Bank and Trust Company of Kalamazoo, **8** 187–88
First National Bank in Albuquerque, **11** 119
First National Bank of Akron, **9** 475
First National Bank of Allentown, **11** 296
First National Bank of Atlanta, **16** 522
First National Bank of Boston, **12** 310; **13** 446
First National Bank of Carrollton, **9** 475
First National Bank of Commerce, **11** 106
First National Bank of Harrington, Delaware *see* J.C. Penny National Bank.
First National Bank of Hartford, **13** 466
First National Bank of Hawaii, **11** 114
First National Bank of Highland, **11** 109
First National Bank of Houma, **21** 522
The First National Bank of Lafayette, **11** 107
First National Bank of Minneapolis, **22** 426–27
First National Bank of Salt Lake, **11** 118
First National Bank of Seattle, **8** 469–70
First National Bankshares, Inc., **21** 524
First National City Bank, **9** 124; **16** 13
First National Holding Corporation, **16** 522
First National Supermarkets, Inc., **II** 641–42; **9** 452
First Nations Gaming, Ltd., **44** 334
First Nationwide Bank, 8 30; **14 191–93**
First Nationwide Holdings Inc., **28** 246
First New England Bankshares Corp., **13** 467
First Nitrogen, Inc., **8** 184
First Nuclear Corporation, **49** 411
First of America Bank Corporation, 8 187–89
First of America Bank-Monroe, **9** 476
First Omni Bank NA, **16** 14; **18** 518; **43** 8
First Options of Chicago, Inc., **51** 148
First Pacific Company Limited, 18 180–82
First Physician Care, Inc., **36** 367
First Pick Stores, **12** 458
First Private Power Corporation, **56** 215
First Quench Retailing Ltd., **52** 416
First Railroad and Banking Company, **11** 111
First Republic Corp., **14** 483
First RepublicBank Corporation, **II** 337; **10** 425–26
First Savings and Loan, **10** 339
First Seattle Dexter Horton National Bank, **8** 470
First Security Bank of Missoula, **35** 197–99
First Security Corporation, 11 117–19; 38 491
First Signature Bank and Trust Co., **III** 268
First Sport Ltd., **39** 60
1st State Bank & Trust, **9** 474
First State Bank Southwest Indiana, **41** 178–79
First SunAmerican Life Insurance Company, **11** 482
First Team Sports, Inc., 15 396–97; **22 202–04**
First Tennessee National Corporation, 11 120–21; 48 176–79 (upd.)
First Trust Bank, **16** 14
First Union Corporation, 10 298–300; 24 482; **37** 148; **57** 415 *see also* Wachovia Corporation.
First USA, Inc., 11 122–24
First USA Paymentech, **24** 393
First Variable Life, **59** 246
First Virginia Banks, Inc., 11 125–26
First Women's Bank of New York, **23** 3
First Worth Corporation, **19** 232
The First Years Inc., 46 191–94
FirstAir Inc., **48** 113
Firstar Corporation, 11 127–29; 33 152–55 (upd.)
FirstBancorp., **13** 467
FirstGroup plc, **38** 321
FirstMiss, Inc., **8** 185
FirstPage USA Inc., **41** 265
Firth Carpet, **19** 275
Fischbach Corp., **III** 198; **8** 536–37
FISCOT, **10** 337
Fiserv Inc., 11 130–32; 33 156–60 (upd.)
Fish & Neave, 54 109–12
Fisher & Company, **9** 16
Fisher Broadcasting Co., **15** 164
Fisher-Camuto Corp., **14** 441
Fisher Companies, Inc., 15 164–66
Fisher Controls International, LLC, 13 224–26; 61 96–99 (upd.)
Fisher Foods, Inc., **II** 602; **9** 451, 452; **13** 237; **41** 11, 13
Fisher Nut, **14** 275
Fisher-Price Inc., 12 167–69; 32 190–94 (upd.)
Fisher Scientific International Inc., 24 162–66
Fishers Agricultural Holdings, **II** 466
Fisk Corporation, 72 132–34
Fiskars Corporation, 33 161–64; 60 351
Fiskeby Board AB, **48** 344
Fisons plc, 9 224–27; 23 194–97 (upd.)
Fitch IBCA Inc., **37** 143, 145
Fitch Investor Services, **65** 243–44
Fitch Lovell PLC, **13** 103
Fitchburg Gas and Electric Light, **37** 406
Fitzsimmons Stores Inc., **16** 452
Fitzwilton Public Limited Company, **12** 529; **34** 496
5 & Diner Franchise Corporation, 72 135–37
Five Bros. Inc., **19** 456
Five Star Entertainment Inc., **28** 241
Five Star Group, Inc., **64** 166
546274 Alberta Ltd., **48** 97
FKI Plc, 57 141–44; 69 52
FKM Advertising, **27** 280
FL Industries Holdings, Inc., **11** 516
Flagler Development Company, **59** 184–85
Flagship Resources, **22** 495
Flagstar Companies, Inc., 10 301–03; 29 150 *see also* Advantica Restaurant Group, Inc.
Flagstone Hospitality Management LLC, **58** 194
Flair Corporation, **18** 467
Flair Fold, **25** 11
Flambeau Products Corporation, **55** 132
Flanders Corporation, 65 149–51
Flanigan's Enterprises, Inc., 60 128–30
Flapdoodles, **15** 291
Flashes Publishers, Inc., **36** 341
Flatiron Mandolin Company, **16** 239
Flatow, Moore, Bryan, and Fairburn, **21** 33
Flavors Holdings Inc., **38** 294
Fleck Controls, Inc., **26** 361, 363
Fleer Corporation, 10 402; **13** 519; **15 167–69; 19** 386; **34** 447; **37** 295
Fleet Aerospace Corporation *see* Magellan Aerospace Corporation.
Fleet Call, Inc., **10** 431–32
Fleet Equity Partners, **62** 325, 327
Fleet Holdings, **28** 503

FleetBoston Financial Corporation, 9 228–30; 36 206–14 (upd.)
Fleetway, **7** 244
Fleetwood Enterprises, Inc., III 484–85; 22 205–08 (upd.)
Fleming Chinese Restaurants Inc., **37** 297
Fleming Companies, Inc., II 624–25; 17 178–81 (upd.)
Fleming Foodservice, **26** 504
Fletcher Challenge Ltd., IV 278–80; 19 153–57 (upd.)
Fletcher Pacific Construction Co. Ltd., **64** 113
Fleury Michon S.A., 39 159–61
Flex Elektrowerkzeuge GmbH, **26** 363
Flex Interim, **16** 421; **43** 308
Flex-O-Lite, **14** 325
Flexi-Van Corporations, **II** 492; **20** 118
Flexsteel Industries Inc., 15 170–72; 41 159–62 (upd.)
Flextronics International Ltd., 38 186–89
Flexys, **16** 462
FLGI Holding Company, **10** 321
Flick Industrial Group *see* Feldmühle Nobel AG.
Flight One Logistics, Inc., **22** 311
Flight Options, LLC, 75 144–46
Flight Refuelling Limited *see* Cobham plc.
FlightSafety International, Inc., 9 231–33; 29 189–92 (upd.)
Flint Ink Corporation, 13 227–29; 41 163–66 (upd.)
Flip Chip Technologies, LLC, **33** 248
FLIR Systems, Inc., 69 170–73
Flo-Pak, Inc., **57** 160
Flora Frey GmbH *see* Vilmorin Clause et Cie
Flora Frey/Sperling *see* Groupe Limagrain
Flora Medicinal J. Monteiro da Silva Ltda., **75** 270
Florafax International, Inc., **37** 162
Floral City Furniture Company *see* La-Z-Boy Incorporated.
Flori Roberts, Inc., **11** 208
Florida Crystals Inc., 35 176–78
Florida Cypress Gardens, Inc., **IV** 623
Florida Distillers Company, **27** 479
Florida East Coast Industries, Inc., 59 184–86
Florida East Coast Railway, L.L.C., **8** 486–87; **12** 278; **59** 184
Florida Flavors, **44** 137
Florida Frozen Foods, **13** 244
Florida Gaming Corporation, 47 130–33
Florida Gas Co., **15** 129
Florida Gas Transmission Company, **6** 578
Florida Panthers Hockey Club, Ltd., **37** 33, 35
Florida Power *see* Progress Energy, Inc.
Florida Power & Light Company *see* FPL Group, Inc.
Florida Presbyterian College, **9** 187
Florida Progress Corp., V 621–22; 23 198–200 (upd.)
Florida Public Utilities Company, 69 174–76
Florida Rock Industries, Inc., 23 326; **46 195–97**
Florida Steel Corp., **14** 156; **76** 129
Florida's Natural Growers, 45 160–62
FloridaGulf Airlines, **11** 300
Florimex Verwaltungsgesellschaft mbH, **12** 109
Florists' Transworld Delivery, Inc., 28 136–38
Florsheim Shoe Group Inc., 9 234–36; 31 209–12 (upd.)
Flour City International, Inc., 44 181–83
Flow International Corporation, 56 132–34
Flow Laboratories, **14** 98
Flow Measurement, **26** 293
Flower Time, Inc., **12** 179, 200
Flowers Industries, Inc., 12 170–71; 35 179–82 (upd.) *see also* Keebler Foods Company.
Flowserve Corporation, 33 165–68; 77 146–151 (upd.)
Floyd West & Co., **6** 290
FLSmidth & Co. A/S, 72 138–40
Fluent, Inc., **29** 4–6
Fluf N'Stuf, Inc., **12** 425
Fluke Corporation, 15 173–75
Flunch, **37** 22
Fluor Corporation, I 569–71, 586; **8 190–93 (upd.); 12** 244; **26** 433; **34 164–69 (upd.); 57** 237–38
Fluor Daniel Inc., **41** 148
The Fluorocarbon Company *see* Furon Company.
Flushing Federal Savings & Loan Association, **16** 346
FlyBE *see* Jersey European Airways (UK) Ltd.
Flying Boat, Inc. (Chalk's Ocean Airways), 56 135–37
Flying Colors Toys Inc., **52** 193
Flying Fruit Fantasy, USA, Inc., **57** 56–57
Flying J Inc., 19 158–60
Flying Tiger Line, **39** 33
FMC Corp., I 442–44; 11 133–35 (upd.)
FMR Corp., 8 194–96; 32 195–200 (upd.)
FMXI, Inc. *see* Foamex International Inc.
FN Manufacturing Co., **12** 71
FNAC, 21 224–26; 26 160
FNC Comercio, **III** 221
FNCB *see* First National City Bank of New York.
FNH USA, Inc., **58** 147
FNK *see* Finance Oil Corp.
FNMA *see* Federal National Mortgage Association.
FNN *see* Financial News Network.
Foamex International Inc., 17 182–85; 26 500
Focal Surgery, Inc., **27** 355
FOCUS, **44** 402
Focus Features, 78 118–122
Fodor's Travel Guides, **13** 429
Fog Cutter Capital Group Inc., **64** 124
Fogdog Inc., **36** 347
Fokker *see* N.V. Koninklijke Nederlandse Vliegtuigenfabriek Fokker.
Fokker Aircraft Corporation of America, **9** 16
Foley & Lardner, 28 139–42
Folksamerica Holding Company, Inc., **48** 431
Follett Corporation, 12 172–74; 39 162–65 (upd.)
Follis DeVito Verdi *see* De Vito/Verdi.
Follum Fabrikker, **63** 314
Fomento de Valores, S.A. de C.V., **23** 170
Fomento Economico Mexicano, S.A. de C.V. *see* Femsa.
Fonda Group, **36** 462
Fondazione Cassa di Risparmio di Venezia, **50** 408
Fondiaria Group, **III** 351
Fonterra Co-Operative Group Ltd., 58 125–27
Food City, **II** 649–50
Food Basics *see* Farmer Jack Supermarkets
The Food Emporium, 64 125–27
Food Fair *see* Farmer Jack Supermarkets
Food For The Poor, Inc., 77 152–155
Food 4 Less Supermarkets, Inc., **17** 558–61
Food Giant, **II** 670
Food Ingredients Technologies, **25** 367
Food King, **20** 306
Food Lion LLC, II 626–27; 7 450; **15 176–78 (upd.),** 270; **18** 8; **21** 508; **33** 306; **44** 145; **66 112–15 (upd.)**
Food Machinery Corp *see* FMC Corp.
Food Source, **58** 290
Food Town Inc., **II** 626–27
Food World, **26** 46; **31** 372
Foodarama Supermarkets, Inc., 28 143–45
FoodBrands America, Inc., 21 290; **22** 510; **23 201–04** *see also* Doskocil Companies, Inc.
FoodLand Distributors, **II** 625, 645, 682
Foodmaker, Inc., 13 152; **14 194–96**
Foodstuffs, **9** 144
Foodtown, **II** 626; **V** 35; **15** 177; **24** 528
FoodUSA.com, **43** 24
Foodways National, Inc., **12** 531; **13** 383
Foot Locker, Inc., 68 157–62 (upd.)
Footaction *see* Footstar, Incorporated.
Foote, Cone & Belding Worldwide, I 12–15; 66 116–20 (upd.)
Foote Mineral Company, **7** 386–87
Footquarters, **14** 293, 295
Footstar, Incorporated, 24 167–69
Foracon Maschinen und Anlagenbau GmbH & Co., **56** 134
Forbes Inc., 30 199–201
The Ford Foundation, 34 170–72
Ford Motor Company, I 164–68; 11 136–40 (upd.); 36 215–21 (upd.); 64 128–34 (upd.)
Ford Motor Company, S.A. de C.V., 20 219–21
Ford New Holland, Inc. *see* New Holland N.V.
Fording Inc., **45** 80
FORE Systems, Inc., 25 161–63; 33 289

Fujisawa Pharmaceutical Company, Ltd., I 635–36; 58 132–34 (upd.)
Fujitsu-ICL Systems Inc., 11 150–51
Fujitsu Limited, III 139–41; 16 224–27 (upd.); 40 145–50 (upd.)
Fujitsu Takamisawa, **28** 131
Fukuoka Mitsukoshi Ltd., **56** 242
Fukuoka Paper Co., Ltd., **IV** 285
Fukutake Publishing Co., Ltd., **13** 91, 93
Ful-O-Pep, **10** 250
Fulbright & Jaworski L.L.P., 22 4; **47 138–41**
Fulcrum Communications, **10** 19
The Fulfillment Corporation of America, **21** 37
Fulham Brothers, **13** 244
Fullbright & Jaworski, **28** 48
Fuller Company *see* FLSmidth and Co. A/S.
Fuller Smith & Turner P.L.C., 38 193–95
Fulton Bank, **14** 40
Fulton Co., **III** 569; **20** 361
Fulton Manufacturing Co., **11** 535
Fulton Performance Products, Inc., **11** 535
Funai Electric Company Ltd., 62 148–50
Funco, Inc., 20 239–41 *see also* GameStop Corp.
Fund American Companies *see* White Mountains Insurance Group, Ltd.
Fundimensions, **16** 337
Funk & Wagnalls, **22** 441
Funnel Cake Factory, **24** 241
Funtastic Limited, **52** 193
Fuqua Enterprises, Inc., 17 195–98
Fuqua Industries Inc., I 445–47; 8 545; **12** 251; **14** 86; **37** 62; **57** 376–77
Furnishings International Inc., **20** 359, 363; **39** 267
Furniture Brands International, Inc., 39 170–75 (upd.)
The Furniture Center, Inc., **14** 236
Furon Company, 28 149–51
Furr's Restaurant Group, Inc., 53 145–48
Furr's Supermarkets, Inc., II 601; **28 152–54**
Furst Group, **17** 106
Furukawa Electric Co., Ltd., III 490–92; 15 514; **22** 44
Futronix Corporation, **17** 276
Future Diagnostics, Inc., **25** 384
Future Graphics, **18** 387
Future Now, Inc., 6 245; **12 183–85**
Future Shop Ltd., 62 151–53; 63 63
FutureCare, **50** 123
Futurestep, Inc., **34** 247, 249
Fuyo Group, **72** 249
FWD Corporation, **7** 513
FX Coughlin Inc., **51** 130
Fyffes Plc, 38 196–99, 201
Fytek, S.A. de C.V., **66** 42

G

G&G Shops, Inc., **8** 425–26
G&K Services, Inc., 16 228–30; 21 115
G&L Inc., **16** 202; **43** 170
G&O Manufacturing Company, Inc. *see* TransPro, Inc.
G&R Pasta Co., Inc., **II** 512
G.B. Lewis Company, **8** 359
G. Bruss GmbH and Co. KG, **26** 141
G.C. Industries, **52** 186
G.C. Murphy Company, **9** 21
G.C. Smith, **I** 423
G.D. Searle & Co., I 686–89; 12 186–89 (upd.); 34 177–82 (upd.)
G. Felsenthal & Sons, **17** 106
G.H. Bass & Co., **15** 406; **24** 383
G.H. Besselaar Associates, **30** 151
G.H. Rinck NV, **V** 49; **19** 122–23; **49** 111
G. Heileman Brewing Co., I 253–55; 10 169–70
G.I.E. Airbus Industrie, I 41–43; 12 190–92 (upd.)
G.I. Joe's, Inc., 30 221–23
G-III Apparel Group, Ltd., 22 222–24
G.J. Coles & Coy. Ltd., **20** 155
G.J. Hopkins, Inc. *see* The Branch Group, Inc.
G.L. Kelty & Co., **13** 168
G.L. Rexroth GmbH, **III** 566; **38** 298, 300
G. Leblanc Corporation, 55 149–52
G.M. Pfaff AG, **30** 419–20
G.P. Group, **12** 358
G.R. Foods, Inc. *see* Ground Round, Inc.
G.R. Herberger's Department Stores, **19** 324–25; **41** 343–44
G.S. Blodgett Corporation, 15 183–85; 22 350 *see also* Blodgett Holdings, Inc.
GABA Holding AG *see* Colgate-Palmolive Company.
Gabelli Asset Management Inc., 13 561; **30 211–14** *see also* Lynch Corporation.
Gables Residential Trust, 49 147–49
GAC *see* The Goodyear Tire & Rubber Company.
GAC Holdings L.P., **7** 204; **28** 164
Gadzooks, Inc., 18 188–90; 33 203
GAF, I 337–40; 22 225–29 (upd.)
Gage Marketing Group, 26 147–49; 27 21
Gaggenau Hausgeräte GmbH, **67** 81
Gagliardi Brothers, **13** 383
Gagnon & Associates, **74** 258
Gaiam, Inc., 41 174–77
Gain Technology, Inc., **10** 505
Gaines Furniture Manufacturing, Inc., **43** 315
Gainsco, Inc., 22 230–32
GalaGen Inc., **65** 216
Galardi Group, Inc., 72 145–47
Galas Harland, S.A., **17** 266, 268
Galavision, Inc., **24** 515–17; **54** 72
Galaxy Aerospace Co. L.P., **69** 216
Galaxy Carpet Mills Inc., **19** 276; **63** 300
Galaxy Energies Inc., **11** 28
Galaxy Nutritional Foods, Inc., 58 135–37
Galbreath Escott, **16** 474
Gale Research Co., *see* The Thomson Corporation
Galen Health Care, **15** 112; **35** 215–16
Galen Laboratories, **13** 160
Galerías Preciados, **26** 130
Galeries Lafayette S.A., V 57–59; 23 220–23 (upd.)
Galey & Lord, Inc., 20 242–45; 66 131–34 (upd.)
Gallaher Group Plc, 49 150–54 (upd.)
Gallaher Limited, V 398–400; 19 168–71 (upd.); 29 195
Gallatin Steel Company, **18** 380; **24** 144
Galleria Shooting Team, **62** 174
Gallo Winery *see* E. & J. Gallo Winery.
Gallop Johnson & Neuman, L.C., **26** 348
The Gallup Organization, 37 153–56; 41 196–97
Galoob Toys *see* Lewis Galoob Toys Inc.
GALP, **48** 117, 119
Galveston Daily News, **10** 3
GALVSTAR, L.P., **26** 530
Galway Irish Crystal Ltd. *see* Belleek Pottery Ltd.
Galyan's Trading Company, Inc., 47 142–44
Gamax Holding, **65** 230, 232
Gamble-Skogmo Inc., **13** 169; **25** 535
The Gambrinus Company, 29 219; **40 188–90**
Gambro AB, 49 155–57
Gamebusters, **41** 409
Gamesa Corporacion Tecnologica S.A., **19** 192; **73** 374–75
GameStop Corp., 69 185–89 (upd.)
GameTime, Inc., **19** 387; **27** 370–71
GAMI *see* Great American Management and Investment, Inc.
Gamlestaden, **9** 381–82
Gamma Capital Corp., **24** 3
Gammalink, **18** 143
Gander Mountain, Inc., 20 246–48
Gannett Company, Inc., IV 612–13; 7 190–92 (upd.); 30 215–17 (upd.); 66 135–38 (upd.)
Gannett Supply, **17** 282
Gantos, Inc., 17 199–201
The Gap, Inc., V 60–62; 18 191–94 (upd.); 55 153–57 (upd.)
GAR Holdings, **19** 78
Garamond Press, **23** 100
Garan, Inc., 16 231–33; 64 140–43 (upd.)
Garanti Bank, **65** 69
Garantie Mutuelle des Fonctionnaires, **21** 225
Garden Botanika, **11** 41
Garden City Newspapers Inc., **38** 308
Garden Escape, **26** 441
Garden Fresh Restaurant Corporation, 31 213–15
Garden of Eatin' Inc., **27** 198; **43** 218–19
Garden Ridge Corporation, 27 163–65
Garden State BancShares, Inc., **14** 472
Garden State Life Insurance Company, **10** 312; **27** 47–48
Garden State Paper, **38** 307–08
Gardenburger, Inc., 33 169–71; 76 160–63 (upd.)
Gardener's Eden, **17** 548–49

Homette Corporation, **30** 423
HomeVestors of America, Inc., **77** **195–198**
Homewood Suites, **9** 425–26
Hominal Developments Inc., **9** 512
Hon Hai Precision Industry Co., Ltd., **59** **234–36**
Hon Industries Inc., **13** **266–69** *see* HNI Corporation.
Honam Oil Refinery, **II** 53
Honda Giken Kogyo Kabushiki Kaisha *see* Honda Motor Company Limited.
Honda Motor Company Limited, **I** **174–76**; **10** **352–54 (upd.)**; **29** **239–42 (upd.)**; **34** 305–06; **36** 243; **55** 326; **59** 393–94, 397
Honey Bear Tree *see* Furth Pharmacy. Inc.
Honeywell Inc., **II** **40–43**; **12** **246–49 (upd.)**; **50** **231–35 (upd.)**
Hong Kong and China Gas Company Ltd., **73** **177–79**
Hong Kong Dragon Airlines Ltd., **18** 114; **66** **192–94**
Hong Kong Fortune, **62** 63
Hong Kong Industrial Co., Ltd., **25** 312
Hong Kong Island Line Co., **IV** 718
Hong Kong Mass Transit Railway Corp., **19** 111
Hong Kong Ming Wah Shipping Co., **52** 80
Hong Kong Resort Co., **IV** 718; **38** 320
Hong Kong Telecommunications Ltd., **6** **319–21**; **18** 114 *see also* Cable & Wireless HKT.
Hong Kong Telephone Company, **47** 177
Hong Leong Group, **26** 3, 5; **71** 231
Hongkong & Kowloon Wharf & Godown Company, **20** 312
Hongkong and Shanghai Banking Corporation Limited, **II** **296–99** *see also* HSBC Holdings plc.
Hongkong Electric Holdings Ltd., **6** **498–500**; **20** 134; **23** **278–81 (upd.)**; **47** 177
Hongkong Land Holdings Ltd., **IV** **699–701**; **47** **175–78 (upd.)**
Honolua Plantation Land Company, Inc., **29** 308
Honshu Paper Co., Ltd., **IV** **284–85**, 292, 297, 321, 326; **57** 274–75
Hood Rubber Company, **15** 488–89
Hood Sailmakers, Inc., **10** 215
Hoogovens *see* Koninklijke Nederlandsche Hoogovens en Staalfabricken NV.
Hook's Drug Stores, **9** 67
Hooker Corp., **19** 324
Hooker Furniture Corp. *see* Bassett Furniture Industries, Inc.
Hooper Holmes, Inc., **22** **264–67**
Hoorcomfort Nederland B.V., **56** 338
Hoosier Insurance Company, **51** 39
Hoosier Park L.P., **29** 118
Hooters of America, Inc., **18** **241–43**; **69** **211–14 (upd.)**
The Hoover Company, **12** 158, **250–52**; **15** 416, 418; **21** 383; **30** 75, 78; **40** **258–62 (upd.)**
Hoover Group Inc., **18** 11
Hoover Treated Wood Products, Inc., **12** 396
Hopkinsons Group *see* Carbo PLC.
Hopkinton LNG Corp., **14** 126
Hopper Soliday and Co. Inc., **14** 154
Hops Restaurant Bar and Brewery, **31** 41; **46** **233–36**
Hopwood & Company, **22** 427
Horace Mann Educators Corporation, **22** **268–70**
Horizon Air Industries, Inc. *see* Alaska Air Group, Inc.
Horizon Corporation, **8** 348
Horizon Group Inc., **27** 221
Horizon Healthcare Corporation, **25** 456
Horizon Holidays, **14** 36
Horizon Industries, **19** 275
Horizon Lamps, Inc., **48** 299
Horizon Organic Holding Corporation, **37** **195–99**
Horizon Travel Group, **8** 527
Horizon/CMS Healthcare Corp., **25** 111, 457; **33** 185
Horizons Laitiers, **25** 85
Hormel Foods Corporation, **18** **244–47 (upd.)**; **54** **164–69 (upd.)**; **59** 102
Horn Venture Partners, **22** 464
Hornbrook, Inc., **14** 112
Horne's, **16** 62
Horsehead Industries, Inc., **51** **165–67**
Horseshoe Gaming Holding Corporation, **62** **192–95**
Horsham Corp. *see* TrizecHahn.
Horst Breuer GmbH, **20** 363
Horst Salons Inc., **24** 56
Horten, **47** 107; **50** 117, 119
Hortifrut, S.A., **62** 154
Horton Homes, Inc., **25** **216–18**
Hoshienu Pharmaceutical Co. Ltd., **58** 134
Hoshino Gakki Co. Ltd., **55** **208–11**
Hosiery Corporation International *see* HCI Direct, Inc.
Hospal SA, **49** 156
Hospira, Inc., **71** **172–74**
Hospital Central Services, Inc., **56** **166–68**
Hospital Corporation of America, **III** **78–80**; **15** 112; **23** 153; **27** 237; **53** 345 *see also* HCA - The Healthcare Company.
Hospital Cost Consultants, **11** 113
Hospital Management Associates, Inc. *see* Health Management Associates, Inc.
Hospital Products, Inc., **10** 534
Hospital Specialty Co., **37** 392
Hospitality Franchise Systems, Inc., **11** **177–79** *see also* Cendant Corporation.
Hospitality Worldwide Services, Inc., **26** **196–98**
Hosposable Products, Inc. *see* Wyant Corporation.
Hoss's Steak and Sea House Inc., **68** **196–98**
Host America Corporation, **79** **202–206**
Host Communications Inc., **24** 404
Hot Dog Construction Co., **12** 372
Hot Dog on a Stick *see* HDOS Enterprises.
Hot Sam Co. *see* Mrs. Fields' Original Cookies, Inc.
Hot Shoppes Inc. *see* Marriott.
Hot Topic, Inc., **33** **202–04**
Hotel Corporation of America, **16** 337
Hotel Corporation of India, **27** 26
Hotel Properties Ltd., **71** **175–77**
Hotel Reservations Network, Inc., **47** 420
Hotels By Pleasant, **62** 276
HotJobs.com, Ltd. *see* Yahoo! Inc.
HotRail Inc., **36** 124
HotWired, **45** 200
Houbigant, **37** 270
Houchens Industries Inc., **51** **168–70**
Houghton Mifflin Company, **10** **355–57**; **26** 215; **36** **270–74 (upd.)**; **46** 441
Houlihan's Restaurant Group, **25** 546
Housatonic Power Co., **13** 182
House of Blues, **32** 241, 244
House of Fabrics, Inc., **21** **278–80**
House of Fraser PLC, **21** 353; **37** 6, 8; **45** **188–91**; **47** 173 *see also* Harrods Holdings.
House of Miniatures, **12** 264
House of Windsor, Inc., **9** 533
Household International, Inc., **II** **417–20**; **21** **281–86 (upd.)**
Household Rental Systems, **17** 234
Housing Development Finance Corporation, **20** 313
Housmex Inc., **23** 171
Houston Airport Leather Concessions LLC, **58** 369
Houston, Effler & Partners Inc., **9** 135
Houston Electric Light & Power Company, **44** 368
Houston Industries Incorporated, **V** **641–44**; **7** 376 *see also* Reliant Energy Inc.
Houston International Teleport, Inc., **11** 184
Houston Oil & Minerals Corp., **11** 440–41
Houston Pipe Line Company, **45** 21
Hoveringham Group, **III** 753; **28** 450
Hoving Corp., **14** 501
Hovnanian Enterprises, Inc., **29** **243–45**
Howard B. Stark Candy Co., **15** 325
Howard Flint Ink Company, **13** 227
Howard H. Sweet & Son, Inc., **14** 502
Howard Hughes Corporation, **63** 341
Howard Hughes Medical Institute, **39** **221–24**
Howard Hughes Properties, Ltd., **17** 317
Howard Humphreys, **13** 119
Howard Johnson International, Inc., **17** **236–39**; **72** **182–86 (upd.)**
Howard Research and Development Corporation, **15** 412, 414
Howard Schultz & Associates, Inc., **73** 266
Howard, Smith & Levin, **40** 126
Howden *see* Alexander Howden Group.
Howdy Company, **9** 177
Howe & Fant, Inc., **23** 82

Howe Sound Co., **12** 253
Howmedica, **29** 455
Howmet Corporation, 12 IV 253–55; **22** 506
Hoyle Products, **62** 384
Hoyt Archery Company, **10** 216
HP *see* Hewlett-Packard Company.
HPI Health Care Services, **49** 307–08
HQ Global Workplaces, Inc., **47** 331
HQ Office International, **8** 405; **23** 364
HRB Business Services, **29** 227
Hrubitz Oil Company, **12** 244
HSBC Holdings plc, 12 256–58; 26 199–204 (upd.)
HSG *see* Helikopter Services Group AS.
Hsiang-Li Investment Corp., **51** 123
HSN, 64 181–85 (upd.)
HSS Hire Service Group PLC, **45** 139–41
HTH, **12** 464
HTM Goedkoop, **26** 278–79; **55** 200
H2O Plus, **11** 41
Hua Bei Oxygen, **25** 82
Hua Yang Printing Holdings Co. Ltd., **60** 372
Hub Group, Inc., 26 533; **38 233–35**
Hub Services, Inc., **18** 366
Hubbard Air Transport, **10** 162
Hubbard, Baker & Rice, **10** 126
Hubbard Broadcasting Inc., 24 226–28; 79 207–212 (upd.)
Hubbard Construction Co., **23** 332
Hubbell Inc., 9 286–87; 31 257–59 (upd.); 76 183–86 (upd.)
Huck Manufacturing Company, **22** 506
Hudepohl-Schoenling Brewing Co., **18** 72; **50** 114
Hudson Automobile Company, **18** 492
The Hudson Bay Mining and Smelting Company, Limited, 12 259–61
Hudson Foods Inc., 13 270–72
Hudson Housewares Corp., **16** 389
Hudson I.C.S., **58** 53
Hudson Pharmaceutical Corp., **31** 347
Hudson River Bancorp, Inc., 41 210–13
Hudson Software, **13** 481
Hudson's *see* Target Corporation.
Hudson's Bay Company, V 79–81; 25 219–22 (upd.)
Hue International, **8** 324
Hueppe Duscha, **III** 571; **20** 362
Huf-North America, **73** 325
Huffman Manufacturing Company, **7** 225–26
Huffy Bicycles Co., **19** 383
Huffy Corporation, 7 225–27; 26 184, 412; **30 239–42 (upd.)**
Hugerot, **19** 50
Hugh O'Neill Auto Co., **12** 309
Hughes Air West, **25** 421
Hughes Aircraft Corporation, **7** 426–27; **9** 409; **10** 327; **13** 356, 398; **15** 528, 530; **21** 201; **23** 134; **24** 442; **25** 86, 223; **30** 175 *see also* GM Hughes Electronics Corporation.
Hughes Communications, Inc., **13** 398; **18** 211
Hughes Corp., **18** 535
Hughes Electronics Corporation, 25 223–25
Hughes Helicopter, **26** 431; **46** 65
Hughes Hubbard & Reed LLP, 44 230–32
Hughes Markets, Inc., 22 271–73
Hughes Network Systems Inc., **21** 239
Hughes Properties, Inc., **17** 317
Hughes Space and Communications Company, **33** 47–48
Hughes Supply, Inc., 14 246–47; 39 360
Hughes Television Network, **11** 184
Hughes Tool Co. *see* Baker Hughes Incorporated.
Hugo Boss AG, 48 206–09
Hugo Neu Corporation, **19** 381–82
Hugo Stinnes GmbH, **8** 69, 494–95; **50** 168
Huhtamäki Oyj, 30 396, 398; **64 186–88**
HUK-Coburg, 58 169–73
The Hull Group, L.L.C., **51** 148
Hulman & Company, 44 233–36; 46 245
Hüls A.G., I 349–50 *see also* Degussa-Hüls AG.
Hulsbeck and Furst GmbH, **73** 325
Hulton, **17** 397
Hulton Getty, **31** 216–17
Human Services Computing, Inc. *see* Epic Systems Corporation.
Humana Inc., III 81–83; 24 229–32 (upd.)
The Humane Society of the United States, 54 170–73
Humanetics Corporation, **29** 213
Humanities Software, **39** 341
Humberside Sea & Land Services, **31** 367
Humble Oil & Refining Company *see* Exxon.
Hummel International A/S, 68 199–201
Hummel Lanolin Corporation, **45** 126
Hummel-Reise, **44** 432
Hummer, Winblad Venture Partners, **36** 157; **69** 265; **74** 168
Hummingbird, **18** 313
Humongous Entertainment, Inc., **31** 238–40
Humps' n Horns, **55** 312
Hunco Ltd., **IV** 640; **26** 273
Hungarian-Soviet Civil Air Transport Joint Stock Company *see* Mal&aacutev Plc.
Hungarian Telephone and Cable Corp., 75 193–95
Hungry Howie's Pizza and Subs, Inc., 25 226–28
Hungry Minds, Inc. *see* John Wiley & Sons, Inc.
Hunt Consolidated, Inc., 7 228–30; 27 215–18 (upd.)
Hunt Manufacturing Company, 12 262–64
Hunt-Wesson, Inc., 17 240–42
Hunter-Douglas, **8** 235
Hunter Fan Company, 13 273–75
Hunting plc, 78 163–166
Huntingdon Life Sciences Group plc, 42 182–85
Huntington Bancshares Inc., 11 180–82
Huntington Learning Centers, Inc., 55 212–14
Huntleigh Technology PLC, 77 199–202
Hunton & Williams, 35 223–26
Huntsman Chemical Corporation, 8 261–63; 9 305
Huntstown Power Company Ltd., **64** 404
Hupp Motor Car Company, **8** 74; **10** 261
Hurd & Houghton, **10** 355
Huron Steel Company, Inc., **16** 357
Hurricane Hydrocarbons Ltd., 54 174–77
Huse Food Group, **14** 352
Husky Energy Inc., 47 179–82; 49 203
Husky Oil Ltd., **IV** 695; **18** 253–54; **19** 159
Husqvarna AB, **53** 126–27
Husqvarna Forest & Garden Company, **13** 564
Hussmann Corporation, **I** 457–58; **7** 429–30; **10** 554; **13** 268; **22** 353–54; **67** 299
Hutcheson & Grundy, **29** 286
Hutchinson-Mapa, **IV** 560
Hutchinson Technology Incorporated, 18 248–51; 63 190–94 (upd.)
Hutchison Microtel, **11** 548
Hutchison Whampoa Limited, 18 252–55; 49 199–204 (upd.)
Huth Inc., **56** 230
Huth Manufacturing Corporation, **10** 414
Hüttenwerke Kayser AG, **62** 253
Huttepain, **61** 155
Huttig Building Products, Inc., 73 180–83
HVB Group, 59 237–44 (upd.)
Hvide Marine Incorporated, 22 274–76
HWI *see* Hardware Wholesalers, Inc.
Hy-Form Products, Inc., **22** 175
Hy-Vee, Inc., 36 275–78; 42 432
Hyatt-Clark Industries Inc., **45** 170
Hyatt Corporation, III 96–97; 16 273–75 (upd.) *see* Global Hyatt Corporation.
Hyatt Legal Services, **20** 435; **29** 226
Hyco-Cascade Pty. Ltd. *see* Cascade Corporation.
Hycor Biomedical Inc. *see* Stratagene Corporation.
Hyde Athletic Industries, Inc., 17 243–45 *see* Saucony Inc.
Hyde Company, A.L., **7** 116–17
Hyder Investments Ltd., **51** 173
Hyder plc, 34 219–21; 52 375
Hydra Computer Systems, Inc., **13** 201
Hydrac GmbH, **38** 300
Hydril Company, 46 237–39
Hydro-Aire Incorporated, **8** 135
Hydro Carbide Corp., **19** 152
Hydro-Carbon Light Company, **9** 127
Hydro Electric, **19** 389–90; **49** 363–64
Hydro-Electric Power Commission of Ontario, **6** 541; **9** 461
Hydro Med Sciences, **13** 367
Hydro-Quebéc, 6 501–03; 32 266–69 (upd.)

J

John Paul Mitchell Systems, 24 250–52
John Pew & Company, **13** 243
John Q. Hammons Hotels, Inc., 24 253–55
John R. Figg, Inc., **II** 681
John Rogers Co., **9** 253
John Sands, **22** 35
John Schroeder Lumber Company, **25** 379
John Sexton & Co., **26** 503
John Strange Paper Company, **8** 358
John Swire & Sons Ltd. *see* Swire Pacific Ltd.
John W. Danforth Company, 48 237–39
John Wanamaker, **22** 110
John Wiley & Sons, Inc., 17 270–72; 65 186–90 (upd.)
John Yokley Company, **11** 194
John Zink Company, **22** 3–4; **25** 403
Johnny Rockets Group, Inc., 31 277–81; 76 220–24 (upd.)
Johns Manville Corporation, **7** 293; **11** 420; **19** 211–12; **61** 307–08; **64 209–14 (upd.)**
Johnsen, Jorgensen and Wettre, **14** 249
Johnson *see* Axel Johnson Group.
Johnson & Higgins, 14 277–80
Johnson and Howe Furniture Corporation, **33** 151
Johnson & Johnson, III 35–37; 8 281–83 (upd.); 36 302–07 (upd.); 75 212–18 (upd.)
Johnson Brothers, **12** 528
Johnson Controls, Inc., III 534–37; 26 227–32 (upd.); 59 248–54 (upd.)
Johnson Engineering Corporation, **37** 365
Johnson Matthey PLC, IV 117–20; 16 290–94 (upd.); 49 230–35 (upd.)
Johnson Outdoors, Inc., **74** 222
Johnson Products Co., Inc., **11** 208; **31** 89
Johnson Publishing Company, Inc., 28 212–14; 72 204–07 (upd.)
Johnson Wax *see* S.C. Johnson & Son, Inc.
Johnson Worldwide Associates, Inc., 24 530; **28 215–17**, 412
Johnsonville Sausage L.L.C., 63 216–19
Johnston Coca-Cola Bottling Company of Chattanooga, **13** 163–64
Johnston Industries, Inc., 15 246–48
Johnston, Lemon & Co., **53** 134
Johnston Press plc, 35 242–44
Johnston Sport Architecture Inc., **63** 91
Johnstown America Industries, Inc., 23 305–07
Johnstown Sanitary Dairy, **13** 393
Joint Environment for Digital Imaging, **50** 322
Joker S.A., **56** 103
Jolly Hotels *see* Compagnia Italiana dei Jolly Hotels S.p.A.
Jolly Time *see* American Pop Corn Company.
Jonathan Logan Inc., **13** 536
Jonell Shoe Manufacturing Corporation, **13** 360
Jones & Babson, Inc., **14** 85
Jones & Johnson, **14** 277
Jones & Laughlin Steel Corp., **I** 489–91; **IV** 228
Jones Apparel Group, Inc., 11 216–18; 39 244–47 (upd.)
Jones Brothers Tea Co., **7** 202
Jones, Day, Reavis & Pogue, 33 226–29
Jones Environmental, **11** 361
Jones Financial Companies, L.P. *see* Edward Jones.
Jones Intercable, Inc., 21 307–09
Jones Janitor Service, **25** 15
Jones Lang LaSalle Incorporated, 49 236–38
Jones Medical Industries, Inc., 24 256–58; 34 460
Jones Motor Co., **10** 44
Jones-Rodolfo Corp. *see* Cutter & Buck, Inc.
Jones Soda Co., 69 218–21
Jonkoping & Vulcan, **12** 462
Jordache Enterprises, Inc., 15 201–02; **23 308–10**
The Jordan Company LP, 70 140–42
Jordan Industries, Inc., 36 308–10
Jordan Valley Electric Cooperative, **12** 265
Jos. A. Bank Clothiers, Inc., II 560; **12** 411; **31 282–85**
The Joseph & Feiss Company, **48** 209
Joseph Leavitt Corporation, **9** 20
Joseph Littlejohn & Levy, **27** 204; **53** 241
Joseph Lumber Company, **25** 379
Joseph Malecki Corp., **24** 444–45
Joseph Schlitz Brewing Company, **25** 281
Joseph T. Ryerson & Son, Inc., 15 249–51; 19 381 *see also* Ryerson Tull, Inc.
Joseph Transportation Inc., **55** 347
Josephson International, **27** 392; **43** 235
Joshin Denki, **13** 481
Joshua's Christian Bookstores, **31** 435–36; **51** 132
Josiah Wedgwood and Sons Limited *see* Waterford Wedgewood plc..
Jostens, Inc., 7 255–57; 25 252–55 (upd.); 73 196–200 (upd.)
Jotcham & Kendall Ltd. *see* Seddon Group Ltd.
JOULÉ Inc., 58 197–200
Journal Register Company, 29 261–63
Journal Star Printing Company, **64** 237
Journey's End Corporation, **14** 107
Jove Publications, Inc., **IV** 623; **12** 224
Jovi, **II** 652
Joy Planning Co., **III** 533
Joy Technologies Inc., **II** 17; **26** 70; **38** 227
Joyce International, Inc., **16** 68
JP Foodservice Inc., **24** 445
JP Household Supply Co. Ltd., **IV** 293
JP Planning Co. Ltd., **IV** 293
JP Realty Inc., **57** 157
JPF Holdings, Inc. *see* U.S. Foodservice.
JPI, 49 239–41
JPS Automotive L.P., **17** 182–84
JPS Textile Group, Inc., 28 218–20
JPT Publishing, **8** 528
JR & F SA, **53** 32
JR Central, **43** 103
Jr. Food Stores, Inc., **51** 170
JR Tokai, **43** 103
JSC MMC Norilsk Nickel, 48 300–02
JSP Corporation, 74 161–64
JT Aquisitions, **II** 661
JTL Corporation, **13** 162–63
JTN Acquisition Corp., **19** 233
JTS Corporation *see* Atari Corporation.
j2 Global Communications, Inc., 75 219–21
Judel Glassware Co., Inc., **14** 502
Judge & Dolph, Ltd. *see* Wirtz Corporation.
The Judge Group, Inc., 51 174–76
Judson Dunaway Corp., **12** 127
Judson Steel Corp., **13** 97
Jugend & Volk, **14** 556
Juice Works, **26** 57
Jujamycn, **24** 439
Jujo Paper Co., Ltd., IV 297–98
JuJu Media, Inc., **41** 385
Julius Baer Holding AG, 52 203–05
Julius Blüthner PianofortefabricGmbH, 78 185–188
Julius Garfinckel & Co., Inc., **22** 110
Julius Meinl International AG, 53 177–80
Jumbo Food Stores *see* Shoppers Food Warehouse Corp.
Jumping-Jacks Shoes, Inc., **17** 390
Junghans Uhren, **10** 152
Juniper Networks, Inc., 43 251–55
Juno Lighting, Inc., 30 266–68
Juno Online Services, Inc., 38 269–72 *see also* United Online, Inc.
Juovo Pignone, **13** 356
Jupiter National, **15** 247–48; **19** 166
Jupiter Partners II, **62** 265
Jupiter Tyndall, **47** 84
Jupitermedia Corporation, 75 222–24
Jurgensen's, **17** 558
Juristförlaget, **14** 556
Jurys Doyle Hotel Group plc, 64 215–17
Jusco Car Life Company, **23** 290
JUSCO Co., Ltd., V 96–99 *see also* AEON Co., Ltd.
Jusco Group, **31** 430
Just Born, Inc., 32 305–07
Just For Feet, Inc., 19 228–30
Just Squeezed, **31** 350
Just Toys, Inc., **29** 476
Justin Industries, Inc., 19 231–33
Juventus F.C. S.p.A, 44 387–88; **53 181–83**
JVC *see* Victor Company of Japan, Ltd.
JW Aluminum Company, **22** 544
JW Bernard & Zn., **39** 203
JWD Group, Inc., **48** 238
JWP Inc., 9 300–02 *see also* EMCOR Group Inc.
JWT Group Inc., I 19–21 *see also* WPP Group plc.

JZC *see* John Zink Company.

K

K&B Inc., 12 286–88
K&F Manufacturing *see* Fender Musical Instruments.
K & G Men's Center, Inc., 21 310–12
K&K Insurance Group, **26** 487
K&K Toys, Inc., **23** 176
K&M Associates L.P., **16** 18; **43** 19
K & R Warehouse Corporation, **9** 20
K&U Enterprise, **75** 230
K-C Aviation, **III** 41; **16** 304; **43** 258
K-Graphics Inc., **16** 306; **43** 261
K-Group, **27** 261
K-H Corporation, **7** 260
K Shoes Ltd., **52** 57–58
K-Swiss, Inc., 33 243–45
K-tel International, Inc., 21 325–28
K-III Holdings *see* Primedia Inc.
K.F. Kline Co., **7** 145; **22** 184
K.H.S. Musical Instrument Co. Ltd., **53** 214
K.H. Wheel Company, **27** 202
K. Hattori & Co., Ltd. *see* Seiko Corporation.
K.J. International Inc., **70** 74, 76
k.k. Staatsbahnen *see* Österreichische Bundesbahnen GmbH.
K Line *see* Kawasaki Kisen Kaisha, Ltd.
K-Line Pharmaceuticals Ltd. *see* Taro Phramaceutical Industries Ltd.
K.O. Lester Co., **31** 359, 361
K.P. American, **55** 305
K.W. Muth Company, **17** 305
KA Teletech, **27** 365
Ka Wah AMEV Insurance, **III** 200–01
Kabelvision AB, **26** 331–33
Kable News Company *see* AMREP Corporation.
Kable Printing Co., **13** 559
Kaepa, **16** 546
Kafte Inc., **28** 63
Kagle Home Health Care, **11** 282
Kagoshima Central Research Laboratory, **21** 330
Kahan and Lessin, **II** 624–25
Kaiser + Kraft GmbH, **27** 175
Kaiser Aluminum & Chemical Corporation, IV 121–23 *see also* ICF Kaiser International, Inc.
Kaiser Foundation Health Plan, Inc., 53 184–86
Kaiser Packaging, **12** 377
Kaiser Permanente Corp. *see* Kaiser Foundation Health Plan, Inc.
Kaiser Steel, **IV** 59
Kaiser's Kaffee Geschäft AG, **27** 461
Kajaani Oy, **IV** 350
Kajima Corporation, I 577–78; 51 177–79
Kal Kan Foods, Inc., 22 298–300
Kalamazoo Limited, **50** 377
Kaldveer & Associates, **14** 228
Kaliningradnefteprodukt, **48** 378
Kalitta Group, **22** 311
Kalua Koi Corporation, **7** 281
Kaman Corporation, 12 289–92; 42 204–08 (upd.)
Kaman Music Corporation, 68 205–07
Kamewa Group, **27** 494, 496
Kaminski/Engles Capital Corp. *see* Suiza Foods Corporation.
Kammer Valves, A.G., **17** 147
Kampgrounds of America, Inc., 33 230–33
Kamps AG, 44 251–54
Kana Software, Inc., 51 180–83
Kanagawa Chuo Kotsu Co., Ltd., **68** 281
Kanan Enterprises Inc., **74** 167
Kanda Shokai, **16** 202; **43** 171
Kanders Florida Holdings, Inc., **27** 50
Kane Foods, **III** 43
Kane-Miller Corp., **12** 106
Kanebo, Ltd., 53 187–91
Kanematsu Corporation, IV 442–44; 24 259–62 (upd.)
Kangaroo *see* Seino Transportation Company, Ltd.
Kanoldt, **24** 75
Kanpai Co. Ltd., **55** 375
The Kansai Electric Power Company, Inc., V 645–48; 62 196–200 (upd.)
Kansai Plast Corporation, **74** 163
Kansallis-Osake-Pankki, II 302–03
Kansas City Ingredient Technologies, Inc., **49** 261
Kansas City Power & Light Company, 6 510–12, 592; **12** 541–42; **50** 38 *see also* Great Plains Energy Incorporated.
Kansas City Securities Corporation, **22** 541
Kansas City Southern Industries, Inc., 6 400–02; 26 233–36 (upd.); 29 333; **47** 162; **50** 208–09; **57** 194
Kansas City White Goods Company *see* Angelica Corporation.
Kansas Fire & Casualty Co., **III** 214
Kansas Public Service Company, **12** 541
Kansas Sand and Concrete, Inc., **72** 233
Kansas Utilities Company, **6** 580
The Kantar Group, **48** 442
Kanzaki Paper Manufacturing Co., **IV** 285, 293
Kao Corporation, III 38–39; 20 315–17 (upd.); 79 225–230 (upd.)
Kaolin Australia Pty Ltd. *see* English China Clays Ltd.
Kapalua Land Company, Ltd., **29** 307–08
Kaplan Educational Centers, **12** 143
Kaplan, Inc., 42 209–12, 290
Kaplan Musical String Company, **48** 231
Kapok Computers, **47** 153
Karan Co. *see* Donna Karan Company.
Karastan Bigelow, **19** 276
Karl Kani Infinity, Inc., 49 242–45
Karl Schmidt Unisia, Inc., **56** 158
Karlsberg Brauerei GmbH & Co KG, 41 220–23
Karmelkorn Shoppes, Inc., **10** 371, 373; **39** 232, 235
Karrosseriewerke Weinsberg GmbH *see* ASC, Inc.
Karstadt Aktiengesellschaft, V 100–02; 19 234–37 (upd.)
Karstadt Quelle AG, 57 195–201 (upd.)
Karsten Manufacturing Corporation, 51 184–86
Kasai Securities, **II** 434
Kasco Corporation, **28** 42, 45
Kash n' Karry Food Stores, Inc., 20 318–20; 44 145
Kashi Company, **50** 295
Kashima Chlorine & Alkali Co., Ltd., **64** 35
Kasmarov, **9** 18
Kaspare Cohn Commercial & Savings Bank *see* Union Bank of California.
Kasper A.S.L., Ltd., 40 276–79
Kasuga Radio Company *see* Kenwood Corporation
Kasumi Co., Ltd., **68** 9
Kat-Em International Inc., **16** 125
Katabami Kogyo Co. Ltd., **51** 179
Kate Industries, **74** 202
kate spade LLC, 68 208–11
Katharine Gibbs Schools Inc., **22** 442
Katherine Beecher Candies, Inc. *see* Warrell Corporation.
Kathy's Ranch Markets, **19** 500–01
Katies, **V** 35
Kativo Chemical Industries Ltd., **8** 239; **32** 256
Katy Industries Inc., I 472–74; 51 187–90 (upd.)
Katz Communications, Inc., 6 32–34
Katz Media Group, Inc., 35 232, **245–48**
Kaufhalle AG, **V** 104; **23** 311; **41** 186–87
Kaufhof Warenhaus AG, V 103–05; 23 311–14 (upd.)
Kaufman and Broad Home Corporation, 8 284–86; 11 481–83 *see also* KB Home.
Kaufmann Department Stores, Inc. *see* The May Department Stores Company.
Kaufring AG, 35 249–52
Oy Kaukas Ab *see* UPM-Kymmene
Kaukauna Cheese Inc., **23** 217, 219
Kauppiaitten Oy, **8** 293
Kawai Musical Instruments Manufacturing Co.,Ltd., 78 189–192
Kawamata, **11** 350
Kawasaki Denki Seizo, **II** 22
Kawasaki Heavy Industries, Ltd., I 75; **III 538–40**, 756; **7** 232; **8** 72; **23** 290; **59** 397; **63 220–23 (upd.)**
Kawasaki Kisen Kaisha, Ltd., V 457–60; 56 177–81 (upd.)
Kawasaki Steel Corporation, IV 30, **124–25**, 154, 212–13; **13** 324; **19** 8
Kawecki Berylco Industries, **8** 78
Kawsmouth Electric Light Company *see* Kansas City Power & Light Company.
Kay-Bee Toy Stores, 15 252–53 *see also* KB Toys.
Kay Home Products, **17** 372
Kay Jewelers Inc., **61** 327
Kaydon Corporation, 18 274–76
Kaye, Scholer, Fierman, Hays & Handler, **47** 436
Kayex, **9** 251
Kaynar Manufacturing Company, **8** 366

Knightway Promotions Ltd., **64** 346
KNILM, **24** 397
Knogo Corp., **11** 444; **39** 78
Knoll Group Inc., **I** 202; **14 299–301**
Knorr-Bremse, **11** 31
Knorr Co *see* C.H. Knorr Co.
Knorr Foods Co., Ltd., **28** 10
The Knot, Inc., 74 168–71
Knott's Berry Farm, 18 288–90; **22** 130
Knowledge Learning Corporation, 51 197–99; **54** 191
Knowledge Systems Concepts, **11** 469
Knowledge Universe, Inc., 54 191–94
KnowledgeWare Inc., 9 309–11; **27** 491; **31 296–98 (upd.)**; **45** 206
Knox County Insurance, **41** 178
Knox Reeves Advertising Agency, **25** 90
Knoxville Glove Co., **34** 159
Knoxville Paper Box Co., Inc., **13** 442
KNP BT *see* Buhrmann NV.
KNP Leykam, **49** 352, 354
KNSM *see* Koninklijke Nederlandsche Stoomboot Maatschappij.
Knudsen & Sons, Inc., **11** 211
Knudsen Foods, **27** 330
Knutson Construction, **25** 331
KOA *see* Kampgrounds of America, Inc.
Koala Corporation, 44 260–62
Kobacker Co., **18** 414–15
Kobe Hankyu Company Ltd., **62** 170
Kobe Shipbuilding & Engine Works, **II** 57
Kobe Steel, Ltd., IV 129–31; **19 238–41 (upd.)**
Kobold *see* Vorwerk & Co.
Kobrand Corporation, **24** 308; **43** 402
Koç Holding A.S., I 478–80; **27** 188; **54 195–98 (upd.)**
Koch Enterprises, Inc., 29 215–17
Koch Industries, Inc., IV 448–49; **20 330–32 (upd.)**; **77 224–230 (upd.)**
Koch-Light Laboratories, **13** 239; **38** 203–04
Kockos Brothers, Inc., **II** 624
Kodak *see* Eastman Kodak Company.
Kodansha Ltd., IV 631–33; **38 273–76 (upd.)**
Koehring Company, **8** 545; **23** 299
Koehring Cranes & Excavators, **7** 513
Koei Real Estate Ltd. *see* Takashimaya Co., Limited.
Koenig & Bauer AG, 64 222–26
Koenig Plastics Co., **19** 414
Kogaku Co., Ltd., **48** 295
Kohl's Corporation, 9 312–13; **30 273–75 (upd.)**; **77 231–235 (upd.)**
Kohl's Food Stores, Inc., **I** 426–27; **16** 247, 249
Kohlberg Kravis Roberts & Co., 24 272–74; **56 190–94 (upd.)**
Kohler Company, 7 269–71; **32 308–12 (upd.)**
Kohler Mix Specialties, Inc. *see*Dean Foods.
Kohn Pedersen Fox Associates P.C., 57 213–16
Kokkola Chemicals Oy, **17** 362–63
Kokomo Gas and Fuel Company, **6** 533
Kokudo Corporation, **74** 301
Kokusai Kigyo Co. Ltd., **60** 301
Kolb-Lena, **25** 85
Kolker Chemical Works, Inc., **7** 308
The Koll Company, 8 300–02
Kollmorgen Corporation, 18 291–94
Kölnische Rückversicherungs- Gesellschaft AG, **24** 178
Komag, Inc., 11 234–35
Komatsu Ltd., III 545–46; **16 309–11 (upd.)**; **52 213–17 (upd.)**
Kompass Allgemeine Vermögensberatung, **51** 23
Konan Camera Institute, **III** 487
KONE Corporation, 27 267–70; **76 225–28 (upd.)**
Kongl. Elektriska Telegraf-Verket *see* Swedish Telecom.
Konica Corporation, III 547–50; **30 276–81 (upd.)**; **43** 284
König Brauerei GmbH & Co. KG, 35 256–58 (upd.)
Koninklijke Ahold N.V., II 641–42; **16 312–14 (upd.)**
Koninklijke Bols Wessanen, N.V., **29** 480–81; **57** 105
Koninklijke Grolsch BV *see* Royal Grolsch NV.
Koninklijke Hoogovens NV *see* Koninklijke Nederlandsche Hoogovens en Staalfabrieken NV.
Koninklijke Java-China Paketvaart Lijnen *see* Royal Interocean Lines.
NV Koninklijke KNP BT *see* Buhrmann NV.
Koninklijke KPN N.V. *see* Royal KPN N.V.
Koninklijke Luchtvaart Maatschappij N.V., I 107–09, 119, 121; **6** 105, 109–10; **14** 73; **28 224–27 (upd.)**
Koninklijke Nederlandsche Hoogovens en Staalfabrieken NV, IV 132–34; **49** 98, 101
Koninklijke Nederlandsche Stoomboot Maatschappij, **26** 241
N.V. Koninklijke Nederlandse Vliegtuigenfabriek Fokker, I 54–56; **28 327–30 (upd.)**
Koninklijke Nedlloyd N.V., 6 403–05; **26 241–44 (upd.)**
Koninklijke Numico N.V. *see* Royal Numico N.V.
Koninklijke Paketvaart Maatschappij, **26** 242
Koninklijke Philips Electronics N.V., 50 297–302 (upd.)
Koninklijke PTT Nederland NV, V 299–301; **27** 471–72, 475 *see also* Royal KPN NV.
Koninklijke Van Ommeren, **22** 275
Koninklijke Vendex KBB N.V. (Royal Vendex KBB N.V.), 62 206–09 (upd.)
Koninklijke Wessanen nv, II 527–29; **54 199–204 (upd.)**
Koninklijke West-Indische Maildienst, **26** 242
Konishiroku Honten Co., Ltd., **III** 487, 547–49
Konrad Hornschuch AG, **31** 161–62
Koo Koo Roo, Inc., 25 263–65
Kookmin Bank, 58 206–08
Koop Nautic Holland, **41** 412
Koor Industries Ltd., II 47–49; **22** 501; **25 266–68 (upd.)**; **54** 363; **68 222–25 (upd.)**
Koors Perry & Associates, Inc., **24** 95
Koortrade, **II** 48
Kop-Coat, Inc., **8** 456
Kopin Corp., **13** 399
Köpings Mekaniska Verkstad, **26** 10
Koppel Steel, **26** 407
Koppers Industries, Inc., I 354–56; **26 245–48 (upd.)**
Koracorp Industries Inc., **16** 327
Koramic Roofing Products N.V., **70** 363
Korbel Champagne Cellers *see* F. Korbel & Bros. Inc.
Körber AG, 60 190–94
Korea Automotive Fuel Systems Ltd., **13** 555
Korea Automotive Motor Corp., **16** 436; **43** 319
Korea Electric Power Corporation (Kepco), 56 195–98
Korea Ginseng Corporation *see* KT&G Corporation.
Korea Independent Energy Corporation, **62** 175
Korea Steel Co., **III** 459
Korea Tobacco & Ginseng Corporation *see* KT&G Corporation.
Korean Air Lines Co. Ltd., 6 98–99; **24** 443; **27 271–73 (upd.)**; **46** 40
Korean Development Bank, **III** 459
Korean Life Insurance Company, Ltd., **62** 175
Koret of California, Inc., 62 210–13
Kori Kollo Corp., **23** 41
Korn/Ferry International, 34 247–49
Koro Corp., **19** 414
Korrekt Gebäudereinigung, **16** 420; **43** 307
KorrVu, **14** 430
Kortbetalning Servo A.B., **II** 353
Kortgruppen Eurocard-Köpkort A.B., **II** 353
Korvettes, E.J., **14** 426
Kos Pharmaceuticals, Inc., 63 232–35
Koss Corporation, 38 277–79
Kosset Carpets, Ltd., **9** 467
Kotobukiya Co., Ltd., V 113–14; **56 199–202 (upd.)**
Kowa Metal Manufacturing Co., **III** 758
Koyland Ltd., **64** 217
KP Corporation, **74** 163
KPM *see* Koninklijke Paketvaart Maatschappij.
KPMG International, 7 266; **10** 115, **385–87**; **29** 176; **33 234–38 (upd.)**
KPN *see* Koninklijke PTT Nederland N.V.
KPR Holdings Inc., **23** 203
KPS Special Situations Fund, L.P., **69** 360–62

L

Lithia Motors, Inc., **41** **238–40**
Lithonia Lighting, Inc., **54** 252, 254–55
LitleNet, **26** 441
Littelfuse, Inc., **26** **266–69**
Little, Brown & Company, **IV** 675; **7** 528; **10** 355; **36** 270
Little Caesar Enterprises, Inc., **7** **278–79**; **24** **293–96 (upd.)** *see also* Ilitch Holdings Inc.
Little General, **II** 620; **12** 179, 200
Little Giant Pump Company, **8** 515
Little League Baseball, Incorporated, **23** 450
Little Leather Library, **13** 105
Little, Royal, **8** 545; **13** 63
Little Switzerland, Inc., **60** **202–04**
Little Tikes Company, **13** **317–19**; **62** **231–34 (upd.)**
Littlewoods Financial Services, **30** 494
Littlewoods plc, **V** **117–19**; **42** **228–32 (upd.)** **Litton Industries Inc.**, **I** **484–86**; **11** **263–65 (upd.)** *see also* Avondale Industries.
Litwin Engineers & Constructors, **8** 546
LIVE Entertainment Inc., **18** 64, 66; **20** **347–49**; **24** 349
LiveAquaria.com., **62** 108
Liverpool Daily Post & Echo Ltd., **49** 405
Liverpool Mexico S.A., **16** 216
Living Arts, Inc., **41** 174
Living Centers of America, **13** 49
Living Videotext, **10** 508
LivingWell Inc., **12** 326
Liz Claiborne, Inc., **8** **329–31**; **25** **291–94 (upd.)**
LKQ Corporation, **71** **201–03**
Lledo Collectibles Ltd., **60** 372
LLJ Distributing Company *see* Spartan Stores Inc.
Lloyd Aereo de Bolivia, **6** 97
Lloyd Creative Staffing, **27** 21
Lloyd George Management, **18** 152
Lloyd Instruments, Ltd., **29** 460–61
Lloyd Italico, **III** 351
Lloyd Thompson Group plc, **20** 313
Lloyd Triestino company, **50** 187
Lloyd-Truax Ltd., **21** 499
Lloyd's, **III** **278–81**; **22** **315–19 (upd.)**; **74** **172–76 (upd.)**
Lloyd's Electronics, **14** 118
Lloyds Chemists plc, **27** 177
Lloyds Life Assurance, **III** 351
Lloyds TSB Group plc, **II** **306–09**; **47** **224–29 (upd.)**
LLP Group plc, **58** 189
LM Ericsson *see* Telefonaktiebolaget LM Ericsson.
LMC Metals, **19** 380
LME *see* Telefonaktiebolaget LM Ericsson.
LNM Group, **30** 252
Lo-Cost, **II** 609
Lo-Vaca Gathering Co., **7** 553
Loblaw Companies Limited, **II** 631–32; **19** 116; **43** **268–72**; **51** 301 *see also* George Weston Limited.
Local Data, Inc., **10** 97
Lockhart Corporation, **12** 564
Lockheed Martin Corporation, **I** **64–66**; **11** **266–69 (upd.)**; **15** **283–86 (upd.)**
Locksmith Publishing Corp., **56** 75
Lockwood Banc Group, Inc., **11** 306
Lockwood Greene Engineers, Inc., **17** 377
Lockwood National Bank, **25** 114
Lockwood Technology, Inc., **19** 179
Loctite Corporation, **8** **332–34**; **30** **289–91 (upd.)**; **34** 209
Lodding Engineering, **7** 521
Lodestar Group, **10** 19
Lodge Plus, Ltd., **25** 430
LodgeNet Entertainment Corporation, **26** 441; **28** **240–42**
The Lodging Group, **12** 297; **48** 245
Loehmann's Inc., **24** **297–99**
The Loewen Group, Inc., **16** **342–44**; **40** **292–95 (upd.)** *see also* Alderwoods Group Inc.
Loewenstein Furniture Group, Inc., **21** 531–33
Loews Cineplex Entertainment Corp., **37** 64
Loews Corporation, **I** **487–88**; **12** **316–18 (upd.)**; **36** **324–28 (upd.)**
LOF Plastics, Inc. *see* Libbey-Owens-Ford.
Loffland Brothers Company, **9** 364
Logan's Roadhouse, Inc., **29** **290–92**
Loganair Ltd., **68** **235–37**
Logic Modeling, **11** 491
Logica plc, **14** **317–19**; **37** **230–33 (upd.)**
Logicon Inc., **20** **350–52**; **45** 68, 310
Logility, **25** 20, 22
Logistics.com, Inc. *see* Manhattan Associates, Inc.
Logistics Data Systems, **13** 4
Logistics Industries Corporation, **39** 77
Logistics Management Systems, Inc., **8** 33
Logitech International S.A., **9** 116; **28** **243–45**; **69** **242–45 (upd.)**
LOGIX Benelux, **74** 143
Logo Athletic, Inc., **35** 363
Logo 7, Inc., **13** 533
Logon, Inc., **14** 377
Lohja Corporation, **61** 295
LoJack Corporation, **48** **269–73**
Lojas Americanas S.A., **77** **240–243**
Lojas Arapuã S.A., **22** **320–22**; **61** **175–78 (upd.)**
Loma Linda Foods, **14** 557–58
Lomak Petroleum, Inc., **24** 380
Lomas & Nettleton Financial Corporation, **III** 249; **11** 122
London & Hull, **III** 211
London & Midland Bank *see* Midland Bank plc.
London & Overseas Freighters plc *see* Frontline Ltd.
London & Rhodesia Mining & Land Company *see* Lonrho Plc.
London and Scottish Marine Oil, **11** 98
London & Western Trust, **39** 90
London Assurance Corp., **55** 331
London Brick Co., **14** 249
London Brokers Ltd., **6** 290
London Buses Limited *see* London Regional Transport.
London Cargo Group, **25** 82
London Central, **28** 155–56
London Drugs Ltd., **46** **270–73**
London East India Company, **12** 421
London Electricity, **12** 443; **41** 141
London Fog Industries, Inc., **29** **293–96**
London Insurance Group, **III** 373; **36** 372
London International Group *see* SSL International plc.
London Precision Machine & Tool, Ltd., **39** 32
London Records, **23** 390
London Regional Transport, **6** **406–08**
London Rubber Co., **49** 380
London Scottish Bank plc, **70** **160–62**
London South Partnership, **25** 497
London Stock Exchange Limited, **34** **253–56**; **37** 131–33
London Transport, **19** 111
Londontown Manufacturing Company *see* London Fog Industries, Inc.
Lone Star Brewing Co., **I** 255
Lone Star Funds, **59** 106
Lone Star Industries, **23** 326; **35** 154
Lone Star Steakhouse & Saloon, Inc., **21** 250; **51** **227–29**
Lone Star Technologies, Inc., **22** 3
Lonely Planet Publications Pty Ltd., **55** **253–55**
Long Distance Discount Services, Inc., **8** 310; **27** 305
Long Distance/USA, **9** 479
Long Island Bancorp, Inc., **16** **345–47**; **44** 33
Long Island Cable Communication Development Company, **7** 63
Long Island College Hospital *see* Continuum Health Partners, Inc.
Long Island Lighting Company, **V** **652–54**; **27** 264
Long Island Power Authority, **27** 265
The Long Island Rail Road Company, **68** **238–40**
Long John Silver's, **57** **224–29 (upd.)**
Long John Silver's Restaurants Inc., **13** **320–22**; **58** 384
Long Lac Mineral Exploration, **9** 282
Long Life Fish Food Products, **12** 230
Long-Term Credit Bank of Japan, Ltd., **II** **310–11**, 338, 369
Long Valley Power Cooperative, **12** 265
The Longaberger Company, **12** **319–21**; **44** **267–70 (upd.)**
Longchamps, Inc., **38** 385; **41** 388
LongHorn Steaks Inc., **19** 341
Longman Group Ltd., **IV** 611, 658
Longs Drug Stores Corporation, **V** **120**; **25** **295–97 (upd.)**
Longview Fibre Company, **8** **335–37**; **37** **234–37 (upd.)**
Lonmin plc, **66** **211–16 (upd.)**
Lonrho Plc, **10** 170; **21** **351–55**; **43** 38; **53** 153, 202 *see also* Lonmin plc.
Lonza Group Ltd., **73** **212–14**
Lookers plc, **71** **204–06**
Loomis Armored Car Service Limited, **45** 378

M

Marcade Group *see* Aris Industries, Inc.
Marcam Coporation *see* MAPICS, Inc.
Marceau Investments, **II** 356
March-Davis Bicycle Company, **19** 383
March of Dimes, 31 322–25
March Plasma Systems, Inc., **48** 299
Marchand, **13** 27
Marchands Ro-Na Inc. *see* RONA, Inc.
Marchesi Antinori SRL, 42 245–48
Marchex, Inc., 72 222–24
marchFIRST, Inc., 34 261–64
Marchland Holdings Ltd., **II** 649
Marchon Eyewear, **22** 123
Marciano Investments, Inc., **24** 157
Marcillat, **19** 49
Marco Acquisition Corporation, **62** 268
Marco Business Products, Inc., 75 244–46
Marcolin S.p.A., 61 191–94; 62 100
Marcon Coating, Inc., **22** 347
Marconi plc, 33 286–90 (upd.)
Marcopolo S.A., 79 247–250
The Marcus Corporation, 21 359–63
Marcy Fitness Products, Inc., **19** 142, 144
Maremont Corporation, **8** 39–40
Margarete Steiff GmbH, 23 334–37
Marge Carson, Inc., **III** 571; **20** 362
Margo's La Mode, **10** 281–82; **45** 15
Marian LLC *see* Charisma Brands LLC.
Marico Acquisition Corporation, **8** 448, 450
Marie Brizard & Roger International S.A., 22 342–44
Marie Callender's Restaurant & Bakery, Inc., 13 66; **28 257–59**
Marina Mortgage Company, **46** 25
Marine Bank and Trust Co., **11** 105
Marine Computer Systems, **6** 242
Marine Harvest, **13** 103; **56** 257
Marine Manufacturing Corporation, **52** 406
Marine Midland Corp., **9** 475–76; **11** 108; **17** 325
Marine Products Corporation, 75 247–49
Marine Transport Lines, Inc., **59** 323
Marine United Inc., **42** 361
Marinela, **19** 192–93
MarineMax, Inc., 30 303–05; 37 396
Marinette Marine Corporation, **59** 274, 278
Marion Brick, **14** 249
Marion Foods, Inc., **17** 434; **60** 268
Marion Laboratories Inc., I 648–49
Marion Manufacturing, **9** 72
Marion Merrell Dow, Inc., 9 328–29 (upd.)
Marionet Corp., **IV** 680–81
Marionnaud Parfumeries SA, 51 233–35; 54 265–66
Marisa Christina, Inc., 15 290–92
Maritime Electric Company, Limited, **15** 182; **47** 136–37
Maritz Inc., 38 302–05
Mark Controls Corporation, **30** 157
Mark Cross, Inc., **17** 4–5
Mark Goldston, **8** 305
Mark IV Industries, Inc., 7 296–98; 21 418; **28 260–64 (upd.); 61** 66
Mark Travel Corporation, **30** 448
Mark Trouser, Inc., **17** 338
Mark's Work Wearhouse Ltd. *see* Canadian Tire Corporation, Limited.
Markborough Properties, **V** 81; **8** 525; **25** 221
Market Development Corporation *see* Spartan Stores Inc.
Market Growth Resources, **23** 480
Market National Bank, **13** 465
Marketing Data Systems, Inc., **18** 24
Marketing Equities International, **26** 136
MarketSpan Corp. *see* KeySpan Energy Co.
Märklin Holding GmbH, 70 163–66
Marks and Spencer p.l.c., V 124–26; 24 313–17 (upd.)
Marks-Baer Inc., **11** 64
Marks Brothers Jewelers, Inc., 24 318–20
Marlene Industries Corp., **16** 36–37
Marley Co., **19** 360
Marley Holdings, L.P., **19** 246
Oy Marli Ab, **56** 103
Marman Products Company, **16** 8
The Marmon Group, Inc., IV 135–38; 16 354–57 (upd.); 70 167–72 (upd.)
The Marmon Group,
Marmon-Perry Light Company, **6** 508
Marolf Dakota Farms, Inc., **18** 14–15
Marotte, **21** 438
Marpac Industries Inc. *see* PVC Container Corporation.
Marquam Commercial Brokerage Company, **21** 257
Marquette Electronics, Inc., 13 326–28
Marquis Who's Who, **17** 398
Marr S.p.A., **57** 82–84
Marriner Group, **13** 175
Marriot Inc., **29** 442
Marriot Management Services, **29** 444
Marriott International, Inc., III 102–03; 21 364–67 (upd.)
Mars, Incorporated, 7 299–301; 22 298, 528; **40 302–05 (upd.)**
Marsh & McLennan Companies, Inc., III 282–84; 45 263–67 (upd.)
Marsh Supermarkets, Inc., 17 300–02; 76 255–58 (upd.)
Marshall & Ilsley Corporation, 56 217–20
Marshall Amplification plc, 62 239–42
Marshall Die Casting, **13** 225
Marshall Field's, 8 33; **9** 213; **12** 283; **15** 86; **18** 488; **22** 72; **50** 117, 119; **61** 394, 396; **63** 242, 244, **254–63** *see also* Target Corporation.
Marshall Industries, **19** 311
Marshalls Incorporated, 13 329–31; 14 62
Marship Tankers (Holdings) Ltd., **52** 329
Marstellar, **13** 204
Marstons, **57** 412–13
The Mart, **9** 120
Martank Shipping Holdings Ltd., **52** 329
Martek Biosciences Corporation, 65 218–20
Marten Transport, **27** 404
Martha Lane Adams, **27** 428
Martha Stewart Living Omnimedia, Inc., 24 321–23; 73 219–22 (upd.)
Martin & Pagenstecher GMBH, **24** 208
Martin-Baker Aircraft Company Limited, 61 195–97
Martin Band Instrument Company, **55** 149, 151
Martin Bros. Tobacco Co., **14** 19
Martin Collet, **19** 50
Martin Dunitz, **44** 416
Martin Gillet Co., **55** 96, 98
Martin Guitar Company *see* C.F. Martin & Co., Inc.
Martin Hilti Foundation, **53** 167
Martin Industries, Inc., 44 274–77
Martin Marietta Corporation, I 67–69 *see also* Lockheed Martin Corporation.
Martin Mathys, **8** 456
Martin Sorrell, **6** 54
Martin Theaters, **14** 86
Martin-Yale Industries, Inc., **19** 142–44
Martin Zippel Co., **16** 389
Martin's, **12** 221
Martindale-Hubbell, **16** 398
Martini & Rossi SpA, 18 41; **63 264–66**
Martinus Nijhoff, **14** 555; **25** 85
Martz Group, 56 221–23
Marubeni Corporation, I 492–95; 24 324–27 (upd.)
Maruetsu, **17** 124; **41** 114
Maruha Group Inc., 75 250–53 (upd.)
Marui Company Ltd., V 127; **62 243–45 (upd.)**
Marusa Co. Ltd., **51** 379
Maruti Udyog Ltd., **59** 393, 395–97
Maruzen Co., Limited, IV 403–04, 476, 554; **18 322–24**
Maruzen Oil Co., Ltd., **53** 114
Marvel Entertainment, Inc., 10 400–02; 78 212–219 (upd.)
Marvin H. Sugarman Productions Inc., **20** 48
Marvin Lumber & Cedar Company, 10 95; **22 345–47**
Marwick, Mitchell & Company, **10** 385
Marx, **12** 494
Mary Ann Co. Ltd., **V** 89
Mary Ann Restivo, Inc., **8** 323
Mary Ellen's, Inc., **11** 211
Mary Kathleen Uranium, **IV** 59–60
Mary Kay Corporation, 9 330–32; 12 435; **15** 475, 477; **18** 67, 164; **21** 49, 51; **30 306–09 (upd.)**
Maryland Cup Company, **8** 197
Maryland Medical Laboratory Inc., **26** 391
Maryland National Corp., **11** 287
Maryland National Mortgage Corporation, **11** 121; **48** 177
Maryland Square, Inc., **68** 69
Marzotto S.p.A., 20 356–58; 67 246–49 (upd.)
Masayoshi Son, **13** 481–82

Midwest Realty Exchange, Inc., **21** 257
Midwest Resources Inc., 6 523–25
Midwest Staffing Systems, **27** 21
Midwest Steel Corporation, **13** 157
Midwest Suburban Publishing Inc., **62** 188
Midwest Synthetics, **8** 553
Midwinter, **12** 529
Miele & Cie. KG, 56 232–35
MIG Realty Advisors, Inc., **25** 23, 25
Migros-Genossenschafts-Bund, 68 252–55
Miguel Galas S.A., **17** 268
MIH Limited, 31 329–32
Mikasa, Inc., 28 268–70
Mike-Sell's Inc., 15 298–300
Mikemitch Realty Corp., **16** 36
Mikohn Gaming Corporation, 39 276–79
Mikon, Ltd., **13** 345
Milac, **27** 259
Milacron, Inc., 53 226–30 (upd.)
Milan AC S.p.A., 79 255–258
Milbank, Tweed, Hadley & McCloy, 27 324–27
Milchem, Inc., **63** 306
Mile-Hi Distributing, **64** 180
Miles Inc., **22** 148
Miles Kimball Co., **9** 393
Miles Laboratories, I 653–55
Milgram Food Stores Inc., **II** 682
Milgray Electronics Inc., **19** 311; **47** 41
Milk Producers, Inc., **11** 24
Milk Specialties Co., **12** 199
Mill-Power Supply Company, **27** 129–30
Millea Holdings Inc., 64 276–81 (upd.)
Millennium & Copthorne Hotels plc, 71 231–33
Millennium Chemicals Inc., **30** 231; **45** 252, 254; **71** 149–50
Millennium Materials Inc. *see* Dyson Group PLC.
Millennium Pharmaceuticals, Inc., 47 249–52
Miller Automotive Group, **52** 146
Miller Brewing Company, I 269–70; 12 337–39 (upd.) *see also* SABMiller plc.
Miller Companies, **17** 182
Miller Container Corporation, **8** 102
Miller Exploration Company *see* Edge Petroleum Corporation.
Miller Freeman, Inc., **IV** 687; **27** 362; **28** 501, 504
Miller Group Ltd., **22** 282
Miller Industries, Inc., 26 293–95
Miller, Mason and Dickenson, **III** 204–05
Miller-Meteor Company *see* Accubuilt, Inc.
Miller, Morris & Brooker (Holdings) Ltd. *see* Gibbs and Dandy plc.
Miller Plant Farms, Inc., **51** 61
Miller Publishing Group, LLC, 57 242–44
Miller, Tabak, Hirsch & Co., **13** 394; **28** 164
Millet, **39** 250
Millet's Leisure *see* Sears plc.
Millicom, **11** 547; **18** 254
Milliken & Co., V 366–68; 17 327–30 (upd.); 29 246
Milliken, Tomlinson Co., **II** 682
Milliman USA, 66 223–26
Millipore Corporation, 25 339–43
Mills Clothing, Inc. *see* The Buckle, Inc.
The Mills Corporation, 77 280–283
Millway Foods, **25** 85
Milne & Craighead, **48** 113
Milne Fruit Products, Inc., **25** 366
Milnot Company, 46 289–91; 51 47
Milpark Drilling Fluids, Inc., **63** 306
Milsco Manufacturing Co., **23** 299, 300
Milton Bradley Company, 21 372–75
Milton Light & Power Company, **12** 45
Milton Roy Co., **8** 135
Milupa S.A., **37** 341
Milwaukee Brewers Baseball Club, 37 247–49
Milwaukee Cheese Co. Inc., **25** 517
Milwaukee Electric Railway and Light Company, **6** 601–02, 604–05
Milwaukee Electric Tool, **28** 40
MIM Holdings, **73** 392
Mimi's Cafés *see* SWH Corporation.
Minatome, **IV** 560
Mindpearl, **48** 381
Mindport, **31** 329
Mindset Corp., **42** 424–25
Mindspring Enterprises, Inc., **36** 168
Mine Safety Appliances Company, 31 333–35
The Miner Group International, 22 356–58
Minera Loma Blanca S.A., **56** 127
Mineral Point Public Service Company, **6** 604
Minerales y Metales, S.A. *see* Industrias Penoles, S.A. de C.V.
Minerals & Metals Trading Corporation of India Ltd., IV 143–44
Minerals and Resources Corporation Limited *see* Minorco.
Minerals Technologies Inc., 11 310–12; 52 248–51 (upd.)
Minerec Corporation, **9** 363
Minerva SA, **72** 289
Minerve, **6** 208
Minet Group, **III** 357; **22** 494–95
MiniScribe, Inc., **10** 404
Minitel, **21** 233
Minivator Ltd., **11** 486
Minneapolis Children's Medical Center, **54** 65
Minneapolis-Honeywell Regulator Co., **8** 21; **22** 427
Minneapolis Steel and Machinery Company, **21** 502
Minnehoma Insurance Company, **58** 260
Minnesota Brewing Company *see* MBC Holding Company.
Minnesota Linseed Oil Co., **8** 552
Minnesota Mining & Manufacturing Company, I 499–501; 8 369–71 (upd.); 26 296–99 (upd.) *see also* 3M Company.
Minnesota Paints, **8** 552–53
Minnesota Power & Light Company, 11 313–16
Minnesota Power, Inc., 34 286–91 (upd.)
Minnesota Sugar Company, **11** 13
Minnetonka Corp., **III** 25; **22** 122–23
Minntech Corporation, 22 359–61
Minn-Dak Farmers Cooperative, **32** 29
Minolta Co., Ltd., III 574–76; 18 93, 186, **339–42 (upd.); 43 281–85 (upd.)**
Minorco, **IV** 97; **16** 28, 293
Minstar Inc., **11** 397; **15** 49; **45** 174
Minton China, **38** 401
The Minute Maid Company, 28 271–74, 473; **32** 116
Minuteman International Inc., 46 292–95
Minyard Food Stores, Inc., 33 304–07
Mippon Paper, **21** 546; **50** 58
Miquel y Costas Miquel S.A., 68 256–58
Miracle Food Mart, **16** 247, 249–50
Miracle-Gro Products, Inc., **22** 474
Miraflores Designs Inc., **18** 216
Mirage Resorts, Incorporated, 6 209–12; 28 275–79 (upd.)
Miraglia Inc., **57** 139
Miramax Film Corporation, 64 282–85
Mirant, **39** 54, 57
MIRAX Corporation *see* JSP Corporation.
Mircali Asset Management, **III** 340
Mircor Inc., **12** 413
Mirror Group Newspapers plc, 7 341–43; 23 348–51 (upd.); 49 408; **61** 130
Misceramic Tile, Inc., **14** 42
Misr Airwork *see* AirEgypt.
Misr Bank of Cairo, **27** 132
Misrair *see* AirEgypt.
Miss Erika, Inc., **27** 346, 348
Miss Selfridge *see* Sears plc.
Misset Publishers, **IV** 611
Mission Group *see* SCEcorp.
Mission Jewelers, **30** 408
Mission Valley Fabrics, **57** 285
Mississippi Chemical Corporation, 8 183; **27** 316; **39 280–83**
Mississippi Gas Company, **6** 577
Mississippi Power Company, **38** 446–47
Mississippi River Corporation, **10** 44
Mississippi River Recycling, **31** 47, 49
Mississippi Valley Title Insurance Company, **58** 259–60
Missoula Bancshares, Inc., **35** 198–99
Missouri Book Co., **10** 136
Missouri Fur Company, **25** 220
Missouri Gaming Company, **21** 39
Missouri Gas & Electric Service Company, **6** 593
Missouri Pacific Railroad, **10** 43–44
Missouri Public Service Company *see* UtiliCorp United Inc.
Missouri Utilities Company, **6** 580
Mist Assist, Inc. *see* Ballard Medical Products.
Mistik Beverages, **18** 71
Misys PLC, 45 279–81; 46 296–99

Mondex International, **18** 543
Mondi Foods BV, **41** 12
Moneris Solutions Corp., **46** 55
Monet Jewelry, **9** 156–57
Money Access Service Corp., **11** 467
Money Management Associates, Inc., **53** 136
Monfort, Inc., 13 350–52
Monitor Dynamics Inc., **24** 510
Monitor Group Inc., **33** 257
Monk-Austin Inc., **12** 110
Monmouth Pharmaceuticals Ltd., **16** 439
Monnaie de Paris, 62 246–48
Monneret Industrie, **56** 335
Monnoyeur Group *see* Groupe Monnoyeur.
Monogram Aerospace Fasteners, Inc., **11** 536
Monogram Models, **25** 312
Monolithic Memories Inc., **16** 316–17, 549
Monon Corp., **13** 550
Monongahela Power, **38** 40
Monoprix *see* Galeries Lafayette S.A.
Monro Muffler Brake, Inc., 24 337–40
Monroe Savings Bank, **11** 109
Monrovia Nursery Company, 70 196–98
Monsanto Company, I 365–67; 9 355–57 (upd.); 29 327–31 (upd.); 77 301–307 (upd.)
Monsoon plc, 39 287–89
Monster Cable Products, Inc., 69 256–58
Monster Worldwide Inc., 74 194–97 (upd.)
Mont Blanc, **17** 5; **27** 487, 489
Montabert S.A., **15** 226
Montan TNT Pty Ltd., **27** 473
Montana Alimentaria S.p.A., **57** 82
Montana Coffee Traders, Inc., 60 208–10
Montana-Dakota Utilities Co., **7** 322–23; **37** 281–82; **42** 249–50, 252
Montana Group, **54** 229
Montana Mills Bread Co., Inc., **61** 153
The Montana Power Company, 6 566; **7** 322; **11 320–22; 37** 280, 283; **44 288–92 (upd.); 50** 367
Montana Refining Company, **12** 240–41
Montana Resources, Inc., **IV** 34
Montaup Electric Co., **14** 125
MontBell America, Inc., **29** 279
Monte Paschi Vita, **65** 71–72
Montedison S.p.A., I 368–69; 14 17; **22** 262; **24 341–44 (upd.); 36** 185–86, 188
Montefina, **IV** 499; **26** 367
Montell N.V., **24** 343
Monterey Homes Corporation *see* Meritage Corporation.
Monterey Mfg. Co., **12** 439
Monterey Pasta Company, 58 240–43
Monterey's Acquisition Corp., **41** 270
Monterey's Tex-Mex Cafes, **13** 473
Monterrey, Compania de Seguros sobre la Vida *see* Seguros Monterrey.
Monterrey Group, **19** 10–11, 189
Montgomery Elevator Company *see* KONE Corporation.
Montgomery Ward & Co., Incorporated, V 145–48; 20 263, **374–79 (upd.)**
Montiel Corporation, **17** 321
Montinex, **24** 270
Montreal Engineering Company, **6** 585
Montreal Mining Co., **17** 357
Montres Rolex S.A., 13 353–55; 34 292–95 (upd.)
Montrose Capital, **36** 358
Montrose Chemical Company, **9** 118, 119
Montupet S.A., 63 302–04
Monumental Corp., **III** 179
Moody's Corporation, 65 242–44
Moody's Investors Service,
Moog Inc., 13 356–58
Moog Music, Inc., 75 261–64
Mooney Aerospace Group Ltd., 52 252–55
Mooney Chemicals, Inc. *see* OM Group, Inc.
Moonlight Mushrooms, Inc. *see* Sylvan, Inc.
Moonstone Mountaineering, Inc., **29** 181
Moore and McCormack Co. Inc., **19** 40
Moore Corporation Limited, IV 644–46
Moore Gardner & Associates, **22** 88
The Moore Group Ltd., **20** 363
Moore-Handley, Inc., 39 290–92
Moore McCormack Resources Inc., **14** 455
Moore Medical Corp., 17 331–33
Moquin Breuil *see* Smoby International SA.
Moran Group Inc., **II** 682
Moran Health Care Group Ltd., **25** 455
Moran Towing Corporation, Inc., 15 301–03
Morana, Inc., **9** 290
More Group plc *see* JCDecaux S.A
Moretti-Harrah Marble Co. *see* English China Clays Ltd.
Morgan & Banks Limited, **30** 460
Morgan Construction Company, **8** 448
Morgan Edwards, **II** 609
Morgan Engineering Co., **8** 545
Morgan Grampian Group, **IV** 687
Morgan Grenfell Group PLC, II 427–29; 59 182–83, 255 *see also* Deutsche Bank AG.
The Morgan Group, Inc., 46 300–02
Morgan Guaranty Trust Company *see* J.P. Morgan & Co. Incorporated.
Morgan, J.P. & Co. Inc *see* J.P. Morgan & Co. Incorporated.
Morgan, Lewis & Bockius LLP, 29 332–34
Morgan, Lewis, Githens & Ahn, Inc., **6** 410
Morgan Schiff & Co., **29** 205
Morgan Stanley Dean Witter & Company, 33 311–14 (upd.); 38 289, 291, 411
Morgan Stanley Group, Inc., II 430–32; 16 374–78 (upd.)
Moria Informatique, **6** 229
Morinaga & Co. Ltd., 61 222–25
Morino Associates, **10** 394
Mormac Marine Group, **15** 302
Morning Star Technologies Inc., **24** 49
Morning Sun, Inc., **23** 66
Morningstar Inc., 68 259–62
Morningstar Storage Centers LLC, **52** 311
Morris Air, **24** 455; **71** 346
Morris Communications Corporation, 36 339–42
Morris Motors, **7** 459
Morris Travel Services L.L.C., 26 308–11
Morrison & Co. Ltd., **52** 221
Morrison & Foerster LLP, 78 220–223
Morrison Homes, Inc., **51** 138
Morrison Knudsen Corporation, 7 355–58; 28 286–90 (upd.) *see also* The Washington Companies.
Morrison Machine Products Inc., **25** 193
Morrison Restaurants Inc., 11 323–25; 18 464
Morse Equalizing Spring Company, **14** 63
Morse Industrial, **14** 64
Morse Shoe Inc., 13 359–61
Morse's Ltd., **70** 161
Mortgage Associates, **9** 229
Mortgage Guaranty Insurance Corp. *see* MGIC Investment Corp.
Mortgage Resources, Inc., **10** 91
MortgageRamp Inc. *see* OfficeTiger, LLC.
Morton Foods, Inc., **27** 258
Morton International Inc., 9 358–59 (upd.)
Morton Thiokol Inc., I 370–72; 19 508; **28** 253–54 *see also* Thiokol Corporation.
Morton's Restaurant Group, Inc., 28 401; **30 329–31**
Mos Magnetics, **18** 140
MOS Technology, **7** 95
Mosby-Year Book, Inc., **IV** 678; **17** 486
Moscow Bank for Reconstruction & Development, **73** 303–04
Moseley, Hallgarten, Estabrook, and Weeden, **III** 389
Mosher Steel Company, **7** 540
Mosinee Paper Corporation, 15 304–06 *see also* Wausau-Mosinee Paper Corporation.
Moskatel's, Inc., **17** 321
Moss Bros Group plc, 51 252–54
Moss-Rouse Company, **15** 412
Mossgas, **IV** 93
Mossimo, Inc., 27 328–30
Mostek Corp., **11** 307–08; **13** 191; **20** 175; **29** 323
Mostjet Ltd. *see* British World Airlines Ltd.
Móstoles Industrial S.A., **26** 129
Mostra Importaciones S.A., **34** 38, 40
Motel 6, 13 362–64; 56 248–51 (upd.) *see also* Accor SA
Mother Karen's, **10** 216
Mothercare plc, 17 334–36; 78 224–227 (upd.)
Mothers Against Drunk Driving (MADD), 51 255–58

N

Nissan Trading Company, Ltd., **13** 533
Nissay Dowa General Insurance Company Ltd., **60** 220
Nisshin Flour Milling Company, Ltd., II 554 *see also* Nisshin Seifun Group Inc.
Nisshin Seifun Group Inc., 66 246–48 (upd.)
Nisshin Steel Co., Ltd., IV 159–60; 7 588
Nissho Iwai K.K., I 509–11
Nissin Food Products Company Ltd., 75 286–88
Nissui *see* Nippon Suisan Kaisha.
Nitches, Inc., 53 245–47
Nitroglycerin AB, **13** 22
Nitroglycerin Ltd., **9** 380
Nittetsu Curtainwall Corp., **III** 758
Nittetsu Sash Sales Corp., **III** 758
Nittsu *see* Nippon Express Co., Ltd.
Niugini Mining Ltd., **23** 42
Nixdorf Computer AG, III 154–55; 12 162; **14** 169; **26** 497 *see also* Wincor Nixdorf Holding GmbH.
Nixdorf-Krein Industries Inc. *see* Laclede Steel Company.
Nizhny Novgorod Dairy, **48** 438
NKI B.V., **71** 178–79
NKK Corporation, IV 161–63, 212–13; **28 322–26 (upd.)**; **53** 170, 172
NL Industries, Inc., 10 434–36; 19 466–68
NLG *see* National Leisure Group.
NLI Insurance Agency Inc., **60** 220
NLM City-Hopper, **I** 109
NM Acquisition Corp., **27** 346
NMC Laboratories Inc., **12** 4
NMT *see* Nordic Mobile Telephone.
NNG *see* Northern Natural Gas Company.
No-Leak-O Piston Ring Company, **10** 492
No-Sag Spring Co., **16** 321
Noah's New York Bagels *see* Einstein/Noah Bagel Corporation.
Nob Hill Foods, **58** 291
Nobel Drilling Corporation, **26** 243
Nobel Industries AB, 9 380–82 *see also* Akzo Nobel N.V.
Nobel Learning Communities, Inc., 37 276–79; 76 281–85 (upd.)
Noble Affiliates, Inc., 11 353–55; 18 366
Noble Broadcast Group, Inc., **23** 293
Noble Roman's Inc., 14 351–53
Nobles Industries, **13** 501
Noblesville Telephone Company, **14** 258
Nobleza Piccardo SAICF, 64 291–93
Noblitt-Sparks Industries, Inc., **8** 37–38
Nobody Beats the Wiz *see* Cablevision Electronic Instruments, Inc.
Nocibé SA, 54 265–68
Nocona Belt Company, **31** 435–36
Nocona Boot Co. *see* Justin Industries, Inc.
Noel Group, Inc., **24** 286–88
NOF Corporation, 72 249–51
NOK Corporation, **41** 170–72
Nokia Corporation, II 69–71; 17 352–54 (upd.); 38 328–31 (upd.); 77 308–313 (upd.)
Nokian Tyres PLC, **59** 91
NOL Group *see* Neptune Orient Lines Limited.
Noland Company, 35 311–14
Nolo.com, Inc., 49 288–91
Nolte Mastenfabriek B.V., **19** 472
Noma Industries, **11** 526
Nomai Inc., **18** 510
Nomura Bank of Japan, **34** 221
Nomura Holdings, Inc., **49** 451
Nomura Securities Company, Limited, II 438–41; 9 383–86 (upd.); 39 109
Nomura Toys Ltd., **16** 267; **43** 232
Non-Fiction Book Club, **13** 105
Non-Stop Fashions, Inc., **8** 323
Noodle Kidoodle, 16 388–91
Noodles & Company, Inc., 55 277–79
Nooter Corporation, 61 251–53
NOP Research Group, **28** 501, 504
Nopco Chemical Co., **7** 308
Nopri *see* GIB Group.
Nor-Cal Engineering Co. GmbH, **18** 162
Nora Industrier A/S, **18** 395
Norampac Inc., **71** 95
Norand Corporation, **9** 411; **72** 189
Noranda Inc., IV 164–66; 7 397–99 (upd.); 9 282; **26** 363; **49** 136; **64 294–98 (upd.)**
Norandex, **16** 204
Norbro Corporation *see* Stuart Entertainment Inc.
Norcal Pottery Products, Inc., **58** 60
Norcal Waste Systems, Inc., 60 222–24
Norcen Energy Resources, Ltd., **8** 347
Norco Plastics, **8** 553
Norcon, Inc., **7** 558–59
Norcore Plastics, Inc., **33** 361
Nordbanken, **9** 382
Norddeutsche Affinerie AG, 62 249–53
Norddeutscher-Lloyd *see* Hapag-Lloyd AG.
Nordea AB, 40 336–39
Nordic Baltic Holding *see* Nordea AB.
Nordica S.r.l., **10** 151; **15** 396–97; **53** 24
NordicTrack, 10 215–17; **22 382–84; 38** 238 *see also* Icon Health & Fitness, Inc.
Nordson Corporation, 11 356–58; 48 296–99 (upd.)
Nordstrom, Inc., V 156–58; 18 371–74 (upd.); 67 277–81 (upd.)
Nordwestdeutsche Kraftwerke AG *see* PreussenElektra AG.
Norelco Consumer Products Co., 26 334–36
Norelec, **27** 138
Norex Leasing, Inc., **16** 397
Norfolk Carolina Telephone Company, **10** 202
Norfolk Shipbuilding & Drydock Corporation, **73** 47
Norfolk Southern Corporation, V 484–86; 29 358–61 (upd.); 75 289–93 (upd.)
Norfolk Steel, **13** 97
Norge Co., **18** 173–74; **43** 163–64
Noric Corporation, **39** 332
Norinchukin Bank, II 340–41
Norlin Industries, **16** 238–39; **75** 262
Norm Thompson Outfitters, Inc., 47 275–77
Norma AS *see* Autoliv, Inc.
Norman BV, **9** 93; **33** 78
Normandy Mining Ltd., **23** 42
Normark Corporation *see* Rapala-Normark Group, Ltd.
Norment Security Group, Inc., **51** 81
Normond/CMS, **7** 117
Norrell Corporation, 25 356–59
Norris Cylinder Company, **11** 535
Norris Grain Co., **14** 537
Norris Oil Company, **47** 52
Norshield Corp., **51** 81
Norsk Aller A/S, **72** 62
Norsk Helikopter AS *see* Bristow Helicopters Ltd.
Norsk Hydro ASA, 10 437–40; 35 315–19 (upd.)
Norsk Rengjorings Selskap a.s., **49** 221
Norske Skog do Brasil Ltda., **73** 205
Norske Skogindustrier ASA, 63 314–16
Norstan, Inc., 16 392–94
Norstar Bancorp, **9** 229
Nortek, Inc., 14 482; **22** 4; **26** 101; **34 308–12; 37** 331
Nortel Inversora S.A., **63** 375–77
Nortel Networks Corporation, 36 349–54 (upd.); 50 130; **72** 129–31
Nortex International, **7** 96; **19** 338
North African Petroleum Ltd., **IV** 455
North American Aviation, **7** 520; **9** 16; **11** 278, 427
North American Carbon, **19** 499
North American Cellular Network, **9** 322
North American Coal Corporation, **7** 369–71
North American Company, **6** 552–53, 601–02
North American Dräger, **13** 328
North American Energy Conservation, Inc., **35** 480
North American InTeleCom, Inc., **IV** 411
North American Light & Power Company, **12** 541
North American Medical Management Company, Inc., **36** 366
North American Mogul Products Co. *see* Mogul Corp.
North American Philips Corporation, **19** 393; **21** 520
North American Plastics, Inc., **61** 112
North American Printing Ink Company, **13** 228
North American Rockwell Corp., **10** 173
North American Site Developers, Inc., **69** 197
North American Systems, **14** 230
North American Training Corporation *see* Rollerblade, Inc.
North American Van Lines *see* Allied Worldwide, Inc.
North American Watch Company *see* Movado Group, Inc.

O

Old Republic International Corporation, 11 373–75; 58 258–61 (upd.)
Old Spaghetti Factory International Inc., 24 364–66
Old Stone Trust Company, **13** 468
Old Town Canoe Company, 74 222–24
Oldach Window Corp., **19** 446
Oldcastle, Inc., **60** 77; **64** 98
Oldover Corp., **23** 225
Ole's Innovative Sports *see* Rollerblade, Inc.
Olean Tile Co., **22** 170
Oleochim, **IV** 498–99
OLEX *see* Deutsche BP Aktiengesellschaft.
Olex Cables Ltd., **10** 445
Olin Corporation, I 379–81; 13 379–81 (upd.); 78 270–274 (upd.)
Olinkraft, Inc., **11** 420; **16** 376
Olive Garden Italian Restaurants, **10** 322, 324; **16** 156–58; **19** 258; **35** 83
Oliver Rubber Company, **19** 454, 456
Olivetti S.p.A., 34 316–20 (upd.); 38 300; **63** 379
Olivine Industries, Inc., **II** 508; **11** 172; **36** 255
Olmstead Products Co., **23** 82
OLN *see* Outdoor Life Network.
Olsten Corporation, 6 41–43; 29 362–65 (upd.); 49 265 *see also* Adecco S.A.
Olympia & York Developments Ltd., IV 720–21; 9 390–92 (upd.)
Olympia Arenas, Inc., **7** 278–79; **24** 294
Olympia Brewing, **11** 50
Olympia Entertainment, **37** 207
Olympiaki, **III** 401
Olympic Courier Systems, Inc., **24** 126
Olympic Fastening Systems, **III** 722
Olympic Insurance Co., **26** 486
Olympic Packaging, **13** 443
Olympic Property Group LLC *see* Pope Resources LP.
Olympic Resource Management LLC *see* Pope Resources LP.
Olympus Communications L.P., **17** 7
Olympus Optical Company, Ltd., **15** 483
Olympus Partners, **65** 258
Olympus Sport *see* Sears plc.
Olympus Symbol, Inc., **15** 483
OM Group, Inc., 17 362–64; 78 275–278 (upd.)
Omaha Public Power District, **29** 353
Omaha Steaks International Inc., 62 257–59
Omega Gas Company, **8** 349
Omega Group *see* MasterBrand Cabinets, Inc.
Omega Protein Corporation, **25** 546
OmegaTech Inc. *see* Martek Biosciences Corporation.
O'Melveny & Myers, 37 290–93
OMI Corporation, **IV** 34; **9** 111–12; **22** 275; **59 321–23**
Omnes, **17** 419
Omni ApS, **56** 338
Omni Construction Company, Inc., **8** 112–13
Omni Hotels Corp., 12 367–69
Omni-Pac, **12** 377
Omni Services, Inc., **51** 76
Omnibus Corporation, **9** 283
Omnicad Corporation, **48** 75
Omnicare, Inc., 13 49 307–10
Omnicom Group Inc., I 28–32; 22 394–99 (upd.); 77 318–325 (upd.)
Omnipoint Communications Inc., **18** 77
OmniSource Corporation, 14 366–67
OmniTech Consulting Group, **51** 99
Omnitel Pronto Italia SpA, **38** 300
OMNOVA Solutions Inc., 59 324–26
Omron Corporation, 28 331–35 (upd.); 53 46
Omron Tateisi Electronics Company, II 75–77
ÖMV Aktiengesellschaft, IV 485–87
On Assignment, Inc., 20 400–02
On Command Video Corp., **23** 135
On Cue, **9** 360
On Demand Group *see* SeaChange International, Inc.
On-Line Systems *see* Sierra On-Line Inc.
Onan Corporation, **8** 72
Onbancorp Inc., **11** 110
Once Upon A Child, Inc., **18** 207–8
Ondulato Imolese, **IV** 296; **19** 226
1-800-FLOWERS, Inc., 26 344–46; 28 137
1-800-GOT-JUNK? LLC, 74 225–27
1-800-Mattress *see* Dial-A-Mattress Operating Corporation.
180s, L.L.C., 64 299–301
One For All, **39** 405
One Price Clothing Stores, Inc., 20 403–05
17187 Yukon Inc., **74** 234
One Stop Trade Building Centre Ltd. *see* Gibbs and Dandy plc.
O'Neal, Jones & Feldman Inc., **11** 142
OneBeacon Insurance Group LLC, **48** 431
Oneida Bank & Trust Company, **9** 229
Oneida County Creameries Co., **7** 202
Oneida Gas Company, **9** 554
Oneida Ltd., 7 406–08; 31 352–55 (upd.)
ONEOK Inc., 7 409–12
Onex Corporation, 16 395–97; 65 281–85 (upd.)
OneZero Media, Inc., **31** 240
Ong First Pte Ltd., **76** 372, 374
Onion, Inc., 69 282–84
Onitsuka Co., Ltd., **57** 52
Online Financial Communication Systems, **11** 112
Only One Dollar, Inc. *see* Dollar Tree Stores, Inc.
Onoda Cement Co., Ltd., III 717–19 *see also* Taiheiyo Cement Corporation.
Onomichi, **25** 469
OnResponse.com, Inc., **49** 433
Onsale Inc., **31** 177
Onstead Foods, **21** 501
OnTarget Inc., **38** 432
Ontario Hydro Services Company, 6 541–42; 9 461; **32 368–71 (upd.)**
Ontario Power Generation, **49** 65, 67
Ontario Teachers' Pension Plan, 61 273–75
OnTrack Data International, **57** 219
OnTrak Systems Inc., **31** 301
Onyx Acceptance Corporation, 59 327–29
Onyx Software Corporation, 53 252–55
O'okiep Copper Company, Ltd., **7** 385–86
Opel AG *see* Adam Opel AG.
Open *see* Groupe Open.
Open Board of Brokers, **9** 369
Open Cellular Systems, Inc., **41** 225–26
Open Market, Inc., **22** 522
Open Text Corporation, 79 301–305
OpenTV, Inc., **31** 330–31
OPENWAY SAS, **74** 143
Operadora de Bolsa Serfin *see* Grupo Financiero Serfin, S.A.
Operation Smile, Inc., 75 297–99
Operon Technologies Inc., **39** 335
Opinion Research Corporation, 46 318–22
Opp and Micolas Mills, **15** 247–48
Oppenheimer *see* Ernest Oppenheimer and Sons.
Oppenheimer & Co., Inc., **17** 137; **21** 235; **22** 405; **25** 450; **61** 50
The Oppenheimer Group, 76 295–98
Oppenheimer Wolff & Donnelly LLP, 71 262–64
Opryland USA, **11** 152–53; **25** 403; **36** 229
Opsware Inc., 49 311–14
Optel S.A., **17** 331; **71** 211
OPTi Computer, **9** 116
Opti-Ray, Inc., **12** 215
Optical Corporation *see* Excel Technology, Inc.
Optical Radiation Corporation, **27** 57
Optilink Corporation, **12** 137
Optima Pharmacy Services, **17** 177
Option Care Inc., 48 307–10
Optische Werke G. Rodenstock, 44 319–23
OptiSystems Solutions Ltd., **55** 67
Opto-Electronics Corp., **15** 483
Optus Communications, **25** 102
Optus Vision, **17** 150
Opus Group, 34 321–23
Oracle Corporation, 6 272–74; 24 367–71 (upd.); 67 282–87 (upd.)
Orange *see* Wanadoo S.A.
Orange and Rockland Utilities, Inc., **45** 116, 120
Orange Glo International, 53 256–59
Orange Julius of America, **10** 371, 373; **39** 232, 235
Orange Line Bus Company, **6** 604
Orange PLC, **24** 89; **38** 300
Orange Shipbuilding Company, Inc., **58** 70
OraSure Technologies, Inc., 75 300–03
Orb Books *see* Tom Doherty Associates Inc.
Orb Estates, **54** 366, 368
ORBIS Corporation, **59** 289

Outpost.com *see* Fry's Electronics, Inc.
Outrigger Enterprises, Inc., 67 291–93
Ovation, **19** 285
Overhead Door Corporation, 70 213–16
Overhill Corporation, 10 382; **51 279–81**
Overland Energy Company, **14** 567
Overland Western Ltd., **27** 473
Overnite Corporation, 58 262–65 (upd.)
Overnite Transportation Co., 14 371–73; 28 492
Overseas-Chinese Banking Corporation, **56** 363
Overseas Insurance Corporation, **58** 272
Overseas Shipholding Group, Inc., 11 376–77
Overseas Telecommunications, Inc., **27** 304
Overseas Union Bank, **56** 362–63
Overstock.com, Inc., 75 307–09
Overture Services, Inc. *see* Yahoo! Inc.
Ovonic Battery Company, Inc. *see* Energy Conversion Devices, Inc.
Ovox Fitness Clubs, **46** 432
Owen Healthcare, **50** 122
Owen Owen, **37** 8
Owen Steel Co. Inc., **15** 117
Owens & Minor, Inc., 16 398–401; 68 282–85 (upd.)
Owens Corning Corporation, III 720–23; 20 413–17 (upd.)
Owens Country Sausage, Inc., **63** 69–70
Owens-Illinois Inc., I 609–11; 26 350–53 (upd.)
Owensboro Municipal Utilities, **11** 37
Owosso Corporation, 29 366–68
Oxdon Investments, **II** 664
Oxfam America, **13** 13
Oxford-AnsCo Development Co., **12** 18
Oxford Bus Company, **28** 155–56
Oxford Financial Group, **22** 456
Oxford Health Plans, Inc., 16 402–04
Oxford Industries, Inc., 8 406–08
Oxford Learning Centres, **34** 105; **76** 240
Oxford Paper Co., **10** 289
Oxford Realty Financial Group, Inc., **49** 26
Oxford University Press, **23** 211
Oxirane Chemical Corporation, **64** 35
OXO International, **16** 234
Oxycal Laboratories Inc., **46** 466
OxyChem, **11** 160
Oxygen Business Solutions Pty Limited *see* Carter Holt Harvey Ltd.
Oxygen Media Inc., **28** 175; **51** 220
Ozark Automotive Distributors, **26** 347–48
Ozark Utility Company, **6** 593; **50** 38
OZM *see* OneZero Media, Inc.

P

P&C Foods Inc., 8 409–11
P&C Groep N.V., **46** 344
P & F Industries, Inc., 45 327–29
P&F Technologies Ltd., **26** 363
P&G *see* Procter & Gamble Company.
P&L Coal Holdings Corporation, **45** 333
P & M Manufacturing Company, **8** 386
P & O *see* Peninsular & Oriental Steam Navigation Company.
P.A. Bergner & Company, **9** 142; **15** 87–88
P.A. Geier Company *see* Royal Appliance Manufacturing Company.
P.A.J.W. Corporation, **9** 111–12
P.A. Rentrop-Hubbert & Wagner Fahrzeugausstattungen GmbH, **III** 582
P.C. Richard & Son Corp., 23 372–74
P.D. Associated Collieries Ltd., **31** 369
P.D. Kadi International, **I** 580
P.E.C. Israel Economic Corporation, **24** 429
P.F. Chang's China Bistro, Inc., 37 297–99
P.G. Realty, **III** 340
P.H. Glatfelter Company, 8 412–14; 30 349–52 (upd.)
P.Ink Press, **24** 430
P.R. Mallory, **9** 179
P.S.L. Food Market, Inc., **22** 549
P.T. Asurasi Tokio Marine Indonesia, **64** 280
P.T. Bridgeport Perkasa Machine Tools, **17** 54
P.T. Darya-Varia Laboratoria, **18** 180
P.T. Gaya Motor, **23** 290
P.T. GOLD Martindo, **70** 235
P.T. Indomobil Suzuki International, **59** 393, 397
P.T. Samick Indonesia, **56** 300
P.T. Satomo Indovyl Polymer, **70** 329
P.T. Unitex, **53** 344
P.V. Doyle Hotels Ltd., **64** 217
P.W. Huntington & Company, **11** 180
P.W.J. Surridge & Sons, Ltd., **43** 132
Paaco Automotive Group, **64** 20
Pabst Brewing Company, **I** 255; **10** 99; **18** 502; **50** 114; **74** 146
Pac-Am Food Concepts, **10** 178; **38** 102
Pac-Fab, Inc., **18** 161
PAC Insurance Services, **12** 175; **27** 258
PACCAR Inc., I 185–86; 26 354–56 (upd.)
PacDun *see* Pacific Dunlop.
The Pace Consultants, Inc. *see* Jacobs Engineering Group Inc.
PACE Entertainment Corp., **36** 423–24
Pace Express Pty. Ltd., **13** 20
Pace Foods Ltd. *see* Campbell Soup Company.
Pace Management Service Corp., **21** 91
PACE Membership Warehouse, Inc. *see* Kmart Corporation.
Pace Pharmaceuticals, **16** 439
Pacemaker Plastics, Inc., **7** 296
Pacer International, Inc., 54 274–76
Pacer Technology, 40 347–49
Pacer Tool and Mold, **17** 310
Pacific Advantage, **43** 253
Pacific Air Freight, Incorporated *see* Airborne Freight Corp.
Pacific Air Transport, **9** 416
Pacific and European Telegraph Company, **25** 99
Pacific Bell *see* SBC Communications.
Pacific Car & Foundry Company *see* PACCAR Inc.
Pacific Coast Feather Company, 67 209, **294–96**
Pacific Communication Sciences, **11** 57
Pacific Destination Services, **62** 276
Pacific Dunlop Limited, 10 444–46 *see also* Ansell Ltd.
Pacific Electric Light Company, **6** 565; **50** 365
Pacific Enterprises, V 682–84; 12 477 *see also* Sempra Energy.
Pacific Finance Corp., **9** 536; **13** 529; **26** 486
Pacific Forest Products Ltd., **59** 162
Pacific Fur Company, **25** 220
Pacific Gamble Robinson, **9** 39
Pacific Gas and Electric Company, V 685–87 *see also* PG&E Corporation.
Pacific Glass Corp., **48** 42
Pacific Guardian Life Insurance Co., **III** 289
Pacific Home Furnishings, **14** 436
Pacific Indemnity Corp., **III** 220; **14** 108, 110; **16** 204
Pacific Integrated Healthcare, **53** 7
Pacific Lighting Corp. *see* Sempra Energy.
Pacific Linens, **13** 81–82
Pacific Link Communication, **18** 180
Pacific Lumber Company, **III** 254; **8** 348–50
Pacific Magazines and Printing, **7** 392
Pacific Mail Steamship Company *see* APL Limited.
Pacific Media K.K., **18** 101
Pacific Monolothics Inc., **11** 520
Pacific National Insurance Co. *see* TIG Holdings, Inc.
Pacific Natural Gas Corp., **9** 102
Pacific Northwest Laboratories, **10** 139
Pacific Northwest Pipeline Corporation, **9** 102–104, 540; **12** 144
Pacific Northwest Power Company, **6** 597
Pacific Petroleums Ltd., **9** 102
Pacific Plastics, Inc., **48** 334
Pacific Power & Light Company *see* PacifiCorp.
Pacific Pride Bakeries, **19** 192
Pacific Publications, **72** 283–84
Pacific Recycling Co. Inc., **IV** 296; **19** 226; **23** 225
Pacific Resources Inc., **IV** 47; **22** 107
Pacific Sentinel Gold Corp., **27** 456
Pacific/Southern Wine & Spirits, **48** 392
Pacific Stock Exchange, **48** 226
Pacific Sunwear of California, Inc., 28 343–45; 47 425
Pacific Telecom, Inc., 6 325–28
Pacific Telesis Group, V 318–20 *see also* SBC Communications.
Pacific Teletronics, Inc., **7** 15
Pacific Towboat *see* Puget Sound Tug and Barge Company.
Pacific Trail Inc., **17** 462; **29** 293, 295–96
Pacific Western Extruded Plastics Company *see* PW Eagle Inc.
Pacific Wine Co., **18** 71; **50** 112

Portways, **9** 92
Posadas *see* Grupo Posadas, S.A. de C.V.
POSCO, 57 287–91 (upd.)
Posful Corporation, **68** 9
Positive Response Television, Inc., **27** 337–38
Post Office Group, V 498–501
Post Properties, Inc., 26 377–79
Postabank és Takarékpénztár Rt., **69** 155, 157
La Poste, V 470–72
Posterscope Worldwide, 70 230–32
Posti- Ja Telelaitos, 6 329–31
PostScript, **17** 177
Potain SAS, **59** 274, 278
Potash Corporation of Saskatchewan Inc., 18 51, **431–33; 27** 318; **50** 90
Potelco, Inc. *see* Quanta Services, Inc.
Potlatch Corporation, 8 428–30; 19 445; **34 355–59 (upd.)**
Potomac Edison Company, **38** 39–40
Potomac Electric Power Company, 6 552–54
Potter & Brumfield Inc., 11 396–98
Pottery Barn, **13** 42; **17** 548–50
Pottsville Behavioral Counseling Group, **64** 311
Poulan/Weed Eater *see* White Consolidated Industries Inc.
PowCon, Inc., **17** 534
Powell Duffryn plc, 31 367–70
Powell Energy Products, **8** 321
Powell Group, **33** 32
Powell's Books, Inc., 37 181; **40 360–63**
Power Applications & Manufacturing Company, Inc., **6** 441
Power Corporation of Canada, 36 370–74 (upd.)
Power-One, Inc., 79 334–337
Power Parts Co., **7** 358
Power Products, **8** 515
Power Team, **10** 492
PowerBar Inc., 44 351–53
Powercor *see* PacifiCorp.
POWEREDCOM Inc., **74** 348
PowerFone Holdings, **10** 433
Powergen PLC, 11 399–401; 12 349; **13** 458, 484; **50** 172, 280–81, **361–64 (upd.)**
Powerhouse Technologies, Inc., 13 485; **27 379–81**
PowerSoft Corp., **11** 77; **15** 374
Powerteam Electrical Services Ltd., **64** 404
Powertel Inc., **48** 130
Powerware Corporation *see* Eaton Corporation.
Pozzi-Renati Millwork Products, Inc., **8** 135
PP&L *see* Pennsylvania Power & Light Company.
PP&L Global, Inc., **44** 291
PPB Group Berhad, 57 292–95
PPG Industries, Inc., III 731–33; 22 434–37 (upd.)
PPI *see* Precision Pattern Inc.
PPI Two Corporation, **64** 334
PPL Corporation, 41 314–17 (upd.)
PPR S.A., 74 244–48 (upd.)
PR Holdings, **23** 382
PR Newswire, 35 354–56
Practical and Educational Books, **13** 105
Practical Business Solutions, Inc., **18** 112
PracticeWorks.com, **69** 33–34
Prada Holding B.V., 45 342–45; 50 215
Pragma Bio-Tech, Inc., **11** 424
Prairie Farms Dairy, Inc., 47 304–07
Prairielands Energy Marketing, Inc., **7** 322, 325
Prakla Seismos, **17** 419
Pranda Jewelry plc, 70 233–35
Prandium Inc., **51** 70
Pratt & Whitney, 7 456; **9** 14, 16–18, 244–46, **416–18; 10** 162; **11** 299, 427; **12** 71; **13** 386; **14** 564; **24** 312; **39** 313
Pratt Hotel Corporation, **21** 275; **22** 438
Pratt Properties Inc., **8** 349
Pratta Electronic Materials, Inc., **26** 425
Praxair, Inc., 11 402–04; 48 321–24 (upd.)
Praxis Biologics, **8** 26; **27** 115
Praxis Corporation, **30** 499
Pre-Fab Cushioning, **9** 93
Pre Finish Metals Incorporated, **63** 270–71
Pre-Paid Legal Services, Inc., 20 434–37
PreAnalytiX, **39** 335
Precept Foods, LLC, **54** 168
Precise Fabrication Corporation, **33** 257
Precise Imports Corp., **21** 516
Precision Castparts Corp., 15 365–67
Precision Engineered Products, Inc., **70** 142
Precision Games, **16** 471
Precision Husky Corporation, **26** 494
Precision IBC, Inc., **64** 20–21
Precision Interconnect Corporation, **14** 27
Precision LensCrafters, **13** 391
Precision Moulds, Ltd., **25** 312
Precision Optical Industry Company, Ltd. *see* Canon Inc.
Precision Pattern Inc., **36** 159
Precision Power, Inc., **21** 514
Precision Response Corporation, **47** 420
Precision Software Corp., **14** 319
Precision Spring of Canada, Ltd., **55** 305
Precision Stainless Inc., **65** 289
Precision Standard Inc. *see* Pemco Aviation Group Inc.
Precision Studios, **12** 529
Precision Tool, Die & Machine Company Inc., **51** 116–17
Precision Tube Formers, Inc., **17** 234
Precisionaire *see* Flanders Corporation.
Precoat Metals, **54** 331
Precor, **III** 610–11
Predica, **II** 266
Predicasts Inc., **12** 562; **17** 254
Prefco Corporation, **57** 56–57
Preferred Medical Products *see* Ballard Medical Products.
Preferred Products, Inc., **II** 669; **18** 504; **50** 454
PREINCO Holdings, Inc., **11** 532
PREL&P *see* Portland Railway Electric Light & Power Company.
Premark International, Inc., III 610–12; 14 548; **28** 479–80 *see also* Illinois Tool Works Inc.
Premcor Inc., 37 309–11
Premier Cement Ltd., **64** 98
Premier Health Alliance Inc., **10** 143
Premier Industrial Corporation, 9 419–21; 19 311
Premier Insurance Co., **26** 487
Premier Medical Services, **31** 357
Premier Milk Pte Ltd., **54** 117
Premier One Products, Inc., **37** 285
Premier Parks, Inc., 27 382–84
Premier Radio Networks, Inc., **23** 292, 294
Premier Rehabilitation Centers, **29** 400
Premier Sport Group Inc., **23** 66
Premiere Labels Inc., **53** 236
Premisteres S.A., **II** 663
Premium Standard Farms, Inc., 30 353–55
PremiumWear, Inc., 30 356–59
Prentice Hall Computer Publishing, **10** 24
Prentice Hall Inc., **I** 453; **IV** 672; **19** 405; **23** 503
Prescott Ball & Turben, **12** 60
Prescott Investors, **14** 303; **50** 311
Prescription Learning Corporation, **7** 256; **25** 253
Présence, **III** 211
Preserver Group, Inc., 44 354–56
President Baking Co., **36** 313
President Casinos, Inc., 22 438–40
President Riverboat Casino-Mississippi Inc., **21** 300
Presidents Island Steel & Wire Company *see* Laclede Steel Company.
Presley Cos., **59** 422
Press Associates, **19** 334
Presses de la Cité *see* Groupe de la Cité.
Pressman Toy Corporation, 56 280–82
Presstar Printing, **25** 183
Presstek, Inc., 33 345–48
Pressware International, **12** 377
Prestage Farms, **46** 83
Prestel Verlag, **66** 123
Prestige et Collections, **III** 48
Prestige Fragrance & Cosmetics, Inc., **22** 158
The Prestige Group plc., **19** 171
Prestige International, **33** 284
Prestige Leather Creations, **31** 435–36
Prestige Properties, **23** 388
Presto Products, Inc., **II** 609–10; **IV** 187; **19** 348; **50** 401
Preston Corporation, 6 421–23; 14 566, 568
Prestone Products Corp., **22** 32; **26** 349
Prestwick Mortgage Group, **25** 187
Pret A Manger, **63** 280, 284–85
Pretty Good Privacy, Inc., **25** 349
Pretty Neat Corp., **12** 216
Pretty Paper Inc., **14** 499
Pretzel Time *see* Mrs. Fields' Original Cookies, Inc.
Pretzelmaker *see* Mrs. Fields' Original Cookies, Inc.
Pretzels Incorporated, **24** 241

R&S Home and Auto, **56** 352
R&S Technology Inc., **48** 410
R. and W. Hawaii Wholesale, Inc., **22** 15
R-Anell Custom Homes Inc., **41** 19
R-B *see* Arby's, Inc.
R-Byte, **12** 162
R-C Holding Inc. *see* Air & Water Technologies Corporation.
R.B. Pamplin Corp., 45 350–52
R.C. Bigelow, Inc., 49 334–36
R.C. Willey Home Furnishings, 72 291–93
R. Cubed Composites Inc., **I** 387
R.E. Funsten Co., **7** 429
R.G. Barry Corp., 17 389–91; 44 364–67 (upd.)
R.G. Dun-Bradstreet Corp. *see* The Dun & Bradstreet Corp.
R. Griggs Group Limited, 23 399–402; 31 413–14
R.H. Donnelley Corporation, **61** 81–83
R.H. Macy & Co., Inc., V 168–70; 8 442–45 (upd.); 30 379–83 (upd.)
R.H. Stengel & Company, **13** 479
R.J. Reynolds, **I** 261, 363; **II** 544; **7** 130, 132, 267, 365, 367; **9** 533; **13** 490; **14** 78; **15** 72–73; **16** 242; **21** 315; **27** 125; **29** 195; **32** 344 *see also* RJR Nabisco.
R.J. Reynolds Tobacco Holdings, Inc., 30 384–87 (upd.)
R.J. Tower Corporation *see* Tower Automotive, Inc.
R.K. Brown, **14** 112
R.L. Crain Limited, **15** 473
R.L. Manning Company, **9** 363–64
R.L. Polk & Co., 10 460–62
R-O Realty, Inc., **43** 314
R.P.M., Inc., **25** 228
R.P. Scherer Corporation, I 678–80
R.R. Bowker Co., **17** 398; **23** 440
R.R. Donnelley & Sons Company, IV 660–62; 38 368–71 (upd.)
R.S.R. Corporation, **31** 48
R.S. Stokvis Company, **13** 499
R. Scott Associates, **11** 57
R-T Investors LC, **42** 323–24
R. Twining & Co., **61** 395
R.W. Beck, **29** 353
R.W. Harmon & Sons, Inc., **6** 410
RABA PLC, **10** 274
Rabbit Software Corp., **10** 474
Rabobank Group, 26 419; **33 356–58**
RAC *see* Ravenswood Aluminum Company; Roy Anderson Corporation.
Racal-Datacom Inc., 11 408–10
Racal Electronics PLC, II 83–84; 11 408, 547; **42** 373, 376; **50** 134
Race Z, Inc. *see* Action Peformance Companies, Inc.
Rachel's Dairy Ltd., **37** 197–98
Racine Hidraulica, **21** 430
Racine Threshing Machine Works, **10** 377
Racing Champions *see* Action Performance Companies, Inc.
Racing Champions Corporation, 37 318–20
Racing Collectables Club of America, Inc. *see* Action Performance Companies, Inc.
Racket Store *see* Duckwall-ALCO Stores, Inc.
Rada Corp., **IV** 250
Radeberger Gruppe AG, 75 332–35
Radian Group Inc., 42 299–301 *see also* Onex Corporation.
Radiant Lamp Corp., **13** 398
Radio & Television Equipment Company (Radio-Tel), **16** 200–01; **43** 168–69
Radio Austria A.G., **V** 314–16
Radio Cap Company *see* Norwood Promotional Products, Inc.
Radio City Productions, **30** 102
Radio Corporation of America *see* RCA Corporation.
Radio Flyer Inc., 34 368–70
Radio-Keith-Orpheum, **9** 247; **12** 73; **31** 99
Radio One, Inc., 67 318–21
Radio Receptor Company, Inc., **10** 319
Radio Shack, **II** 106–08; **12** 470; **13** 174
Radio Vertrieb Fürth *see* Grundig AG.
Radiocel, **39** 194
Radiometer A/S, **17** 287
Radiometrics, Inc., **18** 369
RadioShack Canada Inc., **30** 391
RadioShack Corporation, 36 384–88 (upd.)
Radiotelevision Española, **7** 511
Radisson Hotels Worldwide, **22** 126–27
Radius Inc., 16 417–19
Radix Group, Inc., **13** 20
Radman Inc., **56** 247
RadNet Managed Imaging Services, Inc., **25** 382–84
Radnor Venture Partners, LP, **10** 474
Raet, **39** 177
Raffinerie Tirlemontoise S.A., **27** 436
Raffineriegesellschaft Vohburg/Ingolstadt mbH, **7** 141
RAG AG, 35 364–67; 60 247–51 (upd.)
Rag Shops, Inc., 30 365–67
Ragan Outdoor, **27** 280
Ragazzi's, **10** 331
Ragdoll Productions Ltd., 51 308–11
Ragnar Benson Inc., **8** 43–43
Rail Link, Inc., **27** 181
Rail Van Global Logistics, **54** 276
Railroad Enterprises, Inc., **27** 347
Railtech International *see* Delachaux S.A.
RailTex, Inc., 20 445–47
Railtrack Group PLC, 39 238; **50 369–72**
Railway Maintenance Equipment Co., **14** 43
Rainbow Home Shopping Ltd. *see* Otto-Versand (GmbH & Co.).
Rainbow Media, **47** 421
Rainbow Programming Holdings, **7** 63–64
Rainbow Valley Orchards, **54** 257
RainbowBridge Communications, Inc., **25** 162
Raincoast Book Distribution, **34** 5
Rainer Pulp & Paper Company, **17** 439
Rainfair, Inc., **18** 298, 300
Rainforest Café, Inc., 25 386–88
Rainier Brewing Company, 23 403–05
Rainier Pulp and Paper Company *see* Rayonier Inc.
Rainy River Forest Products, Inc., **26** 445
Rajastan Breweries, Ltd., **18** 502
Raky-Danubia, **IV** 485
Ralcorp Holdings, Inc., **13** 293, 425, 427; **15** 189, 235; **21** 53, 56; **22** 337; **36** 238; **43** 438; **50** 294; **55** 96; **63** 251
Raleigh UK Ltd., 65 295–97
Raley's Inc., 14 396–98; 58 288–91 (upd.)
Ralli International, **IV** 259
Rally's, 25 389–91; 68 313–16 (upd.)
Rallye SA, 12 154; **54 306–09; 59** 107
Ralph & Kacoo's *see* Piccadilly Cafeterias, Inc.
Ralph Lauren *see* Polo/Ralph Lauren Corportion.
The Ralph M. Parsons Company *see* The Parsons Corporation.
Ralph Wilson Plastics, **III** 610–11
Ralph's Industries, **31** 191
Ralphs Grocery Company, 35 368–70
Ralston Purina Company, I 608, **II 561–63; 13 425–27 (upd.)** *see also* Ralcorp Holdings, Inc.
Ramada International Hotels & Resorts, **IV** 718; **9** 426; **11** 177; **13** 66; **21** 366; **25** 309; **28** 258; **38** 320; **52** 281
Rambol, **25** 84
Rampage Clothing Co., **35** 94
Ramparts, Inc., **57** 159
Ramsay Youth Services, Inc., 41 322–24
Ranbar Packing, Inc. *see* Western Beef, Inc.
Ranbaxy Laboratories Ltd., 70 247–49
Ranchers Packing Corp. *see* Western Beef, Inc.
Rand Capital Corp., **35** 52–53
Rand McNally & Company, 28 378–81; 53 122
Randall's Food Markets, Inc., 40 364–67
Randgold & Exploration, **63** 182–83
Random House, Inc., 13 428–30; 31 375–80 (upd.)
Randon Meldkamer, **43** 307
Randon S.A. Implementos e Participações, 79 348–352
Randstad Holding n.v., 16 420–22; 43 307–10 (upd.)
Range Resources Corporation, 45 353–55
The Rank Group plc, II 157–59; 14 399–402 (upd.); 64 317–21 (upd.)
Ranks Hovis McDougall Limited, II 564–65; 28 382–85 (upd.)
Ransburg Corporation, **22** 282
Ransom and Randolph Company, **10** 271
Ransom Industries LP, **55** 266
RAO Unified Energy System of Russia, 45 356–60
Rapala-Normark Group, Ltd., 30 368–71
Rapides Bank & Trust Company, **11** 107
Rapidforms, Inc., **35** 130–31

Reed International PLC, **IV 665–67**; **17 396–99 (upd.)**
Reeder Light, Ice & Fuel Company, **6** 592; **50** 38
Reeds Jewelers, Inc., **22 447–49**
Reese Finer Foods, Inc., **7** 429
Reese Products, **III** 569; **11** 535; **20** 361
Reeves Banking and Trust Company, **11** 181
Reeves Brothers, **17** 182
Reeves Pulley Company, **9** 440
Refco, Inc., **10** 251; **22** 189
Reference Software International, **10** 558
Refinaria de Petróleo Ipiranga S.A., **67** 216
Refineria Metales Uboldi y Cia. S.A., **74** 11
Reflectone Inc. *see* CAE USA Inc.
Reflex Winkelmann & Pannhoff GmbH, **18** 163
Refractarios Mexicanos, S.A. de C.V., **22** 285
Refrigeração Paraná S.A., **22** 27
Refrigerantes do Oeste, SA, **47** 291
Regal-Beloit Corporation, **18 450–53**
Regal Entertainment Group, **59 340–43**
Regal Inns, **13** 364
Regal International, **71** 232
Regal Manufacturing Co., **15** 385
The Regence Group, **74 261–63**
Regency Centers Corporation, **71 304–07**
Regency Health Services Inc., **25** 457
Regency International, **10** 196
Regeneration Technologies, Inc., **68** 379
Regenerative Environmental Equipment Company, Inc., **6** 441
Regeneron Pharmaceuticals Inc., **10** 80
Regent Carolina Corporation, **37** 226
Regent Communications Inc., **23** 294
Regent International Hotels Limited, **9** 238; **29** 200
Régie Autonome des Pétroles, **IV** 544–46; **21** 202–04
Régie des Télégraphes et Téléphones *see* Belgacom.
Régie Nationale des Usines Renault, **I 189–91** *see also* Renault S.A.
Regional Bell Operating Companies, **15** 125; **18** 111–12, 373
Regis Corporation, **18 454–56**; **70 261–65 (upd.)**
Register & Tribune Co. *see* Cowles Media Company.
Regnecentralen AS, **III** 164
Rego Supermarkets and American Seaway Foods, Inc., **9** 451; **13** 237
Rehab Hospital Services Corp., **III** 88; **10** 252
RehabClinics Inc., **11** 367
Rehrig Manufacturing, **51** 35
REI *see* Recreational Equipment, Inc.
REI Ltd. *see* CB Richard Ellis Group, Inc.
Reich, Landman and Berry, **18** 263
Reichart Furniture Corp., **14** 236
Reichhold Chemicals, Inc., **8** 554; **10 465–67**
Reidman Corporation, **41** 65
Reidsville Fashions, Inc., **13** 532
Reiman Publications *see* The Reader's Digest Association, Inc.
Reimersholms, **31** 458–60
Reims Aviation, **8** 92; **27** 100
Rein Elektronik, **10** 459
Reinsurance Agency, **III** 204–05
Reisland GmbH, **15** 340
Reiue Nationale des Usines Renault, **7** 220
Rekkof Restart NV, **28** 327
Relational Courseware, Inc., **21** 235–36
Relational Database Systems Inc., **10** 361–62
Relational Technology Inc., **10** 361
Relationship Marketing Group, Inc., **37** 409
Release Technologies, **8** 484
Reliable Life Insurance Company, **58** 259
Reliable Stores Inc., **14** 236
Reliance Electric Company, **9 439–42**
Reliance Group Holdings, Inc., **III 342–44**
Reliance National Indemnity Company, **18** 159
Reliance Steel & Aluminum Company, **19 343–45**; **70 266–70 (upd.)**
Reliant Energy Inc., **44 368–73 (upd.)**
ReLife Inc., **14** 233; **33** 185
Relìv International, Inc., **58 292–95**
Relocation Central *see* CORT Business Services Corporation.
Rembrandt Group Ltd., **IV** 93, 97; **50** 144
Remedy Corporation, **58 296–99**
RemedyTemp, Inc., **20 448–50**
Remgro, **IV** 97
Remington Arms Company, Inc., **12 415–17**; **40 368–71 (upd.)**
Remington Products Company, L.L.C., **42 307–10**
Remington Rand, **III** 126, 148, 151, 165–66, 642; **10** 255; **12** 416; **19** 430
Remmele Engineering, Inc., **17** 534
Rémy Cointreau S.A., **20 451–53**
Remy Martin, **48** 348–49
REN Corp. USA, Inc., **13** 161
REN Corporation, **49** 156
Renaissance Communications Corp., **22** 522; **63** 393
Renaissance Connects, **16** 394
Renaissance Cosmetics Inc. *see* New Dana Perfumes Co.
Renaissance Energy Ltd., **47** 181
Renaissance Hotel Group N.V., **38** 321
Renaissance Learning Systems, Inc., **39 341–43**
Renal Care Group, Inc., **72 297–99**
Renal Systems, Inc. *see* Minntech Corporation.
Renault Argentina S.A., **67 325–27**
Renault S.A., **26 401–04 (upd.)**; **74 264–68 (upd.)**
Rendeck International, **11** 66
Rendic International, **13** 228
René Garraud *see* Wella AG.
Renfro Corp., **25** 167
Rengo Co., Ltd., **IV 326**
Renishaw plc, **46 358–60**
RENK AG, **37 325–28**
Renner Herrmann S.A., **79 353–356**
Reno Air Inc., **23 409–11**; **24** 400; **28** 25
Reno de Medici S.p.A., **41 325–27**
Réno-Dépôt Inc., **26** 306
Reno Technologies, **12** 124
Rent-A-Center, Inc., **45 365–67**
Rent-Way, Inc., **33 366–68**; **75 336–39 (upd.)**
Rental Service Corporation, **28 386–88**
Renters Choice Inc. *see* Rent-A-Center, Inc.
Rentokil Initial Plc, **34** 43; **47 332–35**; **49** 375–77; **64** 197
Rentrak Corporation, **35 371–74**
Rentz, **23** 219
Renwick Technologies, Inc., **48** 286
Reo Products *see* Lifetime Hoan Corporation.
Repairmaster Canada, Inc., **53** 359
Repco Corporation Ltd., **74 269–72**
Replacement Enterprises Inc., **16** 380
Repligen Inc., **13** 241
Repola Ltd., **19** 465; **30** 325
Repola Oy, **IV** 316, 347, 350
Repsol S.A., **IV 527–29**; **16 423–26 (upd.)**; **49** 211
Repsol-YPF S.A., **40 372–76 (upd.)**
Repubblica, **IV** 587
Republic Airlines, **25** 421; **28** 265
Republic Aviation Corporation, **9** 205–07; **48** 167
Republic Broadcasting Corp., **23** 292
Republic Corp., **I** 447
Republic Engineered Steels, Inc., **7 446–47**; **26 405–08 (upd.)**
Republic Freight Systems, **14** 567
Republic Industries, Inc., **24** 12; **26 409–11**, 501
Republic Insurance, **III** 404
Republic National Bank, **19** 466
Republic New York Corporation, **11 415–19**
Republic Pictures, **9** 75
Republic Powdered Metals, Inc., **8** 454
Republic Steel Corp. *see* Republic Engineered Steels, Inc.
Republic Supply Co., **63** 288
Res-Care, Inc., **29 399–402**
Research Analysis Corporation, **7** 15
Research Cottrell, Inc., **6** 441
Research Genetics, Inc., **52** 183–84
Research in Motion Ltd., **54 310–14**
Research Publications, **8** 526
Réseau Ferré de France, **57** 328, 332; **66 266–68**
Resecenter, **55** 90
Resem SpA, **I** 387
Reserve Mining Co., **17** 356
Reservoir Productions, **17** 150
Residence Inns, **9** 426
Residential Funding Corporation, **10** 92–93
Resin Exchange, **19** 414
ResNet Communications Inc., **28** 241
Resolution Systems, Inc., **13** 201

Ringköpkedjan, **II** 640
Ringling Bros., Barnum & Bailey Circus, **25** 312–13
Ringnes Bryggeri, **18** 396
Rini-Rego Supermarkets Inc., **13** 238
Rini Supermarkets, **9** 451; **13** 237
Rinker Group Ltd., 65 298–301
Rio de Janeiro Refrescos S.A., **71** 140
Rio Grande Industries, Inc., **12** 18–19
Rio Grande Servaas, S.A. de C.V., **23** 145
Rio Sportswear Inc., **42** 269
Rio Sul Airlines *see* Varig, SA.
Rio Tinto plc, IV 58–61, 189–91, 380; **19 349–53 (upd.) 50 380–85 (upd.)**
Riocell S.A. *see* Klabin S.A.
Riordan Freeman & Spogli, **13** 406
Riordan Holdings Ltd., **10** 554; **67** 298
Ripley Entertainment, Inc., 74 273–76
Ripotot, **68** 143
Riser Foods, Inc., 9 451–54; 13 237–38
Risk Management Partners Ltd., **35** 36
Risk Planners, **II** 669
Ritchie Bros. Auctioneers Inc., 41 331–34
Rite Aid Corporation, V 174–76; 19 354–57 (upd.); 63 331–37 (upd.)
Rite-Way Department Store, **II** 649
Riteway Distributor, **26** 183
Rittenhouse Financial Services, **22** 495
Ritter Co. *see* Sybron Corp.
Ritter Sport *see* Alfred Ritter GmbH & Co. KG.
Ritter's Frozen Custard *see* RFC Franchising LLC.
Ritz Camera Centers, 18 186; **34 375–77**
The Ritz-Carlton Hotel Company, L.L.C., 9 455–57; 29 403–06 (upd.); 71 311–16 (upd.)
Ritz Firma, **13** 512
Riunione Adriatica di Sicurtà SpA, III 345–48
Riva Group Plc, **53** 46
The Rival Company, 19 358–60
Rivarossi, **16** 337
Rivaud Group, **29** 370
River Boat Casino, **9** 425–26
River City Broadcasting, **25** 418
River Metals Recycling LLC, **76** 130
River North Studios *see* Platinum Entertainment, Inc.
River Oaks Furniture, Inc., 43 314–16
River Ranch Fresh Foods—Salinas, Inc., **41** 11
River Thames Insurance Co., Ltd., **26** 487
Riverdeep Group plc, **41** 137
Riverside Chemical Company, **13** 502
Riverside Furniture, **19** 455
Riverside Insurance Co. of America, **26** 487
Riverside Iron Works, Ltd., **8** 544
Riverside National Bank of Buffalo, **11** 108
Riverside Press, **10** 355–56
Riverside Publishing Company, **36** 272
Riverwood International Corporation, 7 294; **11 420–23; 48 340–44 (upd.)**
Riviana Foods, 27 388–91
Riviera Holdings Corporation, 75 340–43
Riyadh Armed Forces Hospital, **16** 94
Rizzoli Publishing, **23** 88
RJMJ, Inc., **16** 37
RJR Nabisco Holdings Corp., V 408–10 *see also* R.J Reynolds Tobacco Holdings Inc., Nabisco Brands, Inc.; R.J. Reynolds Industries, Inc.
RK Rose + Krieger GmbH & Co. KG, **61** 286–87
RKO *see* Radio-Keith-Orpheum.
RKO-General, Inc., **8** 207
RLA Polymers, **9** 92
RMC Group p.l.c., III 737–40; 34 378–83 (upd.)
RMH Teleservices, Inc., 42 322–24
RMP International, Limited, **8** 417
Roadhouse Grill, Inc., 22 464–66; 57 84
Roadmaster Industries, Inc., 16 430–33
Roadmaster Transport Company, **18** 27; **41** 18
RoadOne *see* Miller Industries, Inc.
Roadstone-Wood Group, **64** 98
Roadway Express, Inc., V 502–03; 25 395–98 (upd.)
Roanoke Capital Ltd., **27** 113–14
Roanoke Electric Steel Corporation, 45 368–70
Roanoke Fashions Group, **13** 532
Robb Engineering Works, **8** 544
Robbins & Myers Inc., 13 273; **15 388–90**
Robeco Group, **26** 419–20
Roberds Inc., 19 361–63
Robert Allen Companies, **III** 571; **20** 362
Robert Benson, Lonsdale & Co. Ltd. *see* Dresdner Kleinwort Wasserstein.
Robert Bosch GmbH, I 392–93; 16 434–37 (upd.); 43 317–21 (upd.)
Robert E. McKee Corporation, **6** 150
Robert Fleming Holdings Ltd., **I** 471; **11** 495
Robert Gair Co., **15** 128
Robert Garrett & Sons, Inc., **9** 363
Robert Half International Inc., 18 461–63; 70 281–84 (upd.)
Robert Hall Clothes, Inc., **13** 535
Robert Hansen Trucking Inc., **49** 402
Robert Johnson, **8** 281–82
Robert McLane Company *see* McLane Company, Inc.
Robert McNish & Company Limited, **14** 141
Robert Mondavi Corporation, 15 391–94; 39 45; **50 386–90 (upd.); 54** 343
Robert Skeels & Company, **33** 467
Robert Stigwood Organization Ltd., **23** 390
Robert W. Baird & Co. Incorporated, III 324; **7** 495; **67 328–30**
Robert Watson & Co. Ltd., **I** 568
Robert Wood Johnson Foundation, 35 375–78
Robertet SA, 39 347–49
Roberts Express, **V** 503
Roberts Pharmaceutical Corporation, 16 438–40
Roberts Trading Corporation, **68** 99
Robertson Animal Hospital, Inc., **58** 355
Robertson Building Products, **8** 546
Robertson-Ceco Corporation, 8 546; **19 364–66**
Robertson, Stephens & Co., **22** 465
Robin Hood Flour Mills, Ltd., **7** 241–43; **25** 241
Robin International Inc., **24** 14
Robinair, **10** 492, 494
Robinson & Clark Hardware *see* Clarcor Inc.
Robinson Helicopter Company, 51 315–17
Robinson Industries, **24** 425
Robinson Smith & Robert Haas, Inc., **13** 428
Robinson Way, **70** 160–61
Rogue Pictures *see* Focus Features
Rogue Wave Software, Inc. *see* Quovadix Inc.
Robinson's Japan Co. Ltd. *see* Ito-Yokado Co., Ltd.
Robinsons Soft Drinks Limited, **38** 77
Robot Manufacturing Co., **16** 8
Robotic Simulations Limited, **56** 134
Robotic Vision Systems, Inc., **16** 68
ROC *see* Royal Olympic Cruise Lines Inc.
Rocawear Apparel LLC, 77 355–358
Roccade, **39** 177
Roch, S.A., **23** 83
Roche Biomedical Laboratories, Inc., 11 424–26 *see also* Laboratory Corporation of America Holdings.
Roche Bioscience, 14 403–06 (upd.)
Roche Holding AG, **30** 164; **32** 211, 213–14; **37** 113; **50** 421
Rocher Soleil, **48** 315
Rochester Gas And Electric Corporation, 6 571–73
Rochester Group, Inc., **60** 267
Rochester Instrument Systems, Inc., **16** 357
Rochester Telephone Corporation, 6 332–34
Röchling Industrie Verwaltung GmbH, **9** 443
Rock Bottom Restaurants, Inc., 25 399–401; 68 320–23 (upd.)
Rock Island Plow Company, **10** 378
Rock of Ages Corporation, 37 329–32
Rock Systems Inc., **18** 337
Rock-Tenn Company, 13 441–43; 59 347–51 (upd.)
Rockcor Inc., **I** 381; **13** 380
Rockcote Paint Company, **8** 552–53
The Rockefeller Foundation, 34 384–87; 52 15
Rockefeller Group International Inc., 58 303–06
Rocket Chemical Company *see* WD-40 Company.
Rockford Corporation, 43 322–25
Rockford Products Corporation, 55 323–25

Index to Companies

Société Nationale de Programmes de Télévision Française 1 *see* Télévision Française 1.
Société Nationale des Chemins de Fer Français, V 512–15; 57 328–32 (upd.); 67 187–88
Société Nationale des Pétroles d'Aquitaine, **21** 203–05
Société Nationale Elf Aquitaine, IV 544–47; 7 481–85 (upd.)
Société Norbert Dentressangle S.A., 67 352–54
Société Nouvelle d'Achat de Bijouterie, **16** 207
Société Nouvelle des Etablissements Gaumont *see* Gaumont SA.
Société Parisienne d'Achats en Commun, **19** 307
Société Parisienne Raveau-Cartier, **31** 128
Société pour l'Étude et la Realisation d'Engins Balistiques *see* SEREB.
Société pour le Financement de l'Industrie Laitière, **19** 51
Société Samos, **23** 219
Société Savoyarde des Fromagers du Reblochon, **25** 84
Société Succursaliste S.A. d'Approvisonnements Guyenne et Gascogne *see* Guyenne et Gascogne.
Société Suisse de Microelectronique & d'Horlogerie *see* The Swatch Group SA.
Société Tefal *see* Groupe SEB.
Société Tunisienne de l'Air-Tunisair, 49 371–73
Societe Vendeenne des Embalages, **9** 305
Society Corporation, 9 474–77
Socma *see* Sociedad Macri S.A.
SOCO Chemical Inc., **8** 69
Socony *see* Standard Oil Co. (New York).
Socony-Vacuum Oil Company *see* Mobil Corporation.
Socpresse, **60** 281
Sodak Gaming, Inc., **9** 427; **41** 216
Sodexho Alliance SA, 23 154; **29 442–44; 47** 201
Sodiaal S.A., 19 50; **36 437–39 (upd.)**
SODIMA, II 576–77 *see also* Sodiaal S.A.
Sodimac S.A., **69** 312
La Sodis *see* Éditions Gallimard.
Sodiso, **23** 247
Soeker Exploration & Production Pty, Ltd., **59** 336–37
Soekor, **IV** 93
Sofamor Danek Group, Inc. *see* Medtronic, Inc.
Soffo, **22** 365
Soficom, **27** 136
SOFIL *see* Société pour le Financement de l'Industrie Laitière.
Sofimex *see* Sociedad Financiera Mexicana.
Sofitam, S.A., **21** 493, 495
Sofitels *see* Accor SA.
Sofora Telecomunicaciones S.A., **63** 377
Soft Lenses Inc., **25** 55
Soft Sheen Products, Inc., 31 416–18; 46 278
Soft*Switch, **25** 301
Softbank Corporation, 13 481–83; 38 439–44 (upd.); 77 387–395 (upd.)
Softimage Inc., **38** 71–72
SoftKat *see* Baker & Taylor, Inc.
SoftKey Software Products Inc., **24** 276
Softsel Computer Products, **12** 334–35
SoftSolutions Technology Corporation, **10** 558
Software AG, **11** 18
Software Architects Inc., **74** 258
Software Development Pty., Ltd., **15** 107
Software Dimensions, Inc. *see* ASK Group, Inc.
Software, Etc., **13** 545
The Software Group Inc., **23** 489, 491
Software Plus, Inc., **10** 514
Software Publishing Corp., **14** 262
Softwood Holdings Ltd., **III** 688
Sogara S.A., **23** 246–48
Sogedis, **23** 219
Sogo Co., **42** 342
Sohio Chemical Company, **13** 502
Soil Teq, Inc., **17** 10
Soilserv, Inc. *see* Mycogen Corporation.
Sol Meliá S.A., 71 337–39
Sola International Inc., 71 340–42
Solair Inc., **14** 43; **37** 30–31
La Solana Corp., **IV** 726
Solar Electric Corp., **13** 398
Solar Wide Industrial Ltd., **73** 332
Solaray, Inc., **37** 284–85
Solect Technology Group, **47** 12
Solectron Corporation, 12 161–62, **450–52; 38** 186, 189; **46** 38; **48 366–70 (upd.)**
Solera Capital, **59** 50
Solid Beheer B.V., **10** 514
Solid Cement Corporation, **59** 115
Solite Corp., **23** 224–25
Söll, **40** 96, 98
Sollac, **24** 144; **25** 96
Solley's Delicatessen and Bakery, **24** 243
Solo Serve Corporation, 23 177; **28 429–31**
SOLOCO Inc., **63** 305
Soloman Brothers, **17** 561
Solomon Smith Barney Inc., **22** 404
Solomon Valley Milling Company, **6** 592; **50** 37
Solon Automated Services, **II** 607
Solsound Industries, **16** 393
Soltam, **25** 266
Solutia Inc., 29 330; **52 312–15**
Solvay & Cie S.A., I 394–96; 21 464–67 (upd.)
Solvay Animal Health Inc., **12** 5
Solvay S.A., 61 329–34 (upd.)
Solvent Resource Recovery, Inc., **9** 109
Solvents Recovery Service of New Jersey, Inc., **8** 464
SOMABRI, **12** 152
SOMACA, **12** 152
Somali Bank, **31** 220
Someal, **27** 513, 515
Somerfield plc, 47 365–69 (upd.)
Somerville Electric Light Company, **12** 45
Somerville Packaging Group, **28** 420
Sommer-Allibert S.A., 19 406–09
Sommers Drug Stores, **9** 186
Sonat Exploration Company, **63** 366
Sonat, Inc., 6 577–78; 22 68
Sonatrach, 65 313–17 (upd.)
Sonecor Systems, **6** 340
Sonera Corporation, 50 441–44 *see also* TeliaSonera AB.
Sonergy, Inc., **49** 280
Sonesta International Hotels Corporation, 44 389–91
Sonet Media AB, **23** 390
SONI Ltd., **64** 404
Sonic Automotive, Inc., 77 396–399
Sonic Corp., 14 451–53; 37 360–63 (upd.)
Sonic Duo, **48** 419
Sonic Innovations Inc., 56 336–38
Sonic Restaurants, **31** 279
Sonnen Basserman, **II** 475
SonnenBraune, **22** 460
Sonoco Products Company, 8 475–77
Sonofon *see* Telenor ASA.
The Sonoma Group, **25** 246
Sonor GmbH, **53** 216
SonoSite, Inc., 56 339–41
Sony Corporation, II 101–03; 12 453–56 (upd.); 40 404–10 (upd.)
Sony Ericsson Mobile Communications AB, **61** 137
Soo Line Corporation *see* Canadian Pacific Ltd.
Soo Line Mills, **II** 631
Sooner Trailer Manufacturing Co., **29** 367
Soparind, **25** 83–85
Sope Creek, **30** 457
Sophus Berendsen A/S, 49 374–77
SOPORCEL, **34** 38–39
Soporcel-Sociedade Portuguesa de Papel, S.A., **60** 156
Sorbee International Ltd., 74 309–11
Sorbents Products Co. Inc., **31** 20
Sorbus, **6** 242
Soreal, **8** 344
Sorenson Research Company, **36** 496
Sorg Paper Company *see* Mosinee Paper Corporation.
Soriana *see* Organización Soriana, S.A. de C.V.
Sorin S.p.A., **61** 70, 72
Soros Fund Management LLC, 27 198; **28 432–34; 43** 218
Sorrento, Inc., 19 51; **24 444–46; 26** 505
SOS Staffing Services, 25 432–35
Sosa, Bromley, Aguilar & Associates *see* D'Arcy Masius Benton & Bowles, Inc.
Soterra, Inc., **15** 188
Sotetsu Rosen, **72** 301
Sotheby's Holdings, Inc., 11 452–54; 15 98–100; **29 445–48 (upd.); 32** 164; **39** 81–84; **49** 325
Soufflet SA *see* Groupe Soufflet SA.
Sound Advice, Inc., 41 379–82
Sound of Music Inc. *see* Best Buy Co., Inc.
Sound Trek, **16** 74
Sound Video Unlimited, **16** 46; **43** 60
Sound Warehouse, **9** 75

Souplantation Incorporated *see* Garden Fresh Restaurant Corporation.
The Source Enterprises, Inc., 65 318–21
Source Interlink Companies, Inc., 75 350–53
Source One Mortgage Services Corp., **12** 79
Source Perrier, **7** 383; **24** 444
Sourdough Bread Factory *see* Matt Prentice Restaurant Group.
Souriau, **19** 166
South African Airways Ltd., **27** 132 *see also* Transnet Ltd.
The South African Breweries Limited, I 287–89; 24 447–51 (upd.) *see also* SABMiller plc.
South African Transport Services *see* Transnet Ltd.
South Asia Tyres, **20** 263
South Australian Brewing Company, **54** 228, 341
South Beach Beverage Company, Inc., 73 316–19
South Bend Toy Manufacturing Company, **25** 380
South Carolina Electric & Gas Company *see* SCANA Corporation.
South Carolina National Corporation, **16** 523, 526
South Carolina Power Company, **38** 446–47
South Central Bell Telephone Co. *see* BellSouth Corporation.
South Central Railroad Co., **14** 325
South Coast Gas Compression Company, Inc., **11** 523
South Coast Terminals, Inc., **16** 475
South Dakota Public Service Company, **6** 524
South Florida Neonatology Associates, **61** 284
South Fulton Light & Power Company, **6** 514
South Jersey Industries, Inc., 42 352–55
South of Scotland Electricity Board, **19** 389–90
South Overseas Fashion Ltd., **53** 344
South Sea Textile, **III** 705
South Wales Electric Company, **34** 219
South West Water Plc *see* Pennon Group Plc.
South Western Electricity plc, **38** 448; **41** 316
South-Western Publishing Co., **8** 526–28
Southam Inc., 7 486–89; **15** 265; **24** 223; **36** 374
Southco, **II** 602–03; **7** 20–21; **30** 26
Southcorp Holdings Ltd., **17** 373; **22** 350
Southcorp Limited, 54 341–44
Southdown, Inc., 14 454–56; **59** 114–15
Southdown Press *see* PMP Ltd.
Southeast Bank of Florida, **11** 112
Southeast Public Service Company, **8** 536
Southeastern Freight Lines, Inc., **53** 249
Southeastern Personnel *see* Norrell Corporation.
Southern and Phillips Gas Ltd., **13** 485
Southern Australia Airlines, **24** 396
Southern Bank, **10** 426
Southern Bearings Co., **13** 78
Southern Bell, **10** 202
Southern Blvd. Supermarkets, Inc., **22** 549
Southern Box Corp., **13** 441
Southern California Edison Co. *see* Edison International.
Southern California Financial Corporation, **27** 46
Southern California Fruit Growers Exchange *see* Sunkist Growers, Inc.
Southern California Gas Co., **25** 413–14, 416
Southern Casualty Insurance Co., **III** 214
The Southern Company, V 721–23; 38 445–49 (upd.)
Southern Cooker Limited Partnership, **51** 85
Southern Corrections Systems, Inc. *see* Avalon Correctional Services, Inc.
Southern Cotton Co., **24** 488
Southern Cross Paints, **38** 98
Southern Discount Company of Atlanta, **9** 229
Southern Electric PLC, 13 484–86 *see also* Scottish and Southern Energy plc.
Southern Electric Supply Co., **15** 386
Southern Electronics Corp. *see* SED International Holdings, Inc.
Southern Equipment & Supply Co., **19** 344
Southern Financial Bancorp, Inc., 56 342–44
Southern Foods Group, L.P. *see* Dean Foods Company.
Southern Forest Products, Inc., **6** 577
Southern Gage, **III** 519; **22** 282
Southern Graphic Arts, **13** 405
Southern Guaranty Cos., **III** 404
Southern Idaho Water Power Company, **12** 265
Southern Indiana Gas and Electric Company, 13 487–89
Southern Lumber Company, **8** 430
Southern Manufacturing Company, **8** 458
Southern Minnesota Beet Sugar Cooperative, **32** 29
Southern National Bankshares of Atlanta, **II** 337; **10** 425
Southern National Corporation *see* BB&T Corporation
Southern Natural Gas Co., **6** 577
Southern Nevada Power Company, **11** 343
Southern Nevada Telephone Company, **11** 343
Southern New England Telecommunications Corporation, 6 338–40
Southern Oregon Broadcasting Co., **7** 15
Southern Pacific Communications Corporation, **9** 478–79
Southern Pacific Rail Corp. *see* Union Pacific Corporation.
Southern Pacific Transportation Company, V 516–18; **12** 278; **26** 235; **37** 312
Southern Peru Copper Corp.,
Southern Peru Copper Corporation, 40 411–13
Southern Phenix Textiles Inc., **15** 247–48
Southern Poverty Law Center, Inc., 74 312–15
Southern Power Company *see* Duke Energy Corporation.
Southern Recycling Inc., **51** 170
Southern Science Applications, Inc., **22** 88
Southern States Cooperative Incorporated, 36 440–42
Southern Sun Hotel Corporation *see* South African Breweries Ltd.; Sun International Hotels Limited.
Southern Telephone Company, **14** 257
Southern Union Company, **12** 542; **27 424–26**
Southern Video Partnership, **9** 74
Southern Water plc, **19** 389–91; **49** 363, 365–66
Southgate Medical Laboratory System, **26** 391
Southington Savings Bank, **55** 52
The Southland Corporation, II 660–61; 7 490–92 (upd.) *see also* 7-Eleven, Inc.
Southland Mobilcom Inc., **15** 196
Southland Paper, **13** 118
Southland Royal Company, **27** 86
Southland Royalty Co., **10** 190
Southmark Corp., **11** 483; **33** 398
Southport, Inc., **44** 203
Southtrust Corporation, 11 455–57
Southwest Airlines Co., 6 119–21; 24 452–55 (upd.); 71 343–47 (upd.)
Southwest Airmotive Co., **II** 16
Southwest Convenience Stores, LLC, **26** 368
Southwest Converting, **19** 414
Southwest Enterprise Associates, **13** 191
Southwest Forest Industries, **IV** 334
Southwest Gas Corporation, 19 410–12
Southwest Hide Co., **16** 546
Southwest Property Trust Inc., **52** 370
Southwest Sports Group, **51** 371, 374
Southwest Water Company, 47 370–73
Southwestern Bell Corporation, V 328–30 *see also* SBC Communications Inc.
Southwestern Bell Publications, **26** 520
Southwestern Electric Power Co., 21 468–70
Southwestern Explosives, Inc., **76** 34
Southwestern Gas Pipeline, **7** 344
Southwestern Illinois Coal Company, **7** 33
Southwestern Public Service Company, 6 579–81
Southwestern Textile Company, **12** 393
Southwire Company, Inc., 8 478–80; 12 353; **23 444–47 (upd.)**
Souvall Brothers, **8** 473
Souza Cruz S.A., 65 322–24
Souza Pinto Industria e Comercio de Artefatos de Borracha Ltda., **71** 393
Sovereign Corp., **III** 221; **14** 109; **37** 84
Soviba, **70** 322
Sovintel, **59** 209, 211

T

Tellabs, Inc., 11 500–01; 40 426–29 (upd.)
TELMARK, Inc., **57** 284
Telmex *see* Teléfonos de México S.A. de C.V.
Telpar, Inc., **14** 377
Telport, **14** 260
Telstra Corporation Limited, 50 469–72
Telrad Networks Ltd., **68** 222, 225
Teltrend, Inc., **57** 409
Telvent *see* Telecom Ventures.
Telxon Corporation, 10 523–25
Tembec Inc., 66 322–24
Temerlin McClain, **23** 479; **25** 91
TEMIC TELEFUNKEN, **34** 128, 133, 135
Temp Force, **16** 421–22; **43** 308
Temple, Barker & Sloan/Strategic Planning Associates, **III** 283
Temple Frosted Foods, **25** 278
Temple Inks Company, **13** 227
Temple-Inland Inc., IV 341–43; 31 438–42 (upd.)
Templeton, **II** 609
TEMPO Enterprises, **II** 162
Tempo-Team, **16** 420; **43** 307
Tempur-Pedic Inc., 54 359–61
Tempus Expeditions, **13** 358
Tempus Group plc, **48** 442
TemTech Ltd., **13** 326
Ten Cate *see* Royal Ten Cate N.V.
Ten Speed Press, **27** 223
Tenacqco Bridge Partnership, **17** 170
Tenaris SA, 63 385–88
Tenby Industries Limited, **21** 350
Tencor Instruments, Inc. *see* KLA-Tencor Corporation.
Tender Loving Care Health Care Services Inc., **64** 39
Tenet Healthcare Corporation, 55 368–71 (upd.)
TenFold Corporation, 35 421–23
Tengelmann Group, 27 459–62 164
Tengelmann Warenhandelsgesellschaft OHG, **47** 107
Tennant Company, 13 499–501; 33 390–93 (upd.)
Tenneco Inc., I 526–28; 10 526–28 (upd.)
Tennessee Book Company, **11** 193
Tennessee Eastman Corporation *see* Eastman Chemical Company.
Tennessee Gas Pipeline Co., **14** 126
Tennessee Gas Transmission Co., **13** 496; **14** 125
Tennessee Insurance Company, **11** 193–94
Tennessee Paper Mills Inc. *see* Rock-Tenn Company.
Tennessee Restaurant Company, **9** 426; **30** 208–9; **72** 141–42
Tennessee River Pulp & Paper Co., **12** 376–77; **51** 282–83
Tennessee Trifting, **13** 169
Tennessee Valley Authority, 50 473–77
Tennessee Woolen Mills, Inc., **19** 304
TenneT B.V., 78 392–395
Teoma Technologies, Inc., **65** 51–52
TEP *see* Tucson Electric Power Company.
TEPCO Cable Television Inc., **74** 348
TEPPCO Partners, L.P., 73 335–37
Tequila Sauza, **31** 91
Tequilera de Los Altos, **31** 92
Tera Computer Company, **75** 119
TeraBeam Networks Inc., **41** 261, 263–64
Teradata Corporation *see* NCR Corporation.
Teradyne, Inc., 11 502–04
Terex Corporation, 7 513–15; **8** 116; **40 430–34 (upd.)**
Teril Stationers Inc., **16** 36
The Terlato Wine Group, 48 390–92
Terminix International, **11** 433; **25** 16
Terra Industries, Inc., 13 277, **502–04**
Terra Lycos, Inc., 43 420–25; 46 416
Terracor, **11** 260–61
Terragrafics, **14** 245
Terrain King, **32** 26
Terre Haute Electric, **6** 555
Terre Lune, **25** 91
Terrena L'Union CANA CAVAL, 70 320–22
Territory Ahead, Inc., **29** 279
Terumo Corporation, 48 393–95
Tesa, S.A., **23** 82
TESC *see* The European Software Company.
Tesco plc, II 677–78; 24 473–76 (upd.); 68 366–70 (upd.)
Tesoro Petroleum Corporation, 7 516–19; 45 408–13 (upd.)
Tessenderlo Group, 76 345–48
Tesseract Inc., **11** 78; **33** 331
Tessman Seed, Inc., **16** 270–71
The Testor Corporation, 8 455; **51 367–70**
Tetley Group *see* Tata Tea Ltd.
Tetra Pak International SA, 53 327–29
Tetra Plastics Inc. *see* NIKE, Inc.
Tetra Tech, Inc., 29 463–65
Tettemer & Associates *see* The Keith Companies.
Teva Pharmaceutical Industries Ltd., 22 500–03; 47 55; **54 362–65 (upd.)**
Tex-Mex Partners L.C., **41** 270
Texaco Canada Inc., **25** 232
Texaco Inc., IV 551–53; 14 491–94 (upd.); 41 391–96 (upd.) *see also* ChevronTexaco Corporation.
Texas Air Corporation, I 123–24
Texas Almanac, **10** 3
Texas Bus Lines, **24** 118
Texas Coffee Traders, **60** 210
Texas Eastern Corp., **11** 97, 354; **14** 126; **50** 179
Texas Eastern Transmission Company, **11** 28
Texas Farm LLC *see* Nippon Meat Packers Inc.
Texas Gas Resources Corporation, **22** 166
Texas Homecare, **21** 335
Texas Industries, Inc., 8 522–24
Texas Instruments Incorporated, II 112–15; 11 505–08 (upd.); 46 418–23 (upd.)
Texas International Airlines, **21** 142
Texas Metal Fabricating Company, **7** 540
Texas-New Mexico Utilities Company, **6** 580
Texas Pacific Group Inc., 36 472–74
Texas Public Utilities, **II** 660
Texas Rangers Baseball, 51 371–74
Texas Roadhouse, Inc., 69 347–49
Texas Super Duper Markets, Inc., **7** 372
Texas Timberjack, Inc., **51** 279–81
Texas Trust Savings Bank, **8** 88
Texas United Insurance Co., **III** 214
Texas Utilities Company, V 724–25; 25 472–74 (upd.)
Texasgulf Inc., **13** 557; **18** 433
Texboard, **IV** 296; **19** 226
Texstar Petroleum Company, **7** 516
Texstyrene Corp., **IV** 331
Têxtil Santa Catarina Ltda., **72** 68
Textile Diffusion, **25** 466
Textile Paper Tube Company, Ltd., **8** 475
Textile Rubber and Chemical Company, **15** 490
Textron Inc., I 529–30; 34 431–34 (upd.)
Textron Lycoming Turbine Engine, 9 497–99
Texwood Industries, Inc., **20** 363
TFC *see* Times Fiber Communications, Inc.
TFH Publications, Inc., **58** 60
TFM *see* Grupo Transportación Ferroviaria Mexicana, S.A. de C.V.
TFN Group Communications, Inc., **8** 311
TF1 *see* Télévision Française 1
TFP, Inc., **44** 358–59
TFS *see* Total Filtration Services, Inc.
TG Credit Service Co. Ltd., **55** 375
TGEL&PCo *see* Tucson Gas, Electric Light & Power Company.
TH:s Group, **10** 113; **50** 43
Tha Row Records, 69 350–52 (upd.)
Thai Airways International Public Company Limited, 6 122–24; 27 463–66 (upd.)
Thai Lube Blending Co., **56** 290
Thai Nylon Co. Ltd., **53** 344
Thai Union Frozen Products PCL, 75 370–72
Thalassa International, **10** 14; **27** 11
Thales S.A., 42 373–76
Thames Trains, **28** 157
Thames Water plc, 11 509–11; 22 89
Thameslink, **28** 157
THAW *see* Recreational Equipment, Inc.
Theatrical Syndicate, **24** 437
Thelem SA, **54** 267
Therm-o-Disc, **II** 19
Therm-X Company, **8** 178
Thermacore International Inc., **56** 247
Thermador Corporation, **67** 82
Thermadyne Holding Corporation, 19 440–43
Thermal Dynamics, **19** 441
Thermal Energies, Inc., **21** 514
Thermal Power Company, **11** 270
Thermal Snowboards, Inc., **22** 462
Thermal Transfer Ltd., **13** 485
ThermaStor Technologies, Ltd., **44** 366

U

Unigate PLC, II 586–87; 28 488–91 (upd.); 29 150 *see also* Uniq Plc.
Unigesco Inc., **II** 653
Uniglory, **13** 211
Unigro *see* Laurus N.V.
Unigroup, **15** 50
UniHealth America, **11** 378–79
Unijoh Sdn, Bhd, **47** 255
Unik S.A., **23** 170–171
Unilab Corp., **26** 391
Unilever PLC/Unilever N.V., II 588–91; 7 542–45 (upd.); 32 472–78 (upd.)
Unilife Assurance Group, **III** 273
UniLife Insurance Co., **22** 149
Unilog SA, 42 401–03
Uniloy Milacron Inc., **53** 230
UniMac Companies, **11** 413
Unimetal, **30** 252
Uninsa, **I** 460
Union Aéromaritime de Transport *see* UTA.
Union Bag–Camp Paper Corp. *see* Union Camp Corporation.
Union Bank *see* State Street Boston Corporation.
Union Bank of California, 16 496–98 *see also* UnionBanCal Corporation.
Union Bank of New York, **9** 229
Union Bank of Scotland, **10** 337
Union Bank of Switzerland, II 378–79; 21 146 *see also* UBS AG.
Union Bay Sportswear, **17** 460
Union Biscuits *see* Leroux S.A.S.
Union Camp Corporation, IV 344–46
Union Carbide Corporation, I 399–401; 9 516–20 (upd.); 74 358–63 (upd.)
Union Cervecera, **9** 100
Union Colliery Company *see* Union Electric Company.
Union Commerce Corporation, **11** 181
Union Commerciale, **19** 98
Union Corporation *see* Gencor Ltd.
Union des Assurances de Paris, II 234; **III** 201, **391–94**
Union des Coopératives Bressor, **25** 85
Union des Cooperatives Laitières *see* Unicoolait.
Union des Mines, **52** 362
Union des Transports Aériens *see* UTA.
Union Electric Company, V 741–43; 26 451 *see also* Ameren Corporation.
Unión Electrica Fenosa *see* Unión Fenosa S.A.
Union Equity Co-Operative Exchange, **7** 175
Unión Fenosa, S.A., 51 387–90
Union Financiera, **19** 189
Union Financière de France Banque SA, 52 360–62
Union Fork & Hoe Company *see* Acorn Products, Inc.
Union Gas & Electric Co., **6** 529
l'Union Générale des Pétroles, **IV** 560
Union Hardware, **22** 115
Union Laitière Normande *see* Compagnie Laitière Européenne.
Union Levantina de Seguros, **III** 179
Union Light, Heat & Power Company *see* Cincinnati Gas & Electric Company.
Union Minière *see* NV Umicore SA.
Union Mutual Life Insurance Company *see* UNUM Corp.
Union National Bank of Wilmington, **25** 540
Union of European Football Association, **27** 150
Union of Food Co-ops, **II** 622
Union Oil Co., **9** 266
Union Oil Co. of California *see* Unocal Corporation.
Union Pacific Corporation, V 529–32; 28 492–500 (upd.) ; 79 435–446 (upd.)
Union Pacific Resources Group, **52** 30
Union Pacific Tea Co., **7** 202
Union Paper & Co. AS, **63** 315
Union Planters Corporation, 54 387–90
Union Power Company, **12** 541
Union Power Construction Co. *see* Quanta Services, Inc.
Union Pub Company, **57** 411, 413
Union Savings and Loan Association of Phoenix, **19** 412
Union Savings Bank, **9** 173
Union Savings Bank and Trust Company, **13** 221
Union Steamship Co. of New Zealand Ltd., **27** 473
Union Sugar, **II** 573
Union Suisse des Coopératives de Consommation *see* Coop Schweiz.
Union Tank Car Co., **IV** 137
Union Telecard Alliance, LLC, **34** 223
Union Telephone Company, **14** 258
Union Texas Petroleum Holdings, Inc., 7 379; **9 521–23**
Union Trust Co., **9** 228; **13** 222
The Union Underwear Company, **8** 200–01; **25** 164–66
Union Verwaltungsgesellschaft mbH, **66** 123
Unionamerica, Inc., **III** 243; **16** 497; **50** 497
UnionBanCal Corporation, 50 496–99 (upd.)
UnionBay Sportswear Co., **27** 112
Unione Manifatture, S.p.A., **19** 338
Uniphase Corporation *see* JDS Uniphase Corporation.
Uniplex Business Software, **41** 281
Uniq Plc, **52** 418, 420
Unique Casual Restaurants, Inc., 27 480–82
Unique Pub Company, **59** 182
Uniroy of Hempstead, Inc. *see* Aris Industries, Inc.
Uniroyal Chemical Corporation, **36** 145
Uniroyal Corp., **8** 503; **11** 159; **20** 262
Uniroyal Goodrich, **42** 88
Uniroyal Holdings Ltd., **21** 73
Unishops, Inc. *see* Aris Industries, Inc.
Unison HealthCare Corporation, 25 503–05
Unisource Worldwide, Inc., **47** 149
Unistar Radio Networks, **23** 510
Unisys Corporation, III 165–67; 6 281–83 (upd.); 36 479–84 (upd.)
Unit Corporation, 63 407–09
Unit Group plc, **8** 477
Unitech plc, **27** 81
United Acquisitions, **7** 114; **25** 125
United Advertising Periodicals, **12** 231
United AgriSeeds, Inc., **21** 387
United Air Express *see* United Parcel Service of America Inc.
United Air Fleet, **23** 408
United Aircraft and Transportation Co., **9** 416, 418; **10** 260; **12** 289; **21** 140
United Airlines, I 128–30; 6 128–30 (upd.) *see also* UAL Corporation.
United Alaska Drilling, Inc., **7** 558
United Alloy Steel Company, **26** 405
United-American Car, **13** 305
United American Insurance Company of Dallas, **9** 508; **33** 407
United Arab Airlines *see* EgyptAir.
United Artists Corp., **IV** 676; **9** 74; **12** 13; **13** 529; **14** 87; **21** 362; **23** 389; **26** 487; **36** 47; **41** 402 *see also* MGM/UA Communications Company; Metro-Goldwyn-Mayer Inc.
United Artists Theatre Circuit, Inc., **37** 63–64; **59** 341
United Australian Automobile Industries, **62** 182
United Auto Group, Inc., 26 500–02; 68 381–84 (upd.)
United Biscuits (Holdings) plc, II 592–94; 42 404–09 (upd.)
United Brands Company, II 595–97
United Breweries International, Ltd., **60** 207
United Breweries Ltd. *see* Carlsberg A/S.
United Broadcasting Corporation Public Company Ltd., **31** 330
United Building Centers *see* Lanoga Corporation.
United Business Media plc, 52 363–68 (upd.)
United Cable Television Corporation, **9** 74; **18** 65; **43** 431; **76** 75
United Capital Corporation, **56** 136
The United Center *see* Wirtz Corporation.
United Central Oil Corporation, **7** 101
United Cigar Manufacturers Company, *see* Culbro Corporation.
United Cities Gas Company, **43** 56, 58
United Communications Systems, Inc. **V** 346
United Computer Services, Inc., **11** 111
United Consolidated Industries, **24** 204
United Corp., **10** 44
United Dairy Farmers, Inc., 74 364–66
United Defense Industries, Inc., 30 471–73; 66 346–49 (upd.)
United Distillers and Vintners *see* Diageo plc.
United Distillers Glenmore, Inc., **34** 89
United Dominion Industries Limited, 8 544–46; 16 499–502 (upd.); **47** 378; **57** 87
United Dominion Realty Trust, Inc., 52 369–71

Utah Mines Ltd., **IV** 47; **22** 107
Utah Power and Light Company, 9 536; **12** 266; **27 483–86** *see also* PacifiCorp.
UTI Energy, Inc. *see* Patterson-UTI Energy, Inc.
Utilicom, **6** 572
Utilicorp United Inc., 6 592–94 *see also* Aquilla, Inc.
UtiliTech Solutions, **37** 88
Utility Constructors Incorporated, **6** 527
Utility Engineering Corporation, **6** 580
Utility Fuels, **7** 377
Utility Line Construction Service, Inc., **59** 65
Utility Service Affiliates, Inc., **45** 277
Utility Services, Inc., **42** 249, 253
Utility Supply Co. *see* United Stationers Inc.
Utopian Leisure Group, **75** 385
UTStarcom, Inc., 77 458–461
UTV *see* Ulster Television PLC.
Utz Quality Foods, Inc., 72 358–60
UUNET, 38 468–72
UV Industries, Inc., **7** 360; **9** 440
Uwajimaya, Inc., 60 312–14

V

V.L. Churchill Group, **10** 493
VA Linux Systems, **45** 363
VA Systeme *see* Diehl Stiftung & Co. KG
VA TECH ELIN EBG GmbH, 49 429–31
VA Technologie AG, **57** 402
Vacheron Constantin, **27** 487, 489
Vaco, **38** 200, 202
Vaculator Division *see* Lancer Corporation.
Vacuum Metallurgical Company, **11** 234
Vacuum Oil Co. *see* Mobil Corporation.
Vadoise Vie, **III** 273
VAE AG, **57** 402
VAE Nortrak Cheyenne Inc., **53** 352
Vail Associates, Inc., 11 543–46; 31 65, 67
Vail Resorts, Inc., 43 435–39 (upd.)
Vaillant GmbH, 44 436–39
Val Corp., **24** 149
Val-Pak Direct Marketing Systems, Inc., **22** 162
Val Royal LaSalle, **II** 652
Valassis Communications, Inc., 8 550–51; 37 407–10 (upd.); 76 364–67 (upd.)
ValCom Inc. *see* InaCom Corporation.
Valdi Foods Inc., **II** 663–64
Vale do Rio Doce Navegacao SA—Docenave, **43** 112
Vale Harmon Enterprises, Ltd., **25** 204
Vale Power Company, **12** 265
Valenciana de Cementos, **59** 112
Valentine & Company, **8** 552–53
Valentino, **67** 246, 248
Valeo, 23 492–94; 66 350–53 (upd.)
Valero Energy Corporation, 7 553–55; 71 385–90 (upd.)
Valhi, Inc., 10 435–36; **19 466–68**
Valid Logic Systems Inc., **11** 46, 284; **48** 77
Vality Technology Inc., **59** 56
Vallen Corporation, 45 424–26
Valley Bank of Helena, **35** 197, 199
Valley Bank of Maryland, **46** 25
Valley Bank of Nevada, **19** 378
Valley Crest Tree Company, **31** 182–83
Valley Deli Inc., **24** 243
Valley Fashions Corp., **16** 535
Valley Federal of California, **11** 163
Valley Fig Growers, **7** 496–97
Valley Media Inc., 35 430–33
Valley National Bank, **II** 420
Valley of the Moon, **68** 146
Valley-Todeco, Inc., **13** 305–06
Valleyfair, **22** 130
Vallourec SA, 54 391–94
Valmet Corporation, III 647–49; IV 350, 471 *see also* Metso Corporation.
Valmont Industries, Inc., 13 276; **19** 50, **469–72**
Valois S.A. *see* AptarGroup, Inc.
Valores Industriales S.A., 19 10, 12, 189, **473–75; 29** 219
The Valspar Corporation, 8 552–54; 32 483–86 (upd.); 77 462–468 (upd.)
Valtek International, Inc., **17** 147
Value America, **29** 312
Value City Department Stores, Inc., 38 473–75
Value Foods Ltd., **11** 239
Value Giant Stores, **12** 478
Value House, **II** 673
Value Investors, **III** 330
Value Line, Inc., 16 506–08; 73 358–61 (upd.)
Value Merchants Inc., 13 541–43
Value Rent-A-Car, **9** 350; **23** 354
ValueClick, Inc., 49 432–34
Valueland, **8** 482
ValueVision International, Inc., 22 534–36; 27 337
ValuJet, Inc. *see* AirTran Holdings, Inc.
Valvtron, **11** 226
VAMED Gruppe, **56** 141
Van Ameringen-Haebler, Inc., **9** 290
Van Camp Seafood Company, Inc., 7 556–57 *see also* Chicken of the Sea International.
Van Cleef & Arpels Inc., **26** 145
Van de Kamp's, Inc., **7** 430
Van der Moolen Holding NV, **37** 224
Van Dorn Company, **13** 190
Van Houtte Inc., 39 409–11
Van Kirk Chocolate, **7** 429
Van Kok-Ede, **II** 642
Van Lanschot NV, 79 456–459
Van Leer Containers Inc., **30** 397
Van Leer Holding, Inc., **9** 303, 305
Van Leer N.V. *see* Royal Packaging Industries Van Leer N.V.; Greif Inc.
Van Mar, Inc., **18** 88
Van Nostrand Reinhold, **8** 526
Van Ommeren, **41** 339–40
Van Sickle, **IV** 485
Van Waters & Rogers, **8** 99; **41** 340
Van Wezel, **26** 278–79
Van Wijcks Waalsteenfabrieken, **14** 249
Van's Aircraft, Inc., 65 349–51
Vanadium Alloys Steel Company (VASCO), **13** 295–96
Vanant Packaging Corporation, **8** 359
Vance International Airways, **8** 349
Vance Publishing Corporation, 64 398–401
Vanderbilt Mortgage and Finance, **13** 154
Vanessa and Biffi, **11** 226
The Vanguard Group, Inc., 14 530–32; 34 486–89 (upd.)
Vanguard Health Systems Inc., 70 338–40
Vanguard International Semiconductor Corp., **47** 385
Vanity Fair *see* VF Corporation.
Vans, Inc., 16 509–11; 47 423–26 (upd.)
Vanstar, **13** 176
Vantage Analysis Systems, Inc., **11** 490
Vantage Components *see* Bell Microproducts Inc.
Vantive Corporation, **33** 333; **38** 431–32
Varco International, Inc., 42 418–20
Varco-Pruden, Inc., **8** 544–46
Vare Corporation, **8** 366
Vari-Lite International, Inc., 35 434–36
Varian Associates Inc., 12 504–06
Varian, Inc., 48 407–11 (upd.)
Varibus Corporation *see* Gulf States Utilities Company.
Variety Wholesalers, Inc., 73 362–64
Variflex, Inc., 51 391–93
Variform, Inc., **12** 397
VARIG S.A. (Viação Aérea Rio-Grandense), 6 133–35; 26 113; **29 494–97 (upd.); 31** 443–45; **33** 19
Varity Corporation, III 650–52; 7 258, 260; **19** 294; **27** 203, 251
Varlen Corporation, 16 512–14
Varney Speed Lines *see* Continental Airlines, Inc.
Varo, **7** 235, 237
Varsity Spirit Corp., 15 516–18
Varta AG, 23 495–99
VASCO Data Security International, Inc., 79 460–463
Vascoloy-Ramet, **13** 295
Vaserie Trevigiane International S.p.A., **73** 248–49
VASP (Viaçao Aérea de Sao Paulo), **31** 444–45
Vasset, S.A., **17** 362–63
Vast Solutions, **39** 24
Vastar Resources, Inc., 24 524–26; 38 445, 448
Vattenfall AB, 57 395–98
Vaughan Harmon Systems Ltd., **25** 204
Vaughan Printers Inc., **23** 100
Vaungarde, Inc., **22** 175
Vauxhall Motors Limited, 73 365–69
Vax Ltd., **73** 331–32
VBB Viag-Bayernwerk-Beteiligungs-Gesellschaft mbH, **IV** 232; **50** 170
VCA Antech, Inc., 58 353–55
VCH Publishing Group *see* John Wiley & Sons, Inc.
VDM Nickel-Technologie AG, **IV** 89
VEAG, **57** 395, 397

W

Index to Industries

Accounting

American Institute of Certified Public Accountants (AICPA), 44
Andersen, 29 (upd.); 68 (upd.)
Automatic Data Processing, Inc., 47 (upd.)
CROSSMARK 79
Daiko Advertising Inc. 79
Deloitte Touche Tohmatsu International, 9; 29 (upd.)
Ernst & Young, 9; 29 (upd.)
FTI Consulting, Inc., 77
Grant Thornton International, 57
KPMG International, 33 (upd.)
L.S. Starrett Co., 13
McLane Company, Inc., 13
NCO Group, Inc., 42
Paychex, Inc., 46 (upd.)
PKF International 78
Plante & Moran, LLP, 71
PRG-Schultz International, Inc., 73
PricewaterhouseCoopers, 9; 29 (upd.)
Robert Wood Johnson Foundation, 35
StarTek, Inc. 79
Travelzoo Inc. 79
Univision Communications Inc., 24

Advertising & Other Business Services

ABM Industries Incorporated, 25 (upd.)
Ackerley Communications, Inc., 9
ACNielsen Corporation, 13; 38 (upd.)
Acosta Sales and Marketing Company, Inc., 77
Acsys, Inc., 44
Adecco S.A., 36 (upd.)
Adia S.A., 6
Administaff, Inc., 52
The Advertising Council, Inc., 76
Advo, Inc., 6; 53 (upd.)
Aegis Group plc, 6
Affiliated Computer Services, Inc., 61
AHL Services, Inc., 27
Alloy, Inc., 55
Amdocs Ltd., 47
American Building Maintenance Industries, Inc., 6
The American Society of Composers, Authors and Publishers (ASCAP), 29
Amey Plc, 47
Analysts International Corporation, 36
The Arbitron Company, 38
Ariba, Inc., 57
Armor Holdings, Inc., 27
Ashtead Group plc, 34
The Associated Press, 13
Avalon Correctional Services, Inc., 75
Bain & Company, 55
Barrett Business Services, Inc., 16
Barton Protective Services Inc., 53
Bates Worldwide, Inc., 14; 33 (upd.)
Bearings, Inc., 13
Berlitz International, Inc., 13
Big Flower Press Holdings, Inc., 21
Billing Concepts, Inc., 72 (upd.)
The BISYS Group, Inc., 73
Boron, LePore & Associates, Inc., 45
The Boston Consulting Group, 58
Bozell Worldwide Inc., 25
BrandPartners Group, Inc., 58
Bright Horizons Family Solutions, Inc., 31
Broadcast Music Inc., 23
Buck Consultants, Inc., 55
Bureau Veritas SA, 55
Burns International Services Corporation, 13; 41 (upd.)
Cambridge Technology Partners, Inc., 36
Campbell-Mithun-Esty, Inc., 16
Cannon Design, 63
Capita Group PLC, 69
Career Education Corporation, 45
Carmichael Lynch Inc., 28
Cazenove Group plc, 72
CCC Information Services Group Inc., 74
CDI Corporation, 54 (upd.)
Central Parking Corporation, 18
Century Business Services, Inc., 52
Chancellor Beacon Academies, Inc., 53
ChartHouse International Learning Corporation, 49
Chiat/Day Inc. Advertising, 11
Chicago Board of Trade, 41
Chisholm-Mingo Group, Inc., 41
Christie's International plc, 15; 39 (upd.)
Cintas Corporation, 21
COMFORCE Corporation, 40
Command Security Corporation, 57
Computer Learning Centers, Inc., 26
Concentra Inc., 71
Corporate Express, Inc., 47 (upd.)
CoolSavings, Inc., 77
CORT Business Services Corporation, 26
Cox Enterprises, Inc., 22 (upd.)
Creative Artists Agency LLC, 38
CSG Systems International, Inc., 75
Cyrk Inc., 19
Dale Carnegie & Associates Inc. 28; 78 (upd.)
D'Arcy Masius Benton & Bowles, Inc., 6; 32 (upd.)
Dawson Holdings PLC, 43
DDB Needham Worldwide, 14
Deluxe Corporation, 22 (upd.); 73 (upd.)
Dentsu Inc., I; 16 (upd.); 40 (upd.)
Deutsch, Inc., 42
Deutsche Post AG, 29

Aerospace

Airlines

Braathens ASA, 47
Bradley Air Services Ltd., 56
Bristow Helicopters Ltd., 70
British Airways PLC, I; 14 (upd.); 43 (upd.)
British Midland plc, 38
British World Airlines Ltd., 18
Cargolux Airlines International S.A., 49
Cathay Pacific Airways Limited, 6; 34 (upd.)
Ceské aerolinie, a.s., 66
Chautauqua Airlines, Inc., 38
China Airlines, 34
China Eastern Airlines Co. Ltd., 31
China Southern Airlines Company Ltd., 33
Comair Holdings Inc., 13; 34 (upd.)
Continental Airlines, Inc., I; 21 (upd.); 52 (upd.)
Corporación Internacional de Aviación, S.A. de C.V. (Cintra), 20
dba Luftfahrtgesellschaft mbH, 76
Delta Air Lines, Inc., I; 6 (upd.); 39 (upd.)
Deutsche Lufthansa AG, I; 26 (upd.); 68 (upd.)
Eastern Airlines, I
easyJet Airline Company Limited, 39
EgyptAir, 6; 27 (upd.)
El Al Israel Airlines Ltd., 23
The Emirates Group, 39
EVA Airways Corporation, 51
Finnair Oyj, 6; 25 (upd.); 61 (upd.)
Flight Options, LLC, 75
Flying Boat, Inc. (Chalk's Ocean Airways), 56
Frontier Airlines, Inc., 22
Garuda Indonesia, 6
Gol Linhas Aéreas Inteligentes S.A., 73
Groupe Air France, 6
Grupo TACA, 38
Gulf Air Company, 56
HAL Inc., 9
Hawaiian Airlines, Inc., 22 (upd.)
Hong Kong Dragon Airlines Ltd., 66
Iberia Líneas Aéreas de España S.A., 6; 36 (upd.)
Icelandair, 52
Indian Airlines Ltd., 46
Japan Air Lines Company Ltd., I; 32 (upd.)
Jersey European Airways (UK) Ltd., 61
Jet Airways (India) Private Limited, 65
JetBlue Airways Corporation, 44
Kenmore Air Harbor Inc., 65
Kitty Hawk, Inc., 22
Kiwi International Airlines Inc., 20
Koninklijke Luchtvaart Maatschappij, N.V. (KLM Royal Dutch Airlines), I; 28 (upd.)
Korean Air Lines Co., Ltd., 6; 27 (upd.)
Kuwait Airways Corporation, 68
Lan Chile S.A., 31
Lauda Air Luftfahrt AG, 48
Loganair Ltd., 68
LOT Polish Airlines (Polskie Linie Lotnicze S.A.), 33
LTU Group Holding GmbH, 37
Malév Plc, 24
Malaysian Airlines System Berhad, 6; 29 (upd.)
Mesa Air Group, Inc., 11; 32 (upd.); 77 (upd.)
Mesaba Holdings, Inc., 28
Middle East Airlines - Air Liban S.A.L. 79
Midway Airlines Corporation, 33
Midwest Express Holdings, Inc., 35
Northwest Airlines Corporation, I; 6 (upd.); 26 (upd.); 74 (upd.)
Offshore Logistics, Inc., 37
Pakistan International Airlines Corporation, 46
Pan American World Airways, Inc., I; 12 (upd.)
Panalpina World Transport (Holding) Ltd., 47
People Express Airlines, Inc., I
Petroleum Helicopters, Inc., 35
Philippine Airlines, Inc., 6; 23 (upd.)
Pinnacle Airlines Corp., 73
Preussag AG, 42 (upd.)
Qantas Airways Ltd., 6; 24 (upd.); 68 (upd.)
Reno Air Inc., 23
Royal Nepal Airline Corporation, 41
Ryanair Holdings plc, 35
SAA (Pty) Ltd., 28
Sabena S.A./N.V., 33
The SAS Group, 34 (upd.)
Saudi Arabian Airlines, 6; 27 (upd.)
Scandinavian Airlines System, I
Singapore Airlines Ltd., 6; 27 (upd.)
SkyWest, Inc., 25
Société d'Exploitation AOM Air Liberté SA (AirLib), 53
Société Luxembourgeoise de Navigation Aérienne S.A., 64
Société Tunisienne de l'Air-Tunisair, 49
Southwest Airlines Co., 6; 24 (upd.); 71 (upd.)
Spirit Airlines, Inc., 31
Sterling European Airlines A/S, 70
Sun Country Airlines, 30
Swiss Air Transport Company, Ltd., I
Swiss International Air Lines Ltd., 48
TAM Linhas Aéreas S.A., 68
TAP—Air Portugal Transportes Aéreos Portugueses S.A., 46
TAROM S.A., 64
Texas Air Corporation, I
Thai Airways International Public Company Limited, 6; 27 (upd.)
Tower Air, Inc., 28
Trans World Airlines, Inc., I; 12 (upd.); 35 (upd.)
TransBrasil S/A Linhas Aéreas, 31
Transportes Aereos Portugueses, S.A., 6
Turkish Airlines Inc. (Türk Hava Yollari A.O.), 72
TV Guide, Inc., 43 (upd.)
UAL Corporation, 34 (upd.)
United Airlines, I; 6 (upd.)
US Airways Group, Inc., I; 6 (upd.); 28 (upd.); 52 (upd.)
VARIG S.A. (Viação Aérea Rio-Grandense), 6; 29 (upd.)
WestJet Airlines Ltd., 38

Automotive

AB Volvo, I; 7 (upd.); 26 (upd.); 67 (upd.)
Accubuilt, Inc., 74
Adam Opel AG, 7; 21 (upd.); 61 (upd.)
ADESA, Inc., 71
Advance Auto Parts, Inc., 57
Aisin Seiki Co., Ltd., 48 (upd.)
Alfa Romeo, 13; 36 (upd.)
Alvis Plc, 47
America's Car-Mart, Inc., 64
American Motors Corporation, I
Applied Power Inc., 32 (upd.)
Arnold Clark Automobiles Ltd., 60
ArvinMeritor, Inc., 8; 54 (upd.)
Asbury Automotive Group Inc., 60
ASC, Inc., 55
Autobacs Seven Company Ltd., 76
Autocam Corporation, 51
Autoliv, Inc., 65
Automobiles Citroen, 7
Automobili Lamborghini Holding S.p.A., 13; 34 (upd.)
AutoNation, Inc., 50
AVTOVAZ Joint Stock Company, 65
Bajaj Auto Limited, 39
Bayerische Motoren Werke AG, I; 11 (upd.); 38 (upd.)
Belron International Ltd., 76
Bendix Corporation, I
Blue Bird Corporation, 35
Bombardier Inc., 42 (upd.)
Borg-Warner Automotive, Inc., 14; 32 (upd.)
The Budd Company, 8
Canadian Tire Corporation, Limited, 71 (upd.)
CarMax, Inc., 55
CARQUEST Corporation, 29
Caterpillar Inc., 63 (upd.)
Chrysler Corporation, I; 11 (upd.)
CNH Global N.V., 38 (upd.)
Consorcio G Grupo Dina, S.A. de C.V., 36
CSK Auto Corporation, 38
Cummins Engine Company, Inc., I; 12 (upd.); 40 (upd.)
Custom Chrome, Inc., 16
Daihatsu Motor Company, Ltd., 7; 21 (upd.)
Daimler-Benz A.G., I; 15 (upd.)
DaimlerChrysler AG, 34 (upd.); 64 (upd.)
Dana Corporation, I; 10 (upd.)
Danaher Corporation, 77 (upd.)
Deere & Company, 42 (upd.)
Delphi Automotive Systems Corporation, 45
Don Massey Cadillac, Inc., 37
Donaldson Company, Inc., 49 (upd.)
Douglas & Lomason Company, 16
DriveTime Automotive Group Inc., 68 (upd.)
Ducati Motor Holding S.p.A., 30
Eaton Corporation, I; 10 (upd.)
Echlin Inc., I; 11 (upd.)
Edelbrock Corporation, 37

Beverages

Bio-Technology

Medtronic, Inc., 30 (upd.)
Millipore Corporation, 25
Minntech Corporation, 22
Mycogen Corporation, 21
New Brunswick Scientific Co., Inc., 45
Qiagen N.V., 39
Quintiles Transnational Corporation, 21
Seminis, Inc., 29
Serologicals Corporation, 63
Sigma-Aldrich Corporation, 36 (upd.)
Starkey Laboratories, Inc., 52
STERIS Corporation, 29
Stratagene Corporation, 70
Tanox, Inc., 77
TECHNE Corporation, 52
TriPath Imaging, Inc., 77
Waters Corporation, 43
Whatman plc, 46
Wisconsin Alumni Research Foundation, 65
Wyeth, 50 (upd.)

Chemicals

A. Schulman, Inc., 8
Aceto Corp., 38
Air Products and Chemicals, Inc., I; 10 (upd.); 74 (upd.)
Airgas, Inc., 54
Akzo Nobel N.V., 13
Albemarle Corporation, 59
AlliedSignal Inc., 22 (upd.)
American Cyanamid, I; 8 (upd.)
American Vanguard Corporation, 47
Arch Chemicals Inc. 78
ARCO Chemical Company, 10
Asahi Denka Kogyo KK, 64
Atanor S.A., 62
Atochem S.A., I
Avantium Technologies BV 79
Avecia Group PLC, 63
Baker Hughes Incorporated, 22 (upd.); 57 (upd.)
Balchem Corporation, 42
BASF Aktiengesellschaft, I; 18 (upd.); 50 (upd.)
Bayer A.G., I; 13 (upd.); 41 (upd.)
Betz Laboratories, Inc., I; 10 (upd.)
The BFGoodrich Company, 19 (upd.)
BOC Group plc, I; 25 (upd.); 78 (upd.)
Brenntag AG, 8; 23 (upd.)
Burmah Castrol PLC, 30 (upd.)
Cabot Corporation, 8; 29 (upd.)
Calgon Carbon Corporation, 73
Caliper Life Sciences, Inc., 70
Cambrex Corporation, 16
Catalytica Energy Systems, Inc., 44
Celanese Corporation, I
Celanese Mexicana, S.A. de C.V., 54
Chemcentral Corporation, 8
Chemi-Trol Chemical Co., 16
Church & Dwight Co., Inc., 29
Ciba-Geigy Ltd., I; 8 (upd.)
The Clorox Company, 22 (upd.)
Croda International Plc, 45
Crompton Corporation, 9; 36 (upd.)
Cytec Industries Inc., 27
Degussa-Hüls AG, 32 (upd.)
DeKalb Genetics Corporation, 17
The Dexter Corporation, I; 12 (upd.)
Dionex Corporation, 46
The Dow Chemical Company, I; 8 (upd.); 50 (upd.)
DSM N.V., I; 56 (upd.)
Dynaction S.A., 67
E.I. du Pont de Nemours & Company, I; 8 (upd.); 26 (upd.)
Eastman Chemical Company, 14; 38 (upd.)
Ecolab Inc., I; 13 (upd.); 34 (upd.)
Elementis plc, 40 (upd.)
Engelhard Corporation, 72 (upd.)
English China Clays Ltd., 15 (upd.); 40 (upd.)
Enterprise Rent-A-Car Company, 69 (upd.)
Equistar Chemicals, LP, 71
ERLY Industries Inc., 17
Ethyl Corporation, I; 10 (upd.)
Ferro Corporation, 8; 56 (upd.)
Firmenich International S.A., 60
First Mississippi Corporation, 8
Formosa Plastics Corporation, 14; 58 (upd.)
Fort James Corporation, 22 (upd.)
G.A.F., I
The General Chemical Group Inc., 37
Georgia Gulf Corporation, 9; 61 (upd.)
Givaudan SA, 43
Great Lakes Chemical Corporation, I; 14 (upd.)
Guerbet Group, 46
H.B. Fuller Company, 32 (upd.); 75 (upd.)
Hauser, Inc., 46
Hawkins Chemical, Inc., 16
Henkel KGaA, 34 (upd.)
Hercules Inc., I; 22 (upd.); 66 (upd.)
Hoechst A.G., I; 18 (upd.)
Hoechst Celanese Corporation, 13
Huls A.G., I
Huntsman Chemical Corporation, 8
IMC Fertilizer Group, Inc., 8
Imperial Chemical Industries PLC, I; 50 (upd.)
International Flavors & Fragrances Inc., 9; 38 (upd.)
Israel Chemicals Ltd., 55
Kemira Oyj, 70
Koppers Industries, Inc., I; 26 (upd.)
L'Air Liquide SA, I; 47 (upd.)
Lawter International Inc., 14
LeaRonal, Inc., 23
Loctite Corporation, 30 (upd.)
Lonza Group Ltd., 73
Lubrizol Corporation, I; 30 (upd.)
Lyondell Chemical Company, 45 (upd.)
M.A. Hanna Company, 8
MacDermid Incorporated, 32
Mallinckrodt Group Inc., 19
MBC Holding Company, 40
Melamine Chemicals, Inc., 27
Methanex Corporation, 40
Minerals Technologies Inc., 52 (upd.)
Mississippi Chemical Corporation, 39
Mitsubishi Chemical Corporation, I; 56 (upd.)
Mitsui Petrochemical Industries, Ltd., 9
Monsanto Company, I; 9 (upd.); 29 (upd.)
Montedison SpA, I
Morton International Inc., 9 (upd.)
Morton Thiokol, Inc., I
Nagase & Company, Ltd., 8
Nalco Chemical Corporation, I; 12 (upd.)
National Distillers and Chemical Corporation, I
National Sanitary Supply Co., 16
National Starch and Chemical Company, 49
NCH Corporation, 8
Nisshin Seifun Group Inc., 66 (upd.)
NL Industries, Inc., 10
Nobel Industries AB, 9
NOF Corporation, 72
Norsk Hydro ASA, 35 (upd.)
Novacor Chemicals Ltd., 12
NutraSweet Company, 8
Occidental Petroleum Corporation, 71 (upd.)
Olin Corporation, I; 13 (upd.); 78 (upd.)
OM Group, Inc., 17; 78 (upd.)
OMNOVA Solutions Inc., 59
Penford Corporation, 55
Pennwalt Corporation, I
Perstorp AB, I; 51 (upd.)
Petrolite Corporation, 15
Pfizer Inc. 79 (upd.)
Pioneer Hi-Bred International, Inc., 41 (upd.)
Praxair, Inc., 11
Quantum Chemical Corporation, 8
Reichhold Chemicals, Inc., 10
Renner Herrmann S.A. 79
Rhodia SA, 38
Rhône-Poulenc S.A., I; 10 (upd.)
Robertet SA, 39
Rohm and Haas Company, I; 26 (upd.); 77 (upd.)
Roussel Uclaf, I; 8 (upd.)
RPM, Inc., 36 (upd.)
RWE AG, 50 (upd.)
The Scotts Company, 22
SCP Pool Corporation, 39
Sequa Corp., 13
Shanghai Petrochemical Co., Ltd., 18
Sigma-Aldrich Corporation, 36 (upd.)
Solutia Inc., 52
Solvay S.A., I; 21 (upd.); 61 (upd.)
Stepan Company, 30
Sterling Chemicals, Inc., 16; 78 (upd.)
Sumitomo Chemical Company Ltd., I
Takeda Chemical Industries, Ltd., 46 (upd.)
Terra Industries, Inc., 13
Tessenderlo Group, 76
Teva Pharmaceutical Industries Ltd., 22
Tosoh Corporation, 70
Total Fina Elf S.A., 24 (upd.); 50 (upd.)
Ube Industries, Ltd., 38 (upd.)
Union Carbide Corporation, I; 9 (upd.); 74 (upd.)
United Industries Corporation, 68
Univar Corporation, 9

Conglomerates

Construction

Containers

Drugs/Pharmaceuticals

Electrical & Electronics

Engineering & Management Services

Entertainment & Leisure

Financial Services: Banks

Financial Services: Excluding Banks

Food Products

Food Services & Retailers

John Lewis Partnership plc, 42 (upd.)
Johnny Rockets Group, Inc., 31; 76 (upd.)
KFC Corporation, 7; 21 (upd.)
King Kullen Grocery Co., Inc., 15
Koninklijke Ahold N.V. (Royal Ahold), II; 16 (upd.)
Koo Koo Roo, Inc., 25
The Kroger Co., II; 15 (upd.); 65 (upd.)
The Krystal Company, 33
Kwik Save Group plc, 11
La Madeleine French Bakery & Café, 33
Landry's Restaurants, Inc., 15; 65 (upd.)
The Laurel Pub Company Limited, 59
Laurus N.V., 65
LDB Corporation, 53
Leeann Chin, Inc., 30
Levy Restaurants L.P., 26
Little Caesar Enterprises, Inc., 7; 24 (upd.)
Loblaw Companies Limited, 43
Logan's Roadhouse, Inc., 29
Lone Star Steakhouse & Saloon, Inc., 51
Long John Silver's, 13; 57 (upd.)
Luby's, Inc., 17; 42 (upd.)
Lucky Stores, Inc., 27
Lund Food Holdings, Inc., 22
Madden's on Gull Lake, 52
Maid-Rite Corporation, 62
Maines Paper & Food Service Inc., 71
Marie Callender's Restaurant & Bakery, Inc., 28
Marsh Supermarkets, Inc., 17; 76 (upd.)
Matt Prentice Restaurant Group, 70
Max & Erma's Restaurants Inc., 19
Mayfield Dairy Farms, Inc., 74
Mazzio's Corporation, 76
McAlister's Corporation, 66
McCormick & Schmick's Seafood Restaurants, Inc., 71
McDonald's Corporation, II; 7 (upd.); 26 (upd.); 63 (upd.)
Megafoods Stores Inc., 13
Meijer Incorporated, 7
The Melting Pot Restaurants, Inc., 74
Metcash Trading Ltd., 58
Métro Inc., 77
Metromedia Companies, 14
Mexican Restaurants, Inc., 41
The Middleby Corporation, 22
Minyard Food Stores, Inc., 33
MITROPA AG, 37
Monterey Pasta Company, 58
Morrison Restaurants Inc., 11
Morton's Restaurant Group, Inc., 30
Mrs. Fields' Original Cookies, Inc., 27
Musgrave Group Plc, 57
Nash Finch Company, 8; 23 (upd.); 65 (upd.)
Nathan's Famous, Inc., 29
National Convenience Stores Incorporated, 7
New Seasons Market, 75
New World Restaurant Group, Inc., 44
New York Restaurant Group, Inc., 32
Noble Roman's Inc., 14
Noodles & Company, Inc., 55
NPC International, Inc., 40
O'Charley's Inc., 19; 60 (upd.)
Old Spaghetti Factory International Inc., 24
The Oshawa Group Limited, II
Outback Steakhouse, Inc., 12; 34 (upd.)
P&C Foods Inc., 8
P.F. Chang's China Bistro, Inc., 37
Palm Management Corporation, 71
Pancho's Mexican Buffet, Inc., 46
Panda Management Company, Inc., 35
Panera Bread Company, 44
Papa John's International, Inc., 15; 71 (upd.)
Papa Murphy's International, Inc., 54
Pappas Restaurants, Inc., 76
Pathmark Stores, Inc., 23
Peapod, Inc., 30
Penn Traffic Company, 13
Performance Food Group Company, 31
Perkins Family Restaurants, L.P., 22
Peter Piper, Inc., 70
Petrossian Inc., 54
Phillips Foods, Inc., 63
Picard Surgeles, 76
Piccadilly Cafeterias, Inc., 19
Piggly Wiggly Southern, Inc., 13
Pizza Hut Inc., 7; 21 (upd.)
Planet Hollywood International, Inc., 18; 41 (upd.)
Players International, Inc., 22
Ponderosa Steakhouse, 15
Portillo's Restaurant Group, Inc., 71
Provigo Inc., II; 51 (upd.)
Publix Super Markets Inc., 7; 31 (upd.)
Pueblo Xtra International, Inc., 47
Quality Dining, Inc., 18
Quality Food Centers, Inc., 17
The Quizno's Corporation, 42
Rally's, 25; 68 (upd.)
Ralphs Grocery Company, 35
Randall's Food Markets, Inc., 40
Rare Hospitality International Inc., 19
Raving Brands, Inc., 64
Red Robin Gourmet Burgers, Inc., 56
Restaurant Associates Corporation, 66
Restaurants Unlimited, Inc., 13
RFC Franchising LLC, 68
Richfood Holdings, Inc., 7
Richtree Inc., 63
The Riese Organization, 38
Riser Foods, Inc., 9
Roadhouse Grill, Inc., 22
Rock Bottom Restaurants, Inc., 25; 68 (upd.)
Romacorp, Inc., 58
Roundy's Inc., 58 (upd.)
RTM Restaurant Group, 58
Rubio's Restaurants, Inc., 35
Ruby Tuesday, Inc., 18; 71 (upd.)
Ruth's Chris Steak House, 28
Ryan's Restaurant Group, Inc., 15; 68 (upd.)
Safeway PLC, II; 24 (upd.); 50 (upd.)
Santa Barbara Restaurant Group, Inc., 37
Sbarro, Inc., 16; 64 (upd.)
Schlotzsky's, Inc., 36
Schultz Sav-O Stores, Inc., 21
Schwan's Sales Enterprises, Inc., 26 (upd.)
Seaway Food Town, Inc., 15
Second Harvest, 29
See's Candies, Inc., 30
Seneca Foods Corporation, 17
Service America Corp., 7
SFI Group plc, 51
Shaw's Supermarkets, Inc., 56
Shells Seafood Restaurants, Inc., 43
Shoney's, Inc., 7; 23 (upd.)
ShowBiz Pizza Time, Inc., 13
Skyline Chili, Inc., 62
Smart & Final, Inc., 16
Smith's Food & Drug Centers, Inc., 8; 57 (upd.)
Sodexho Alliance SA, 29
Somerfield plc, 47 (upd.)
Sonic Corporation, 14; 37 (upd.)
The Southland Corporation, II; 7 (upd.)
Spaghetti Warehouse, Inc., 25
SPAR Handels AG, 35
Spartan Stores Inc., 8
Starbucks Corporation, 77 (upd.)
Stater Bros. Holdings Inc., 64
The Steak n Shake Company, 41
Steinberg Incorporated, II
Stew Leonard's, 56
The Stop & Shop Supermarket Company, II; 68 (upd.)
Subway, 32
Super Food Services, Inc., 15
Supermarkets General Holdings Corporation, II
Supervalu Inc., II; 18 (upd.); 50 (upd.)
SWH Corporation, 70
SYSCO Corporation, II; 24 (upd.); 75 (upd.)
Taco Bell Corporation, 7; 21 (upd.); 74 (upd.)
Taco Cabana, Inc., 23; 72 (upd.)
Taco John's International, Inc., 15; 63 (upd.)
TelePizza S.A., 33
Tesco PLC, II
Texas Roadhouse, Inc., 69
Timber Lodge Steakhouse, Inc., 73
Tops Markets LLC, 60
Total Entertainment Restaurant Corporation, 46
Toupargel-Agrigel S.A., 76
Trader Joe's Company, 13; 50 (upd.)
Travel Ports of America, Inc., 17
Tree of Life, Inc., 29
Triarc Companies, Inc., 34 (upd.)
Tubby's, Inc., 53
Tully's Coffee Corporation, 51
Tumbleweed, Inc., 33
TW Services, Inc., II
Ukrop's Super Market's, Inc., 39
Unique Casual Restaurants, Inc., 27
United Dairy Farmers, Inc., 74
United Natural Foods, Inc., 32; 76 (upd.)
Uno Restaurant Corporation, 18
Uno Restaurant Holdings Corporation, 70 (upd.)
Uwajimaya, Inc., 60
Vail Resorts, Inc., 43 (upd.)
VICORP Restaurants, Inc., 12; 48 (upd.)
Village Super Market, Inc., 7

Health & Personal Care Products

Health Care Services

Hotels

Information Technology

Insurance

Legal Services

Fish & Neave, 54
Foley & Lardner, 28
Fried, Frank, Harris, Shriver & Jacobson, 35
Fulbright & Jaworski L.L.P., 47
Gibson, Dunn & Crutcher LLP, 36
Greenberg Traurig, LLP, 65
Heller, Ehrman, White & McAuliffe, 41
Hildebrandt International, 29
Hogan & Hartson L.L.P., 44
Holland & Knight LLP, 60
Holme Roberts & Owen LLP, 28
Hughes Hubbard & Reed LLP, 44
Hunton & Williams, 35
Jenkens & Gilchrist, P.C., 65
Jones, Day, Reavis & Pogue, 33
Kelley Drye & Warren LLP, 40
King & Spalding, 23
Kirkland & Ellis LLP, 65
Latham & Watkins, 33
LeBoeuf, Lamb, Greene & MacRae, L.L.P., 29
The Legal Aid Society, 48
Mayer, Brown, Rowe & Maw, 47
Milbank, Tweed, Hadley & McCloy, 27
Morgan, Lewis & Bockius LLP, 29
Morrison & Foerster LLP 78
O'Melveny & Myers, 37
Oppenheimer Wolff & Donnelly LLP, 71
Orrick, Herrington and Sutcliffe LLP, 76
Patton Boggs LLP, 71
Paul, Hastings, Janofsky & Walker LLP, 27
Paul, Weiss, Rifkind, Wharton & Garrison, 47
Pepper Hamilton LLP, 43
Perkins Coie LLP, 56
Pillsbury Madison & Sutro LLP, 29
Pre-Paid Legal Services, Inc., 20
Proskauer Rose LLP, 47
Ropes & Gray, 40
Saul Ewing LLP, 74
Shearman & Sterling, 32
Sidley Austin Brown & Wood, 40
Simpson Thacher & Bartlett, 39
Skadden, Arps, Slate, Meagher & Flom, 18
Snell & Wilmer L.L.P., 28
Southern Poverty Law Center, Inc., 74
Stroock & Stroock & Lavan LLP, 40
Sullivan & Cromwell, 26
Troutman Sanders L.L.P. 79
Vinson & Elkins L.L.P., 30
Wachtell, Lipton, Rosen & Katz, 47
Weil, Gotshal & Manges LLP, 55
White & Case LLP, 35
Williams & Connolly LLP, 47
Wilson Sonsini Goodrich & Rosati, 34
Winston & Strawn, 35
Womble Carlyle Sandridge & Rice, PLLC, 52

Manufacturing

A-dec, Inc., 53
A. Schulman, Inc., 49 (upd.)
A.B.Dick Company, 28
A.O. Smith Corporation, 11; 40 (upd.)
A.T. Cross Company, 17; 49 (upd.)
A.W. Faber-Castell Unternehmensverwaltung GmbH & Co., 51
AAF-McQuay Incorporated, 26
AAON, Inc., 22
AAR Corp., 28
Aarhus United A/S, 68
ABB Ltd., 65 (upd.)
ABC Rail Products Corporation, 18
Abiomed, Inc., 47
ACCO World Corporation, 7; 51 (upd.)
Accubuilt, Inc., 74
Acme United Corporation, 70
Acme-Cleveland Corp., 13
Acorn Products, Inc., 55
Acushnet Company, 64
Acuson Corporation, 36 (upd.)
Adams Golf, Inc., 37
Adolf Würth GmbH & Co. KG, 49
Advanced Circuits Inc., 67
Advanced Neuromodulation Systems, Inc., 73
AEP Industries, Inc., 36
Ag-Chem Equipment Company, Inc., 17
Aga Foodservice Group PLC, 73
AGCO Corporation, 13; 67 (upd.)
Agfa Gevaert Group N.V., 59
Agrium Inc., 73
Ahlstrom Corporation, 53
Airgas, Inc., 54
Aisin Seiki Co., Ltd., III
AK Steel Holding Corporation, 41 (upd.)
AKG Acoustics GmbH, 62
Aktiebolaget Electrolux, 22 (upd.)
Aktiebolaget SKF, III; 38 (upd.)
Alamo Group Inc., 32
ALARIS Medical Systems, Inc., 65
Alberto-Culver Company, 36 (upd.)
Aldila Inc., 46
Alfa Laval AB, III; 64 (upd.)
Allen Organ Company, 33
Allen-Edmonds Shoe Corporation, 61
Alliant Techsystems Inc., 8; 30 (upd.); 77 (upd.)
The Allied Defense Group, Inc., 65
Allied Healthcare Products, Inc., 24
Allied Products Corporation, 21
Allied Signal Engines, 9
AlliedSignal Inc., 22 (upd.)
Allison Gas Turbine Division, 9
Alltrista Corporation, 30
Alps Electric Co., Ltd., 44 (upd.)
Alticor Inc., 71 (upd.)
Aluar Aluminio Argentino S.A.I.C., 74
Alvis Plc, 47
Amer Group plc, 41
American Axle & Manufacturing Holdings, Inc., 67
American Biltrite Inc., 43 (upd.)
American Business Products, Inc., 20
American Cast Iron Pipe Company, 50
American Greetings Corporation, 59 (upd.)
American Homestar Corporation, 18; 41 (upd.)
American Locker Group Incorporated, 34
American Power Conversion Corporation, 67 (upd.)
American Seating Company 78
American Standard Companies Inc., 30 (upd.)
American Technical Ceramics Corp., 67
American Tourister, Inc., 16
American Woodmark Corporation, 31
Ameriwood Industries International Corp., 17
Amerock Corporation, 53
Ameron International Corporation, 67
AMETEK, Inc., 9
AMF Bowling, Inc., 40
Ampacet Corporation, 67
Ampco-Pittsburgh Corporation 79
Ampex Corporation, 17
Amway Corporation, 30 (upd.)
Analogic Corporation, 23
Anchor Hocking Glassware, 13
Andersen Corporation, 10
The Andersons, Inc., 31
Andreas Stihl AG & Co. KG, 16; 59 (upd.)
Andritz AG, 51
Ansell Ltd., 60 (upd.)
Anthem Electronics, Inc., 13
Apasco S.A. de C.V., 51
Apex Digital, Inc., 63
Applica Incorporated, 43 (upd.)
Applied Films Corporation, 48
Applied Materials, Inc., 10; 46 (upd.)
Applied Micro Circuits Corporation, 38
Applied Power Inc., 9; 32 (upd.)
AptarGroup, Inc., 69
ARBED S.A., 22 (upd.)
Arc International, 76
Arctco, Inc., 16
Arctic Cat Inc., 40 (upd.)
Ariens Company, 48
The Aristotle Corporation, 62
Armor All Products Corp., 16
Armstrong World Industries, Inc., III; 22 (upd.)
Artesyn Technologies Inc., 46 (upd.)
ArthroCare Corporation, 73
ArvinMeritor, Inc., 54 (upd.)
Asahi Glass Company, Ltd., 48 (upd.)
Ashley Furniture Industries, Inc., 35
ASICS Corporation, 57
ASML Holding N.V., 50
Astec Industries, Inc. 79
Astronics Corporation, 35
ASV, Inc., 34; 66 (upd.)
Atlas Copco AB, III; 28 (upd.)
Atwood Mobil Products, 53
AU Optronics Corporation, 67
Aurora Casket Company, Inc., 56
Austal Limited, 75
Austin Powder Company, 76
Avedis Zildjian Co., 38
Avery Dennison Corporation, 17 (upd.); 49 (upd.)
Avocent Corporation, 65
Avondale Industries, 7; 41 (upd.)
AVX Corporation, 67
B.J. Alan Co., Inc., 67
Badger Meter, Inc., 22
BAE Systems Ship Repair, 73
Baker Hughes Incorporated, III

Materials

Mining & Metals

Newmont Mining Corporation, 7
Neyveli Lignite Corporation Ltd., 65
Niagara Corporation, 28
Nichimen Corporation, IV
Nippon Light Metal Company, Ltd., IV
Nippon Steel Corporation, IV; 17 (upd.)
Nisshin Steel Co., Ltd., IV
NKK Corporation, IV; 28 (upd.)
Noranda Inc., IV; 7 (upd.); 64 (upd.)
Norddeutsche Affinerie AG, 62
North Star Steel Company, 18
Nucor Corporation, 7; 21 (upd.); 79 (upd.)
Oglebay Norton Company, 17
Okura & Co., Ltd., IV
Oregon Metallurgical Corporation, 20
Oregon Steel Mills, Inc., 14
Outokumpu Oyj, 38
Park Corp., 22
Peabody Coal Company, 10
Peabody Energy Corporation, 45 (upd.)
Peabody Holding Company, Inc., IV
Pechiney SA, IV; 45 (upd.)
Peter Kiewit Sons' Inc., 8
Phelps Dodge Corporation, IV; 28 (upd.); 75 (upd.)
The Pittston Company, IV; 19 (upd.)
Placer Dome Inc., 20; 61 (upd.)
Pohang Iron and Steel Company Ltd., IV
POSCO, 57 (upd.)
Potash Corporation of Saskatchewan Inc., 18
Quanex Corporation, 13; 62 (upd.)
RAG AG, 35; 60 (upd.)
Reliance Steel & Aluminum Co., 19
Republic Engineered Steels, Inc., 7; 26 (upd.)
Reynolds Metals Company, IV
Rio Tinto PLC, 19 (upd.); 50 (upd.)
RMC Group p.l.c., 34 (upd.)
Roanoke Electric Steel Corporation, 45
Rouge Steel Company, 8
The RTZ Corporation PLC, IV
Ruhrkohle AG, IV
Ryerson Tull, Inc., 40 (upd.)
Saarberg-Konzern, IV
Salzgitter AG, IV
Sandvik AB, IV
Saudi Basic Industries Corporation (SABIC), 58
Schnitzer Steel Industries, Inc., 19
Severstal Joint Stock Company, 65
Shanghai Baosteel Group Corporation, 71
Siderar S.A.I.C., 66
Smorgon Steel Group Ltd., 62
Southern Peru Copper Corporation, 40
Southwire Company, Inc., 8; 23 (upd.)
Steel Authority of India Ltd., IV
Stelco Inc., IV
Stillwater Mining Company, 47
Sumitomo Metal Industries, Ltd., IV
Sumitomo Metal Mining Co., Ltd., IV
Tata Iron & Steel Co. Ltd., IV; 44 (upd.)
Teck Corporation, 27
Tenaris SA, 63
Texas Industries, Inc., 8
Thyssen AG, IV
The Timken Company, 8; 42 (upd.)
Titanium Metals Corporation, 21
Tomen Corporation, IV
Total Fina Elf S.A., 50 (upd.)
U.S. Borax, Inc., 42
Ugine S.A., 20
NV Umicore SA, 47
Universal Stainless & Alloy Products, Inc., 75
Usinor SA, IV; 42 (upd.)
Usinor Sacilor, IV
VIAG Aktiengesellschaft, IV
Voest-Alpine Stahl AG, IV
Vulcan Materials Company, 52 (upd.)
Walter Industries, Inc., 22 (upd.)
Weirton Steel Corporation, IV; 26 (upd.)
Westmoreland Coal Company, 7
Wheeling-Pittsburgh Corp., 7
WMC, Limited, 43
Worthington Industries, Inc., 7; 21 (upd.)
Xstrata PLC, 73
Zambia Industrial and Mining Corporation Ltd., IV

Paper & Forestry

Abitibi-Consolidated, Inc., IV; 25 (upd.)
Albany International Corporation, 51 (upd.)
Amcor Ltd, IV; 19 (upd.); 78 (upd.)
American Greetings Corporation, 59 (upd.)
American Pad & Paper Company, 20
Aracruz Celulose S.A., 57
Arjo Wiggins Appleton p.l.c., 34
Asplundh Tree Expert Co.,20; 59 (upd.)
Avery Dennison Corporation, IV
Badger Paper Mills, Inc., 15
Beckett Papers, 23
Bemis Company, Inc., 8
Bohemia, Inc., 13
Boise Cascade Corporation, IV; 8 (upd.); 32 (upd.)
Bowater PLC, IV
Bunzl plc, IV
Canfor Corporation, 42
Caraustar Industries, Inc., 19; 44 (upd.)
Carter Lumber Company, 45
Cascades Inc., 71
Champion International Corporation, IV; 20 (upd.)
Chesapeake Corporation, 8; 30 (upd.)
Consolidated Papers, Inc., 8; 36 (upd.)
Crane & Co., Inc., 26
Crown Vantage Inc., 29
CSS Industries, Inc., 35
Daio Paper Corporation, IV
Daishowa Paper Manufacturing Co., Ltd., IV; 57 (upd.)
Deltic Timber Corporation, 46
Dillard Paper Company, 11
Doman Industries Limited, 59
Domtar Inc., IV
DS Smith Plc, 61
Empresas CMPC S.A., 70
Enso-Gutzeit Oy, IV
Esselte Pendaflex Corporation, 11
Federal Paper Board Company, Inc., 8
FiberMark, Inc., 37
Fletcher Challenge Ltd., IV
Fort Howard Corporation, 8
Fort James Corporation, 22 (upd.)
Georgia-Pacific Corporation, IV; 9 (upd.); 47 (upd.)
Groupe Rougier SA, 21
Grupo Portucel Soporcel, 60
Guilbert S.A., 42
Hampton Affiliates, Inc., 77
Holmen AB, 52 (upd.)
Honshu Paper Co., Ltd., IV
International Paper Company, IV; 15 (upd.); 47 (upd.)
James River Corporation of Virginia, IV
Japan Pulp and Paper Company Limited, IV
Jefferson Smurfit Group plc, IV; 49 (upd.)
Jujo Paper Co., Ltd., IV
Kimberly-Clark Corporation, 16 (upd.); 43 (upd.)
Kimberly-Clark de México, S.A. de C.V., 54
Klabin S.A., 73
Kruger Inc., 17
Kymmene Corporation, IV
Longview Fibre Company, 8; 37 (upd.)
Louisiana-Pacific Corporation, IV; 31 (upd.)
M-real Oyj, 56 (upd.)
MacMillan Bloedel Limited, IV
Matussière et Forest SA, 58
The Mead Corporation, IV; 19 (upd.)
MeadWestvaco Corporation, 76 (upd.)
Mercer International Inc., 64
Metsa-Serla Oy, IV
Miquel y Costas Miquel S.A., 68
Mo och Domsjö AB, IV
Monadnock Paper Mills, Inc., 21
Mosinee Paper Corporation, 15
Nashua Corporation, 8
National Envelope Corporation, 32
NCH Corporation, 8
Norske Skogindustrier ASA, 63
Oji Paper Co., Ltd., IV
P.H. Glatfelter Company, 8; 30 (upd.)
Packaging Corporation of America, 12
Papeteries de Lancey, 23
Plum Creek Timber Company, Inc., 43
Pope & Talbot, Inc., 12; 61 (upd.)
Pope Resources LP, 74
Potlatch Corporation, 8; 34 (upd.)
PWA Group, IV
Rayonier Inc., 24
Rengo Co., Ltd., IV
Reno de Medici S.p.A., 41
Rexam PLC, 32 (upd.)
Riverwood International Corporation, 11; 48 (upd.)
Rock-Tenn Company, 13; 59 (upd.)
Rogers Corporation, 61
St. Joe Paper Company, 8
Sanyo-Kokusaku Pulp Co., Ltd., IV
Sappi Limited, 49
Schweitzer-Mauduit International, Inc., 52
Scott Paper Company, IV; 31 (upd.)
Sealed Air Corporation, 14
Sierra Pacific Industries, 22
Simpson Investment Company, 17
Specialty Coatings Inc., 8

Personal Services

Petroleum

Publishing & Printing

Real Estate

Retail & Wholesale

Rubber & Tire

Telecommunications

Wanadoo S.A., 75
Watkins-Johnson Company, 15
The Weather Channel Companies, 52
West Corporation, 42
Western Union Financial Services, Inc., 54
Western Wireless Corporation, 36
Westwood One, Inc., 23
Williams Communications Group, Inc., 34
The Williams Companies, Inc., 31 (upd.)
Wipro Limited, 43
Wisconsin Bell, Inc., 14
Working Assets Funding Service, 43
XM Satellite Radio Holdings, Inc., 69
Young Broadcasting Inc., 40
Zoom Technologies, Inc., 53 (upd.)

Textiles & Apparel

Abercrombie & Fitch Company, 35 (upd.); 75 (upd.)
adidas Group AG, 75 (upd.)
adidas-Salomon AG, 14; 33 (upd.)
Adolfo Dominguez S.A., 72
Alba-Waldensian, Inc., 30
Albany International Corp., 8
Algo Group Inc., 24
American Safety Razor Company, 20
Amoskeag Company, 8
Angelica Corporation, 15; 43 (upd.)
AR Accessories Group, Inc., 23
Aris Industries, Inc., 16
ASICS Corporation, 57
Authentic Fitness Corporation, 20; 51 (upd.)
Banana Republic Inc., 25
Bata Ltd., 62
Benetton Group S.p.A., 10; 67 (upd.)
Bill Blass Ltd., 32
Birkenstock Footprint Sandals, Inc., 12
Blair Corporation, 25
Brazos Sportswear, Inc., 23
Brioni Roman Style S.p.A., 67
Brooks Brothers Inc., 22
Brooks Sports Inc., 32
Brown Group, Inc., V; 20 (upd.)
Bugle Boy Industries, Inc., 18
Burberry Ltd., 17; 41 (upd.)
Burke Mills, Inc., 66
Burlington Industries, Inc., V; 17 (upd.)
Calcot Ltd., 33
Calvin Klein, Inc., 22; 55 (upd.)
Candie's, Inc., 31
Canstar Sports Inc., 16
Capel Incorporated, 45
Capezio/Ballet Makers Inc., 62
Carhartt, Inc., 30, 77 (upd.)
Cato Corporation, 14
Chargeurs International, 21 (upd.)
Charming Shoppes, Inc., 8
Cherokee Inc., 18
Chic by H.I.S, Inc., 20
Chico's FAS, Inc., 45
Chorus Line Corporation, 30
Christian Dior S.A., 19; 49 (upd.)
Christopher & Banks Corporation, 42
Cia Hering, 72
Cintas Corporation, 51 (upd.)
Claire's Stores, Inc., 17
Coach Leatherware, 10
Coats plc, V; 44 (upd.)
Collins & Aikman Corporation, 13
Columbia Sportswear Company, 19; 41 (upd.)
Companhia de Tecidos Norte de Minas - Coteminas, 77
Concord Fabrics, Inc., 16
Cone Mills LLC, 8; 67 (upd.)
Converse Inc., 31 (upd.)
Cotton Incorporated, 46
Courtaulds plc, V; 17 (upd.)
Croscill, Inc., 42
Crown Crafts, Inc., 16
Crystal Brands, Inc., 9
Culp, Inc., 29
Cygne Designs, Inc., 25
Dan River Inc., 35
Danskin, Inc., 12; 62 (upd.)
Deckers Outdoor Corporation, 22
Delta and Pine Land Company, 59
Delta Woodside Industries, Inc., 8; 30 (upd.)
Designer Holdings Ltd., 20
The Dixie Group, Inc., 20
Dogi International Fabrics S.A., 52
Dolce & Gabbana SpA, 62
Dominion Textile Inc., 12
Donna Karan International Inc., 15; 56 (upd.)
Donnkenny, Inc., 17
Duck Head Apparel Company, Inc., 42
Dunavant Enterprises, Inc., 54
Dyersburg Corporation, 21
Ecco Sko A/S, 62
The Echo Design Group, Inc., 68
Edison Brothers Stores, Inc., 9
Eileen Fisher Inc., 61
Ellen Tracy, Inc., 55
Eram SA, 51
Ermenegildo Zegna SpA, 63
ESCADA AG, 71
Esprit de Corp., 8; 29 (upd.)
Etam Developpement SA, 44
Etienne Aigner AG, 52
Evans, Inc., 30
Fab Industries, Inc., 27
Fabri-Centers of America Inc., 16
Fat Face Ltd., 68
Fieldcrest Cannon, Inc., 9; 31 (upd.)
Fila Holding S.p.A., 20
Florsheim Shoe Group Inc., 31 (upd.)
Fossil, Inc., 17
Frederick's of Hollywood Inc., 16
French Connection Group plc, 41
Fruit of the Loom, Inc., 8; 25 (upd.)
Fubu, 29
G&K Services, Inc., 16
G-III Apparel Group, Ltd., 22
Galey & Lord, Inc., 20; 66 (upd.)
Garan, Inc., 16; 64 (upd.)
Gerry Weber International AG, 63
Gianni Versace SpA, 22
Giorgio Armani S.p.A., 45
The Gitano Group, Inc. 8
Greenwood Mills, Inc., 14
Groupe DMC (Dollfus Mieg & Cie), 27
Groupe Yves Saint Laurent, 23
Gucci Group N.V., 15; 50 (upd.)
Guess, Inc., 15; 68 (upd.)
Guilford Mills Inc., 8; 40 (upd.)
Gymboree Corporation, 15; 69 (upd.)
Haggar Corporation, 19; 78 (upd.)
Hampton Industries, Inc., 20
Happy Kids Inc., 30
Hartmarx Corporation, 8
The Hartstone Group plc, 14
HCI Direct, Inc., 55
Healthtex, Inc., 17
Helly Hansen ASA, 25
Hermès S.A., 14
The Hockey Company, 34
Hugo Boss AG, 48
Hummel International A/S, 68
Hyde Athletic Industries, Inc., 17
I.C. Isaacs & Company, 31
Industria de Diseño Textil S.A., 64
Interface, Inc., 8; 29 (upd.); 76 (upd.)
Irwin Toy Limited, 14
Items International Airwalk Inc., 17
J. Crew Group, Inc., 12; 34 (upd.)
JLM Couture, Inc., 64
Jockey International, Inc., 12; 34 (upd.); 77 (upd.)
Johnston Industries, Inc., 15
Jones Apparel Group, Inc., 39 (upd.)
Jordache Enterprises, Inc., 23
Jos. A. Bank Clothiers, Inc., 31
JPS Textile Group, Inc., 28
K-Swiss, Inc., 33
Karl Kani Infinity, Inc., 49
Kellwood Company, 8
Kenneth Cole Productions, Inc., 25
Kinney Shoe Corp., 14
Klaus Steilmann GmbH & Co. KG, 53
Koret of California, Inc., 62
L.A. Gear, Inc., 8; 32 (upd.)
L.L. Bean, Inc., 10; 38 (upd.)
LaCrosse Footwear, Inc., 18; 61 (upd.)
Laura Ashley Holdings plc, 13
Lee Apparel Company, Inc., 8
The Leslie Fay Company, Inc., 8; 39 (upd.)
Levi Strauss & Co., V; 16 (upd.)
Liz Claiborne, Inc., 8
London Fog Industries, Inc., 29
Lost Arrow Inc., 22
Maidenform, Inc., 20; 59 (upd.)
Malden Mills Industries, Inc., 16
Marzotto S.p.A., 20; 67 (upd.)
Milliken & Co., V; 17 (upd.)
Mitsubishi Rayon Co., Ltd., V
Mossimo, Inc., 27
Mothercare plc, 17; 78 (upd.)
Movie Star Inc., 17
Mulberry Group PLC, 71
Naf Naf SA, 44
Nautica Enterprises, Inc., 18; 44 (upd.)
New Balance Athletic Shoe, Inc., 25; 68 (upd.)
NIKE, Inc., V; 8 (upd.); 75 (upd.)
Nine West Group, Inc., 39 (upd.)
Nitches, Inc., 53
The North Face Inc., 18; 78 (upd.)
Oakley, Inc., 18
OshKosh B'Gosh, Inc., 9; 42 (upd.)

Tobacco

Transport Services

Dollar Thrifty Automotive Group, Inc., 25
Dot Foods, Inc., 69
East Japan Railway Company, V; 66 (upd.)
EGL, Inc., 59
Emery Air Freight Corporation, 6
Emery Worldwide Airlines, Inc., 25 (upd.)
Enterprise Rent-A-Car Company, 6
Eurotunnel Group, 37 (upd.)
EVA Airways Corporation, 51
Evergreen International Aviation, Inc., 53
Evergreen Marine Corporation (Taiwan) Ltd., 13; 50 (upd.)
Executive Jet, Inc., 36
Exel plc, 51 (upd.)
Expeditors International of Washington Inc., 17; 78 (upd.)
Federal Express Corporation, V
FedEx Corporation, 18 (upd.); 42 (upd.)
Forward Air Corporation, 75
Fritz Companies, Inc., 12
Frontline Ltd., 45
Frozen Food Express Industries, Inc., 20
Garuda Indonesia, 58 (upd.)
GATX Corporation, 6; 25 (upd.)
GE Capital Aviation Services, 36
Gefco SA, 54
General Maritime Corporation, 59
Genesee & Wyoming Inc., 27
Geodis S.A., 67
The Go-Ahead Group Plc, 28
The Greenbrier Companies, 19
Greyhound Lines, Inc., 32 (upd.)
Groupe Bourbon S.A., 60
Grupo TMM, S.A. de C.V., 50
Grupo Transportación Ferroviaria Mexicana, S.A. de C.V., 47
Gulf Agency Company Ltd. 78
GulfMark Offshore, Inc., 49
Hanjin Shipping Co., Ltd., 50
Hankyu Corporation, V; 23 (upd.)
Hapag-Lloyd AG, 6
Harland and Wolff Holdings plc, 19
Harper Group Inc., 17
Heartland Express, Inc., 18
The Hertz Corporation, 9
Holberg Industries, Inc., 36
Hospitality Worldwide Services, Inc., 26
Hub Group, Inc., 38
Hvide Marine Incorporated, 22
Illinois Central Corporation, 11
International Shipholding Corporation, Inc., 27
J.B. Hunt Transport Services Inc., 12
John Menzies plc, 39
Kansas City Southern Industries, Inc., 6; 26 (upd.)
Kawasaki Kisen Kaisha, Ltd., V; 56 (upd.)
Keio Teito Electric Railway Company, V
Keolis SA, 51
Kinki Nippon Railway Company Ltd., V
Kirby Corporation, 18; 66 (upd.)
Knight Transportation, Inc., 64
Koninklijke Nedlloyd Groep N.V., 6
Kuehne & Nagel International AG, V; 53 (upd.)
La Poste, V; 47 (upd.)
Landstar System, Inc., 63
Leaseway Transportation Corp., 12
London Regional Transport, 6
The Long Island Rail Road Company, 68
Maine Central Railroad Company, 16
Mammoet Transport B.V., 26
Martz Group, 56
Mayflower Group Inc., 6
Mercury Air Group, Inc., 20
The Mersey Docks and Harbour Company, 30
Metropolitan Transportation Authority, 35
Miller Industries, Inc., 26
Mitsui O.S.K. Lines, Ltd., V
Moran Towing Corporation, Inc., 15
The Morgan Group, Inc., 46
Morris Travel Services L.L.C., 26
Motor Cargo Industries, Inc., 35
National Car Rental System, Inc., 10
National Express Group PLC, 50
National Railroad Passenger Corporation (Amtrak), 22; 66 (upd.)
Neptune Orient Lines Limited, 47
NFC plc, 6
Nippon Express Company, Ltd., V; 64 (upd.)
Nippon Yusen Kabushiki Kaisha (NYK), V; 72 (upd.)
Norfolk Southern Corporation, V; 29 (upd.); 75 (upd.)
Oak Harbor Freight Lines, Inc., 53
Ocean Group plc, 6
Odakyu Electric Railway Co., Ltd., V; 68 (upd.)
Oglebay Norton Company, 17
Old Dominion Freight Line, Inc., 57
OMI Corporation, 59
The Oppenheimer Group, 76
Österreichische Bundesbahnen GmbH, 6
OTR Express, Inc., 25
Overnite Corporation, 14; 58 (upd.)
Overseas Shipholding Group, Inc., 11
Pacer International, Inc., 54
The Peninsular and Oriental Steam Navigation Company, V; 38 (upd.)
Penske Corporation, V
PHH Arval, V; 53 (upd.)
Pilot Air Freight Corp., 67
Plantation Pipe Line Company, 68
Polar Air Cargo Inc., 60
The Port Authority of New York and New Jersey, 48
Port Imperial Ferry Corporation, 70
Post Office Group, V
Preston Corporation, 6
RailTex, Inc., 20
Railtrack Group PLC, 50
Réseau Ferré de France, 66
Roadway Express, Inc., V; 25 (upd.)
Royal Olympic Cruise Lines Inc., 52
Royal Vopak NV, 41
Ryder System, Inc., V; 24 (upd.)
Santa Fe Pacific Corporation, V
Schenker-Rhenus AG, 6
Schneider National, Inc., 36; 77 (upd.)
Securicor Plc, 45
Seibu Railway Company Ltd., V; 74 (upd.)
Seino Transportation Company, Ltd., 6
Simon Transportation Services Inc., 27
Smithway Motor Xpress Corporation, 39
Société Nationale des Chemins de Fer Français, V; 57 (upd.)
Société Norbert Dentressangle S.A., 67
Southern Pacific Transportation Company, V
Stagecoach Holdings plc, 30
Stelmar Shipping Ltd., 52
Stevedoring Services of America Inc., 28
Stinnes AG, 8; 59 (upd.)
Stolt-Nielsen S.A., 42
Sunoco, Inc., 28 (upd.)
Swift Transportation Co., Inc., 42
The Swiss Federal Railways (Schweizerische Bundesbahnen), V
Swissport International Ltd., 70
Teekay Shipping Corporation, 25
Tibbett & Britten Group plc, 32
Tidewater Inc., 11; 37 (upd.)
TNT Freightways Corporation, 14
TNT Post Group N.V., V; 27 (upd.); 30 (upd.)
Tobu Railway Co Ltd, 6
Tokyu Corporation, V
Totem Resources Corporation, 9
TPG N.V., 64 (upd.)
Trailer Bridge, Inc., 41
Transnet Ltd., 6
Transport Corporation of America, Inc., 49
TTX Company, 6; 66 (upd.)
U.S. Delivery Systems, Inc., 22
Union Pacific Corporation, V; 28 (upd.); 79 (upd.)
United Parcel Service of America Inc., V; 17 (upd.)
United Parcel Service, Inc., 63
United Road Services, Inc., 69
United States Postal Service, 14; 34 (upd.)
USA Truck, Inc., 42
Velocity Express Corporation, 49
Werner Enterprises, Inc., 26
Wincanton plc, 52
Wisconsin Central Transportation Corporation, 24
Yamato Transport Co. Ltd., V; 49 (upd.)
Yellow Corporation, 14; 45 (upd.)
Yellow Freight System, Inc. of Delaware, V

Utilities

AES Corporation, 10; 13 (upd.); 53 (upd.)
Aggreko Plc, 45
Air & Water Technologies Corporation, 6
Alberta Energy Company Ltd., 16; 43 (upd.)
Allegheny Energy, Inc., V; 38 (upd.)
Ameren Corporation, 60 (upd.)
American Electric Power Company, Inc., V; 45 (upd.)
American States Water Company, 46
American Water Works Company, Inc., 6; 38 (upd.)
Aquila, Inc., 50 (upd.)
Arkla, Inc., V

Public Service Company of New Hampshire, 21; 55 (upd.)
Public Service Company of New Mexico, 6
Public Service Enterprise Group Inc., V; 44 (upd.)
Puerto Rico Electric Power Authority, 47
Puget Sound Energy Inc., 6; 50 (upd.)
Questar Corporation, 6; 26 (upd.)
RAO Unified Energy System of Russia, 45
Reliant Energy Inc., 44 (upd.)
Rochester Gas and Electric Corporation, 6
Ruhrgas AG, V; 38 (upd.)
RWE AG, V; 50 (upd.)
Salt River Project, 19
San Diego Gas & Electric Company, V
SCANA Corporation, 6; 56 (upd.)
Scarborough Public Utilities Commission, 9
SCEcorp, V
Scottish and Southern Energy plc, 66 (upd.)
Scottish Hydro-Electric PLC, 13
Scottish Power plc, 19; 49 (upd.)
Seattle City Light, 50
SEMCO Energy, Inc., 44
Sempra Energy, 25 (upd.)
Severn Trent PLC, 12; 38 (upd.)
Shikoku Electric Power Company, Inc., V; 60 (upd.)
SJW Corporation, 70
Sonat, Inc., 6
South Jersey Industries, Inc., 42
The Southern Company, V; 38 (upd.)
Southern Electric PLC, 13
Southern Indiana Gas and Electric Company, 13
Southern Union Company, 27
Southwest Gas Corporation, 19
Southwest Water Company, 47
Southwestern Electric Power Co., 21
Southwestern Public Service Company, 6
Suez Lyonnaise des Eaux, 36 (upd.)
TECO Energy, Inc., 6
Tennessee Valley Authority, 50
Tennet BV 78
Texas Utilities Company, V; 25 (upd.)
Thames Water plc, 11
Tohoku Electric Power Company, Inc., V
The Tokyo Electric Power Company, 74 (upd.)
The Tokyo Electric Power Company, Incorporated, V
Tokyo Gas Co., Ltd., V; 55 (upd.)
TransAlta Utilities Corporation, 6
TransCanada PipeLines Limited, V
Transco Energy Company, V
Trigen Energy Corporation, 42
Tucson Electric Power Company, 6
UGI Corporation, 12
Unicom Corporation, 29 (upd.)
Union Electric Company, V
The United Illuminating Company, 21
United Utilities PLC, 52 (upd.)
United Water Resources, Inc., 40
Unitil Corporation, 37
Utah Power and Light Company, 27
UtiliCorp United Inc., 6
Vattenfall AB, 57
Vereinigte Elektrizitätswerke Westfalen AG, V
VEW AG, 39
Viridian Group plc, 64
Warwick Valley Telephone Company, 55
Washington Gas Light Company, 19
Washington Natural Gas Company, 9
Washington Water Power Company, 6
Westar Energy, Inc., 57 (upd.)
Western Resources, Inc., 12
Wheelabrator Technologies, Inc., 6
Wisconsin Energy Corporation, 6; 54 (upd.)
Wisconsin Public Service Corporation, 9
WPL Holdings, Inc., 6
WPS Resources Corporation, 53 (upd.)
Xcel Energy Inc., 73 (upd.)

Waste Services

Allied Waste Industries, Inc., 50
Allwaste, Inc., 18
American Ecology Corporation, 77
Appliance Recycling Centers of America, Inc., 42
Azcon Corporation, 23
Berliner Stadtreinigungsbetriebe, 58
Brambles Industries Limited, 42
Browning-Ferris Industries, Inc., V; 20 (upd.)
Chemical Waste Management, Inc., 9
Clean Harbors, Inc., 73
Copart Inc., 23
E.On AG, 50 (upd.)
Ecology and Environment, Inc., 39
Industrial Services of America, Inc., 46
Ionics, Incorporated, 52
ISS A/S, 49
Kelda Group plc, 45
MPW Industrial Services Group, Inc., 53
Newpark Resources, Inc., 63
Norcal Waste Systems, Inc., 60
1-800-GOT-JUNK? LLC, 74
Pennon Group Plc, 45
Philip Environmental Inc., 16
Philip Services Corp., 73
Roto-Rooter, Inc., 15; 61 (upd.)
Safety-Kleen Corp., 8
Sevenson Environmental Services, Inc., 42
Severn Trent PLC, 38 (upd.)
Shanks Group plc, 45
Shred-It Canada Corporation, 56
Stericycle, Inc., 33; 74 (upd.)
TRC Companies, Inc., 32
Veit Companies, 43
Waste Connections, Inc., 46
Waste Holdings, Inc., 41
Waste Management, Inc., V
Wheelabrator Technologies, Inc., 60 (upd.)
Windswept Environmental Group, Inc., 62
WMX Technologies Inc., 17

Geographic Index

Azerbaijan

Bahamas

Bahrain

Bangladesh

Belgium

Belize

Bermuda

Brazil

Canada

Cayman Islands

Chile

China

Colombia

Croatia

Czech Republic

Germany

Ghana

Greece

Hong Kong

Hungary

Iceland

India

Indonesia

Iran

Ireland

Israel

Italy

Jamaica

Japan

Kanebo, Ltd., 53
Kanematsu Corporation, IV; 24 (upd.)
The Kansai Electric Power Company, Inc., V; 62 (upd.)
Kao Corporation, III; 20 (upd.); 79 (upd.)
Kawai Musical Instruments Mfg Co. Ltd. 78
Kawasaki Heavy Industries, Ltd., III; 63 (upd.)
Kawasaki Kisen Kaisha, Ltd., V; 56 (upd.)
Kawasaki Steel Corporation, IV
Keio Teito Electric Railway Company, V
Kenwood Corporation, 31
Kewpie Kabushiki Kaisha, 57
Kikkoman Corporation, 14; 47 (upd.)
Kinki Nippon Railway Company Ltd., V
Kirin Brewery Company, Limited, I; 21 (upd.); 63 (upd.)
Kobe Steel, Ltd., IV; 19 (upd.)
Kodansha Ltd., IV; 38 (upd.)
Komatsu Ltd., III; 16 (upd.); 52 (upd.)
Konica Corporation, III; 30 (upd.)
Kotobukiya Co., Ltd., V; 56 (upd.)
Kubota Corporation, III; 26 (upd.)
Kumagai Gumi Company, Ltd., I
Kumon Institute of Education Co., Ltd., 72
Kyocera Corporation, II; 21 (upd.); 79 (upd.)
Kyokuyo Company Ltd., 75
Kyowa Hakko Kogyo Co., Ltd., III; 48 (upd.)
Kyushu Electric Power Company Inc., V
Lion Corporation, III; 51 (upd.)
Long-Term Credit Bank of Japan, Ltd., II
Mabuchi Motor Co. Ltd., 68
Makita Corporation, 22; 59 (upd.)
Marubeni Corporation, I; 24 (upd.)
Maruha Group Inc., 75 (upd.)
Marui Company Ltd., V; 62 (upd.)
Maruzen Co., Limited, 18
Matsushita Electric Industrial Co., Ltd., II; 64 (upd.)
Matsushita Electric Works, Ltd., III; 7 (upd.)
Matsuzakaya Company Ltd., V; 64 (upd.)
Mazda Motor Corporation, 9; 23 (upd.); 63 (upd.)
Meiji Milk Products Company, Limited, II
The Meiji Mutual Life Insurance Company, III
Meiji Seika Kaisha Ltd., II; 64 (upd.)
Mercian Corporation, 77
Millea Holdings Inc., 64 (upd.)
Minolta Co., Ltd., III; 18 (upd.); 43 (upd.)
The Mitsubishi Bank, Ltd., II
Mitsubishi Chemical Corporation, I; 56 (upd.)
Mitsubishi Corporation, I; 12 (upd.)
Mitsubishi Electric Corporation, II, 44 (upd.)
Mitsubishi Estate Company, Limited, IV; 61 (upd.)
Mitsubishi Heavy Industries, Ltd., III; 7 (upd.); 40 (upd.)
Mitsubishi Materials Corporation, III
Mitsubishi Motors Corporation, 9; 23 (upd.); 57 (upd.)
Mitsubishi Oil Co., Ltd., IV
Mitsubishi Rayon Co., Ltd., V
The Mitsubishi Trust & Banking Corporation, II
Mitsui & Co., Ltd., 28 (upd.)
The Mitsui Bank, Ltd., II
Mitsui Bussan K.K., I
Mitsui Marine and Fire Insurance Company, Limited, III
Mitsui Mining & Smelting Co., Ltd., IV
Mitsui Mining Company, Limited, IV
Mitsui Mutual Life Insurance Company, III; 39 (upd.)
Mitsui O.S.K. Lines, Ltd., V
Mitsui Petrochemical Industries, Ltd., 9
Mitsui Real Estate Development Co., Ltd., IV
The Mitsui Trust & Banking Company, Ltd., II
Mitsukoshi Ltd., V; 56 (upd.)
Mizuho Financial Group Inc., 58 (upd.)
Mizuno Corporation, 25
Morinaga & Co. Ltd., 61
Nagasakiya Co., Ltd., V; 69 (upd.)
Nagase & Co., Ltd., 8; 61 (upd.)
NEC Corporation, II; 21 (upd.); 57 (upd.)
NGK Insulators Ltd., 67
NHK Spring Co., Ltd., III
Nichii Co., Ltd., V
Nichimen Corporation, IV; 24 (upd.)
Nichirei Corporation, 70
Nidec Corporation, 59
Nihon Keizai Shimbun, Inc., IV
The Nikko Securities Company Limited, II; 9 (upd.)
Nikon Corporation, III; 48 (upd.)
Nintendo Co., Ltd., III; 7 (upd.); 28 (upd.); 67 (upd.)
Nippon Credit Bank, II
Nippon Express Company, Ltd., V; 64 (upd.)
Nippon Life Insurance Company, III; 60 (upd.)
Nippon Light Metal Company, Ltd., IV
Nippon Meat Packers Inc., II, 78 (upd.)
Nippon Oil Corporation, IV; 63 (upd.)
Nippon Seiko K.K., III
Nippon Sheet Glass Company, Limited, III
Nippon Shinpan Co., Ltd., II; 61 (upd.)
Nippon Steel Corporation, IV; 17 (upd.)
Nippon Suisan Kaisha, Limited, II
Nippon Telegraph and Telephone Corporation, V; 51 (upd.)
Nippon Yusen Kabushiki Kaisha (NYK), V; 72 (upd.)
Nippondenso Co., Ltd., III
Nissan Motor Company Ltd., I; 11 (upd.); 34 (upd.)
Nisshin Seifun Group Inc., II; 66 (upd.)
Nisshin Steel Co., Ltd., IV
Nissho Iwai K.K., I
Nissin Food Products Company Ltd., 75
NKK Corporation, IV; 28 (upd.)
NOF Corporation, 72
Nomura Securities Company, Limited, II; 9 (upd.)
Norinchukin Bank, II
NTN Corporation, III; 47 (upd.)
Obayashi Corporation 78
Odakyu Electric Railway Co., Ltd., V; 68 (upd.)
Ohbayashi Corporation, I
Oji Paper Co., Ltd., IV; 57 (upd.)
Oki Electric Industry Company, Limited, II
Okuma Holdings Inc., 74
Okura & Co., Ltd., IV
Omron Corporation, II; 28 (upd.)
Onoda Cement Co., Ltd., III
ORIX Corporation, II; 44 (upd.)
Osaka Gas Company, Ltd., V; 60 (upd.)
Paloma Industries Ltd., 71
Pearl Corporation 78
Pentax Corporation 78
Pioneer Electronic Corporation, III; 28 (upd.)
Rengo Co., Ltd., IV
Ricoh Company, Ltd., III; 36 (upd.)
Roland Corporation, 38
Ryoshoku Ltd., 72
Sankyo Company, Ltd., I; 56 (upd.)
Sanrio Company, Ltd., 38
The Sanwa Bank, Ltd., II; 15 (upd.)
SANYO Electric Company, Ltd., II; 36 (upd.)
Sanyo-Kokusaku Pulp Co., Ltd., IV
Sapporo Breweries, Ltd., I; 13 (upd.); 36 (upd.)
SEGA Corporation, 73
Seibu Department Stores, Ltd., V; 42 (upd.)
Seibu Railway Company Ltd., V; 74 (upd.)
Seiko Corporation, III; 17 (upd.); 72 (upd.)
Seino Transportation Company, Ltd., 6
The Seiyu, Ltd., V; 36 (upd.)
Sekisui Chemical Co., Ltd., III; 72 (upd.)
Sharp Corporation, II; 12 (upd.); 40 (upd.)
Shikoku Electric Power Company, Inc., V; 60 (upd.)
Shimano Inc., 64
Shionogi & Co., Ltd., III; 17 (upd.)
Shiseido Company, Limited, III; 22 (upd.)
Shochiku Company Ltd., 74
Showa Shell Sekiyu K.K., IV; 59 (upd.)
Snow Brand Milk Products Company, Ltd., II; 48 (upd.)
Softbank Corp., 13; 38 (upd.)
Sony Corporation, II; 12 (upd.); 40 (upd.)
The Sumitomo Bank, Limited, II; 26 (upd.)
Sumitomo Chemical Company Ltd., I
Sumitomo Corporation, I; 11 (upd.)
Sumitomo Electric Industries, Ltd., II
Sumitomo Heavy Industries, Ltd., III; 42 (upd.)
Sumitomo Life Insurance Company, III; 60 (upd.)

The Sumitomo Marine and Fire Insurance Company, Limited, III
Sumitomo Metal Industries, Ltd., IV
Sumitomo Metal Mining Co., Ltd., IV
Sumitomo Mitsui Banking Corporation, 51 (upd.)
Sumitomo Realty & Development Co., Ltd., IV
Sumitomo Rubber Industries, Ltd., V
The Sumitomo Trust & Banking Company, Ltd., II; 53 (upd.)
Suntory Ltd., 65
Suzuki Motor Corporation, 9; 23 (upd.); 59 (upd.)
Taiheiyo Cement Corporation, 60 (upd.)
Taiyo Fishery Company, Limited, II
The Taiyo Kobe Bank, Ltd., II
Takara Holdings Inc., 62
Takashimaya Company, Limited, V; 47 (upd.)
Takeda Chemical Industries, Ltd., I; 46 (upd.)
TDK Corporation, II; 17 (upd.); 49 (upd.)
TEAC Corporation 78
Teijin Limited, V; 61 (upd.)
Terumo Corporation, 48
Tobu Railway Co Ltd, 6
Toho Co., Ltd., 28
Tohoku Electric Power Company, Inc., V
The Tokai Bank, Limited, II; 15 (upd.)
The Tokio Marine and Fire Insurance Co., Ltd., III
The Tokyo Electric Power Company, 74 (upd.)
The Tokyo Electric Power Company, Incorporated, V
Tokyo Gas Co., Ltd., V; 55 (upd.)
Tokyu Corporation, V; 47 (upd.)
Tokyu Department Store Co., Ltd., V; 32 (upd.)
Tokyu Land Corporation, IV
Tomen Corporation, IV; 24 (upd.)
Tomy Company Ltd., 65
TonenGeneral Sekiyu K.K., IV; 16 (upd.); 54 (upd.)
Toppan Printing Co., Ltd., IV; 58 (upd.)
Toray Industries, Inc., V; 51 (upd.)
Toshiba Corporation, I; 12 (upd.); 40 (upd.)
Tosoh Corporation, 70
TOTO LTD., III; 28 (upd.)
Toyo Sash Co., Ltd., III
Toyo Seikan Kaisha, Ltd., I
Toyoda Automatic Loom Works, Ltd., III
Toyota Motor Corporation, I; 11 (upd.); 38 (upd.)
Ube Industries, Ltd., III; 38 (upd.)
Unitika Ltd., V; 53 (upd.)
Uny Co., Ltd., V; 49 (upd.)
Victor Company of Japan, Limited, II; 26 (upd.)
Wacoal Corp., 25
Yamaha Corporation, III; 16 (upd.); 40 (upd.)
Yamaichi Securities Company, Limited, II
Yamato Transport Co. Ltd., V; 49 (upd.)
Yamazaki Baking Co., Ltd., 58
The Yasuda Fire and Marine Insurance Company, Limited, III
The Yasuda Mutual Life Insurance Company, III; 39 (upd.)
The Yasuda Trust and Banking Company, Ltd., II; 17 (upd.)
The Yokohama Rubber Co., Ltd., V; 19 (upd.)

Kuwait

Kuwait Airways Corporation, 68
Kuwait Petroleum Corporation, IV; 55 (upd.)

Latvia

A/S Air Baltic Corporation, 71

Lebanon

Middle East Airlines - Air Liban S.A.L. 79

Libya

National Oil Corporation, IV; 66 (upd.)

Liechtenstein

Hilti AG, 53

Luxembourg

ARBED S.A., IV; 22 (upd.)
Cargolux Airlines International S.A., 49
Espírito Santo Financial Group S.A. 79 (upd.)
Gemplus International S.A., 64
RTL Group SA, 44
Société Luxembourgeoise de Navigation Aérienne S.A., 64
Tenaris SA, 63

Malaysia

Berjaya Group Bhd., 67
Genting Bhd., 65
Malayan Banking Berhad, 72
Malaysian Airlines System Berhad, 6; 29 (upd.)
Perusahaan Otomobil Nasional Bhd., 62
Petroliam Nasional Bhd (Petronas), IV; 56 (upd.)
PPB Group Berhad, 57
Sime Darby Berhad, 14; 36 (upd.)
Telekom Malaysia Bhd, 76
Yeo Hiap Seng Malaysia Bhd., 75

Mauritius

Air Mauritius Ltd., 63

Mexico

Alfa, S.A. de C.V., 19
Altos Hornos de México, S.A. de C.V., 42
Apasco S.A. de C.V., 51
Bufete Industrial, S.A. de C.V., 34
Casa Cuervo, S.A. de C.V., 31
Celanese Mexicana, S.A. de C.V., 54
CEMEX S.A. de C.V., 20; 59 (upd.)
Cifra, S.A. de C.V., 12
Consorcio ARA, S.A. de C.V. 79
Consorcio G Grupo Dina, S.A. de C.V., 36
Controladora Comercial Mexicana, S.A. de C.V., 36
Corporación Internacional de Aviación, S.A. de C.V. (Cintra), 20
Desc, S.A. de C.V., 23
Editorial Television, S.A. de C.V., 57
Empresas ICA Sociedad Controladora, S.A. de C.V., 41
Ford Motor Company, S.A. de C.V., 20
Gruma, S.A. de C.V., 31
Grupo Aeropuerto del Sureste, S.A. de C.V., 48
Grupo Carso, S.A. de C.V., 21
Grupo Casa Saba, S.A. de C.V., 39
Grupo Cydsa, S.A. de C.V., 39
Grupo Elektra, S.A. de C.V., 39
Grupo Financiero Banamex S.A., 54
Grupo Financiero Banorte, S.A. de C.V., 51
Grupo Financiero BBVA Bancomer S.A., 54
Grupo Financiero Serfin, S.A., 19
Grupo Gigante, S.A. de C.V., 34
Grupo Herdez, S.A. de C.V., 35
Grupo IMSA, S.A. de C.V., 44
Grupo Industrial Bimbo, 19
Grupo Industrial Durango, S.A. de C.V., 37
Grupo Industrial Saltillo, S.A. de C.V., 54
Grupo Mexico, S.A. de C.V., 40
Grupo Modelo, S.A. de C.V., 29
Grupo Posadas, S.A. de C.V., 57
Grupo Televisa, S.A., 18; 54 (upd.)
Grupo TMM, S.A. de C.V., 50
Grupo Transportación Ferroviaria Mexicana, S.A. de C.V., 47
Hylsamex, S.A. de C.V., 39
Industrias Bachoco, S.A. de C.V., 39
Industrias Penoles, S.A. de C.V., 22
Internacional de Ceramica, S.A. de C.V., 53
Kimberly-Clark de México, S.A. de C.V., 54
Organización Soriana, S.A. de C.V., 35
Petróleos Mexicanos, IV; 19 (upd.)
Pulsar Internacional S.A., 21
Real Turismo, S.A. de C.V., 50
Sanborn Hermanos, S.A., 20
Sears Roebuck de México, S.A. de C.V., 20
Telefonos de Mexico S.A. de C.V., 14; 63 (upd.)
Tubos de Acero de Mexico, S.A. (TAMSA), 41
TV Azteca, S.A. de C.V., 39
Valores Industriales S.A., 19
Vitro Corporativo S.A. de C.V., 34
Wal-Mart de Mexico, S.A. de C.V., 35 (upd.)

Nepal

Royal Nepal Airline Corporation, 41

Netherlands

ABN AMRO Holding, N.V., 50
AEGON N.V., III; 50 (upd.)
Akzo Nobel N.V., 13; 41 (upd.)
Algemene Bank Nederland N.V., II

Netherlands Antilles

New Zealand

Nigeria

Norway

Oman

Pakistan

Panama

Peru

Philippines

Poland

Portugal

Puerto Rico

Qatar

Romania

Russia

Saudi Arabia

Scotland

Singapore

South Africa

South Korea

Spain

Sweden

United States

Dan River Inc., 35
Dana Corporation, I; 10 (upd.)
Danaher Corporation, 7; 77 (upd.)
Daniel Industries, Inc., 16
Daniel Measurement and Control, Inc., 74 (upd.)
Dannon Co., Inc., 14
Danskin, Inc., 12; 62 (upd.)
Darden Restaurants, Inc., 16; 44 (upd.)
Darigold, Inc., 9
Dart Group Corporation, 16
Data Broadcasting Corporation, 31
Data General Corporation, 8
Datapoint Corporation, 11
Datascope Corporation, 39
Datek Online Holdings Corp., 32
Dauphin Deposit Corporation, 14
Dave & Buster's, Inc., 33
The Davey Tree Expert Company, 11
The David and Lucile Packard Foundation, 41
The David J. Joseph Company, 14; 76 (upd.)
David's Bridal, Inc., 33
Davis Polk & Wardwell, 36
DaVita Inc., 73
DAW Technologies, Inc., 25
Dawn Food Products, Inc., 17
Day & Zimmermann Inc., 9; 31 (upd.)
Day Runner, Inc., 14; 41 (upd.)
Dayton Hudson Corporation, V; 18 (upd.)
DC Comics Inc., 25
DC Shoes, Inc., 60
DDB Needham Worldwide, 14
Dean & DeLuca, Inc., 36
Dean Foods Company, 7; 21 (upd.); 73 (upd.)
Dean Witter, Discover & Co., 12
Dearborn Mid-West Conveyor Company, 56
Death Row Records, 27
Deb Shops, Inc., 16; 76 (upd.)
Debevoise & Plimpton, 39
Dechert, 43
Deckers Outdoor Corporation, 22
Decora Industries, Inc., 31
Decorator Industries Inc., 68
DeCrane Aircraft Holdings Inc., 36
DeepTech International Inc., 21
Deere & Company, III; 21 (upd.); 42 (upd.)
Defiance, Inc., 22
DeKalb Genetics Corporation, 17
Del Laboratories, Inc., 28
Del Monte Foods Company, 7; 23 (upd.)
Del Taco, Inc., 58
Del Webb Corporation, 14
Delaware North Companies Incorporated, 7
dELiA*s Inc., 29
Delicato Vineyards, Inc., 50
Dell Inc., 9; 31 (upd.); 63 (upd.)
Deloitte Touche Tohmatsu International, 9; 29 (upd.)
DeLorme Publishing Company, Inc., 53
Delphi Automotive Systems Corporation, 45
Delta Air Lines, Inc., I; 6 (upd.); 39 (upd.)
Delta and Pine Land Company, 33; 59
Delta Woodside Industries, Inc., 8; 30 (upd.)
Deltec, Inc., 56
Deltic Timber Corporation, 46
Deluxe Corporation, 7; 22 (upd.); 73 (upd.)
DEMCO, Inc., 60
DeMoulas / Market Basket Inc., 23
DenAmerica Corporation, 29
Denbury Resources, Inc., 67
Dendrite International, Inc., 70
Denison International plc, 46
Dentsply International Inc., 10
Denver Nuggets, 51
DEP Corporation, 20
Department 56, Inc., 14; 34 (upd.)
Deposit Guaranty Corporation, 17
DePuy Inc., 30; 37 (upd.)
Deschutes Brewery, Inc., 57
Designer Holdings Ltd., 20
Destec Energy, Inc., 12
Detroit Diesel Corporation, 10; 74 (upd.)
The Detroit Edison Company, V
The Detroit Lions, Inc., 55
The Detroit Pistons Basketball Company,41
Detroit Red Wings, 74
Detroit Tigers Baseball Club, Inc., 46
Deutsch, Inc., 42
Developers Diversified Realty Corporation, 69
Devon Energy Corporation, 61
DeVry Incorporated, 29
Dewberry 78
Dewey Ballantine LLP, 48
Dex Media, Inc., 65
The Dexter Corporation, I; 12 (upd.)
DFS Group Ltd., 66
DH Technology, Inc., 18
DHL Worldwide Express, 6; 24 (upd.)
Di Giorgio Corp., 12
Diagnostic Products Corporation, 73
The Dial Corp., 8; 23 (upd.)
Dial-A-Mattress Operating Corporation, 46
Dialogic Corporation, 18
Diamond of California, 64 (upd.)
Diamond Shamrock, Inc., IV
DiamondCluster International, Inc., 51
Dibrell Brothers, Incorporated, 12
dick clark productions, inc., 16
Dick Corporation, 64
Dick's Sporting Goods, Inc., 59
Dictaphone Healthcare Solutions 78
Diebold, Incorporated, 7; 22 (upd.)
Diedrich Coffee, Inc., 40
Dierbergs Markets Inc., 63
Digex, Inc., 46
Digi International Inc., 9
Digital Equipment Corporation, III; 6 (upd.)
Digital River, Inc., 50
Dillard Paper Company, 11
Dillard's Inc., V; 16 (upd.); 68 (upd.)
Dillingham Construction Corporation, I; 44 (upd.)
Dillon Companies Inc., 12
Dime Savings Bank of New York, F.S.B., 9
DIMON Inc., 27
Dionex Corporation, 46
Dippin' Dots, Inc., 56
Direct Focus, Inc., 47
DIRECTV, Inc., 38; 75 (upd.)
Discount Auto Parts, Inc., 18
Discount Drug Mart, Inc., 14
Discovery Communications, Inc., 42
Discovery Partners International, Inc., 58
The Dixie Group, Inc., 20
Dixon Industries, Inc., 26
Dixon Ticonderoga Company, 12; 69 (upd.)
DMI Furniture, Inc., 46
Do it Best Corporation, 30
Dobson Communications Corporation, 63
Doctor's Associates Inc., 67 (upd.)
The Doctors' Company, 55
Documentum, Inc., 46
Dolby Laboratories Inc., 20
Dole Food Company, Inc., 9; 31 (upd.); 68 (upd.)
Dollar Thrifty Automotive Group, Inc., 25
Dollar Tree Stores, Inc., 23; 62 (upd.)
Dominick's Finer Foods, Inc., 56
Dominion Homes, Inc., 19
Dominion Resources, Inc., V; 54 (upd.)
Domino Sugar Corporation, 26
Domino's Pizza, Inc., 7; 21 (upd.)
Domino's, Inc., 63 (upd.)
Don Massey Cadillac, Inc., 37
Donaldson Company, Inc., 16; 49 (upd.)
Donaldson, Lufkin & Jenrette, Inc., 22
Donatos Pizzeria Corporation, 58
Donna Karan International Inc., 15; 56 (upd.)
Donnelly Corporation, 12; 35 (upd.)
Donnkenny, Inc., 17
Donruss Playoff L.P., 66
Dorsey & Whitney LLP, 47
Doskocil Companies, Inc., 12
Dot Foods, Inc., 69
Double-Cola Co.-USA, 70
DoubleClick Inc., 46
Doubletree Corporation, 21
Douglas & Lomason Company, 16
Dover Corporation, III; 28 (upd.)
Dover Downs Entertainment, Inc., 43
Dover Publications Inc., 34
The Dow Chemical Company, I; 8 (upd.); 50 (upd.)
Dow Jones & Company, Inc., IV; 19 (upd.); 47 (upd.)
Dow Jones Telerate, Inc., 10
DPL Inc., 6
DQE, Inc., 6
Dr Pepper/Seven Up, Inc., 9; 32 (upd.)
Drackett Professional Products, 12
Drake Beam Morin, Inc., 44
DreamWorks SKG, 43
The Drees Company, Inc., 41
The Dress Barn, Inc., 24; 55 (upd.)

General Mills, Inc., II; 10 (upd.); 36 (upd.)
General Motors Corporation, I; 10 (upd.); 36 (upd.); 64 (upd.)
General Nutrition Companies, Inc., 11; 29 (upd.)
General Public Utilities Corporation, V
General Re Corporation, III; 24 (upd.)
General Signal Corporation, 9
General Tire, Inc., 8
Genesco Inc., 17
Genesee & Wyoming Inc., 27
Genesis Health Ventures, Inc., 18
Genetics Institute, Inc., 8
Geneva Steel, 7
Genmar Holdings, Inc., 45
Genovese Drug Stores, Inc., 18
GenRad, Inc., 24
Gentex Corporation, 26
Gentiva Health Services, Inc. 79
Genuardi's Family Markets, Inc., 35
Genuine Parts Company, 9; 45 (upd.)
Genzyme Corporation, 13; 38 (upd.); 77 (upd.)
The Geon Company, 11
George A. Hormel and Company, II
The George F. Cram Company, Inc., 55
George P. Johnson Company, 60
George S. May International Company, 55
Georgia Gulf Corporation, 9; 61 (upd.)
Georgia-Pacific Corporation, IV; 9 (upd.); 47 (upd.)
Geotek Communications Inc., 21
Gerald Stevens, Inc., 37
Gerber Products Company, 7; 21 (upd.)
Gerber Scientific, Inc., 12
German American Bancorp, 41
Getty Images, Inc., 31
Gevity HR, Inc., 63
Ghirardelli Chocolate Company, 30
Giant Cement Holding, Inc., 23
Giant Food Inc., II; 22 (upd.)
Giant Industries, Inc., 19; 61 (upd.)
Gibraltar Steel Corporation, 37
Gibson Greetings, Inc., 12
Gibson Guitar Corp., 16
Gibson, Dunn & Crutcher LLP, 36
Giddings & Lewis, Inc., 10
Gilbane, Inc., 34
Gilead Sciences, Inc., 54
Gillett Holdings, Inc., 7
The Gillette Company, III; 20 (upd.); 68 (upd.)
Gilman & Ciocia, Inc., 72
Girl Scouts of the USA, 35
The Gitano Group, Inc., 8
Glacier Bancorp, Inc., 35
Glacier Water Services, Inc., 47
Glamis Gold, Ltd., 54
Gleason Corporation, 24
The Glidden Company, 8
Global Berry Farms LLC, 62
Global Crossing Ltd., 32
Global Hyatt Corporation, 75 (upd.)
Global Imaging Systems, Inc., 73
Global Industries, Ltd., 37
Global Marine Inc., 9
Global Outdoors, Inc., 49
Global Power Equipment Group Inc., 52
GlobalSantaFe Corporation, 48 (upd.)
Gluek Brewing Company, 75
GM Hughes Electronics Corporation, II
Godfather's Pizza Incorporated, 25
Godiva Chocolatier, Inc., 64
Gold Kist Inc., 17; 26 (upd.)
Gold'n Plump Poultry, 54
Gold's Gym International, Inc., 71
Golden Belt Manufacturing Co., 16
Golden Books Family Entertainment, Inc., 28
Golden Corral Corporation, 10; 66 (upd.)
Golden Enterprises, Inc., 26
Golden Krust Caribbean Bakery, Inc., 68
Golden State Foods Corporation, 32
Golden State Vintners, Inc., 33
Golden West Financial Corporation, 47
The Goldman Sachs Group Inc., II; 20 (upd.); 51 (upd.)
The Golub Corporation, 26
Gonnella Baking Company, 40
The Good Guys, Inc., 10; 30 (upd.)
Good Humor-Breyers Ice Cream Company, 14
Goodby Silverstein & Partners, Inc., 75
Goodman Holding Company, 42
GoodMark Foods, Inc., 26
Goodrich Corporation, 46 (upd.)
GoodTimes Entertainment Ltd., 48
Goodwill Industries International, Inc., 16; 66 (upd.)
Goody Products, Inc., 12
Goody's Family Clothing, Inc., 20; 64 (upd.)
The Goodyear Tire & Rubber Company, V; 20 (upd.); 75 (upd.)
Google, Inc., 50
Gordmans, Inc., 74
Gordon Food Service Inc., 8; 39 (upd.)
The Gorman-Rupp Company, 18; 57 (upd.)
Gorton's, 13
Goss Holdings, Inc., 43
Gottschalks, Inc., 18
Gould Electronics, Inc., 14
Goulds Pumps Inc., 24
Goya Foods Inc., 22
GP Strategies Corporation, 64 (upd.)
GPU, Inc., 27 (upd.)
Graco Inc., 19; 67 (upd.)
Graham Corporation, 62
GranCare, Inc., 14
Grand Casinos, Inc., 20
Grand Piano & Furniture Company, 72
The Grand Union Company, 7; 28 (upd.)
Granite Broadcasting Corporation, 42
Granite Construction Incorporated, 61
Granite Industries of Vermont, Inc., 73
Granite Rock Company, 26
Granite State Bankshares, Inc., 37
Grant Prideco, Inc., 57
Grant Thornton International, 57
Graphic Industries Inc., 25
Gray Communications Systems, Inc., 24
Graybar Electric Company, Inc., 54
Great American Management and Investment, Inc., 8
The Great Atlantic & Pacific Tea Company, Inc., II; 16 (upd.); 55 (upd.)
Great Harvest Bread Company, 44
Great Lakes Bancorp, 8
Great Lakes Chemical Corporation, I; 14 (upd.)
Great Lakes Dredge & Dock Company, 69
Great Plains Energy Incorporated, 65 (upd.)
Great Western Financial Corporation, 10
Greatbatch Inc., 72
Grede Foundries, Inc., 38
The Green Bay Packers, Inc., 32
Green Mountain Coffee, Inc., 31
Green Tree Financial Corporation, 11
Greenberg Traurig, LLP, 65
The Greenbrier Companies, 19
Greene, Tweed & Company, 55
GreenPoint Financial Corp., 28
Greenwood Mills, Inc., 14
Greg Manning Auctions, Inc., 60
Greif Inc., 15; 66 (upd.)
Grey Advertising, Inc., 6
Grey Global Group Inc., 66 (upd.)
Grey Wolf, Inc., 43
Greyhound Lines, Inc., I; 32 (upd.)
Griffin Industries, Inc., 70
Griffin Land & Nurseries, Inc., 43
Griffon Corporation, 34
Grill Concepts, Inc., 74
Grinnell Corp., 13
Grist Mill Company, 15
Gristede's Foods Inc., 31; 68 (upd.)
Grolier Incorporated, 16; 43 (upd.)
Grossman's Inc., 13
Ground Round, Inc., 21
Group 1 Automotive, Inc., 52
Group Health Cooperative, 41
Grow Biz International, Inc., 18
Grow Group Inc., 12
Grubb & Ellis Company, 21
Grumman Corporation, I; 11 (upd.)
Gruntal & Co., L.L.C., 20
Gryphon Holdings, Inc., 21
GSD&M Advertising, 44
GSI Commerce, Inc., 67
GT Bicycles, 26
GT Interactive Software, 31
GTE Corporation, V; 15 (upd.)
GTSI Corp., 57
Guangzhou Pearl River Piano Group Ltd., 49
Guccio Gucci, S.p.A., 15
Guess, Inc., 15; 68 (upd.)
Guest Supply, Inc., 18
Guidant Corporation, 58
Guilford Mills Inc., 8; 40 (upd.)
Guitar Center, Inc., 29; 68 (upd.)
Guittard Chocolate Company, 55
Gulf & Western Inc., I
Gulf Island Fabrication, Inc., 44
Gulf States Utilities Company, 6
GulfMark Offshore, Inc., 49
Gulfstream Aerospace Corporation, 7; 28 (upd.)

Mackie Designs Inc., 33
Macmillan, Inc., 7
The MacNeal-Schwendler Corporation, 25
Macromedia, Inc., 50
Madden's on Gull Lake, 52
Madison Gas and Electric Company, 39
Madison-Kipp Corporation, 58
Mag Instrument, Inc., 67
Magma Copper Company, 7
Magma Design Automation Inc. 78
Magma Power Company, 11
MagneTek, Inc., 15; 41 (upd.)
MAI Systems Corporation, 11
Maid-Rite Corporation, 62
Maidenform, Inc., 20; 59 (upd.)
Mail Boxes Etc., 18; 41 (upd.)
Mail-Well, Inc., 28
Maine & Maritimes Corporation, 56
Maine Central Railroad Company, 16
Maines Paper & Food Service Inc., 71
The Major Automotive Companies, Inc., 45
Malcolm Pirnie, Inc., 42
Malden Mills Industries, Inc., 16
Mallinckrodt Group Inc., 19
Malt-O-Meal Company, 22; 63 (upd.)
Management and Training Corporation, 28
Mandalay Resort Group, 32 (upd.)
Manhattan Associates, Inc., 67
The Manitowoc Company, Inc., 18; 59 (upd.)
Mannatech Inc., 33
Manning Selvage & Lee (MS&L), 76
Manor Care, Inc., 6; 25 (upd.)
Manpower Inc., 9; 30 (upd.); 73 (upd.)
Manufactured Home Communities, Inc., 22
Manufacturers Hanover Corporation, II
Manville Corporation, III; 7 (upd.)
MAPCO Inc., IV
MAPICS, Inc., 55
March of Dimes, 31
Marchex, Inc., 72
marchFIRST, Inc., 34
Marco Business Products, Inc., 75
The Marcus Corporation, 21
Marie Callender's Restaurant & Bakery, Inc., 28
Marine Products Corporation, 75
MarineMax, Inc., 30
Marion Laboratories, Inc., I
Marisa Christina, Inc., 15
Maritz Inc., 38
Mark IV Industries, Inc., 7; 28 (upd.)
Marks Brothers Jewelers, Inc., 24
The Marmon Group, IV; 16 (upd.)
The Marmon Group, Inc., 70 (upd.)
Marquette Electronics, Inc., 13
Marriott International, Inc., III; 21 (upd.)
Mars, Incorporated, 7; 40 (upd.)
Marsh & McLennan Companies, Inc., III; 45 (upd.)
Marsh Supermarkets, Inc., 17; 76 (upd.)
Marshall & Ilsley Corporation, 56
Marshall Field's, 63
Marshalls Incorporated, 13
Martek Biosciences Corporation, 65
Martha Stewart Living Omnimedia, Inc., 73 (upd.)
Martha Stewart Living Omnimedia, L.L.C., 24
Martin Industries, Inc., 44
Martin Marietta Corporation, I
Martz Group, 56
Marvel Entertainment Inc., 10; 78 (upd.)
Marvin Lumber & Cedar Company, 22
Mary Kay Corporation, 9; 30 (upd.)
Masco Corporation, III; 20 (upd.); 39 (upd.)
Mashantucket Pequot Gaming Enterprise Inc., 35
Masland Corporation, 17
Massachusetts Mutual Life Insurance Company, III; 53 (upd.)
Massey Energy Company, 57
MasTec, Inc., 19; 55 (upd.)
Master Lock Company, 45
MasterBrand Cabinets, Inc., 71
MasterCard International, Inc., 9
Material Sciences Corporation, 63
Matria Healthcare, Inc., 17
Matrix Service Company, 65
Matrixx Initiatives, Inc., 74
Matt Prentice Restaurant Group, 70
Mattel, Inc., 7; 25 (upd.); 61 (upd.)
Matthews International Corporation, 29; 77 (upd.)
Maui Land & Pineapple Company, Inc., 29
Mauna Loa Macadamia Nut Corporation, 64
Maverick Tube Corporation, 59
Max & Erma's Restaurants Inc., 19
Maxco Inc., 17
Maxicare Health Plans, Inc., III; 25 (upd.)
The Maxim Group, 25
Maxim Integrated Products, Inc., 16
MAXIMUS, Inc., 43
Maxtor Corporation, 10
Maxus Energy Corporation, 7
Maxwell Shoe Company, Inc., 30
MAXXAM Inc., 8
Maxxim Medical Inc., 12
The May Department Stores Company, V; 19 (upd.); 46 (upd.)
Mayer, Brown, Rowe & Maw, 47
Mayfield Dairy Farms, Inc., 74
Mayflower Group Inc., 6
Mayo Foundation, 9; 34 (upd.)
Mayor's Jewelers, Inc., 41
Maytag Corporation, III; 22 (upd.)
Mazel Stores, Inc., 29
Mazzio's Corporation, 76
MBC Holding Company, 40
MBIA Inc., 73
MBNA Corporation, 12; 33 (upd.)
MCA Inc., II
McAlister's Corporation, 66
McCarthy Building Companies, Inc., 48
McCaw Cellular Communications, Inc., 6
McClain Industries, Inc., 51
McClatchy Newspapers, Inc., 23
McCormick & Company, Incorporated, 7; 27 (upd.)
McCormick & Schmick's Seafood Restaurants, Inc., 71
McCoy Corporation, 58
McDATA Corporation, 75
McDermott International, Inc., III; 37 (upd.)
McDonald's Corporation, II; 7 (upd.); 26 (upd.); 63 (upd.)
McDonnell Douglas Corporation, I; 11 (upd.)
The McGraw-Hill Companies, Inc., IV; 18 (upd.); 51 (upd.)
MCI WorldCom, Inc., V; 27 (upd.)
McIlhenny Company, 20
McJunkin Corporation, 63
McKee Foods Corporation, 7; 27 (upd.)
McKesson Corporation, I; 12; 47 (upd.)
McKinsey & Company, Inc., 9
McLane Company, Inc., 13
McLeodUSA Incorporated, 32
McMenamins Pubs and Breweries, 65
MCN Corporation, 6
MCSi, Inc., 41
McWane Corporation, 55
MDU Resources Group, Inc., 7; 42 (upd.)
The Mead Corporation, IV; 19 (upd.)
Mead Data Central, Inc., 10
Meade Instruments Corporation, 41
Meadowcraft, Inc., 29
MeadWestvaco Corporation, 76 (upd.)
Measurement Specialties, Inc., 71
Mecklermedia Corporation, 24
Medco Containment Services Inc., 9
Media Arts Group, Inc., 42
Media General, Inc., 7; 38 (upd.)
Mediacom Communications Corporation, 69
MediaNews Group, Inc., 70
Medical Information Technology Inc., 64
Medical Management International, Inc., 65
Medicis Pharmaceutical Corporation, 59
MedImmune, Inc., 35
Medis Technologies Ltd., 77
Meditrust, 11
Medline Industries, Inc., 61
Medtronic, Inc., 8; 30 (upd.); 67 (upd.)
Medusa Corporation, 24
Megafoods Stores Inc., 13
Meier & Frank Co., 23
Meijer Incorporated, 7; 27 (upd.)
Mel Farr Automotive Group, 20
Melaleuca Inc., 31
Melamine Chemicals, Inc., 27
Mellon Bank Corporation, II
Mellon Financial Corporation, 44 (upd.)
Mellon-Stuart Company, I
The Melting Pot Restaurants, Inc., 74
Melville Corporation, V
Melvin Simon and Associates, Inc., 8
Memorial Sloan-Kettering Cancer Center, 57
Memry Corporation, 72
The Men's Wearhouse, Inc., 17; 48 (upd.)
Menard, Inc., 34
Menasha Corporation, 8; 59 (upd.)
Mendocino Brewing Company, Inc., 60
The Mentholatum Company Inc., 32

Niagara Corporation, 28
Niagara Mohawk Holdings Inc., V; 45 (upd.)
Nichols Research Corporation, 18
Nicklaus Companies, 45
NICOR Inc., 6
NIKE, Inc., V; 8 (upd.); 36 (upd.); 75 (upd.)
Nikken Global Inc., 32
Niman Ranch, Inc., 67
Nimbus CD International, Inc., 20
Nine West Group, Inc., 11; 39 (upd.)
99> Only Stores, 25
NIPSCO Industries, Inc., 6
Nitches, Inc., 53
NL Industries, Inc., 10
Nobel Learning Communities, Inc., 37; 76 (upd.)
Noble Affiliates, Inc., 11
Noble Roman's Inc., 14
Noland Company, 35
Nolo.com, Inc., 49
Noodle Kidoodle, 16
Noodles & Company, Inc., 55
Nooter Corporation, 61
Norcal Waste Systems, Inc., 60
NordicTrack, 22
Nordson Corporation, 11; 48 (upd.)
Nordstrom, Inc., V; 18 (upd.); 67 (upd.)
Norelco Consumer Products Co., 26
Norfolk Southern Corporation, V; 29 (upd.); 75 (upd.)
Norm Thompson Outfitters, Inc., 47
Norrell Corporation, 25
Norstan, Inc., 16
Nortek, Inc., 34
North Atlantic Trading Company Inc., 65
The North Face, Inc., 18; 78 (upd.)
North Fork Bancorporation, Inc., 46
North Pacific Group, Inc., 61
North Star Steel Company, 18
Northeast Utilities, V; 48 (upd.)
Northern States Power Company, V; 20 (upd.)
Northern Trust Company, 9
Northland Cranberries, Inc., 38
Northrop Grumman Corporation, I; 11 (upd.); 45 (upd.)
Northwest Airlines Corporation, I; 6 (upd.); 26 (upd.); 74 (upd.)
Northwest Natural Gas Company, 45
NorthWestern Corporation, 37
Northwestern Mutual Life Insurance Company, III; 45 (upd.)
Norton Company, 8
Norton McNaughton, Inc., 27
Norwood Promotional Products, Inc., 26
NovaCare, Inc., 11
Novell, Inc., 6; 23 (upd.)
Novellus Systems, Inc., 18
Noven Pharmaceuticals, Inc., 55
NPC International, Inc., 40
The NPD Group, Inc., 68
NRG Energy, Inc. 79
NRT Incorporated, 61
NSF International, 72
NSS Enterprises Inc. 78
Nu Skin Enterprises, Inc., 27; 76 (upd.)
Nu-kote Holding, Inc., 18
Nucor Corporation, 7; 21 (upd.); 79 (upd.)
Nutraceutical International Corporation, 37
NutraSweet Company, 8
NutriSystem, Inc., 71
Nutrition for Life International Inc., 22
NVIDIA Corporation, 54
NVR Inc., 8; 70 (upd.)
NYMAGIC, Inc., 41
NYNEX Corporation, V
O.C. Tanner Co., 69
Oak Harbor Freight Lines, Inc., 53
Oak Industries Inc., 21
Oak Technology, Inc., 22
Oakhurst Dairy, 60
Oakley, Inc., 18; 49 (upd.)
Oaktree Capital Management, LLC, 71
Oakwood Homes Corporation, 15
Obie Media Corporation, 56
Occidental Petroleum Corporation, IV; 25 (upd.); 71 (upd.)
Ocean Beauty Seafoods, Inc., 74
Ocean Spray Cranberries, Inc., 7; 25 (upd.)
Oceaneering International, Inc., 63
O'Charley's Inc., 19; 60 (upd.)
Octel Messaging, 14; 41 (upd.)
Ocular Sciences, Inc., 65
Odetics Inc., 14
ODL, Inc., 55
Odwalla, Inc., 31
OEC Medical Systems, Inc., 27
Office Depot, Inc., 8; 23 (upd.); 65 (upd.)
OfficeMax, Inc., 15; 43 (upd.)
OfficeTiger, LLC, 75
Offshore Logistics, Inc., 37
Ogden Corporation, I; 6
The Ogilvy Group, Inc., I
Oglebay Norton Company, 17
Oglethorpe Power Corporation, 6
The Ohio Art Company, 14; 59 (upd.)
Ohio Bell Telephone Company, 14
Ohio Casualty Corp., 11
Ohio Edison Company, V
Oil-Dri Corporation of America, 20
Oil States International, Inc., 77
The Oilgear Company, 74
Oklahoma Gas and Electric Company, 6
Olan Mills, Inc., 62
Old America Stores, Inc., 17
Old Dominion Freight Line, Inc., 57
Old Kent Financial Corp., 11
Old National Bancorp, 15
Old Navy, Inc., 70
Old Orchard Brands, LLC, 73
Old Republic International Corporation, 11; 58 (upd.)
Old Spaghetti Factory International Inc., 24
Old Town Canoe Company, 74
Olin Corporation, I; 13 (upd.); 78 (upd.)
Olsten Corporation, 6; 29 (upd.)
OM Group Inc. 17; 78 (upd.)
Omaha Steaks International Inc., 62
O'Melveny & Myers, 37
OMI Corporation, 59
Omni Hotels Corp., 12
Omnicare, Inc., 49
Omnicom Group, Inc., I; 22 (upd.); 77 (upd.)
OmniSource Corporation, 14
OMNOVA Solutions Inc., 59
On Assignment, Inc., 20
180s, L.L.C., 64
One Price Clothing Stores, Inc., 20
1-800-FLOWERS, Inc., 26
Oneida Ltd., 7; 31 (upd.)
ONEOK Inc., 7
Onion, Inc., 69
Onyx Acceptance Corporation, 59
Onyx Software Corporation, 53
Operation Smile, Inc., 75
Opinion Research Corporation, 46
Oppenheimer Wolff & Donnelly LLP, 71
Opsware Inc., 49
Option Care Inc., 48
Opus Group, 34
Oracle Corporation, 6; 24 (upd.); 67 (upd.)
Orange Glo International, 53
OraSure Technologies, Inc., 75
Orbital Sciences Corporation, 22
Orbitz, Inc., 61
Orchard Supply Hardware Stores Corporation, 17
Ore-Ida Foods Inc., 13; 78 (upd.)
Oregon Chai, Inc., 49
Oregon Dental Service Health Plan, Inc., 51
Oregon Freeze Dry, Inc., 74
Oregon Metallurgical Corporation, 20
Oregon Steel Mills, Inc., 14
O'Reilly Automotive, Inc., 26; 78 (upd.)
Organic Valley (Coulee Region Organic Produce Pool), 53
Orion Pictures Corporation, 6
Orleans Homebuilders, Inc., 62
Orrick, Herrington and Sutcliffe LLP, 76
Orthodontic Centers of America, Inc., 35
The Orvis Company, Inc., 28
Oryx Energy Company, 7
Oscar Mayer Foods Corp., 12
OshKosh B'Gosh, Inc., 9; 42 (upd.)
Oshkosh Truck Corporation, 7
Oshman's Sporting Goods, Inc., 17
Osmonics, Inc., 18
O'Sullivan Industries Holdings, Inc., 34
Otis Elevator Company, Inc., 13; 39 (upd.)
Otis Spunkmeyer, Inc., 28
OTR Express, Inc., 25
Ottaway Newspapers, Inc., 15
Otter Tail Power Company, 18
Outback Steakhouse, Inc., 12; 34 (upd.)
Outboard Marine Corporation, III; 20 (upd.)
Outdoor Research, Incorporated, 67
Outdoor Systems, Inc., 25
Outlook Group Corporation, 37
Outrigger Enterprises, Inc., 67
Overhead Door Corporation, 70
Overhill Corporation, 51
Overnite Corporation, 14; 58 (upd.)

Piggly Wiggly Southern, Inc., 13
Pilgrim's Pride Corporation, 7; 23 (upd.)
Pillowtex Corporation, 19; 41 (upd.)
The Pillsbury Company, II; 13 (upd.); 62 (upd.)
Pillsbury Madison & Sutro LLP, 29
Pilot Air Freight Corp., 67
Pilot Corporation, 49
Pinkerton's Inc., 9
Pinnacle Airlines Corp., 73
Pinnacle West Capital Corporation, 6; 54 (upd.)
Pioneer Hi-Bred International, Inc., 9; 41 (upd.)
Pioneer Natural Resources Company, 59
Pioneer-Standard Electronics Inc., 19
Piper Jaffray Companies Inc., 22
Pitman Company, 58
Pitney Bowes Inc., III; 19; 47 (upd.)
Pittsburgh Brewing Company, 76
Pittsburgh Steelers Sports, Inc., 66
The Pittston Company, IV; 19 (upd.)
Pittway Corporation, 9; 33 (upd.)
Pixar Animation Studios, 34
Pixelworks, Inc., 69
Pizza Hut Inc., 7; 21 (upd.)
Pizza Inn, Inc., 46
Plains Cotton Cooperative Association, 57
Planar Systems, Inc., 61
Planet Hollywood International, Inc., 18; 41 (upd.)
Plantation Pipe Line Company, 68
Plante & Moran, LLP, 71
Platinum Entertainment, Inc., 35
PLATINUM Technology, Inc., 14
Plato Learning, Inc., 44
Play by Play Toys & Novelties, Inc., 26
Playboy Enterprises, Inc., 18
PlayCore, Inc., 27
Players International, Inc., 22
Playskool, Inc., 25
Playtex Products, Inc., 15
Pleasant Company, 27
Pleasant Holidays LLC, 62
Plexus Corporation, 35
Plum Creek Timber Company, Inc., 43
Pluma, Inc., 27
Ply Gem Industries Inc., 12
The PMI Group, Inc., 49
PMT Services, Inc., 24
The PNC Financial Services Group Inc., II; 13 (upd.); 46 (upd.)
PNM Resources Inc., 51 (upd.)
Pogo Producing Company, 39
Polar Air Cargo Inc., 60
Polaris Industries Inc., 12; 35 (upd.); 77 (upd.)
Polaroid Corporation, III; 7 (upd.); 28 (upd.)
Policy Management Systems Corporation, 11
Policy Studies, Inc., 62
Polk Audio, Inc., 34
Polo/Ralph Lauren Corporation, 12; 62 (upd.)
PolyGram N.V., 23
PolyMedica Corporation, 77
Pomeroy Computer Resources, Inc., 33
Ponderosa Steakhouse, 15
Poof-Slinky, Inc., 61
Poore Brothers, Inc., 44
Pope & Talbot, Inc., 12; 61 (upd.)
Pope Resources LP, 74
Popular, Inc., 41
The Port Authority of New York and New Jersey, 48
Port Imperial Ferry Corporation, 70
Portal Software, Inc., 47
Portillo's Restaurant Group, Inc., 71
Portland General Corporation, 6
Portland Trail Blazers, 50
Post Properties, Inc., 26
Potlatch Corporation, 8; 34 (upd.)
Potomac Electric Power Company, 6
Potter & Brumfield Inc., 11
Powell's Books, Inc., 40
Power-One, Inc. 79
PowerBar Inc., 44
Powerhouse Technologies, Inc., 27
PPG Industries, Inc., III; 22 (upd.)
PPL Corporation, 41 (upd.)
PR Newswire, 35
Prairie Farms Dairy, Inc., 47
Pratt & Whitney, 9
Praxair, Inc., 11; 48 (upd.)
Pre-Paid Legal Services, Inc., 20
Precision Castparts Corp., 15
Premark International, Inc., III
Premcor Inc., 37
Premier Industrial Corporation, 9
Premier Parks, Inc., 27
Premium Standard Farms, Inc., 30
PremiumWear, Inc., 30
Preserver Group, Inc., 44
President Casinos, Inc., 22
Pressman Toy Corporation, 56
Presstek, Inc., 33
Preston Corporation, 6
PRG-Schultz International, Inc., 73
Price Communications Corporation, 42
The Price Company, V
Price Pfister, Inc., 70
PriceCostco, Inc., 14
Priceline.com Incorporated, 57
PriceSmart, Inc., 71
PricewaterhouseCoopers, 9; 29 (upd.)
Pride International Inc. 78
Primark Corp., 13
Prime Hospitality Corporation, 52
Primedex Health Systems, Inc., 25
Primedia Inc., 22
Primerica Corporation, I
Prince Sports Group, Inc., 15
Princess Cruise Lines, 22
The Princeton Review, Inc., 42
Principal Mutual Life Insurance Company, III
Printpack, Inc., 68
Printrak, A Motorola Company, 44
Printronix, Inc., 18
Prison Rehabilitative Industries and Diversified Enterprises, Inc. (PRIDE), 53
The Procter & Gamble Company, III; 8 (upd.); 26 (upd.); 67 (upd.)
Prodigy Communications Corporation, 34
Professional Bull Riders Inc., 55
The Professional Golfers' Association of America, 41
Proffitt's, Inc., 19
Progress Energy, Inc., 74
Progress Software Corporation, 15
The Progressive Corporation, 11; 29 (upd.)
ProLogis, 57
Promus Companies, Inc., 9
Proskauer Rose LLP, 47
Protection One, Inc., 32
Provell Inc., 58 (upd.)
The Providence Journal Company, 28
The Providence Service Corporation, 64
Provident Life and Accident Insurance Company of America, III
Providian Financial Corporation, 52 (upd.)
The Prudential Insurance Company of America, III; 30 (upd.)
PSI Resources, 6
Psychiatric Solutions, Inc., 68
Pubco Corporation, 17
Public Service Company of Colorado, 6
Public Service Company of New Hampshire, 21; 55 (upd.)
Public Service Company of New Mexico, 6
Public Service Enterprise Group Inc., V; 44 (upd.)
Public Storage, Inc., 52
Publishers Clearing House, 23; 64 (upd.)
Publishers Group, Inc., 35
Publix Supermarkets Inc., 7; 31 (upd.)
Pueblo Xtra International, Inc., 47
Puget Sound Energy Inc., 6; 50 (upd.)
Pulaski Furniture Corporation, 33
Pulitzer Inc., 15; 58 (upd.)
Pulte Corporation, 8
Pulte Homes, Inc., 42 (upd.)
Pumpkin Masters, Inc., 48
Pure World, Inc., 72
Purina Mills, Inc., 32
Puritan-Bennett Corporation, 13
Purolator Products Company, 21; 74 (upd.)
Putt-Putt Golf Courses of America, Inc., 23
PVC Container Corporation, 67
PW Eagle, Inc., 48
Pyramid Breweries Inc., 33
Pyramid Companies, 54
Q.E.P. Co., Inc., 65
QSC Audio Products, Inc., 56
Quad/Graphics, Inc., 19
Quaker Fabric Corp., 19
Quaker Foods North America, 73 (upd.)
The Quaker Oats Company, II; 12 (upd.); 34 (upd.)
Quaker State Corporation, 7; 21 (upd.)
QUALCOMM Incorporated, 20; 47 (upd.)
Quality Chekd Dairies, Inc., 48
Quality Dining, Inc., 18
Quality Food Centers, Inc., 17
Quanex Corporation, 13; 62 (upd.)
Quanta Services, Inc. 79

Vatican City

Venezuela

Vietnam

Virgin Islands

Wales

Zambia